*Essential Guide to PeopleSoft
Development and Customization*

Essential Guide to PeopleSoft Development and Customization

TONY DELIA
GALINA LANDRES
ISIDOR RIVERA
PRAKASH SANKARAN

MANNING

Greenwich
(74° w. long.)

For electronic browsing and ordering of this and other Manning books, visit http://www.manning.com. The publisher offers discounts on this book when ordered in quantity. For more information, please contact:

Special Sales Department
Manning Publications Co.
209 Bruce Park Avenue   Fax: (203) 661-9018
Greenwich, CT 06830   email: orders@manning.com

Manning Publications Co.   Copyeditor: Adrianne Harun
209 Bruce Park Avenue   Typesetter: Dottie Marsico
Greenwich, CT 06830   Cover designer: Leslie Haimes

Printed in the United States of America
2 3 4 5 6 7 8 9 10 – VH – 03 02

brief contents

contents

Part 3   PeopleCode: an in-depth look   257

Part 7   *Using Application Engine 769*

about this book

The *Essential Guide to PeopleSoft Development and Customization* is an exhaustive, as well as practical, guide covering PeopleSoft 7.5 and many new features in release 8.0. Both novice and experienced programmers will benefit from the detailed coverage of topics ranging from the basics of Application Designer to the proper use of PeopleCode within the Application Processor. The book serves as both a reference and a tutorial and covers advanced topics that other books avoid. The reader can gain valuable expertise by following the exercises and building sample applications and utilities. Extensive coverage of PeopleCode, including scroll and function library examples, can be found as well as the methodology behind customization and upgrades. Discover how to effectively utilize SQR and Process Scheduler. Master various levels of PeopleSoft security. Most developers won't touch PeopleSoft COBOL programs with a ten foot pole. Expand your horizons by uncovering the secrets of PeopleSoft COBOL and the PTPSQLRT module and even walk through a sample customization. Application Engine is a powerful PeopleTool—but one of the least understood. Through a series of simple but effective exercises, the reader can learn Application Engine concepts such as dynamic SQL, decision logic, and dynamic sections. A useful Application Engine utility is produced which will enhance the delivered Process Scheduler panels. This book takes a soup-to-nuts approach leading the reader through the full cycle of application development.

The four authors provide the reader with the skills necessary to compete in the PeopleSoft marketplace for years to come. Special sections are included which provide detailed information on new features in PeopleSoft release 8. The reader should gain valuable insight into the next generation of PeopleTools. Exciting new features such as the new PeopleCode Debugger and PeopleCode dot notation, using a new series of object classes, are revealed. Also covered are Application Designer enhancements and improved Process Scheduler design and SQR support. See firsthand how Application Engine has been turbo-charged with a new line of meta-constructs, PeopleCode actions, and file handling capability, as well as a new integrated design. The authors' primary goal was not to be the first book on the market ... it was to be the best.

INTENDED AUDIENCE

This book is intended for both beginner and experienced PeopleSoft support personnel including:

- technical developers and consultants who develop, customize, or support PeopleSoft applications
- functional consultants and users who would like greater insight into the realm of PeopleSoft application development
- project leaders and managers responsible for PeopleSoft implementations, customizations, and upgrades.
- database administrators, network technicians, programmers, and all other technical personnel involved in PeopleSoft implementations and support
- computer specialists who would like to learn how to use the PeopleSoft development toolset through self-study.
- those who enjoyed *SQR in PeopleSoft and Other Applications* and would like to pick up where the book left off

HOW THIS BOOK IS ORGANIZED

There are seven major parts to this book. The reader will find it to be most effective by following the examples and exercises provided. Special chapters appear in some sections describing new features in PeopleSoft release 8. These include details on Application Designer, PeopleCode, SQR, Process Scheduler, and Application Engine.

Part 1 gives an overview of PeopleSoft architecture including comparisons between two-tier, three-tier, and web based architecture and their functions. Also included is an introduction to the PeopleSoft environment. Part 1 also describes development and administrative tools such as Application Designer, Data Mover, Security Administrator, and Tree Manager. The reader will become familiar with records, fields, panels, and menus as well as PeopleCode, projects, and upgrades.

Application Development comprises part 2 of the book. The reader will gain valuable insight while building a sample Problem Tracking application. Critical design elements and components are discussed and incorporated into your application. We apply enhancements using search records, derived work fields, PeopleCode, and push buttons. We also discover panel design features such as scroll bars, subpanels, secondary panels, and grids. We learn the difference between PeopleSoft and database objects. We also cover the application processor as it performs during search processing, data retrieval, and PeopleCode events. New Application Designer features found in PeopleSoft release 8 are presented.

Part 3 is an in-depth look at PeopleCode. Here the reader can find a basic overview along with detailed descriptions of the PeopleCode language and related components. Follow the examples which reveal the proper technique for accessing panel buffer fields, working with scroll bars and effective dates, using embedded SQL, and performing error handling procedures. Additional topics such as Security, Meta-SQL, and function libraries are discussed along with debugging techniques. New PeopleCode features found in PeopleSoft release 8 are presented.

Part 4 deals with customizing PeopleSoft-delivered applications. In this section, we determine when to customize and what impact customization has on future upgrades. Tips on performing an upgrade are given along with a discussion on the proper use of projects. Walk through several sample customizations and the steps required to successfully implement your derived modifications.

Part 5 discusses the use of SQR in PeopleSoft applications. Here we see how SQR programs are set up and run in the PeopleSoft environment. We find comprehensive coverage when using run control records and communicating with Process Scheduler and Process Monitor. Unearth the secrets behind implementing security levels and scheduling recurring jobs. New SQR and Process Scheduler features found in PeopleSoft release 8 are also presented.

Part 6 is an explanation of PeopleSoft COBOL and it's unique structure. Differences between conventional COBOL programming and PeopleSoft's particular flavor is discussed. Learn the fundamentals behind the PTPSQLRT module which is the driving force behind PeopleSoft COBOL. Individual PTPSQLRT actions are examined along with the required parameters for each. A realistic modification is performed demonstrating the concepts behind PeopleSoft COBOL. Additional facets such as Process Scheduler API, Configuration Manager and using trace files are discussed.

Part 7 serves as both a reference and tutorial into the world of Application Engines. After an overview describing the basic components and functionality of an Application Engine, the section offers the reader a series of exercises designed to demonstrate each A/E concept. During these simple exercises we cover decision logic and loop control, as well as how to access cache records, effectively utilize dynamic sections, and more. Additional topics are presented describing trace files, restart capability, and analysis of Application Engine programs. New Application Engine features found in PeopleSoft release 8 are also presented.

The appendices found in the book consist of descriptions of the Problem Tracking application (appendix A), Locations by Operator Class application (appendix B), a listing of PeopleSoft system tables (appendix C), Application Engine examples (appendix D), a list of commonly used built-in PeopleCode functions (appendix E), and a list of Application Engine functions (appendix F).

CODE DOWNLOAD

All source code presented in this book is available from the Manning website. The URL www.manning.com/delia includes a link to the source code files.

about the authors

TONY DELIA has over fifteen years' experience working with mainframe, client/server, and relational database applications, including PeopleSoft HR, Payroll, and Financial applications. He specializes in custom application development. Tony enjoys roller hockey, weight lifting, and most other physical activities. He seldom travels far without a sketchbook and crayons. Some of his artwork and technical creations can be seen on his website http://www.sqrtools.com.

GALINA LANDRES has been working in the field of computer science for more than twenty years. Galina has been involved in the development and customization of PeopleSoft applications since PeopleSoft's release 3.0. She is a co-author of *SQR in PeopleSoft and Other Applications* (Greenwich, CT: Manning Publications, 1999). Galina is a founder of SQRLand (www.sqrland.com), a consulting company specializing in PeopleSoft, SQR, and relational database applications.

ISIDOR RIVERA has been in the field of software development for twenty years. His background includes Mainframe and Client/Server applications. He has worked on systems in areas such as Financial Modeling, Accounting, and more recently, Human Resources and Payroll applications. Isidor has much experience converting legacy data to PeopleSoft for distinct business units of a major corporation and has in-depth knowledge of the globalization of PeopleSoft applications.

PRAKASH SANKARAN has been working with client/server applications for the past twelve years. During that time, he has been involved in implementing PeopleSoft applications for the past ten years. He has been working with the PeopleSoft application since release 1. Prakash has extensive experience in converting legacy systems to PeopleSoft as well as upgrading existing PeopleSoft applications to newer releases. Some clients which contributed to Prakash's development and growth in the PeopleSoft field are the International Monetary Fund, Wakefern Food Corporation, Best Foods, St. Francis and Bristol Hospitals, Seagram, and SPX Corporation.

The authors share several common threads. Besides having a considerable amount of PeopleSoft experience, each of them has consistently exhibited a willingness to share this experience with others. It is this spirit of helping others which has served as the motivating factor in producing this book.

acknowledgments

Many people deserve special recognition for their part in the making of this book. First and foremost, our appreciation goes to the people at Manning Publications who made this book a reality. Not only were they professional and supportive, but very patient and understanding as well. Our special thanks goes to Marjan Bace, Ted Kennedy, Mary Piergies, Adrianne Harun, Dottie Marsico, Leslie Haimes, and Sharon Mullins.

We would like to thank the following people who participated in the technical review of this book: Ahmet Emre, Peter Choi, Andrew Gatti, Buddy MacDonald, Cary Cloud, Celia Hyman, Cindy Finnigan, David and Lisa Hill, David Hardacker, Del Iglesia, Doug Cha, JR Growney, Peter Choi, Richard Reid, Steve Britt, and Steve Gill

A special note of gratitude goes to Chris Heller, the Director of PeopleTools Product Strategy, for supplying release 8.0 information and also reviewing much of our material. His contributions to this book have been greatly appreciated.

Tony DeLia would like to thank his family for their support and acceptance of occasional neglect. Additionally he'd like to thank his wife Tanya, who has been an inspiration and a beacon, carefully guiding the direction of his career. She has also given him the greatest gift imaginable, his daughter Katie. His dog Devon deserves some praise for quietly waiting to be let out while Tony finished some of these chapters. Tony would also like to thank Galina, Isidor, and Prakash for the opportunity to be a part of this book.

Galina Landres would like to thank her husband Vlad for his enormous help in the review process. This whole project was his idea and Vlad helped tremendously to bring it to life. Many thanks go to her son Gene and her daughter Inna for their love and support as well as their help in the book's creation. Galina thanks her dear parents for being very understanding and patient. Special thanks go to Irina, Arkady, Ester, and Leon for their continuous love and support. Many thanks to the entire team at Seagrams (her best and favorite client). Huge appreciation goes to her fellow co-authors Tony, Isidor, and Prakash for their excellent work and great friendship.

Isidor Rivera writes: This is for the memory of my father Isidro, Sr. Your illness and subsequent passing in the spring of '99 was very unexpected. We had so many plans early last year, just as this book project was beginning. In the months following your passing, it became so difficult to come home and work on this project. The weekends and late evenings were spent thinking about all the wonderful things you did for Sonia and me. How we marvel at your work and miss you deeply. Thanks to the co-authors, Galina, Tony, and Prakash for helping me find the strength and will to continue.

Prakash would like also to thank his book colleagues, Galina, Tony, and Isidor for putting up with his work schedule and his endless (not anymore!) delays with his part of the book. He also thanks his primary clients in the past five years—Wakefern Food Corporation, Best Foods, St. Francis and Bristol Hospitals, Seagram, and SPX—for giving him an opportunity to acquire the experience he needed to write this book. Finally, he would like to thank his father for always supporting him in whatever he has done in his life.

about the cover illustration

The cover illustration of this book is from the 1805 edition of Sylvain Maréchal's four-volume compendium of regional dress customs. This book was first published in Paris in 1788, one year before the French Revolution. Its title alone required no fewer than 30 words:

> *Costumes Civils actuels de tous les peuples connus dessinés d'après nature gravés et coloriés, accompagnés d'une notice historique sur leurs coutumes, moeurs, religions, etc., etc., redigés par M. Sylvain Maréchal*

The four volumes include an annotation on the illustrations: "gravé à la manière noire par Mixelle d'après Desrais et colorié." Clearly, the engraver and illustrator deserved no more than to be listed by their last names—after all they were mere technicians. The workers who colored each illustration by hand remain nameless.

The colorful variety of this collection reminds us vividly of how culturally apart the world's towns and regions were just 200 years ago. Dress codes have changed everywhere and the diversity by region, so rich at the time, has faded away. It is now hard to tell the inhabitant of one continent from another. Perhaps we have traded cultural diversity for a more varied personal life—certainly a more varied and exciting technological environment. At a time when it is hard to tell one computer book from another, Manning celebrates the inventiveness and initiative of the computer business with book covers based on the rich diversity of regional life of two centuries ago, brought back to life by Maréchal's pictures. Just think, Maréchal's was a world so different from ours people would take the time to read a book title 30 words long.

An introduction to PeopleSoft and PeopleTools

PeopleSoft has been very successful in the ERP marketplace for many years. An obvious reason for this has been PeopleSoft's ability to provide solid packaged solutions for a wide range of business functions. Equally important is PeopleSoft's commitment to incorporating the latest advances in technology into its software. Each release of PeopleSoft has kept stride with the best that technology has to offer. For instance, PeopleSoft's architecture has evolved from a traditional two-tier to three-tier in release 7.0 to web-based architecture in the current 7.5 release and in the not-too-distant future, *n*-tier architecture will arrive in the upcoming 8.0 release. In addition, PeopleSoft provides an extensive toolset called PeopleTools, which allows customers to easily modify existing applications or develop new ones. Third-party software such as SQR and Crystal Reports are bundled into the PeopleSoft package for increased functionality.

In the pages ahead we take a look at the evolution of client/server architecture. We consider its components and how client/server architecture specifically relates to PeopleSoft. We then perform a general walkthrough of the PeopleSoft software, discussing some of its basic capabilities. You'll find a description of Configuration Manager and learn how it is used to control your PeopleSoft environment. An overview of many tools used within PeopleSoft—including Application Designer, Data Mover, Security Administrator, and Tree Manager are also presented. As you proceed through the chapters, you'll see that PeopleTools is very robust yet easy to use—and, yes, fun!

C H A P T E R   1

PeopleSoft fundamentals

PeopleSoft has evolved from the traditional client/server architecture to the multi-tier architecture in PeopleSoft 7.0. In this chapter we will discuss the components that are part of this evolution and describe the functions of the individual tiers that form this architecture.

1.1 PEOPLESOFT ARCHITECTURE

1.1.1 Two-tier architecture

Traditional client/server installations are defined as two-tier architecture, which means that two components exist in a two-tier structure, Client and Server. Client refers to the workstation used to access the application; Server refers to either a database server or some other type application server. In PeopleSoft, Server, in client/server architecture, always implies the database server which hosts the application database.

The following illustration can help us understand the two components and how they communicate between each other.

Client Workstation

Figure 1.1   Two-tier architecture

The client workstation converts the client request into SQL statements and communicates to the database server using database connectivity tools. The client workstation processes all user requests and transmits them across the network to the database server. Some advantages of a two-tier architecture are as follows:

- simple architecture
- easier administration
- cost reduction

A two-tier architecture is ideal when the client is connected to the server on a local area network, but SQL transmissions are voluminous and, as a result, efficient transmissions are not possible across the wide area network. PeopleSoft and other client/server software applications wanted to overcome this challenge and make it possible for client workstations across wide area networks to have faster access to the application.

1.1.2 Three-tier architecture

Citrix Systems introduced an application server, which runs processes that would otherwise run on a client workstation. Users log in to the application server and sessions are run on the remote application server. Users transmit keystrokes and mouse-clicks to the application server which then transmits images back to the client workstation.

The application server acts as the third tier. The key advantage in configuring a third tier is that it is physically located near the database server. Communication between the database server and the application server is within a local area network or better. Data transmitted between the client and the application server is less voluminous than sending SQL requests across the wide area network directly to the database server. This concept reduces the size of data transmitted on the wide area network. Application servers provide a central point of administration as well. They are usually configured to have more processing power and memory. Multiple application servers can be configured to share loads from numerous clients accessing applications across the wide area network. Citrix servers are physical application servers, and there is always a cost involved in maintaining hardware.

PeopleSoft joined with BEA Systems to introduce a transaction-based application server called Tuxedo. Tuxedo application server is a collection of server processes that communicate to the database server. On the server side, workstation listeners are listening to client Tuxedo requests and sending them to the appropriate server process. These server processes request individual services, which can handle jobs such as SQL calls, panel group build, panel group save, and so forth.

Some advantages in a physical three-tier architecture include:

- remote session capabilities near the database server
- reduction of network traffic by transmitting only keystrokes, mouse-clicks, and images across the wide area network
- single point of administration and monitoring per application server
- single point of installation per application server
- load balancing using multiple application servers

Some advantages in a Tuxedo-based three-tier architecture include:

- the ability to transmit more requests using Tuxedo services than using SQL on a network
- the ability to process Tuxedo requests close to where data resides
- the ability to reduce bottleneck in the database server because Tuxedo requests are queued in the application server and transmitted to the database using Tuxedo services as they become available
- the ability to achieve a minimum installation of clientside software, thereby resulting in thin clients
- load balancing by installing many application servers that process data requests from clients
- the ability to encrypt data transmitted from the database server to the client
- the scalability of Tuxedo application servers, which support a wide range of operating systems, databases, and hardware platforms
- the ability to install application software in a single server, thus resulting in easier software maintenance and upgrades

In both Citrix and Tuxedo implementations, more than one application server can be installed depending on the number of clients accessing the database. Some implementations use Tuxedo clients on Citrix Metaframe systems which take advantage of both systems. Users access the three-tier client software on Citrix application servers using remote sessions. PeopleSoft application software is installed/replicated on one or more Citrix application servers.

Note, that a Tuxedo application server can either be a logical or physical configuration.

Logical Application Server　In a logical application server configuration, Tuxedo application software is installed on the same physical machine as the database server. In this case, only two physical machines exist in the whole configuration: the client workstation and the database server, which hosts both the database and Tuxedo.

Physical Application Server　In a physical application server configuration, Tuxedo application software is installed on a separate physical machine, one different from the database server. In this case, three physical machines exist in the configuration: the client workstation, the application server, and the database server. The physical application server and the database server are either connected on the same network backbone or within the local area network.

The illustrations in figures 1.2 and 1.3 can help us understand both the physical and logical three-tier architectures in PeopleSoft.

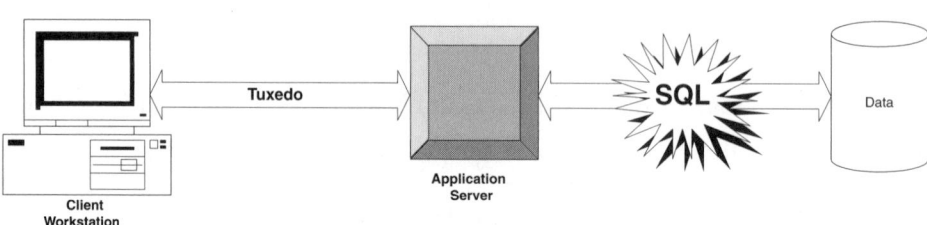

Figure 1.2　Physical three-tier architecture

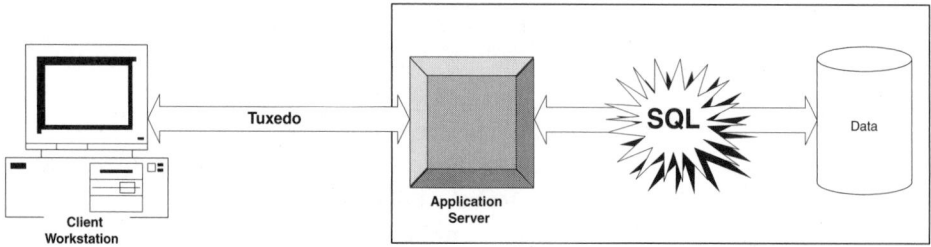

Figure 1.3　Logical three-tier architecture

Notice that the only difference between these three-tier architectures is the number of physical machines configured.

With the arrival of electronic commerce and the recognition of the advantages of accessing applications on the Internet, the next step toward expanding the PeopleSoft architecture was to create a web client.

1.1.3 Web architecture

PeopleSoft introduced a web client which can access a web server that hosts PeopleSoft HTML files and Java applets. The web server communicates with the application server using a BEA System product, called Jolt, that supports web client connections. Jolt interprets HTML and Java applet requests from the web server to the application server. Jolt acts as the translator of Java and HTML codes into C++ codes.

The web server architecture can be either a physical or logical architecture. In a physical architecture installation, Jolt Internet Relay (JRLY) and Jolt Relay Adapter (JRAD) software are required. JRLY and JRAD are products supplied by BEA Systems to secure transactions transmitted on an Internet or Intranet connection. JRLY is installed on the web server placed outside the firewall, and JRAD is installed on the same machine as the application server. Figure 1.4 illustrates the web architecture in a PeopleSoft 7.5 installation.

In figure 1.4, we notice that the web server is an additional tier to a logical three-tier architecture. The web client uses a web browser to access the application. Java applets and HTML files loaded on the web server are used to access the application. The web server connects to the application server with the help of Jolt.

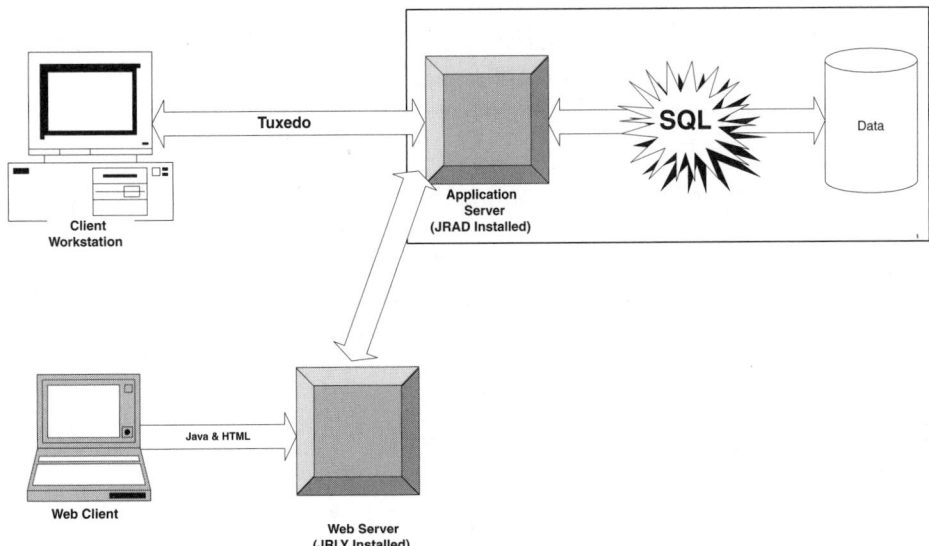

Figure 1.4   Web architecture

1.1.4 *n*-tier architecture

So far, we have discussed the evolution of PeopleSoft architecture in the previous sections. We should realize by now endless possibilities exist for expanding this architecture to service various types of clients. PeopleSoft 7.5 serviced Windows clients, three-tier clients and web clients. PeopleSoft 8 will be released with the deployment of a number of tiers which service many types of clients. The number of tiers that can be deployed is expandable, hence it is called the *n*-tier Architecture.

PeopleSoft 8 also introduces the Internet client which can access the PeopleSoft application using the HTTP protocol via a web browser. PeopleSoft 8 will still support the Windows client and the three-tier client. Additional features such as the Directory Server, Application Messaging and PSWebDeploy will be available with PeopleSoft 8. Directory Server provides a single point of user ID and password administration for users logging into multiple databases. Integration with third party applications using XML/HTTP based messaging will be available using Application Messaging and Publish/Subscribe concepts. PSWebDeploy helps a large number of users access the PeopleSoft application with minimum installation required on their workstations. The client workstation is installed with an executable called PSLaunch that accesses the PeopleSoft application server and downloads the components required to access a PeopleSoft application panel. The PSLaunch software can be launched using a link from a web browser. PSLaunch software can also be launched from an email attachment or from a file stored on the user workstation.

The *N*-tier architecture is advantageous in that it:
- introduces the Internet client that can access the PeopleSoft application using a web browser
- offers minimum workstation installation and thin client
- reduces network traffic by accessing the application using Tuxedo requests that are smaller than an SQL request
- deploys and adds components to this architecture to service more types of clients than before

Figure 1.5 provides an insight into the *n*-tier architecture, illustrating the types of clients that this architecture can service.

As you can see in figure 1.5, multiple application servers and web servers are deployed accessing the same database. In the same installation, Windows clients, Tuxedo clients, and Internet clients are deployed. Windows clients can access the PeopleSoft application using traditional two-tier access.

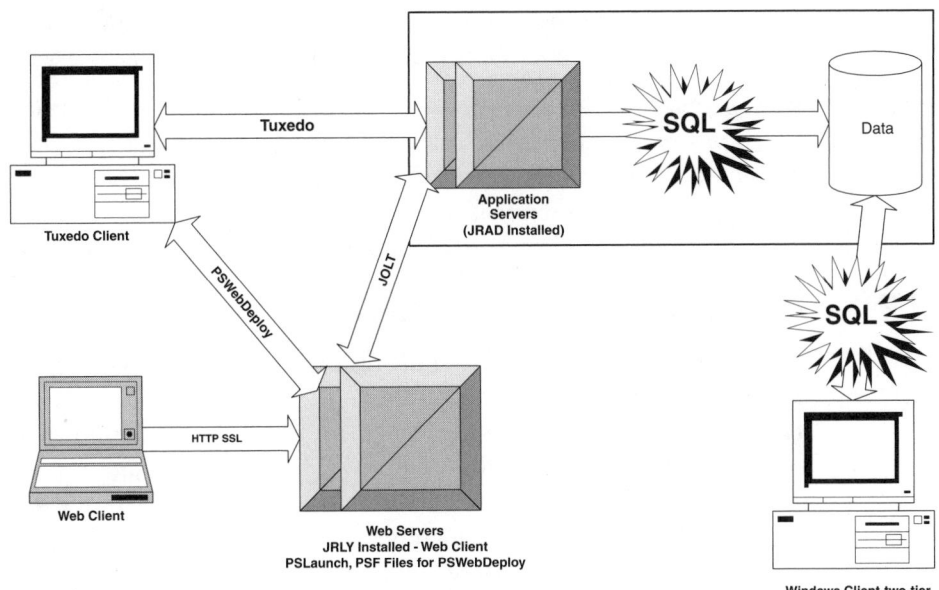

Figure 1.5 *n*-tier architecture

1.1.5   Tiers and their functions

The following important tiers are pertinent only to the PeopleSoft architecture.

Client   A client is the tier which facilitates the user to access the server. A client can be a user workstation which runs a Windows 95 or Windows NT operating system. The client can access PeopleSoft using a traditional two-tier connection using SQL, a three-tier connection using Tuxedo, or a four-tier connection using a web browser.

Database server   The database server hosts the PeopleSoft application database. The application can be hosted on a variety of relational database platforms such as Oracle, Microsoft SQL Server, Sybase, DB2, and so forth. The database server can also be hosted on a variety of operating systems such as Windows NT, Unix, MVS, and so forth. In addition, the database server hosts the SQL connectivity software which communicates with the client and the application server.

Application server   The application server, an intermediate tier which connects the client, the web server, and the database server, can be run on a Unix or Windows NT operating system. The application server runs the Tuxedo and Jolt middle-ware applications and can either be a logical server—which resides on the same machine as the database server—or a physical server—which resides on a different machine than the database server. The application server can also be a Citrix server which runs remote client sessions. Some installations deploy both Citrix servers and Tuxedo application servers which help create remote client access for tools and database access for data.

Web server Web servers service web clients which access the PeopleSoft application using a web browser. The web server contains HTML and Java applets which the web clients access using a web browser. The web server can either be a physical or logical server. When the web server is installed on a separate physical machine, it also contains the Jolt Internet Relay, used for communicating to the application server.

1.2 A USER'S VIEW TO PEOPLESOFT

PeopleSoft Applications offer an array of functionality, tools, and reporting features. The current technology is based on relational database and client/server architecture. The back end or database can reside on many platforms. Platform/database combinations such as UNIX/Oracle, MVS/DB2, Windows/SQLBase, and NT/SQL Server are just some of the many platforms and databases supported by PeopleSoft Applications.

As the new millennium progresses, the move toward web-based technology is becoming ever more pronounced. PeopleSoft e-Business and Enterprise Performance Management applications are also gaining momentum using web technology.

1.2.1 Signing onto PeopleSoft

Our journey into PeopleSoft begins with a sign-on into the application. The example in figure 1.6 illustrates the PeopleSoft sign-on panel for a two-tier connection. Figure 1.7 illustrates a three-tier sign-on.

The sign-on panel identifies several items:

Connection type PeopleSoft applications support connectivity on both two-tier and three-tier client/server configurations. When a client signs onto the application using a two-tier connection, the client connects directly to the database server. In a

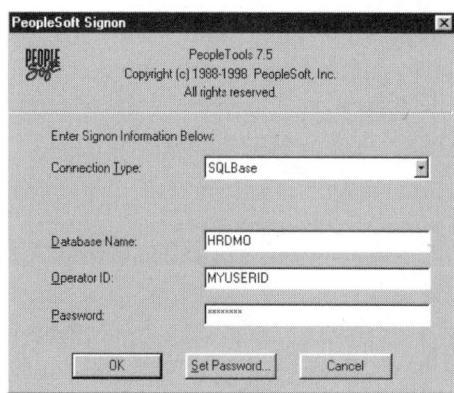

Figure 1.6
PeopleSoft sign-on (two-tier)

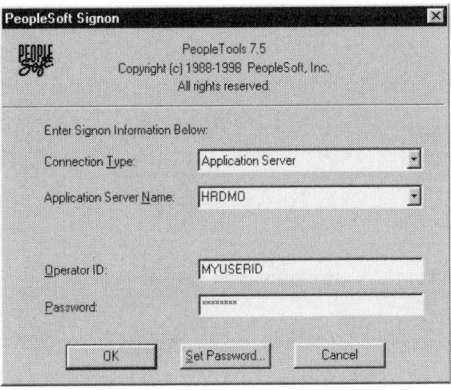

Figure 1.7
PeopleSoft sign-on (three-tier)

three-tier connection, the client is connected to an application server that maintains connections to the database server

Database name   The database name is simply the name of the database to which we are connecting.

Operator ID   The operator ID is the ID used to enter the PeopleSoft application. The ID is generally set up by the security administrator. PeopleSoft IDs are linked to an operator class which has specific functionality privileges allocated to it. In addition to English, the operator ID can have other languages such as Dutch, French, German, Japanese, Portuguese, and Spanish linked to it. Two users who have unique IDs but are linked to the same operator class can view the same panels in their own language.

Password   The password is initially established by the security administrator, but can subsequently be changed by the end user. This can be accomplished by clicking the Set Password button. Some items on the sign-on panel do not have to be keyed in every time we logon. Unless we are transitioning from one platform and/or database type to another, or we support applications on varying platforms and databases, the connection type parameter can be set one time. The database name, application server name, and ID can also be set. As a result, these parameters do not have to be entered at each login. The Startup tab of the Configuration Manager panel enables defaults and overrides during the PeopleSoft login process. An example of the Configuration Manager panel is shown in figure 1.8.

1.2.2   Configuration Manager

The Configuration Manager (figure 1.8) enables PeopleSoft settings to be administered from a central site. These settings, however, are based on how the application is implemented. Registry settings impact a workstation setup and can be shared by an entire group. Therefore, a change to one setting may impact all users in the group. This is common in a Citrix environment or when users share a common file server which contains the executables and runtime Dynamic Link Libraries (DLLs). The Configuration Manager contains tab settings which can be used to tailor specific environmental conditions. Configuration Manager can be entered using the Edit → Preferences → Configuration menu navigation from either the various applications or from a PeopleTool such as Utilities, Process Scheduler, Application Engine, Mass Change, or Translate.

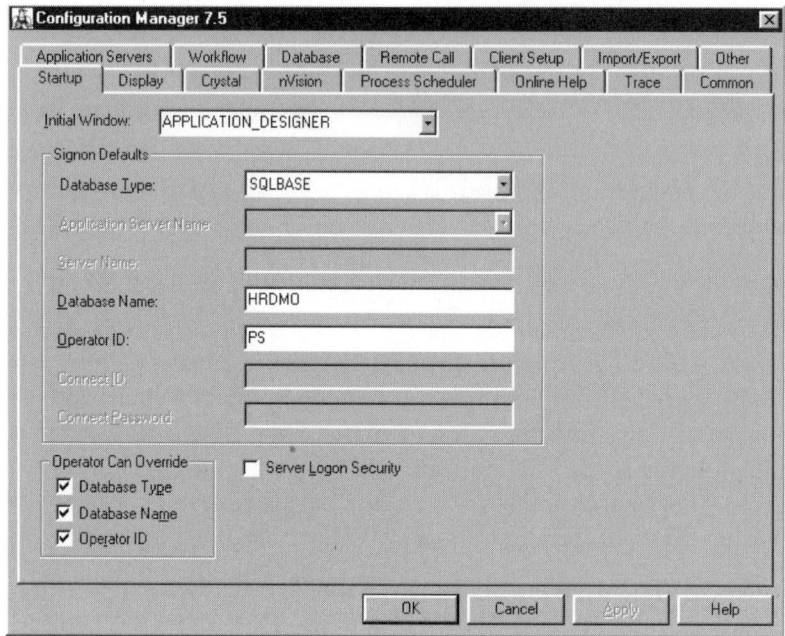

Figure 1.8 Configuration Manager

Startup The Startup tab allows for the entry of default values for database type, database name, and operator ID. In the startup tab, additional parameters exist which can be defaulted but they are more platform-specific. These parameters include the current ID/password for DB2 and Informix. MS SQL Server, and Oracle platforms do not use these options. The lower left portion of the panel enables us to override the database type, name, and operator ID. These parameters can then be modified during sign-on.

Display The Display tab enables the modification of the PeopleSoft application panels to be adjusted, based on desktop needs. These modifications include changes to panel height and width.

The Navigator display options can be set so that the navigator is displayed once during PeopleSoft startup each time a menu group is opened or not displayed.

Crystal The Crystal tab provides the Crystal executable path and default location of Crystal Reports. Additional Crystal options include using trace during execution as well as the subsequent logging to a trace file.

nVision The *n*Vision settings are linked to PeopleSoft queries which are sent to an Excel spreadsheet. The number of blank Excel columns between output data on a spreadsheet can be specified. If no blank separator columns are required, the "Space Between Query Columns" parameter can be set to zero.

Process Scheduler The Process Scheduler settings enable us to specify the directory search path for SQR programs and COBOL executables. This tab setting also identifies any PeopleTools and MS Word executable directory.

Online help Any online documentation associated with Windows help or People-Books can be defined based on function keys and PeopleBooks search order.

Trace Several types of settings can be used during an online session. Trace can include PeopleCode trace, SQL trace, and message agent trace. The default online trace file is DBG1.tmp, which can be overridden by specifying an online trace file.

Common This tab specifies the language setting used on panels and related objects. The Cache file directory can also be specified on this tab. Data Mover, which is a database administration tool used to migrate application data and objects, requires an input, output, and log file. The directories for Data Mover files can be specified on this tab.

Application servers Any configured application server to which a client is allowed to connect to can be specified on this tab. Additional parameters are Application Server Name, Machine Name or IP Address, Port Number, Tuxedo Connect String. The Set and Delete buttons enable the entry and removal of Application Server Names.

Workflow Under the Workflow tab you specify the options and locations related to the Workflow implementation at your site.

PeopleSoft Workflow allows tasks to be automated into flexible business processes. From a technical perspective, the options required to use Workflow can be identified on this tab. Some items, which can be specified on this tab, include Message Agent, Forms, and Mail Protocol.

Database Databases such as DB2 and Sybase may require additional settings that can be used to improve or monitor the system operations. Some parameters include DB2 message size, Sybase packet size, and Application Designer image conversion which enables the conversion of images to a new format during upgrades.

Remote Call   The options on the Remote Call tab are related to the Tuxedo Remote Call. Transactions that require intensive memory and CPU resources can be run on a remote server. The parameters include the timeout, the debugging options, and the appearance on the desktop of a child COBOL process.

Client Setup   The Client Setup tab identifies the options which impact workstations as well as invoke the Client Setup process. The settings include Shortcut Links, 3-Tier Minimal Install, and ODBC Setup. When checked, the Install Workstation option connects the Client Setup function.

Import/Export   The environment settings established can be exported to or imported from a file using the information specified on the Import/Export tab.

Other   These settings impact the environment used to run the PeopleSoft quality server for manufacturing applications. These settings require two parameters, which identify the local data directory and SQR Output.

1.2.3   Navigation in PeopleSoft

Once you logon to PeopleSoft, the panels you see displayed depend on several factors:

- PeopleSoft products installed on your system
- the initial window default in the Configuration Manager
- the security profile of your operator ID, which allows you to view only certain panels

For example, a typical Human Resources user would have access to the Administer Workforce panels, illustrated in figure 1.9.

The panels and menus used in the delivered PeopleSoft applications can be easily navigated with proper knowledge of function keys and toolbar icons. Custom applications should also use the same convention as standard PeopleSoft applications. Throughout this book, you'll see figures which reference two small custom applications used to present the topics discussed. One application is used for problem tracking and the other links operator classes to office locations.

Let's discuss the objects found on a PeopleSoft application panel.

Menus are used to group functionally-related panels and panel groups. A typical menu in the HRMS system is illustrated in figure 1.10. The menu identifies the bar items contained in the menu. The menu navigation required to display the panel group illustrated in figure 1.9 can be written as

Navigation: Go → Administer Workforce (GBL) → Use → Hire

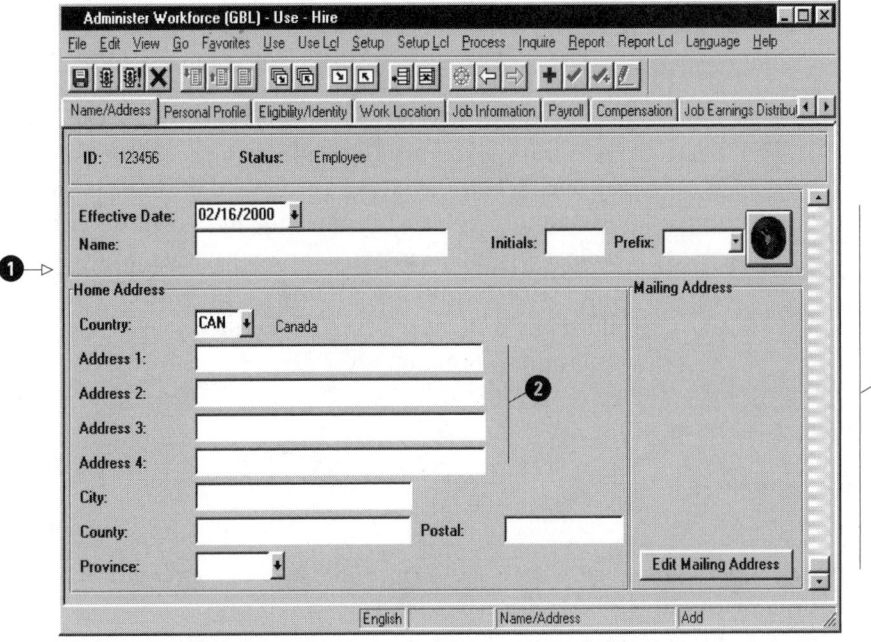

Figure 1.9   Administer Workforce panels

❶ Panel

❷ Record Fields

❸ Scroll Bar

Navigation: Administer Workforce (GBL) → Use → Hire

Figure 1.10   Menu portion of toolbar

❶ Menu Label

❷ Menu Bar Label

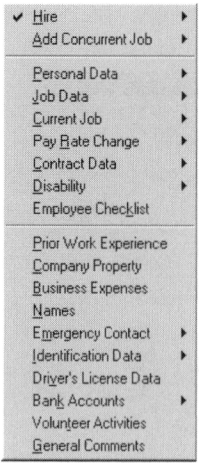

Figure 1.11   Menu items under the Use menu bar label

After the menu is displayed, each menu bar item may contain one or more menu items to which the operator has access. The menu items associated with the Use menu bar label are shown in figure 1.11.

Features, such as the toolbar, are common to PeopleSoft Applications. Specific panel functionality allows us to use the toolbar for saving data, submitting a process or canceling out of a panel. When a list is present, several list toolbar buttons can be used to display a list or move up and down the list. Additional toolbar buttons can be used to navigate from one panel to another or to insert/delete rows from a scroll bar. Figure 1.12 illustrates a standard toolbar available with most PeopleSoft applications using release 7.xx.

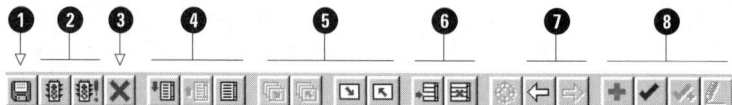

Figure 1.12   Typical PeopleSoft application toolbar

❶ Save button

❷ Run, Run with Defaults

❸ This cancels a panel

❹ Next in List, Previous in List, List

❺ Next Panel in Group, Previous Panel in Group, Next Panel, Previous Panel

❻ Insert Row (F7) Delete Row (F8)

❼ Change Window content, Back ⇐, Forward ⇒

❽ Add, Update/Display, Update/Display All, Correction

If you are familiar with Windows applications you know that the Save button is enabled after a change has been made to a panel. A save operation on a panel or panel group can also be performed by pressing the ENTER key.

Run and Run with Defaults are used to submit processes to the Process Scheduler. The Process Scheduler can submit a process such as an Application Engine, an SQR, or a COBOL program to be run on a client workstation or server.

The Cancel button is used to cancel activity on a panel.

Next in List, Previous in List, and List are activated when a partial key value is entered into a search dialog and the results of the search return more than one record. These buttons enable a list to be displayed and navigated upward or downward.

Next Panel in Group, Previous Panel in Group, Next Panel, and Previous Panel allow for movement between panels or panel groups.

Records which contain effective-dated rows or are part of a parent/child key hierarchy can be presented on panels that utilize scroll bars. The use of scroll bars enables us to work effectively with multiple record hierarchies. At the same time, however, scroll bars present unique challenges to both the developer and end user. (In subsequent chapters throughout this book, scroll bars will be discussed and explained in more detail.) Figure 1.9 is an example of a panel that contains one scroll bar. A panel with scroll bars may use the Insert Row and Delete Row icons. These icons are used to insert or delete effective-dated rows. Function key F7 can be used to insert data, while F8 deletes data.

The Change Window Content button is used to toggle on and off the business process maps. The Back and Forward buttons are used when navigation display is used with menus.

Additional buttons such as Add, Update/Display, Update/Display All, and Correction are used when data consisting of new keys are added or when data are updated.

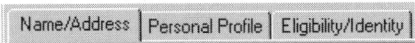

Figure 1.13 Tabs in a panel group

Panel tab labels identify the panels in a panel group and are used to move from one panel to another. An example of panel tab labels is shown in figure 1.13.

KEY POINTS

1 PeopleSoft has evolved from a traditional two-tier client server architecture in the earlier years, to a web based *n*-tier architecture in PeopleSoft.

2 PeopleSoft *n*-tier architecture enables various types users to access PeopleSoft applications. Application owners, end users, employees, and vendors can access PeopleSoft applications using various architectures and tools.

3 PeopleSoft provides applications that are robust, full of tools, and functionality.

4 The PeopleSoft sign-on process requires a connection type, database name or application server, operator ID, and password. These options can be set once using the Configuration Manager.

5 Menus, toolbars, and panels vary, based on the functionality assigned to an operator class.

6 Toolbar buttons as well as menu actions and function keys enable the end-user to save, cancel, insert, or delete data on a panel.

C H A P T E R   2

Development tools

In this chapter, we cover some basic concepts surrounding the primary development tools used in PeopleSoft. The Application Designer is a conglomeration of the primary development tools that design a PeopleSoft application. Prior to release 7 of PeopleSoft, objects were built using individual tool menus for each object. For example PeopleSoft 6 has Data Designer to develop record definitions, translate values, and so on; Panel Designer was used to build panels; and Menu Designer was used to build menus. Starting from release 7, however, PeopleSoft integrated all the development tools into an integrated menu, the Application Designer.

2.1 FIELDS

Fields are at the lowest level in the totem pole of objects in PeopleSoft. Fields are individual objects defined in a PeopleSoft system. One or more fields are assembled to form a record definition, and fields can be shared across record definitions. In other words, the same field can be used in more than one record definition. The basic attribute of a field is the same across all these record definitions. For example, a field defined as character field is always a character field across all record definitions.

The following field attributes are shared across all record definitions in the system.

- field type
- field length
- field decimal places
- translate values (optional)
- long and short names
- field formats

The field type, length, decimals (if any), long names, short names and field formats are the same across all record definitions. Translate values, although attached to a field, can be used optionally in record definitions. Fields on record definitions can be defined not to use the translate values attached to fields.

Field types allowed in PeopleSoft include the following:

- *Character* fields are usually used for codes in PeopleSoft.
- *Long Character* fields are used to store comments in PeopleSoft.
- *Number* fields can hold positive integers and decimal numbers.
- *Signed Number* fields can hold negative integers and decimals.
- *Date* fields can hold dates and is always represented in a "MM/DD/YYYY" format online regardless of how they are stored in the database.
- *Time* fields can hold time and are represented in a "HH:MI:SS.999999" format. Seconds and subseconds are optional and can be suppressed.
- *DateTime* fields can hold both date and time in one field. They are represented in the same format as date and time fields put together. They can be used to store date and time stamps in PeopleSoft.
- *Image* fields are used to store pictures in PeopleSoft. Some formats in which images can be stored are bitmaps, JPEG, Postscript, and so on. Employee photos are stored using Image fields in a PeopleSoft HRMS system.

Fields attributes are stored in a database table called PSDBFIELD, the catalog table, which is populated as fields are created and changed in a PeopleSoft system. All field definitions in a PeopleSoft system can be listed from this catalog table. During an application upgrade, this catalog table is used to compare and list out differences in fields across databases.

PSDBFIELDLANG   This language-related catalog table stores field long and short descriptions in alternate languages. The long and short descriptions can be used when a user, who has a default language other than English, accesses the field online.

When fields are used in record definitions, they are stored in a catalog table called PSRECFIELD. By querying this table we can find out all the records that use a certain field in the system. (See chapter 4 for more about creating fields in PeopleSoft.)

2.2   RECORDS

A record definition is a collection of fields. A record definition in PeopleSoft can be an SQL table, an SQL view, a Sub record, a Derived/Work record, a query view or a dynamic view. SQL tables and SQL views also exist in the database. Other types of record definitions are stored only in the PeopleSoft system.

Record definitions may possess a variety of attributes, but they can be categorized into three properties. The list of properties for a record definition include General properties, Use properties, and Type properties.

General properties contains a description of the record definition, the last date and time the record definition was updated, and the ID of the operator who updated it. Use properties defines the key fields, search fields, list fields, query security record, related language record, parent record, and the audit properties for the record definition. Type properties defines the type for the record definition. We define whether the record definition is an SQL table, an SQL view, and so on. under the Type properties. Let us look at some of the catalog tables that store properties of a record definition.

PSRECDEFN   Record definitions in PeopleSoft are stored in a catalog table called PSRECDEFN. This table stores all the primary attributes for a record definition. It holds attributes such as record type, audit record name, related language record, parent record name, query security record, index count, field count, and others. This table also holds the table space name for record definitions defined as an SQL table. All record definitions that are SQL tables or views are stored with a prefix of 'PS_'; all PeopleTools record definitions are defined with a non-standard SQL table name. The SQLTABLE-NAME field is an override to the 'PS_' prefix. In the database, the table name is stored with the value entered in the SQLTABLENAME field without the 'PS_' prefix.

PSRECFIELD   The PSRECFIELD table stores the fields that the record definition contains. Each field in the record can have its own edit properties. It can either have translate value edits, prompt table edits, or a Yes/No edit. These attributes are specific to the record definition field. Each field can also hold default values and PeopleCode events specific to the record definition. A field in this catalog table, called PROG-COUNT, contains the number of PeopleCode events for the record field. If this program count does not match the actual number of PeopleCode events for a given field, the record definition cannot be opened.

PSINDEXDEFN   The PSINDEXDEFN table contains a row for each index for the record definition. This table is populated only if the record definition is an SQL table or an SQL view.

PSKEYDEFN   The PSKEYDEFN table contains all the fields that the PSINDEXDEFN holds. All the record fields that compose the index are stored with the key sequence.

PSRECDDLPARM   The PSRECDDLPARM table has all the DDL parameters for the record definition. This is stored only if the record definition is an SQL table or an SQL view.

As you can see, record definitions serve as building blocks with fields assembled in them. It is important to remember that record definitions defined as SQL tables or views are also stored in the back end database. Other types of record definitions are stored only in PeopleSoft and are not database objects. Record definitions that are database objects have to be built in the database as well. Chapter 8 describes the process of building database objects from PeopleSoft record definitions.

PSRECDEFNLANG   This language-related catalog table stores long and short descriptions of record definitions. When a user has a default language other than English, the user can see record descriptions in his/her own default language. Developers can login to the system using alternate languages and enter descriptions in that language.

Other types of record definitions are Derived/Work records, query views, dynamic views, and subrecords. The use of Derived/Work records and subrecords are explained in chapter 6.

2.3   PANELS

Panels serve as user interface to the application. Panels are built using field and record definitions. Panels are a collection of record fields adhering to certain rules. Panels vary from simple panels, panels with scroll bars, panels with subpanels and secondary panels, and panel groups.

Let us look at all the panel field types used in PeopleSoft:

- *Frames* group fields logically. For example, fields used to hold an address can be grouped into a frame for clarity.
- *Group boxes* are similar to frames in the sense that they are also used to group fields. The difference is that group boxes are used to group the same field with translate values. Group boxes group the same record field with radio buttons representing different translate values. An example of a panel with group boxes is the PAYROLL_DATA2 panel in a PeopleSoft HRMS system.
- *Static Text* fields are used to hold free form text.
- *Static Image* fields store images that remain static and do not change at any point of time.
- *Checkboxes* store fields that either accept 'Yes' or 'No' for input. They can also be used to store fields that contain only two translate values. They can be turned on or off to store two different values in them.

- *Dropdown list boxes* are used for any field that has a prompt record. By clicking on the drop-down button, the user can invoke the prompt to produce a list of valid values.
- *Edit boxes* are very similar to drop-down list boxes except that they do not have a prompt list. Edit box is the most common panel field type in PeopleSoft. When a field that has a prompt record is defined as an edit box, the panel designer automatically changes the field into a drop down list box. The prompt button can be hidden using the Panel Field Properties screen.
- *Images* stores images in the database. Unlike static image fields, image fields can hold dynamic images. Images can be inserted into the panel field by either choosing the F5 key or by choosing "Edit/Insert Image" from the application menu.
- *Long Edit boxes* are used for long fields that are, in turn, used to enter comments. They can be sized to the desired height and length, and they scroll as more data are input into them.
- *Push Buttons* are used to invoke a command, bring up a secondary panel, or invoke a process. We will learn more about push buttons in chapter 6.
- *Radio Buttons* are fields that can contain a value from the translate table. They are used for record fields which have translate values in them. PeopleSoft has changed most of its radio button fields to drop-down list boxes in release 7. This makes a lot of sense because radio buttons restrict the values that can be entered into an application panel. Since radio buttons can hold only one translate value from a field, a radio button must exist for each translate value. In contrast, one drop-down list box shows all the translate values in a list.
- *Trees* represent data in a tree format. For example, departments can be entered using a tree format in a PeopleSoft HRMS system.
- *Grids* are used instead of scroll bars. They can replace single level scroll bars to represent data in a spreadsheet format. (See chapter 7 for more information relative to Grids.)
- *Scroll Bars* store multiple rows of data into the same record definition. Scroll bars can also be used to store effective dated rows in the system. (See chapter 7 for more information about scroll bars.)
- *Secondary Panels* are used to organize fields in a separate panel. When a panel has optional fields, those fields can be stored using a secondary panel. For example, in the PeopleSoft HRMS system, secondary panels are used to enter mailing addresses for employees. Secondary panels are invoked using push button fields. (See chapter 7 for more information about secondary panels.)
- *Subpanels* are used to organize fields from a subrecord. They are used as an input mechanism for repetitive fields. Addresses in any record definition contain standard fields such as street address, city, county, state, zip code, and country. A subpanel, which contains all these fields from a subrecord, can be built and used in more than one panel.

The following catalog tables are used to store panel definitions in PeopleSoft:

PSPNLDEFN   The PSPNLDEFN catalog table stores panel descriptions, field counts, panel types, and grid definitions. Panels are built using the same panel name in different languages. LANGUAGE_CD is part of this catalog table and stores one row for each language, if needed.

PSPNLFIELD   The PSPNLFIELD table stores the attributes of all fields in the panels. Some attributes stored in this table include the panel field type, the record name, the field name, the field labels, and so on. This catalog table also stores rows for panel fields in different languages, if necessary. Attributes such as Related Display and Control Display items are also stored in this catalog table. This catalog table has the most number of rows stored in the database among all PeopleSoft catalog tables because, for every panel field, one row exists in this table. Even if the same record field is used in ten different panels, ten rows are stored in the database.

2.4   PANEL GROUPS

Panel groups contain a series of panels that are either organized functionally or contain many record definitions. A single panel group can be used to store data into multiple records. Panel groups are ideal for records that have more than one child record. For example, in the PeopleSoft HRMS system PERSONAL_DATA is used to store personal information for an employee. JOB, EMPLOYMENT, and BEN_PROG_PARTIC are tables that store employment and benefit information for the employee. These tables are placed in a series of panels into a panel group called JOB_DATA.

Individual panels are attached to form a panel group. All the panels in a panel group use the same search record. Also, a search record can be defined when the ADD action is used. Panel groups can also contain work panels that can be hidden. In other words, the hidden panels will be invisible when the panel group is accessed online.

Panel groups were part of the menu object prior to PeopleSoft release 7. Starting from release 7, panel groups are objects themselves. Panel groups can be attached to more than one menu item. Panel groups are stored in their own catalog tables. Panel groups were part of the menu object prior to PeopleSoft release 7. Thus, as stated, starting from release 7, panel groups are objects themselves which means panel groups can be attached to more than one menu item.

PSPNLGRPDEFN   The PSPNLGRPDEFN table stores the panel group description, search records, processing location, and market definitions. Markets are used to store the same panel group using different market locations. For example, suppose we want to build different conditional logic for the same panel group for different user regions. The market field makes this possible.

Let's say that we want to use one panel group with two different market definitions for users in United Kingdom and the U.S. We want to have descriptions written using U.K. English conventions or U.S. English conventions depending on the market definition defined in the panel group. In this case, we first build the panel group with 'USA' as the market definition, then clone it by changing the market definition to

GBR. Logic can be built by using the system variable %MARKET%, available during panel processing.

PSPNLGROUP   The PSPNLGROUP table stores all the panels contained in the panel group. Each panel can have its own name and label. Item Name uniquely identifies the panel, and Item Label shows in the application menu. Panels can also be hidden within a panel group. All these definitions are stored in this catalog table.

PSPNLGDEFNLANG   This catalog table stores language-related descriptions for a panel group.

PSPNLGROUPLANG   This catalog table stores panel item names and labels in languages other than English.

2.5   *MENUS*

Menus serve as gateways to the application. Menus store panel groups that in turn hold application panels which help the user access data from the database. Menu items are individual items which hold a panel group and provide access to an application panel. Users have to be given access to a menu item to access an application panel. Panel level security can be managed using the Security Administrator menu in PeopleSoft.

Menus can be either "standard" or "pop-up" menus. Standard menus, used to create application panels, come with pre-defined menu items. File, Edit, View, Go, Favorites, and Help are the bar items that come predefined in a standard menu. Standard menus are included in a menu group, a collection of like menus grouped by function. When we create a Menu definition, we can specify the menu group for the menu. We can also specify the sequence for the menu within the menu group. We can likewise specify the sequence for the menu group, which can either be sorted numerically or alphabetically.

Pop-up menus are attached to panel fields and function as context sensitive menus. When the user right-clicks on a panel field, pop-up menus are activated. Pop-up menus are defined as a panel field attribute in the panel definition and do not have any predefined menu items. Pop-up menus, useful in bringing up help when the user needs it, can also be used to facilitate look-ups of related information for panels in a standard menu. Panel Fields can be highlighted to indicate the existence of an associated pop-up menu for the panel field by activating the Highlight Pop-up Menu Fields checkbox under the Display tab in the Configuration Manager. The following catalog tables store menu definitions:

PSMENUDEFN   This catalog table stores the menu definition. It contains the menu group name, the menu label, the menu sequence, the menu group sequence, and the menu type.

PSMENUITEM This catalog table holds the individual items in a standard or pop-up menu. It contains the panel group, the bar name, the item name, the item label, and the override search record name.

PSMENUDEFNLANG The PSMENUDEFNLANG table stores menu descriptions and labels in languages other than English.

PSMENUITEMLANG The PSMENUITEMLANG table stores menu item names, labels, and bar names in languages other than English.

Menus, when migrated to other databases, are migrated as a whole. Individual menu items cannot be marked for migration. For this reason, when menus are being developed by more than one developer, caution has to be exercised in moving these menus to other databases.

2.6 PEOPLECODE

Activated at different points of panel processing, PeopleCode events are used to control logic during panel processing. Some PeopleCode events are activated before a panel is brought up online; other PeopleCode events are activated during save time. The following PeopeCode events are available in PeopleSoft:

- `FieldDefault` PeopleCode is used to default values into a panel field.
- `FieldEdit` is used to edit values entered into a panel field.
- `FieldChange` is used to perform actions upon entry into a panel field. Other fields can be populated, depending on values entered into a panel field. Functions held in `Field Formula` PeopleCode can be called from `Field Change` PeopleCode.
- `FieldFormula` usually holds functions called from other PeopleCode events. `Field Formula` can also be used to perform logic based on values entered on several fields in the panel.
- `RowInit` is used to initialize fields in a panel before they are displayed.
- `RowInsert` is used to perform logic when rows are inserted on a scroll bar.
- `RowDelete` is used to perform logic when rows are deleted from a scroll bar.
- `RowSelect` PeopleCode is used to drop records on a scroll bar before they are displayed on the panel.
- `SaveEdit` is used to edit fields in the panel at save time. `Save Edit` can also be used to edit several fields in the panel.
- `SavePreChg` is performed before the data are stored in the database. It can be used to change values in panel fields just before they are saved in the database.
- `SavePostChange` is performed after the data are stored in the database. It can be used to insert values into other tables after save time.
- `SearchInit` PeopleCode is used to populate values into fields used as input fields for the application panel. Fields in search records which appear in the input dialog box contain the `Search Init` PeopleCode event.
- `SearchSave` is used to edit values entered in the input dialog box.

- `WorkFlow` events are used to create work flow to other users based on functions performed by the current user.
- `PrePopup` PeopleCode is activated before a panel is brought up on a pop-up menu.

The following catalog tables store PeopleCode events in PeopleSoft:

PSPROGNAME   This catalog table stores one row per PeopleCode event. It contains the record name and the field name that holds the PeopleCode event as well as the type for the PeopleCode event.

PSPCMNAME   This table stores references to other fields in PeopleCode events.

PSPCMPROG   This catalog table stores the actual PeopleCode text. It also holds the count of number of references made to other fields from the PeopleCode event.

2.7   PROJECTS AND UPGRADES

Projects are a collection of objects developed to build an application. Let's say we are developing a time and attendance system. We can include all fields, records, panels, panel groups, menus and PeopleCode used to develop this application. Projects are useful when you want to organize objects and migrate them to other databases. Projects can also be used for change control purposes.

Objects can be inserted into a project by either pressing the F7 key or by choosing "Insert/Objects into Project" from the Application Designer menu. Projects are stored in the following catalog tables:

PSPROJECTDEFN   This catalog table stores the project definition and also holds attributes such as commit levels, copy options, target database name, operator ID necessary to sign on to the target database, and report filter options.

PSPROJECTITEM   This catalog table stores all the objects included in the project as well as the object type, the action to be taken on the object during upgrade, and the copy status.

PSPROJECTMSG   The PSPROJECTMSG table holds error/status messages when projects are upgraded from the source to the target database.

2.7.1   Upgrades

Projects can be upgraded by accessing the Upgrade option from the Tools menu. Objects in projects are pushed from the source database to the target database. Prior to release 7, objects were pulled from the source database into the target database. In order to migrate objects, it was necessary to log into the target database. Starting from release 7, however, objects are pushed from the source database. This makes a whole lot of sense, especially in the implementation stage of a project. Usually, test and production databases exist in every implementation. As soon as development is finished, projects can be pushed to the test database for testing. Once the application is tested, the project can be moved to the production database.

2.8 CROSS-REFERENCE UTILITIES

Utilities, built inside the Application Designer and Utilities menus, are helpful during development in PeopleSoft. Let's take a look at these utilities and consider how we can use them.

2.8.1 Find object references

In the Application Designer, we can find where a particular object is being used by choosing "Edit/Find Object References" from the Application Designer menu. The object should be open first in order to find its object references. The result is then shown in the output window in the bottom of the Application Designer screen. Double-clicking on any of the resulting reference objects will open that particular object in the screen (figure 2.1).

Notice how the five objects which refer to MY_APPLICATION_ID field are shown on the output window in the bottom of the screen. We can find references for any object in the Application Designer by following the same procedure.

Navigation: Open → Field → MY_APPLICATION_ID → Edit → Find Object References

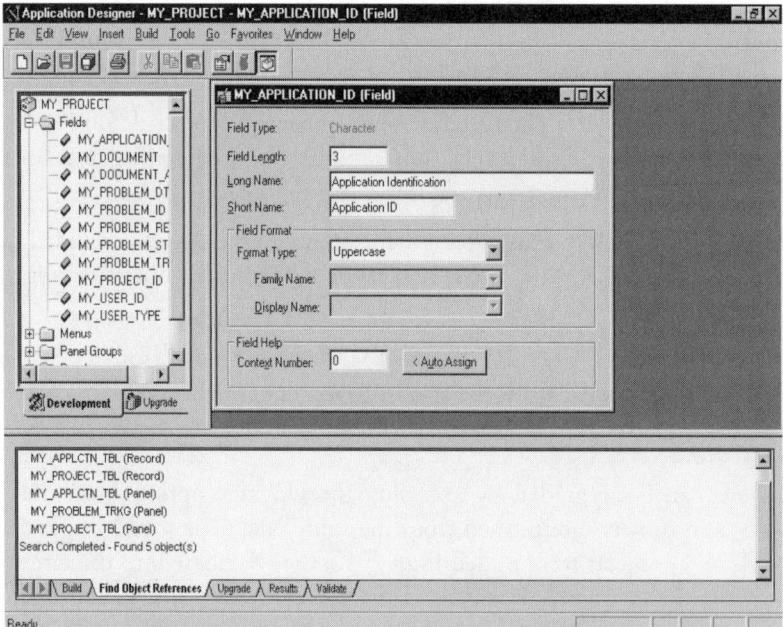

Figure 2.1   Find object references using the Application Designer

2.8.2 Find string In PeopleCode

Navigation: Edit → Find in PeopleCode

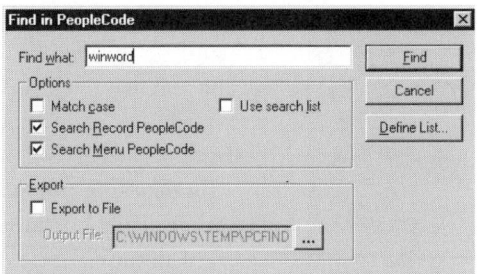

Figure 2.2 Find string in PeopleCode

Navigation: Define List (Find in PeopleCode)

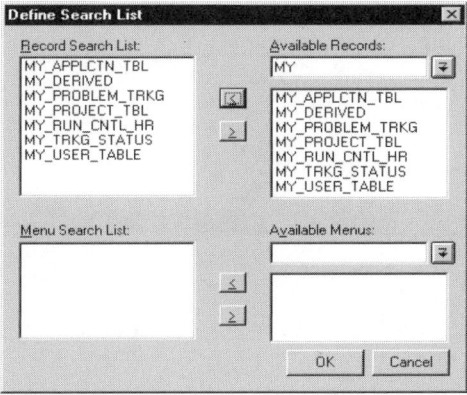

Figure 2.3 Define list of object to search

We can also search PeopleCode text in PeopleSoft to search for a string. This feature is useful for finding customized PeopleCode in the system. We should follow a convention in developing custom PeopleCode. We mark custom PeopleCode with a standard comment and use this comment as the string to search for all occurrences of custom PeopleCode. To search the PeopleCode for text, choose "Edit/Find in PeopleCode" from the Application Designer screen (figure 2.2).

We enter text as a search string in the box labeled "Find what." We also define a list of record definitions for search by clicking on the Define List push button. In figure 2.3 we define the list of record definitions and push them to the left-hand side of the screen. We click on "OK" to complete the list for search, and the output is displayed in the output windows of the Application Designer screen. When a list is not defined, all PeopleCode events in the database are searched for the occurrence of the text string.

The results of the PeopleCode search can also be exported into a file by choosing the Export to File option and specifying an output destination. The Match Case checkbox will match the string exactly for upper and lowercase characters.

2.8.3 Record Cross References

Navigation: Go → Utilities → Use → Record Cross Reference

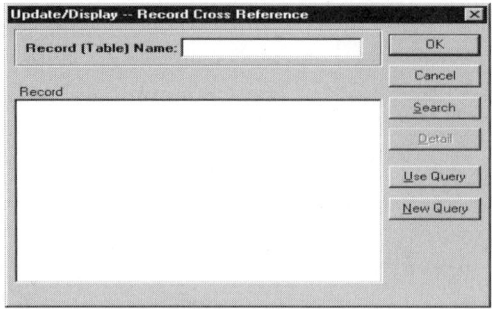

Figure 2.4   Record Cross Reference

We can find the Cross References for a record definition across all objects in the database by choosing "Use/Record Cross Reference" from the Utilities menu.

By choosing the record name in the input dialog box in Figure 2.4 we can find all the objects in the database that refer to the record definition.

In figure 2.5, two tabs exist which show information on objects that refer to the MY_PROJECT_TBL record definition. The first tab shows all the panels, views, and menu items that use the record definition. The second tab shows prompt definitions, field defaults, and PeopleCode events that use the record definition. The Record Cross Reference is a great tool to use to determine where a particular record definition is being used.

Navigation: Use → Record Cross Reference (from the UTILITIES menu)

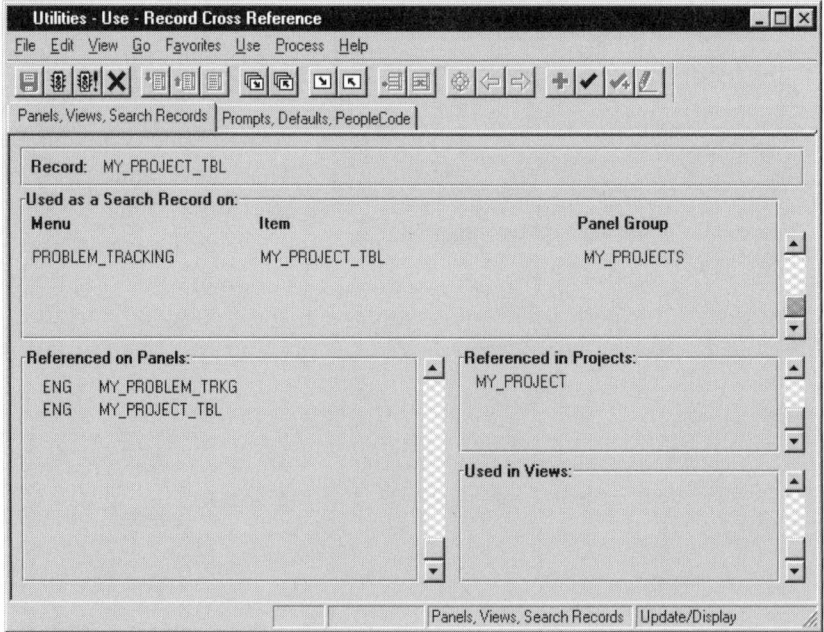

Figure 2.5   Record Cross Reference

All these utilities work using SQL views delivered with the PeopleSoft system. These views refer to the catalog tables that we have been visiting throughout this chapter. Some SQR programs, which come delivered with the system, also serve as cross reference utilities. These SQR programs start with an XRF prefix. For example, XRFFLPN.SQR shows references to fields from panels.

C H A P T E R   3

Administration tools

In addition to the tools discussed in chapter 2, PeopleTools provides mechanisms to load and unload data across database platforms. Simple prompt tables can be loaded using the Import Manager tool.

The Security Administrator provides a tool to manage PeopleSoft operator IDs. The ability to group many users into an operator class enables the individual(s) administering security to grant or revoke access to panels and processes much faster when the IDs are linked to a particular class.

Tree Manager is another tool that can be used for reporting security. This chapter presents an overview of these tools and will complement the information obtained in the chapters ahead.

3.1 DATA MOVER

Data Mover is a PeopleTool utility that enables the developer to move data from one database to another. Data Mover can also be used to move tables from one PeopleSoft platform to another. Most organizations have multiple databases such as production, QA, and development. Consequently, the need to move or unload data from one environment to another is a necessity.

3.1.1 Data Mover overview

Data Mover uses commands which can be entered ad-hoc or from predefined script files.

The scripts generated by Application Designer can be used in Data Mover to execute SQL statements against database tables without regard to database platform. Data Mover also uses scripts to load and unload data and to perform table manipulation. These scripts can be made up of Data Mover commands, SQL statements, or a combination of both.

Let's define a simple Data Mover script which unloads data from one environment and then loads the data into another.

Our first step is to sign onto the database. The sign-on process is similar to the PeopleSoft application sign-on described in chapter 1. After sign-on, the Data Mover window is displayed. This window is the mechanism used to process Data Mover scripts.

NOTE   Data Mover scripts do not necessarily have to be defined in the Data Mover window. Scripts are generated by Application Designer during create and alter table actions. Scripts can also be developed using a text editor.

In figure 3.1 the assumption is made that the script is defined in the Data Mover window. After Data Mover is launched, a new script can be defined.

The Data Mover window consists of an input window and an output window. Statements are entered into the input window and processed by the Data Mover PeopleTool. The data are captured on a file that can be supplied to another Data Mover script during a migration of data to another database or platform. Data Mover is extensively used during upgrades and specific system updates such as patches and fixes. Additional applications of Data Mover can be used for backups and restores or the movement of setup data. In the PeopleSoft HRMS application, the use of setup data such as Company, Department, and Locations can be moved to another database on a regular basis. This is very useful during testing or when it is necessary to have an environment similar to production. Reusable scripts can be developed to unload data from one database and load it into another.

Navigation: File → New

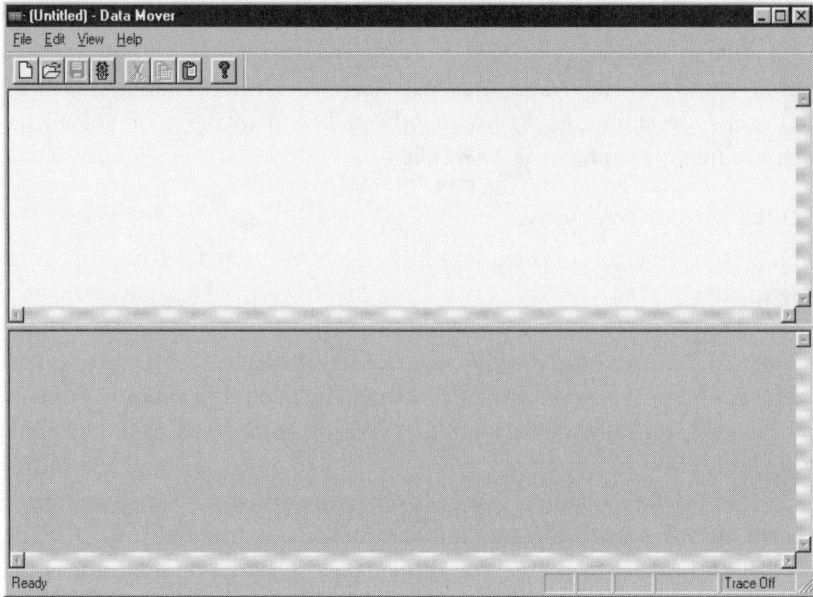

Figure 3.1   Data Mover window

NOTE   The use of Data Mover may not always be feasible when very large tables are moved. For large tables, database specific utilities such as Oracle Export/Import or DB2 SQL loader may be used. The disadvantage is that those tools have specific platform and database dependencies.

We've developed an application called Problem Tracking, to illustrate the tools and concepts used in PeopleSoft. In figure 3.2, Data Mover scripts are used to export several tables from the Problem Tracking system.

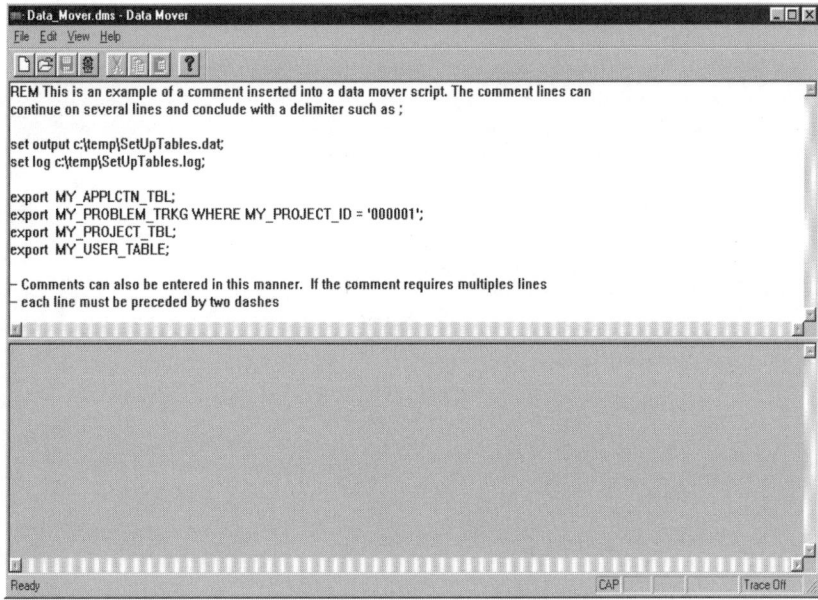

Figure 3.2   Data Mover commands

3.1.2   Examining the Data Mover script

Let's examine our Data Mover script. The first statement is a remark. In Data Mover, a remark can be entered by coding REMARK, REM or - -. The next two statements are Set commands, which are used to identify the environmental settings with which Data Mover will work. In the example, the first SET OUTPUT statement identifies an output file. When tables are unloaded, the specified output file will contain the exported data. The next Set statement represents a log file which records Data Mover activity. The activity is also displayed in the output window.

The Export statements are used to write the specified records to the file identified by the SET OUTPUT statement. The Export statement can accept an optional WHERE block, which can be used to limit the selected data to specific values. The contents of the WHERE block can be any valid SQL statements. In the example, Data Mover will only export entries from MY_PROJECT_TBL which have a MY_PROJECT_ID field containing '000001'. The other tables are exported in their entirety. Data Mover commands are delimited using a semicolon (;).

To run the script, click on the traffic light or select File → Run Script (figure 3.3).

The log file contains statistics such as run date, data mover release, and number of records exported for each table. The output file SetUpTables.dat contains the exported table entries and data. In a real world example (and depending on the number and size of tables exported), a file such as SetUpTables.dat can become very large.

Navigation: File → Run Script

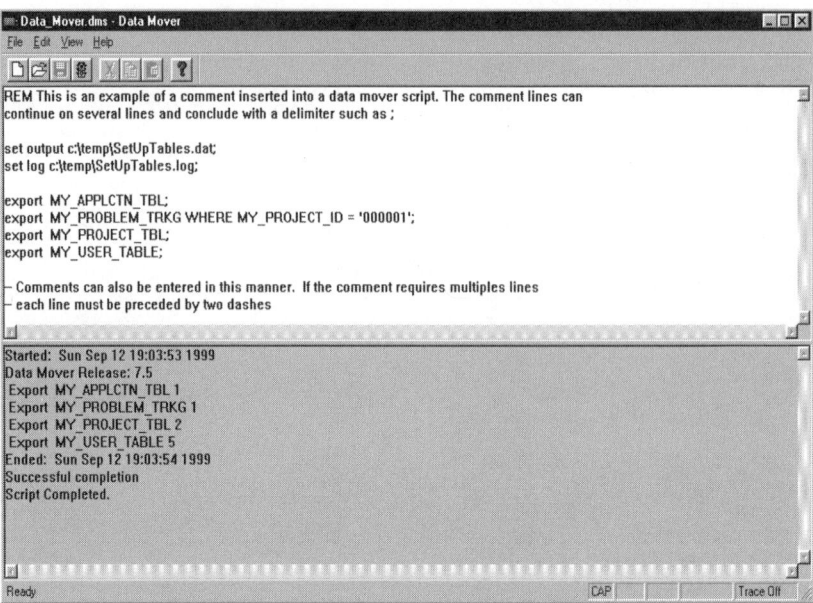

Figure 3.3 Data Mover windows after execution

This data can be saved for backup purposes or can be migrated to another database. Let's continue with the example and assume that the data will be loaded onto another database. Our next task is to load the data into another database. The statements used to accomplish this task are illustrated in figure 3.4.

The SET INPUT statement identifies the name of the input file for this script. In this example, the input file is the output file used in figure 3.3. The SET LOG statement refers to the file used in the export operation. The log file is written over and contains the results of the data load.

The next statement in the script is REPLACE_ALL. This statement drops the specified table and any associated indexes. The table and indexes are then created using the characteristics that appear in the input file. The data are then loaded into the specified table.

This example contains an embedded SQL statement. When the export operation is run as shown in figure 3.3, the Where statement is used to select only those rows in MY_PROBLEM_TRKG that contain a '000001' in the MY_PROJECT_ID field. This is done in order to preserve any existing data for MY_PROJECT_ID values other than '000001' on the target record. The Delete statement removes any '000001' values before the subsequent Import statement is processed. The Import statement does not alter existing table characteristics or data. For an existing

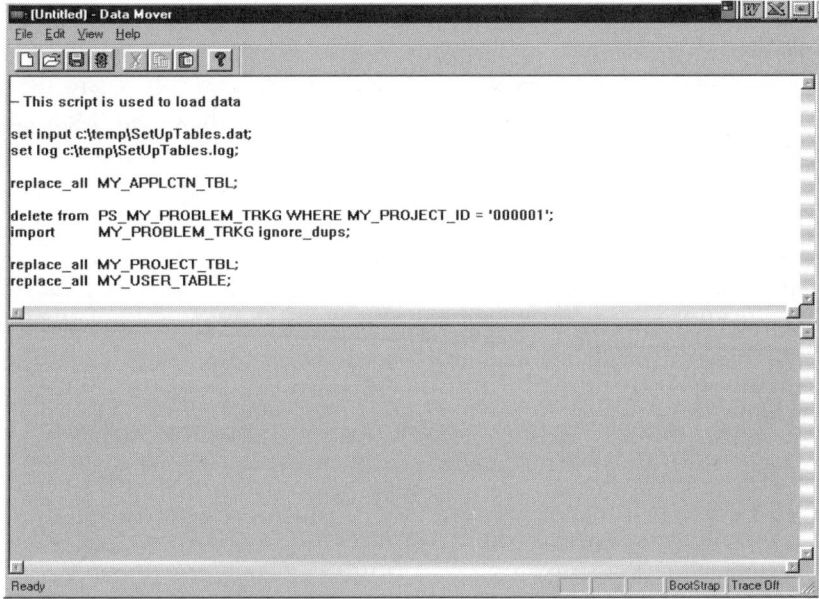

Figure 3.4   Data Mover script to load

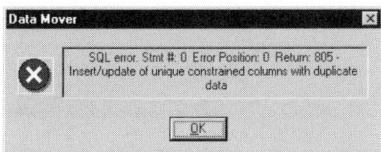

Figure 3.5   Data Mover duplicate data

table, `Import` inserts non-duplicate rows only. Duplicate entries generate an error message similar to the one illustrated in figure 3.5. Duplicate entries can be ignored using the `IGNORE_DUPS` parameter. `IGNORE_DUPS` permits duplicate row messages without abnormally terminating the import operation. In the example, the `IGNORE_DUPS` parameter is redundant because of the preceding `Delete` statement. The parameter should be used with caution because there may be instances where duplicate rows might indicate design errors in the export and import process. `REPLACE_DATA` is a version of the `Import` statement. The difference is that `REPLACE_DATA` first deletes data from the table and then inserts the corresponding data referenced on the input file.

3.2   IMPORT MANAGER

Import Manager is another tool that can be used to load Application data. A popular use of Import Manager is the conversion of data from one system to another or from one set of codes to a format compatible with PeopleTools tables. One unique feature of Import Manager is that, while data are loading, system edits are being performed as if the data were entered from a PeopleSoft application panel. Edits can also include

PeopleCode programs if necessary, and PeopleCode programs can contain code to execute when they are run during the Import Manager process only.

Import Manager works very closely with PeopleTools record definitions. The fields on the record definition are mapped to data on the Import Manager upload file. A great way to learn Import Manager is by example, so let's begin.

3.2.1   Defining an import definition

The following example loads data obtained from an existing legacy application to a soon-to-be implemented PeopleSoft HRMS system. The data are loaded into the Department table, and our objective is to build as much of the record information as possible. After the departments are loaded, the end user can complete the record with additional information.

The input file exists as an ASCII file with a fixed length format. (These are file requirements for Import Manager.)

Let's begin the Import Manager session:

Navigation: PeopleTools → Import Manager → File → New

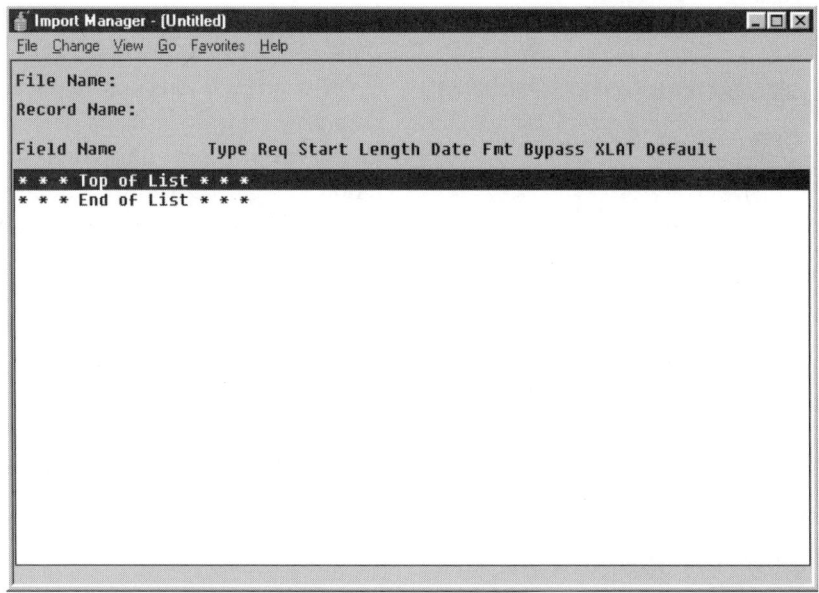

Figure 3.6   Import Manager window

Our next step is to assign a file name and record name to the Import Manager definition.

Navigation: Change → Header

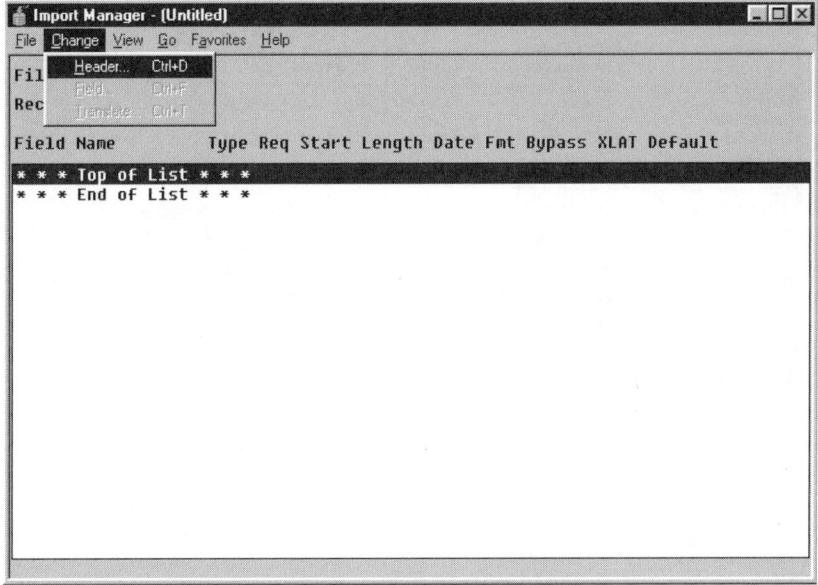

Figure 3.7   Header menu option

The Import Header information is displayed (figure 3.7). The record name is selected from a list box containing all available record names as shown in figure 3.8.

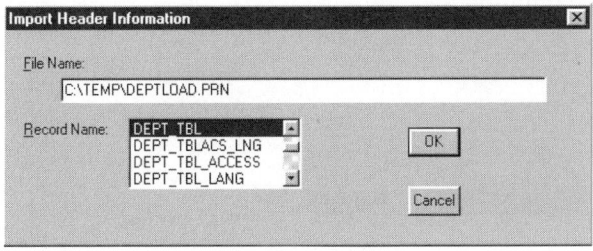

Figure 3.8
Defining header information

After the Import Header information is entered, we click OK and are presented with a list of field names from the DEPT_TBL record definition. The record field names are then available in the Import Manager window (figure 3.9).

```
 Import Manager - (Untitled)                                          _ □ ✕
 File  Change  View  Go  Favorites  Help

 File Name:
 Record Name: DEPT_TBL

 Field Name          Type Req Start Length Date Fmt Bypass XLAT Default
 * * * Top of List * * *
 SETID            |Char|Yes|   0 |  5   |            |  No  |  No  |
 DEPTID           |Char|Yes|   0 | 10   |            |  No  |  No  |
 EFFDT            |Date|Yes|   0 | 10   |YYYYMMDD    |  No  |  No  |%date
 EFF_STATUS       |Char|Yes|   0 |  1   |            |  No  |  No  |A
 DESCR            |Char|Yes|   0 | 30   |            |  No  |  No  |
 DESCRSHORT       |Char|No |   0 | 10   |            |  No  |  No  |
 COMPANY          |Char|No |   0 |  3   |            |  No  |  No  |
 SETID_LOCATION   |Char|No |   0 |  5   |            |  No  |  No  |
 LOCATION         |Char|No |   0 | 10   |            |  No  |  No  |
 TAX_LOCATION_CD  |Char|No |   0 | 10   |            |  No  |  No  |
 MANAGER_ID       |Char|No |   0 | 11   |            |  No  |  No  |
 MANAGER_POSN     |Char|No |   0 |  8   |            |  No  |  No  |
 BUDGET_YR_END_DT |Nbr |No |   0 |  4   |            |  No  |  No  |
 BUDGET_LVL       |Char|Yes|   0 |  1   |            |  No  |  No  |N
 GL#_EXPENSE      |Char|No |   0 | 35   |            |  No  |  No  |
 EEO4_FUNCTION    |Char|No |   0 |  2   |            |  No  |  No  |
 CAN_IND_SECTOR   |Char|No |   0 |  3   |            |  No  |  No  |
 ACCIDENT_INS     |Char|No |   0 |  3   |            |  No  |  No  |
 SI_ACCIDENT_NUM  |Char|No |   0 | 15   |            |  No  |  No  |
 HAZARD           |Char|No |   0 |  4   |            |  No  |  No  |
 ESTABID          |Char|No |   0 |  5   |            |  No  |  No  |
 RISKCD           |Char|No |   0 |  6   |            |  No  |  No  |
 * * * End of List * * *
```

Figure 3.9   Record Definition window

In this example, the Import Manager upload file contains basic information. To load a "stripped down" version of the department table record, three data elements in the input file are all that are required. By combining default values and one People-Code program, data can be loaded into the department table using the small input file illustrated in figure 3.10.

The mapping process can now begin. During this process we have several options. We can:

- point fields to columns on the input file,
- default fields by supplying default values in the Import Field definition, or
- provide no specific reference to fields. (The assumption is that this category of fields can either be populated later or will not require a value at all.)

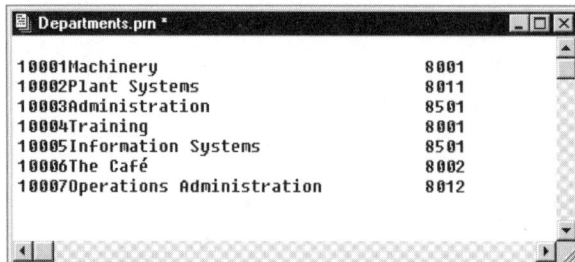

**Figure 3.10
Import Manager data file**

CHAPTER 3   ADMINISTRATION TOOLS

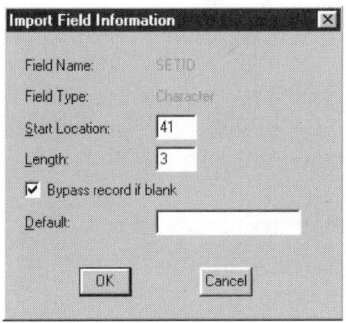

Figure 3.11   Field information window

The first field on the record is SETID. We double-click and enter the starting location and length on the corresponding input record. The dialog box to enter this information is illustrated in figure 3.11.

The default starting location is zero, and the default length is obtained from the record. In the example, SETID and COMPANY use the same value. This enables us to map these two fields to one specific column on the upload file.

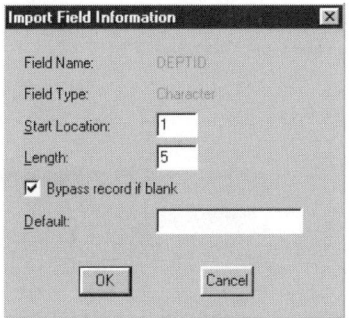

Figure 3.12   Assign department ID

The next field is DEPTID. DEPTID is the field which appears in column 1 on the upload file. The assignment for DEPTID is shown in figure 3.12.

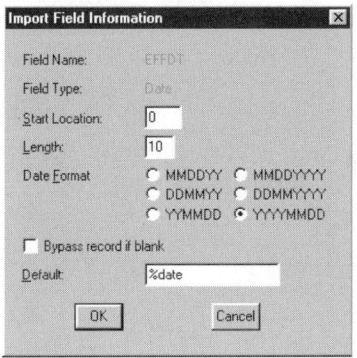

Figure 3.13   Date formats allowed

The next field is the Effective date. EFFDT is defaulted to the current date (figure 3.13).

Import Manager default values are taken from the default value setting in the Application Designer Record Field properties. When an actual date value is loaded, Import Manager allows date formats to be specified.

Another feature of Import Manager is that field contents can be translated from one value to another. The translation process occurs before the record is inserted into the database. This is useful when data are being converted from a legacy application. In the example, column 39 on the upload file contains a comparable effective status value as it exists on the legacy application. We know that, in PeopleSoft, the EFF_STATUS field Xlat values are A and I, which represent Active and Inactive respectively. The legacy application equivalents are 1 and 2. The EFF_STATUS field information appears in figure 3.14.

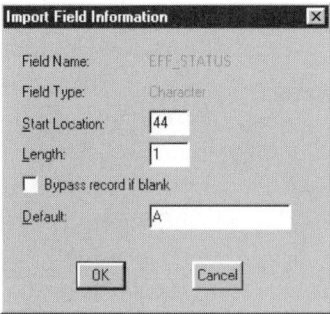

Figure 3.14   EFF_STATUS

When loading the effective status, blank values are not bypassed; they are defaulted to A. To set up translate values for EFF_STATUS, the field is highlighted in the Import Manager window followed by the corresponding menu action.

The Translate Values dialog box (figure 3.15) enables the entry of old and new values. Figure 3.16 illustrates how old and new values are entered into the dialog box.

Navigation: Change → Translate

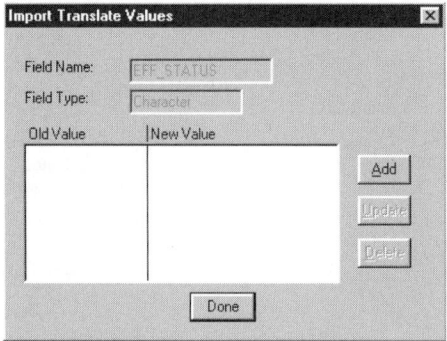

Figure 3.15   Translate values dialog

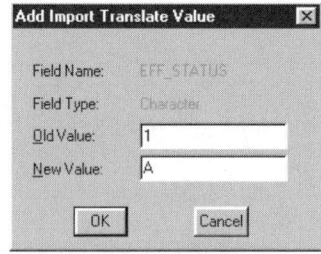

Figure 3.16   Entering translate values

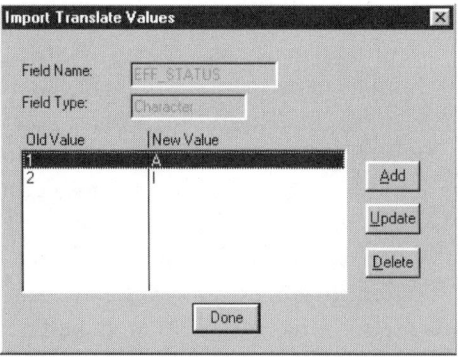

Figure 3.17   Completed translate values

The completed translate values are identified in figure 3.17.

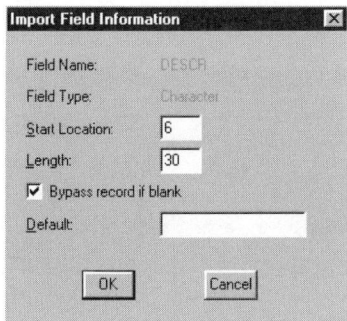

Figure 3.18 Department description

The next two fields, DESCR and DESCR-SHORT, contain the full department description as well as a short description. On the upload file, the description appears in column 6. Because the next field on the upload file begins in column 36, we allow a 30 character length for DESCR and 10 for DESCRSHORT. The field information for DESCR is illustrated in figure 3.18.

The start and end columns of data on the upload file must be tracked carefully. It is possible to load the contents of one field into an incorrect column on the record. This is particularly true for fields that do not contain edits.

The "Bypass record if blank" box is checked for COMPANY, SETID, and DESCR. For EFF_STATUS, blank fields are allowed and are subsequently defaulted to A. Fields considered important, such as descriptions, key fields, or codes, should not be passed as blank whenever possible. In our example, we are loading "skeleton" records onto the department table which contains the significant data elements (SETID, DEPTID, DESCR). The EFF_STATUS is defaulted to Active if the data are not available. Some end-user involvement may exist after the process is completed. For this example, identifying departments as active or inactive can be one of these tasks.

The next field, COMPANY, shares the same position on the upload file as SETID. All other remaining fields are either defaulted based on the record definition or are left blank.

Navigation: Import Manager → File → Save

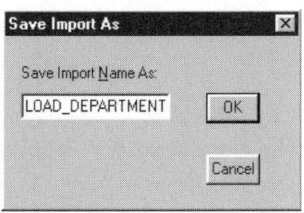

Figure 3.19 Import Manager save dialog

After these tasks are completed, our next step is to save the import definition (figure 3.19).

The Import Manager definition is now completed (figure 3.20). To view the definition based on the input order on the file, use the view menu option.

Navigation: View → Input Order

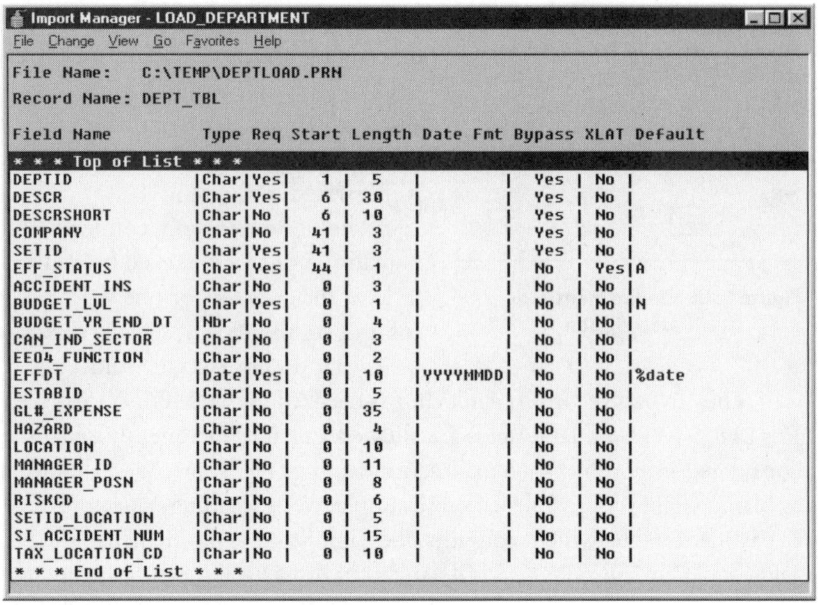

Figure 3.20   Completed Import Manager definition

When viewing the import definition fields we can see that Import Manager has several menu options available:

Navigation: View → Record Order	This is the default. Fields are displayed as they appear on the record definition.
Navigation: View → Input Order	Fields are displayed based on starting column positions of the upload file.
Navigation: View → Alpha Order	Record is displayed based on alphabetical field names.

One additional item which can play a role during the Import Manager process is People-Code. When the import definition is run, the following PeopleCode events are executed:

- RowInit
- FieldEdit
- FieldFormula
- SaveEdit
- SavePreChg
- WorkFlow
- SavePostChg

Based on the PeopleCode events identified, let's insert a small piece of code that concatenates the company into the description field. This will help identify departments which were migrated from the legacy system. The code is inserted into the SaveEdit event:

```
If %Import = True Then
   DESCR = RTrim(DESCR, " ") | " (" | COMPANY | ")";
End-If;
```

The %Import system variable is verified for a return value of True. The system variable indicates this is an Import Manager session. During non-Import Manager sessions the variable returns False. As a result, any code in the context of the If statement is not executed.

NOTE	PeopleCode is discussed in part 3 and appendix E also contains a selected list of PeopleCode built-in functions.

3.2.2 Running the Import Manager

At this point, we are now ready to run the import. The run import dialog box, shown in figure 3.21, contains a list of import definitions, run types, and report parameters.

Navigation: File → Run

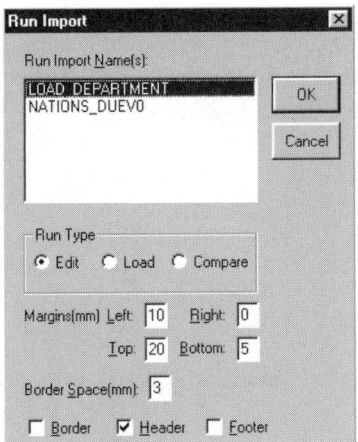

Import Manager can be run in one of three modes:

Edit	Generates a report based on the data in the upload file. No database inserts are performed.
Load	Attempts to write to the database. Edits are also performed against record keys, and translate and prompt tables. Effective date processing is implicitly performed.
Compare	Performs the same function as Edit. This is reserved for future use.

Figure 3.21   Run Import window

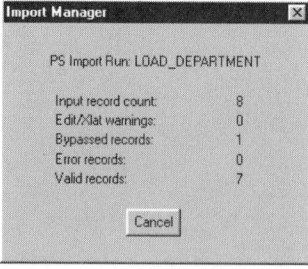

Import Manager displays a run status window (figure 3.22) that indicates the number of input records processed. For very large input files, we can identify the number of valid records or records that generate errors as Import Manager is processed.

Import Manager produces a report containing the record counts (figure 3.23).

Figure 3.22   Import Manager run status

```
Printed: 09/12/99  8:02:08PM   Database: HRDMO   PS Import Run: LOAD_DEPARTMENT   Version: 26   Page: 1

Record Name: DEPT_TBL
Run Type:    Edit

End of run.
     Input record count:  8
     Edit/Xlat warnings:  0
     Bypassed records:    1
     Error records:       0
     Valid records:       7
```

Figure 3.23   Import Manager report

Finally, let's look at the end results. The department profile within PeopleSoft is illustrated in figure 3.24. Note the embedded company code in the description field. This is accomplished using the small piece of PeopleCode inserted into the `SaveEdit` event.

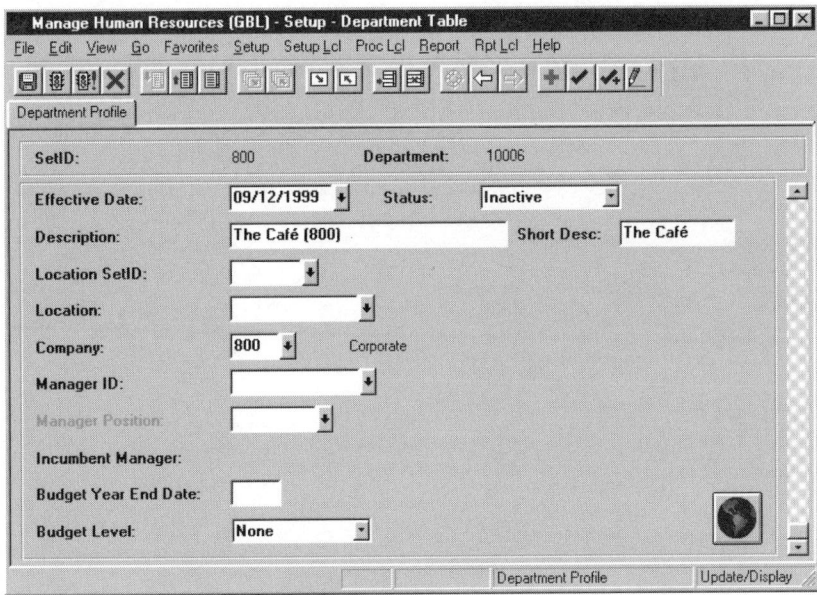

Figure 3.24   Results of Import Manager run

3.3   SECURITY ADMINISTRATOR

PeopleSoft security is comprised of operators and classes of operators. An operator is the individual ID assigned to a user. A class of operators is a profile that includes the menu items and type access each operator assigned to the class will have.

3.3.1   Defining an operator class

In this section we define a simple operator class and assign an operator ID to it.

The Security Administrator can be entered using the menu (figure 3.25).

Navigation: Go → PeopleTools → Security Administrator → File → New

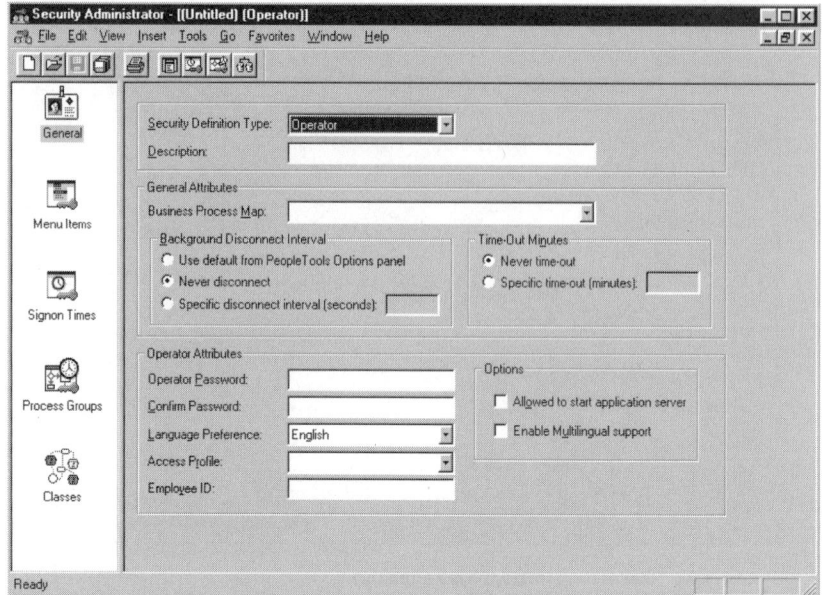

Figure 3.25   Security Administrator panel

Several options are available based on whether the security definition type is operator or class of operators:

- General
- Menu items
- Sign-on times
- Process groups
- Classes

General

First, we define a class of operators. To define a class, select "Class of Operators" from the Security Definition Type list box. An optional 30 character description can be entered. The General Attributes section contains several settings. Business Process Map identifies the path within the business process to which the operator class will have access to when using the Navigator. In HRMS, business processes are events such as New Hires and Terminations. These events are graphically represented in the business process.

The Background Disconnect Interval uses the default from the PeopleTools option panel. This feature enables a database connection to be released when the instance is moved to the background or is minimized as an icon. The connection is reestablished when a database call is required for SQL statements.

The Time-Out feature specifies the amount of inactivity allowed in minutes. The system signs off the ID after the threshold period has been exceeded. The General options are illustrated in figure 3.26.

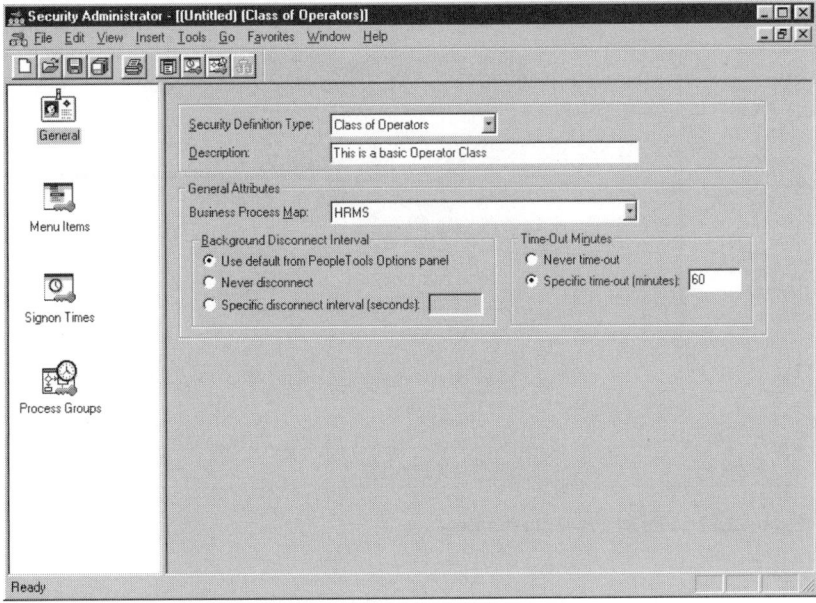

Figure 3.26   General Security options

At this point, we can save the panel by supplying an operator class name, then proceed to insert menu items.

Menu Items

Menu Items are the main components of an operator class. Here we select menus and make specific menu items accessible to each operator class. Click on the Menu Items icon within the Security Administrator window.

Our next step is to insert a menu (figure 3.27).

A list of available menus is provided. In the example, we select the ADMINISTER_WORKFORCE_(GBL) menu by double-clicking on its name. A list of associated menu items is displayed (figure 3.28).

When the Select Menu Items window is presented, we can either press the Select All button or select only those menu items the operator class is allowed. View Only security can be given by clicking on a menu item and then clicking the Change Display-Only button. The DispOnly column will then contain the value Yes. Display Only security

Navigation: Insert → Menu Name

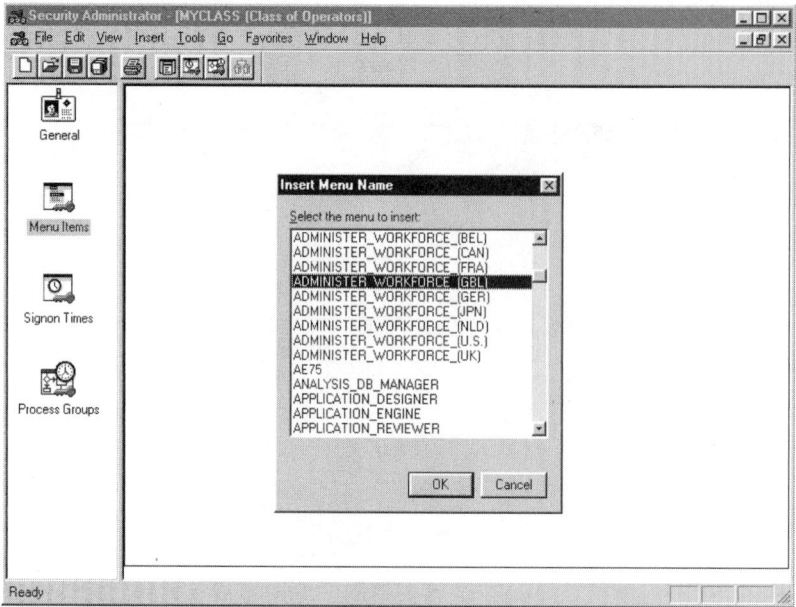

Figure 3.27 List of available menus

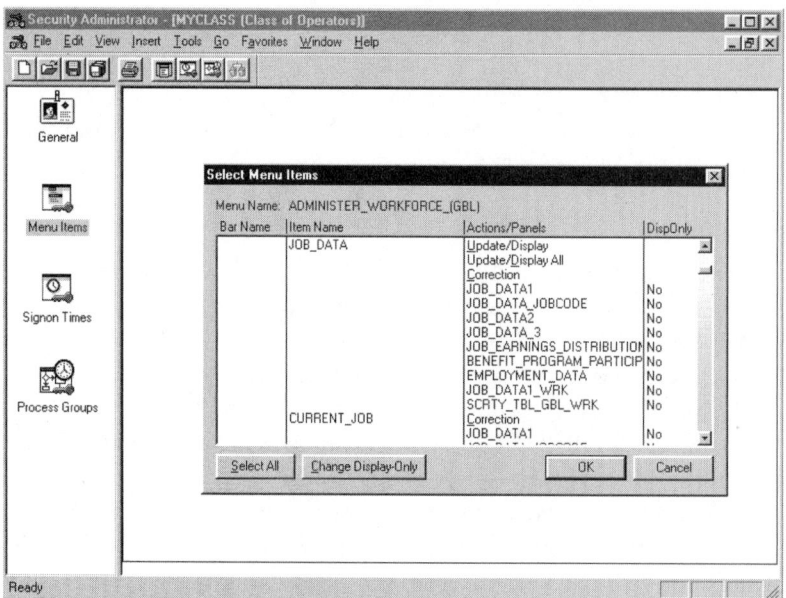

Figure 3.28 Select menu items window

permits the operator to view data, but does not allow changes. Figure 3.29 identifies the menu items selected for the ADMINISTER_WORKFORCE_(GBL) menu.

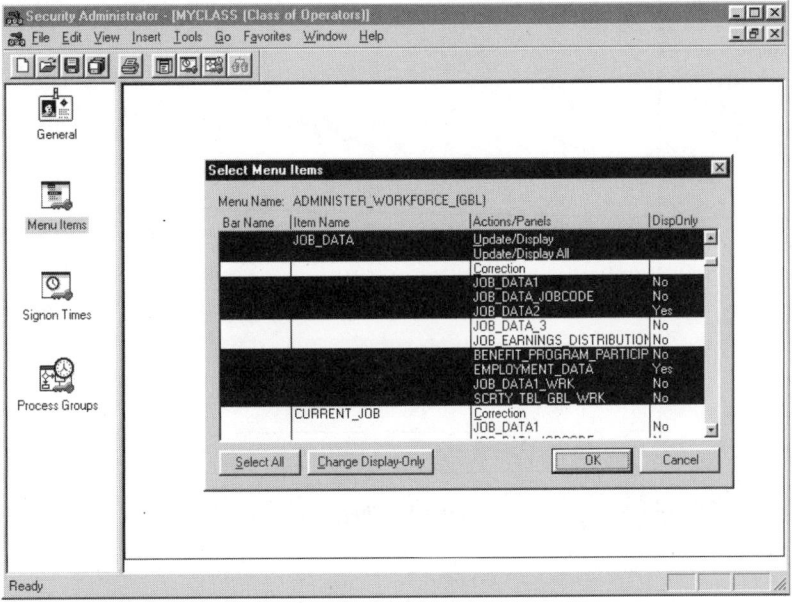

Figure 3.29   Menu Items selected. Note DispOnly option Yes

Note the DispOnly column for the JOB_DATA2 and EMPLOYMENT panels. Based on the menu items selected, any operator IDs assigned to this class have access to the JOB_DATA panels as follows:

- JOB_DATA1   Update/Display, Update/Display All
- JOB_DATA_JOBCODE   Update/Display, Update/Display All
- JOB_DATA2   Display Only
- BENEFIT_PROGRAM   Update/Display, Update/Display All
- EMPLOYMENT_DATA   Display Only

To enable the operator class to run queries, the Query menu is inserted into the profile as well. The operator class now contains two menus (figure3.30).

Signon times

To display sign-on times, click on Signon Times or select View → Signon Times (figure 3.31):

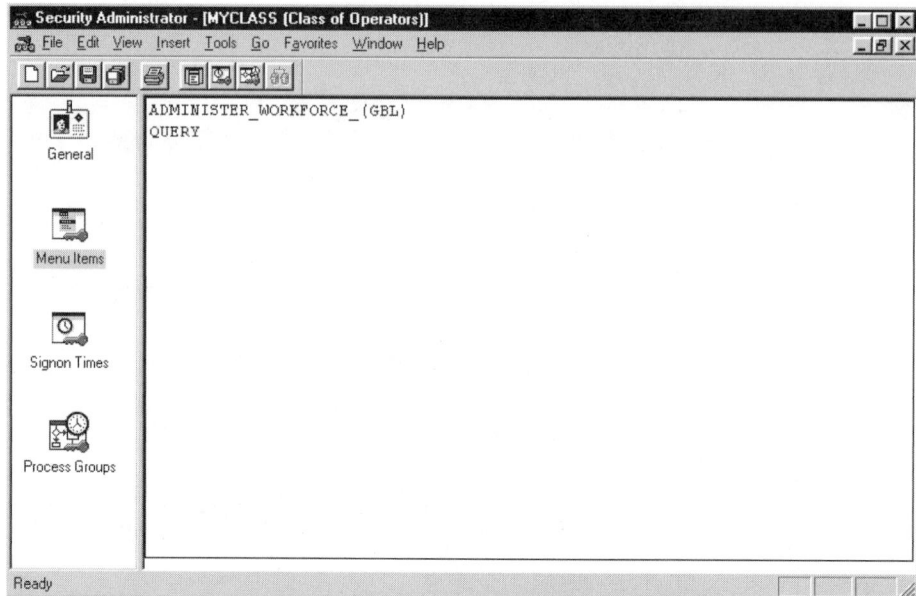

Figure 3.30   Menus allocated to operator class

Navigation: View → Signon Times

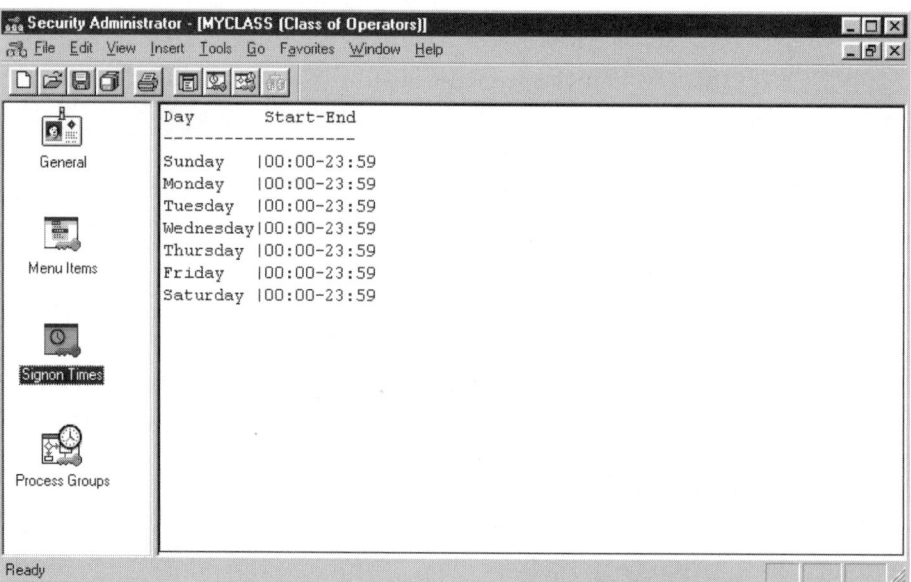

Figure 3.31   Authorized sign-on times

Figure 3.32 Modify authorized sign-on time

Navigation: Insert →
                Signon Times

Figure 3.33 Second time period

Navigation: Insert →
                Process Group

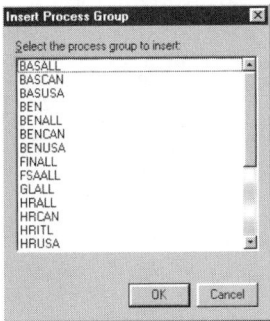

Figure 3.34 Adding a process group

Sign-on times identify what days of the week (and hours within those days) during which a user is authorized to logon. In some organizations sign-on times are restricted to prevent updates during batch cycle runs such as Payroll. Occasions also exist when activities such as database reorganizations or data migrations occur, which may require limited access for specific periods of time.

The authorized sign-on times display consists of two columns, Day and Time, representing the allowed sign-on times for each day of the week. To change the sign-on times, double-click on the day of the week.

We can have multiple sign-on times during the day, provided the time ranges do not overlap. Let's assume, for example, that Saturday is the system maintenance window, and, with the exception of a few IDs, no one else should be on the system between 17:01 and 21:30. To enforce this, we can change the time range for Saturday and then insert an additional time period which allows for sign-on after the maintenance window.

To change the Saturday sign-on time, double-click on Saturday and change the time as shown in figure 3.32.

This change enables the user to be logged on between 00:00 and 17:00. To add additional time periods, select Insert → Signon Times (figure 3.33).

Modifying the sign-on time ensures that our users are not on the system during the Saturday time period 17:01–21:29. This information may help provide clues when a help desk report reads `User mysteriously disconnected from system`.

Process groups

The next available item in the Security Administrator window is process groups. When process definitions are set up using the Process Scheduler PeopleTool, the definitions are linked to one or multiple process groups. When a process is defined and attached to a process group, that process cannot be run by an operator until the class contains the process group as part of its definition. A process group can contain many process definitions.

To add a process group, select Insert → Process Group (figure 3.34).

At this point we have an operator class with two menus. The class is disconnected after sixty minutes of inactivity. With the exception of the Saturday 17:01–21:29 time period, the operator class can be logged onto the system at all other times.

3.3.2   Linking operator IDs to an operator class

Now that an operator class has been defined, we need to define an operator ID and link it to the class. Before proceeding, do not forget to save the operator class settings.

To establish an operator ID, click on the General icon in the Security Administrator window or select the View, General menu item.

The next step is to change the security definition type to Operator and enter an optional description. The General Attributes section is required when an operator ID is not linked to an operator class.

The operator attributes are defined as follows:

- *Operator Password*   The Operator Password is the password the operator will require during sign-on.
- *Confirm Password*   This field is compared to the operator password and must match its value.
- *Language Preference*   This option overrides the base language setting defined in the configuration manager. The option can be left blank to use the default setting. The language preference can be overridden using the Configuration Manager as discussed in part 1.
- *Access Profile*   After the operator has been validated during logon, this parameter identifies the ID and password used to connect to the database. A typical access profile is SYSADM.
- *Employee ID*   The Employee ID field contains the operator's PeopleSoft EMPLID, which is compared against the database and prevents users from changing their own data.

Additional options also exist. They include:

- *Start the application server*   This option indicates whether or not the user is allowed to start the application server. Access to this option is commonly limited to system administrators.
- *Multilingual support*   This option permits the user to work in multiple languages. The user does not have to log off or change his/her language preference setting.

The appropriate fields are entered and saved. The operator ID profile is illustrated in figure 3.35.

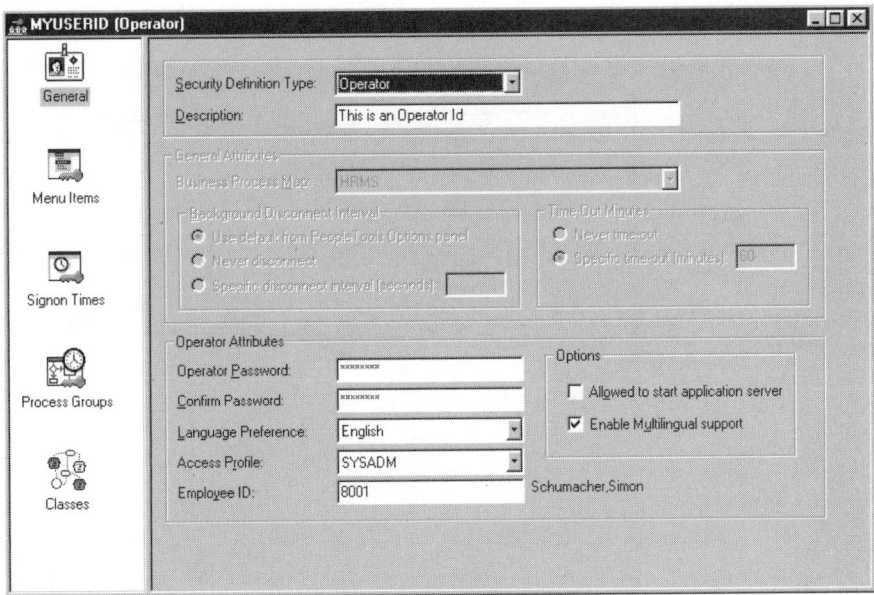

Figure 3.35 Operator ID attributes for MYUSERID

In this example, the operator ID is linked to the MYCLASS profile which implies that the menu items, sign-on times, and process groups will be defaulted from the class profile.

To link the operator ID to one or more classes, click on the Classes icon in the Security Administrator window or select View → Classes From the Menu (figure 3.36).

Navigation: View → Classes

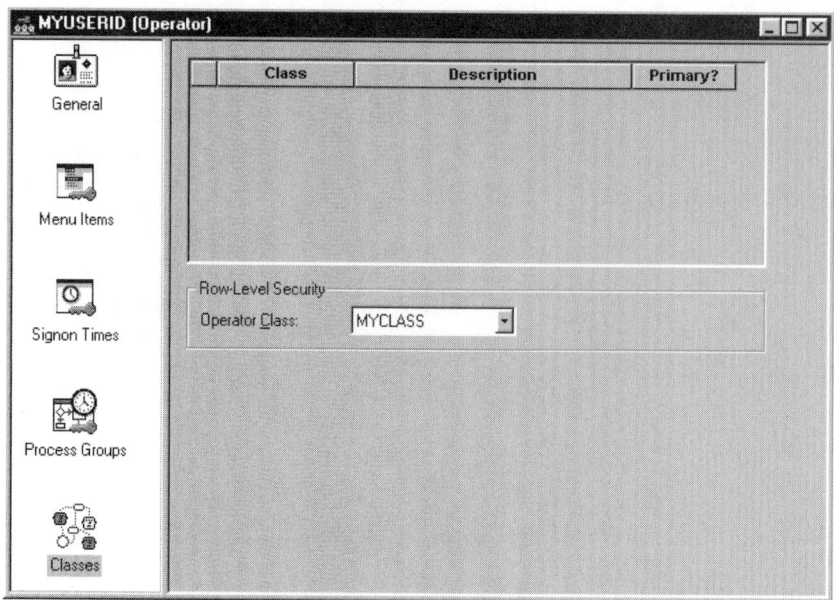

Figure 3.36   Viewing operator classes linked to an ID

Navigation: Insert → Class

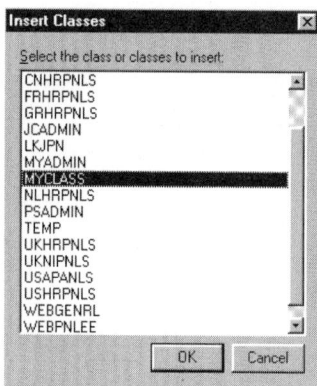

Figure 3.37   Attaching operator class

To attach one or more operator classes to an ID, we can select Insert → Class (figure 3.37).

The operator ID MYUSERID is now linked to the class MYCLASS and is authorized to use the menu items selected.

Operator classes serve an important function, particularly from a table space and system administration perspective. The System Administrator allows operator IDs to be defined without a link to an operator class. This may be useful for a handful of IDs, but when hundreds or thousands of IDs are necessary, quite a large amount of system resources and administration time are involved. The one-to-many ratio between a class and many operator IDs reduces the number of rows in the PSAUTHITEM system table. This tool table contains the authorized menu items allocated to an operator ID or class. Without classes, a system with one hundred users would require at least one hundred times the amount of rows in the PSAUTHITEM table. System resources are improved, for example, when ten distinct classes of operators are allocated among the one hundred operator IDs. From an administration perspective, security is facilitated when IDs are grouped into classes.

When it becomes necessary to add additional operator classes, we use the Insert Classes menu and select the appropriate classes. An example of MYUSERID with additional classes allocated is illustrated in figure 3.38.

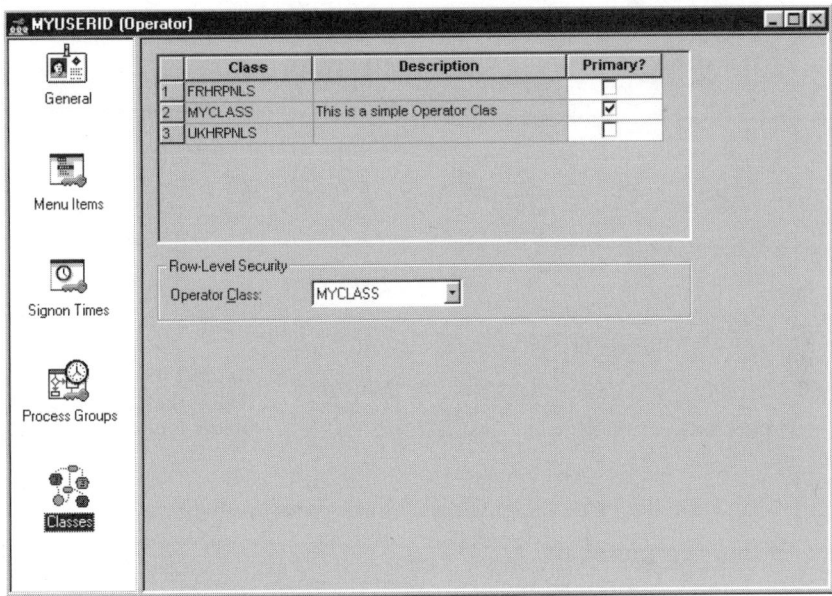

Figure 3.38   Allocating classes to an ID

The example in figure 3.38 identifies MYCLASS as the primary operator class. Any menu items associated with the two additional classes are made available to MYUSERID. Row level security is used to limit access to specific data linked to the security search views.

3.3.3   Restricting Application Designer Access

An IS organization can include developers and functional analysts supporting or implementing a PeopleSoft application. Sometimes a rift between developers and functional staff, and even among developers themselves, may arise when the issue of security is addressed. The question of who has access to specific tools is often a touchy subject. Some developers do not want undocumented changes made to objects. This is a justified argument, particularly when the changes cause production problems or do not appear until the next upgrade, during which time the culprits have either moved on or developed short-term amnesia.

When a group requires restricted access to an entire object type, such as panels and menus in the Application Designer, the access can be restricted using the Application Designer Access feature shown in figure 3.39.

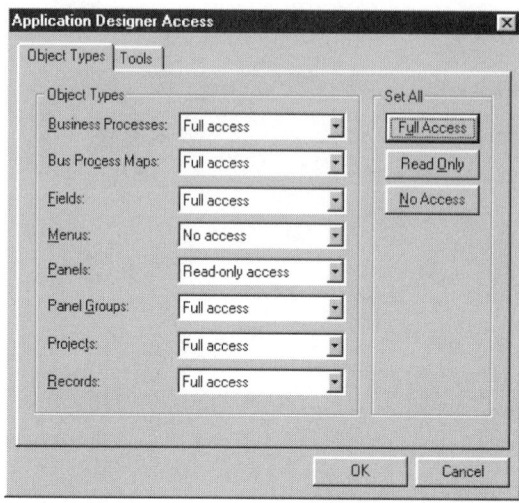

**Figure 3.39
Restricting access to an entire
object type**

In release 7.xx of PeopleTools, object types are defined as:

- business processes
- business process maps
- fields
- menu definitions
- panel/panel group definitions
- project definitions
- record definitions

The example in figure 3.39 does not allow menu access in Application Designer and enables read-only access to panels. Now, let's assume we have someone who is assigned to work on specific functionality but requires access to update menus and panels. This can cause a dilemma. On the one hand, we want the person to make the necessary changes to a specific set of panels and menus. Alternatively, we have to change the settings to Full Access for menu and panel objects. How can this quandary be solved? The answer is Object Security, our next topic of discussion.

3.4   OBJECT SECURITY

Object security is an additional layer of security which can be used to restrict access to PeopleTools objects such as record definitions, panel definitions, menus, and others.

Object security is also used at the field level. When a modification to a field on a record is required, object security access is necessary. A change that involves the modification of a field label or field attribute will require access to every record that contains the field.

3.4.1 Object groups

Object groups are the entities defined using object security linked to security administrator profiles. The object group can be comprised of objects related to specific applications such as Human Resources or General Ledger. The object group can also include PeopleTool objects such as records, menus, and panels. Object security is applied to object groups only and not to individual objects.

Let's define a simple object and attach it to a security profile. The initial object security window is shown in figure 3.40.

Navigation: Go → PeopleTools → Object Security → File → New Group

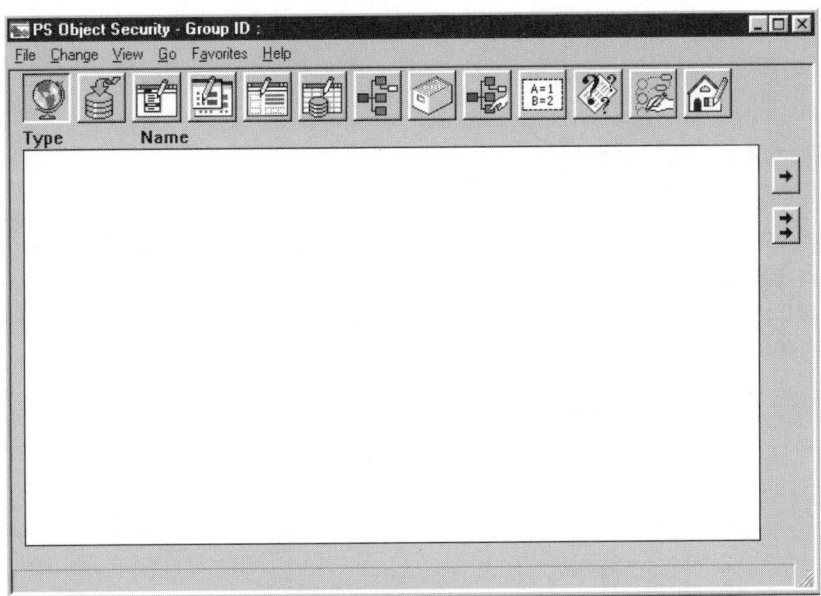

Figure 3.40 Object Security panel

Let's assume that we are working with a developer to enhance a few of our custom applications. These applications include some HRMS objects. The developer is allowed access to these objects only. To define an object group, we must select which objects to add or remove from the group. When defining a new object group, the objects associated with the object type are selected using the toolbar or menu. To select record objects, select View → Records From the Object Security Menu (figure 3.41).

Navigation: Object Security → View → Records

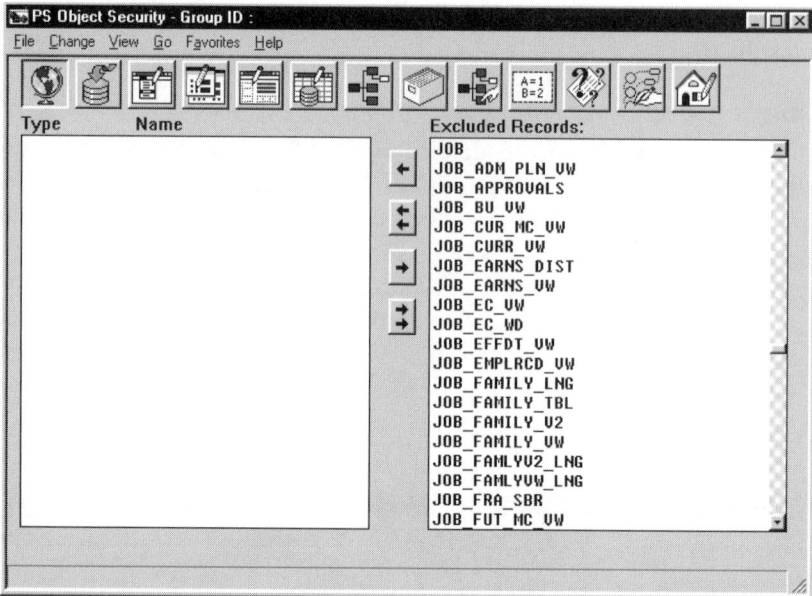

Figure 3.41 View record definition objects

For this example, we can choose the records prefixed with JOB and move them to the left side of the panel. The left side indicates the objects included in the object group and the right side represents the excluded objects. The arrows can be used as follows:

← moves selected object(s) to the left side

⇐ adds all objects in the excluded group to the left side

→ moves the select object(s) to the excluded group

⇉ moves all objects to the excluded group

The selected records and panels related to specific HRMS functionality are also added to the object group. The object group build is completed with the addition of panel groups and menus. After all the objects are added, the object group can be saved.

After the object group is saved, the objects can be viewed using the View All menu selection. The selected objects and related types are displayed in the panel (figure 3.42). The Type column contains an identifier for the object type as follows:

- P=Panel
- B=Business Process

- Q=Query
- E=Tree
- R=Record
- G=Panel Group
- S=Tree Structure
- I=Import
- U=Business Process Map
- J=Project
- X=Translate Table
- M=Menu

Navigation: Object Security → File → Save

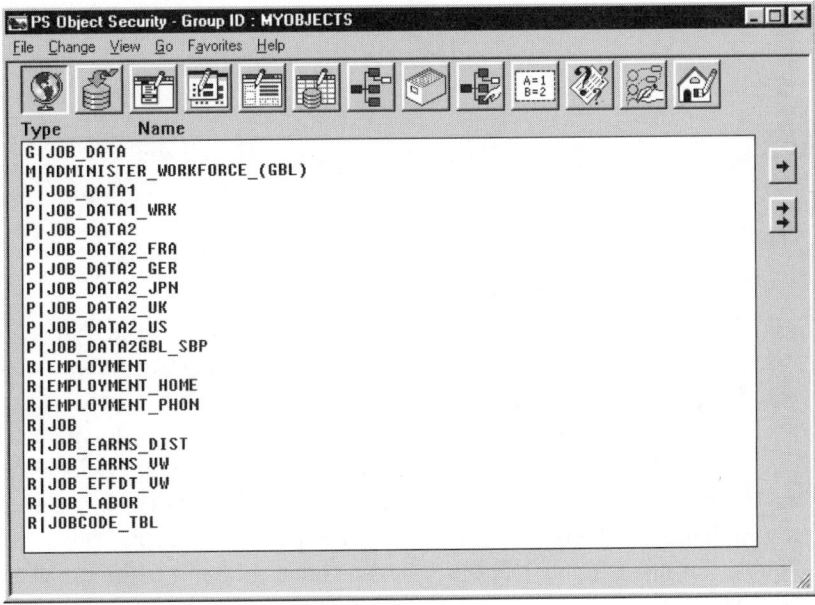

Figure 3.42   Completed object group

3.4.2   Linking object groups to security classes

After the object group is defined, it is then allocated to security class profiles. To assign an object group to a security class, it is necessary to open the class profile (see figure 3.43).

Navigation: Object Security → File → Open → Operator

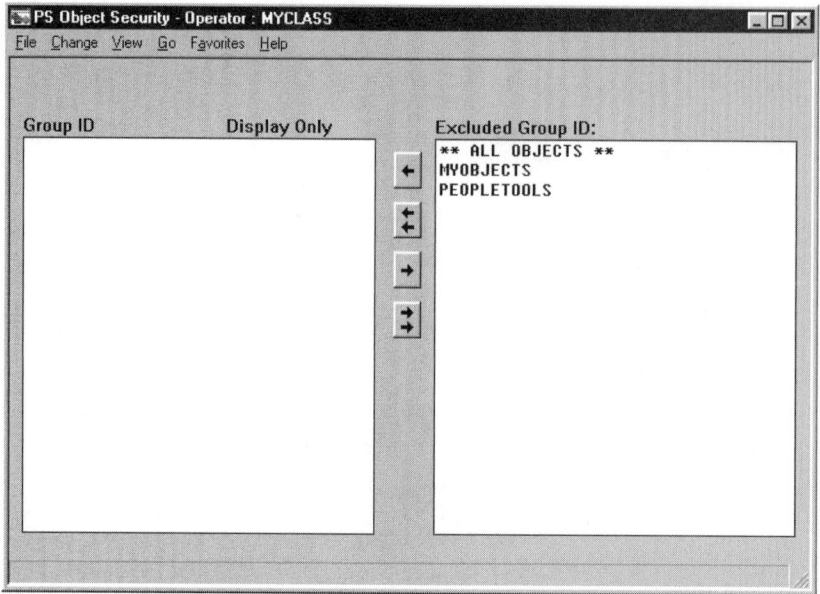

Figure 3.43   Assigning object group to class profile

The arrow buttons can be used to move object groups to the left side. The arrows work in the same manner as when they are used to allocate specific objects, such as records and panels. The left side indicates the group IDs allocated to the class.

To enable view only, select Change, Display Only from the menu. This displays the Object Security list dialog that contains the object groups allocated to the class. An individual object group can be selected or all the groups can be selected by pressing the All button. When objects in a group are specified as display only, it is a cliché for "Look, but don't touch." This implies the objects cannot be modified.

The completed object group and link to class MYCLASS are shown in figure 3.44.

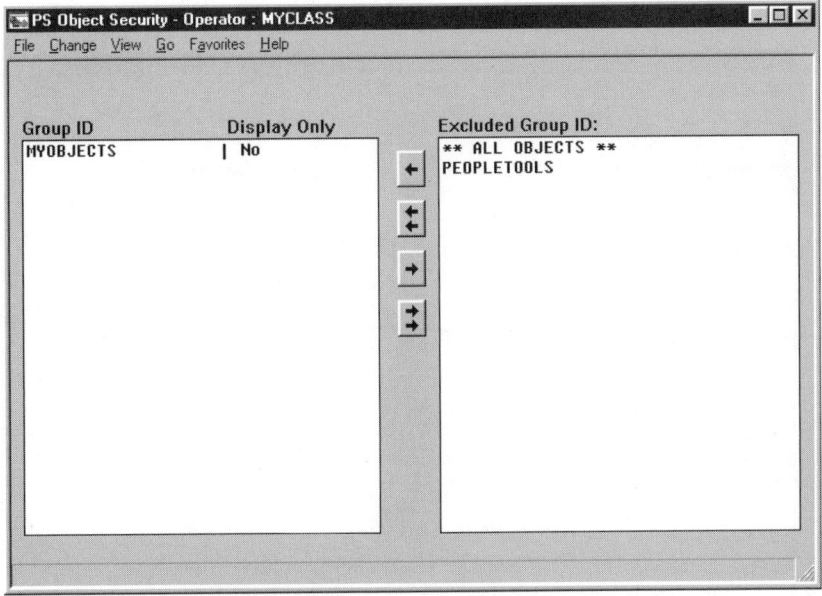

Figure 3.44   Completed object group and class profile

3.5   OPERATOR PREFERENCES

After an operator ID has been established, the Operator Preferences panel can be used to specify defaults such as Business Unit, SetID, Company Code, Country, and Currency Code. Additional settings include standard hours and payroll system. When the operator logs on to the application, default values specified on this panel will be used when necessary. This facilitates global implementations and reduces some level of functionality which is used to provide specific defaults such as country or currency code, based on system identifiers (menu, operator class).

To display the Operator Preferences panel, we can use the menu.

Navigation: Define General Options → Setup → Operator Preferences

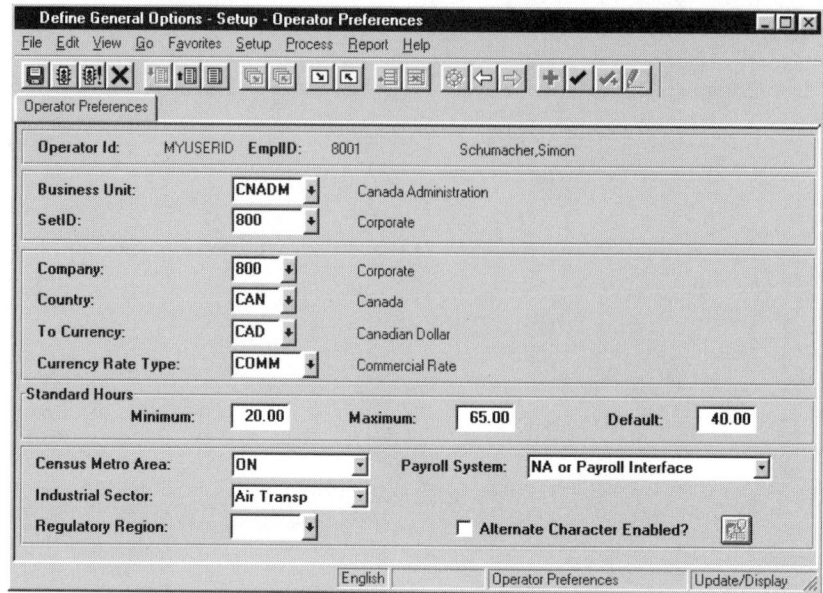

Figure 3.45   Operator preferences

3.6   TREE MANAGER

Tree Manager is a tool that can be used to graphically represent a hierarchy such as the departmental structure within an organization or the relationship between tables in a database. Tree branches or nodes can be traveled up or down, expanded, collapsed, and used to drive processes such as reporting and security. A tree can be used to produce a report identifying the tables an operator class can query.

The illustration in figure 3.46 is an example of a tree and the nodes, branches, and other components that make up a tree.

The following list describes the icons used to represent the structures contained in a tree similar to the one in figure 3.46:

This icon defines the top of the tree.

This icon identifies a category that is used to group similar data elements together at a high level. An example of a category in figure 3.46 is TOOLS.

This icon represents a tree structure. A tree structure represents a hierarchy within a category. ACCESS_GROUP is an example of a tree structure in figure 3.46.

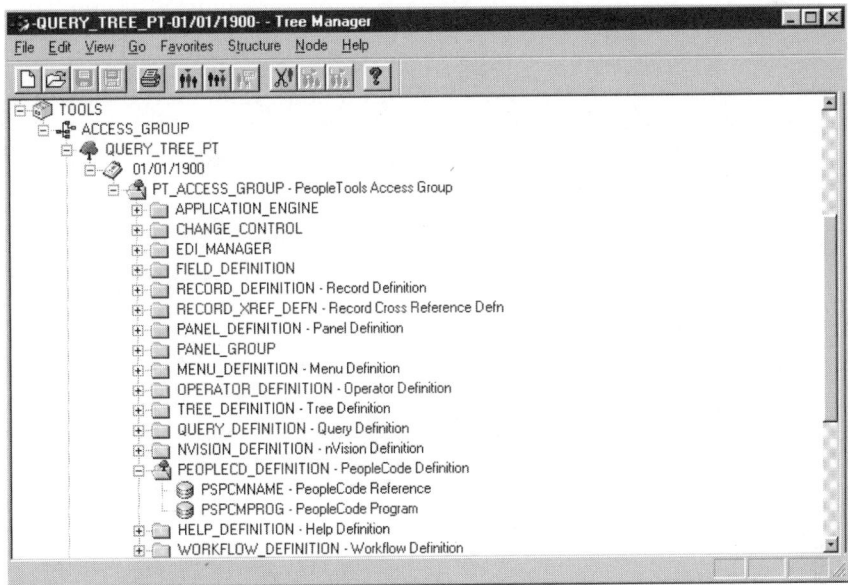

Figure 3.46   A tree and its components

🌳   A tree definition consists of a description, higher level category, use of levels section and status. Figure 3.47 illustrates the tree definition for QUERY_TREE_PT. The menu item to access this panel is Edit → Tree Definition.

🗂   SetID/Effective Date are the key fields in a tree definition. This information is required when a Tree is opened.

🔨   This icon identifies the Tree Branch. When a tree is branched, it is actually divided into two objects. One object is for the new branch and contains the remaining tree components. Within PeopleSoft, not every tree will require or contain branches. When a tree is branched, some improvement in efficiency may exist because less data are available to load. A more important application of tree branches is for security.

🌿   This icon represents a branch node.

📂   This icon identifies an expanded node. In figure 3.46, the PT_ACCESS_GRP is an example of an expanded node. In the illustration, many nodes report to it.

📂   This is also an expanded node in which levels are skipped.

🗒   This icon represents a collapsed node. When a node is collapsed, the box next to the node contains a "+," indicating nodes are reporting to the collapsed node but are not displayed by Tree Manager. In figure 3.46 PANEL_GROUP is an example of a collapsed node.

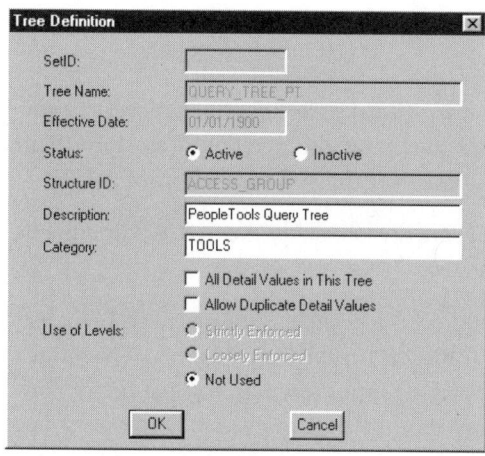 This icon represents a collapsed node. (However, the levels represented by this icon are skipped.)

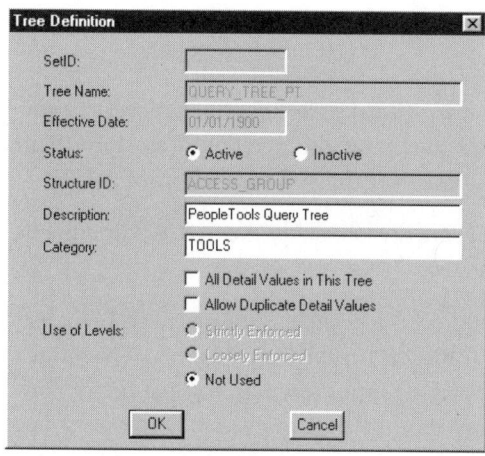 This icon applies to detail/summary trees.

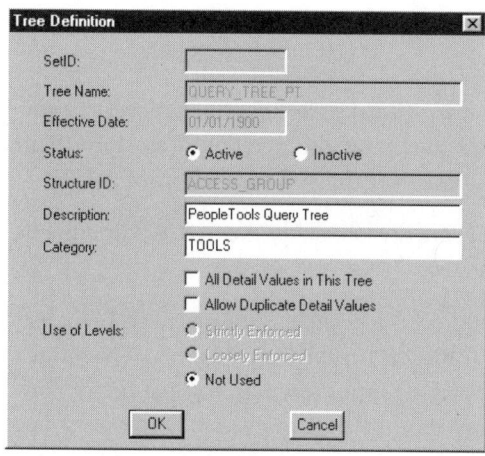 The icon represents a record definition. In the example (figure 3.46) PSPCMPROG is a record definition. It can also be collapsed or expanded to reveal child nodes.

TIP   When changes are made to the departmental security tree, a process is required to update the security profile for operator and operator classes. This process, called PER505, confirms that operators will have access to the modified tree structure.

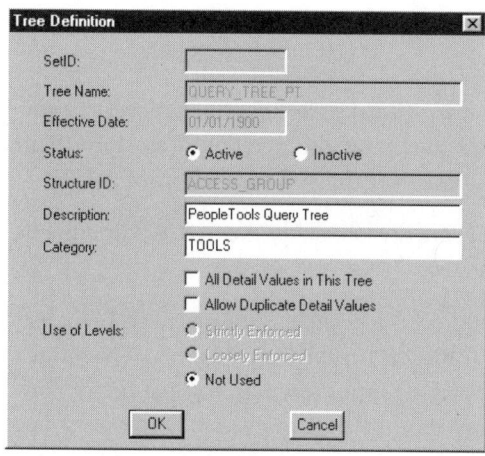

Figure 3.47
Tree definition for QUERY_TREE_PT

Tree can be categorized into four groups: Detail Trees, Summary Trees, Node Oriented Trees, and Query Access Trees.

Detail trees are considered the most basic type of tree. A detail tree rolls up to detail values comprised of tree nodes that combine the detail values and roll up to higher level tree nodes.

Summary trees enable us to re-arrange or re-group nodes from a detail tree. The detail tree itself is not copied in its entirety. Detail values in a summary tree are tree nodes from another detail tree, not values from database fields.

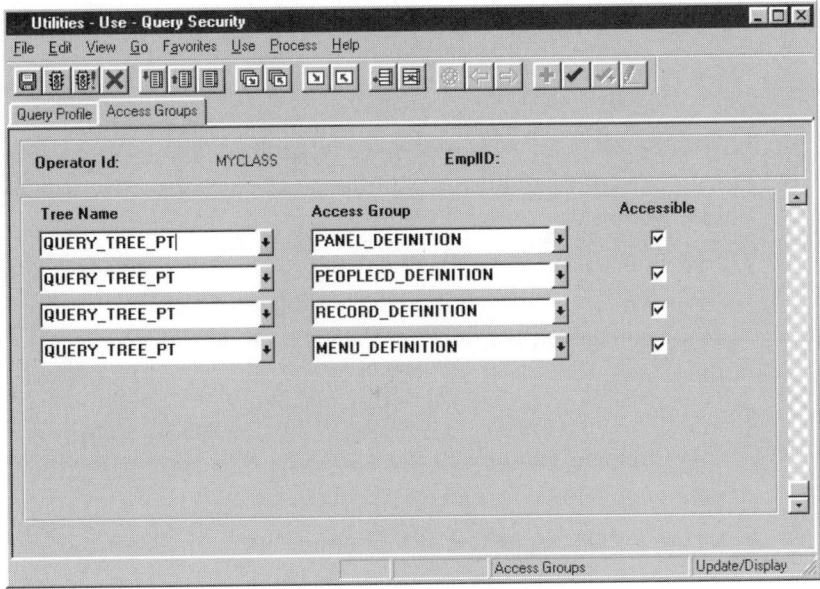

Figure 3.48　Query access trees used with query security

Node oriented trees contain nodes which depict database field values. Node Oriented trees can be used in applications such as HRMS Departmental Security.

Query trees are used in conjunction with PeopleSoft Query. Query trees combine database record definitions into entities identified as access groups. Access groups are used with the Query Security panel where we link an operator ID or class to one or more access groups. Each tree name can contain one or more access groups. A user cannot query records not contained in the access groups linked to their operator class. Figure 3.48 illustrates the use of query access tress with query security.

1 Data mover is a PeopleTool that is used to load and unload data from one environment to another. Data Mover can be used to load data across database platforms.

2 Import Manager is another tool that can be used to load data to tables defined by the Application Designer. Import Manager uses the record definition and an ASCII fixed file. The fields on the file are mapped to fields on the record.

3 Security Administrator is used to define Classes of Operators containing access to menus and menu items. An Operator Class is also linked to process groups defined by process scheduler.

4 Operator IDs can be linked to multiple operator classes and one class profile for row level security.

5 Object security is a tool that can be used to limit access to specific objects contained in an object group.

6 Tree Manager is a tool that can be used graphically represent departments within an organization or relationships between database tables.

PART 2

Application development

Application development in PeopleSoft begins with Application Designer. Once the requirements have been specified you can begin building your application in a logical sequence. Here's a simplified example of this sequence. First you define and create any custom field definitions you may need. The field definitions can then be utilized in a record. You can create online applications by placing these records with their associated fields on a panel. Panels can be placed in a panel group and added to a menu. Security access is assigned to operators who will utilize the new panel on the menu. If the new panel is used as a front-end to a batch process, a process definition is created and linked to the panel. These basic tasks can be accomplished very easily using Application Designer, Security Administrator and Process Scheduler. Additional enhancements, simple or complex, may be made as well. We'll demonstrate the use of these and other People-Tools by building a Problem Tracking application, gradually introducing more advanced features as our development progresses. Some advanced panel design features include working with scroll bars, effective dates, sub and secondary panels and using grid objects. The key to online development in PeopleSoft is the Application Processor which dynamically governs data retrieval and event processing. PeopleCode, PeopleSoft's proprietary language, should always be written to fully exploit the capabilities of the Application Processor. By carefully following along with the Problem Tracking application you'll see all of these exciting features unfold before you. As I mentioned earlier, this is some very fun stuff!

C H A P T E R   4

Building your first application

PeopleSoft uses a bottom-to-top methodology to build applications. A bottom-to-top method involves individually collecting all the components used to build higher level components, eventually arriving at a fully developed application. In this chapter, we look at how this methodology is used to design and develop an application.

4.1 IDENTIFYING THE APPLICATION

Our first step in application development is to collect development specifications. The user requesting the application may provide the initial specification. Then, the developer creates technical specifications for user review. To facilitate our discussion on basic functions used in collecting user specifications, we will develop a Problem Tracking application. Our Problem Tracking application will function within People-Soft and track both user-reported problems as well as developed solutions in a project life cycle. Hundreds of PeopleSoft implementations require such an application to efficiently track problems and resolutions. We'll build the underlying data model for our application in such a way that the project team can use a variety of search mechanisms to identify resolutions to new incidents. This application will be particularly useful as a production tool to provide customer support in a live environment. Note that, while endless possibilities exist for enhancing this application, we'll limit our discussion here to basic functions, leaving more advanced development concepts for a later review.

4.1.1 Fit/Gap analysis

We begin by identifying our business needs and then evaluating those needs against the PeopleSoft software application package. This process, called Fit Analysis, identifies functions in the PeopleSoft application that fit the business needs. It also helps identify any Gaps that the application package cannot accommodate. We identify Fits and Gaps in a Fit/Gap analysis document, which is then used to build our project plans and delineate development efforts toward successful implementation. Tools provided by PeopleSoft are so easy to use that even new applications can be built with relative ease. In our case, Problem Tracking is a brand new application not available in PeopleSoft. Hence, we need to gather business needs to develop the application from scratch. Let us look at the business functions that should be available in a common Problem Tracking application.

4.1.2 Gathering user requirements

In all the projects in which we have ever been involved, user specifications have proven to be extremely important. User specifications show us how the user sees the end result. Specifications are developed both by the technical and functional users. Several iterations of the specifications are exchanged back and forth between the technical and functional users, depending upon the complexity of the application. Technical users must assist the functional user in identifying the application fields that are utilized in a user panel or report. Specifications also help the developer to stay on track so far as the business needs are concerned and develop for those needs. Even though we won't discuss the stage where specifications are developed in this book, we cannot emphasize enough how important it is to develop with written specifications.

Let's suppose that our functional and technical users get together, discuss the business functions that should be available in the application, and arrive at the following requirements for the application:

- All problems reported should be categorized into a set number of applications such as Human Resources, Payroll, Benefits, Accounts Payable, General Ledger, and so on.
- All problems reported should identify the end user that reported them.
- All problems reported should have a status for tracking purposes.
- The problems and resolutions should be stored in a public domain so that all users have access to the resolutions.
- The application should be able to identify and prioritize commonly reported problems.
- The basic design of this application should facilitate problem tracking in new and future projects.

Figure 4.1 illustrates some inputs and outputs to and from our application.

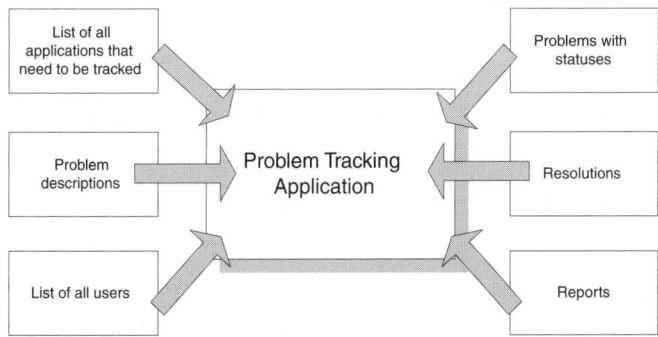

Figure 4.1   Problem Tracking application—Input/Output diagram

4.1.3   Identifying the objects to be developed

Now that we have compiled all the user requirements that we need to build our application, we can create a list of objects that need to be developed in PeopleSoft. How do we go about doing this? Data design is a term that comes to mind. Using PeopleSoft's integrated application development tool, Application Designer, we can build all the objects for our application by following these steps:

1. develop all record definitions that will be used in our application,
2. identify database keys for SQL tables and views,

3 develop all the user interface screens (otherwise known as panels) in PeopleSoft,

4 develop all the panel groups that provide a gateway to our application panels,

5 develop menu items that will hold the application panels and present them to the user, and

6 provide user access to menu items.

4.1.4 Prototype

While gathering user requirements, it is always useful to create a prototype of the application. A prototype allows us to walk the users through the application panels to give them an idea relative to data input and output. Prototypes are also used to gather additional user inputs on data elements missed during the Fit/Gap analysis. Prototypes help in creating final user specifications for development. Figure 4.2 shows the relationships between different objects in a PeopleSoft application.

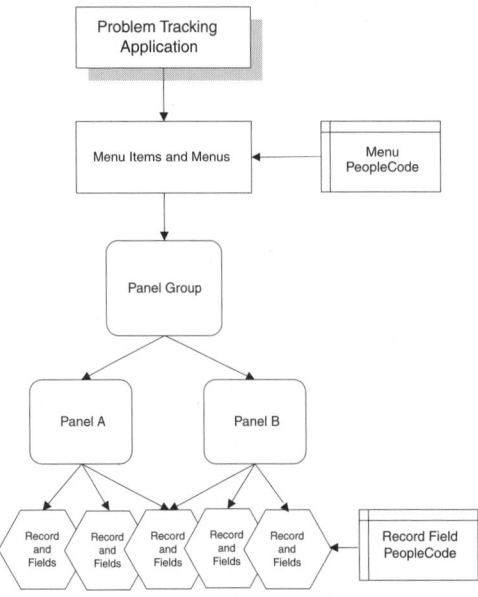

Figure 4.2
PeopleSoft Object Relationships

In this case, the Problem Tracking application is a new application in PeopleSoft. Here we ask the user to walk us through the current system. If this process can be performed during the Fit Analysis stage, then the prototype stage is skipped, and we proceed to the design, development, and unit testing stages.

As you can see in figure 4.2, design is usually performed starting from the top (represented by our application). On the contrary, development is performed from bottom up with objects assembled individually to achieve the end result. The bottom then refers to all the individual objects, and the top refers to the application. First, we start from the top, designing our application's presentation to the user including all user interface objects such as panels and menus. Then we design and develop the Record definitions, views, PeopleCode, and panel groups, which are building blocks for the user interface. The panels and the panel groups, together with application menus, will provide the user interface to our Problem Tracking application.

We can now start building development specifications. These specifications are incorporated into the project time line in a project plan document. During stages in projects, new problems arise and these problems can be tracked using our application. As mentioned before, we will use the Application Designer tool to develop our application.

4.2   USING THE APPLICATION DESIGNER

Application Designer, is a comprehensive design tool used to build applications in PeopleSoft. Ideally, we want to build all the objects related to this application into a PeopleSoft Project. A Project is a collection of PeopleSoft objects developed to serve a common function. In our case, the purpose of developing objects is to build a Problem Tracking application. Therefore, we collect all objects we develop and include them in one project. Let us take a look at the Application Designer screen before we can start our development (figure 4.3).

Navigation: Go → PeopleTools → Application Designer

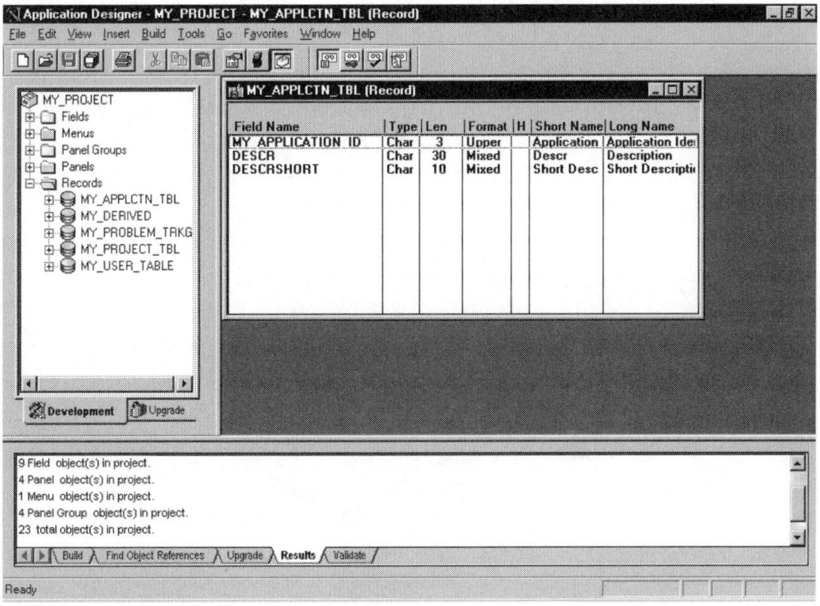

Figure 4.3   Application Designer screen

The left side of the Application Designer screen is called the Project Workspace. When we open projects (*Navigation:* File → Open → Project), all objects in the project are displayed in the Project Workspace. The right side, the Object Workspace, is the actual development area. The bottom tab portion of the screen serves as an output window for showing development progress, object reference searches, and so forth. For example, if we search for object references in the whole database (*Navigation:* Edit → Find Object References), the output appears in the bottom window. In figure 4.3 we can see that a project is already open. The objects in MY_PROJECT are all displayed in the Project Workspace. We can also see the number of objects in our project in the Output Window. The right side is used for development of these objects. Let's go through the process of developing these objects, inserting them into MY_PROJECT as we finish.

The icons that we see in the Application Designer menu bar are all short cuts used for various tasks. When we move the mouse pointer over these icons, a tab appears, denoting the tasks these icons perform. Let's look at all the icons available in the Application Designer screen.

4.2.1 General icons

- *New*—creates new objects.
- *Open*—opens existing objects.
- *Save*—saves the current object. In other words, if we have multiple objects open and we are working on one particular object, only the current object that we are working on will be saved when we choose the Save button.
- *Save All*—saves all objects that are open in the Application Designer screen.
- *Print*—prints the current object.
- *Cut*—deletes and stores the selected item in the clipboard.
- *Copy*—copies the selected item into the clipboard.
- *Paste*—pastes the copied item into the selected area.
- *Properties*—brings up the Properties window for the current object.
- *Build Current*—helps build SQL tables and views in the database. (We will learn more about this in chapter 8.)
- *Project Workspace*—is a toggle to hide or show the project workspace in the Application Designer screen.

4.2.2 Record display icons

These icons appear only when a record definition is open and is the current object in focus:

- *Field Display*—displays all record fields, their attributes, short name, and long name.
- *Use Display*—displays all the search keys, list box items, and defaults for the record definition.
- *Edits Display*—displays all the edits for the record definition.
- *PeopleCode Display*—displays all record fields and their associated PeopleCode events.

4.2.3 Panel design icons

These icons are available only when a panel definition is open and is the current object in focus:

- *Select Group*—selects a group of panel fields for cut, paste, and move operations.
- *Order*—displays the Order panel that is used to change the order of panel fields.
- *Test*—is a toggle that switches between test and design mode.
- *Object Inspector*—is a toggle that hides or shows the Object Inspector tool.
- *Panel Size*—controls the panel sizing properties.
- *Grid*—is a toggle that hides or shows a grid in the Object Workspace.
- *Label Position*—moves the field label to its default position.

- *Text*—adds a static text field into the panel.
- *Frame*—adds a frame into the panel.
- *Group Box*—adds a group box into the panel.
- *Static Image*—adds a static image into the panel.
- *Edit Box*—adds an edit box into the panel.
- *Drop-Down List*—adds a drop down list into the panel.
- *Long Edit Box*—adds a long edit box into the panel.
- *Check Box*—adds a check box into the panel.

- *Radio Button*—adds a radio button into the panel.
- *Image*—adds an image into the panel.
- *Scroll Bar*—adds a scroll bar into the panel.
- *SubPanel*—adds a subpanel into the panel.
- *Push Button*—adds a push button into the panel.
- *Secondary Panel*—adds a secondary panel into the panel.
- *Tree Control*—adds a tree control into the panel.
- *Grid Control*—adds a grid control into the panel.

4.2.4   Panel group icons

- *Insert Panel*—inserts a panel into the panel group.
- *Validate Panel Group*—validates the panel group.

If we double-click on any object that appears in the Project Workspace, the object is opened in the Object Workspace. When we click on the object using the right mouse button, a standard pop-up menu appears showing tasks that can be performed on the object. We can customize the Application Designer by accessing Options from the View menu. We can also customize or resize components of the Application Designer by dragging the edges of Project Workspace, Object Workspace, and Output Window using the mouse.

And, as we also noted under the general icons, the Project Workspace icon is a toggle that shows or hides the Project Workspace.

4.3   CREATING FIELD DEFINITIONS

Let's start by looking at the schema—e.g., the structure—for the first record in our application. We will call this record MY_USER_TABLE and start here for simplicity reasons:

```
Record Name     MY_USER_TABLE

Field Names     MY_USER_ID
                NAME
                EMPLID
                PHONE
                MY_USER_TYPE
```

We have five fields in this record. The first and the last fields are new fields we need to create before we can start building our Record definition. The other three fields are already available in a PeopleSoft HRMS application. Fields in PeopleSoft are defined, as well, not within the scope of a record, but globally throughout the entire database.

Navigation: File → New (From Application Designer)

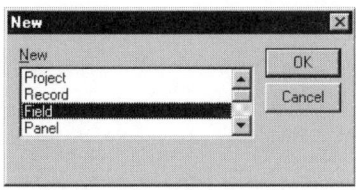

Figure 4.4   Create a new object

Figure 4.5   Selecting the field attribute

Fields are objects and they can be shared across record definitions. For this purpose, let us suppose that we are working in a PeopleSoft HRMS application. First, we create a new field (figure 4.4).

We choose `Field` as the new object type. Then we choose `Character` as the field type in the New field window as illustrated in figure 4.5.

In the Field Attributes screen (figure 4.6) we specify the field length, long name, and the short name for the field. We also specify the field format as `Uppercase`. We associate the field with a particular field format by defining the family name and the display name for the format (figure 4.5).

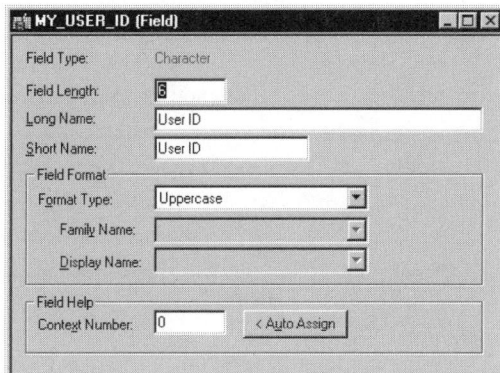

Figure 4.6
Field Attributes Screen

NOTE   Fields are individual objects. When field attributes are changed, they are changed throughout the system. The same field can be used across many record definitions.

Field Help Context Number is a number we can use to associate the field with a help text in a Windows-based help file. We click on Auto Assign to automatically assign the next available Context Number from the system. WINHELP can be used to create a Windows-based help file. Since PeopleSoft has reserved context numbers up to 10,000,000, we must use numbers higher than this to associate our fields with Windows-based help.

We can also create the MY_USER_TYPE field by following the same instructions. Let us see how numeric, date, and other types of fields are created in PeopleSoft. In order to do so, let us take a look at other fields available in our application. The navigation is the same except that the correct field type has to be chosen as illustrated in figure 4.5.

PRIORITY is a number field that we will use in MY_PROBLEM_TRKG table. Since this field exists in a PeopleSoft HRMS system, we are going to make use of this field in our record definition. Take a look at the field attribute for this field (figure 4.7).

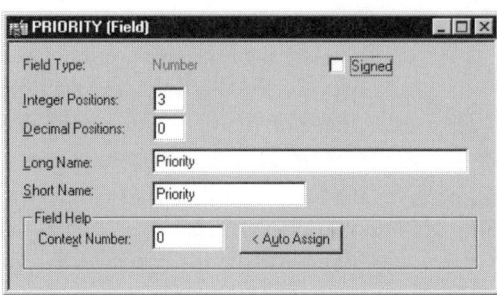

Figure 4.7
Number and Signed Number—
Field Attributes screen

We have to specify the Integer and Decimal positions for number fields. The attributes screen is the same for both Number and Signed Number field types except that the Signed checkbox is turned on for a signed number.

Figure 4.8 illustrates the attributes defined for MY_PROBLEM_RESOLTN field, a long character field. We define a maximum length for the long character field by entering a '0' to use the maximum length that the database can accommodate. This can be anywhere from 2000 to 64000 characters, depending upon the database platform. We also define whether the field is to be stored in Raw Binary or Text format. Raw Binary can be used to store embedded Nulls in our field.

Figure 4.9 illustrates a Date field in PeopleSoft. For this purpose, we use the INCIDENT_DT field in our application.

In order to resolve Y2K issues, PeopleSoft has presented all dates with inclusive century dates. If the user enters a date without the century, the Default Century

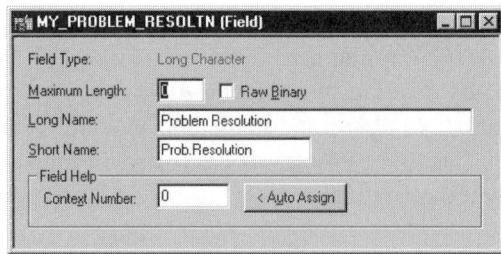

Figure 4.8
Long Character Field Attributes

attribute comes into play. We can enter a number here that determines the century for the date. If a century is not entered, and the two-character year is greater than the number specified in this box, the Application Processor uses the current century for the date; otherwise, it defaults to the next century.

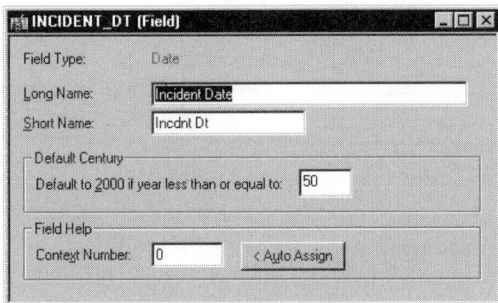

Figure 4.9
Date Field Attributes screen

Figure 4.10 illustrates attributes defined for a Date/Time field in PeopleSoft. The MY_PROBLEM_DTTM field used in our application is a Date/Time field.

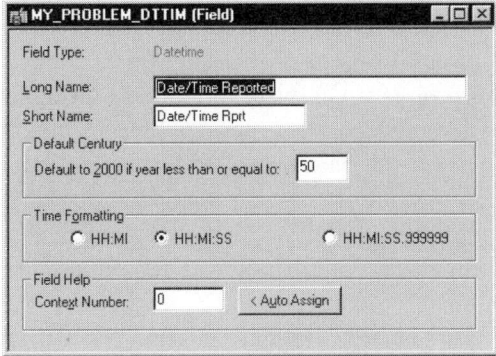

Figure 4.10
Date/Time Field Attributes screen

The Date/Time field attributes are the same as the Date field attributes. The Date/Time field has an additional attribute for the time part. "HH" refers to the hour portion of time, "MI" refers to the minute portion, "SS" refers to the second portion; and "999999" refers to the subsecond portion. We choose "HH:MI:SS" for MY_PROBLEM_DTTM field.

Let us take a look at a Time field in PeopleSoft. Notice in figure 4.11 that the attribute screen only has the time attributes.

By the end of this section, we should have created all the custom fields needed for our application. We can accomplish this task by building a schema for all records

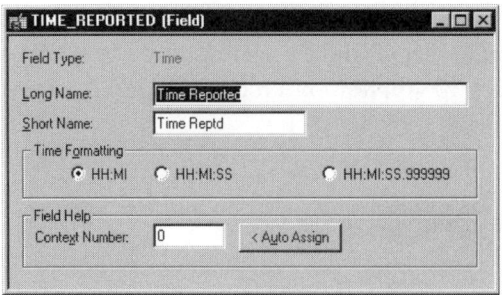

Figure 4.11
Time Field Attributes screen

that will be used in our application. Since fields are building blocks used to build Record definitions, it is convenient to have all the fields in the system ready for inclusion when records are built. Another way of accomplishing this task is to add the new fields when building the Record definition. By creating a schema for all records in our application, we can easily identify the custom fields as opposed to the fields delivered in a PeopleSoft system.

Now that we have started creating custom objects in the system, it is only logical to create a Project that will hold all the objects used in creating our application.

4.4 WORKING WITH PROJECTS

A project is a collection of objects used to develop an application or a subsystem. It's a good habit to save into a project all objects that belong to an application or subsystem. This ensures that the project is complete for application upgrade to other databases. In our case, we are developing a whole new application, and all the objects which we create for our application will be collected and stored as a project. We just created all our custom fields, so now it's time to save them to a project.

By default the Application Designer screen always displays an untitled project upon startup. We had previously saved a number of field definitions. These fields can be inserted into the untitled project either by pressing F7 or choosing "Insert/Current Object into Project" from the Application Designer screen. (We use this last option to insert objects currently open in the Application Designer screen.)

Alternatively, we can bring up a list of objects and then insert them into the project. We can accomplish this by pressing CTRL-F7 or by choosing "Insert/Objects into Project" from the Application Designer screen. We can also insert a whole project into our current project by choosing "insert/Projects into Project" from the Application Designer screen.

Finally, we save this Project by choosing the Save icon from the Application Designer screen. We are then prompted to name the project as illustrated in figure 4.12.

We use MY_PROJECT to insert the other objects we create for our application. Let's take a look at how we define project properties using the Application Designer.

Navigation: File → Save Project from Application Designer

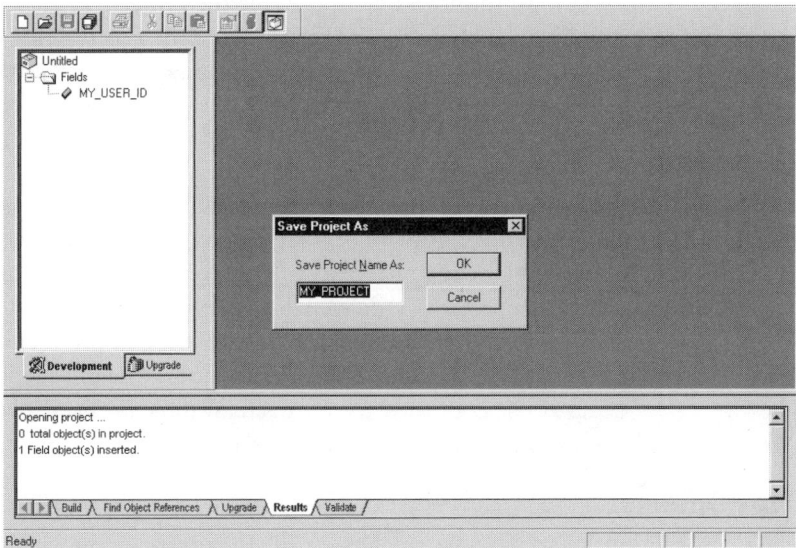

Figure 4.12   Saving a project

The Project Properties window has three different tabs: the General, the Report filter, and the Copy Options (figure 4.13).

Navigation: File → Project Properties (MY_PROJECT is open)

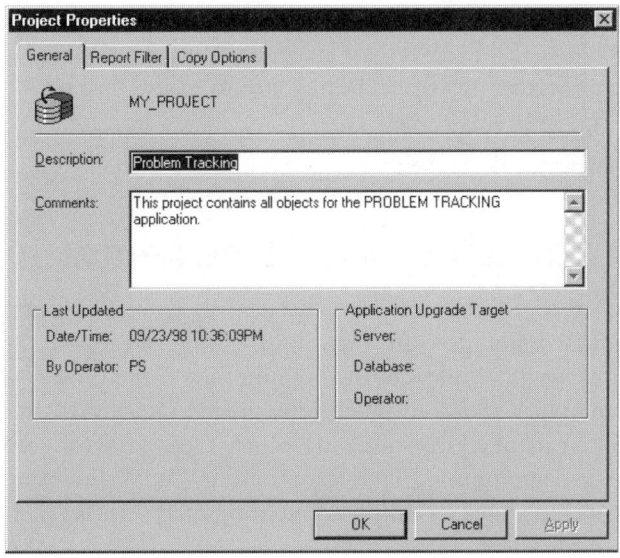

**Figure 4.13
Project Properties screen,
General tab**

4.4.1 General

Under the General tab, we specify a description for the project. The Comments section is used to maintain a log of changes to the project. The LAST UPDATED section displays the date and time when the project was last updated as well as the ID of the operator who last updated the project.

4.4.2 Report Filter

During a major application or tools upgrade, all objects identified as custom objects during the `Upgrade Comparison` process are tagged as CUSTOM. We can use the Application Upgrader tool to migrate objects from one database to another. The `Upgrade Comparison` process is a delivered PeopleSoft process used to compare objects between two databases. For example, development and production databases can be compared to identify newly developed objects not in the production database. The `Upgrade Comparison` process uses a database link between two databases. (We will describe more about the `Upgrade Compare` process in chapter 20.)

4.4.3 Copy Options

The Copy Options tab defines parameters for the `Upgrade Copy` process in PeopleSoft. After database objects are compared, the target database can be upgraded to match the source database by running the `Upgrade Copy` process (see chapter 20).

After defining Project Properties, click on the Apply push button to save the properties. MY_PROJECT is complete so far as the properties are concerned. We can add more objects to this project, and the Project Properties will still apply to all the objects in the project.

After saving the project, all objects in the project appear on the left side of the Application Designer screen.

| TIP | All objects used in developing an application can be inserted into a project. The project as a whole can be migrated to other databases. |
| NOTE | All objects in PeopleSoft contain a Date/Time stamp for their last update as well as the ID of the operator who updated them. |

4.5 CREATING A PEOPLESOFT RECORD DEFINITION

A record definition is a collection of fields that defines data storage in the database and data presentation online. Record definitions can be categorized as tables, SQL views, Derived/Work records, Subrecords, Dynamic views, and Query views. We will discuss the different types of record definitions more later in this section. For our application we will create one Derived/Work record. Derived/Work records are only relevant to the online application. They exist only in PeopleTools and not in the database. Derived records, used as temporary holding spaces during panel execution, can also be used to hold fields that are counters, calculation fields, or command fields. In our case, we will use the Derived record field as a command field to open a document. In chapter 6 we will add more fields to this Derived record to show how the derived fields are used as counters and calculated fields. First, let's consider in detail the steps necessary to create a PeopleSoft record definition:

- create a schema
- identify and create custom fields
- create a record definition
- define Record Definition properties
- define Record Field properties
- perform Data Administration, if necessary

4.5.1 Create a schema

Remember, a schema acts as a structure and is developed before SQL tables and views are built. Similarly, we can create a schema for each record definition used in our application. Our application is built using individual objects. In this case, these individual objects are fields, which are assembled into record definitions using the schema. Listed immediately following are the fields that we will use to build the record definitions for our application:

```
Record Name     MY_USER_TABLE
Field Names     MY_USER_ID
                NAME
                EMPLID
                PHONE
                MY_USER_TYPE

Record Name     MY_PROJECT_TBL
Field Names     MY_PROJECT_ID
                DESCR
                MY_APPLICATION_ID
                START_DATE
                END_DATE
                CONTACT_NAME
                CONTACT_PHONE

Record Name     MY_APPLCTN_TBL
Field Names     MY_APPLICATION_ID
                DESCR
                DESCRSHORT

Record Name     MY_PROBLEM_TRKG
Field Names     MY_PROBLEM_ID
                INCIDENT_DT
                MY_PROJECT_ID
                MY_PROBLEM_STATUS
                PRIORITY
```

```
                            MY_USER_ID
                            MY_PROBLEM_TRACKER
                            CLOSE_DT
                            MY_DOCUMENT_ATTACH
                            DESCRLONG
                            MY_PROBLEM_RESOLTN
                            MY_PROBLEM_DTTIM

        Record Name         MY_DERIVED
        Field Names         MY_DOCUMENT
                            MY_USER_ID
```

4.5.2   Identify and create custom fields

We have two custom fields in the first record definition. We identify these custom fields by the prefix "MY," which we use to identify the custom objects in our application. In order to build the first record, we first create the two new fields by accessing the Application Designer "File" menu and choosing "New" option. Then we choose `Field` as the object type. Once we have created these fields in the database, we can start building our record definition. We create field definitions by using the techniques described in section 4.3.

4.5.3   Creating a record definition

The PeopleSoft catalog table which stores record definitions is called PSRECDEFN. SQL tables and SQL views, which are record definitions, are database objects as well. SQL tables store permanent data in the database, and SQL views helps us in presenting this data in different ways. For this simple reason, SQL tables and SQL views are the only built-in types of record definitions within the database.

To create a record definition, we start by clicking on the New icon from the Application Designer screen and choosing `Record` as the object type. A new screen appears where we can insert the necessary fields.

Figure 4.14 illustrates a blank record definition. We insert fields into this record definition by first selecting the key fields, which are always the first fields in the field order.

Navigation: File → New → Record

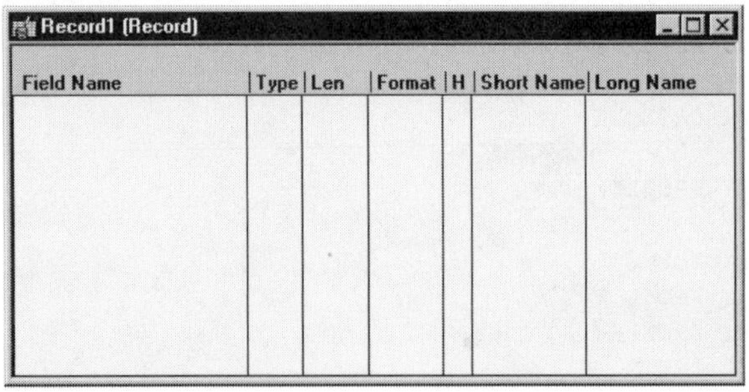

**Figure 4.14
New Record screen in the
Application Designer**

Figure 4.15 illustrates the screen used to insert fields into record definitions. We can either type in the field name or search for the field name by entering the first few characters of the field name and clicking on the Insert push button. When we specify the full field name, the field is inserted into the blank Record screen (figure 4.14). When we search for a field by providing the first few characters of the field name, all field objects matching the selection criteria appear in the bottom. We then highlight the correct field and click on Insert to include the field to the record definition.

Navigation: Insert → Field (Blank Record Definition is open)

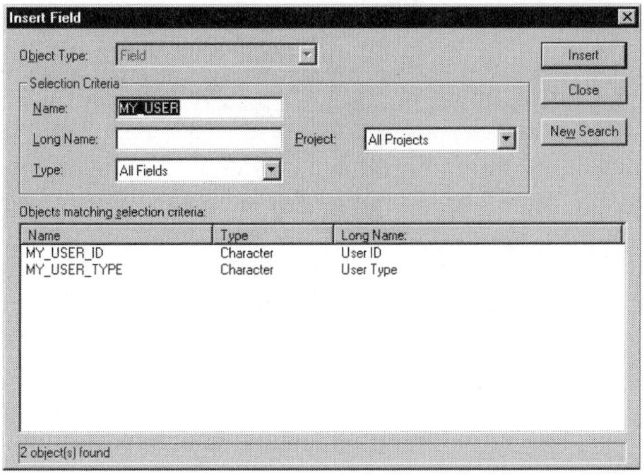

Figure 4.15
Inserting a field into a record definition

TIP Fields are placed next to each other when we start from a blank record screen. When inserting a field into an already existing record definition, determine the field that will be the previous field after the new field is inserted. Highlight that field, then proceed with the insertion. The new field will be placed right after the highlighted field.

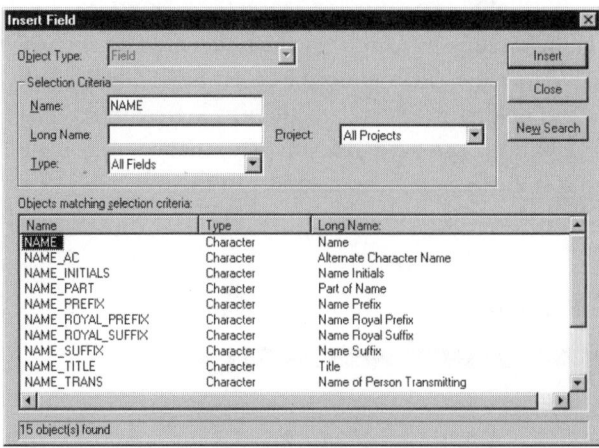

Figure 4.16
Inserting a field into a record definition

After all fields are inserted (figure 4.16), choose Close to finish the selection, then File/Save from the Application Designer screen to save, the record definition. During save time we will be prompted for a record name so name this record MY_USER_TABLE. Notice that we have used a prefix of MY_ to identify that the record definition is a custom one. The record definition for MY_USER_TABLE appears as illustrated in figure 4.17.

Field Name	Type	Len	Format	H	Short Name	Long Name
MY_USER_ID	Char	6	Upper		User ID	User ID
NAME	Char	50	Name		Name	Name
EMPLID	Char	11	Upper		ID	EmplID
PHONE	Char	24	Custm		Phone	Telephone
MY_USER_TYPE	Char	1	Upper		User Type	User Type

Figure 4.17
A saved record definition screen

Now we need to insert this record definition into our project. We accomplish this by choosing "Insert/Current Object into Project" from the Application Designer menu. Since we have added all the fields that comprise this record, we now define the record attributes required to complete the record definition.

Under the Tools/Options menu, we can specify default options for a project, including a setting for inserting objects into the project. We can choose the option that results in the automatic insertion of an object after the object is modified and saved. As an alternative, the manual insertion option gives us better control regarding objects inserted into the project.

4.5.4   Defining record definition properties

We can also bring up the Record Properties screen illustrated in figure 4.18 by pressing ALT-ENTER from the keyboard. The record definition itself should be open at this time. We complete defining Record Definition properties by entering parameters in the three different tabs—the General tab, the Use tab, and the Type tab—available in the Record Properties screen.

Navigation: File → Object Properties (MY_USER_TABLE is open)

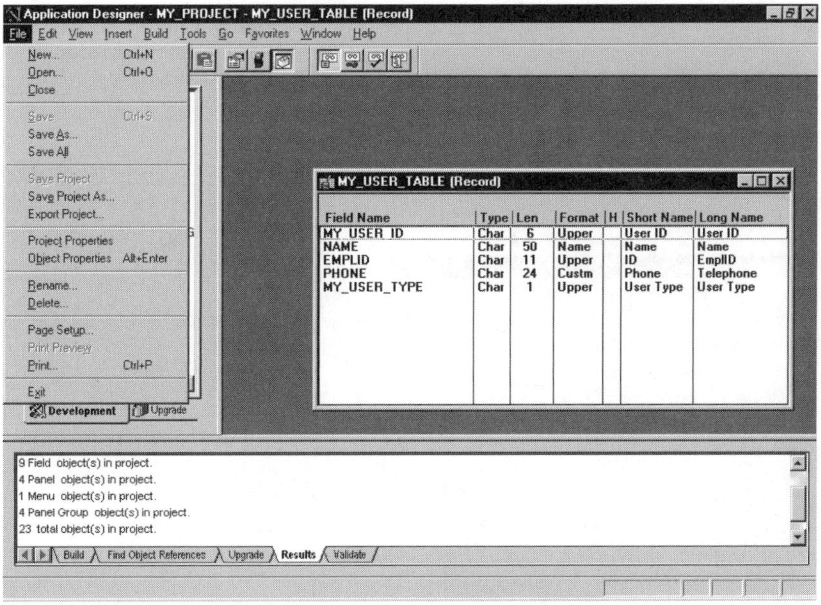

Figure 4.18   Record properties screen in Application Designer

General tab

In figure 4.19 we can see the General tab where we describe the record definition. We can also maintain a log of changes made to the record definition here in the Comments section. Notice that the Last Updated section helps us identify the date and time the record definition was last updated as well as the ID of the operator who last updated it.

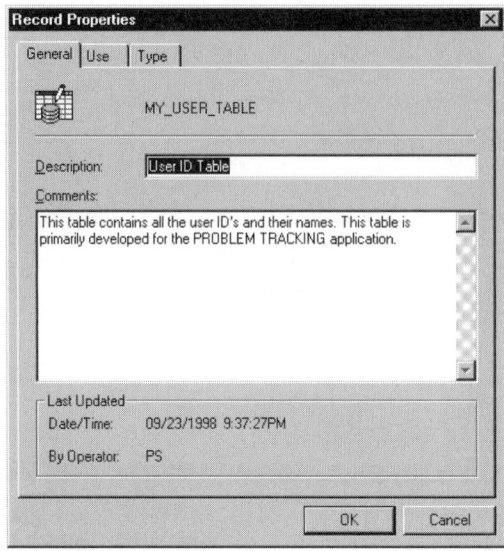

Figure 4.19
Record definition properties—
General tab

Figure 4.20 illustrates the Use tab under the Record Properties screen.

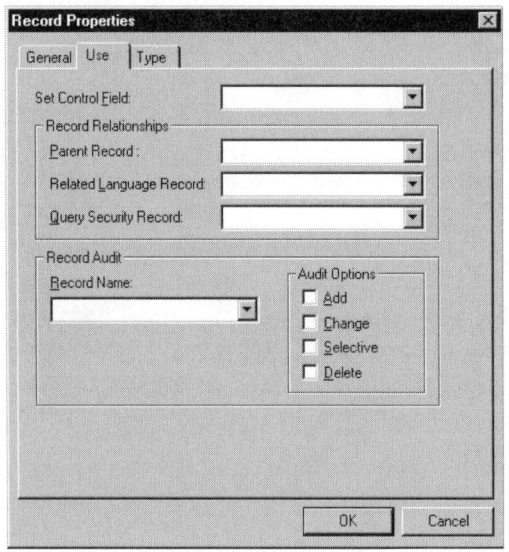

Figure 4.20
Record definition properties—Use tab

Use tab

Let's go through the properties defined in the Use tab. Although we won't be using these features in MY_USER_TABLE, let's quickly walk through these features and briefly explain their usage.

Set Control field   The Set Control field is used in a multi-company environment. You can use Set Control field to share this particular table across companies. For example, MY_USER_TABLE can be shared between companies by simply adding SETID to the MY_USER_TABLE definition. The SETID field is a delivered field in PeopleSoft. This field has to be both the first field in the record definition and a search key. We can specify another field from the system as the Set Control field. The value of the Set Control field will be compared to the value of SETID field from MY_USER_TABLE. This comparison controls the selection of data from MY_USER_TABLE. Organizations with multiple companies can use the same record definition we create here to access user definitions for other applications in the PeopleSoft database. So COMPANY field can be the Set Control field that will control the display and access of user definitions from MY_USER_TABLE.

Parent record   In the Parent record, you define a record definition that can serve as a Parent record to MY_USER_TABLE. Parent/Child relationships help create automatic hierarchical joins using the PS/Query tool delivered in PeopleSoft. For example, in a PeopleSoft HRMS application, the PERSONAL_DATA record is the Parent record for EMPLOYMENT. Common search keys between these two record definitions define the Parent/Child relationship between them.

Related Language record   The Related Language record is used in a multilingual PeopleSoft application. Let's use MY_PROJECT_TBL as an example to better explain this process. Suppose that, MY_PROJECT_TBL is accessed from offices all over the world, and access to this table must be provided in multiple languages. We can create a Related Language record that stores project information in different languages. The Related Language record contains all search keys from the primary record definition as well as LANGUAGE_CD field as an additional key. All other fields entered and stored in multiple languages are also included in the record definition. As a user logs into the application, the user options define the Base Language Code for the user. This allows the user to enter language-specific information stored in the Related Language record. This function is most commonly used in Human Resources applications where users from different countries access employee information in different languages.

Query Security record   The Query Security record provides row level security for record definitions in PS/Query. When a Query is created using a record definition, the record definition is automatically joined with the Query Security record to secure the data that the user can view. For example, access to personnel information in a

PeopleSoft Human Resources database can be controlled using PERS_SRCH_GBL as a Query Security record.

Record audit   The Record Audit facilitates auditing online updates to data stored in a record definition. By turning on the audit flags in a record definition, we can record all inserts, updates, and deletes. You can either specify a record name defined as a database table to hold the audit information, or if you do not specify a record name and audit flags are turned on, PeopleSoft stores the audit information in a generic audit table called PSAUDIT. Four audit flags may be activated. Each initiates that audit based on user action:

- *Add*   triggers the system to populate the audit table when new rows are added to the audited table.
- *Change*   triggers the system to populate the audit table when any row in the audited table is changed.
- *Selective*   triggers the system to populate the audit table when any one of the fields in the audited table is changed.
- *Delete*   triggers the system to populate the audit table when any row in the audited table is deleted.

When we create our own audit table, we have to add three relevant fields to the audit table. They are AUDIT_OPRID, AUDIT_STAMP, and AUDIT_ACTN fields. In addition to these fields, any other field in the audited record definition can be added to the audit table, but the default PSAUDIT table captures enough information required for an audit.

MY_USER_TABLE does not contain any properties defined under the Use tab.

Type tab

Record Type   The Record Type tab (figure 4.21) is where we define whether the record definition is an SQL table, SQL view, Dynamic view, Derived/Work, Sub-record, or a Query view. MY_USER_TABLE will be defined as an SQL table.

SQL View Select statement   On the right hand side of the properties screen, we define the SQL `Select` statement for an SQL view definition. (We will learn more about SQL views in chapter 7 when we define an SQL view for use in inquiry panels.)

Non-standard SQL Table Name   Through the non-standard SQL Table Name option, we give the record definition a non-standard name, one that differs from the normal PeopleSoft standard. PeopleSoft prefixes all tables with a "PS_" prefix. We can override this standard by entering a non-standard SQL table name. All PeopleTools tables follow a non-standard naming convention. The PeopleTools tables and views with non-standard names are referred without the "PS_" prefix. The name still starts with "PS" to identify it as a PeopleSoft catalog table. For example, PSRECDEFN is a PeopleSoft catalog table where record definitions are stored. We will set the record type as an SQL table for our MY_USER_TABLE definition.

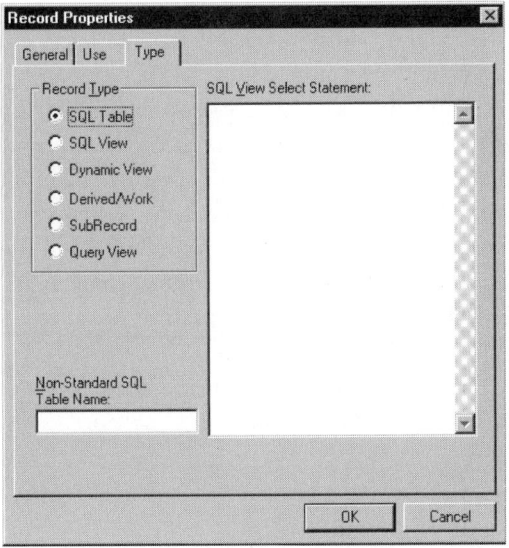

Figure 4.21
Record definition properties—Type tab

4.5.5   Define record field properties

The next step in creating a record definition is to define record field properties. Record field properties contain search key, list box, audit, and default information for a particular record field. We click on Edit/Record Field Properties to define properties for all the fields in our record. Record Field properties apply to fields only within the purview of this record definition. When used in other record definitions, these fields do not share the properties defined here. The record field must be highlighted before we can edit record field properties. The record field properties screen contains two tabs: the Use and Edits tabs.

NOTE   Properties defined for a record field apply to the field only within the purview of that record definition. The same field used in another record definition will not necessarily share the same properties.

Use tab

Keys   Figure 4.22 illustrates the Use tab under the Record Field Properties screen. Using the following options, a list of keys can be defined for the record field:

- *Key*   defines a record field as a database key only.
- *Duplicate Order Key*   defines a record field as a duplicate order key in the database.
- *Alternate Search Key*   defines a record field as an alternate search key in PeopleSoft. Alternate Search Keys are automatically selected as list box items. A non-unique index is created in the database for all alternate search keys.

- *Descending Key* makes a database key a descending key. Usually the EFFDT and EFFSEQ fields are defined as descending keys to view the latest effective-dated rows in the top of the scroll bar.
- *Search Key* defines the record field as a search key. All fields defined as search keys are also defined as list box items. When the record definition is used as a search record, all Search and Alternate search keys appear on the input dialog box.
- *List Box Item* defines the record field as a list box item. When search key values yield multiple rows, the values of all list box item fields appear in the list box.
- *From Search Field* defines the record field as a From Search field. The search process yields all entries that have values greater than or equal to the value supplied in this field.
- *Through Search Field* defines the record field as a Through Search field. The search process yields all entries that have values less than or equal to the value supplied in this field.

Navigation: Edit → Record Field Properties from the Application Designer

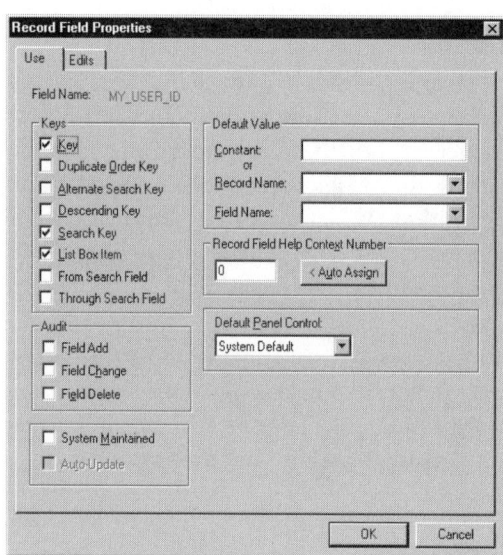

Figure 4.22
Record Field Properties screen—
Use tab

We define MY_USER_ID field as a key, a search key and a list box Item. We define NAME and EMPLID fields, from MY_USER_TABLE as alternate search keys. This automatically defines them as list box items as well.

Figure 4.23   Input Dialog box during Add

Let's look at the Input dialog box for our application. Figure 4.23 illustrates the input or search dialog box that appears when users access MY_USER_TABLE using our application. Notice that we are adding users here, hence we have to specify a value for the MY_USER_ID field defined as a search key.

In figure 4.24, you can see how alternate search key fields and list box items appear when we try to access the application panel online using Update/Display action. The list box provides users with values of key fields before they choose the item that they want to view and edit.

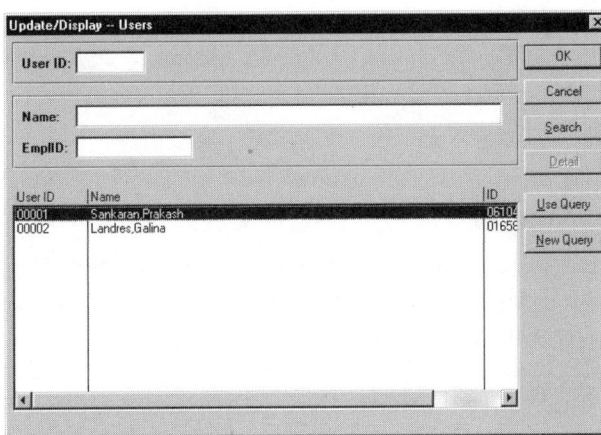

Figure 4.24
Input dialog box and list box during Update/Display

We'll discuss From and Through search keys in greater detail in chapter 6.

Default Value   We can specify defaults in the Record Field Properties screen (figure 4.22) for a particular record field. We can either use a constant as the default value or assign a value from another record field. Default values are populated into a field only when the field is blank or zero. We can also use the `FieldDefault` PeopleCode event to provide default values.

NOTE   Default values specified in record fields are processed first before `Field-Default` PeopleCode is executed.

Record Field Help Context Number   The Record Field Help Context Number is similar to the Field Help Context Number. The help text can be summoned when the record field is accessed online. (The Help text explains the usage of a field within a record definition.) The Help Context Number associates this record field to a Windows-based Help text. As we mentioned previously, PeopleSoft reserves Help Context Numbers up to 10,000,000, so we must use a number higher than 10,000,000. We can also assign this number automatically by using the Auto Assign button.

Default Panel Control   The Default Panel Control controls the appearance of the record field on a panel. The options available here are Edit Box, Drop-Down List, and System Default. If we choose System Default, the system selects the default panel field type for this record field.

Audit   Changes to the record field can be audited online using the Audit option. When the Field Add option is chosen, any new values entered in record fields are audited. When the Field Change option is chosen, any changes to record fields are audited. When the Field Delete option is chosen, all deletes are audited. All audit information is populated into a delivered audit table called PSAUDIT. The audit record name can be overridden by specifying an audit record attached to record definition properties (figure 4.20).

System Maintained   The System Maintained field is used for reporting purposes only. We turn on this checkbox if we want the record field to be updated by the system.

Auto Update   The Auto Update option is used for Date/Time fields. The system updates the record field to the current date and time. Any user-changes to a field defined for Auto Update will be overwritten with the current date and time. We can use this option for the MY_PROBLEM_DTTIM field in the MY_PROBLEM_TRKG record definition to automatically store the system Date/Time into that field.

Edits tab

After the options under the Use tab are completed, we can proceed to the Edits tab under the Record Field Properties Screen (figure 4.25).

Navigation: Edit → Record Field Properties from the Application Designer → Edits

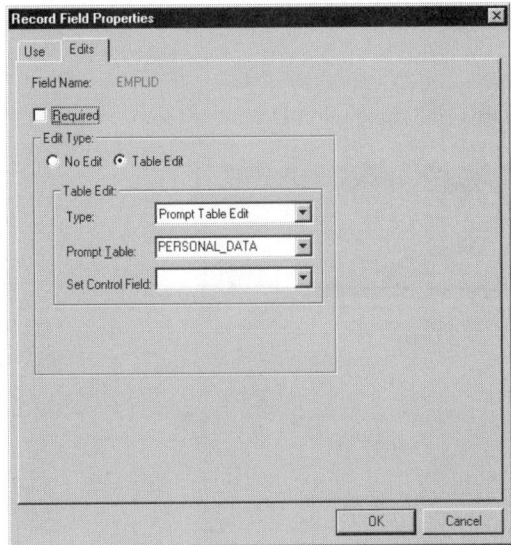

Figure 4.25
Record Field Properties screen,
Edits tab

Required   This option makes the field a "Required" field, meaning that the user has to enter a value into this field on an application panel that contains this record field. We will make MY_USER_ID a required field in MY_USER_TABLE.

Edit Type   The Edit Type option edits the value entered in this field. If we specify No Edit, then the field is not edited. If we choose the option Table Edit, then we have to specify the edit type. Four different types of edits are associated with a record field.

- *Prompt Table Edit*   The record field is attached to a prompt record that has the list of valid values. The user is not allowed to choose any value outside the list of valid values. EMPLID field in MY_USER_TABLE uses PERSONAL_DATA as the prompt record. (To learn more about Prompt Processing, refer to chapter 6.)
- *Prompt Table with No Edit*   This is the same as Prompt Table Edit except that this option allows the user to enter values not in the list of valid values.
- *Translate Table Edit*   This option edits the value entered into this field against the XLATTABLE. Translate values are attached to field definitions. These translate values are activated for the particular record by using this option. If this option is not chosen, translate values attached to a particular field definition is not used in editing. MY_USER_TYPE field has translate values that are activated for MY_USER_TABLE record definition. (To learn more about translate values, refer to chapter 6.)
- *Yes/No Table Edit*   This is used for fields that contain a Yes or No value. Usually record fields defined as checkboxes in panels use this option.

In figure 4.25, you can see the prompt record attached to the EMPLID field in MY_USER_TABLE. Figure 4.26 illustrates the translate values attached to MY_USER_TYPE field in MY_USER_TABLE.

Navigation: View → Translate from the Application Designer Menu

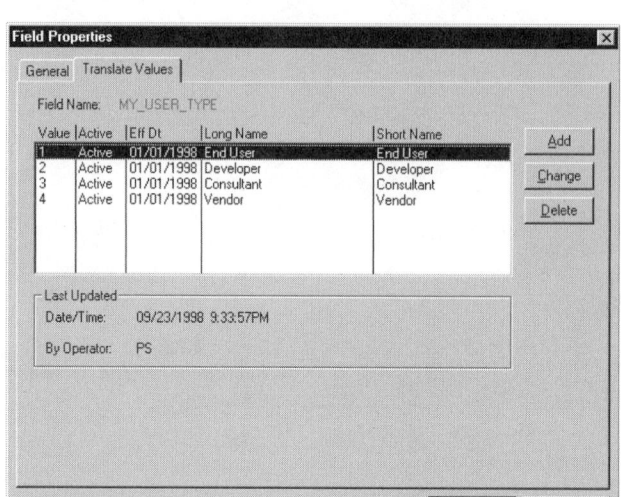

Figure 4.26
Translate values

Set Control Fields   Set control fields can be used only with prompt table edits. The set control field specified here will override the set control field defined for the record definition containing this field. The value of the set control field will be used in prompt processing. The prompt record contains the SETID field and the value in the set control field on the panel will be compared to the value of the SETID field from the prompt record.

In PeopleSoft, Record Field Properties are shown in four display formats: Field Display, Use Display, Edit Display, and PeopleCode Display. Figures 4.27 through 4.30 show all four display views as well as a brief description of their content.

Field Display shows the field type, field length, field format, short name, and long name for the record fields.

Navigation: View → Field Display (MY_USER_TABLE is open)

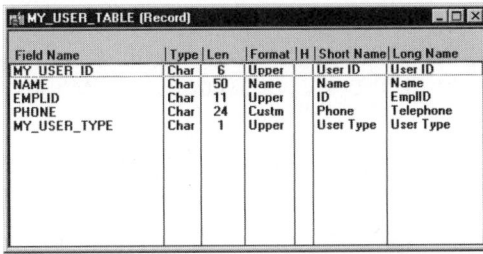

Figure 4.27
Record definition, Field Display

Use Display shows all the properties we entered under the Use tab using the Record Field Properties screen.

Navigation: View → Use Display (MY_USER_TABLE is open)

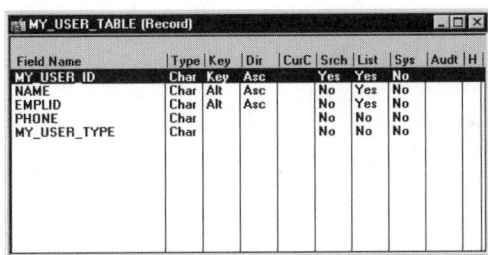

Figure 4.28
Record definition, Use Display

Edits Display shows all properties we entered under the Edits tab using the Record Field Properties screen.

Navigation: View → Edit Display (MY_USER_TABLE is open)

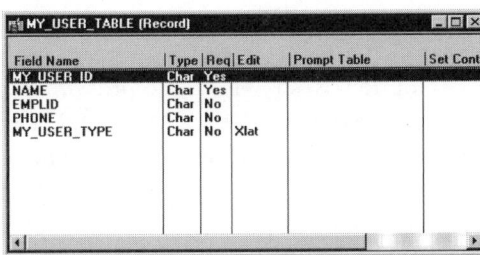

Figure 4.29
Record definition, Edits Display

CREATING A PEOPLESOFT RECORD DEFINITION

PeopleCode Display shows all Record Field PeopleCode in the record definition. (We will discuss adding PeopleCode to record fields in part 3.) A record field which contains a PeopleCode program attached to one of its PeopleCode events will show a Yes against the PeopleCode event. In figure 4.30, you can see a PeopleCode program attached to the FieldChange PeopleCode event of the EMPLID field.

Navigation: View → PeopleCode Display (MY_USER_TABLE is open)

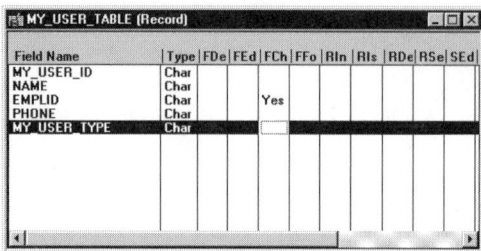

Figure 4.30
Record Definition, PeopleCode Display

4.5.6 Perform Data Administration

Data Administration, a precursor to building an object in the database, is performed in the database. SQL tables and SQL views are database objects and must be built in the database. We use record definitions specified as SQL tables and SQL views to do so. Database objects are built using scripts that use the Data Definition Language (DDL) Model defaults. DDL is used to create data dictionaries in relational databases. It is good practice to generate scripts to build objects and save the scripts in your dictionary of DDL scripts. Not only will this practice prove useful if the record definitions have to be rebuilt in the database, it also provides a record of all DDL statements executed in the database.

Build objects

Let's look at how we build SQL tables and SQL views using record definitions. Figure 4.31 illustrates the screen in the Application Designer tool used to build database objects.

When the Build → Project option is chosen, all records in the project are included in the build scope list. In our example, we open MY_USER_TABLE through the Application Designer, then choose Build → Current Object from the menu.

In the Build screen, we choose the Create Tables action. MY_USER_TABLE is defined as an SQL table and included in build process. We choose the Execute SQL Now option for MY_USER_TABLE. MY_USER_TABLE is a new object, therefore, it does not yet exist in the database as a table. When we choose the Create Tables

Navigation: Build → Project or Current Object

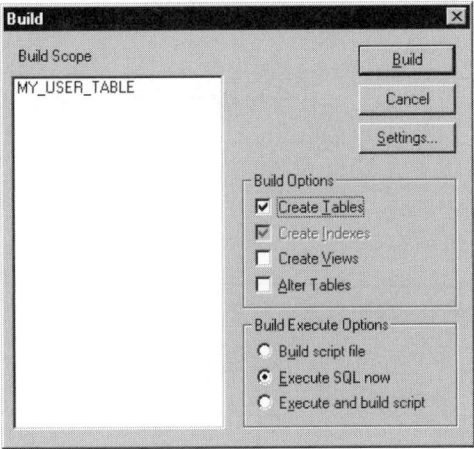

Figure 4.31
Building an object in the database

action, the Create Indexes option is also turned on automatically. This creates all indexes for PS_MY_USER_TABLE in the database.

NOTE   SQL tables and views are prefixed with the letters PS_. The MY_USER_TABLE record is called PS_MY_USER_TABLE in the database for example. This unique prefix helps the database administrator identify PeopleSoft tables and views easily.

We will learn more about building SQL tables, views, and indexes in chapter 8.

4.6   CREATING A PEOPLESOFT PANEL DEFINITION

Panel design is a crucial step in building an application. Panels have to be designed to facilitate easier and faster input online. While record design is important for storing data and for data integrity, panel presentation is the primary evaluation factor for the online application. To build an application panel, we need to perform the following steps:

- assemble record fields in the panel.
- define panel field attributes.
- check the panel layout.
- define panel properties.
- save the panel

Let's start by building a simple presentation panel to enter users through the Problem Tracking application.

4.6.1 Assembling record fields in the panel

We open our project and choose File → New from the Application Designer menu. We can then choose `Panel` as the object type.

Figure 4.32 shows the blank panel that we use to assemble record fields. We begin by placing fields in the order of input, starting with the highest level key from the record definition. Since we are building a panel to enter users for our application, we start by choosing fields from MY_USER_TABLE.

Navigation: File → New → Panel

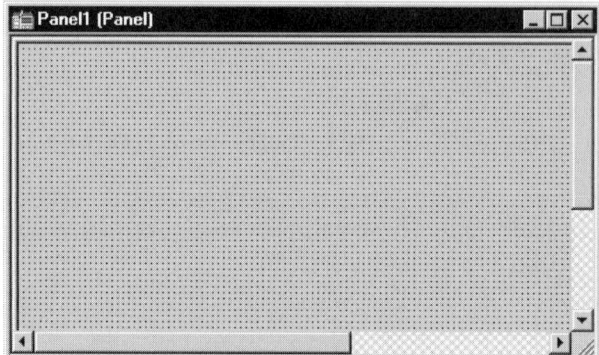

**Figure 4.32
Panel designer screen in
Application Designer**

We insert fields into our blank panel by choosing Insert from the Application Designer menu and choosing the correct panel field type. The first field in MY_USER_TABLE is the MY_USER_ID field that is an Edit Box field.

We choose the panel field type based on how the field will be used functionally. In this example, we either add or update user IDs through our panel. The EMPLID field will be a drop-down list panel field type simply because we attached a prompt record to this field. Because MY_USER_TYPE has translate value attached to it, it can be defined as a drop-down list panel field type. NAME and PHONE are Edit Box panel field types. Let us take a look at how the panel appears with all the five fields from MY_USER_TABLE placed in input order.

In figure 4.33, we have defined MY_USER_ID field as a display-only field. This is because MY_USER_ID is used as the search field to access the panel. EMPLID and MY_USER_TYPE fields have a drop-down arrow indicating that they are drop-down list fields. This means that, by simply clicking on the drop-down arrow, a list of valid values will be presented to the user.

In addition to the five different fields, a Static Text field exists in the panel. This is the example telephone number format shown next to the PHONE field in figure 4.33.

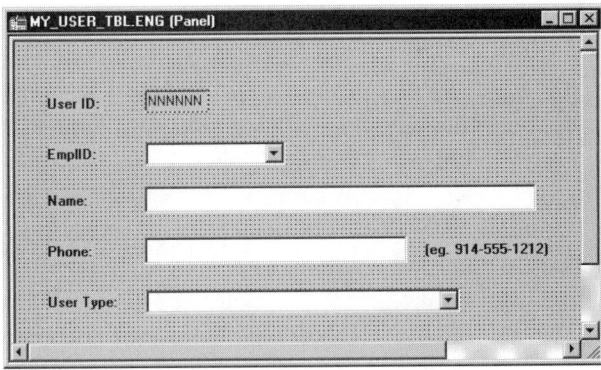

Figure 4.33
Assembled record fields
on a panel

4.6.2 Define panel field properties

After placing the fields in a blank panel, we then define panel field properties. Default panel field properties can be changed using three different tabs: the Record, the Label, and the Use tabs. (See figure 4.34.)

To change the Panel Field properties for each panel field, highlight the panel field and bring up the Panel Field Properties screen either by choosing Edit → Panel Field Properties from the Application Designer menu or pressing CTRL-F from the keyboard.

Record tab

Navigation: Right Click on the panel field → Panel Field Properties

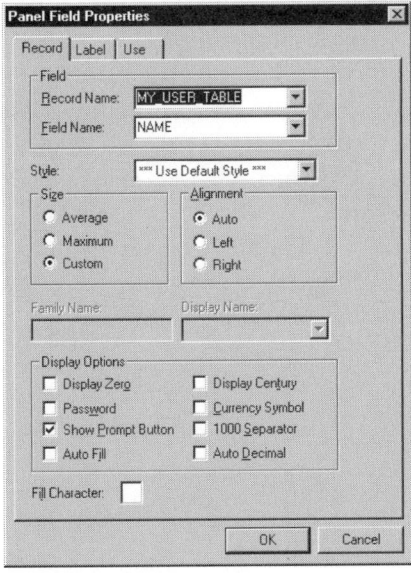

The Record tab (figure 4.35) defines the source, size, and display options for our panel field. The record name is MY_USER_TABLE, and the field name is NAME (figure 4.34). We can also control the size of panel fields under this tab. The NAME field is defined as Custom. This enables us to adjust the size of the field on the panel. Panel field size can be adjusted by using the right corners and dragging them to the left to reduce the size or to the right to increase the size.

Figure 4.34 Panel Field Properties
screen—Record tab

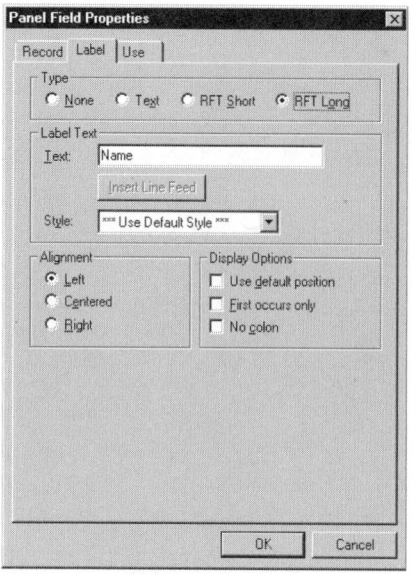

Figure 4.35 Panel Field Properties Screen—Label tab

Label tab

The Label tab (figure 4.35) defines the properties for panel field labels. There are two components to a panel field: one is the panel field itself, and the other is the label for the panel field. Let's take a look at the Label tab for the panel field EMPLID from MY_USER_TBL panel.

In figure 4.35, we have defined the Label type to use the Long name from EMPLID field definition. We can also choose to use Short name, or Text as the panel field label or define the panel field not to use any label. Panel field labels can be aligned to the panel field itself by using the Alignment option.

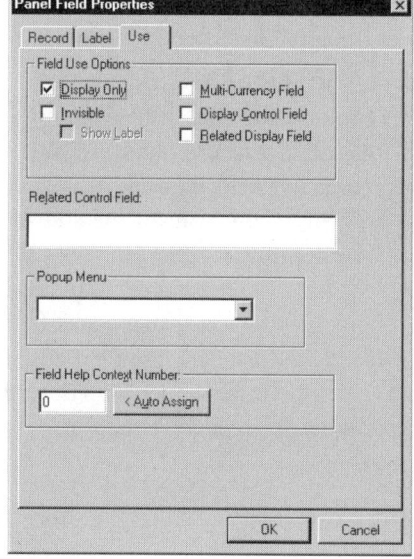

Figure 4.36 Panel Field Properties screen—Use tab

Use tab

The Use tab defines the panel field usage properties. Figure 4.36 illustrates the Panel Field properties for the EMPLID field from MY_USER_TBL panel.

Look back to figure 4.33. Notice that MY_USER_ID field is a display-only field in the panel. We were able to define that under the Use tab for that panel field.

For more about defining Panel Field Properties, see chapter 7.

4.6.3 Checking the panel layout

Once all the fields are laid out on a panel, and the panel field properties have been defined, it is time to check the layout of the fields in the panel. Checking the layout of fields helps:

- check the input order of fields
- check if all key fields are assembled first before other non-key fields
- check if all Related Display fields are placed after their respective Display Control fields (For example, if EMPLID is the Display Control field and NAME is the Related Display field, we have to make certain that EMPLID is before the NAME field in the panel field layout.)
- (if there is a scroll bar in the panel) be sure all fields inside the scroll bar are from one record definition except for Related Display and Derived fields
- make certain that key fields that facilitate prompts on prompted fields in the panel are before the prompted fields themselves. (For example, in a PeopleSoft HRMS application, there is a table called PAY_CALENDAR that contains payroll calendars to process payrolls. This table has three key fields: COMPANY, PAYGROUP, and PAY_END_DT fields. In order to prompt on the PAY_END_DT field, values for COMPANY and PAYGROUP must be available to facilitate the prompt.)

When we save the panel, these checks are enforced, and a message appears if the panel is invalid. We can always change the layout of fields if the panel is invalid at save time.

4.6.4 Define panel properties

Navigation: File → Object Properties

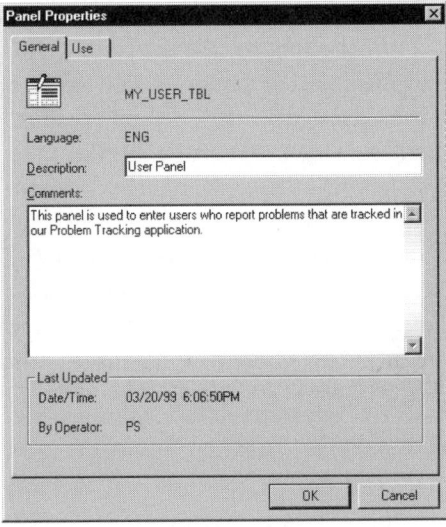

**Figure 4.37   Panel Properties screen—
General tab**

The Panel Properties screen can be brought up either by choosing File/Object Properties from the Application Designer menu or right-clicking on any one of the panel fields and choosing Panel Properties from the pop-up menu. Two different tabs exist in the Panel Properties screen: the General tab and the Use tab. Figures 4.37 and 4.38 illustrate the two tabs in the Panel Properties screen.

General tab

The General tab displays the language, a brief description, comment, and last updated date/time/operator ID for the panel. PeopleSoft allows language versions of panels. Panels can be stored in languages other than English. The

Comments section can be used to maintain a log of changes to the panel. All People-Soft objects maintain the last updated date/time and the ID for the operator that last updated the object.

Use tab

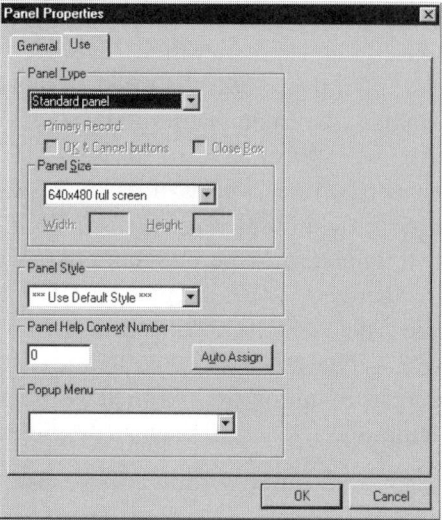

The Use tab contains the panel type, panel size, panel style and pop-up menu attributes. The panel can be defined as a standard panel, SubPanel or a secondary panel. Panel size attributes control the panel resolution. We can design the panel to suit VGA or SVGA resolutions. We can define a style for the panel. The whole panel will inherit the style defined here. Panel Help Context Number is used to link the panel with online help. A pop-up menu can be attached to the panel. When the user right clicks anywhere in the panel, the pop-up menu is activated.

**Figure 4.38   Panel Properties screen—
Use tab**

4.6.5   Saving the panel

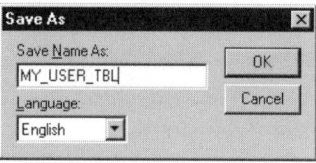

Our final step is to save the panel definition. We can save the panel by choosing File/Save from the Application Designer menu or by clicking on the Save tool bar icon. Figure 4.39 illustrates the screen brought up to save the panel definition.

Figure 4.39   Save a panel

We enter a name for the panel and click on OK to save the panel. The Language drop-down list box allows us to save panels in other languages for multilingual access. The base language appears on this drop-down list. Panel definitions can be saved in languages other than English by logging into the system as a user whose base language is the language in which you want to save the panel.

1 PeopleSoft development is performed from bottom-to-top (i.e., People-Tools objects are developed to reach the top—the fully developed application of sub-systems).

2 User specifications and technical specifications are extremely useful for the development process.

3 The Application Designer tool is an integrated tool delivered with People-Soft applications to help in application development.

4 Projects are used to include all objects used to develop an application or sub-system.

5 Fields are individual PeopleSoft objects.

6 Record can be specified as SQL tables, SQL views, Derived/Work records, Query Views, Dynamic Views and Subrecords. Only SQL tables and views are built in the database as objects.

7 Field attributes are the same across all record definitions. Record field attributes apply only to a particular record definition.

8 A panel can be a standard panel, a subpanel, or a secondary panel.

9 Secondary panels are used to organize fields by their function. Subpanels are used to separate repetitive fields, like address fields into a subpanel. Both subpanels and secondary panels can be included in a standard panel.

C H A P T E R   5

Providing user access to the application

We have created all objects required to build the user interface and provide access to our application. (Note, that panel groups and application menus can be termed as user interface in PeopleSoft.)

A panel group can have one or more panels in it. Menu items provide user access to functions available under an application menu. Panel groups are attached to menu items. While providing access to a particular Menu Item, any one or all of the panels in the panel group can be chosen. It is important to also note that other aspects of security exist apart from the menu items that this chapter will discuss.

5.1   CREATING PANEL GROUPS IN PEOPLESOFT

PeopleSoft panels are attached to application menus using panel groups. Prior to PeopleSoft version 7, panel groups were part of the menu definition, but starting from PeopleSoft version 7, panel groups are separate objects which nonetheless serve the same purpose of linking panels to application menus.

Panel groups contain one or more panels. They can be created to make panels look more organized. Instead of crowding a panel with fields, multiple panels can be created and attached to a panel group. Panel groups can also be created to organize fields by function. JOB DATA in the PeopleSoft HRMS application is a classic example of one such panel group. Panel groups can be shared across menu items as long as the menu items share the same panel. To create a panel group, we move through the following steps:

1   create a new panel group
2   insert panels into the panel group
3   define panel group properties
4   save the panel group definition

5.1.1   Create a new panel group

We create a new panel group by choosing File/New from the Application Designer screen and choosing panel group as the object. Figure 5.1 shows the blank Panel Group screen that results.

Navigation: File → New → Panel Group

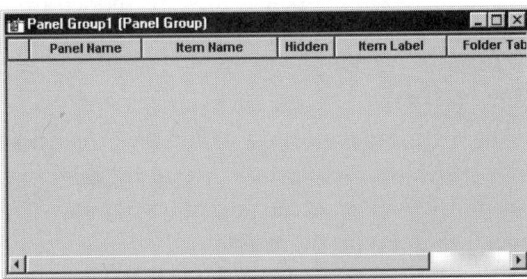

Figure 5.1
New Panel Group screen

5.1.2   Insert panels into the panel group

We start by adding an already-built panel into our new panel group. We insert a panel into the panel group by choosing Insert/Panel from the Application Designer screen. Figure 5.2 illustrates this process.

All panels that match the selection criteria are displayed in the screen. Once we finish inserting all the required panels into the panel group, we close the Insert Panel screen

Navigation: Insert → Panel into Group

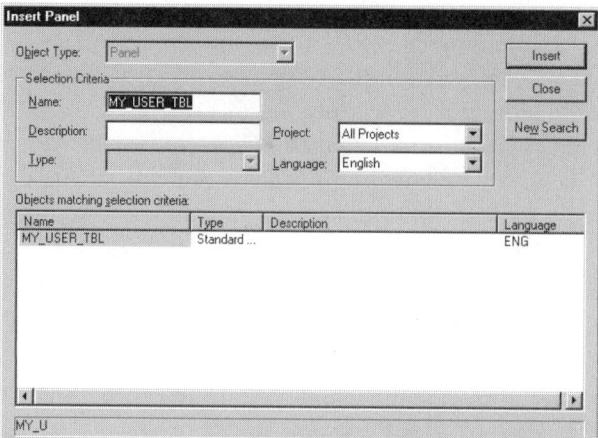

Figure 5.2
Insert panel into panel group

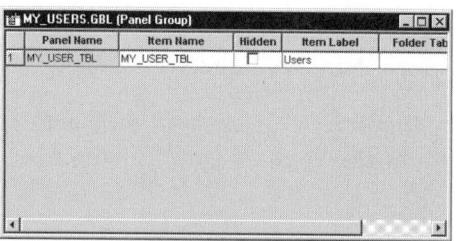

Figure 5.3   Panel inserted in a panel group

by clicking the Close button. Figure 5.3 illustrates the screen as it appears after the panel is inserted into the panel group.

Item Name and Item Label can be changed to fit the functional description of the panel group. The Hidden flag is used to hide panels in a panel group, a useful option when more than one panel exists in the panel group and one of those panels must be hidden from user access.

The Folder tab is the label for the folder after the panel group has been brought up.

5.1.3   Define Panel Group properties

Before we save the panel group definition, we must define the properties for the panel group. The Panel Group Properties window is brought up by choosing Edit/Object Properties from the Application Designer menu. In figures 5.4 and 5.5, you can see the two tabs under the Panel Group Properties window.

General tab

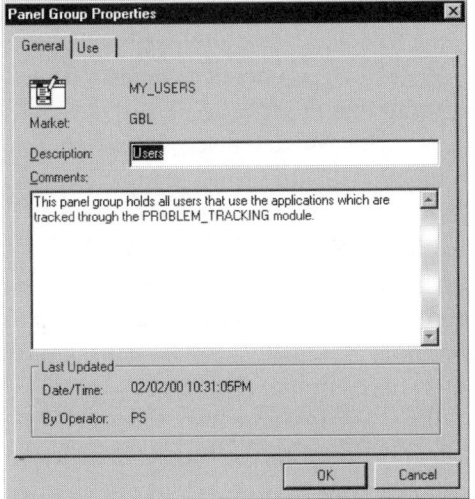

Figure 5.4   Panel Group Properties—General tab

Under the General tab, we enter a brief description and comments for the panel group. The Comments section is used as a modification log for the panel group. The last updated Date/Time as well as the ID of the operator who last updated the panel group is also displayed in the General tab.

Use tab

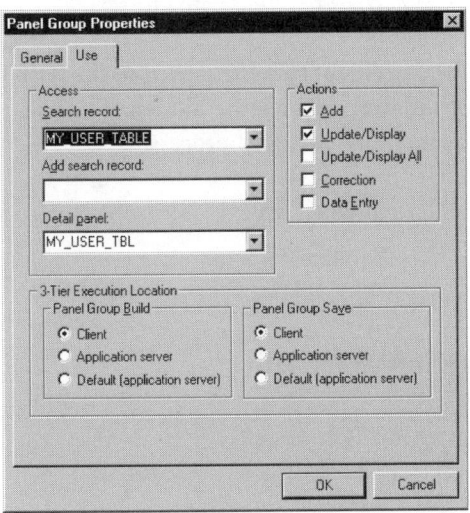

Figure 5.5   Panel Group Properties—Use tab

The Use tab holds the `Search Record`, `Add Search Record`, `Detail Panel Name`, `Actions`, `Build`, and `Save` locations for the panel group. In our example, we define MY_USER_TABLE as the search record. Because we won't specify an Add Search Record, MY_USER_TABLE will be used for `Add` action as well. Authorized actions are `Add` and `Update/Display` for our panel group. `Update/Display All` and `Correction` actions are used for panel groups which access effective-dated record definitions. When using the Tuxedo Application Server in a 3-tier environment, the `Panel Group Build` and the `Panel Group Save` locations come into play. These two parameters determine where the panel group is built and saved during online access.

5.1.4   Save the panel group definition

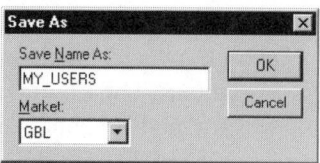

Figure 5.6   Panel Group save

We can now save the panel group definition by choosing File/Save from the Application Designer menu. We will be prompted to enter a name for the panel group (figure 5.6).

The Market field is used to provide custom functionality to a panel group. The same panel group can be saved for two different markets that serve two different functions. For example, in a PeopleSoft HRMS application, the New Hire process can provide the same functionality but with subtle differences in different countries. We can create one panel group using different Markets to suit those subtle differences. Essentially, the two panel groups are two different objects that serve a common function but in different ways.

Let's look at a panel group which contains more than one panel. For this purpose, we use the JOB_DATA_HIRE panel group from the PeopleSoft HRMS system. This panel group has several panels which use the same search record, but display portions of data from tables separated by functional areas. This allows the user to access fields separated by function. Multiple records are also updated through this panel group. The SQL tables updated using this panel group are PERSONAL_DATA, JOB, JOB_EARNS_DIST, BEN_PROG_PARTIC, and EMPLOYMENT. These individual panels contain fields from these records. The user is able to save all the information for an employee in the database.

In figure 5.7, you can see the number of panels attached to the JOB_DATA_HIRE panel group. Notice that two of the twelve panels are hidden. These are used to hold Work/Derived fields used for calculation and panel processing. The user does not see the hidden panels in the application menu. The Item Label is displayed as a subitem under the Menu Item and as folder tab labels unless folder tab Labels are filled.

Navigation: File → Open → Panel Group → JOB_DATA_HIRE

JOB_DATA_HIRE.GBL [Panel Group]

	Panel Name	Item Name	Hidden	Item Label	Folder Tab Label
1	PERSONAL_DATA1	PERSONAL_DATA_1	☐	&Name/Address	
2	PERSONAL_DATA2	PERSONAL_DATA_2	☐	Personal &Profile	
3	PERSONAL_DATA3	PERSONAL_DATA_3	☐	&Eligibility/Identity	
4	JOB_DATA1	JOB_DATA1	☐	&Work Location	
5	JOB_DATA_JOBCO	JOB_DATA_JOBCODE	☐	&Jobcode	Job Information
6	JOB_DATA2	JOB_DATA2	☐	&Payroll	
7	JOB_DATA3	JOB_DATA_3	☐	&Compensation	Compensation
8	JOB_DATA_ERNDIS	JOB_EARNINGS_DISTRI	☐	Job Earnings &Distri	
9	JOB_DATA_BENPR	BENEFIT_PROGRAM_P	☐	&Benefit Program P	
10	EMPLOYMENT_DTA	EMPLOYMENT_DATA1	☐	&Employment Data	
11	JOB_DATA1_WRK	JOB_DATA_1_WORK	☑	Job Data 1 Work	
12	SCRTY_TBL_GBL_	SCRTY_TBL_GBL_WRK	☑	Scrty Tbl Gbl Wrk	

**Figure 5.7
JOB_DATA_HIRE panel group
definition**

5.1.5 Panel groups and process definitions

Process definitions are used to identify batch processes in PeopleSoft, which are executed using the Process Scheduler. Just as menu item definitions are attached to panel groups, so are process definitions. When the user chooses the Run icon (Traffic Light) from an application menu, the Application Processor attempts to match the panel group from the application menu item with Process definitions which contain the same panel group. All matching process definitions are then presented to the user in a list on a Process Scheduler Request panel. A panel group, therefore, is the common link between a process definition and a menu item definition.

(To learn more on how to attach Process definitions to application menus, refer to chapter 27.)

5.2 CREATING APPLICATION MENUS IN PEOPLESOFT

Application menus serve as a gateway to the online application. Application menus can either be data entry panels, inquiry panels, or process panels. Panels that deliver common functions are usually linked to the same application menu. For example, all panels related to setting up payroll tables are linked to a menu called Define Payroll Process in a PeopleSoft Human Resources application. To create an application menu, we

- create a new menu definition
- create new bar items
- create new Menu Items
- define Menu Item Properties
- define Menu properties
- Save the menu definition

5.2.1 Create a new menu definition

Navigation: File → New → Menu

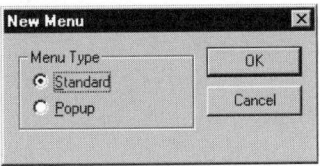

Figure 5.8   New menu

We create a new menu definition as illustrated in figure 5.8.

Standard menus are application menus while pop-up menus are linked to a panel or a panel field. We choose "Standard" for our application menu, bringing up a blank Menu Definition screen (figure 5.9).

Navigation: File →New → Menu → OK

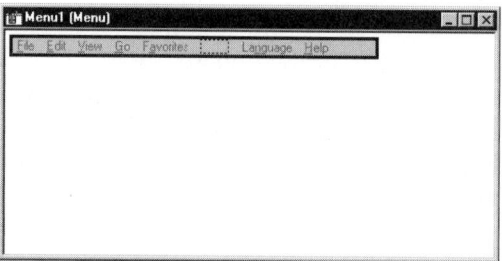

Figure 5.9
New standard menu screen

5.2.2 Create new bar items

The dotted lines, which appear on the blank screen in figure 5.9, represent a bar item. Bar items are groupings of individual menu items. Let's start by defining a bar item and its properties.

By default, a standard menu contains some standard bar items which are components of every application menu. These bar items serve as general purpose items that the end user can use when accessing the application menus. For example, the bar item File is used for saving and canceling panels. The bar item Edit is used for editing functions and other hot key functions used in the application panel. Go serves as a gateway to other application menus in PeopleSoft.

Navigation: Double Click on the dotted lines from a Standard menu screen

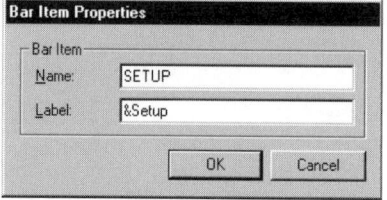

Figure 5.10   Bar Item Properties

Let's consider how we can define a custom bar item attached to an application menu. We define Bar Item properties by double-clicking between the dotted lines.

In figure 5.10 we define a bar item named SETUP with a label of &Setup. The character "&" denotes the hot key letter that accesses the menu item using the keyboard without using a mouse. In this example, by pressing ALT-S from the keyboard, the user can access the Setup bar item.

5.2.3 Create new menu items

Once we create a bar item we can add menu items under that bar item by double-clicking on the dotted lines below the Setup bar item. Figure 5.11 illustrates the dotted lines for new Menu Items. The Setup bar item is used to create setup tables for our application. Likewise, we use the Tracking bar item to track all incidents and resolutions in our application. We can create all the menu items that functionally fall under the Setup bar item (figure 5.12).

Navigation: Go → File → Open → Menu → Problem Tracking

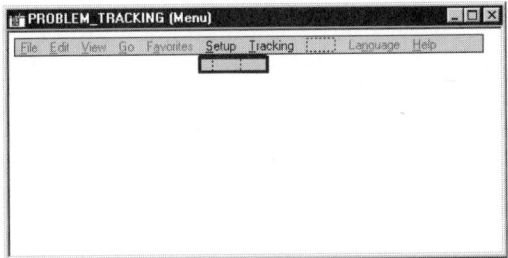

Figure 5.11
Menu item properties screen

Navigation: Double-clicking on the dotted lines for Menu Items

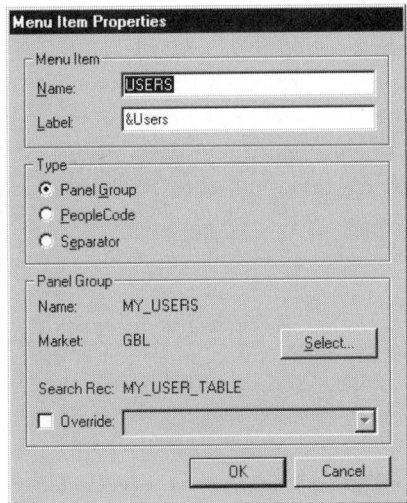

Figure 5.12
Menu item properties screen

5.2.4   Define Menu Item properties

Figure 5.13 illustrates the Menu Item Properties screen. We start by giving the menu item a name and a label. Then we define the menu item as a panel group item.

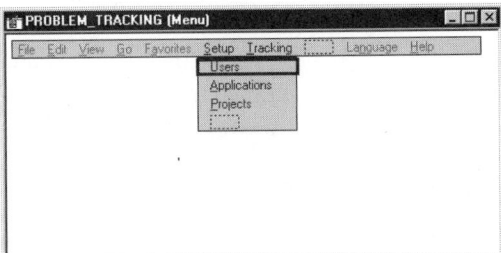

Figure 5.13
Standard menu screen with bar and menu items

Menu items can either be panel groups, Menu PeopleCode, or separator items. When we define the Menu Items as Panel Groups or as PeopleCode items we have to associate the menu items with a panel group. We can choose a panel group associated with the menu item by clicking on the Select button from the Menu Item Properties screen. In our example, we choose MY_USERS as the panel group. We can also override the search record associated with the panel group by clicking the override search record checkbox on and entering an override search record from the Menu Item Properties screen.

TIP   We can add more than one menu item under a bar item, and we can add more than one bar item to an application menu.

Before we start adding new menu items to our application menu, we have to add fields, records, panels, and panel groups to build the menu item. Once we design and develop all these objects, we are ready to assemble them into a new menu item for the user.

Menu definitions are stored in tables which are language-related. For each language used in the system, the bar item and menu item descriptions are stored separately. This enables users to view these application menus in different languages.

NOTE   Application menus are migrated as a whole from one database to another. The individual bar and menu items cannot be chosen for migration. For this reason, when application menus are migrated across databases, one has to be careful not to overwrite another developer's work in the same menu.

5.2.5   Define menu properties

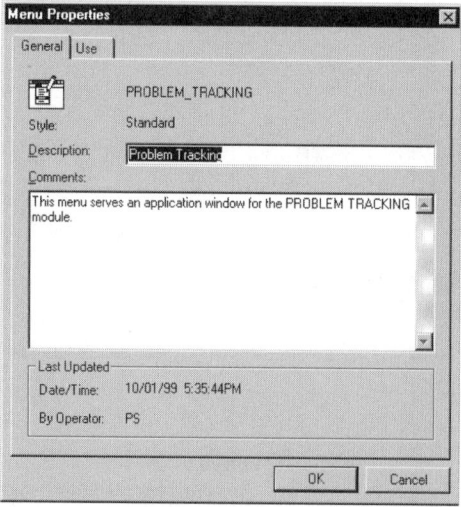

Figure 5.14   Menu Properties—General tab

Now that we have attached menu items to the application menu, it's time to define properties for the application menu as a whole. Figures 5.14 and 5.15 illustrate the tabs under the Menu Item Properties screen.

The Menu Properties window can be brought up by choosing File/Object Properties from the Application Designer menu. The application menu should be open to perform this operation.

General tab

The General tab contains a brief description and Comments for the application menu. The Comments section can be used to maintain a modification log for the application menu. The General tab displays the last Date/Time the menu was updated and the ID of the operator who updated it.

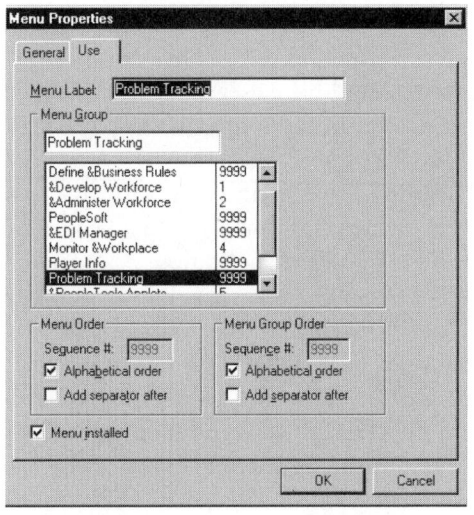

Figure 5.15   Menu Properties—Use tab

Use tab

Under the Use tab, we can provide a label for the menu. This label will be seen under the Go menu online. We can also group one or more application menus together in a menu group. The menu groups appear as the first list when we choose the Go menu. When the names for the menu and the menu group are the same, the menu appears as part of the list under the Go menu. We can also provide a sequence for how the menu groups appear under the Go menu. In addition, the sort order for both the menu and the menu group can be specified under the Use tab.

5.2.6   Save the menu definition

Figure 5.16   Menu definition save

We are now ready to save our menu definition. Figure 5.16 illustrates the Save Panel window for a menu definition.

We can name our application menu PROBLEM_TRACKING and click the OK button to save the menu definition.

5.2.7   Pop-up menus

Pop-up menus are used to access context sensitive information. For example, in fields defined as dates, we can provide a calendar that will pop-up when the user right-clicks on the Date field. Pop-up menus can either be attached to panels or panel fields. The attached pop-up menu is activated when the user right-clicks on the panel field.

Pop-up menus can either be used for panel transfers or for executing PeopleCode. Panel transfers require parameters such as menu name, panel group, panel, and action which are required when transferring to a panel. PeopleCode is attached to the panel field and the PrePopup PeopleCode event is executed before the pop-up menu is shown.

To bring up another panel using PeopleCode, we define the pop-up menu as PeopleCode and attach a PrePopup PeopleCode event to the record field. When you define the pop-up menu as a transfer, only one transfer panel can be defined. This is a Non-Modal transfer definition. When the pop-up menu is defined as PeopleCode, the DOMODAL PeopleCode function can be used to transfer focus to different panels for different panel field values. This is a Modal transfer definition. (To learn more about PrePopup PeopleCode events, refer to part 3 herein.)

5.3 AUTHORIZING USERS

After we build menu items, we have to authorize user access to these menu items. We can do so by using the Security Administrator tool in PeopleSoft (found in the PeopleTools menu group under the Go menu).

Operator security in PeopleSoft is driven using two fields: the OPRID and the OPRCLASS fields. OPRID is a unique identification given to a PeopleSoft user. Every operator must have a password to log on to the application. An operator may belong to one group or many groupings of operators, otherwise known as operator classes.

Prior to PeopleSoft release 7, an operator could be assigned only to one particular operator class. This made it difficult for system administrators to define unique groupings of operators. System administrators either had to change the business needs or create more classes. Starting with PeopleSoft release 7, an operator can be associated with more than one operator class. All the security attributes of the operator classes translate down to the operator. In other words, if the operator belongs to two operator classes, attributes of both these classes are attached to the operator profile.

Attributes control the creation of operator classes. Every user needs an operator ID to use the PeopleSoft application. It's often a difficult task to find an operator class that fits the user's security profile. Let us look at the attributes attached to an operator class to better understand the previous statement.

The following criteria are used to determine the creation of operator classes in the system:

- *Menu items*   Menu items that the operator can access determine the operator class for the user. If a group of operators has the same set of menu items they can access, then they can potentially be under the same operator class, provided all the other criteria are similar.
- *Sign-on times*   If the operators can have access to the system at similar time durations, then they can belong to the same operator class. Sign-on times control the time when a user can log on to the PeopleSoft application.
- *Process groups*   Process groups are identifiers by which batch processes are differentiated. These identifiers can either be functional identifiers or any other identifier by which the processes are separated. For example, identifiers in a PeopleSoft Human Resources system can be PAYALL, HRALL, BENALL, and so forth, differentiating the processes into functional areas. Hence, operators who run similar processes can belong to the same operator class. When an operator has security to a particular process group, that does not necessarily mean that the operator can run all processes under that process group. The operator has to have access to the menu items that run these processes as well.

- *Functional security* Functional security is row-level security which secures application data in the PeopleSoft system. In a PeopleSoft HRMS application certain fields such as Department, Business Unit and Pay Groups can be used to provide row level security. Likewise in a PeopleSoft General Ledger application, fields like Business Unit, Product, and Location may be used for functional security. Each operator is able to access data based on these functional attributes. For example, a group of operators in the Michigan plant can only access employees who work in the paygroup which has all employees from the Michigan plant. So all operators who have similar access based on functional criteria can belong to the same operator class.

Now that we know the criteria by which operator classes are determined, let's build these classes using the Security Administrator tool.

5.3.1 General attributes

Let's create an operator class called MYADMIN, which will be used to create operators who can access our Problem Tracking application menu. We have defined the Security definition type as Class of Operators. We can provide a Business process map for the operator class under the General attributes. Business process maps are graphical representations of application menus which the users can view to access panels. We can control how the user views a Navigator display of menu items using the Configuration Manager.

We can define the Background Disconnect Interval and Online Time-out minutes in the General Attributes screen. Background Disconnect Interval controls the disconnection of icons which stay in the background and use system resources by not getting disconnected. Online Time-out Minutes control the time out of the PeopleSoft session as a whole after a certain amount of idle time. We now save this operator class by choosing File/Save from the menu in the Security Administrator screen. When we are prompted for a name, we name our operator class MYADMIN.

5.3.2 Menu items

By clicking on the Menu Items icon on the left side (figure 5.17), we start authorizing user access to menu items. Select the menu which the user can access by choosing Insert/Menu Name from the Security Administrator screen. All menu items which belong to the user application menu appear on a list box. In our example, we choose PROBLEM_TRACKING as the menu item. Then we can highlight the menu items which the user can access or choose Select All to select all menu items in the application menu. We can also provide Display Only access to a particular menu item by clicking on the Change Display-Only button. Once we have chosen all menu items which the user can access, we click OK to close the Select Menu Items window (figure 5.18).

Navigation: Go → PeopleTools → Security Administrator → File → New

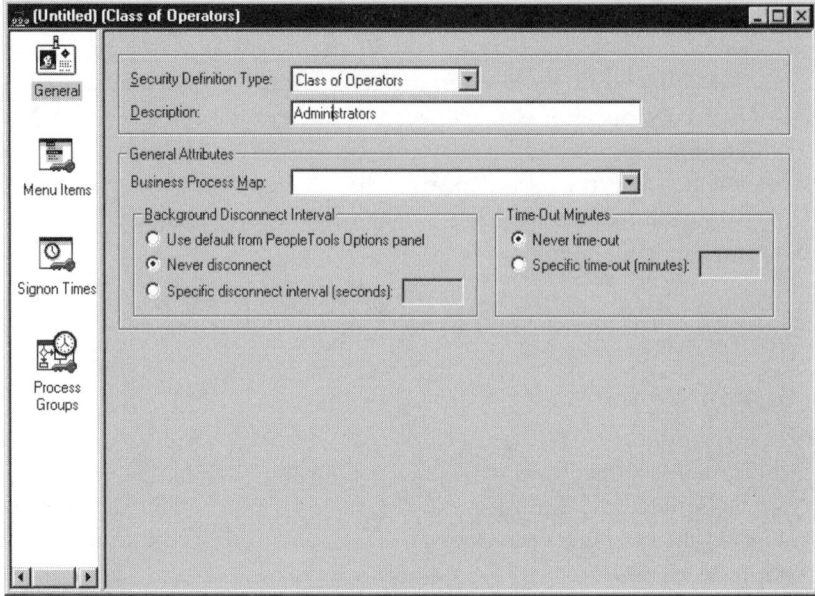

Figure 5.17   Operator Security window—General view

Navigation: Insert/Menu Name under the Menu Items tab

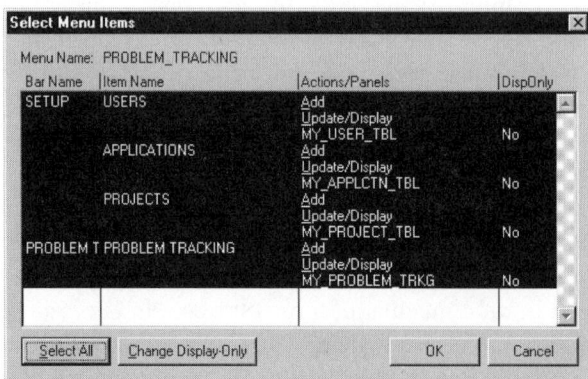

Figure 5.18
Menu items selection screen

Notice all the menu items (figure 5.18) have been highlighted for user access, and the DispOnly column reads "No" on all the selected items. We can add more application menus and menu items for user access by repeating the same steps using other application menus from the Security Administrator screen.

5.3.3   Sign-On Times

By choosing the Signon Times icon from the left side (figure 5.19), we can enter logon times for users. Basically, we enter a sign-on time for each day of the week by using Insert/Signon Times from the Security Administrator screen. Let us take a look at the sign-on times for MYADMIN operator class. We can add more than one interval of time when the user can access the system. For example, we can add 00:00 hours as the starting time and 10:00 as the ending time on Sunday, and also add 13:00 and 15:00 as the starting and ending time on Sunday. This allows the user to access the system only between those times on Sundays.

Navigation: Click on the Signon Times tab

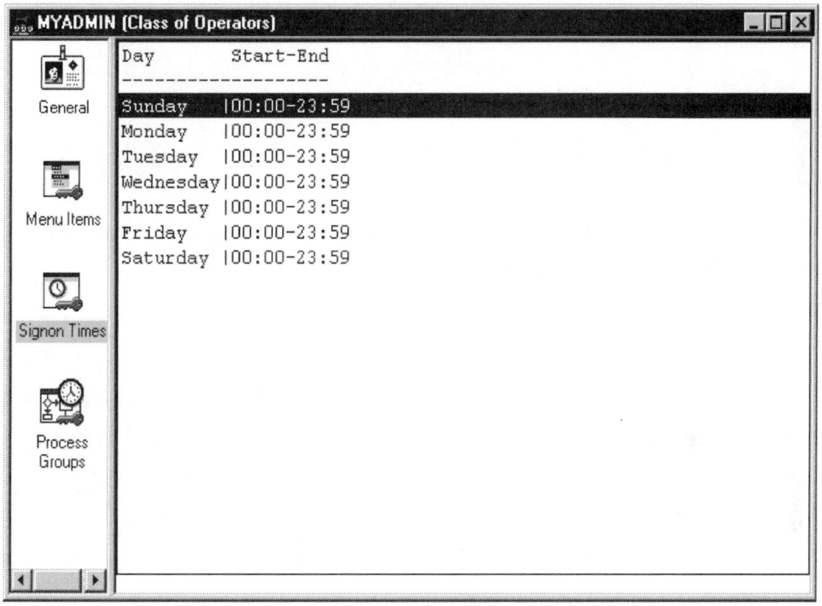

Figure 5.19   Operator Security window—Signon Times view

5.3.4   Process groups

Process groups are groups of processes that identify process definitions in PeopleSoft. Process groups control process security in PeopleSoft. For example, let's say a process named PER005 belongs to the HRALL Process Group. All operator classes, which have access to the HRALL Process Group, will be able to run that process provided they have access to the menu item that runs the process. So we include all the process groups that the operator class can access by using Insert/Process Groups from the Security Administrator screen.

In figure 5.20 we can see the process groups for the MYADMIN operator class.

Navigation: Click on the Process Groups tab

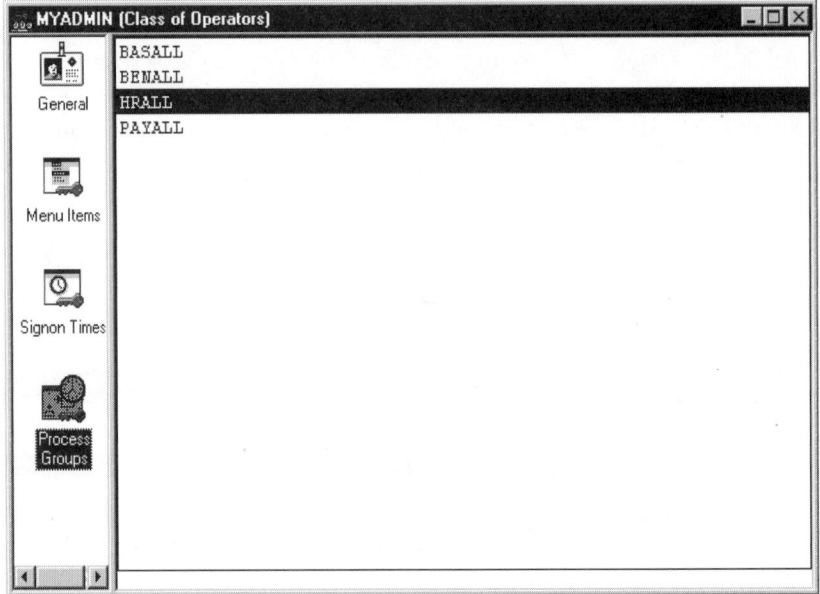

Figure 5.20 Operator Security window—Process Groups view

Figure 5.20 indicates that the MYADMIN operator class can access all processes defined under BASALL, BENALL, HRALL, and PAYALL process groups. The operator class also needs access to the menu items that run these processes. If a hundred processes are defined under the HRALL process group, the user does not always have access to all the menu items that initiate the hundred processes, so menu item access and process group access work hand-in-hand to determine what processes a user can run.

Figure 5.21 illustrates how a process definition is defined and how the process definition attributes are linked to operator security.

The process definition in figure 5.21 belongs to the HRALL and HRCAN process groups. Also the panel groups which are attached to menu items are defined. The combination of both these attributes gives the user access to this process.

Navigation: Go → PeopleTools → Process Scheduler → Use-Process Definitions

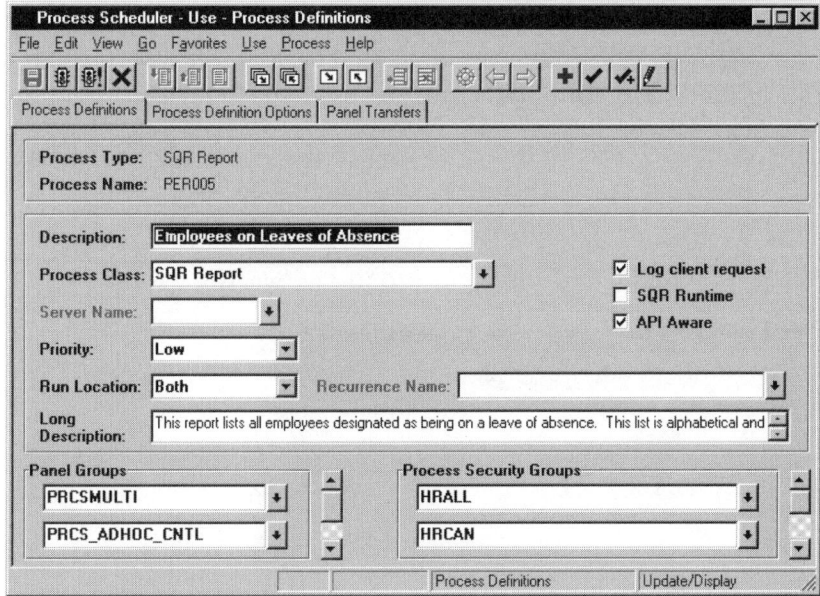

Figure 5.21   Process definition

5.3.5   Process profiles

Every operator class has a process profile which controls certain processing parameters. We can change the process profile for an operator class by choosing Edit/Process Profile from the Security Administrator screen.

Process profiles control printer, output destinations, and process view/update parameters for an operator class. These are default parameters for an operator class, and the operator can override these parameters at the time of running a process. Let us take a look at the process profile screen for MYADMIN operator class (figure 5.22).

In figure 5.22, we can notice that the file and printer destinations are separated by Client and Server destinations. The Server destination is the server where the PeopleSoft Process Scheduler is currently running. Let's review the parameters which control how the operators who belong to this operator class view and update processes and run controls:

- *Allow Process Request—View By*—controls the processes that the operator class can view on the Process Monitor.
- *Allow Process Request—Update By*—controls the processes that the operator class can update on the Process Monitor.
- *Allow Requestor to Override Output Destination*—allows the operator class to override the default output destination in a process request.

- *Allow Requestor to Override Server Parameters*—allows the operator to override the Server parameters in which the process runs.
- *Allow Requestor to View Server Status*—allows the operator class to view the status of the Process Scheduler.
- *Allow Requestor to Update Server Status*—allows the operator class to stop, suspend, or restart the Process Scheduler.
- *Allow Requestor to Update Recurrence Definition*—allows the operator class to define and update Recurrence in a process request.

Navigation: Edit → Process Profile (MYADMIN operator class is open)

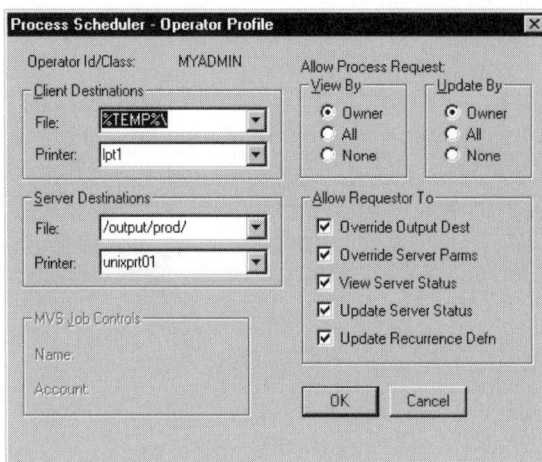

Figure 5.22
Operator Process Scheduler profile screen

Now we need to save the operator class once again. We do so by choosing File/Save from the Security Administrator screen. All attributes defined are now attached to MY_ADMIN operator class.

5.3.6 Creating operators using operator class definitions

From now on, MYADMIN operator class can be used as a template to create actual operators in the system. We can bring up a new screen by choosing File/New from the Security Administrator screen, but first we have to make sure the security definition type is set to Operator in order to save an operator definition (figure 5.23).

Only the General tab and the Classes tab are necessary to create an operator definition. The other tabs translate from the operator class attributes for the operator. We now enter the operator attributes to complete the operator definition. Some attributes are required in order to save the operator definition.

Navigation: File → Open → MYOPER

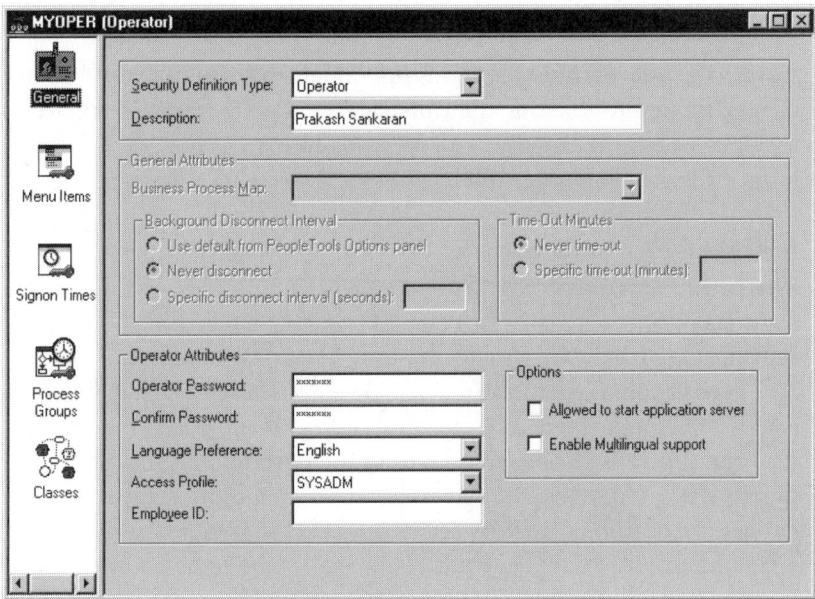

Figure 5.23   Operator definition for MYOPER

General tab

Operator Password   The password that the operator uses to sign on to PeopleSoft.

Confirm Password   A confirmation to save the password for the operator.

Language Preference   The base language with which the operator signs on to PeopleSoft. This plays a significant role, controlling the language used to display descriptions when the operator signs on to PeopleSoft.

Access Profile   The access ID the operator needs to login to the database. PeopleSoft uses the access ID to create a session in the database. Access IDs are the only IDs which have access to database tables and views. Using the access ID, operators in the system can access database tables and views. One access ID can be used to provide entry by all users in the system. Therefore, the Database Administrator needs to maintain grants and permissions only for that one access ID in the system. When the operator logs into the system, the operator's access to the system is verified, after which the access ID is used to retrieve data from tables and views.

Employee ID   If the operator is also an employee and the Human Resources system is maintained using PeopleSoft, then we can enter the Employee ID for the operator here. In a PeopleSoft Human Resources system, entering the Employee ID prevents operators from changing their own data.

Allowed to Start application server This option allows the operator to start a PeopleSoft application server. For example, a Tuxedo server is an application server running the PeopleSoft application.

Enable Multilingual Support This option lets the operator edit data in multiple languages. By simply accessing the Language menu item from any application menu, the user can switch the language to edit fields in panels that are stored in multiple language or related language tables.

Classes tab

This attribute is used only for operator definitions. As mentioned before, starting from PeopleSoft release 7, an operator can be included in more than one operator class, making it easy for system administrators to create operator classes.

System administrators can create operator classes which define panel access separately. They can also create operator classes which define function security. Then, they can attach these operator classes to the operator. The operator class that defines the panel access provides the operators with the appropriate menu items. The class that defines the functional security secures the data that they will access. For example, in a PeopleSoft HRMS implementation, we can create an operator class which has menu items/panels which a typical HR user can access. This one class provides panel access to all HR users throughout the system. At the same time, we also need to create individual classes that contain the appropriate application security for these users. Let's take a look at the following matrix to better understand this process. We assume that all these users are HR users, and that they belong to different locations processing various paygroups and departments.

In table 5.1, the column on the left contains the actual operator IDs in the system. All three users access the same set of panels and menu items. Hence, they are attached to the HRADMIN class. They will, however, be able to access only the departments and paygroups in their respective locations. So they are also each attached to individual classes (NYCHR, SFOHR, and WDCHR) which contain the respective departments that they are able to access. The same theory can be used across all PeopleSoft applications to arrive at the number of operator classes needed in the system.

Table 5.1 Operator security

Operators	Location	Panel Class	Security Class
SOSGOOD	New York	HRADMIN	NYCHR
CFINNIGA	San Francisco	HRADMIN	SFOHR
GMORDIN	Washington, D.C	HRADMIN	WDCHR

To attach the operator to an operator class we choose Insert/Classes from the Security Administrator screen. We also choose the primary operator class for the operator by clicking on the Primary checkbox (figure 5.24).

Navigation: Click on the Classes tab

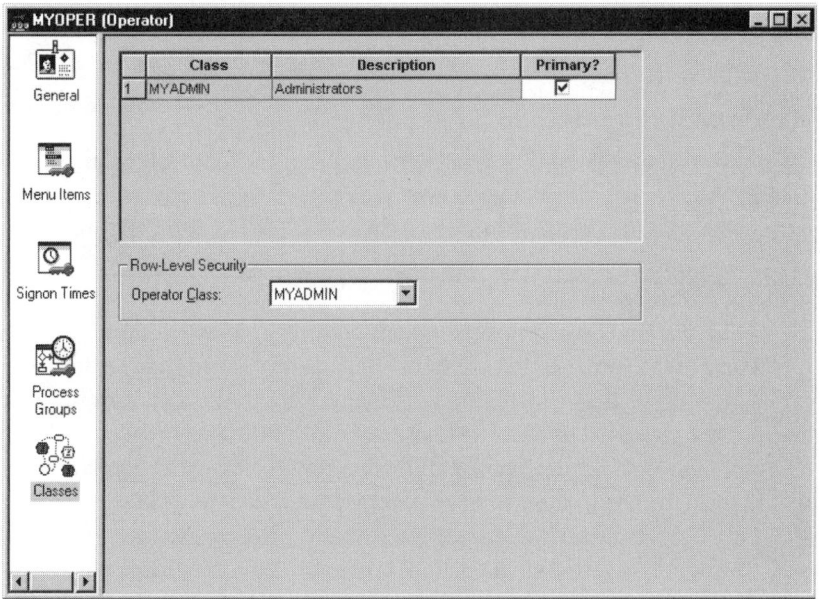

Figure 5.24   Operator Security window—Classes view

The primary operator class controls the application data security for the operator. The primary operator class can also provide panel and menu access for the operator. If we follow this path, we will end up creating more operator classes than necessary, but if we can separate the application data security and the panel security attributes, we can reduce the number of operator classes created in the system.

Row-level security

Navigation: File → Save

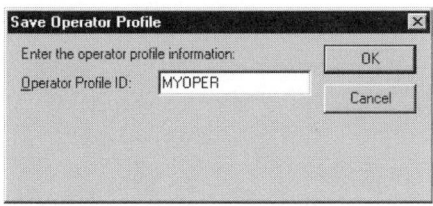

Figure 5.25   Save an operator definition

To secure data, PeopleSoft uses the primary operator class for the user. PeopleSoft release 7 offers a new feature, ROWSECCLASS. This is the row-level security class for the operator. ROWSECCLASS requires a change in the search view definitions that PeopleSoft delivers in its application. Currently, all search views contain either OPRID or OPRCLASS fields. PeopleTools automatically uses the primary operator class at search time. It attaches an extra condition to the WHERE clause of the search view to control the selection of data from the system. If we replace the OPRCLASS or OPRID fields in security views with the field ROWSECCLASS, PeopleTools now uses that class for the operator to control data access.

We now save the operator definition by providing a name. In our example, we provide MYOPER as the name for the operator (figure 5.25).

5.3.7 Understanding functional security (Trees)

We have discussed creating functional security and controlling the data the user can see in the system. Now let's see how we can define the data which the operator class can access. We do this by using the ADMINISTER HR SYSTEM menu in a PeopleSoft HRMS application. In PeopleSoft HRMS, the DEPARTMENT field is used as a key field to control data access.

The system contains a department security tree which contains the organization structure. This security tree contains organization groupings of departments.

A group of departments may report to a location, and a group of locations may report to a divisional office. The divisional office ultimately reports to a corporate office. This organizational hierarchy is built using the tree manager, which, in turn, is used to build the department table in PeopleSoft HRMS. Each node in the tree is an entry in the PS_DEPT_TBL record. All employees in the system are assigned to a department.

Before we see how we can define the departments which an operator class can access, let's look at the department security tree in a PeopleSoft HRMS system (figure 5.26).

Navigation: Go → PeopleTools → Tree Manager

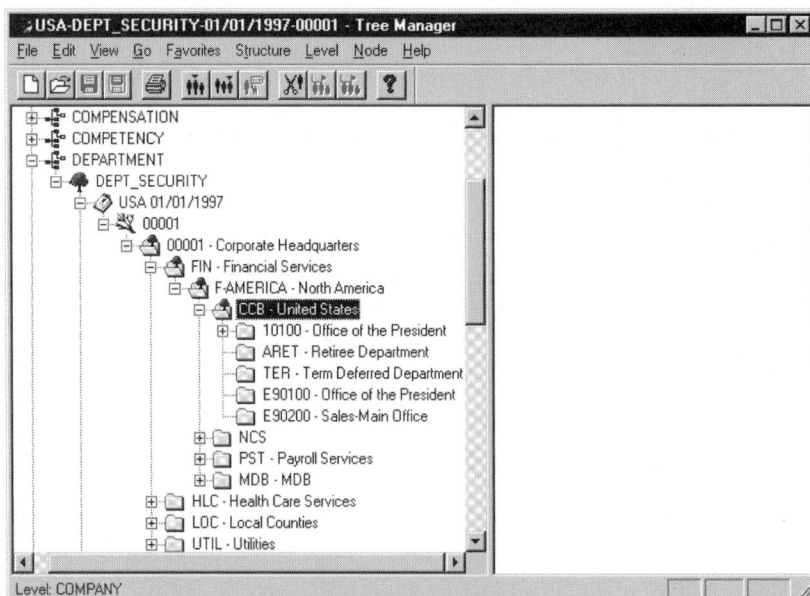

Figure 5.26 Department security tree in PeopleSoft HRMS

If we look at the tree in figure 5.26, we see that it has a structure called DEPARTMENT, which contains the DEPT_SECURITY trees. `00001` denotes corporate headquarters, and FIN, HLC, LOC, and UTIL represent different divisions providing different services within the organization. USA is the set ID for corporate headquarters and all the divisions (services) and departments underneath them.

Now, let's look at the data security screen where we define these values to control data access for an operator class. The Maintain Data Security screen in figure 5.27 has two rows for operator class MYADMIN. The first row provides MYADMIN access to all services, divisions, and departments under `00001` (Corporate). The second row excludes access only to department `10100` (Office of the President). This means MYADMIN can access all employee records for employees who report to `00001` (Corporate), except for those employees who report to `10100` (Office of the President).

These values are saved in PS_SCRTY_TBL_DEPT. This table is used in all the search views in PeopleSoft HRMS which control department security.

Navigation: Go → Administer HR System → Use → Maintain Data Security

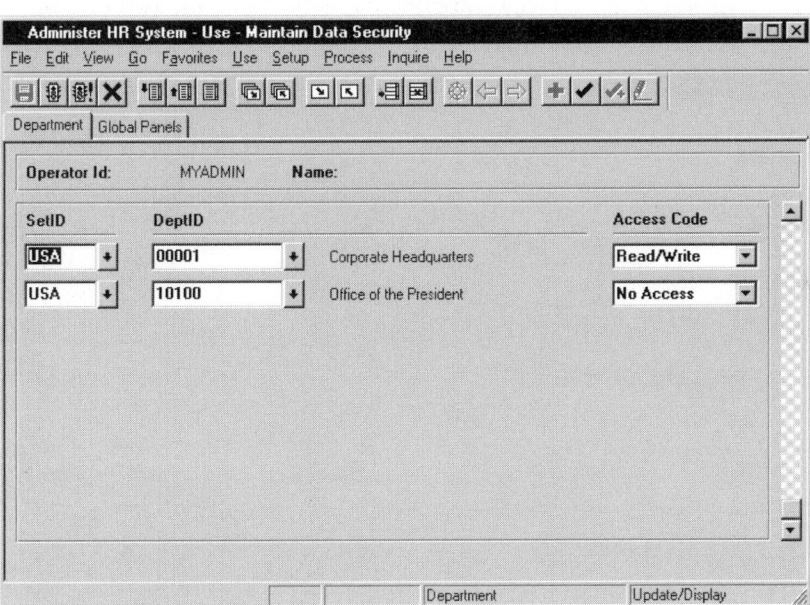

Figure 5.27 Maintain data security in PeopleSoft HRMS

1 Panel Groups can contain one or more panels in them. Panel Groups are used to separate panel fields by function. Panel Groups are also used to update multiple record definitions at the same time.

2 Panel Groups attach an application panel to a menu item.

3 Menus can be standard or pop-up menus. Standard menus come delivered with standard bar items. More bar items and menu items can be added to the standard application menu.

4 A menu item is a single unit used to provide access to applications.

5 A panel group containing one or more panels is attached to a menu item. Access can be provided to any one or all of the panels in the panel group.

6 The Security Administrator tool is used to authorize users for access to menu items. OPRID and OPRCLASS fields are the two primary fields used to define Operator Security.

CHAPTER 6

Enhancing your application

6.1 CREATING AND USING PROMPT RECORDS

Prompt records can be either database tables or database views. We utilize a prompt record to create a drop-down list that contains the possible list of values for a field. A user entering values into such a field will be restricted to the values produced by the prompt record. Drop-down lists work only on character fields. (Usually fields that are used as codes have drop down lists behind them.)

Prompt records are attached to record fields, which means only one prompt record can be used for a record field at a given time. This is important because prompt records for a record field can be changed dynamically during panel processing. Before we learn more about dynamic prompt records, let's cover the basics.

Prompt records, which are similar to search records, are primarily put to work using search and database keys. A key difference between prompt records and search records is the input mechanism. While prompt records are supplied with inputs from fields in the panel, search records are supplied with inputs from input dialog boxes. Nevertheless, the principle behind the workings of prompt and search records is the same.

6.1.1 Principles of prompt records

Prompt records contain fields defined as key fields. The fields prompted are defined as key fields in the prompt records. The prompted field can either be the first key field in the prompt record or any other field in the key field list. When the prompted field is not the first key field on the prompt record, the fields that precede the prompted field must be populated for the prompt to work. Since prompt fields are database keys, they facilitate faster searching during prompt processing. Let's consider a few examples:

6.1.2 Prompt records with a single search key

Prompt records with a single search key are simple enough to understand. The prompted field is the only search key on the prompt record. In this case, no reason exists to supply an input to the prompt record. The prompt list is brought up by clicking on the drop-down arrow or by pressing F4.

In our application, we can create a single key prompt field. In MY_PROJECT_TBL, we can define a prompt record behind MY_APPLICATION_ID field.

Let's walk through this process of defining the prompt record in MY_PROJECT_TBL. First, we have to open the record definition for MY_PROJECT_TBL using the Application Designer (figure 6.1).

Navigation: Edit → Record Field Properties

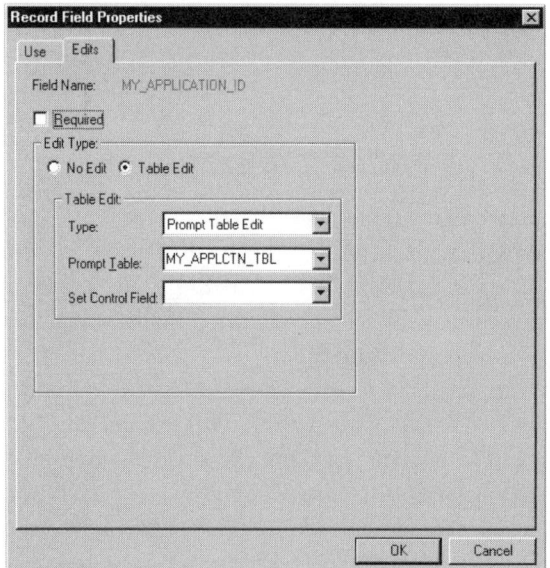

Figure 6.1
Defining prompt records

We used MY_APPLCTN_TBL as the prompt record, so let's take a quick look at the search key definition for this prompt record. In figure 6.2, we can see that the only search key in the prompt record is the MY_APPLICATION_ID field. This is an example of a simple prompt record: the prompt list appears without any input from the panel, and once the prompt record is defined for a record field, the prompt record can be used on any panel that contains that record field.

In figure 6.2, we can see that MY_APPLICATION_ID is marked as a search field on MY_APPLCTN_TBL. All fields that are marked as List Items also appear on the prompt list. Now, let's look at the prompt field and the prompt list as they appear on an online application panel.

Figure 6.3 illustrates the drop-down arrow on MY_APPLICATION_ID field.

Navigation: File → Open → Record → MY_APPLCTN_TBL

MY_APPLCTN_TBL (Record)

Field Name	Type	Key	Dir	CurC	Srch	List	Sys	Audt	H
MY_APPLICATION_ID	Char	Key	Asc		Yes	Yes	No		
DESCR	Char	Alt	Asc		No	Yes	No		
DESCRSHORT	Char				No	No	No		

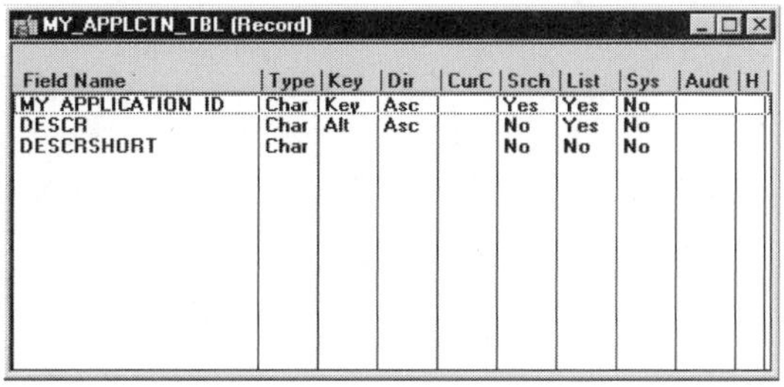

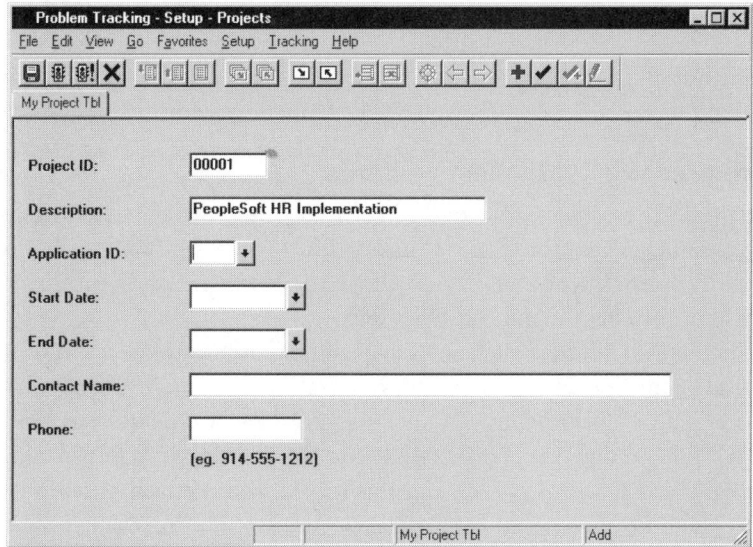

Figure 6.2
Prompt record—Key display

Navigation: Go → Problem Tracking → Setup → Projects (User Application)

Figure 6.3 Prompt records on an application panel

We press F4 from the field to bring up the prompt list. Now, consider the actual prompt list generated from this field (figure 6.4).

Navigation: F4 from the field (or) Clicking on the drop down arrow

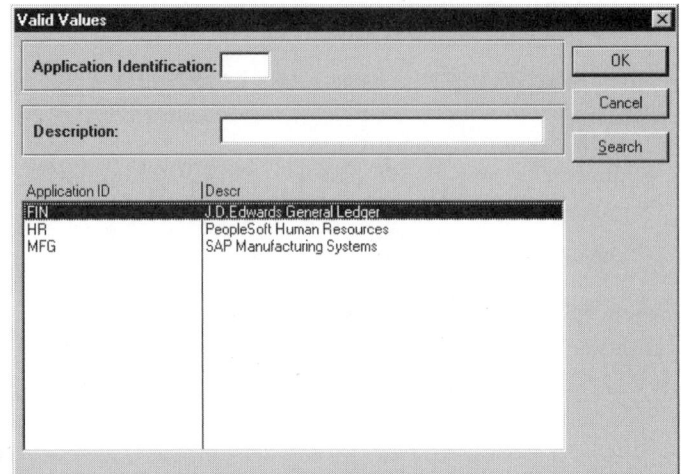

Figure 6.4
Prompt list from the
Projects panel

In the prompt list of valid values, both the search key and all the list box items appear. In figure 6.2 we saw the key definition for MY_APPLCTN_TBL. In addition to the MY_APPLICATION_ID field defined as the search key, the DESCR field is defined as a list box item. Since MY_APPLICATION_ID is a code, the DESCR field provides a description to help the user choose the correct application ID from the prompt list. By highlighting any one of the valid values from the prompt list and choosing OK, we are able to populate the panel field with that value.

6.1.3   Prompt records with effective dates

Some prompt records are effective-dated. Every time the characteristics of the stored information changes, a new row is inserted in the prompt table with a new effective date. In PeopleSoft, the Application Processor automatically returns the list of valid values as of the effective date on the panel.

Since we do not have such an example in our application, let's look at an example from the PeopleSoft HRMS application. Let's say that employee job-related information is stored in a record named JOB. This record has two fields in particular that store the COMPANY and the PAYGROUP for the employee. The prompt record for COMPANY is COMPANY_TBL, and this record has an effective date and an effective status. These fields—special fields that the Application Processor treats differently—are named EFFDT and EFF_STATUS in PeopleSoft. The COMPANY field is prompted from the JOB DATA panel group. Let's take a look at the panel for further explanation on how the EFFDT field affects the prompt.

The panel in figure 6.5 has an effective date which controls the prompt list on the COMPANY field. The effective date on this panel is compared with the effective date on COMPANY_TBL to provide the prompt list. All companies active and effective as of 9/1/1996 appear in the prompt list. EFF_STATUS field on the COMPANY_TBL controls the active and inactive status of the company, and EFFDT field controls the effective date. Now let's look at the key definition for COMPANY_TBL (figure 6.6).

Navigation: Go → Administer Workforce (U.S) → Use → Job Data (PeopleSoft HRMS)

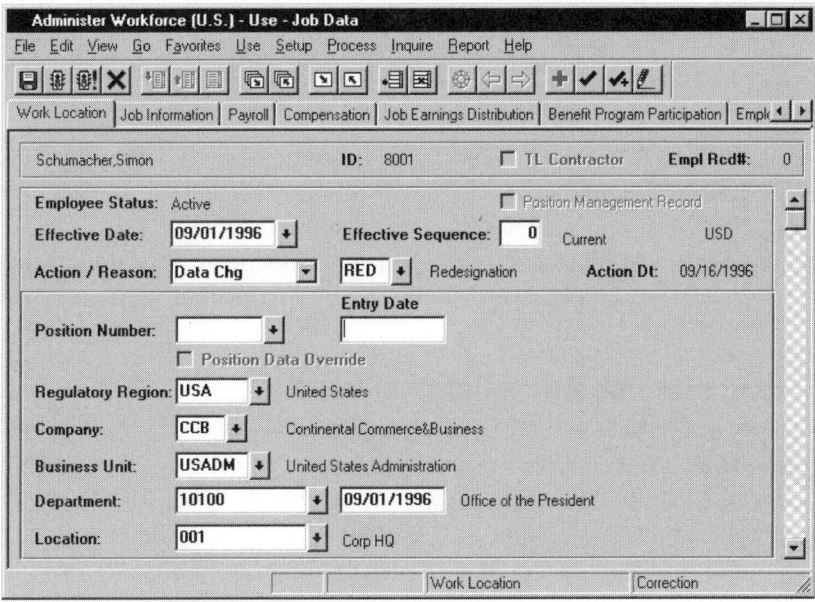

Figure 6.5 PeopleSoft HR panel—Prompt record with EFFDT

Navigation: File → Open → Record → COMPANY_TBL (Application Designer)

COMPANY_TBL (Record)

Field Name	Type	Key	Dir	CurC	Srch	List	Sys	Audt
COMPANY	Char	Key	Asc		Yes	Yes	No	
EFFDT	Date	Key	Desc		No	No	No	
EFF_STATUS	Char				No	No	No	
DESCR	Char	Alt	Asc		No	Yes	No	
DESCR_AC	Char				No	No	No	
DESCRSHORT	Char				No	No	No	
ADDRESS_SBR	SRec				No	No	No	
ADDRESS1_AC	Char				No	No	No	
ADDRESS2_AC	Char				No	No	No	
ADDRESS3_AC	Char				No	No	No	
CITY_AC	Char				No	No	No	
FEDERAL_EIN	Nbr				No	No	No	

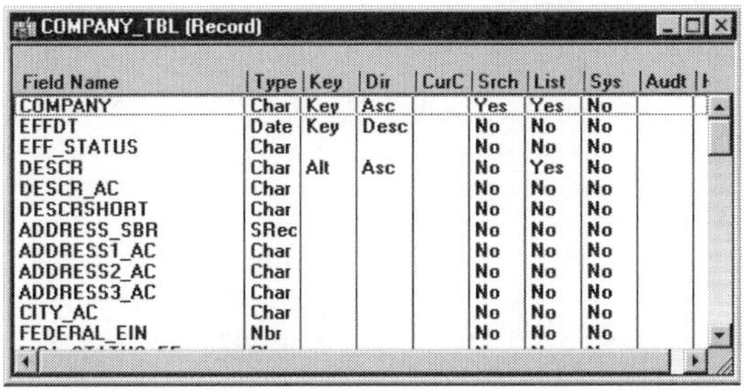

Figure 6.6
Search keys of a prompt record with EFFDT and EFF_STATUS

Notice that COMPANY is the only search key in this prompt record. The effective date on the JOB DATA panel is compared with the effective date on the COMPANY_TBL. Also, the effective status on COMPANY_TBL should be active as of the effective date on JOB DATA. In table 6.1, we can see combinations of EFFDT from JOB and EFFDT, EFF_STATUS from the COMPANY_TBL. The last column on the matrix here denotes whether the company appears on the prompt list.

Table 6.1   Effective date comparison

COMPANY	COMPANY EFFDT	COMPANY EFF. STATUS	JOB EFFDT	Prompt List
CCB	1/1/1996	Active	9/1/1996	Yes
CCB	5/1/1996	Active	9/1/1996	Yes
CCB	11/1/1996	Inactive	9/1/1996	No
CCB	1/1/1997	Active	9/1/1996	No

The first two combinations satisfy the prompt list; the last two entries do not. The COMPANY_TBL entries for the last two entries are either inactive, or, the effective date is in the future. We can deduce that the row in the prompt record should be active on or before the effective date on the panel that contains the prompt field. *If there is no effective date on the panel that contains the prompt field, then the system date is used for comparison.*

6.1.4   Prompt records with multiple search keys

Now, let's consider a situation where a prompt record has more than one search key; using the PAYGROUP field from the JOB DATA panel as an example. This field has the PAYGROUP_TBL as the prompt record. Let us take a look at the search keys on the PAYGROUP_TBL (figure 6.7).

The rules for effective date and effective status still apply to this prompt record. The only difference is the additional search key. PAYGROUP is the field being

Navigation: File → Open → Record → PAYGROUP_TBL (Application Designer)

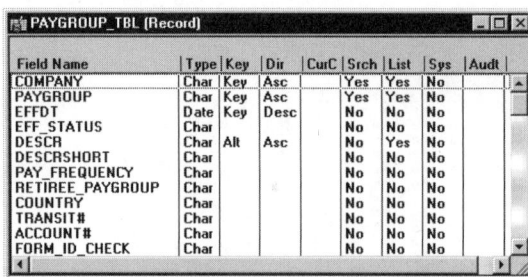

**Figure 6.7
Prompt records with
multiple search keys**

prompted, and it is not the first key on this prompt record. COMPANY is the first search key here.

It is a simple task to make this prompt record work efficiently. The COMPANY field has to be populated with a valid value for the prompt on the PAYGROUP field to work correctly. For this reason, the panel fields have to be laid out in such a way that the search keys appear in the correct order. The COMPANY field can be an input field, a display-only field, or even a hidden field in the panel. Simply by populating the COMPANY field, we are supplying an input to the prompt. The prompt search uses the value entered in COMPANY and produces a list of PAYGROUPS that belong to the COMPANY.

The same rules apply for any number of search keys. All high level keys have to be populated in order for a prompt field to work correctly. In PeopleSoft HRMS, another record, the PAY_CALENDAR, is used as a prompt record to produce a list of payroll end dates. Let's look at the keys on this record to understand how a prompt list is provided for the PAY_END_DT field.

In figure 6.8, we see three search keys: COMPANY, PAYGROUP, and PAY_END_DT fields. In order for the prompt to work correctly on the PAY_END_DT field, the COMPANY and PAYGROUP fields have to be populated with valid values.

Navigation: File → Open → Record → PAY_CALENDAR (Application Designer)

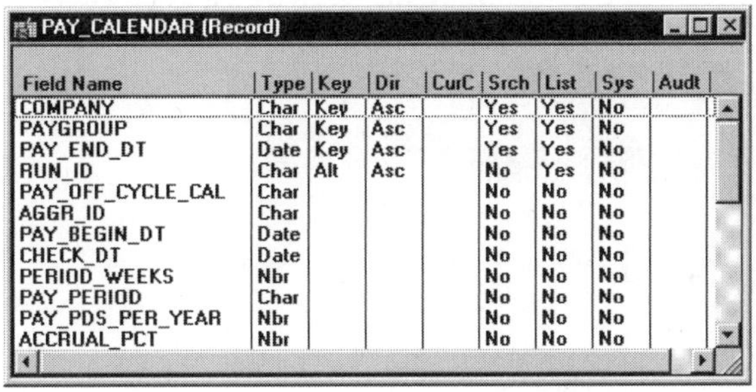

Field Name	Type	Key	Dir	CurC	Srch	List	Sys	Audt
COMPANY	Char	Key	Asc		Yes	Yes	No	
PAYGROUP	Char	Key	Asc		Yes	Yes	No	
PAY_END_DT	Date	Key	Asc		Yes	Yes	No	
RUN_ID	Char	Alt	Asc		No	Yes	No	
PAY_OFF_CYCLE_CAL	Char				No	No	No	
AGGR_ID	Char				No	No	No	
PAY_BEGIN_DT	Date				No	No	No	
CHECK_DT	Date				No	No	No	
PERIOD_WEEKS	Nbr				No	No	No	
PAY_PERIOD	Char				No	No	No	
PAY_PDS_PER_YEAR	Nbr				No	No	No	
ACCRUAL_PCT	Nbr				No	No	No	

Figure 6.8
Prompt records with multiple search keys (more than two)

TIP Values for all higher level key fields must be supplied for a prompt list to work. If the prompted field is the third key on the search record, the first two key fields must have values for prompt processing. The Application Processor verifies whether any rows in the prompt record satisfy the values in the key fields. If rows are found, a prompt list is provided to the user.

6.1.5 Dynamic prompt records

Sometimes, the prompt record behind a field cannot be determined until runtime. The data contained in the panel dictates the prompt record to be used. The prompt record has to then be chosen dynamically through a PeopleCode event. Let's walk through an example from the PeopleSoft HRMS application, a variable prompt record defined on the HEALTH_BENEFIT record. This record stores health benefits enrollments. The field that uses the variable prompt is BENEFIT_PLAN.

The first prompt record is an SQL view that contains all benefit plans not defined for COBRA. The second prompt record is also an SQL view that has all benefit plans defined for COBRA. A flag called COBRA_PLAN (in the BEN_DEFN_PLAN record) is set to a value of `Y` for COBRA. Both the SQL views are built using the BEN_DEFN_PLAN record.

We set the variable prompt records using a `RowInit` PeopleCode event in HEALTH_BENEFIT. Any field from the DERIVED record can be placed on the panel, and this field will be populated with the actual prompt record name through a PeopleCode event. The prompt record name on the record field definition is a % sign and the actual field name from the DERIVED record.

For example, if the field name on the DERIVED record is EDITTABLE, then the prompt record name is defined as `%EDITTABLE`. The % sign is recognized as a field from the DERIVED record. As long as this field is populated with the correct record name, the prompt list works correctly. Let's look at how the prompt record is defined on the HEALTH_BENEFIT record (figure 6.9).

Navigation: File → Open → Record → HEALTH_BENEFIT (Application Designer)

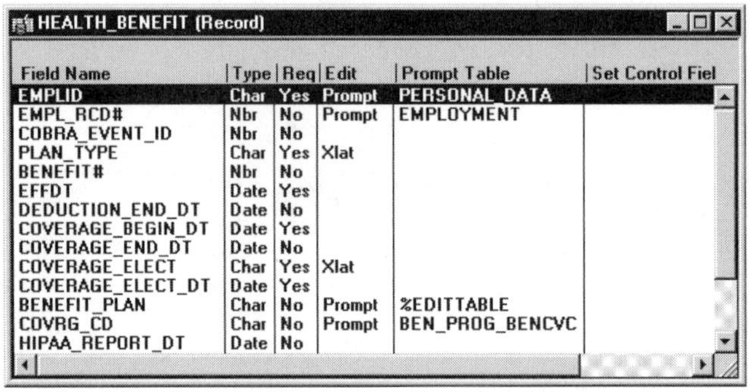

HEALTH_BENEFIT (Record)

Field Name	Type	Req	Edit	Prompt Table	Set Control Fiel
EMPLID	Char	Yes	Prompt	PERSONAL_DATA	
EMPL_RCD#	Nbr	No	Prompt	EMPLOYMENT	
COBRA_EVENT_ID	Nbr	No			
PLAN_TYPE	Char	Yes	Xlat		
BENEFIT#	Nbr	No			
EFFDT	Date	Yes			
DEDUCTION_END_DT	Date	No			
COVERAGE_BEGIN_DT	Date	Yes			
COVERAGE_END_DT	Date	No			
COVERAGE_ELECT	Char	Yes	Xlat		
COVERAGE_ELECT_DT	Date	Yes			
BENEFIT_PLAN	Char	No	Prompt	%EDITTABLE	
COVRG_CD	Char	No	Prompt	BEN_PROG_BENCVC	
HIPAA_REPORT_DT	Date	No			

Figure 6.9 Variable prompt record definition

The prompt record is defined as `%EDITTABLE`, which means that the field EDITTABLE from the DERIVED record has to be placed on the panel for the prompt to work correctly. The PeopleCode event that populates this work field appears in figure 6.10.

Figure 6.10 illustrates how the PeopleCode event populates the EDITTABLE field with two different values based on the panel name being used. Also, notice that the `RowInit` event populates this field before the user gets a chance to access the prompt list.

Navigation: File → Open → Record → HEALTH_BENEFIT → View → PeopleCode Display

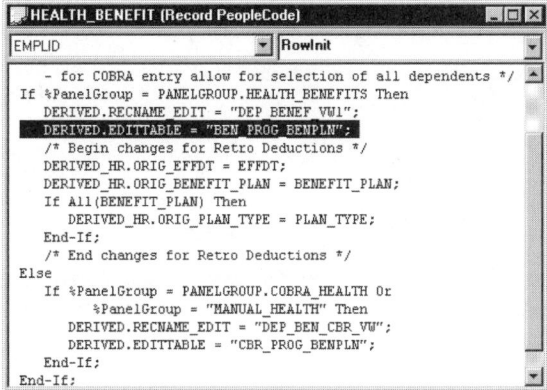

```
HEALTH_BENEFIT (Record PeopleCode)                    _ □ ×
EMPLID                        ▼   RowInit                  ▼
    - for COBRA entry allow for selection of all dependents */  ▲
If %PanelGroup = PANELGROUP.HEALTH_BENEFITS Then
    DERIVED.RECNAME_EDIT = "DEP_BENEF_VW1";
    DERIVED.EDITTABLE = "BEN_PROG_BENPLN";
    /* Begin changes for Retro Deductions */
    DERIVED_HR.ORIG_EFFDT = EFFDT;
    DERIVED_HR.ORIG_BENEFIT_PLAN = BENEFIT_PLAN;
    If All(BENEFIT_PLAN) Then
        DERIVED_HR.ORIG_PLAN_TYPE = PLAN_TYPE;
    End-If;
    /* End changes for Retro Deductions */
Else
    If %PanelGroup = PANELGROUP.COBRA_HEALTH Or
         %PanelGroup = "MANUAL_HEALTH" Then
        DERIVED.RECNAME_EDIT = "DEP_BEN_CBR_VW";
        DERIVED.EDITTABLE = "CBR_PROG_BENPLN";
    End-If;
End-If;                                                    ▼
```

Figure 6.10
**RowInit PeopleCode event to set
variable prompt record**

The search keys on the prompt record still work the same way as we have seen before. The search keys have to be the same on all prompt records. The rows returned in the prompt list are different. Let's finish this section by looking at the search key definition for the two prompt records used in the example (figures 6.11 and 6.12).

Navigation: File → Open → Record → CBR_PROG_BEN_PLN

Field Name	Type	Key	Dir	CurC	Srch	List	Sys	Audt	H
BENEFIT_PROGRAM	Char	Key	Asc		No	Yes	No		
PLAN_TYPE	Char	Key	Asc		No	Yes	No		
BENEFIT_PLAN	Char	Key	Asc		No	Yes	No		
EFFDT	Date	Key	Desc		No	Yes	No		
DESCR	Char	Alt	Asc		No	Yes	No		
DESCRSHORT	Char				No	No	No		
PROGRAM_TYPE	Char				No	No	No		
OPTION_CD	Char				No	No	No		
DEPENDENT_MARRIAGE	Char				No	No	No		
DEP_AGE_LIMIT	Nbr				No	No	No		
EXCL_DISABLED_AGE	Char				No	No	No		
STUDENT_AGE_LIMIT	Nbr				No	No	No		

Figure 6.11
**Variable prompt record—
Key display**

Navigation: File → Open → Record → BEN_PROG_BENPLN

Field Name	Type	Key	Dir	CurC	Srch	List	Sys	Audt	H
BENEFIT PROGRAM	Char	Key	Asc		No	No	No		
EFFDT	Date	Key	Desc		No	No	No		
PLAN_TYPE	Char	Key	Asc		No	No	No		
BENEFIT_PLAN	Char	Key	Asc		No	Yes	No		
DESCR	Char	Alt	Asc		No	Yes	No		
DESCRSHORT	Char				No	No	No		
PROGRAM_TYPE	Char				No	No	No		
OPTION_CD	Char				No	No	No		
DEPENDENT_MARRIAGE	Char				No	No	No		
DEP_AGE_LIMIT	Nbr				No	No	No		
EXCL_DISABLED_AGE	Char				No	No	No		
STUDENT_AGE_LIMIT	Nbr				No	No	No		

Figure 6.12 Variable prompt record—Key display

The key structures are exactly the same on both prompt records. Because the SQL views return different rows based on application context, a variable prompt record is necessary.

TIP Variable prompt records are used with the help of a field from the DERIVED record. For example, if the field from DERIVED record is called RECNAME_EDIT, the prompt record is defined as %RECNAME_EDIT in the record that uses the prompt record. A PeopleCode event will populate the variable prompt record name at run time.

6.2 CREATING AND MAINTAINING TRANSLATE VALUES

PeopleSoft provides objects that can be used to store a list of valid values for a field. Translate values are different from prompt values in the sense that translate values do not need an individual database table for storage. While each prompt list has its own record, all translate values are stored in one PeopleSoft tool table, called the XLATTABLE. Let's take a look at the fields from XLATTABLE to see how they store translate values (figure 6.13).

XLATTABLE has four database keys to store unique translate values. Let us describe the fields in XLATTABLE.

- FIELDNAME   The actual field name in PeopleSoft for which translate values are stored.
- LANGUAGE_CD   The language in which translate descriptions are stored,
- FIELDVALUE   This is the actual translate value code.
- EFFDT   The effective date for the translate value.
- VERSION   PeopleSoft maintains version number for caching and upgrading translate values.
- EFF_STATUS   Denotes the active or inactive status of the translate value

- XLATLONGNAME   The location where a long description can be stored for the translate value.
- XLATSHORTNAME   The location where a short description can be stored for the translate value.
- LASTUPDDTTM   The last Date/Time the translate value was updated.
- LASTUPDOPRID   The ID of the operator that last updated the translate value.

Navigation: Go → Open → Record → XLATTABLE

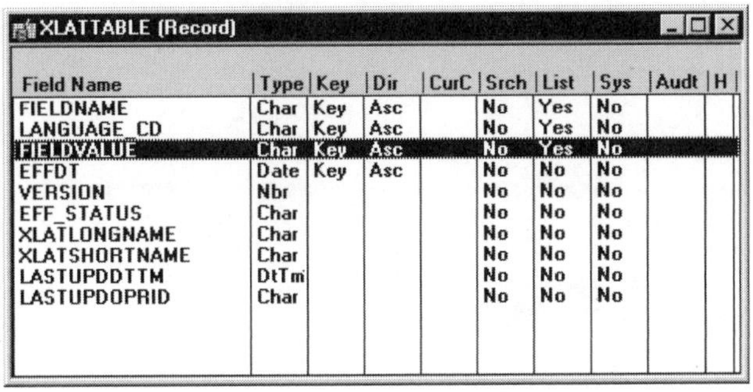

Figure 6.13
Key structure of XLATTABLE

Translate values can be a maximum of four characters. So fields that are one to four characters long and used as codes can be stored in the translate table. Translate values are also effective-dated. The long and short descriptions can be different on different effective dates.

Translate values are associated with a field object. After you have created character fields, you attach translate values to them. Let's look at how we can attach translate values to a field (figure 6.14).

A field must be open in order to add, change, or delete its translate values. The buttons Add, Change, and Delete are used to add, change, and delete translate values respectively.

We also see the last updated Date/Time and the operator ID. Even though translate values are attached to a field object, this does not mean translate values are always used for a field when it is attached to a record definition. The translate values edit can either be turned on or off for a record field. This can be accomplished using the Edits tab in the Record Field Properties screen. Figure 6.15 illustrates the edits defined for fields from MY_USER_TABLE record.

Xlat in the Edit column indicates that the translate values edit has been turned on for the record field MY_USER_TYPE in the record definition MY_USER_TABLE. The same field can be used in another record definition without the translate values edit. Figure 6.16 illustrates how translate table edit is turned on for MY_USER_TYPE field in MY_USER_TABLE

Navigation: File → Object Properties → Translate Values tab (MY_USER_TYPE field is open)

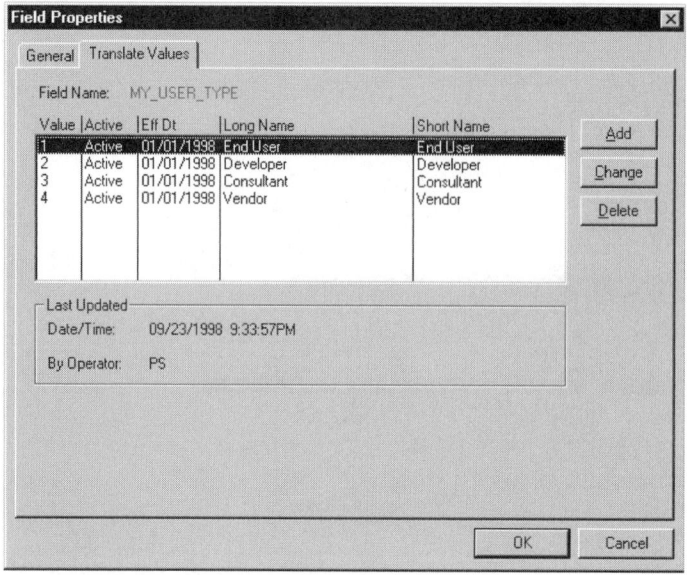

Figure 6.14   Translate Values for a field

Navigation: File → Open → Record → MY_USER_TABLE → View → Edit Display

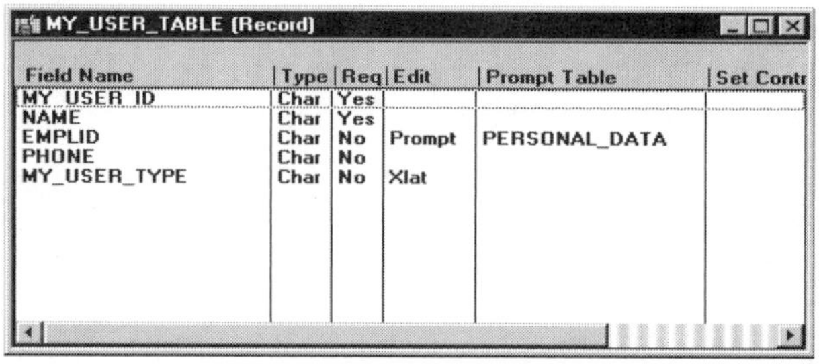

**Figure 6.15
Edits display for a record
definition**

Translate values can appear on a panel either as an edit box or a drop-down list box. Drop-down list boxes can display the Translate long name and short name in the drop-down list. If an edit box is used, then the Translate short or long names can be displayed using a related display field. Figure 6.17 illustrates how translate values appear on a drop-down list within the online application.

Navigation: Highlight Field → Edit → Record Field Properties

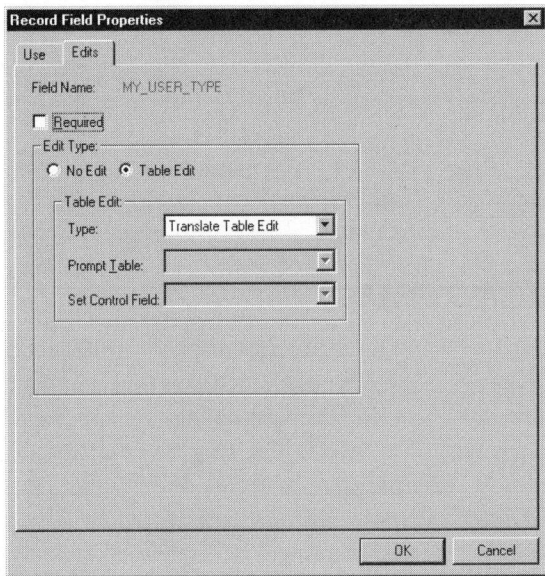

Figure 6.16
Record Field Properties—Edits tab

Navigation: Go → Problem Tracking → Setup → Users

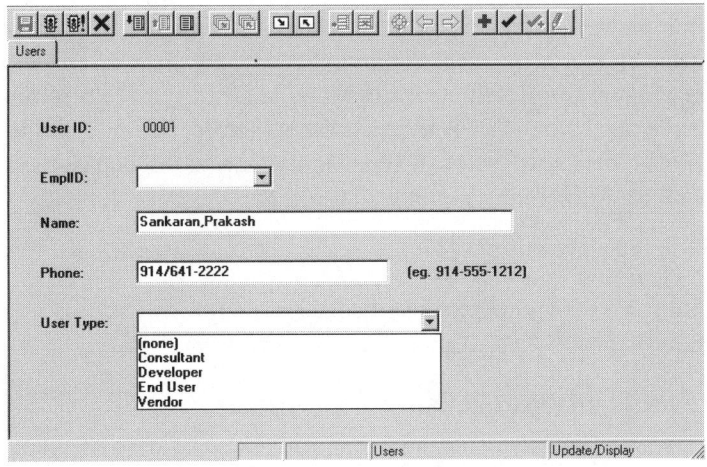

Figure 6.17
User panel with a
drop-down list box
for translate values

TIP	Effective dates on translate tables work the same way as in prompt records. The value of the effective date in the application panel is compared to the effective date in XLATTABLE. All translate values for the record field that are active on or before the effective date in the application panel are included in the translate list.
NOTE	Translate values are attached to field definitions. They can be included in records with or without the Translate Table Edit.

6.3   CREATING AND USING SEARCH RECORDS

Search records are used to control and limit the data displayed on a user panel. Search records can be either SQL tables or SQL views. When you create a panel group, you must specify the search record to be used. A search dialog box appears when the user tries to access the panel group, and search values may be entered into fields from search records designated as a search keys or alternate search keys. After the search keys are entered, any matching entries from the search record are displayed in a list box. Besides the search keys themselves, additional fields defined as list box items also appear in the list box.

Search records are specified in panel groups. A panel group, no matter how many panels it contains, needs a search record. The same search record can be specified in more than one panel group. For example, in PeopleSoft HRMS, the same search record is used for employee lookup. These panel groups are designed to look up employees either by using an employee ID or employee's last name. Search records are designed to limit the number of rows the user can access at any given point of time.

As we saw in chapter 4, a field has to be a database key in order to be a search key. Also, not all database keys are defined as search keys in PeopleSoft. This concept leaves us with four different types of search records:

- search records without any keys
- search records with search keys
- search records with search keys and database keys
- search records with From and Through search keys

6.3.1   Search records without keys

Sometimes, search records do not have any search keys or database keys. We see this only in instances when we do not want users to be prompted for any input. This means data selection can be performed without any input.

INSTALLATION table (from the PeopleSoft HRMS application which contains general information about the application) is an excellent example. It has fields such as the last employee ID assigned, default country, default currency code, commit counts, and so forth. This table has only one row and does not contain any database keys or search keys, making it possible to look up data from the INSTALLATION table without any input. We may encounter other instances where we may want to bring up panels without providing any input. In such instances, we can use the INSTALLATION table as the search record. One example in the PeopleSoft Benefits Administration application is the BAS ACTIVITY panel. This panel retrieves all rows from the BAS_ACTIVITY table without any input.

6.3.2   Search records with search keys

Search keys are fields that appear on the input dialog box. Fields from the input dialog box determine the rows that appear as list box items. Fields from the Input dialog box may be display-only items on the panel.

If values are entered on all search keys, and an entry is found in the search record matching those values, the Application Processor brings up the panel directly without providing a list box. If values are entered only in certain fields, then a list box appears matching the items entered in the search fields. Fields defined as search keys are always defined as list box items, but list box items are not all search keys. List box items help the user identify data that will appear on the panel.

Let's take a look at how search records are built and how they control the data selection. To do so, we will take a look at our Problem Tracking application and see how users are added and updated. By looking at the underlying table, we can easily determine the keys that can be used in the search.

In figure 6.18, MY_USER_TABLE is used as a search record to add and update users. Here we are using the data record itself as the search record. We see that MY_USER_ID is the only search key field in this search record. When we perform a partial search on the MY_USER_ID field, the Application Processor retrieves all entries that match the value entered in MY_USER_ID field. NAME and EMPLID fields are used as alternate search keys. Alternate search keys work the same way as search keys, except that they are not unique.

In figure 6.19, we input a "0" in the MY_USER_ID field. We have all entries that matched the partial key search in the list box. Let us try the same search with no input.

Navigation: File → Open → Record → MY_USER_TABLE

MY_USER_TABLE (Record)

Field Name	Type	Key	Dir	CurC	Srch	List	Sys	Audt	H
MY_USER_ID	Char	Key	Asc		Yes	Yes	No		
NAME	Char	Alt	Asc		No	Yes	No		
EMPLID	Char	Alt	Asc		No	Yes	No		
PHONE	Char				No	No	No		
MY_USER_TYPE	Char				No	No	No		

**Figure 6.18
Search keys on a
search record**

Navigation: Go → Problem Tracking → Setup → Users

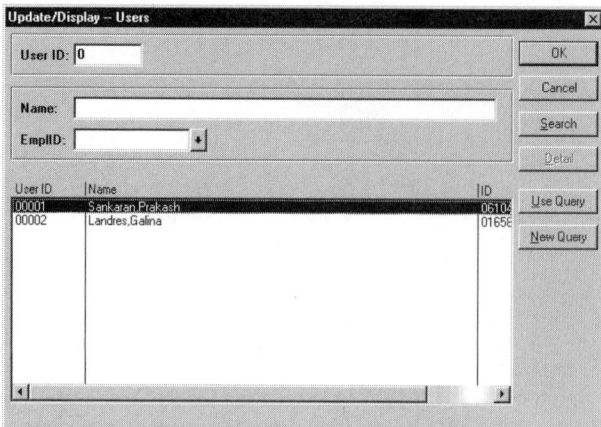

Figure 6.19
Search keys and list box
items (partial search)

When no input is supplied, all rows from MY_USER_TABLE are listed in the list box (figure 6.20).

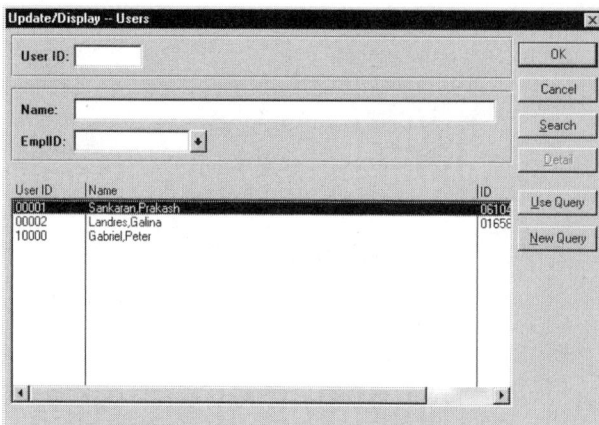

Figure 6.20
Search keys and list box
items (no input)

NOTE The number of entries retrieved for the list box is limited to the first 256 rows returned by the Application Processor. Only the first 256 rows are displayed in the list box. When the number of entries exceeds the limit, message is issued to the user specifying that there are more than 256 rows that match the input supplied.

Now let's look at a search record that has more than one search key. In PeopleSoft HRMS the pay calendar table uses more than one search key as input.

Only the COMPANY field was entered in the search dialog box. The Application Processor retrieved all pay calendar entries that belong to company CCB. The message at the bottom in figure 6.21 indicates that more matching entries exist than those displayed in the list box.

Navigation: Go → Define Business Rules → Define Payroll Process →
Setup 2 → Pay Calendar Table

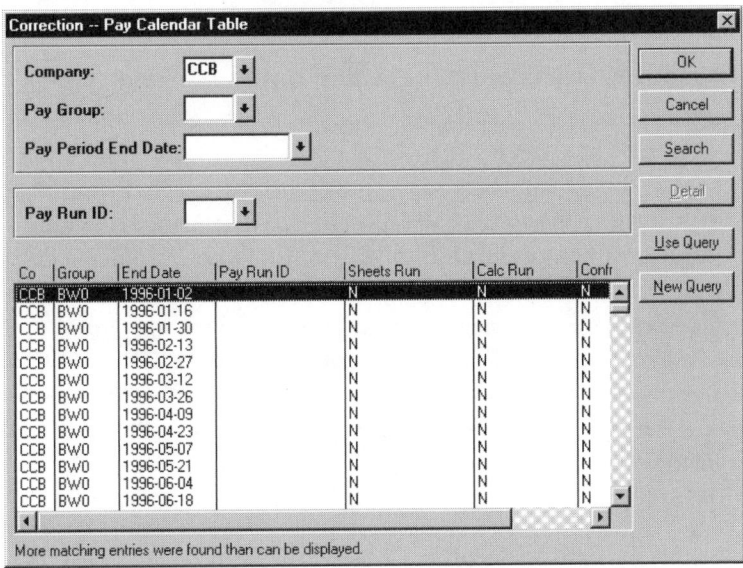

Figure 6.21 Search records with more than one search key

We can narrow the search by inputting a value into the PAYGROUP field. When a value is input into the COMPANY, PAYGROUP, and PAY_END_DT fields, the Application Processor attempts to match the values with entries in the search record. If a match is found, the Application Processor proceeds to display the panel without providing a list box.

RUN_ID field is an alternate search key field. It is a duplicate key that may list more than one entry in the list box. Let us take a look at the key definition for the PAY_CALENDAR record (figure 6.22).

Navigation: File → Open → Record → PAY_CALENDAR

Field Name	Type	Key	Dir	CurC	Srch	List	Sys	Audt
COMPANY	Char	Key	Asc		Yes	Yes	No	
PAYGROUP	Char	Key	Asc		Yes	Yes	No	
PAY_END_DT	Date	Key	Asc		Yes	Yes	No	
RUN_ID	Char	Alt	Asc		No	Yes	No	
PAY_OFF_CYCLE_CAL	Char				No	No	No	
AGGR_ID	Char				No	No	No	
PAY_BEGIN_DT	Date				No	No	No	
CHECK_DT	Date				No	No	No	
PERIOD_WEEKS	Nbr				No	No	No	
PAY_PERIOD	Char				No	No	No	
PAY_PDS_PER_YEAR	Nbr				No	No	No	
ACCRUAL_PCT	Nbr				No	No	No	

Figure 6.22
Search record with search keys

6.3.3 Search records with search keys and database keys

Some search records use search keys as well as database keys that are not defined as search keys in the search. In the PeopleSoft HRMS application, the record EMPL_COMP_SRCH is used to look up employee details based on the company for which they work. All payroll balances and tax data panels use this as the search record. This search record, in addition to two search keys, also has a database key that controls the search. This database key is the OPRCLASS field which narrows down the search based on the department security setup for the operator.

Figure 6.23 illustrates the key definition for EMPL_COMP_SRCH record. The Application Processor automatically includes certain fields in the search criteria. Two such fields, the OPRID and the OPRCLASS fields, when included in a search record, are automatically included in the search.

Navigation: File → Open → Record → EMPL_COMP_SRCH

Field Name	Type	Key	Dir	CurC	Srch	List	Sys	Audt	H
EMPLID	Char	Key	Asc		Yes	Yes	No		
COMPANY	Char	Key	Asc		Yes	Yes	No		
OPRCLASS	Char	Key	Asc		No	No	No		
ACCESS_CD	Char				No	No	No		
NAME	Char	Alt	Asc		No	Yes	No		
NAME_AC	Char				No	No	No		
LAST_NAME_SRCH	Char				No	No	No		
NID_COUNTRY	Char				No	No	No		
NATIONAL_ID_TYPE	Char				No	No	No		
NID_DESCRSHORT	Char				No	No	No		
NATIONAL_ID	Char				No	No	No		

Figure 6.23
Search records with search keys and database keys

PeopleSoft uses OPRID and OPRCLASS fields to provide application security. Department security in a PeopleSoft HRMS application is controlled using these two fields. Security definitions are attached to the OPRCLASS field, while search views include the tables that store these security definitions. When the Application Processor automatically includes OPRCLASS in the search, security definitions for that particular OPRCLASS secure the data which the user can access. Each PeopleSoft user, or OPRID, is attached to an operator class or OPRCLASS.

Since OPRCLASS and OPRID fields are available as system variables during the panel session, it makes sense to use them automatically in the search. In figure 6.24, we can see that OPRCLASS does not appear in the input dialog box.

Navigation: Go → Compensate Employees → Maintain Payroll Data U.S. → Use →
Employee Tax Data

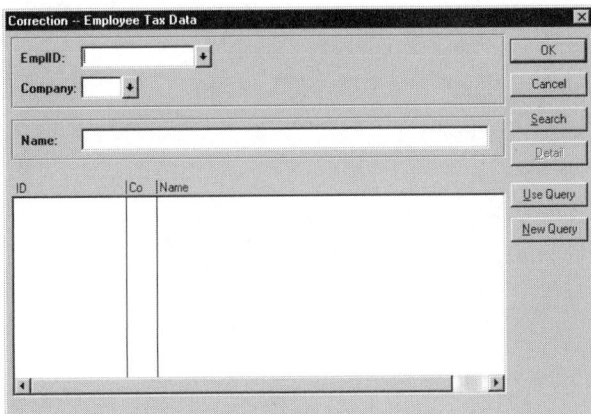

Figure 6.24
Search records that use search keys and database keys

6.3.4   Search records with From and Through search keys

PeopleSoft 7 introduced a new feature that allows From and Through search keys to be defined in search records. All rows that are greater than or equal to the From value and lesser than or equal to the Through value are fetched from the search record. For example, we can define the MY_PROBLEM_STATUS field from MY_PROBLEM_TRKG record as a From or Through search key.

The MY_PROBLEM_STATUS field is defined as an alternate search key. Figure 6.25 illustrates the results returned in the list box when a value of 3 is entered in that field.

The Application Processor found an exact match and displayed the application panel directly without providing a list box. Let's define the MY_PROBLEM_STATUS field as a Through search key in MY_PROBLEM_TRKG record (figure 6.26).

Under the Edits tab in Record Field Properties, we can define the MY_PROBLEM_STATUS field as a Through search field. Figure 6.27 illustrates the rows retrieved using the same input value of 3.

The Application Processor retrieves all entries from MY_PROBLEM_TRKG record which have a value less than or equal to 3 in the MY_PROBLEM_STATUS field. Because MY_PROBLEM_STATUS field is defined as a Through search key, more than one entry is found to match the entries in the search record. The Application Processor provides a list box with all matching entries.

Navigation: Go → Problem Tracking → Tracking → Track Problems → Update/Display

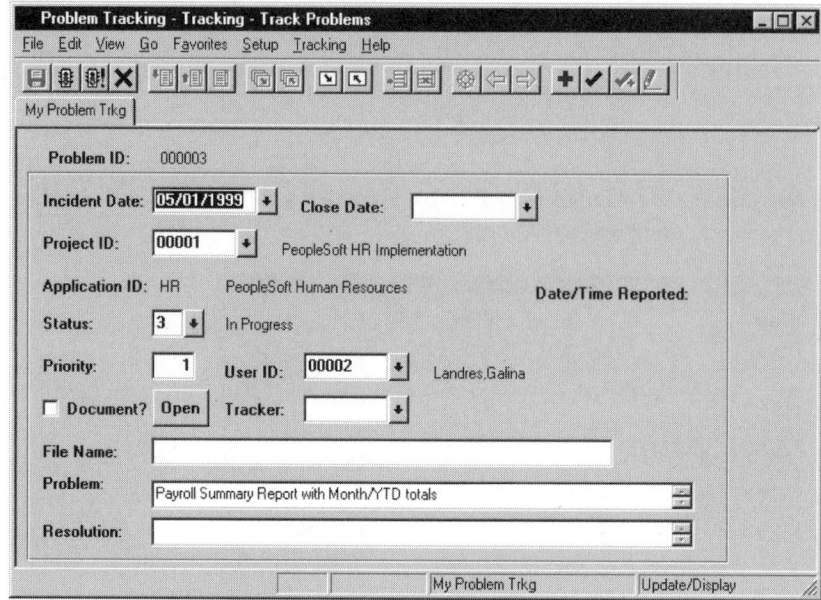

Figure 6.25   Search key—exact match

Navigation: File → Open → Record → MY_PROBLEM_TRKG →
HighLight MY_PROBLEM_STATUS → Edit → Record Field Properties

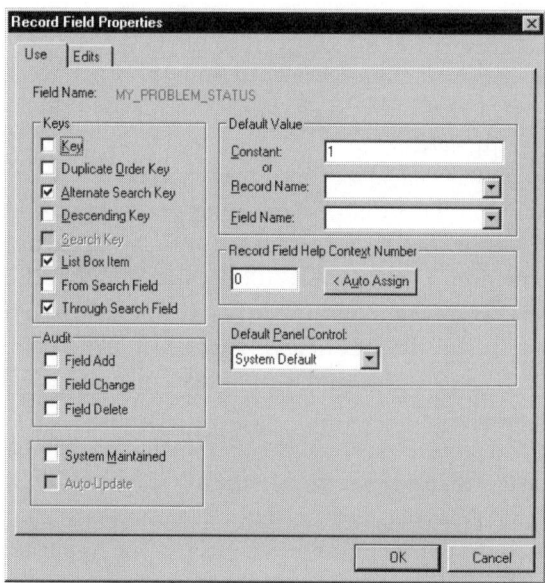

**Figure 6.26
Search record with
Through search key**

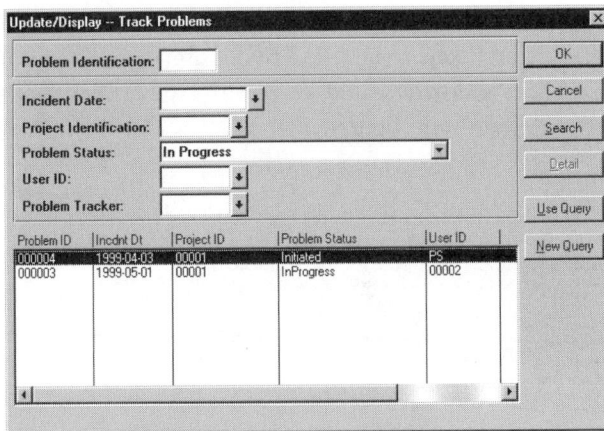

Figure 6.27
Through search key results

6.3.5 Create and define search records

To create and define search records, we must:

- create a record definition for the search record
- define search keys and list box items
- build the search record definition in the database as a table or view
- attach search records to panel groups

Let's create and define a search record, using the Problem Tracking application. We will add and update incidents and problems using the application. The database table that is being updated is the MY_PROBLEM_TRKG table. We already created the MY_PROBLEM_TRKG record prior to this. Let's look at the search keys for this table and determine if we can use it as a search record.

Navigation: File → Open → Record → MY_PROBLEM_TRKG

Field Name	Type	Key	Dir	CurC	Srch	List	Sys	Audt	H
MY_PROBLEM_ID	Char	Key	Asc		No	No	No		
INCIDENT_DT	Date	Alt	Asc		No	No	No		
MY_PROJECT_ID	Char	Alt	Asc		No	No	No		
MY_PROBLEM_STATUS	Char	Alt	Asc		No	No	No		
PRIORITY	Nbr				No	No	No		
MY_USER_ID	Char	Alt	Asc		No	No	No		
MY_PROBLEM_TRACKEI	Char	Alt	Asc		No	No	No		
CLOSE_DT	Date				No	No	No		
MY_DOCUMENT_ATTACI	Char				No	No	No		
DESCRLONG	Long				No	No	No		
MY_PROBLEM_RESOLTI	Long				No	No	No		
MY_PROBLEM_DTTIM	DtTm				No	No	No		

Figure 6.28
Record definition showing database keys

MY_PROBLEM_ID is the only unique key field in MY_PROBLEM_TRKG record. We define this field as a search key. In addition to defining search fields, a number of other fields can be used as alternate search keys in this table. You can see the final search key and list box definition in figure 6.29.

Navigation: File → Open → Record → MY_PROBLEM_TRKG

MY_PROBLEM_TRKG (Record)

Field Name	Type	Key	Dir	CurC	Srch	List	Sys	Audt	H
MY_PROBLEM_ID	Char	Key	Asc		Yes	Yes	No		
INCIDENT_DT	Date	Alt	Asc		No	Yes	No		
MY_PROJECT_ID	Char	Alt	Asc		No	Yes	No		
MY_PROBLEM_STATUS	Char	Alt	Asc		No	Yes	No		
PRIORITY	Nbr				No	No	No		
MY_USER_ID	Char	Alt	Asc		No	Yes	No		
MY_PROBLEM_TRACKEF	Char	Alt	Asc		No	Yes	No		
CLOSE_DT	Date				No	No	No		
MY_DOCUMENT_ATTACI	Char				No	No	No		
DESCRLONG	Long				No	No	No		
MY_PROBLEM_RESOLTI	Long				No	No	No		
MY_PROBLEM_DTTIM	DtTm				No	No	No		

Figure 6.29
Record definition showing search keys and list box items

Let's look at how we defined the search keys and the list box items.

Navigation: Highlight Field → File → Edit → Record Field Properties → Use Tab

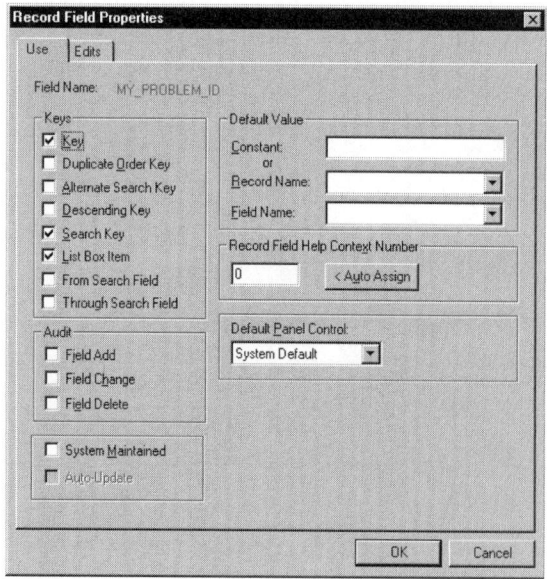

Figure 6.30
Define Record Field properties

All the fields can be highlighted one at a time, and the properties can be defined under the Use tab.

Our next step is to build the search record in the database. If the search record is an SQL table and the table already has data, we do not want to recreate the table. If the search record definition is an SQL view, however, then we can go ahead and recreate the SQL view any time.

In this next step, we attach the search record to the panel group definition using the panel group MY_PROBLEM_TRKG. After opening the panel group, we define the search record for that panel group under the Use tab.

Navigation: File → Open → Panel Group → MY_PROBLEM_TRKG → File → Object Properties

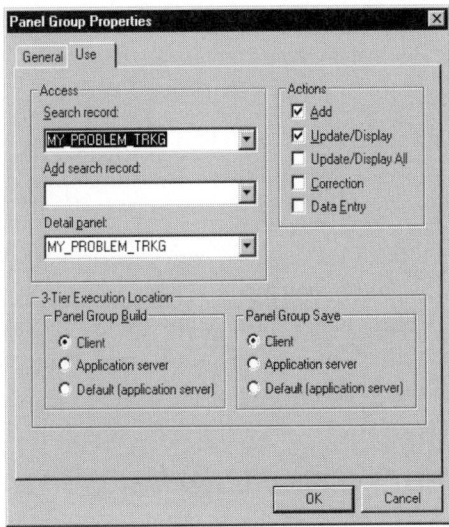

Figure 6.31
Panel Group Properties—Use tab

We attach two search records to the panel group definition. Add Search Record is used for Add action and the regular search record is used for Update/Display, Update/Display All, and Correction. If the Add search record is not specified, the regular search record is used for Add action as well.

When the panel group is attached to a menu item, the search record can be overridden at that time using the Menu Item Properties screen to accomplish this task. Figure 6.32 illustrates how we can override search records defined in panel groups. By turning on the Override checkbox, we can define the override search record on the drop-down box located to the right of the checkbox.

Navigation: Edit → Menu Item Properties (PROBLEM_TRACKING menu is open)

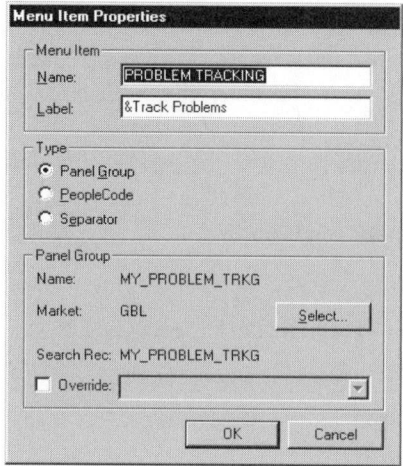

Figure 6.32
Menu Item Properties

NOTE Search keys are database keys as well. Alternate search keys are defined as non-unique database keys.

NOTE Values input in search fields are matched with entries in the search record. When only one entry is found matching the input, the Application Processor displays the application panel without providing a list box. When the number of entries found matching the input is more than one, then a list box is provided with the matching entries.

6.4 WORKING WITH DERIVED/WORK RECORDS

Derived/Work records are used as temporary storage records during Application Processing. Derived records can be used for a number of other purposes such as:

- counters and totals
- push buttons and command fields
- display messages
- temporary holding fields
- to define dynamic prompt records

The most common uses of Derived/Work records, however, are as command fields, counter fields, and total fields. Derived records are also called work records. For the purpose of this section, we will refer to them as derived records.

Derived records are record definitions which are relevant only to the online application. They do not exist in the database as an object. Only records defined as SQL tables and views are stored in the database. Derived records are populated only during the panel session. Once the panel is cancelled, data stored in the derived record is lost. Derived records may be shared across application panels. Because they are not stored in the database, they can also be used across multiple panel sessions at the same time. Only the field placed on the application panel remains in memory. The other fields from the derived record are not available in the panel buffer. Let's look at a few examples of derived records in use.

6.4.1 Using derived records as counters and totals

Fields in derived records can be used as counters and totals. The fields can either be displayed on the panel or hidden and used only for calculations. PeopleCode events can be attached to these derived fields just like any other record field. We have a panel that shows totals by status in our Problem Tracking application. Figure 6.33 illustrates an application panel from our Problem Tracking application that makes use of derived records.

Navigation: Go → Problem Tracking → Tracking → Problems—Totals by Status

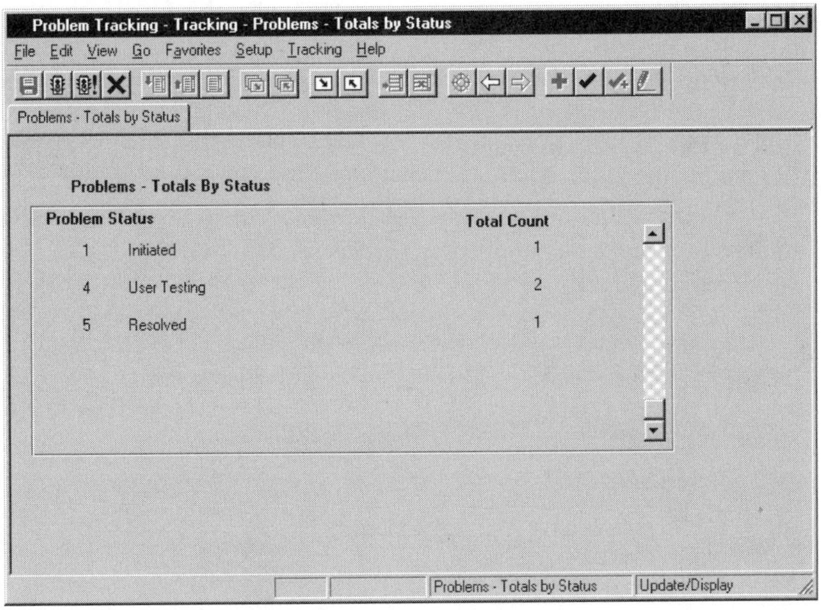

Figure 6.33   Application panel using a derived record

Fields from derived records can be used across multiple panels. Only the fields that are placed in the application panel are available in the panel buffer. Other fields from the derived record are not available for access. One instance of a derived field in a panel session does not interfere with another instance of the same field in another panel session.

The panel in figure 6.33 shows the total number of problems by status code. We can use a derived field to compute the total number of problems/incidents tracked using our application by following these steps:

- add a derived field that can hold the grand total to MY_DERIVED record
- place the derived field in MY_TRKG_STATUS panel
- create a PeopleCode event to compute the grand total

These three simple steps will give us the total number of problems/incidents tracked in the system. In PeopleSoft, already defined fields can be reused. We can add any field that accommodates totals to our derived record. We do not have to necessarily create a new field in the system. Let's see how we can find such a field in the system. First, we open the MY_DERIVED record definition. We then retrieve a list of fields (defined in the system) that start with the letters TOT. Figure 6.34 illustrates this process.

We can use any field already available in the system. We choose TOTAL_COUNT field for this purpose. In figure 6.35, we can see the TOTAL_COUNT field included in MY_DERIVED record definition.

In our example, we use a record defined as an SQL view to compute the total number of problems by problem status. Let's take a look at the definition for the SQL view used in our example (figure 6.36).

Navigation: Insert/Field (MY_DERIVED Record Definition Open)

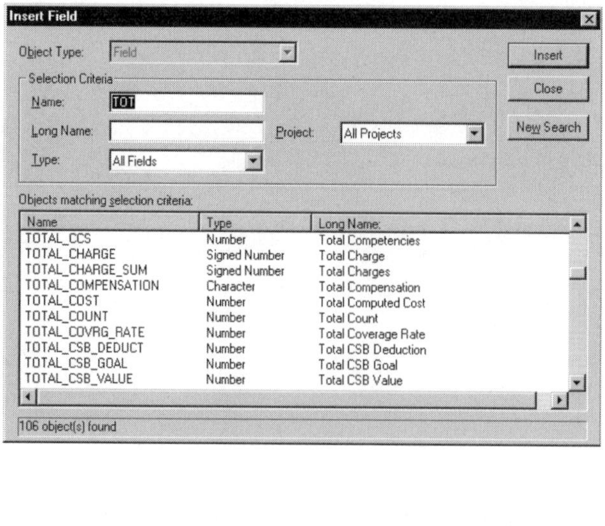

Figure 6.34
Fields defined in the system

Navigation: File → Open → Record → MY_DERIVED

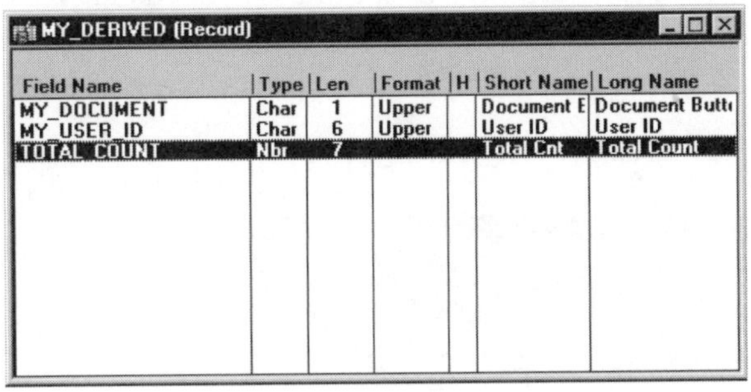

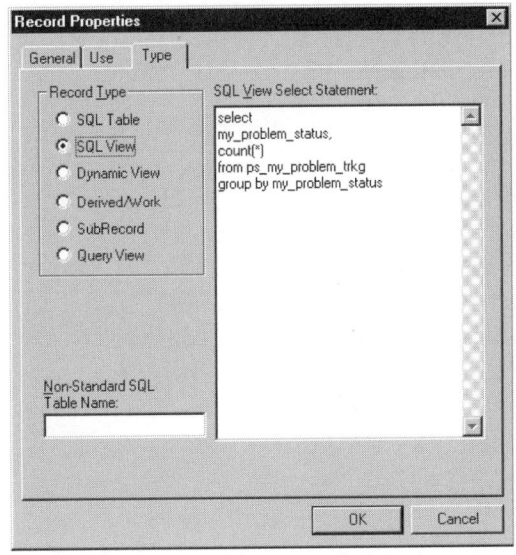

Figure 6.35
Adding a derived field

Navigation: File → Open → MY_TRKG_STATUS

Figure 6.36
SQL view definition

MY_TRKG_STATUS has a TOTAL_COUNT field that contains totals by problem status. Our goal is to produce a grand total of all problems/incidents tracked in the system.

In order to compute the grand total, the individual totals from the scroll bar have to be added together. We can populate the computed grand total into the TOTAL_COUNT field from MY_DERIVED record. First we need to place the field from the derived record on our panel.

> **TIP** The same field definition can be used in multiple record definitions. A field from different record definitions can be used in the same application panel as well.

In figure 6.37, we see an additional field in the bottom of the panel. This is the physical location of the TOTAL_COUNT field from MY_DERIVED record where the field is displayed when the panel is brought up.

Navigation: File → Open → Panel → MY_TRKG_STATUS

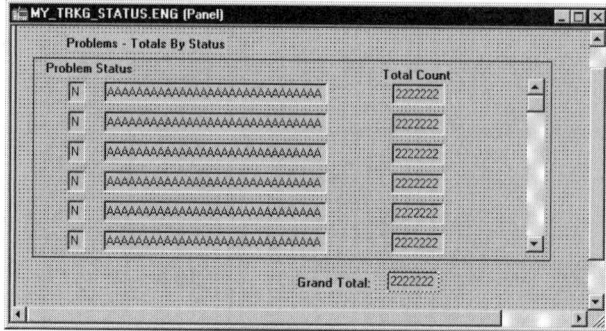

Figure 6.37
Panel definition with derived record field

Because we are using this field as the grand total, we need only one instance of this field. If we place it below the scroll bar in the panel field layout, we will have many instances of this field. (Figure 6.38 illustrates how the TOTAL_COUNT field from MY_DERIVED record is placed above the scroll bar.)

Now let's create a `RowInit` PeopleCode event on MY_TRKG_STATUS record to populate the grand total field. As rows are loaded on the scroll bar, we can add the totals from each row in the scroll bar to the TOTAL_COUNT field in MY_DERIVED record. We access level zero fields from inside the scroll bar by referring to them with

Navigation: Layout → Order (MY_TRKG_STATUS panel is open)

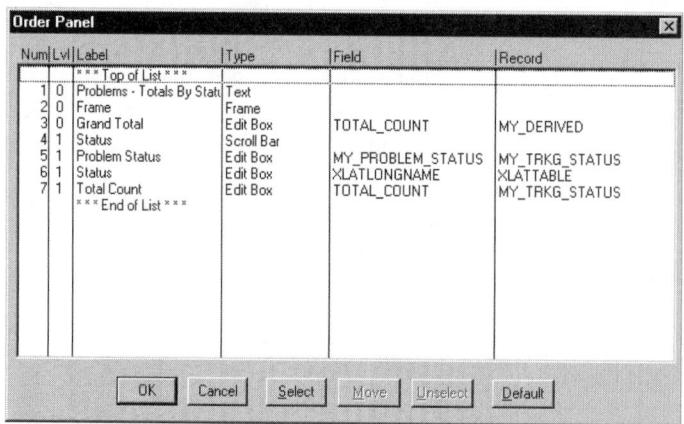

Figure 6.38
Panel field layout for MY_TRKG_STATUS panel

the proper record name prefix. (Figure 6.39 illustrates the PeopleCode program that computes the grand total.)

Navigation: Highlight TOTAL_COUNT → View → View PeopleCode
(MY_TRKG_SATUS record is open)

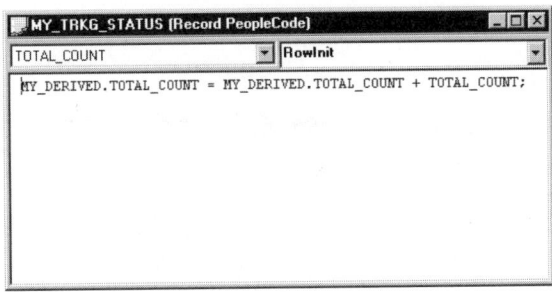

**Figure 6.39
PeopleCode which computes
grand total**

We refer to the field in MY_DERIVED record as MY_DERIVED.TOTAL_COUNT. Notice that the TOTAL_COUNT field from MY_TRKG_STATUS record appears without any record prefix. PeopleCode can refer to all fields from one record without using any record prefix. (Figure 6.40 illustrates the application panel with the grand total field.)

Navigation: Go → Problem Tracking → Tracking → Problems—Totals By Status

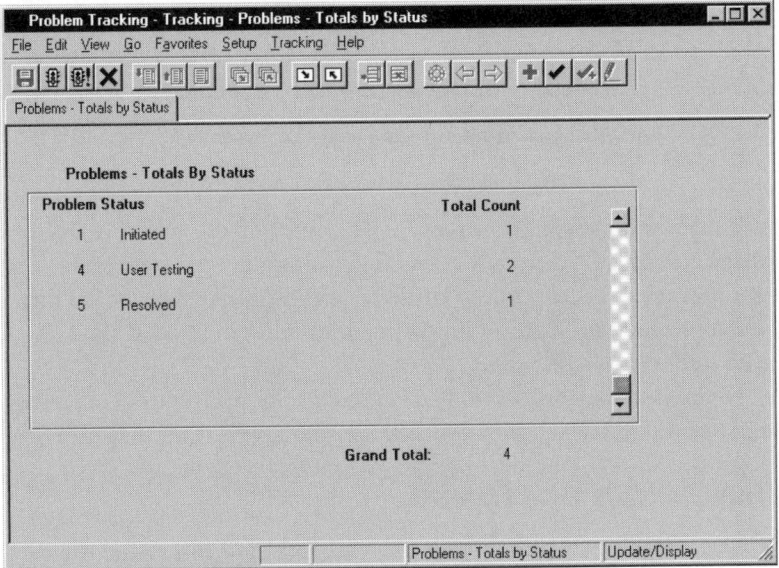

Figure 6.40   Application panel using derived record

6.4.2 Using derived records to display messages

In our next example, we see how a derived field is used as a message text field. The JOB_DATA1 panel in PeopleSoft's HRMS application contains the JOB_PANEL_MSG field from the DERIVED_HR record. This field helps the user determine whether the row being displayed is a current, a future, or a historical row. In figure 6.41, this display message appears in the application panel.

Navigation: Go → Administer Workforce U.S. → Use → Job Data → Correction

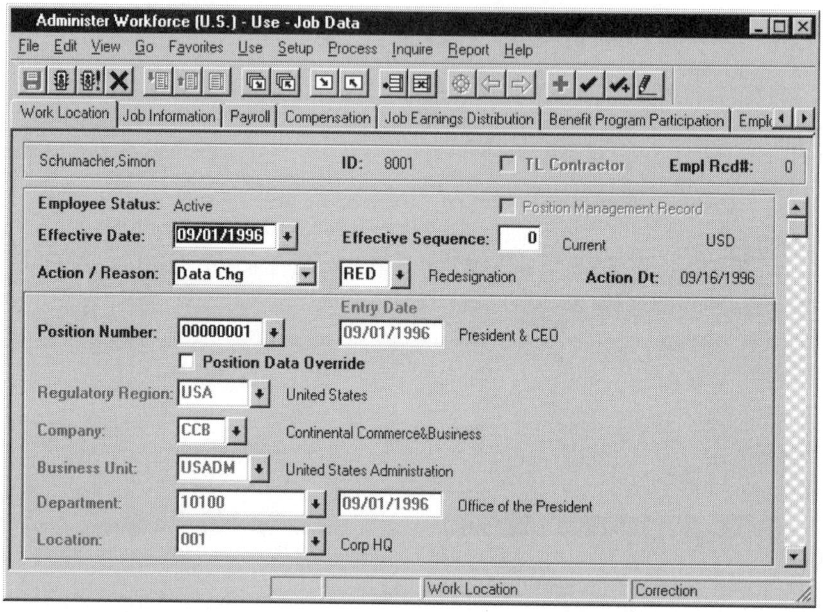

Figure 6.41   Job Data panel using a derived field as a message field

Notice the message "Current" to the right of the effective sequence field. This message is populated into the derived field using a PeopleCode event. The Application Processor executes a RowInit PeopleCode event as rows are loaded into the scroll bar. The PeopleCode program performs logic to determine what message should be displayed in the derived field.

In the next section, we will learn how to use push buttons in PeopleSoft. In the process of doing so, we will also learn another application that uses derived records.

6.5   USING PUSH BUTTONS

Push buttons are panel fields which can be activated to execute events. Push buttons are also called command buttons. Push buttons can be defined as command buttons, secondary panels or processes. When push buttons are defined as commands, they execute a `FieldChange` PeopleCode event attached to the panel field. When they are defined as secondary panels, they activate a secondary panel. When they are defined as a process, they execute a batch process.

Let us look at our Problem Tracking application again. In MY_PROBLEM_TRKG panel, we added a panel field called MY_DOCUMENT from MY_DERIVED record. This derived field can be used to display documents associated with the problem being tracked.

In our example, we use Microsoft Word as the document type to document problems. We can add a field to the MY_PROBLEM_TRKG record which holds the full path and filename for the Microsoft Word document. We use the field, FILENAME, which already exists in the system (figure 6.42).

Navigation: Go → File → Open → Record → MY_PROBLEM_TRKG

Field Name	Type	Len	Format	H	Short Name	Long Name
MY_PROBLEM_ID	Char	6	Upper		Problem ID	Problem Ide
INCIDENT_DT	Date	10			Incdnt Dt	Incident Da
MY_PROJECT_ID	Char	6	Upper		Project ID	Project Idei
MY_PROBLEM_STATUS	Char	1	Upper		Problem Sta	Problem Sta
PRIORITY	Nbr	3			Priority	Priority
MY_USER_ID	Char	6	Upper		User ID	User ID
MY_PROBLEM_TRACKEI	Char	6	Upper		Problem Tra	Problem Tra
CLOSE_DT	Date	10			Close Date	Date Closei
MY_DOCUMENT_ATTACI	Char	1	Upper		Document?	Document /
DESCRLONG	Long	0			Descr	Description
MY_PROBLEM_RESOLTI	Long	0			Prob.Resol	Problem Re
MY_PROBLEM_DTTIM	DtTm	26	Scnds		Date/Time	Date/Time
FILENAME	Char	80	Mixed		File Name	File Name

**Figure 6.42
Adding a field to a record
definition**

Figure 6.43 illustrates how the push button is added into the MY_PROBLEM_TRKG panel.

First, we define panel field properties for the push button. Two tabs exist where we define the properties for a push button.

Under the Record tab, we define whether the push button is a command, process or, secondary panel. In this example, the push button is a command button. We specify MY_DERIVED as the record and MY_DOCUMENT as the field for the push button.

Under the Label tab, we specify a label for the push button. We also define the font for the label under this tab. Figure 6.44 and 6.45 illustrates the Panel Field Properties screen for the push button.

After saving the panel definition we are ready to take a look at the push button as it appears in the application panel (figure 6.46).

Navigation: Insert → Push Button (MY_PROBLEM_TRKG panel is open)

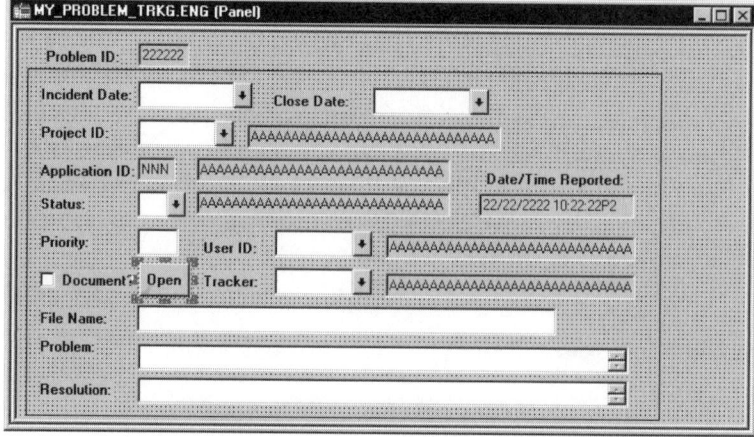

Figure 6.43   Inserting a push button in an application panel

Navigation: Edit → Panel Field Properties (MY_DOCUMENT field is highlighted)

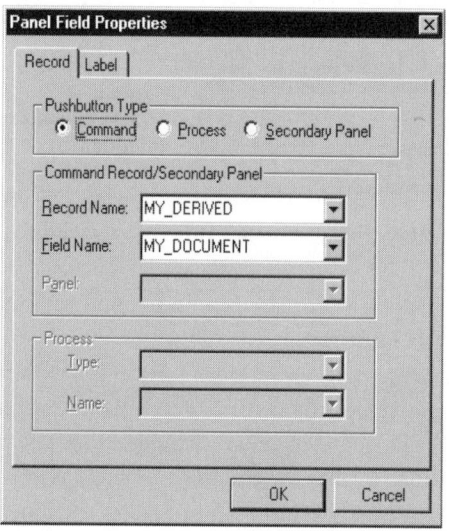

**Figure 6.44   Push button properties—
Record tab**

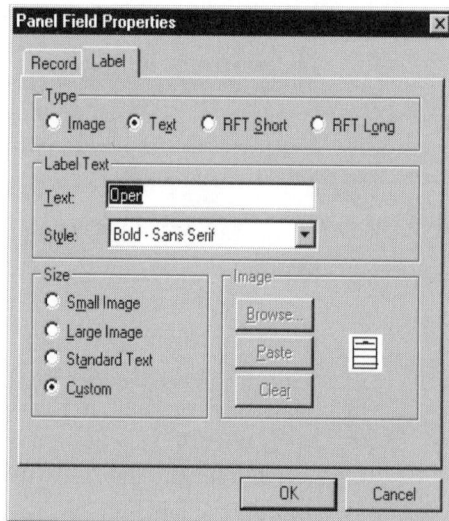

**Figure 6.45   Push button properties—
Label tab**

Navigation: Go → Problem Tracking → Tracking → Track Problems

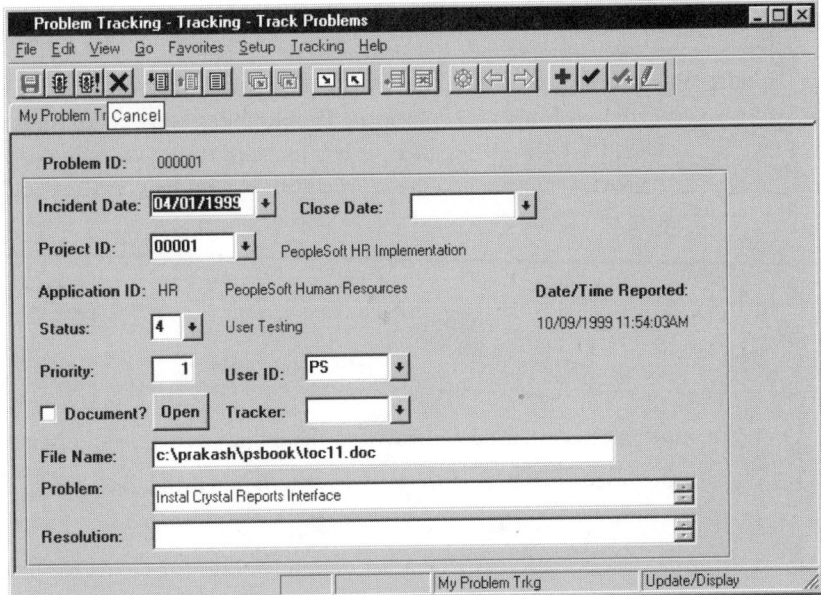

Figure 6.46   Push button field in an application panel

As soon as the user activates the push button, the PeopleCode program attached to MY_DOCUMENT field's `FieldChange` PeopleCode event is executed. This PeopleCode event executes Microsoft Word along with the full path and filename. Figure 6.47 illustrates the PeopleCode event which accomplishes this task.

Navigation: File → Open → MY_DERIVED → View → View PeopleCode Display

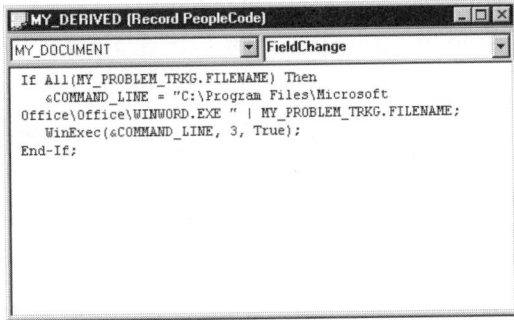

**Figure 6.47
PeopleCode event attached to
a push button**

This PeopleCode event uses the `WinExec` function. This is a synchronous operation. The Application Processor will wait for the user to view and close the document before it continues to process other events.

| NOTE | When push buttons are used as command buttons, they are always associated with a `FieldChange` PeopleCode event. When push buttons are used as secondary panels, it is important to note that the actual secondary panel has to be placed after the push button field in the panel field layout. |

KEY POINTS

1 Prompt records are used to provide a list of valid values for a panel field.

2 Prompt processing is performed with the help of database and search keys on the prompt record.

3 Translate values also provide a list of valid values for character fields one to four characters in length. All translate values in the system are stored in one record called the XLATTABLE.

4 Search records are used to control and limit the data displayed on a user panel.

5 Search fields and alternate search fields on a search record are displayed in a dialog box during search processing.

6 When the Application Processor finds an exact match for values entered in search fields, it displays the panel without providing a list box. When the number of rows that match the values entered in search fields is more than one, the Application Processor provides a list box with matching entries.

7 Derived/Work records are used in applications which require Total fields, Push Button fields, message fields, dynamic prompt records, etc.

8 Push Buttons are used as commands, processes, or secondary panels.

C H A P T E R   7

Advanced panel design features

This chapter covers some advanced features used when building a panel in PeopleSoft. Panels serve as user interfaces to the application. A number of added features in PeopleSoft 7 help the developer build powerful application panels that can perform a variety of tasks.

7.1 WORKING WITH SCROLL BARS

It is safe to say that over half the panels in a PeopleSoft application are built with scroll bars. In some cases, scroll bars are used to display multiple rows of data from the same Record definition. This is the simplest way to describe it. Scroll bars are also used to display records that have a Parent/Child relationship and to maintain historical data using effective dates.

Scroll bars have counts that determine the number of rows displayed on the scroll and define the panel buffer information. For example, if one scroll bar is on a panel, then the level above the scroll bar is referred to as level 0 while the scroll itself is referred to as level 1. Several "level 1" scroll bars can exist on the same panel, most probably displaying data from multiple record definitions. Each one of these "level 1" scroll bars can have scroll bars below them.

Scroll bars from the same record definition can span multiple panels (also known as panel groups). Each of these panels contains a group of fields from the same Record definition. Fields are grouped by functions within these panels. JOB DATA is an example of a group of panels that display fields from the same record definition across multiple panels on the same scroll level.

Scroll bars—usually hidden scrolls built from work records—can also be used as work scrolls. Sometimes work scrolls are used to update an SQL table. The scroll bar contains fields from an SQL view and, during save time, those fields update the underlying SQL table. The POSITION_DATA group of panels in PeopleSoft HRMS performs updates on incumbents from changes made to positions.

Scroll bars can be used in a panel to:

- display multiple rows of data from one record definition uniquely identified by one or more key fields
- display effective-dated rows
- display records with parent/child relationships
- act as work scrolls

7.1.1 Multiple rows on scroll bars

By simply building a panel with a single scroll bar and assembling the required fields from the record definition we can use scroll bars to display multiple rows of data from the same record definition. We have an example in our Problem Tracking application built in chapter 6. This panel shows the total number of problems by problem status.

Figure 7.1 shows a panel that displays the problem status and the total number of problems. The panel has a related display field that shows the translate description of the problem status field. The Grand Total field is placed on level zero before the scroll bar in the order of fields because only one occurrence of the grand total field can exist on the panel. Inside the scroll bar, however, we have multiple occurrences of the problem status field showing on the scroll bar.

Navigation: File → Open → Panel → MY_TRKG_STATUS

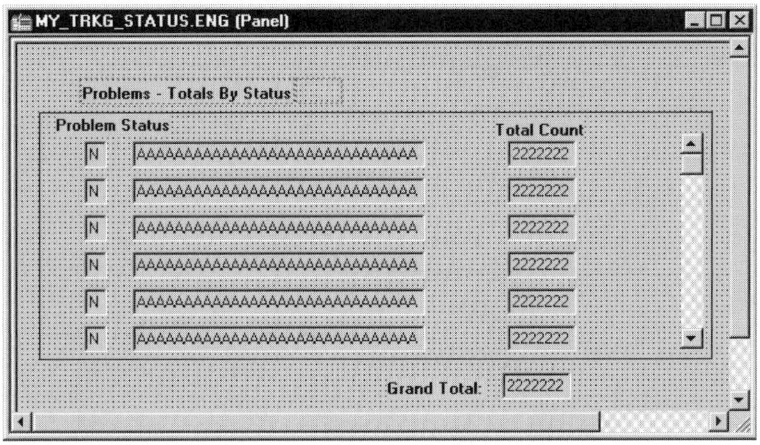

Figure 7.1   Panel displaying multiple rows on the scroll bar

---

NOTE   On a scroll bar, only fields from one record definition can exist unless they are related display or derived fields. This limitation forces us to create multiple scroll bars or build a group of panels.

Given that a scroll bar can contain fields from only one record definition, we assemble record definitions, which are child records, on a lower level scroll. The description field in figure 7.1 is a related display field. All related display fields have an associated control display field. In this example, the problem status field controls the value displayed as the description. Let's look at the panel field layout to better understand what we've just described.

Looking at the panel fields layout (figure 7.2) we notice three things described in the previous section.

- All the fields below the scroll bar are either from the MY_TRKG_STATUS record definition or they are related display fields such as XLATLONGNAME from the XLATTABLE.

- The MY_PROBLEM_STATUS field from the MY_TRKG_STATUS record definition is placed before the XLATLONGNAME field from XLATTABLE. This is because MY_PROBLEM_STATUS field is the Display Control field, and XLATLONGNAME is the Related Display field.

- The TOTAL_COUNT field from the MY_DERIVED record definition is placed before the scroll bar. This will help us show one grand total of all the problems/incidents in our application. Of course, PeopleCode has to be used to show the grand total field in this work field as illustrated in figure 6.39.

Navigation: Layout → Order (MY_TRKG_STATUS panel is open)

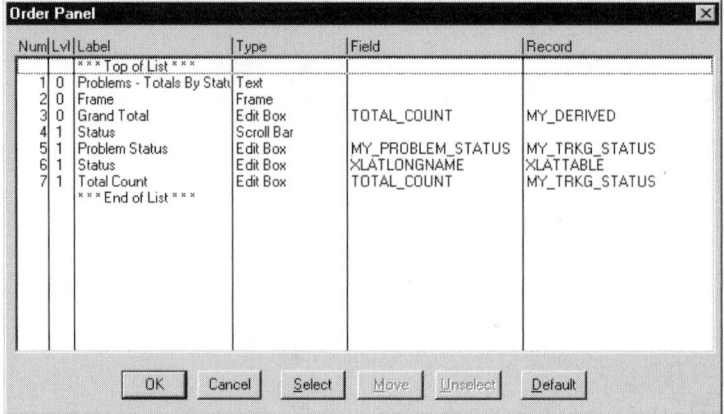

Figure 7.2 Panel fields layout

NOTE A scroll bar has an occurs level and an occurs count. Occurs level is the scroll level number. Occurs count is the number of rows that can be displayed when the panel is brought up. Fields are placed after the scroll bar in the panel field layout so that multiple occurrences of data can be displayed on the scroll bar. Any field that should be displayed only once on the panel must be placed before or above the scroll bar in the panel field layout.

7.1.2 Parent and child records on scrolls

In our Problem Tracking application, we do not have a parent and child record assembled on a panel with a scroll bar. Let's look instead at the PeopleSoft HRMS application where we have examples we can review to learn more about Parent and Child records on a scroll. One good example is the deduction table, which contains three different Child records. The deduction table is populated using a group of panels. Let us look at the key structure of the DEDUCTION_TBL (figure 7.3) and its child record, the DEDUCTION_CLASS table (figure 7.4).

DEDUCTION_TBL has three key fields. If we look at the DEDUCTION_CLASS table, we notice that it has two more keys than the DEDUCTION_TBL.

From figure 7.4 we can deduce that, for a row of data in the DEDUCTION_TBL, we can possibly have multiple rows of data in the DEDUCTION_CLASS table. Of course, we assume that these record definitions are going to be viewed and updated using the same panel group. These tables are actually updated using a group of five panels in the PeopleSoft HRMS system.

Navigation: File → Open → Record → DEDUCTION_TBL

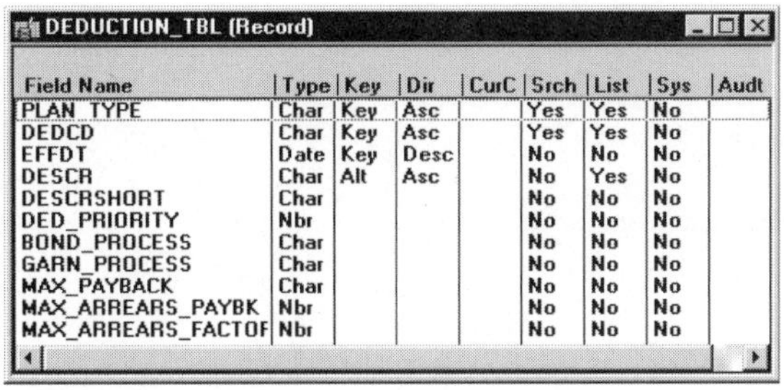

DEDUCTION_TBL (Record)

Field Name	Type	Key	Dir	CurC	Srch	List	Sys	Audt
PLAN_TYPE	Char	Key	Asc		Yes	Yes	No	
DEDCD	Char	Key	Asc		Yes	Yes	No	
EFFDT	Date	Key	Desc		No	No	No	
DESCR	Char	Alt	Asc		No	Yes	No	
DESCRSHORT	Char				No	No	No	
DED_PRIORITY	Nbr				No	No	No	
BOND_PROCESS	Char				No	No	No	
GARN_PROCESS	Char				No	No	No	
MAX_PAYBACK	Char				No	No	No	
MAX_ARREARS_PAYBK	Nbr				No	No	No	
MAX_ARREARS_FACTOF	Nbr				No	No	No	

Figure 7.3
Key structure of a parent record

Navigation: File → Open → Record → DEDUCTION_CLASS

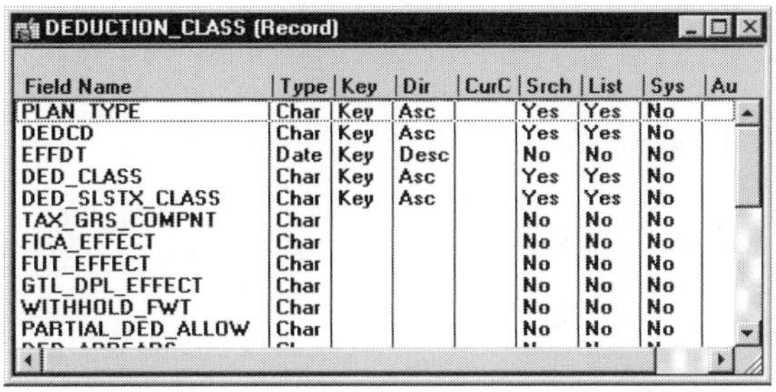

DEDUCTION_CLASS (Record)

Field Name	Type	Key	Dir	CurC	Srch	List	Sys	Au
PLAN_TYPE	Char	Key	Asc		Yes	Yes	No	
DEDCD	Char	Key	Asc		Yes	Yes	No	
EFFDT	Date	Key	Desc		No	No	No	
DED_CLASS	Char	Key	Asc		Yes	Yes	No	
DED_SLSTX_CLASS	Char	Key	Asc		Yes	Yes	No	
TAX_GRS_COMPNT	Char				No	No	No	
FICA_EFFECT	Char				No	No	No	
FUT_EFFECT	Char				No	No	No	
GTL_DPL_EFFECT	Char				No	No	No	
WITHHOLD_FWT	Char				No	No	No	
PARTIAL_DED_ALLOW	Char				No	No	No	

Figure 7.4
Key sctructure of a child record

Because DEDUCTION_CLASS is a child record to DEDUCTION_TBL, they can be placed on panels which contain scroll bars. There can be multiple rows of data in the DEDUCTION_CLASS table for a unique combination of PLAN_TYPE, DEDCD, and EFFDT fields from the DEDUCTION_TBL. The first three keys in both the tables have the same value.

Let's look at the panels that contain these record definitions (figure 7.5). DEDUCTION_TABLE2 panel contains fields from DEDUCTION_TBL and DEDUCTION_CLASS record definitions. DEDUCTION_TBL is on the level one scroll bar, and DEDUCTION_CLASS is on the level two scroll bar.

For a particular deduction code with an effective date, multiple deduction classes can be entered using the level two scroll bar. If there are multiple records on the level one scroll bar with different effective dates, then multiple rows in DEDUCTION_CLASS table are associated with every effective-dated row in DEDUCTION_TBL.

Navigation: File → Open → Panel → DEDUCTION_TABLE2

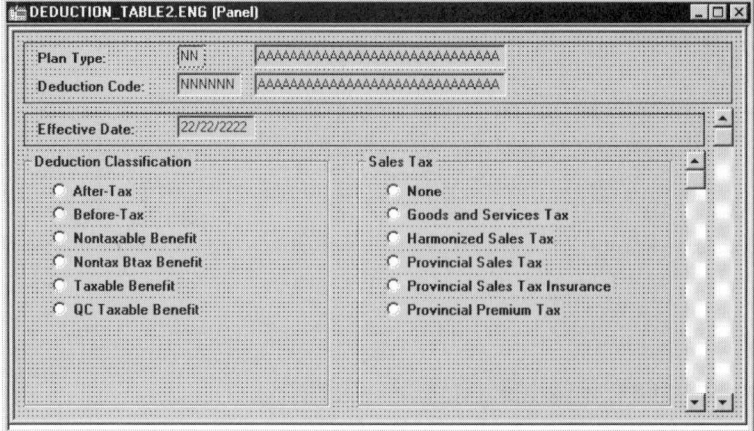

Figure 7.5   Panel with parent and child records on scrolls

Look at the panel layout and check the order in which the fields were laid out when the panel was built (figure 7.6).

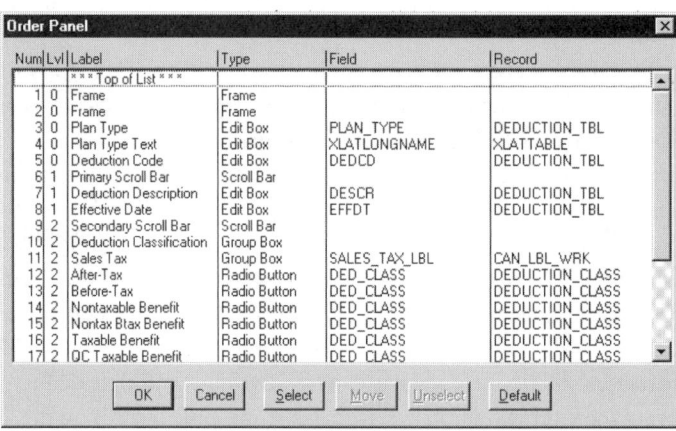

**Figure 7.6
Panel layout with parent and child records**

Fields from the DEDUCTION_TBL record are placed inside the level one scroll bar, and fields from the DEDUCTION_CLASS record are placed inside the level two scroll bar. The key fields—PLAN_TYPE and DEDCD—are seen only once in this panel and belong to level 0. Level 0 fields are usually populated from the search dialog box. The key fields automatically propagate from level 0 to other scroll levels during save time. Using the level one scroll bar, we can easily enter multiple rows into DEDUCTION_TBL for the same PLAN_TYPE and DEDCD fields, but for different effective dates. Likewise, using the level two scroll bar, we can enter multiple rows into DEDUCTION_CLASS for a particular PLAN_TYPE, DEDCD, and EFFDT combination.

NOTE   The level above the level one scroll bar is called level zero. Any field that has a single occurrence is placed on this level. Usually fields from search/input dialog boxes are placed on level zero. The search key fields are placed once on level zero, and the values in these fields automatically propagate to child records in other scroll levels satisfying the parent/child relationship.

7.1.3   Scroll bars used as work scrolls

Scroll bars can be used as work scrolls in PeopleSoft for two main purposes: to load multiple rows of data from application tables for access and reference; and to update one or more rows of data from the work scroll into database tables and views. Work scrolls are usually hidden scroll bars or placed in a hidden panel within a panel group.

In PeopleSoft HRMS, one example of a work scroll resides in the JOB DATA group of panels. Let's look at the JOB DATA panel group definition to see how the whole panel containing work scrolls is hidden.

The panel group in figure 7.7 in fact has two hidden panels, both containing work scrolls. For our purposes, we will look at the JOB_DATA1_WRK panel which contains multiple work scrolls.

Navigation: File → Open → Panel Group → JOB_DATA

JOB_DATA.GBL (Panel Group)

	Panel Name	Item Name	Hidden	Item Label	Folder Tab Label
1	JOB_DATA1	JOB_DATA1	☐	&Work Location	
2	JOB_DATA_JOBCO	JOB_DATA_JOBCODE	☐	&Job Information	Job Information
3	JOB_DATA2	JOB_DATA2	☐	&Payroll	
4	JOB_DATA3	JOB_DATA_3	☐	&Compensation	Compensation
5	JOB_DATA_ERNDIS	JOB_EARNINGS_DISTRI	☐	Job Earnings &Distri	
6	JOB_DATA_BENPR	BENEFIT_PROGRAM_P	☐	&Benefit Program P	
7	EMPLOYMENT_DTA	EMPLOYMENT_DATA	☐	&Employment Data	
8	JOB_DATA1_WRK	JOB_DATA1_WRK	☑	Job Data1 Wrk	
9	SCRTY_TBL_GBL_	SCRTY_TBL_GBL_WRK	☑	Scrty Tbl Gbl Wrk	

Figure 7.7
Panel groups with hidden panels

TIP   You can place work scrolls in hidden panels within a panel group. Alternatively, you can make the work scrolls themselves invisible.

Look at the number of scroll bars this panel contains (figure 7.8). This panel accesses more record definitions than all the other panels in this panel group combined. In PeopleSoft HRMS, when an employee is hired, a number of related tables have to be populated during save time. These work scrolls help perform that task.

Navigation: File → Open → Panel → JOB_DATA1_WRK

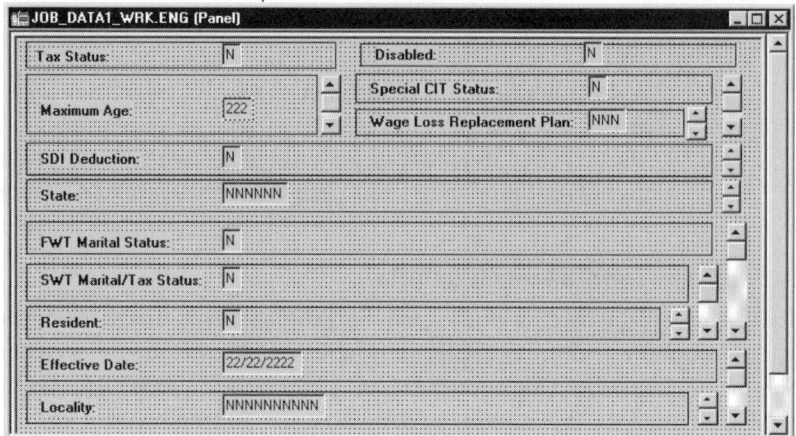

Figure 7.8   Hidden panel with work scrolls

TIP   When a field from a record definition is placed on a scroll bar, all the other fields from that record definition are also available in the panel buffer. This is true for record definitions that are SQL tables and view. This means any field from that record definition can be accessed directly using PeopleCode. This does not apply to derived records.

The work scrolls on the JOB_DATA1_WRK panel contain only one field from each record that they update. Because all fields from a record in a work scroll are available in the panel buffer, the Application Processor is able to update all of them. The field labeled "Maximum Age" in figure 7.8 belongs to the record CAN_TAX_TBL, which is placed on scroll level number one. Let's look at the properties for this scroll bar.

Notice in figure 7.9 that this scroll bar is defined as No Auto Select. This means data are populated into the scroll using a PeopleCode event, not the Application Processor. Based on an action, a PeopleCode event populates data into CAN_TAX_TBL scroll bar. When the panel is saved, this data are automatically saved into the database table.

Now let's look at the field from figure 7.8 labeled "State" (in the center of the panel). This field is from the TAX_LOCATION2 record definition and is also in scroll level one. Let us take a look at the properties of the scroll bar which contains this field.

Navigation: Edit → Panel Field Properties (JOB_DATA1_WRK Panel is open)

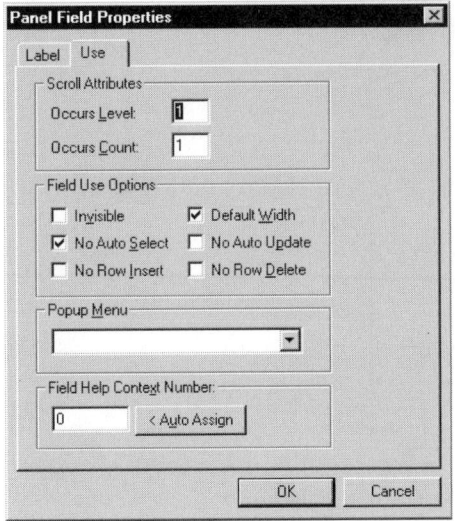

Figure 7.9
Scroll bar properties

TIP   Use the No Auto Select feature under Scroll Bar properties to disable the Application Processor from populating data into scrolls automatically. Similarly, use the No Auto Update feature to disable the Application Processor from saving data in scrolls to the database.

In figure 7.10, the scroll bar is set for auto select. As soon as the TAX_LOCATION_CD is filled up with a value on JOB_DATA1 panel, this scroll will be populated in the panel buffer. Also, for every effective-dated row in the JOB record, corresponding values will be built into this scroll bar.

Let us take a look at the definition for the TAX_LOCATION2 record. In figure 7.11 we see that TAX_LOCATION_CD field is a search key on TAX_LOCATION2. As soon as TAX_LOCATION_CD field is available in the panel buffer the Application Processor automatically selects data into the work scroll. Prompt records follow the same concept, using search key values to produce a prompt list.

NOTE   When the No Auto Select option is turned off, scroll bars are set for auto select. If a record in such a scroll bar has key fields, the Application Processor populates the fields from the record as soon as values for these key fields are available in the panel buffer. The key fields must be either in the same scroll level or in higher level scrolls.

Navigation: Edit → Panel Field Properties (JOB_DATA1_WRK Panel is open)

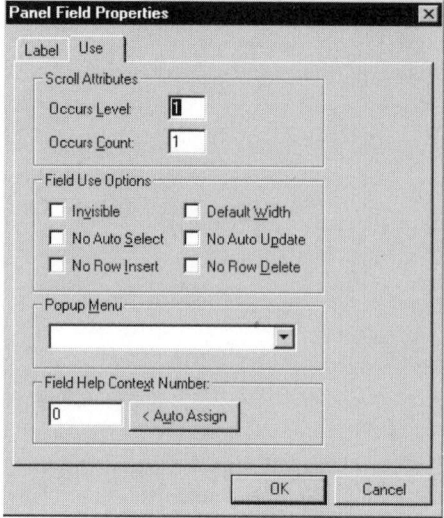

Figure 7.10
Scroll bar properties

Navigation: File → Open → Record → TAX_LOCATION2

Field Name	Type	Key	Dir	CurC	Srch	List	Sys	Audt	H	D
TAX_LOCATION_CD	Char	Key	Asc		Yes	Yes	No			
STATE	Char	Key	Asc		No	No	No			
LOCALITY	Char	Key	Asc		No	No	No			
LOCALITY_LINK	Char				No	No	No			

Figure 7.11
Key structure of TAX_LOCATION2

Now let's look at the panel field layout for the JOB_DATA1_WRK panel (figure 7.12).

All the work scrolls in this panel (figure 7.12) are level one scroll bars. Some are set for No Auto Select and are populated by a PeopleCode event. For most work scrolls in the panel, No Auto Update option is turned off. This enables the Application Processor to save data from the scroll buffer to the underlying database table during save time.

PeopleCode functions that update scrolls are `InsertRow`, `UpdateValue`, `ScrollSelect`, `ScrollSelectNew`, and so on. (We discuss these PeopleCode functions in chapter 16.) Let us take a quick look at the PeopleCode program that populates the FED_TAX_DATA scroll bar.

As illustrated in figure 7.12 only the FWT_MAR_STATUS field from FED_TAX_DATA record is placed on the panel. But, take a look at the PeopleCode

Navigation: Layout → Order (JOB_DATA1_WRK panel is open)

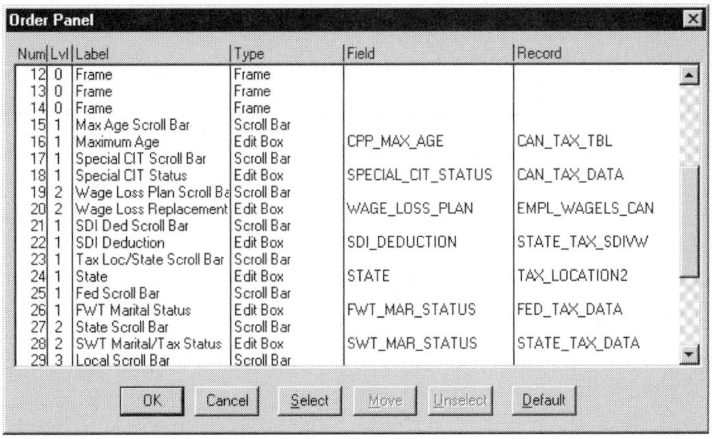

Figure 7.12   Panel field layout of a hidden panel with work scrolls

program shown in figure 7.13. Here you can see other fields from FED_TAX_DATA being referenced and populated. The entire FED_TAX_DATA record definition is available for reference in the panel buffer.

Navigation: File → Open → Record → FUNCLIB_PAY → Highlight Field → View PeopleCode

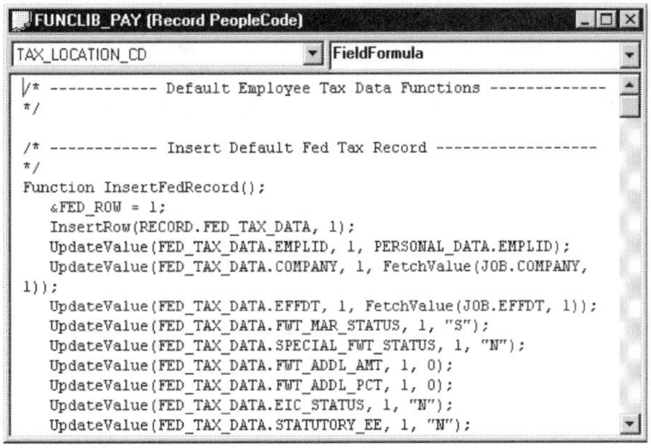

**Figure 7.13
PeopleCode event that updates
work scrolls**

This PeopleCode program is written as a function and included in a function library. This function is also stored in a derived record that contains many payroll functions. The two key PeopleCode functions used to insert and populate rows on the scroll bar are `InsertRow` and `UpdateValue`. Similarly, STATE_TAX_DATA and LOCAL_TAX_DATA scrolls are populated using the same PeopleCode functions.

When the panel is saved, the Application Processor automatically populates the underlying database tables.

7.2   WORKING WITH EFFECTIVE DATES

Effective date and effective sequence are two of the most important fields used in a PeopleSoft application. Effective Date and Effective Sequence fields are used to maintain historical data in PeopleSoft. These two fields create an audit trail of changing application data. They also enable PeopleSoft batch applications to perform retroactive and future-dated processing. Effective-dated data rows are accessed in PeopleSoft using scroll bars. The effective date field is usually the first field on the scroll bar in the panel field layout. Effective dated processing is based on menu item actions. Menu item actions are Add, Data Entry, Update/Display, Update/Display All, and Correction.

Based on the action chosen by the user, the number of rows fetched from the database varies. Let us see how menu item actions affect the number of rows selected.

Add   When an Add action is used to access a panel group, the Application Processor checks for the existence of rows in the search record with keys in the input dialog box. If the row already exists in the database table, a message is issued to the user (figure 7.14).

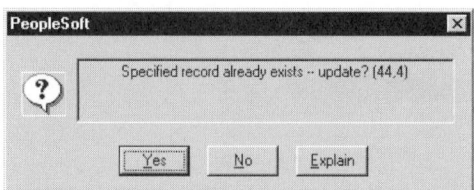

Figure 7.14
Record exists during Add action

In the event that record already exists and if the user chooses "Yes" to the message in figure 7.14, menu item action is automatically changed to Update/Display.

Update/Display   When the Update/Display action is used to access a panel group, only the current and future dated rows are selected from the table. In the Update/Display mode, data on the current effective-dated row cannot be changed. With the exception of the effective date field itself, other data on a future dated row may be changed.

Update/Display All   When the Update/Display All action is used to access a panel group, all the effective-dated rows from the table are selected. As with Update/Display, data on the current effective-dated row cannot be changed. With the exception of the effective date field, all other fields may be changed.

Correction   When the `Correction` action is used to access a panel group, all effective-dated rows from the table are selected. All the selected rows can be changed including the effective date field. For this reason, `Correction` must be authorized only to users who are administrators and understand the implications of correcting data.

Let us look at a sample set of data to understand historical, current, and future-dated rows in a table. We can use the DEPARTMENT table from the PeopleSoft HRMS application to illustrate the concept (figure 7.15).

Navigation: Go → Define Business Rules → Manage Human Resources U.S.
            → Use → Department Table → Correction

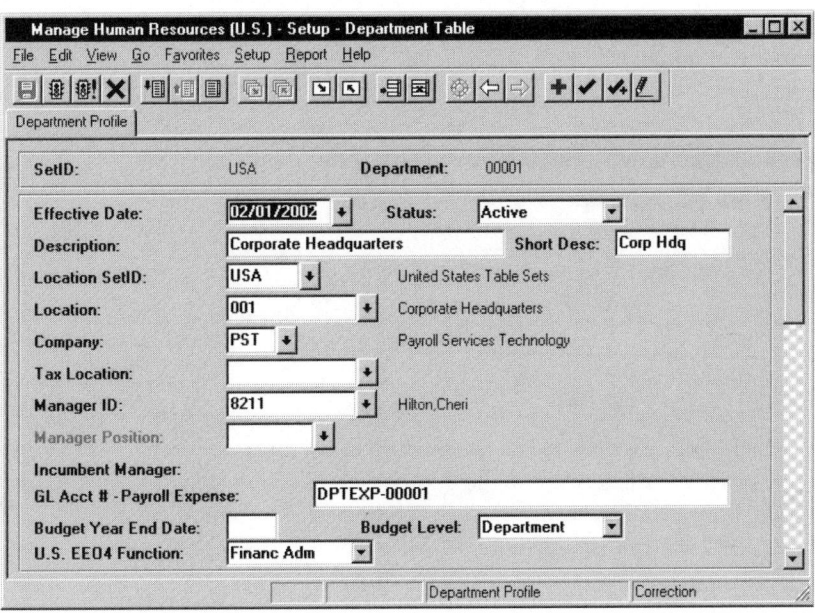

Figure 7.15   Panel with effective dates on scrolls

We brought up the panel in figure 7.15 using the `Correction` action. This loads all the effective-dated rows on the scroll bar. Notice that EFFDT is the first field inside the scroll bar. Let's take a closer look at the effective dates from all rows from the DEPARTMENT table loaded in the scroll bar. The rows are sorted in a descending sequence on the scroll bar (table 7.1).

Effective dates are used to maintain historical data. Scroll bars are used in panels to view historical effective-dated rows.

Table 7.1   Effective dates from the DEPARTMENT table

Effective Date	Definition	Description
02/01/2002	Future	This date is in the future compared to the current date.
06/15/1996	Current	This date is current and effective as of today.
01/01/1960	History	This date is in history.

Let us see what happens when current and history rows are changed using the Update/Display and Update/Display All actions.

A message (figure 7.16) is issued.

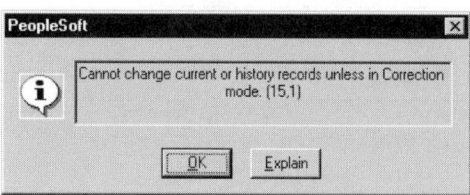

Figure 7.16
Changing data using Update/Display

TIP   We can prevent users from correcting current and history rows by disabling their access to the Correction action in menu items. This can be accomplished with the help of the Security Administrator tool.

7.2.1   PeopleCode functions for effective-dated processing

Some delivered PeopleCode functions are built into PeopleTools. Most of these functions are used to fetch the effective dates or the row numbers which contain the effective dates from the scroll bar. All these functions work only on effective-dated records. Let us look at some of these functions and how they can be used.

CurrEffDt returns the effective date from the current row on the scroll bar. Regardless of where the cursor is on the scroll bar, this function will return the value of the current effective date.

CurrEffSeq returns the value of the effective sequence field from the current row on the scroll bar.

CurrEffRowNum returns the row number that contains the current effective-dated row on the scroll bar.

`NextEffDt` returns the value of a field on the next effective-dated row. This function takes a fieldname as a parameter.

`NextRelEffDT` returns the value of a related display field from the next effective-dated row. The input parameter to this function is usually a panel field defined as a Display Control item. The output field is defined as a "Related Display" field.

`PriorRelEffDt` returns the value of a "Related Display" field from the prior effective-dated row. The parameters are the same as the `NextRelEffDt` function.

(Please refer to part 3 of this book for more detailed descriptions about these built-in PeopleCode functions.)

NOTE The `Update/Display` action selects only current and future effective dated rows. The `Update/Display All` and `Correction` actions select all rows from the database table.

NOTE The Effective Sequence field is used in conjunction with the Effective Date field. We can use Effective Sequence to distinguish history rows with the same effective date. For example, in PeopleSoft HRMS, JOB record has both EFFDT and EFFSEQ as key fields. When the user enters a promotion and pay rate increase using the same EFFDT for an employee, the EFFSEQ field is used to distinguish the two rows.

7.3 WORKING WITH SUBPANELS AND SECONDARY PANELS

Subpanels are used to populate repetitive sets of fields using a subrecord. Alternatively, secondary panels are used to organize panel fields based on functionality. Both subpanels and secondary panels are used to organize panel fields and make them easier for input.

7.3.1 Subpanels

Subrecords play a key part in building subpanels. Let's look at a record definition which contains a subrecord, the PERSONAL_DATA record from the PeopleSoft HRMS system (figure 7.17).

Navigation: File → Open → Record → PERSONAL_DATA

Field Name	Type	Len	Format	H	Short Name	Long Name
EMPLID	Char	11	Upper		ID	EmplID
NAME	Char	50	Name		Name	Name
NAME_PREFIX	Char	4	Mixed		Prefix	Name Prefix
NAME_SUFFIX	Char	15	Mixed		Suffix	Name Suffix
LAST_NAME_SRCH	Char	30	Upper		Last Name	Last Name
FIRST_NAME_SRCH	Char	30	Upper		First Name	First Name
ADDRESS_SBR	SRec					
ADDR_OTR_SBR	SRec					
PHONE_SBR	SRec					
PER_STATUS	Char	1	Upper		Per Status	Personnel Status
ORIG_HIRE_DT	Date	10			Hire Date	Original Hire Date
SEX	Char	1	Upper		Sex	Gender
AGE_STATUS	Char	1	Upper		Age 18+	Age 18 or Older
MAR_STATUS	Char	1	Upper		Mar Status	Marital Status
BIRTHDATE	Date	10			Birthdate	Date of Birth
BIRTHPLACE	Char	30	Mixed		Birthplace	Birth Location
BIRTHCOUNTRY	Char	3	Upper		Country	Birth Country

Figure 7.17
Record definition with subrecords

ADDRESS_SBR is a great example of the use of subrecords and subpanels. Consider now the definition of ADDRESS_SBR subrecord (figure 7.18).

Navigation: File → Open → Record → ADDRESS_SBR

Field Name	Type	Len	Format	H	Short Name	Long Name
COUNTRY	Char	3	Upper		Cntry	Country
ADDRESS1	Char	35	Mixed		Address 1	Address Line 1
ADDRESS2	Char	35	Mixed		Address 2	Address Line 2
ADDRESS3	Char	35	Mixed		Address 3	Address Line 3
ADDRESS4	Char	35	Mixed		Address 4	Address Line 4
CITY	Char	30	Mixed		City	City
NUM1	Char	6	Mixed		Nbr 1	Number 1
NUM2	Char	4	Mixed		Nbr 2	Number 2
HOUSE_TYPE	Char	2	Upper		House	House Type
COUNTY	Char	30	Mixed		County	County
STATE	Char	6	Upper		St	State
POSTAL	Char	12	Custm		Postal	Postal Code
GEO_CODE	Char	11	Upper		Geo Code	Tax Vendor Geograph
IN_CITY_LIMIT	Char	1	Upper		In Cty Lmt	In City Limit

Figure 7.18
Definition of a subrecord

All the fields in ADDRESS_SBR are standard fields that can be used to update address information. Many record definitions in PeopleSoft contain ADDRESS_SBR in its definition. In the database, the subrecord does not actually exist as an SQL table. Only the online application recognizes the subrecord. In the database, the fields from the SubRecord are automatically expanded and stored as individual fields. Because ADDRESS_SBR is used in multiple record definitions, the address fields in all these tables can be updated using the ADDRESS_SBP panel (figure 7.19).

The ADDRESS_SBP subpanel can be placed into any other panel (containing record definitions), using the ADDRESS_SBR subrecord. Notice that the panel field labels are also specified as panel fields. Even though the fields can be the same, the label for these fields can be different based on the context of the application panel. Take a

Navigation: File → Open → Panel → ADDRESS_SBP

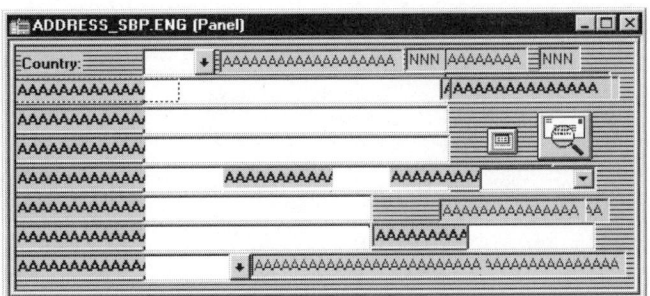

Figure 7.19
ADDRESS_SBP subpanel

look at the PERSONAL_DATA1 panel which has the ADDRESS_SBP subpanel in it (figure 7.20).

Navigation: File → Open → Panel → PERSONAL_DATA1

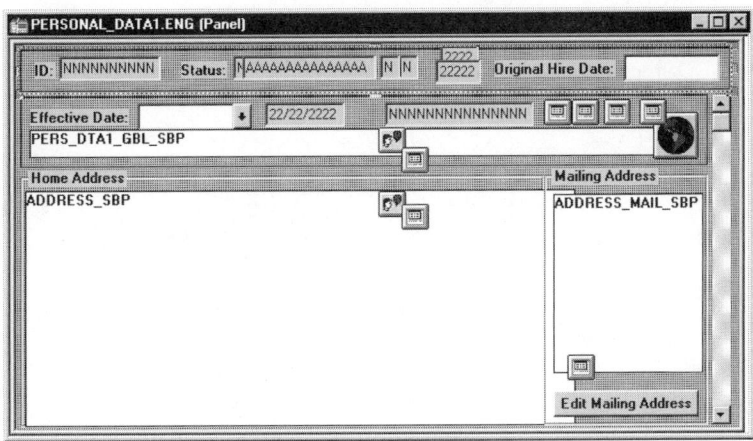

Figure 7.20   Application panel using a subpanel

TIP   Record fields can be used as panel field labels. This technique is used to provide context sensitive field labels for Subrecord fields. Subrecord fields are pre-designed in a subpanel and field labels cannot be changed when these subpanels are included in a main panel. Record fields can be used as field labels so that they can be populated based on the context of the main panel (which includes the subpanel in question).

The difficult part in designing a subpanel is the placement of fields on the subpanel. Fields have to suit all the application panels that use them. A potential problem also arises when subpanels must fit into application panels. Usually, fields on the main application panels are rearranged to fit the subpanel properly. The ADDRESS_SBP subpanel in the PERSONAL_DATA1 panel contains all those fields from the ADDRESS_SBR subrecord. At save time, these fields are updated into the PS_PERSONAL_DATA table.

Subpanels can be inserted into an application panel by choosing Insert/ SubPanel from the Application Designer menu.

The same subpanel, when placed on LOCATION_TABLE1 panel, accesses the address fields from the LOCATION_TBL record. Another popular subpanel in all PeopleSoft applications is the Process Run Control subpanel.

Navigation: File → Open → Panel → PRCSRUNCNTL_SBP

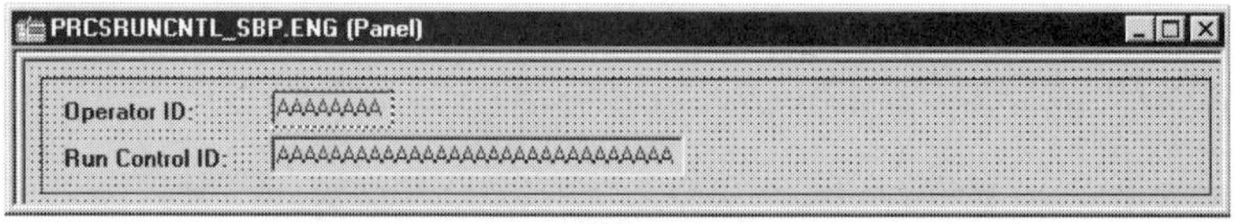

Figure 7.21 Process Run Control subpanel

All Run Control panels, which initiate a batch process, require the operator ID and Run Control ID fields in their record definition. The Process Run Control subpanel helps the Run Control panels by providing these two fields.

7.3.2 Secondary panels

Secondary panels are used to segregate functionally such as fields into a separate panel. Optional fields are separated out into a secondary panel. Secondary panels are accessed using a push button. Both the push button and the secondary panel are placed on the main application panel, one after another. Push button fields are always placed before the secondary panels in the panel layout.

Secondary panels can be inserted into a main application panel by choosing Insert/Secondary Panel from the Application Designer menu. In figure 7.20, the PERSONAL_DATA1 panel also includes secondary panels.

The push button labeled Edit Mailing Address is a derived field which activates the secondary panel. The secondary panel appears as a small hidden icon in the main application panel. Let's look at the definition of this secondary panel (figure 7.22).

Navigation: File → Open → Panel → ADDRESS_OTHER_SEC

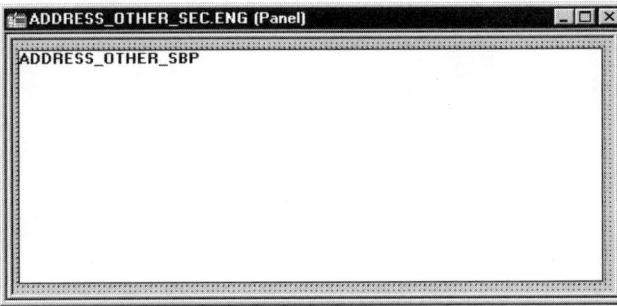

Figure 7.22
Secondary panel definition

> **TIP** Secondary panels have an advantage over subpanels. Secondary panels do not have to be designed to accommodate the main application panel. They are brought up online by pushing a button from the main panel. When secondary panels are brought up, they appear on top of the main panel. They can be closed once data are entered into the fields after focus is transferred back to the main panel.

This secondary panel also uses a subpanel. Subpanels are pre-developed panels which contain certain fields. As soon as the subpanel is placed in an application or a secondary panel, all fields from the subpanel are automatically included inside them. This secondary panel is used to edit the mailing address for an employee. Since address fields are already built into ADDRESS_SBP and ADDRESS_OTHER_SBP subpanels available in the system, this secondary panel makes use of the ADDRESS_OTHER_SBP subpanel.

> **TIP** If a SubPanel design is not suitable to fit the main application panel, the SubPanel can be included in a Secondary Panel and then the Secondary Panel can in turn be included in the main panel.

Let's look at the PeopleCode event which brings up this secondary panel (figure 7.23).

The DoModal PeopleCode function is used to bring up the secondary panel online. Instead of cluttering the panels with fields used to enter optional mailing addresses, PeopleSoft has built this secondary panel, which contains these fields. The secondary panel can be summoned on an as-needed basis by activating a push button.

Navigation: File → Open → Record → DERIVED_HR → View → PeopleCode Display,

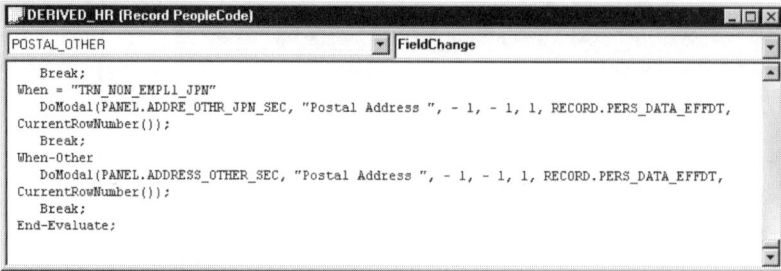

Figure 7.23   PeopleCode program that activates a secondary panel

In figure 7.24, the secondary panel appears on top of the main application panel:

Navigation: Activate Push Button

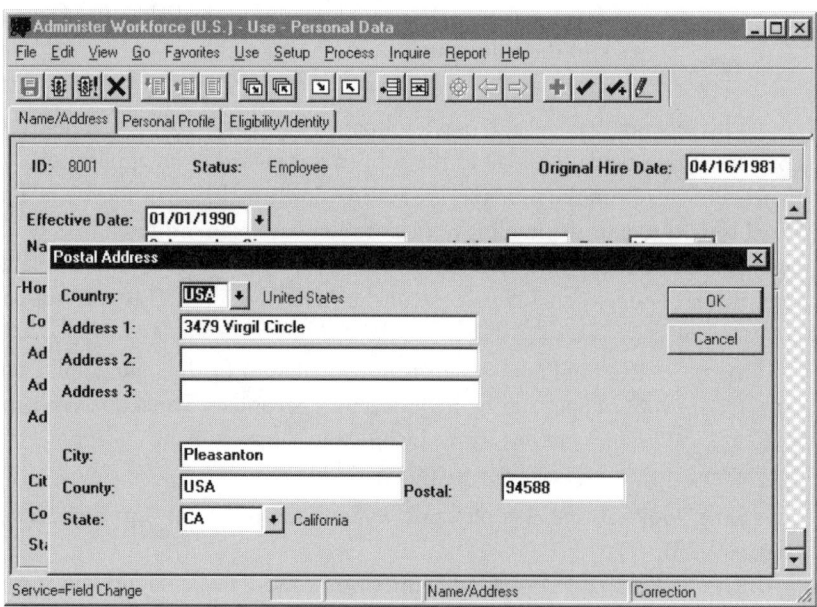

Figure 7.24   Secondary panels on an application panel

7.4   *DESIGNING INQUIRY PANELS*

Inquiry panels are display panels that cannot update data. Used as organized queries to the database, inquiry panels are easy to build. They consist of several record fields assembled on a panel adhering to panel design rules. Inquiry panels are also used to by-pass some complex PeopleCode events in record definitions and help in quick inquiry of data. The Application Processor populates information from database tables into the online panel.

In our Problem Tracking application, we designed an inquiry panel which shows us totals by problem status. Let's look at the definition for MY_TRKG_STATUS panel (figure 7.25).

Navigation: File → Open → Panel → MY_TRKG_STATUS

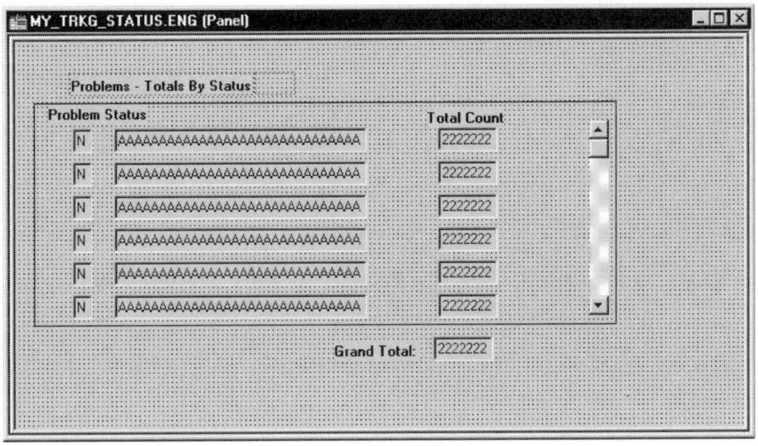

Figure 7.25   Inquiry panel

This simple example of an inquiry panel makes use of an SQL view to display information online. The description field is a related display field from the XLATTABLE. The TOTAL_COUNT field inside the scroll bar is the result of the aggregate SUM function used in the SQL view. The grand total field is populated by a simple PeopleCode event adding all the individual totals from inside the scroll bar and displaying the grand total using a derived field.

By building an SQL view definition and using fields from the view definition on the inquiry panel, all PeopleCode events from MY_PROBLEM_TRKG record are bypassed (figure 7.26):

Navigation: File → Open → Record → MY_TRKG_STATUS → File → Object Properties

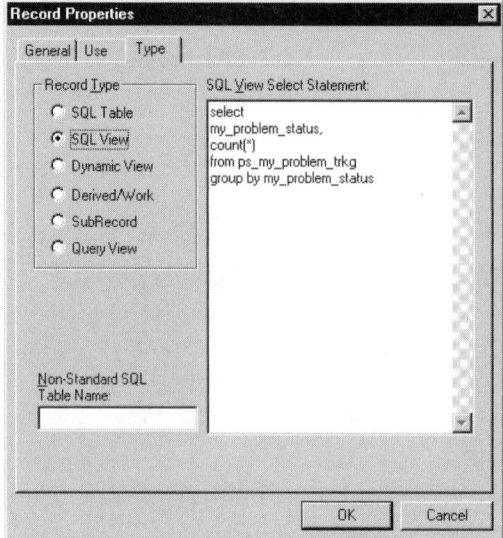

Figure 7.26
SQL view definition

Take a look, too, at the record definition of MY_TRKG_STATUS SQL view (figure 7.27).

Navigation: File → Open → Record → MY_TRKG_STATUS

Field Name	Type	Len	Format	H	Short Name	Long Name
MY_PROBLEM_STATUS	Char	1	Upper		Problem Sta	Problem Status
TOTAL_COUNT	Nbr	7			Total Cnt	Total Count

Figure 7.27
Record definition
of an SQL view

The inquiry panel has the two fields from the SQL view definition and a related display field from the XLATTABLE. Let's look at the panel field layout and see how the grand total field is derived (figure 7.28).

Notice that the grand total field is a derived field from the MY_DERIVED record definition. As the rows are populated inside the scroll, the totals by individual statuses are added and can be displayed in the grand total field. Now, consider the PeopleCode event from the MY_TRKG_STATUS record definition which sums up the individual totals and

Navigation: Layout → Order (MY_TRKG_STATUS panel is open)

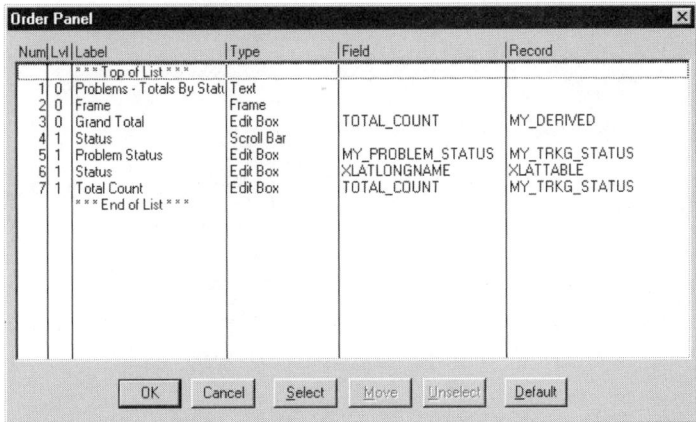

Figure 7.28   Panel layout of an inquiry panel

populates that sum into the TOTAL_COUNT field from the MY_DERIVED record definition (figure 7.29).

Navigation: View → PeopleCode (MY_TRKG_STATUS PeopleCode Display)

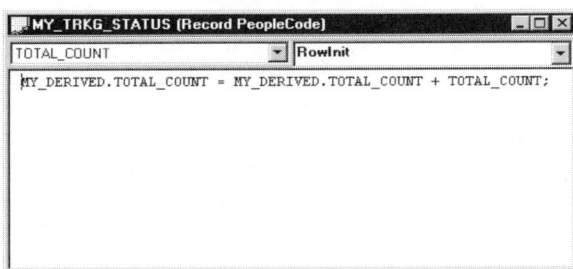

**Figure 7.29
PeopleCode event that
populates a derived field**

In figure 7.30, we see a more complex inquiry panel from the PeopleSoft HRMS system. This panel uses derived fields as switches to change the fields being displayed on the panel. In other words, the panel has key fields from the Job record assembled very close to each other. Based on the choice that the user makes, some fields are hidden and others are shown on the panel. Figure 7.30 shows the definition of this panel.

It may seem that this panel is cluttered with fields, but the four display switches on the top control the display and hiding of fields, using PeopleCode events built behind these display switches. Take a look at the actual online panel (figure 7.31). The online panel appears far more organized than the actual panel design, because certain fields have been hidden based on the choice of switches selected by the user.

Navigation: File → Open → Panel → JOB_SUMMARY

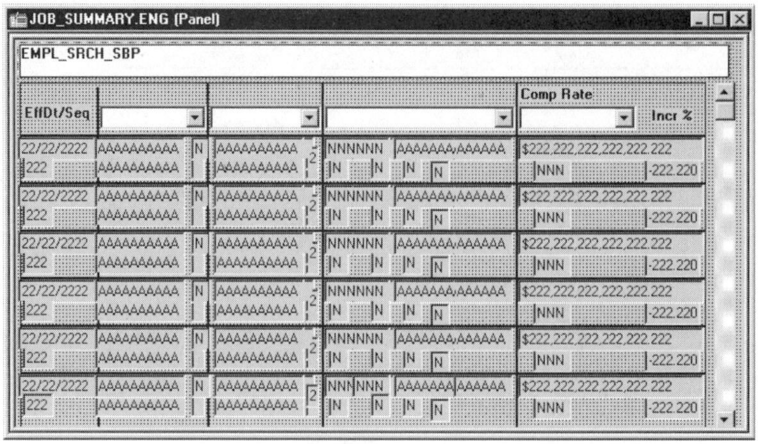

Figure 7.30 Definition of a complex inquiry panel

Navigation: Go → Administer Workforce U.S. → Inquire → Job Summary

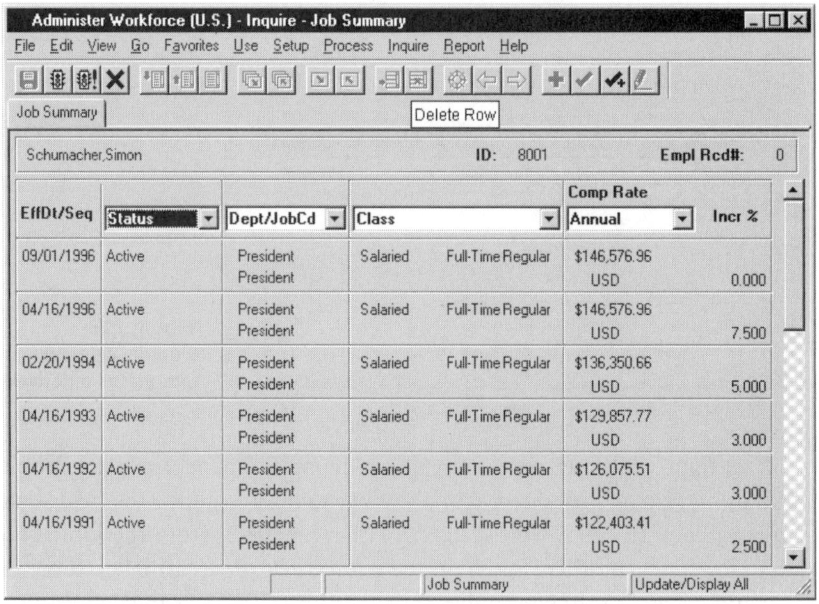

Figure 7.31 Online view of an inquiry panel

The online panel also uses an SQL view definition to display all the fields from the database. The panel uses JOB_VW, an SQL view based on the JOB table. JOB_VW does not have any of the PeopleCode events from the Job record. The inquiry panel is displayed without processing any PeopleCode event from the Job record. This inquiry panel fetches rows from the database faster than the JOB DATA panels, saving inquiry time.

The same rules apply for scroll bars on an inquiry panel. A scroll bar can contain only fields from one record definition (except for related display and derived fields).

7.5   USING A GRID ON A PANEL

Grids are spreadsheet-like displays on an application panel. As do spreadsheets, grids have cells that can be expanded and contracted. Columns can be frozen to fit more columns into a panel; data from grids can be copied into spreadsheets, and vice versa. Grids are also similar to single level scroll bars. Using grids, we can insert, delete, and change rows.

Grids cannot be used as alternatives to multiple level scroll bars. Basic panel field objects are accommodated on a grid. Objects such as edit boxes, push buttons, check boxes, drop-down list boxes, and long edit boxes are allowed on grids. Note, too, that grids have to be the last control on the panel, and only one grid is allowed in a panel.

In figure 7.32, we see a PeopleSoft HRMS panel that uses a grid for data entry.

Navigation: Go → Compensate Employees → Administer Automated Benefits

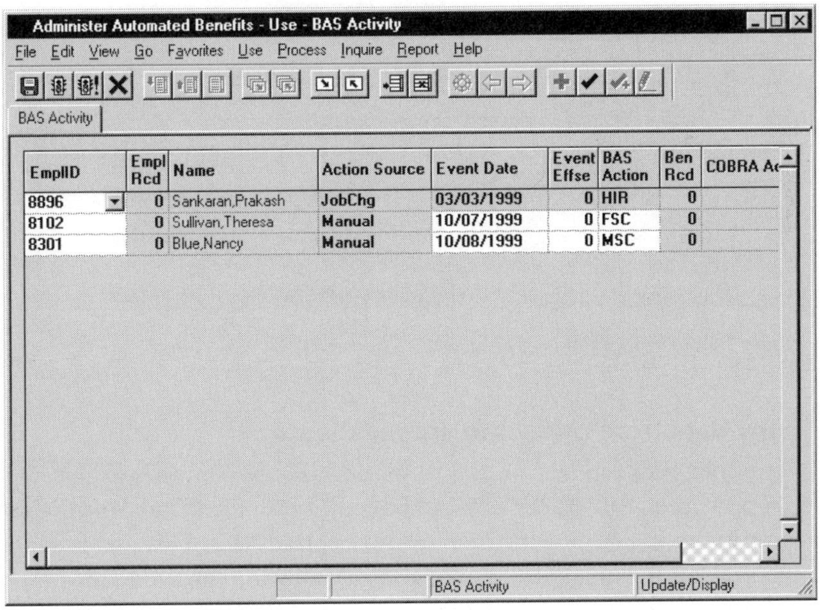

Figure 7.32   Panel with a grid

We can see that some fields here are display fields, others are input fields. The two Manual lines were manually inserted into the grid in a fashion similar to that of `row-insert` function in a scroll bar.

When grids are used, we can:

- sort the grid on any column by clicking on the column heading like a spreadsheet
- copy columns from the grid and paste them into a spreadsheet
- copy columns from a spreadsheet and paste them into the grid
- adjust row height and column width on the grid
- freeze columns on the grid like a spreadsheet

Using the panel from figure 7.32, let's demonstrate all the foregoing features of a grid:

7.5.1   Sorting the grid on its columns

`Employee ID` is the primary key on the main record in this panel. When we bring up the panel, the grid is sorted on the EMPLID field (figure 7.32). After clicking on the column heading for the NAME field (figure 7.33), the grid is sorted on an ascending order of that field. When the column heading is clicked again, the grid will be sorted on a descending order of that field.

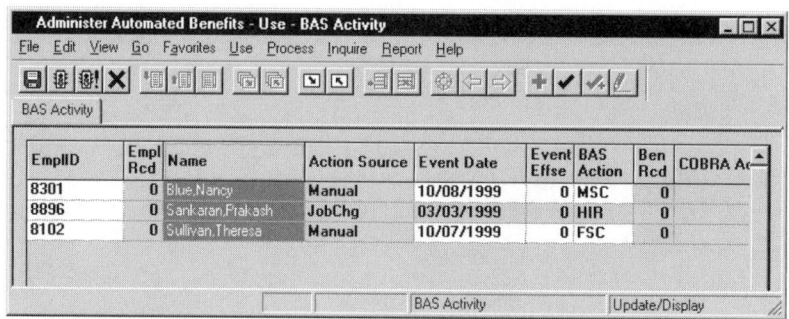

Figure 7.33   Grid sorted on a column

7.5.2   Copy data from grids into spreadsheets

Data from grids can be copied into spreadsheets. When we highlight the cells on the grid and press CTRL-C, the cells can be copied into the Window's clipboard. Then we can paste them into a text editor or into a spreadsheet. This is a useful feature which allows a user to input data into the grid and copy the entire grid into a spreadsheet for a variety of reasons. The user can perform calculations on numeric fields, copy data into spreadsheets for documentation purposes, and so forth. Let's explore this by copying data from the grid into the spreadsheets.

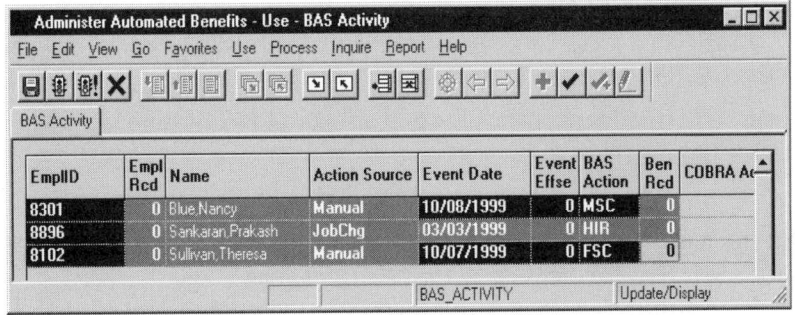

Figure 7.34 Copying data from a grid to the clipboard

Using the mouse—or the shift keys—and highlighting the cells, we copy the cells into the clipboard (figure 7.34). Figure 7.35 illustrates how this data appears when pasted on a spreadsheet.

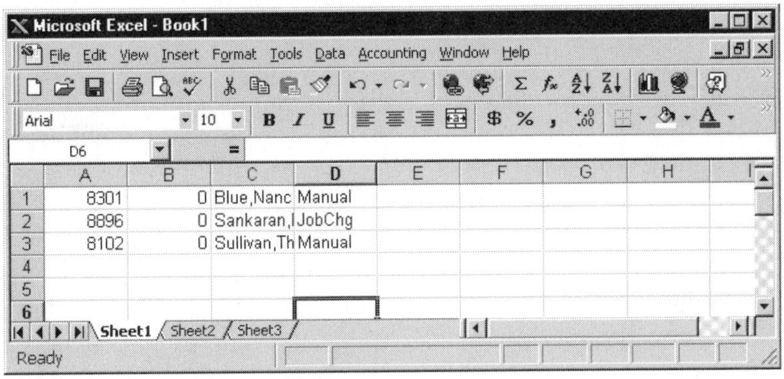

Figure 7.35 Data from grid copied into a spreadsheet

7.5.3   Copy data from spreadsheets into grids

To copy the data from the spreadsheet back to the same grid, we highlight all the cells from the Excel spreadsheet and copy them into the clipboard. Then, we paste right into the grid. Although data can be pasted into one row on the grid, limitations exist on pasting data copied from spreadsheets into grids that have keys. Database key constraints will restrict us from copying multiple rows of data into Grids.

It is possible to copy multiple rows into grids which use derived records. We can create a work grid with derived fields, insert the necessary number of rows into the grid, and paste multiple rows of data into it. Data can be saved in database tables using the SQLEXEC PeopleCode function.

7.5.4   Adjust row heights and column widths

By grabbing the edges of a column or a row and dragging them to the appropriate width or height, we can control column and row sizes just as we can in a spreadsheet. In figure 7.36, we can see how the grid appears after adjusting the column width and the row height.

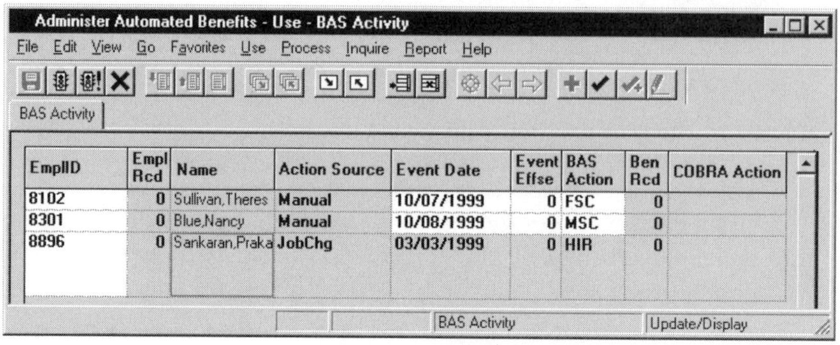

Figure 7.36   Adjust column width and row height on a grid

We increased the row height of the last row on the grid. We also reduced the column width of the NAME column. As you reduce the column width, more columns from the right side appear on the screen.

7.5.5   Freezing columns on a grid

Freezing columns on a grid is not dynamic as on a spreadsheet. The grid must be defined to contain frozen columns, and, unlike in spreadsheets, columns cannot be frozen on the application panel. How do frozen columns appear on the application panel? Figure 7.37 shows our previous grid frozen on the NAME column. When the panel is scrolled to the right, the columns to the right of the frozen column disappear, and the columns hidden on the right side of the panel become visible.

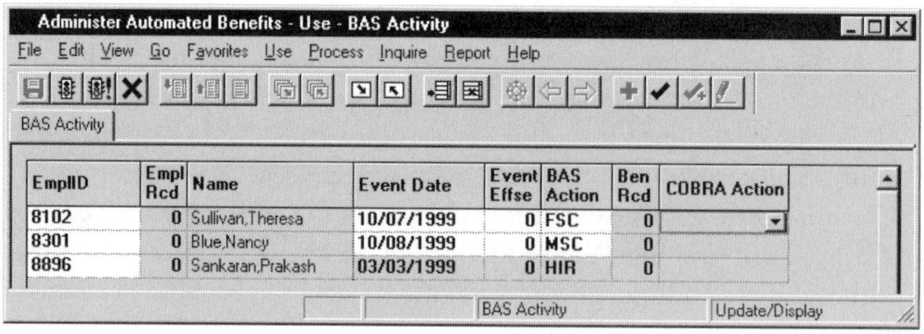

Figure 7.37   Frozen columns on a grid

The Action Source field is hidden and the Cobra Action field appears on the application panel. Previously, this field was not visible, and the whole grid would have scrolled to the left side hiding the EMPLID column. Because the grid was frozen at the NAME column, however, everything to the right of that field scrolls, moving either to the right or the left.

7.5.6 Creating a grid on a panel

Let's take a look at the steps to insert a grid into an application panel. We will present the MY_USER_TBL in a grid-like display, starting by creating a new panel and inserting a grid object into the panel (figure 7.38).

Navigation: File → New → Panel → Insert → Grid

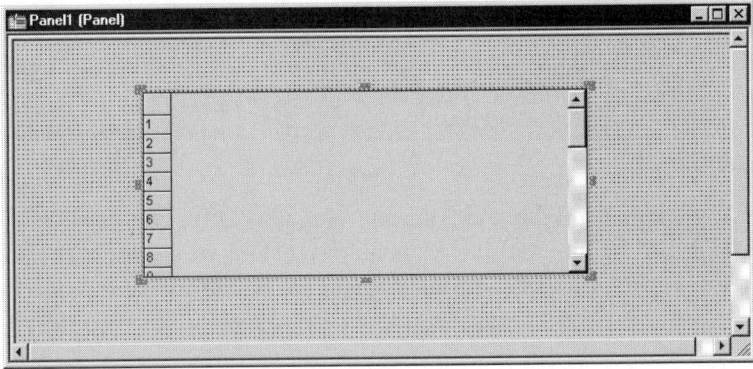

Figure 7.38 Inserting a grid into a new panel

The grid is like any other panel field. We edit the properties for the grid by choosing Panel Field properties like any other panel field. Figure 7.39 illustrates the Grid Properties screen.

We have to define a main record for the grid. Here we define MY_USER_TABLE as the main record. We also define the Occurs Level just as we did on a scroll bar. We insert grids on any level on the scroll bar. In other words, a grid can be placed inside a regular scroll bar.

Under the Columns tab, we add the fields that appear on the grid. We click on the Add button to add columns on the grid. We choose the panel field type and the record field that we want to add to the grid. The properties of each field on the grid are edited using the Panel Field Properties screen.

Under the Labels tab, we add a label to the whole grid. This tab is also used to control the display of row and column headings.

Under the Use tab, we control the properties of the scroll on the grid. We can also attach a pop-up menu to the grid using this tab. Figures 7.40, 7.41, and 7.42 illustrate the other tabs in the Grid Properties screen.

Navigation: Edit → Panel Field Properties (Grid should be highlighted)

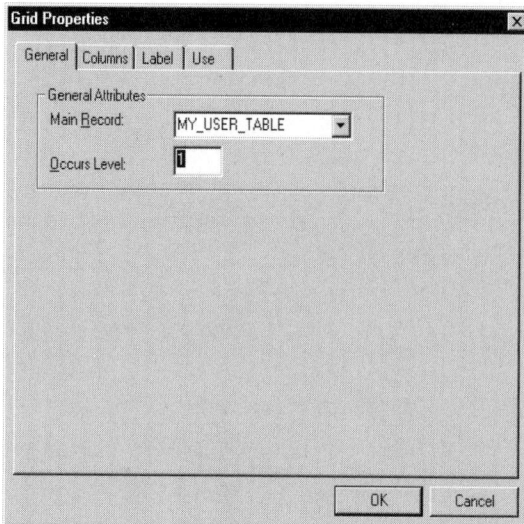

Figure 7.39
Grid Properties—General tab

By clicking on the Add button (figure 7.40), we add any field from MY_USER_TABLE into the grid. As mentioned before, we can use only edit boxes, drop-down list, checkboxes, push button, long edit boxes, and secondary panel field types.

Navigation: Edit → Panel Field Properties (Grid should be highlighted)

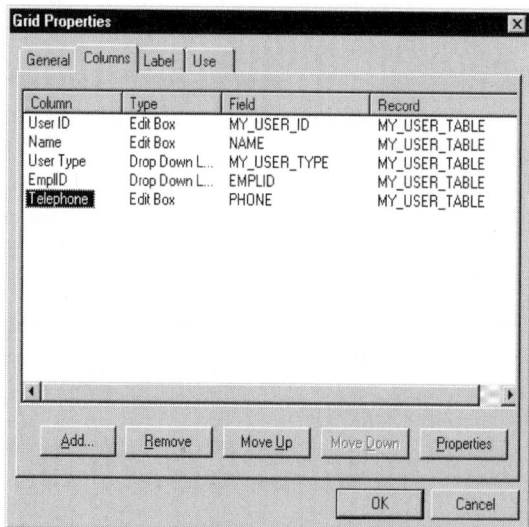

Figure 7.40
Grid Properties—Columns tab

Navigation: Edit → Panel Field Properties (Grid should be highlighted)

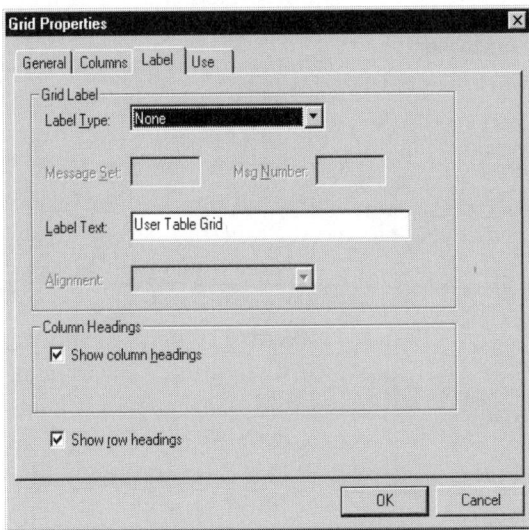

Figure 7.41
Grid Properties—Label tab

Navigation: Edit → Panel Field Properties (Grid should be highlighted)

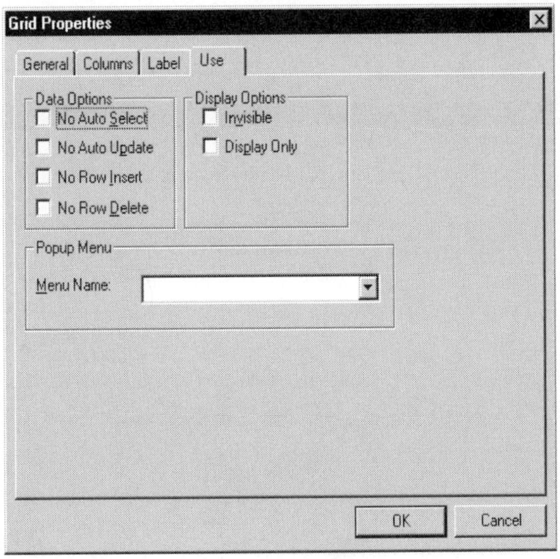

Figure 7.42
Grid Properties—Use tab

By highlighting MY_USER_ID field from the Columns tab in figure 7.40 and clicking on the Properties button, we edit field properties for that individual field within the grid. Here we can specify the panel field properties (as covered in chapter 4).

One key feature, in the Panel Field properties screen is the Freeze Grid Column option (figure 7.43). Choosing this option, we freeze columns on the grid just as we

Navigation: Properties (From Columns tab in Grid Properties screen)

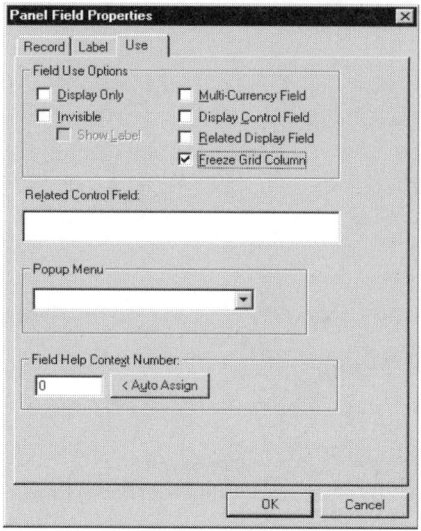

can on a spreadsheet. All columns to the left of the column chosen for the freeze are frozen as well. We can also remove columns from the grid by choosing the Remove button under the Columns tab (figure 7.40). We order the sequence of the fields on the grid by choosing the Move Up or Move Down buttons from the Columns tab of the Grid Properties screen.

After attaching the grid panel to a panel group, adding a menu item to our Problem Tracking menu, and providing security to the new menu item, we can view the grid panel online. Figure 7.44 shows how the grid appears in the application.

The columns in a grid panel can be resized online. Columns defined as frozen fields do not scroll when the scroll bar is used to move to the right or the left side.

Figure 7.43   Freeze grid column

Navigation: Go → Problem Tracking → Setup → User Table Grid

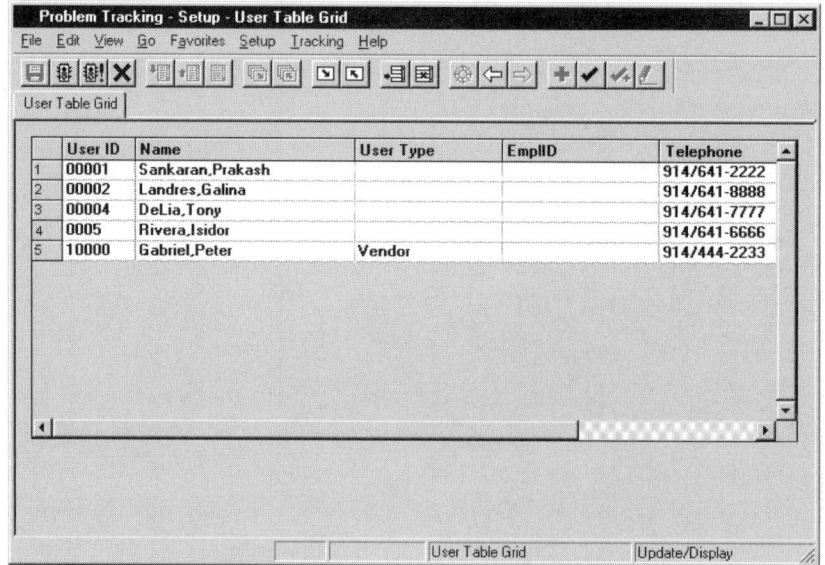

Figure 7.44   Grid application panel

KEY POINTS

1 Scroll bars are used to display multiple rows of data from the same record on one application panel.

2 Scroll bars are also used to maintain historical data using the EFFDT and EFFSEQ fields.

3 The level above the level one scroll bar is called level 0. Level 0 fields are usually fields from the search dialog box. These fields automatically propagate to child scroll levels to satisfy Parent/Child relationships.

4 The `Update/Display` action displays only current and future effective-dated rows from the database table.

5 The `Update/Display All` and `Correction` actions display all effective-dated rows from the database table.

6 Subpanels and secondary panels are used to organize panel fields. Subpanels can be built using subrecords which contain repetitive fields that can be shared across many panels. Secondary panels separate panel fields by function. Optional fields which are seldom entered can be included into a secondary panel.

7 Inquiry panels can be designed to facilitate faster access to data. PeopleCode programs in records defined as SQL tables can be bypassed by building clone records that are defined as SQL views. The fields from the SQL view can be used in the inquiry panels.

8 A grid can be used to replace a single-level scroll bar on a panel.

9 A grid can be used in a panel to facilitate easier data entry. It also provides the user with capabilities such as resizing row and column size, freezing columns, and copying data into spreadsheets.

CHAPTER 8

Building database objects

8.1 TABLES AND VIEWS IN PEOPLESOFT

PeopleSoft applications are table-based systems. PeopleTools, which runs the online application, is stored in database tables and views. A PeopleSoft application, which runs using PeopleTools, contains three distinct sets of SQL tables and views—Database catalog tables and views, PeopleTools tables and views, as well as Application tables and views.

The tables in each set perform unique functions to run the application. They are also distinguished by the manner in which they are created, modified, deleted, and likewise populated.

8.1.1 Database catalog tables and views

Database catalog tables and views are system tables which store attributes for all PeopleTools and Application tables and views in the database. Database catalog tables vary across database platforms; database catalog views are representations of data stored in the database catalog tables.

The database engine uses data attributes to access and store application data. Database catalog tables store field attributes, table attributes, index attributes, table spaces, view definitions, and so on. Installed when the database is created, database catalog tables and views are updated when the PeopleTools and application tables are created, modified, or deleted. When a PeopleSoft application is installed, both PeopleTools tables/views and Application tables/views are created in the database. Let's look at a few examples of database catalog tables (table 8.1).

Table 8.1 Database catalog table

Database Platform	Database Object	Catalog Table
Oracle	Tables	DBA_TABLES
	Columns	DBA_TAB_COLUMNS
SQLBase	Tables	SYSTABLES
	Columns	SYSCOLUMNS

8.1.2   PeopleTools tables and views

PeopleTools tables and views are part of the PeopleSoft application and are delivered along with the PeopleSoft system. They are application catalog tables which store attributes for fields, records, panels, panel groups, menus, PeopleCode, and other PeopleSoft objects. PeopleTools catalog tables and views are updated when a developer creates, modifies, or deletes a PeopleSoft object. Remember, PeopleSoft objects are building blocks for the online system. The Application Processor assembles these building blocks by accessing data from PeopleTools tables and presents the information in a graphical representation online.

Table 8.2 PeopleTools catalog tables

Objects	PeopleTools Table
Fields	PSDBFIELD
Records	PSRECFIELD, PSRECDEFN, PSINDEXDEFN, PSKEYDEFN, PSRECDDLPARM, PSIDXDDLPARM
Panels	PSPNLFIELD, PSPNLDEFN
Panel Groups	PSPNLGRPDEFN, PSPNLGROUP
Menus	PSMENUDEFN, PSMENUITEM
PeopleCode	PSPCMPROG, PSPROGNAME, PSPCMNAME

These PeopleTools catalog tables listed in table 8.2 are stored in the database as well. Let's look at how these PeopleTools catalog tables are updated.

Suppose a developer creates a record definition by performing the following tasks:

- create the schema for the record
- create fields, if necessary for the record
- define record properties

- define record field properties
- save the record definition
- build the record in the database (tables and views)

When the developer saves the record definition, the definition is stored in PeopleTools catalog tables.

The following PeopleTools tables are updated in this process:

- *PSDBFIELD* is the PeopleTools table that stores field definitions. A row is added into this SQL table each time the developer creates a new field.
- *PSRECDEFN* is the PeopleTools table that stores record definitions. A row is added into this SQL table each time the developer creates a new record.
- *PSRECFIELD* is the PeopleTools table that stores record field definitions. A row is added into this SQL table for each field in the record definition.
- *PSINDEXDEFN* is the PeopleTools table that stores index definitions for SQL tables. A row is added into this SQL table for each index defined for the record.
- *PSKEYDEFN* is the PeopleTools table that stores definitions of columns that are defined as indexed fields. A row is added for each column that is defined as indexed columns for each index.
- *PSRECDDLPARM* is the PeopleTools table that stores database specific parameters for the database table.
- *PSIDXDDLPARM* is the PeopleTools table that stores database specific parameters for the table indexes.

NOTE   PeopleTools tables and views are not prefixed with PS_ because PeopleTools tables and views are given a non-standard SQL table name in the Type tab under the record properties. Application tables and views are prefixed with PS_ when the corresponding SQL table or view is created in the database. For example, if the record is named PERSONAL_DATA in PeopleSoft, the corresponding SQL table in the database is called PS_PERSONAL_DATA.

8.1.3   Application tables and views

Users maintain business data in the application. User data are stored in application tables and views. When the user accesses the online application, data from application tables and views are presented online. Application tables and views are created as database objects.

Definitions for application tables and views are stored in PeopleTools catalog tables. The PeopleTools object definitions for application tables and views are called records. Records can also be query views, dynamic views, subrecords, and derived/work records.

Records defined as SQL tables and views are built into the database simply because tables store application data, and views are representations of data. Other PeopleSoft objects—such as panels, panel groups, menus, PeopleCode, and so on—process and present application data online. Every time the users access the online application, these objects are built online. They do not exist in the database.

Records defined as SQL tables permanently store data in the database. Record definitions are created online using PeopleTools. At this point, the record exists in PeopleSoft, but is not yet a database table. As it is, the record definition cannot store any data in the database. When the developer builds the record, a database table which can store data entered using the online application is created. Similarly, records defined as SQL views are created using PeopleTools as well.

The developer must define parameters before records can be built in the database. Records defined as SQL tables contain build parameters used in the build process. Build parameters vary across database platforms.

TIP DDDAUDIT is an SQR process which identifies records defined as tables and views, which do not exist in the database and vice versa.

Let's look at the definition for MY_PROBLEM_TRKG record (figure 8.1).

MY_PROBLEM_TRKG is defined as an SQL table in the application. In the database, the corresponding database table is named PS_MY_PROBLEM_TRKG. When the developer builds the actual SQL table in the database, other related database objects

Navigation: File → Open → Record → MY_PROBLEM_TRKG → File → Object Properties

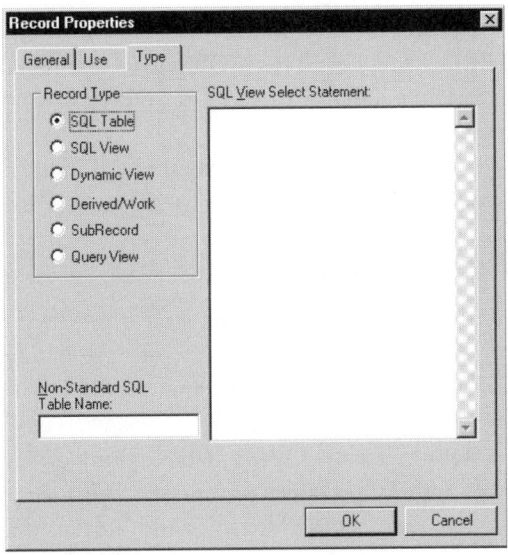

Figure 8.1
Record definition (SQL Table)—
Type tab

are created as well. SQL tables also have indexes to facilitate faster access to data stored in them. Indexes are also database objects. When database objects are created, they update database catalog tables.

Now let's take a look at the definition for MY_TRKG_STATUS record (figure 8.2).

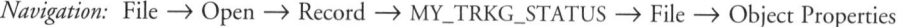

Navigation: File → Open → Record → MY_TRKG_STATUS → File → Object Properties

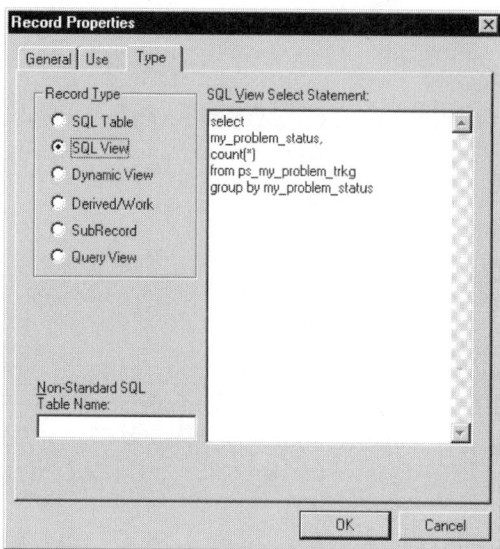

Figure 8.2
Record definition (SQL View)—Type tab

MY_TRKG_STATUS is a record defined as an SQL view. In the database, this object is called PS_MY_TRKG_STATUS. This SQL view represents data from PS_MY_PROBLEM_TRKG table in a Totals format. The SQL view is built using the SQL View `Select` Statement.

Before we describe how application tables and views are built in the database, let's consider the data modeling tools that PeopleSoft delivers as part of PeopleTools.

8.2   *DATABASE OBJECT MODELING*

PeopleSoft delivers tools which allow a database administrator to define data models. PeopleSoft objects which are stored as database objects, use the defined models as defaults. The database administrator can change the defaults and override parameters based on application needs.

When the PeopleSoft system is installed, these database models are updated to suit the defaults for majority of application tables and indexes. This way, the database administrator has to override parameters only for tables and indexes that cannot use the default storage parameters. Data models are different across database platforms. PeopleSoft delivers platform-specific parameters based on the platform of installation. If, for example, the installation is an Oracle installation, the modeling tools automatically supply parameters used in an Oracle database.

Let's look at the tools used for data modeling in PeopleSoft. Figures 8.3 and 8.4 illustrate data modeling defaults for SQL tables and indexes in an Oracle platform.

Navigation: Go → PeopleTools → Utilities → Use → DDL Model Defaults

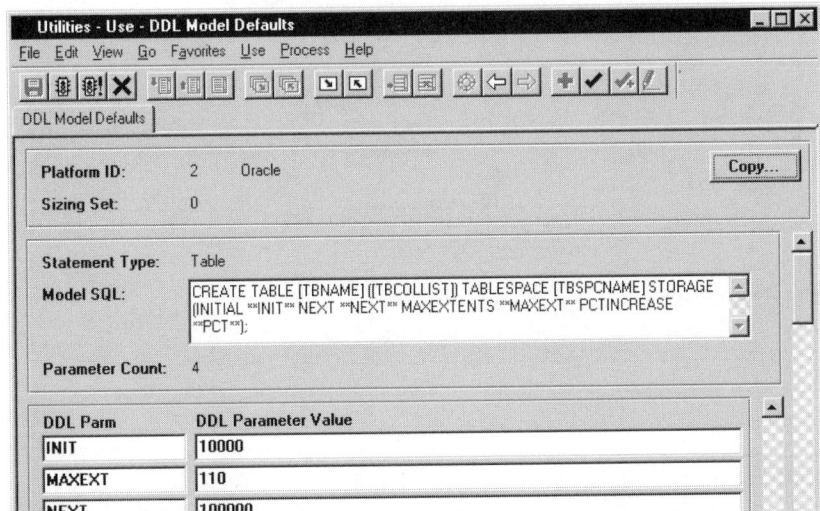

Figure 8.3   DDL model default—table

Platform ID is unique for each database platform. PeopleSoft supplies the following platforms for data modeling:

    0 - SQLBase
    1 - DB2
    2 - Oracle
    3 - Informix
    4 - DB2/Unix
    5 - Allbase
    6 - Sybase
    7 - Microsoft SQL Server
    8 - DB2/AS400

In figure 8.4 the first scroll bar contains data modeling parameters for *all* database objects. The second scroll bar contains individual parameters used for modeling *each* database object. These parameters come predefined, and the DDL parameter value can be changed for each parameter.

Navigation: Go → PeopleTools → Utilities → Use → DDL Model Defaults

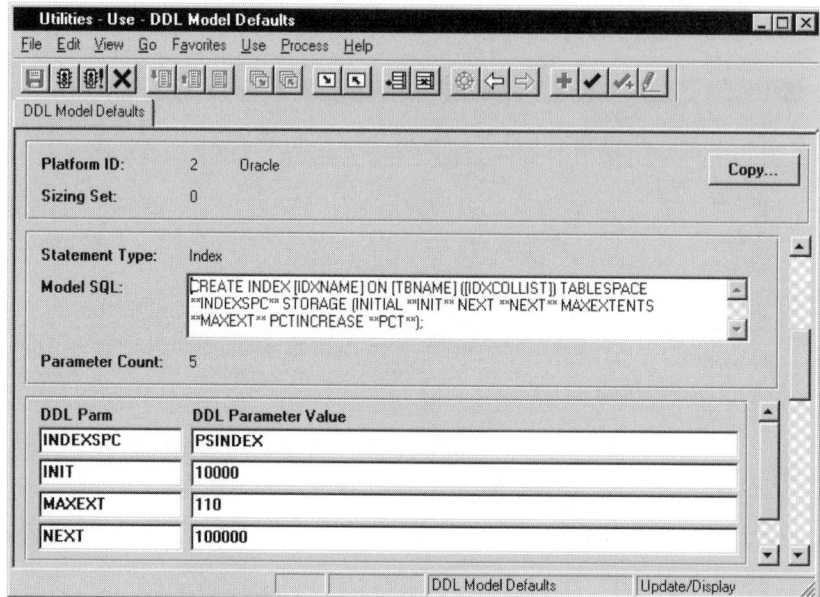

Figure 8.4   DDL model default—index

Data modeling parameters can be overridden for each record definition using the Data Administration option in Application Designer. The database administrator has to estimate data storage parameters for individual application tables and indexes and, if default parameters are not suitable, override them.

8.3   BUILDING DATABASE TABLES AND VIEWS

Record definitions defined as SQL tables or views can be built in the database using the Application Designer. A record definition must be built in the PeopleSoft system first before it can be built as a database object.

Record definitions are defined as SQL tables or views through the Use tab in the Record Properties screen, and attributes defined before an SQL table or view can be built in the database. Let's use the MY_PROBLEM_TRKG record from our Problem Tracking application to understand this progression (figure 8.5).

Navigation: File → Open → Record → MY_PROBLEM_TRKG → File → Object Properties

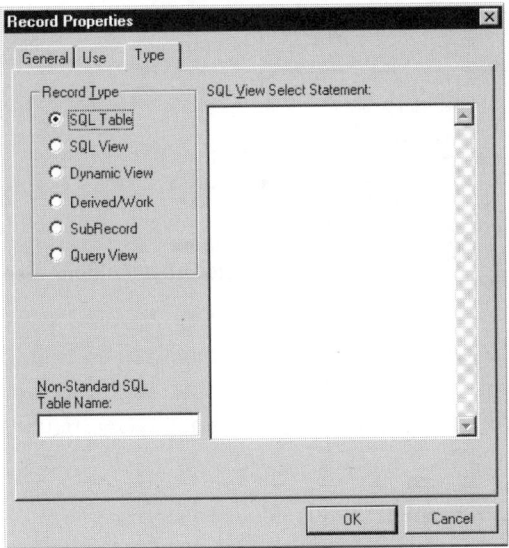

Figure 8.5
Record Properties—Use tab

First we list the steps required to build a PeopleSoft record definition in the database:

- define the record definition type
- define the database keys
- define DDL parameters for the table
- define DDL parameters for indexes
- build the object in the database

8.3.1   Define the record definition type

As we can see in figure 8.5, the Record definition must be defined as an SQL table or an SQL view. We do this through the Use tab in the Record Properties screen. When the record definition is defined as an SQL view, the record definition can be built in the database at any time without any fear of losing data because SQL views are just representations of data from SQL tables. They do not store actual data in the database.

8.3.2   Define the database keys

Our next step is to define the database keys for the SQL table or view. We do this using the Application Designer tool. Remember, the record definition must be open to perform this step (figure 8.6).

When the record definition is first built using fields from the PeopleSoft system, the developer should have an idea of the fields that will be used to build the database index. Database keys perform best when they are placed one after another. For this

Navigation: File → Open → Record → MY_PROBLEM_TRKG

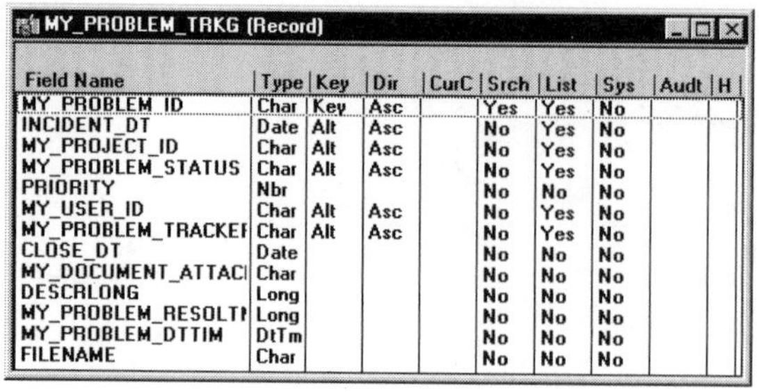

Figure 8.6
Record definition—Use display

reason, we place the database keys in sequence in the record definition. By highlighting each field and choosing Edit/Record field Properties from the Application Designer menu, we can define a record field as the database key (figure 8.7).

Navigation: Highlight Record Field → Edit → Record Field Properties

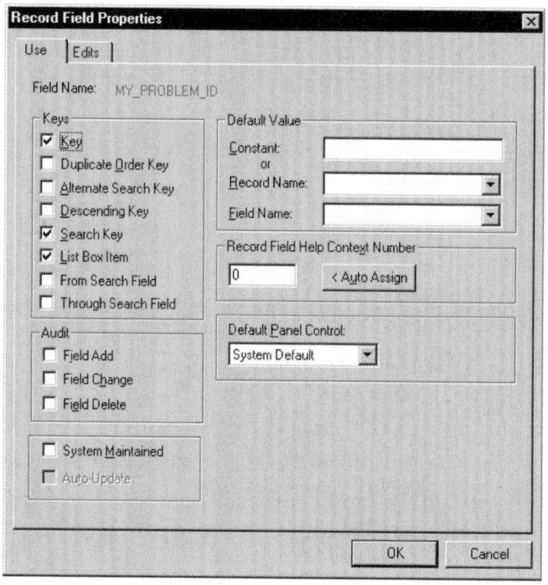

Figure 8.7
Record Field Properties

Record fields can be defined as database keys by clicking on the Key checkbox. The other options are Duplicate Order Key for non-unique indexes, Alternate Search Key, and Descending Key. Alternate Search Keys are also used to create non-unique indexes in the database. They appear in the online application in list boxes as well. Descending Keys are simply database keys presented in a descending order. They can be part of either a unique or a non-unique index. All the record fields, which are

CHAPTER 8 BUILDING DATABASE OBJECTS

database keys can be defined as such by highlighting the appropriate field and choosing "Edit → Record Field Properties" from the Application Designer menu.

8.3.3 Define DDL parameters for the table

Data Definition Language (DDL) defines the parameters needed to create the object in the database. Parameters such as storage parameters, data increments, and table space parameters are defined in this step. DDL parameters vary according to database platforms. We will use Oracle as the database platform for our purposes. Figure 8.8 illustrates the Maintain Record DDL screen where DDL parameters are entered.

Navigation: Tools → Data Administration → Record DDL (Record Definition is open)

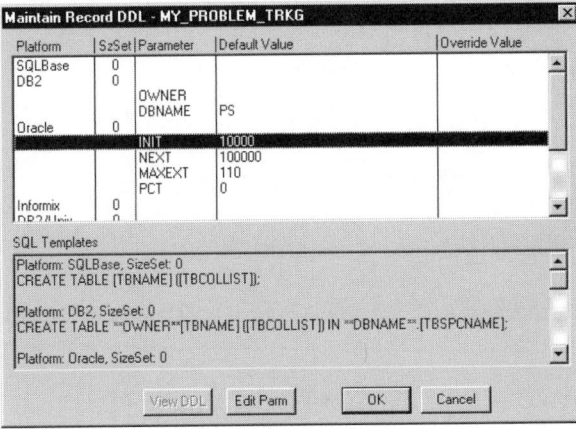

Figure 8.8
Record DDL Parameters

Navigation: Double Click on a DDL Parameter (From Maintain Record DDL screen

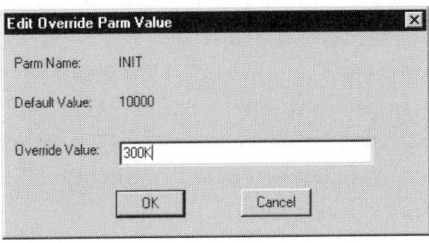

Figure 8.9   Override DDL parameter

Oracle database requires parameters such as `Initial Extent`, `Next Extent`, `Maximum Extents` and `Percentage of Increase`. They can be defined by double-clicking on each of those parameters under the Oracle section (figure 8.8). The default values seen in figure 8.8 are defined in the DDL Model Defaults panel under the Utilities menu. The defaults are not, however, always suitable for all tables in the database. We can enter an override to these parameters before the object is created in the database.

All DDL parameters can be overridden by entering the override value, choosing the OK button, and saving the record definition (figure 8.9). DDL parameters are saved in the PSRECDDLPARM PeopleTools catalog table. As we said, DDL parameters vary across database platforms, so only parameters applicable to your database should be changed before the object is created.

8.3.4 Define DDL parameters for indexes

Index DDL parameters can be changed as illustrated in figure 8.10.

Navigation: Tools → Data Administration → Indexes (Record Definition is open)

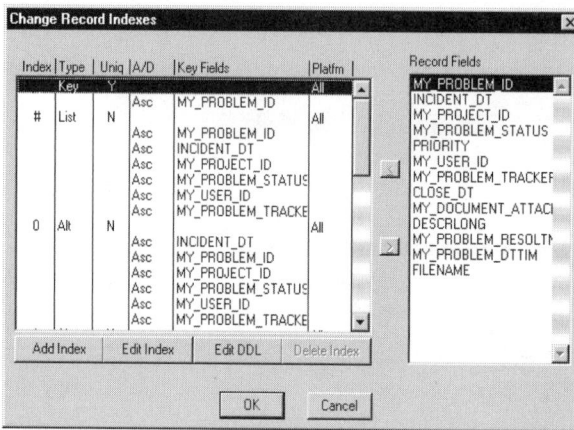

Figure 8.10
Change index DDL parameters

Based on the key defined for the record definition, PeopleTools determines the number of database indexes that must be created in the database. Primary indexes are given the same name as the table name. Other indexes are named with a numerical sequence added. In our example, the primary index for MY_PROBLEM_TRKG table is named PS_MY_PROBLEM_TRKG. The other indexes are named PS0MY_PROBLEM_TRKG, PS1MY_PROBLEM_TRKG, and so on.

By choosing the Edit DDL button, we can override DDL parameters for each of these indexes. Before the Edit DDL button is pushed, each index is highlighted. Index DDL parameters also vary across database platforms (figure 8.11). The Edit Index button can be used to change the index uniqueness. The index can also be turned off on some database platforms using the Edit Index button.

Navigation: Edit DDL (From Change Record Indexes screen)

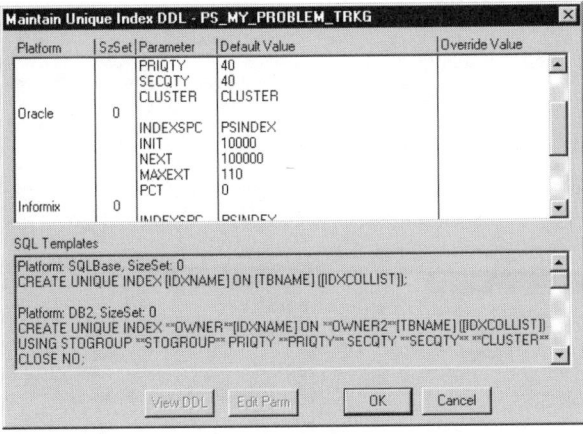

Figure 8.11
Index DDL parameters

Navigation: View DDL (From Index DDLParameters Screen)

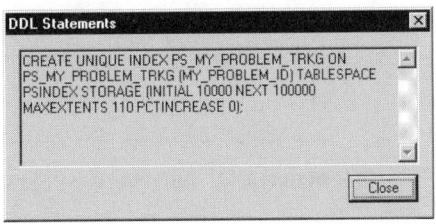

Figure 8.12   View DDL

The parameters in figure 8.11 are the same as the DDL parameters for tables—with one exception. The table spaces for indexes are overridden here. Each of these parameters can be overridden either by double-clicking on the parameter or highlighting the parameter and choosing the Edit Parm button. We can use the View DDL button to look at the actual DDL statement that will be used to create the index in the database (figure 8.12).

8.3.5   Build the object in the database

Once we specify the record definition as an SQL table or view, we must build the record in the database. Since we have defined the database keys and DDL parameters, it's time to build the record in the database. Before we can do so, we still have to define the table space parameter for an SQL table. This parameter is not required in all database platforms.

The table space parameter can be changed as illustrated in figure 8.13.

All tables built under the table space chosen are displayed in the list. Before we build the object in the database, we must save the record definition by clicking on the Save icon from the Application Designer menu.

We build the current open object by choosing Build → Current Object from the Application Designer menu. Two options appear on the Build Object screen. They are Build Options and Build Execute Options. Build Options is used to control the types of database objects built; Build Execute Options controls how the database objects are built.

Now let's consider the options—and the reasons we'd choose them—under Build and Build ExecuteOptions (figure 8.14).

Navigation: Tools → Data Administration
               → Set Table Space
               (Record Definition is open)

Navigation: Build → Current Object
                    (Record Definition is open)

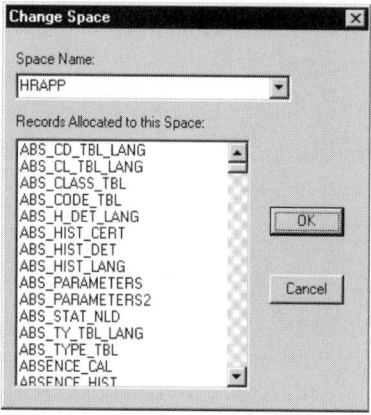

Figure 8.13   Set table space

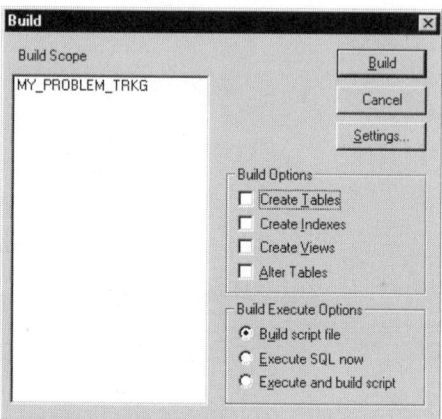

Figure 8.14   Build objects

Build options

- *Create Tables*   Choose this option to build all records defined as SQL tables in the Build Scope list.
- *Create Indexes*   Choose this option to build all indexes for SQL tables in the Build Scope list.
- *Create Views*   Choose this option to build all records defined as SQL views in the Build Scope list.
- *Alter Tables*   Choose this option to alter schema for records defined as SQL tables in the Build Scope list.

TIP   When the Alter Tables option is chosen, only those SQL tables that require an alter in the Build Scope list will be altered. Tables which require alteration are determined by comparing the record and database definitions for the tables.

Build Execute options

- *Build Script File*   Choose this option to build a script file before executing the SQL script to create or alter the database object.
- *Execute SQL Now*   Choose this option to execute DDL SQL statements and create or alter the database object immediately. This option may not be available for SQL Alters in some database platforms.
- *Execute and Build Script*   Choose this option if you want to execute and build the DDL SQL statements at the same time.

TIP   It is prudent to always build a script file before execution. The script files can be used for review before execution. The script files can also be used as change documents.

Figure 8.14 shows the Settings button used to control recreate options, script creation options, and logging options. Figures 8.15 through 8.18 illustrate all four tabs in the Build Settings screen.

Under the Create tab, (figure 8.15) we either choose to recreate the object if it already exists or skip re-creation. This option is applicable to objects already present in the database. Use Table Creation Options for SQL tables and View Creation Options for SQL views.

Navigation: Settings (From the Build Object screen)

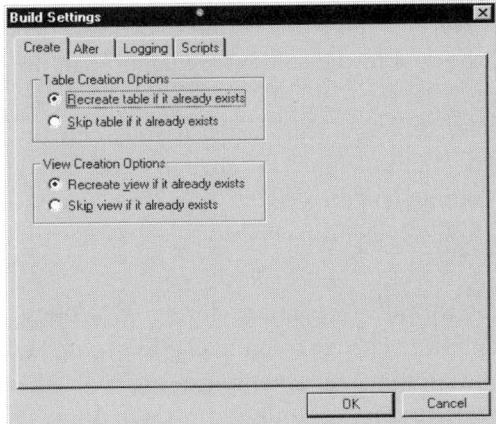

Figure 8.15
Build Settings—Create tab

Under the Alter tab (figure 8.16), we enter settings specific to altering SQL tables.

Navigation: Settings (From the Build Object screen)

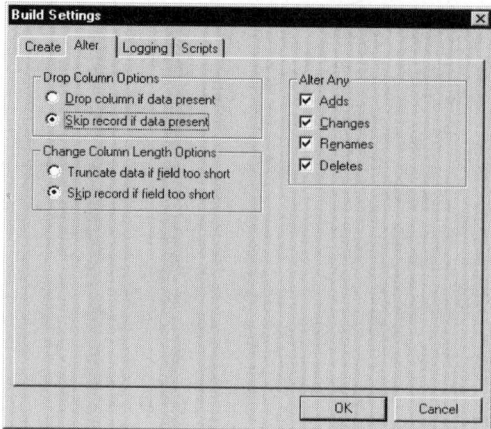

Figure 8.16
Build Settings—Alter Tab

Drop Column Options

- *Drop column if data present*   Choose this option if you want to delete a column as part of SQL Alter, even if the column contains data in it.
- *Skip record if data present*   Choose this option if you want to skip altering a table when data are present in a column and the column is being dropped.

Change Column Length Options

- *Truncate data if field too short*   Choose this option to truncate data when a field length is changed, and, the data in the column are larger than the new column length.
- *Skip record if field too short*   Choose this option if you want to skip the SQL Alter for the record when column lengths are changed, and data in the column are larger than the new column length.

Alter Any

- *Adds*   Choose this option to add new columns during SQL Alters.
- *Changes*   Choose this option to change column lengths during SQL Alters.
- *Renames*   Choose this option to rename columns during SQL Alters.
- *Deletes*   Choose this option to drop columns during SQL Alters.

During SQL Alter, the Build Settings specific to the Alter process is verified to determine whether to proceed to alter a record or to skip the record.

NOTE   Alter Any settings vary across database platforms. Some database platforms do not allow changing of column lengths without re-creation of tables.

Under the Logging tab, we specify options for logging the results from the Build process (figure 8.17).

Navigation: Settings (From the Build Object screen)

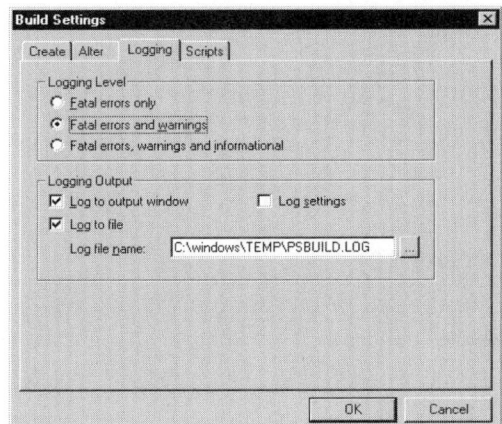

Figure 8.17
Build Settings—Logging tab

Logging level

- *Fatal Errors Only*   Choose this option when you want only the fatal errors to be logged during the process.
- *Fatal Errors and Warnings*   Choose this option when you want both fatal errors and warnings to be logged during the Build process.
- *Fatal errors, warnings, and informational*   Choose this option to log all results during the Build process.

Logging output

- *Logging to Output Window*   Choose this option if you want the log to be displayed on an output window.
- *Log to File*   Choose this option to log files to a text file. You can specify the full path and the file name for the log file in the Log file name box.
- *Log settings*   Choose this option to log all settings at the time the Build process was executed.

Under the Scripts tab (figure 8.18), we specify options to build a script file.

Navigation: Settings (From the Build Object screen)

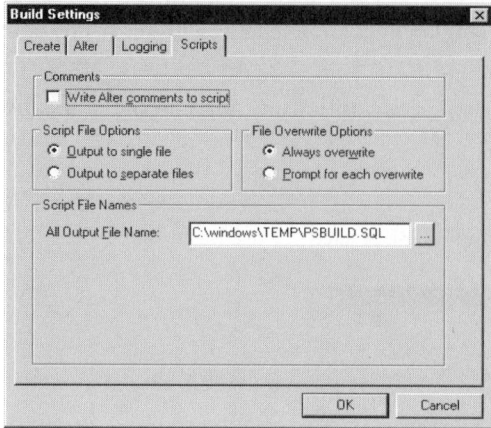

Figure 8.18
Build Settings—Scripts tab

Write Alter comments to script

Choose this checkbox to see Alter comments in the script file. During the Build process, information is written about changes to individual fields right above the actual Alter SQL statement. This checkbox is useful especially when we need to alter a number of columns in the same SQL table.

Script File Options

- *Output to single file*   Choose this option if you want to build a single script file for SQL Table Creates, SQL Table Alters, SQL View Creates, and Index Creates.
- *Output to separate files*   Choose this option if you want to create separate files for SQL Table Creates, SQL Table Alters, SQL View Creates, and Index Creates. When this option is chosen, four boxes appear under the Script File Names option to accommodate separate filenames.

File Overwrite Options

- *Always overwrite*   Choose this option if you want to overwrite existing Build scripts with the same name.
- *Prompt for each overwrite*   Choose this option if you want to be prompted during the build process, before scripts are overwritten.

TIP   Because SQL views do not store actual data, they can be re-created whenever necessary.

NOTE   PeopleSoft performs SQL Alters by re-creation in some database platforms. During this process, PeopleSoft creates a table called PS_1 used to temporarily hold data from the SQL table being altered. The SQL Alter process may fail if the table being altered consumes considerable storage space. Review the `Build` script to ensure that the SQL table PS_1 can hold data from the SQL table being altered.

TIP   Record DDL parameters have to be constantly evaluated and updated as data grow in the database. It is prudent to keep record DDL parameters in PeopleSoft in sync with the storage parameters for the corresponding SQL tables in the database.

KEY POINTS

1 Records defined as SQL tables or SQL views are also database objects and have to be created in the database.

2 Table and Index DDL parameters have to be set before the object can be built in the database.

3 When altering tables, we recommend that you build a script file. The script file has to be reviewed before execution in the database.

4 SQL views can be re-created at any time.

5 DDL Model defaults are used as default DDL parameters to build objects in the database.

CHAPTER 9

PeopleSoft Application Processor

In the previous chapters, we described concepts behind the development of a PeopleSoft application panel. We also explained how security is provided to users to access application panels. This chapter primarily focuses on how PeopleTools processes an application panel.

Application Processor organizes the numerous individual processes that occur from the time a panel group is requested to the time the panel group is saved. It is important to understand these individual processes and the sequence in which the Application Processor organizes them. This knowledge helps us design and develop objects more intuitively to suit business needs.

In each stage of the Application Processor (figure 9.1) a number of PeopleCode events are executed. In this chapter, we will walk through the Application Processor stages using the Track Problems menu item from our Problem Tracking application as an example. As we do, the sections will switch back and forth between Add and Update/Display modes. The reader will need to correlate screens in the correct order to follow an entire mode from start to finish. (Part 3 describes in detail the individual PeopleCode events as well as more about sequences in which these events are executed.)

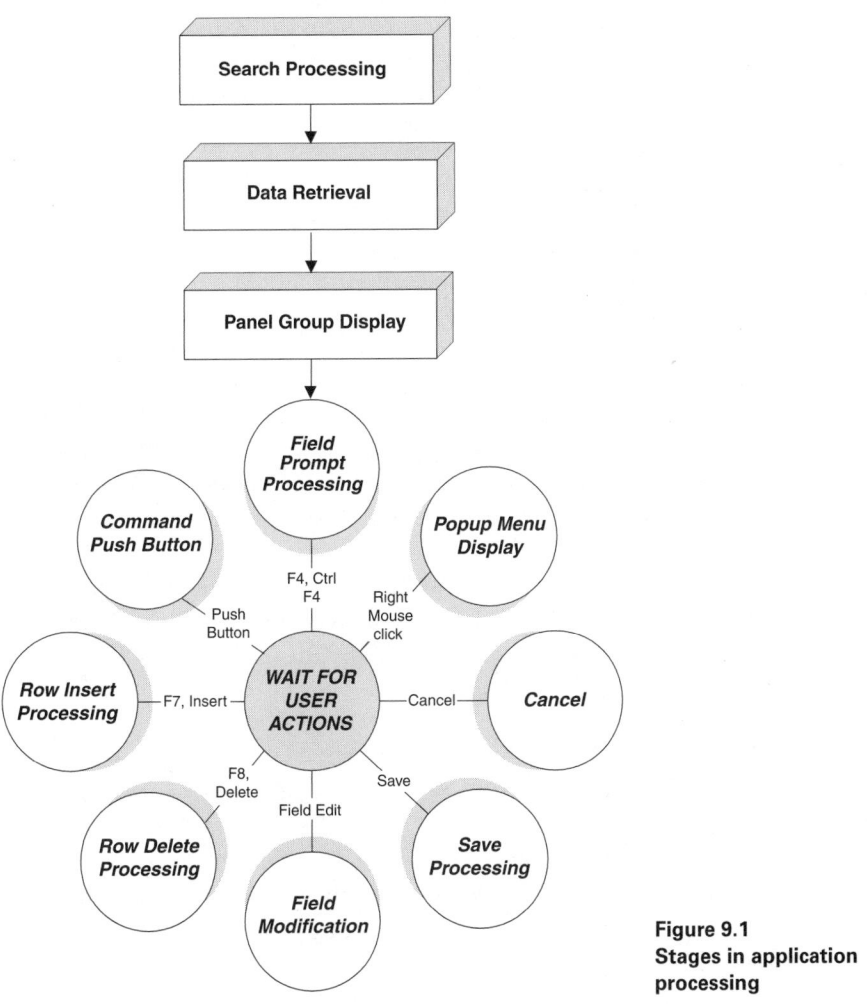

Figure 9.1
Stages in application processing

NOTE   The key to application processing is the panel group object. The panel group definition provides vital information throughout all stages to process the application panel.

9.1 SEARCH PROCESSING

Search Processing takes place when the user chooses the menu item that accesses the application panel group. This stage begins by building the search dialog box used to access the panel group and ends after fields for data retrieval are populated and saved into the search fields. The Search Processing stage can be further divided into multiple steps. Let's walk through all possible steps that can occur during this stage.

- determine mode of access
- retrieve panel group definition
- determine search fields
- populate and display search record fields
- edit user inputs into search dialog fields
- populate search buffer for data retrieval

9.1.1 Determine mode of access

The Application Processor determines the mode in which the user accesses the panel group. All authorized modes necessary to access the panel group are pre-determined when the application menu is brought up. Users can view only authorized panel group actions when they access the application menu. The Application Processor determines authorized panel group actions from a PeopleTools catalog table called PSAUTHITEM. Let's look at our example and find out what the authorized actions are for the menu item.

In figure 9.2, this user has two different actions/modes authorized for this menu item. The panel group definition screen will show all the authorized actions for the menu item. Based on the action chosen by the user, the Application Processor determines the record used for search processing.

9.1.2 Retrieve panel group definition

Search records are attached to panel group definitions. Therefore, the Application Processor has to retrieve the panel group definition to determine the search record. PSPNLGRPDEFN is the PeopleTools catalog table which contains the search records for a panel group. We can define two different search records for a panel group: a search record used in Add mode and a search record for all other modes. Figure 9.3 shows the panel group properties screen. Here we can see how search records and authorized actions are attached to panel groups.

The Panel Group Properties screen contains the two search records and the authorized actions available for the panel group. When Add search record is left blank, the regular search record is used for all authorized actions. Add and Update/Display are the two authorized actions available for this panel group. A panel group, however, can have more authorized actions than a user can see when the actual application menu item is accessed. Security to the menu item and corresponding actions are provided using the Security Administrator screen. In the example, we access this

Navigation: Go → Problem Tracking → Tracking → Track Problems

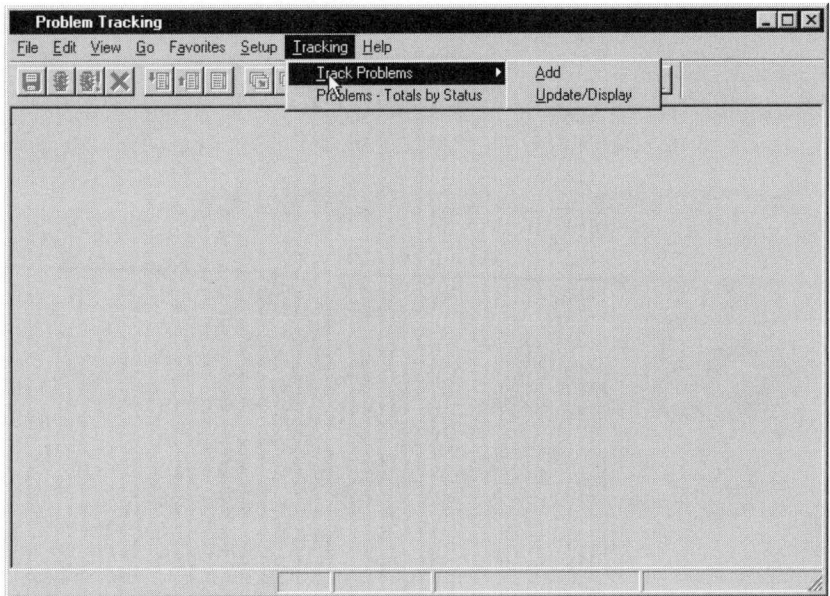

Figure 9.2   Authorized action for a panel group

Navigation: File → Object Properties (MY_PROBLEM_TRKG panel group is opened first)

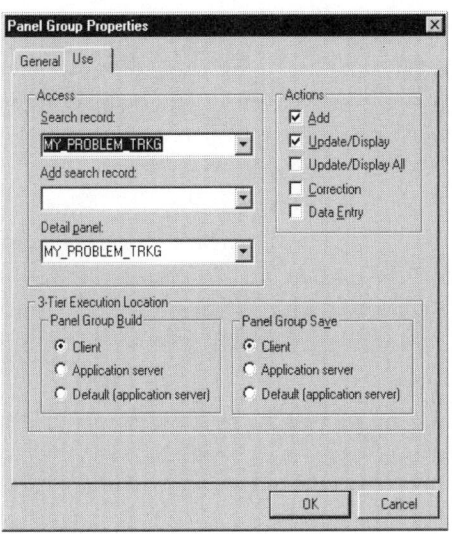

Figure 9.3
Panel Group Properties—Use tab

menu item using the PS operator that belongs to the ALLPANLS operator class. Figure 9.4 shows the Security Administrator screen where security is provided to ALLPANLS to access this menu item.

Navigation: File → Open → ALLPANLS (From Security Administrator screen)
Double-click on PROBLEM_TRACKING line item under the Menu Items tab

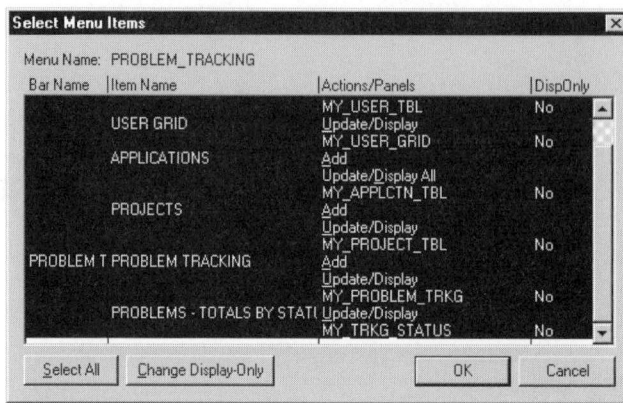

Figure 9.4
Authorized menu items
and actions

All authorized menu items are highlighted in figure 9.4. In our example, we can either choose Add or Update/Display actions. Next, we will see how the Application Processor reacts when either action is selected.

9.1.3   Determine search fields

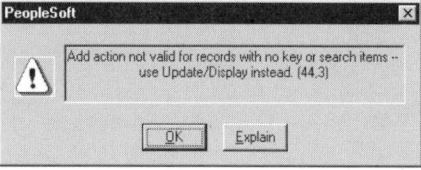

Figure 9.5   Search records with no search keys

The Application Processor determines the search fields that should appear on the input dialog box. Fields defined as search keys in the search record are assembled on the input dialog box. Fields defined as alternate search keys in the search record are also assembled on the input dialog box in all modes except Add mode. When no search keys are defined, the Application Processor proceeds directly to the data retrieval stage after verifying that the user is accessing the application panel in Add mode. When a mode other than Add is selected, the error message in figure 9.5 is issued.

In PeopleSoft HRMS, the INSTALLATION record can be used as the search record to access the panel group directly, without an input dialog box. As we saw in the previous error message, we cannot use Add mode to access panel groups which contain search records with no search keys.

TIP	Search records that do not have search keys can be processed using `Update/Display` mode only. This is useful when you want to bring up an application panel without an input dialog box.

Before we continue with our application panel example, let's look at the definition for MY_PROBLEM_TRKG record.

Navigation: File → Open → Record → MY_PROBLEM_TRKG → View → Use Display

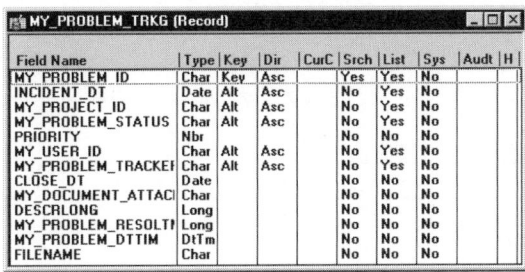

Figure 9.6
Search key definition for a search record

Navigation: Go → Problem Tracking → Tracking → Track Problems → Add

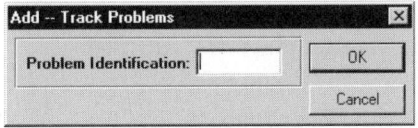

Figure 9.7 Search fields in Add mode

In our record definition, we have one field defined as the search key and five fields defined as alternate search keys. The panel processor fetches the search record definition in order to determine the search keys that will be presented on the input dialog box. In figure 9.7, we can see which fields are brought up on an input dialog box when the menu item is accessed in `Add` mode.

In `Add` mode, all fields defined as search keys are presented to the user in the input dialog box. MY_PROBLEM_ID is the only field defined as a search key. Now let us access the menu item using `Update/Display` mode (figure 9.8).

In addition to search fields, alternate search fields are also presented on the input dialog box in `Update/Display` mode. We notice another difference in the input dialog box between `Add` and `Update/Display` modes: a list box is provided to display search results, once search field values are saved.

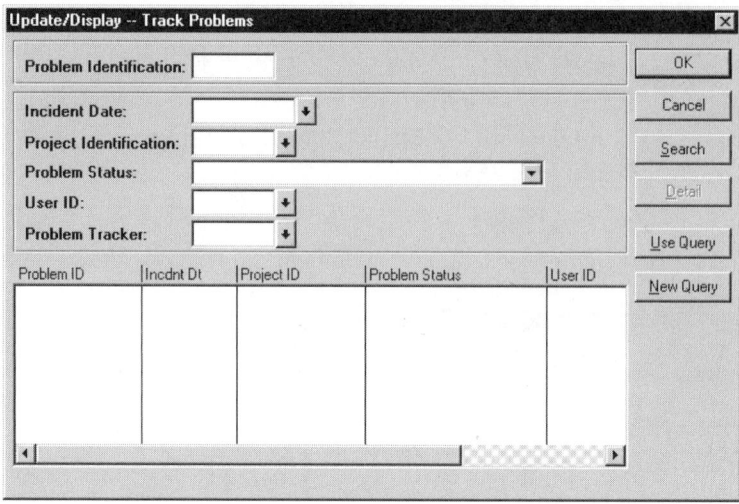

Figure 9.8   Search fields using Update/Display

9.1.4   Populate and display search fields

Before the Application Processor brings up the search/input dialog box, it executes certain PeopleCode events, which populate default values into the search fields. Any default values that are attached to fields in search records are used.

In Add mode FieldDefault, RowInit, and SearchInit PeopleCode events are executed (in that order) for search and alternate search fields. In other modes, SearchInit PeopleCode events are executed, and values are populated into search fields. We can attach PeopleCode to these events on the search record to see how they populate search fields before displaying them.

Figure 9.9 illustrates how PeopleCode is added to the FieldDefault event for MY_PROBLEM_ID field.

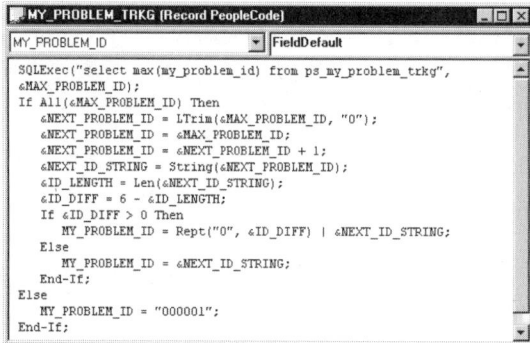

Figure 9.9
FieldDefault PeopleCode event on a search field

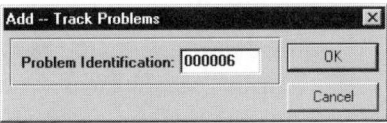

Figure 9.10 FieldDefault PeopleCode event in Add mode

This PeopleCode increments the MY_ PROBLEM_ID field automatically. We only want to increment MY_PROBLEM_ID field in Add mode. FieldDefault is executed on a search record only in the Add mode. We do not want to default anything to MY_PROBLEM_ID in other modes. We use the Update/Display mode to update problem IDs which have been already created using the application. Let us see how the Application Processor executes this PeopleCode event and displays it on the input dialog box (figure 9.10).

We see that FieldDefault was executed and the next problem ID is now displayed on the input dialog box. FieldDefault is an iterative event that is constantly processed. FieldDefault PeopleCode event executes any time the field is blank. RowInit PeopleCode event executes any time the field is displayed either on the input dialog box or on the panel.

9.1.5   Edit search fields

The next step in search processing occurs when the user enters or overrides values in the search fields. The Application Processor performs internal field format-checking upon data entry into search fields. For example, when the user enters characters into fields defined as numeric, the Application Processor issues a message to the user. When search fields are defined as required fields on the search record, the user must enter values into such fields before saving the input. The following types of edits take place when data are entered into search fields:

- field format edits
- required field edits
- field modification PeopleCode edits (Field Edit)
- search/save PeopleCode edits (Save Edit, Search Save)

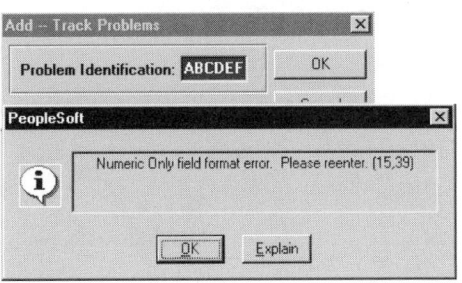

Figure 9.11   Field format edits

We will illustrate a few types of PeopleCode edits in this section. We'll also show you all the non-PeopleCode edits that the Application Processor validates.

Figure 9.11 illustrates how field formats are verified by the Application Processor. Similarly, other format types like date, time, name, and so on, are edited.

In figure 9.12, the Application Processor issues a message when a required field is blanked out. All search key fields presented on the input dialog box are usually defined as required fields. This is especially useful when the search field appears on the panel as a display field. However, when the field is displayed as an input field or when

Figure 9.12 Required field edit

a PeopleCode event populates the field, a required field edit is not necessary.

Again, certain PeopleCode events are executed in this step.

In `Add`, when the user enters values into the search fields, `FieldEdit` and `FieldChange` PeopleCode events from search fields are executed. When the user saves the input by clicking on the OK button, `SaveEdit` and `SearchSave` PeopleCode events are executed from search fields.

TIP   Search fields that are not input fields on the panel can be defined as Required fields. This prevents the user from saving the panel with empty keys in `Add` mode.

In `Update/Display`, when the user enters values into search fields, no PeopleCode events are executed. However, when the user saves the input, `Search-Save` PeopleCode event is executed. In `Update/Display` mode, events are processed for both search fields and alternate search fields.

Suppose we want to issue a warning message when the user tries to override the problem ID assigned by the system. How can we do this? We can add a `SearchSave` PeopleCode to one of the search fields. In this case, the only search field in our search record is the MY_PROBLEM_ID field. Let us take a look at the PeopleCode we can write to perform this function (figure 9.13).

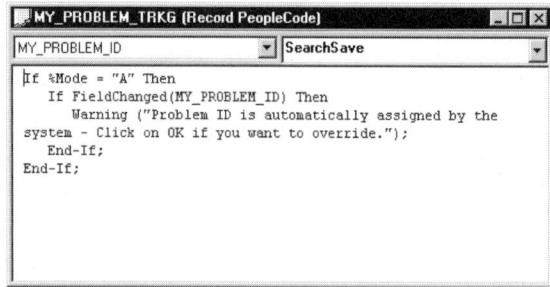

**Figure 9.13
SearchSave PeopleCode**

Because `SearchSave` PeopleCode event is executed in all modes, we use the `%Mode` system variable to execute this PeopleCode event in `Add` mode only. This PeopleCode event will issue a warning message when the user tries to change the problem ID assigned by the `FieldDefault` PeopleCode event.

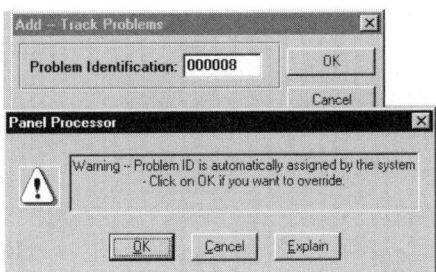

Figure 9.14 SearchSave PeopleCode event in Add mode

In figure 9.14, a warning message is provided with options to continue or to cancel. When the user chooses the OK button, the Application Processor proceeds to the next step for data retrieval. When the user chooses the Cancel button, the Application Processor brings the user back to the input dialog box for re-entry.

In chapter 13, "PeopleCode and the Application Processor," PeopleCode events in search processing are discussed in detail.

9.2   DATA RETRIEVAL

Data retrieval starts when the user populates the search dialog box and clicks OK. At this point, all edits, default processing, and search save processing has taken place, and the Application Processor uses the search keys to retrieve data.

What happens when the Search record does not have any search keys defined? In that case, all rows from the database are retrieved for panel group display. An example of this is the INSTALLATION table panel group in all PeopleSoft applications. The INSTALLATION table only has one row in it with no database keys defined.

The Application Processor performs the following operations during the data retrieval stage:

- verifies mode with data from search record
- prepares fields for the list box based on search keys
- prepares a list of panels that builds the panel group
- prepares a list of tables and views necessary to display the panel group in Update/Display, Update/Display All, and Correction modes
- retrieves data from the database for the complete list of tables and views

9.2.1   Verify mode with data from search record

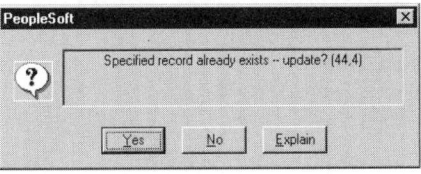

Figure 9.15   Validate mode with data in the database

The Application Processor validates the menu action (Add, Update/Display, and so on) that the user chooses with data from the search record. If the user chooses Add mode and the search record already has data matching the search fields, the Application Processor issues a message to that effect. If we choose Add mode and then choose 000001 as the problem ID, the Application Processor checks whether the search record has data matching those keys. In this case, the search record is MY_PROBLEM_TRKG. In the database, this table has a row that matches that problem ID. The Application Processor issues a message as illustrated in figure 9.15.

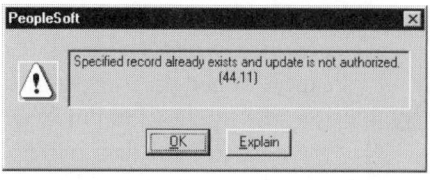

Figure 9.16 Update action not authorized

The message, however, enables the user to bring up the panel group in Update/Display mode. If the user is not authorized to choose Update/Display mode for the panel group, the Application Processor again issues an error message (figure 9.16).

In modes other than Add, the Application Processor proceeds directly to the next step to prepare list box items.

9.2.2   Prepare the list box

A list box is the result of search processing and data retrieval. All rows in the search record—in other words, the underlying database table or view—are presented on the list box. The list box is provided only when the Data Retrieval finds more than one row that matches the search fields. The Application Processor provides a list box when more than one row is found matching search fields; a partial search results in multiple rows; or no input is supplied for search.

We should be aware that when discussing search fields, we imply Primary Search Fields and Alternate Search Fields. The data retrieval stage attempts to match rows using both types. The results on the list box enable us to choose the data we want to view or update. Search fields and alternate search keys are automatically defined as list box items, but we can override this by turning off the definition for the list box. Any field from the search record except for Long Edit Boxes can be defined as a list box item.

In figure 9.17, all fields marked as list box items appear on the list box.

NOTE   Search records can either be SQL tables or views. When search records are SQL views, the Application Processor accesses data from tables that were used to build the views.

Navigation: File → Open → Record → MY_PROBLEM_TRKG

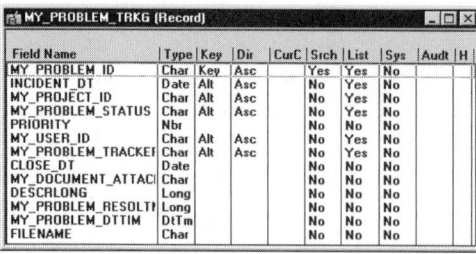

Figure 9.17
Definition of search record

Figure 9.18 illustrates a list box with all rows in the database table. We did not provide any input on the search dialog box. All rows from MY_PROBLM_TRKG table are displayed in the list box, a useful feature when the user is not sure what to enter for input.

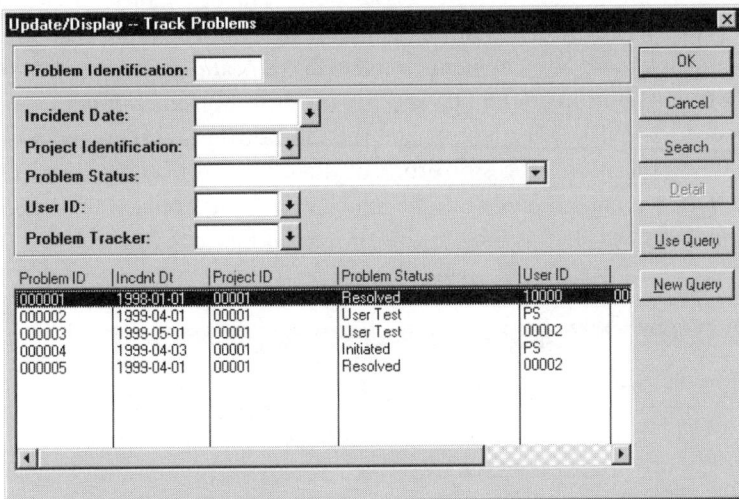

**Figure 9.18
List box display
with no input**

Now, let's provide input on the input dialog box and see how the Application Processor selects rows in the list box (figure 9.19).

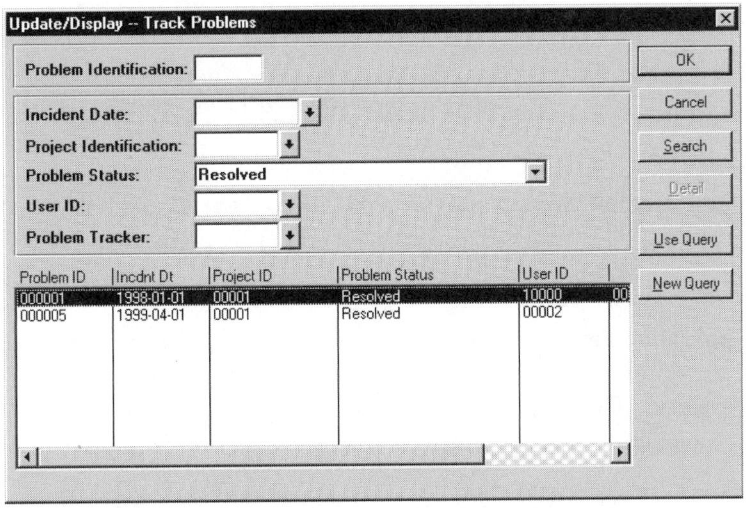

**Figure 9.19
List box display
with full key
input**

The example lists resolved incidents. Notice how the Application Processor uses the Problem Status field as input and displays all rows which match the status. We can also provide partial input in a search field. The Application Processor matches partial input and displays rows which match the partial input.

To perform this task, the Application Processor reads the record definition, and it retrieves information from PeopleSoft catalog tables, PSRECDEFN and PSRECFIELD. These catalog tables contain details on search fields and list box fields. The user can choose any line item from the list box and then view data on the panel.

Two push buttons—the OK and Search push buttons—trigger the Application Processor to populate a list box. When the OK button is chosen and a unique match exists, the Application Processor proceeds directly to displaying the panel. When the Search button is chosen and a unique match exists, the Application Processor displays the list box instead. Let us look at this process in figure 9.20.

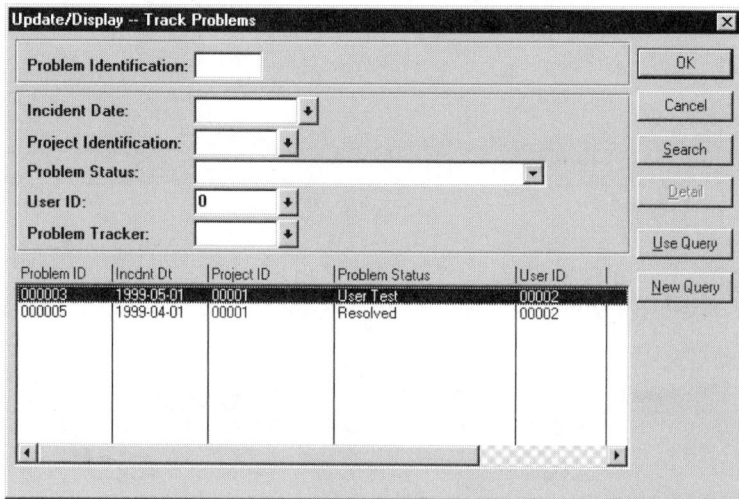

Figure 9.20
List box display with partial key input

In the example, we just provide a "0" in the User ID field, and the Application Processor finds all the rows that contained a User ID prefixed with a "0."

9.2.3 Prepare a list of panels

The Application Processor must still retrieve data to display on the panel. In order to do so, the Application Processor must access the panel group definition and prepare a list of panels. The Application Processor retrieves this information from a PeopleSoft catalog table called PSPNLGROUP. Remember, one or more panels may be in a panel group.

In this step, the Application Processor determines the order in which panels are displayed, the field layouts in a panel, the control display fields, the related display fields, the secondary panels, the subpanels, and so on. All these related objects are attached to the panel definition. The PeopleSoft catalog table which stores this definition is called PSPNLFIELD.

In our example, the panel group MY_PROBLEM_TRKG contains only one panel. Figure 9.21 shows the number of panels in the panel group.

Navigation: File → Open → Panel Group → MY_PROBLEM_TRKG

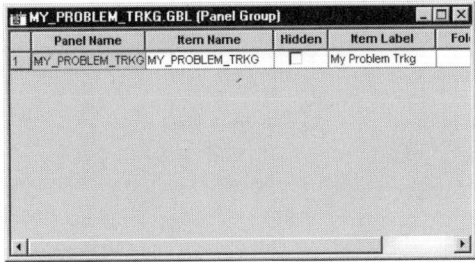

Figure 9.21
Panel group definition

After the Application Processor has prepared a list of panels and related objects, it proceeds to the next step.

9.2.4   Prepare a list of records and fields

The Application Processor starts preparing the records needed to build the panels. The records can be SQL tables, SQL views, or derived records.

In Add mode, the Application Processor retrieves less data from the database when compared to other modes. This is because, in Add mode the Application Processor invokes a new panel group. In Add mode, too, the Application Processor may need to retrieve values for related display fields, which are descriptions for search key fields.

In Update/Display, the Application Processor has to retrieve data for tables and views on the panel.

Derived records do not exist in the database. They are work records either populated by record field defaults or PeopleCode events. We can get a list of the records that MY_PROBLEM_TRKG panel contains by looking at the panel field layout. The panel field layout contains records and fields that make a panel.

In figure 9.22, we can see that MY_PROBLEM_TRKG panel displays fields from SQL tables and derived records. Some of these fields are related display fields which show descriptions for control display fields.

Navigation: File → Open → Panel → MY_PROBLEM_TRKG → Layout → Order

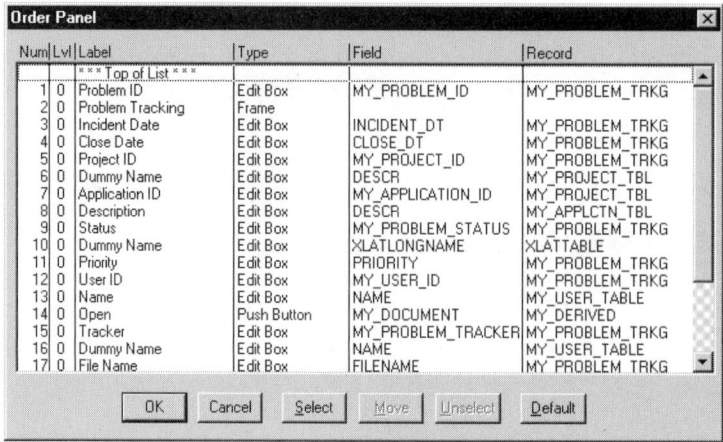

Figure 9.22
Panel field layout

9.2.5 Retrieves data from the database

In our next step, the Application Processor begins retrieving data for the list of tables and views on the panel. In Add, the Application Processor does not retrieve any data for our example. This is because the Application Processor displays a new panel and no related display descriptions are necessary on this new panel.

In Update/Display, the Application Processor retrieves data from MY_PROBLEM_TRKG table because, in modes other than Add, the Application Processor has to retrieve existing data for viewing and update from the database.

In Add, the table MY_PROBLEM_TRKG is accessed from the database.

In Update/Display, the following tables are accessed from the database:

* MY_PROBLEM_TRKG
* MY_PROJECT_TBL
* MY_APPLCTN_TBL
* XLATTABLE
* MY_USER_TABLE

The tables MY_PROJECT_TBL, MY_APPLCTN_TBL, XLATTABLE, and MY_USER_TABLE are all accessed to retrieve information for related display fields. In Add, because the control display fields do not have any values and are new, values for these related display fields are not necessary.

Let us take a look at the panel display in the Add (figure 9.23) and Update/Display (figure 9.24) modes to better understand this concept.

All panel fields are new here and do not have any values. The Problem ID field is populated because it was entered using the search dialog box.

Navigation: Go → Problem Tracking → Tracking → Track Problems → Add

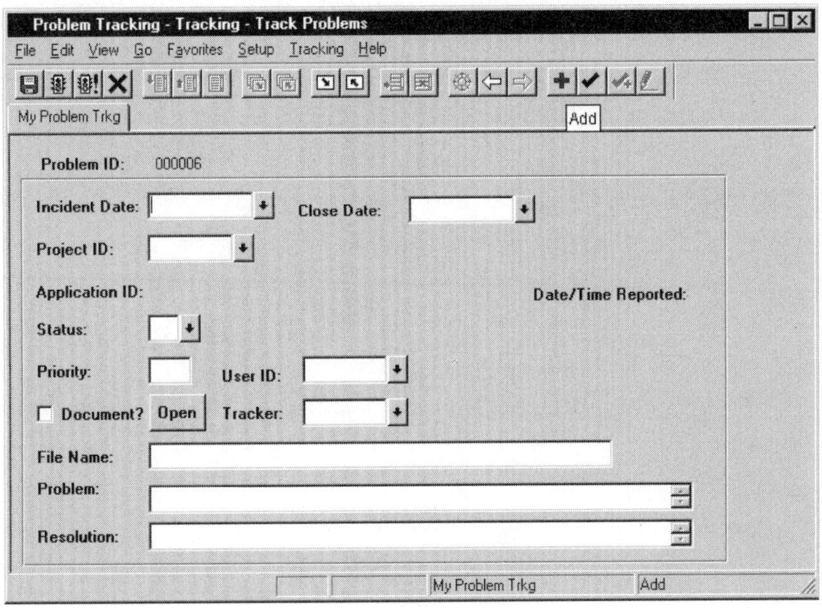

Figure 9.23 Application panel group in Add mode

In figure 9.24, notice some of the differences in the `Update/Display` mode. The data row that matches the Problem ID, `000001` is retrieved from the database. Data for all related display fields are also retrieved from the database. Project Description, Application Description, Status Description, User Name, and Tracker Name are some of the related display fields in the panel.

In `Add`, none of the related display fields have corresponding control display fields. However, if the values from search fields have corresponding related display fields, data for these fields are retrieved in `Add`.

The Application Processor uses search key values to retrieve information from MY_PROBLEM_TRKG table. So it uses MY_PROBLEM_ID field as the key field to retrieve data from this table. Information is retrieved from MY_PROJECT_TBL using MY_PROJECT_ID field from MY_PROBLEM_TRKG table. The Application Processor constructs SQL statements based on these parameters. In the database, table indexes are built using search fields defined in record definitions. The Application Processor can retrieve information from database tables and views more efficiently when key fields are available. Then, the Application Processor proceeds to the panel group display stage.

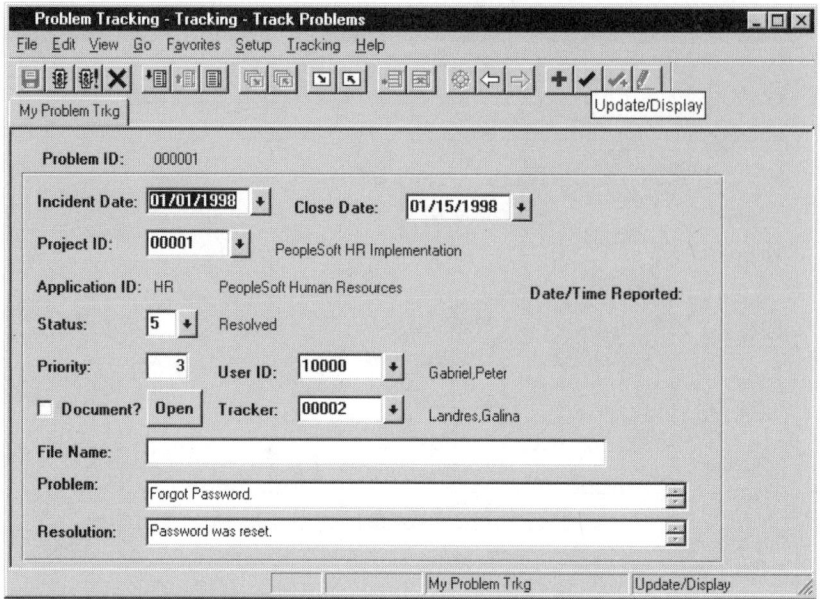

Figure 9.24   Application panel group in Update/Display mode

9.3   PANEL GROUP DISPLAY

After the Application Processor has collected data for panel group display, it performs row select and default processing on fields in the panel group. PeopleCode events are used to perform row select and default processing before the final data buffer is prepared for panel group display. The Application Processor then begins displaying panel fields by populating input fields, display fields, related display fields, and so forth. The Application Processor also has to determine the field labels and field layout before it can display the panel group. During the panel group display stage, the Application Processor performs row select and default processing (Iterative), displays panel group, and waits for user action.

9.3.1   RowSelect processing

In the Add mode, the Application Processor does not perform any row select processing. Row select processing discards rows from the buffer based on RowSelect PeopleCode event. In Add, no rows are selected or retrieved from the database.

In Update/Display, the Application Processor performs row select processing using the RowSelect PeopleCode event. After data retrieval, the Application Processor discards rows from the panel buffer. Row select processing is only performed on panels with scroll bars. During panel group display, the Application Processor discards the rows from the buffer based on PeopleCode logic and will not display any discarded rows of data on the panel. The `RowSelect` PeopleCode event can be used to discard rows from the buffer and stop loading data into the panel.

| NOTE | Row select processing is only performed on panels with scroll bars. The `RowSelect` PeopleCode event is used to discard rows from scroll bar buffers before the final panel group display. Data discarded using row select processing is not available in the buffer. |

9.3.2   Default processing (iterative)

Default processing is performed using the `FieldDefault` and `FieldFormula` PeopleCode events. All fields that are not related display fields go through default processing which occurs both in `Add` and `Update/Display` modes. Default processing is an iterative process which constantly checks for blank fields in the panel group. A PeopleCode event may blank out a field that has field level default assigned to it. In this situation, the Application Processor performs default processing for the blank field. Any time the value of a field in the panel group changes, default processing is performed for other blank fields in the panel group.

Default processing is also processed using default values defined in record field properties. First, all defaults attached to record fields are processed, then `FieldDefault` and `FieldFormula` PeopleCode events are processed.

The Application Processor performs default processing on panel fields when the panel field is blank after data retrieval, the panel field is blanked out by a PeopleCode event, or the user blanks out a panel field.

Chapter 13, "PeopleCode and the Application Processor," covers default processing PeopleCode events as well as the sequence in which they are executed in greater depth. In this section, we want to illustrate how record field level defaults are processed. First, let's look at how default values appear on the record definition screen (figure 9.25).

Navigation: File → Open → Record → MY_PROBLEM_TRKG → View → Use Display

Field Name	Type	Key	Dir	CurC	Srch	List	Sys	Audt	H	Default
MY_PROBLEM_ID	Char	Key	Asc		Yes	Yes	No			
INCIDENT_DT	Date	Alt	Asc		No	Yes	No			
MY_PROJECT_ID	Char	Alt	Asc		No	Yes	No			
MY_PROBLEM_STATUS	Char	Alt	Asc		No	Yes	No			'1'
PRIORITY	Nbr				No	No	No			
MY_USER_ID	Char	Alt	Asc		No	Yes	No			
MY_PROBLEM_TRACKE	Char	Alt	Asc		No	Yes	No			
CLOSE_DT	Date				No	No	No			
MY_DOCUMENT_ATTAC	Char				No	No	No			
DESCRLONG	Long				No	No	No			
MY_PROBLEM_RESOLTI	Long				No	No	No			
MY_PROBLEM_DTTIM	DtTm				No	No	No			
FILENAME	Char				No	No	No			

Figure 9.25
Record definition—field defaults

If MY_PROBLEM_STATUS field is blank at the time the panel group is displayed, the default value defined in that record field is used to populate the field. Record field defaults are used in all modes as long as the field is blank. Let us look at the application panel in the Add mode to see how default values are used during display (figure 9.26).

Navigation: Go → Problem Tracking → Tracking → Track Problems

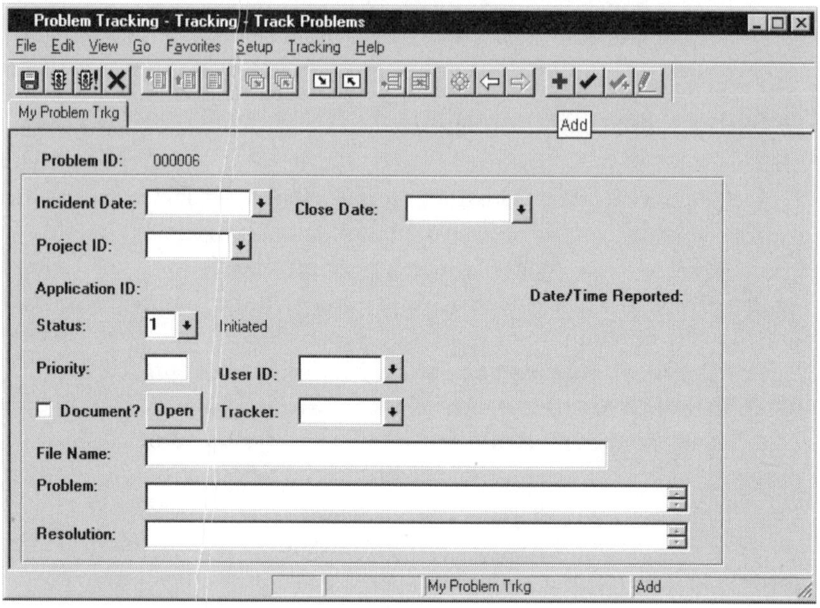

Figure 9.26 Record field default processing

Similarly, in modes other than Add, record field defaults are processed as well. Usually, however, when the application panel is processed in modes other than Add, field values from the database are retrieved and displayed. In instances where these fields are blank, record field defaults are used as display values.

9.3.3   Display panel group

During a panel group display, the Application Processor assembles fields in the order in which they are defined in the panel field layout. In this process, the Application Processor also displays field labels for panel fields. After performing all necessary items for display, the Application Processor then executes the RowInit PeopleCode event that may change the value of a panel field.

We also saw that default processing occurs when a panel field is blanked out. The RowInit PeopleCode event can potentially blank out a panel field, and the Application

Processor immediately performs default processing. Let us take a look at the panel field layout one more time to see the order in which fields are displayed (figure 9.27).

Navigation: File → Open → Panel → MY_PROBLEM_TRKG → Layout → Order

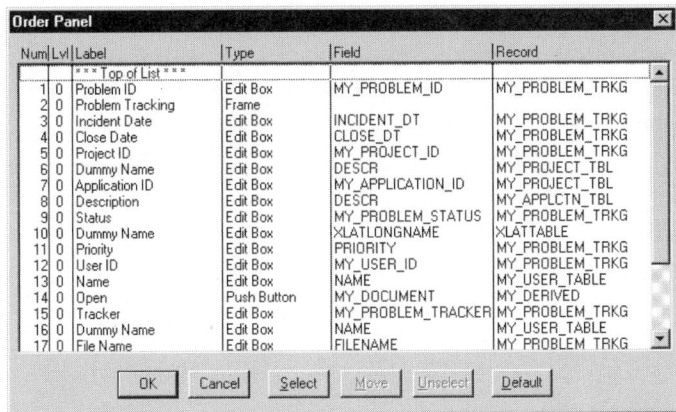

Figure 9.27
Panel field layout

Usually, search fields appear first in the order in which fields are displayed. Alternate search keys can be placed anywhere in the panel layout.

TIP   Display control fields are always placed before their corresponding related display fields. In order for the Application Processor to successfully retrieve values for related display fields, values in the corresponding display control fields must be populated first.

After all fields are displayed, `RowInit` PeopleCode events are executed. At this point, all derived fields are also populated with PeopleCode events. After data retrieval and row select processing, derived fields are populated along with all other fields in the panel. Derived fields also go through default processing and display processing PeopleCode events.

TIP   All default processing and display processing PeopleCode events from panel fields are processed during panel display. Even if a field is not present in the panel, PeopleCode events are triggered from that field. One exception to this rule is fields from derived records. PeopleCode is processed from derived fields only when they are present in the panel. For this reason, the same derived record can be shared across multiple panel sessions without interfering with each other.

In instances where multiple panels are present in a panel group, each panel is displayed in sequence within the panel group. The focus is on the panel the user chooses while accessing the panel group. The Application Processor now waits for user action.

9.4 DATA ENTRY OR INQUIRY

The Application Processor displays field values in the panel group and waits for user action. User actions can be adding, updating, or deleting data and saving them to the database. Some panel groups consist of inquiry panels that do not require any data entry. After the panel group is displayed, the user can perform the following list of actions in the data entry or inquiry stage:

- field modifications
- rowInsert
- rowDelete
- prompt processing
- command or push buttons
- pop-up menus
- save processing
- Cancel

9.4.1 Field modification

The user can modify any input field on the panel. When the user modifies the value on a panel field, the Application Processor performs field edit processing. The following processes are executed when a user modifies a panel field:

- internal PeopleTools edits
- field edit
- field change
- default processing

PeopleTools edits the value entered in the field with the field format defined for the field and it issues a message to the user. For example, when the user enters a non-numeric character into a field that can accept only numeric values, the Application Processor issues a message (figure 9.28).

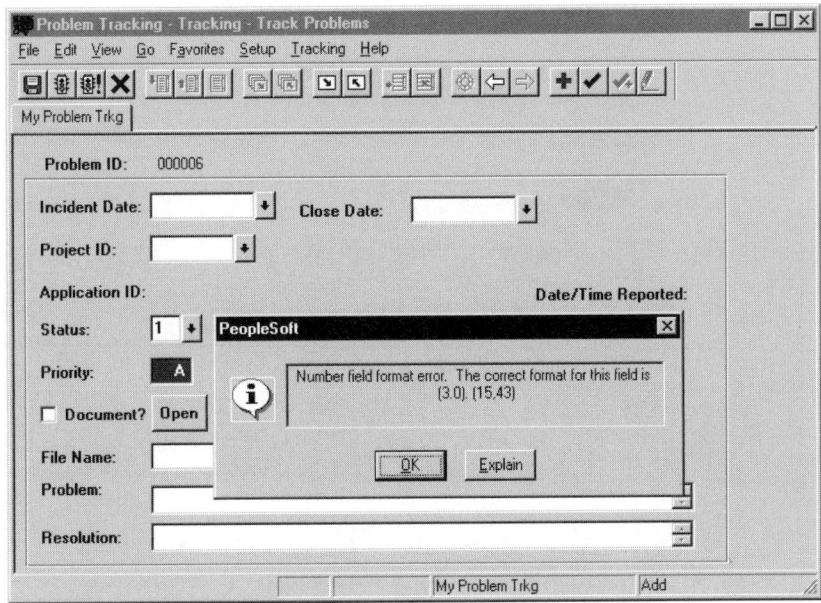

Figure 9.28   Field format edits

Similarly, the Application Processor performs other types of edits by comparing the values entered with record field attributes. Let us look at the record field attributes for the INCIDENT_DT field (figure 9.29).

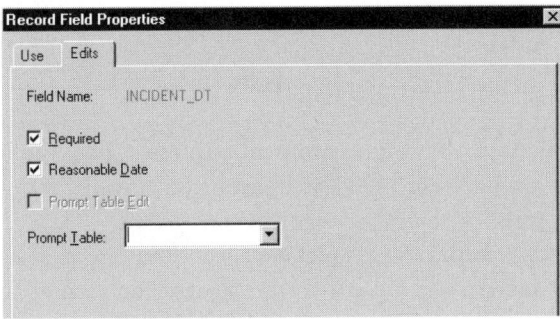

Figure 9.29
Record Field Properties

The INCIDENT_DT field is edited and defined as a required field. The Reasonable Date checkbox is enabled as well. Let us see how the Application Processor behaves when the value entered into this field fails the edit (figure 9.30).

Because we entered a past date, the Application Processor issues a warning message indicating that the date is out of range. The Application Processor issues this

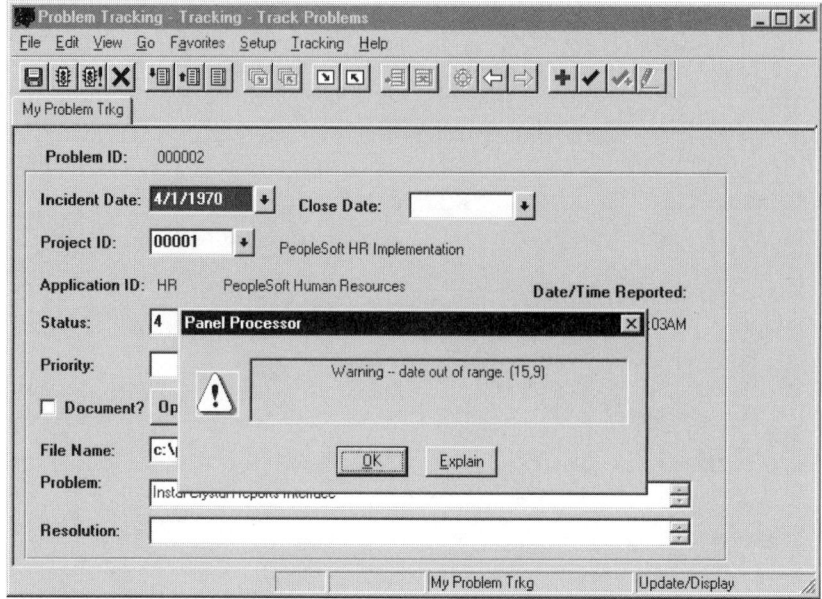

Figure 9.30 Reasonable Date checkbox

message when the date is over thirty days in the past or future and the reasonable date check is enabled. The following types of PeopleTools edits are available in PeopleSoft:

- Field Format
- Required Field
- Reasonable Date
- Prompt Table Edits
- Yes/No Table Edits
- Translate Table Edits

All these edits are performed using record field attributes. The Application Processor retrieves information on record field attributes from PeopleSoft catalog tables PSRECFIELD and PSDBFIELD.

`FieldEdit` and `FieldChange` PeopleCode events are also processed once the Application Processor successfully processes the PeopleTools edits. Chapter 13, "PeopleCode and the Application Processor," explains these PeopleCode events in a thorough fashion.

And, as we discussed earlier, any time a panel field is changed, the Application Processor performs default processing.

9.4.2   RowInsert

We use the `RowInsert` function on panels that have scroll bars. We can either press the F7 key or choose the row insert icon from the application menu. When a row is inserted into a scroll bar, the following events take place:

- A new row is inserted in the current scroll area and all dependent scroll areas.
- The `RowInsert` PeopleCode event is executed.
- Default processing occurs for fields on the new scroll row.
- The `RowInit` PeopleCode events are processed for fields on the new scroll row.

The Application Processor automatically inserts a row into the current scroll bar and child scroll bars. After the new rows are created, `RowInsert` event is executed from all fields in the scroll bars. As previously discussed, the Application Processor performs iterative default processing on all fields in the scroll bar. Default values are used only when the fields are blank or zero for numeric fields. Finally, `RowInit` is triggered from all the fields on the scroll bar.

When the primary record on the scroll bar is effective-dated, the Application Processor copies values of fields from the current row to the new row. (`Current` does not imply the current effective-dated row. It means the row from which the user chooses to perform the row insert.) This feature is built internally into PeopleTools to accommodate maintenance of history data in PeopleSoft. This enables the user to override only the fields that are different on the new row.

TIP   When the primary record on the scroll bar is effective-dated during `RowInsert`, the Application Processor automatically copies data into the new row.

TIP   We can disable the `RowInsert` function on a scroll bar by editing scroll bar properties in panels.

9.4.3   RowDelete

We can use the `RowDelete` function on panels that have scroll bars. This function is used to delete rows from the scroll bar. The `RowDelete` function can be performed by either pressing the F8 Key or by choosing the row delete icon from the application menu. When the `RowDelete` function is chosen, the `RowDelete` PeopleCode event is executed from fields on the scroll area; a warning message is issued to verify the `RowDelete`; and rows are deleted from the current scroll area and all child scroll areas.

The Application Processor executes the `RowDelete` PeopleCode event from fields on the scroll area. This PeopleCode event can be used to verify whether the user can delete this row, and an error or warning message can be issued to either prevent or warn the user.

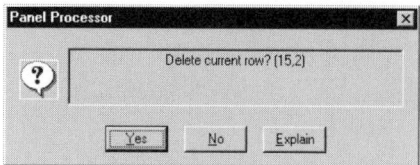

Figure 9.31 PeopleTools message during RowDelete

By default, the Application Processor automatically issues the message in figure 9.31 when a row is deleted from the scroll bar.

If the user chooses to proceed with RowDelete, the Application Processor deletes rows from the current scroll area as well as all dependent scroll areas. It is important to note that the rows are not physically deleted from the database until the panel is saved. The deleted row is still available for access until save time.

TIP	Scroll bar functions such as TotalRowCount and ActiveRowCount treat rows marked as deleted in scroll bars differently. The TotalRow-Count function adds all rows including deleted rows on the scroll bar. The ActiveRowCount function adds all rows except the deleted rows.
TIP	We can disable the RowDelete function on a scroll bar by editing scroll bar properties in panels.

9.4.4 Prompt processing

A prompt is a list of valid values for a Panel field. Prompt processing is activated under record field properties. When the user presses the F4 Key or clicks on the drop-down list, the Application Processor provides a list of valid values for the panel field. Prompt processing is performed using keys from the prompt table.

For the prompt to be processed correctly, key fields from the prompt table have to be present on the panel group. Let's take a look at how prompt processing works in the MY_PROBLEM_TRKG panel (figure 9.32).

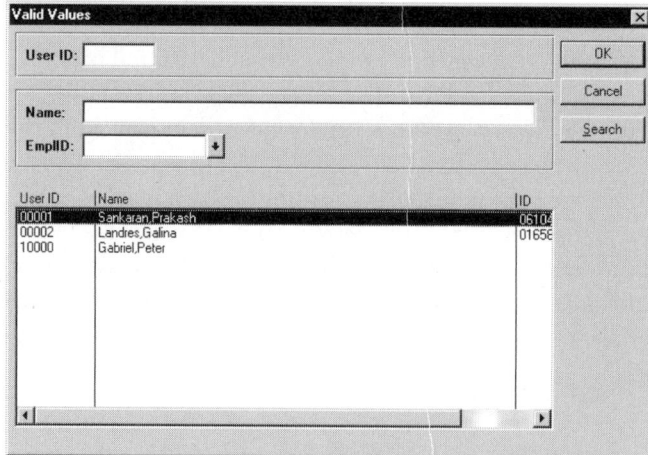

**Figure 9.32
Prompt processing**

Here, we activated the prompt on the User ID field, and the Application Processor produced a list of valid users from MY_USER_TABLE. MY_USER_TABLE is the prompt record for the MY_USER_ID field on the MY_PROBLEM_TRKG record.

Observe how the Application Processor displays all list box fields from the Prompt record in the prompt list. (To learn more about prompt records and prompt processing refer to chapter 6.)

9.4.5 Command or push buttons

When command or push buttons are pressed, the Application Processor executes the `FieldChange` PeopleCode event for the panel field. Push buttons can be defined as a command button, a process, or a secondary panel.

When the push button is defined as a command button, the Application Processor executes `FieldChange` PeopleCode event from the record field. When the push button is defined as a process, the batch process attached to the push button definition is run. When the push button is defined as a secondary panel, the secondary panel attached to the push button definition is brought up. Consider the example from our application panel shown in figure 9.33.

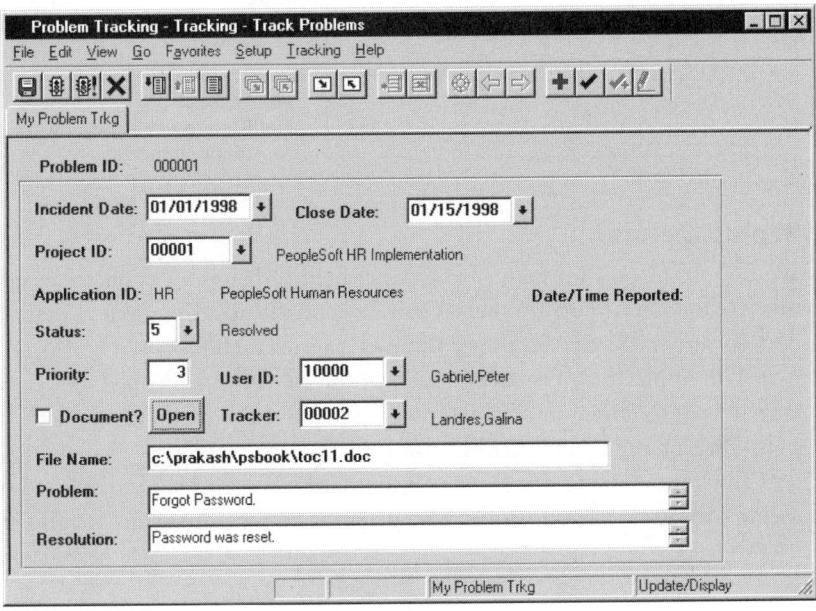

Figure 9.33   Push buttons on application panels

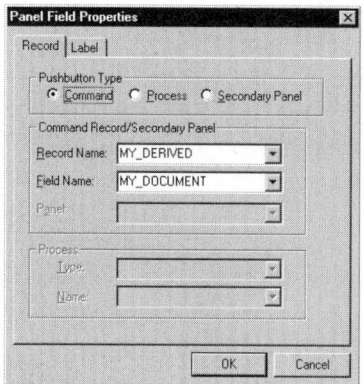

Figure 9.34 Push Button Properties

When the Open push button is activated, the `FieldChange` PeopleCode event is processed. Let's look at the definition for the push button and the `FieldChange` PeopleCode event attached to it (figures 9.34 and 9.35).

The push button is defined as a command button, and the field MY_DOCUMENT is from MY_DERIVED record. The `FieldChange` PeopleCode event from this record field opens a Microsoft Word document with the filename as the parameter. The Application Processor automatically executes the `FieldChange` PeopleCode event to bring up the Word document. (To learn more about push buttons, refer to chapter 6.)

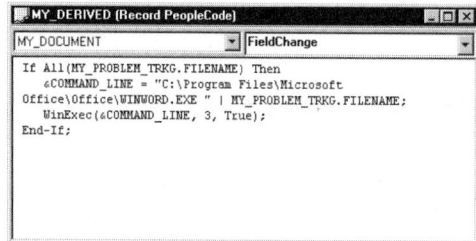

**Figure 9.35
FieldChange PeopleCode
for the push button**

9.4.6 Pop-up menus

We can attach pop-up menus to a panel field to bring up context-sensitive information. Two types of pop-up menus can be brought up from a panel field: the standard pop-up menu and the developer-defined pop-up menu.

The Application Processor executes the `PrePopup` PeopleCode event when the user activates a developer-defined pop-up menu. Pop-up menus are activated either by right-clicking on a panel field or using the SHIFT-F10 Key.

In figure 9.36, we can see how a standard pop-up menu is displayed by the Application Processor. We can use any field in our application panel for this purpose.

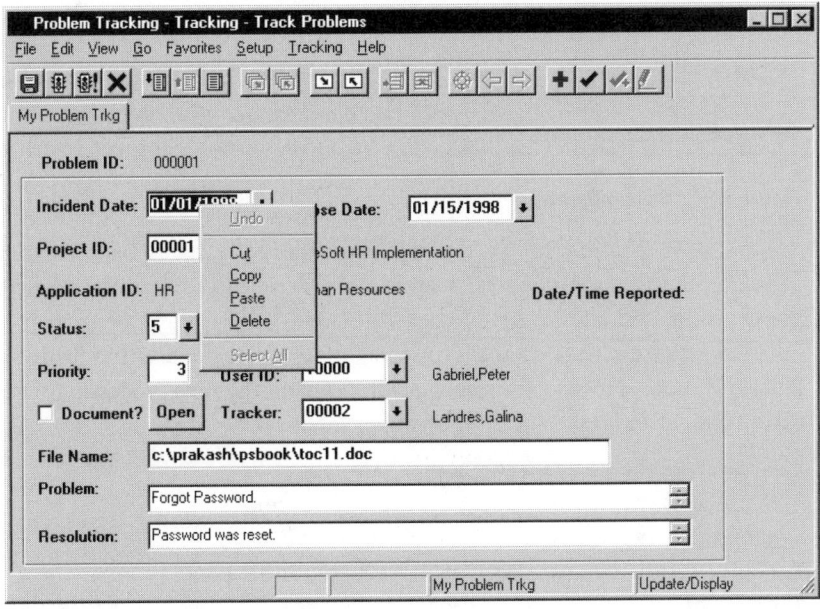

Figure 9.36   Standard pop-up menu for a panel field

9.4.7   Save processing

When the user chooses to save the panel group by pressing on the Save button, the Application Processor begins the save processing stage. We start with any one of the following actions:.

- choose File → Save from the application menu
- press ENTER using the keyboard
- choose the Save button

When the user performs the following actions, the Application Processor issues a message to the user, as illustrated in figure 9.37.

- choose Next in List
- choose Previous in List
- choose List
- choose another panel group
- choose another application menu without starting a new window
- close the application panel window

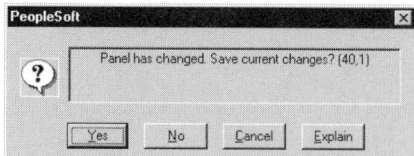

Figure 9.37 Save message

The message in figure 9.37 is just a reminder to the user that data has been changed in the application panel and the changes are not saved yet. When the user chooses "Yes" to proceed with the save, the save processing stage begins. When the user chooses "No," the Application Processor transfers the focus back to the application panel. When the user chooses "Cancel," the Application Processor cancels the whole panel group, and all changes are lost.

Let's go back to our panel group example where the user has made some changes and now chooses to save the panel group. During the save processing stage, the Application Processor triggers the following events:

- executes the `SaveEdit` PeopleCode event
- executes the `SavePreChg` PeopleCode event
- executes the `WorkFlow` PeopleCode event
- updates the database with changes made in the panel group
- executes `SavePostChg` PeopleCode event
- saves the data to the database

Execute SaveEdit PeopleCode event

The Application Processor executes `SaveEdit` PeopleCode events from all records in the panel group except records which contain related display fields. Let us look at the panel field layout for MY_PROBLEM_TRKG panel to identify related display and non-related display fields (figure 9.38).

Navigation: Layout → Order (MY_PROBLEM_TRKG panel is open)

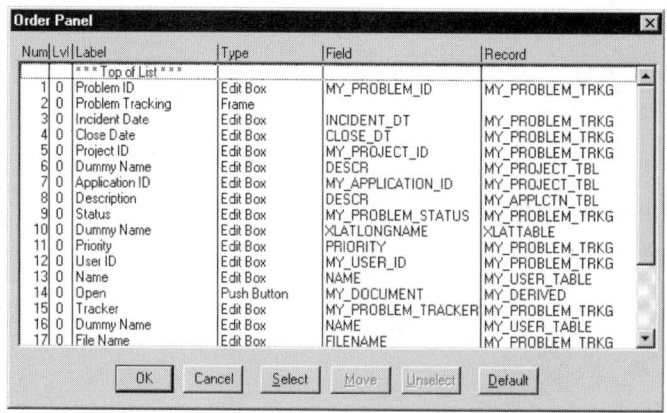

**Figure 9.38
Panel fields layout**

In figure 9.38, we notice that fields exist from more than one record definition. MY_PROJECT_TBL, MY_APPLCTN_TBL, XLATTABLE, and MY_USER_TABLE are records that contain the related display fields in the panel. The only other record that does not contain related display fields is the MY_PROBLEM_TRKG record.

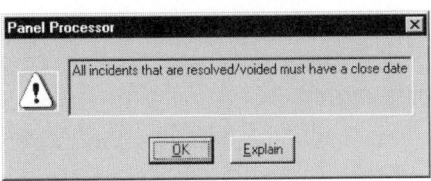

Figure 9.39 Error message

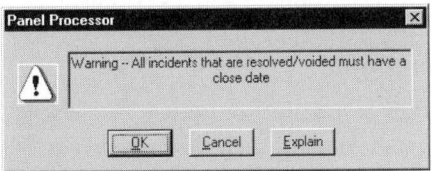

Figure 9.40 Warning message

Only the `SaveEdit` PeopleCode events from MY_PROBLEM_TRKG record are going to be executed by the Application Processor. `SaveEdit` PeopleCode events are used to validate user data entry before saving them to the database. Error and warning messages can be added to `Save-Edit` PeopleCode events to either prevent or warn the user after validation. Let's go back to our example and look at the difference between an error message and a warning message (figures 9.39 and 9.40).

An error message prevents the user from saving the panel group. The Application Processor then returns the focus to the application panel to allow the user to rectify the error. A warning message allows the user to override the validation and save the panel group. The user can choose the OK button to override the message and save the panel group. On the other hand, the user can choose the Cancel button to get back to the panel group and correct the problem causing the Application Processor to issue the warning message. `SaveEdit` events are processed in the order in which fields are laid out in the record definition. (Part 3 will explain more about the usage of `SaveEdit` PeopleCode events.)

TIP   `SaveEdit` events are processed in the order in which fields are laid out in the record definition. `SaveEdit` events in records that are present in panels with scroll bars are processed starting from level zero.

Execute SavePreChg PeopleCode event

The Application Processor executes all `SavePreChg` PeopleCode events from records in the application panel with the exception of records which contain related display fields. `SavePreChg` PeopleCode events are used to process data after user input—before the data are saved to the database. A perfect use for `SavePreChg` PeopleCode event would be to populate certain fields which are not input fields on the panel, based on other fields which *are* input fields. The Application Processor executes the `SavePreChg` PeopleCode events in the order in which the fields are laid out in the record definition. The Application Processor errors out with a runtime error when an error or warning message is used in `SavePreChg` PeopleCode events. (Part 3 explains `SavePreChg` PeopleCode events in greater detail.)

TIP   An error or warning message can be used only in `SaveEdit` PeopleCode event during save processing.

Execute WorkFlow PeopleCode event

After all panel fields are populated for saving, the Application Processor then executes `WorkFlow` PeopleCode events. `WorkFlow` PeopleCode events are used to trigger business events which either update a work list or execute a message agent. `WorkFlow` PeopleCode events are executed in the order in which fields are laid out in the record definition. (Again see part 3 for more discussion on `WorkFlow` PeopleCode events.)

Update the database with changes

The Application Processor then builds SQL scripts to update database tables based on changes made to the panel. Some database platforms allow updates to SQL views that in turn update the underlying database tables from which the views were built. It is important to note that the data are not saved in the database yet. In other words, the Application Processor does not perform any commits to the database in this step. In the `Add` mode, the Application Processor determines that it must perform an SQL insert. In other modes, the Application Processor determines that an update is necessary. In panel groups with scroll bars, the Application Processor performs an SQL insert for rows added into the scroll bar and SQL deletes for rows deleted from the scroll bar.

TIP   Rows that are deleted from the scroll bar are available in the panel buffer until the Application Processor issues an SQL commit to the database.

Execute SavePostChg PeopleCode event

The Application Processor executes all `SavePostChg` PeopleCode events from records in the panel group. `SavePostChg` PeopleCode events are not executed from records which contain related display fields in the panel group. `SavePostChg` PeopleCode events can be used to perform updates to other related application tables based on information entered in the panel group. As with the preceeding PeopleSoft events, `SavePostChg` PeopleCode events are executed in the order in which fields are laid out in the record definition. (See part 3 for more information about `SavePostChg` PeopleCode events.)

Saves the data to the database

The Application Processor is now ready to save the changes permanently to the database. The Application Processor issues an SQL commit to the database to accomplish this. At this time, all rows deleted from scroll bars are no longer available in the panel buffer. The Application Processor, after successfully saving data, returns the focus back to the panel group in a static state.

NOTE   The Application Processor can error out with a runtime error after Save-Edit PeopleCode events are executed. Runtime errors can occur as a result of errors in SQLExec statements, database index constraints, data storage parameters, network connection loss, and so forth.

Navigation: File → Object Properties (Panel Group is open)

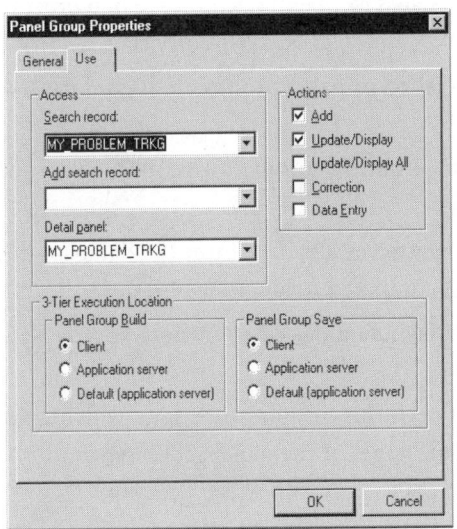

Figure 9.41   Panel Group build and save parameters

The panel group definition contains two parameters which help the Application Processor determine both where to build the panel group and where to perform save processing (figure 9.41).

Figure 9.41 illustrates the two parameters in the panel group definition which the Application Processor uses to build and save the panel group. When Client is chosen either for Panel Group Build or Panel Group Save, the Application Processor is going to process both stages on the client workstation. When Application Server is chosen, the Application Processor is going to process both stages in the machine which hosts the Application Server. The Application Server is physically closer to where data reside than the client workstation.

During save processing, all PeopleCode events except for the SaveEdit PeopleCode event can be executed on the Application Server.

In a three-tier installation which runs using a Tuxedo Application Server configuration, it is prudent to process both these stages close to the database server. (For a detailed description on two-tier and three-tier installations, refer to chapter 1.)

9.4.8 Cancel

Finally, the user can choose to cancel all changes made to the fields in the panel group by simply choosing the Cancel button from the application menu. The user can also choose "No" to the message illustrated in figure 9.37 to cancel all changes.

KEY POINTS

1 The Application Processor organizes numerous individual steps from the time the user accesses an application panel to the time the user saves the changes to the database.

2 The Application Processor stages can be divided into search processing, data retrieval, panel group display, and data entry/inquiry stages.

3 Search records that are attached to panel groups are used during the search processing stage.

4 The Application Processor executes a number of PeopleCode events during all stages.

5 The Application Processor retrieves less data from the database in Add and Data Entry modes when compared to all other modes.

6 Panel field definitions and layouts are used to retrieve and display fields in the panel group.

7 The Application Processor performs default processing, which is an iterative process performed during all stages of the panel group session.

8 During the data entry/inquiry stage, the Application Processor performs validations, executes field modification PeopleCode events and row modification PeopleCode events, and performs save processing.

9 Save processing starts when the user chooses to save the panel group session.

10 In a three-tier installation, the Application Processor looks at the Panel Build parameter and the Panel Save parameter in the panel group definition in order to determine where to build and save the panel group.

C H A P T E R   1 0

Application Designer— PeopleSoft 8

PeopleSoft 8 contains exciting new features that enhance the types of end users who can access a PeopleSoft application. One such feature is the Internet Client. Almost all the new features that are available in the Application Designer tool are focused to service the Internet Client. While the Application Designer tool in this new release is similar to that in release 7.5, some enhancements are available in PeopleSoft 8. Let's have a look at what's new in PeopleSoft 8.

10.1 DEVELOPMENT OBJECTS

A number of new objects can be developed using the Application Designer tool in PeopleSoft 8. Objects such as the Application Engine Program and Approval Rule Sets, developed using a tool menu outside of the Application Designer tool in release 7, are now integrated with the Application Designer tool. The following is a list of objects that can be developed using the Application Designer. New objects in PeopleSoft 8 are mentioned in *Italics*:

- Activity
- Application Engine Program
- Approval Rule Set
- *Business Component*
- *Business Interlink*
- *File Layout*
- *HTML Definition*
- *Image*
- *Message Definition*
- *Message Channel*
- *Message Node*
- *SQL*
- *Style Sheet*

10.1.1 Application Engine program

Application Engine is a PeopleTools object that provides an alternative to using COBOL and SQR for batch applications. Application Engine is now integrated within the Application Designer tool and can be upgraded between databases. To learn more about new features in Application Engine in release 8, see chapter 45 in this book.

10.1.2 Business components

Business components are individual business transactions. Business transactions such as Purchase Orders, New Hires, and Journal Entries can be encapsulated into a business component. Business Components are single instances of a panel group session and can be invoked from external applications as well as from PeopleCode. The whole idea behind business component definitions is to provide external access to PeopleSoft applications. Business Components expand the possibilities of the user types who can access the system.

Business component definitions are divided into three parts:

- Search Keys are from the search records defined in panel groups.
- Methods are processes that take place when the business component is invoked.
- Properties refers to a single instance of data in the panel group. For example, data stored in a field in the panel group constitutes a property.

Figure 10.1 illustrates a business component definition in PeopleSoft 8.

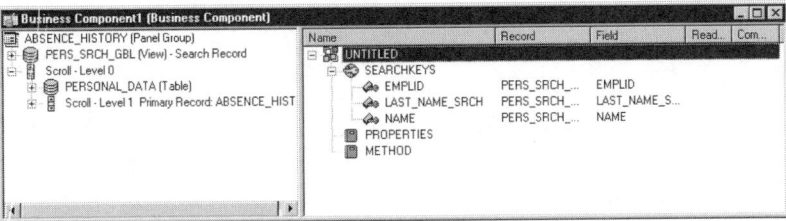

Figure 10.1 Business component definition

The business component API is used by external applications to access the PeopleSoft business component and supports the following environments:

- Microsoft COM (Visual Basic)
- PeopleCode

Figure 10.2 is an illustration from PeopleBooks 8 on business component architecture.

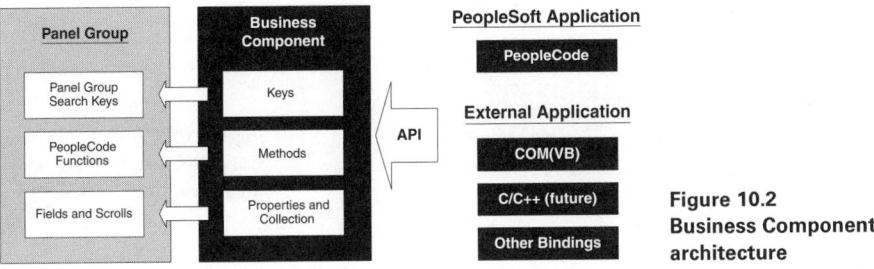

**Figure 10.2
Business Component
architecture**

10.1.3   Business interlink

A business interlink allows you to integrate your software system with PeopleSoft. Business Interlink is a gateway to your software system from PeopleSoft. You can invoke a business interlink from your PeopleSoft application. The external software system is integrated by using a business interlink plug-in which provides a framework to that system. The business interlink plug-in allows you to invoke the external software system using PeopleCode.

Basically, the business interlink plug-in accesses the PeopleSoft Application Server, which then initiates a business interlink object which resides in the PeopleSoft application. The business interlink plug-in can be located in the same machine as the

PeopleSoft Application Server to enable access to software systems within your company. On the other hand, the business interlink plug-in can be located outside the firewall on a web server to access third-party software applications from within PeopleSoft.

The business interlink plug-in exposes the external software system to PeopleSoft as sets of input/output transactions or data classes for query and updates. For example, your PeopleSoft Payroll application can transact with your Oracle General Ledger system to feed in journal entries using data classes which represent the data structure in the external database. Similarly, your PeopleSoft Benefits application can feed enrollment transactions to vendors which manage employee benefits. Figure 10.3 illustrates the business interlink architecture with the plug-in located on a web server.

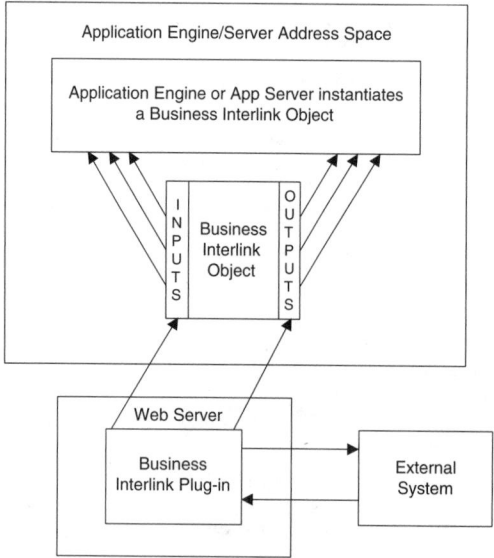

Figure 10.3
Business interlink architecture—plug-in located on the web server

10.1.4 File Layout

File Layout maps fields in a file. It basically describes the location of columns in a file. Using the file layout definition, PeopleCode can either read from or write into a file. Figure 10.4 illustrates a simple file layout definition in PeopleSoft 8.

One or more record definitions may be used in building a file layout. Fields from the record definitions are automatically expanded into the file layout. The record fields are only used as templates for columns in the file. No correlation exists between record fields and the file layout. Changes to record field attributes will not be reflected in the file layout.

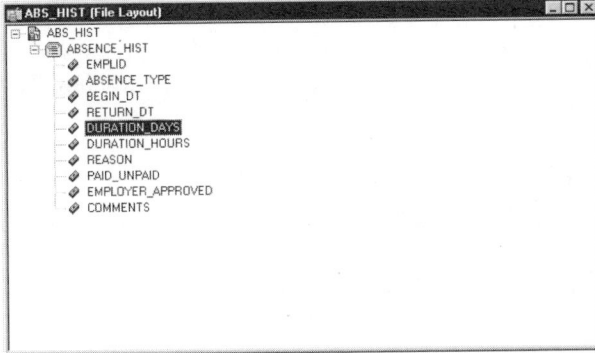

Figure 10.4
File layout definition

10.1.5 HTML definitions

HTML area control can be inserted into any PeopleSoft panel. It can be viewed only from an Internet Client. The Internet Client automatically converts the panel into HTML tags. The HTML area control can be inserted into any level in the panel as a rectangular box which can be reshaped and resized.

An HTML area can be populated using static texts and images or dynamic record fields. The HTML area control is different from other Internet Client controls. While the Internet Client translates other controls such as check boxes, prompt lists, and so forth. into HTML tags in the HTML area control, the developer writes HTML code used as is during runtime, but HTML tags <body>, <frame>, <frameset>, <form>, <head>, <html>, <meta>, and <title> are not supported in the HTML area control.

10.1.6 Image definition

Images are converted into image definitions and stored in a repository. In PeopleSoft 7.5, images were associated to panels and defined as panel fields. In PeopleSoft 8, image files are converted into image definitions and stored within PeopleTools as objects.

The following image types can be stored as image definitions:.

- BMP—Bitmap
- DIB—Device independent Bitmap
- JPEG
- GIF—Only for Internet Client

10.1.7 Message definition

Message definition is used in the Application Messaging system in PeopleSoft. Message definitions store information on how a single message is passed using the Application Messaging system. Messages are objects formatted in XML. In PeopleSoft 8, messages are used as a single unit of transaction in the Publish and Subscribe process.

10.1.8 Message channel definition

Message channels group individual message definitions and organize their transmission. They route messages between nodes across your network and they define how each single message definition in the group should process.

10.1.9 Message node definition

Message nodes are physical systems connected to the messaging network. Subscribers subscribe to a Message node, which can be an Application Server or a database, and the Application Server or the database publishes a message, which is transmitted to the subscriber using message channel definitions. Message channel definitions include information on how to route messages from the publishing node to the subscribing node. Figure 10.5 illustrates how messages are published and subscribed using these three new object types.

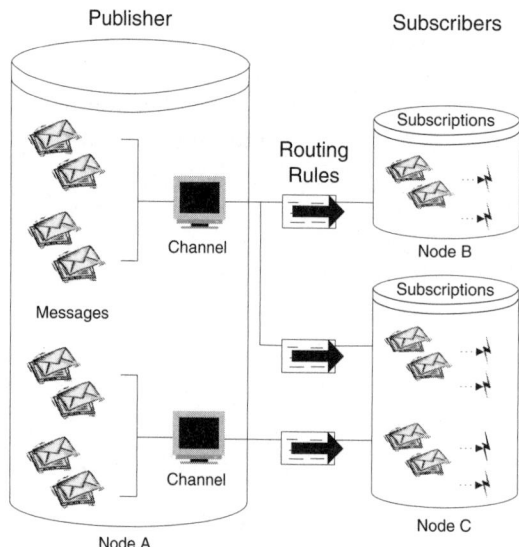

**Figure 10.5
Publishing and subscribing
messages—application messaging**

10.1.10 SQL definition

We can store SQL statements in PeopleTools using the Application Designer. An SQL definition can be a section of an entire SQL statement that you want to reuse or multiple SQL statements. The SQL definition can be accessed using PeopleCode SQL-Class. Unlike SQLEXEC functions, an SQLClass allows selection of all rows using an SQL statement. You can also create an SQL definition using PeopleCode, then store it in PeopleTools. The SQL definition contains the SQL statement, the database type, and an effective date.

PeopleCode functions associated with the SQL definitions are `CreateSQL`, `DeleteSQL`, `FetchSQL`, and `GetSQL`.

10.1.11 Style sheet

Web development needs style attributes beyond foreground, background, and fonts. In PeopleSoft 8, a new development object, the Style Sheet, can be created using the Application Designer. A style sheet is a collection of styles that can be used on a webpage. A style sheet can be displayed only on the Internet Client and is attached to the properties of a PeopleSoft Panel definition. PSSTYLEDEF is the default style sheet that is delivered in PeopleSoft 8. This default style sheet already contains classes that define style attributes in a webpage.

10.2 OTHER FEATURES

Other new features are available in PeopleSoft 8 under the Application Designer tool. They can be categorized into:

- general environment
- field definitions
- record definitions
- panel definitions
- panel groups

10.2.1 General environment

- The PeopleCode Debugger can be accessed using the new Debug menu from the Application Designer tool.
- Language translations can be performed from the Tools menu using the Translate menu item.
- A new Internet Options menu item is available under the View menu from the Application Designer tool.
- Additional password controls are available in PeopleSoft 8. Minimum length, password expiry, and special character requirements are some features which control user passwords.

10.2.2 Field definitions

- Multiple labels can be attached to field definitions in PeopleSoft 8. A default label can be indicated in the field definition. Any one of the labels can be used as the record field label or panel field label.
- Numeric fields can accommodate thirty-one decimals in PeopleSoft 8.

10.2.3 Record definitions

- You can sort fields within a record definition by clicking on the column headings.

- Subrecords attached to record definitions can be expanded and viewed.
- A new record type called the Temporary Table is now available in PeopleSoft 8.

10.2.4   Panel definitions

- Under the panel field layout screen, scroll levels are now displayed. Control Display and Related Display fields can also be seen in the panel field layout screen.
- Required fields appear with an '*' at runtime in panels.
- Multiple grids can be included in the same panel in PeopleSoft 8.
- Grids can be hidden or shown using a PeopleCode object.

10.2.5   Panel group definitions

- Panel groups are displayed in a tabbed interface in the object workspace.
- Two new PeopleCode events associated with panel groups—the `PreBuild` and `PostBuild` PeopleCode events—are available in PeopleSoft 8.
- A new option is available to disable saving the panel group in PeopleSoft 8.
- Internet Client attributes are available in the panel group definition to support the new Internet Client.

PART 3

PeopleCode: an in-depth look

One of the most powerful PeopleTools is the proprietary language called PeopleCode, which is used in conjunction with the Application Processor to control an application's behavior. The fundamental elements in the PeopleCode language are similar to those found in other programming languages such as SQR, Visual Basic, and PowerBuilder. In addition, PeopleCode has an extensive set of functions and syntax conventions designed specifically for PeopleSoft object types such as scroll bars. Some readers may be familiar with event-driven languages like Visual Basic where code is attached to action events such as mouse-clicking or tabbing from one field to another. As we discovered in part 2, the Application Processor differs in that it generally maintains events at the record and field levels. For example, when a panel is initially populated, the fields may be initialized through PeopleCode designated in the RowInit event. When an attempt is made to save the information on a panel, the Application Processor calls any SaveEdit PeopleCode that may exist. Since all the events and execution of PeopleCode are regulated by the Application Processor, the developer is free to concentrate on the functional aspects of the program. PeopleCode language elements, syntax, variables, and field references will be covered along with further explanation of event processing and program execution flow. To demonstrate a few advanced features of PeopleCode, we continue to examine and enhance our Problem Tracking application as well as present other pertinent examples. One of the most difficult PeopleCode techniques to master is working with scroll bars. To emphasize scroll handling, we create a slick little application which links employees to operator classes/locations. We also cover topics such as function libraries, error handling, debugging, and embedded SQL. The section concludes with an overview of new PeopleCode features in release 8.0.

C H A P T E R   1 1

Introduction to PeopleCode

Using Application Designer, we can build records and panel functionality that are quite eclectic. The PeopleCode language offers a wide range of features including the ability to manipulate variables, panels, and scrollbars. PeopleCode is accessed from the Application Designer, which contains the PeopleCode editor.

259

11.1 WHAT IS PEOPLECODE?

PeopleCode is a PeopleSoft proprietary programming language used with People-Tools applications. It is an interpreted scripting language and works as part of Application Designer in conjunction with the Application Processor. PeopleCode programs are linked to applications through record fields or menu items.

Let's assume that an application is distributed to various clients. Some of these clients would like to fully utilize the application, and others require limited functionality or fewer fields on panels than what would normally be displayed. One option would be to develop two panels: one panel can contain all the delivered fields; and the other panel would contain a limited number of fields. Maintaining two panels would not be difficult, but if a multitude of panels existed requiring similar designs, our panel maintenance would increase. This would also impact future upgrades, menu maintenance, and security—the potential for a tumultuous undertaking!

If the objective is to be more efficient within certain standards and utilize the Application Designer environment to a fuller extent, PeopleCode can be used to hide fields on the same panel. This approach saves the replication of panels. We can identify the user in an efficient manner so that the PeopleCode can operate on the correct fields by using operator classes, panel groups, menus, or language code. Once this information is known to the program, the manipulation of the PeopleTools environment can be done by hiding fields on panels and setting varying default values and edit controls using PeopleCode. Although several panels may not be required, the trade-off is additional PeopleCode that can, however, be localized to specific records and events.

As we've said, PeopleCode is a programming language which enables developers to extend the functionality of PeopleTools applications. An application can be refined or made more efficient through the use of PeopleCode. These refinements can take many forms including:

- hiding and un-hiding values on a panel
- defaulting values based on some common identifier
- editing values entered on a panel
- submitting jobs to the Process Scheduler
- enabling/disabling menu items
- calling functions from various events. (possibly leading to code efficiency and reusability)

Familiarity with structured programming languages such as C++, Visual Basic, SQR, and knowledge of relational data base concepts and SQL provide a foundation for a better understanding of PeopleCode. PeopleCode's syntax is similar to some structured languages but the events, rules, and general behavior of PeopleCode are directly linked to the Application Designer and PeopleTools environment. Panels, menus, records, and fields are all interwoven into the application of the PeopleCode language.

PeopleCode programs are joined with record fields and triggered by events such as record initialization, tabbing out of a field, saving a record, or other events generated by the Application Processor. Think of the Application Processor as a traffic officer who coordinates the efforts between the end-user, panels, PeopleCode, and other PeopleTools objects. Variables appearing on panels and work fields may be initialized or manipulated using PeopleCode. Other features include message functions used to communicate with the end user as well as features which handle panel scroll bars and their data contents.

11.2 PEOPLECODE EVENTS

In PeopleTools 7 every PeopleCode program is associated with both objects and events. PeopleCode events occur when specific actions take place. These actions can take place when a panel is initially displayed or when the value of a field on a panel is changed. Two types of PeopleCode exist within Application Designer. The first type is tied to events and occurs within record fields. The other type of PeopleCode is tied to menu items. These are referred to as record PeopleCode and menu PeopleCode, respectively. Collectively, we can refer to both types as PeopleCode event sets.

11.2.1 Record PeopleCode events

PeopleTools terminology defines a record as an SQL table, a view, or a derived/work record. Fields are a subset of records and they contain over ninety percent of People-Code. Each field can have an event, and each event can trigger PeopleCode. Some code is more efficient when contained in specific events; however, the same code placed into other events can generate runtime errors.

The illustration in figure 11.1 demonstrates the relationship between records, fields, and their corresponding PeopleCode events.

As figure 11.1 illustrates, records are comprised of fields. A record can contain one to many fields. Each field contained in a record has events and may have PeopleCode linked to one or more events. Events enable the developer to interact with the PeopleTools environment at key points during a working session. These events can include PeopleCode to initialize values and perform specific actions when a row is selected or when data are changed on a panel. PeopleCode can also be used to interact with events during panel save operations. We can categorize events into those that occur before data are retrieved from a record, during the maintenance phase when data are changed, and at the time data are saved to a record.

Record PeopleCode events include:

- `FieldDefault`
- `FieldEdit`
- `FieldChange`
- `FieldFormula`
- `RowInit`

- RowSelect
- RowInsert
- RowDelete
- PrePopup
- SaveEdit
- SavePreChg
- WorkFlow
- SavePostChg
- SearchInit
- SearchSave

These events occur during actions related to fields. PeopleCode can be attached to these events and can range from simple to complex. Hypothetically, PeopleCode can be inserted into each of the events for a given field. Not every PeopleCode event plays a role, so it may not be relevant or necessary to insert PeopleCode into each

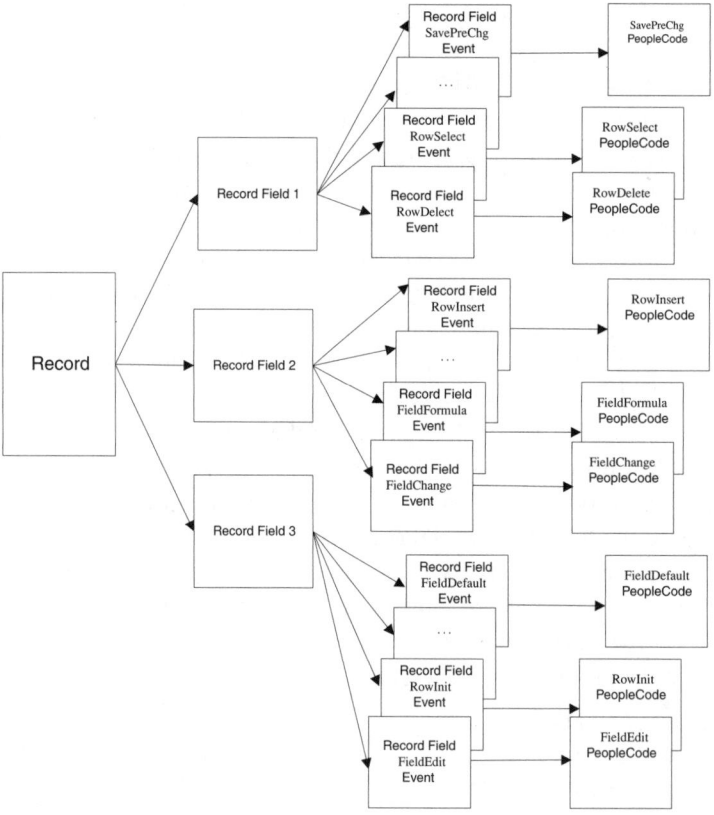

Figure 11.1 Relationship between records, fields, and PeopleCode events

event. Some PeopleCode events are triggered based on factors such as scroll bars and pop-up menus that appear on a panel. For example, in the Problem Tracking application, the panel MY_PROBLEM_TRKG does not contain a scroll bar. If we insert `RowInsert` or `RowDelete` PeopleCode, the programs in the events are never executed because `RowInsert` and `RowDelete` are related to scroll bar actions.

11.2.2   Menu PeopleCode events

Only one Menu PeopleCode event exists:

* `ItemSelected`

Menu PeopleCode is linked to the selection of a menu item from a standard or pop-up menu item.

11.3   USING APPLICATION DESIGNER TO DEVELOP PEOPLECODE

The Application Designer enables the insertion or editing of PeopleCode from points within the project workspace. PeopleCode can be accessed:

* from a record field definition
* by double-clicking on the lightening bolt "⚡" in the project workspace
* from a menu item
* within the panel definition

PeopleCode is commonly added and modified from the Application Designer through record field definitions. To add record PeopleCode to the Problem Tracking application, the first step required is to open the project definition from the Application Designer.

The Problem Tracking application, when viewed from the project workspace, contains objects such as menus, panel groups, records, and fields (figure 11.2). When we view projects and more specifically objects such as records, we see they contain a "+" on the left side. Clicking on the "+" for records displays all the records contained in the project. A subsequent click to a record such as MY_PROBLEM_TRKG displays the fields contained in the record. Figure 11.3 ❶, illustrates the record fields for MY_PROBLEM_TRKG record in MY_PROJECT.

Navigation: File → Open → Project → My Project

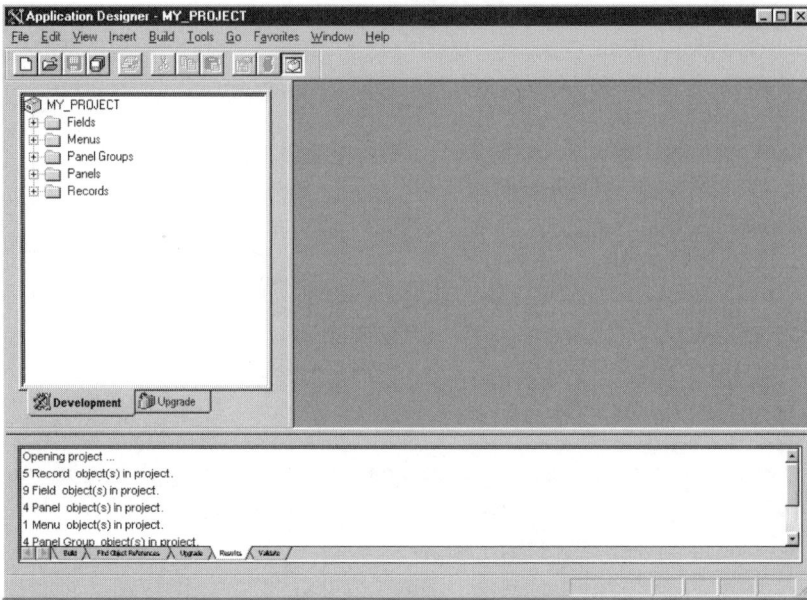

Figure 11.2 Initial project workspace

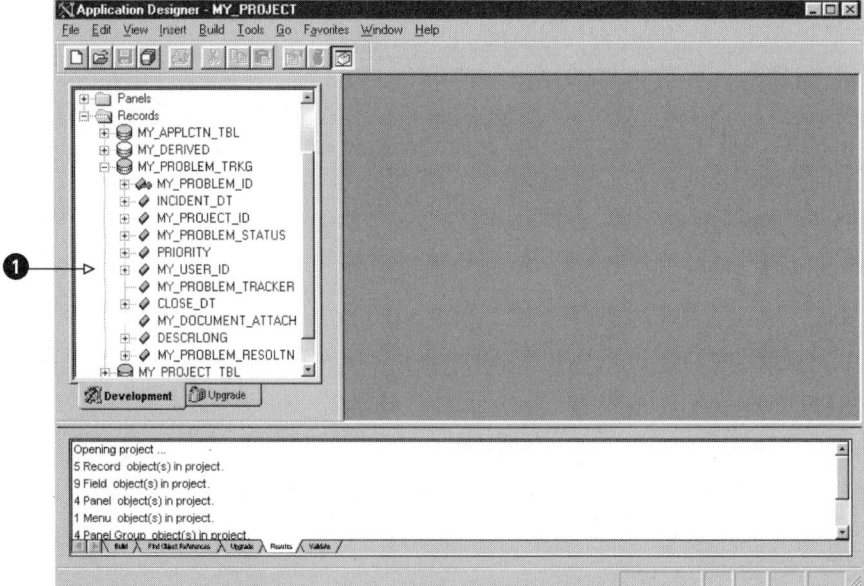

Figure 11.3 Record fields in the project workspace

The "+" next to the record field indicates that PeopleCode exists for that field. In figure 11.3 the record field MY_PROBLEM_TRKG.MY_USER_ID contains People-Code as indicated by the "+." When we click on the "+" for MY_USER_ID, any PeopleCode associated with the field is identified by the ⚡ symbol for that event. The example in figure 11.4, ❶ indicates that the field MY_USER_ID contains several record PeopleCode events.

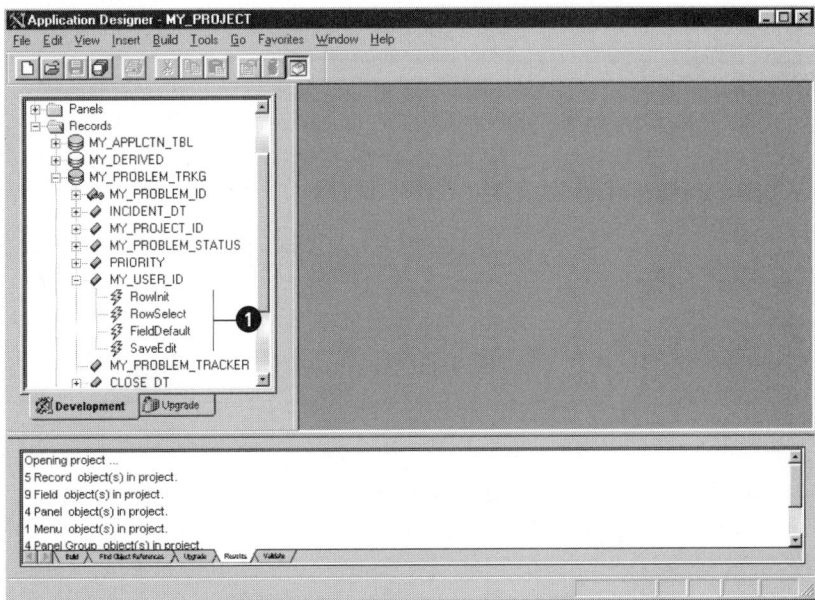

Figure 11.4   Record fields with PeopleCode

To view the record definition, double-click on the record name. We can also click on the desired record name within the workspace and, using the right mouse button, click on View Definition. An alternative method of viewing the record definition can be accomplished by double-clicking on the appropriate record name, which then enters the field display mode. After the record definition is displayed, we can view any associated PeopleCode from the PeopleCode display panel that displays the fields and corresponding events.

Another manner by which we can identify where PeopleCode exists for a record is to use the PeopleCode Display toolbar icon as illustrated by ❶ in figure 11.5. When viewing the PeopleCode Display panel, any field containing PeopleCode will have "Yes" displayed at the intersection of the fieldname and event.

Navigation: View → PeopleCode Display

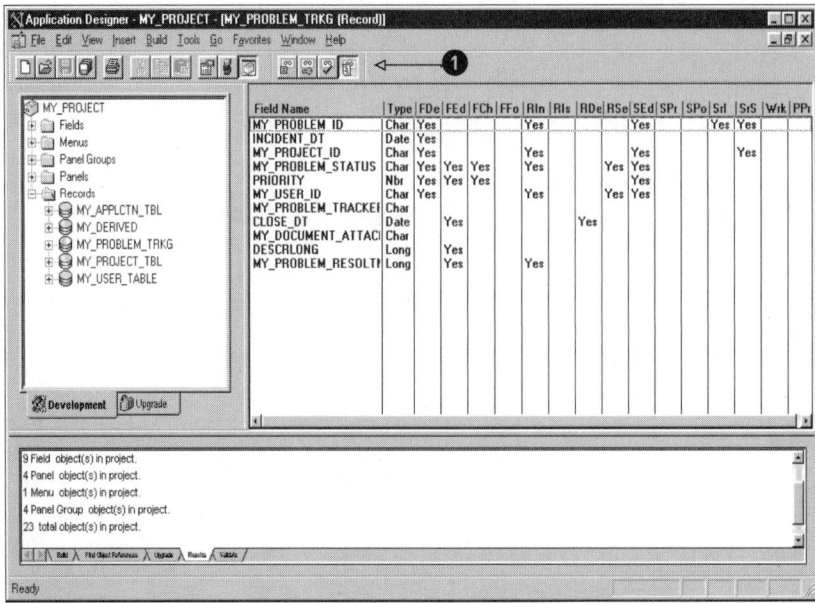

Figure 11.5   PeopleCode display view

To access PeopleCode through a panel definition, click on the field to which the code is to be added or modified. As illustrated in figure 11.6 the right mouse button is used to view PeopleCode for the Close Date field.

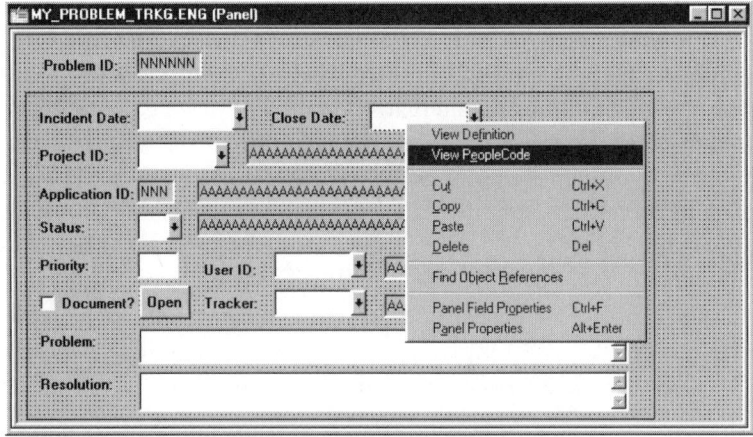

Figure 11.6   Accessing PeopleCode through a panel definition

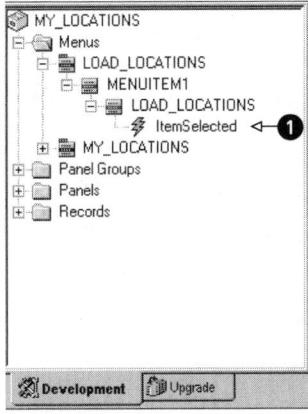

Figure 11.7   Accessing Menu
PeopleCode

Menu PeopleCode can be accessed in a similar manner to record PeopleCode from the menu definition. Figure 11.7, ❶ illustrates the menu used for a small application used to link security operator classes and locations. Menu PeopleCode can be accessed using the right mouse button on the menu item or by double-clicking on the "⚡".

With a basic understanding of PeopleCode and how to access it, we are now ready to become familiar with the syntax, the rules, and the statements required to successfully implement applications that utilize PeopleCode.

KEY POINTS

1 PeopleCode is a programming language, which enables developers to extend the functionality of PeopleTools applications.

2 The Application Designer is used to insert or update PeopleCode statements.

3 PeopleCode events enable the developer to interact with the PeopleTools environment at key points during a work session.

4 Events occur during actions related to record fields. PeopleCode attached to all or some of these events is referred to as record PeopleCode.

5 Menu PeopleCode consists of the ItemSelected event and is linked to the selection of an item from a menu.

C H A P T E R   1 2

PeopleCode language elements

The objective of this chapter is to introduce some of the fundamentals and basic building blocks of the PeopleCode language. In addition to the language constructs, the chapter illustrates how PeopleCode can be used to build simple programs using the materials presented in part 2.

12.1 PEOPLECODE AND RECORD FIELDS

In part 2, a record and it's associated fields were identified and built. The section "Creating a PeopleSoft panel definition" illustrates how fields are added to a panel with basic prompts and PeopleTools edits. Beyond the range of these edits is where knowledge and application of PeopleCode becomes a key element in the development and implementation of PeopleSoft applications. PeopleCode is linked to record fields, unlike fields in Application Designer that have the same characteristics, regardless of the records on which they exist. When a field named MY_PROBLEM_STATUS is defined, the field may appear on several different records. When the characteristics of the field are changed, the change is reflected throughout the database. If the field description or data type is changed, the modification is reflected on every table and panel containing the field MY_PROBLEM_STATUS. PeopleCode, on the other hand, is linked to fields through the record field definition. As an example, let's assume we've added PeopleCode to the RowInit event of the MY_PROBLEM_TRKG record, MY_USER_ID field. Using dot notation, it can also be specified as MY_PROBLEM_TRKG.MY_USER_ID.RowInit. The field MY_USER_ID also exists on the record MY_DERIVED; however MY_DERIVED.MY_USER_ID.RowInit does not contain this PeopleCode. Alternatively, when the length of the field MY_USER_ID is changed, the new length is reflected in both the MY_PROBLEM_TRKG and MY_USER_ID records.

12.2 PEOPLECODE EDITOR

In chapter 11 we discussed how PeopleCode can be viewed from a record field definition: by double-clicking on the lightening bolt "⚡" in the project workspace, from a menu item, or within the panel definition. The PeopleCode editor provides a facility to insert and maintain PeopleCode. Language statements, comments, and expressions entered are saved into the PeopleTools system table PSPCMPROG. This record is linked to the record containing record field definitions, PSRECFIELD. The PeopleCode editor performs syntax checking during save. Explicit syntax checking can be performed using a handy feature that validates syntax, available with release 7. Validate syntax is represented by the toolbar button ☑ and verifies syntax without having to enable the save button. Records and fields used as bind variables in embedded SQL and scroll functions are also validated at this time. The syntax check edits a large percentage of code, but some rules in PeopleCode however are not strictly enforced. These errors can "slip by" and result in runtime error messages which can halt the processing of a panel—for example, an error might be a reference to a non-existing record enclosed within the quotes of a SQLExec statement or an invalid usage of scroll levels.

Navigation: Tools → Options → PeopleCode

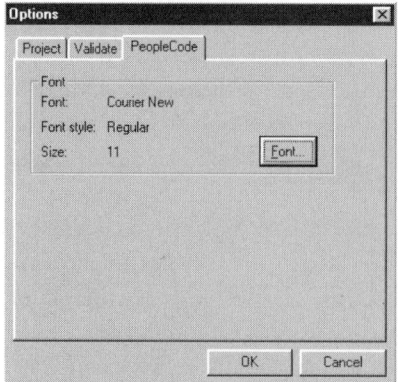

Figure 12.1 Customization of PeopleCode editor font settings

Additional PeopleCode editor features include:

- customization of font settings, which can be changed by selecting Options → PeopleCode from the menu (figure 12.1)
- integration with Application Designer toolbar, menus, and accessibility via a pop-up window
- support for drag-and-drop PeopleCode text between independent programs

Let's view the PeopleCode for MY_PROBLEM_TRKG.MY_USER_ID.RowInit as illustrated in figure 12.2.

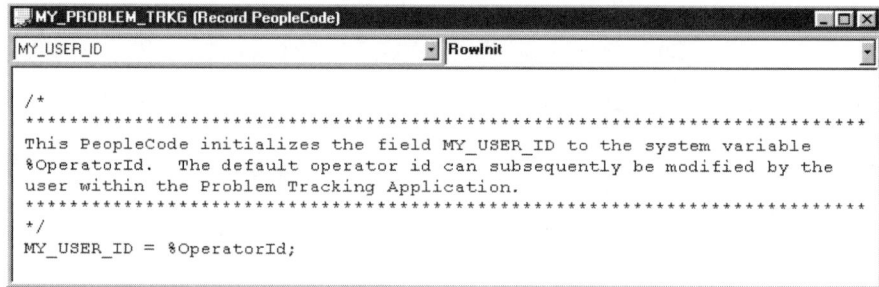

Figure 12.2 PeopleCode characteristics

The illustration in figure 12.2 identifies some PeopleCode characteristics:

- The header area identifies the record name and identifies this as PeopleCode attached to the MY_PROBLEM_TRKG record. In PeopleTools there are two types of PeopleCode: record and menu. The example identifies record PeopleCode.
- The area below the header displays the fieldname (MY_USER_ID) and the type of PeopleCode event (`RowInit`).
- Finally, the actual PeopleCode statements.

When new PeopleCode is added to or removed from a record, the record definition must be saved prior to exiting the PeopleTools session. A record definition does not have to be saved when existing PeopleCode is changed. The PeopleCode itself is saved to the appropriate PeopleCode tools tables.

12.3 PEOPLECODE COMMENTS

Figure 12.2 contains an example of PeopleCode statements. The first several lines contain comments. Comments provide an excellent method of internal code documentation. Information such as the date, the author, and the purpose of the code can be detailed in comments. Comments can exist anywhere in a PeopleCode program. They are not executed and can also be helpful during upgrades. If all our code were documented with a common text literal such as company name, we could conceivably search PeopleCode for the string and identify customizations. Two methods of inserting comments into a PeopleCode program are available. One form is to enclose comments with a leading /* and trailing */. This can be useful when testing code or debugging. It can also be helpful when one wishes to prevent PeopleSoft-delivered code from executing, but does not want to delete the code. The REM statement can also be used for comments. The REM or REMark statement is terminated with a semicolon (;). Comments beginning with a /* generate an error message when an attempt to validate syntax or a save operation is performed and the closing */ statement is missing. A misplaced semicolon (;) in a REM statement does not generate a message. It is possible that comments as well as PeopleCode statements are both treated as comments, because the scope of the REM statement terminates with the semicolon. Figure 12.3 shows some examples of valid comments and others that are not coded correctly. In the example, &STRING_FIELD2 is preceded by a REM statement. The second REM is not terminated by a semi-colon and, therefore, &STRING_FIELD2 initialization is treated as part of the comments.

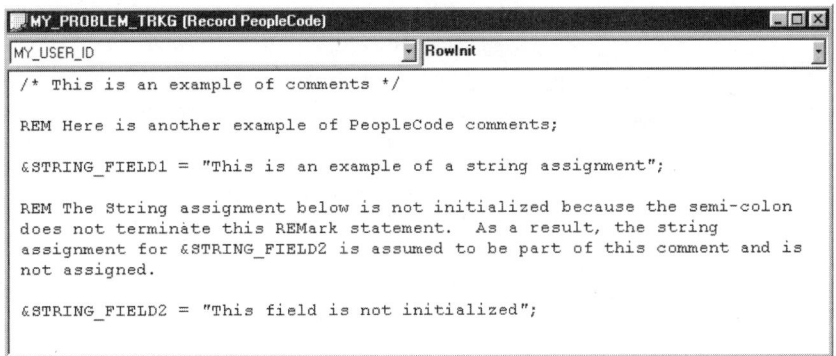

Figure 12.3   PeopleCode comments

12.4 DATA TYPES

The PeopleCode language contains several data types that permit operations on all categories of database fields. The examples that follow initialize variables. A

PeopleCode temporary variable is preceded by an ampersand ("&"), which assumes the data type of the assignment statement.

STRING	Strings are made up of any combination of characters that can be numeric, alphabetic, or special characters. A string can be initialized by enclosing the combination of characters in either single (') or double (") quotation marks. When one type of delimiter, either a single quote or double quote, is part of the string, it can be enclosed by the other delimiter type. Our first code example below is an example of single and double quotation marks used in string data types. PeopleCode functions exist, which operate on strings. Some are used to convert strings to numbers, combine or concatenate two or more strings, and trim a string either on the right or left. String functions will be reviewed as we progress through the chapters.
NUMBER	A number is any decimal value including integers and decimal points. A large percentage of the data types used in PeopleCode are either of the string or numeric type. As with strings, there are many functions that operate on the Number data type. Our second example below is an example of numbers in PeopleCode.
DATE	Dates are stored internally in the YYYY-MM-DD format. It is important to note that each platform and type of database stores dates differently, based on how the date is used. The Application Processor converts dates when they are loaded into a PeopleCode program. However, functions such as SQLExec, which operate directly on database tables and fields do not automatically convert dates. There are a number of built-in and Meta-SQL functions that work with dates and can be used to convert the formats.
DATETIME	A DateTime data type contains a date and a time expressed as YYYY-MM-DD-HH.MI.SS.SSSSSS. PeopleCode functions such as DatePart and TimePart extract the date or time portion. Functions such as DateTime6 and DateTimeValue generate a DATETIME data type.
TIME	Expressed as HHMISS. Functions involving TIME data type return numeric values expressed as seconds and sub-seconds.
BOOLEAN	A Boolean data type can have one of two values, TRUE or FALSE.
OBJECT	This data type is used with functions such as CreateObject. Word documents or Excel spreadsheets are examples of OLE objects.
ANY	This data type may contain any of the other data types. A field defined as ANY takes on the characteristics of the field with which it is initialized. A variable having no explicit data type declaration is ANY by default. PeopleCode determines the data type based on circumstances. It is therefore possible to have an undeclared field that can be used interchangeably by various data types and functions. The third example below provides us with a flavor of how ANY data types can be used.

The following is an example of single and double quotation marks used in string data types:

```
/* Here is an example of a string */
&STRING_FIELD1 = "This is a basic PeopleCode string";
&STRING_FIELD2 = "This is a string that contains a 'single quote'  delimiter
character";
&STRING_FIELD3 = "This string is enclosed within single quotes and contains
a string ""enclosed in double quotes""";
```

Where possible, enclose strings in double quotation marks and represent any embedded strings using single quotes.

Below, we can see examples of numbers in PeopleCode:

```
/* Examples of Numbers in PeopleCode */
&NUMBER_FIELD1 = 12345;
&NUMBER_FIELD2 = 123.45;
&NUMBER_FIELD3 = 0.12345;
&NUMBER_FIELD4 = - 123.45;
```

Let's look at an example of ANY data type:

```
/* Definition of an ANY data type */
Local any &WORK_FIELD;

/* ANY data type being set to a STRING */
&WORK_FIELD = " ";

REM  &Work_Field now becomes a NUMBER;
&WORK_FIELD = &NUMBER_FIELD * 100;

REM This concatenates two strings. &WORK_FIELD is a string again;
&WORK_FIELD = &STRING_FIELD1 | &STRING_FIELD2;

REM What datatype will the following statement return ? ;
&WORK_FIELD = %Date - &MY_BIRTHDATE;
/* If you guessed Number, you are correct. A number expressed as days is the
result. However, the ANY data type can also contain a date.  Below,
&WORK_FIELD is set to the current date;*/
&WORK_FIELD = %Date;
```

12.5   *PEOPLECODE DATA ELEMENTS*

12.5.1   Record field references

As we've already discussed in part 2, records are comprised of fields. How a field is referenced, retrieved, and initialized is of particular importance when the fieldname exists on various records accessible to a PeopleCode program. The syntax of a record field is as follows:

```
[RecordName].FieldName
```

Three components make up a record field name:

RecordName

RecordName is required when the PeopleCode program is in a record field other than the record where the PeopleCode resides. The name can contain from one to fifteen characters. At the database level, PeopleTools prefixes application tables with PS_. Within Application Designer however, the PS_ prefix is not used. When a record is opened or referred to in a panel, the prefix must be omitted. If specified, the presence of the prefix actually results in an 'Invalid record name' error message when used on a panel. The exception is the SQLExec statement that contains embedded SQL statements.

Period separator

The period is used when the record name prefix is required. When a PeopleCode program refers to a field on the same record as the program, the record name prefix is not required and is actually removed by the PeopleCode editor.

Fieldname

Both Fieldname and RecordName are not case sensitive and are converted to UPPERCASE by the PeopleCode editor. A fieldname can consist of one to eighteen characters and can include special characters such as @, _, $ and #. When used in field names, some of these special characters such as the # may be platform dependent. The RecordName.FieldName convention becomes more important when using specific functions that require an explicit RecordName.FieldName definition. Functions that use RecordName.FieldName are described throughout this book and in appendix E. More specific examples include:

```
FetchValue
FieldChanged
GetStoredFormat
Gray
Hide
PriorValue
SetCursorPos
SetDefault
SetDefaultAll
SetDefaultNext
SetDefaultPrior
SortScroll
SQLExec
Transfer
Ungray
Unhide
UpdateValue
```

12.5.2 Temporary variables

Temporary variables use the prefix '&' as part of their naming convention. Names can range from one to seventeen characters in length and consist of letters A–Z (a–z), digits 0–9 and special characters @, _, $ and #. Record field names can consist of one to eighteen characters, one more than variables because of the '&' prefix. The following illustrates the use of temporary variables and field names:

```
/* These are PeopleCode temporary Variables */
&STRING_FIELD1 = "This is a string temporary variable";

/* This is a numeric temporary variable */
&NUMBER_FIELD1 = 100;

&SPECIAL_2@10# = "This field name contains special characters";
```

> **TIP**   Although special characters can be included in record field names and variable names, they are not recommended except for the underscore character ('_').

12.5.3 Constants

Within PeopleCode, numeric, string, and Boolean constants are available. Numeric constants may be expressed as any number and can be included in assignments such as

```
&NUMBER_FIELD1 = 12345;
&NUMBER_FIELD2 = 123.45;
&NUMBER_FIELD13 = - 123.45;
&NUMBER_FIELD14 = 0.12345;
&NUMBER_FIELD5 = - 0.12345;
```

String constants are enclosed within single or double quotation marks. To enclose a single quotation as part of a string, we can place double quotation marks around it. Alternatively, we can enclose double quotations within single quotation marks:

```
&STRING1 = "Example of a basic string";
&STRING2 = "This is 'One string within another string'";
&STRING3 = "This is ""Another string within another""";
```

Boolean constants can be represented as True or False.

The following example verifies the Boolean return value issued by a function call:

```
If &RETURN_VALUE = True Then
   SetDefault(MY_PROBLEM_RESOLTN);
   SetDefault(CLOSE_DT);
End-If;
```

An alternative method of verifying a Boolean value is to omit the comparison operator:

```
If &RETURN_VALUE Then
   SetDefault(MY_PROBLEM_RESOLTN);
   SetDefault(CLOSE_DT);
End-If;
```

When &RETURN_VALUE returns False, the statements in the context of If are not executed.

12.5.4   System variables

Unlike temporary variables that can be defined by the developer, system variables are predefined and available within PeopleCode programs to access system information. System variables are prefixed with "%" whenever they are referenced in a program. Information such as date, time, current language, panel name, and additional information can be retrieved through system variables. System variables can be used in place of a constant or as part of an expression when assigning variables. They can also be passed to functions as parameters such as SQL strings passed to the SQLExec function. A list of system variables and descriptions follow.

%BPName	Returns a string containing the name of the Business Process from a worklist entry when accessed from a panel within a worklist. If the current panel group is not accessed from a worklist, an empty string is returned.
%Date	Returns the current date in YYYY-MM-DD format.
%DateTime	Returns the date and time as a Date/Time value in YYYY-MM-DD-HH.MI.SS.SSSSSS format.
%DbName	Returns the name of the current database.
%DbType	Type of database expressed as a string. Some database types include SQLBase, DB2, Oracle, or Microsoft.
%EmployeeId	Returns the employee ID of the operator currently logged on. This can be used to limit access to an employee's own data, but is only effective when the employee ID on the operator security record is populated correctly.
%Import	During Import Manager sessions this variable is returned as True. All other times it is False. This variable can be referenced if we wish to execute PeopleCode during import manager sessions only.
%Language	A character string is returned indicating the operator language preference.
%Market	Returns a string representing the Market property of the current panel group.
%Menu	Returns the current menu name. This uppercase string can be used to process actions based on menu. Specific edit or function calls can be controlled by menu name.
%MessageAgent	Contains a string representing the current message definition name when the current panel is invoked by a message agent routine. An empty string is returned when the panel is not initiated by a message agent routine.

%Mode	When an operator initiates a panel group associated with a menu item, this field will contain the menu action selected. The values can be: • "A" Add • "U" Update • "L" Update All • "C" Correction • "E" Data Entry
%OperatorClass	Returns the primary operator class for the current operator.
%OperatorRowLevelSecurityClass	
	Returns the row-level security class of the current operator. The row-level security class is different from the operator's primary class.
%OperatorId	The ID of the current user logged on. This entry exists on the PSOPRDEFN table.
%Panel	Returns the current panel name.
%PanelGroup	Name of the current panel group. As with %Menu, this variable can be used to control program flow or take specific actions according to the panel group. A panel group contains the panels associated within the group and can be used to identify panels to a PeopleCode program. The difference between %Panel and %Panel-Group is that %Panel identifies only the current panel on which the cursor is focused. Let's assume we have three panels, PANEL_A, PANEL_B, and PANEL_C. They belong to a panel group named PANEL_ABC. If our code reads as if %Panel = Panel.PANEL_B and the cursor is on PANEL_A, the If statement condition returns False. When the intent is to take action during FieldChange events on any of these panels, the code should read if %PanelGroup = PANEL_ABC.
%SQLRows	When using the SQLExec in conjunction with an UPDATE, DELETE, or INSERT operation, the number of rows affected by such a statement is returned in this variable. During the SELECT operation, this variable returns zero when no rows are selected and non-zero if one or more rows are selected. Unlike the other operations, the non-zero value does not indicate the number of rows returned for a SELECT.
%Time	Returns the current time in HH.MI.SS.SSSSSS format.
%WLInstanceID	When accessing a panel from a worklist, this variable contains the name of the worklist instance ID. The variable will contain blanks when the panel is not accessed from a worklist.
%WLName	Contains the name of the worklist. A blank is returned when the current panel is not accessed within a worklist.

The next example is used in the PeopleSoft HRMS application. This example verifies the %PanelGroup variable for the JOB_DATA_HIRE that is used in the new hire process. The example also references the %Mode variable.

```
If %PanelGroup = PANELGROUP.JOB_DATA_HIRE Then
    If %Mode = "A" Then
        FUNCLIB_HR.DEFAULT_SETID = &SETID;
    End-If;
End-If;
```

12.5.5   Global and local variables

Variables can be defined as global or local. By default, all variables are defined as local and do not necessarily need the Local prefix. In release 7 of PeopleTools, a local variable, the variable name, and its contents cease to exist at the conclusion of the PeopleCode event. As with function definitions and declarations, variable declarations must be placed above the main body of a PeopleCode program. A variable declared as ANY (or one that doesn't have an explicit declaration) will have the data type chosen by PeopleCode based on field contents. An ANY data type can store various data types such as String and Number. Some risk exists when a field is used for various data types. A function that requires a number to be passed to it may actually receive a string or date field, which can result in unpredictable errors when a field defined as ANY is passed to a function.

Global variables remain in effect during a PeopleSoft session and maintain their value from one panel group or PeopleCode event to another. The alternative is to pass values using derived/work record fields where possible. Passing and maintaining variables in a derived/work record allows us to share PeopleCode as well as work fields. In the Problem Tracking system, the table MY_DERIVED is an example of a derived/work record. This type record does not exist at the database level as a table. The fields on this type record can be shared across panels. Another useful application for derived/work records is the use of function libraries. (Function libraries will be discussed in chapter 16.) Examples of variable declarations are shown as follows:

```
/* Examples of variable declarations: */
Local string &NAME;
Local number &DEPARTMENT_COUNT;
Global number &TOTAL_COUNT;
Local any &ANY_TYPE;
```

TIP Global variables must be defined in every PeopleCode program that uses the variables. The PeopleSoft recommendation is to use global variables sparingly.

12.6 STATEMENTS AND EXPRESSIONS

This section examines how PeopleCode programs are constructed using various types of statements. PeopleCode statements include code that controls execution flow and can range from a simple If-Then-Else to complex loops. A statement can also be a simple expression. Let's examine statements and expressions and see how they work in unison.

12.6.1 Statements

Statements consist of data assignments, program language constructs, declarations, and subroutine calls.

A semicolon (;) is used to separate PeopleCode statements. The PeopleCode Editor disregards extra blank lines and spaces within the code. When a program is saved to the database, excess spaces or blank lines are removed automatically by the editor. Let's consider some examples of PeopleCode statements:

```
/* This is a comment before a Declare Function Statement */
REM This is another comment before a Declare Function Statement;
/*This is an example of a function declaration statement */
Declare Function My_Schedule_Function PeopleCode MY_DERIVED.MY_USER_ID
FieldFormula;

&WORK_FIELD = "This is an example of a string assignment statement";

REM  This is a number assignment based on an "expression";
&RESULT_FIELD = &NUMBER_OF_ITEMS * &PRICE_PER_ITEM;

/* This is a function return statement */
&WORKSHEET_FIELD = CreateObject("Excel.Sheet");
```

Assignment statements, as represented by &WORK_FIELD above are the most basic types of statements within PeopleCode.

12.6.2   Control statements

Another type of PeopleCode statement is a control statement. A control statement is involved in the execution flow of a PeopleCode program and includes the following:

- If-Then-Else
- Evaluate
- For
- Loops with condition statements (Repeat, While)

If-Then-Else

When we write a PeopleCode program or any program for that matter, do we simply enter a bunch of statements and assume the program will figure it all out? If your answer to this is yes, then you've been watching too much science fiction (for the time being). Controlling the execution flow of a PeopleCode program is accomplished using branching statements, For loops and conditional loops. Basic examples of branching are illustrated below, using the If-Then-Else statement. The statement compares two strings and returns a message:

```
if &Text1 <> &Text2 then
   WinMessage ("Strings are not not the same");
 else
   WinMessage ("Strings, match!");
 end-if;
```

If-Then-Else construct statements are a key piece of program code that you will use often. The expression following the If keyword is evaluated as a logical True or False. If the evaluated expression is True (non-zero), PeopleCode executes all the statements following then until an Else or End-If statement is encountered. These statements may also contain their own If-Then-Else statements. When the expression evaluated is False, the statements following the Else clause are executed. An End-if is required for every If statement.

The Else statement is not always required for an If statement. Else is specified when it is necessary to perform additional actions when an If condition is not satisfied.

The following is another example of an If-Then-Else statement used to identify the value of the Problem Status field:

```
If MY_PROBLEM_STATUS = "1" Then
   WinMessage("This incident is in an initiated status");
Else
   WinMessage("This incident is not in an initiated status");
End-If;
```

A nested If-Then-Else statement contains more than one If statement and may also contain more than one Else statement. The following is an example of nested If statements. Note, that for every If statement there is a corresponding End-If:

```
If MY_PROBLEM_STATUS = "1" Then
   WinMessage("This incident is in an initiated status");
Else
   If MY_PROBLEM_STATUS = "2" Then
      WinMessage("This incident has been assigned");
   Else
      If MY_PROBLEM_STATUS = "3" Then
         WinMessage("This incident is in progress");
      End-If;
   End-If;
End-If;
```

In the example below each If statement has a corresponding End-If. The placing of an End-If is important, because it defines the scope of an If statement:

```
If MY_PROBLEM_STATUS = "1" Then
   If MY_USER_ID = " " Then
      WinMessage("This incident is in an initiated status, but has no
assigned user");
   Else
      If MY_PROBLEM_STATUS = "2" Then
         WinMessage("This incident has been assigned");
      Else
         If MY_PROBLEM_STATUS = "3" Then
            WinMessage("This incident is in progress");
         End-If;
      End-If;
   End-If;
End-If;
```

The example above appears intact, but upon closer examination we see that the statements checking for a value of "2" or "3" will never be executed because the code is interpreted as follows:

If MY_PROBLEM_STATUS is "1" and MY_USER_ID is blank, send a message, otherwise, if MY_PROBLEM_STATUS is "2", send a message. As you can see, the second message, based on a value of "2" will never be sent because it is also based on the field MY_PROBLEM_STATUS having a value of "1". Because these two conditions can never co-exist (except in science fiction), the PeopleCode statements require some adjustment. The corrected code is shown below:

```
If MY_PROBLEM_STATUS = "1" Then
   If MY_USER_ID = "" Then
      WinMessage("This incident is in an initiated status, but has no
assigned user");
   End-If;
Else
   If MY_PROBLEM_STATUS = "2" Then
      WinMessage("This incident has been assigned");
   Else
      If MY_PROBLEM_STATUS = "3" Then
         WinMessage("This incident is in progress");
      End-If;
   End-If;
End-If;
```

TIP   String comparisons are always case-sensitive.

Evaluate

Another form of branching is done using the Evaluate statement. This statement can be used when multiple conditions exist. The syntax of the Evaluate statement can be written as follows:

```
Evaluate Expression
      When Comparison
         [statements]
         Break
      When Comparison
         [more statements]
         Break
      When-Other [Optional]
End-Evaluate;
```

The Evaluate statement, in conjunction with When, compares an expression using relational operators in a series of When clauses. In a fashion similar to If-Then-Else statements, when the result of the comparison is True, the statements in the When clause are executed. Once these statements are completed, the operation moves on to evaluate the comparison in a subsequent When clause. In a nutshell, the statements in which the When comparison results in a True condition are executed. The optional When-Other clause is executed after any previous When comparisons in the Evaluate statement are False. An Evaluate statement can be exited by using the Break statement. A good practice is to include the Break statement when the intent is to prevent subsequent When statements from executing. The following illustrates the use of the Evaluate statement and sends a message based on the contents of the %Language system variable.

```
Evaluate %Language
When = "ENG"
   &MESSAGE = "We are using English";
When = "ESP"
   &MESSAGE = "We are using Spanish";
When = "FRA"
   &MESSAGE = "We are using French";
When = "GER"
   &MESSAGE = "We are using German";
When = "INE"
   &MESSAGE = "We are using International English";
When-Other
   &MESSAGE = "We are using another language";
End-Evaluate;
```

The statements used above can be rewritten using nested If statements (such as those below). Notice the additional statements required to accomplish the same task using the Evaluate statement.

```
If %Language = "ENG" Then
   &MESSAGE = "We are using English";
Else
   If %Language = "ESP" Then
      &MESSAGE = "We are using Spanish";
   Else
      If %Language = "FRA" Then
         &MESSAGE = "We are using French";
      Else
         If %Language = "GER" Then
            &MESSAGE = "We are using German";
         Else
            If %Language = "INE" Then
               &MESSAGE = "We are using International English";
            Else
               &MESSAGE = "We are using another language";
            End-If;
         End-If;
      End-If;
   End-If;
End-If;
```

`Evaluate` statements may behave differently in other programming languages. The following example contains a small piece of code. In the example, the variable &A is evaluated. Assuming the value of &A is 1 at the time of the `Evaluate` statement, the value is then changed to 2. At the time PeopleCode executes the second `When` statement, which compares the value &A to 2, the original value of &A is evaluated. We can therefore state that the results of each `When` statement are based on the condition in place at the time of the `Evaluate`.

```
Evaluate &A
When = 1
&A = 2;
When = 2
&A = 3;
End-Evaluate;
```

SQR users may be aware that `Evaluate` statements work differently. If the field being evaluated has its value changed within the `When` statement, it is possible that the newly changed value will impact subsequent `When` statements because the new value is evaluated in each `When` statement. In SQR, the second `When` statement would have been executed assuming the initial value is "1" and then is changed to "2". A good practice to avoid these pitfalls is to use the `Break` statement. While this does not occur within PeopleCode, we can rewrite the `Evaluate` statement below to develop good programming habits:

```
Evaluate &A
When = 1
   &A = 2;
   Break;
When = 2
   &A = 3;
   Break;
End-Evaluate;
```

Because the `Break` statement transfers control to the `End-Evaluate`, any remaining `When` statements are bypassed, which also improves performance.

For

`For` can be a useful statement when the need to execute statements repetitively becomes necessary. The statement works in conjunction with an initial setting of a variable that is subsequently incremented by a value—after the statements in the scope loop are executed. The format of the `For` statement is as follows:

```
For count = expression1 to expression2
      [Step i];
      PeopleCode Statements
    End-For;
```

The statements in the loop are continuously executed until `expression2` is `true`. `Step` represents the increment value that is added to the count field each time the loop is executed. When Step is omitted, the default increment is 1. When we wish to decrement by 1 or count backwards, use `Step -1` as `expression2`.

Loops can be nested—that is, they can contain other `For` or `While` loops as well as other types of PeopleCode statements. The `Break` statement terminates the current active loop. When the current loop is part of a nested loop, any higher level loops are returned following the `Break` statement. The higher level loops can be subsequently terminated with a `Break` statement or when the value of count is equal to `expression2`. If no higher level loop exists, processing continues with the statement following the end of the loop.

The following is an example of a `For` loop which contains an update to a field on a scroll area. The loop begins on row number one and continues until all the number of active rows in the scroll are processed. The scroll function `ActiveRowCount` is used to obtain the number of active rows. The variable `&I` is incremented by 1 based on the rules of the `For` statement.

```
For &I = 1 To ActiveRowCount(RECORD.MY_LOCATIONS);
   UpdateValue(MY_LOCATIONS.EFFDT, &I, &EFFDT);
End-For;
```

The next example combines the decrement feature with an `If` statement. The loop begins with the highest active row and is processed from highest to lowest using the `Step -1` statement.

```
If %Panel = "MY_LOCATIONS" Then
   For &I = ActiveRowCount(RECORD.MY_LOCATIONS) To 1 Step - 1;
      DeleteRow(RECORD.MY_LOCATIONS, &I);
   End-For;
End-If;
```

Repeat

The `Repeat` statement initiates a loop and executes the statements within the scope of the loop until the PeopleCode expression is `True`. These statements can be other loops or other PeopleCode statements and function calls. In a manner similar to loop statements such as `For` and `While`, a `Break` statement within a `Repeat` loop returns control to the next higher level loop. When the current loop is not part of a higher level loop, processing continues with the statement following the end of the loop.

The format of the `Repeat` statement is as follows:

```
Repeat
     [Statement List]
Until
     [expression]
```

The example below illustrates the use of Repeat to obtain the effective date and remove the row from a scroll area. The function ActiveRowCount is used to obtain the number of rows the loop will process. The FetchValue function obtains the effective date, and the subsequent RowFlush removes the row from the scroll area.

```
&I = 0;
/* Obtain number of active rows */
&ROW_COUNT = ActiveRowCount(RECORD.MY_LOCATIONS);
Repeat
    &I = &I + 1;
    &EFFDT = FetchValue(EFFDT, &I);
    If &EFFDT < %Date Then
        RowFlush(RECORD.MY_LOCATIONS, &I);
    End-If;
Until &I = &ROW_COUNT;
```

TIP   The Break statement—not an If statement—terminates the loop.

While

The While control statement initiates a loop and is repeated until the PeopleCode expression is False. This can be somewhat misleading because many loop statements terminate when the condition is True. The While statement, however, terminates when the condition is False.

And you thought this was going to be another clone of the Repeat and For statements! In many aspects the statements are the same, including the execution of the statements within the scope of the loop. These statements can be other loops or other PeopleCode statements and function calls. As with other loop statements, a Break within a loop returns control to the next higher level loop or processing continues with the statement following the end of the loop. The difference and inherent danger particularly with the While statement is the potential for a runaway loop. Because the statement is terminated as a result of a False condition, improper wording often leads to more runaway loops with the While statement than with other loop statements.

The format of the While control statement is:

```
While
    [PeopleSoft expression]
    [Statement List]
End-While;
```

Following is an example of a While statement that displays a message and numeric data type variable several times.

```
&MAX_LOOP = 0;
While &MAX_LOOP < 5
```

```
    WinMessage("This is pass number " | &MAX_LOOP);
    &MAX_LOOP = &MAX_LOOP + 1;
End-While;
```

The following is an example of what NOT to do when using the `While` statement. The example results in a runaway loop, because in this sample the value of &MAX_LOOP is always going to be greater than zero.

```
&MAX_LOOP = 1;
While &MAX_LOOP > 0
    WinMessage("This is pass number " | &MAX_LOOP);
    &MAX_LOOP = &MAX_LOOP + 1;
End-While;
```

12.6.3   Expressions

PeopleCode expressions

Basic PeopleCode expressions can be written as:

```
        &WORK_FIELD = Expression;
```

In the example, the result of the expression to the right is placed into a variable named &WORK_FIELD. The target of an expression is either a variable or a record field. In their most basic form, expressions are characterized by one or more data elements on either side of the assignment operator. The assignment operation in the example below is used to initialize the record field MY_USER_ID with the current operator ID.

```
MY_USER_ID = %OperatorId;
```

Expressions can combine any of the following:

- constants
- temporary variables
- system variables
- record fields
- other expressions
- function parameters

Simple expressions can be combined into compound expressions using math operators:

```
&X = (&A + &B) * ((&D - &C) / &E);
```

In PeopleCode the equal sign (=) has a dual purpose. It behaves as an assignment operator, in the preceding example or as a comparison operator. (Remember our example that combined the decrement feature with an `If` statement.) On one line, the equal sign is used as a comparison operator, and on the following line, as an assignment operator. The context of the equal sign is dependent on how a particular expression is used and the PeopleCode statements that contain the expression. A simple assignment operation contains a variable to the left and another variable, constant or literal, to the right. A comparison operation may use a statement such as If, which implies that the equal sign is being used as a comparison operator.

Putting PeopleCode expressions to work

Now that we have a basic understanding of PeopleCode, we can begin to put together simple statements and expressions using strings, dates, and operators for statements using comparison, math, and Boolean expressions.

The combining of two or more strings can be accomplished using the vertical bar symbol (|) which acts as a concatenation operator. Operands supplied to the concatenation operator are automatically converted to strings. An example of string concatenation is illustrated below:

```
&TEXT_MESSAGE = "Hello " | %OperatorId | "The current time is " | (%Time);
WinMessage(&TEXT_MESSAGE);
```

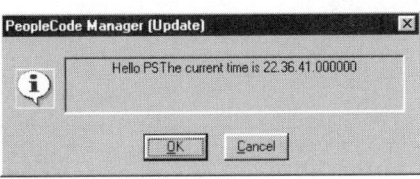

Figure 12.4   Contents of concatenated string

In the example, we see that the statement is a string assignment. Two string literal types and two system variable types exist here. The expression on the right of the equal sign is a concatenation expression. The statement is terminated with a semi-colon.

The string variable &TEXT_MESSAGE contains the concatenation results displayed in the message in figure 12.4.

NOTE   All data types used in concatenation expressions are converted to string.

Expressions using Date/Time values can be constructed to perform date arithmetic. Dates/Time values can be added or subtracted resulting in a number. The result is a value expressed as number of days. When working with time variables, the number result is a value expressed in seconds. Constants, variables, and record fields containing numbers can be added to Date/Time values. The resulting number will be days or seconds.

As an example, to determine the number of elapsed days since the initial reporting of a problem in the Problem Tracking system, we could construct the statement shown below.

```
&DAYS_ELAPSED = (%Date - MY_PROBLEM_TRKG.INCIDENT_DT);
```

Here, the variable &DAYS_ELAPSED contains a number that represents the difference between the system variable %Date and the date value contained in MY_PROBLEM_TRKG.INCIDENT_DT.

Comparison operators are used when we wish to compare two expressions containing the same data type. A Boolean value is returned as a result of the comparison. Comparison operators are represented by the following symbols:

=	equal
<>	not equal
>	greater than
<	less than
>=	greater than or equal to
<=	less than or equal to

Let's now take a look at some comparison operators. When comparing strings, comparisons are always case-sensitive. The following compares two strings that contain the same words. Do you know what message is displayed?

```
&TEXT1 = "TODAY IS A FINE DAY";
&TEXT2 = "Today is a fine day";
If &TEXT1 <> &TEXT2 Then
   WinMessage("Strings are not not the same");
Else
   WinMessage("Strings, match!");
End-If;
```

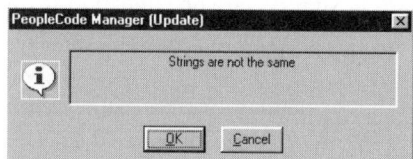

Figure 12.5   Result of string comparison

Figure 12.5 indicates that although the strings contain the same words, one string is uppercase and the other string is mixed case. The comparison results in a `False` condition when both strings are compared. Math Operators are your normal everyday arithmetic operators. The following represents the arithmetic operators used in PeopleCode:

+	addition
-	subtraction
*	multiplication
/	division
**	exponential

In PeopleCode, math operations are performed within a hierarchy as illustrated. The hierarchy of operations is specified explicitly. When used in an operation, parentheses override the hierarchy.

Highest

Unary operator	+ B or - C
Exponeniate	(A ** B)
Multiply, Divide	(A * B / C)
Add, Subtract	(A + B - C)
Relational, sign, conditions	(A > B)
Logical NOT	NOT (A > B)
Logical AND	(A AND B)

Lowest

Logical OR	(A OR B)	
(A * B * C)	[Same as]	(A * B) * C
(A + B - C ** D)	[Same as]	(A + B) - (C ** D)

TIP   Operations having equal hierarchy are evaluated from left to right

---

Boolean operators are formed by the logical operators And, Or, and Not. Examples of Boolean operators are shown below. As with mathematical operators, parentheses can be used to override precedence.

```
/* Example of Boolean operators and expected results */
If &A > &C And
     &B > &A Or
     &C < &B Then
   &MESSAGE = "This is an example of Boolean operators and is TRUE when the
value of &A is greater than &C  and the value of &B is greater than &A Or
the value of &C is less than &B.  Our example can be rewritten with paren-
theses";
End-If;

If (&A > &C And
     &B > &A) Or
     &C < &B Then
   &MESSAGE = "This example is TRUE when the value of &A is greater than &C
AND the value of &B is greater than &A. The example is also TRUE if the
value of &C is less than &B ";
End-If;
```

12.7 PEOPLECODE TOOLS TABLES

After inserting or modifying PeopleCode statements, it is necessary to save the code. When the save button is pressed, the related PeopleCode system tables that are updated include:

PSPCMNAME is the PeopleCode reference table. It contains the internal name assigned by PeopleTools and all other record fields referred from a PeopleCode event. As an example, the panel MY_PROBLEM_TRKG contains data elements from the record MY_PROJECT_TBL. When a reference is made to fields on MY_PROJECT_TBL from a PeopleCode program which resides on the MY_PROBLEM_TRKG record, a row exists for each field referred to on MY_PROJECT_TBL, from PeopleCode in MY_PROBLEM_TRKG. Figure 12.6 contains a query of the PSPCMNAME table contents for MY_PROBLEM_TRKG.MY_USER_ID. We see that PCM105665 is the internal name, ❶ assigned by the system to an event for the field MY_USER_ID.

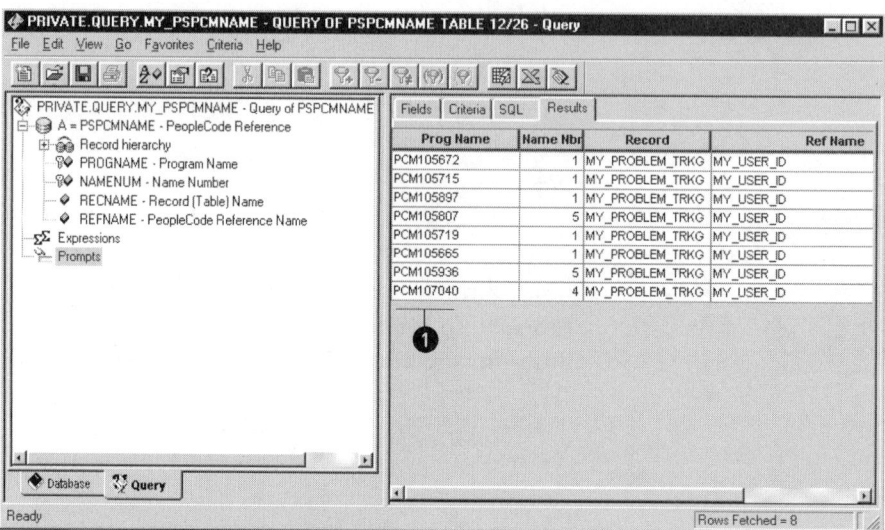

Figure 12.6   Contents of PSPCMNAME

PSPCMPROG contains the internal PeopleCode name and Date/Time stamp of the last update including the user ID. The table also contains the actual PeopleCode program text.

PSPROGNAME contains the internal PeopleCode name, fieldname and record name. Figure 12.7 contains the table entries for internal program name PCM105665.

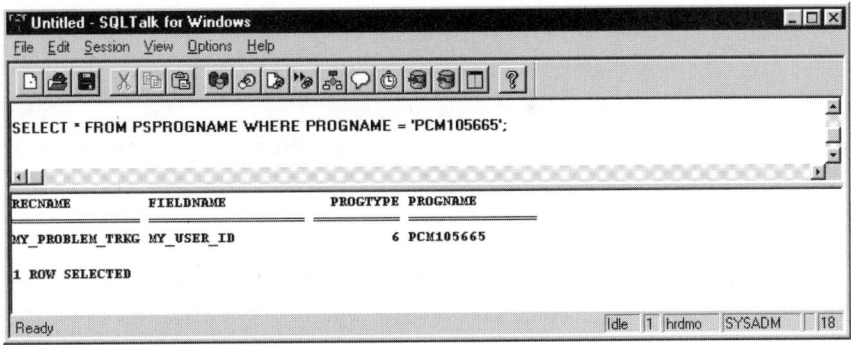

Figure 12.7   Contents of PSPROGNAME

PSRECFIELD contains records and their associated field definitions. One important field on this table is PROGCOUNT which contains the number of events for a record field that contains PeopleCode. A SQL SELECT statement (figure 12.8) for the record field MY_PROBLEM_TRKG.MY_USER_ID indicates a PROGCOUNT value of 4, which identifies PeopleCode existing in several events for the record field.

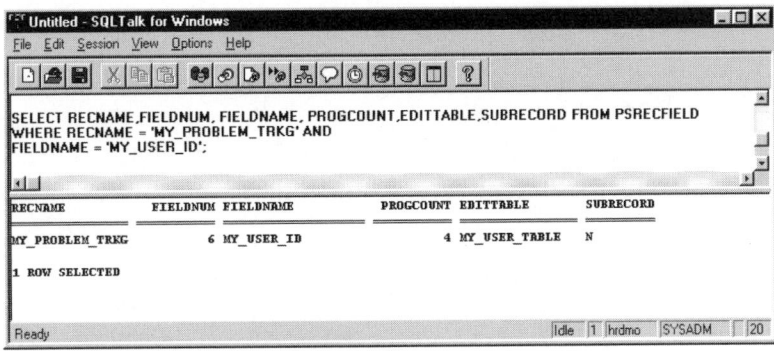

Figure 12.8   Contents of PSRECFIELD

1 The PeopleCode editor provides us with a facility to insert and maintain PeopleCode statements.

2 PeopleCode comments allow for internal code documentation.

3 PeopleCode handles various data types such as String, Numeric, Date, Time, and Object. A Boolean data type can only have a `True` or `False` value.

4 Record Field naming standards enable the PeopleCode program to access the contents of fields. The [RecordName].FieldName format is used to access fields in records other than the record in which the PeopleCode resides.

5 System variables are available to PeopleCode programs to access system information such as current date, database type, operator ID, and operator security class.

6 PeopleCode recognizes global and local variables. Global variables remain in effect during a PeopleSoft panel session but use more overhead. Local variables only exist during the PeopleCode event.

7 Statements include data assignments, declarations, and subroutine calls. Expressions can be constants, variables, record fields, or values passed to functions.

8 PeopleCode execution flow can be handled using `If-Then-Else`, `Evaluate`, `For`, `Repeat`, and `While` statements.

C H A P T E R   1 3

PeopleCode & the Application Processor

The Application Processor is the system tool responsible for carrying out tasks such as displaying selected panels and panel groups, invoking PeopleCode at various events and controlling updates to database records. Having a good understanding of how the Application Processor interacts with PeopleCode is important when designing an application or determining where to insert custom code.

13.1   THE APPLICATION PROCESSOR

Imagine, if you will, a busy intersection with no traffic lights at the height of rush hour on the Friday afternoon of a long holiday weekend. No traffic lights or traffic officer! This is a scene of chaos if ever there were one.

When an end user sits in front of his/her terminal during a PeopleSoft session, there can be much confusion from the perspective of the operating system and PeopleTools environment. All those mouse clicks and menu selections have to be controlled and guided somehow. The PeopleTools Application Processor performs just such a function. When the end user requests information or wishes to update information, the panels, menus and panel groups are controlled by... you guessed it, the Application Processor! The Application Processor also interacts with PeopleCode programs, and this interaction is the cornerstone of PeopleCode within the PeopleTools environment. During the course of an online request, events are triggered which may result in the execution of PeopleCode programs tied to such events.

PeopleCode programs are tied to an event and either a record (record PeopleCode) or a menu item (menu PeopleCode). If, during the course of a work session, an event is triggered that is tied to PeopleCode, the statements within that event are executed. The Application Processor ensures that each event is allowed its fair share of memory and an "at bat" in the event line-up. Menu PeopleCode operates when menu items are selected. Record PeopleCode operates on data rows associated with record objects and is normally triggered during events in an online session.

PeopleCode events are utilized during the phases of an online session. Chapter 9 discussed The Application Processor and how it interacts within the following stages:

- search processing
- data retrieval
- panel group display
- data entry or inquiry

During these stages, PeopleCode programs can be inserted to enhance an application or perform required tasks that cannot be easily accomplished using basic Application Designer panel functionality. Knowing where to insert code is just as important as knowing how to write code. Events exist which may not be triggered based on specific actions. Some events are based on actions that occur before a panel group is displayed. These events are related to search processing, interpretation of search key values, and default processing. When new data are added, certain events and actions occur that do not occur when existing data are displayed for update. Whether data are being added or displayed for update, PeopleCode can be inserted into these events to establish default values or control the look and feel of menus, panels, and scroll areas as well as to submit batch processes when necessary.

13.2 SEARCH PROCESSING

When a menu item is selected, the Application Processor interacts with PeopleCode events based on the menu action requested. Where PeopleCode is placed is important because some events do not permit specific actions. For example, a SQLExec SELECT statement that enables the execution of SQL statements against a database table can be placed in any event. SQLExec statements containing database updates, however, are only allowed during events such as SavePreChg, WorkFlow, and SavePostChg. Similarly, message functions containing more than one button are not allowed during "Think Time" PeopleCode events. Think Time PeopleCode events are actions that interrupt processing and wait for a user reply to a message box containing more than one push button. A message box with multiple buttons can impact the course of a program's flow.

13.2.1 Menu item is chosen

A panel session is commonly initiated with the selection of an item from a menu. As discussed in part 2, menu actions can be Add, Update/Display, Update/Display All, or Correction.

When a menu item is selected, the Application Processor loads into its memory buffers the panel group definition and search records associated with the selected menu item. Included in these objects are the records and events containing People-Code associated with the Application Processor's flow of execution. Within these events, the Application Processor retrieves the necessary database keys for the records contained in the panel group. Records that make up the panels in a panel group are retrieved and presented to the end user on one or multiple panels.

13.2.2 Search processing—Add mode

Panel group startup process and associated PeopleCode events are triggered, depending upon the menu action selected. We have developed a small application which links security operator classes and office locations. This application is used to link employees to the operator class/location combination, primarily for reporting purposes. Let's assume the menu contains two actions, Add and Update/Display. After selecting Add from a menu, an end-user is presented with an Add dialog box. Fields defined as search keys in the search record are assembled on the input dialog box. In Add mode, however, fields defined as alternate search keys in the search record do not appear on the input dialog box. To a user, an Add dialog box is automatically displayed; but to the Application Processor and any associated PeopleCode, it's another Friday afternoon on the freeway!

Before an Add dialog box is displayed several PeopleCode events occur. The events are

- FieldDefault
- FieldFormula

- RowInit
- SearchInit

FieldDefault

The event is triggered before the panel is displayed to the user. As discussed in part 2, field values can be defaulted in the Application Designer and can also be defaulted from the `FieldDefault` event. The Application Processor examines the fields in a panel group and, if the field is blank (character field) or zero (numeric field), the Application Processor sets the field to any value specified in the Application Designer Record Field Properties. When no default value is specified, any `FieldDefault` PeopleCode associated with the field is executed. It is important to note that, if a field has been assigned a default value in the Record Field Properties, and we also happen to include a neat little piece of `FieldDefault` PeopleCode, the Application Processor determines if the field is blank or zero before any `FieldDefault` program execution. Because the default value from the record definition already filled the field, the Application Processor does not execute the `FieldDefault` PeopleCode.

`FieldDefault` is an iterative event that constantly checks for blank (character field) or zero (numeric field) in the panel group. When a field does not have a default value in its Record Field Properties and does not have a value as a result of data entry or some other PeopleCode event, the `FieldDefault` event executes as a result of another event occurring. The other events can include fields on a panel. Figure 13.1 is an example of `FieldDefault` PeopleCode used in the Problem Tracking application. Note that more than one field can be defaulted. This enables us to consolidate code rather than spreading it across fields.

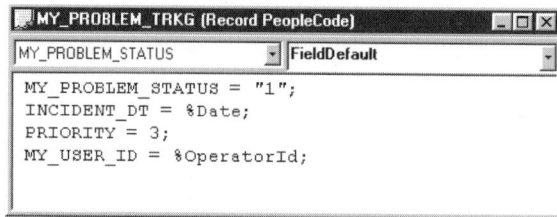

**Figure 13.1
Example of FieldDefault
PeopleCode**

FieldFormula

Each time an event is triggered by the Application Processor, the `FieldFormula` event is also triggered. As a result, the PeopleCode contained in `FieldFormula` is executed in between the execution of other events. Any PeopleCode contained in the `FieldFormula` event of a panel field is executed regardless of the field in which the PeopleCode resides. Due to its high performance overhead and potential system degradation, the use of `FieldFormula` is used primarily in function libraries where stored PeopleCode can be shared across many records and varying panel groups.

RowInit

`RowInit` PeopleCode can be used to control the initial appearance of a field or panel group control. The event is triggered each time the Application Processor encounters a row of data before the panel is displayed. `RowInit` PeopleCode is executed on all fields and rows in the panel buffer. The operator class/location contains two panels that use a common derived/work record. PeopleCode is inserted into the `RowInit` event of the derived/work record to display the number of rows in a scroll area. Because the code operates on two different panels and is contained in the same Record.Field, the code uses an `If` conditional statement (discussed in chapter 12). This code (figure 13.2) will work in `Add` as well as `Update/Display` modes.

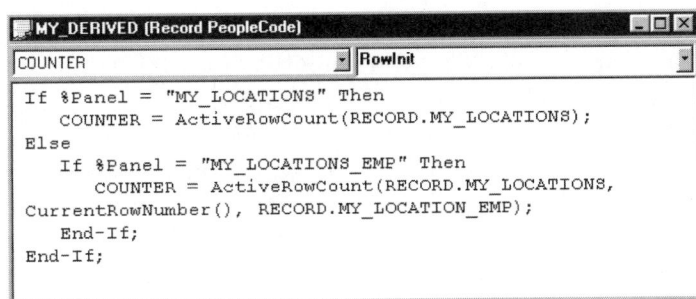

Figure 13.2
Shared RowInit
PeopleCode for
two panels

SearchInit

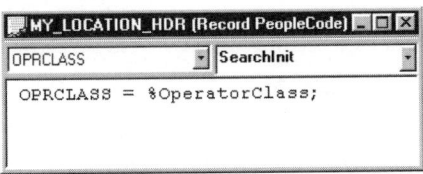

Figure 13.3   SearchInit PeopleCode

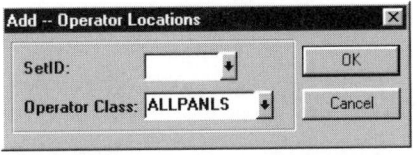

Figure 13.4   Add mode dialog box

In `Add` mode, the SearchInit event is triggered prior to display of the `Add` dialog. It enables the developer to prepopulate search fields. Under certain circumstances it may be necessary to populate a search dialog based on the action mode. This can be accomplished using the `%Mode` system variable discussed in chapter 12.

In the operator class/location example, the `%OperatorClass` system variable can be used to prepopulate the input dialog box. The `SearchInit` code returns the primary operator class for the current operator. The `Add` dialog is populated with this value.

However, the user still has the option of modifying the operator class before pressing OK. The `SearchInit` PeopleCode and subsequent `Add` dialog box are illustrated in figures 13.3 and 13.4 respectively.

| TIP | SearchInit PeopleCode is only executed for search key fields. Any SearchInit PeopleCode attached to a non-search key field is ignored. |

In the operator class/locations, SETID is an identifier that is five characters in length and Operator Class is eight characters. For this application, SETID and Operator Class are basic components required during initialization of the panel and are used to kick off the related Application Processor events. The events executed following the display and subsequent data entry into an Add dialog box are as follows:

- FieldEdit
- FieldChange
- SaveEdit
- SearchSave

FieldEdit

One of the most commonly used PeopleCode events is FieldEdit. Typical FieldEdit code includes edits such as date verification, hide/unhide of fields, and message displays to the operator when necessary. Figure 13.5 is an example of FieldEdit PeopleCode (applied to Problem Tracking) which generates an error message when the incident close date (CLOSE_DT) contains a date value prior to the incident date (INCIDENT_DT). FieldEdit is triggered when the user edits a field then tabs out or clicks on another field, edits a field and, without tabbing out, attempts to save the panel, changes the condition of a radio button, or clicks on a command push button.

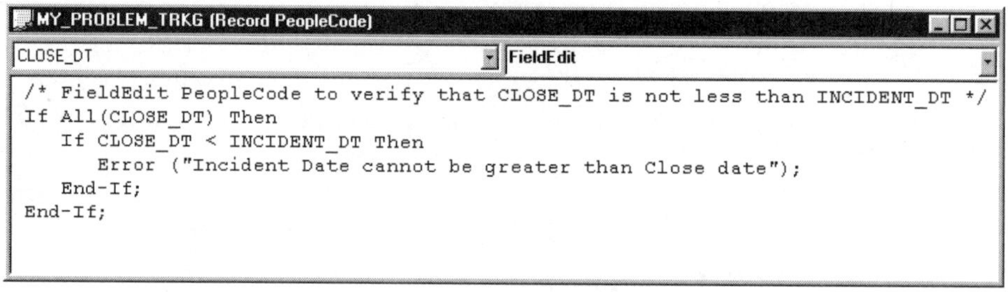

```
MY_PROBLEM_TRKG (Record PeopleCode)                                    _ □ ×
CLOSE_DT                                 ▼  FieldEdit                          ▼
/* FieldEdit PeopleCode to verify that CLOSE_DT is not less than INCIDENT_DT */
If All(CLOSE_DT) Then
   If CLOSE_DT < INCIDENT_DT Then
      Error ("Incident Date cannot be greater than Close date");
   End-If;
End-If;
```

Figure 13.5   FieldEdit PeopleCode

When PeopleCode is added to validate fields, we can use the Error or Warning statement to display a message. Both statements highlight the field in red. The Error statement does not permit entering data into another field or attempting to save the changes after an error message has been displayed. The Warning statement notifies the user with a message but permits work to continue. Any PeopleCode in `FieldEdit` is only triggered following Application Processor edits that include data type/format checking, prompt table verification, or Yes/No and translate table edits.

When the `FieldEdit` event is triggered from an `Add` dialog box, only the search fields that appear in the Add dialog box will have any associated `FieldEdit` PeopleCode executed. `FieldEdit` PeopleCode for non-search key fields which appear on a panel is executed after the panel is displayed and the `FieldEdit` actions take place.

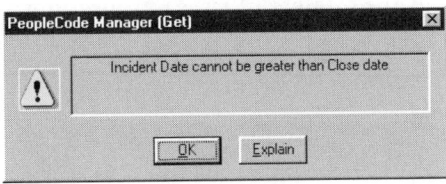

An error message similar to the one displayed in figure 13.6 prevents the panel or panel group from being saved. In the example, if an incident close date less than the incident date is entered, the `Field-Edit` event is triggered, regardless of whether or not we tab out of the field. When an error message is displayed, the choices available to the user are to correct the error or cancel the panel.

Figure 13.6 Error Message generated during FieldEdit

The example in figure 13.5 verifies that CLOSE_DT has a value before performing additional edits. This is accomplished using the `All` PeopleCode function.

FieldChange

The `FieldChange` event follows `FieldEdit` and occurs after the contents of a field have been modified and `FieldEdit` PeopleCode has been accepted. `Field-Change` is available to all modes (`Add`, `Update/Display`,`Correction`, `Data Entry`). As the name suggests, the event is triggered when a field on a panel is changed. After `FieldEdit`, the Application Processor then writes the changed field to the panel buffer and triggers the `FieldChange` event. PeopleCode in this event is commonly used to recalculate field values on a panel or to change the appearance of fields, buttons, or other controls on a panel.

SaveEdit

`SaveEdit` is another important event. After an Add dialog box is filled, and all edits have occurred for the search fields entered, any `SaveEdit` PeopleCode related only to the search fields is executed.

Because `SaveEdit` is used in all modes, an additional description will be presented in the section Data Entry or Inquiry.

SearchSave

PeopleCode in this event is executed for search key fields on a dialog (Add, Search and Data Entry dialogs). While `SearchInit` enables us to control processing before search keys are populated, `SearchSave` is used after the search keys are populated and the user has clicked OK. If we want to ensure that the user enters at least one value into a search field, we can do so with PeopleCode in this event. Figure 13.7 is an example of code used to require at least one key field. A partial key value is acceptable because it can be used to limit the number of rows returned in tables that contain large amounts of data.

Figure 13.7   SearchSave code to require at least one search key

13.3   DATA RETRIEVAL

13.3.1   Search processing—Update mode

Choosing `Update/Display` from a menu generates a search dialog box. The search fields displayed are those defined as list box items in Application Designer. Before the Search Dialog box is displayed, the Application Processor triggers the following events:

- `SearchInit`
- `SearchSave`
- `RowSelect`

SearchInit

PeopleCode behaves the same regardless of mode. Therefore, it is important to know when and under what circumstances the code will be executed. Because `SearchInit` PeopleCode can be executed from `Add` as well as `Update/Display`, a common practice is to reference the `%Mode` system variable. A search dialog for the operator class/location panels is illustrated by figure 13.8.

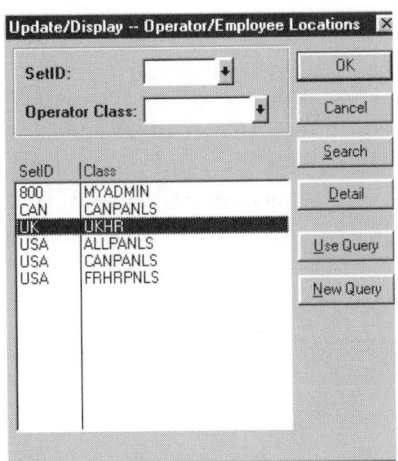

SetID	Class
800	MYADMIN
CAN	CANPANLS
UK	UKHR
USA	ALLPANLS
USA	CANPANLS
USA	FRHRPNLS

Figure 13.8   Search Dialog—Update mode

SearchSave

`SearchSave` is used after the search keys are populated and the user has clicked OK. The event behaves the same as in `Add` mode following the display and subsequent data entry into a dialog box.

RowSelect

This event occurs at the start of the Panel Build process when data are read into the panel group. `RowSelect` PeopleCode can be used to prevent the Application Processor from loading data, based on specific criteria. PeopleCode can also be used to stop the Application Processor from loading further rows of data. Without `RowSelect` PeopleCode, the Application Processor inserts data into the panel group when the database record key matches the designated search key.

How do we stop at a certain row or prevent more rows from being loaded once a certain condition has been met? In earlier releases of PeopleCode, the `Warning` and `Error` statements could have been used. Placing these statements in the `RowSelect` event has the effect of rejecting the row before it is displayed. Although not recommended, these statements can still be used. We can now, however, code a `DiscardRow` or a `StopFetching` function statement to achieve these tasks. The `DiscardRow` skips the current row of data and processing continues with any subsequent rows. Using the `StopFetching` function enables the Application Processor to select the current row of data and terminate reading any subsequent rows.

Here's a question: Would you code a `RowSelect` event with the knowledge that users may be loading many rows onto their clients? And, more importantly, what if the client is on the other side of the planet from the database server? Take note: `DiscardRow` or `StopFetching` discards rows or stops the selection process after rows have been accepted by the Application Processor. As a result, some overhead exists, as does the potential for inefficient coding with the implementation of `RowSelect` using these two functions. A small application may work well with these statements. However, a heavily used application would fare better with record views and effective dated tables where historical data could be separated before getting to the client.

In our application linking operator classes to office locations, we need to remove any employees who have an `EMPLID` starting with `'L'`. This process can be accomplished by inserting the `DiscardRow` function into the `RowSelect` event (figure 13.9). Because the operator class/location panel is not a heavily used application, the concern over inefficient code is not as important as in some heavily used applications.

During the panel group build phase, Update action modes incorporate some events used during Add. The Application Processor can either add data to the panel group or retrieve data from database tables. Based on panel display control fields and related display fields, the Application Processor determines when to retrieve data from other records. As discussed in chapter 9, when building panels, the records can be SQL tables, SQL views, or derived/work records.

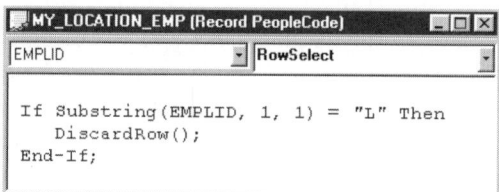

Figure 13.9
Using DiscardRow in RowSelect

During the data retrieval stage, there is little PeopleCode involvement. The Application Processor constructs SQL statements based on search key values provided previously, records defined as related display, and, more importantly, the mode in which the Application Processor is operating. During Add mode, less data are retrieved from the database than in modes such as Update/Display and Correction. After the Application Processor has retrieved the data necessary, it is ready to go into the panel group display stage.

13.4 PANEL GROUP DISPLAY

During Panel Group display, the following PeopleCode events are executed:

- FieldDefault (Iterative)
- RowInit

The previous section, "Search processing—Add mode" (13.2.2) covers FieldDefault and FieldFormula events. These events are categoried as Default processing. "Search processing—Add mode" also discusses RowInit in depth.

At this juncture, the Application Processor has selected (and possibly removed) records using DiscardRow in the RowSelect. The RowInit event has also occurred for the selected rows. The panel is now ready to be presented to the user. After the panel group is displayed, the Application Processor exits from the freeway and into a rest area where it waits for operator actions.

NOTE   When selecting data in a scroll area, RowSelect and RowInit PeopleCode events occur for each row that is read into the scroll.

All default processing and display processing PeopleCode events from panel fields, except related display fields, are processed during panel display. Even if a field is not present in the panel, PeopleCode events are triggered from that field. One exception to this rule is fields from Derived/Work records. PeopleCode is processed from derived fields only when they are present in the panel. For this reason the same Derived/Work record can be shared across multiple panel sessions without interfering with each other.

13.5 DATA ENTRY AND INQUIRY

13.5.1 Modifying data on a panel

From a PeopleCode perspective, the majority of events and activities take place during data entry and save processing. Save processing events begin when the user clicks the save toolbar icon or selects File, Save from the menu. When the panel group is displayed the user is presented with information based on his/her security profile. If the user has view capability only, then no adding or updating can be performed. Given the proper security, however, the user can perform activities that trigger PeopleCode events. These events include:

- FieldEdit
- FieldChange
- RowInsert
- RowDelete

NOTE   When entering data on a panel, the F4 and CTRL+F4 prompt does not trigger any PeopleCode events.

FieldEdit and FieldChange

During data entry, when the user edits a field on the panel and then tabs out of the field or clicks on another field, the FieldEdit PeopleCode event is triggered. Please refer to section 13.2.2 for more information regarding FieldEdit and FieldChange.

RowInsert

When a RowInsert activity is performed (F7), the Application Processor adds a row of data to the active scroll area. In Problem Tracking, the panel MY_PROBLEM_TRKG is not a scroll panel and, therefore, PeopleCode events such as RowInsert and RowDelete are not executed. This is important because we could add lines and lines of RowInsert PeopleCode containing the fanciest routines, functions and edits, but, if our screen does not contain a scroll bar, then our People-Code will never get executed!

The Application Processor first inserts an empty row into the active scroll area. The RowInsert event is then executed, and PeopleCode operates on the fields in the newly inserted row. A successful RowInsert event is followed by the Application Processor events FieldDefault, FieldFormula, and RowInit. RowInsert PeopleCode operates on rows containing a scroll area on the panel. These events are executed before the panel is redisplayed so if RowInsert code is replicated in the RowInit event, the code is triggered twice because RowInit follows RowInsert. RowInsert PeopleCode can be used primarily for specific processing when new rows are inserted into a scroll area. RowInit PeopleCode is used when rows of data are loaded into a panel buffer. RowInit is triggered for both scroll and nonscroll data, whereas RowInsert is only triggered for panels containing scroll data.

The Error and Warning statements should not be used in RowInsert PeopleCode. The Application Processor runtime error will force the user to cancel the panel group without saving it.

RowDelete

RowDelete results in removal of data from a scroll area and, subsequently, from the database during save operations. This event is triggered when the user deletes a row of data by pressing the row delete button or the F8 function key. Before the Application Processor removes a row from the buffer, fields on the deleted row can be referenced from PeopleCode in the RowDelete event. The Application Processor marks the rows as deleted, but the actual delete does not take place until save processing. The RowDelete event is executed following the "Delete current row?" verification message issued by the Application Processor. When a No reply is given, any code associated with RowDelete is not triggered. An application of the use of RowDelete can be used to update the Scroll Count field on the panel illustrated in figure 13.10. Figure 13.11 represents a simple line of code which updates the scroll count during a RowDelete event. The ActiveRowCount function is used to produce a count of the number of active rows in the panel scroll area. Rows marked for deletion are not included in the count.

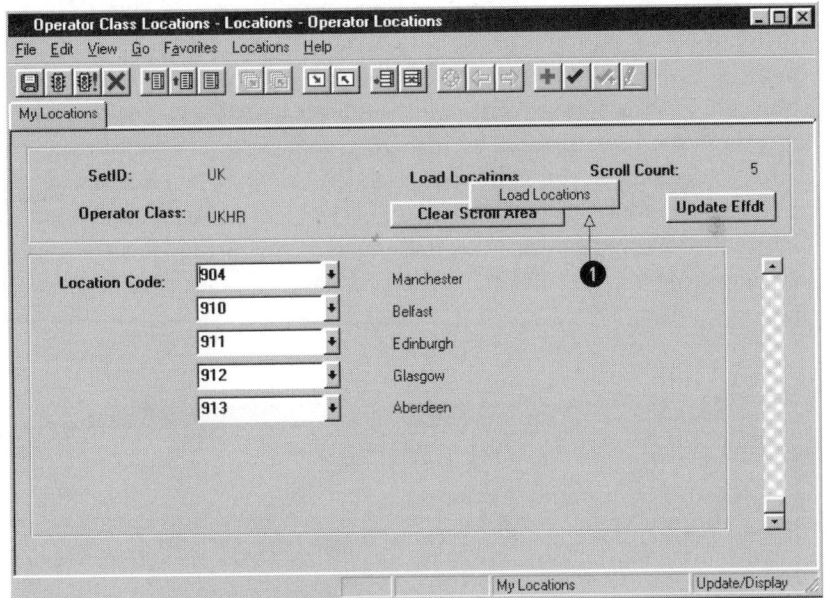

Figure 13.10   RowInsert and RowDelete processing is only possible on panels containing scrolls.

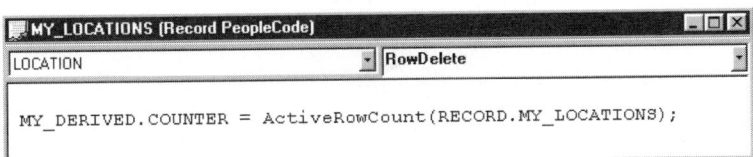

Figure 13.11   RowDelete code used to update counter

PrePopup

As developers, we can attach a pop-up menu to a panel field, which is displayed at runtime when the user clicks the right mouse button of the corresponding field. The PrePopup event is triggered immediately before the display of the pop-up menu. When we compare PeopleCode in pop-up menus to PeopleCode in standard menus, we see limitations to the standard menu PeopleCode that do not exist in pop-up menu PeopleCode. If we do not wish to add command push buttons to our panel, pop-up menus can be used instead. As an example, let's refer to figure 13.10 and, more specifically, the label titled "Load Locations," ❶. This field is associated with a pop-up menu which loads locations associated with the SETID field. For this process we have defined a pop-up menu named LOAD_LOCATIONS. To illustrate the PrePopup event, let's assume that after we right-click the field labeled "Load Locations," the

PeopleCode associated with this pop-up menu is executed (figure 13.12). Each time the right mouse button is clicked, the scroll area fills with data. An unsuspecting end-user can perform this several times before activating the save button. This type action generates an error message indicating duplicate keys. We can be pro-active and prevent this duplicate key situation by including code to delete data before populating the scroll buffer area. In this example, the code to clear the scroll area and related database records is inserted into the PrePopup event (figure 13.13). As a result of implementing the PrePopup code, when the user right-clicks the "Load Locations" field, the PrePopup event executes the associated code and clears the scroll area before it is filled with data.

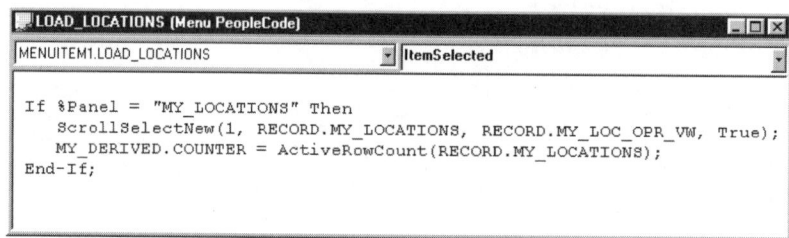

Figure 13.12   PeopleCode associated with a pop-up menu

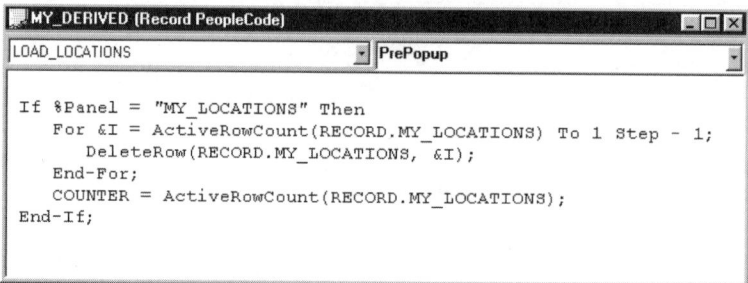

Figure 13.13   PrePopup code to clear scroll buffer area

Pop-up menu PeopleCode could also be used to calculate field values, trigger Workflow events, or run a modal transfer.

NOTE   The DeleteRow function used in figure 13.13 could have been combined with the code in figure 13.12. It has been placed into the event to demonstrate PrePopup.

13.6 SAVE PROCESSING

After data entry is completed and all `FieldEdit` PeopleCode events are executed, the user can either save the panel or cancel it. As a result of canceling a panel, no save processing is performed. All those elegant routines written for execution during a save process are overlooked by the Application Processor, which resets the status of the panel group following a cancel. When the save button is activated, the Application Processor then triggers four events associated with save. The events are:

- `SaveEdit`
- `SavePreChg`
- `Workflow`
- `SavePostChg`

SaveEdit

The PeopleCode associated with this event is executed after the operator saves the panel group. This event allows the developer to verify data consistency across fields and records.

After the user has clicked the save button or pressed enter, the `SaveEdit` event is triggered. Any PeopleCode in this event is executed after the Application Processor performs edits of its own. `SaveEdit` PeopleCode can be used when more than one field in the panel group is required to perform validity checking or a consistency edit. The `SaveEdit` event enables us to verify fields after they have all been keyed into a panel group. We could use `FieldEdit` PeopleCode, but if there are ten fields on a panel group that require some form of editing, a user would not want to enter a field, have a message appear, and correct the field only to repeat the same sequence on the next field. `SaveEdit` is not related to any specific field and, except for deleted rows, is triggered on every row of data in the panel group buffer. This can be tricky at times. As an example, let's assume that we have an employee's JOB history panel, which is effective-dated. Let's also assume that we've made changes to the current effective-dated row. Coincidentally, a record somewhere in the scroll contains bad data. The data are probably the result of a conversion program that did not perform edits on every field. When the user clicks "Save," the associated PeopleCode will be triggered for every row in the scroll. Any errors encountered somewhere in the stack of JOB data will require correction when the error prevents a save operation.

Our friends, the `Error` and `Warning` statements, can be used in `SaveEdit` PeopleCode. The `Error` statement displays a message, but prevents the user from saving any data while the `Warning` statement displays a message and presents the user with the option to save the data via an OK or to Cancel without saving. If the PeopleCode program can determine which field requires correction, the PeopleCode function `SetCursorPos` can be called before `Error` or `Warning`. Figure 13.14 illustrates PeopleCode in the `SaveEdit` event. The code verifies for changed fields using the built-in function `FieldChanged` and calls an External PeopleCode function named

MyAuditFunction. Putting this code into an event such as FieldEdit or FieldChange represents a bit more of a challenge because the function would be called each time the event is generated. Think of the user who changes a field many times before pressing save.

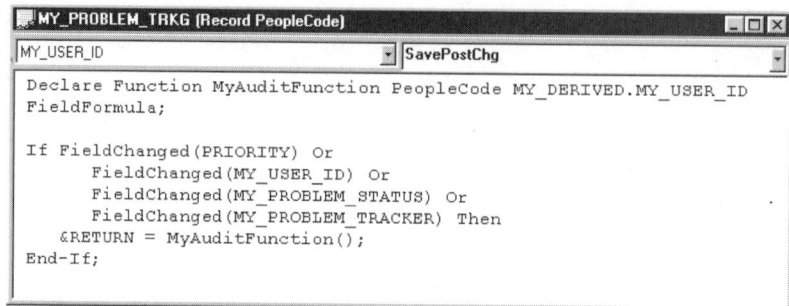

```
MY_PROBLEM_TRKG (Record PeopleCode)                              _ □ ×
MY_USER_ID                              ▾   SavePostChg                        ▾
Declare Function MyAuditFunction PeopleCode MY_DERIVED.MY_USER_ID
FieldFormula;

If FieldChanged(PRIORITY) Or
     FieldChanged(MY_USER_ID) Or
     FieldChanged(MY_PROBLEM_STATUS) Or
     FieldChanged(MY_PROBLEM_TRACKER) Then
   &RETURN = MyAuditFunction();
End-If;
```

Figure 13.14   SaveEdit PeopleCode

SavePreChg

SavePreChg occurs after the SaveEdit event terminates successfully. SavePreChg enables the PeopleCode program to modify data one last time before the Application Processor updates the database. Upon successful completion of a SavePreChg event, the WorkFlow event is then executed. WorkFlow is triggered before the Application Processor generates the corresponding database updates, such as INSERT, UPDATE, and DELETE.

WorkFlow

This event follows SavePreChg and is executed before any of the database updates are performed. The database updates are then followed by the SavePostChg event. Workflow PeopleCode is separated from PeopleCode in the other events and should be designed so that Workflow executes when all SaveEdit and SavePreChg code have been completed. Workflow programs should include PeopleCode related to Workflow and linked to business processes only. At the time a business process is defined, we also include the panels that trigger any related business events. The combination workflow panels and PeopleCode programs are considered application agents and are loaded as part of the panel group.

Workflow PeopleCode includes either the TriggerBusinessEvent() a PeopleCode function that triggers events, or Virtual_Router(), which is linked to the Virtual Approver.

SavePostChg

After `SavePreChg`, the Application Processor executes PeopleCode in the `Workflow` event. The Application Processor then executes any database updates (`INSERT`, `UPDATE`, `DELETE`), followed by the `SavePostChg` event. Records that require updating, but are not included in the current panel group, can be updated in this event using the `SQLExec` statement. Be aware that if the `SavePostChg` event fails to execute correctly, the Application Processor will not issue a SQL commit. Similarly, the use of `Error` and `Warning` statements in `SavePostChg` PeopleCode issues a runtime error that forces the user to cancel the panel group without saving it.

13.6.1   Adding PeopleCode to save processing

Some code added to the Problem Tracking application makes it more efficient, but there is always room for improvement. It is not always a good idea to add "bells and whistles" to an application just because we have the tools. It is also not feasible to add complex code to satisfy one user when there are hundreds of other users that will not benefit from the added code. The application presented is a small application, and some "loop holes" are opened up, as we will illustrate.

When a problem has been resolved, certain housekeeping steps should be completed. These steps include entering the Problem Resolution text and entering a Close date.

In its current form, the application will accept a problem status value of 5 (Resolved) without validating that the resolution text field is entered. Because we cannot change the Record Field Properties of the MY_PROBLEM_RESOLTN field and make it required, PeopleCode can be added to accomplish this task for us. The code shown (figure 13.15) will accomplish the task and require that the resolution text field is entered for resolved issues.

The next step is to ensure that the Close Date field is entered when the problem status has been resolved. The code in figure 13.16 will check for a status of 5 and then require that the CLOSE_DT field contain a valid date value. Because CLOSE_DT is defined as a `Date` data type, the Application Processor performs the standard date checking for us.

One additional piece of code we would like to add is related to the following scenario. Let's say the problem is reported and entered into the system. The problem status is subsequently assigned, tested and resolved; and at the time of resolution, the

```
MY_PROBLEM_TRKG (Record PeopleCode)
MY_PROBLEM_STATUS          SaveEdit

If MY_PROBLEM_STATUS = "5" Then
   If None(MY_PROBLEM_RESOLTN) Then
      Error ("Please enter problem resoution text");
   End-If;
End-If;
```

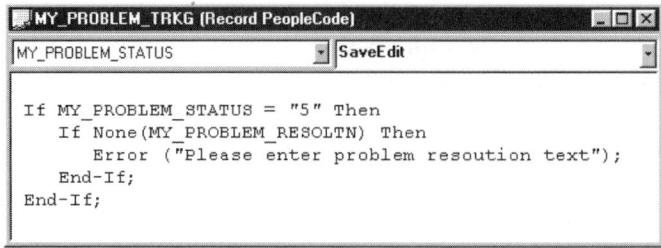

Figure 13.15 Using PeopleCode to verify a field is entered

```
MY_PROBLEM_TRKG (Record PeopleCode)
MY_PROBLEM_STATUS          SaveEdit

If MY_PROBLEM_STATUS = "5" Then
   If None(MY_PROBLEM_RESOLTN) Then
      Error ("Please enter problem resoution text");
   End-If;
Else
   If None(CLOSE_DT) Then
      Error ("Problem status is resolved, enter a Close Date");
   End-If;
End-If;
```

Figure 13.16 Verify that Close Date is entered

Problem Resolution text field is entered, along with a close date. It is then determined that the problem was not resolved and the status should be set to "In Progress," to indicate that it is being handled by a developer.

This issue requires that we reset the Problem Resolution text field and the Close date. Our program logic has now changed from reactive to proactive. The code to accomplish this task is illustrated in figure 13.17. The PeopleCode function `SetDefault` is used to set the field to a `NULL` value. During the next `FieldDefault` event, MY_PROBLEM_RESOLTN and CLOSE_DT are set to their appropriate default values. After the user has clicked the save button or pressed the ENTER key, the `SaveEdit` event is triggered. The last several examples were placed into the `SaveEdit` event of the field MY_PROBLEM_STATUS. The code is placed into `SaveEdit` to ensure that is it executed after the Application Processor performs its own edits. Additionally, `SaveEdit` PeopleCode is used when more than one field in the panel group is required to perform validity checking. Another less strategic reason to include the code in `SaveEdit` is that some end-users will automatically remove the resolution text field and close date then reset the problem status to "2." This action will bypass the edit in figure 13.17.

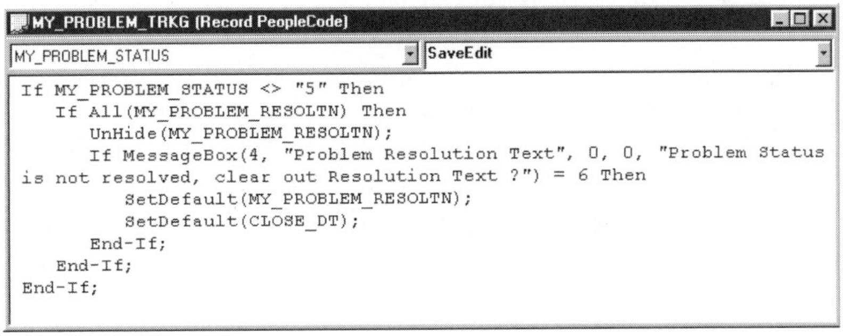

MY_PROBLEM_TRKG (Record PeopleCode)
MY_PROBLEM_STATUS
SaveEdit
If MY_PROBLEM_STATUS <> "5" Then
   If All(MY_PROBLEM_RESOLTN) Then
      UnHide(MY_PROBLEM_RESOLTN);
      If MessageBox(4, "Problem Resolution Text", 0, 0, "Problem Status is not resolved, clear out Resolution Text ?") = 6 Then
         SetDefault(MY_PROBLEM_RESOLTN);
         SetDefault(CLOSE_DT);
      End-If;
   End-If;
End-If;

Figure 13.17 Code to reset data

Figure 13.18 illustrates the completed panel with some bells and whistles added for additional editing features.

Problem Tracking - Tracking - Track Problems
File Edit View Go Favorites Setup Tracking Help
My Problem Trkg
Problem ID: 000001
Incident Date: 03/05/1999
Close Date: 03/07/1999
Project ID: 000001
Upgrade to 7.5
Application ID: 000
My Problem Tracking
Status: 5
Resolved
Priority: 3
User ID: PS
Document?
Open
Tracker: TEST1
Tester,Oliver
Problem: Upgrade compare reports are not being generated.
Resolution: Reports were being sent to a list file rather than the printer. Parameters were changed and reports are now printing.
My Problem Trkg
Update/Display

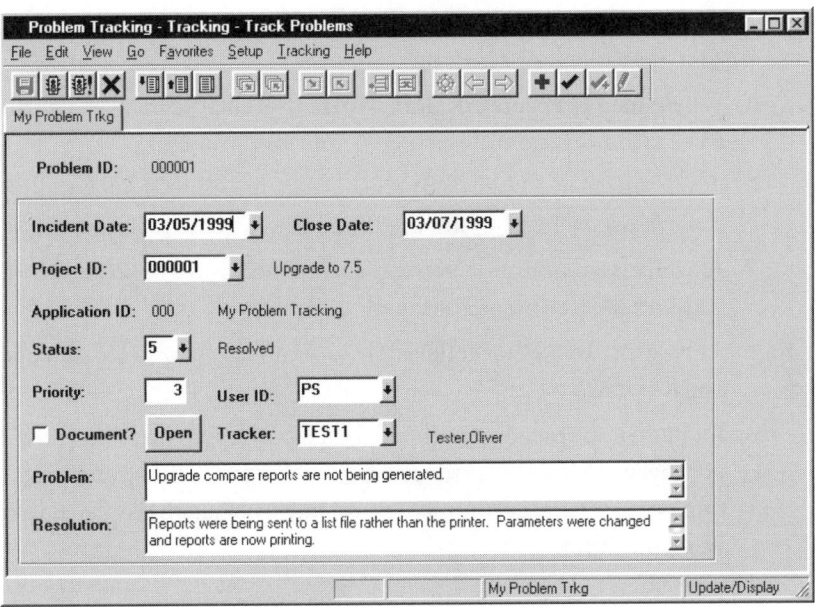

Figure 13.18 Completed panel with custom PeopleCode

1 The Application Processor acts as a traffic agent on a busy street. It controls everything from the time the user selects a menu item until all save processing has been completed as well as everything in between.

2 Event Processing is the cornerstone of PeopleCode programs. Code can be inserted before a search dialog is displayed, at every step in between, and after all database updates have been performed.

3 Some events such as `FieldDefault` and `RowInit` occur before data are displayed on the panel.

4 `FieldFormula` is an event that occurs after each and every event that contains PeopleCode is executed. A lot of overhead is associated with `Field-Formula` and its use has been left mostly to function libraries on Derived/Work records. `FieldEdit` also executes for each field on a panel which contains a blank or zero value.

5 When data are entered into a panel, events such as `FieldEdit` and `FieldChange` can be executed before save processing.

6 `RowInsert` and `RowDelete` are events linked to the F7 and F8 function keys, respectively. They are used primarily on panels containing scroll bars.

7 After the save button is pressed, events such as `SaveEdit`, `SavePreChg`, and `SavePostChg` are executed.

8 The `WorkFlow` event follows `SavePreChg` just prior to all database table updates.

9 Any `PrePopup` code associated with a pop-up menu is executed before the pop-up menu is displayed. If we do not wish to add command push buttons to a panel, pop-up menus and any associated PeopleCode can always be used instead.

C H A P T E R   1 4

Messages and error handling

Communication between a PeopleSoft application and an end-user is key to a successful implementation. PeopleCode message functions enable the application to send messages containing a simple OK push button or an Error message that will prevent further processing of a panel, until data on the panel has been corrected. In between these extremes, messages can be sent in varying detail containing custom messages. Utilizing the PeopleTools Message Catalog, these messages can be sent to a worldwide audience in a variety of languages. With no changes to a PeopleCode program and a change to the language code, cataloged messages can be "cloned" for every language required.

14.1 USING THE MESSAGEBOX FUNCTION

The MessageBox function is one of the more important PeopleCode built-in functions. MessageBox enables PeopleCode programs to communicate with an end-user via a message box window. PeopleCode program flow can then be controlled based on the push button return values selected. (The syntax and rules of MessageBox can be found in appendix E.)

One of the parameters used by MessageBox is style. The style parameter enables the construction of a message box window with a blend of icons and push buttons. An optional default button can also be specified. Table 14.1 identifies the values required for buttons, default buttons, and icons.

Table 14.1 Style parameter combinations

Value	Push buttons	Default button	Type of icon
0	One push button containing OK	First button in the message box is the default	None
1	Two buttons containing OK and Cancel		
2	Three buttons containing Abort, Retry and Ignore		
3	Three buttons containing Yes, No and Cancel		
4	Two buttons containing Yes and No		
5	Two buttons containing Retry and Cancel		
16			Icon contains a stop sign.
32			Icon contains a question mark.
48			Icon contains an exclamation point.
64			Contains a small letter "i".
256		Second button in the message box is the default.	
512		Third button in the message box is the default.	

In addition to the button combinations illustrated in table 14.1, the `MessageBox` window also contains an Explain button. As the name implies, the Explain button provides a more detailed explanation of the message text.

Some important rules regarding the use of `MessageBox` concern the buttons that can be used during certain PeopleCode events. The OK and Explain buttons do not interrupt processing. However, when any other type of button displayed in a message box interrupts processing, the system waits until one of the buttons is clicked. The function then becomes "user think-time," which indicates the button action returns a value to the function. As a result of awaiting a reply, the Application Processor suspends the PeopleCode program until the user clicks on one of the buttons contained in the message. A program in this manner cannot be used in the following events:

- `RowSelect`
- `SavePreChg`
- `WorkFlow`
- `SavePostChg`

When the OK button is the only button represented by the style parameter, the function can then be used in all PeopleCode events. The style parameter does not control the Explain button and is not indicative of whether `MessageBox` is considered think-time.

Based on table 14.1, if a message box contains an OK and Cancel button as the default, along with a question mark icon, what would the value of style have to be? If you guessed 289, you win the prize! The following PeopleCode statement produces the message box shown in figure 14.1.

```
MessageBox (289,"Example", 0, 0, "MessageBox example");
```

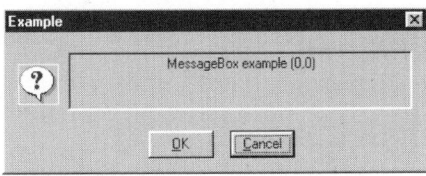

Figure 14.1 A standard MessageBox window

Using table 14.1 as a reference, let's examine the `MessageBox` window in figure 14.1. The `MessageBox` contains two buttons, OK and Cancel (style value = 1). The second button represents the default (style value = 256), and the question mark icon appears in the message box (style value = 32). The sum of these values is 289, which is the style used for this example.

Let's assume the numbers were not added correctly and, rather than using 289, we supplied 288 as the style to `MessageBox` instead. How will the message box appear? When the following statement is executed, the message box appears as shown in figure 14.2.

```
MessageBox (288,"Example", 0, 0, "MessageBox example");
```

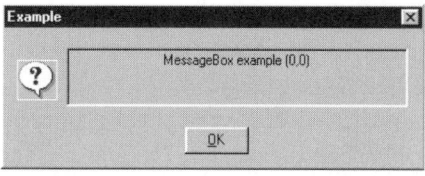

Figure 14.2 MessageBox window using erroneous style

Because the style parameter is incorrect by a value of 1, the message box contains an OK push button only. The message box contains this single push button because zero is the value used to represent a single button containing OK (as described in table 14.1). A value of 288 indicates that any additional buttons are not factored into the required style value equation.

The next parameter is the title of the message box. The title is defaulted when a null string is passed. For example, the following statement produces a null title in the MessageBox window:

```
MessageBox (289,"", 0, 0, "MessageBox example");
```

The statement produces the message box shown in figure 14.3 with a defaulted title.

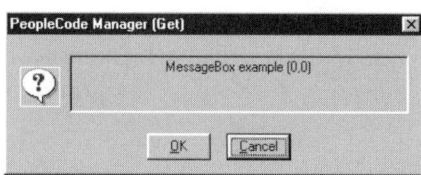

Figure 14.3 MessageBox with defaulted title

The next parameter is the message_set number of the message catalog. The Message Catalog enables us to store messages for retrieval using functions such as MessageBox. We can either set up our own custom messages or use the existing ones. To define a custom cataloged message, we can select Use → Message Catalog from the Utilities menu.

Navigation: Utilities → Use → Message Catalog → Add

Figure 14.4 Adding Message Catalog entries

The illustration in figure 14.4 indicates message set number 20001 in English will be added to the catalog. Message sets 1 through 19,999 are reserved for PeopleSoft application use. Message sets 20,0000 through 29,000 are available for custom use.

We populate the panel in figure 14.5 and then proceed to add the same message in Spanish, as illustrated by figure 14.6.

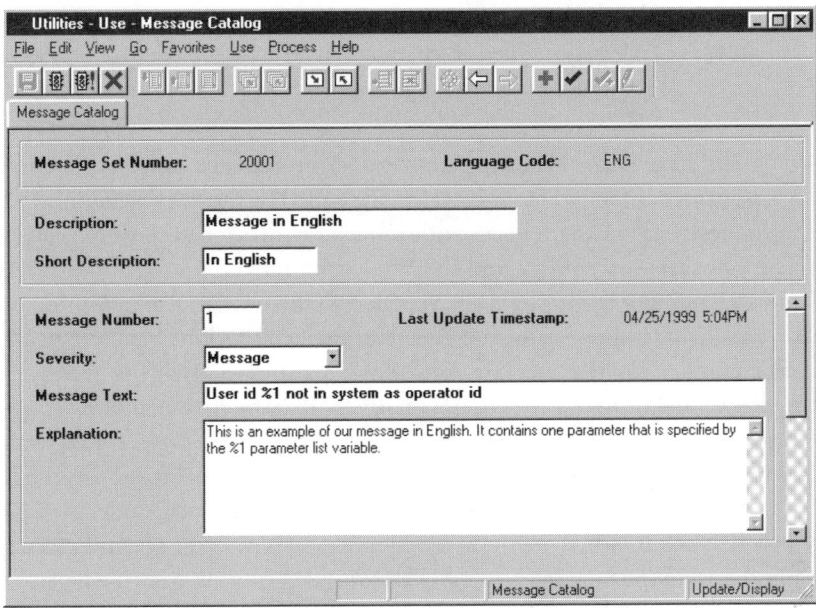

Figure 14.5 Message in English

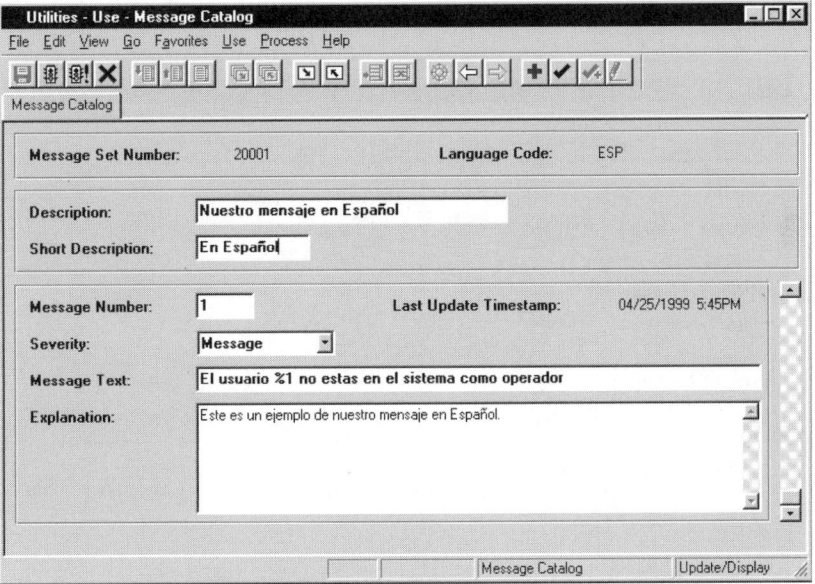

Figure 14.6 Same message number in Spanish

Messages added to the range used by PeopleSoft (1–19,999) or messages customized in this range may be impacted by future releases of the product.

The next `MessageBox` parameter is the message number. Each message set is accompanied by one or more messages identified by the message number. The examples in figures 14.5 and 14.6 begin with message number 1 (a most logical starting place). The language, description, and short description fields are part of the message set. The message number is automatically assigned to the next available number in the message set and includes the severity, message text, and explanation. To insert an additional message number for the message set 20001, we first display the message displayed in figure 14.5. The next step is to use the Insert Row toolbar icon or F7 function key. The Insert Row augments the message number and presents a panel that enables the entry of message severity, text, and explanation. A similar panel is shown in figure 14.7.

Default text is the next parameter and it is displayed under two circumstances. The first occurs when the message identified by message set and message number is not found in the message catalog. The second condition occurs when a value less than 1 is supplied in the message set field. A `MessageBox` as outlined in the following statement uses the default text because of the zero passed in the message set number.

```
MessageBox(289, "", 0, 0, "");
```

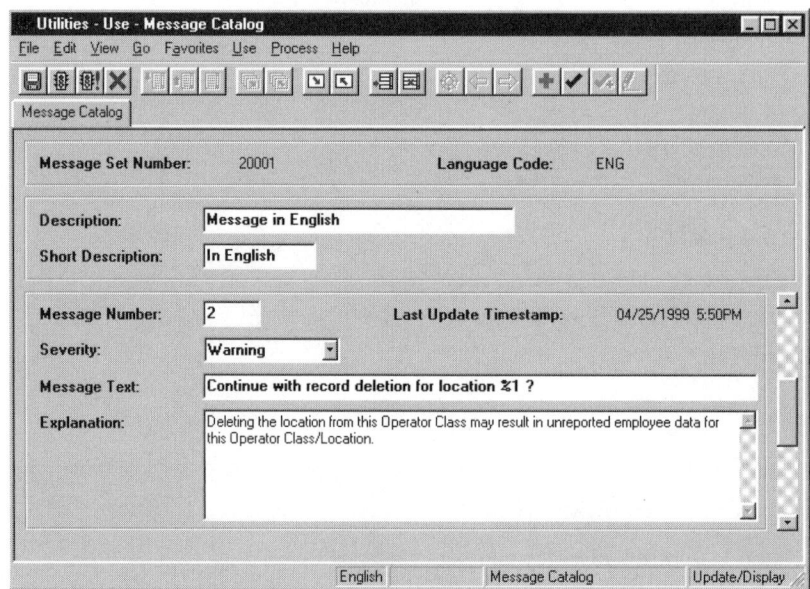

Figure 14.7   Inserting additional message number

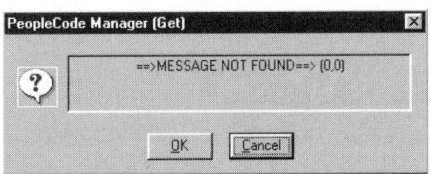

Figure 14.8 Missing default text

The preceding example specifies a null default text. As a result, the Application Processor issues the message shown in figure 14.8.

As illustrated by figure 14.8, Message-Box uses the style parameter and replaces the title with a default value. MessageBox then fills in the default text with its own MESSAGE NOT FOUND verb.

The next and last parameter is the parameter list. It may sound somewhat redundant, but these are the optional parameters that appear in the message or default text. Variables cannot simply be imbedded into messages, they must be passed as parameters to the message text. The parameters are referenced using the '%' character and an integer that corresponds to the sequence in which the parameter appears in the message text. To include the literal '%' in the text use '%%'.

MessageBox return value

MessageBox returns a value based on which push button is pressed. The return values are listed in table 14.2. A value of zero returned by MessageBox indicates that there is insufficient memory to create the message box. A message box containing a Cancel button returns the same value as when the ESC key is pressed or Cancel button is selected

Table 14.2 MessageBox return values

Returns	Description
0	Insufficient memory
-1	Warning
1	OK button was pressed
2	Cancel
3	Abort
4	Retry
5	Ignore
6	Yes
7	No

Message severity

When used with cataloged messages, MessageBox can specify a message severity. Message severity is a parameter entered into the message catalog. By specifying the message severity, a message can be transformed from a warning into an error message without a change to the PeopleCode that generates the message. To modify the message severity for a cataloged message, use the Utilities menu.

The illustration in figure 14.9 indicates that there are four message severity categories and outcomes:

- *Message*   Output is displayed as a message only.
- *Warning*   Message text is sent as a warning and requires user response.
- *Error*   The message is displayed with an error, which implies that further processing is halted until the error is corrected.
- *Cancel*   After the message is displayed, cancellation of the current panel is forced.

Navigation: Utilities → Use → Message Catalog → Update/Display

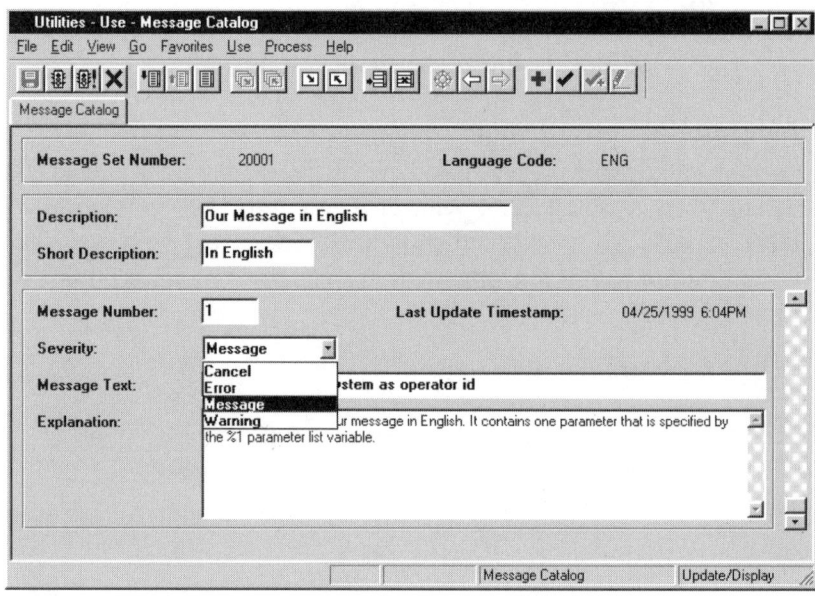

Figure 14.9   Message severity levels

Utilizing MessageBox in PeopleCode

The following example performs some verification and generates the message that was added in figure 14.5. The `MessageBox` portion of the code contains a style of 289. As we learned, a style of 289 includes an OK and default Cancel button in addition to a question mark icon. When the message set number is specified and is not less than 1, the Explain button is also displayed. This occurs even when the message does not appear in the message catalog. When a non-zero message set number is supplied, the message stored in the catalog table is displayed in the message window. However, if the message is not stored in the catalog, the default text is then substituted. The message text parameter list contains one parameter identified by '%1'. When the message is displayed, '%1' contains the value of the field MY_USER_ID. This PeopleCode example is utilized when setting up users in the current Problem Tracking application.

The code surrounding MessageBox verifies the existence of the user ID field on the PSOPERDEFN record. The panel field MY_USER_ID is compared to the contents of the system variable %OperatorId, which contains the uppercase string of the operator ID logged on. Assuming the %OperatorId variable contains the value PS, the following code generates the message displayed in figure 14.10 when executed on the panel:

```
If MY_USER_ID <> %OperatorId Then
   If (SQLExec("Select  'x' from PSOPRDEFN where OPRID = :1", MY_USER_ID,
&OPRID)) = True Then
      If %SqlRows = 0 Then
         MessageBox(289, "Verify", 20001, 1, "User id %1 not in system as
operator id", MY_USER_ID);
      End-If;
   End-If;
End-If;
```

Using the example in figure 14.10, under a similar circumstance a Spanish language user in Latin America who has a Spanish language setting receives the message shown

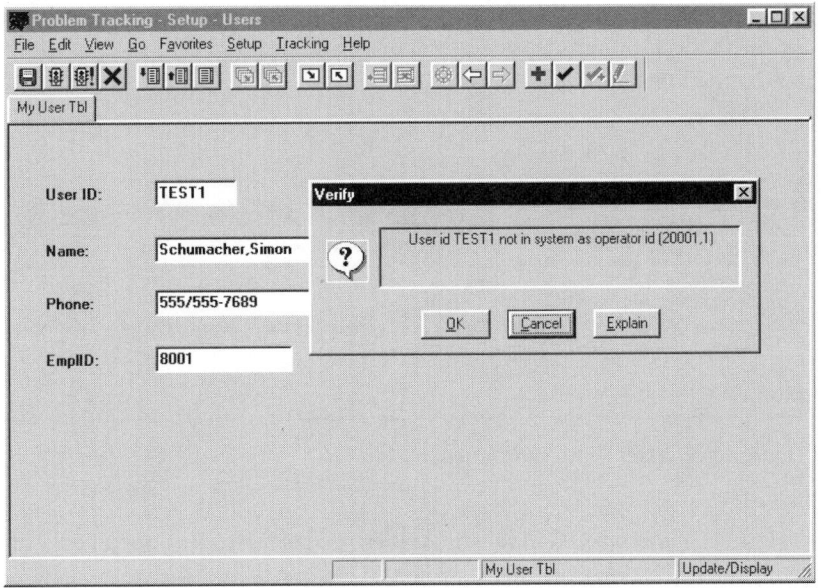

Figure 14.10   Our MessageBox in action

in figure 14.11. The beauty of this is that no additional changes are made to the PeopleCode program.

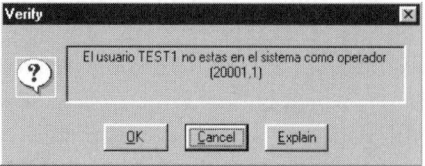

Figure 14.11 Display cataloged Spanish message

The message in figure 14.11 is message set 20001, message number 1. The Spanish language message text reflects the language code ESP. When a message number is duplicated in varying languages, all the other parameters including push buttons, defaults, and the question mark icon are identical to the original language message. The possibility exists that when a message is translated from one language to another, the entire message can be different. The example in figure 14.11 could relay a completely different message than the original intended message in figure 14.10. For implementations with a worldwide audience, some type of audit should be in place when messages are entered in different languages.

User Think-Time

At the beginning of this section, we discussed the incidence of User Think-Time. This can occur during specific PeopleCode events and can be characterized by a message box containing buttons other than OK and Explains. These "other" buttons interrupt system processing and wait until some action is performed with reference to the buttons. Because the system is in a wait mode, Application Processor suspends the PeopleCode program. `SavePostChg` is one event that does not allow user think-time functions.

Figure 14.12 is an example of a User Think-Time function.

Figure 14.12 User Think-Time function

This is the type of code which does not get noticed immediately, but lurks until a Problem Tracking incident is resolved. When a problem has finally been resolved and all the information in the resolution text is entered, a message is displayed following save action. The message, shown in figure 14.13 is not the message expected by the user.

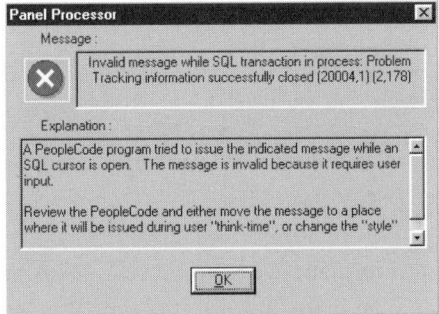

This is not the type of message that the developer who implemented the `SavePostChg` PeopleCode had in mind when it was coded. The error occurs because the style parameter contains three buttons: Yes, No, and Cancel. The PeopleCode can be corrected as follows:

Figure 14.13   User Think-Time message

```
If MY_PROBLEM_STATUS = "5" Then
    MessageBox(0, "Problem Tracking information sucessfully closed", 20004,
1, "Update Complete");
End-If;
```

The message box can now be displayed (figure 14.14). Because this is a problem tracking application, the users were kind enough to enter this into the system as well.

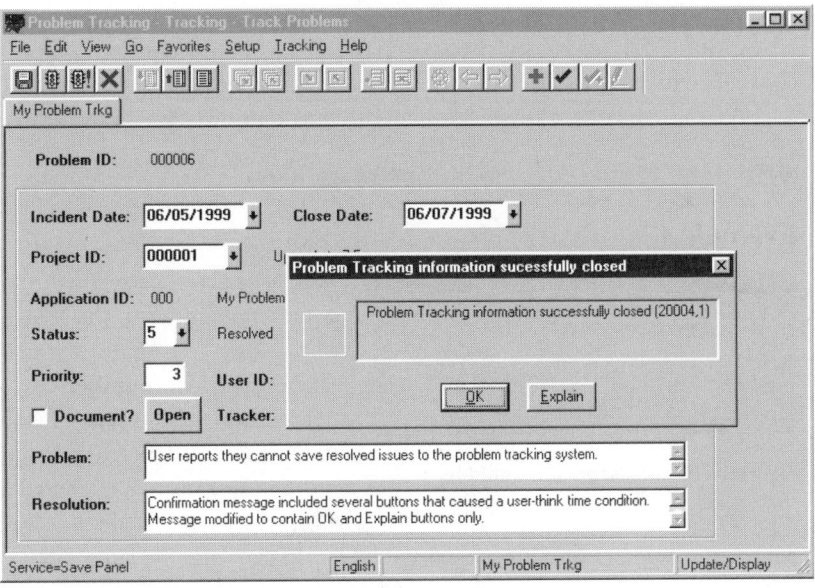

Figure 14.14   Successful display of message during SavePostChg

14.2 USING *WINMESSAGE*

Another common method of communicating messages is through the use of the `WinMessage` function. `WinMessage` can be used to send messages in a manner similar to `MessageBox`. As we will see in a later chapter, WinMessage can also be used as a debugging tool.

14.2.1 WinMessage

`WinMessage` is used to display an informational message box. With the use of the style parameter, two or more buttons can be included in the message, but their use is limited to certain PeopleCode events. When the style parameter is left out of the function call or contains more than one button, the function becomes `user think-time`, which indicates the button action returns a value to the function. As a result of awaiting a reply, the Application Processor suspends the PeopleCode program until the user clicks on one of the buttons contained in the message. A program in this manner cannot be used in the following PeopleCode events:

- `SavePreChg`
- `WorkFlow`
- `RowSelect`
- `SavePostChg`

From a debugging perspective, `WinMessage` can also be used to display field contents while allowing us to "inch" our way through PeopleCode when necessary.

A simple `WinMessage` can be written as follows:

```
WinMessage ("This is a basic WinMessage example");
```

Example 1

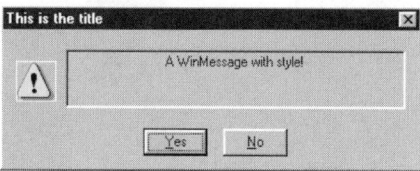

Figure 14.15 Message generated by WinMessage

`WinMessage` can also accept a style parameter similar to the style used in `MessageBox`. The parameter is optional and, when used, the number of push buttons, default button and type of icon that appear in the message box can be controlled based on the value passed. (Refer to table 14.1 for a list of style categories and values.) A third parameter, which contains a message box title, can also be supplied. The following code generates the message shown in figure 14.15:

```
WinMessage("A WinMessage with style!", 52, "This is the title");
```

CHAPTER 14   MESSAGES AND ERROR HANDLING

Example 2

Let's assume we are examining a PeopleCode program in HRMS and want to know the values of three fields. The fields are COMPRATE, COMP_FREQUENCY, and STD_HRS. WinMessage can then be used to concatenate and display fields, variables, and literal strings. The PeopleCode utilizing WinMessage might be similar to the illustration in figure 14.16. The resulting message is in figure 14.17.

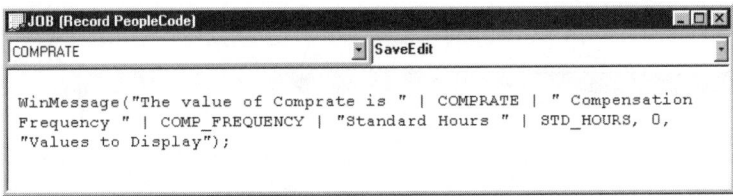

Figure 14.16   WinMessage used to display field values

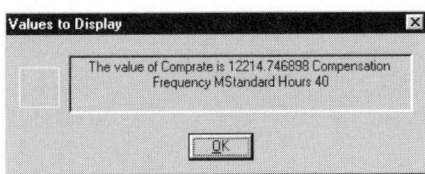

**Figure 14.17
Concatenated message using fields
and literal strings**

14.2.2   Additional examples

When fully utilized, the WinMessage function takes three parameters. The example in figure 14.16 cannot contain a comma in the message portion of the text string. Any record fields or variables displayed are concatenated with the message text. In the example, there are three text strings and three record fields. Initially, you may decide to code the statement differently. Here are some examples of what to expect:

If you separate the message text components with commas as illustrated by figure 14.18, expect the PeopleCode editor to return a message (figure 14.19) when performing a syntax check.

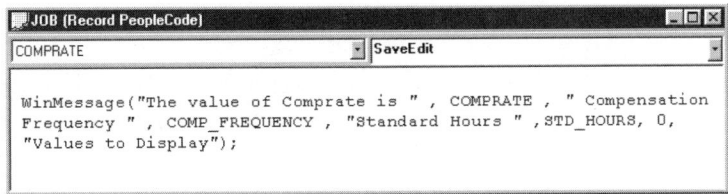

Figure 14.18   Incorrect use of commas in message parameter

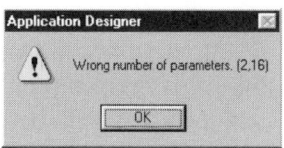

Figure 14.19 Message returned by PeopleCode editor

You may decide to enclose the message text, record fields or variables within one string. If the code is written as outlined in figure 14.20, you will then be able to perform the syntax check correctly, save your PeopleCode, and move on to another task. However, when this is tested—or if you are the type of developer who moves work to production without testing (shame on you)—then expect a similar message to the one shown in figure 14.21.

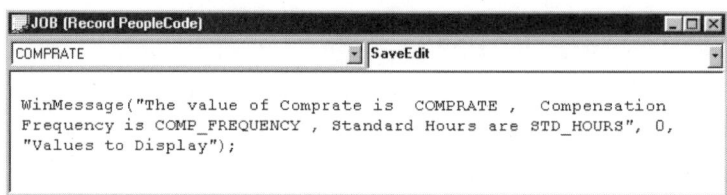

Figure 14.20 Invalid concatenation of fields and variables

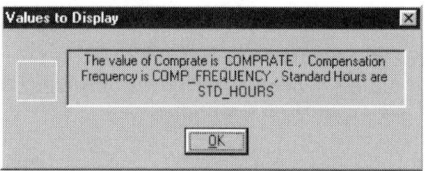

Figure 14.21 Incorrect message string

In the message displayed by figure 14.21, the Application Processor could not distinguish between record fields, variables, and text strings in the message parameter. This is why the concatenation character ' | ' is utilized to include strings and variables when used in such message.

TIP All data types are converted to `String` when used in `WinMessage`.

14.3 ERROR AND WARNING

When performing data validation it is sometimes necessary to stop a program and display a message. Among the various methods used to display messages, PeopleCode provides two functions that enable us to communicate with the end user. The `Error` and `Warning` functions can be used to perform these tasks.

14.3.1 Error

The `Error` function is used to display an error message and stop processing of the active panel. In a manner similar to `MessageBox`, `Error` works with messages stored in the Message Catalog or with a text string supplied to the Error function.

A basic `Error` statement can be written:

```
Error ("This is an example of an error message");
```

The value contained in `String` can be a literal text message or a message stored in the Message Catalog. A stored message must be retrieved using the `MsgGet` or `MsgGetText` function. This is important when using translated text messages as in figure 14.6. The `Error` function, when executed, terminates the PeopleCode program and prevents further statements from being executed. `Error`, however, produces varying results from one PeopleCode event to another. The events in which `Error` is usually incorporated include `FieldEdit` and `SaveEdit`. When executed in these events, the message is displayed and processing is halted. In `FieldEdit`, the field containing the PeopleCode event is highlighted. When used in `SaveEdit`, no fields are highlighted. One way we can work around this in the `SaveEdit` event is to use the `SetCursorPos` function for the field, prior to calling the `Error` function. `RowDelete` is another PeopleCode event in which `Error` is sometimes used. When `Error` is called from `RowDelete`, the message is displayed, and the row is not deleted.

The use of `Error` in other PeopleCode events is not recommended. These events include:

- `FieldDefault`
- `FieldFormula`
- `RowInit`
- `FieldChange`
- `Prepopup`
- `RowInsert`
- `SavePreChg`
- `SavePostChg`

The following illustrates the use of `Error`:

```
If MY_USER_ID <> %OperatorId Then
    If (SQLExec("Select  'x' from PSOPRDEFN where OPRID = :1", MY_USER_ID,
&OPRID)) = True Then
        If %SqlRows = 0 Then
            Error (MsgGet(20001, 1, "User id %1 not in system as operator id",
MY_USER_ID));
        End-If;
    End-If;
End-If;
```

14.3.2   Warning

The `Warning` function is used to display a warning type message. `Warning` differs from `Error` because processing is not halted by a warning message. The user is presented with OK and Explain buttons, then has the opportunity to correct or change data. `Warning` works with messages stored in the Message Catalog or a text string supplied to the `Warning` function.

A basic `Warning` statement can be written as:

```
Warning ("This is an example of a warning message");
```

The value contained in the string passed to `Warning` can be a literal text message or a message stored in the Message Catalog. The stored message must be retrieved using `MsgGet` or `MsgGetText`. `Warning` produces varying results from one PeopleCode event to another. The events in which `Warning` is commonly used include `FieldEdit` and `SaveEdit`. When used in `FieldEdit`, the message is displayed and the field that contains the PeopleCode is highlighted. Placing the `Warning` statement in `SaveEdit` displays the message but does not highlight fields. One way we can work around this in the `SaveEdit` event is to use the `SetCursorPos` function for the field prior to the `Warning` function call. `RowDelete` is another PeopleCode event in which `Warning` is sometimes used. When `Warning` is called in `RowDelete`, the message is displayed with OK and Cancel buttons. The user then has the option to either delete the row by pressing OK or to back out of the delete by pressing Cancel.

The use of `Warning` in other PeopleCode events is not recommended. These events include:

- `FieldDefault`
- `FieldFormula`
- `RowInit`
- `FieldChange`
- `RowInsert`
- `SavePreChg`
- `SavePostChg`

Figure 14.22 illustrates the use of the `Warning` statement in the Operator Class/ Location panel. The resulting warning message text and subsequent explanation are shown in figures 14.23 and 14.24. The definition for message set 20001, message number 2 is shown in figure 14.25. `Warning` is called from the `RowDelete` event and contains an OK, a Cancel, and an Explain button.

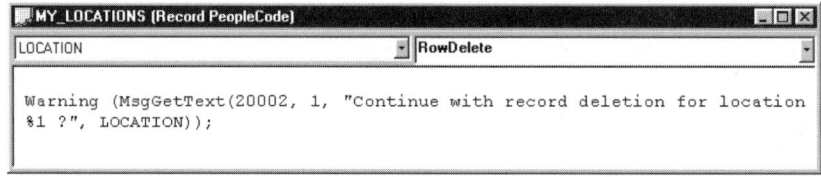

Figure 14.22   Using the Warning statement

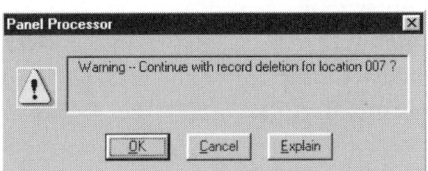

Figure 14.23   Warning message text

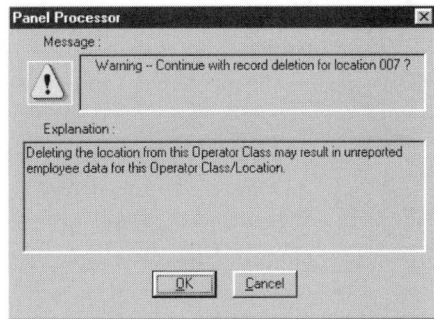

Figure 14.24   Explanation associated with Warning

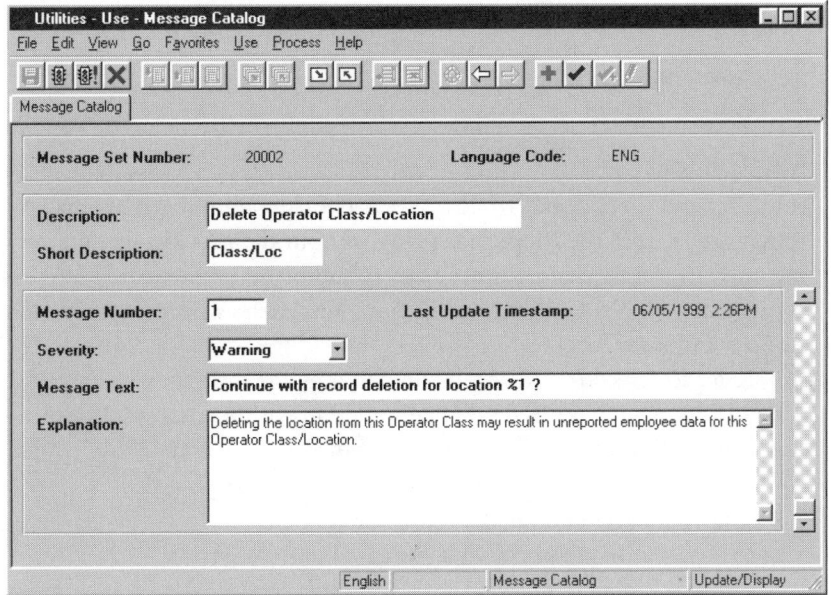

Figure 14.25   Message Number 2 definition

14.4   *MSGGET* AND *MSGGETTEXT*

Various PeopleCode message functions can be used to display messages that are stored in the Message Catalog table. Retrieving stored messages can be accomplished using the `MsgGet` and `MsgGetText` functions. As you will remember from an earlier discussion, the Message Catalog enables us to define the same message in various languages. These functions become an invaluable tool when working on a global application.

14.4.1   MsgGet

MsgGet has two primary tasks: to retrieve messages from the Message Catalog; and to substitute the value of each parameter contained in the message text identified by %1, %2, %3.

MsgGet is used in conjunction with Error, Warning, MessageBox, and WinMessage to retrieve the corresponding message text from the Message Catalog. When a message set number less than 1 is supplied or the message is not in the catalog, the default message text is substituted. An example using MsgGet can be written as follows:

```
MsgGet(20003, 1, "Problem Id %1, is not resolved", MY_PROBLEM_ID)
```

MsgGet is not a function which can be run on its own. Without a preceding MessageBox, WinMessage, or Error, an 'Invalid Function Statement' message is issued by the syntax check. The MsgGet function call statement can be completed with a corresponding WinMessage:

```
WinMessage(MsgGet(20003, 1, "Problem Id %1, is not resolved",
MY_PROBLEM_ID));
```

14.4.2   MsgGetText

MsgGetText is similar to MsgGet. The key difference is that MsgGetText retrieves text from the Message Catalog without the message set and message number included in the message. MsgGetText cannot be implemented alone. It is used in conjunction with the other message functions such as WinMessage, MessageBox, Error, and Warning.

Refer to the code and accompanying message in figures 14.22 and 14.23. In the example, MsgGetText is used in conjunction with Warning. The message box does not display the message set and message number, which are 20002 and 1 respectively.

NOTE   Fields and variables with a Number or Date/Time data type are converted to String when displayed in messages.

---

1 The `MessageBox` function is used to display messages from within PeopleCode programs.

2 The parameters used in `MessageBox` control the buttons, default button and icons in the message box window.

3 Messages can be defined by message set and message number, to the PeopleCode Message Catalog. These messages are then displayed by PeopleCode functions.

4 Messages can appear in various languages and are displayed in a chosen language, if the user profile is set up with the corresponding language code.

5 The `Error` and `Warning` functions work in conjunction with a `MsgGet` or `MsgGetText`, when displaying messages from the Message Catalog.

6 The difference between `Error` and `Warning` is that `Error` terminates the PeopleCode program and subsequent processing. `Warning` allows the user to continue after clicking the OK button.

7 `MsgGet` and `MsgGetText` retrieve messages from the Message Catalog. `MsgGetText` does not display the message set and message number.

C H A P T E R   1 5

Embedded SQL

PeopleCode enables the developer to execute SQL statements for data access and update. SQL statements submitted from a SQLExec statement do not interact with the Application Processor. The statements are executed directly on the database server. Using SQLExec raises inherent issues such as security and the potential for runtime errors, which may not be identified by the PeopleCode editor.

15.1 WHEN TO USE EMBEDDED SQL

Application Designer and PeopleCode built-in functions offer several methods of retrieving and updating data. A panel can contain a field defined as a display control field. A display control field is used to establish a link to a related display field. The related display field usually contains some type of description loaded from a prompt or translation table. Retrieving values from a corresponding table requires that some type of common key is present. The subsequent data retrieval can only be completed when the panel is loaded into the buffer area.

Additional strategies that can be implemented to update and retrieve data include the UpdateValue function, which updates a value on a record, and FetchValue, which retrieves data from a record. UpdateValue and FetchValue are commonly used with scroll data. These functions, however, have their limitations.

15.2 THE SQLEXEC FUNCTION

When it is necessary to retrieve, update, or delete data outside of the common panel processor, PeopleCode provides the SQLExec function. SQLExec is a function which receives an SQL string, circumvents the Application Processor, and works directly with the database server to perform operations. Rather than selecting an entire row of data, as the Application Processor does, SQLExec only selects the field(s) specified. Not unlike other built-in functions, SQLExec has its limitations and drawbacks and it should be used with discretion. SQLExec can be a powerful ally to the developer when used correctly and efficiently.

15.2.1 SQLExec

SQLExec executes an SQL command passed as a string from a PeopleCode program. The SQL string can contain bind variables, subselects, and joins. Data elements appearing in a Select statement are returned to the PeopleCode program as output and can be stored in variables or record fields.

A SQLExec statement can be written as follows:

```
SQLExec("Select  NAME from PS_PERSONAL_DATA where EMPLID = :1",
&EMPLID, &NAME);
```

The preceeding example selects the name field from the HRMS PERSONAL_DATA record and stores it into a variable called &NAME. The :1 represents a bind variable that contains an employee ID value used in the search criteria. Bind variables are the data elements referenced in the SQL string. Two types of bind variables exist: regular and inline. When regular bind variables used, each requires a corresponding variable name which replaces the :n reference in the SQL string. These variables appear outside the double quotes. In the preceding example, the bind variable :1 is substituted by the &EMPLID variable at runtime.

SQLExec is one function where unpredictable results can occur if rules are not followed. Because SQLExec bypasses the Application Processor and heads directly to the database, no evaluation of the SQL string contained in quotes is performed. Record fields used as inline bind variables or output variables are evaluated by the PeopleCode editor when they are not contained in the SQL string. When PeopleCode containing SQLExec statements are entered into the PeopleCode editor, any undefined record fields generate an error message during the syntax check or PeopleCode save operation. SQLExec statements containing inline bind variables are the exception. An incorrectly coded SQL statement that contains inline bind variables generates a runtime error message. Remember, the inline bind variables are enclosed within quotes. A previously undefined output variable such as &NAME is created at runtime and does not generate an error.

A SQLExec SELECT statement retrieves one row of data only. When multiple rows are selected, the data associated with the first row is the only data returned. What if the example above were rewritten as

```
SQLExec("Select  NAME from PS_PERSONAL_DATA where EMPLID <> :1",
&EMPLID, &NAME);
```

Only the first employee whose EMPLID does not match the contents of &EMPLID will have his/her name returned and stored in the &NAME output variable. The maximum number of output variables when using SELECT is 64.

With SQLExec, UPDATES, INSERTS, and DELETES can be performed, but can only be done in the following events:

- SavePreChg
- WorkFlow
- SavePostChg

SQLExec returns an optional Boolean. A value of True indicates that the function was successfully executed.

Let's now review a statement that contains a SQLExec function call. The PeopleCode is shown in figure 15.1. This statement is used in Problem Tracking to verify the MY_USER_ID field against the PeopleTool security record.

The SQLExec in this example is part of a nested If statement. In the example, we are verifying that the value contained in the record field MY_USER_ID exists on the PSOPRDEFN table. PSOPRDEFN is a Tools table which contains the operator definition (see chapter 3 for a description of the operator ID and class of operators). On the PSOPRDEFN table, we are comparing the OPRID column, which is the PeopleSoft operator ID, to the user ID entered into the Problem Tracking application panel. The bind variable represented as :1 is the first parameter to follow the SQL string. It is substituted with the contents of the field MY_USER_ID at runtime. If other bind variables were used, they would follow MY_USER_ID in the order in which they appeared in

```
MY_USER_ID                                    ▼ │FieldEdit                                      ▼

If MY_USER_ID <> %OperatorId Then
   If (SQLExec("Select  'x' from PSOPRDEFN where OPRID = :1", MY_USER_ID,
&OPRID)) = True Then
      If %SqlRows = 0 Then
         Error (MsgGet(20001, 1, "User id %1 not in system as operator id",
MY_USER_ID));
      End-If;
   End-If;
End-If;
```

Figure 15.1 SQLExec statement

the SQL string and would subsequently be identified as :2, :3, and so on as required. A bind variable cannot reference a LONG data type.

In the example, the next parameter that follows MY_USER_ID is an output variable. This can also be a record field. The example uses an output variable named &OPRID which does not require pre-definition. Upon closer examination, however, the output variable &OPRID does not contain the results of the Select. In this example we use a convention that substitutes a literal for the OPRID field. This is done to verify that the value contained in MY_USER_ID exists on the table. Selecting the actual value into &OPRID is redundant but acceptable. Any references to &OPRID, however, are not accurate if we select the literal 'x' into the variable.

SQLExec returns an optional Boolean. In the example, the code checks for a value of True to indicate a successful function call. In the context of this example we are using the Boolean return value to determine if the next statement will be executed. In the example, the function return value is verified before executing the next statement. An alternative method of writing the SQLExec portion is:

```
If MY_USER_ID <> %OperatorId Then
   If (SQLExec("Select  'x' from PSOPRDEFN where OPRID = :1", MY_USER_ID,
&OPRID)) Then
      If %SqlRows = 0 Then
         Error (MsgGet(20001, 1, "User id %1 not in system as operator id",
MY_USER_ID));
      End-If;
   End-If;
End-If;
```

Because SQLExec returns a Boolean value, the comparison operator is not necessary. People who are new to development may find this convention somewhat strange. The If statement evaluates the expression in parenthesis. When the expression is True, any subsequent statements are executed.

The next statement is interesting: SQLExec uses the system variable %SQLRows to identify the number of rows impacted by the most current SQLExec. The number of rows affected by an UPDATE, INSERT, or DELETE statement is reflected in the %SQLRows system variable. A SELECT statement, however, returns zero when no rows are selected and returns a non-zero value if one row is selected.

> **NOTE** When performing a Select, the non-zero value returned in %SQLRows does not reflect the total number of rows selected. The non-zero value is a return code, not the actual number of rows selected.

15.3 USING INLINE BIND VARIABLES

Refer to the example in figure 15.1. When an inline bind variable is used to represent the field MY_USER_ID, the PeopleCode appears as shown in figure 15.2.

```
MY_USER_TABLE (Record PeopleCode)                          _ □ ×
MY_USER_ID                        ▼  FieldEdit                        ▼

If MY_USER_ID <> %OperatorId Then
   If (SQLExec("Select  'x' from PSOPRDEFN where OPRID =
:MY_USER_TABLE.MY_USER_ID", &OPRID)) Then
      If %SqlRows = 0 Then
         Error (MsgGet(20001, 1, "User id %1 not in system as operator
id", MY_USER_ID));
      End-If;
   End-If;
End-If;
```

Figure 15.2   Inline Bind variables

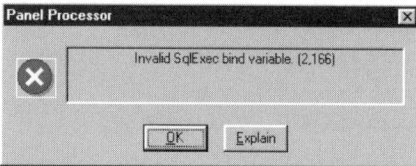

Figure 15.3   Runtime error using incorrect bind variable

The inline bind variable requires full record field qualification. A runtime error message is issued when the bind variable is coded as :MY_USER_ID. An error message however is not issued during the PeopleCode editor session. No error is generated because the inline bind variable appears within the SQL string, and no edits are performed against it until runtime. When regular bind variables are used, the PeopleCode editor verifies that the correct record and field combination are defined to the Application Designer. An example of a runtime error message is displayed in figure 15.3.

Conversely, if we erroneously code the inline bind variable illustrated in figure 15.2 as :OUR_USER_TABLE.MY_USER_ID, the PeopleCode editor does not generate an error during a syntax check or when the code is saved. Instead, we receive a runtime error as illustrated by figure 15.4.

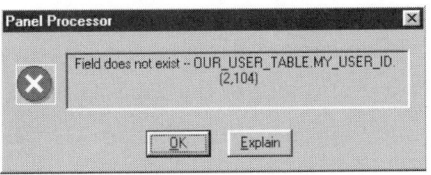

Figure 15.4 Incorrect record field used as inline bind variable

We should consider several items when using inline bind variables. The PeopleCode editor does not check for incorrect record names or field names referenced as inline variables in the SQL string. These names are resolved at runtime. If you are part of a development team using custom tables, the possibility exists that someone may rename a table or a field referenced as an inline bind variable. In the example in figure 15.2, if the table were actually renamed to OUR_USER_TABLE by someone who thought it more appropriate than MY_USER_TABLE, the PeopleCode would produce a runtime error. This assumes that, after the renaming was accomplished, syntax checking was performed against the PeopleCode. Similarly, a PeopleTools upgrade may also contain table name changes bundled into the upgrade. If you have developed custom code, the references to these tables or fields within an SQL string are not updated automatically by the upgrade process. Any syntax checking will flag record and fields that do not exist, provided they are not contained in the SQL string as inline bind variables.

15.4 DATES AND META-SQL

There are platform limitations to using embedded SQL particularly for Date/Time values. Each platform has its own unique method when it comes to handling dates. The methods are not dramatically different, but the differences are enough so that in order to remain platform independent, PeopleTools uses its own date formatting. In PeopleCode programs, the Application Processor converts data for use in PeopleTools applications. Data that may appear different from one platform to another can include dates and data types such as LONG. The Application Processor performs these conversions when data are loaded into buffers for input processing or when the data are moved from the buffer to the database. The SQLExec statement does not perform this type of data conversion. In essence, when using SQLExec, what is read in as a result of a Select is what appears in the output value.

The Application Processor stores dates as YYYY-MM-DD. When a SQLExec loads a date value stored on the database as DD-Mon-YYYY, a subsequent comparison between the two dates will always result in False.

One method that enables us to get around these platform specific issues is the Meta-SQL function. Meta-SQL functions are imbedded into statements that receive an SQL string such as SQLExec. Most Meta-SQL functions can be categorized into two types, either as an in function or an out function.

There are however some functions such as TrimSubStr and SubString that serve dual roles.

At runtime, In functions containing UPDATE, SELECT, or INSERT statements extend to become platform specific SQL. These functions generate SQL statements containing variables that are passed to the database. `In` functions can be used, for example, when a date is used in the `WHERE` clause of a `Select` or `Update` statement. `In` functions can also be used when a date is sent to the database via an Insert statement. `Out` functions also extend at runtime to become platform-specific SQL which appear in `Select` statements.

Definitions of `Meta-SQL` functions are listed in appendix E.

The examples below compare a `SQLExec` statement using the platform-specific ORACLE/DB2 substring against the PeopleCode platform independent `%Substring` `Meta-SQL`. In both examples we are selecting the first ten characters from the NAME field of the PERSONAL_DATA record. The first example uses the platform-specific `SUBSTR` function:

```
SQLExec("Select  SUBSTR (NAME,1,10) from PS_PERSONAL_DATA
    where EMPLID = :1", &EMPLID, &NAME)
```

While this example uses the %Substring Meta-SQL function:

```
SQLExec("Select  %Substring(NAME,1,10) from PS_PERSONAL_DATA
    where EMPLID = :1", &EMPLID, &NAME)
```

The statements are similar but the benefit of the statement in the second example is platform independence. The `SUBSTR` function uses the same basic parameters as the `Meta-SQL`. The argument string, starting position, and length are even in the same order. Nothing is as easy as it appears, however, and this is no exception. Suppose we are using ORACLE specific functions and the MIS management has decided to migrate functionality to SQLBase. If we were to use platform-dependent functions, our code would appear as:

```
SQLExec("Select  @SUBSTRING(NAME,0,10) from PS_PERSONAL_DATA
    where EMPLID = :1", &EMPLID, &NAME)
```

We can immediately see that the function is `@SUBSTRING`. Another and more potentially risky result is that, when using the `@SUBSTRING` function, the first character in the string begins at position 0. The ORACLE, DB2, and Meta-SQL start at position 1. Without careful analysis, these types of changes can lead to major problems later on.

Let's look at another example using dates. With no edits, dates are selected in formats, depending on the database type. Some databases select dates as YYYYMMDD, and others select dates as DD-MON-YYYY. In the following example, we are looking for a total of all employees in PERSONAL_DATA who have a BIRTHDATE <= January 1st 1970. The count is placed into a variable called &SUM. A database specific piece of code may appear as:

```
&COMPARE_DATE = "1970-01-01";
SQLExec("Select  COUNT(*) from PS_PERSONAL_DATA  where BIRTHDATE <=  TO_
DATE(:1,'YYYY-MM-DD')", &COMPARE_DATE, &SUM);
```

Using an `In` Meta-string, we can obtain platform independence. The example below uses the `%DateIn` function and receives a date in the format `YYYY-MM-DD`.

```
&COMPARE_DATE = "1970-01-01";
SQLExec("Select  COUNT(*) from PS_PERSONAL_DATA  where BIRTHDATE <=
%DateIn(:1)", &COMPARE_DATE, &SUM);
```

15.5 SECURITY AND MAINTENANCE CONSIDERATIONS

When using `SQLExec` with inline bind variables, we need to keep in mind that future upgrades may rename tables or fields. Syntax checks of inline bind variables will not indicate this type of discrepancy. Inconsistencies can also occur when a custom table is modified and any corresponding code does not reflect the change.

More importantly, we need to know that the use of `SQLExec` has the potential to allow the end-user to update or delete data. Assuming the user has database privileges, coding `SQLExec` without giving consideration to security can result in a user unknowingly changing data. This can most likely occur when the `SQLExec` statement has been coded incorrectly, without verifying security. Perhaps the `SQLExec` updates data to which the user would not normally have access.

KEY POINTS

1. `SQLExec` is a function that allows the developer to execute SQL statements directly on the database server.

2. Bind variables can be passed two ways: regular and inline.

3. `Meta-SQL` enables `SQLExec` to work with `Date`, `Time`, and `String` parameters. This allows some level of platform independence.

4. Of utmost importance is that the use of `SQLExec` bypasses the standard PeopleSoft security. The security in place may limit the user access to specific data. Unless `SQLExec` code mimics the security functionality, improper use of `SQLExec` can result in a security breach.

CHAPTER   16

Working with scrolls

This chapter discusses the methods used to process panels that contain scrolls. Data consisting of multiple rows may occupy the same panel and include various primary record definitions. Knowledge of how system buffers are processed is necessary for panels or panel groups containing multiple occurs levels, because the Application Processor utilizes PeopleCode in the same order. Not every panel contains or requires a scroll bar. For panels that do contain scroll bars, specific terminology, functions, and methods are often used to reference data in the panel buffers. Topics aimed at providing an understanding of how to use PeopleCode in multiple occurs levels include:

- the relationship between records on different scroll levels
- the order in which the system processes buffers
- PeopleCode functions used with scrolls
- the SQL string within scroll functions

In part 2, Advanced Panel Design Features, we discussed how to add scroll bar objects to panels. A panel containing scroll bars may include multiple occurs levels and occurs count. At the PeopleCode level, a large amount of code can be devoted to working within multiple occurs levels. Multiple occurs levels impact PeopleCode execution because the order in which the Application Processor handles scroll buffer areas and the manner in which PeopleCode is written must work together. Understanding the relationship between records at varying occurs levels is important for writing efficient code.

16.1 PARENT/CHILD RELATIONSHIP

According to PeopleTools terminology, a record at the highest level in a panel is referred to as the level zero record. From a multiple level perspective, a panel containing only one record and no scroll bars is elementary. On a panel containing one scroll bar, two occurs levels exist: zero and one. What we have at occurs level zero is one or more record definitions that contain one or multiple fields, used to link data in subsequent levels. The level zero record is considered the Parent row, and level one is the Child. When data buffers are processed, level zero records are handled before level one records. When a panel contains two scroll bars, the level zero records are processed first and are then followed by one row of level one data. When there are two occurrence levels, the level one record is parent to level two. After a single level one record is processed, the system then processes level two records. The cycle is then repeated; the next level one row of data are processed, then followed by all associated level two records.

Table 16.1 illustrates parent and child keys:

Table 16.1   Relationship between Parent and Child rows

SETID	OPRCLASS	Location	Emplid
USA	ALLPANLS	001	6601
USA	ALLPANLS	001	7705
USA	ALLPANLS	001	6603
USA	ALLPANLS	002	8101
USA	ALLPANLS	002	8102
USA	ALLPANLS	002	8105
USA	ALLPANLS	003	8201
USA	ALLPANLS	003	8651
USA	ALLPANLS	003	8773

The parent and child keys are SETID, OPRCLASS, and Location. An additional child key is Emplid.

A selected parent row contains three key values. Child rows also contain the same three key values plus an additional key. In this example EMPLID is the additional child key. A parent key containing '001' as the third key value may have one or more child rows that contain the same key values. On a panel containing two scrolls representing the data illustrated in table 16.1, when parent key 001 is encountered, the child keys 6601, 7705, and 6603 are processed before parent key 002 and its corresponding child key values 8101, 8102, and 8105.

When scroll bars are defined with AutoSelect, all data are retrieved with one Select statement, regardless of the number of scrolls. The Select is performed after a search key is chosen. The Application Processor then manages the buffers by processing level zero records first, then all subsequent levels as discussed previously.

TIP   Level zero fields are usually based on search records.

Using the knowledge obtained in part 2, it is possible to build a panel containing two scroll bars and no PeopleCode. We could define a level zero record, a level one record, and a level two record. Without PeopleCode, however, the functionality is limited to certain panel processor functions and to end-user actions such as Insert Row (F7) and Delete Row (F8). At this basic level, we could define a panel, add scroll bars, and establish the parent/child relationships. When the panel is processed, any scroll areas would be populated automatically. There are circumstances, however, under which we, as the developers, would have to programmatically control the processing of panel scroll areas. Our work becomes complex and, therefore, more interesting when PeopleCode is added to enhance the processing behind panel scroll areas.

The objective of this chapter is to enable the reader to develop panels using scroll bars and, more importantly, to add the necessary PeopleCode that will interact with data contained in these scrolls. This includes the following items:

- loading data into a scroll
- removing data from a scroll
- removing scroll data from a database table
- determining the number of records in a scroll
- retrieving or updating data in a scroll buffer area

To begin our tour of scroll functionality, we will use two panels containing scrolls. The concept behind the panels is to link operator security classes and office locations that are on the LOCATION_TBL record. We then link the employees in the specified locations to the operator class/location combination. Figure 16.1 illustrates the Operator Class/Location panel, and figure 16.2 is the panel that links the operator class/locations to employee data.

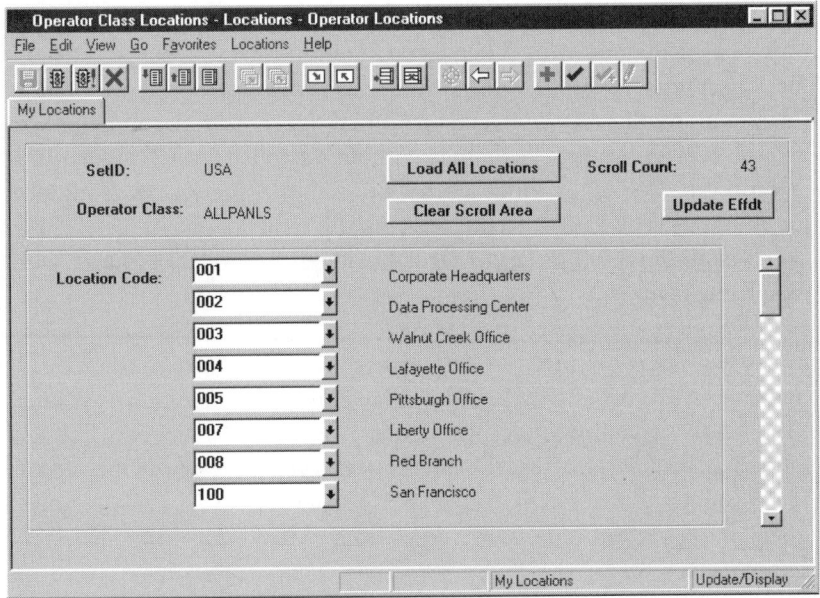

Figure 16.1   Operator Class/Location panel

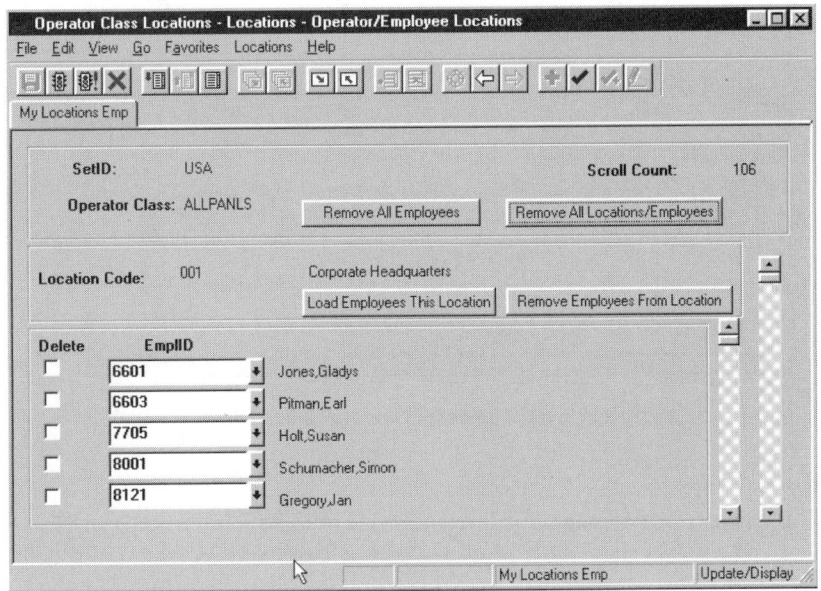

Figure 16.2   Link employees to operator/class locations

As we can see by the illustrations, one panel contains a single scroll bar, and the other panel contains two. When using functions that operate on scroll areas, the number of parameters passed to these functions varies based on the number of scrolls. The maximum number of scroll levels permitted is three. When adding a scroll to a panel, a scroll at level 3 cannot be defined without a scroll at level 2. Similarly, a scroll at level 2 cannot be defined without a scroll at level 1. A hierarchy among keys should also be followed. The level 2 record requires the same key fields as level 1 in addition to its own unique key. The level 1 record requires the level 0 key fields, with the addition of a unique key value.

Referring to figure 16.1, we can see several record definitions in the panel because it is a panel with one scroll containing two primary records. The level 0 primary record is MY_LOCATION_HDR. This record contains two keys, SETID and OPRCLASS. The primary record at level 1 is MY_LOCATIONS. This record is a child of MY_LOCATION_HDR. The order and level of fields for the operator class/locations panel is illustrated by figure 16.3. MY_LOCATION_HDR is considered the primary scroll record, because the keys from this table control the data selected into subsequent scrolls.

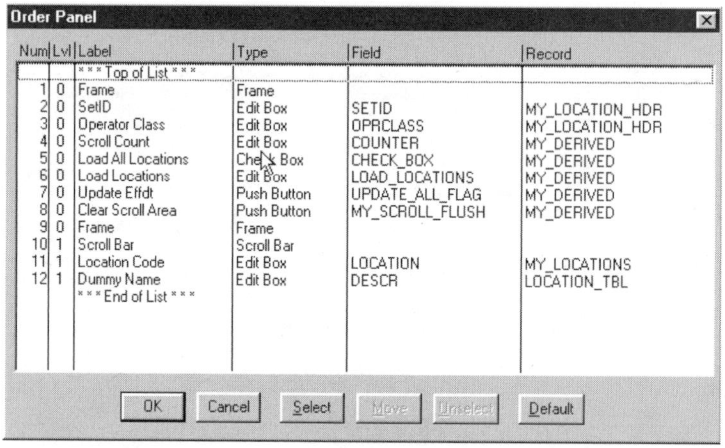

Figure 16.3   Order and level of fields for Operator Class/Location panel

---

NOTE   For each scroll level, only one primary scroll record can exist. Other records can be those of related display fields and Derived/Work fields.

The illustration in figure 16.3 also identifies an additional record at level 0, MY_DERIVED. This record contains the PeopleCode linked to the push buttons on the panel. At level 1, we have the record MY_LOCATIONS and the location table

(LOCATION_TBL). The location table is used to retrieve the location description and effective date.

The record definitions and key fields for the three primary records used in figures 16.1 and 16.2 are shown in figures 16.4, 16.5 and 16.6.

MY_LOCATION_HDR (Record)

Field Name	Type	Key	Dir	CurC	Srch	List	Sys	Audt	H	Default
SETID	Char	Key	Asc		Yes	Yes	No			OPR DEF TBL HR.SETID
OPRCLASS	Char	Key	Asc		Yes	Yes	No			

Figure 16.4   Fields for MY_LOCATION_HDR

MY_LOCATIONS (Record)

Field Name	Type	Key	Dir	CurC	Srch	List	Sys	Audt	H	Default
SETID	Char	Key	Asc		Yes	Yes	No			OPR DEF TBL HR.SETID
OPRCLASS	Char	Key	Asc		Yes	Yes	No			
LOCATION	Char	Key	Asc		Yes	No	No			
EFFDT	Date				No	No	No			

Figure 16.5   Fields for MY_LOCATIONS

MY_LOCATION_EMP (Record)

Field Name	Type	Key	Dir	CurC	Srch	List	Sys	Audt	H	Default
SETID	Char	Key	Asc		Yes	Yes	No			OPR DEF TBL HR.SETID
OPRCLASS	Char	Key	Asc		Yes	Yes	No			
LOCATION	Char	Key	Asc		Yes	No	No			
EMPLID	Char	Key	Asc		No	No	No			

Figure 16.6   Fields for MY_LOCATION_EMP

NOTE   Only one row of data for each level 0 record is allowed on a panel. Other rows are displayed on a list box.

Now that we are better acquainted with the panels, records, and parent/child relationships involved in the scroll demonstration, we can begin to review the functions and apply them to the panels in figures 16.1 and 16.2.

Navigation: Locations → Operator Locations → Add

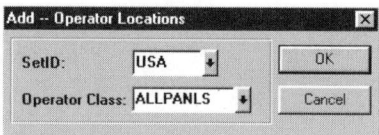

Figure 16.7   Establish the operator class header

From a functional perspective, when an operator class is linked to one or more locations, a location header record has to be initially established. We can use the menu to select the SETID and OPRCLASS.

After the operator class header is established, the PeopleCode behind the push button is ready to load data into the scroll area (figure 16.8).

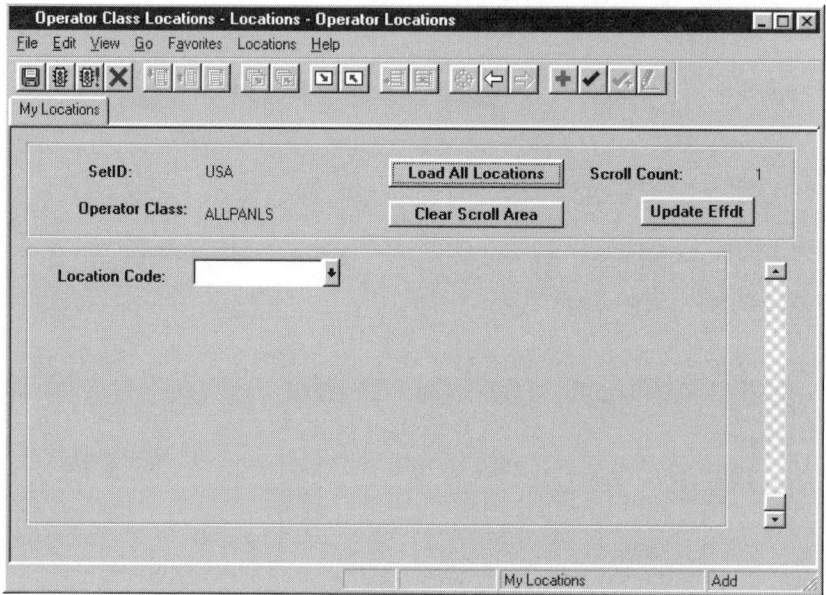

Figure 16.8   Initial Operator Class/Location panel

The panel shown in figure 16.8 refers to information for MY_LOCATION_HDR but contains no data in the scroll area referencing MY_LOCATIONS. The objective here is to load all location codes from the location table for this particular SETID. Several methods can be used to accomplish this task. One method involves the use of People-Code Scroll functions.

16.2   *PEOPLECODE FUNCTIONS USED WITH SCROLLS*

The first function that will be applied is ScrollSelect. Functions that operate on data contained in a scroll use the ScrollPath to reference the individual row or scroll levels at which the functions are targeted. ScrollPath defines the records at each scroll level as well as the target record name. When we reference a scroll at level 1, `ScrollPath` is comprised of the target record only. A reference to data at scroll level 2 requires specification of the level 1 record and the target record name. When referring to rows or data on scroll level 3, level 1 and level 2 records are required, in addition to the target record name.

16.2.1 ScrollSelect

The `ScrollSelect` function selects records from a table and loads them into the scroll buffer area of a panel. In terms of Parent/Child relationships, `ScrollSelect` chooses all corresponding child rows and inserts them under the next higher level row. The function requires the specification of the target scroll area, a source record from which to select rows and an optional SQL string. The parameters passed to `ScrollSelect` vary based on the scroll level at which the function is targeted:

Level 1

```
ScrollSelect (1, RECORD.target_recname, RECORD.sel_recname);
```

Level 2

```
ScrollSelect (2, RECORD.level1_recname, RECORD.target_recname,
RECORD.sel_recname);
```

Level 3

```
ScrollSelect (3, RECORD.level1_recname, RECORD.level2_recname,
RECORD.target_recname, RECORD.sel_recname);
```

In addition to the parameters required to reference data at the various scroll levels, the optional SQL string and Turbo parameters can be specified. (Refer to appendix E for syntax description of `ScrollSelect`.) Let's apply `ScrollSelect` to the panels presented in figures 16.1 and 16.2.

Example 1

Figure 16.8 contains a push button—Load All Locations. We can use `ScrollSelect` to load all location codes from the location table for the SETID contained in the record MY_LOCATION_HDR. The code using `ScrollSelect` is illustrated in figure 16.9.

The code in figure 16.9 first verifies that the panel name is MY_LOCATIONS. This is necessary because the code is executed from a Derived/Work record (MY_DERIVED), which can be used on different panels. The `DeleteRow` statement is used to delete rows from the scroll and database table. In this example, (`DeleteRow` is used in a loop. Rows are processed from high to low, because rows are renumbered each time they are deleted.) The `ScrollSelect` parameters identify that the target

```
  MY_DERIVED (Record PeopleCode)                                        _ □ ×
 LOAD_LOCATIONS                          ▼  FieldChange                      ▼
 /*
 *********************************************************************************
 ** ScrollSelect example for a panel containing 1 scroll bar
 *********************************************************************************
 */
 If %Panel = "MY_LOCATIONS" Then
    For &I = ActiveRowCount(RECORD.MY_LOCATIONS) To 1 Step - 1;
       DeleteRow(RECORD.MY_LOCATIONS, &I);
    End-For;
    ScrollSelect(1, RECORD.MY_LOCATIONS, RECORD.MY_LOC_OPR_VW, True);
    COUNTER = ActiveRowCount(RECORD.MY_LOCATIONS); ◄─────┐
 End-If;                                                 ❶
```

Figure 16.9   ScrollSelect at level 1 scroll

scroll area is at level 1. Based on the scroll level, `target_recname` and `sel_recordname` parameters are required. MY_LOCATIONS is the target record name and the select scroll area. Data are retrieved from MY_LOC_OPR_VW, which is a view that selects locations with the most current effective date from the LOCATION_TBL record. This parameter can be the same as the target record name, but in this example, we are selecting from a view and loading the selected fields into a different target record. The COUNTER field, ❶, contains the number of active rows in the scroll area and is reflected on the panel. The `True` parameter at the end of the function call indicates that we are using the `Turbo` feature. When specified in Scroll functions such as `ScrollSelect` and `ScrollSelectNew`, `Turbo` improves performance of `ScrollSelect`.

(Refer to figure 16.1 for an illustration of how the panel appears after the `ScrollSelect` PeopleCode is executed.)

Example 2

The next panel links employees to the operator class/locations.

The panel illustrated by figure 16.10 contains a push button—Load Employees This Location. The code behind this button is used to populate the scroll area with employee IDs that have a current location code equal to the value of the location on the current level 1 scroll. The code to accomplish this task on scroll level 2 is shown in figure 16.11.

In addition to `ScrollSelect`, other functions and statements are used to accomplish the task of loading employee data for the location at scroll level 1. The code verifies the panel name is MY_LOCATIONS_EMP. This is necessary because the code is executed from a Derived/Work record and can be used on different panels. Conceptually, the code used to load the scroll on MY_LOCATIONS and MY_LOCATIONS_EMP panels can be localized on the same record and fieldname in the Derived/Work record. The `DeleteRow` statement is used to delete rows from the

Navigation: Locations → Operator/Employee Locations

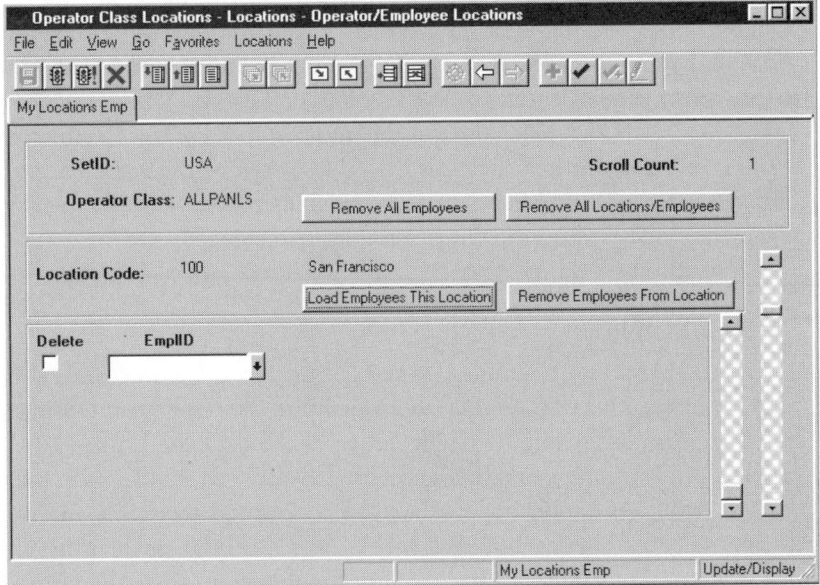

Figure 16.10   Panel to link operator class/locations and employees

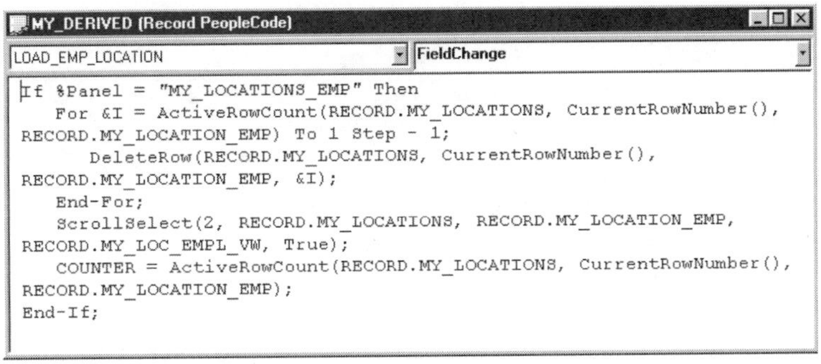

```
MY_DERIVED (Record PeopleCode)                                    _ □ X
LOAD_EMP_LOCATION                          ▼  FieldChange                ▼
If %Panel = "MY_LOCATIONS_EMP" Then
   For &I = ActiveRowCount(RECORD.MY_LOCATIONS, CurrentRowNumber(),
RECORD.MY_LOCATION_EMP) To 1 Step - 1;
      DeleteRow(RECORD.MY_LOCATIONS, CurrentRowNumber(),
RECORD.MY_LOCATION_EMP, &I);
   End-For;
   ScrollSelect(2, RECORD.MY_LOCATIONS, RECORD.MY_LOCATION_EMP,
RECORD.MY_LOC_EMPL_VW, True);
   COUNTER = ActiveRowCount(RECORD.MY_LOCATIONS, CurrentRowNumber(),
RECORD.MY_LOCATION_EMP);
End-If;
```

Figure 16.11   ScrollSelect at level 2 scroll

scroll area and database table. The `DeleteRow` is used in a loop. Rows are processed from high to low, because rows are renumbered each time they are deleted. `DeleteRow` will be discussed later in this chapter. The `ScrollSelect` parameters identify that the target scroll area is at level 2. This scroll level will contain the selected employee IDs. Because the target record is at level 2, the level1_recname parameter is required. In the example the level 1 record name is coded as RECORD.MY_LOCATIONS. The target record is MY_LOCATION_EMP and resides at level 2. In the example the select record (sel_recordname) is represented by a view. A view is used to extract the most current effective-dated Job rows and join them with the corresponding location table entry. The optional Turbo parameter is set to TRUE so that performance of ScrollSelect can be improved. Because the potential to load many rows of employee IDs at scroll level 2 exists, the use of this parameter is vital. The COUNTER field contains the number of active rows in the scroll area. This count is reflected on the panel as is the value passed by the ActiveRowCount function. This function will be discussed later, but it is worthwhile to mention that its parameters are based on the target scroll level referenced.

A function similar to ScrollSelect is ScrollSelectNew.

16.2.2   ScrollSelectNew

ScrollSelectNew resembles ScrollSelect except that ScrollSelectNew marks records as New when they are loaded into the scroll area. During save processing, these records are automatically added to the database. ScrollSelect is used to select pre-existing rows into a scroll area. Because ScrollSelect does not mark rows as New, some other type of activity is required to enable the save button. A DeleteRow used in combination with ScrollSelect enables the save button for new rows. ScrollSelectNew requires the specification of the target scroll area, a source record from which to select rows, and an optional SQL string. The parameters passed to ScrollSelectNew vary based on the scroll level at which the function is targeted.

Level 1

```
ScrollSelectNew (1, RECORD.target_recname, RECORD.sel_recname);
```

Level 2

```
ScrollSelectNew (2, RECORD.level1_recname, RECORD.target_recname,
RECORD.sel_recname);
```

Level 3

```
ScrollSelectNew (3, RECORD.level1_recname, RECORD.level2_recname,
RECORD.target_recname, RECORD.sel_recname);
```

In addition to the parameters required to reference data at the various scroll levels, the optional SQL string and Turbo parameters can be specified.

Example

The code in figure 16.12 applies ScrollSelectNew to the level 1 scroll that appears on the panel MY_LOCATIONS.

As we can see by the sample code, ScrollSelectNew is essentially the same as ScrollSelect. The parameters and their use are identical. In the example,

```
MY_DERIVED (Record PeopleCode)                                    _ □ ×
LOAD_LOCATIONS                          ▼  FieldChange                  ▼
/*
** **************************************************************************
** ScrollSelectNew example for a panel containing 1 scroll bar
** **************************************************************************
*/
If %Panel = "MY_LOCATIONS" Then
   For &I = ActiveRowCount(RECORD.MY_LOCATIONS) To 1 Step - 1;
      DeleteRow(RECORD.MY_LOCATIONS, &I);
   End-For;
   ScrollSelectNew(1, RECORD.MY_LOCATIONS, RECORD.MY_LOC_OPR_VW, True);
   COUNTER = ActiveRowCount(RECORD.MY_LOCATIONS);
End-If;
```

Figure 16.12   Using ScrollSelectNew at level 1

ScrollSelectNew operates on target scroll level 1. The key difference is that the Location Table entries matching the SETID at level 0 are loaded into the scroll buffer and are marked as NEW. During save processing, they are added to the database.

The panel in figure 16.1 can be used to illustrate the results of ScrollSelect-New if it were used in place of ScrollSelect.

This panel also contains additional characteristics due to its ability to utilize the F7 and F8 function keys.

Locations can also be added by using the F7 Insert Row key and the Location prompt table, rather than using the "Load All Locations" push button. The F8 Delete Row key can also be used to remove unwanted rows. To give a real world example, let's say that the user has elected to load all locations automatically, using the push buttons, but then decides to enter the locations manually. At this point, the user can cancel out and start again. We can however, make the process more efficient by providing the ability to clear the scroll area before it is saved. This can be done using the ScrollFlush function.

16.2.3   ScrollFlush

ScrollFlush is used to remove records from a target scroll area. The function requires the specification of the target scroll area as the ScrollPath. The parameters passed to ScrollFlush are based on the scroll level from where the rows are to be removed.

Level 1

```
ScrollFlush (RECORD.target_recname);
```

Level 2

```
ScrollFlush (RECORD.level1_recname, level1_row, RECORD.target_recname);
```

Level 3

```
ScrollFlush (RECORD.level1_recname, level1_row, RECORD.level2_recname,
level2_row,  RECORD.target_recname);
```

Rows flushed from the target scroll area are not removed from the database.

Example 1

Figure 16.8 contains a push button labeled "Clear Scroll Area." The PeopleCode is shown in figure 16.13. When activated, the PeopleCode behind the push button clears the target scroll area using ScrollFlush.

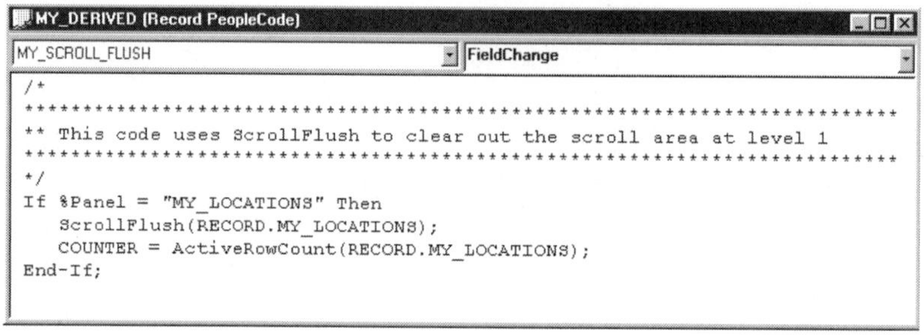

```
MY_DERIVED (Record PeopleCode)
MY_SCROLL_FLUSH                                    FieldChange
/*
 *************************************************************************
 ** This code uses ScrollFlush to clear out the scroll area at level 1
 *************************************************************************
 */
If %Panel = "MY_LOCATIONS" Then
   ScrollFlush(RECORD.MY_LOCATIONS);
   COUNTER = ActiveRowCount(RECORD.MY_LOCATIONS);
End-If;
```

Figure 16.13   ScrollFlush at level 1

A field named MY_SCROLL_FLUSH is added to MY_DERIVED and then placed on the panel. Because MY_DERIVED is a work record, there is no need to alter or recreate the table after the field is added to the record. The code to accomplish the ScrollFlush is placed in the FieldChange event. The example takes one parameter because we are clearing rows at scroll level 1. As a result, only the target record name is specified.

Example 2

Figure 16.10 contains a push button labeled "Remove Employees From Location." The button can be used to clear out the scroll area after employee data has been loaded. The PeopleCode utilizes ScrollFlush at the level 2 scroll. The example is illustrated in figure16.14.

A review of the PeopleCode in figure 16.14 indicates the panel name is verified as MY_LOCATIONS_EMP. The ScrollFlush parameters use level1_recname. This parameter is required because the target record is at level 2. The example specifies the level 1 record name as RECORD.MY_LOCATIONS. ScrollFlush is targeted at scroll level 2 and as a result, the level1_row parameter is required. The CurrentRowNumber function is used to identify the row number at scroll level 1. The target record is MY_LOCATION_EMP, which resides at level 2.

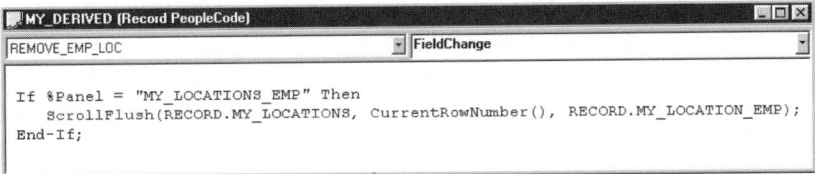

```
MY_DERIVED (Record PeopleCode)                                    _□×

REMOVE_EMP_LOC                            ▼  FieldChange           ▼

If %Panel = "MY_LOCATIONS_EMP" Then
    ScrollFlush(RECORD.MY_LOCATIONS, CurrentRowNumber(), RECORD.MY_LOCATION_EMP);
End-If;
```

Figure 16.14   ScrollFlush at Scroll level 2

NOTE   The `ScrollFlush` function does not delete records from the database. It removes them from the target scroll and related buffer areas only.

16.3   ADDITIONAL SCROLL FUNCTIONS

At this point, the reader should have a better understanding of scrolls and some of the functions used to process them, as discussed in the previous sections. The following additional scroll functions use parameters similar to those discussed previously.

It is sometimes necessary to identify the number of rows in a scroll area. PeopleCode uses several functions to count records in a target scroll area. Several count functions are available because data marked for deletion may not be required in some routines. `ActiveRowCount` is one such function:

16.3.1   ActiveRowCount

`ActiveRowCount` returns a number representing the sum of active rows in a given scroll area. Records marked as deleted are not included in the count. `ActiveRowCount` is often used when we are looping and examining each row in the target scroll area. The parameters used by `ActiveRowCount` are based on the scroll level in which a count of active rows is required.

Level 1

```
ActiveRowCount (RECORD.target_recname);
```

Level 2

```
ActiveRowCount (RECORD.level1_recname, level1_row, RECORD.target_recname);
```

Level 3

```
ActiveRowCount (RECORD.level1_recname, level1_row, RECORD.level2_recname,
level2_row,  RECORD.target_recname);
```

Example 1

The Operator Class/Location panel in figure 16.1 can be used to illustrate `ActiveRowCount` at scroll level 1. The panel contains a label named "Scroll Count," used to indicate the number of non-deleted rows in the scroll area. The COUNTER field on MY_DERIVED contains the return value from the `ActiveRowCount` function that appears on the panel.

The use of `ActiveRowCount` to display the number of rows in a scroll requires that it be placed strategically in various events, in order for the count to reflect inserts and deletes correctly.

The two panels used in the Operator Class/Location application can use `ActiveRowCount` in the following events or actions:

- `RowInit`
- `ScrollSelect/ScrollSelectNew`
- `ScrollFlush`
- `RowInsert (F7)`
- `RowDelete (F8)`

The example below can be applied to the panel in figure 16.1, which contains one scroll level. Each time any push button is activated, the "Scroll Count" field is updated. The field named COUNTER reflects the number of active rows in the scroll area.

```
COUNTER = ActiveRowCount(RECORD.MY_LOCATIONS);
```

The preceding code can be applied to scroll level 1. At scroll level 2, the following code returns the number of active rows. The count is applied to the panel illustrated in figure 16.2.

```
COUNTER = ActiveRowCount(RECORD.MY_LOCATIONS, CurrentRowNumber(),
RECORD.MY_LOCATION_EMP);
```

Example 2

The use of `ActiveRowCount` can be applied during loop processing. The example below uses `ActiveRowCount` when using the `DeleteRow` function. In the example, the variable `&I` initially contains the number of active rows, which enables the loop to work from the highest to the lowest row in the scroll.

```
For &I = ActiveRowCount(RECORD.MY_LOCATIONS) To 1 Step - 1;
   DeleteRow(RECORD.MY_LOCATIONS, &I);
End-For;
```

Functions such as `ActiveRowCount` and `ScrollFlush` require a level row number as part of the `ScrollPath`. A scroll area can contain one or many rows. Each row has a number associated with it which indicates its place in the scroll area. The number can be used to identify a parent row to its corresponding child rows. A function that returns the number associated with a row in a scroll area is `CurrentRowNumber`.

16.3.2   CurrentRowNumber

The `CurrentRowNumber` function is used when it is necessary to identify the row number of the current row in a scroll area. The function takes a parameter which represents the level where the row number is retrieved. When the level parameter is not specified, the function uses the current scroll level from where the function is called as the default level. `CurrentRowNumber` is sometimes used with `ActiveRowCount` to limit the number of times a loop is processed based on the active rows in the scroll area.

Example

The following example uses `CurrentRowNumber` during execution of the `ActiveRowCount` and `DeleteRow` functions. When used in conjunction with `ActiveRowCount` and `DeleteRow`, `CurrentRowNumber` returns the parent row number as a path to the child row MY_LOCATION_EMP. In this context, the parent row may reference one or more child rows.

```
For &I = ActiveRowCount(RECORD.MY_LOCATIONS, CurrentRowNumber(),
   RECORD.MY_LOCATION_EMP) To 1 Step - 1;
   DeleteRow(RECORD.MY_LOCATIONS, CurrentRowNumber(),
     RECORD.MY_LOCATION_EMP, &I);
End-For;
```

16.3.3   DeleteRow

A number of PeopleCode programs imitate user actions performed using toolbar icons or function keys. The `DeleteRow` function can be used to delete records from a scroll area and database.

The `DeleteRow` function enables rows to be deleted by a PeopleCode program. The function triggers the `RowDelete` event that mimics the F8/Delete Row operation. `DeleteRow` removes records from the target scroll as well as from the database. `DeleteRow` requires the specification of the `ScrollPath` and the target row number to delete. The parameters passed to `DeleteRow` are based on the scroll level and target record number from where rows are to be removed. Using the `DeleteRow` function at various levels can be written as follows:

Level 1

```
DeleteRow (RECORD.target_recname, target_row);
```

Level 2

```
DeleteRow (RECORD.level1_recname, level1_row, RECORD.target_recname,
target_row);
```

Level 3

```
DeleteRow (RECORD.level1_recname, level1_row, RECORD.level2_recname,
level2_row,  RECORD.target_recname, target_row);
```

NOTE   DeleteRow cannot be called from the same scroll level as that of the target scroll area.

Example 1

The panel in figure 16.10 used to link operator classes to employees contains a button labeled "Remove All Employees." When activated, the PeopleCode removes employee data only and removes it from every record at scroll level 1. The code utilizes two loops. The outer loop retrieves the number of active rows for scroll level 1. The inner loop references the child rows that contain employee data and deletes them. The code to accomplish this task is shown in figure 16.15. Data for the parent record MY_LOCATIONS remains intact after the code completes execution.

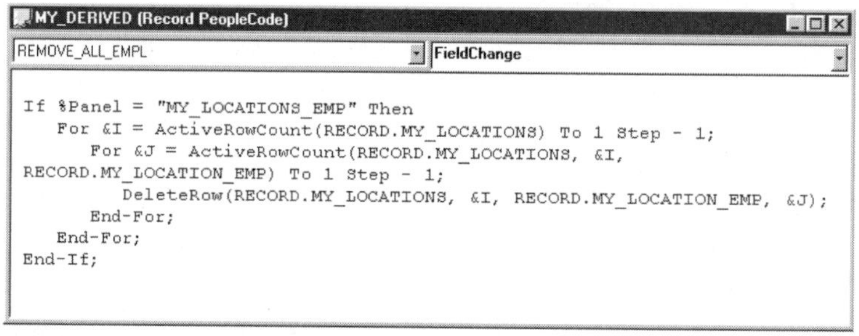

```
MY_DERIVED (Record PeopleCode)                                    _ □ ×
REMOVE_ALL_EMPL                          ▼  FieldChange                  ▼

If %Panel = "MY_LOCATIONS_EMP" Then
   For &I = ActiveRowCount(RECORD.MY_LOCATIONS) To 1 Step - 1;
      For &J = ActiveRowCount(RECORD.MY_LOCATIONS, &I,
RECORD.MY_LOCATION_EMP) To 1 Step - 1;
         DeleteRow(RECORD.MY_LOCATIONS, &I, RECORD.MY_LOCATION_EMP, &J);
      End-For;
   End-For;
End-If;
```

Figure 16.15   DeleteRow at scroll level 2

Example 2

Another push button on the panel in figure 16.10 is labeled "Remove Employees From Location." The code behind this button (figure 16.16) removes employee data from the current scroll level 1 row.

Example 3

An additional button on the panel is labeled "Remove All Locations/Employee." This piece of code removes all locations as well as all the employee data associated with the

```
MY_DERIVED (Record PeopleCode)                              _ □ ×
REMOVE_EMP_LOC                          ▼  FieldChange                    ▼

If %Panel = "MY_LOCATIONS_EMP" Then
   For &I = ActiveRowCount(RECORD.MY_LOCATIONS, CurrentRowNumber(),
RECORD.MY_LOCATION_EMP) To 1 Step - 1;
      DeleteRow(RECORD.MY_LOCATIONS, CurrentRowNumber(),
RECORD.MY_LOCATION_EMP, &I);
   End-For;
End-If;
```

Figure 16.16   DeleteRow at scroll level 2

locations. From a conceptual perspective, it appears that the code to complete this task would be complex. Actually the code (figure 16.17) is not as intricate as one might expect.

```
MY_DERIVED (Record PeopleCode)                              _ □ ×
REMOVE_ALL_LOC_EMP                      ▼  FieldChange                    ▼

If %Panel = "MY_LOCATIONS_EMP" Then
   For &I = ActiveRowCount(RECORD.MY_LOCATIONS) To 1 Step - 1;
      DeleteRow(RECORD.MY_LOCATIONS, &I);
   End-For;
End-If;
```

**Figure 16.17
Using DeleteRow to
remove all rows from
both scrolls**

The `DeleteRow` function is used in a loop and removes all active records at scroll level 1. Because the record MY_LOCATIONS is parent to the data at scroll level 2, `DeleteRow` removes all lower child level records. The removal of child rows is done automatically by `DeleteRow` as each scroll level 1 record is deleted.

The `ActiveRowCount` function is used to compute the number of active rows. The `DeleteRow` function works from the bottom of the scroll bar and is illustrated by the `Step -1` parameter in the `For` statement.

NOTE   `DeleteRow` marks records as deleted. During save processing, rows marked for deletion are removed from the database. `ScrollFlush` clears data from the scroll buffer area only and does not routinely delete rows from the database.

16.3.4   FetchValue

When working with scrolls, it is sometimes necessary to reference data which appears in the individual rows located in the panel scroll buffer. A function used to extract data from these rows is `FetchValue`.

The `FetchValue` function retrieves the value of a field from a row stored in the panel buffer of a scroll area and places it into a variable or fieldname. In addition to the `ScrollPath` parameter, `FetchValue` requires `target_row` and `recordname.fieldname` parameters as well. To use `FetchValue` at the various levels, the following syntax is used:

Level 1

```
FetchValue (RECORD.target_recname, target_row, [recordname.] fieldname);
```

Level 2

```
FetchValue (RECORD.level1_recname, level1_row, RECORD.target_recname,
target_row, [recordname.]fieldname);
```

Level 3

```
FetchValue (RECORD.level1_recname, level1_row, RECORD.level2_recname,
level2_row, RECORD.target_recname, target_row, [recordname.]fieldname);
```

Example

Using figure 16.10 let's assume that employee IDs contain a specific level of information based on the type of ID. An ID beginning with the letter "L" represents employee populations excluded from the Operator Class/Location functionality. As a result, the code should prevent any employee ID, which has a leading "L," from appearing on the panel. To accomplish this task, the PeopleCode associated with the "Load All Locations" push button can be rewritten as shown in figure 16.18.

FetchValue is used after the scroll area has been populated using ScrollSelect. In the example, FetchValue is used in a loop that is executed at scroll level 1. FetchValue takes five parameters; MY_LOCATIONS is the level 1

```
/*
****************************************************************
** Using FetchValue for selection criteria at scroll level 2
****************************************************************
*/
If %Panel = "MY_LOCATIONS_EMP" Then
   ScrollSelect(2, RECORD.MY_LOCATIONS, RECORD.MY_LOCATION_EMP,
RECORD.MY_LOC_EMPL_VW, True);
   For &I = ActiveRowCount(RECORD.MY_LOCATIONS, CurrentRowNumber(),
RECORD.MY_LOCATION_EMP) To 1 Step - 1;
      &EMPLID = FetchValue(RECORD.MY_LOCATIONS, CurrentRowNumber(),
RECORD.MY_LOCATION_EMP, &I, MY_LOCATION_EMP.EMPLID);
      If Substring(&EMPLID, 1, 1) = "L" Then
         DeleteRow(RECORD.MY_LOCATIONS, CurrentRowNumber(),
RECORD.MY_LOCATION_EMP, &I);
      End-If;
   End-For;
   COUNTER = ActiveRowCount(RECORD.MY_LOCATIONS, CurrentRowNumber(),
RECORD.MY_LOCATION_EMP);
End-If;
```

Figure 16.18   Using FetchValue to exclude Emplids

record name. The level 1 row is supplied by the `CurrentRowNumber` function. The third parameter is the target record name, MY_LOCATION_EMP. The fourth parameter is the variable &I, which contains the row number in the target scroll area. The fifth parameter, [record name.] fieldname is also required. The record name prefix is used because the `FetchValue` call is made from the MY_DERIVED record, which is different from the record that contains the EMPLID fieldname.

After the call to `FetchValue`, the variable &EMPLID contains the result and is tested using the `SubString` function to determine if the first character is an "L." In the example, `DeleteRow` is used to remove rows that match the selection criteria.

One additional bit of information regarding `FetchValue` is the empty scroll area. Because the `ActiveRowCount` function returns 1 when there are no rows in a target scroll, `FetchValue` may return erroneous data. The PeopleCode in figure 16.18 can be written to include a verification for &EMPLID by adding the following PeopleCode before the `If SubString` statement.

```
If ActiveRowCount(RECORD.MY_LOCATIONS, CurrentRowNumber(),
    RECORD.MY_LOCATION_EMP) = 1 Then
        If None(&EMPLID) Then
            /*  Scroll is Empty */
            Break;
        End-If;
```

In this example, the verification of an empty scroll is not vital. Other applications using `FetchValue`, however, may require empty scroll verifications before additional operations are performed.

When working with scrolls, it sometimes becomes necessary to hide rows of data rather than delete or flush them from the scroll area. PeopleCode contains two functions that are used to hide specific rows or an entire scroll area. The functions are `HideRow` and `HideScroll`.

16.3.5 HideRow

`HideRow` is used to hide a specific row and any child rows in subordinate scroll levels. The parameters passed to `HideRow` are based on the scroll level and target record number where rows are to be hidden. The syntax for `HideRow` at various levels can be written as follows:

Level 1

```
HideRow (RECORD.target_recname, target_row);
```

Level 2

```
HideRow (RECORD.level1_recname, level1_row, RECORD.target_recname,
target_row);
```

Level 3

```
HideRow (RECORD.level1_recname, level1_row, RECORD.level2_recname,
level2_row,  RECORD.target_recname, target_row);
```

Example

The example presented in figure 16.18 can be rewritten using `HideRow` in place of the `RowFlush` function. `HideRow` does not remove rows from a scroll. The code shown in figure 16.19 hides the target row ❶, but, during save processing, any hidden rows are written to the database.

```
MY_DERIVED (Record PeopleCode)                                    _ □ ✗
LOAD_EMP_LOCATION                              ▼  FieldChange                ▼
/*
**********************************************************************
** Using FetchValue for selection criteria at scroll level 2
**********************************************************************
*/
If %Panel = "MY_LOCATIONS_EMP" Then
   ScrollSelect(2, RECORD.MY_LOCATIONS, RECORD.MY_LOCATION_EMP,
RECORD.MY_LOC_EMPL_VW, True);
   For &I = ActiveRowCount(RECORD.MY_LOCATIONS, CurrentRowNumber(),
RECORD.MY_LOCATION_EMP) To 1 Step - 1;
      &EMPLID = FetchValue(RECORD.MY_LOCATIONS, CurrentRowNumber(),
RECORD.MY_LOCATION_EMP, &I, MY_LOCATION_EMP.EMPLID);
      If Substring(&EMPLID, 1, 1) = "L" Then
         HideRow(RECORD.MY_LOCATIONS, CurrentRowNumber(),    ◄——❶
RECORD.MY_LOCATION_EMP, &I);
      End-If;
   End-For;
   COUNTER = ActiveRowCount(RECORD.MY_LOCATIONS, CurrentRowNumber(),
RECORD.MY_LOCATION_EMP);
End-If;
```

Figure 16.19   HideRow function

In addition to hiding rows of data in a scroll area, it is sometimes necessary to hide an entire scroll bar. Hiding a scroll changes the look of a panel because the scroll bar cannot be viewed. The `HideScroll` function is used to hide a scroll bar and its corresponding data.

16.3.6   HideScroll

`HideScroll` is similar to `HideRow` except that instead of hiding a row, the complete scroll area is hidden, including all data in the scroll and the scroll bar. For each scroll level, the syntax for `HideScroll` can be written as follows:

Level 1

```
HideScroll (RECORD.target_recname);
```

Level 2

```
HideScroll (RECORD.level1_recname, level1_row, RECORD.target_recname);
```

Level 3

```
HideScroll (RECORD.level1_recname, level1_row, RECORD.level2_recname,
level2_row,  RECORD.target_recname);
```

Example

On some occasions, work scrolls are used to store rows of data subsequently used elsewhere in a routine. Work scrolls do not usually appear on a panel; they can be hidden using `HideScroll`. The objective is to hide the entire scroll for selected locations at level 2. Level 2 contains employee data and is hidden following the `HideScroll`. Figure 16.20 contains the panel without the implementation of `HideScroll`.

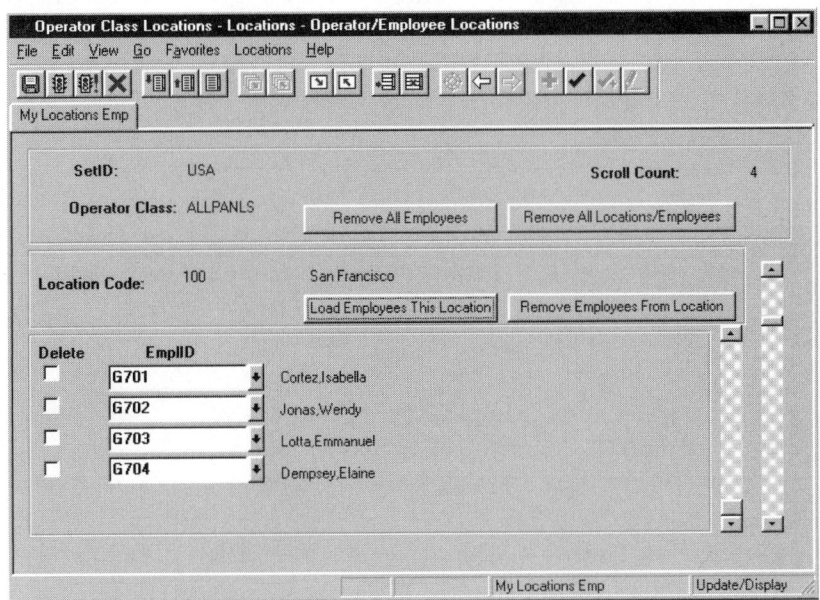

Figure 16.20   Level 2 scroll data

The following example (figure 16.21) contains the necessary PeopleCode required to hide the child scroll area at level 2 for location codes 100 and 300.

The panel illustrating the hidden scroll area for location 100 is shown in figure 16.22. The Delete label that appears on the scroll level 2 area is static text and is not impacted by `HideScroll`.

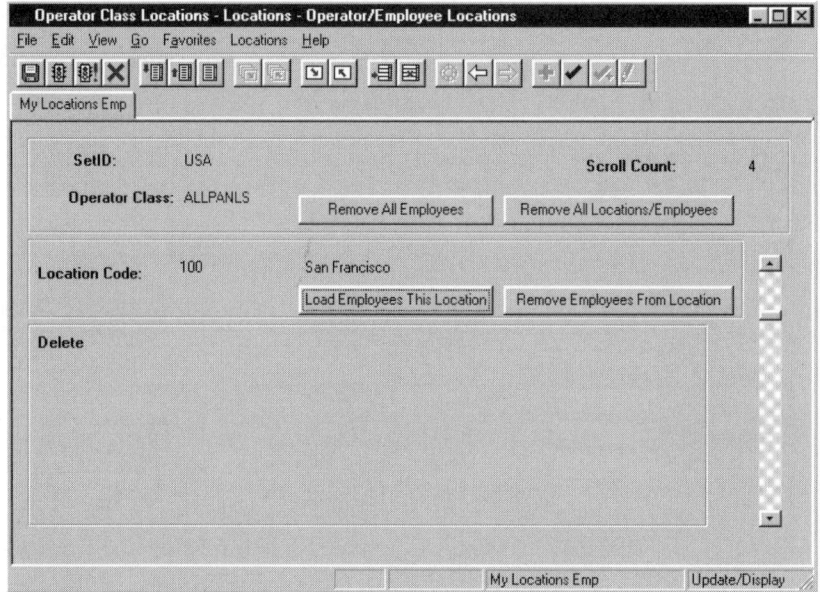

```
MY_DERIVED (Record PeopleCode)                                    _□ ×
LOAD_EMP_LOCATION                            ▼  FieldChange                ▼
/*
**********************************************************************
** HideScroll implemented at Scroll Level 2
**********************************************************************
*/
If %Panel = "MY_LOCATIONS_EMP" Then
   Evaluate MY_LOCATIONS.LOCATION
   When = "100"
   When = "300"
      HideScroll(RECORD.MY_LOCATIONS, CurrentRowNumber(),
RECORD.MY_LOCATION_EMP);
      Break;
   End-Evaluate;
End-If;
```

Figure 16.21   Using HideScroll on specific locations

Figure 16.22   Panel after HideScroll is executed

16.3.7   RowScrollSelect

The `ScrollSelect` and `ScrollSelectNew` functions read data from the specified
`Select` record into a scroll area and distribute child keys based on their corresponding
parent key values. The PeopleCode functions `RowScrollSelect` and `RowScroll-`
`SelectNew` are similar to their counterparts `ScrollSelect` and `ScrollSelect-`
`New`. The difference is that `RowScrollSelect` and `RowScrollSelectNew` do not
automatically allocate child rows to their corresponding parent rows.

To illustrate, refer to figure 16.20. When implemented correctly, `ScrollSelect` and `ScrollSelectNew` automatically load child keys `G701`, `G702`, and `G703` on a panel containing two scroll levels when parent key `100` is encountered. Conversely, `RowScrollSelect` and `RowScrollSelectNew` require that the SQL string be used to limit the keys of the rows loaded, to those of the parent row. `RowScrollSelect` requires the specification of the target scroll area, a source record from which to select rows, and the SQL string. The parameters passed to `RowScrollSelect` vary based on the scroll level at which the function is targeted:

Level 1

```
RowScrollSelect (1, RECORD.target_recname, RECORD.sel_recname);
```

Level 2

```
RowScrollSelect (2, RECORD.level1_recname, level1_row,
RECORD.target_recname, RECORD.sel_recname);
```

Level 3

```
RowScrollSelect (3, RECORD.level1_recname, level1_row,
RECORD.level2_recname, level2_row,  RECORD.target_recname,
RECORD.sel_recname);
```

Example

The following code (figure 16.23) demonstrates the use of `RowScrollSelect` at the level 2 scroll. It operates on the panel illustrated by figure 16.10.

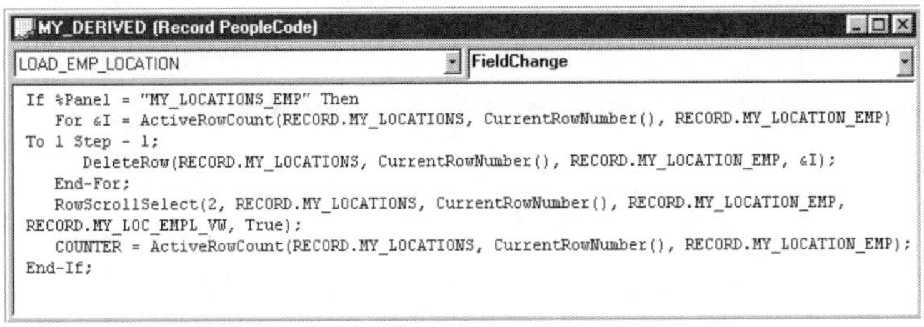

Figure 16.23 RowScrollSelect at level 2

The populated panel using `RowScrollSelect` is shown in figure 16.24.

The example has one flaw. The panel illustrated in figure 16.24 contains more data than the number of employees for the location at level 1. Note the scroll count field and compare it to figure 16.20. A big difference! In the example, the code erroneously does not contain a `WHERE` statement and results in all level 2 rows being loaded into the scroll level 2 buffer, for ALL employees! Without limiting the scroll

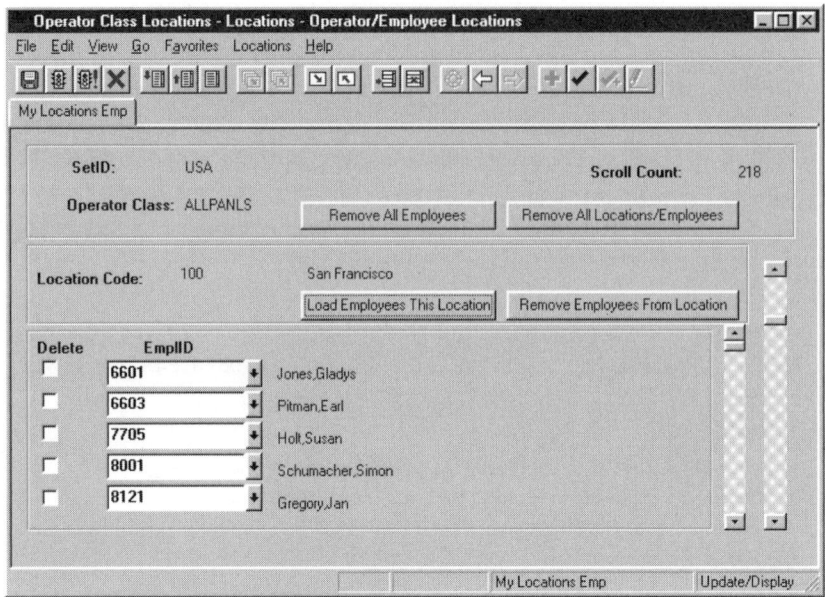

Figure 16.24   Panel using RowScrollSelect

level 2 rows to those of the parent at level 1, data for all employees in the
`sel_recordname` are loaded into the scroll buffer.

The correctly coded `RowScrollSelect` function is illustrated in figure 16.25.
The `WHERE` SQL clause is inserted to limit keys to those of the parent, ❶. The code
produces the same results as those in figure 16.20.

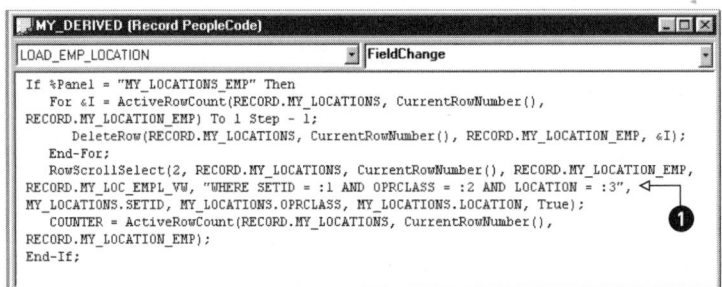

Figure 16.25   Correctly coded RowScrollSelect

A review of the PeopleCode in the example illustrates how `RowScrollSelect`
is used with the other PeopleCode statements. First, the panel is verified so that the
statements within the scope of the `If` statement are executed when the panel name is

MY_LOCATIONS_EMP. This is necessary because the code is executed from a Derived/Work record, which may contain code used on different panels. The `DeleteRow` statement is used to delete rows from the scroll and database table. In this example, `DeleteRow` is used in the context of a loop. Rows are processed from high to low, because rows are renumbered each time they are deleted. The level number identifies the target scroll area is at level 2. The level1_recname parameter is required because the target record is a level 2. `CurrentRowNumber` is used to obtain the level 1 row. Level 1 row is required when the target record is at level 2. The target record-name is MY_LOCATIONS_EMP and represents the target record into which data will be selected. The sel_recordname parameter is identified by MY_LOC_EMPL_VW, which is a view used to extract the most current effective-dated JOB rows and join them with the corresponding location table entry. This parameter can be the same as the target record name, but, in the example, we are selecting from a view and loading the selected fields into the MY_LOCATIONS_EMP target record. The COUNTER field contains the number of active rows in the scroll area. This count is reflected on the panel.

TIP   Understanding the record key definitions for parent and child records facilitates the construction of SQL strings for `RowScrollSelect` and `RowScrollSelectNew` functions.

16.3.8   RowScrollSelectNew

`RowScrollSelectNew` resembles `RowScrollSelect` the only exception being that `RowScrollSelectNew` marks records as NEW when they are loaded into the scroll area. `RowScrollSelectNew` does not automatically place child rows under the corresponding parent data within the scroll buffer. It requires that the SQL string be used to limit the rows loaded into the scroll to those of the parent row. `RowScrollSelectNew` requires the specification of the target scroll area, a source record from which to select rows and an SQL string. The parameters passed to `RowScrollSelectNew` vary based on the scroll level at which the function is targeted:

Level 1

```
RowScrollSelectNew (1, RECORD.target_recname, RECORD.sel_recname);
```

Level 2

```
RowScrollSelectNew (2, RECORD.level1_recname, level1_row,
RECORD.target_recname, RECORD.sel_recname);
```

Level 3

```
RowScrollSelectNew (3, RECORD.level1_recname, level1_row,
RECORD.level2_recname, level2_row,  RECORD.target_recname,
RECORD.sel_recname);
```

Example

The PeopleCode example for RowScrollSelectNew (figure 16.26) loads the selected data into MY_LOCATIONS using MY_LOC_OPR_VW as the sel_recordname. In the example, sel_recordname is a view used to select the most current effective dated LOCATION_TBL entry for the specified SETID field. Because the records selected into the target scroll are marked as NEW, they are inserted into the database during save processing. For this example, another SETID value has been selected. The panel is shown in figure 16.27.

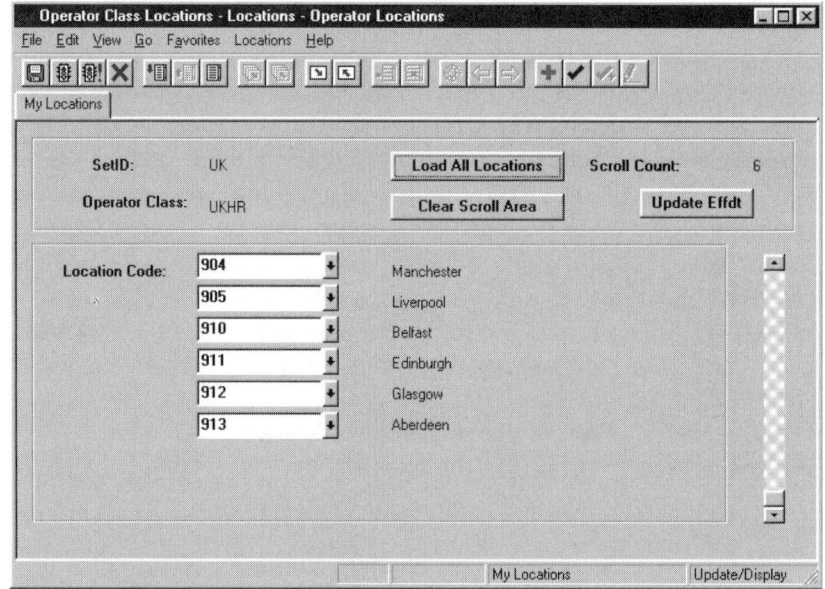

```
MY_DERIVED (Record PeopleCode)
LOAD_LOCATIONS                                          FieldChange
/*
*********************************************************************************
** RowScrollSelectNew example for a panel containing 1 scroll bar              *
*********************************************************************************
*/
If %Panel = "MY_LOCATIONS" Then
   For &I = ActiveRowCount(RECORD.MY_LOCATIONS) To 1 Step - 1;
      DeleteRow(RECORD.MY_LOCATIONS, &I);
   End-For;
   RowScrollSelectNew(1, RECORD.MY_LOCATIONS, RECORD.MY_LOC_OPR_VW, "WHERE SETID = :1",
MY_LOCATION_HDR.SETID, True);
   COUNTER = ActiveRowCount(RECORD.MY_LOCATIONS);
End-If;
```

Figure 16.26   RowScrollSelectNew at the level 1 scroll

Figure 16.27   Operator/Class locations using RowScrollSelectNew

16.3.9 RowFlush

RowFlush is a scroll function used to remove a particular row of data from the panel scroll and scroll buffer area. RowFlush does not delete rows from the database. RowFlush requires the specification of the target ScrollPath and the target row. The parameters passed to RowFlush vary based on the scroll level at which the function is targeted. To use RowFlush on specific levels, it can be coded as follows:

Level 1

```
RowFlush (RECORD.target_recname, target_row);
```

Level 2

```
RowFlush (RECORD.level1_recname, level1_row, RECORD.target_recname,
target_row);
```

Level 3

```
RowFlush (RECORD.level1_recname, level1_row, RECORD.level2_recname,
level2_row,  RECORD.target_recname, target_row);
```

Example

The level 2 scroll area in figure 16.24 contains a checkbox labeled Delete. RowFlush can be used after the push button labeled "Load Employees This Location" has been activated. The associated employee data are selected into the scroll area and can subsequently be saved. If the need to delete employee data are required, the Delete Row (F8) toolbar option can be used. The F8 or Delete Row however requires that we confirm the delete, thereby adding an additional step for the user. The Delete checkbox can be applied during save processing to use RowFlush, which removes the identified rows prior to their insertion into the database table. Figure 16.28 illustrates the use of the panel before it is saved.

The illustration identifies two rows that have the Delete checkbox indicator turned on. During save processing, the code shown in figure 16.29 is executed. For rows having the DELETE_ROW field set to "Y", the PeopleCode calls the RowFlush function. The result of the RowFlush function is illustrated in figure 16.30.

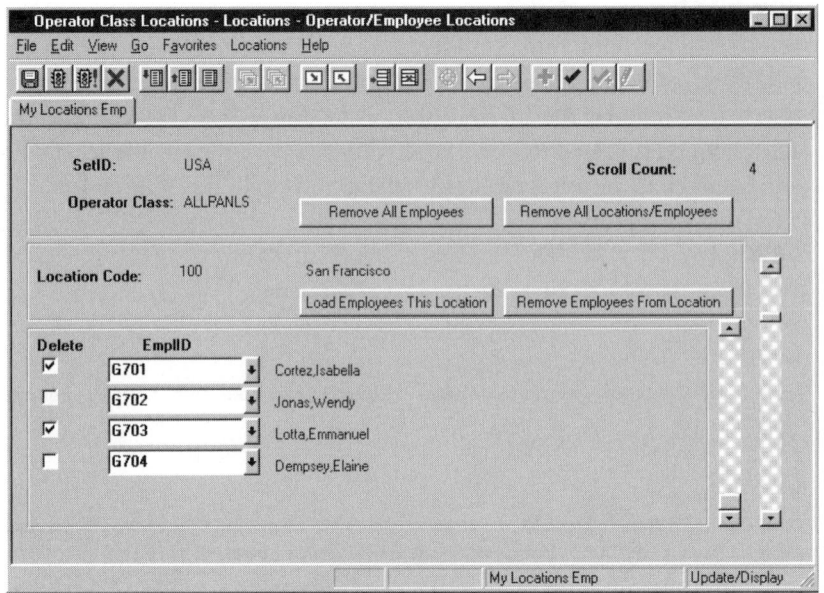

Figure 16.28　Using RowFlush to remove scroll data

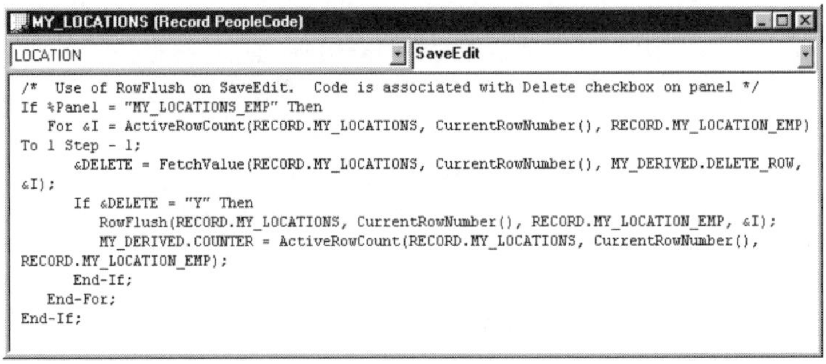

```
MY_LOCATIONS (Record PeopleCode)                                    _ □ ✕
LOCATION                           ▼  SaveEdit                              ▼
/*  Use of RowFlush on SaveEdit.  Code is associated with Delete checkbox on panel */
If %Panel = "MY_LOCATIONS_EMP" Then
    For &I = ActiveRowCount(RECORD.MY_LOCATIONS, CurrentRowNumber(), RECORD.MY_LOCATION_EMP)
To 1 Step - 1;
        &DELETE = FetchValue(RECORD.MY_LOCATIONS, CurrentRowNumber(), MY_DERIVED.DELETE_ROW,
&I);
        If &DELETE = "Y" Then
            RowFlush(RECORD.MY_LOCATIONS, CurrentRowNumber(), RECORD.MY_LOCATION_EMP, &I);
            MY_DERIVED.COUNTER = ActiveRowCount(RECORD.MY_LOCATIONS, CurrentRowNumber(),
RECORD.MY_LOCATION_EMP);
        End-If;
    End-For;
End-If;
```

Figure 16.29　RowFlush PeopleCode at level 2

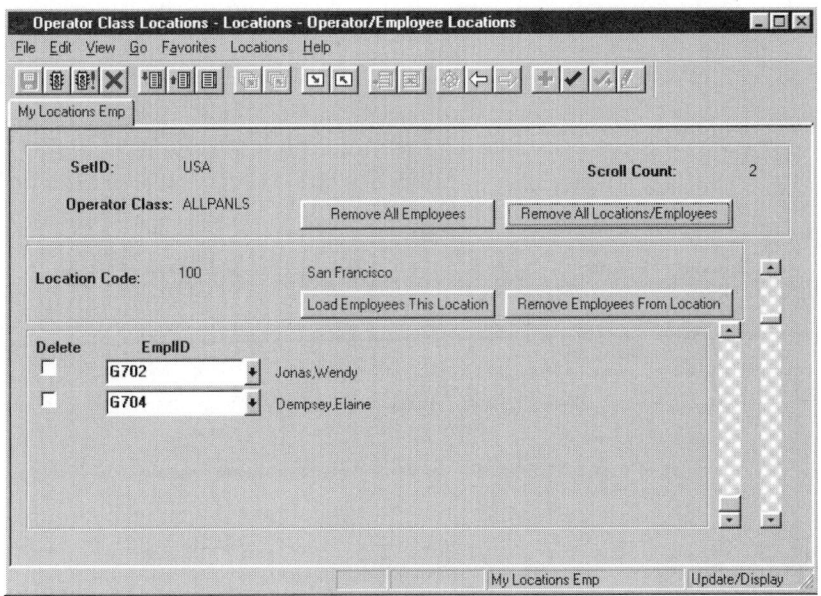

Figure 16.30   Resulting panel with selected rows removed

The PeopleCode surrounding `RowFlush` in figure 16.29 contains verification of the panel name MY_LOCATIONS_EMP. In the example, the code is executed from the `SaveEdit` event of the record MY_LOCATIONS. `FetchValue` is used to retrieve the indicator field MY_DERIVED.DELETE_ROW. The field is checked for a value "Y". A `True` condition causes the `RowFlush` function to be called. The `RowFlush` parameters include level1_recname. This parameter is required because the target record is at level 2. The parameter is specified as `RECORD.MY_LOCATIONS`. Because the target record is at level 2, the level1_row parameter is also required. `CurrentRowNumber` is used to obtain the level 1 row. The target record name is specified as MY_LOCATIONS_EMP. At level 2 the last parameter passed to `RowFlush` is target_row. The variable &I, which is used to loop through the data at scroll level 2, identifies the row number to be removed from the specified target scroll area. An additional line of code references MY_DERIVED.COUNTER, which is updated after `RowFlush` so that the panel contains the actual number of active rows following save processing.

It is important to note that `RowFlush` does not remove rows from the database; it only removes them from the panel scroll buffer. In the example presented, `RowFlush` does not work for data that has been saved to the database, then subsequently deleted using the Delete indicator. Let's review again. Refer to figure 16.20 and assume the data on that panel has now been saved. The panel is then subsequently retrieved, and two rows are checked off (figure 16.28) with the assumption that the rows will be deleted during save processing. Following save processing, the rows marked for deletion will be gone and will appear to have been deleted. However, when the scroll buffer is reloaded with data from the table or view, the "deleted" rows reappear. For this reason, RowFlush is limited to specific applications. It is more common to use DeleteRow because data are removed from the scroll and deleted from the database.

Figure 16.31 illustrates the DeleteRow function as a replacement for RowFlush.

```
MY_LOCATIONS (Record PeopleCode)                                    _ □ ×
LOCATION                            ▼  SaveEdit                           ▼
/*  Using DeleteRow to remove data from scroll area and database table */
If %Panel = "MY_LOCATIONS_EMP" Then
    For &I = ActiveRowCount(RECORD.MY_LOCATIONS, CurrentRowNumber(), RECORD.MY_LOCATION_EMP)
To 1 Step - 1;
        &DELETE = FetchValue(RECORD.MY_LOCATIONS, CurrentRowNumber(), MY_DERIVED.DELETE_ROW,
&I);
        If &DELETE = "Y" Then
            DeleteRow(RECORD.MY_LOCATIONS, CurrentRowNumber(), RECORD.MY_LOCATION_EMP, &I);
            MY_DERIVED.COUNTER = ActiveRowCount(RECORD.MY_LOCATIONS, CurrentRowNumber(),
RECORD.MY_LOCATION_EMP);
        End-If;
    End-For;
End-If;
```

Figure 16.31   Using DeleteRow in place of RowFlush

TIP   The RowFlush example does not necessarily have to be replaced with DeleteRow to obtain the desired functionality. The use of the Delete Row toolbar icon or F8 also removes rows from the scroll area while maintaining the RowFlush PeopleCode. This will require an additional step for the user, however.

16.3.10   UpdateValue

The UpdateValue function works in a similar manner to FetchValue to update the value of a field using the value parameter passed to the function. UpdateValue requires the target_row and recordname.fieldname parameters as well as a value that can be specified as a variable, constant, or record field. To use UpdateValue at various levels, the following syntax is used:

Level 1

```
UpdateValue (RECORD.target_recname, target_row, [recordname.] fieldname,
value);
```

Level 2

```
UpdateValue (RECORD.level1_recname, level1_row, RECORD.target_recname,
target_row, [recordname.]fieldname, value);
```

Level 3

```
UpdateValue (RECORD.level1_recname, level1_row, RECORD.level2_recname,
level2_row,  RECORD.target_recname, target_row, [recordname.]fieldname,
value);
```

Example

The Operator Class/Locations panel contains a button labeled "Update Effdt." When the button is activated, a secondary panel is displayed which accepts a date value. The date entered from the secondary panel is used to update an effective date field located on MY_LOCATIONS record. The effective date is used for reporting and internal tracking purposes, but does not appear on the panels illustrated. Figure 16.32 illustrates the secondary panel.

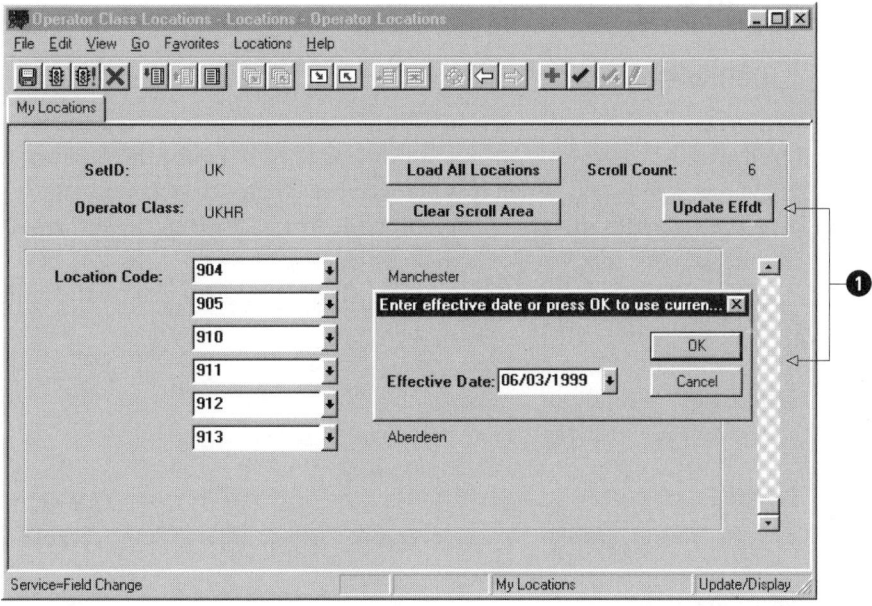

Figure 16.32   Update Effdt secondary panel associated with UpdateValue

The PeopleCode utilizing UpdateValue is shown in figure 16.33. This code works in conjunction with the Update Effdt push button (❶ in figure 16.32) and uses the date entered from the secondary panel.

The UpdateValue parameters specify target record name as RECORD.MY_LOCATIONS. The target_row parameter is specified as a variable &I, which is incremented using the For statement. The variable &I represents the row numbers in the target scroll area. Record name is required as a prefix to fieldname

```
MY_DERIVED (Record PeopleCode)                    _ □ X
EFFDT                          ▼  FieldChange              ▼
For &I = 1 To ActiveRowCount(RECORD.MY_LOCATIONS);
   UpdateValue(RECORD.MY_LOCATIONS, &I, MY_LOCATIONS.EFFDT, EFFDT);
End-For;
```

Figure 16.33
UpdateValue PeopleCode

because the PeopleCode is executed from the MY_DERIVED record. As a result, the target fieldname is prefixed with MY_LOCATIONS. The last parameter received by UpdateValue is a value. In the example, the value is entered into the secondary panel and contained in the work field MY_DERIVED.EFFDT.

TIP   Regular data assignment can be used instead of UpdateValue when the field to be updated appears on the same record as the PeopleCode.

16.3.11   TotalRowCount

As previously discussed, it is sometimes necessary to identify the number of rows in a scroll area. ActiveRowCount is a function used to count the number of active rows in a target scroll area. When it is necessary to count active as well as deleted rows, the TotalRowCount function can be used. TotalRowCount returns the aggregate number of rows in a scroll area including deleted rows.

The parameters required by TotalRowCount are based on the target scroll level for which a count is required:

Level 1

```
TotalRowCount (RECORD.target_recname);
```

Level 2

```
TotalRowCount (RECORD.level1_recname, level1_row, RECORD.target_recname);
```

Level 3

```
TotalRowCount (RECORD.level1_recname, level1_row, RECORD.level2_recname,
level2_row,  RECORD.target_recname);
```

Example 1

To obtain the total number of rows contained in the scroll area of the Operator Class/ Location panel, the following code using TotalRowCount can be used:

```
MY_DERIVED.COUNTER = TotalRowCount(RECORD.MY_LOCATIONS);
```

Example 2

The following example uses `TotalRowCount` on the level 2 scroll to count the number of child rows containing employee data:

```
MY_DERIVED.COUNTER = TotalRowCount (RECORD.MY_LOCATIONS,
CurrentRowNumber(), RECORD.MY_LOCATION_EMP);
```

TIP	Rows marked as "deleted" remain in the buffer until an SQL commit is issued after the `SavePostChg` PeopleCode event.

KEY POINTS

1 A panel can contain up to three scroll levels. A panel with two scroll levels contains primary records at occurs level zero, occurs level 1, and occurs level 2.

2 The level zero record is considered the parent row and level 1 is the child. A level 1 row is parent to a level 2 row. Each level can contain multiple records, but only one primary record can exist for each level specified.

3 During processing of data buffers, records at occurs level zero are handled before occurs level 1. A panel containing two occurs levels will process the level zero records first, then a single row of level 1 data, and all level 2 rows which are children of the level 1 row.

4 Some PeopleCode functions used to operate on scrolls include `ScrollSelect`, `ScrollSelectNew`, and `ScrollFlush`. Additional functions such as `RowSelect`, `RowSelectNew`, and `RowFlush` require the use of the WHERE block in the SQL string to match parent keys.

5 Other functions used to complement scroll processing include `FetchValue`, `UpdateValue`, `ActiveRowCount`, and `CurrentRowNumber`. These functions allow us to process specific data with a scroll area.

C H A P T E R   1 7

Function libraries

A Function Library is a collection of one or more routines that can be called from another program. Function Libraries offer us the opportunity to reuse code and to write special routines which can be shared by applications running under People-Tools. In addition to writing and calling functions written in the PeopleCode language, we can also call external programs written in languages such as C/C++. A function usually accepts one or more values and can either return a value or not.

17.1 FUNCTION OVERVIEW

Functions are pieces of code that, in their most basic form, accept a string of parameters and can either return a value, return no value or in some instances call another function and eventually return home. Functions are everywhere and not only in PeopleCode. An SQL `Select` statement that utilizes specialized date functions will enable formats to be used as input and output based on patterns passed to the functions. Similarly, the SQR statement `RTRIM` is also a function. COBOL has functions such as `NUMVAL`, which work in conjunction with a `Move` or `Compute` statement. All types of functions share these characteristics:

- They can be called from almost anywhere in a program.
- They may be called once or thousands of times by a program.
- They perform a specific task that can be shared by systems. Some functions are bundled into software packages and are used to make the software more efficient or to relieve the application developer from writing redundant routines.
- They do not have to be written in the same language as the calling routine. PeopleCode can call C functions as well as C++. If we are daring enough, we can also write callable Assembler routines.

An important requirement of a function is that it establishes a calling convention to allow parameters to be passed back and forth. A function which formats dates could be written to accept one format and pass back another format. The function must know what the input format is and what the output format will be. Assume we have a function called `DATE_FUNCTION`, which accepts a Julian date in the form `YYDDD` and returns the value `YYYYMMDD`. Such a function will be flawed in several ways. First, the function should be flexible enough that it can accept a variety of formats and output them in the manner desired by the calling program. So while we may have some issues with a `YYDDD` format we could also accept `D/M/Y`, `MMDDYY`, or `dd-Mon-YYYY` where `Mon` is a three character representation of Month. January 1, 2000 would be `01-JAN-2000`. The routine would also require indicators to identify the input and output formats. This style of coding helps eliminate redundancy and allows for the localization of functions.

NOTE   PeopleCode functions cannot be called by any other type of programs written in a language other than PeopleCode.

PeopleCode programs utilize various types of functions. The function types are as follows:

- built-in
- internal
- external PeopleCode
- external non-PeopleCode

17.2 PEOPLECODE BUILT-IN FUNCTIONS

Built-in functions are the standard PeopleCode functions developed by PeopleSoft which can be called without being declared. Built-in functions are used to manipulate dates, strings, scrolls, and messages. Functions can be grouped into functional categories. Built-in functions differ from Internal and External PeopleCode functions because they do not necessarily have to be written in PeopleCode. Many built-in functions are written in C++.

Functions, by definition, are basically routines that can be shared among different programs or, at the very least, among programs common to an application. A good example of such a function is the PeopleCode built-in function RTrim. This is a great little built-in function that removes characters, usually blanks, from the rightmost portion of a string. You pass it the string or list of strings you wish to remove from the source string, and it works just fine. Most of the PeopleCode built-in functions can be used by other PeopleCode programs when necessary.

PeopleCode built-in functions can be grouped into functional categories. For the current release of PeopleTools, some of the most frequently used categories and corresponding functions are:

- Conversion
- Date/Time
- Effective Date/Sequence
- Logical
- Mail
- Math
- Message Catalog/Display
- Panel Buffer
- Panel Control
- Process Scheduler
- Save/Cancel
- Scroll Functions
- SQL
- String
- Transfers
- Validation

Many of the frequently used functions in these categories are listed in appendix E. Some have been discussed in previous chapters. For example, Message functions are discussed in chapter 14 and the SQLExec function is illustrated in chapter 15. In chapter 16, we examined scroll functions and how they can be applied to panels containing multiple scroll levels. A discussion of a few more frequently used categories follows.

17.2.1 Conversion functions

Functions categorized as conversion are primarily used to translate data values from one character set or data type to another. Some functions belong to more than one category. An example of this is the `String` function, which can be used to convert from a non-string data type to a string. The `String` function is categorized as both a `String` and `Conversion` function.

Another example of a conversion function is `Char`. The `Char` function is used to convert numeric values to their corresponding character values. An example of the `Char` function follows:

```
&CHAR_STRING = Char(72) | Char(69) | Char(76) | Char(76) | Char(79);
```

The target variable contains HELLO based on the ASCII number values passed to the `Char` function.

17.2.2 Date/Time functions

PeopleCode provides a number of date and time handling functions categorized as Date/Time. Functions in this category can be used to convert dates represented by numbers into a `Date` data type. Date/Time functions can also be used to extract the date or time portion of a `DateTime` data type. An example of a Date/Time function is `Date`. The `Date` function converts a numeric date into a `Date` data type. An example of `Date` follows:

```
&DATE_NUMBER = 20000122;
&DATE_OUT = Date(&DATE_NUMBER);
```

The variable `&DATE_OUT` contains a date represented as 2000-01-22.

The `DateValue` function is another Date/Time function that accepts a date in the Windows regional format setting and returns a `Date` data type. Assuming the Windows regional date setting is `yy/mm/dd`, the `DateValue` function can be applied in this manner:

```
&DATE_FORMAT = "000122";
&THIS_DATE = DateValue(&DATE_FORMAT);
```

After the `DateValue` function is called, the variable `&THIS_DATE` contains a `Date` data type containing 2000-01-22.

`Time` is a function which receives a number representing a time value and obtains a `Time` data type. The parameter passed to the `Time` function is a number based on a 24-hour clock with the format `HHMMSS[.SSSSSS]`.

```
&REPORT_TIME = 143041.000001;
&TIME_VALUE = Time(&REPORT_TIME);
```

The `Time` function obtains a time value from the numeric variable `&REPORT_TIME` and stores it in `&THIS_TIME`, which now contains the value `14.30.41.000001`. Notice that the precision goes out to .000001 seconds.

Additional built-in functions that operate on date or time values can be used to perform arithmetic on date or time variables. `AddToDate` is a function which receives a date parameter and three values representing number of years, months, and days. The values are added to the date value supplied and a `Date` value is returned which contains the original date and the aggregate value represented by years, months, and days. Here is an example of `AddToDate`.

```
&RETURN_DATE = AddToDate(%Date, 5, - 4, 3);
```

Based on the preceding example, when the `AddToDate` function receives control, the function receives the current system date, the number of years represented as 5, number of months as –4, and number of days as 3. Assuming the current date is 2000-01-22, the value of `&RETURN_DATE` is now 2004-09-26. This represents a date five years in the future, less four months, plus three days from the current date.

NOTE   Passing negative numbers to represent years, months, or days has the effect of subtracting from the date value passed.

17.2.3   Effective Date/Sequence functions

In PeopleSoft, most applications are built around the concept of Effective Date and Effective Sequence. With effective-dated records, data can be managed chronologically in the order of events. Under varying circumstances, the need for multiple records with the same effective date is inevitable. To handle such conditions, the Effective sequence key field is utilized. The combination of Effective Date (`EFFDT`) and Effective Sequence (`EFFSEQ`) enables the existence of unique rows with the same effective date. Functions categorized as Effective Date/Sequence operate primarily on scroll areas containing effective-dated rows or tables which contain Effective Date and Effective Sequence as part of their key structure.

The `CurrEffdt` function is used to return the effective date of the current record on the specified scroll level. The function can be used to extract the effective date, which is returned as a `Date` value or used in a conditional statement.

To extract the effective date of the current record we can code:

```
&RETURN_DATE = CurrEffDt(CurrentLevelNumber());
```

The function can also be used in a conditional context. For example, when specific processes are performed based on effective date values, the following can be used:

```
If CurrEffDt(CurrentLevelNumber()) < %Date Then
   Audit_Changes(EMPLID);
End-If;
```

In this example, the `Audit_Changes` function is executed when the effective date of the current record is less than the `%Date` system variable, which stores the current system date.

The `CurrEffSeq` function is used to obtain the effective sequence of a specified scroll level. The following example grays out the Account Code field on a panel when the current Effective Sequence contains a higher value than the prior record:

```
If CurrEffSeq(1) > PriorEffdt(EFFSEQ) Then
   Gray(ACCT_CD);
End-If;
```

Based on data in table 17.1, let's assume that the HRMS application contains a current record with an effective date of 1999-07-01 and an ACTION_REASON of XFR. When the ACTION_REASON value for the next record is required, the `NextEffDt` function can be used. `NextEffDt` returns the value of the specified record field which exists in the next effective-dated row. To obtain the next ACTION_REASON, the function call can be written as:

```
&NEXT_ACTION_REASON = NextEffdt(ACTION_REASON);
```

After the function call, the variable `&NEXT_ACTION_REASON` contains PRO. Using table 17.1, when the current record's Effective Date is 2000-01-05, the `NextEffDt` function call is skipped because a next record does not exist.

Another function categorized as Effective Date/Sequence is `PriorEffDt`. This function works in contrast to `NextEffDt` and is used to return the contents of the specified field from the prior effective-dated row. Using table 17.1, the following statement retrieves the XFR ACTION_REASON when the current effective-dated row is 2000-01-05.

```
&PRIOR_ACTION_REASON =PriorEffdt(ACTION_REASON);
```

A statement using `PriorEffdt` is ignored when the current effective-dated row is 1996-01-01.

Table 17.1 Effective Date and Action/Reasons

EFFDT	ACTION_REASON
2000-01-05	PRO
1999-07-01	XFR
1998-06-30	MER
1996-01-01	HIR

17.2.4 Logic functions

Functions in this category are used to test for the existence of blank values. The commonly used All function is used to determine whether one or more fields contain a value. The All function statement is useful in the SaveEdit PeopleCode event if we wish to verify that one or more fields have been entered. For the Problem Tracking application, the All function can be used to determine if specific fields have been entered. The All function can be used to test several fields with one call. The following code can be placed into the SaveEdit event for one of the specified fields; it verifies that the three fields passed as parameters each contain a value before calling MyScheduleFunction function:

```
If All(PRIORITY, MY_USER_ID, MY_PROBLEM_TRACKER) Then
   MyScheduleFunction();
End-If;
```

An additional logic function used to test for the existence of values is None. The function returns TRUE if the field or list of fields supplied do not contain a value. A Boolean FALSE is returned when one or more fields contain a value. A variation on the All function can be written using None to test for the existence of specific values.

```
If None(PRIORITY, MY_USER_ID, MY_PROBLEM_TRACKER) Then
   Error ("Enter all required fields");
End-If;
```

BEST PRACTICE PeopleCode programs can be reduced in terms of lines of code by combining multiple fields when using Logic functions such as All or None.

17.2.5 Math functions

Functions categorized as Math operate primarily on numeric data and can be used to assist with complex calculations. Some of these functions are invaluable when using PeopleSoft Financials, Payroll, or Manufacturing applications. When assigning numeric data elements that result from a multiplication or division operation, it is sometimes necessary to obtain a specific number of decimal positions before inserting values into a database table. One function used to accomplish this task is Round. The Round function returns a decimal number rounded up to the number of positions specified by the second parameter. If we are required to round the HRMS data element COMPRATE to three decimal positions, the following statement can be used:

```
JOB.COMPRATE = Round(JOB.COMPRATE, 3);
```

An additional function, which operates on numeric data but is not interested in decimal positions, is the Int function. The Int function removes decimal positions from a number and returns an integer value. As an example let's assume one of the payroll subroutines calculates hours worked, based on whole hours only. The following code can be used to calculate overtime hours using the Int function:

```
If &HOURS_WORKED > JOB.STD_HOURS Then
    &OVERTIME_HOURS = Int(&HOURS_WORKED) - JOB.STD_HOURS;
End-If;
```

Based on that Int example, employees working overtime hours that are not whole hours will not be too happy on payday. That is because the Int function does not perform any rounding. In the example, when the value of &HOURS_WORKED is 65.753 the Int function uses 65.

When dividing numbers, it is sometimes necessary to interpret the value of the remainder field. This can be accomplished using the Mod function. Mod divides one number by another and returns a value representing the remainder. We can see an application of the Mod function when a specified number is divided by number of years. Let's assume we have shares of stock and wish to allocate them evenly in whole numbers over a period of seven years. One rule is that, when the number cannot be divided evenly, the first year contains one additional share. This may appear complicated at first but can be facilitated using Mod:

```
&YEARLY_STOCK = (&STOCK_SHARES / 7);
&YEARLY_STOCK = Int(&YEARLY_STOCK);
&REMAINING_SHARES = Mod(&STOCK_SHARES, 7);
If &REMAINING_SHARES <> 0 Then
    &FIRST_YEAR_STOCK = &YEARLY_STOCK + 1;
End-If;
```

Observe how the routine uses both Mod and Int to determine the yearly stock and any remaining shares.

17.2.6 Panel buffer functions

Functions in this category are used to identify changes to records residing in panel buffers. A panel buffer can contain scroll data as well as non-scroll data. Panel Buffer functions can also be used to mimic operator functionality such as InsertRow (F7) and DeleteRow (F8). These functions are essential during save processing because they can be used to perform specific routines based on user actions.

The Problem Tracking application referred to throughout this book uses a main data entry panel (figure 17.1) which contains several editable fields. The task of identifying changes made to fields can be accomplished by including PeopleCode which tests each record field for changes. Such a task requires several lines of code. A more efficient method can be applied by incorporating the `RecordChanged` panel buffer function. The function returns a Boolean (`TRUE`) when the contents of a record have been changed on a panel or modified programmatically since being retrieved from the database.

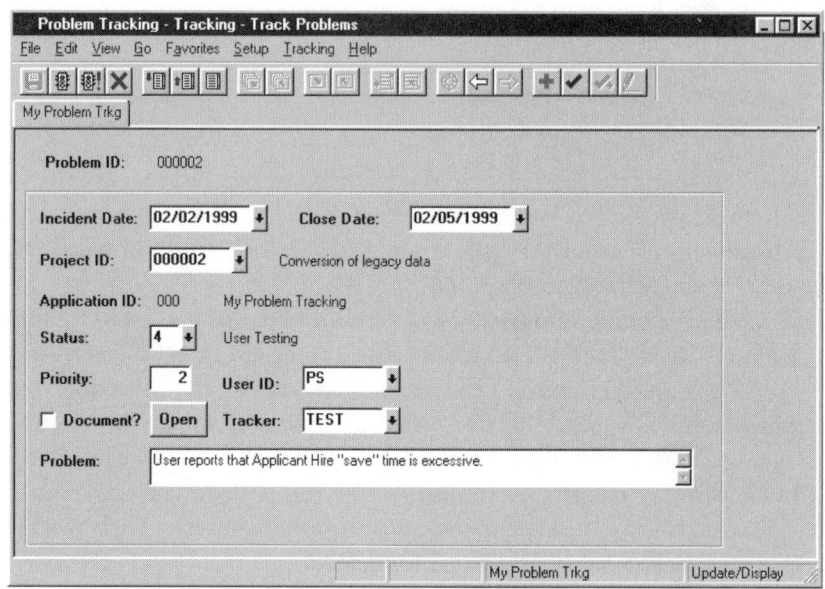

Figure 17.1   Problem Tracking panel

An example of `RecordChanged` can be applied as follows:

```
If RecordChanged(RECORD.MY_PROBLEM_TRKG) Then
    &RETURN_VALUE = MyScheduleFunction();
End-If;
```

`FieldChanged` is another panel buffer function. However, unlike `RecordChanged` which operates on the entire record, `FieldChanged` can be used to identify if one or more fields have been modified The function thereby operates at the field level. To test specific fields in Problem Tracking, a statement can be written as illustrated by the following example:

```
If FieldChanged(MY_PROBLEM_TRKG.PRIORITY) Or
       FieldChanged(MY_PROBLEM_TRKG.MY_USER_ID) Or
```

```
        FieldChanged(MY_PROBLEM_TRKG.MY_PROBLEM_STATUS) Or
        FieldChanged(MY_PROBLEM_TRKG.MY_PROBLEM_TRACKER) Then
    &RETURN_VALUE = MyScheduleFunction();
End-If;
```

Additional panel buffer functions can be used to delete records or identify records marked for deletion. When it is necessary to delete a record, the `DeleteRecord` panel buffer function can be used. The function deletes a level zero record and any associated child rows. The records are marked for deletion and are removed from the database during save processing. The function accepts any field values from the target record to be marked for deletion:

```
If &DELETE = "Y" Then
    DeleteRecord(MY_LOCATIONS.OPRCLASS)
End-If;
```

This example deletes the corresponding record from the table MY_LOCATIONS as well as any associated child rows.

Records marked for deletion by a panel buffer function such as `DeleteRecord` can be identified using the `RecordDeleted` function. An example of how `RecordDeleted` can be applied to scroll data at level 2 follows:

```
If RecordDeleted(RECORD.MY_LOCATIONS, CurrentRowNumber(),
RECORD.MY_LOCATION_EMP) Then
    &RETURN = My_Audit_Function();
End-If;
```

Panel buffer functions can also be used to insert records into a scroll or to identify records as new to the database. The `InsertRow` function is used to insert a new row of data into the scroll buffer. The operation is followed by the `RowInsert` PeopleCode event. `InsertRow` mimics the F7 operator function. To insert data at the level 2 scroll, `InsertRow` can be written in the following manner:

```
InsertRow(RECORD.MY_LOCATIONS, CurrentRowNumber(), RECORD.MY_LOCATION_EMP);
```

During save processing, records added to the database can be identified using the `RecordNew` panel buffer function. When used in `SaveEdit` before the record is inserted into the database, `RecordNew` is used to identify new records. This can be useful when special routines are necessary for newly added data. It is important to identify new data which can be added using F7 (Row Insert) or the `InsertRow` function. In order to recognize a new record at scroll level 1 for the table MY_LOCATIONS, the following code can be used:

```
If RecordNew(RECORD.MY_LOCATIONS) Then
    &RETURN = My_Audit_Function();
End-If;
```

17.2.7   Panel control functions

Consider the following scenario: we have implemented the HRMS module among a large number of users, many having access to the same panels. There are, however, some clients who do not require access to a number of fields distributed throughout the panel group. The objective is to allow access to these panels without displaying the fields. Several methods exist for accomplishing this task. One method involves creating several panels without the specified fields. We then have to create a new panel group and add the corresponding panel group to a menu. This approach requires additional panels. An alternative and more efficient method is to use PeopleCode. Using system variables and specific PeopleCode panel control functions, the selected fields can be hidden or made inaccessible on selected panels. One panel control function that can be utilized is the Hide function. Hide can render the specified panel fields invisible. Assuming the panels containing these fields are on a specific panel group, the following code can be applied to accomplish this task:

```
If (Substring(%PanelGroup, 1, 8) = "SPECIAL_DATA") Then
    Hide(COMPRATE);
    Hide(SAL_ADMIN_PLAN);
    Hide(GRADE);
    Hide(HOURLY_RT);
    Hide(ANNUAL_RT);
    Hide(MONTHLY_RT);
End-If;
```

Other circumstances exist in which hiding fields in not necessary. If we simply wish to prevent certain editable fields from being written over, the panel control function, Gray can be used. The Gray function is commonly used in the RowInit event and can also be used in events such as FieldChange after the contents of a field are modified.

In the Problem Tracking application, when an issue is considered closed, certain fields can be presented as display only using the Gray built-in function contained in the following code:

```
If MY_PROBLEM_STATUS = "5" Then
    Gray(PRIORITY);
    Gray(MY_USER_ID);
    Gray(MY_PROBLEM_TRACKER);
    Gray(DESCRLONG);
End-If;
```

Additional Panel Control functions can be used to make panel fields visible again. The UnHide function can be used for this task, but only works on fields that were hidden using the Hide function. Fields initially set to invisible, based on the panel field properties tab, are not impacted by UnHide. The following example is used to Hide or UnHide a field on the Problem Tracking panel:

```
If MY_PROBLEM_STATUS <> "5" Then
    Hide(MY_PROBLEM_RESOLTN);
```

```
Else
   UnHide(MY_PROBLEM_RESOLTN);
End-If;
```

The UnGray function can be used to make a previously protected field editable using Gray. UnGray is commonly used in the RowInit event and can also appear in events such as FieldChange after the contents of a field are modified.

In the Problem Tracking application we can see the UnGray function when a Problem Status is changed from resolved back to another status:

```
If PriorValue(MY_PROBLEM_STATUS) = "5" And
      MY_PROBLEM_STATUS <> "5" Then
   UnGray(PRIORITY);
   UnGray(MY_USER_ID);
   UnGray(MY_PROBLEM_TRACKER);
   UnGray(DESCRLONG);
End-If;
```

17.2.8   Save/Cancel functions

Functions in the Save/Cancel category enable the PeopleCode program to force a cancel from an active panel or to save the contents of a panel. The DoCancel function is used to cancel the activity on a panel and imitate the Esc or Cancel ✖ toolbar. Figure 17.2 illustrates the use of DoCancel after a Warning statement has been issued. The panel is canceled after the user replies OK to the warning message.

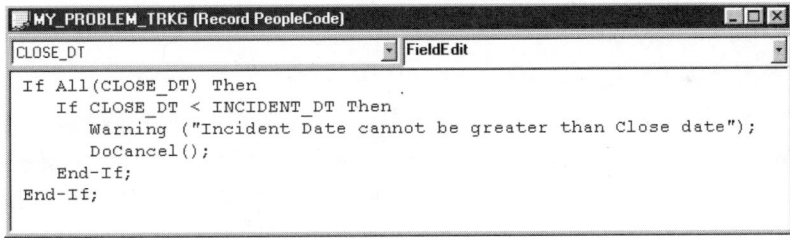

Figure 17.2   Using the DoCancel function

NOTE   If Error were used in place of Warning, the DoCancel function would have no effect, because the Error function negates any further processing until the error has been corrected.

In addition to providing the ability to cancel a panel, PeopleCode functions enable save processing to be performed without a user save action. This can be accomplished using the DoSave function which can be executed from specific PeopleCode events. DoSave performs save processing at the conclusion of the current PeopleCode program in the `FieldEdit`, `FieldChange`, and `MenuItemSelect` events. Any statements following `DoSave` are executed through the remainder of the program and then the associated save events are triggered. These events include `SaveEdit`, `SavePreChg`, `WorkFlow`, and `SavePostChg`. An example of `DoSave` in the Problem Tracking application is illustrated by figure 17.3.

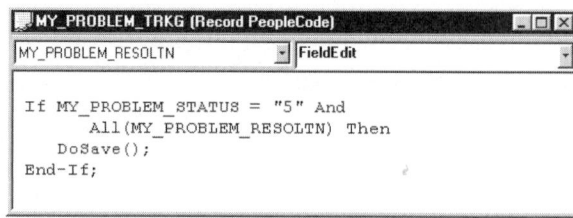

Figure 17.3
Using DoSave function

17.2.9 String functions

String functions enable the developer to manipulate `String` data types. This category of functions can be used to extract portions of a string, determine the length of a string, or to remove specified leading and trailing characters.

The `Substring` function references a string for a specified length and starting position. The following example uses `Substring` to verify a portion of the `%PanelGroup` system variable and to hide a panel field:

```
If (Substring(%PanelGroup, 1, 8) = "SPECIAL_DATA") Then
    Hide(COMPRATE);
End-If;
```

`LTrim` and `RTrim` are functions that can be used to remove specified leading or trailing characters respectively. Both functions accept up to two parameters. When the second parameter is specified, any characters appearing in the parameter string are removed from the first string parameter. If the second parameter is not supplied, any leading or trailing blanks are removed by default. MY_PROBLEM_RESOLTN is a field that contains a text field. To remove any unwanted trailing asterisks from this field, `RTrim` can be applied as follows:

```
MY_PROBLEM_RESOLTN = RTrim(MY_PROBLEM_RESOLTN, "*");
```

It sometimes becomes necessary to represent data in one common format or case. This may be necessary when data are maintained for interface purposes and are sent to a third party application. Some of these third party applications may require that alphabetic data sent in a specific case only. PeopleCode functions `Lower` and `Upper` can be used to convert alphabetic characters to lower case or upper case, respectively.

The following example illustrates how the field MY_PROBLEM_RESOLTN can be converted to uppercase:

```
MY_PROBLEM_RESOLTN = Upper(MY_PROBLEM_RESOLTN);
```

Alternatively, we can convert the text in the field MY_PROBLEM_RESOLTN to all lowercase using the Lower function:

```
MY_PROBLEM_RESOLTN = Lower(MY_PROBLEM_RESOLTN);
```

Another application of the Upper function can be illustrated when comparing two fields which may contain mixed case data. The following example compares two Name fields and performs a function call when the names match:

```
If Upper(PERSONAL_DATA.NAME) = Upper(&EXTRACT_NAME) Then
    ProcessVerification(PERSONAL_DATA.NAME);
Else
    WinMessage("Names are not equal");
End-If;
```

Another commonly used string function is Len, which determines how many characters are contained in a string. To find out the number of characters stored in the field MY_PROBLEM_RESOLTN, the Len function can be used in the following manner:

```
&FIELD_LENGTH = Len(DESCRLONG);
```

17.2.10   Panel transfer functions

Functions in this category are associated with the transfer of control from one panel to another. PeopleCode programs using functions related to Transfer can be used to steer clients through related panels without prompting for key values. AddKeyListItem is a transfer function that can be used to help clients move around related panels without prompting for key values. Let's assume we are using the Operator Class/Locations application. The user links operator classes to locations and then links the operator classes to employee data. In order to set up a list of keys to facilitate transferring control to the next panel, AddKeyListItem can be implemented as follows:

```
AddKeyListItem(MY_LOCATION_EMP.SETID, MY_LOCATIONS.SETID);
AddKeyListItem(MY_LOCATION_EMP.OPRCLASS, MY_LOCATIONS.OPRCLASS);
AddKeyListItem(MY_LOCATION_EMP.LOCATION, MY_LOCATIONS.LOCATION);
```

A function used to transfer control when the operator presses F6 or presses the Next-Panel toolbar icon is the SetNextPanel function. Continuing with the previous example, SetNextPanel can be used to transfer control to the panel MY_LOCATION_EMP after data on the operator class location panel is saved. The function verifies that the panel name appears on the current menu:

```
SetNextPanel("MY_LOCATION_EMP");
```

SetNextPanel identifies the panel to which control will be transferred following user actions such as F6 or activation of the NextPanel toolbar icon. The TransferPanel function is not activated based on user actions; it transfers control to the next panel in the panel group, the panel name supplied to the function, or the panel identified by a previous SetNextPanel. To illustrate the use of the SetNextPanel and TransferPanel functions, we make the assumption that the operator class location panels reside in the same panel group as the departmental security panels. The following statement transfers control to either the panel used to link locations and employees or the standard departmental security panel:

```
If %Panel = "MY_LOCATIONS" Then
    SetNextPanel("MY_LOCATIONS_EMP");
Else
    SetNextPanel("SCRTY_TABL_DEPT");
End-If;
TransferPanel();
```

An alternative method in which to code the TransferPanel function can be written using a variable set based on a conditional statement:

```
If %Panel = "MY_LOCATIONS" Then
    &NEXT_PANEL_NAME = "MY_LOCATIONS_EMP";
Else
    &NEXT_PANEL_NAME = "SCRTY_TABL_DEPT";
End-If;
TransferPanel(&NEXT_PANEL_NAME);
```

The example passes a variable to the TransferPanel function rather than using SetNextPanel to identify the next panel name.

17.2.11 Process Scheduler functions

PeopleCode can be used to submit a batch process that will run on a client or server location. A process can be associated with an SQR or a COBOL program and can be used to generate reports or processes, such as payroll batch cycles. ScheduleProcess is a function used to submit processes to the PeopleSoft Process Scheduler. The function accepts a number of parameters and stores a row of data into the process request table (PSPRCSRQST), which enables the system to schedule the process or job. The following example establishes the required and optional parameters to call the ScheduleProcess function. The example submits an SQR Report and identifies the process as INSERTS:

```
&PRCSTYPE = "SQR Report";
&PRCSNAME = "INSERTS";
&RUNLOCATION = "2";
```

```
&RUNCNTLID = "INSERTS";
&PRCSINSTANCE = "";
&RUNDTTM = %Datetime;
&RECURNAME = " ";
&SERVERNAMERUN = "PSUNX";
&RETURN_VALUE = ScheduleProcess(&PRCSTYPE, &PRCSNAME, &RUNLOCATION,
&RUNCNTLID, &PRCSINSTANCE, &RUNDTTM, &RECURNAME, &SERVERNAMERUN);
```

17.3 PEOPLECODE INTERNAL FUNCTIONS

An internal PeopleCode function is defined and used within the same PeopleCode program. The function can be declared in any PeopleCode program event, and the actual function definition requires that it be placed at the beginning of a program. Multiple functions can be defined within the same program, provided they are defined before any PeopleCode statements. In some functions, return values can be passed back to the calling program. Other types of functions perform some kind of operation on one or more fields.

17.3.1 Defining an internal function

An internal function is defined using the Function statement, which identifies the function name, parameters, and return value. A simple function definition can be written as follows:

```
Function MyFunction(&PARAMETER1, &PARAMETER2) Returns string;
End-Function;
```

The Function statement identifies the function name and any parameters passed to it. In the preceding example, the function MyFunction receives two parameters and returns a string. When a return value is specified, the data type of the returned value must also be specified. These return values can be any of the supported data types.

Example

An internal PeopleCode function can be defined and used in the Problem Tracking application. This internal function, illustrated by figure 17.4, will "live" in the SaveEdit event of the field MY_PROBLEM_STATUS. The purpose of the function is to verify that some text has been entered into the problem resolution field, when an issue has been resolved (&MY_PROBLEM_STATUS = "5"). The function also initializes the contents of the resolution text field (MY_PROBLEM_RESOLTN) when a value other than 5 is entered, and a Yes reply is entered from the message box.

The Function statement defines the function name as MyTextFunction. This function receives two parameters, &PROBLEM_STATUS and &TEXT. In the example, the fields passed are MY_PROBLEM_STATUS and MY_PROBLEM_RESOLTN. MyTextFunction returns a Boolean back to the calling routine as a return value.

The actual code contained in the function verifies if the variable &PROBLEM_STATUS has a value of 5 (resolved). If the value is resolved, the code then

```
MY_PROBLEM_TRKG (Record PeopleCode)                           _ □ X

MY_PROBLEM_STATUS                    ▾ │ SaveEdit                      ▾

Function MyTextFunction(&PROBLEM_STATUS, &TEXT) Returns boolean;
   If &PROBLEM_STATUS = "5" Then
      If Len(&TEXT) <= 10 Then
         Return False;
      End-If;
   Else
      If MessageBox(4, "Problem Resolution Text", 0, 0, "Problem Status is
not resolved, clear out Resolution Text ?") = 6 Then
         &TEXT = "";
         Return True;
      End-If;
      Return False;
   End-If;
End-Function;
```

Figure 17.4   Internal PeopleCode function

checks the length of the variable &TEXT. Any length less than or equal to 10 produces an error message, which requires that a problem resolution text be entered. A length of 10 is used because there should be some type of dialogue that can be followed when reviewing problems and resolutions.

The other part of this function is enabled when a user had previously entered a problem resolution text and the problem is actually not resolved. With good intention, the user may have thought everything was working correctly, changed the problem status to 5, and entered comments into the resolution text field. Upon later review, however, this problem has not been resolved and requires additional analysis. When the value of MY_PROBLEM_STATUS is changed from resolved to another value, the user has the option of allowing the function to clear out the resolution text field or leaving it intact.

Figure 17.5 illustrates the use of MyTextFunction in the Problem Tracking application panel.

After the problem has been resolved, the problem status is changed to 5, and the problem resolution text is verified. The PeopleCode in the function statement verifies that a resolution text has been entered. An example of a resolved problem status is displayed in figure 17.6.

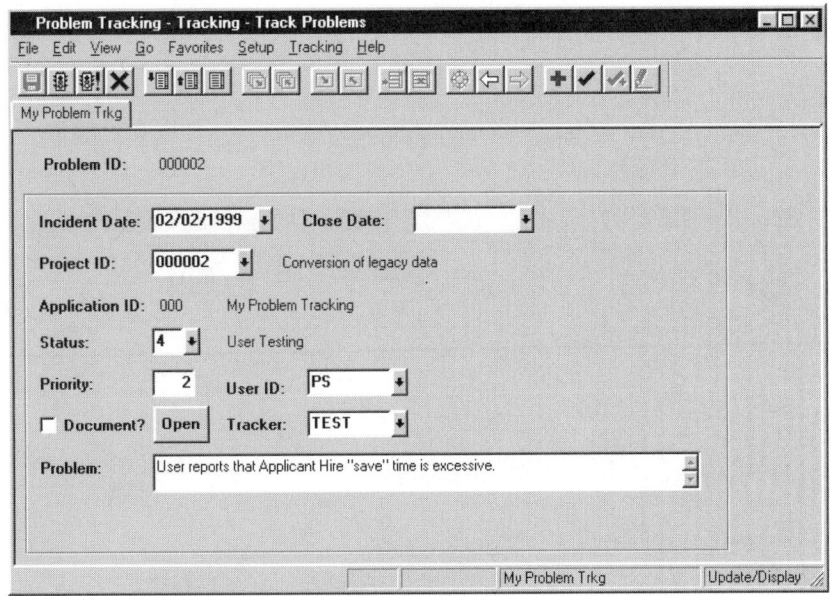

Figure 17.5   Example of an unresolved problem status

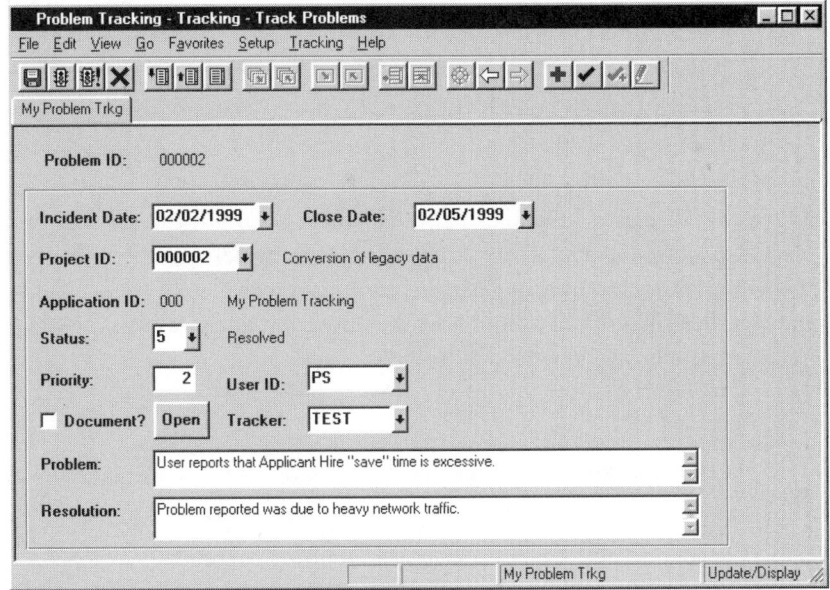

Figure 17.6   Resolved incident and resolution text

An additional feature of `MyTextFunction` provides the ability to clear out the problem resolution text when the status is prematurely set to 5 and subsequently set to another value at a later time. In the example, if the problem is not actually resolved and is changed to 4 (User Testing), a message (figure 17.7) is presented to the operator.

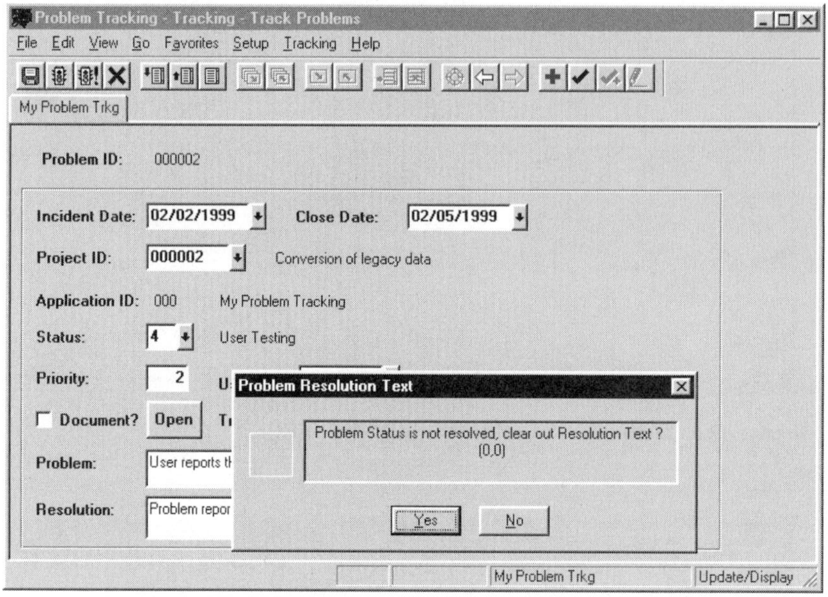

Figure 17.7 Internal PeopleCode function at work

Now that the problem status is no longer resolved, the existing problem resolution text may not necessarily apply after a final resolution. The PeopleCode in the function allows the user to keep the resolution text or remove it. The statement following the function call should reset the resolution text as well as the CLOSE_DT field. The statement can be written as follows:

```
If &RETURN_VALUE = True Then
   SetDefault(MY_PROBLEM_RESOLTN);
   SetDefault(CLOSE_DT);
End-If;
```

For PeopleCode internal and external functions, parameters are passed by reference. The `MyTextFunction` example in figure 17.4 contains the function call as follows:

```
&RETURN_VALUE = MyTextFunction (MY_PROBLEM_STATUS, MY_PROBLEM_RESOLTN);
```

The calling program passes the fields MY_PROBLEM_STATUS and MY_PROBLEM_RESOLTN. Because PeopleCode function parameters are passed by reference, any modification to the contents of either field contained in `MyTextFunction` are reflected in the calling program upon completion of the call. While the variables `&PROBLEM_STATUS` and `&TEXT` have unique names, they are actually pointers to the address of the fields MY_PROBLEM_STATUS and MY_PROBLEM_RESOLTN.

The internal function example presented in figure 17.6 is limited to the Problem Tracking application and, more specifically, to the MY_PROBLEM_STATUS.`SaveEdit` event for the problem resolution text field. A preferred objective is to write functions that can be used by more than one PeopleCode record field event. Nothing is lost when a function such as `MyTextFunction` is used, but there is also little to gain. Greater efficiencies can be realized by writing External PeopleCode functions, which are the next topic of discussion.

17.4   PEOPLECODE EXTERNAL FUNCTIONS

PeopleCode external functions do not have to be stored in the same record event as internal functions. The PeopleCode convention of storing functions places the code in Derived/Work records with either of two prefixes, FUNCLIB_ or DERIVED_. Generally, these functions by convention are stored in the `FieldFormula` event. Two key items to understand when working with PeopleCode functions are defining a function and declaring one. A function such as `MyTextFunction` is defined in figure 17.4. Because the function is an internal PeopleCode function, it cannot be called from another PeopleCode program. However, if the function in figure 17.4 were an external PeopleCode function and called from another PeopleCode program, it would still be defined in the same manner. A PeopleCode function not defined in the calling program must be declared before it can be called.

Functions are useful when repetitive code is required and, more importantly, when the function can be called from various programs.

To effectively use external PeopleCode functions several steps must be followed:

1 Define the external function.

2 Declare the function.

3 Call the function.

4 Interpret any return values when necessary.

17.4.1 Define the External function

In figure 17.8 we have defined an external PeopleCode function. An externally defined function is defined in the same manner as a function called internally from the same Recordname.Fieldname.Event.

```
MY_DERIVED (Record PeopleCode)                                              _ □ ×
MY_USER_ID                                      ▼  FieldFormula                   ▼
/ *
**************************************************************************************
** This is an example of an External PeopleCode Function that schedules a
** process.  The process produces a report.
**
**************************************************************************************
*/
Function MyScheduleFunction() Returns number;
    If %Mode <> "A" Then
        Return 0;
    End-If;
    &PRCSTYPE = "SQR Report";
    &PRCSNAME = "INSERTS";
    &RUNLOCATION = "1";
    &RUNCNTLID = "INSERTS";
    &PRCSINSTANCE = "";
    &RUNDTTM = %Datetime;
    &RECURNAME = " ";
    &SERVERNAMERUN = "PSUNX";
    &RETURN_VALUE = ScheduleProcess(&PRCSTYPE, &PRCSNAME, &RUNLOCATION,
&RUNCNTLID, &PRCSINSTANCE, &RUNDTTM, &RECURNAME, &SERVERNAMERUN);
    Return &RETURN_VALUE;
End-Function;
```

Figure 17.8   External PeopleCode function definition

A review of the code in figure 17.8 identifies the following:

- The function statement names the function MyScheduleFunction and indicates that the function receives no parameters but returns a number value.
- The statements contained within the function verify that the current mode is Add before continuing.
- A function can call another function. In the example, MyScheduleFunction is calling the built-in function ScheduleProcess and passes parameter values initialized by the statements preceding the call.
- The function returns a zero when the mode is not Add. The ScheduleProcess function returns a value that is also the return value passed back by MyScheduleFunction.
- End-Function signals the end of the PeopleCode function. This statement is required for both internal and external function definitions.

17.4.2 Declare the function

Now that we have a function defined, it would be great to call it occasionally. Before a PeopleCode function can be called, however, it must be declared in the calling program. A `Declare Function` statement is required for each unique function that it calls. If a program calls five distinct functions it will require five function declarations. The function declaration identifies the function name—and where it resides—in terms of record name, field name, and event. A `Declare Function` statement can be written as follows:

```
Declare Function MyFunction PeopleCode MY_DERIVED.MY_USER_ID FieldFormula;
```

A PeopleCode function can be defined on any record definition. All PeopleCode function declaration statements must appear at the top of the calling program before any of the regular program code.

Example

For the Problem Tracking application, we would like to execute a process each time a new user is added to the database.

The external function is defined in figure 17.8. With the exception of comments, which can appear anywhere in a program, the `Declare Function` statement(s) must be at the top of the calling program. When adding new users to MY_USER_TBL, the function call can be inserted into the `SavePostChg` event and written as shown figure 17.9.

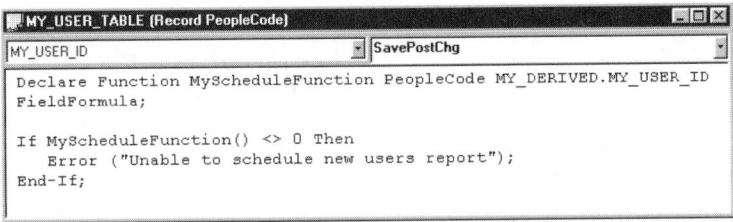

Figure 17.9   Declaring and calling the external function

The code illustrated in figure 17.9 uses the `Declare Function` statement to identify the function name as `MyScheduleFunction`. The additional parameters specify that it is a PeopleCode function and resides in the record field MY_DERIVED.MY_USER_ID. The function is stored in the `FieldFormula` event. The function call statement is used in the context of a conditional `If`, which interprets the function call return value. A non-zero value issued by the function call implies an unsuccessful call, which generates an error message.

17.4.3 Call the function

In the example presented in figure 17.9, the `MyScheduleFunction` call does not pass any parameters. An external PeopleCode function call can simply be written as `Function_Name()`. Any parameters passed are enclosed in parentheses.

17.4.4 Interpret return values

Many circumstances require that the return value of a function be interpreted before proceeding with the remaining code. A return value can be any data type. A common convention is to return zero when the function call is successful or neutral. The example used in figure 17.9 utilizes the return value in the context of an `If` statement. The external function `MyScheduleFunction` returns a zero when the mode is not `Add`. This type of verification could certainly be done before the function is called, so that no function call is made from modes such as `Update/Display` or `Correction`. When writing functions, however, it is important to be prepared for all types of parameters and circumstances. While one developer may call `MyScheduleFunction` during `Add` mode only, other developers may call it, regardless of mode. Similarly, some functions may require data types such as `Number` or `String` exclusively. Such functions should be written in a manner that can handle incorrect data and pass the appropriate return codes that can be useful when the need for debugging arises.

The `Return` statement is used to transfer control from the current active function back to the calling program. After the calling program has received control, program execution resumes with the next logical statement following the function call.

17.5 EXTERNAL NON-PEOPLECODE FUNCTIONS

Another type of function to consider is an external Non-PeopleCode function. This type function is declared differently from a PeopleCode function and is stored in a C-callable library. PeopleCode can call an external program, which may be useful to us when a required complex function already exists in a C-library or when we wish to interface with Windows (DLL) or equivalent UNIX accessible Dynamic Link Libraries (shared libraries/shared objects). The idea here is to take advantage of these libraries when the function already exists outside of PeopleCode or when the need for performing unusual or behind-the-scene types of tasks becomes necessary. Some of these functions can interact with the operating system, system hardware, or perform operations that require programs at levels such as C++, JAVA, or Assembler. When calling external Non-PeopleCode functions, the `Declare Function` statement is somewhat different than the external PeopleCode declaration.

Example

An External non-PeopleCode function declaration can be written as:

```
Declare Function OpenTextFile Library "My_Lib.dll" Alias "OpenFile"
     (string, integer) Returns integer;
```

The `Declare Function` statement identifies the function name as `OpenTextFile`. The function resides in a Dynamic Link Library named My_Lib.dll. The optional Alias name is `OpenFile`.

In the example, the `ext_datatype` parameters which refer to the data types the function expects are identified as `String` and `Integer`. Any parameters passed to the external function are enclosed within one set of parentheses. The `Return` statement indicates the function returns an integer.

The function declaration example can be written in a more complex manner by identifying optional parameters:

```
Declare Function OpenTextFile Library "My_Lib.dll" Alias "OpenFile"
     (string Ref As string, integer Value As number) Returns integer As
number;
```

The preceding example contains additional parameters. One parameter in particular may impact program results. The parameter list identifies the first parameter expected by the called function to be a `String`. Additionally, REF indicates it is passed by reference, which implies that the address of the data element is passed to the called function. The `pc_type` of the first parameter identifies it as being a `String` data type in the calling PeopleCode program. The called function expects the second parameter to be an integer. Its `pc_type` is a number in the calling program. The potential impact is that the second parameter is passed by `Value`. As previously discussed, passing a parameter by `Value` signals that the actual value is passed to the called function. How can this impact a program? When a value is passed by reference (REF), the address of the data element is passed to the called function. Any subsequent modifications made to that data element in the called function are reflected when control is returned to the calling program. Specifying `Value` passes the actual value of the data element; however, any changes made to the data element in the called function are not reflected in the calling program after control is returned to it. Consequently, a calling program which expects modified data following a function call, will not receive modified data when the parameters are passed by `Value`.

A non-PeopleCode external function call is identical to the other types of PeopleCode function calls. For the code presented in the preceding examples, the first parameter represents a file name and its corresponding path, passed as a string. The second parameter identifies the manner in which the file will be opened. The `'1'` represents Open for Input and a `'2'` represents Open for Output. The function call is shown as:

```
&FILENAME = "MyInput.txt";
&IO_TYPE = 1;
&RETURN_VALUE = OpenTextFile(&FILENAME, &IO_TYPE);
Rem  Verify Return Value 0 = Ok;
If &RETURN_VALUE <> 0 Then
    Error ("File " | &FILENAME | " Cannot be opened");
End-If;
```

1 A function is a collection of programs or subroutines which, when called, perform a specific task.

2 A PeopleCode function can be stored on any record event.

3 Internal PeopleCode functions are defined within the same record event in which they are called.

4 Callable PeopleCode functions are referred to as external PeopleCode functions and are defined in a record event. The function call passes any variables to the called function.

5 PeopleCode external functions can be shared by different programs and can improve efficiency by reducing program code.

6 All functions are defined with a `Function` statement, regardless of whether they are internal or external.

7 The `Declare Function` statement is required when calling a PeopleCode or non-PeopleCode external function.

8 External non-PeopleCode functions are not commonly used, but can help to perform tasks that cannot be easily done by standard PeopleCode functions.

C H A P T E R   1 8

PeopleCode debugging tools

If you are new to PeopleTools and have read, understood, and applied the techniques and information provided thus far, then you are on your way to becoming a PeopleTools developer. Of course, your introduction will not be complete and should not be complete until you have encountered problems with records, panels, and PeopleCode. A good developer is one who writes code that works, is efficient, and can be reused. A great developer is one who can use debugging tools and knows how and where to look for bugs.

18.1 THE FIRST BUG

According to computer industry folklore, the first stored program computer was invented in 1944 by the U.S. Army; it was called EDVAC. As fate would have it, the first reported computer "bug" was a moth, which was caught up in the computer and discovered by a U.S. naval officer and mathematician, Grace Murray Hopper. Webster's *New World Dictionary of Computer Terms* defines a bug as "a mistake in a computer program or system, or a malfunction in a computer hardware component. To DEBUG means to remove mistakes and correct malfunctions."

As with nature, computer bugs come in all sizes. Minor computer bugs cause little inconvenience; more serious bugs can impact a payroll or financial posting process; and real serious bugs can create catastrophes similar to the NASA Mars Climate Orbiter lost in 1999. That problem was initially reported as either human error or software error. Most likely, there is no difference. At this point in time, computer programs which can "think" for themselves are quite basic and mostly left to Hollywood films. To some extent, computer bugs will always exist. Even HAL 9000 was (or will be?) bug-ridden. Our objective as developers is to minimize bugs, and when they do arise, limit their impact and know how to go about resolving them. Knowing how to detect bugs and use debugging tools are most important.

18.2 USING WINMESSAGE

WinMessage can be a useful debugging tool because it can be used to display information in a message box window. A WinMessage statement containing an OK button can be used in any PeopleCode event. If more than one button is used, the function becomes a user think-time function limited to specific PeopleCode events only. With the exception of an Object data type, WinMessage converts any data type into a string and displays it in the message box window.

NOTE   Refer to chapter 14 and appendix E for additional information regarding WinMessage.

Debugging a program using WinMessage enables PeopleCode to display the contents of variables, system variables, and record fields. A constant can be displayed alone or concatenated with multiple data elements.

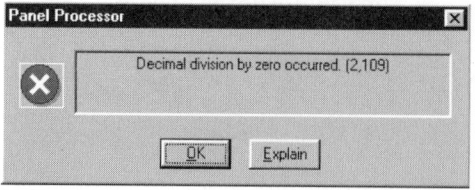

Figure 18.1   Error message returned

Let's assume we have a panel group comprised of six panels. Each panel requires multiple data elements and fires off many calculations. When an error message similar to the one in figure 18.1 is issued, WinMessage can be used to help locate the code and data responsible.

The suspect code can be identified by inserting `WinMessage` statements into the PeopleCode programs linked to the events in question. This can be accomplished by inserting a simple message to identify the program and event.

To identify the suspect code, `WinMessage` statements can be written as follows:

```
WinMessage("This is JOB.COMPRATE.SaveEdit");
WinMessage("Now in DERIVED_HR.COMPRATE.FieldFormula");
```

After the program is identified, `WinMessage` can then be used to narrow down the set of statements generating the error. Let's assume the following statements are suspect:

```
If &A > &OLD_RATE Then
    &NEW_RATE = ((&X + &Y) / (&Z * &OLD_RATE));
End-If;
```

`WinMessage` can be used to combine string constants and variables into one statement.

For example:

```
WinMessage("The value of &X is " | &X | " Y = " | &Y | "  Z= " | &Z);
```

From a debugging perspective, `WinMessage` is a simple debugging tool used to locate and identify PeopleCode programs and data elements. In some applications of `WinMessage`, however, the process of identifying and localizing bugs may appear redundant and sometimes tedious. Complex functionality which involves many PeopleCode programs, functions, and data elements may be more difficult to track using `WinMessage`. A more intuitive debugging PeopleTool which is flexible and takes some of the guesswork out of tracking down errors, is the Application Reviewer, which is the next topic of discussion.

18.3   THE APPLICATION REVIEWER

The Application Reviewer is used to trace the path of PeopleCode programs as they execute. It enables the developer to stop a program at a specific point in its execution, list the contents of variables, and trace external or internal function calls. Program return values and PeopleCode function parameters can also be logged. Features of Application Reviewer include establishing breakpoints, viewing data elements, and tracing programs, data, and program calls.

After acquiring a good working knowledge of Application Reviewer, the task of debugging can be simplified.

18.3.1   Breakpoints

A breakpoint is a preset area of code where the program will stop execution. When setting breakpoints with Application Reviewer, we have the opportunity to inspect code and view the contents of variables or record fields. Stepping through

PeopleCode and identifying what effect each statement has on variables and fields can be easily accomplished using Application Reviewer. Alternatively, we can review all the PeopleCode associated with a particular panel group. This can be done using the Break at Start menu option.

The Application Reviewer works on one panel group at a time. As a result, the Application Reviewer is opened after the panel group that needs to be debugged has been started.

The modification of a user name in Problem Tracking can be used to track PeopleCode programs using Application Reviewer. First, start the menu of the application to be debugged. In this example, the Problem Tracking menu is started (figure 18.2).

Navigation: Go → Problem Tracking

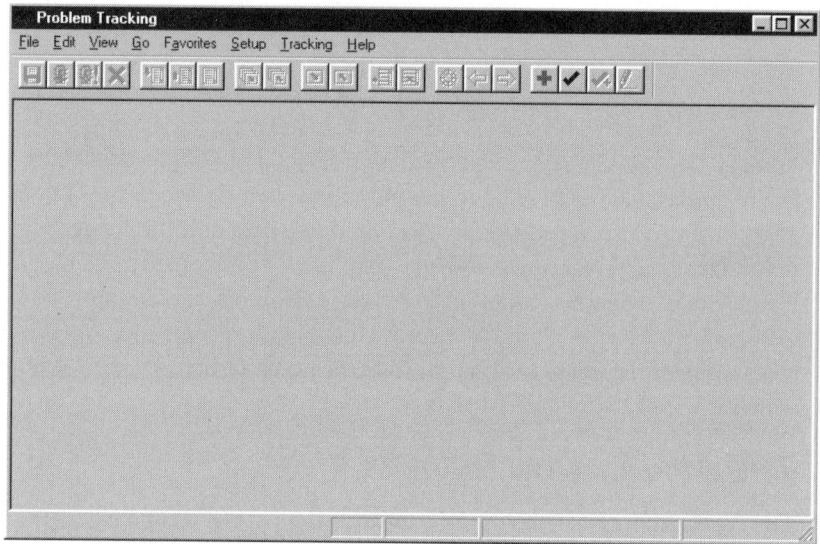

Figure 18.2   Start panel before application reviewer

The display of the Problem Tracking menu is then followed by the display of the Application Reviewer menu (figure 18.3).

NOTE   The Application Reviewer panel is not available in the PeopleTools menu until after an application has been started

Navigation: Go → PeopleTools → Application Reviewer

Figure 18.3   Initial Application Reviewer panel

Break at Start

**Figure 18.4
Break at Start**

To establish a generic breakpoint after the Application Reviewer menu is displayed, choose Break, Break at Start as shown in figure 18.4.

The next step is to enter the specific application panel group that is being debugged. When Break at Start is selected from the Application Reviewer menu, any PeopleCode executed at panel startup is displayed. This includes PeopleCode events such as SearchSave and SearchInit.

TIP   For a better understanding of PeopleCode and event processing, refer to chapter 13.

The steps required to use break are now set. Be aware, however, that if the break is set correctly and no PeopleCode break point is detected, it is possible the People-Code programs may only execute after the panel is displayed. Events executed after the panel group is displayed include FieldEdit and FieldChange. Consequently, the Application Reviewer is displayed when the first PeopleCode program is detected and not necessarily when the application panel is displayed.

Navigation: Problem Tracking → Setup → Users

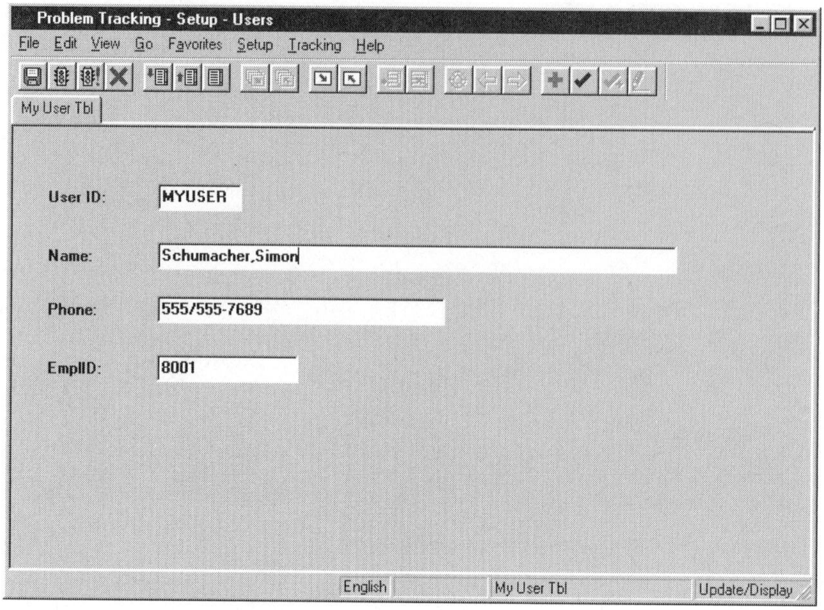

Figure 18.5 Setup Users Panel

For the example presented, no breaks have been encountered so far. We can see by the illustration in figure 18.6 that PeopleCode exists for this record in `FieldEdit`, `SaveEdit`, and `SavePostChg`.

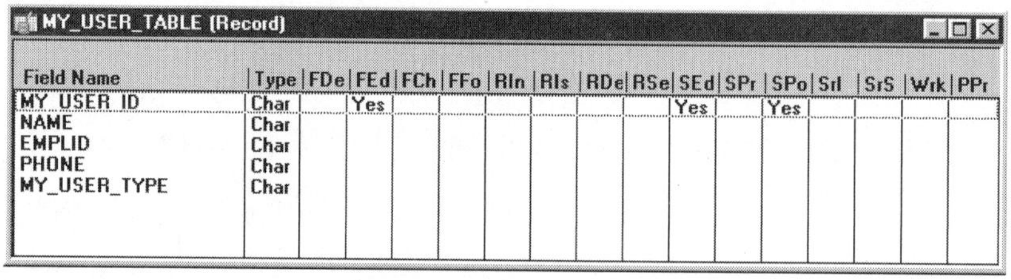
MY_USER_TABLE (Record)

Field Name	Type	FDe	FEd	FCh	FFo	RIn	RIs	RDe	RSe	SEd	SPr	SPo	SrI	SrS	Wrk	PPr
MY_USER_ID	Char		Yes							Yes		Yes				
NAME	Char															
EMPLID	Char															
PHONE	Char															
MY_USER_TYPE	Char															

Figure 18.6 PeopleCode events for MY_USER_TABLE

The PeopleCode illustrated in figure 18.6 explains why no breaks have been displayed up to this point. It is worth mentioning that, when PeopleCode exists in an event such as `FieldDefault`—where we expect to have a break before the panel is displayed—the PeopleCode may not necessarily get displayed. Recall that any `FieldDefault` PeopleCode is not executed for record fields containing data when a record is subsequently displayed. `FieldDefault` PeopleCode is, however, an iterative process that continues to execute until a field has a value.

We have changed the name field for user `MYUSER`. After tabbing out of the field or pressing the save button, the Application Reviewer screen is displayed as shown in figure 18.7.

```
MY_USER_TABLE.MY_USER_ID-FieldEdit
IF MY_USER_ID <> %OperatorId Then
   If (SQLExec("Select 'x' from PSOPRDEFN where OPRID = :1", MY_USER_ID, &OPRID)) Then
      If %SqlRows = 0 Then
         MessageBox(289, "Verify", 20001, 1, "User id %1 not in system as an operator", MY_USER_ID);
      End-If;
   End-If;
End-If;
```

Figure 18.7   Application Reviewer window

Several options are available after the Application Reviewer panel is displayed. Pressing F4 or using the View, Show Panel menu item enables a jump between the user panel and Application Reviewer.

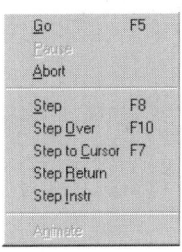

Go	F5
Pause	
Abort	
Step	F8
Step Over	F10
Step to Cursor	F7
Step Return	
Step Instr	
Animate	

Figure 18.8 Application Reviewer Run menu items

The Run menu option, shown in figure 18.8 contains several Step features which add flexibility when stepping through PeopleCode.

When Break at Start is used, F5 or Run → Go enables the current program to execute until the next PeopleCode program is detected. After breakpoints have been specified throughout the program, pressing F5 resumes processing until the next break in the program is found.

The F7 or Run → Step to Cursor steps through the PeopleCode until the cursor location.

The F8 or Run → Step is used to execute the current line of PeopleCode and step into functions. In the example in figure 18.7, the PeopleCode verifies if MY_USER_ID, entered from the User ID panel (figure 18.5), exists as a valid ID on the Operator security record. If the ID does not exist, as detected by the `SQLExec` statement, the PeopleCode sends out a message using `MessageBox`. When stepping through code, the message is displayed, and no more stepping is allowed until the message box is closed. In the example, we have an OK and Cancel button based on the style parameter. Pressing OK allows the Application Reviewer to continue.

The F10 or Run → Step Over option steps through the line of code but does not step into functions. The functions are still executed, but with this option they are not stepped into.

The Run → Step Return menu option stops after the current function has returned.

Run → Step Instr is used with the Log view and allows simulated machine code instructions to be processed.

Break at Start is one method of setting breakpoints. Establishing one or multiple breakpoints in one or more PeopleCode programs can be accomplished using the Application Reviewer.

Break at Cursor

Using Break at Start on a panel with many fields and corresponding PeopleCode programs may require stepping through a range of programs and events. A specific breakpoint can be set in one or more programs using Break at Cursor. This can be accomplished as follows:

Navigation: Application Reviewer → File → Open → MY_USER_TABLE

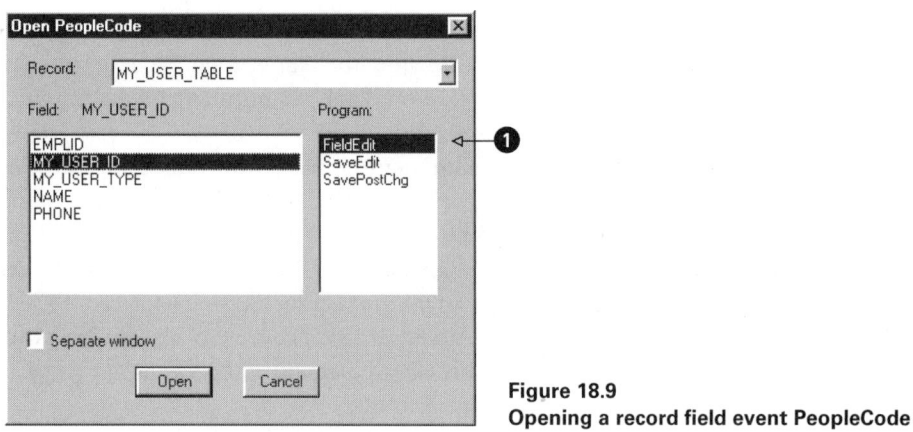

Figure 18.9
Opening a record field event PeopleCode

The PeopleCode events associated with MY_USER_ID are shown in figure 18.9, ❶. For this example, the MY_USER_TABLE.MY_USER_ID.FieldEdit event is selected. The PeopleCode for the event is presented in figure 18.10.

```
MY_USER_TABLE.MY_USER_ID-FieldEdit
If MY_USER_ID <> %OperatorId Then
   If (SQLExec("Select  'x' from PSOPRDEFN where OPRID = :1", MY_USER_ID, &OPRID)) Then
      If %SqlRows = 0 Then
         MessageBox(289, "Verify", 20001, 1, "User id %1 not in system as an operator", MY_USER_ID)
      End-If;
   End-If;
End-If;
```

Figure 18.10   PeopleCode opened for Break at Cursor

To establish a breakpoint, move the cursor to the line of PeopleCode on which to break. Breakpoints can then be set using one of the following methods:

- double-clicking on the cursor line,
- pressing F9, or
- selecting Break at Cursor from the Application Reviewer menu.

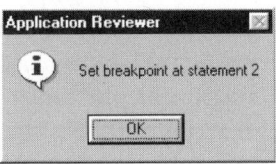

Figure 18.11
Breakpoint confirmation

In the example, the breakpoint is set on the second line of the program. The message in figure 18.11 is issued, which indicates the breakpoint is set on the second statement. When a breakpoint is set, the same options available when using Break at Start apply to Break at Cursor as well. These include stepping through the PeopleCode after a break is encountered.

Navigation: Application Reviewer → Break → List

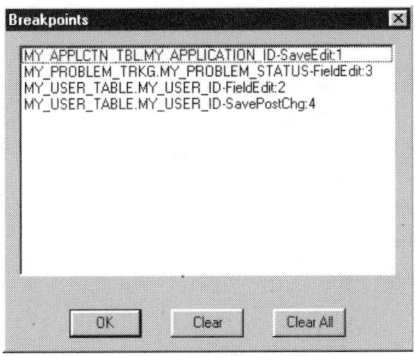

Figure 18.12 Breakpoint dialog box

Additional breakpoints set in the current PeopleCode program or other events in the Problem Tracking panel group can be identified using the Break, List option. List is used to display the breakpoint dialog box, which contains the breakpoints for records, fields, and events contained in the panel group.

Breakpoints can be cleared in two ways. One manner is to clear all breakpoints using the menu Break, Clear All, which removes all breakpoints. To clear one or more particular breakpoints and keep the remaining ones intact, use the Breakpoints dialog box.

18.3.2 Viewing data

Navigation: Application Reviewer → Data → PeopleCode Variable

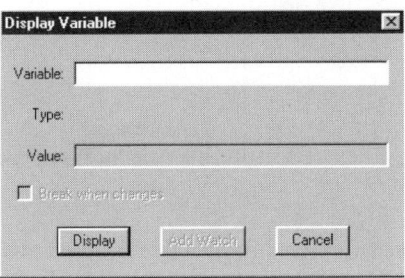

Figure 18.13 PeopleCode variable dialog box

Viewing data elements can also be accomplished using Application Reviewer. This is very useful when debugging because it enables us to see the impact that PeopleCode statements and functions have on data. Some functions have a black box effect, but with Application Reviewer, the return values of functions can be examined. After a break is executed, data can be viewed using the Application Reviewer menu shown in figure 18.13.

The previous section illustrated how to set breakpoints in a PeopleCode program. A breakpoint was set on statement 2 (figure 18.11), which is the SQLExec.

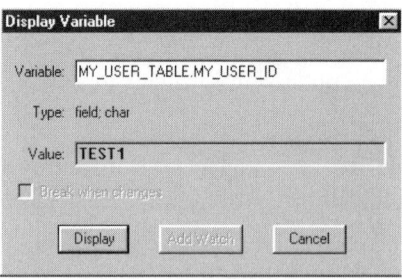

Figure 18.14   Value of MY_USER_ID field

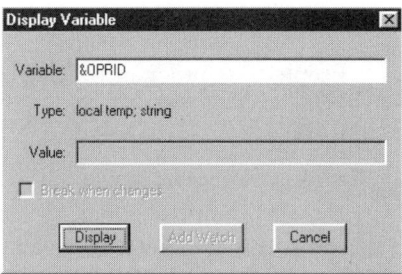

Figure 18.15   Value of &OPRID variable

To view the value of the record field MY_USER_ID, the display variable dialog box can be entered as shown in figure 18.14.

Characteristics of the Display Variable dialog box include the record fieldname, data type, and value of the field. Upon conclusion of the SQLExec statement, the contents of variable &OPRID can also be displayed. What is the value of the variable &OPRID after SQLExec?

The &OPRID variable (figure 18.15) does not contain a value because SQLExec selects the literal x and, therefore, the variable is not populated even when the Select statement finds a match. Using a literal in a Select statement is a common practice when all that is required is the verification of data without the need for return values. This is pointed out because it is important to understand what the PeopleCode statements and function calls are doing. In this particular example, knowledge of SQL is important to avoid inaccurate conclusions when it is discovered that &OPRID does not contain a value.

18.3.3   Additional Application Reviewer options

Local or global variables can be viewed using the View Locals menu option, which displays the Local Temps screen illustrated in figure 18.16.

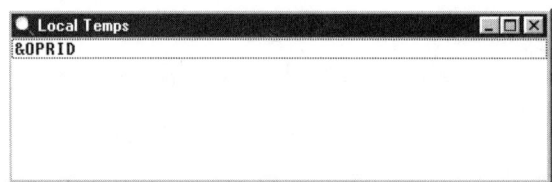

**Figure 18.16
Viewing local variables**

Application Reviewer can be used to view log files which reflect selected system activity. This can be set by selection of the menu option as shown in figure 18.17.

Navigation: Application Reviewer → Options → Log

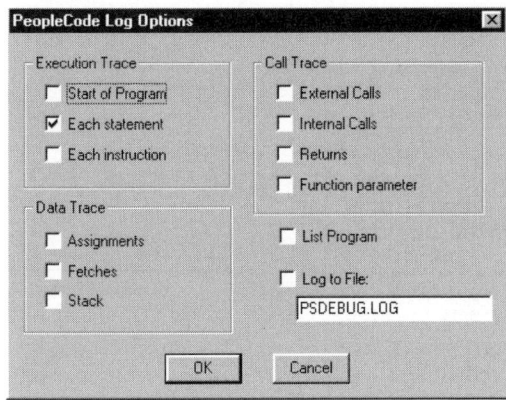

Figure 18.17
PeopleCode log options

As illustrated in figure 18.17, PeopleCode log options are divided into three categories:

- Execution Trace
- Data Trace
- Call Trace

The Execution Trace option enables PeopleCode programs to be traced at the start of each program, each program statement, or each program instruction. The default is set to each statement.

The next option available is Data Trace. The options are Assignments, Fetches, and Stack. Assignments log all data assignments made to variables or record fields. The log window in Application Reviewer must be open to log data assignment activity to a file. Some caution must be used when logging activity. It is possible to generate very large log files during a PeopleSoft session. Logged traced data assignments are written to the default file PSDEBUG.log. A typical log window may look like the following:

```
7
  0 If MY_USER_ID <> %OperatorId Then
>> Begin MY_USER_TABLE.MY_USER_ID-FieldEdit
^^^^^^^^^^ PeopleCode Program Listing End
 396, stop
 377, statement Next=396
 376, pop
 364, builtin    - MessageBox #Parms=6
 348, fetch      MY_USER_TABLE.MY_USER_ID
 298, push       User id %1 not in system as an
 274, push       1
 251, push       20001
 234, push       Verify
 212, push       289
```

```
 202, branch <>  377
 180, push        0
 164, fetch      Builtin - %SqlRows
 152, br  False  377
 140, builtin     - SQLExec #Parms=3
 126, push       &OPRID (temp #0)
 112, push       MY_USER_TABLE.MY_USER_ID
  60, push       Select  'x' from PSOPRDEFN whe
  52, branch =   377
  36, fetch      Builtin - %OperatorId
  20, fetch      MY_USER_TABLE.MY_USER_ID
   1, statement Next=377
   0, start      Field=MY_USER_TABLE.MY_USER_ID-FieldEdit Temps=1 Stack=6
vvvvvvvvvv PeopleCode Program Listing:
```

The panel activity is displayed in the log window. To write the contents to a file, a File Save operation is required before closing the Application Reviewer. Depending on the log options set, a significant amount of information is stored in a trace log file. Some of this information requires further interpretation.

A log file can be viewed using an ASCII text editor such as PFE. The components in a log file include

- line number in the file
- internal tracing reference numbers
- address of instructions in a program
- operation code
- operation operands represent information used by each operation

The operation code and operation operands work in conjunction with one another and are available to the list and trace options. The operation code refers to the internal operation performed by the program. The operand is the value required by the specific operation. Some operation codes and operands used in the preceding code example are as illustrated in table 18.1:

Table 18.1 Operation codes and operands

Operation	Operands	Description
Start		identifies the beginning of a PeopleCode program
Push	constant	pushes the operand into the stack
BR True	location	This instruction works with the internal program stack. It checks the current item on the stack for a Boolean return value. When the value is True, program control is transferred to the operand location.
Branch	location	Program control is transferred to the operand location. No return value is tested.
Fetch	Record.field	retrieves a record field value and pushes it onto the stack
BR False	location	works with the internal program stack (It checks the current item on the stack for a Boolean return value. When the value is False, program control is transferred to the operand location.)

Table 18.1 Operation codes and operands (continued)

Operation	Operands	Description
BuiltIn	Function	executes the specified function
	#Parameters	represents the number of parameters
Call	DLL	calls a routine stored in a Dynamic Link Library
	Internal function	calls an internal PeopleCode function
	External function	calls an external PeopleCode function stored in record.fieldname
Error		halts the PeopleCode program
Exit		exits the PeopleCode program
Return		returns control to the next higher level program
Store	record.field	stores the top stack item into the operand record field
Stop		identifies the end of a PeopleCode program
Pop		Removes top item from the stack

We can use the information in table 18.1 to examine selected log file entries found in the preceding code example.

Line #	Details of operation performed
348	The Fetch Operand retrieves the record.field operand and pushes it onto the stack. In this example, the record.field is `MY_USER_TABLE.MY_USER_ID`
298	The `Push` statement is used to move the constant to the stack.
202	The branch <> statement compares the two top items on the stack. In this example, control is passed to line 377. This specifies the location of the next statement, which is a `Stop` operation.

18.4 SEARCH IN PEOPLECODE

Application Designer contains a search facility that can be used to look for strings contained in PeopleCode programs. Search can be performed against record PeopleCode, menu PeopleCode, or both. The search can be tailored to look in a specific record or several records. The search can also be used to search all PeopleCode programs. When searching for an exact string a Match Case option exists. The results are sent to a search output window, with the additional option of sending the output to a file. To begin searching, select Edit → Find in PeopleCode from the menu.

The dialog box (figure 18.18) is used when searching the entire database for the `MessageBox` string. Searching the entire database is necessary when no additional information is known about the location of the PeopleCode string. Clicking on the Define List button can be used to narrow a search. This produces the Define Search List window (figure 18.19) where the number of records or menus to search can be limited to specific records or prefixes. Using this feature produces more efficient results.

Navigation: Application Designer → Edit → Find in PeopleCode

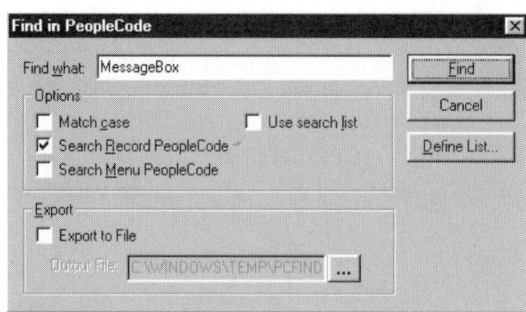

Figure 18.18
Find in PeopleCode dialog box

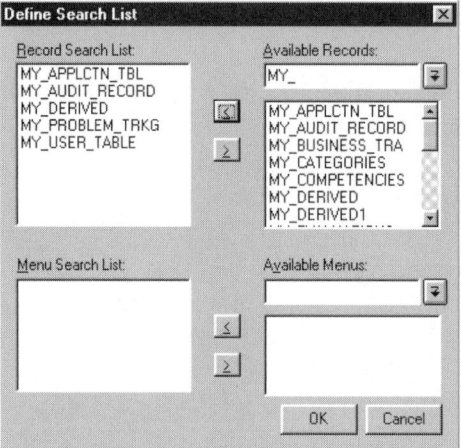

Figure 18.19   Define Search List dialog

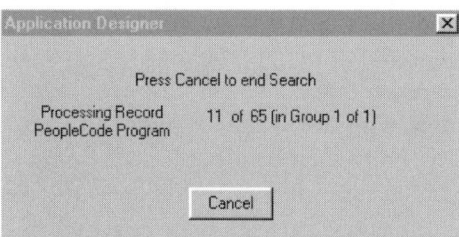

Figure 18.20   Search status

The search can be narrowed to a specific record key—in this example, record names that begin with MY_. A list of available records containing MY_ as the record name prefix is used. The selected records are moved to the left side of the dialog box. Clicking OK closes the Define Search List dialog. The Find button is then pressed, and the search begins. The status is displayed in figure 18.20.

When a search list is not specified, the search may run for several minutes, depending on the number of records searched. A search which specifies a list containing many records may also require additional time. Pressing the Cancel button while performing a search can stop the search process.

The search results are displayed in the Find in PeopleCode output window. The results of the search can also be sent to a file for later viewing. This can be done by clicking the "Export to File" checkbox in the Find in PeopleCode dialog box.

18.5 PEOPLECODE TRACE

PeopleCode Trace is another tool used for debugging. Trace produces an output file defined in the trace page of Configuration Manager. Two methods of producing a PeopleCode Trace file exist: the Trace PeopleCode menu option and the `SetTracePC` Function.

18.5.1 Trace PeopleCode utility

The Trace PeopleCode feature enables the tracing of PeopleCode programs using preset options in the Trace PeopleCode panel.

The illustration in figure 18.21 identifies how several trace options can be set before beginning a Problem Tracking panel session. The trace file is a standard text file that can be opened and read with a file editor such as PFE or Notepad. The trace file contains the operation codes and operands generated by the program. The file is similar to the log file discussed in the Application Reviewer section. There is good reason for this similarity: the trace utility can be replaced by the Application Reviewer trace without losing trace option functionality.

A second trace method is the `SetTracePC` function. This function helps control PeopleCode Trace settings from one or more PeopleCode programs.

Navigation: Utilities → Use → Trace PeopleCode

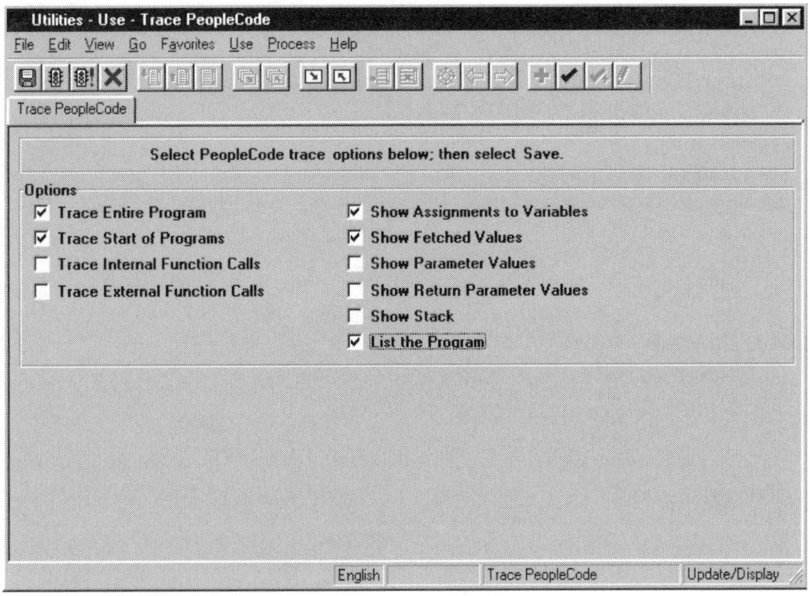

Figure 18.20   Trace PeopleCode utility

18.5.2 SetTracePC

The `SetTracePC` function controls PeopleCode Trace, based on parameter values passed to the function. The function takes one parameter, which represents the trace settings used in producing the output trace file. If multiple trace options are required, each option number is added, and the sum is passed to the `SetTracePC` function.

`SetTracePC` produces a file named DBG1.tmp in the Windows Temp directory. We can specify a unique name if necessary and this can be done from within the configuration manager trace option. The Set Trace options are as follows:

Table 18.2 SetTrace PC options

Value	Option description
1	This option traces the program that is executed. It includes options 64, 128 and 256 specified below.
2	Lists the entire program.
4	Displays the outcomes of assignments made to variables.
8	Identifies the values retrieved for all variables.
16	Identifies the contents used in the internal stack.
64	This trace option identifies when each program is started.
128	Identifies the calls made to external PeopleCode routines.
256	Identifies the calls made to internal PeopleCode routines.
512	Displays the value of parameters passed to a function.
1024	This option displays the values of parameters at the conclusion of a function call.

Based on the values identified in table 18.2, a statement using `SetTracePC` can be written as follows:

```
&OPTION_VALUE = 14;
SetTracePC(&OPTION_VALUE);
```

In the example, the option value passed to `SetTracePC` generates a file containing the following:

- Program listing   +2
- Results of variable assignments +4
- Values of variables fetched   +8

At this point, we have a better understanding of how to use PeopleCode program debugging tools.

1 WinMessage is a function which can be used to help in debugging by displaying the contents of variables and record fields. WinMessage can be used in any PeopleCode event provided only one button exists in the message box.

2 The Application Reviewer is a key tool used in debugging PeopleCode programs. With Application Reviewer we can set breakpoints and examine the results of PeopleCode statements and function calls. The value of record fields and variables can also be displayed.

3 The Application Reviewer can be used to identify local and global variables.

4 Trace options in Application Reviewer can be applied to program execution, data, and function calls.

5 Search PeopleCode is an Application Designer tool that enables the search of strings contained in PeopleCode programs. The search can be done across the entire database or against specific records.

6 PeopleCode Trace is a utility that can also trace PeopleCode programs. It produces a report and can be initiated from the Utilities menu option or from within a PeopleCode program using the SetTracePC option.

C H A P T E R   1 9

PeopleCode— PeopleSoft 8

With release 8 of PeopleTools and, more specifically, PeopleCode, we have vast amounts of new knowledge to acquire. In regard to PeopleCode, features in release 7.5 are not lost. Backward compatibility and the integration of new PeopleCode functionality enables PeopleCode to work with features available in release 8. Release 8 contains key enhancements to the PeopleCode language and the environment in which these new tools are used.

In this chapter, we briefly discuss some new items which make the development and implementation of PeopleCode more exciting and challenging than ever before. As the World Wide Web becomes a major player in business and personal use, PeopleCode is there with Web Client and Internet Client design.

An attempt to list and describe the new features in PeopleCode release 8 would practically require a small book on its own. Some of the topics selected for this discussion of release 8 were reviewed in previous chapters. This should provide the reader some perspective between releases 7 and 8. PeopleCode release 8 is also very object oriented. As a result, the File and SQL objects are briefly illustrated. Additional topics include new panel events, enhanced scroll processing and working with arrays. In release 8, a tool that we will use at one time or another is the PeopleCode Debugger. The debugger includes increased functionality and can be entered directly from the Application Designer.

19.1 FILE OBJECT

One of the more important features in PeopleTools 8 is PeopleCode object syntax. Standard classes and the use of dot notation enable us to access functions and objects contained in these classes. The use of object syntax allows PeopleCode to execute in Application Engine programs not linked to panel groups. This signals a move away from the relationship between PeopleCode and panel groups. PeopleCode can now be written so that it is run in a stand-alone mode. This C++ type syntax also contains classes comprised of methods (which are the functions contained in a class). One such class is the File class, which contains methods (functions) and properties (fields) that can be used to open, read, and write to external or "flat" files. If you are a C++ or Visual Basic developer, you'll appreciate these classes.

To define a File object, the statement can be coded as:

```
Local File &MyTextFile;
```

This example creates a file object named &MyTextFile, which is a pointer to an object that contains file-handling methods. Because the variable is a pointer, the file object is passed by reference to PeopleCode functions and methods. Now, let's assign the File object an address of a file contained on a floppy disk:

```
&MyTextFile = GetFile (a:\"Interface.txt", "R");
```

The statement calls the GetFile function used to create a new instance of a file object based on the File class. The function links the file object with an external file and then opens the file Interface.txt. After the file is opened, additional methods contained in the File class can be used to read from or write to the file. In the example, the second parameter passed to the GetFile function represents the mode in which the file is read. An "R" indicates the file is opened for Reading.

We now wish to read the file into a string using the ReadLine method. ReadLine is a File object-associated method that reads a line of text from the file object. In the following example, text is read into the string &Interface_Record and passed to an external PeopleCode function named ProcessInterfaceData:

```
Local String &Interface_Record;
While &MyTextFile.ReadLine(&Interface_Record);
```

```
                &RETURN_VALUE = ProcessInterfaceData(&Interface_Record);
        End-While;
```

To close and unlink the file object &MyTextFile from the external file Interface.txt, we can use the Close method, which frees up all resources connected with the file object:

```
&MyTextFile.Close();
```

19.2 SQL OBJECT

Earlier releases of PeopleCode used the SQLExec statement to perform database operations such as Select or Update. For release 8 of PeopleTools, SQL definitions can be created in the Application Designer and can subsequently be used as SQL programs. Components of the SQL statements can subsequently be re-used. In PeopleCode 8, programs can now access SQL definitions through the SQL class. While the SQLExec function can still be used in release 8, the SQL class has added functionality which enables multiple rows to be selected. When performing a Select using SQLExec, the function only selects the first row. The SQL class is similar to SQLExec because it supports bind values and output variables.

The following example defines an SQL object named &MySQL. The CreateSQL statement is used to create an instance of an SQL object, which is opened based on the values passed in the SQL string.

CreateRecord is a method associated with a Record object. Data rows will be selected from the record in this example:

```
/*  Define SQL and Record objects */
Local SQL &MySQL;
Local Record &MyRecord;

&MyRecord = CreateRecord(Record.MY_LOCATIONS);
&MySQL = CreateSQL ("%Selectall (:1) where SETID = :2 and OPRCLASS = :3");
```

Our next step is to execute the SQL statement of the object &MySQL. This statement Selects from the record MY_LOCATIONS and loads the corresponding fields into &MyRecord, which is an object of MY_LOCATIONS:

```
/* Execute the attached statement */
&MySQL.Execute (&MyRecord, &SETID, &OPRCLASS);
```

The next statement is Fetch, which is a method associated with an SQL object. The Select statement in the preceding example retrieves the rows, based on the value of bind variables supplied during execution of the statement. The following Fetch operation retrieves each subsequent row processed by the Select statement associated with &MySQL objects.

```
/* Fetch from the select row */

If &MySQL.Fetch(&MyRecord) Then
 ProcessMyLocationRecord(&MyRecord);
 End-if;
```

After data rows have been processed, it is necessary to close the SQL statement. The `Close` method associated with an SQL object disconnects `&MySQL` from the `Select` statement. The `Close` statement is illustrated as follows:

```
/* Close the SQL object */
&MySQL.Close();
```

19.3 ASSOCIATING PEOPLECODE WITH PANEL GROUPS

Some PeopleCode used throughout this book—more specifically, the programs contained in fields shared between two or more panels—may contain statements which identify the panel name. These statements are executed before any processing is performed. The code used by a particular panel must first be prefixed with an `If` statement:

```
If %Panel = "MY_LOCATIONS" Then
/* Statements associated with this panel */
End-if;
```

The preceding code is associated with specific functionality for the panel only. A similar `If` statement, related to another panel with a different set of statements, can also reside in the same record field event. This approach works but is usually not efficient, particularly in terms of record reusability. In release 8, PeopleCode can be linked to panel groups and the elements that make up a panel group such as panels, panel records, and panel fields. The PeopleCode associated with panel groups and their corresponding components include:

- Panel group record field PeopleCode
- Panel group record PeopleCode
- Panel group PeopleCode
- Panel PeopleCode
- Panel field control PeopleCode

This type of PeopleCode is only available from a panel group definition and the events for the specific panel group components. Panel group record field PeopleCode is different from record field PeopleCode because the former is associated with record fields which exist on a panel group and its related events. Panel group PeopleCode is not available from a record definition; it can only be retrieved through a panel group's structure. An example of a panel group structure and corresponding panel group record field PeopleCode is illustrated in figure 19.1.

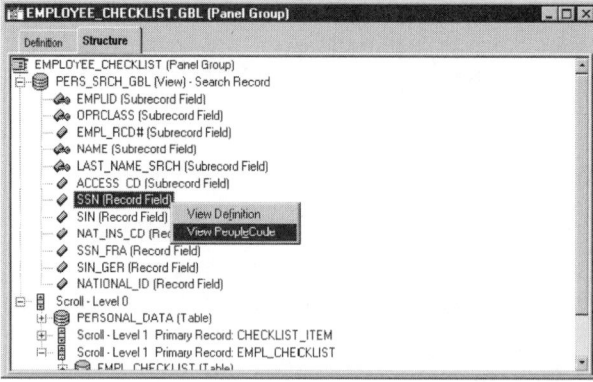

Figure 19.1
Panel group record field PeopleCode from the panel group structure

Panel groups contain several new events associated with panels and panel groups. The events are `Activate`, `PreBuild`, and `PostBuild`.

19.3.1 Activate event

When a panel is initially displayed the `Activate` event is triggered. The event is also generated when tabbing between panels contained in a panel group. PeopleCode which resides in this event is specific only to the panel and can include some of the functionality related to panel display, such as `Hide` and `UnHide`. Each panel contains its own `Activate` event. PeopleCode in this event can only be linked to panels.

19.3.2 PreBuild

`PreBuild` PeopleCode is related to panel groups only and is triggered before the remaining panel group build events are executed. PeopleCode in this event can be used to hide or unhide panels.

19.3.3 PostBuild

PeopleCode in this event is triggered after the other panel group build events have been generated. Programs in this event are linked to panel groups only and can be used to set panel group variables.

19.4 ENHANCED SCROLL FUNCTIONS

In chapter 16, we learned how to implement PeopleCode scroll functions such as `ScrollSelect` and `RowScrollSelect`. In release 8, the new `Rowset` class can be used to work with `ScrollSelect` or `RowScrollSelect` using the class methods, `Select` and `SelectNew`. These class methods enable the PeopleCode program to control the selection of data into panel scroll areas. `Select` and `SelectNew` are used with a `Rowset`, which is equivalent to a scroll area. The level zero area of a panel is also the level zero `Rowset`. The level zero `Rowset` also contains data in the panel buffers. In chapter 16, we learned about parent and child relationships.

Release 8 uses child `Rowsets` controlled by a higher level `Rowset` known as the parent `Rowset`. The process of selecting into `Rowsets` also includes child `Rowsets` when autoselect is enabled. Child `Rowsets`, however, are processed in a manner similar to `RowScrollSelect` and utilize a `WHERE` to limit child `Rowsets` to that of the parent `Rowset`.

19.4.1   Using Select

The `Select` method associated with a `Rowset` class is used to retrieve rows from an SQL table or view. The record definition of the SQL table or view from which rows are retrieved is referred to as the select record. The top level `Rowset` containing the PeopleCode which executes the `Select` is referred to as the default scroll record. `Select` automatically positions child `Rowsets` under the corresponding parent row executing the method. As with `ScrollSelect` and `RowScrollSelect`, `Select` also accepts an optional SQL string which can include a `WHERE` block used to limit the rows into the scroll area.

Let's apply the `Rowset` class and its corresponding `Select` method to the level 2 `ScrollSelect` example presented in chapter 16.

The first step creates an instance of a record object named &MY_LOCATIONS_REC and a `Rowset` object, based on the MY_LOCATIONS record. The PeopleCode is shown as follows:

```
Local Record  &MY_LOCATIONS_REC;
Local Rowset  &MY_LOCATIONS;
```

The next step (illustrated following) uses `GetRecord` to create a record object which references the MY_LOCATIONS record. The `GetRowSet` method is used to create a `Rowset` object and the current MY_LOCATIONS row.

```
&MY_LOCATIONS_REC = GetRecord(RECORD.MY_LOCATIONS);
&MY_LOCATIONS = GetRowSet (SCROLL.MY_LOCATIONS);
```

The `Select` method is implemented using the child `Rowset` MY_LOCATION_EMP, which is passed as the first parameter to the `Select` method. The next parameter is the select record represented by the view MY_LOC_EMPL_VW. The new Meta-SQL function `%KeyEqual` extends into a conditional phrase that can be used in the `WHERE` clause. When more than one key exists in the record, the phrase will include an `AND` for each of the record keys. `%KeyEqual` performs the task of automatically applying the Meta-SQL functions `%Datein()`, `%TimeIn()` and `%DateTimeIn()`, based on the data type of the field. When the value is a string it will be enclosed in quotes. A `NULL` value will be replaced with `"IS  NULL"`. The bind variable (`:1`) passed to `%KeyEqual` is the record object &MY_LOCATIONS_REC.

```
&MY_LOCATIONS.Select (SCROLL.MY_LOCATION_EMP, RECORD.MY_LOC_EMPL_VW, "WHERE
%KeyEqual(:1)", &MY_LOCATIONS_REC);
```

19.5   ARRAY CLASS

The PeopleCode Array class enables the definition of array objects without necessarily specifying a fixed size. The array size expands and contracts based on whether data are added to or removed from the object. A simple array can be declared as:

```
Local Array of String &MyStringArray;
```

Multi-dimensional arrays can also be specified. A two-dimensional array comprised of numbers can be declared as:

```
Local Array of Array of Number &MyNumberArray;
```

Referencing elements in an array can be accomplished using indexes. The array &MyStringArray can be referenced as follows:

```
&String_Element = &MyStringArray[5];
```

19.5.1   Populating an array

An array can be populated several ways. On method uses CreateArrary when the array is initially created and can be written as:

```
&MyStringArray = CreateArray("String 1","String 2","String 3");
```

An array can also be populated by assigning values to the individual array elements:

```
&MyStringArray = CreateArray();
&MyStringArray [1] = "String 1";
&MyStringArray [2] = "String 2";
&MyStringArray [3] = "String 3";
```

Push is a method associated with an array class:

```
&MyStringArray.Push("String 1");
&MyStringArray.Push("String 2");
&MyStringArray.Push("String 3");
```

Unshift is another method associated with an array class. It can be used to add items to the beginning of the array:

```
&MyStringArray.Unshift ("String 1");
&MyStringArray.Unshift ("String 2");
&MyStringArray.Unshift ("String 3");
```

19.5.2 Removing items from an array

Two methods associated with an array class include `Pop` and `Shift`. To select and remove array items from the end of an array using `Pop`, the code can be written in the following manner:

```
&String_Field = &MyStringArray.Pop();
```

In the preceding example, the value of `&String_Field` is "String 3" after using the `Pop` method.

The `Shift` method can be used to select and remove items from the beginning of an array:

```
&String_Field = &MyStringArray.Shift();
```

Because `Shift` targets the beginning of an array, the value of `&String_Field` is "String 1" following execution of the `Shift` method.

19.5.3 Using an array in a loop

A basic PeopleCode `For` loop can be written to reference the values in an array. A numeric data element can be utilized as an index to reference array items. The code can be written as follows:

```
For &I = 1 to  &MyStringArray.Len;
   &String_Field = &MyStringArray [&I];
End-For;
```

`Len` is an array class property that represents the current number of items in an array.

19.6 PEOPLECODE DEBUGGER

The PeopleCode Debugger, formerly known as Application Reviewer, offers increased functionally and simplicity of use. In release 7, the Application Reviewer is entered using Go → Application Reviewer. Now, the PeopleCode Debugger is included in the Application Designer. A panel group can now be started, and the PeopleCode Debugger can be entered from Application Designer. Alternatively, another panel group can be entered and automatically run in debug mode.

19.6.1 Improved visual support

In chapter 18, we saw how Application Reviewer enables breakpoints to be set so that PeopleCode statements can be tracked. The PeopleCode Debugger includes a visual indicator of breakpoints and an arrow that identifies the current line of code. Figure 19.2 shows an arrow which illustrates how the current line of code is identified, ❶.

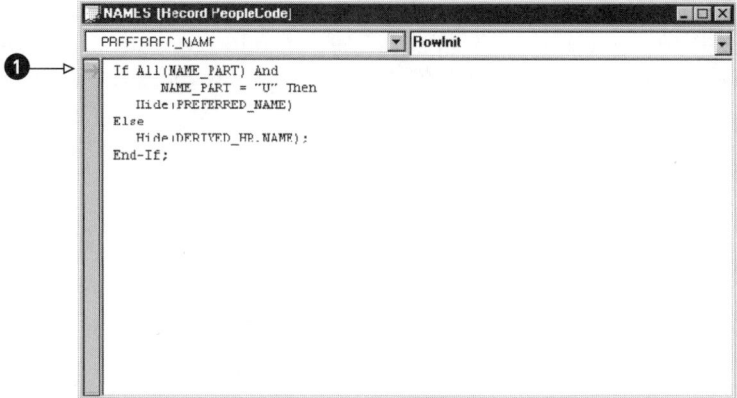

Figure 19.2 Identification of current line executing

The PeopleCode Debugger also visually identifies breakpoints using indicators as shown by ❶ in figure 19.3.

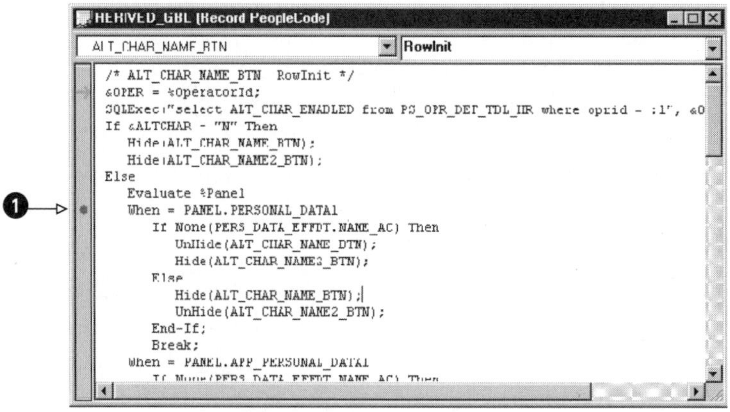

Figure 19.3 Visual indicator of breakpoint

Another great feature of the PeopleCode Debugger is referred to as "Hover Inspect." This feature enables the visual inspection of simple variable or field contents displayed in a pop-up window. An example of using Hover Inspect is illustrated in figure 19.4. The contents of the variable after the data assignment is denoted by ❶.

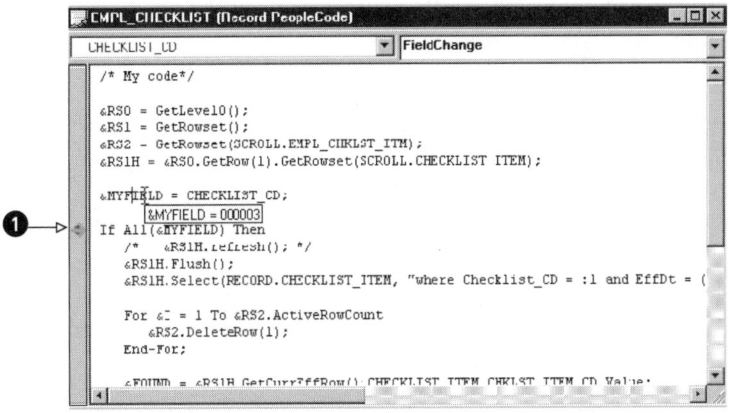

Figure 19.4 Using Hover Inspect

Variables can now be viewed from different windows based on the type. These variable types and their associated window include Local, Global, Panel Group, and Parameter. The Parameter window can be used to view user-specified parameters included in function calls. An example of a Local variable window is shown in figure 19.5.

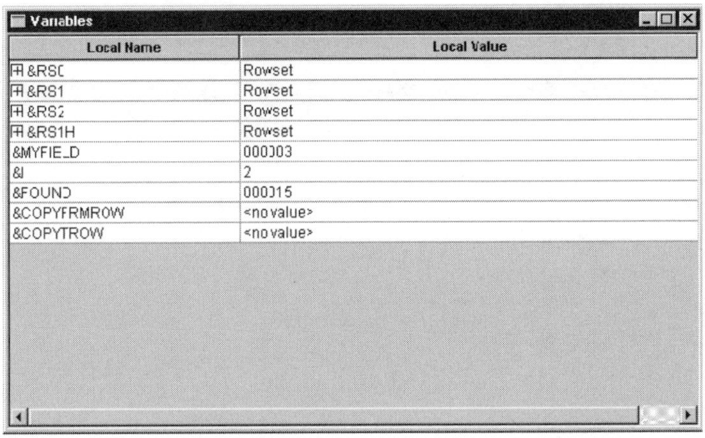

Figure 19.5 Local variable window

The visual representation of objects can be extended to display the object properties. The "+" convention is used and appears next to the variable name. The example in figure19.5 identifies Rowsets at several levels. The level 1 Rowset is expanded (figure 19.6) to reveal properties that comprise the `Rowset`. Some properties include Effdt, Name, and `ActiveRowCount`.

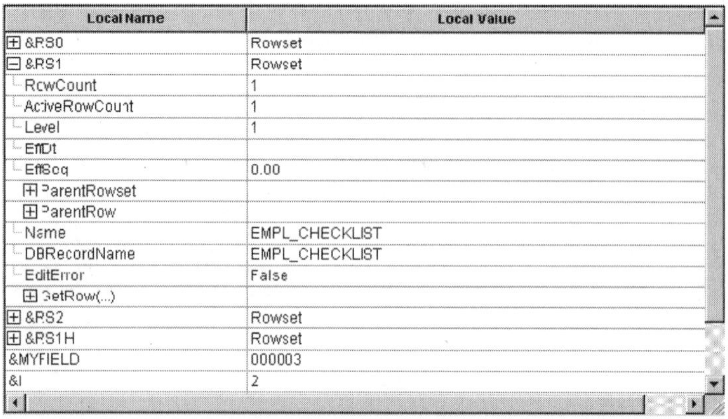

Local Name	Local Value
⊞ &RS0	Rowset
⊟ &RS1	Rowset
└ RowCount	1
└ ActiveRowCount	1
└ Level	1
└ EffDt	
└ EffSeq	0.00
⊞ ParentRowset	
⊞ ParentRow	
└ Name	EMPL_CHECKLIST
└ DBRecordName	EMPL_CHECKLIST
└ EditError	False
⊞ GetRow(...)	
⊞ &RS2	Rowset
⊞ &RS1H	Rowset
&MYFIELD	000003
&I	2

Figure 19.6 Expanded Rowset object

Field object values are listed under the value column when viewed in the debugger. The field value can now be viewed without having to navigate to the value properties. Figure 19.7 illustrates how the PERSONAL_DATA record and its associated fields can be viewed.

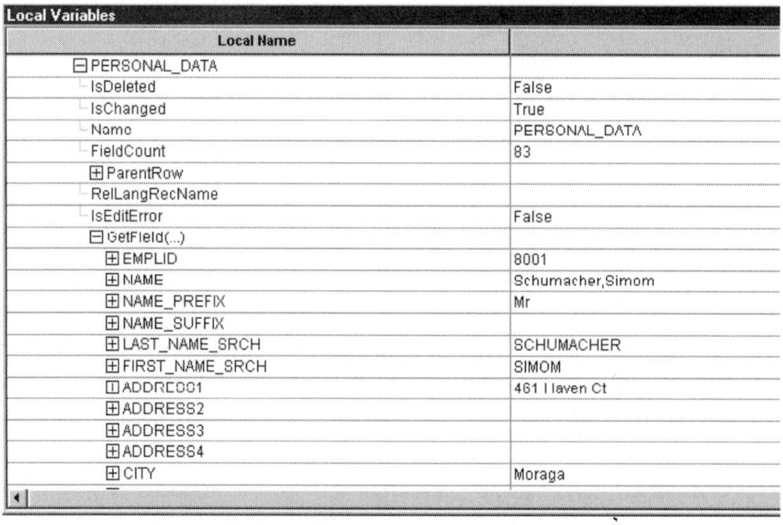

Local Variables

Local Name	
⊟ PERSONAL_DATA	
└ IsDeleted	False
└ IsChanged	True
└ Name	PERSONAL_DATA
└ FieldCount	83
⊞ ParentRow	
└ RelLangRecName	
└ IsEditError	False
⊟ GetField(...)	
⊞ EMPLID	8001
⊞ NAME	Schumacher,Simom
⊞ NAME_PREFIX	Mr
⊞ NAME_SUFFIX	
⊞ LAST_NAME_SRCH	SCHUMACHER
⊞ FIRST_NAME_SRCH	SIMOM
⊞ ADDRESS1	461 Ilaven Ct
⊞ ADDRESS2	
⊞ ADDRESS3	
⊞ ADDRESS4	
⊞ CITY	Moraga

Figure 19.7 Viewing record field values

19.6.2 Additional options

Additional options which can be selected after the debugger is running include:

- Exit Debug Mode
- Abort Running Program
- Edit Breakpoints

The Exit Debug Mode option automatically saves all breakpoints before leaving debug mode. The PeopleCode program currently running can be terminated using the Abort Running Program option. The Edit Breakpoints option displays a menu identifying the lines containing breakpoints (figure 19.8).

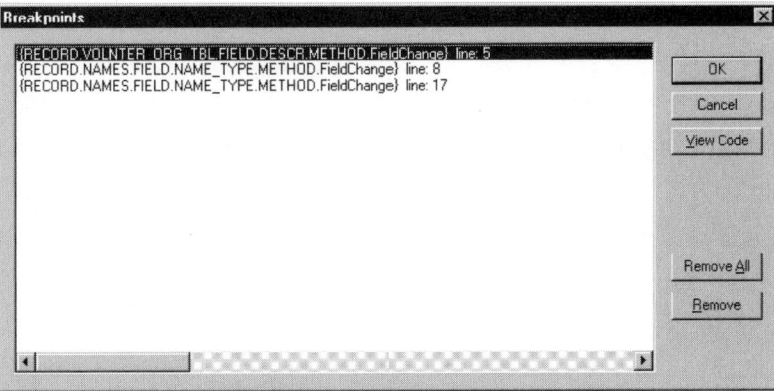

Figure 19.8   Edit breakpoints menu

This menu enables us to remove specific breakpoints or to remove all breakpoints. The View Code button will display the code containing the breakpoint. The menu also identifies the line number in the PeopleCode program which contains the breakpoint.

PART 4

Customizing PeopleSoft-delivered applications

To be recognized as one of the leading contenders in the ERP arena is no small feat. Each packaged application produced by the ERP vendor must have functionality to accommodate a wide range of companies with varying business requirements. Some requirements may be dictated by the particular laws of a given state or even country. With the expansion of companies into the global marketplace, the challenge to provide complete ERP solutions is greater than ever. PeopleSoft has responded to these challenges and has produced an impressive set of functional applications in areas such as Finance, Human Resource Management, Manufacturing, and Student Administration. These applications may provide customers with all the functionality they need right-out-of-box. This is known as running plain "vanilla" PeopleSoft. Some companies, especially the larger variety, are inundated with rules, regulations, and requirements unique to their businesses. These companies are faced with a decision: to either re-engineer their business processes or customize the PeopleSoft applications. The philosophies and perceptions toward customization vary. Some companies avoid customization at all costs while others embrace the opportunity. In many cases, you will find no other alternative exists but to customize the delivered applications.

PeopleSoft provides a full set of tools to create and manage these customizations. We discuss these tools in detail while providing information on the customization process, project management, and software upgrades. The reader can follow along with sample customizations while maintaining a project that contains all of the modified objects. Through the use of PeopleTools, customers are also afforded the opportunity to create application extensions and sub-systems which provide increased functionality while having relatively little impact on upgrades. It is always in your best interest to fully understand the impact and management of customizations to get the most out of PeopleSoft.

CHAPTER 20

"Vanilla" vs. customized

20.1 WHAT IS CUSTOMIZATION?

As you've seen in the previous chapters, PeopleSoft delivers a great suite of tools that are simple to use and that allow for speedy development cycles. Some of our readers are probably anxious to start the development and customization using PeopleTools. But is this always necessary? And what kind of considerations should we always keep in mind?

All of us in the PeopleSoft world have probably heard the frequently used term "Vanilla." Strictly speaking, this means no customizations are allowed to the delivered system. In a more liberal interpretation, this means you should customize only when necessary. The perpetual dilemma—to customize or not to customize—remains. Both approaches present advantages and disadvantages (which we will discuss) but as always in real life, a reasonable compromise, in most cases, is the best way to go. Our goal after all is to make the new system functional, convenient, and user-friendly. First let's agree on what is considered a customization, what kind of customizations may be necessary, and what kind of customizations are better to avoid.

A customization is any change to a delivered application. Let's divide the entire pool of all customizations into additions to the PeopleSoft-delivered application (or system extensions); and true modifications to these applications.

Imagine a situation when your old system had a functionality not present in the PeopleSoft-delivered system. You have the following choices to consider:

- change your company business practice and drop the old functionality
- develop a manual desk procedure to support the old functionality
- create an external (Excel, Access, Visual Basic, and so forth) application that can interface with the delivered PeopleSoft application
- change PeopleSoft-delivered objects and programs to incorporate the desired functionality into the delivered application
- develop an addition to the delivered application by creating your own menus, panels, records, and processes utilizing PeopleTools.

Let's first briefly characterize each option. Later, we will discuss some of these alternatives in greater detail.

20.1.1   Changing your company business practice

Often (this is more common to small and midsize companies), management tries to save on both system development and future maintenance by changing the current business rules and processes in order to fit the PeopleSoft-delivered system. Generally speaking, implementing PeopleSoft creates a good opportunity to review current processes and procedures and bring them up to industry standards. PeopleSoft has done considerable research and has built systems that are supposed to address all possible needs of an average company. In reality, not all businesses are able to fully adapt the delivered applications. The problem is that this "average" company is an abstraction. It simply does not exist. Real companies have traditions. They may follow unique business practices that separate them from other businesses in the industry and (who knows?) may help them to compete on both labor and primary business markets. Implementing PeopleSoft-delivered systems already means big changes and a tremendous psychological impact, but it should not also involve cutting off important and healthy business functionality just because aspects don't fit the "Vanilla" option.

20.1.2   Developing a manual desk procedure

Can we keep the good old functions and still spare ourselves the development cost? Let's make every function that is not available in the delivered system a manual desk procedure! This may be the perfect approach for seldom-used tasks, but if the function has to be performed on a regular basis, automation is the way to go.

20.1.3 Creating a satellite application with interface to PeopleSoft

Oftentimes, the management realizes that changes are inevitable, but may still insist on keeping the system "Vanilla." They may then try to augment the PeopleSoft-delivered modules with satellite applications using available desktop computing tools such as Microsoft Excel, Access, and so on. Developing satellite applications just to avoid any changes to the PeopleSoft system may not always be the best choice. Instead of maintaining one centralized PeopleSoft system, you may end up maintaining a number of different applications and interfaces between them. On the other hand, if a satellite system already exists and has all the functionality that users need, developing an interface to PeopleSoft may be a good idea.

20.1.4 Changing PeopleSoft-delivered objects and programs

In some cases, changes to the PeopleSoft-delivered objects are absolutely necessary to suit business needs. This option comes with a hidden price tag. Later in this chapter, we will discuss in greater detail the considerations you would have to bear in mind to minimize the impact on a delivered application. The most important consideration is a future upgrade. What happens when PeopleSoft delivers a new release? Your changes then have to be merged with the new application release. Some changes may be straightforward, and others may be more complex. A simple task such as adding a new field to an existing PeopleSoft table, for example, may be a dangerous exercise. In the subsequent chapters we'll discuss what to look for as well as how to minimize impact on the delivered application.

20.1.5 Developing additions with PeopleTools

If added functionality can be independent of the PeopleSoft-delivered system, our preference would be choice number five: Developing a subsystem by using PeopleTools. With PeopleTools, you can develop entire subsystems to supplement the "Vanilla" application while keeping them separate from the delivered application. Why is it so important to keep new objects isolated from the delivered ones? Well, one reason is to minimize the impact on future application upgrades. Another reason is to prevent changes made to the application from interfering with the delivered PeopleSoft application.

20.2 UPGRADE CONSIDERATIONS

What is an upgrade to a new PeopleSoft release, and why should this be an important consideration when making changes to the delivered application?

We all know that software applications constantly go through upgrades, improvements, and even total restructuring and redesign to be competitive, but how do these changes affect customizations? Usually, a good software package makes its releases backward-compatible. The problem is that PeopleSoft not only delivers software development tools, it also delivers an entire suite of applications. In addition, PeopleSoft usually delivers a new major PeopleTools and application release once a year. Sometimes, a PeopleTools release is delivered twice a year in order to compete with other software companies. PeopleSoft has a strict schedule that you would have to follow in order to keep your software package current and be supported by PeopleSoft.

It is important to understand the concept of upgrade procedure in order to make good and educated decisions on customizations.

PeopleSoft did its best to develop good tools that are designed to perform upgrades to new releases. Nevertheless, the process of upgrades remains cumbersome. The most difficult part of the upgrade process is usually comparing the currently used application to the base application of the same release and to the new release of the application. Even though the compare programs will identify the differences for you, you still have to go over every change and decide—and this is an extremely important decision—whether to carry a change over to the new release, drop the change, or merge the change with the PeopleSoft changes. This last option is the most difficult. It happens when the changes to the object are done by both you and PeopleSoft.

All in all, the fewer changes you make to the delivered application, the less time required to perform an upgrade.

Although a detailed discussion of all steps involved in a release upgrade is not in the scope of this book, we want to describe ways to make the maintenance of PeopleSoft applications easier.

Rule 1. When performing system modifications, document every change. For example, if you have changed an existing Record definition or created a new one, put your initials, Date/Time stamp, type of modifications (New, Change), and a brief explanation in the comments section (figure 20.1).

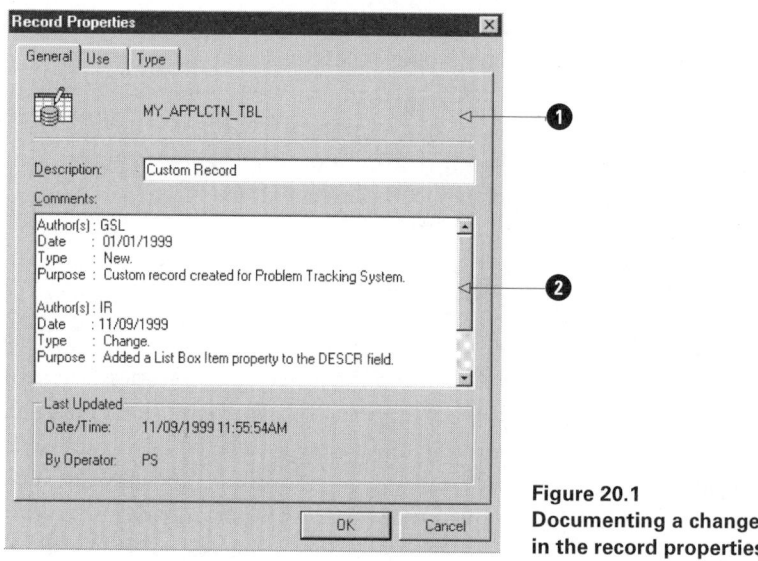

**Figure 20.1
Documenting a change
in the record properties**

CHAPTER 20 "VANILLA" VS. CUSTOMIZED

❶ The record has a prefix of `MY_` to identify a customization.

❷ The header specifies the initials, the Date/Time of customization, the modification type, and the short description.

Always insert extensive comments when changing PeopleCode programs. It is a good idea to develop a standard change header and use it all the time when performing customizations. It should include the developer's name, date/time, reason for change, and any other useful information. Developers must also put in trailers to mark the end of any changes they have made when customizing PeopleCode or any other program (figure 20.2).

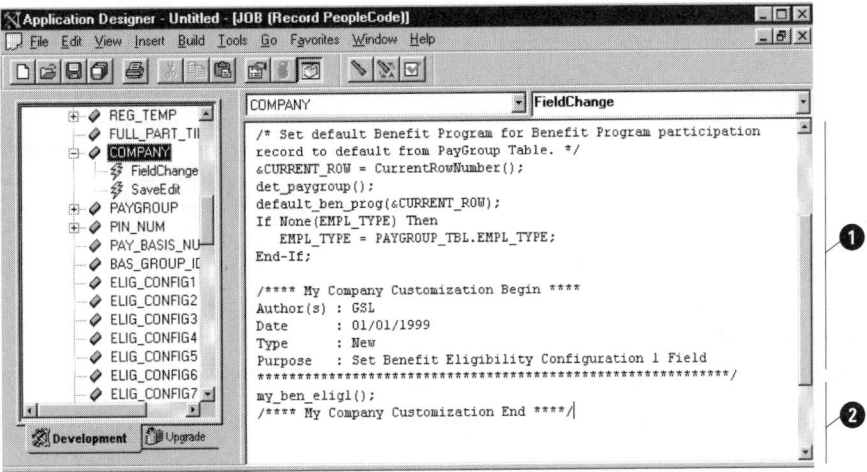

Figure 20.2   Documenting PeopleCode changes

❶ The header marking the beginning of PeopleCode customizations.

❷ The trailer marking the end of PeopleCode customizations.

When you prefix changed objects with certain characters, such as your company name or abbreviation, you can easily identify all the changes you or your colleagues have ever made. You can use any prefix letters that suit your needs.

In our Problem Tracking application developed in part 2, we used the prefix `MY_` to identify all custom records, fields, panels, and so on. A new record definition may include both the existing and custom fields. Hence, if you prefix all custom fields, you can identify the changes immediately.

Rule 2. Use a prefix to identify your custom objects. For example, in figure 20.3 you can see that we named our custom record as MY_APPLCTN_TBL and the custom field as MY_APPLICATION_ID. The other two fields in this record are PeopleSoft-delivered fields (figure 20.3).

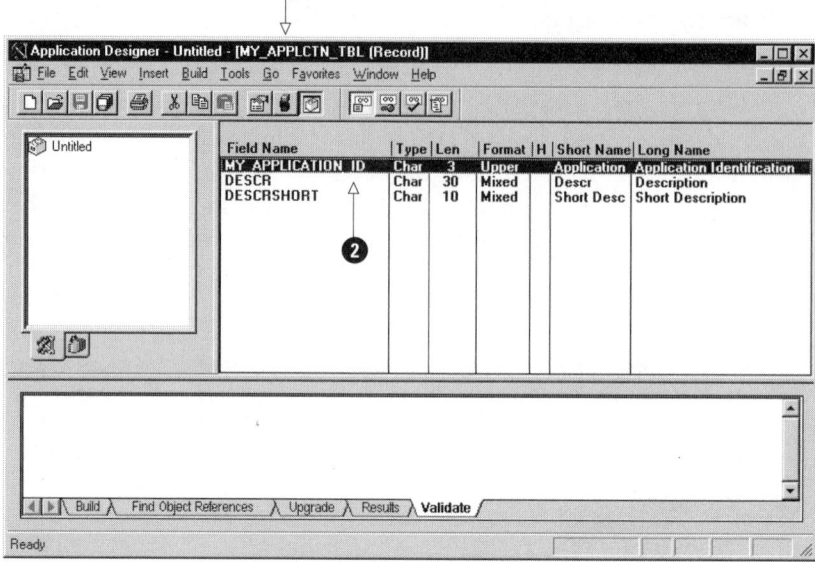

Figure 20.3   Using a prefix to identify custom objects

❶ Prefix "MY" is used to identify custom record
❷ Prefix "MY" is used to identify custom field.

Carefully examine the change requirements and always consider different ways to accomplish the customizations. If there is a way to isolate the changes, consider making them an addition to the system rather than changing the delivered system.

Let's suppose a user requests that a new field be added to an existing panel. As a PeopleSoft developer, you know that the related record may have to be modified as well. Be careful. A simple change like this can sometimes lead to major problems once a new version of PeopleSoft is released. Consider a situation when you just need to add one custom field to an existing record definition. During an upgrade to a new PeopleSoft release, you would have to add this field to the Record definition and alter the table. But this is not the only thing you would have to consider. What if the new release includes an SQR or COBOL program that uses the same table and inserts a record into this table? Since all fields in PeopleSoft tables (except date fields) are defined as NOT NULL fields, the SQR or COBOL program delivered by PeopleSoft will result in the following database error: 'Inserting a NULL value to a column where NOT NULL specified'. Here's why: When the above-mentioned program inserts a record into the modified table, it does not know anything about your modifications. As a result, the program only inserts the values into the specified table columns, causing the database engine to insert NULL values into the custom columns. To avoid this problem, you have to search all programs for any possible inserts into the changed table and modify the programs as necessary.

Another way to perform the same changes is to create a new custom record and add a custom panel to an existing panel group. In this case, the initial work requires more effort, but later during the upgrade you only need to be concerned with adding another panel to the panel group. Is this the recipe for all customizations? Not necessarily, because every particular case may have its own twists and each should be considered individually. If, for example, you have simple panel changes to apply, it may make more sense to perform modifications in place. In this case, you can take advantage of the Upgrade Compare process that identifies the changes you performed. (We will discuss all of these and more in the subsequent chapters.)

Rule 3. Add rather than modify when you need to perform extensive changes to the delivered system.

If you are utilizing PeopleSoft-delivered fields, don't change their properties. Changing field properties may affect all other objects where the field is used. If you cannot find existing fields with characteristics that you need, you are better off creating new ones.

Rule 4. Do not change properties of PeopleSoft-delivered fields.

Avoid moving fields around in panels just for cosmetic reasons. Even if you just click on a panel field and move it inadvertently and then save the panel, the system considers this a change, and reports it during the upgrade, thereby adding to the upgrade effort.

Rule 5. Do not move fields in delivered panels just for cosmetic reasons.

The next and final rule is simple and obvious.

Rule 6. Never delete any fields from delivered records or panels. You can always use PeopleCode to hide fields in panels, if necessary.

- document every change
- use prefix letters to identify your custom objects
- add rather than modify when you need to perform extensive changes to the delivered system
- do not move fields in delivered panels just for cosmetic reasons
- never delete any fields from delivered records or panels

20.3 IDENTIFYING OBJECTS FOR CUSTOMIZATION

PeopleSoft allows you to modify the existing system. The important questions to ask are "what are the objects that have to be modified?" and "what is the best way to perform the modifications?" As we have already discussed in the previous chapter, you should always keep upgrade considerations in mind. At the same time, you should think of other implications, such as development time, ease of maintenance, possible impact on response time, panel design constraints, coordination with other sub-systems, and so on.

In order to customize a PeopleSoft-delivered application, you need to identify all objects that will be impacted by your changes. Since in real life there are usually several approaches to the same task, we will present different methods of customization in the next chapters, discussing the pros and cons of each approach.

You've already learned that a simple request to add a field to a panel may not be as simple as it appears at first glance. Therefore, when you are getting a request or even a simple question about what will be involved in the customization, do not rush to reply. Gather requirements and assess the situation by looking at the objects involved. Consider all the alternatives and select the most appropriate one. Depending on the method you selected for your customization, there may be one object or a multitude of objects that have to be customized.

Also, while deciding on the best way of customization, do not forget about the major constraint in PeopleSoft panel development: you cannot have multiple records within the same scroll bar. The only exceptions are fields from Derived/Work records and the related display fields. Based on your specific requirements, you may need to add another panel to your existing panel group.

In subsequent chapters, we will present examples of the most frequently used customizations. We'll not only discuss those examples, we'll customize the delivered PeopleSoft application using real life situations.

20.4 PERFORMING AN UPGRADE

When performing customizations to PeopleSoft-delivered applications, knowledge of the upgrade process is crucial. A good understanding of the long-term consequences of a particular change to the delivered system puts you in a better position to make a more intelligent decision on how customizations should be performed.

Let's highlight some important upgrade concepts and demonstrate them on simple examples. (Please refer to the PeopleSoft-delivered technical documentation and to the upgrade instructions when performing an upgrade process.)

First, to avoid any confusion in the upgrade's terminology, let's take a look at the PeopleSoft's definitions of different types of upgrades.

PeopleSoft categorizes upgrades into three types: *PeopleTools upgrade*, *Application upgrade*, and *Customization upgrade*.

During the PeopleTools upgrade, you move to a new PeopleTools release. This type upgrade requires installing new software and usually involves upgrading PeopleTools database objects. PeopleSoft provides database scripts to perform this type upgrade, which also involves copying new executables and dynamic link libraries delivered by PeopleSoft.

During the Application upgrade, you move to a new PeopleSoft application release. It can either be a minor application release upgrade or a major application release upgrade. Periodically, PeopleSoft delivers application updates and fixes that you'll need to apply to your database. You use the Data Mover tool to import update projects into a stand-alone, application update database (AUDB). After that, you copy the objects into your database using Application Designer. PeopleSoft always provides the documentation (associated with a particular fix or update) that you need to follow. For the latest information on updates and fixes for PeopleSoft products, you should check the updates and fixes database in Customer Connection at www.peoplesoft.com.

When you need to migrate your newly developed or customized PeopleSoft objects from one database to another (for example, from development to production), you are performing the Customization type of upgrade within the same release level.

The aforementioned upgrades are performed differently, depending on the type of upgrade (PeopleTools, Application, or Customization) and the level of your current and the future releases.

Usually, however, you'll go through the following steps while performing any type of upgrade:

- *Populate a project*   As discussed in part 2 of this book, a project is a set of records, panels, fields, and other objects grouped together to help you in application development, customization, and upgrade. A project is populated either manually while performing a customization or automatically by the Upgrade Compare and Report process.

- *Perform a comparison*   Execute the Compare and Report process. Depending on the Compare Type you select, this process either compares objects in your project to the corresponding objects in your target database or compares all objects in your source and target databases and repopulates your project.

- *Change or verify the upgrade settings*   The system assigns the default settings for each object in your project for the source and target databases based on the result of comparison. You can specify whether or not to upgrade each object by changing the object's Upgrade flag.

- *Perform a copy*   Execute the Upgrade Copy process to copy objects from the source database to the target database or delete objects in the target database. Only objects with the Upgrade flag set to On are added, replaced, or deleted in the target database.

- *Execute any* Alter/Create *scripts as necessary*   If your project contains any records that are specified as SQL tables or views you should execute the proper SQL scripts to synchronize the underlying database structure with PeopleTools records and index definitions.

- *Stamp the target database*   The target database is usually "stamped" to indicate that it has changed from its previous release level. When upgrading to a new PeopleSoft release, this step is required. The target database should be stamped with the PeopleSoft release level, specified in the upgrade instructions.

Let's illustrate the Customization type of upgrade using a simple example of modifying a record definition:

Suppose we need to modify our custom MY_COMPANY_TBL record by adding a custom field, MY_COMP_BUSINESS, to it. Let's assume that this record was created as a child to COMPANY_TBL some time ago and already resides in the development, test, and production databases.

First, we create a new custom field (figure 20.4).

Navigation: GO → Application Designer → File → New → Field

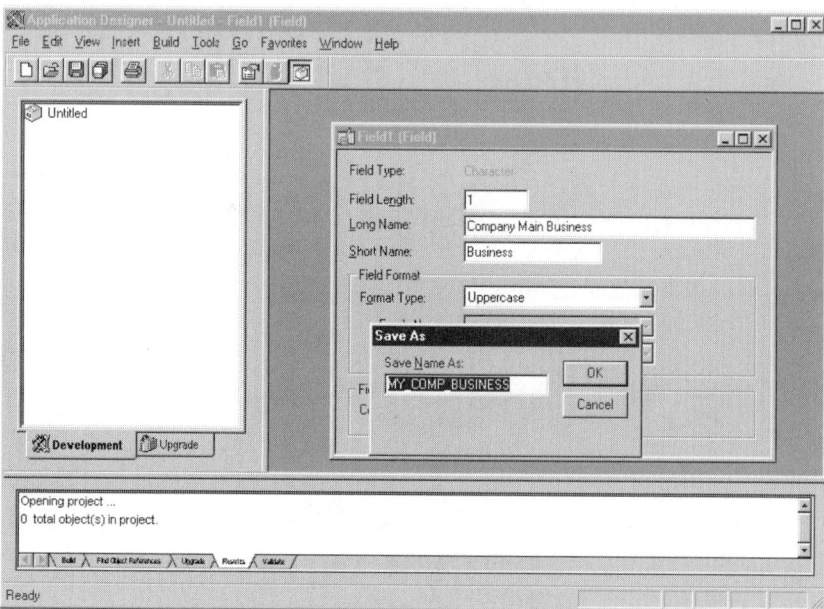

Figure 20.4 Creating a custom field MY_COMP_BUSINESS

After saving the field, let's add the new field to a new project by pressing the F7 function key or selecting Insert → Insert Current Object into Project from the Application Designer tool bar menu (figure 20.5).

Navigation: Insert → Insert Current Object into Project

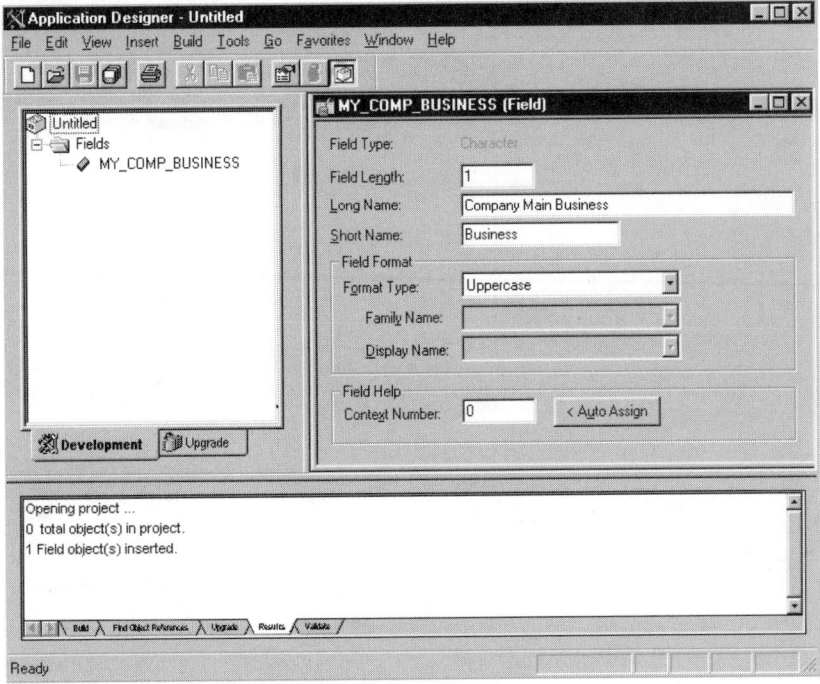

Figure 20.5   Adding a new object to a project.

Our next step is to add this field to the MY_COMPANY_TBL record definition. From the Application Designer menu, select File → Open → Record and type MY_COMPANY_TBL. After the record is displayed, highlight the field after which you want the new field to be inserted, then select Insert → Field → MY_COMP_BUSINESS. Save the record definition and add the modified object to our project by pressing the F7 function key (figure 20.6).

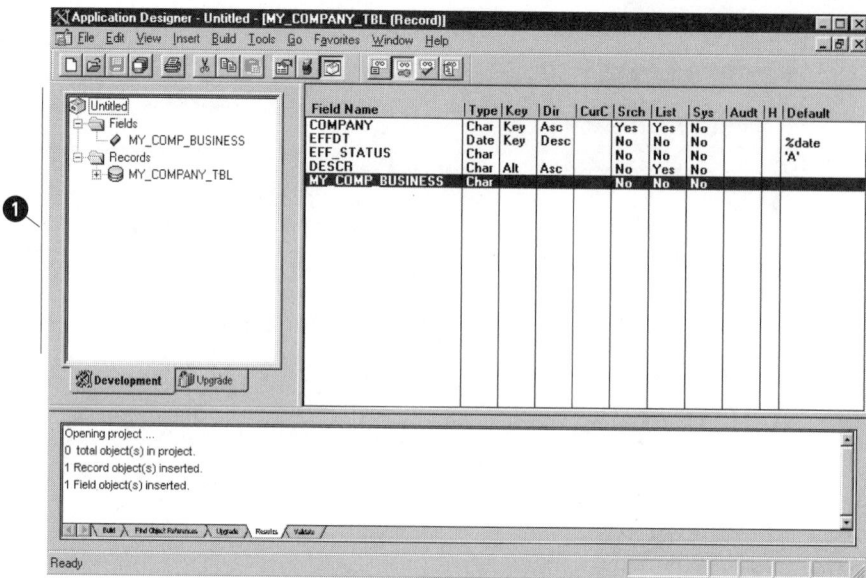

Figure 20.6   Adding the modified table to a project

As you can see from figure 20.6 ❶, all our modified objects are listed in the Application Project workspace. Let's save this project as MY_COMPANY_CHG by selecting File → Save Project As.

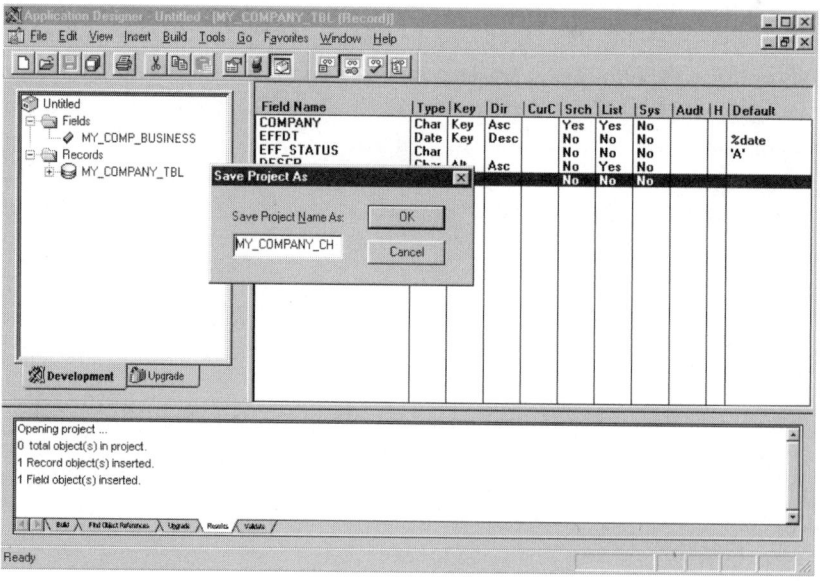

Figure 20.7   Saving our new project

Two tabs exist in the Application Designer project panel: the Development tab and the Upgrade tab. These allow you to work with the project in two different modes. The Development tab helps you perform operations on objects listed in the project. It allows you to see the object's dependencies and lists all the objects by their type. You can simply double-click on an object in the project workspace to bring the object up for any further modifications or review.

The Upgrade tab displays all objects available for upgrade from one database (source) to another (target). Let's switch from the Development tab to the Upgrade tab in our project and double-click on the field folder in the Project workspace (figure 20.8.)

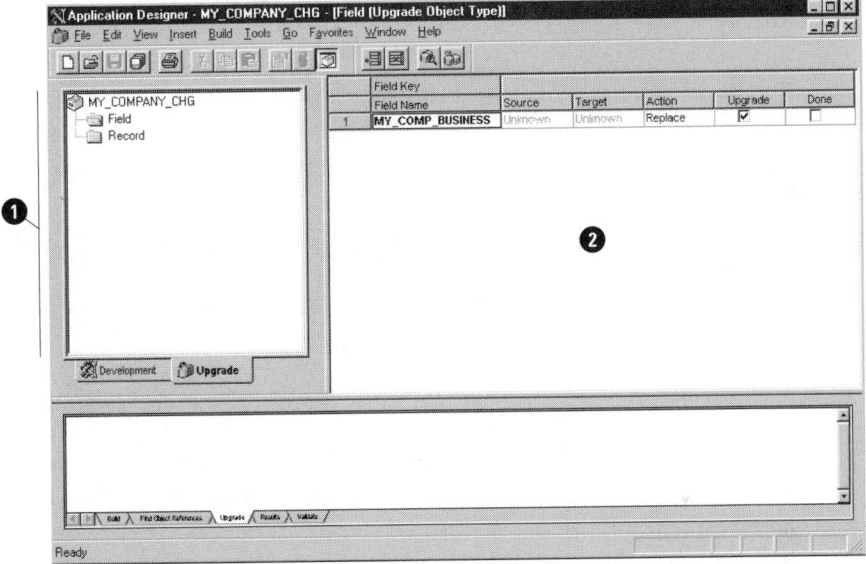

Figure 20.8 Reviewing a project in the Upgrade mode. The MY_COMP_BUSINESS field default upgrade options.

❶ Project Workspace. The Upgrade View.

❷ The Upgrade Definition window.

The Upgrade Definition window, which appears in the object workspace, displays the upgrade options available for the MY_COMP_BUSINESS field. The options displayed for this particular object are just the default options that have been initially set by the system automatically. In our example, we have two objects that have to be migrated to the target database, the MY_COMP_BUSINESS field and the MY_COMPANY_TBL record. The MY_COMP_BUSINESS field is a custom object that we just created. Therefore, it is safe to copy this object to the target database without fear of overlaying any existing objects.

Another object, the MY_COMPANY_TBL record, is an example of an existing object modification. Let's double-click on the record and display the record's upgrade default options (figure 20.9).

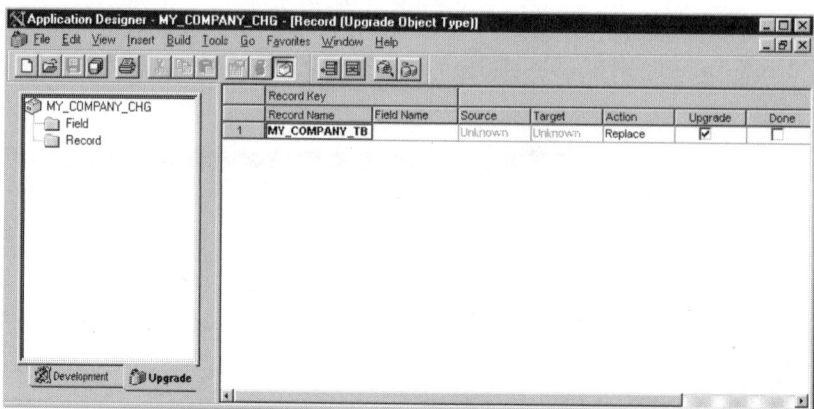

Figure 20.9   The MY_COMPANY_TBL record default options before the comparison

Using this simple example of customizing a record definition, we can demonstrate all the steps involved in the customization type of upgrade process.

Usually, all customizations and initial testing are done in the development database. The next step is the migration of modified objects to the test database for more thorough testing. And the last step is the migration of the project that includes all the changes to the production database. A migration of modified objects from one database to another is considered a Customization type of upgrade.

During the Customization Upgrade, you usually populate a project with the modified objects and copy the objects from your project to the test and production databases. Before copying the modified objects, you can execute the Upgrade Compare and Report process to compare all objects in your project with the corresponding objects in the target database.

Please note that, when executing a Customization Upgrade, it is not always necessary to execute the Compare and Report process. We can run the Compare process for our record modifications just to verify if this table has been modified by a concurrent development while we were testing it in the test database. However, if you have a strict mechanism for locking the objects before any customization, (which is always advisable), it may be safe to execute the Upgrade Copy process right away.

Let's run the comparison process (figure 20.10).

Navigation: Tools → Upgrade → Compare and Report

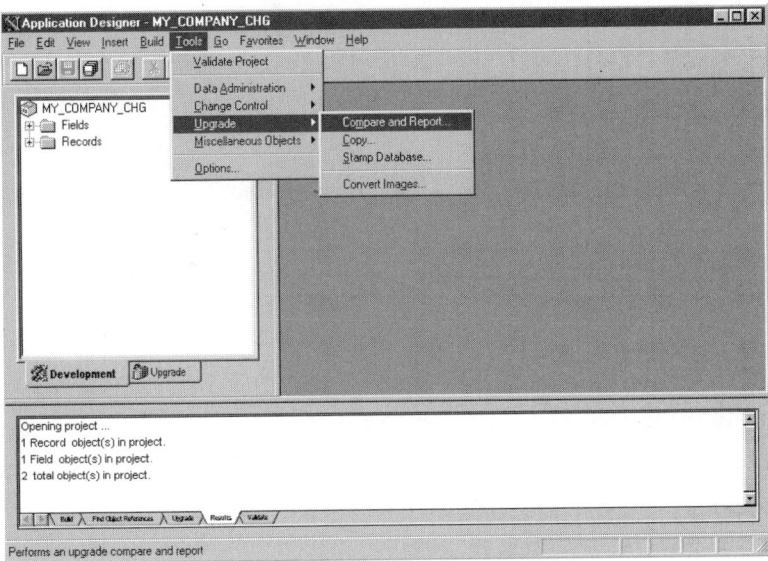

Figure 20.10   Executing the Upgrade Compare and Report process

The system asks us to sign on to the target database (figure 20.11).

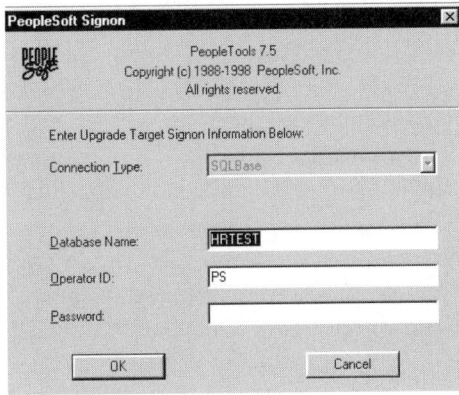

Figure 20.11
Log in to the Target database

After connecting to our test database, we are presented with the Compare and Report panel, which is a key panel in the upgrade process (figure 20.12). You can find a multitude of parameters in this panel that we will explain in more detail.

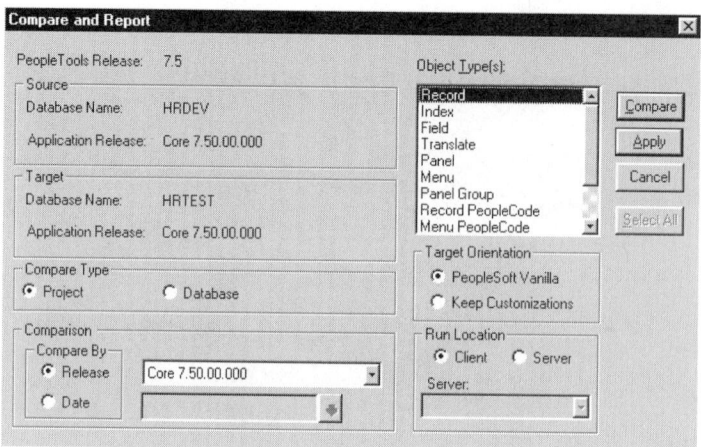

Figure 20.12   The Compare and Report panel

In the panel shown in figure 20.12, we see all parameters required for our Compare process. The first thing we need to verify is if the source and the target databases are specified correctly. In our example, we are comparing the objects in the HRDEV database to the objects in the HRTEST database.

The Compare Type can be either *Project* or *Database*. If a Project comparison is selected, only the objects in the current project are compared (of the types specified in the Object Type(s) box). The contents of the project do not change.

When a Database comparison is chosen, all objects selected in the Object Type(s) box are compared. Unlike the Project type comparison, if you choose the Database comparison, the contents of the current project are replaced with objects found during the comparison.

You can specify if you want to compare either by the release common to your source and target databases or by a particular date. The comparison process labels objects as Changed or Custom/Changed if they've been changed since the Date/Time stamp for that release level or since the date that you specify.

Depending on where you execute your comparison process, on Client or Server, you can select either one or multiple types of objects to compare. If you execute the process on Client, you can only select one object type at a time, due to locking constraints.

TIP   Execute your Comparison process on Server (set Run Location to Server) in order to compare multiple objects at the same time. In this case, you should select more than one object type or select all from the Object Type(s) group box .

If you chose to select all object types, you can deselect any unwanted object types pressing the CTRL key and using the left mouse pointer simultaneously.

CHAPTER 20   "VANILLA" VS. CUSTOMIZED

In our example, we execute the Upgrade type of Customization and compare only one object type, the record. Therefore, we can run our process on the Client.

The *target orientation* allows you to select either the PeopleSoft Vanilla orientation or Keep Customizations option. The target orientation tells the system how to set the upgrade checkboxes in the Upgrade Definition window for objects that were last modified by the customer in one database and last modified by PeopleSoft in the other database. If you select the PeopleSoft Vanilla orientation, the upgrade checkboxes in the Upgrade Definition window will be set to preserve PeopleSoft's changes. If you select the Keep Customizations option, the checkboxes will be set to preserve your changes. We'll talk more about the target orientation later in this chapter.

Let's now execute the Compare and Report process by clicking on the Compare button. The Upgrade Compare and Report process is initiated. You can verify the status of the job on your Process Monitor screen. The process name for the Record type of compare that we selected is UPGCREC.

If you open your project again in the Upgrade mode and double-click on the record in the project workspace window, you can see the online comparison messages in the lower part of the panel in your output window (figure 20.13). You can also print the messages by right-clicking in the output window and selecting the Print option.

Are you surprised to see two lines in our Upgrade Definition window after the record comparison is executed? The Compare process recognized that the MY_COMP_BUSINESS field is absent in the target database and repopulated our project with the new MY_COMPANY_TBL. MY_COMP_BUSINESS record field. Note that this is the only situation in which the Compare and Report process will repopulate a project during a Project type comparison.

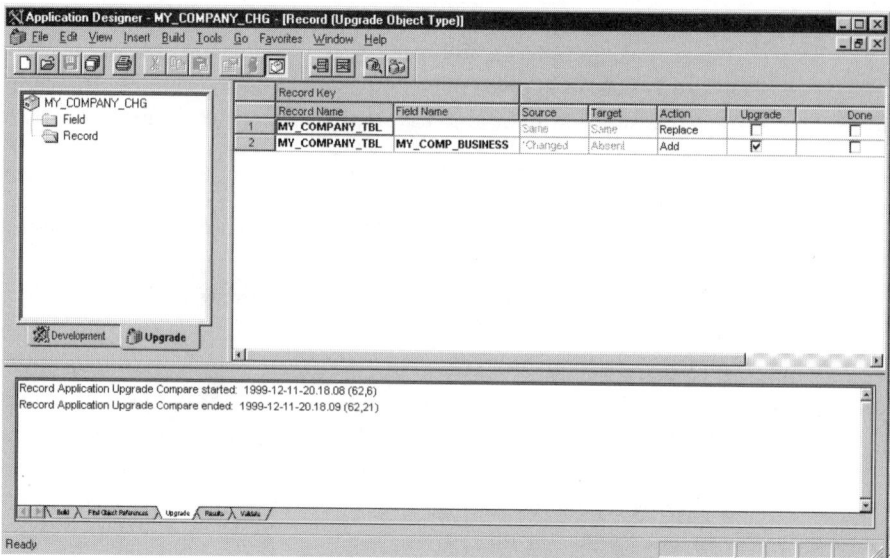

Figure 20.13   Viewing the results of the Record Comparison

NOTE   When records are compared either during a database or a project comparison, any differences found in record fields will be populated into the project.

Why did the process turn on the Upgrade flag only for the second line in our project? We'll explain this in the next subsection.

20.4.1   Understanding how the Upgrade Compare process works

In the Upgrade Compare process, PeopleSoft first compares the object definition in the source database to the object definition of the target. If it recognizes a difference, it checks to see if either of these objects had changed since the comparison release.

PeopleSoft tracks the object's Date/Time stamp (LASTUPDDTTM) value stored in the PeopleTools System Catalog tables. For example, it stores this value in the PSRECFIELD and PSDBFIELD tables for our custom field MY_COMP_BUSINESS. Since we added a new field, MY_COMP_BUSINESS, to these catalog tables, the compare program identifies the change and marks this field as Custom Changed in our source database and as Absent in our target database.

Another system catalog table, the PSRECDEFN table, contains the Date/Time stamp equal to the last time we modified the MY_COMPANY_TBL record definition. It is stamped by the system only if any of the record properties (such as the record description, a query search record, a parent record, and so forth.) are modified. Since, in our example, we have not modified any of the record properties, the system is not going to update the PSRECDEFN table in the target database and, therefore, the first line in figure 20.13 has not been marked for upgrade.

Please refer to appendix C of this book for a list of the PeopleSoft System Catalog tables. A familiarity with these tables will definitely help you to understand the PeopleSoft system from inside and will no doubt make you a better developer.

Another important component of the compare process is the release date/time value for the comparison release level. This value, RELEASEDTTM, is stored in another PeopleSoft table, PSRELEASE.

PeopleSoft then compares the date our object was last modified with the release date. If the date of the object is greater than the release date, PeopleSoft considers this object changed.

In addition to the date comparison, the system checks the last operator ID that modified the object. It then considers the object changed if it was modified by someone other than PeopleSoft (LASTUPDOPRID <> 'PPLSOFT').

During the Comparison Upgrade process, the system determines Status, Action, and Upgrade values for each object. The Status value is defined for both the source and target objects.

Status may have the following values: Unknown, Absent, Changed, Unchanged, Changed * , Unchanged *, Same.

As you can see from figure 20.9, the status values for our source and target databases are Unknown. This is a default status, and it means that the object has not been compared. This is also a temporary status, assigned when an object is manually inserted into a project. As soon as the compare process is executed, this status is replaced with the appropriate status.

The Absent status value means that the object was found in the other database, but not in this one. In our example, as you can see in figure 20.13, after we ran the compare process, the status value of Absent is specified for the target database.

The status value Changed/Unchanged means that the object was changed/unchanged by PeopleSoft (PSOFT user) since the last comparison release.

The status value Changed * means that the object was modified by someone other than PeopleSoft (the LASTUPDOPRID value is not PPLSOFT) since the last comparison release. That is exactly why we can see the value of Changed* in figure 20.13 for our source database modified object.

The status value Unchanged * means that the object was modified by the customer (LASTUPDOPRID is not PPLSOFT) prior to the comparison release.

Finally, the status value Same means that the object has not been modified. This status appears only as a result of a Project type of compare and not a Database type of compare.

When upgrading to a new PeopleSoft release, all custom objects developed by users should have the Absent status in the source (new release) database. On the other hand, all of the new objects developed by PeopleSoft should have the Absent status in the target (your Production) database.

The Upgrade process assigns one of the following Actions to each object: Add, Delete, or Replace, based on the comparison process.

Action Add means that the object will be added to the target database. Action Delete means that the object will be deleted from the target database. Action Replace means that the object in the target database will be replaced with the corresponding object in the source.

In our example, the record field object MY_COMP_BUSINESS has Action = Add, because this field will be added to the target database.

You would be able to decide whether to execute the Action during the Upgrade Copy process, which is the actual migration. Take a look at the next value, the Upgrade. This value could be set to Y or N, which indicates to the Copy process whether the corresponding Action should or should not be executed. During the new release upgrade, it is the upgrade team's responsibility to make certain that all the values are set correctly. The system can only set the Upgrade values to Y or N based on the comparison results and the target orientation. The target orientation allows the user to either choose the upgrade to keep PeopleSoft changes or retain custom changes in the target database.

Suppose the new release came with some modifications to the PERSONAL_DATA record. Let's assume that we also modified this record. During the Upgrade Compare and Report process, the status of this object will be Changed in the source database (the PeopleSoft's new release database) and Changed * in the target database. The Action will be Replace, and the Upgrade value will be set to Y or to N, depending on the orientation that is selected for our upgrade. If we choose to take PeopleSoft's objects when both have been changed, then our modifications will be overwritten. If we choose to keep the target unchanged, then PeopleSoft's changes will be dropped. In cases such as this, the customizations have to be examined, and the decision made on whether to keep the customizations, abandon them, or merge with the new PeopleSoft-delivered modifications. Each case should be looked up separately in situations similar to the one described.

Let's get back now to our Compare process. Since we execute our process on the Client, we should perform the compare for each object type separately. Our Upgrade project contains two objects: a record and a field. We just executed the record comparison. Should we now compare the field? In this particular case, it is not necessary since we created a new field, and we know that this field does not exist in the target database. We can go directly to the Copying process.

20.4.2 Copying a project to the target database

When you have completed all your upgrade settings, the next step is to copy the project into your target database. It is a good idea to check the Change Control locking status of your target database and check your copy options before initiating a Copy process. (Please refer to PeopleSoft technical documentation for information about Locking and Upgrades.)

Let's select File → Project Properties to verify our Copy options.

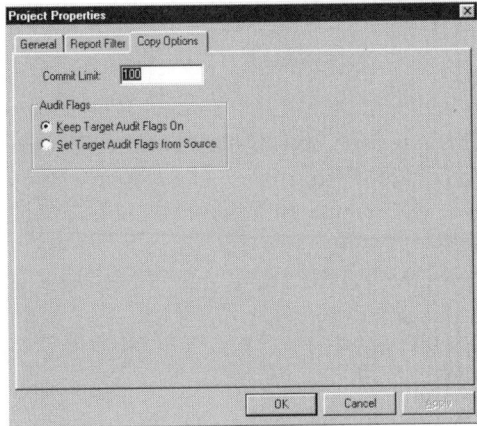

Figure 20.14
Verifying the project's Copy Options

As you can see from figure 20.14, the default commit limit is set to 100. You can modify this number based on the amount of time it takes you to complete the process. Increasing this number speeds up your process. Be careful: if something goes wrong, it may increase the amount of work in your recovery process. Always consult your Database Administrator before you change the commit limit.

In the Audit Flags box, you specify the Audit Flags setting to either Keep Target Audit Flags On or Set Target Audit Flags from Source. This allows you to preserve your target database audit (PSAUDIT) settings if you choose the default option or to bring flags from the source database to the target.

For our task, let's leave all the default options on, click on the Cancel button, and initiate a Copy process.

The system asks you to sign on to the target database. Let's sign on to our HRTEST database and click on the OK button.

The system displays the Copy dialog panel (figure 20.15).

Navigation: Tools → Upgrade → Copy

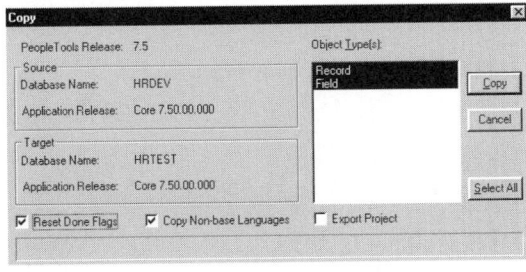

Figure 20.15   The Upgrade Copy dialog panel

If you have the option of Reset Done Flags turned on, the system will reset
all done flags for selected objects before performing a copy. If you have not selected
Reset Done Flags, it will only copy the objects with Done flags turned off.

When Copy Non-base Languages option is on, the system copies all base and
related language objects to the target database. Otherwise, it copies only base language
version tables.

You can also check the Export Project box ON to copy the current project to your
target database before copying any other objects.

Now we can perform the actual copy process. Just click on the Copy button from
the Upgrade Copy dialog panel.

When the Copy process is executed, it displays the messages on the Upgrade
Project output window. You can click on each object to check the messages and to verify if the Done flag is set to Y as shown in figure 20.16.

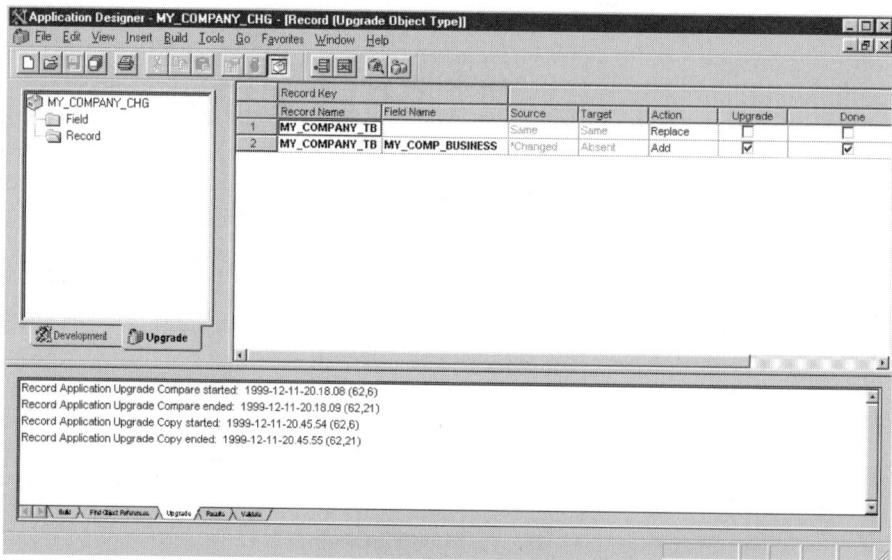

Figure 20.16   Verifying the results of the Upgrade Copy process

Just as with the panel shown in figure 20.16, if you click on field in your project
workspace, you see that the Done flag is ON for field copy as well.

20.4.3   Executing Alter/Create scripts

Since we modified the record definition in the target database, we should create and execute the SQL necessary to synchronize the underlying database structure with the PeopleTools record.

Navigation: Build → Current Object

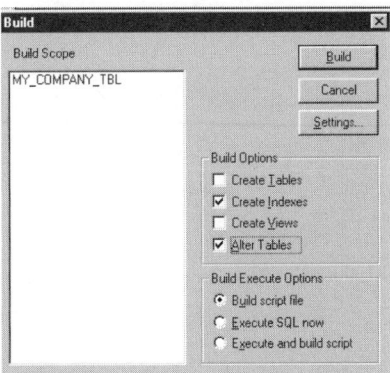

Figure 20.17   Building a script to alter the MY_COMPANY_TBL table

Let's login to the HRTEST database, open our project, and switch to the Development tab. Double-click on the MY_COMPANY_TBL table in the project workspace to display the record definition.

Since MY_COMPANY_TBL already exists in the target database, we use the Alter Tables as our Build Options, and Build Script file as Build Execute Options. The results of the Build operation are written to a script file that our Database Administrator can execute.

After MY_COMPANY_TBL is altered, we move to the next step. Our last step in the Upgrade process is to stamp the target database.

20.4.4   Stamping the database

After copying a project into the target database, you can change the customer release number to specify that it has changed from its previous customer release level. This process, called "stamping the database," helps you keep track of all customer releases to this version of your database.

This step is necessary only for PeopleTools and Application types of upgrade.

NOTE   In order to stamp your database with the customer release number, you have to be logged on to this database.

Navigation: Tools → Upgrade → Stamp Database

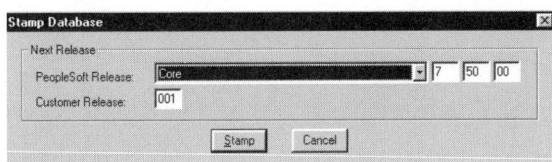

**Figure 20.18
Stamping the database**

The stamping of your database is optional when you change your customer release, but it is required by PeopleSoft when upgrading to another PeopleSoft release level. It is usually included in the upgrade instructions.

KEY POINTS

1 A customization is any change to a delivered application.

2 When performing customizations, try to minimize the impact on the future system upgrades.

3 Document every change.

4 Use prefix letters to identify your custom objects.

5 Use "add" vs. "modify" approach when performing the extensive changes to the delivered PeopleSoft system.

6 Avoid changing PeopleSoft-delivered field properties and cosmetic changes in the delivered panels.

7 Do not delete any fields from the delivered panels and records.

8 PeopleSoft divides all upgrades into three types: PeopleTools Upgrade, Application Upgrade, and Customization Upgrade.

9 The following steps are usually performed in any kind of upgrade:
   - populating a project
   - performing a comparison
   - changing or verifying the upgrade settings
   - performing a copy
   - executing `Alter/Create` scripts as necessary
   - stamping the target database

C H A P T E R   2 1

Customizing delivered panels

Adding a field to a panel is one of the most frequent requests PeopleSoft developers receive. This task can be greatly simplified if the added field already exists in one of the records attached to the panel. We'll start with the simplest example, one which PeopleSoft marketing representatives usually use to demonstrate how easy it is to customize delivered PeopleSoft applications using PeopleTools. Our goal is not only to show you how to do customizations, but to discuss different ways to perform customizations. We also want to stress the importance of thinking about the impact of a particular change on future upgrades.

We'll begin with exercise 1:

> Add a field to the Personal Profile panel to specify whether the employee belongs to the Highly Compensated Employee category.

Our objective here is to customize a delivered PeopleSoft panel to achieve the panel illustrated in figure 21.1.

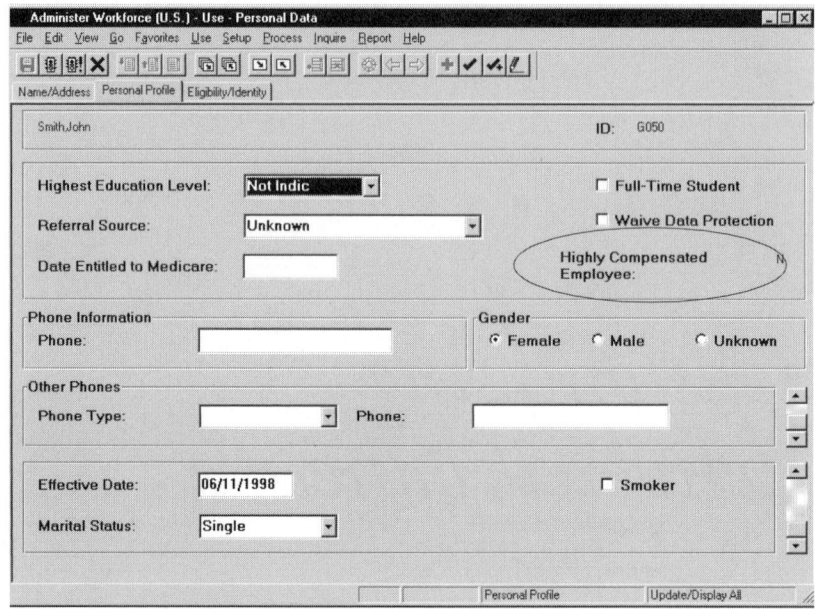

Figure 21.1   The Personal Profile panel that includes a new field

If you have some experience with PeopleSoft, you may know which of the PeopleSoft objects (fields, records, and panels) are involved in this change. PeopleSoft has so many records and fields that it's impossible to remember everything. We will discuss some handy PeopleTools techniques that can be used in order to obtain this information.

21.1   WHAT OBJECTS SHOULD BE CUSTOMIZED?

Let's do a little research here. Open a panel that your user wants to customize and find out what records are linked to this panel. Before we open the Personal Profile panel, let's also turn on the option of displaying the panel name (figure 21.2).

Now we can access our panel and find the physical object name of the Personal Profile panel.

Navigation: GO → Administer Workforce → Administer Workforce (U.S) →
            Use → Personal Data.

Let's select `Update/Display` and enter a part of an employee name, for example, "Smith." The system presents you with a list of all employees whose last name starts with "Smith." Let's select "Smith, John" and bring up the Personal Profile panel for the selected employee (figure 21.3).

Navigation: View → PanelName

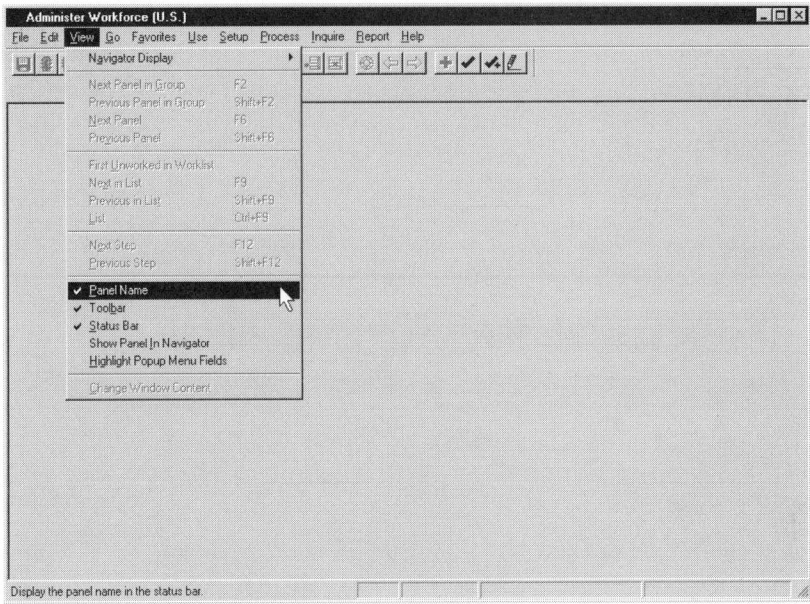

Figure 21.2   How to display the actual panel name

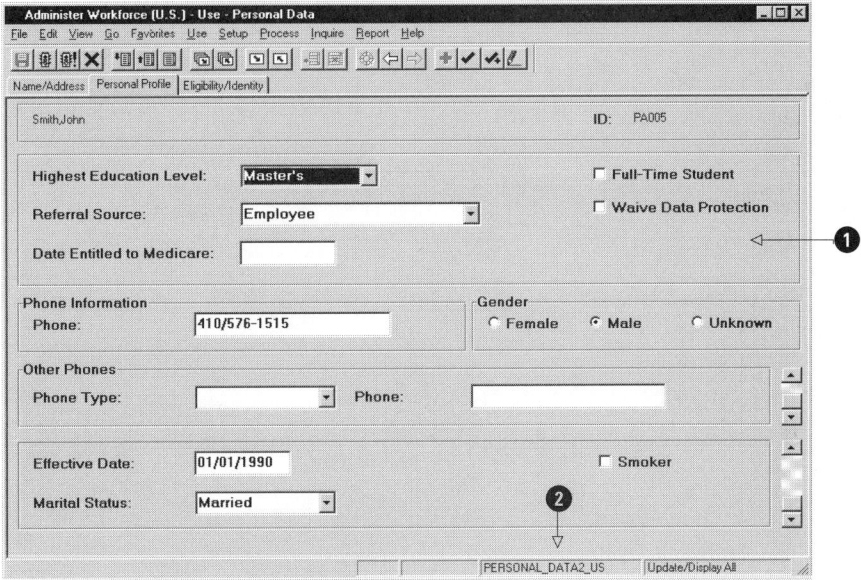

Figure 21.3   The Personal Profile panel

1 Add Highly Compensated Employee field to this sub panel

2 Panel Name as it is referenced in PeopleTools

As you can see in figure 21.3, the system displays the panel name at the bottom of the screen. Now that we know the name of the panel, our next step is to look at the panel via the Application Designer and find out what records are used by this panel (figure 21.4).

Navigation: Go → PeopleTools → Application Designer → File → Open → Panel →
PERSONAL_DATA2_US

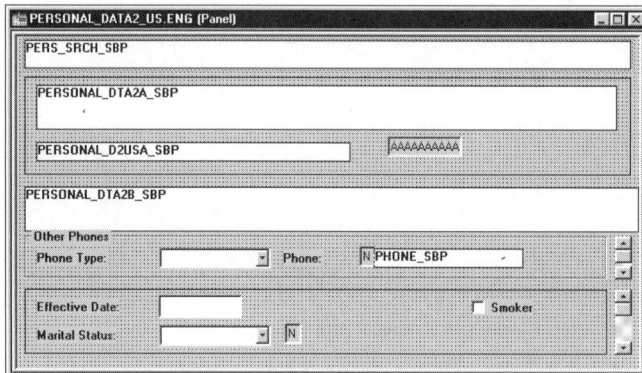

Figure 21.4   The Personal Profile panel (PERSONAL_DATA2_US) displayed via the Application Designer

To see the records and fields used in this panel, click on Layout and select Order.

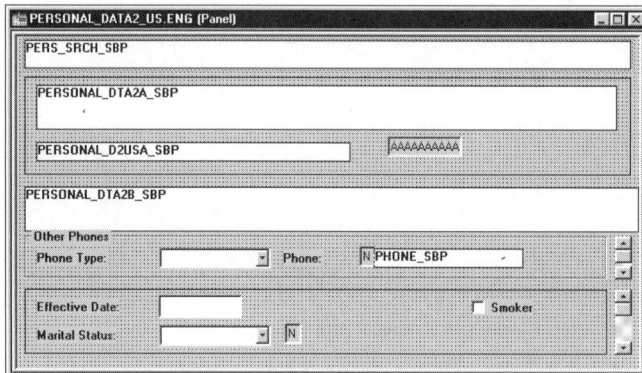

Figure 21.5   Subpanels, records, and fields that are used in the PERSONAL_DATA2_US panel

As we scroll through the panel shown in figure 21.5, we can see all the records used in the PERSONAL_DATA2-US panel and its subpanels. Let's examine records in this panel and see if the Highly Compensated Employee field belongs to any of them. The PERSONAL_DATA is one of the core records in the HRMS database. Let's open it in the Application Designer.

Navigation: Go → PeopleTools → Application Designer → File → Open → Record →
PERSONAL_DATA

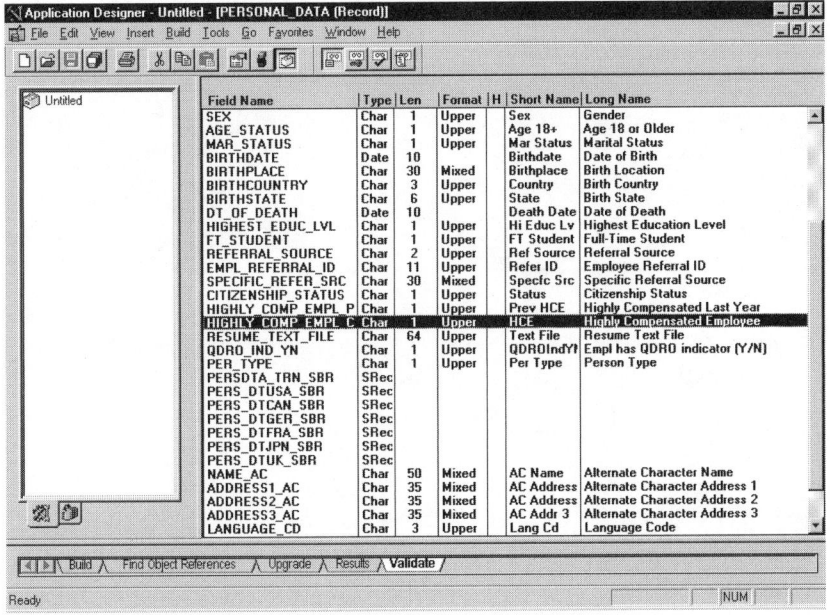

Figure 21.6   The PERSONAL_DATA table

Two fields exist which may be used for our purposes: The first is Highly Compensated for the previous and current year. After verifying requirements with our user, we decide to use the second one.

Stay in touch with your users during all stages of development. Do not wait until the end of your implementation to find the answers to your questions.

This makes our task simple. We just need to add the field to the panel. Take a look again at the panel in figure 21.4. Our users want to add a new field to the upper portion of the panel. As you can see, we need to modify the PERSONAL_DTA2A_SBP subpanel.

21.2 MODIFYING A PANEL

We already know that in order to add the required field to the Personal Data panel, we need to customize the PERSONAL_DTA2A_SBP subpanel. Let's open it and perform the actual modification.

Navigation: Go → PeopleTools → Application Designer → File → Open → Panel →
PERSONAL_DTA2A_SBP

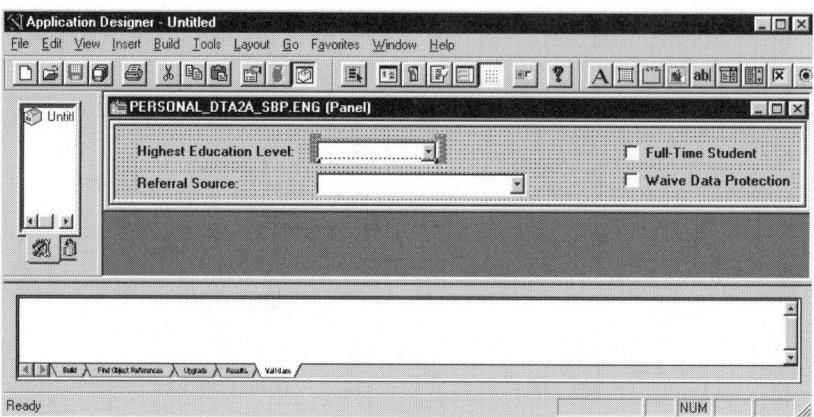

Figure 21.7   Modifying PERSONAL_DTA2A_SBP. Step 1: Opening a panel

Let's resize the subpanel a little bit and add a field to the panel by clicking on the Insert menu item and selecting an appropriate panel field type from the Application Designer tool bar. What type panel field are we going to add to our panel? As you can see in figure 21.8, different types are available: `Edit Box`, `Check Box`, `Drop Down List`, and so on.

Generally, the following guidelines are used for selecting a field type. (Please refer to part 2 of this book to learn more about panel design.)

- `Edit Box` is used for text data entry.
- `Drop Down List` is usually used to allow data selection from a list of translate value descriptions, or a prompt list.
- `Long Edit Box` is associated with long character fields from a Record definition.
- `Check Box` is used for data entry fields that can have one of two values: on or off. Y/N fields are usually the best candidates for the check boxes.
- `Radio Button` represents one value for a field with multiple defined values.

TIP   Use Edit Box as a general purpose panel field type for display fields.

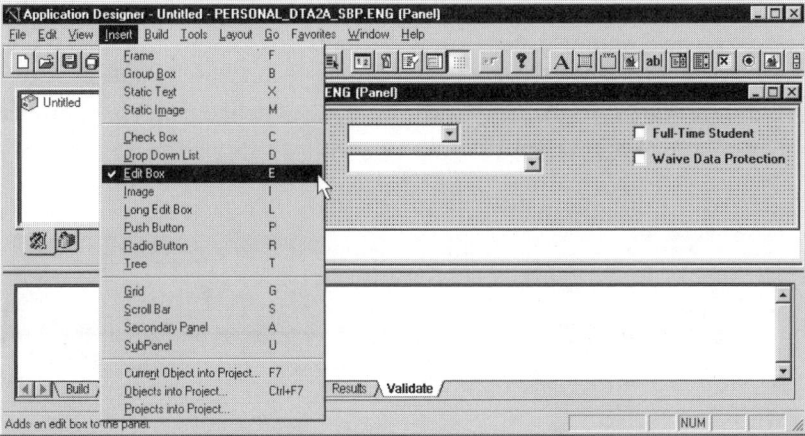

Figure 21.8   Selecting an appropriate field type

In order to select the right option, we need to see the properties of the HIGHLY_COMP_EMPL_C field. You can either open the HIGHLY_COMP_EMPL_C field from the Application Designer menu or right mouse click on the field in the record as shown in figure 21.9.

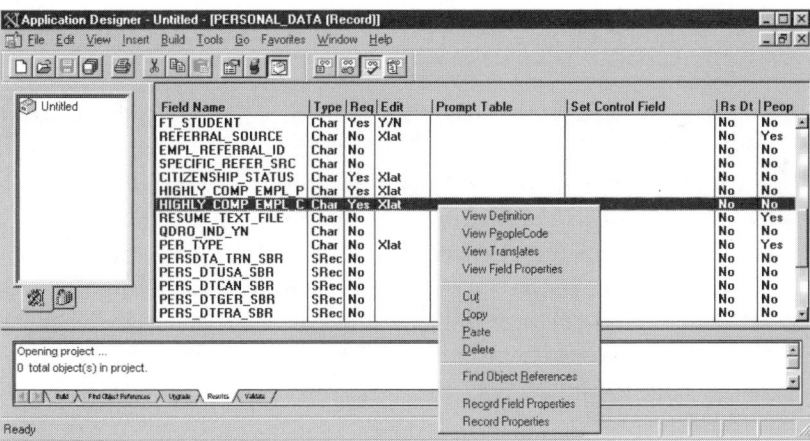

Figure 21.9   Inspecting the field's properties

From figure 21.9 we can see that our field has some translate values. Also, we have to keep in mind that users do not want to make this field a data entry field. Since they will be using it for information purposes only, we can assume that the Edit Box will work fine to represent this field in the panel.

Getting back to the panel in figure 21.8, let's select the `Insert/Edit Box` and place the field on our panel.

After placing the selected field on the panel (by default, the system assigned "Dummy Name" to the new field), we need to define panel field properties. Using a right mouse click on the field, select Panel Field Properties.

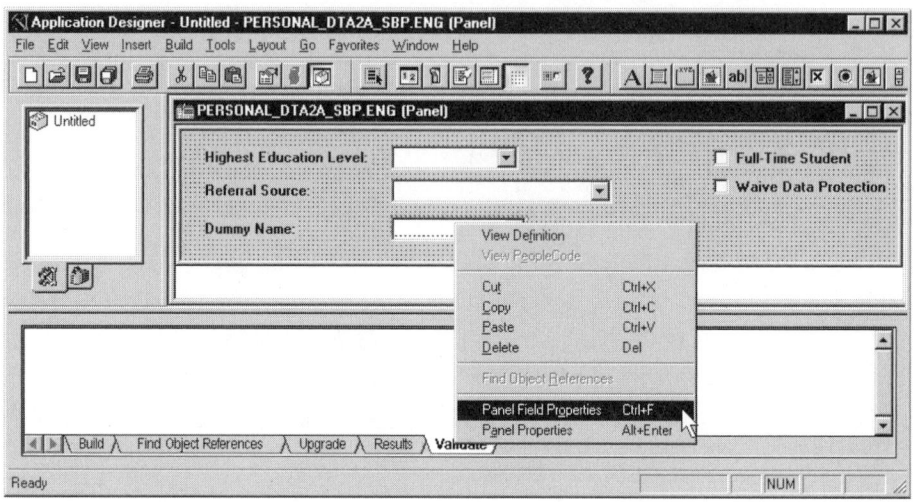

Figure 21.10   Assigning the newly added field its properties

Now we can specify the record, PERSONAL_DATA and the field, HIGHLY_ COMP_EMPL_C (figure 21.11).

On the second tab of the Panel Field Properties panel, the Label tab, we need to select the field label. Keeping in mind that this panel may be used in different languages, it's always better to select the `RFT Short` or `Long` rather than `Text`. Why? If you specify `Text` in the label field, and the panel is using languages other than your base language, the label will still appear in your base language. When you specify the `RFT Short` or `Long` description, the label is taken from the corresponding related language table (figure 21.12).

CHAPTER 21   CUSTOMIZING DELIVERED PANELS

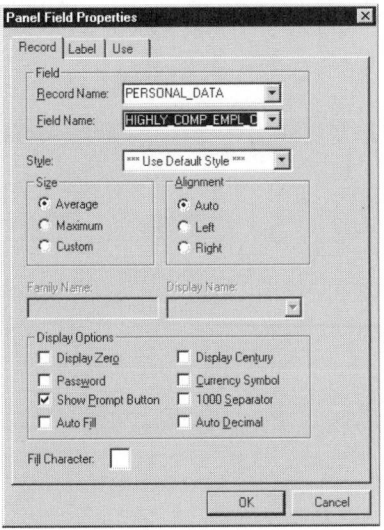

Figure 21.11 Specifying the record and the field

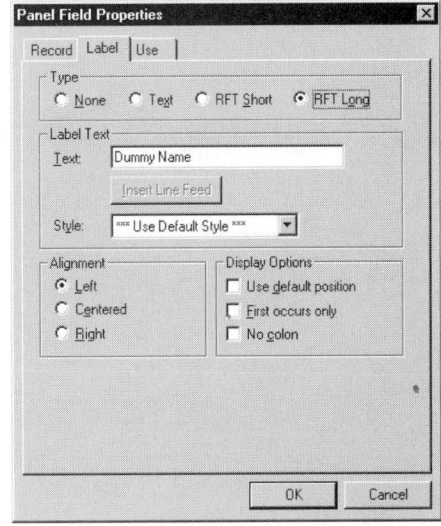

Figure 21.12 Selecting a label for our field

TIP   In global development projects, always specify the Label type as RFT Short or RFT Long

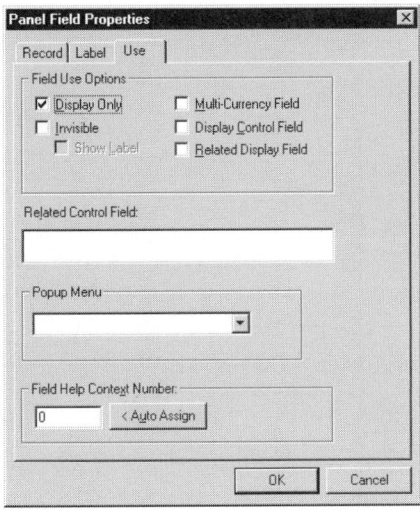

Figure 21.13 Defining our field as Display Only

On the Use tab of this panel, we mark this field as Display Only. This means that the field is used for information only as our users requested, since they do not plan to update this field on the panel.

Clicking on the OK button results in adding the new field to the subpanel (figure 21.14).

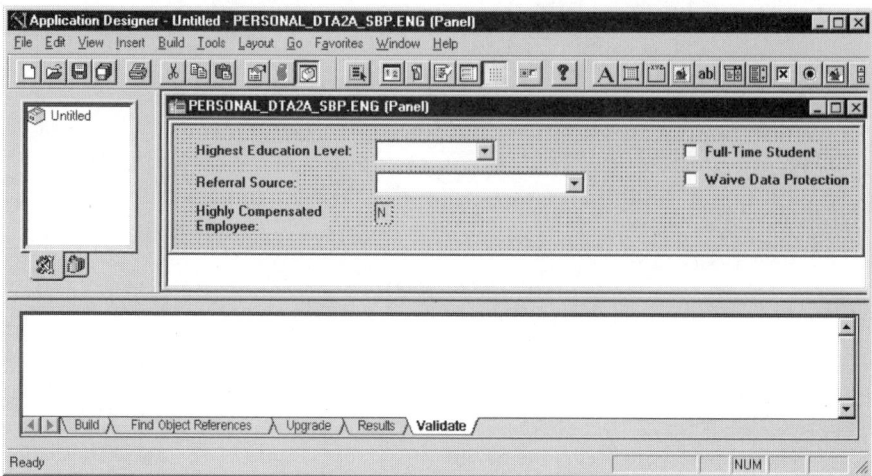

Figure 21.14   Adding the Highly Compensated Employee field to the subpanel

Save the modified panel and select File → Object Properties or ALT-ENTER to document the changes.

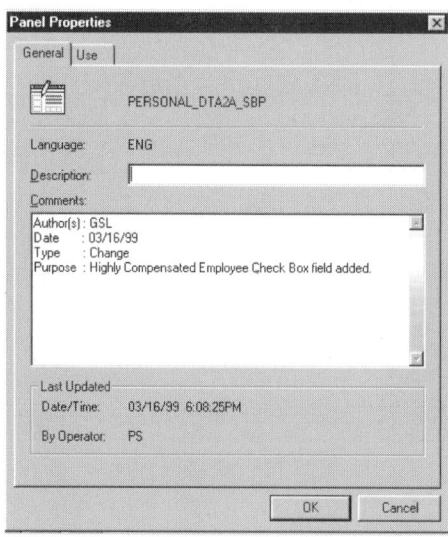

**Figure 21.15
Documenting our changes
on the Panel Properties**

Our comments will be useful during the upgrade so we save them by clicking on the OK button. Now we can test the change.

21.3 TESTING THE MODIFICATIONS

Let's first click on the [🔲] button or select Layout → Test Mode to ensure that the field really is accurately placed.

Navigation: GO → Administer Workforce → Administer Workforce (U.S) →
Use → Personal Data.

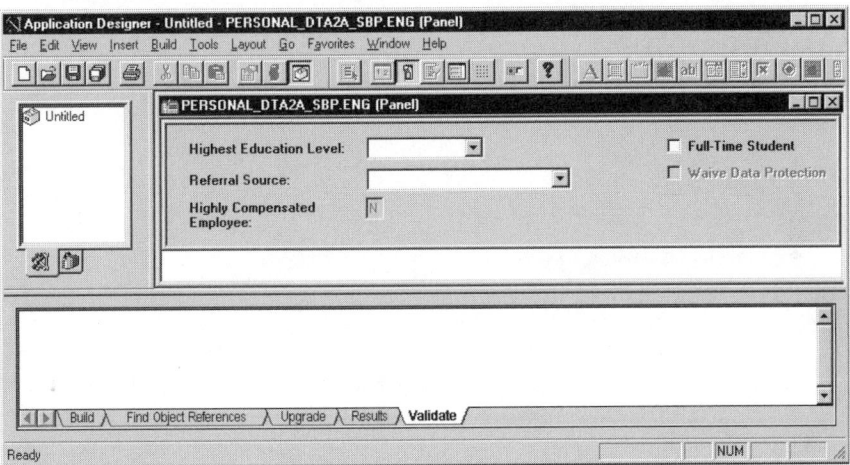

Figure 21.16   Testing the subpanel

The panel looks good in test mode. Now, we can perform a real test.

Let's select Update/Display and enter the same name, "Smith." After selecting an employee—for example, "John Smith"—our newly modified panel appears as shown in figure 21.17.

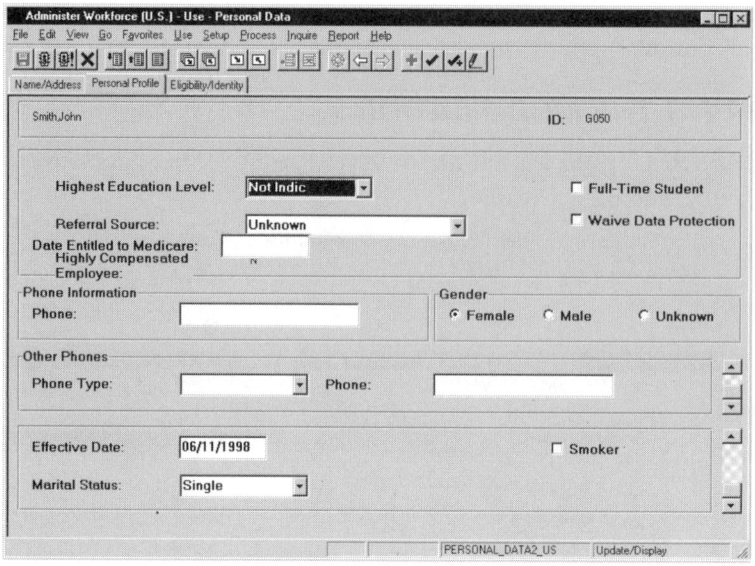

Figure 21.17 Testing the modified panel

As you can see, our new field is barely visible on the panel. It is blocked by another field. What happened? That's not what we expected, but that's exactly what testing is for! What could have possibly gone wrong? Remember that we added our new field to a subpanel and viewed the subpanel in test mode. It's obvious now that we overlaid other parts of the panel. Let's take a look at our panel again.

The panel in figure 21.18 consists of a number of subpanels. One of the subpanels, PERSONAL_D2USA_SBP, is placed over the PERSONAL_DTA2A_SBP subpanel. Also, if you compare this figure with the panel on figure 21.4, you notice that the PERSONAL_DTA2A_SBP subpanel occupies much more space now. Remember that we resized this subpanel in order to fit the new field into it but we forgot about other subpanels. This is exactly what caused our problem. Therefore, careful planning has to be done in order to find the correct placement in the panel for our new field. In our development, we were actually concentrating on finding the correct field and record. The test shows that space planning is equally important. If you display the panel (shown in figure 21.18) in test mode, you realize that the better choice is to place our field in the right corner of this subpanel where it is not blocked by other subpanels. Let's open our subpanel again and move the field to the right by dragging it to the desired position on the subpanel (figure 21.19).

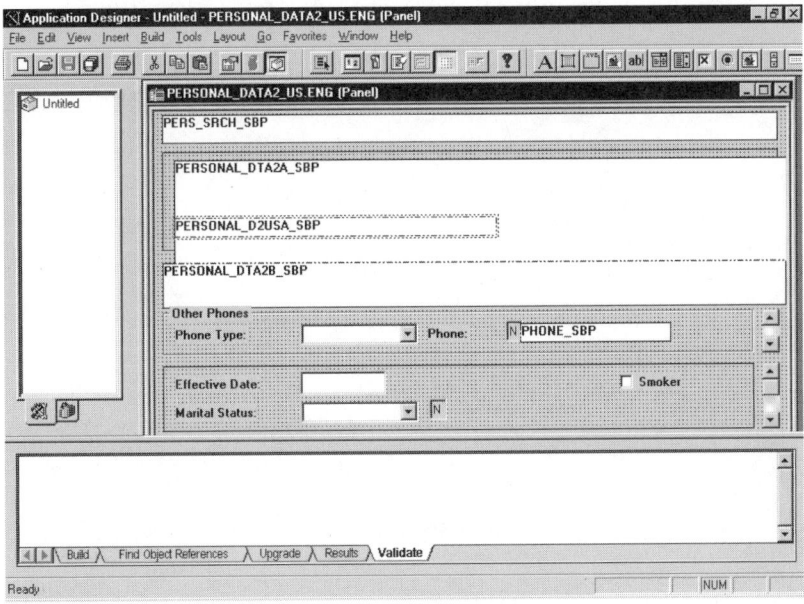

Figure 21.18   Inspecting the PERSONAL_DATA2_US panel

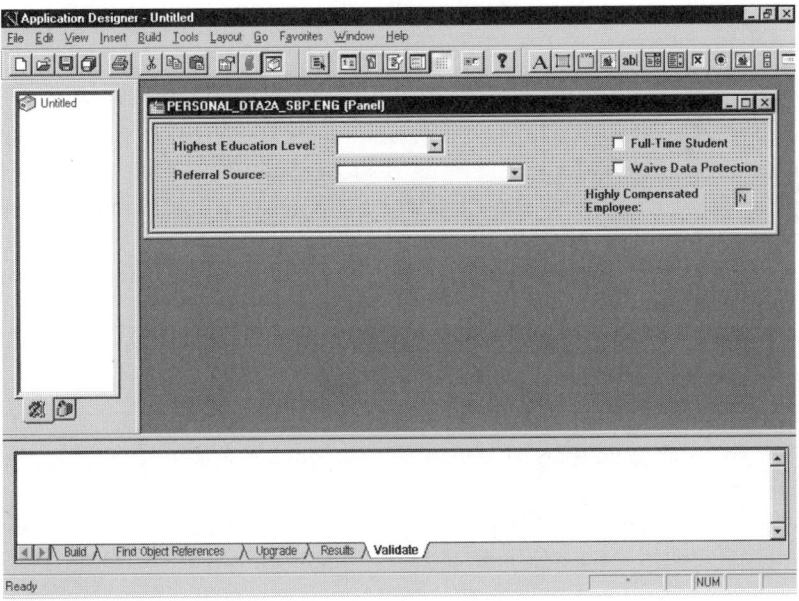

Figure 21.19   The modified PERSONAL_DTA2A_SBP subpanel

After the change to the panel is saved, let's test it again (figure 21.20).

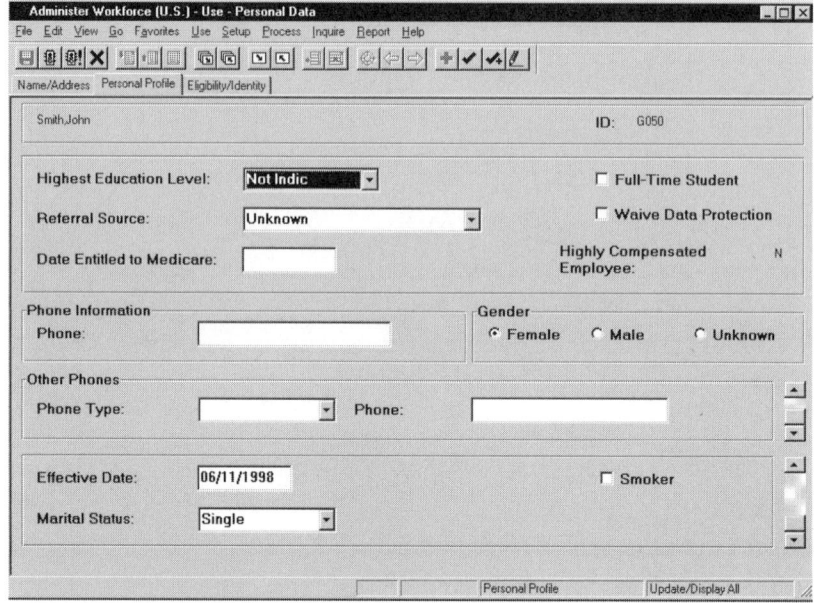

Figure 21.20   Testing the modified panel

Our new field is in place, and it looks as if it has always been there. It will help users to identify highly compensated employees as requested. We performed our modification just by adding an existing field to a subpanel. One other important point must be made: Since we added a field to the subpanel, all panels using this subpanel now display the new field. Therefore, let's first find out which other panels include the modified subpanel, then we can decide if our changes are still appropriate.

TIP   Use the Find Object References utility to find all the objects that reference a modified subpanel.

In order to do that, let's open our subpanel in Application Designer and request the Object References.

As shown in figure 21.21, two more panels use our subpanel. These two panels will definitely have a new look after our modifications are performed. If our users do not want to see a new field on the other panels, we can hide this field by using a simple PeopleCode statement based on the panel name.

Navigation: Edit → Find Object References

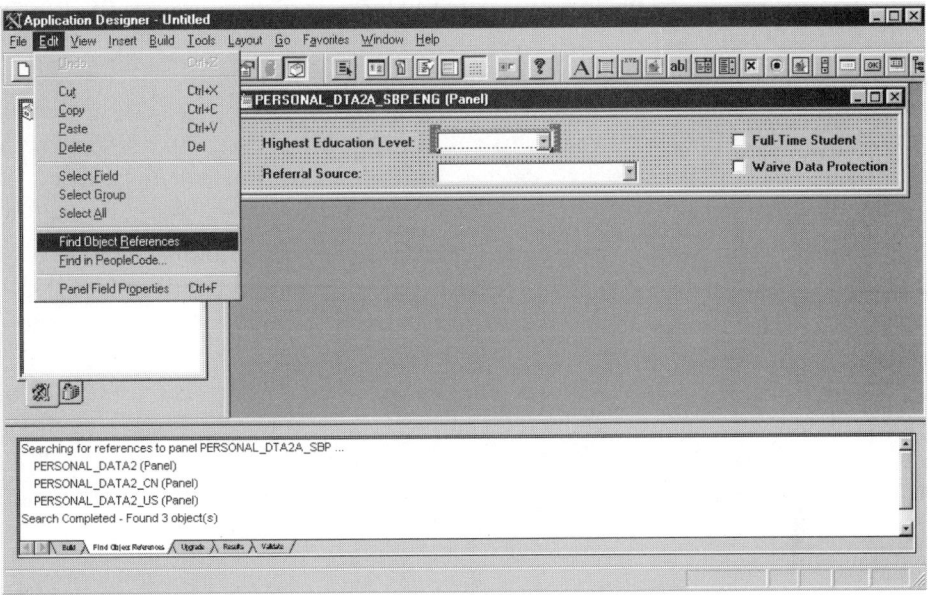

Figure 21.21   Finding all panels that use the PERSONAL_DTA2A_SBP subpanel

21.4   *POSSIBLE IMPACTS ON FUTURE UPGRADES*

Since our customization was simple, we chose to modify the delivered panel. Another alternative could be to copy the delivered panel under a different name and then apply all customizations. In this case, we would have to modify a panel group to replace the delivered panel with our newly customized one. There are pros and cons in each approach. In subsequent chapters, we'll demonstrate other approaches as well and let our readers decide which method of customization they prefer.

The only modified object in our customization was a delivered panel, and we documented our change in the Panel Object Properties Comment box. Will this little change really impact the new release upgrade? To answer this question, let's consider the following situations:

1   The Personal Profile panel in the new release has not been changed by use of PeopleSoft.

2   Another field has been added by PeopleSoft to the same panel in the new release.

3   The same field (Highly Compensated Employee) has been added by PeopleSoft to another panel in the same panel group.

In case 1, the Upgrade Compare and Report process identifies the change. After reviewing the modification, you can drop the panel delivered by the new PeopleSoft release, thus preserving your modified panel in your production database.

NOTE   Please bear in mind that when upgrading to a new application release, the source database usually contains all PeopleSoft new release objects, while the target database is a copy of your production database.

In case 2, the Upgrade Compare and Report process tells you that both objects have actually been changed. Your task, therefore, becomes more complex, since you have to review all the changes and merge your modifications with the new PeopleSoft-delivered panel.

Case 3 is even more complex. Beside recognizing that PeopleSoft actually delivered the same or similar functionality, you have to decide which modification to leave and which one to drop. In cases like this, we recommend adapting PeopleSoft's way, even though your users may already have become accustomed to the change you delivered and may find PeopleSoft's change less convenient.

BEST PRACTICE   If PeopleSoft delivers the same or similar functionality in the new release, try to use the PeopleSoft objects and drop the customization.

Good communication may be needed to explain that, by adapting PeopleSoft's solution, we bring our system closer to "Vanilla." In cases like these, it is also important to ensure that the upgrade team is familiar with all customizations made to the application. Good documentation certainly helps. It may also be a good idea to involve the people who made the customizations in the upgrade project.

1 Do not forget to document all changes.

2 When modifying a subpanel, keep in mind that this modification will affect any panel to which the customized subpanel belongs.

3 In the global development environment use RFT Short or Long descriptions when assigning a label to a panel field.

4 It is always important to test all modifications.

5 Even a simple addition to the delivered panel will impact future application release upgrades.

C H A P T E R   2 2

Adding new fields and panels

In the previous chapter, we discussed how to add a field to a panel when the field already exists in the PeopleSoft-delivered application and belongs to the record linked to this panel. We also discussed possible implications on future upgrades.

What if the new field does not exist in your current system? When adding such a field to a delivered panel group, you have to make an important decision about the best way to perform your customizations. We have already discussed the advantages of the "Add vs. Modify" approach. Let's now consider practical examples and talk about our customizations in details.

Let's turn to exercise 2:

> Add three custom fields to the employee's Job Data and Job Data Hire panel groups.

Let's say we have three new fields: the Acquisition Date, the Union Seniority Sequence, and the Badge ID. The fields will be populated by data entry via an effective-dated on-line panel.

Let's assume, too, that the team involved in a Fit/Gap analysis has already recognized the fact that the required fields were not delivered by PeopleSoft.

In order to perform this customization we first must identify objects that have to be customized or created. We already know that our task will include creating three custom fields. Our next step is to figure out where to place these fields and what alternatives we may have in implementing this task.

22.1 WHAT OBJECTS SHOULD BE CUSTOMIZED OR ADDED?

From the user requirements, we know that the new fields should belong to the Job Data panel group. Let's open this panel group from the Application Designer and inspect the records linked to the panels in this panel group.

Navigation: GO → PeopleTools → Application Designer → Open → Panel Group → JOB_DATA

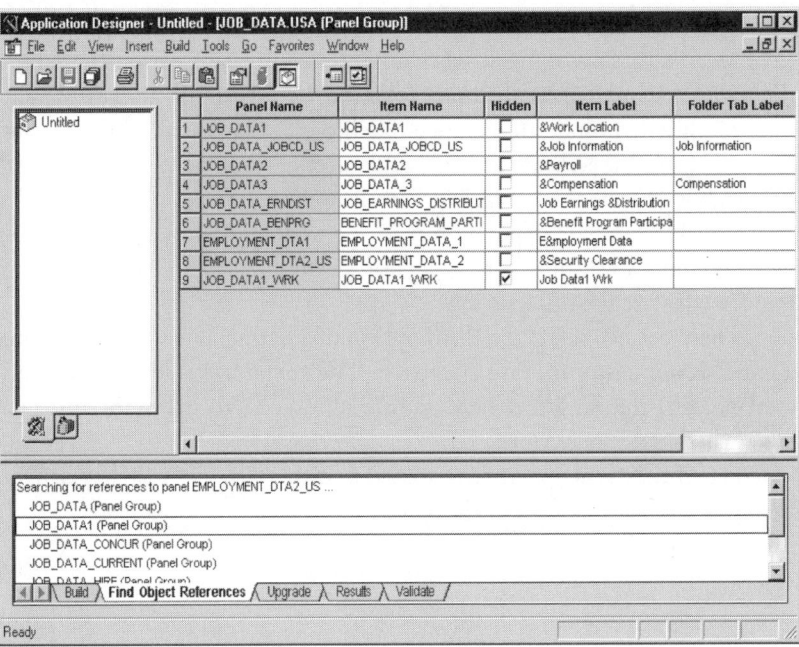

Figure 22.1 Inspecting the JOB_DATA panel group

As you can see from figure 22.1, the JOB_DATA panel group consists of nine panels. This panel group contains employee job history, employment, payroll, compensation, and other information. If you open these panels one by one, you see that the first six panels in this panel group are effective-dated (they include EFFDT as a high-order key field), which supports the maintenance of the employee's job history. Since our new fields should belong to effective-dated panels, we have the following alternatives:

- add the new fields to an existing effective-dated record and the corresponding panel
- create a custom effective-dated record and add this record to one of the existing effective-dated panels in the JOB_DATA panel group
- create a custom effective-dated record and a new panel, and add the new panel to the JOB_DATA panel group

Let's discuss each option:

The first option is probably best from the user's point of view, but as we already discussed in chapter 20, we should stay away from customizing major PeopleSoft-delivered records.

The second option is as good as the first one from the user's point of view if we can find a panel that is not overly crowded and is logically suitable to hold the new fields. There is, however, one important drawback. We know that our fields should belong to an effective-dated panel. We also know that PeopleSoft does not allow multiple records (besides derived/work and related display) within the same scroll bar on the panel. (See part 2 of this book for more details about designing panels with multiple scroll bars.) Since all effective-dated panels have scroll bars, the task becomes a bit more complex. We can possibly add another scroll bar to one of the effective-dated panels, but this involves extensive panel modifications.

Considering the impact on future upgrades, it is simpler and cleaner just to create and maintain a custom panel that houses all current and future custom fields that require effective date processing.

Therefore, we select the third option of creating a new effective-dated record and a panel as our customization approach. The advantage is less customizations to delivered objects; the drawbacks are additional objects to maintain and one more panel with which users may work.

Let's find out what records are used in the JOB_DATA1 panel. Double-click on the JOB_DATA1 panel from the screen in figure 22.1 and click on the ![button] button or select Layout → Order.

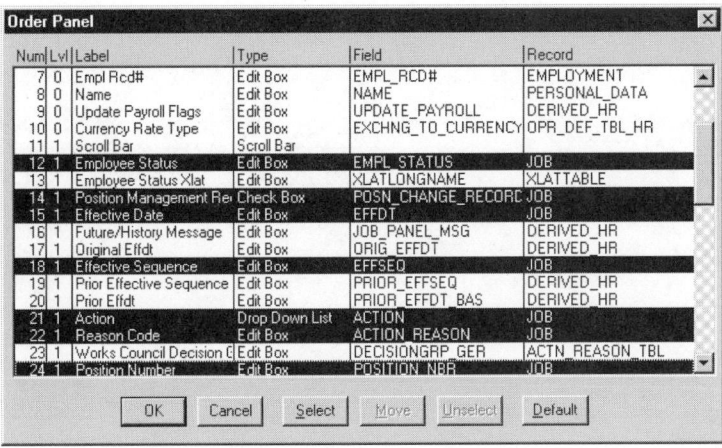

Figure 22.2   **Identifying records used in the JOB_DATA1 panel**

Since the JOB record is an effective-dated record, it can be used to create our new record definition. We don't necessarily need to find a record to clone. It's just sometimes easier and faster, especially when you know that your new record will have the same key structure as the existing one. We can use a similar approach when cloning effective-dated panels.

To summarize, we identified five new objects: three new custom fields, one custom effective dated record to house these fields, and a custom panel.

After creating a new panel, we need to modify all the related panel groups used to access a new panel. Also, since the new panel is added to these panel groups, the appropriate security access has to be granted to users of the new panel.

22.2   CREATING NEW CUSTOM FIELDS

Let's create our new objects in the Application Designer. We start with the Acquisition Date field (figure 22.3).

After selecting Date as a field type for our new field, we are ready to enter other field characteristics as shown in figure 22.4, then save the newly created field as "MY_ACQUISITN_DT."

When a new field is added, don't forget to insert the field into a project by using F7 key or Insert → Current Object into Project. You can also turn on the option to automatically insert a new or modified object to your project as shown in figure 22.5.

Since we want to keep track of all the customizations, we leave this option turned on.

Navigation: Go → PeopleTools → Application Designer → New → Field

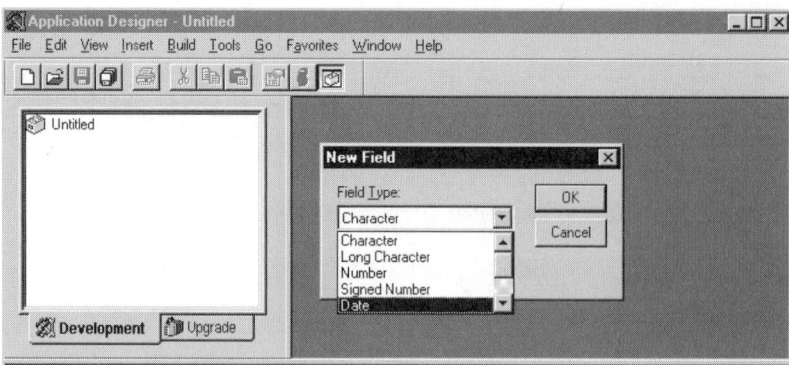

Figure 22.3   Creating a new Date-type field

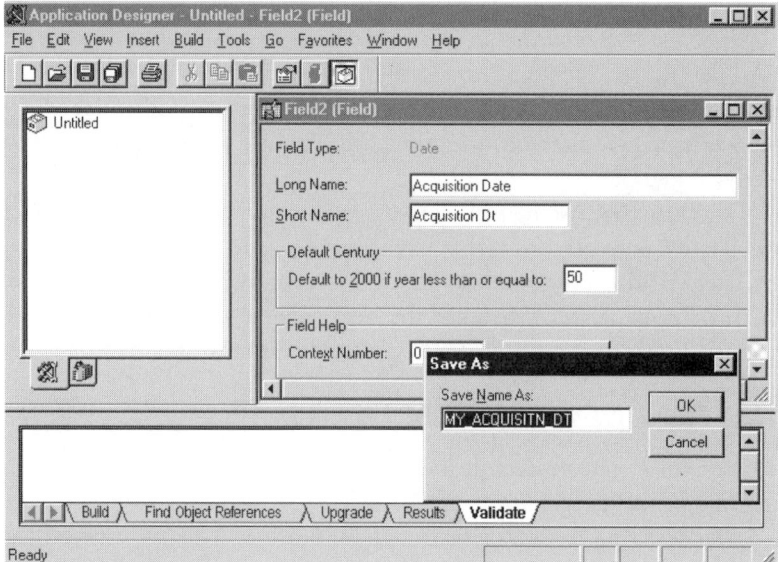

Figure 22.4   Adding new field properties and saving the field as
MY_ACQUISITN_DT

Also, since this is the first object in our project, let's save our new project as
MY_CUSTOM_02 by selecting File → Save Project As (figure 22.6).

Navigation: Tools → Options

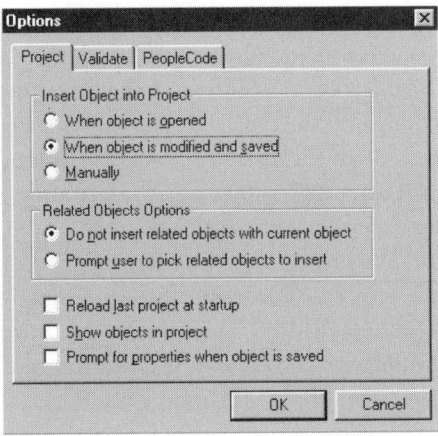

Figure 22.5
This option allows you to automatically insert into the current project any object you save

BEST PRACTICE

When working with a single project, use the Automatic Insert option to ensure all customized objects are added to your project.

Do not use the Automatic Insert option if you are simultaneously working on objects that should be placed into different projects. The Automatic Insert option will insert your object into the project currently open.

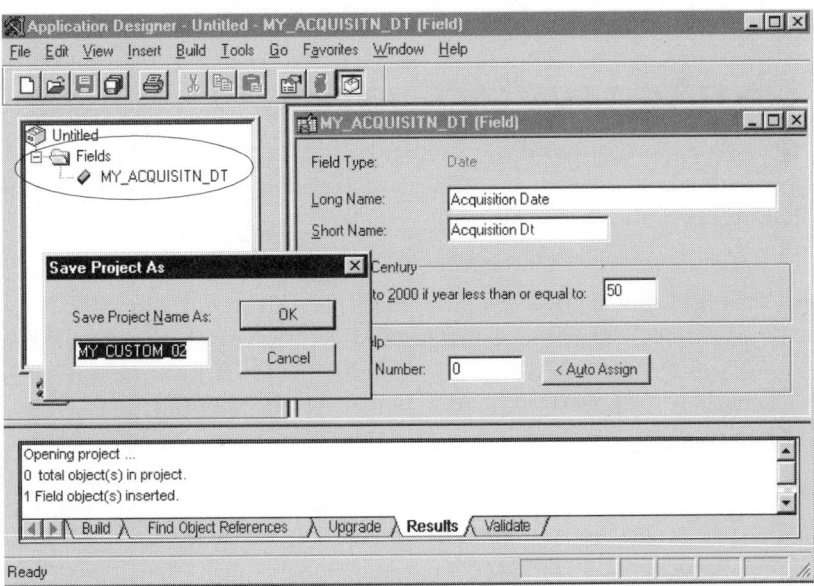

Figure 22.6   Adding a new field to a project and saving the project as MY_CUSTOM_02

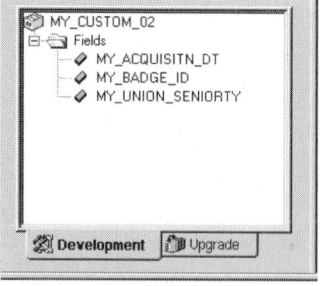

Figure 22.7 All the new fields are in the project

Our next task is to create the other two fields by performing the same steps used to create the first field. This time, we create the Union Seniority Sequence field as `Number`, and the Badge ID as `Character`. After creating the new objects, we place them into our MY_CUSTOM_02 project to keep track of all the customizations performed. The panel on figure 22.7 shows our project after we complete these steps.

We just created three new fields and added them to a project. Was it absolutely necessary to create all these new fields? The answer is "No." We could have found some PeopleSoft-delivered fields with the same data types and reused them for our needs. For example, instead of creating the Acquisition Date field, we could have used the FROM_DATE field, and, instead of creating a new Union Seniority Sequence field, we could have reused the SEQ_NBR field.

Both techniques present advantages and disadvantages. If you create custom fields and prefix their names with some specific letters, they can be easily identified as new objects. Also, you can give them meaningful descriptions that can be used in the panels where these fields are placed. This is especially important when dealing with multilingual environments. On the other hand, it's a good idea, if you can, to simply reuse the delivered fields with their properties, since it decreases the number of customized objects, thus saving upgrade efforts. In our particular case, since we wanted to use distinguished labels on the panels, and because this panel will be used with other languages, we purposely created three new custom fields.

22.3 CREATING A CUSTOM RECORD

Creating a custom record is a simple task. Since we've already done all the groundwork and decided to use the JOB record as a candidate for cloning, let's just open the JOB record and save it as MY_JOB_INFO.

Navigation: GO → PeopleTools → Application Designer → Open → Record

Type JOB and press ENTER. Select the Job record and save it immediately as MY_JOB_INFO. After the record is saved, let's leave only the key fields in the record and delete all the fields we are not planning to use. Now is the time to add the three new custom fields to the MY_JOB_INFO Record definition and save it again. It will also be automatically added to the MY_CUSTOM_02 project.

TIP   Fields can be deleted from a record definition by highlighting the field and choosing Edit → Delete or pressing the delete key.

The new record definition is created (figure 22.8).

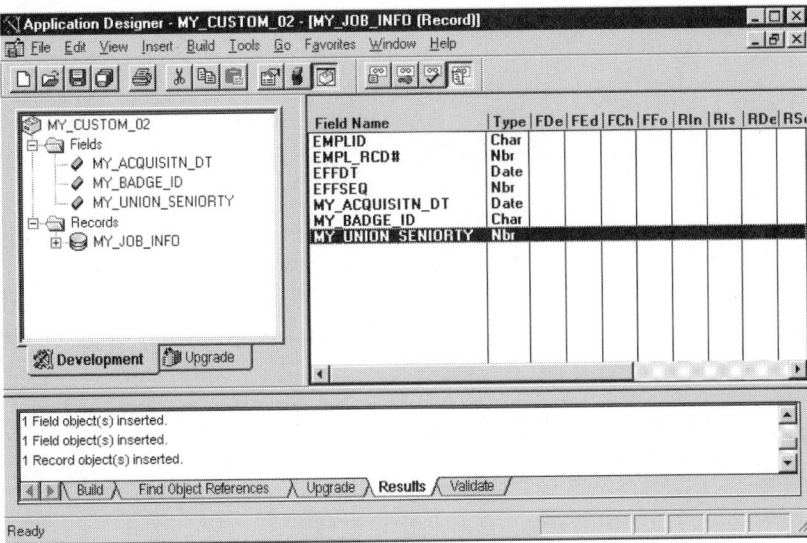

Figure 22.8 Creating a new record definition by cloning the Job record and adding custom fields

As we discussed in part 2, after a record definition is created, the next step is to build a corresponding table in the database. Select Build → Current Object from the Application Designer Menu. Specify Create Tables and Execute SQL now as shown in figure 22.9.

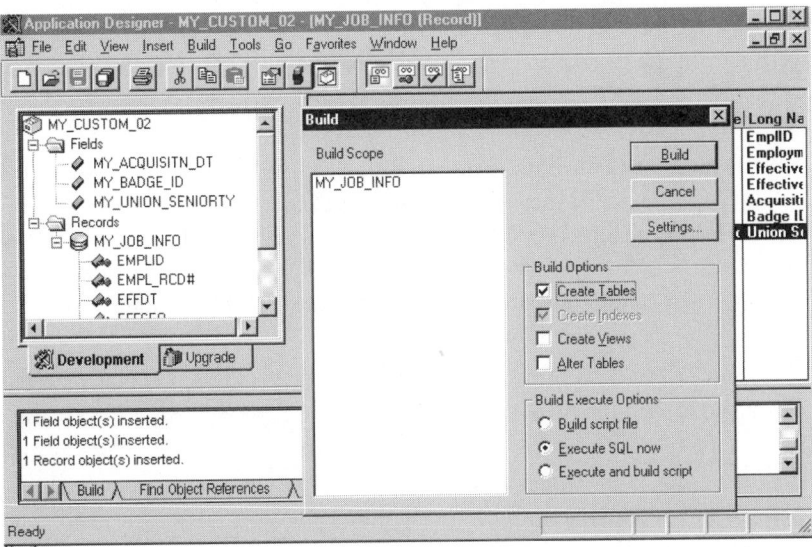

Figure 22.9 Creating a database level table

Since we are creating a brand-new table, it is safe to use the Create Tables and Execute SQL now options.

Since we just created this table, we should not worry about the data. Therefore, after clicking on the Build button, our new table MY_JOB_INFO is created. Please note that you may not have the authority to execute an SQL directly. In this case, you can use the option of building a script file, and your database administrator will execute it for you.

22.4 *CREATING A CUSTOM PANEL*

We've already decided to create a custom panel named MY_JOB. Using our preferred technique of cloning PeopleSoft-delivered objects, let's find an appropriate panel to clone. It sometimes may take you more time in searching for an appropriate object to clone than to create an object from scratch. Each particular case, creating from scratch or cloning, has its pros and cons. When adding a new panel to a panel group, there is an advantage to cloning an existing panel. First of all, you already know all panels in the panel group. Secondly, your new panel must have the same Level 0 record as the other panels in the panel group to be able to use the same search record specified for all panels in the panel group. Since we've decided to make our new panel effective-dated, our record should also have the same Level 1 record as other effective-dated records in the panel group.

Therefore, in our particular case, we'll clone one of the panels from the JOB_DATA panel group. Let's open, for example, an effective-dated panel named JOB_DATA_JOBCD_US and save it as MY_JOB panel.

We leave all Level 0 fields plus all Level 1 fields in the panel. In our particular case, the EMPLID and EMPL_RCD# are Level 0 fields, while the EFFDT and EFFSEQ are Level 1 fields. All other fields should be deleted.

Let's add our three new fields—the Acquisition Date, the Union Seniority Sequence, and the Badge ID—to the panel (figure 22.10).

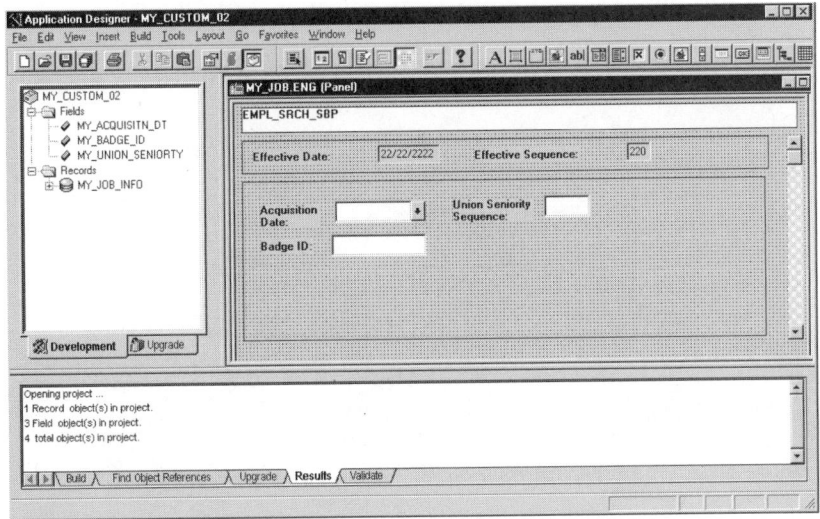

Figure 22.10   Adding custom fields to the new MY_JOB panel

Figure 22.11   Trying to save the newly created custom panel

Once we have all the required fields in our new panel, let's save the panel. After clicking on the button, or selecting File → Save, the Panel Processor displays the error message shown in figure 22.11.

Don't panic! Let's examine the panel layout and fix the problem.

BP
**BEST
PRACTICE**

After a panel is created or modified, it is always a good habit to verify the Order panel by clicking on the ▮▮ button or by selecting Layout → Order from the Application Designer Menu.

The Order panel shows all the fields and records as well as the levels to which these fields belong. It also displays the tab order (figure 22.12).

Now it's clear what the Panel Processor did not like about our panel. The JOB and the MY_JOB_INFO records are both located under the same scroll bar. How are we going to correct this? We know that our new fields belong to the MY_JOB_INFO record. This record also has EFFDT and EFFSEQ as its key fields. Should we just change the record behind the EFFDT and EFFSEQ fields from the JOB record to MY_JOB_INFO record?

Don't rush to a solution. In fact, this is a common problem for new PeopleSoft developers. Let's discuss this situation. Suppose we do this change, and now all the

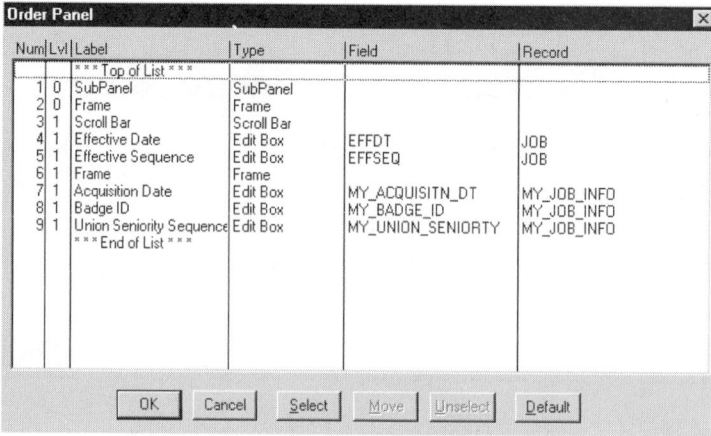

Figure 22.12   The Order Panel for our newly created MY_JOB panel

records in the scroll Level 1 belong to MY_JOB_INFO. The Panel Processor sees no problems and allows you to save this panel. But when you add this panel to the JOB_DATA panel group and start testing, you immediately spot that this panel does not work as it should. It acts as a stand-alone panel, while our users wanted it to be a part of the Job history. Take a look at the panels in the JOB_DATA panel group. All effective-dated panels have the same dates. Why? Because all Level 1 information comes from the same JOB record. If we make our Level 1 record different from the JOB record, our panel will maintain its own dates, one that would have nothing to do with the effective date of the JOB record.

Therefore, the correct solution is to add one more scroll bar and make our new fields belong to the Scroll Level 2. Let's do it. Select Insert → Scroll Bar from the Application Designer menu and place it next to our new fields as shown in figure 22.13.

After the new scroll bar is inserted, we need to set its Occurs level to 2. Let's click on the new scroll bar and, with a right mouse click, select Panel Field Properties. Specify the label of the new scroll bar as Scroll bar MY_JOB (figure 22.14).

The next step is to switch to the Use tab of this panel and specify the MY_JOB scroll bar properties (figure 22.15).

Since we created the scroll bar for the sole purpose of maintaining another record under a different level, we don't really need to show this scroll bar to our users. Therefore, we'll make it invisible. Also, it is a good idea to select the No Row Insert and No Row Delete options. While this functionality is not needed for our panel, if not turned off, it may still be used by mistake. After saving the Panel Field Properties information, we have to make sure that all our new fields belong to this scroll bar level.

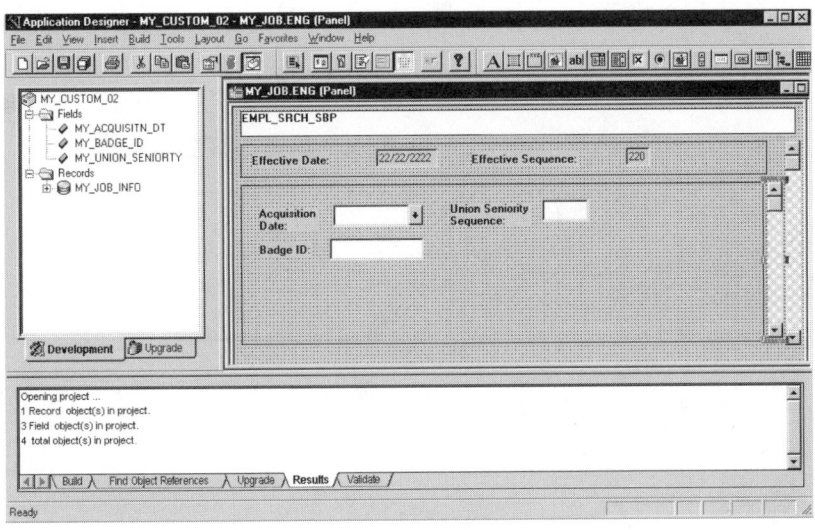

Figure 22.13 Adding a Level 2 scroll bar to a panel

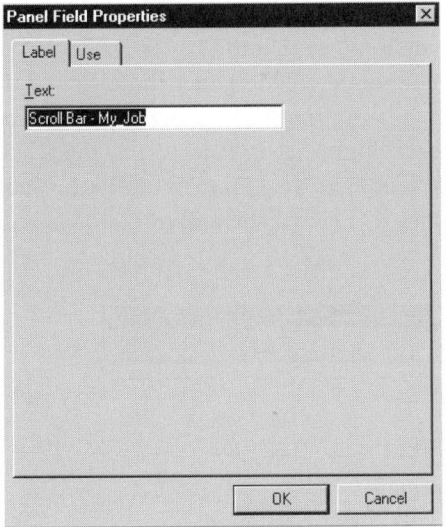

Figure 22.14 Specifying a label for a new scroll bar

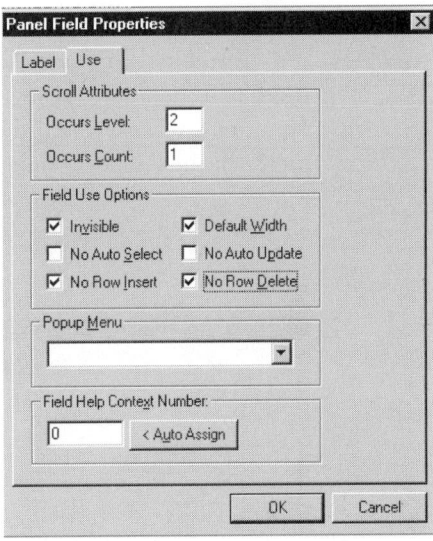

Figure 22.15 Specifying the Occurs Level 2 for our new scroll bar

---

TIP   Placing a scroll bar right above the group of fields makes all the fields that follow the scroll bar belong to the same scroll level.

Figure 22.16 shows that fields number 8, 9, and 10 as well as the scroll bar itself, now belong to Level 2.

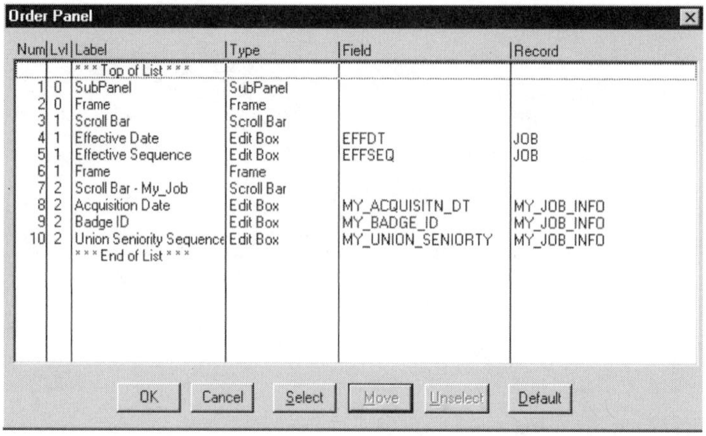

Figure 22.16   The scroll bar My_Job is located right above all the custom fields

If you look at figure 22.16, you'll notice that the Badge ID field is located above the Union Seniority Sequence field, while on the panel the order of these fields is opposite. To make the order of tabulation the same as the field order on the panel, highlight the Badge ID field and click on the Select button. The field disappears from the screen. Don't be alarmed. Just highlight the Union Seniority Sequence field and click on the Move button. Our Badge ID field will be moved as shown in figure 22.17.

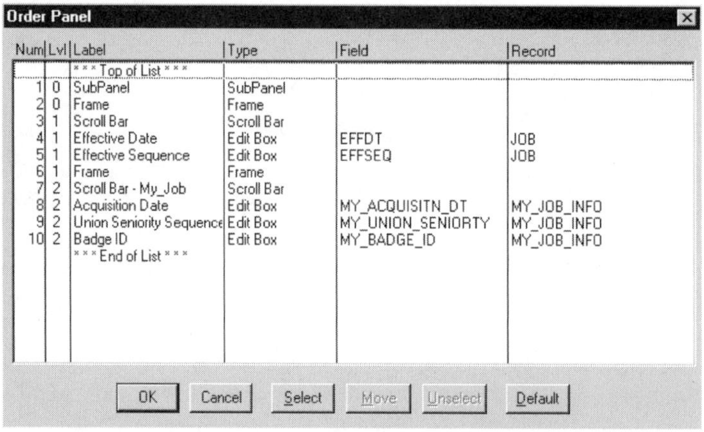

Figure 22.17   Changing the field order in the Order Panel

After all is done, let's save our new panel; it will be added to the MY_CUSTOM_02 project.

Now it is time to test the panel. Just click on the 🔲 button or select Layout → Test Mode, and you can see how the panel looks. You can also perform a preliminary tab order test by entering values and using the tab key to switch between the fields (figure 22.18).

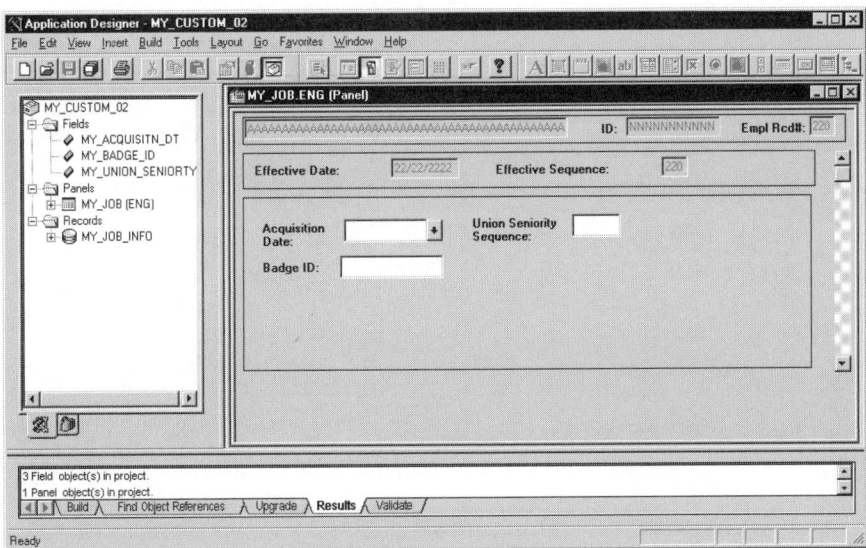

Figure 22.18   Using Test Mode to test the new panel

In order to perform a real test of the panel, we would need to finish all other related modifications.

22.5   ADDING A NEW PANEL TO THE EXISTING PANEL GROUP

Based on the original request, the new panel should be accessed from both the JOB_DATA panel group and the JOB_DATA_HIRE panel group.

First, let's open the JOB_DATA panel group.

We add our new panel at the end of all effective-dated panels, right above EMPLOYMENT_DTA1. In order to add our panel, highlight the EMPLOYMENT_DTA1 panel, and select Insert → Panel Into Group from the Application Designer menu. Type MY_JOB panel name, highlight the panel, click on Insert, and then click on Close. Our new panel is inserted into the JOB_DATA panel group (figure 22.20).

Navigation: Go → Application Designer → Open → Panel Group → JOB_DATA

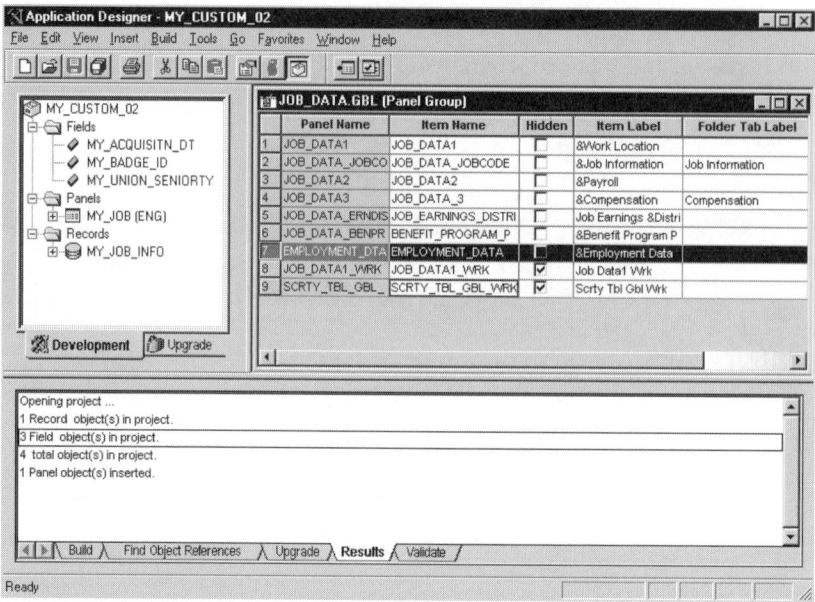

Figure 22.19   The JOB_DATA panel group

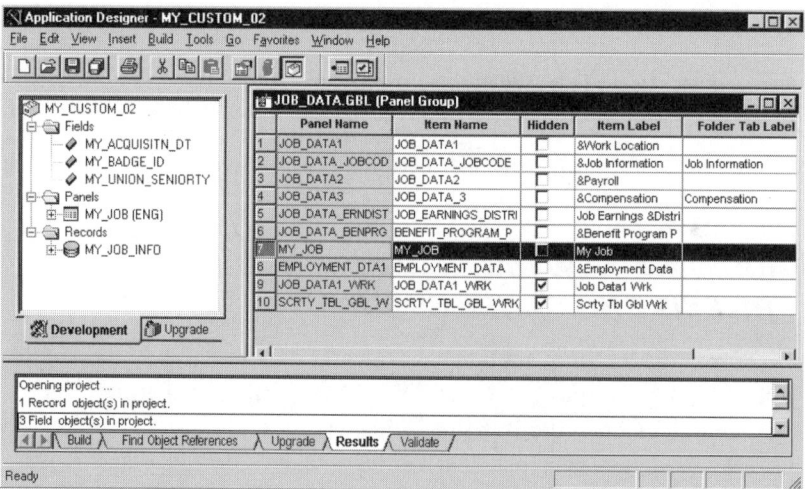

Figure 22.20   Inserting the MY_JOB panel into the JOB_DATA panel group

After the panel is inserted, we save the modified panel group, and it is inserted into our project.

Our next step is to add the panel to the JOB_DATA_HIRE panel group. We can demonstrate another method of adding a panel to a panel group by dragging the panel from the project workspace. Let's open the JOB_DATA_HIRE panel group, select the MY_JOB panel from the project workspace, and drag it to the panel group (figure 22.21).

TIP   The drag-and-drop method inserts your panel (from the left side on your screen) right before the highlighted panel (on the right side of the screen). If no panels are highlighted, the panel is added to the end.

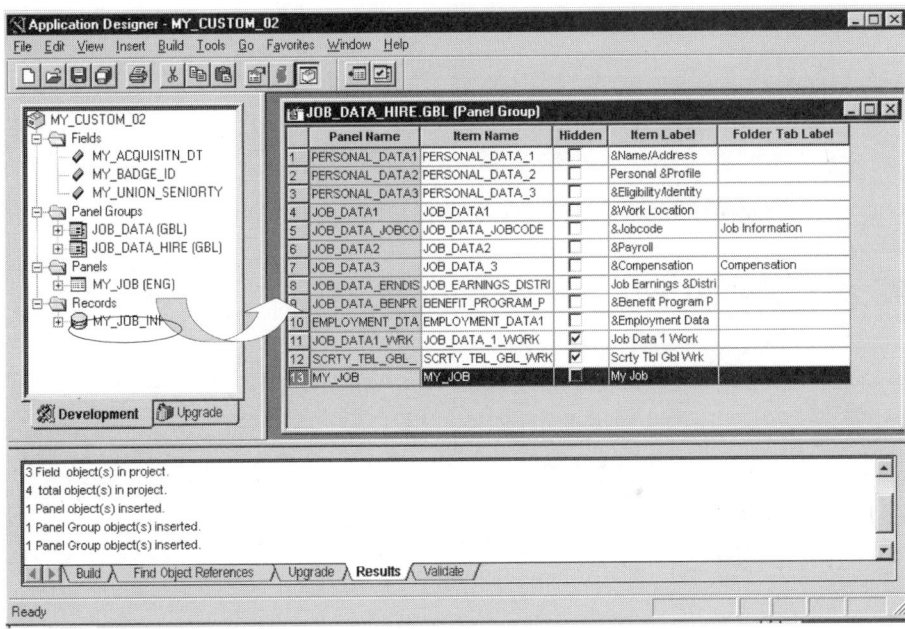

Figure 22.21   Using the drag-and-drop method to insert a panel to a panel group

Since we have not specified the exact place in the JOB_DATA_HIRE panel group where we wanted the MY_JOB panel to be inserted, the system simply placed our panel at the end as number 13 (figure 22.21). You can change the order of panels in the panel group by dragging the panel to the place you need it to be.

When all is done, let's save our modified panel group. Our project will look as shown in figure 22.22.

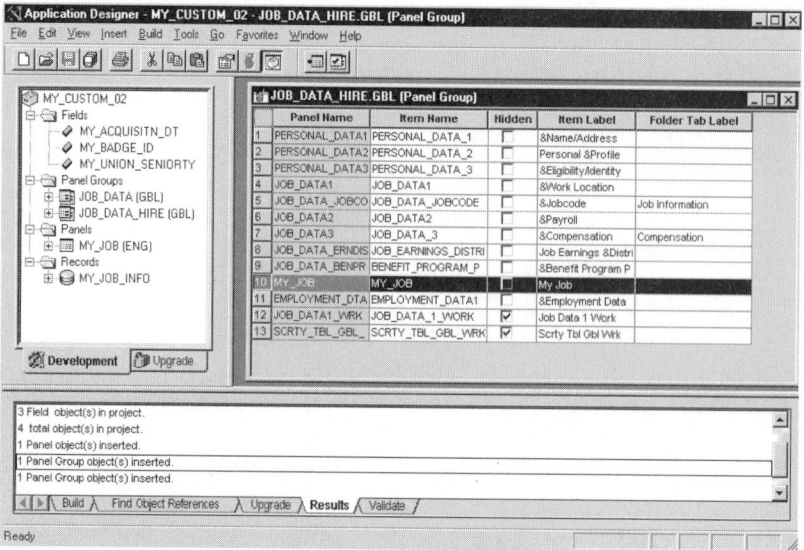

Figure 22.22   Our project contains two modified panel groups

22.6   GRANTING SECURITY ACCESS

Since we changed the existing panel group by adding a new panel to it, we have to grant security access to all users who would need to work with this new panel. First, we grant security access to the ALLPANLS operator class that will be used to test our customizations.

Select Menu Items, and double-click on the ADMINISTER_WORKFORCE_(GBL) menu (figure 22.23).

Navigation: Go → PeopleTools → Security Administration → Open → ALLPANLS

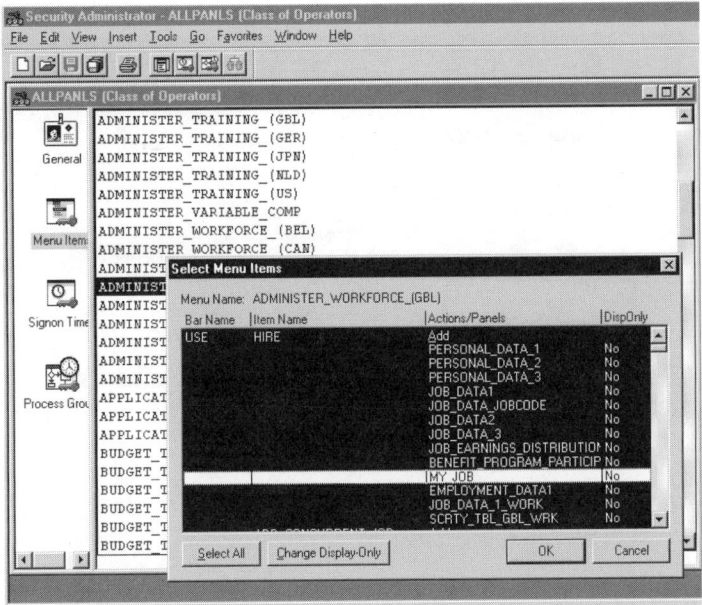

Figure 22.23   Selecting ADMINISTER_WORKFORCE_(GBL) menu item

Highlight the MY_JOB panel group under the bar name USE and item name HIRE. Repeat the same process with the JOB DATA item name, press OK and then, save the modified security. Now security access has been granted to all users who need to use this panel.

22.7 TESTING OUR CHANGES

We need to make certain that all our modifications work correctly. Remember, we created a new panel and a new record. We also added a new panel to the existing panel group. Our goal is not only to verify that the new functionality is in place, but also to ensure that it works perfectly with the delivered objects.

Let's start by testing the Job Data panel group.

Navigation: Go → Administer Workforce → Administer Workforce (GBL) → Use → Job Data
→ My Job → Update/Display All

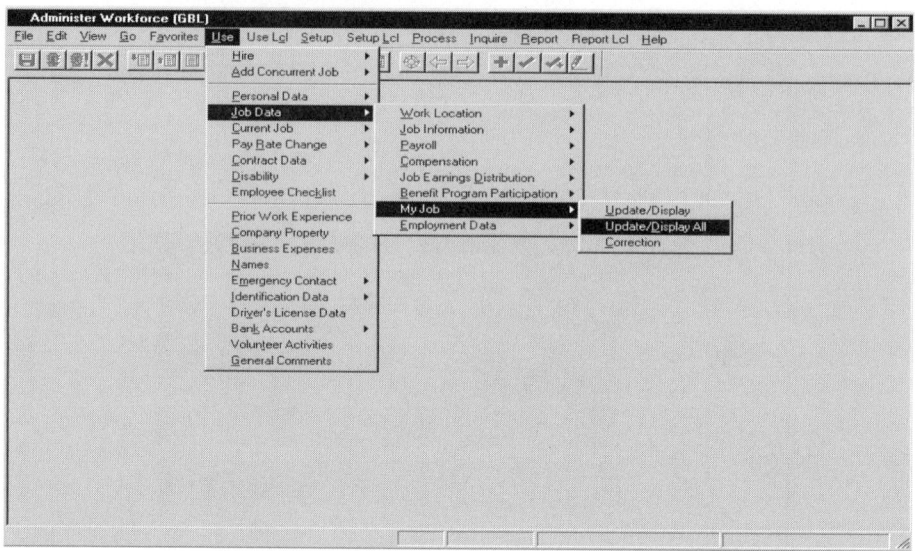

Figure 22.24   Testing the Job Data panel group

Let's select an employee—for example, "Smith, Lily"—and fill in our new panel as shown in figure 22.25.

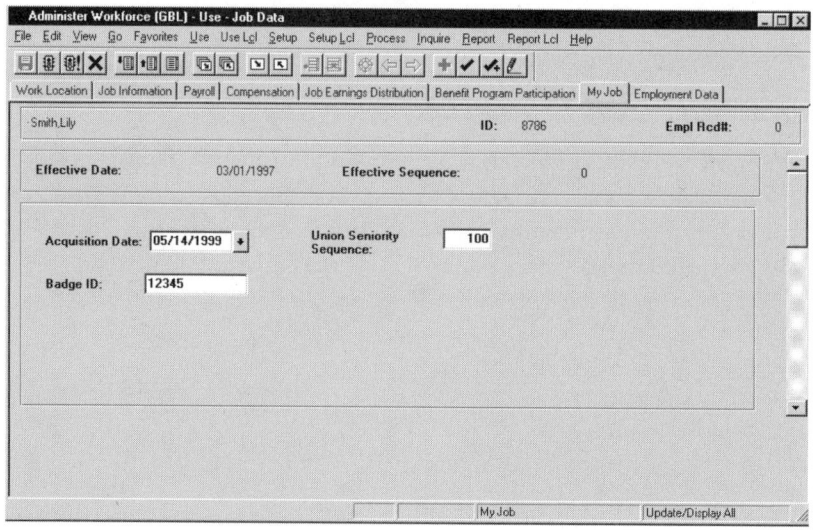

Figure 22.25   Entering information into the new panel

Pay attention to the Effective Date and Effective Sequence fields. These fields have exactly the same data as that in the JOB record. If we insert another JOB record with another effective date, the data in our panel should also change. Let's test this. Figure 22.26 shows that when a new JOB record is inserted, the effective date on MY_JOB panel is also changed while the rest of the data are carried over from the previous record.

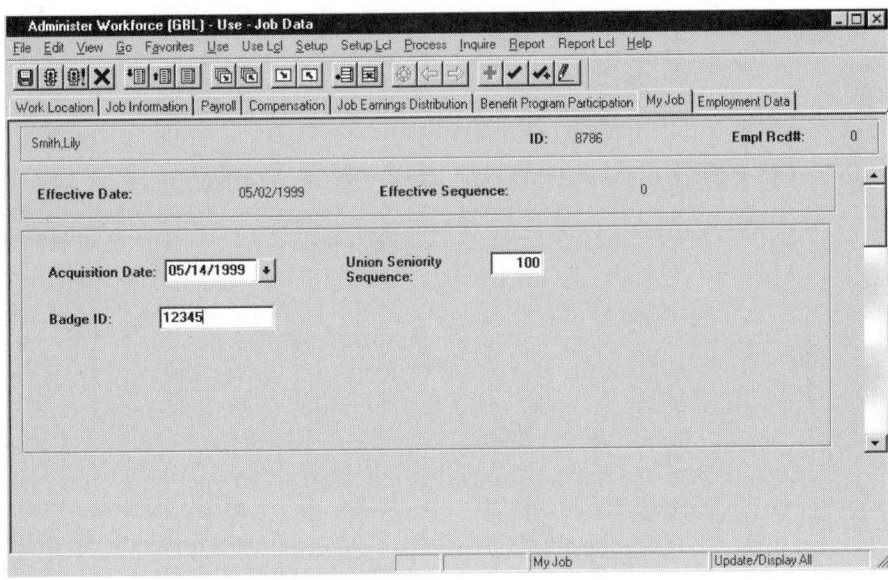

Figure 22.26   **Inserting a JOB row leads to the insertion of another row in the MY_JOB panel as well**

Since we know that we created a new custom record MY_JOB_INFO to save information on the panel, let's verify that the information is saved correctly and that it is also effective-dated. In order to do this, we just execute a simple `Select` statement (figure 22.27).

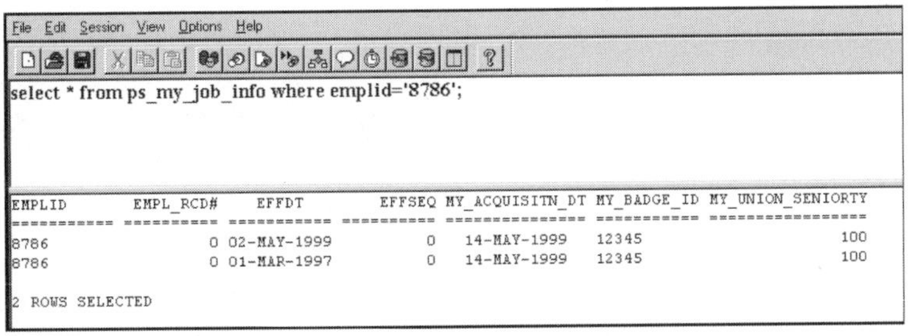

Figure 22.27   Verifying that the panel information was saved correctly in the underlying MY_JOB_INFO table

BEST PRACTICE
Use your SQL tools to verify that the underlying table is properly updated by any online panel operations.

In order to verify all possible situations, a complete test plan would have to be created and executed. For example, we would need to test our customizations in all available modes: `Update`, `Update/Display`, and `Corrections`. The new fields' boundaries would have to be verified as well.

To test the Job Data Hire panel group, we would follow the same testing sequence that we used for the Job Data panel group.

22.8 POSSIBLE IMPACT ON FUTURE UPGRADES

As our readers may have already noticed, we tried to minimize the impact on future upgrades during all stages of our development. We used distinctive names for all of our objects, documented our changes, and created a project to keep track of all customizations. We also avoided the temptation to customize the delivered JOB record. However, some of the changes to the delivered system were not avoidable. For example, we modified the delivered Panel Groups: JOB_DATA and JOB_DATA_HIRE. Therefore, with the new release, we will either have to re-apply our changes if PeopleSoft delivers any new functionality to these panel groups, or to accept our customized version if PeopleSoft makes no changes to them. Also, as we already emphasized in our previous discussion, there is always a possibility that PeopleSoft may deliver similar or even the same functionality. In this case, PeopleSoft's new features should take precedence over ours.

1 When creating a custom record, you can either re-use the existing fields or create custom ones.

2 You can insert an object into a project by using the F7 key or Insert → Current Object into Project. You can also turn on the option in the Application Designer to automatically insert a new or modified object to your project.

3 The Application Processor will not allow you to save a panel with more than one data record in a scroll. Exceptions are fields from Derived records and related display fields.

4 When modifying panels, always examine the Order Panel to ensure that all the fields are located in the correct places and belong to all the proper scroll bars.

5 All panels in the panel group should have the same Level 0 records.

6 When adding an effective-dated panel to a panel group where all panels have the same effective date, make certain that the effective date field belongs to the same record in all the panels.

7 While testing panel modifications, it is essential to verify (with the help of your SQL tools) that the underlying table is properly updated by any online operations.

C H A P T E R   2 3

Adding new functionality to PeopleSoft-delivered applications

In this chapter, we will show you how you can add new functionality to an existing application by cloning PeopleSoft-delivered objects. Some knowledge of the PeopleSoft Benefits Administration module will help our readers understand the business reason for the modification under discussion. For those readers not familiar with Benefits Administration, this exercise may be useful from a purely technical development perspective.

Again, let's turn to an example, exercise #3:

> Allow users to delete the Benefits Administration Event from an online panel based on the user's selection. Only events that are not finalized should be allowed for deletion.

494

Our task here is to allow users to delete certain rows from the database. Only super-users with special security access will be allowed to perform this function.

Why would we need to develop a process that allows the deletions of the Benefit Administration events? Let's examine the background of this problem.

Benefits Administration is a PeopleSoft application that helps administer employee benefits in an automated fashion. Benefit tables are populated with eligible benefits for employees through a batch process, and employees are then allowed to make their choice. The Benefits Eligibility process makes use of related employee information from the PeopleSoft Human Resources application. In this process, a user can correct or delete information that was incorrectly entered into an HR application. Such actions can result in incorrect benefit eligibility information that was prepared based on the original HR information. PeopleSoft Benefits Administration process disconnects when the HR information is deleted, or does not reprocess the event correctly when key HR information is changed. Therefore, if we allow our Benefit super-users to delete an incorrect event and then reprocess the event, the benefit eligibility information will be corrected.

23.1 WHAT OBJECTS SHOULD BE CUSTOMIZED OR ADDED?

Since this functionality is not currently available within the Benefits Administration module, we will create a custom panel to allow our users to perform the changes online. A custom record should also be created and linked to the new panel. When a user selects a particular event for deletion, SQL delete commands will be executed. We'll place these commands into appropriate record field events, thus creating a custom PeopleCode program.

23.2 CREATING A CUSTOM RECORD BY CLONING AN EXISTING ONE

As usual, it is useful to find an appropriate record from which to clone. Since we are developing this project for Benefits Administration, let's take a look at the main Benefits Administration table, BAS_PARTIC (figure 23.1).

This table contains the information about employee's benefit events. Since our task is to show users all available events for a particular employee and allow them to select from a list of events, we create a view from this table.

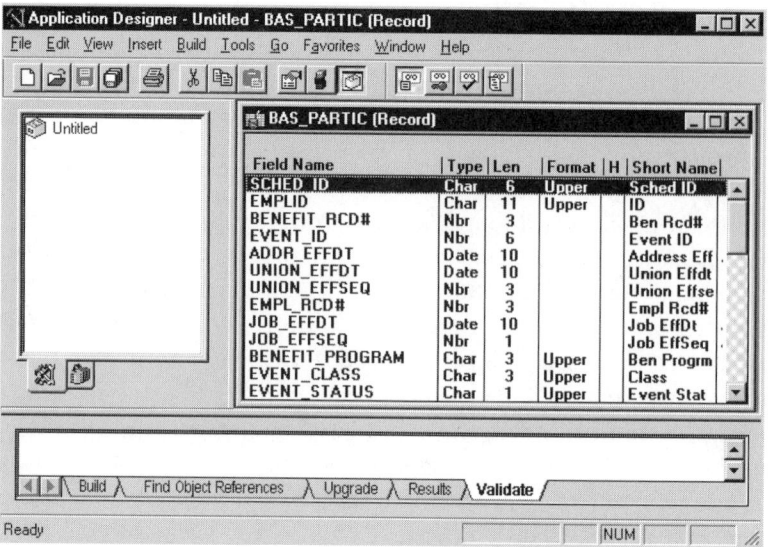

Figure 23.1   Selecting the BAS_PARTIC record as a source for cloning

Let's first save this record as MY_BAS_DEL_VW and then delete all the fields we don't need to use. Our next step is to change the record's property to SQL View. The SQL View `Select` statement looks as shown in figure 23.2.

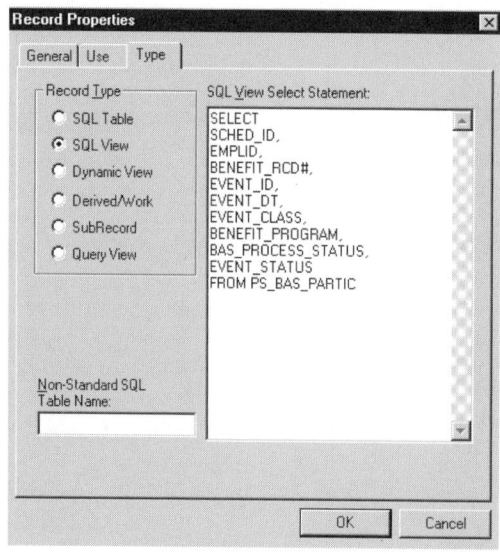

Figure 23.2
Creating a custom view definition

Before saving our new record definition, let's compare all the fields we specified in the view definition to the fields in our record definition. Please remember that the field order in the `Select` statement shown in figure 23.2 should exactly match the order of fields in our new record definition. Let's also not forget to put a useful description for our new view definition in the General tab of Record Properties.

It is important to define the key fields for the view. Here we defined SCHED_ID, EMPLID, BENEFIT_RCD#, and EVENT_ID as key fields.

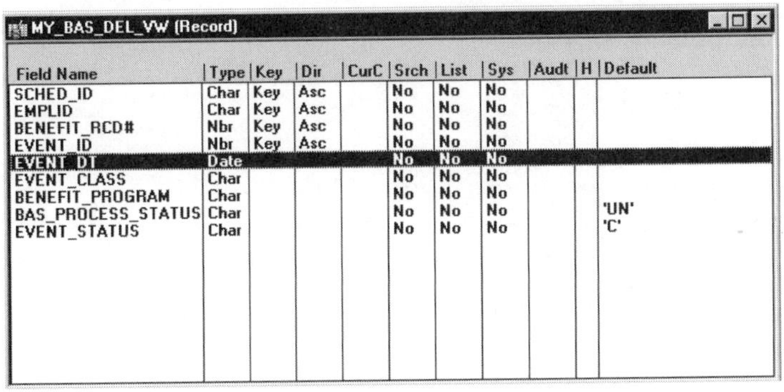

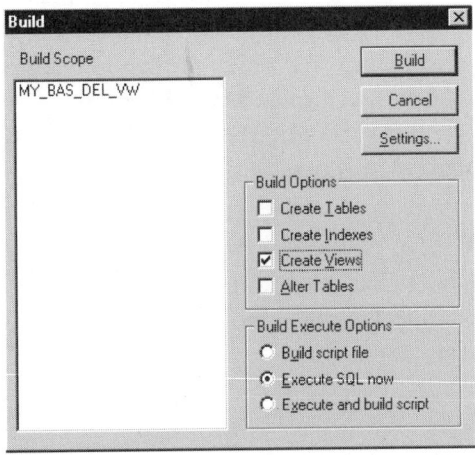

Figure 23.3   Defining the key fields

Let's save our record definition. After the record definition is created, we need to build the actual view in the database. Let's build it by clicking on the 🔧 tool bar button or selecting Build → Current Object from the Application Designer Menu (figure 23.4).

**Figure 23.4
Creating a database level View**

Select the Create Views checkbox from the Build Options group box. Also click on the Execute SQL now radio button from the Build Execute Options group box. Then, click on the Build button to execute the SQL and create the view. The view is created, and the information about the Build process is displayed on the Application Designer output window, as shown in figure 23.5.

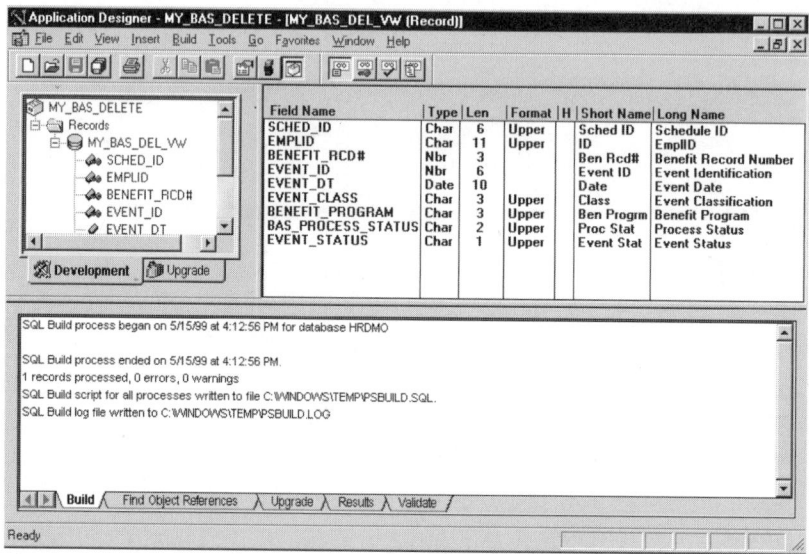

Figure 23.5   The information about the Build process is displayed

---

TIP   You can create an SQL View at any point in time without any fear of data loss.

As you can see from figure 23.5, our first object created for exercise 3 is added to a project automatically because we specified an automatic insert to a project in the Tools → Options. We also saved our new project as MY_BAS_DELETE.

Now that the view is created, we can construct a custom panel.

23.3   CREATING A CUSTOM PANEL

Let's look at the PeopleSoft-delivered Benefits Administration application and find a panel that may be used for cloning. Bear in mind that our new panel must be an employee-level panel and should contain the information about various employees' benefit events.

As a basis for cloning, choose an application panel that resembles the functionality required for the customizations.

Let's open the Event Status Update panel to see if this panel could be used as a basis for cloning.

Navigation: Go → Compensate Employees → Administer Automated Benefits → Use → Event Status Update.

Select any employee ID—for example, 8845—and press the ENTER key. The system will display the employee's Event Status Update panel. BAS_PARTIC_STS panel is used as indicated by ❶.

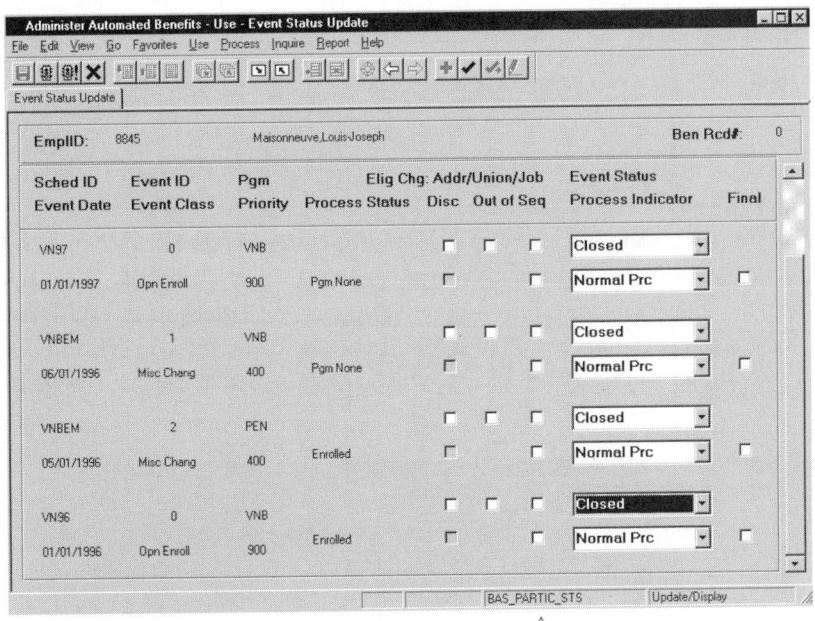

Figure 23.6   The Event Status Update panel

❶

Let's open the BAS_PARTIC_STS panel used in this screen.

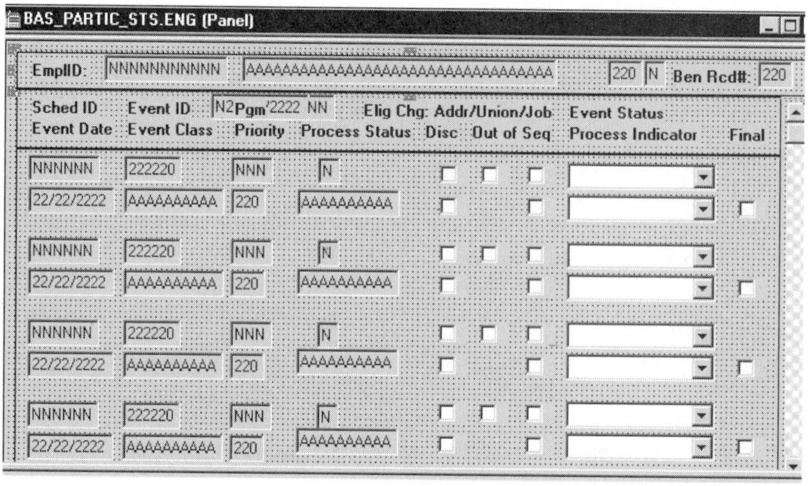

BAS_PARTIC_STS.ENG (Panel)

| EmplID: | NNNNNNNNNNN | AAAAAAAAAAAAAAAAAAAAAAAAAAAAAAAAA | | 220 | N | Ben Rcd#: | 220 |

Sched ID	Event ID:	N2Pgm'2222 NN		Elig Chg: Addr/Union/Job	Event Status	
Event Date	Event Class	Priority	Process Status	Disc Out of Seq	Process Indicator	Final
NNNNNN	222220	NNN	N	☐ ☐ ☐	▾	
22/22/2222	AAAAAAAAAA	220	AAAAAAAAAA	☐ ☐	▾	☐
NNNNNN	222220	NNN	N	☐ ☐ ☐	▾	
22/22/2222	AAAAAAAAAA	220	AAAAAAAAAA	☐ ☐	▾	☐
NNNNNN	222220	NNN	N	☐ ☐ ☐	▾	
22/22/2222	AAAAAAAAAA	220	AAAAAAAAAA	☐ ☐	▾	☐
NNNNNN	222220	NNN	N	☐ ☐ ☐	▾	
22/22/2222	AAAAAAAAAA	220	AAAAAAAAAA	☐ ☐	▾	☐

Figure 23.7 The BAS_PARTIC_STS panel

As you can see, the panel in figure 23.7 can be easily used for this task. Let's first save the panel as MY_BAS_DEL_EVNT and then customize it. You have to be really careful when deleting all fields that are not going to be used and replacing the records behind the fields with our custom MY_BAS_DEL_VW record. Sometimes, cloning a panel may become so cumbersome that it may be easier just to create your own panel from scratch. No matter what method you use to create your custom panel—cloning or creating from scratch—your new panel will look like the one shown in figure 23.8.

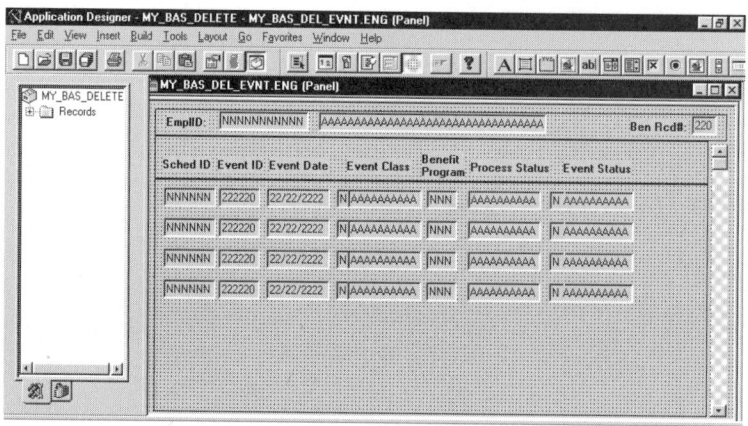

Figure 23.8 Creating a custom panel by cloning the BAS_PARTIC_STS delivered panel

Let's verify that all fields in our panel are in the right order and belong to the correct records. Click on the [1 2] button or select Layout → Order and examine the field order in our new panel (figure 23.9).

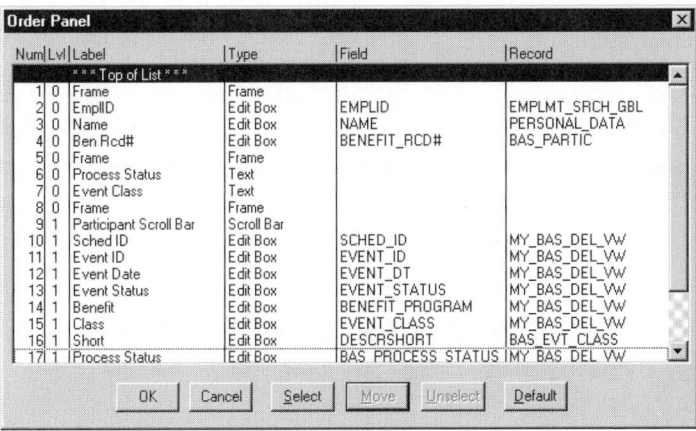

Figure 23.9   The Order panel for MY_BAS_DEL_EVNT

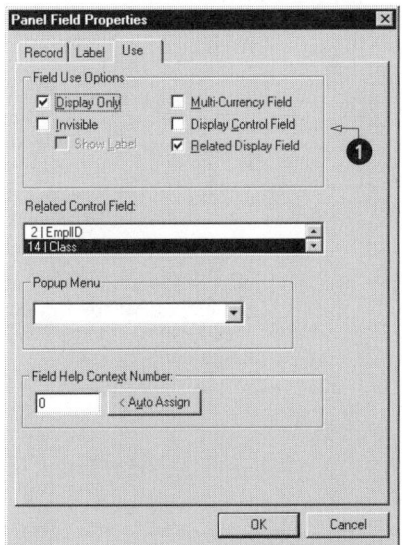

Figure 23.10   Making sure that the DESCRIPTION is a Related Display field

Pay attention to all the levels used in this panel (shown in the second column) and all corresponding records. Our panel consists of two levels. Level 0 houses the EMPLID, NAME, BENEFIT_RCD#, as well as text fields used as headers for the Level 1 columns. Multiple records on Level 0 are allowed since we don't have a scroll bar at this level.

Level 1 requires more attention. We can see two records that belong to this level, MY_BAS_DEL_VW and BAS_EVT_CLASS. Is this a mistake? Take a look at the field column in figure 23.9. The field that belongs to BAS_EVT_CLASS is the DESCRSHORT field. Based on the Display Control and Related Display rule discussed in part 2 of this book, you can include a field from another record under the same scroll bar if the field is specified as a Related Display field. This is, most probably, the case here. Let's verify this by selecting the Event Class description field on the panel and keying CTRL+F or using the right mouse button on the field and selecting

Panel Field Properties (figure 23.10). The DESCRSHORT field is a Related Display field with the Event Class as its Display Control field (❶).

As we expected, the DESCRSHORT field is specified as a Related Display field and has a reference to the EVENT_CLASS field as a Display Control field.

Let's get back to the Order panel in figure 23.9. We also need to verify that all fields listed in this panel are in the correct order. The number in the first column of the Order panel indicates the tab order. Notice that field Event Status is not in the right place. If you use the TAB key, it will position a cursor on the Event Status field right after the Event Date field is tabbed out. According to our panel design, this field should be the last field in a row for the panel. This problem is very simple to fix. Just highlight the field you need to move—in our case, it's field 13—and press the Select button as shown in figure 23.11.

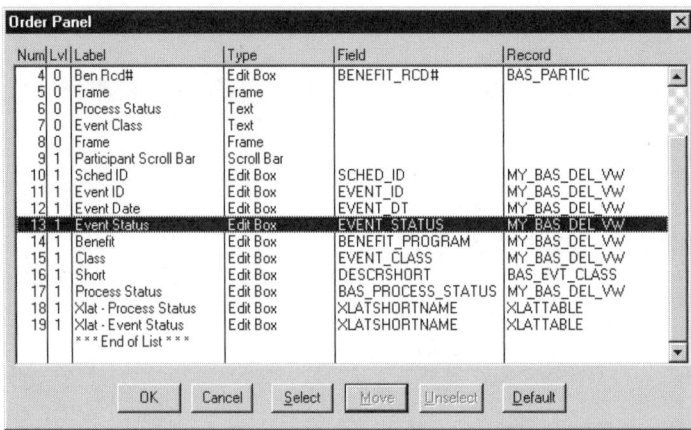

**Figure 23.11
Selecting a field to
be moved to another
place on the panel**

Then highlight the field to which you want to move the selected field—in this example, it's field 17—and click on Move. Now the Event Status field is in the right place, located below the Process Status field.

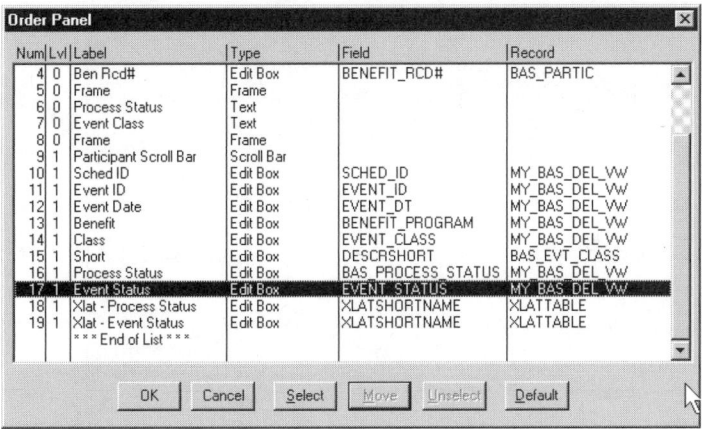

Figure 23.12   Repositioning the Event Status field

Let's take another look at our Order panel. Is everything correct? Looks fine at first glance. Now, let's save our panel changes again (figure 23.13).

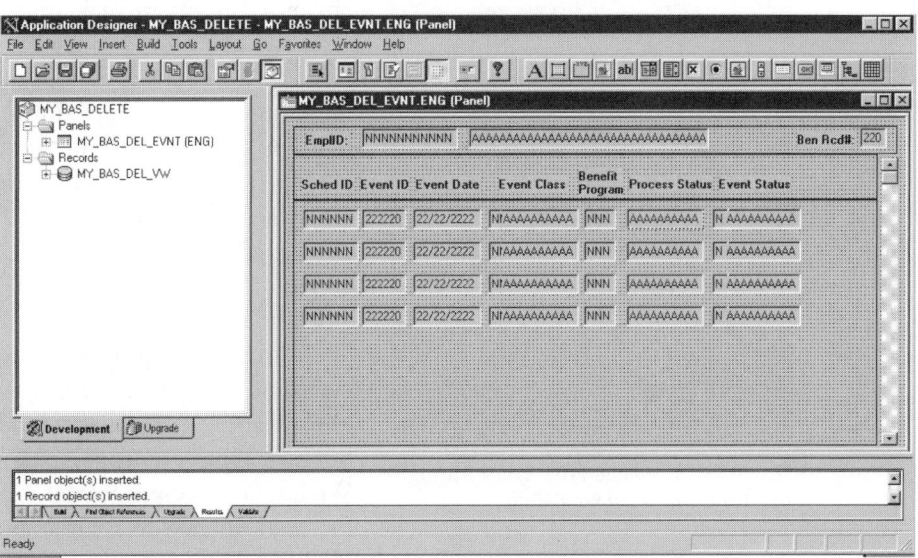

Figure 23.13   The MY_BAS_DEL_EVNT panel is added to our project

Now we can use Test Mode by clicking on the 🔳 tool bar button or selecting Layout → Test Mode from the menu.

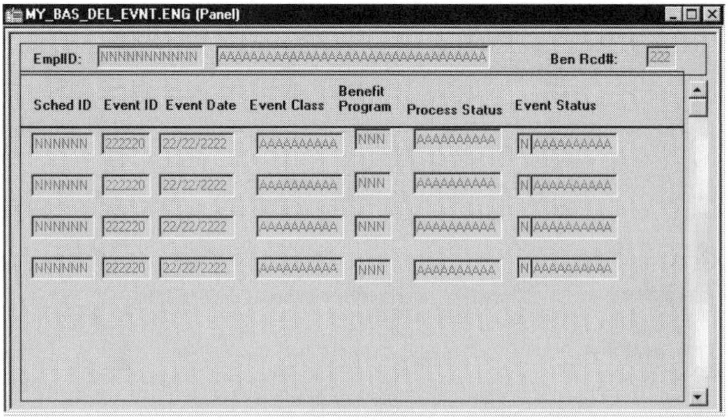

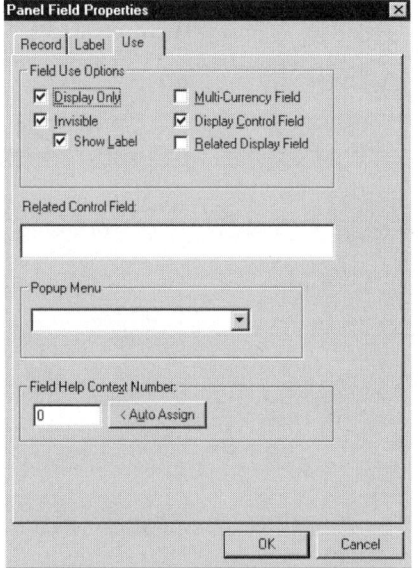

Figure 23.14 Looking at our new panel in test mode

Notice that there are two fields under the Event Status column on the panel: the Event Status Display Control field and the Event Status Description (figure 23.14). We obviously forgot to make our Event Status field invisible. Let's perform this change. First, we have to exit the test mode by clicking on the 🔲 tool bar button again. Then, right-click on the Event Status field and select the Panel Field Properties. Mark the Event Status Display Control field invisible (figure 23.15). Don't forget, however, to click on the Show Label option; otherwise, it will become invisible as well.

After pressing the OK button, let's test our panel again (figure 23.16).

Figure 23.15 Making the Event Status Display Control field invisible

The Event Status field looks fine now, but how are our users going to delete events? We display all the information about events for users to decide what events should be deleted. Now we need to give them the ability to do so. This is a good time to use a Derived/Work record field as a placeholder for additional functionality.

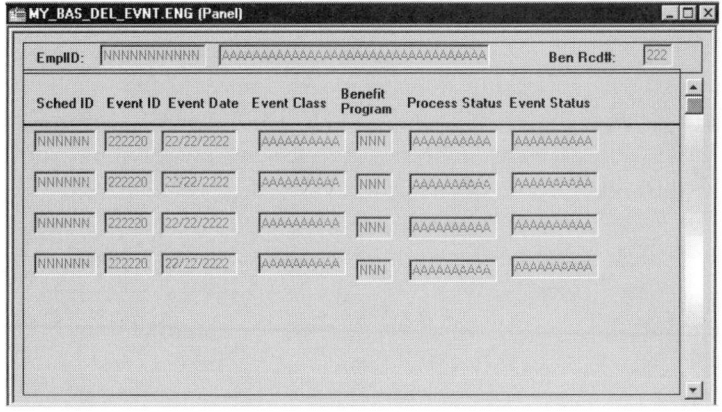

Figure 23.16   The MY_BAS_DEL_EVNT panel in test mode

23.3.1   Creating custom fields for a Derived/Work record

Let's create a custom field MY_EVENT_DELETE as a Yes/No field to be used in the panel for every event selected for deletion.

Navigation: Go → Application Designer → Select New → Field

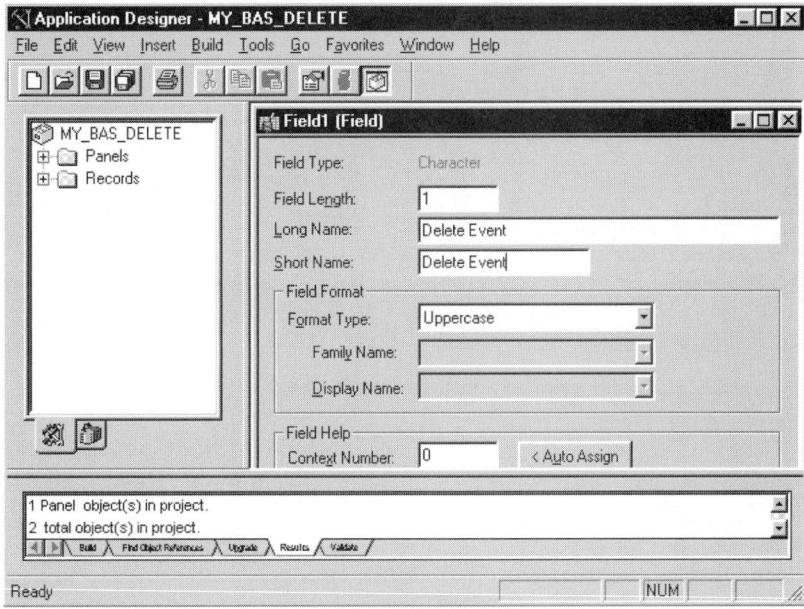

Figure 23.17   Creating a custom field for a Derived/Work record

Let's save the field as MY_EVENT_DELETE. It will be automatically added to our project.

Soon we'll plug special functionality into this field and discuss it in detail, but now, we need to create one more field, MY_DELETE_PROCESS. Why another field? The MY_EVENT_DELETE field will be displayed for each event on the panel. Some events will be marked for deletion, others won't. Users will be able to scroll down the panel and review all the events. When necessary, they will uncheck some events chosen for deletion. After all events on the panel are reviewed, users will need a way to indicate that the deletion process can occur. This is why we need another field.

We repeat the steps described above and create another one character field as a placeholder for our Delete script.

Navigation: Go → Application Designer → Select New → Field

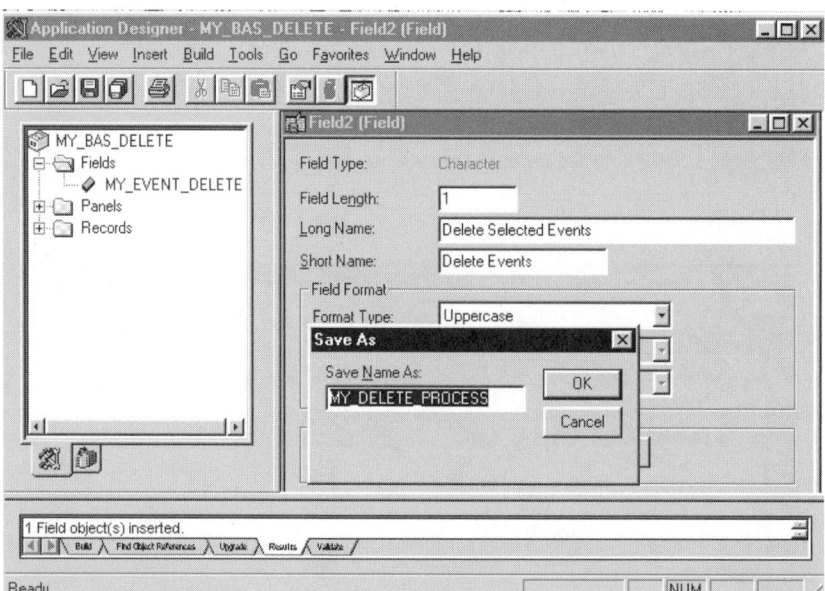

Figure 23.18   Creating the MY_DELETE_PROCESS field

We are now ready to create a custom Derived/Work record to hold our newly created fields.

23.3.2   Creating a custom Derived/Work record

As we discussed in part 2, Derived/Work records are often used to display temporary values on a panel. You can also use them to store temporary values from user input. Since the Application Processor will retrieve only the fields from the Derived/Work

CHAPTER 23 ADDING NEW FUNCTIONALITY

record that are explicitly referenced by the particular panel into a record buffer, you can keep all your work fields for multiple projects in one custom record. Fields in such records are often used to store and trigger PeopleCode programs. Let's create a Derived/Work record MY_WORK.

Insert our two custom fields MY_EVENT_DELETE and MY_DELETE_PROCESS to the record as shown in figure 23.19.

Navigation: Go → Application Designer → New → Record

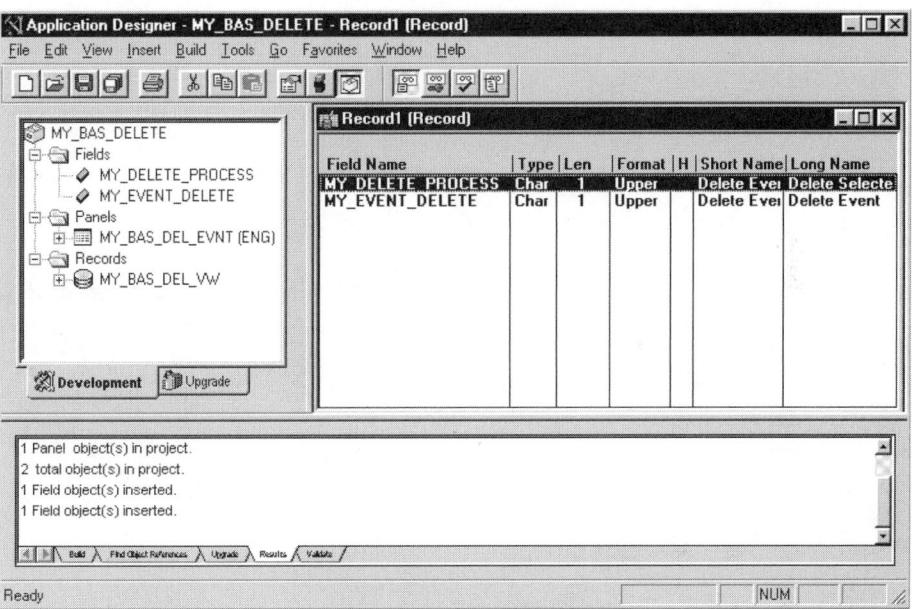

Figure 23.19   Creating a custom Derived/Work record

After the fields are inserted into the record, make certain that the Edit type for MY_EVENT_DELETE field is specified as a Yes/No table edit. Let's save the new record as MY_WORK. Now we need to define the record properties. We have to specify the type record as Derived/Work record (figure 23.20).

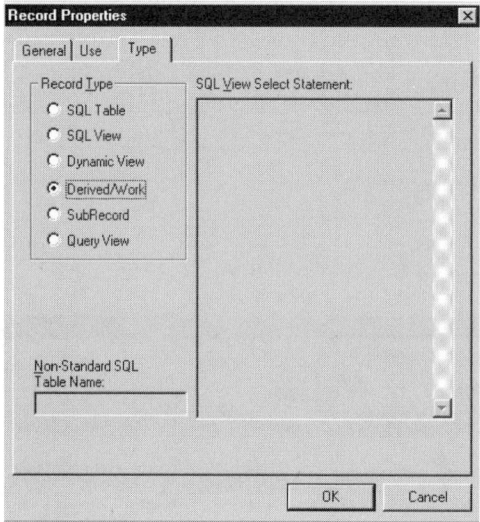

Figure 23.20
Specifying the proper record type
for our custom work record

**Figure 23.21   The MY_WORK
record is created as a
Derived/Work record**

After filling in the record description in the General tab, we save our new record, and it is automatically added to our project (figure 23.21).

Since the Derived/Work records are usually used as placeholders for different PeopleCode events, there is no need to create a database level table.

23.3.3   Adding Derived/Work fields to our panel

Our next step is to add the newly created derived fields to our panel. We start with the MY_DELETE_EVENT field and place it on the panel as shown in figure 23.22.

Let's also add the MY_DELETE_PROCESS field to our panel. This field is used to initiate the deletion process. This time, we use a push button field type as shown in figure 23.23.

As discussed in part 2 of this book, command push buttons are associated with a Record.Field. When a user presses a push button, the corresponding `FieldChange` PeopleCode event is triggered.

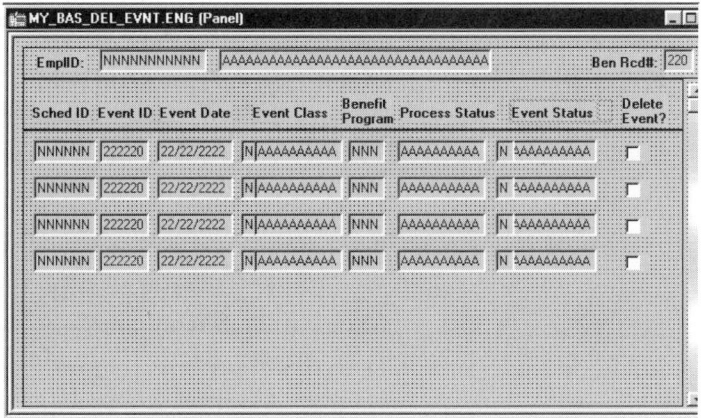

Figure 23.22   Adding Derived/Work field to a panel

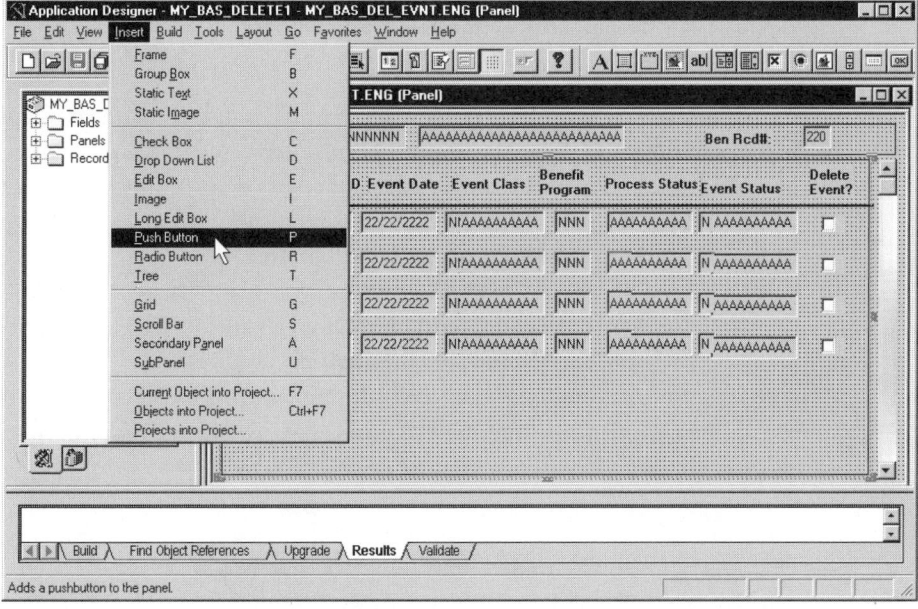

Figure 23.23   Adding a push button field to the panel

We place this field at the bottom of the panel as a stand-alone field, so users can click on it when they decide to execute the Delete script. If you look at the panel in figure 23.24, you'll notice that the newly added button looks a little awkward: it has multiplied into four copies.

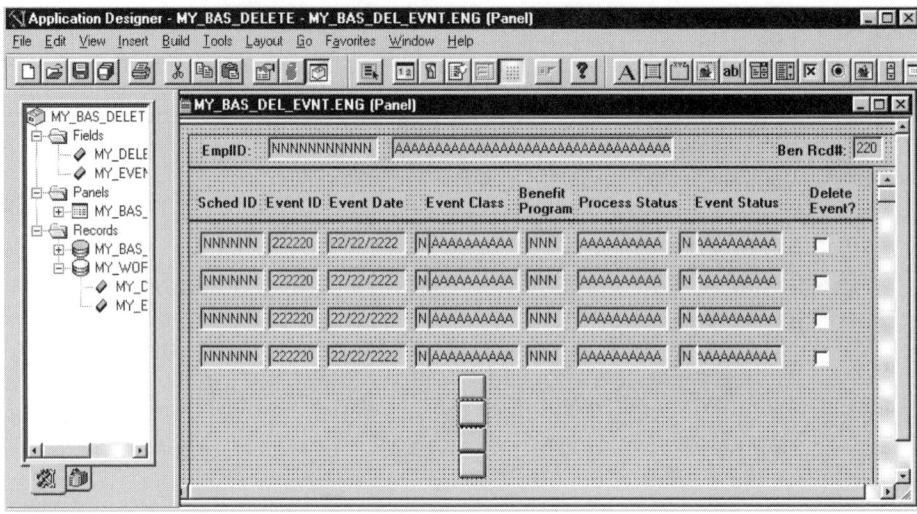

Figure 23.24   The new push button field looks awkward

The reason why we have the four push buttons instead of one is that this field now belongs to the scroll bar area with four occurrences. Any field that belongs to this scroll bar area will be shown in as many occurrences, as defined in the scroll bar properties. Before linking the push button field to our Derived/Work record, let's open the panel order and move the field out of the scroll bar area.

TIP   When creating a push button for an entire panel, be certain it is placed outside of the scroll bar with multiple occurrences.

Let's select the highlighted field and move it to the Level 0 area of the panel (figure 23.26.

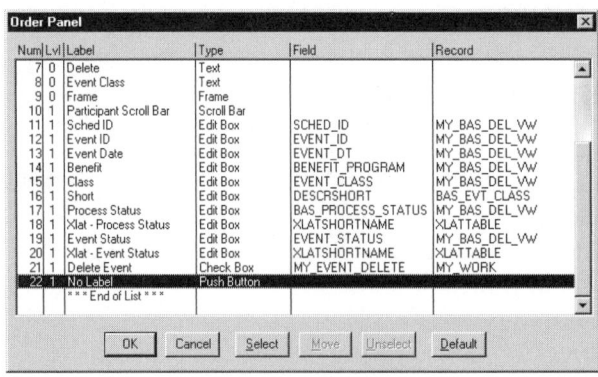

Figure 23.25
At this moment the new push button field belongs to the scroll bar level 1 area

CHAPTER 23   ADDING NEW FUNCTIONALITY

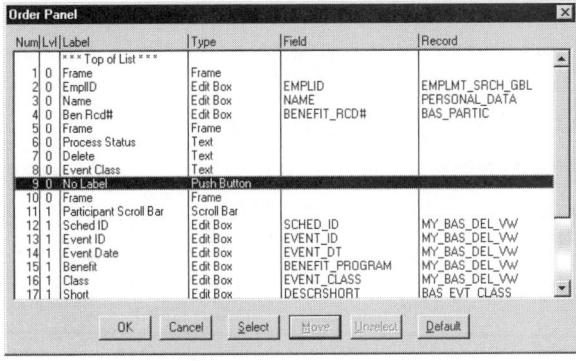

Figure 23.26
Moving the push button field to Level 0

After clicking on the OK button, our panel looks as shown in figure 23.27.

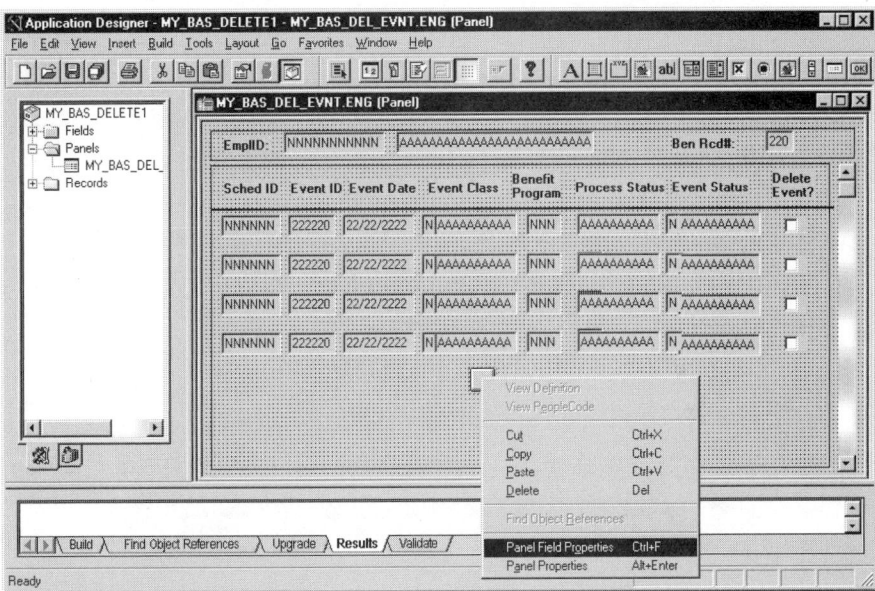

Figure 23.27   Now the push button has been moved out of the scroll bar area

Now we need to set up the push button field properties. This is a special field. It allows you to execute a command or process or call a secondary panel. We already discussed the usage of push buttons in part 2 of this book. Since we will be using this field in order to execute our PeopleCode `Delete` script, the type of push button must be specified as Command. When the user presses the push button, the PeopleSoft Application Processor automatically triggers the PeopleCode script associated with the `FieldChange` event for the MY_DELETE_PROCESS field (figure 23.28). After all the panel's setup is done, we can work on creating our PeopleCode event scripts.

In this panel, we also link our Derived/Work record MY_WORK and the MY_DELETE_PROCESS field with the push button. Let's switch to the second panel in this panel group and specify the label for our new field (figure 23.29).

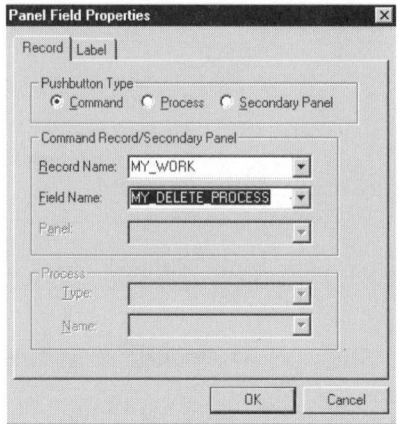

Figure 23.28   Specifying the push button type as Command

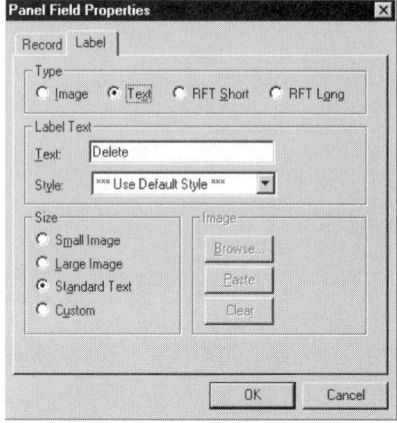

Figure 23.29   Specifying a label for our push button

Note that we used Text as the label type for our push button and specified it as Delete.

TIP   PeopleSoft recommends using short names for push buttons. The long description of the field itself will be shown as a push button tools tip.

After clicking on the OK button, our panel looks as shown in figure 23.30.

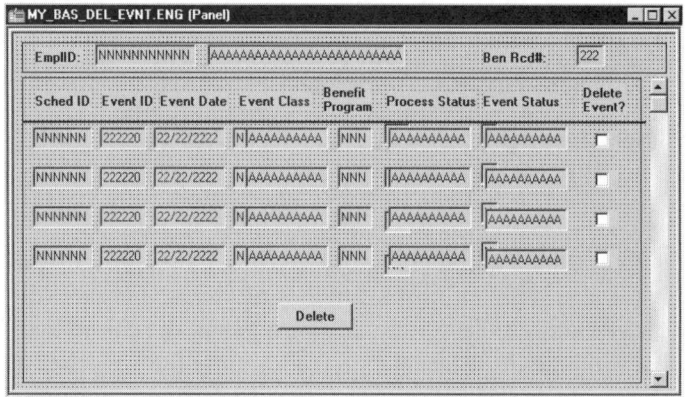

Figure 23.30   Push button Delete is added to the panel

It looks as though we now have all the fields we need. We can test the panel once again in the test mode, to be certain that all fields are aligned, but in order to comprehensively test our new panel, it should be placed into a panel group and menu.

23.4 CREATING A CUSTOM PANEL GROUP

Let's select File → New → Panel Group from the Application Designer and add our panel to the panel group (Insert → Panel) (figure 23.31).

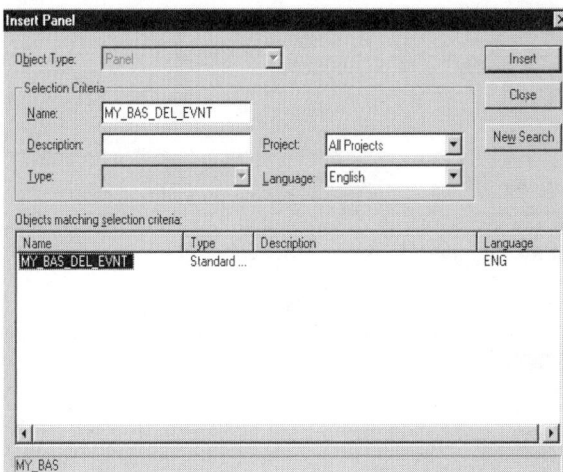

Figure 23.31
Adding the MY_BAS_DEL_EVNT panel to a panel group

After the panel is added, don't forget to click on the Close button. You get a panel group with the default Item Name and Item Label. These values may be changed. Let's set the Item Label to Event Delete as shown in figure 23.32.

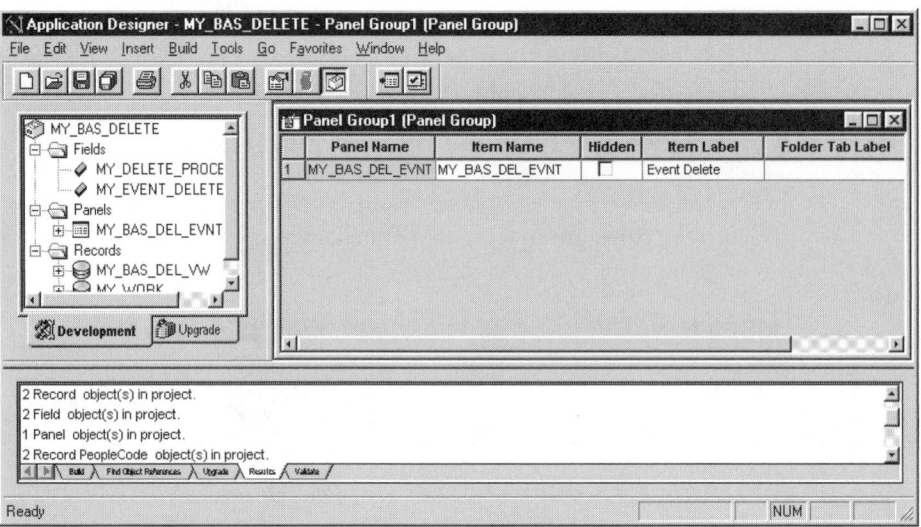

Figure 23.32 Specifying the Item label in the new panel

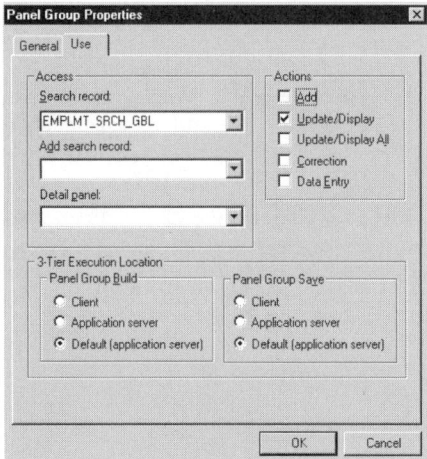

Figure 23.33 Specifying panel group properties

Our next step is to set the panel's properties. Click on the tool bar button and fill in the Panel Group Description and Comments fields in the General tab of the Panel Group Properties panel (figure 23.33). Switch to the Use tab and select the proper search record. Since our header information on the panel is the employee's information, it makes sense to select the EMPLMT_SRCH_GBL view as our search record.

Now we can save the panel group as MY_BAS_DEL_EVNT (figure 23.34).

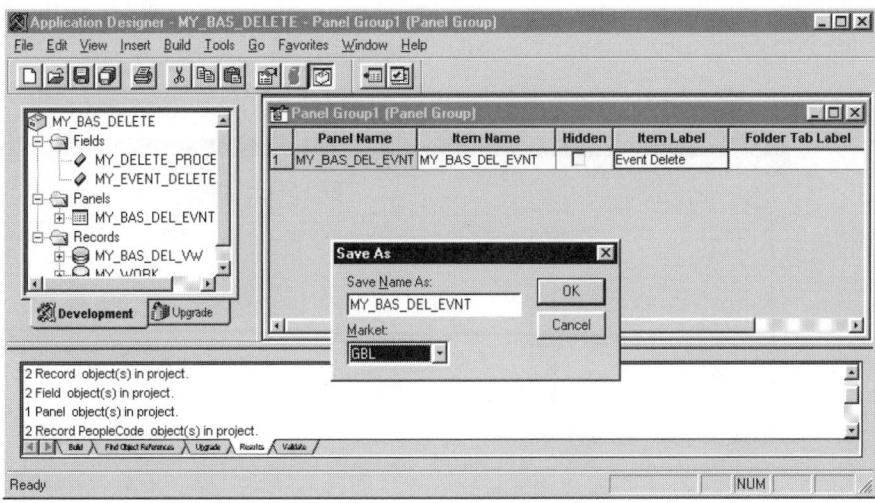

Figure 23.34   Saving the new panel group as MY_BAS_DEL_EVNT

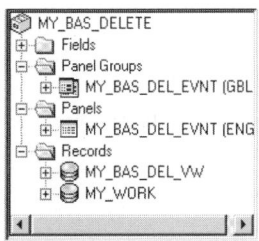

Figure 23.35   The new panel group is added to our project

After our new panel group is saved, the MY_BAS_DELETE project looks like that shown in figure 23.35.

23.5 MODIFYING A MENU

Since our new panel is a part of Benefits Administration, we attach the new custom panel group to the Administer Automated Benefits menu.

Let's open Menu → Administer Automated Benefits. Click on the Process menu bar and select an empty rectangle (figure 23.36).

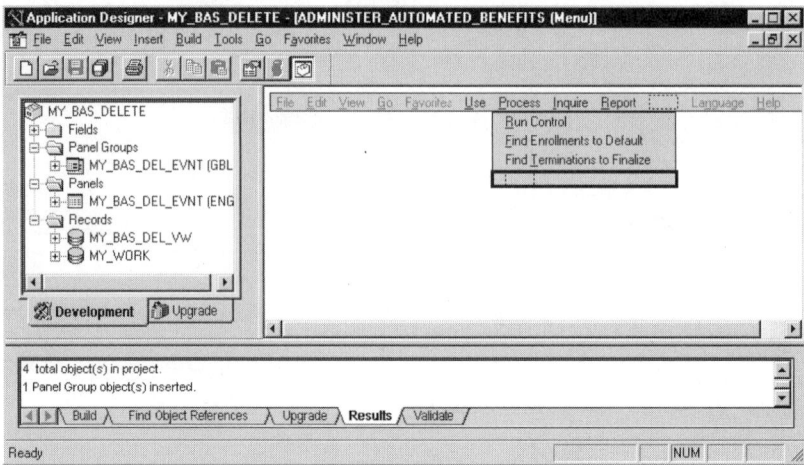

Figure 23.36   Selecting a menu to customize

Double-click on the empty rectangle and specify the new menu item properties (figure 23.37).

Figure 23.37
Specifying menu item properties

Click on the Select button to attach our custom panel to the new menu item.

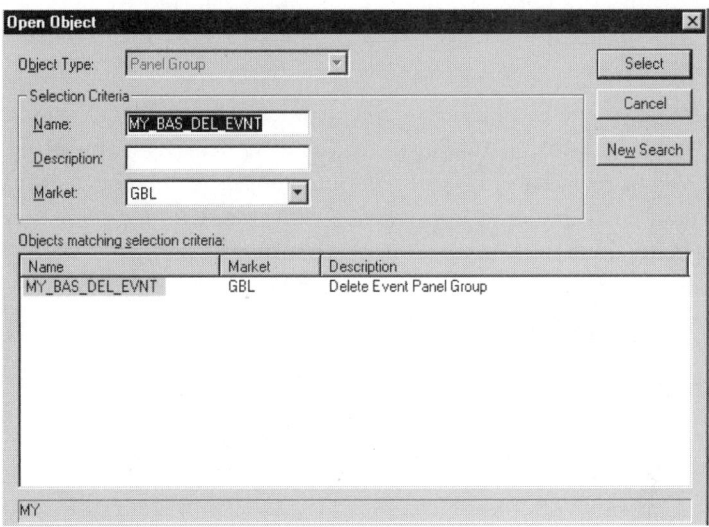

Figure 23.38   Selecting the proper panel group for a new menu item

After clicking on the Select button, the new menu item is inserted into the menu as shown in figure 23.39.

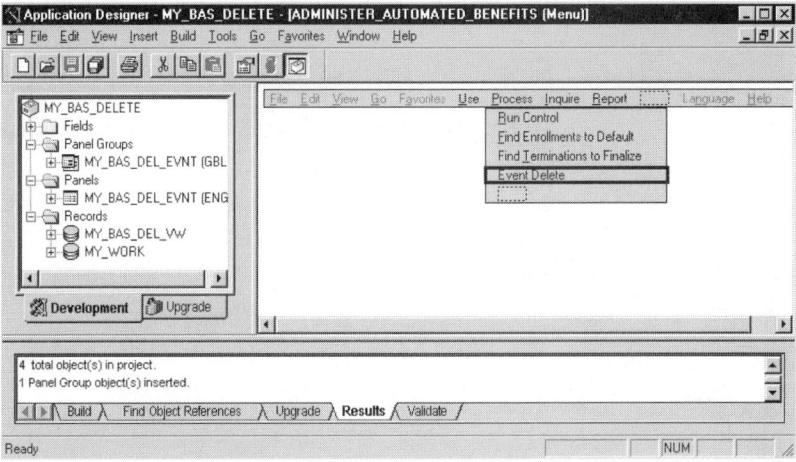

Figure 23.39   The Event Delete menu item is added to the Administer Automatic Benefits menu

When the menu is saved, it is automatically added to our project.

WARNING You can only add an entire menu to your project and not an individual menu item.

When the upgrade project gets executed, let's say, to migrate your modifications to production, the entire Administer Automated Benefits menu in the production database will be replaced with the menu from your development environment. If your development environment is not in synch with production, or concurrent modifications are being done to the menu, this exercise may be dangerous because your entire menu will overlay the production version. Of course, if you execute the Compare and Report process before migration, such an exercise would identify the differences.

23.6   *ADDING A PEOPLECODE SCRIPT*

Our customizations are almost done, and you may be wondering how we are actually going to delete the selected Benefits Administration events. Remember that we just created a Derived/Work record and added the two fields from this record to our custom panel. Now is the time to write a PeopleCode script that will perform the deletion of the marked records.

Let's open the MY_WORK record by double-clicking on the record in the project and view the PeopleCode events by clicking the ⬚ tool bar button, or selecting View → View PeopleCode from the Application Designer Menu (figure 23.40).

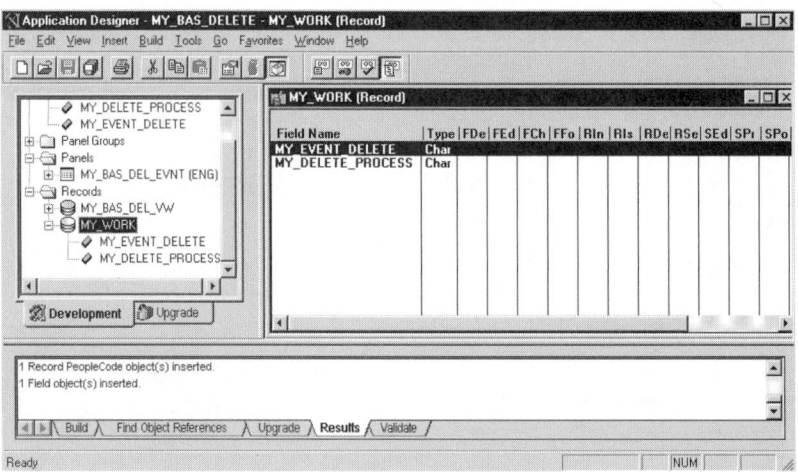

Figure 23.40   The PeopleCode events of the MY_WORK record

We have to accomplish two tasks here. The first is to allow a preliminary selection of events for the potential deletion of all records associated with each selected event. The second task is the actual deletion of the events marked by our users.

Let's start with the first task. Recall that only nonfinalized events can be deleted. In order to distinguish between finalized and non finalized events, we need to check the BAS_PROCESS_STATUS field of the MY_BAS_DEL_VW record. We'll place our code into the RowInit event of the MY_EVENT_DELETE field. The PeopleCode program shown in figure 23.41 should be sufficient to perform the task.

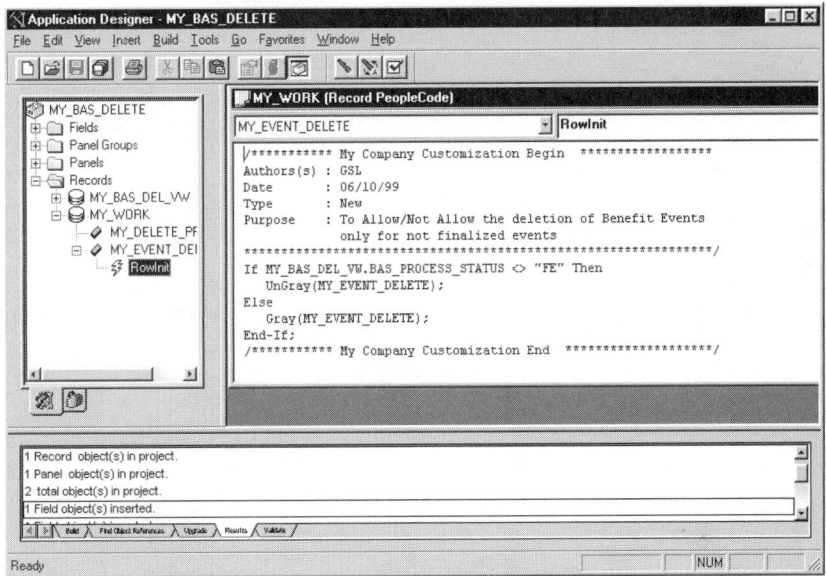

Figure 23.41   Adding a PeopleCode to the RowInit event

As you can see from figure 23.41, this simple code is saved and added to our project. It checks if the BAS_PROCESS_STATUS is equal to 'FE' (Finalized-Enrolled) and based on the result of the comparison, it either grays out (disables) or makes the Event Delete field available to users.

Our second task is a bit more complex. When users select an event for deletion, we have to delete all records associated with this event (e.g., all rows added to the database when the event was created). Therefore, detailed knowledge of the Benefits Administration module is necessary. Assuming that we, as developers, are familiar with this product, our next PeopleCode program will look like this:

```
For &ROW = ActiveRowCount(MY_BAS_DEL_VW.EMPLID) To 1 Step - 1
   &DELETE = FetchValue(MY_EVENT_DELETE, &ROW);
   &SCHED_ID = FetchValue(MY_BAS_DEL_VW.SCHED_ID, &ROW);
```

```
    &EMPLID = FetchValue(MY_BAS_DEL_VW.EMPLID, &ROW);
    &BENEFIT_RCD# = FetchValue(MY_BAS_DEL_VW.BENEFIT_RCD#, &ROW);
    &EVENT_ID = FetchValue(MY_BAS_DEL_VW.EVENT_ID, &ROW);
    If &DELETE = "Y" Then
        DeleteRow(RECORD.MY_BAS_DEL_VW, &ROW);
        SQLExec("delete from ps_bas_partic  where sched_id = :1 and emplid =
:2 and benefit_rcd# = :3 and event_id = :4", &SCHED_ID, &EMPLID,
&BENEFIT_RCD#, &EVENT_ID);


        SQLExec("delete from ps_bas_partic_plan where sched_id = :1 and emplid
= :2 and benefit_rcd# = :3 and
event_id = :4", &SCHED_ID, &EMPLID, &BENEFIT_RCD#, &EVENT_ID);
        SQLExec("delete from ps_bas_partic_optn where sched_id = :1 and emplid
= :2 and benefit_rcd# = :3 and event_id = :4", &SCHED_ID, &EMPLID,
&BENEFIT_RCD#, &EVENT_ID);
        SQLExec("delete from ps_bas_partic_cost where sched_id = :1 and emplid
= :2 and benefit_rcd# = :3 and event_id = :4", &SCHED_ID, &EMPLID,
&BENEFIT_RCD#, &EVENT_ID);
        SQLExec("delete from ps_bas_partic_dpnd where sched_id = :1 and emplid
= :2 and benefit_rcd# = :3 and event_id = :4", &SCHED_ID, &EMPLID,
&BENEFIT_RCD#, &EVENT_ID);
        SQLExec("delete from ps_bas_partic_invt where sched_id = :1 and emplid
= :2 and benefit_rcd# = :3 and event_id = :4", &SCHED_ID, &EMPLID,
&BENEFIT_RCD#, &EVENT_ID);
    End-If;
End-For;
```

Let's examine our PeopleCode. Our goal here is to delete records from the following BenAdmin tables:

- PS_BAS_PARTIC
- PS_BAS_PARTIC_PLAN
- PS_BAS_PARTIC_OPTN
- PS_BAS_PARTIC_COST
- PS_BAS_PARTIC_DPND
- PS_BAS_PARTIC_INVT

Since we need to delete only records selected by our user, the first part of the code selects the MY_EVENT_DELETE field from every row (in the For loop) and checks if it is marked by users for deletion. It also fetches key fields such as SCHED_ID, EMPLID, BENEFIT_RCD#, and EVENT_ID for each record and uses these fields as bind variables in the database Delete statements.

Please note that we are performing the deletions by using the SQLExec commands because there are a multitude of tables that contain information for each Benefit event.

Now we need to make a decision on where to place this PeopleCode program. In other words, what PeopleCode event should the program belong to? The first thought would be to place it in the `FieldChange` event of the MY_DELETE_PROCESS record. After all, we created the push button field in the panel to do just that. We also know that push button commands should have their processes in the `FieldChange` event, because this event is triggered when the button is pushed. But if you recall our PeopleCode discussions in part 3 of this book, since our PeopleCode contains the SQLExec statements, they could only be issued in the `SavePreChg`, `WorkFlow`, or `SavePostChg` events. In order to resolve this conflict, let's use a trick here. As soon as the push button is activated, it will trigger the PeopleCode from the `FieldChange` event (figure 23.42).

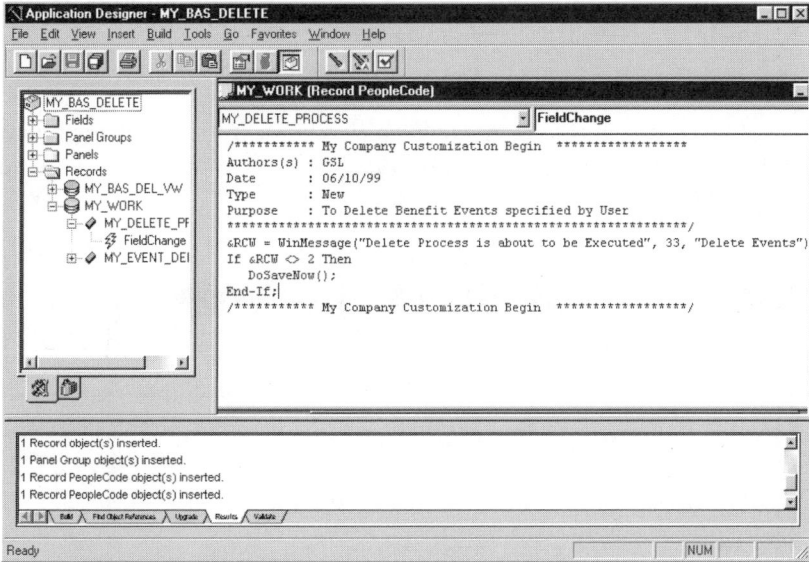

Figure 23.42 The FieldChange event PeopleCode script executed when the Delete push button is clicked on.

In the PeopleCode shown in figure 23.42, we first provide our users with a facility to cancel the `Delete` request by prompting them to accept or cancel their request. It's always a good idea to give your users a second chance to decide if they really want to delete the records. If they decide to go on, we execute the PeopleCode `DoSaveNow()` function. This function, in turn, triggers the execution of all `Save` events. Therefore, if we place our PeopleCode program described in the previous page into the `SavePostChg` event, it will be executed immediately after the user clicks on the OK button of the prompt box.

Let's select the `SavePostChg` event (figure 23.43).

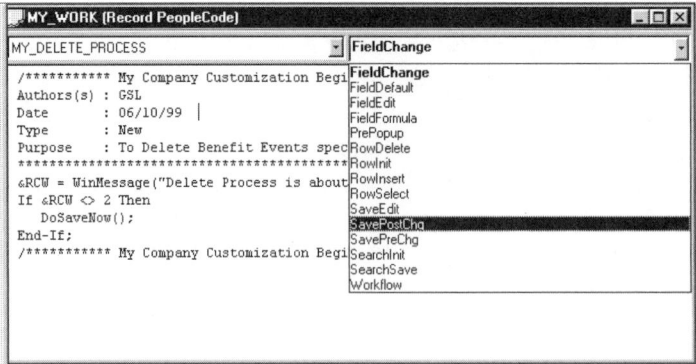

Figure 23.43   Selecting the SavePostChg event

Our next step is to copy the PeopleCode we created earlier and paste it into the `SavePostChg` event. We also add some comments as a standard header (figure 23.44).

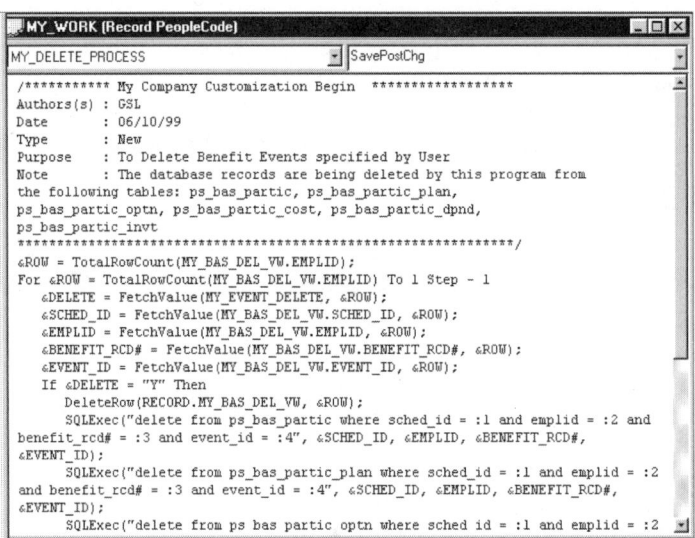

Figure 23.44   Adding a PeopleCode program to delete all selected events.

After saving the PeopleCode script and adding it to our project, we just need to grant security access to our users and ourselves before testing.

23.7 GRANTING SECURITY ACCESS

Navigation: Go → PeopleTools → Security Administrator → Open → ALLPANLS
→Menu Items

Select the ADMINISTER_AUTOMATIC_BENEFITS menu.

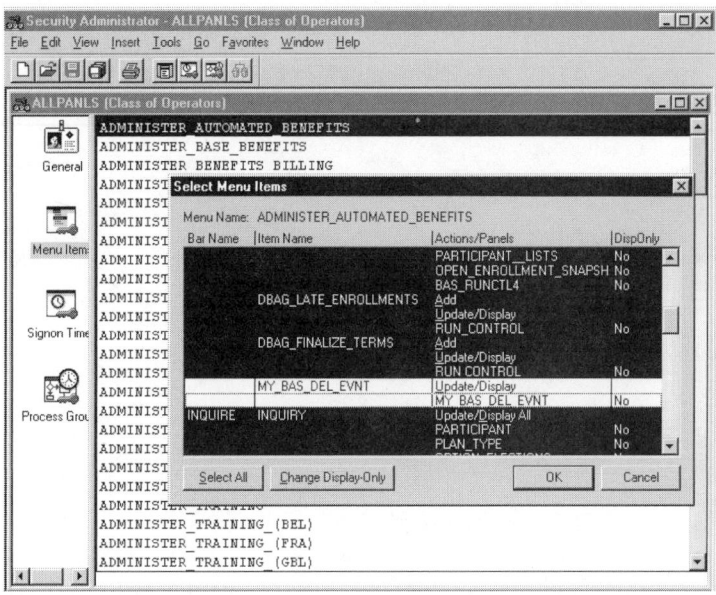

Figure 23.45   Granting security access to MY_BAS_DEL_EVT menu item

Highlight the two lines that belong to the MY_BAS_DEL_EVNT menu item, press OK, and save the security changes for operator class ALLPANLS. Repeat the same steps for your BenAdmin user's access.

Now is the time for a real test.

23.8 TESTING OUR CHANGES

Navigation: Go → Compensate Employees → Administer Automated Benefits → Use → Event Delete

Let's select the same employee ID, 8845, as we did at the beginning of our chapter.

Our new Event Delete panel appears showing all BenAdmin events associated with the selected employee. When scrolling through the records, we can see that for all `Finalized/Enrolled` events (Process Status= `Enrolled`) our Delete Event checkboxes are correctly grayed out, not allowing users to delete these events. Three events remain available for deletion: VN97, VN98, and VNBEM. Click on the Delete Event checkbox for these three open events, then click on the Delete push button as shown in figure 23.46.

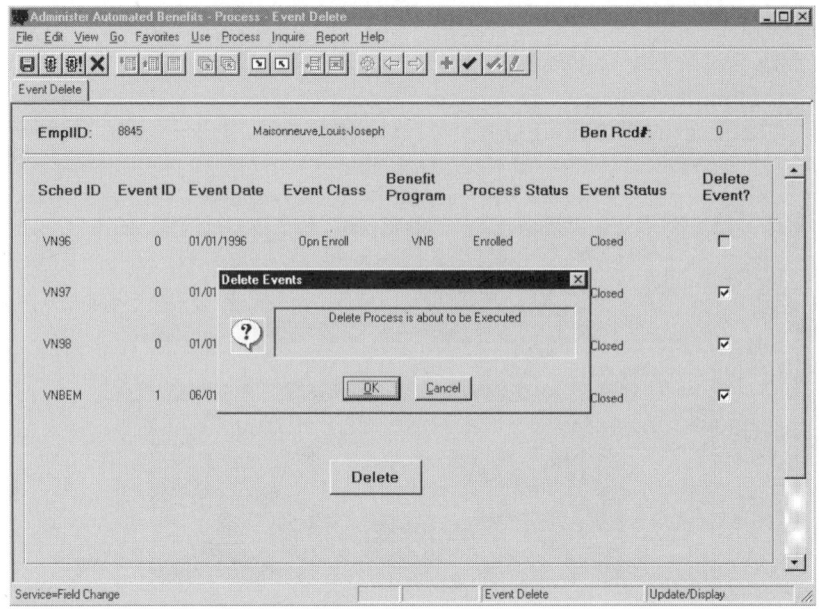

Figure 23.46   Deleting three open events

So far, the PeopleCode that we placed in our events worked just fine. We've got a prompt that gave us an opportunity to cancel the Delete process if necessary. Let's say we want to go ahead and click on the OK button. The results of our `Delete` script execution from the `SavePostChg` PeopleCode event will be as displayed in figure 23.47.

We see only two events now. These two events were not targeted for deletion. It looks like all our changes are working. Since our modification involved a database update, it is necessary to verify if the records have been actually deleted from the tables. Using database tools such as SQLPlus for Oracle or SQL Talk in SQL Server or any other tool that is available in your environment, you can simply select the information from the tables specified in our `Delete` PeopleCode script and make certain that the records are not there.

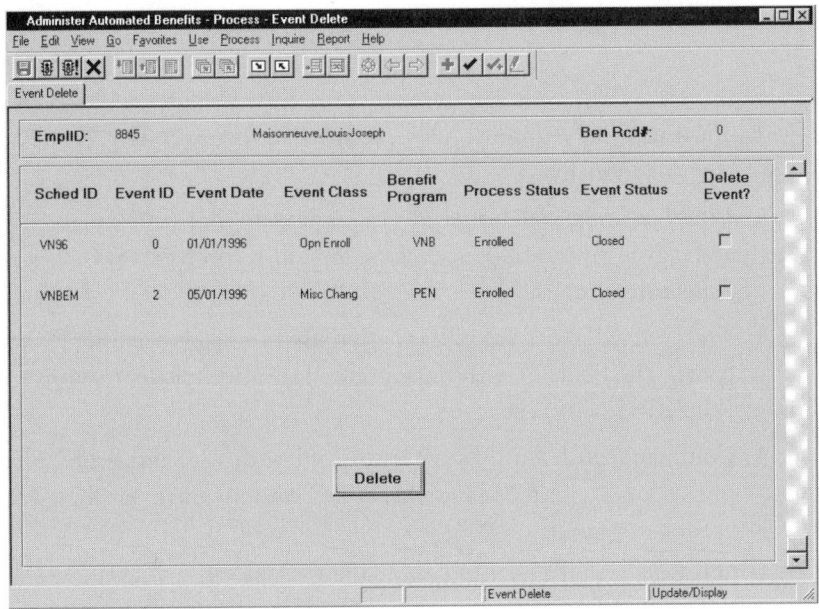

Figure 23.47   All three selected events have been deleted from the screen and from the database

23.9   *POSSIBLE IMPACT ON FUTURE UPGRADES*

In this chapter we illustrated a classical example of enhancing user functionality by using the "Add" as opposed to the "Modify" approach. During our development process we were trying to minimize the impact on future upgrades. We developed our own custom records, panel, PeopleCode programs, panel group, and menu item. As in the previous chapter, we used distinctive names for all of our objects, documented our changes, and created a project to keep track of all customizations. The only modified PeopleSoft-delivered object was the Administer Automated Benefits menu to which we added our newly created menu item, linking it to our custom panel group.

Still, as we have already discussed, there is always a possibility that PeopleSoft delivers the similar or same functionality. In this case, you have to evaluate the PeopleSoft changes. If PeopleSoft's new features are in fact similar to ours, they should take precedence over our own.

1 You can greatly improve user productivity by extending PeopleSoft-delivered functionality

2 When creating your panel by cloning a delivered panel, make certain that all fields in your new panel belong to your records. Always check the Order panel carefully.

3 The Derived/Work records are often used to display temporary values on a panel. The fields in such records are ideal placeholders to store and trigger PeopleCode programs.

4 Command push buttons are associated with a record.field. When a user presses on a push button, the corresponding Field Change PeopleCode event is triggered.

5 When your panel has a functionality to delete data from database tables, it is a good idea to give your users an option to confirm or cancel the deletion.

Customizing security search records, PeopleCode, and menus

In the previous chapter, we discussed the customization of PeopleSoft-delivered objects and creation of new objects such as fields, records, panels, panel groups, and some PeopleCode scripts. In the next example, we will demonstrate how to change the behavior of PeopleSoft's record selection mechanism by simply modifying the delivered search record. Please keep in mind that this exercise requires a good understanding of PeopleSoft's department security and security search records.

Let's turn to exercise 4:

Allow users to access records of employees transferred to another department.

527

Many PeopleSoft HRMS developers have often heard their users in HR departments complain that they can not access the records of their former employees who had been transferred to different departments. In fact, often a business reason exists for such requests. Of course, security must be in place to prevent users from having access to unauthorized information. Consequently, an HR manager can have access to the records of only those employees who belong to the department to which the HR manager is presently assigned. In this exercise, we need to find a way to allow HR managers access to the records of their former employees assigned to different departments. First, let's identify the objects that need to be customized or created.

24.1 WHAT OBJECTS SHOULD BE CUSTOMIZED OR ADDED?

Let's refresh our knowledge on what exactly prevents users from seeing their former employee's records.

As discussed in part 2 of this book, some panels in PeopleSoft are accessed with the help of special search views. These views are designed to restrict the user's access to unauthorized data. In HRMS, for example, employee information is protected based on the Department Security delivered by PeopleSoft.

When we select a particular employee's record by entering full or partial information in the search box, the PeopleSoft Application Processor builds a `Select` statement according to the information entered by the user, and based on the search record specified for the particular Panel Group. Our goal, therefore, is to look at the security search record and figure out how to modify it.

In order to understand how PeopleSoft's Application Processor works, and what exactly happens when a user enters the particular selection criteria, let's use the PeopleSoft `Trace` utility.

First we need to check if the trace filename is specified in the Configuration Manager panel (figure 24.1).

After the trace is activated, the system will write the trace file to the specified directory. In our case the directory for the trace output file is specified by the environment variable `%TEMP%`. The default filename for the trace file is DBG1.tmp. You can verify the settings for your Windows `Temp` directory in the Process Scheduler tab of the Configuration Manager.

Navigation: Edit → Preferences → Configuration

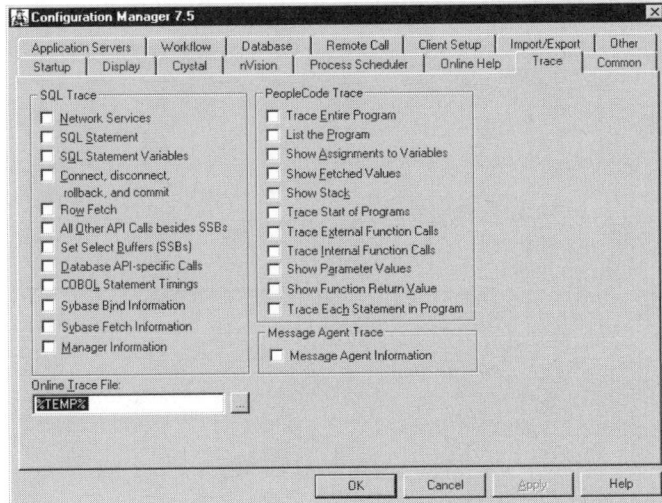

Figure 24.1
Verifying the
Trace filename

Our next step is to activate the trace (figure 24.2).

Navigation: Go → PeopleTools → Utilities

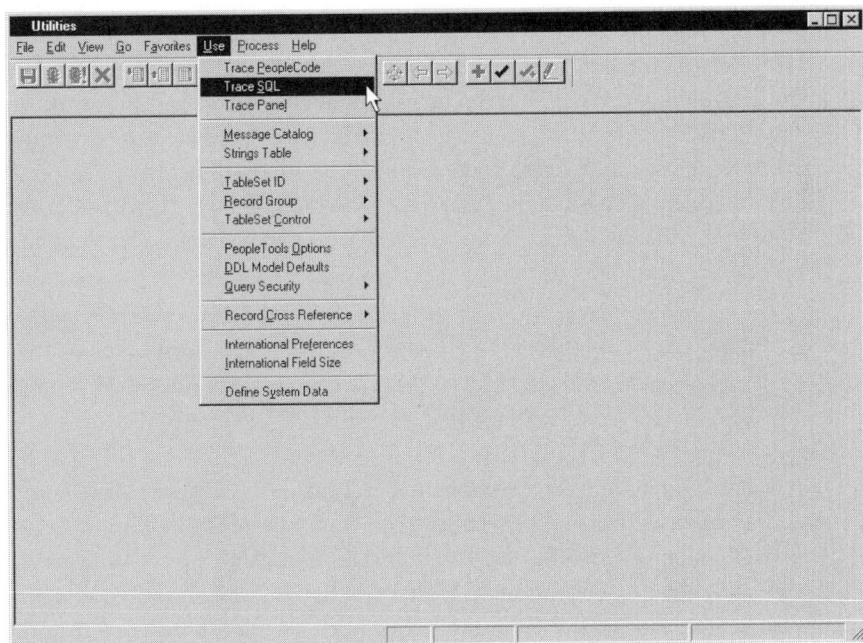

Figure 24.2   Selecting the Trace SQL utility

From the Utilities Menu, select Use → Trace SQL.

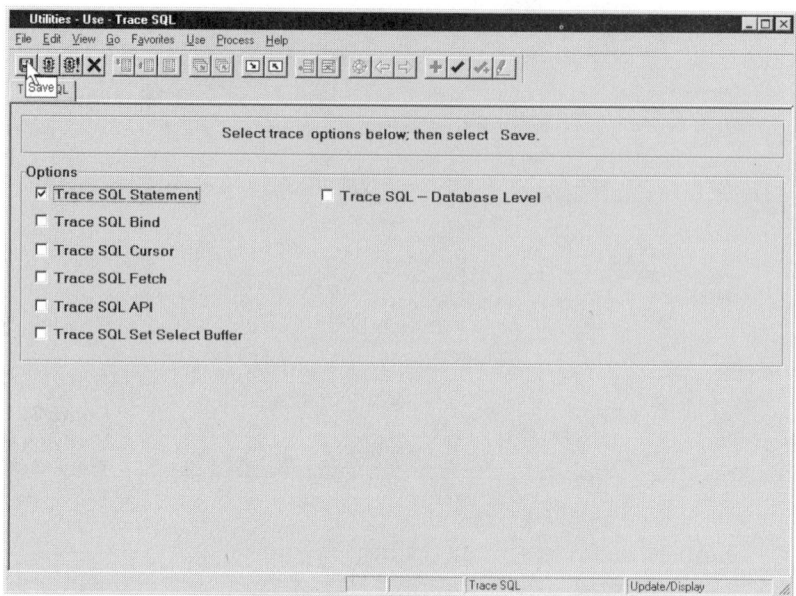

Figure 24.3   The Trace SQL Utility panel

On the panel (in figure 24.3), we can select any combination of traces we need. For our purposes, we select only the first one since we only need to see the SQL statement that Application Processor constructs based on the parameters in our request. Make sure you save the selection. This panel is a bit misleading. When you first open it, the panel already has the `Trace SQL` statement checked on. This is the panel default option. The trace will not be activated until you actually save the selection. Please note that after you activate the trace, all your following steps will be recorded in the trace file.

TIP   In order to make the trace file reasonably small, activate the trace right at the point where you need it and stop the trace as soon as your testing is over. It's always easier to work with smaller files.

After saving the trace options, we minimize the Utilities panel and go through a couple of steps that will provide the information we are looking for.

We type "Smith" as our search criteria name and press OK (figure 24.4).

At this particular moment, we already have all the requested records selected. We should stop the trace, then examine our trace log file. In order to stop the trace, maximize the Utilities panel, unclick the trace selections, then save the panel (figure 24.5).

CHAPTER 24   CUSTOMIZING COMPONENTS

Navigation: Go → Administer_Workforce_(U.S.) → Use → Job Data →
Update/Display All

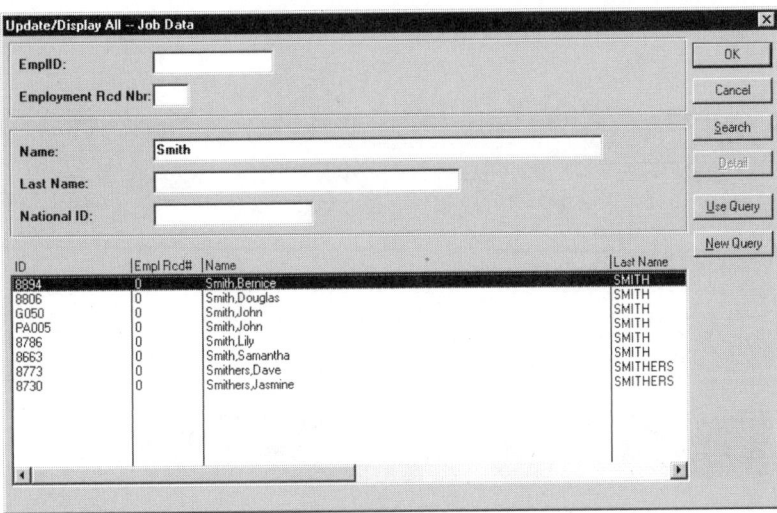

Figure 24.4   Selecting Smith with a trace activated behind the scene

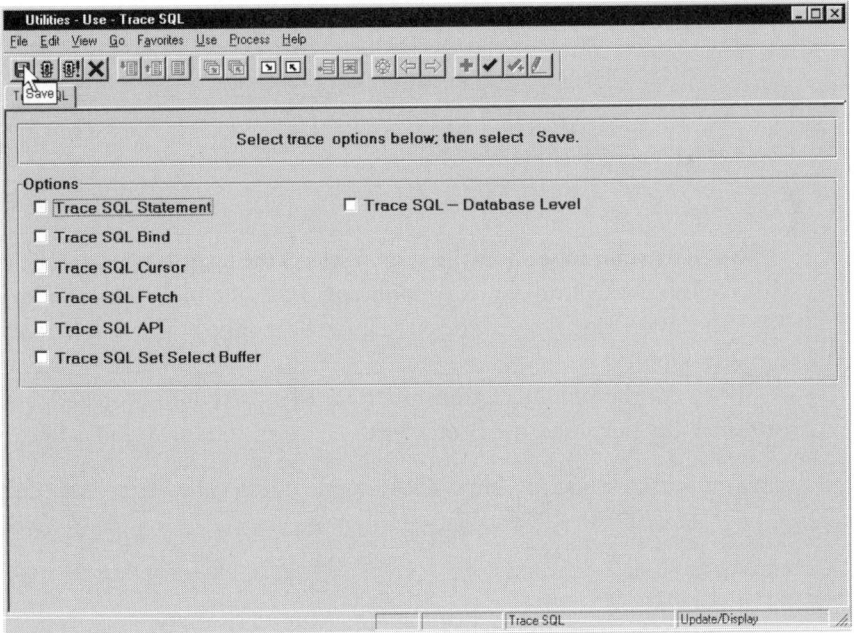

Figure 24.5   Deactivating the Trace utility

TIP	Do not forget to deactivate the Trace utility as soon as the test is done.

Now we can take a look at our trace file.

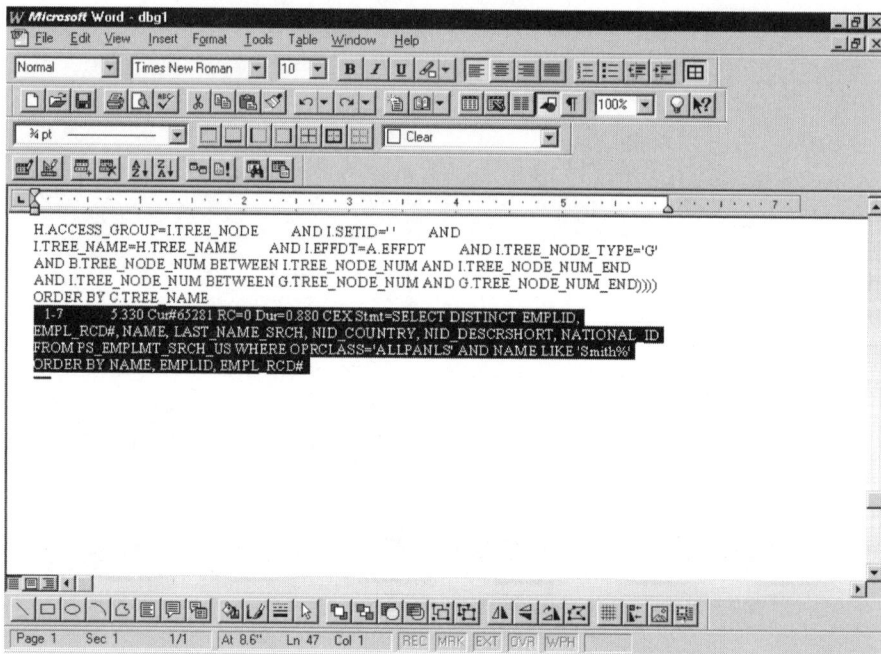

Figure 24.6 A portion of the Trace file

Since we want to see how the system selects the records with the last name starting with "Smith," let's find the corresponding SQL statement in our file. It should be either the last one or close to the end, since we stopped our trace as soon as the selection was done.

If we cut the statement from the trace file, paste into Notepad, and reformat it for readability purposes, the PeopleSoft's Select statement looks like the following:

```
SELECT DISTINCT EMPLID, EMPL_RCD#, NAME, LAST_NAME_SRCH, NID_COUNTRY,
NID_DESCRSHORT, NATIONAL_ID
FROM PS_EMPLMT_SRCH_US
WHERE OPRCLASS='ALLPANLS'
AND NAME LIKE 'Smith%'
ORDER BY NAME, EMPLID, EMPL_RCD#
```

As you can see, the `Select` statement built to get records from the database looks pretty simple. The records are selected from the PS_EMPLMT_SRCH_US table, which is a search record specified for the Job Data panel group. This tells us that this record is responsible for selecting the requested information. The selection is limited to the search criteria ("Smith") and the operator class (ALLPANLS). Since PS_EMPLMT_SRCH_US is a security search view, our `Select` statement only returns the records that the ALLPANLS operator class is allowed to see. Note the `DISTINCT` keyword in the `Select` statement. This way the `Select` returns distinct rows and builds a list box for the operator's further selection. If the operator has an appropriate access to the record, this record is displayed in the list box.

Do we always need to activate the trace in order to figure out what search record is used? No, we demonstrated this as a convenient way to learn what is actually going on behind the scene. The next time you need to deal with search records, you will remember how it works, and the only thing you need to verify then is the security search record used for a particular panel group.

Let's now make certain that the PS_EMPLMT_SRCH_US record is, in fact, the search record for the JOB_DATA panel group. Selections from the PS_EMPMT_SRCH_US record is indicated by ❶.

Navigation: GO → PeopleTools → Application Designer → Open → Pane Group
   → JOB_DATA

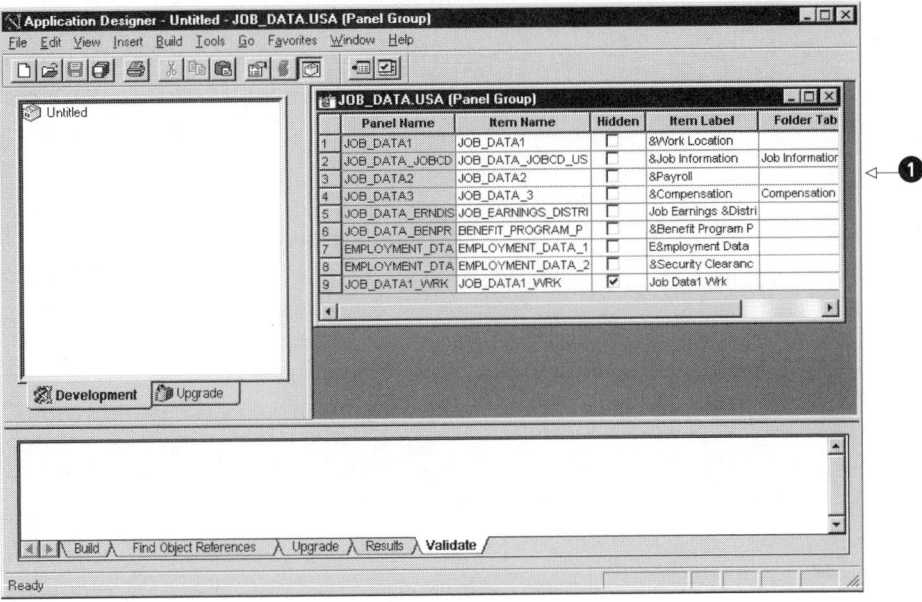

Figure 24.7   Examining the JOB_DATA panel group

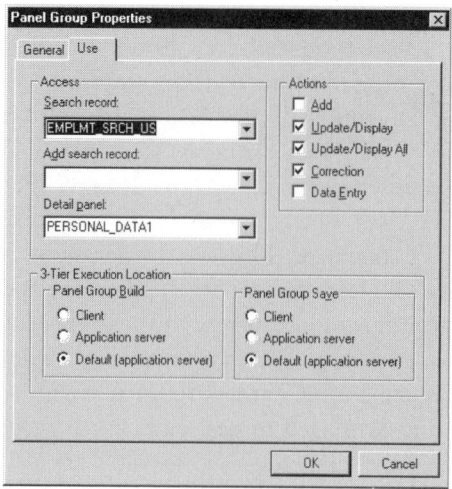

Figure 24.8   Looking for the Search record

In order to find out what search record is attached to this panel group, click on the 🔲 button or select File → Object Properties.

The screen in figure 24.8 appears.

The search record that is used for the JOB_DATA panel group is the EMPLMT_SRCH_US record. In our next step we will open and examine this search record.

Navigation: GO → PeopleTools → Application Designer → Open → Record → EMPLMT_SRCH_US.

After opening the record, let's take a look at its properties. Click on the 🔲 button, then select the Type tab.

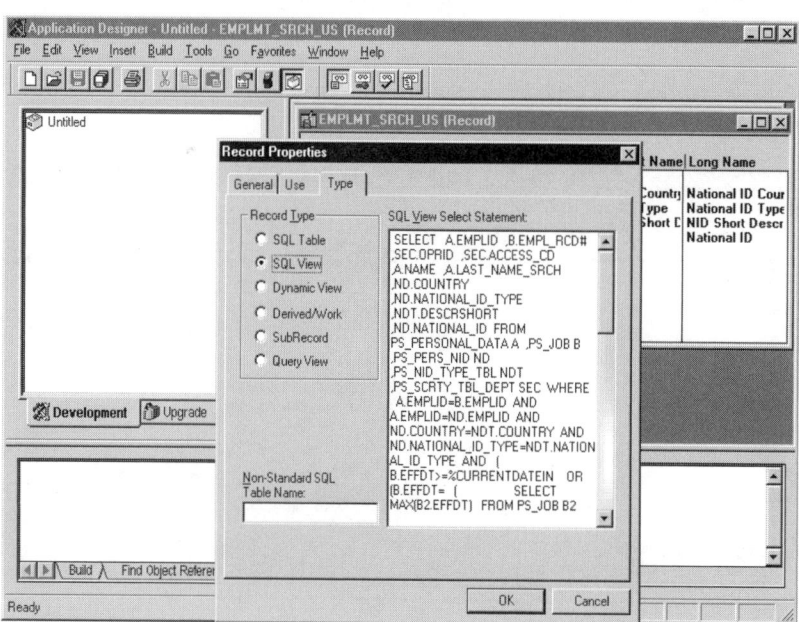

Figure 24.9   The Type tab of the EMPLMT_SRCH_US record properties

Let's copy and paste the SQL view definition, so we can see it better:

Listing 24.1

SQL View Select statement for the EMPLMT_SRCH_US record

```
SELECT A.EMPLID, B.EMPL_RCD#, SEC.OPRID, SEC.ACCESS_CD, A.NAME,
A.LAST_NAME_SRCH, ND.COUNTRY, ND.NATIONAL_ID_TYPE, NDT.DESCRSHORT,
ND.NATIONAL_ID
FROM
PS_PERSONAL_DATA A,
PS_JOB B,
PS_PERS_NID ND,
PS_NID_TYPE_TBL NDT,
PS_SCRTY_TBL_DEPT SEC
WHERE
    A.EMPLID              = B.EMPLID
AND A.EMPLID              = ND.EMPLID
AND ND.COUNTRY            = NDT.COUNTRY
AND ND.NATIONAL_ID_TYPE = NDT.NATIONAL_ID_TYPE
AND (B.EFFDT >= %CURRENTDATEIN
    OR
    (B.EFFDT  =
        (SELECT MAX(B2.EFFDT)
         FROM PS_JOB B2
         WHERE B.EMPLID   = B2.EMPLID
   AND B.EMPL_RCD# = B2.EMPL_RCD#
   AND B2.EFFDT    <= %CURRENTDATEIN)
     AND B.EFFSEQ     =
         (SELECT MAX(B3.EFFSEQ)
          FROM PS_JOB B3
          WHERE B.EMPLID     = B3.EMPLID
             AND B.EMPL_RCD# = B3.EMPL_RCD#
             AND B.EFFDT     = B3.EFFDT )
    )
    )
AND SEC.ACCESS_CD = 'Y'
AND EXISTS
    (SELECT 'X'
    FROM PSTREENODE SEC3
    WHERE SEC3.SETID    = SEC.SETID
    AND SEC3.SETID      = B.SETID_DEPT
    AND SEC3.TREE_NAME = 'DEPT_SECURITY'
    AND SEC3.EFFDT      = SEC.TREE_EFFDT
    AND SEC3.TREE_NODE = B.DEPTID
    AND SEC3.TREE_NODE_NUM BETWEEN
        SEC.TREE_NODE_NUM AND SEC.TREE_NODE_NUM_END
    AND NOT EXISTS
        (SELECT 'X'
         FROM PS_SCRTY_TBL_DEPT SEC2
         WHERE SEC.OPRID  = SEC2.OPRID
         AND   SEC.SETID  = SEC2.SETID
         AND   SEC.TREE_NODE_NUM <> SEC2.TREE_NODE_NUM
```

```
AND     SEC3.TREE_NODE_NUM BETWEEN
        SEC2.TREE_NODE_NUM AND SEC2.TREE_NODE_NUM_END
AND     SEC2.TREE_NODE_NUM BETWEEN
        SEC.TREE_NODE_NUM AND SEC.TREE_NODE_NUM_END
    )

)
```

■

As you may have noticed in listing 24.1, this view definition is fairly complex. Our goal is not to completely redesign this view, but to understand how it can be customized to allow our users access to the required information. This view selects the employee records in departments that a particular operator class is allowed to access. Take a closer look at the view. It selects the latest (EFFDT is in descending order) record from the PS_JOB table, based on the department found in this record and the operator class. What if, instead of selecting the top PS_JOB record, we allow the selection of any record from the department in which the employee used to work in the past or is currently employed? This will allow our users to access employee's records as required. We will perform the actual modifications in the next subchapters. Here, we just have to figure out what objects to modify. Now that we found what object is responsible for the security access, the question is: "Is it safe just to go ahead and change the security view?" And the answer is "Absolutely NOT." This view is used not only in a multitude of panels, but also as a query security record. Changing this view may result in an incorrect panel access as well as inaccurate reporting. Let's find all the objects that use this view.

TIP   Use the Find Object References PeopleSoft utility to identify all the on-line objects that might be affected by your customization.

After the record is displayed, click on Edit → Find Object References (figure 24.10).

At the end of the search for object references, PeopleSoft displays the count of objects found. There are 123 objects currently using the EMPLMT_SRCH_US record. Therefore, if you change the EMPLMT_SRCH_US record, all 123 objects will be affected in one way or another.

A better and safer way to perform our customization would be to create a new custom view based on this record and modify it to satisfy the user's requirements.

What about the panel and the panel group? We have to create a custom panel group with the new security search view attached. In addition, a new menu item must be added to the existing menu. Is that all? Let's take a look at our requirements again. Our users would like to have access to the records of their former employees, but they should not see the salary sensitive information for departments to which they are not supposed to have access. How do we do this? PeopleCode program can help us hide salary-related fields.

CHAPTER 24   CUSTOMIZING COMPONENTS

Navigation: GO → Application Designer → Open → Record → EMPLMT_SRCH_US

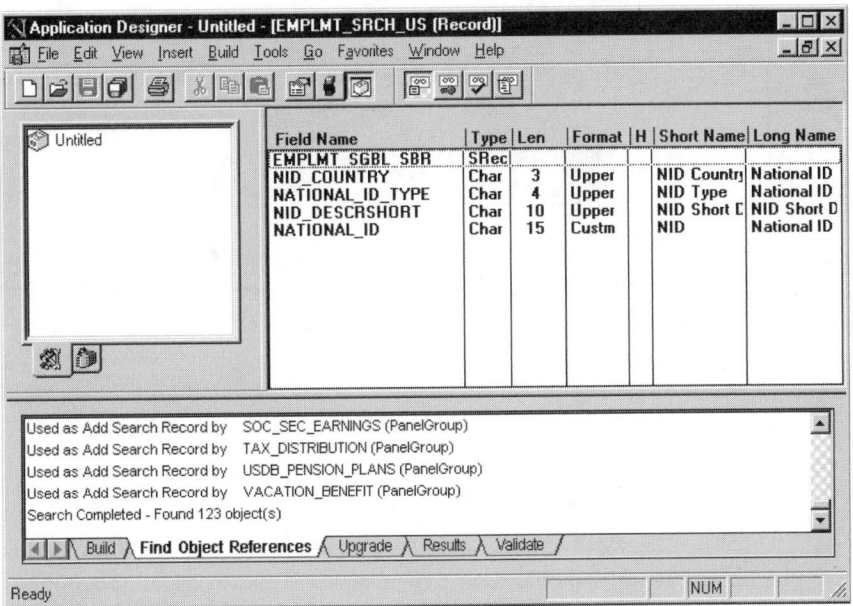

Figure 24.10 Displaying all objects that use the EMPLMT_SRCH_US record

To summarize, we have identified the following objects that must be customized or created:

- a custom security search view
- a panel group with this new view attached
- a menu item
- a PeopleCode script

24.2 CREATING A CUSTOM SECURITY RECORD

Our task is pretty simple. We already learned that our new record should be cloned from the PeopleSoft-delivered EMPLMT_SRCH_US record. Let's open this record and save it as MY_EMPLMT_XFER (figure 24.11).

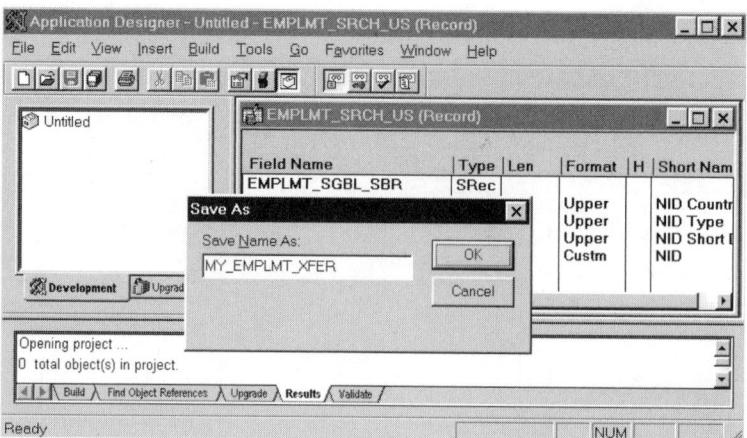

Figure 24.11 Creating the MY_EMPLMT_XFER search view by cloning the
EMPLMT_SRCH_US record

When saving the record, we get a warning message asking if the PeopleCode should be copied along with the record (figure 24.12). Since we are planning to modify the existing SQL view definition, let's answer "Yes," and copy all the PeopleCode events.

Figure 24.12
**Saving PeopleCode programs along
with the record definition**

Since we just created and saved our new object, it is added to a project. Let's save the project as MY_JOB_XFER (figure 24.13).

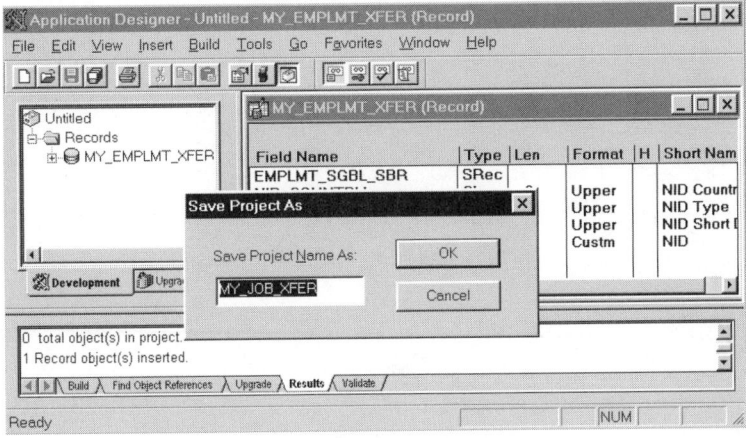

Figure 24.13   Adding the MY_EMPLMT_XFER record to a project

So far, we've created the record definition. Our next task is to modify the actual SQL view definition. Let's press the Alt → Enter and customize our search record.

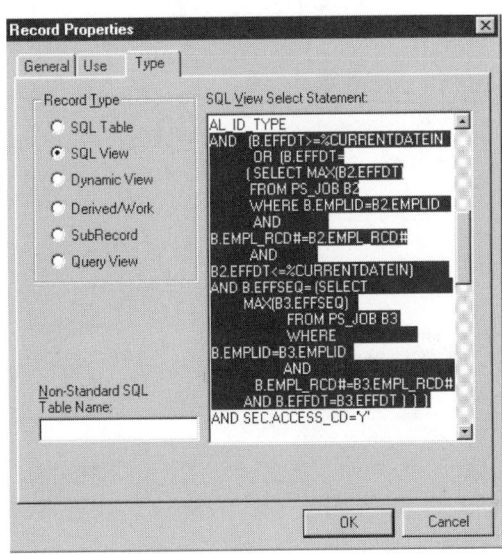

**Figure 24.14
An SQL View definition for the
EMPLMT_SRCH_US record**

As discussed earlier in this chapter, this view is responsible for allowing users access to particular information. The highlighted portion of the view represents the SQL logic that selects the current PS_JOB record. This is exactly a portion of the SQL that we were planning to replace. After deleting the highlighted portion of the Select statement, our new view definition appears as shown in figure 24.15.

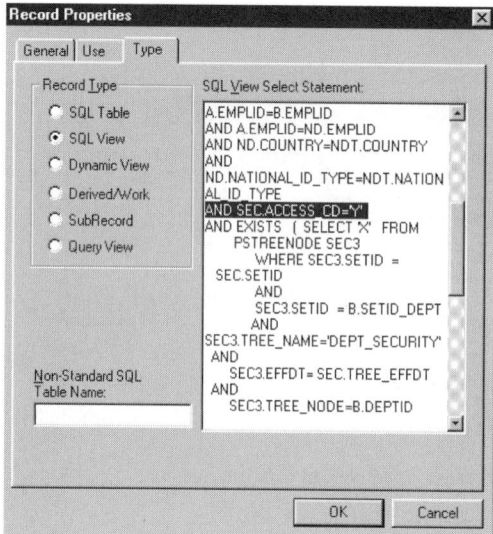

Figure 24.15
The SQL view after deleting the EFFDT logic

After pressing the OK button to accept our changes, let's switch to the first tab of the panel group and document our modifications (figure 24.16).

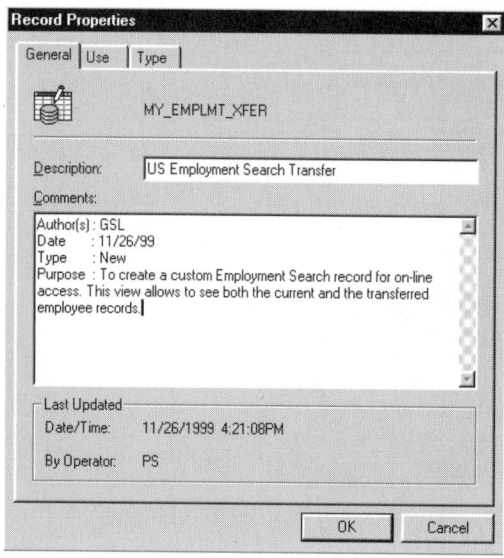

Figure 24.16
Documenting our changes in the General tab of the Record Properties

Our next step is to create a database level view.

Navigation: Build → Current Object

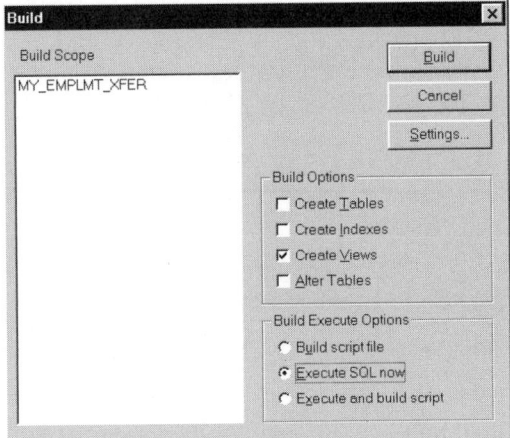

Figure 24.17
Building the database level view

Select Create Views and Execute SQL now options and click on the Build button (figure 24.17).

Our view is ready. We did not get syntax errors which means that the view is valid. Will it work as expected? We'll find this out soon. First, we need to create a new panel group and a new menu item.

24.3 *CREATING A CUSTOM PANEL GROUP*

As you may have already guessed, we are going to clone an existing panel group in order to create our own. Let's find the name of the panel group used in the Administer_Workforce_US menu (figure 24.18).

We open this menu and click on the Use menu bar.

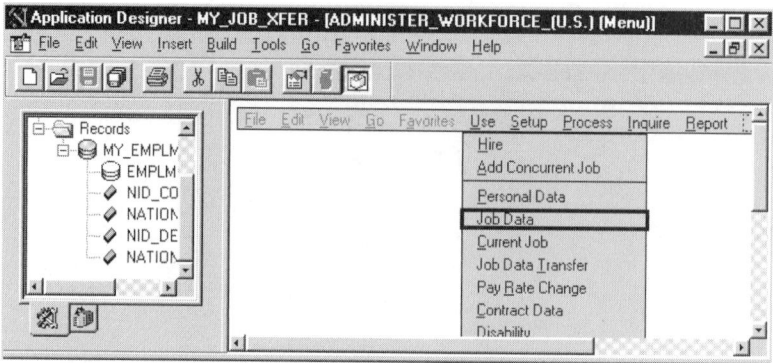

Figure 24.18 Finding the name of a panel group

If we double-click on the Job Data menu item, we see the panel group name and the search record used for this panel group in the Menu Item Properties panel (figure 24.19).

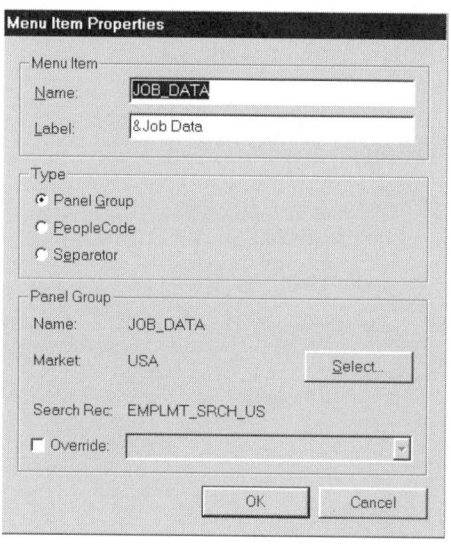

Figure 24.19
The JOB_DATA panel group is used to access the Job Data menu item

Let's open the JOB_DATA panel group and save it as MY_JOB_DATA_XFER (figure 24.20).

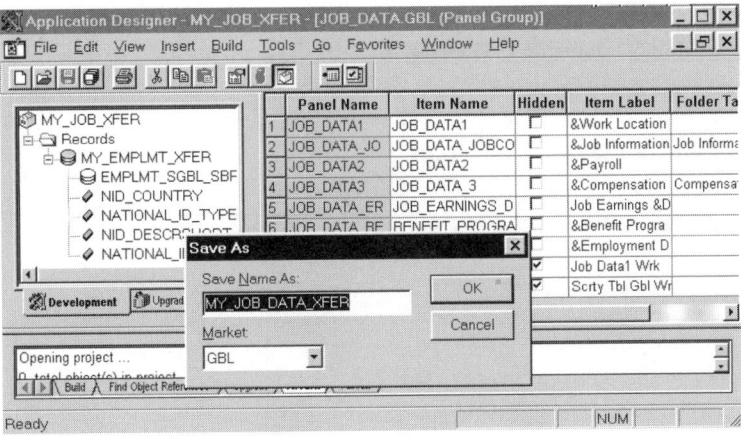

Figure 24.20   Saving the MY_JOB_DATA_XFER panel group

Since we just created another custom object, it is added to our project. The MY_JOB_XFER project now contains two of our custom objects (figure 24.21).

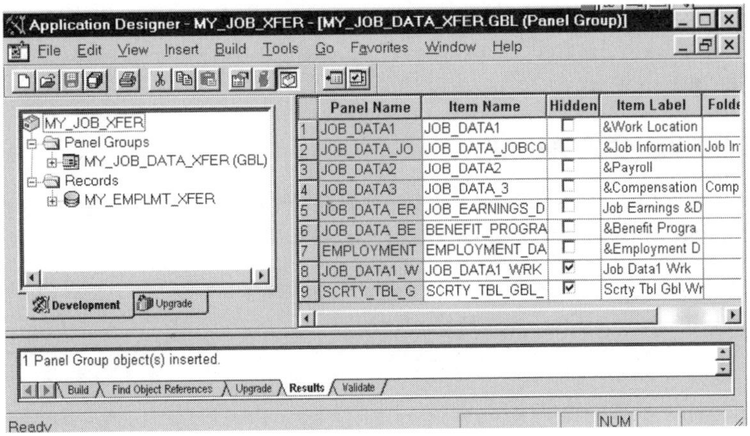

Figure 24.21   A new panel group is added to our project

Even though we added the new panel group to a project, we haven't finished customizing our panel group yet. We just wanted to save our work. Now we'll proceed with the rest of our modifications. Our next step is to modify the panel group properties. We type some useful description in the General tab, then switch to the Use tab of the Panel Group Properties. Let's specify the search record as MY_EMPLMT_XFER (figure 24.22).

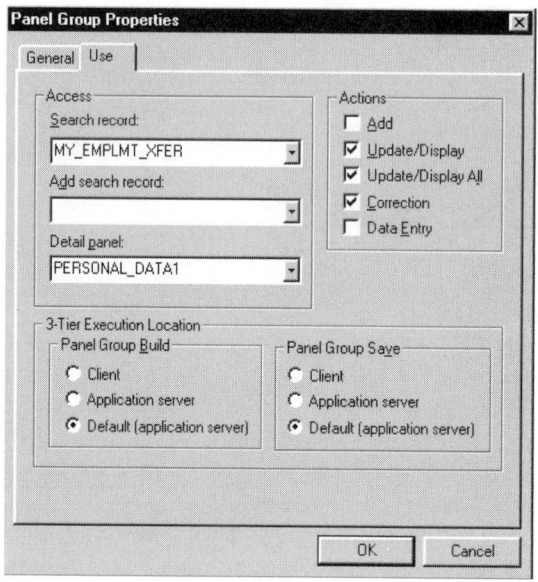

Figure 24.22
Specifying the search record for our custom panel group

Click on the OK button and save our changes. By executing this step, we actually linked the newly created custom search record to the panel group.

We are now ready to modify the menu.

24.4 MODIFYING A MENU

Since our users want the new Job Data Transfer panel group to be accessed from the same menu as the Job Data, we open the ADMINISTER_WORKFORCE_(US) menu (figure 24.23).

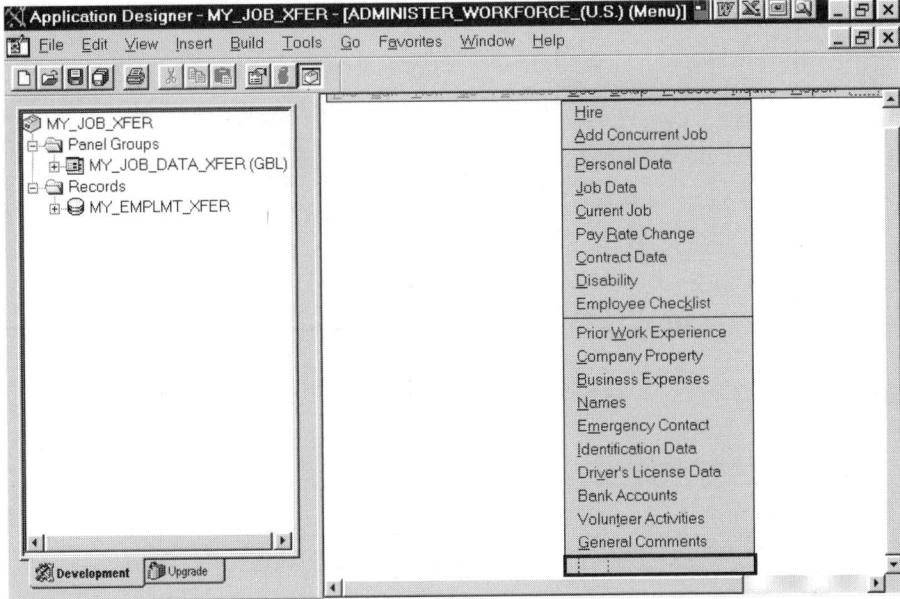

Figure 24.23 **Modifying the delivered menu**

We double-click on the empty rectangle and specify our own menu item name, a label, and a panel group. This menu should be linked to the MY_JOB_DATA_XFER panel group (figure 24.24).

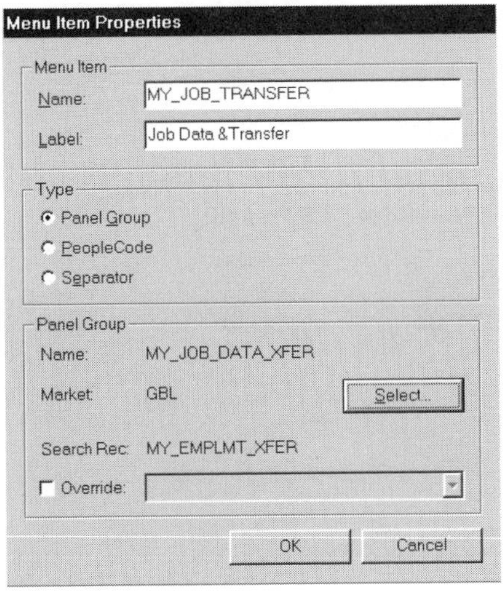

Figure 24.24
Creating a custom menu item

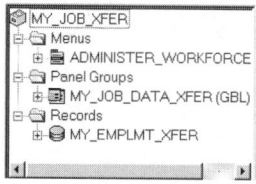

Figure 24.25   Adding the Administer Workforce US menu to the project.

Type in the menu item name and label that will be displayed for users. Select the panel group MY_JOB_DATA_XFER for this menu and specify the MY_EMPLMT_XFER as a search record. Let's move the new menu item next to the delivered Job Data menu item by dragging and dropping the object. After completing the menu changes, we save it. Our project is shown in figure 24.25.

24.5   *GRANTING SECURITY ACCESS*

Navigation: Go → PeopleTools → Security Administrator → Open → ALLPANLS
→ Menu Items

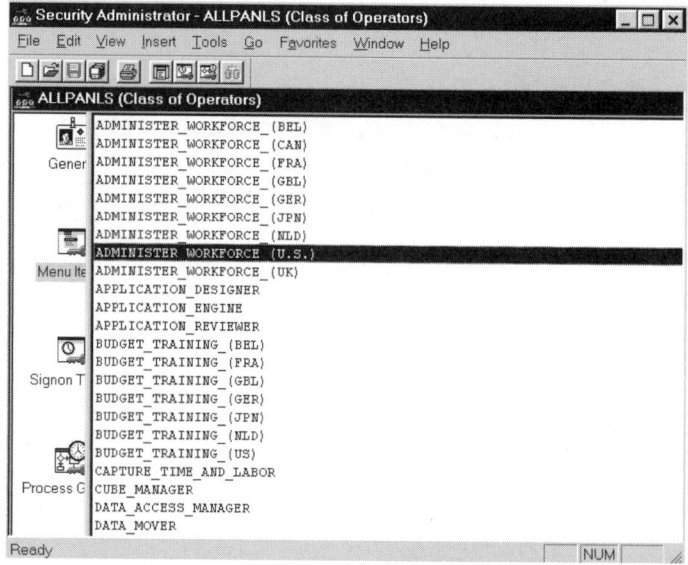

Figure 24.26   Selecting the Administer Workforce (U.S.) menu

After selecting the Administer Workforce (U.S.) menu, the security panel looks as shown in figure 24.27

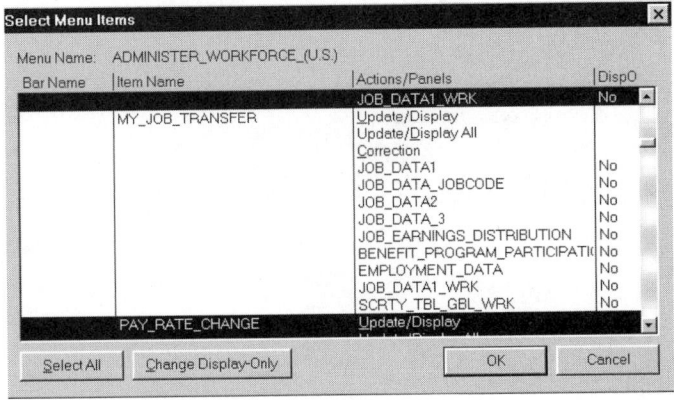

Figure 24.27   Granting user's security to the Job Transfer menu item

Highlight every line that belongs to the MY_JOB_TRANSFER Menu Item and then click the OK button.

24.6   *TESTING OUR CHANGES*

Before we start testing, let's state the expected results. Our goal was to allow end users access to their transferred employee's records. In other words, if an employee were transferred to another department, and if we have no access to the employee's new department records, we should still be able to see the transferred employee records using our newly created objects. At the same time, if we try to access the same records via the regular PeopleSoft-delivered Job Data panel group, the employee records will not be available.

At first, let's examine the department security access for the ALLPANLS operator class, since this is the class we use for our testing purposes (figure 24.28).

After selecting the ALLPANLS operator class and clicking on the OK button, we get a list of departments with their respective access codes (figure 24.29).

Navigation: Go → Define Business Rules → Administer HR System → Use →
Maintain Data Security

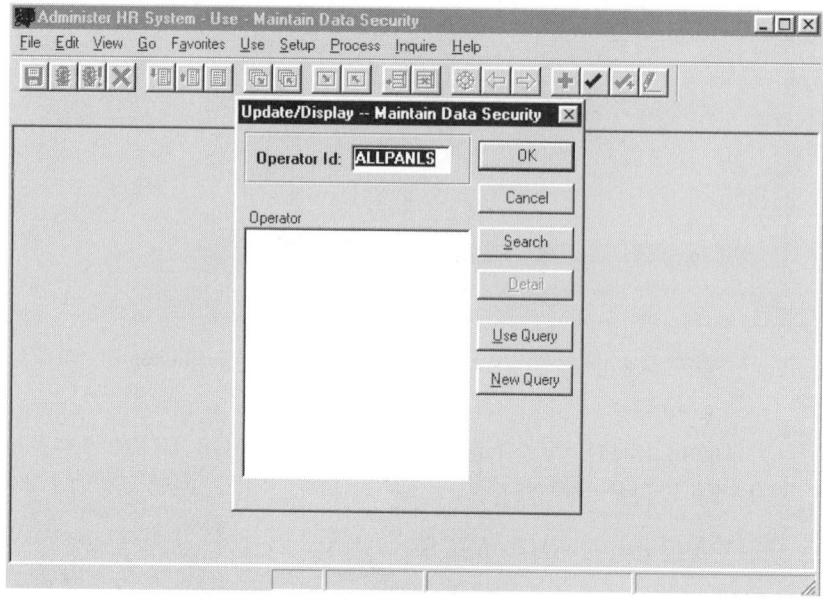

Figure 24.28   Selecting the ALLPANLS operator class

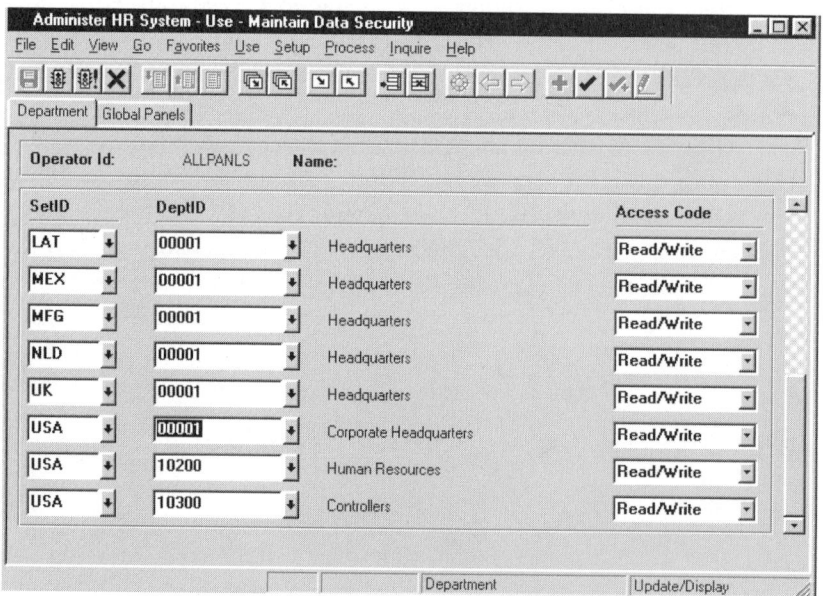

Figure 24.29   Department security for the ALLPANLS operator class

CHAPTER 24   CUSTOMIZING COMPONENTS

For our test purposes, let's modify the ALLPANLS operator class and deny access to one of the departments—for example, department 10200, Human Resources—as shown in figure 24.30.

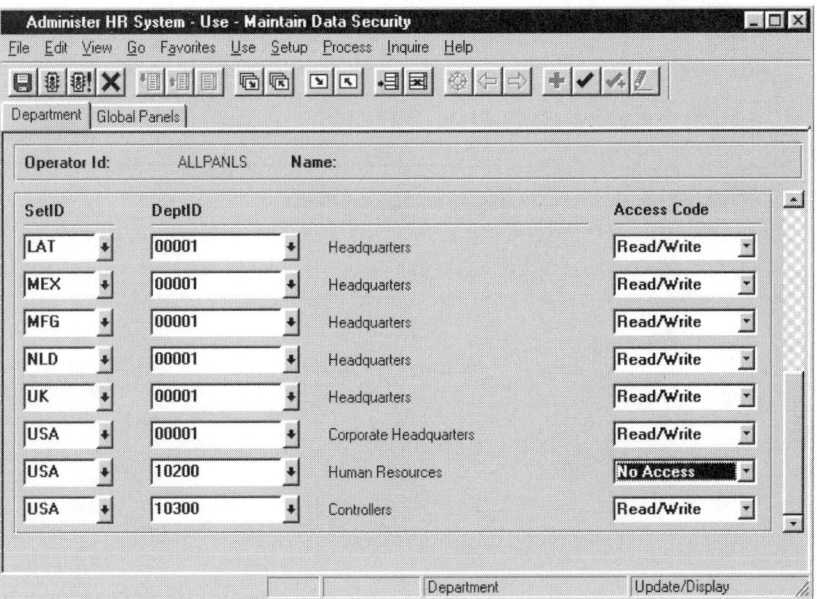

Figure 24.30 Changing the access code for the Human Resources Department to No Access

Our next step is to transfer an employee to department 10200, Human Resources.

Navigation: GO → Administer Workforce(U.S.) → Use → Job Data → Work Location →
Update/Display All

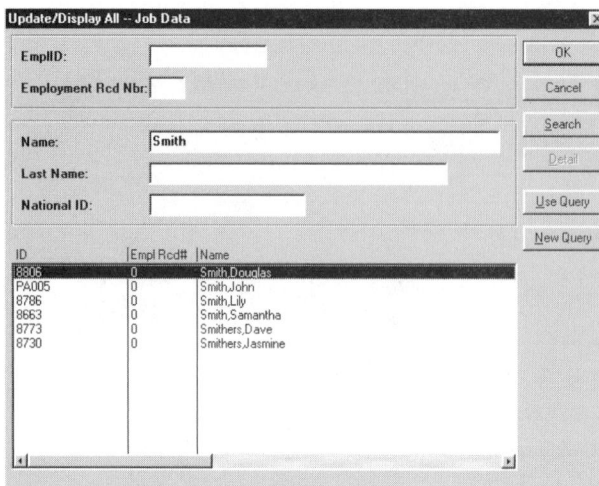

**Figure 24.31
Selecting an employee
to be transferred to another
department**

     After selecting "Smith, Douglas," the first employee in the list, we transfer this
employee to department 10200 by inserting a new row (figure 24.32).

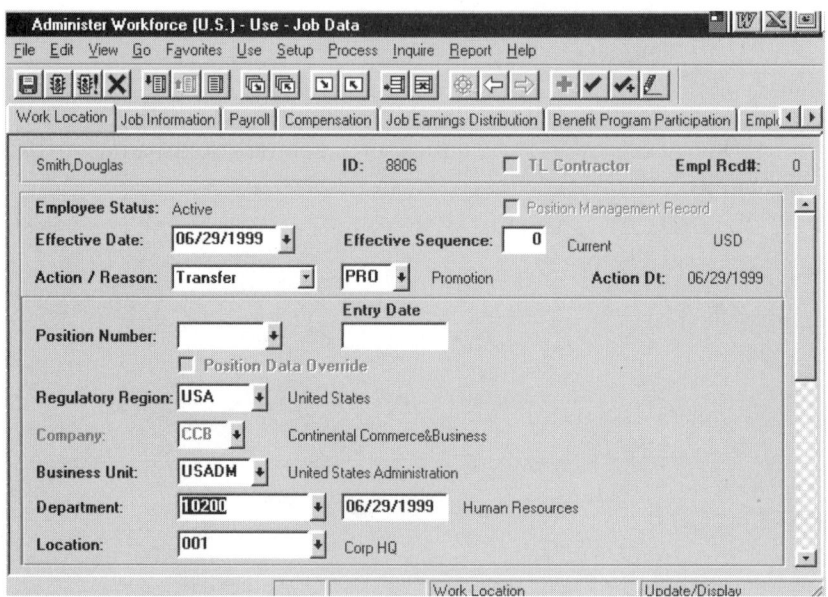

Figure 24.32   Transferring Smith Douglas to department 10200

After saving the record, we can try to access it again. Let's enter "Smith" again as a partial key in the Job Data search box.

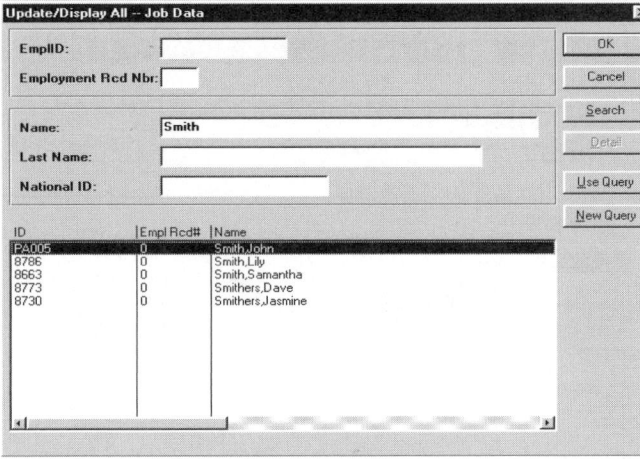

Figure 24.33
Selecting the records of all employees with last names starting with "Smith..."

As you can see from our selection list, the record of "Smith, Douglas" is not found. Of course, we know the reason. This employee has been transferred to a department to which our operator class does not have security access.

Now, let's see how our modifications work. We select the same employee, but this time from our new menu item.

Navigation: GO → Administer Workforce(U.S.) → Use → Job Data Transfer →
Work Location → Update/Display All

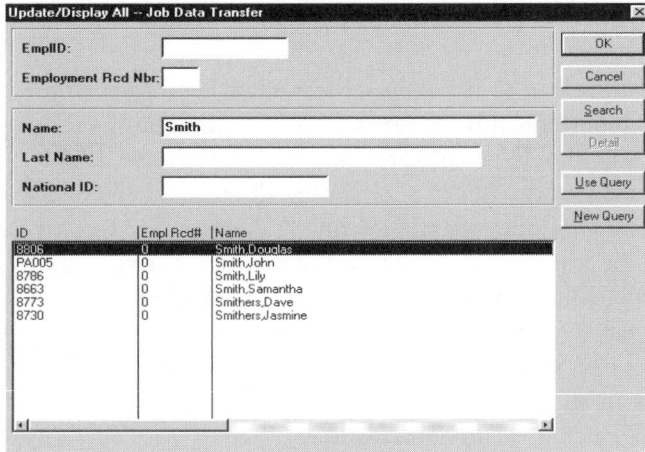

Figure 24.34
Selecting all Smith's records from the Job Data Transfer menu

The record of "Smith, Douglas" is in the list. This means that our new security search record, which is solely responsible for selecting items in the list, is working. Let's select this employee and verify his records (figure 24.35).

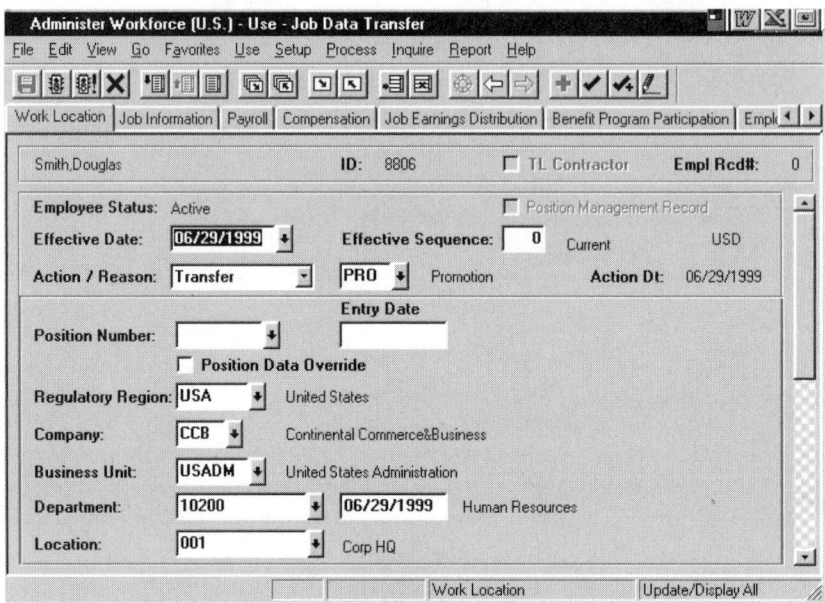

Figure 24.35   "Smith, Douglas" record selected from the new menu item

Let's recall that our users should have access to the records of their former employees, but they should not see the compensation information for the departments to which they don't have access. Switch to the compensation tab to see if this requirement is met (figure 24.36).

We allowed our user to access the records of his/her former employee, but at the same time we compromised the security itself. According to the security that we set up earlier, our user should not have access to the Department 10200 and, therefore, should not see the sensitive information for this department. To resolve the problem, we can write a PeopleCode program to either hide the entire records for the department to which the user does not have access or hide all sensitive fields in these records.

We have to go back to the drawing board (which often happens in the real life development), talk to our users again, present them with some options, and decide on the strategy. Let's suppose that our users decided to go with the second option—i.e., to allow access to all the records, but hide the sensitive salary information in the departments to which users do not have access.

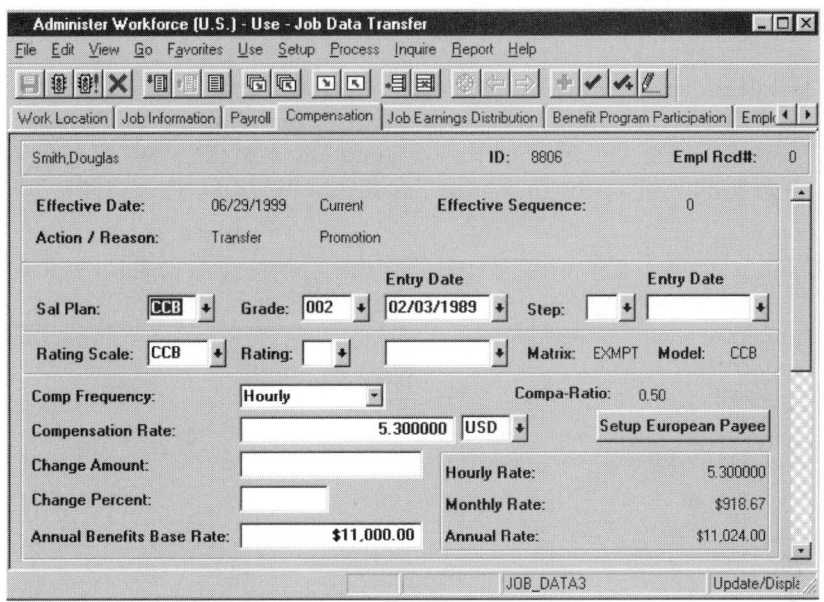

Figure 24.36   The Compensation Tab for Douglas Smith's record contains all the employee's salary-related information

24.7   DEVELOPING A PEOPLECODE PROGRAM

Our goal is to create a PeopleCode program that enables us to hide salary information in the JOB records to which users do not have access. How do we know which user has access to a particular department? Our knowledge about the Department security that we gained during our trace activity at the beginning of this chapter will help us to do this. When an end user enters the search key (full or partial) for the employee record, the Application Processor retrieves all matching records into the buffer based on the selection criteria and our redesigned search record. Then, before the records are displayed on the screen, all PeopleCode programs from the `FieldDefault`, `RowInit`, and `RowSelect` events are fired for every record behind the panels in the panel group. If we want to display only the records to which our user has access and discard the others, the `RowSelect` event with a DiscardRow command will help us make the Application Processor skip the current row of data and continue processing other rows. Since our task is to hide certain sensitive fields, we use another PeopleCode event, the `RowInit` event. The `RowInit` programs are responsible for setting up the initial display of data.

Now that we've decided in what event to place our code, we need to think of how to best achieve this. Our program should analyze the operator class that accesses the panel group, then, for each selected employee record, get the department code, and verify if the operator class has access to this department. In order to do so, we need to create a PeopleCode program with SQLExec statements similar to the SQL in the search record. When dealing with SQL statements in PeopleCode, it is always a good idea to create your SQL statements outside of PeopleCode and test them using your database manipulation tools. Take a look at the security view SQL at the beginning of this chapter. Let's just copy a portion of the SQL that deals with department security. This time we will look at the lower portion of this view:

```
AND SEC.ACCESS_CD = 'Y'
AND EXISTS
   (SELECT 'X'
    FROM PSTREENODE SEC3
    WHERE SEC3.SETID     = SEC.SETID
    AND SEC3.SETID       = B.SETID_DEPT
    AND SEC3.TREE_NAME = 'DEPT_SECURITY'
    AND SEC3.EFFDT       = SEC.TREE_EFFDT
    AND SEC3.TREE_NODE = B.DEPTID
    AND SEC3.TREE_NODE_NUM BETWEEN
        SEC.TREE_NODE_NUM AND SEC.TREE_NODE_NUM_END
    AND NOT EXISTS
        (SELECT 'X'
         FROM PS_SCRTY_TBL_DEPT SEC2
         WHERE SEC.OPRID  = SEC2.OPRID
         AND    SEC.SETID = SEC2.SETID
         AND    SEC.TREE_NODE_NUM <> SEC2.TREE_NODE_NUM
         AND    SEC3.TREE_NODE_NUM BETWEEN
                SEC2.TREE_NODE_NUM AND SEC2.TREE_NODE_NUM_END
         AND    SEC2.TREE_NODE_NUM BETWEEN
                SEC.TREE_NODE_NUM AND SEC.TREE_NODE_NUM_END
        )
   )
```

Note, that the portion of SQL enclosed in parenthesis uses columns from the PS_JOB table (with the table name alias B) such as SETID_DEPT and DEPTID and from the SCRTY_TBL_DEPT (with the table name alias SEC) such as SETID and TREE_EFFDT. For testing purposes, we can plug in specific values relevant to our test employee ("Smith, Douglas") into this SQL code. Let's put our SQL together and execute it (figure 24.37).

As you can see, we plugged in the following values: the OPRID='ALLPANLS', SETID='USA', TREE_NODE='10200'. Using these values, our SQL did not return any rows (figure 24.38). This is exactly what we expected, since we turned off access to this department earlier in our test. Just to make sure that our SQL is working correctly, let's plug in another department—this time the one to which the ALLPANLS operator class has access—and run it again.

Our test SQL returned one row. We now know that our SQL is working correctly.

The next step is to decide where we should place our RowInit PeopleCode event. We also need to know the names of the fields we need to hide. First, let's find the panel name where the salary-related information for the employee must be hidden.

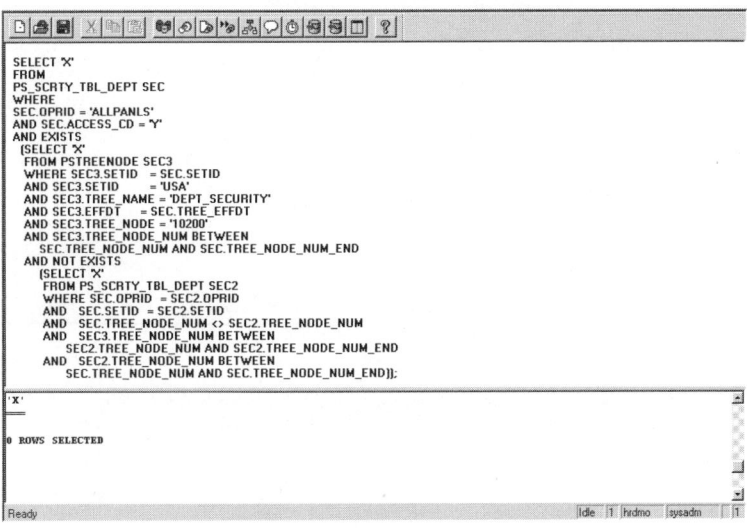

```
SELECT 'X'
FROM
PS_SCRTY_TBL_DEPT SEC
WHERE
SEC.OPRID = 'ALLPANLS'
AND SEC.ACCESS_CD = 'Y'
AND EXISTS
 (SELECT 'X'
  FROM PSTREENODE SEC3
  WHERE SEC3.SETID   = SEC.SETID
  AND SEC3.SETID      = 'USA'
  AND SEC3.TREE_NAME = 'DEPT_SECURITY'
  AND SEC3.EFFDT     = SEC.TREE_EFFDT
  AND SEC3.TREE_NODE = '10200'
  AND SEC3.TREE_NODE_NUM BETWEEN
     SEC.TREE_NODE_NUM AND SEC.TREE_NODE_NUM_END
  AND NOT EXISTS
    (SELECT 'X'
     FROM PS_SCRTY_TBL_DEPT SEC2
     WHERE SEC.OPRID  = SEC2.OPRID
     AND   SEC.SETID  = SEC2.SETID
     AND   SEC.TREE_NODE_NUM <> SEC2.TREE_NODE_NUM
     AND   SEC3.TREE_NODE_NUM BETWEEN
        SEC2.TREE_NODE_NUM AND SEC2.TREE_NODE_NUM_END
     AND   SEC2.TREE_NODE_NUM BETWEEN
        SEC.TREE_NODE_NUM AND SEC.TREE_NODE_NUM_END)];

'X'

0 ROWS SELECTED
```

Figure 24.37   Executing the SQL statements outside PeopleSoft for testing purposes

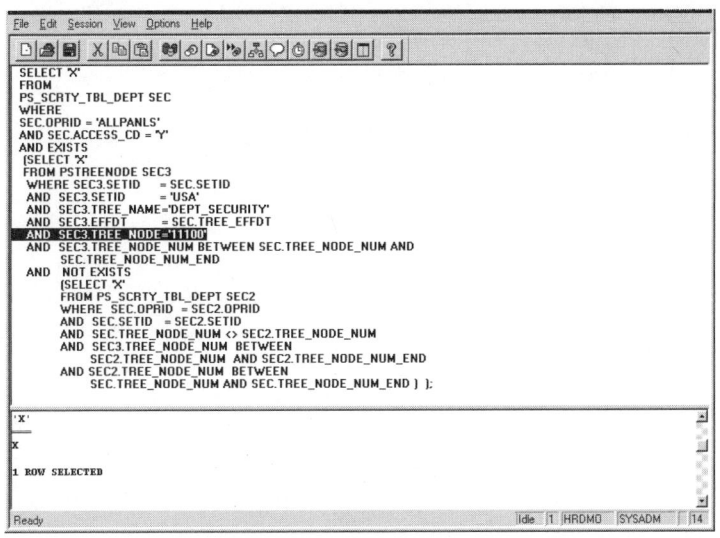

```
SELECT 'X'
FROM
PS_SCRTY_TBL_DEPT SEC
WHERE
SEC.OPRID = 'ALLPANLS'
AND SEC.ACCESS_CD = 'Y'
AND EXISTS
 (SELECT 'X'
  FROM PSTREENODE SEC3
  WHERE SEC3.SETID   = SEC.SETID
  AND SEC3.SETID     = 'USA'
  AND SEC3.TREE_NAME='DEPT_SECURITY'
  AND SEC3.EFFDT     = SEC.TREE_EFFDT
  AND SEC3.TREE_NODE='11100'
  AND SEC3.TREE_NODE_NUM BETWEEN SEC.TREE_NODE_NUM AND
      SEC.TREE_NODE_NUM_END
  AND  NOT EXISTS
     (SELECT 'X'
      FROM PS_SCRTY_TBL_DEPT SEC2
      WHERE  SEC.OPRID  = SEC2.OPRID
      AND  SEC.SETID    = SEC2.SETID
      AND  SEC.TREE_NODE_NUM <> SEC2.TREE_NODE_NUM
      AND  SEC3.TREE_NODE_NUM BETWEEN
         SEC2.TREE_NODE_NUM AND SEC2.TREE_NODE_NUM_END
      AND SEC2.TREE_NODE_NUM BETWEEN
         SEC.TREE_NODE_NUM AND SEC.TREE_NODE_NUM_END ) ];

'X'

x

1 ROW SELECTED
```

Figure 24.38   Testing SQL with department 11100

If you look back at figure 24.36, you can see that the Compensation tab panel name is JOB_DATA3.

Now we can open the JOB_DATA3 panel and determine the names of all the fields we are planning to hide. After the panel is opened, let's examine the Order panel (figure 24.39).

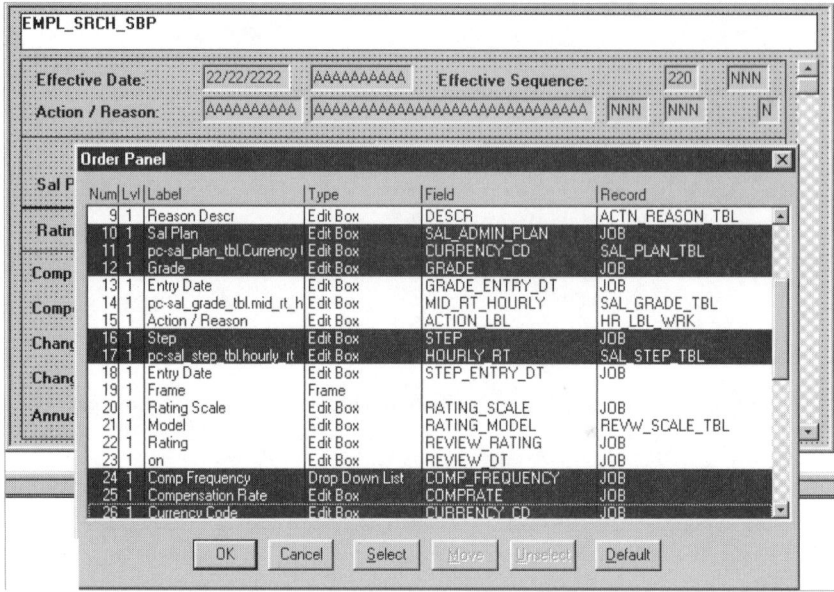

Figure 24.39 Examining the Order Panel for the JOB_DATA3 Panel

As you can see from figure 24.39, all salary-related fields belong to the JOB record. These fields need to be hidden in our customized panel. Let's place the PeopleCode script that hides the salary-related fields to the JOB.EMPLID `RowInit` event. In order to minimize the necessary customizations to PeopleSoft-delivered PeopleCode, let's create a function outside the JOB record.

PeopleSoft, by convention, usually places its functions in the `FieldFormula` event of the derived FUNCLIB records. These records (FUNCLIB_HR, FUNCLIB_BEN, FUNCLIB_PAY, and so forth.) are used as placeholders for the external functions called from different record field events. Generally, a function may belong to any record event. (Please see part 3 of this book for more details about function libraries.) We'll create our own derived record here to hold our first function, as well as any others that may follow.

24.7.1   Creating a derived Funclib record and PeopleCode

Let's create a record named MY_FUNCLIB and add one field to it. Let's re-use the existing EMPLID field. Remember, the purpose of this record is just to hold PeopleCode functions.

Before the record is saved, do not forget to change its properties, add some useful comments, and define this record as a Derived/Work record. We don't need to use the Build option, since this record is not going to be created at the database level.

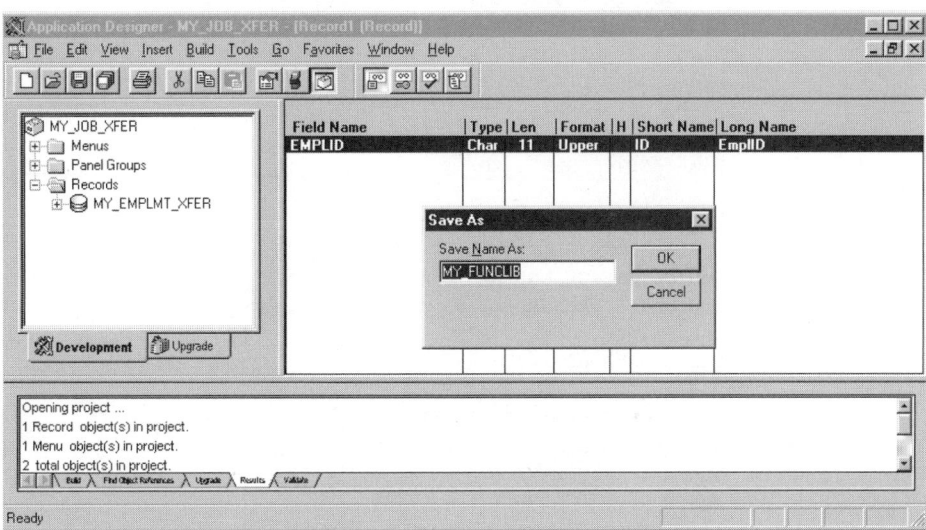

Figure 24.40 Creating a derived record for our custom function library

Now we can start by creating a function named MY_CHECK_SECURITY. This function will control the user's access to departments for each JOB record in the buffer. We place this function in our newly created MY_FUNCLIB derived record, EMPLID FieldFormula event (figure 24.41).

Since our PeopleCode function has grown quite big, let's display it separately in order to understand how it works:

```
Function my_check_security(&SETID_DEPT, &DEPTID);
    &OPERATOR = %OperatorClass;
    SQLExec("SELECT 'X' FROM PS_SCRTY_TBL_DEPT SEC WHERE SEC.OPRID=:1 AND
SEC.ACCESS_CD='Y' AND EXISTS (SELECT 'X' FROM PSTREENODE SEC3 WHERE
SEC3.SETID = SEC.SETID AND SEC3.SETID = :2 AND
SEC3.TREE_NAME='DEPT_SECURITY' AND SEC3.EFFDT= SEC.TREE_EFFDT AND
SEC3.TREE_NODE=:3 AND SEC3.TREE_NODE_NUM BETWEEN SEC.TREE_NODE_NUM AND
SEC.TREE_NODE_NUM_END AND NOT EXISTS (SELECT 'X' FROM PS_SCRTY_TBL_DEPT
SEC2 WHERE SEC.OPRID = SEC2.OPRID AND SEC.SETID = SEC2.SETID AND
SEC.TREE_NODE_NUM <> SEC2.TREE_NODE_NUM AND SEC3.TREE_NODE_NUM BETWEEN
SEC2.TREE_NODE_NUM AND SEC2.TREE_NODE_NUM_END AND SEC2.TREE_NODE_NUM
BETWEEN SEC.TREE_NODE_NUM AND SEC.TREE_NODE_NUM_END))", &OPERATOR,
&SETID_DEPT, &DEPTID, &SELECTED);
    If None(&SELECTED) Then
```

```
            Hide(JOB.COMP_FREQUENCY);
            Hide(JOB.COMPRATE);
            Hide(JOB.CHANGE_PCT);
            Hide(JOB.CHANGE_AMT);
            Hide(JOB.ANNUAL_RT);
            Hide(JOB.MONTHLY_RT);
            Hide(JOB.HOURLY_RT);
            Hide(JOB.ANNL_BENEF_BASE_RT);
            Hide(JOB.SAL_ADMIN_PLAN);
            Hide(JOB.GRADE);
            Hide(JOB.STEP);
            Hide(JOB.CURRENCY_CD);
        Else
            UnHide(JOB.COMP_FREQUENCY);
            UnHide(JOB.CHANGE_PCT);
            UnHide(JOB.CHANGE_AMT);
            UnHide(JOB.ANNUAL_RT);
            UnHide(JOB.MONTHLY_RT);
            UnHide(JOB.HOURLY_RT);
            UnHide(JOB.ANNL_BENEF_BASE_RT);
            UnHide(JOB.SAL_ADMIN_PLAN);
            UnHide(JOB.GRADE);
            UnHide(JOB.STEP);
            UnHide(JOB.CURRENCY_CD);
        End-If;
End-Function;
```

■

You can see the EMPLID `FieldFormula` function here. Testing PeopleCode programs within the PeopleSoft system is relatively easy. As we discussed in part 3 of this book, the PeopleCode editor catches your syntax and compilation errors while saving your program, or you can use the Validate Syntax option of the Application Designer menu. You can also use the Application Reviewer, which is a powerful PeopleCode online debugging tool.

Let's take a close look at our PeopleCode program. The function name is placed in the beginning after the `Function` keyword. Any function in PeopleCode has to start with the word `Function` and end with `End-Function`. Our function accepts two parameters: `&SETID_DEPT` and `&DEPTID`. These two variables hold the values of the corresponding JOB record SETID_DEPT and DEPTID fields. These parameters along with the operator ID are used as bind variables in our SQLExec `Select` statement. As we have seen earlier, the SQLExec returns the 'X' as the result of its execution if the operator has access to the particular department. If the operator has no access, the SQLExec returns nothing. The next statement checks the selected variable and either hides or unhides the salary-related fields, based on the result of SQLExec.

Usually, you don't have to fully design your PeopleCode program in order to test it. It is always a good idea to test it by pieces or blocks. In our case, however, we can't test this particular PeopleCode program because we just created a function, and we

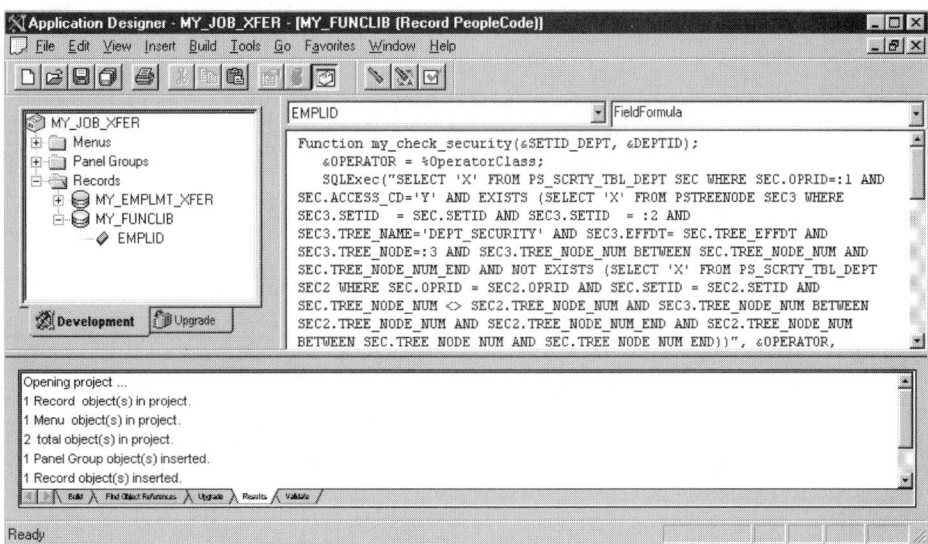

Figure 24.41   Creating a function and placing it in the EMPLID, FieldFormula event

need to write a code to call this function. Let's do this. As we have already discussed, we are going to place our function call in the PeopleSoft-delivered JOB record, EMPLID `RowInit` event. In PeopleCode, an external function must be declared in the event where the call is coded. Figure 24.42 illustrates how to code a custom function declaration.

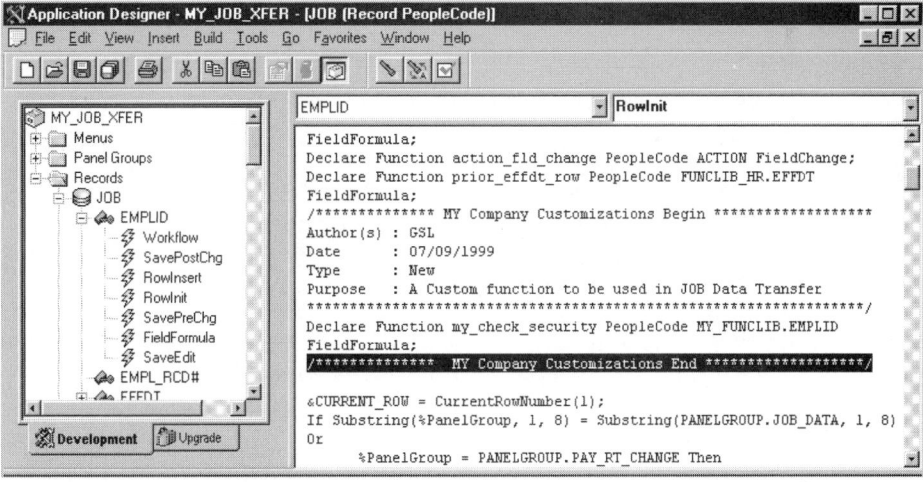

Figure 24.42   The function declaration is added to the JOB.EMPLID RowInit PeopleCode.

When we declared our function, we specified the following relative declaration parameters:

- *The function name* `my_check_security`
- *Record_name.field_name* MY_FUNCLIB.EMPLID (this is the place where our function resides)
- *Event Type* `FieldFormula`

We also specified that this external function is a PeopleCode function, to distinguish it from other types of external non-PeopleCode (for example, "C") functions.

After the function is declared, we want to add simple code to execute the function. Remember, we need to pass two parameters: `SETID_DEPT` and `DEPTID` to our function. These are the actual JOB record field values. Since the `RowInit` event will be triggered for each JOB record fetched from the database, our function will be called for every fetched row. Figure 24.43 shows the function call.

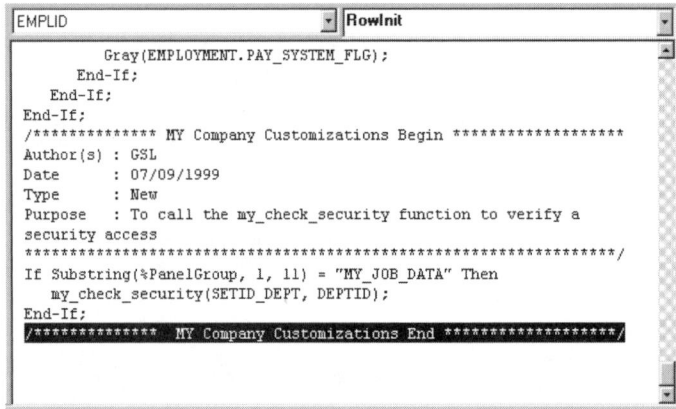

```
EMPLID                        ▼  RowInit                      ▼
            Gray(EMPLOYMENT.PAY_SYSTEM_FLG);
      End-If;
   End-If;
End-If;
/************** MY Company Customizations Begin ******************
Author(s) : GSL
Date      : 07/09/1999
Type      : New
Purpose   : To call the my_check_security function to verify a
security access
*********************************************************************/
If Substring(%PanelGroup, 1, 11) = "MY_JOB_DATA" Then
   my_check_security(SETID_DEPT, DEPTID);
End-If;
/************** MY Company Customizations End ******************/
```

Figure 24.43   Calling our custom MY_CHECK_SECURITY function

Our PeopleCode script is done, a function is created, and a function call is placed to the `RowInit` event of JOB.EMPLID. Let's test our PeopleCode programs.

24.8   TESTING PEOPLECODE MODIFICATIONS

Let's repeat some of the steps that we've performed during our first round of testing, but this time with our PeopleCode modifications at work.

Let's select the same employee, "Smith, Douglas." We'll display the most current record and its department number first.

Navigation: Go → Administer Workforce (U.S.) → Use → Job Data Transfer → Work Location
→ Update Display All

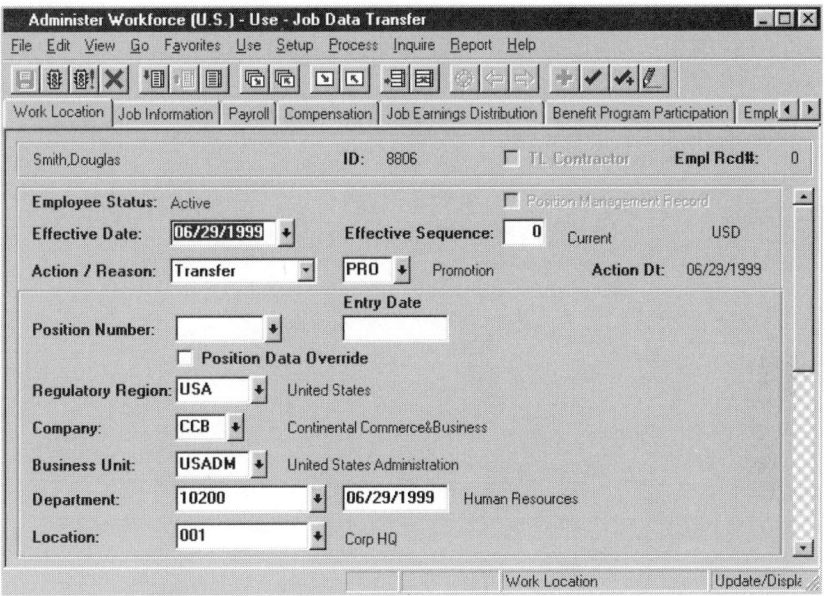

Figure 24.44   Testing the PeopleCode modifications. The record belongs to department 10200

If we switch to the Compensation panel, all salary-related information must be hidden. Let's select the Compensation tab (see figure 24.45).

As you can see from figure 24.45, our PeopleCode program did its job. All salary-related fields that we identified before are hidden. The panel may look a little awkward. Usually, the final look of any customized panel is discussed between the end users and developers. From the programming point of view, however, our code worked perfectly. To make sure that our users can still see the information for the departments to which they have access, we go back to the Work Location panel and click on the scroll bar to see the previous record for this employee (figure 24.46).

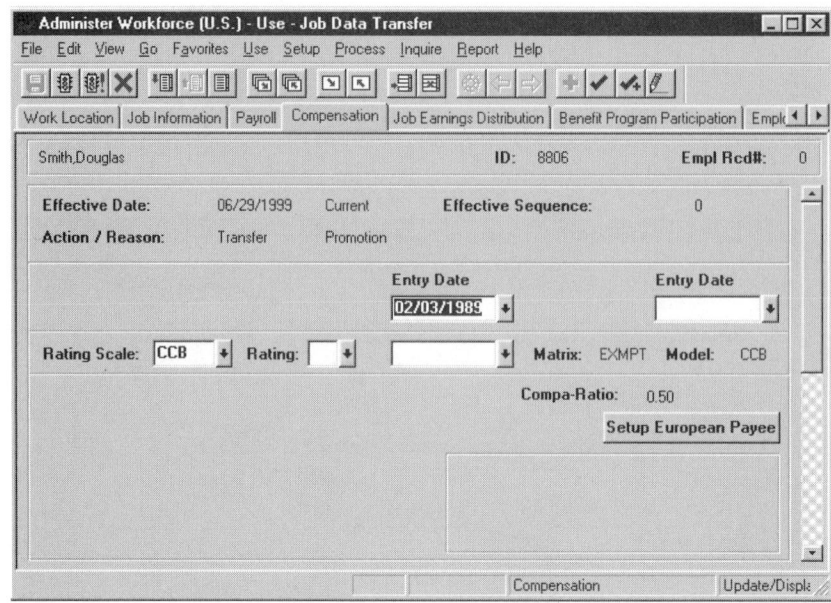

Figure 24.45   All salary-related fields on the Compensation panel are hidden

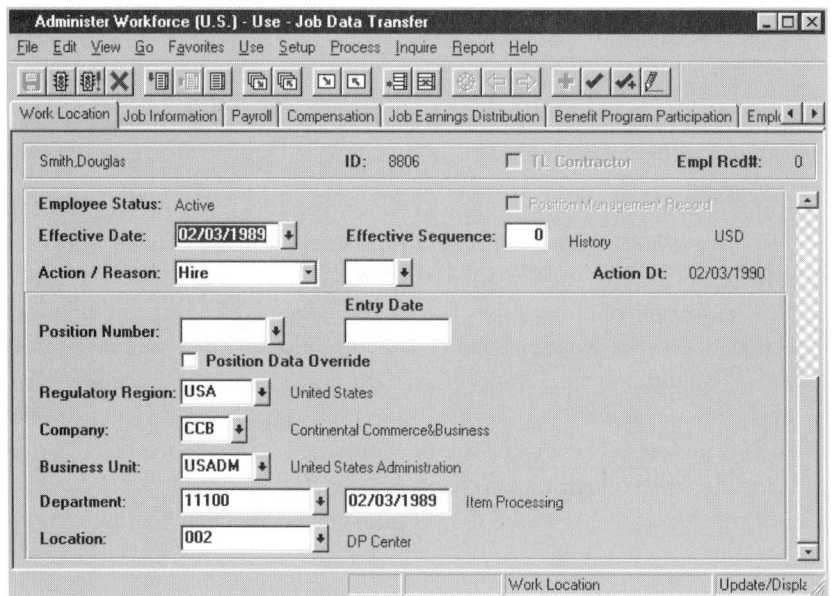

Figure 24.46   Examining the previous record of transferred Employee

CHAPTER 24   CUSTOMIZING COMPONENTS

This record belongs to Department 11100, to which our ALLPANLS operator class currently has access. Let's switch to the Compensation panel to be certain that none of the salary-related fields are hidden (figure 24.47).

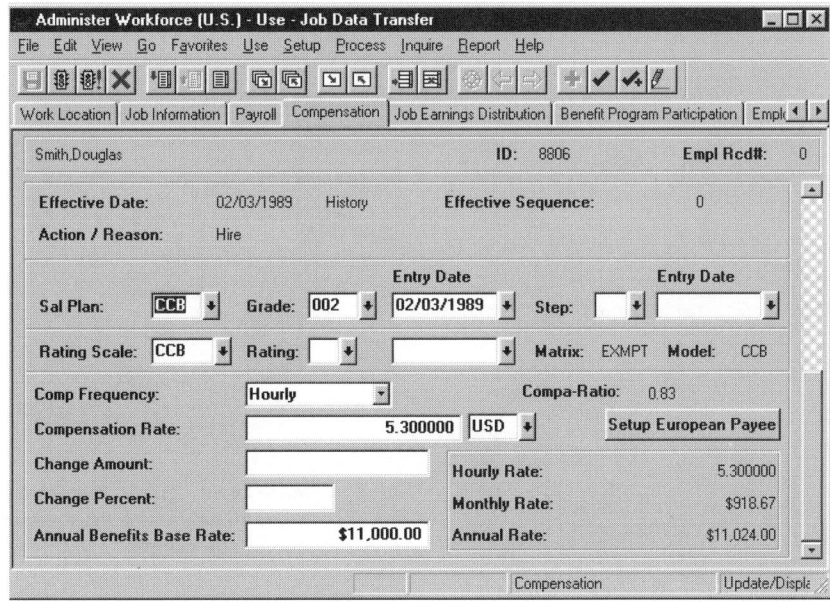

Figure 24.47   The salary-related information is available for ALLPANLS operator for the previous employee record

Our basic testing is done. Of course, we need to do more testing to ensure that our code did not cause any problems in the delivered application. For example, we need to test the non-customized Job Data panels, since we implemented our PeopleCode in the JOB record. We also have to test it for the operators that do not belong to the ALLPANLS operator class with different department security access. You should develop a test plan for all possible situations and execute it before moving these modifications to the production database.

24.9   POSSIBLE IMPACT ON FUTURE UPGRADES

As in our previous chapters, in order to fully understand the possible impact of our customizations on future application release upgrades, we want to summarize all the modifications we performed in this project. This time we will use our project MY_JOB_XFER, which we have been updating all along during our development. It will help us not to miss any modifications. Let's open the project. We know that the project panel has two tabs: the Development tab and the Upgrade tab. During our development, we used the Development tab only.

Take a look at the Development tab of our project in figure 24.48. It includes all the objects that we modified—and even more. If you click, for example, on the plus sign next to the Job record, you can see all the fields with their respective PeopleCode events (figure 24.49).

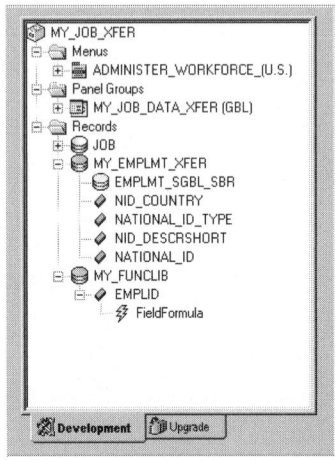

Figure 24.48   The Development tab of our project

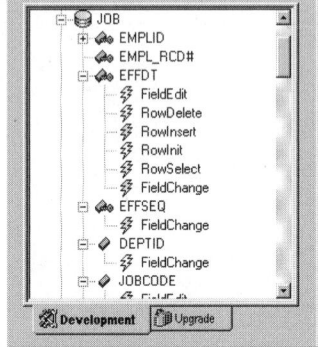

Figure 24.49   The Development tab shows all fields with their respective PeopleCode events

Does this mean that we modified all these PeopleCode programs? As you may guess, the answer is "No." The Development tab displays all related objects for your convenience in case you need to modify or review them.

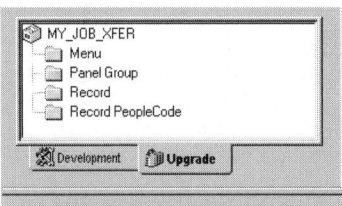

Figure 24.50   The Upgrade tab

When migrating your changes to another database or preparing for an Application Upgrade, the best way is to switch to the Upgrade tab (figure 24.50).

Our Upgrade project tab consists of all the objects that we have modified. Let's double-click on each of the folders that represent our modified objects one by one. Please keep in mind that the Upgrade projects are used for two purposes: an upgrade to the next release level and a simple migration to any target database. Even though our goal in this section is to discuss possible future upgrade implications, we first need to migrate the modifications to our test and production databases. Therefore, we'll look at the project from the migration point of view first and examine all the objects that must be migrated. Then we can discuss the possible implications on future release upgrades.

Take a look at the Menu Upgrade shown in figure 24.51.

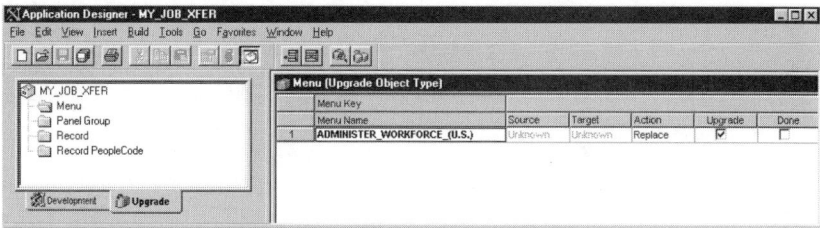

Figure 24.51   The Menu upgrade panel

NOTE   Please remember that during the upgrade to a new release level, your Target database is actually a copy of your production database. The Source database is your new release database. Therefore, you can do one of the following with your modifications in the Target database: preserve them, delete them or replace your modified objects with the new release objects.

As you can see, on the right side of our project in figure 24.51, the ADMINISTER_WORKFORCE_(U.S.) menu is prepared for migration to the target database. Action = `Replace` is specified, and the Upgrade flag is turned on. As we already discussed in chapter 20, these are the default options. After execution of the Upgrade Compare and Report process, the real options replace the default ones. When copying the menu object, be careful. The project, as we have already mentioned before, copies, not just the menu item that you added or modified, but the entire ADMINISTER_WORKFORCE_(U.S.) menu. Make sure that this object (Menu) is up-to-date in your development environment before you make any changes to it. The alternative is to turn off the Upgrade flag and modify the menu in the target environment manually. You can use the "copy and paste" technique successfully on the menus in this case.

How will this object change affect our future upgrades? This is a delivered object, and there is a good chance that in the future you will have to merge the modifications with the new release menu if some of the items in this menu are changed by PeopleSoft. If PeopleSoft's menu stays the same in the next release, we could safely leave the modified menu in the target database.

Let's move on to our next object, the panel group. Figure 24.52 shows the panel group upgrade.

Unlike the menu upgrade where we modified an existing object, the MY_JOB_DATA_XFER object was created by us. You can easily see it by its prefix "MY." Even though the default action is specified as `Replace`, this object is added to the target database. The `Replace` action is changed to `Add` after the Upgrade

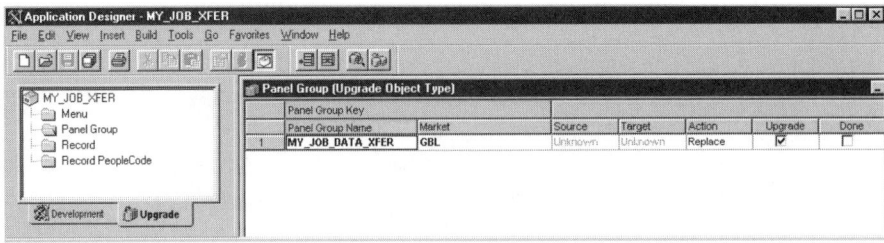

Figure 24.52   A panel group upgrade

Compare and Report process runs and identifies that the object is missing from the target database.

During the new application release upgrade it is safe to preserve this custom object in the target database.

Our next object is Record (figure 24.53).

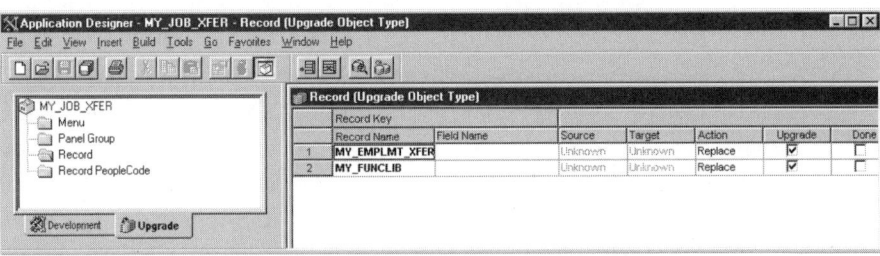

Figure 24.53   A record upgrade

As you can see from figure 24.53, we have two new custom records: MY_EMPLMT_XFER and MY_FUNCLIB. During the upgrade to a new application release, these records should be preserved in your target database. Note that, even though the JOB record was listed in our Development tab, it is not listed in the Upgrade tab since we did not modify this record.

Similar to the panel group, these two objects are just additions to the system, and, therefore, we should not have any problems when the new release comes.

The Record PeopleCode Upgrade (figure 24.54) shows only those PeopleCode Events that were customized or added. In our example, the JOB.EMPLID RowInit event PeopleCode program will be replaced (if we choose to) in the target database during our migration to the Production database. The MY_FUNCLIB.EMPLID FieldFormula event PeopleCode program will be added to the target database.

Here we have a combination of the two previously discussed cases of future upgrade implications. The MY_FUNCLIB.EMPLID FieldFormula event PeopleCode program

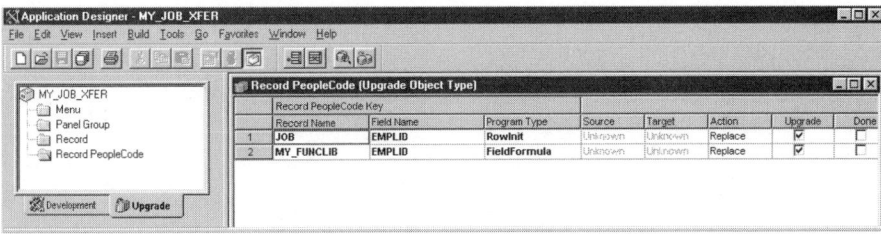

Figure 24.54   The Record PeopleCode Upgrade

can be preserved in the target database. The PeopleCode program from the JOB.EMPLID `RowInit` event must be compared to the new release `RowInit` event PeopleCode. If the changes are only ours, it's safe to have our customized object in the new release target database. Otherwise, the old and the new PeopleCode programs have to be manually merged.

In addition, always consider a case when a similar change is delivered in the new release. Our recommendation then would be to replace your customizations with the PeopleSoft version.

KEY POINTS

1　Many panels in PeopleSoft are accessed with the help of special search views that provide row-level security.

2　The Trace utility helps to understand how the Panel Processor works behind the scenes.

3　When modifying an SQL view definition, it is a good idea to test SQL statements by using your database manipulation tools outside PeopleSoft.

4　All PeopleCode programs from the `FieldDefault`, `RowInit`, and `RowSelect` events are fired for every record behind the panels in the panel group.

5　The `RowInit` event PeopleCode programs are responsible for setting up the initial display of data.

6　Always add all your modified objects to the project. It will greatly help you during the upgrade and migration to your Test and Production databases.

Using SQR in PeopleSoft applications

Structured Query Report Writer (SQR) is a programming language currently owned and supported by BRIO Technology. SQR, one of many third-party tools that comes packaged with PeopleSoft, combines the power of SQL, the sophistication of procedural logic, and the freedom of multiple-platform development. PeopleSoft has used SQR extensively for many of their batch, reporting, and upgrade applications. Because PeopleSoft was deliberately designed to perform against a variety of operating systems and databases, it is no surprise the makers of PeopleSoft chose SQR for many of their programming requirements. SQR is a powerful and flexible language that can run on multiple platforms and supports almost all relational databases. Operating systems include Windows, DOS, Unix, and MVS. Some examples of supported databases are Oracle, DB2, SQLBase, and Informix.

Contrary to what its name may suggest, SQR is much more than a reporting tool. Using SQR we can write sophisticated and robust applications that perform data manipulation, file handling, data extraction, data loading, and, of course, reporting. *SQR in PeopleSoft and Other Applications* (Landres, Galina and Vlad Landres. Greenwich, CT: Manning Publications, 1999.) is a comprehensive guide that covers all aspects of SQR development. The authors summed up SQR quite succinctly in their introductory section when they proclaimed: "(SQR) is a serious tool for serious people." Once you have used SQR for even a short period of time, you will no doubt agree with them. The chapters ahead pick up where Galina and Vlad Landres left off in their book. More emphasis is placed here on integrating SQR with PeopleSoft components such as Process

Scheduler, Process Monitor, and Run Controls. We further enhance our Problem Tracking application by creating custom SQR reports that are executed via Process Scheduler. The reader can explore the full SQR development cycle, which includes creating the Run Control record, panel, and panelgroup; adding the panel to a menu; assigning operator security to the new menu item; and creating the process definition for the SQR program. In addition, we cover topics such as implementing security in SQR and scheduling recurring jobs. We end the section with an overview of new SQR and Process Scheduler features in release 8.0.

Running SQR programs in PeopleSoft applications

PeopleSoft applications offer a wide range of query and reporting tools which enable users to access the necessary information for both day-to-day and long-term business decisions. For each product (HRMS, Payroll, Financials, and so forth), PeopleSoft delivers a set of standard canned reports as a part of its basic package. At the same time, PeopleSoft offers a number of tools designed to help developers customize existing reports as well as create new ones.

PeopleSoft has selected Structured Query Report Writer (SQR) as one of its main reporting and processing tools because SQR provides a flexible and robust report-writing environment. SQR works beautifully when your report needs complex procedural logic or tricky database manipulation; when you need to run your report on multiple platforms; when your report structure is complex with multiple breaks; or when you need to combine data base retrieval with special row processing.

SQR programs are not distributed in the form of platform-dependent executables. They can be easily moved between platforms, either at source level or as pre-compiled pseudo-code modules. All SQR commands, directives, and operators are platform-transparent and require no changes when the programs are moved across platforms. At the same time, programmers are free to invoke any operating system's specific commands or utilities if they feel the benefits of platform independence are outweighed by other considerations such as performance, ease of maintenance, or the need to integrate their programs into certain specific environments.

25.1 HOW SQR PROGRAMS RUN UNDER PEOPLESOFT

Let's start by discussing the way PeopleSoft interacts with SQR programs at a conceptual level without going into many details.

In most cases, PeopleSoft users initiate their requests for reports via PeopleSoft online panels. These panels can be delivered by PeopleSoft or developed by application programmers.

When online panel information is filled in, PeopleSoft generates process request parameters. These parameters usually include the operator ID, Run Control ID, run location, output destination, file/printer name, plus application-specific parameters, for example, `Company ID`, `From Date`, `To Date`, and so on.

After the process request parameters have been read from an online panel, PeopleSoft passes them to the Process Scheduler.

The Process Scheduler is a tool that enables users of the PeopleSoft system to manage PeopleSoft batch processes. Any program that runs under the PeopleSoft Process Scheduler is called a process. It can be a reporting program, a file generation program, an interface to another system, a database update program, and such. You can run processes on your workstation or on the server. You can also combine several processes into job streams and schedule them for a subsequent execution. (We will discuss this later in chapter 30.)

The Process Scheduler generates the SQR command line with flags and arguments required to run the requested SQR program, invokes SQR, and passes the flags and arguments to SQR. When the input from the online panel is saved, the system updates a number of tables that are used by SQR to communicate with the Process Scheduler and the Process Monitor via the special PeopleSoft API.

The requested SQR program is executed. It may generate reports, update the database, create flat files, or print its reports directly on the specified printer. Users are kept informed about the program status with the help of the PeopleSoft Process Monitor. The Process Monitor receives the program feedback via the PeopleSoft API parameters and displays the program status on the Process Monitor panel.

25.2 SELECTING A REPORT FROM A MENU

PeopleSoft-delivered reports are usually displayed under the Report or Process menu bar item. In most cases, programs that generate output for printing or displaying are listed under Report, while programs that manipulate the database records or generate flat files are listed under Process. Many programs do several jobs: print reports, update the databases, and generate files.

To run a report, select it from the appropriate menu: the Report menu or the Process menu. First, you have to know, of course, which report you need to execute. Let's take a look at all available reports within the Administer Workforce U.S. menu.

To begin, let's open for example, the Administer Workforce U.S. menu panel, click on the Report menu bar, and select the Years of Service report to run (figure 25.1).

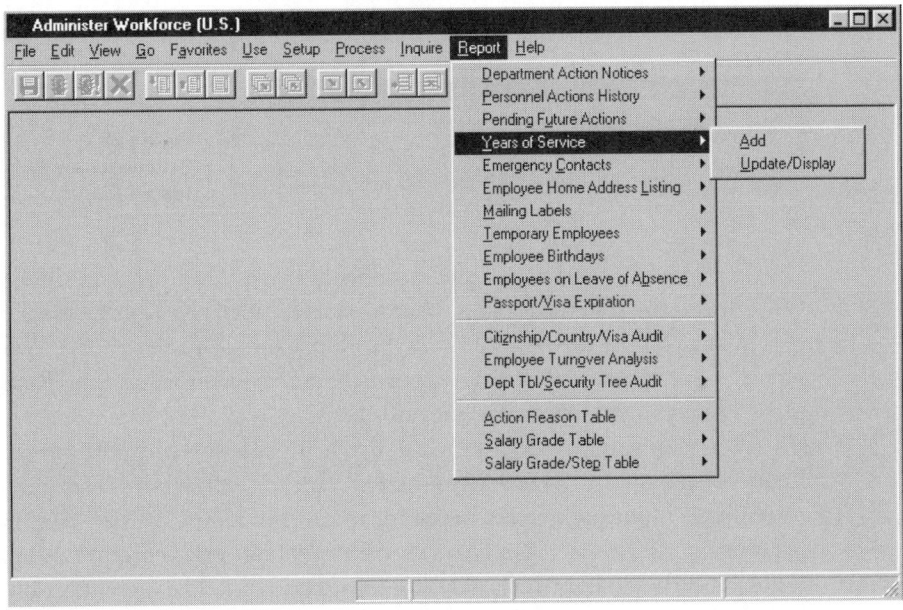

Figure 25.1   Selecting a report to run under the Process Scheduler

The system asks you to choose between the Add and Update/Display options. The Add or Update action does not indicate adding or updating a report; it means adding or updating a special Run Control ID associated with each process request.

25.3 USING THE RUN CONTROL

When we run a process via the Process Scheduler, we need to supply it with a number of parameters such as Run Location, Output Destination, File/Printer name, and so on. This information is stored in the PeopleTools Run Control record PSPRCSRUNCNTL.

In addition, each process maintains its own application Run Control record to store the process-specific input run-time parameters, for example, As-Of-Date, Company Code, or State. The Run Control ID along with the Operator ID are the key fields in both application Run Control records and PeopleTools Run Control records.

Let's get back to our previous panel (figure 25.1). In this panel, the system asks you to create a new PeopleTools Run Control record or select an existing one. If an existing record fits your process execution requirements, you can select the Update/ Display option, find the proper record, and reuse it. Otherwise, you need to select the Add action and add a new Run Control ID for a new record. We create a new Run Control by selecting the Add action (figure 25.2).

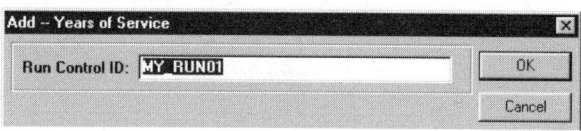

Figure 25.2
Adding a new Run Control record

We enter MY_RUN01 on the system's prompt. After pressing the ENTER key or OK button, the system displays the next screen called the Run Control panel.

What you see in figure 25.3 is the Run Control panel for the Years of Service report. The Operator ID value is your PeopleSoft logon value. The Run Control ID is the value you entered in the previous panel.

Please note that this panel includes a process-specific portion called "Report Request Parameters," which may look different for each report. This part of the panel contains all input parameters necessary to run the report. In our case, there are two parameters: As Of Date and Years of Service. Let's enter 01/01/2000 as the value for the first parameter and 10 for the second one. The upper portion of the panel is a standard subpanel usually included in most Run Control panels. It contains the Operator ID, the Run Control ID, and the Language. A similar subpanel without the Language is also available.

As soon as this panel is saved, an application Run Control record is created. This record, identified by the Run Control ID and the Operator ID, stores the report input parameters. It will allow you to reuse these parameters in the next report runs. The next time you need to run this report, you simply select the proper Run Control ID (in our case, it is MY_RUN01), and the system automatically retrieves the settings. (Note that some HRMS applications may delete their application Run Control records upon successful execution).

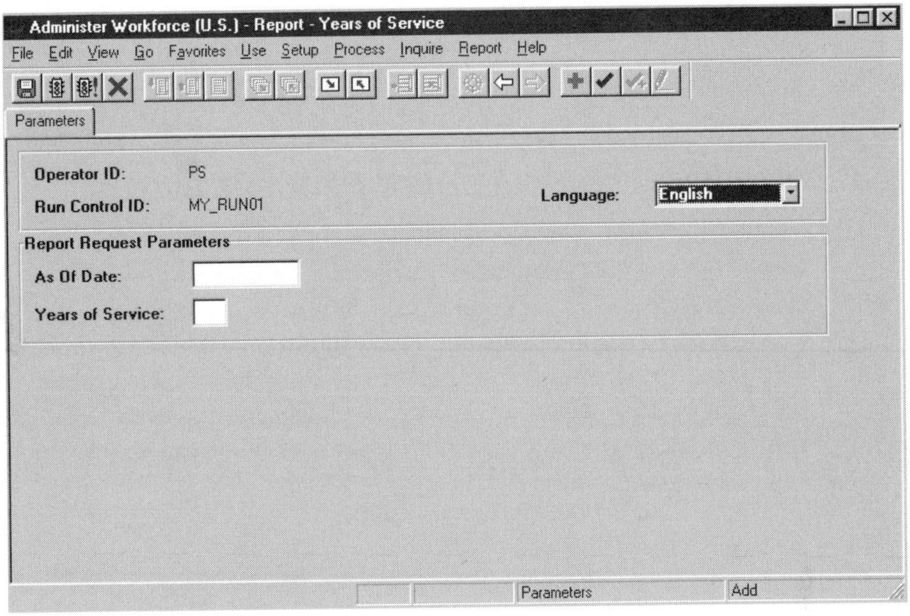

Figure 25.3   The Run Control panel for the Years of Service report

In order to run the report, click on the Traffic Light ▓ button or select File, Run. You will go to the next panel, which displays the Process Scheduler Request dialog panel, where you can specify when and where to run the report (figure 25.4).

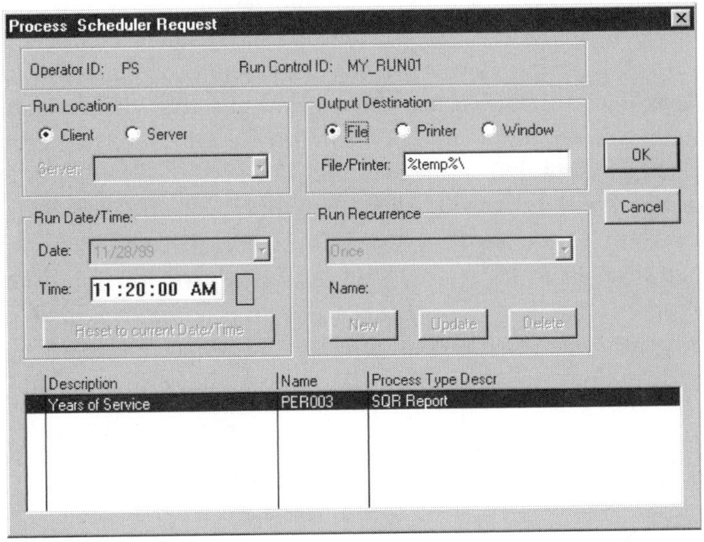

**Figure 25.4
The Process Scheduler Request dialog panel**

After you select all the settings on the Process Scheduler Request dialog panel, the PeopleTools Run Control record (PSPRCSRUNCNTL) is updated. This gives the PeopleSoft Process Scheduler the necessary information to run and monitor the process request.

25.4 THE PROCESS SCHEDULER REQUEST DIALOG

The Process Scheduler Request dialog panel (shown in figure 25.4) is used to specify where you want to run your report, the destination of your report's output, and the time of the actual run. Let's take a closer look at these parameters.

The Run Location group box allows you to choose between running your report on Client or Server. If you select Server, you have to select the server name from the list of available servers. If you want to schedule your process to run at a later time, you must select Server because your process scheduling can only be done on a server, and not on your client machine.

TIP   Always select a server name when Run Location is Server.

The Output Destination of your report may be File or Printer. The Window output is available only for Crystal Report programs, not for SQR programs. If you want to direct your output to a file, you need to enter the filename and a complete path for the file in the Printer/File text box. If you enter an existing file name, the system will overlay the old file.

If you need to print a hard copy of the report, select Printer and specify which printer port to use in the Printer/File text box.

The Run Recurrence and Run Date/Time parameters are only available if you select Server as the run location. The Run Recurrence parameter allows you to define your process as a recurring process that may be executed on a periodic basis.

Run Date/Time defaults to the current date and time. If you plan to schedule only one report run, select the Once option in the Run Recurrence selection and enter the desired run date and time in the Date and Time boxes. If you select a Run Recurrence value other than the default value Once, and specify the proper run recurrence definition, it will override any Run Date/Time you may have previously set.

Let's see how you arrange to run your process at a specific time. Remember, you can use this option only by specifying the run location as Server. If, for example, you want to run your report every Sunday, weekly at 7 AM, you have to create a new Run Recurrence definition (if one has not been set up already): click on the New button and name it WEEKLY AT 7 AM (figure 25.5).

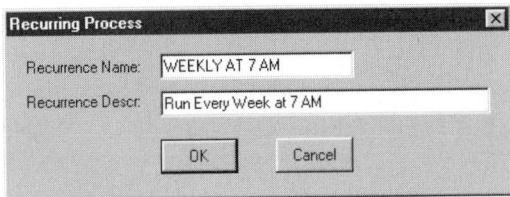

Figure 25.5
creating a new Run Recurrence definition

When you press the OK button, the Recurrence Definition panel appears (figure 25.6). This panel allows you to define the starting date and time, the run frequency, and all other necessary scheduling information.

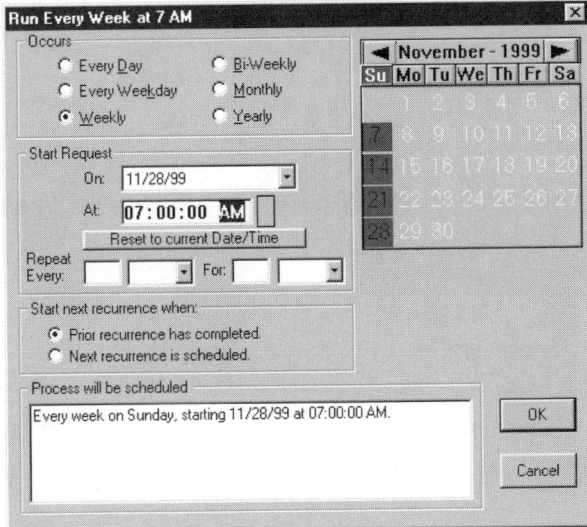

Figure 25.6
The Recurrence Definition panel

It is important to keep in mind that all the report-run schedule information is entered for a specific Run Control record, identified by a combination of the Run Control ID and operator ID. You should not use this Run Control ID to run or schedule other processes. Technically, the system will allow you to do this, but all your previous settings will then be overlaid with the new settings.

TIP   Use meaningful Run Control IDs.

For example, the Years of Service report may be scheduled to run every Sunday using a Run Control ID named Sunday_Run. If, in addition to this run schedule, you want to run the report at the end of the month, another Run Control ID must be used; otherwise, the every Sunday run schedule will be overlaid.

Now that you know how to schedule report runs, let's go back to figure 25.4 and review the run parameters on the Process Scheduler Request Dialog panel for the Years of Service report. We select the Run Location as Client and the Output Destination as File. We need to make sure that the output file goes to the proper directory. Since we run the report on the client machine and cannot schedule it to run at a specified time, the run time defaults to the current time. The only thing you need to do is to press OK. Another PeopleSoft tool, called Process Monitor, can help you monitor your process. (Remember, every report run under the Process Scheduler is a *process!*)

25.5 VIEWING THE STATUS OF YOUR REPORT VIA THE PROCESS MONITOR

The Process Monitor not only allows you to check the status of your process, but also permits you to see the report run parameters, delete the report from input or output queue, and perform other tasks (figure 25.7).

Navigation: Go → PeopleTools → Process Monitor

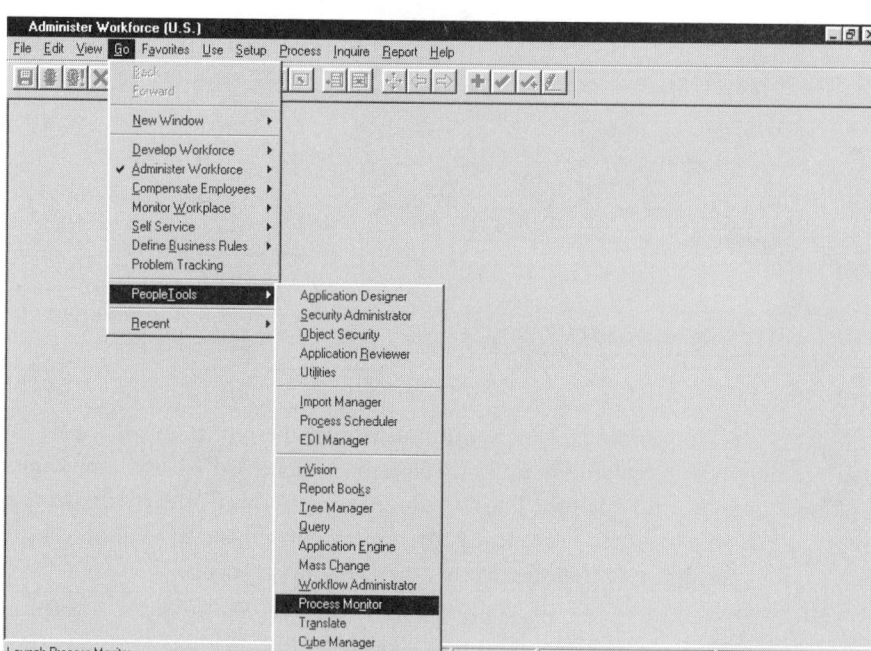

Figure 25.7 Invoking the Process Monitor

After selecting the Process Monitor, the system displays the Process Monitor panel (figure 25.8).

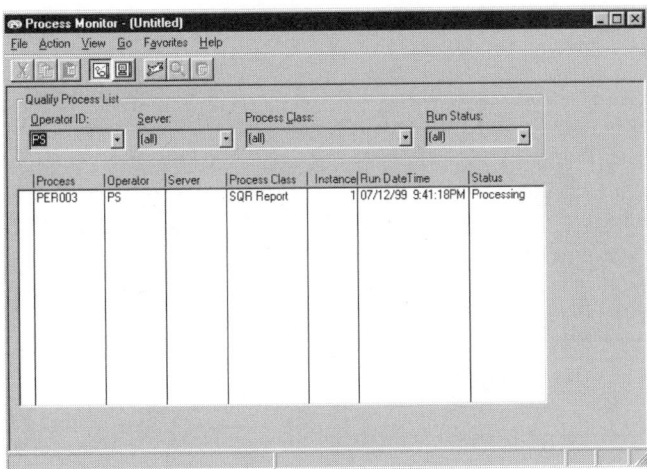

Figure 25.8
The Process Monitor
panel with Process
Status = Process

The Process Monitor panel in figure 25.8 displays the information about all processes by the operator ID. You can easily modify the view by narrowing the selection down to a specific operator ID, server, process class, and run status. The last column in this panel (named "Status") shows the status of your process. The status could be one of the following: `Success`, `Initiated`, `Hold`, `Queued`, `Processing`, `Canceled`, `Error`.

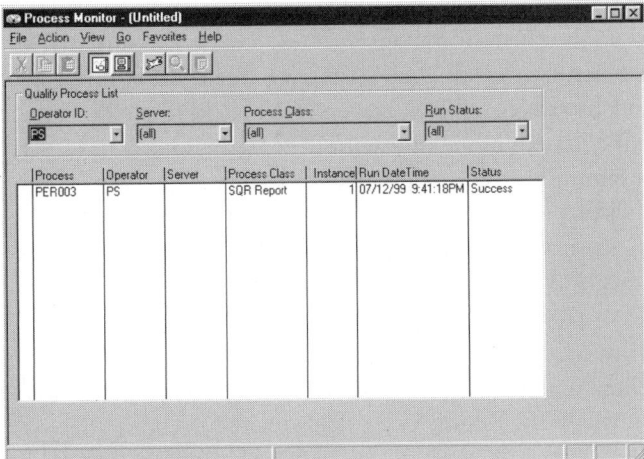

Figure 25.9
The Process Monitor
panel with Process
Status = Success

Let's double-click on your process. The system displays the Process Request Detail panel group, which consists of two panels: Process Detail and Request Parameters (figure 25.10).

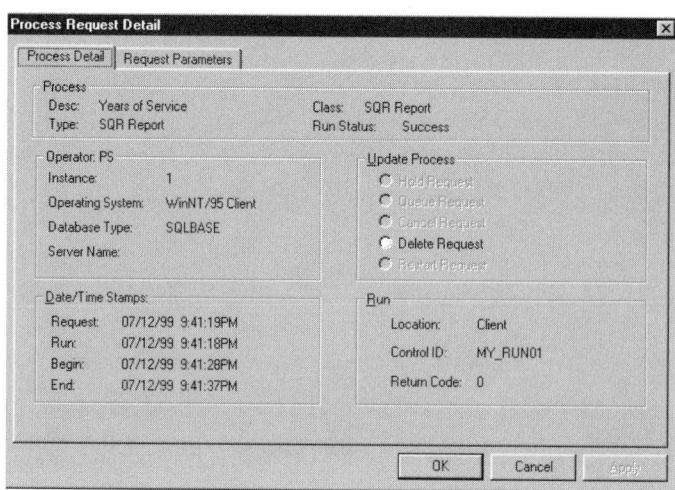

Figure 25.10
The Process Detail panel

The Process Detail panel shows the process information including the process description, type, and run status, the ID of the operator who initiated the process; the operating system under which the process is run; the database type; and the server name if the process is run on a server. You can check to see how long your report took to run by looking at the beginning and ending date/time stamps. Knowing these details can be useful in troubleshooting. Sometimes, if the process you started just sits in the input queue with its status equal to Initiated or Queued, and you wonder what's going on, the first thing to do is check the Process Detail panel to see whether the process was initiated on the client or the server. If the process was initiated on a server, was the correct server name entered? You can check to see if the appropriate Server Agent is up and running by selecting View, Servers or by clicking on ▤ in the main Process Monitor panel. If you need more information, go to the second Process Request Detail sub panel and examine the request parameters (figure 25.11).

This panel displays all parameters passed to your process, as well as the command line used during the execution. You can also use the Copy to Clipboard push button if you need to save and review your process request parameters.

TIP   If you forget the destination of your output report file, you can always check it in the Request Parameters panel. The output destination will be shown in the Parameter list following the –f flag.

Figure 25.11
The Request
Parameters panel

25.5.1 Controlling your processes via the Process Monitor

The Process Monitor panel gives you complete control over your process. You can cancel, delete, or put the process on hold. Depending on the current status of your process, the system will allow you to select a valid action. For example, if the process has finished, you can delete it from the Process Monitor panel. If the process was just initiated, you can cancel the process, and then delete the process status record from the panel (figure 25.12).

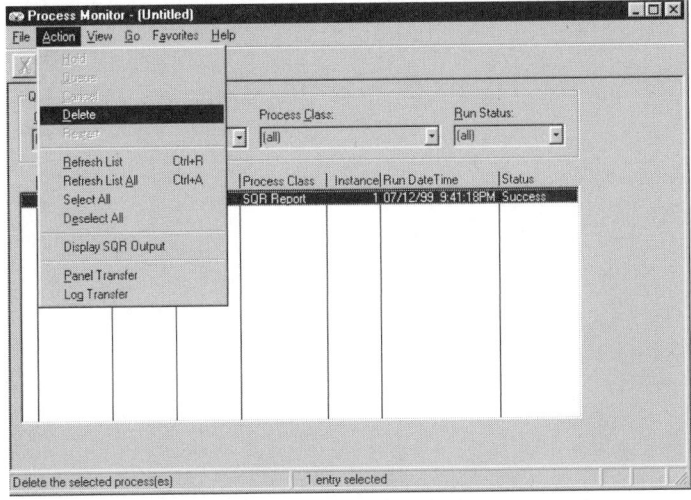

Figure 25.12 Deleting the process status record from the Process Monitor panel

25.6   VIEWING THE REPORT OUTPUT

When you run your report on the client, you can display your report output from the Process Monitor panel. Click on your process, then select Action, and Display SQR Output (figure 25.13).

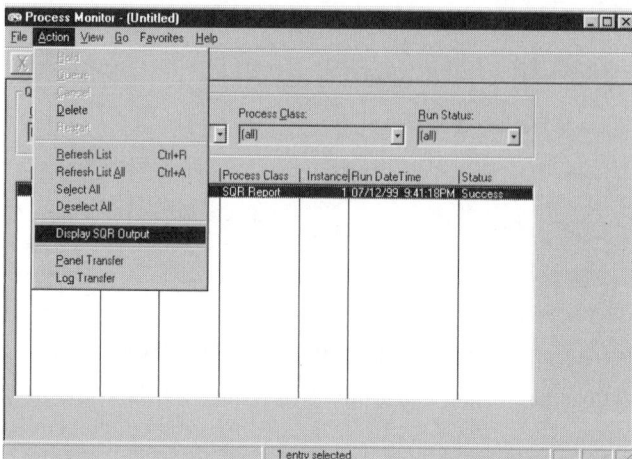

Figure 25.13
Displaying SQR output

You can see the output of your program displayed on Windows Notepad (or WordPad if the output is too large). Note that, if the output is in the .lis format, you see the special print control characters on the first line of your report, (figure 25.14). When you print the report on a printer, the report comes out without the special characters in the format specified by your program.

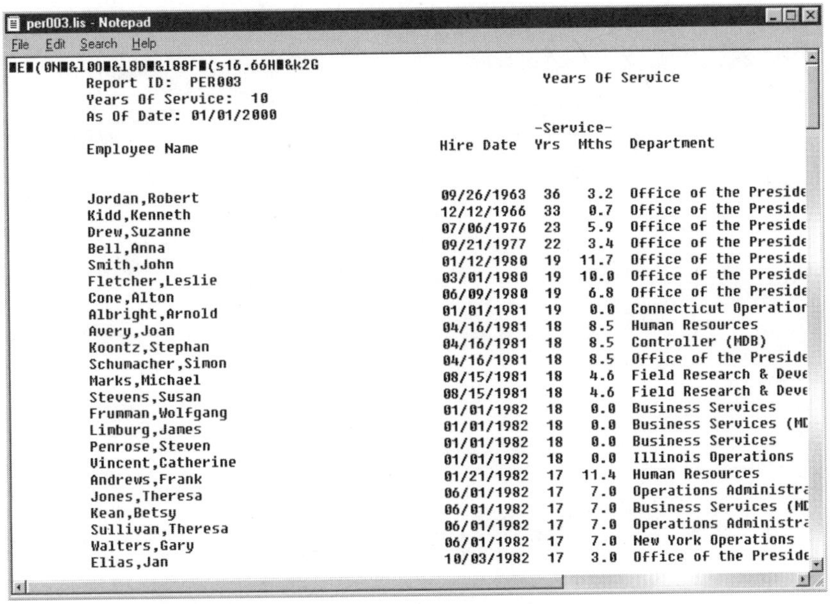


```
■E■(0N■&l00■&l8D■&l88F■(s16.66H■&k2G
        Report ID:  PER003                                              Years Of Service
        Years Of Service:  10
        As Of Date: 01/01/2000
                                                                     -Service-
        Employee Name                                     Hire Date  Yrs  Mths  Department


        Jordan,Robert                                     09/26/1963  36   3.2  Office of the Preside
        Kidd,Kenneth                                      12/12/1966  33   0.7  Office of the Preside
        Drew,Suzanne                                      07/06/1976  23   5.9  Office of the Preside
        Bell,Anna                                         09/21/1977  22   3.4  Office of the Preside
        Smith,John                                        01/12/1980  19  11.7  Office of the Preside
        Fletcher,Leslie                                   03/01/1980  19  10.0  Office of the Preside
        Cone,Alton                                        06/09/1980  19   6.8  Office of the Preside
        Albright,Arnold                                   01/01/1981  19   0.0  Connecticut Operatior
        Avery,Joan                                        04/16/1981  18   8.5  Human Resources
        Koontz,Stephan                                    04/16/1981  18   8.5  Controller (MDB)
        Schumacher,Simon                                  04/16/1981  18   8.5  Office of the Preside
        Marks,Michael                                     08/15/1981  18   4.6  Field Research & Deve
        Stevens,Susan                                     08/15/1981  18   4.6  Field Research & Deve
        Frumman,Wolfgang                                  01/01/1982  18   0.0  Business Services
        Limburg,James                                     01/01/1982  18   0.0  Business Services (MD
        Penrose,Steven                                    01/01/1982  18   0.0  Business Services
        Vincent,Catherine                                 01/01/1982  18   0.0  Illinois Operations
        Andrews,Frank                                     01/21/1982  17  11.4  Human Resources
        Jones,Theresa                                     06/01/1982  17   7.0  Operations Administra
        Kean,Betsy                                        06/01/1982  17   7.0  Business Services (MD
        Sullivan,Theresa                                  06/01/1982  17   7.0  Operations Administra
        Walters,Gary                                      06/01/1982  17   7.0  New York Operations
        Elias,Jan                                         10/03/1982  17   3.0  Office of the Preside
```

Figure 25.14 SQR output displayed via the Process Monitor panel

If you run your report on the server, you cannot see the report output from the Process Monitor panel. You can use FTP or another available tool to copy your report output from the server to the client. Another option is to print your report directly from the server to your network printer.

25.7 Editing Run Control records

You already know that any process execution is controlled by two types of records: the PeopleTools Run Control record and the application Run Control record. Both records have the same key identifier, a combination of the Run Control ID and the operator ID.

The PeopleTools Run Control record stores the generic report control information: where to run the report and where to direct the report output. Additional information related to the process run request specifics, is stored in the Process Request system table.

In order to see the PeopleTools Run Control record, select Edit/Preference/Run Control from the Administer Workforce (U.S.) panel (figure 25.15).

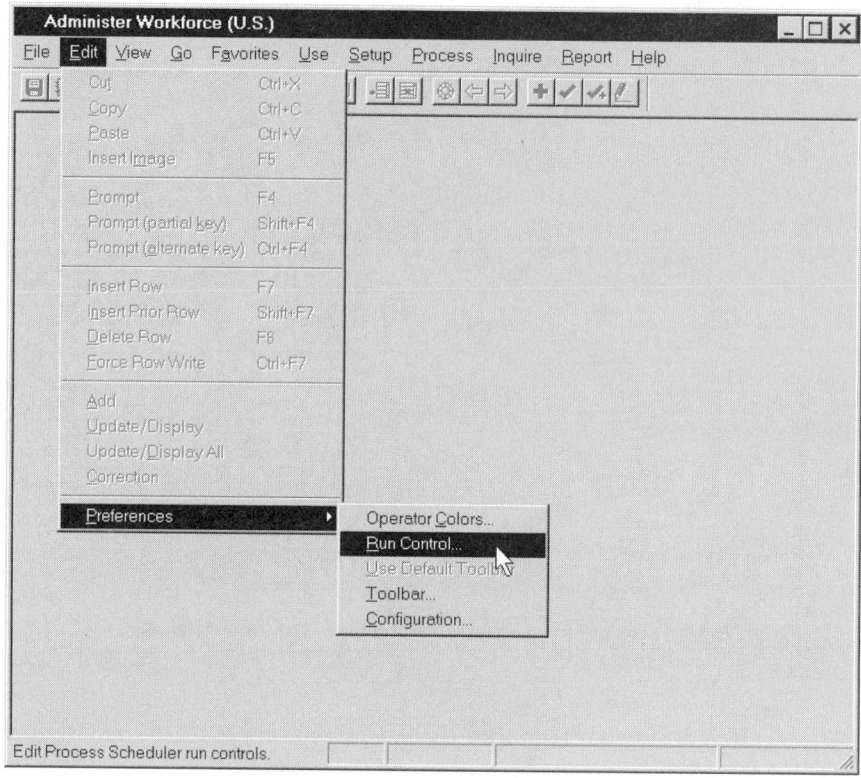

Figure 25.15   Selecting the Run Control Edit panel

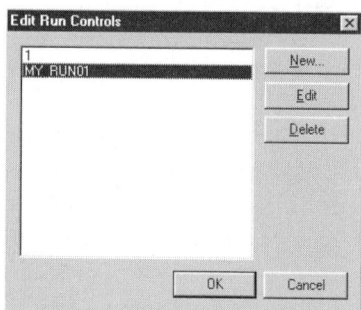

Figure 25.16   Edit Run Controls dialog

The system displays the Edit Run Controls dialog window shown in figure 25.16.

You can see all the Run Control record IDs that you are allowed to access based on your security, including the one you just created: MY_ RUN01. Select this ID and press the OK button to see the record details. The system brings the Edit Run Control panel shown in figure 25.17.

As you can see, the predefined settings for this Run Control ID are displayed on the panel. The panel shows the run location as Client and the output directed to File.

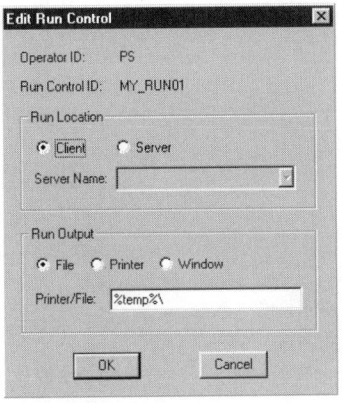

Figure 25.17 The Edit Run Control panel

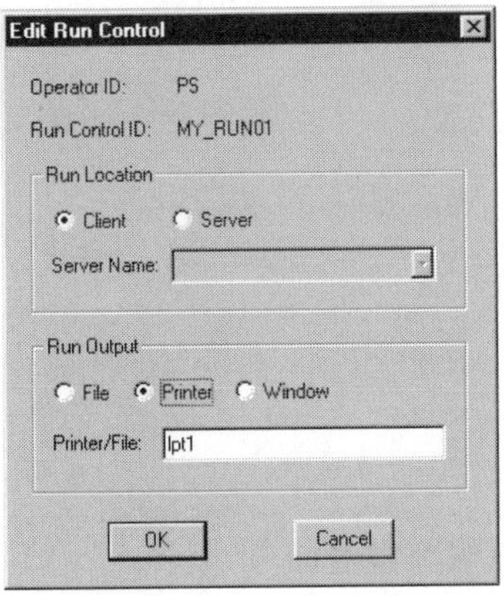

Figure 25.18 Changing the Run Control settings

Press the CANCEL button and return to the previous window (figure 25.16). As you can see from the dialog panel, you have the ability to create new Run Control records, edit existing records, or even delete records you no longer need. Keep in mind that, if you delete a Run Control record, only the PeopleTools Run Control record will be deleted. All Application Run Control records with the same key values remain in the system. These records can be deleted via a database management tool outside of PeopleSoft. Depending on your database, you can use products like SQL*Plus for Oracle, SQL Programmer for Sybase, QMF for DB2, or similar ones.

Let's see what would happen if you changed some of the Run Control parameters. On the Edit Run Controls dialog (figure 25.16), select MY_RUN01 again and press the EDIT button.

The system brings back the Edit Run Control panel with all the previously specified settings. Now change the Run Output setting from File to Printer and press the OK button to save the changes (figure 25.18).

Now that we have figured out how to see and change the PeopleTools Run Control records, let's see if you can do the same with the application Run Control records.

The application Run Control record contains all application-specific report input parameters. In order to see this record on the Administer Workforce (U.S.) window (figure 25.19), select Report/Years Of Service and, this time, select the Update/Display option.

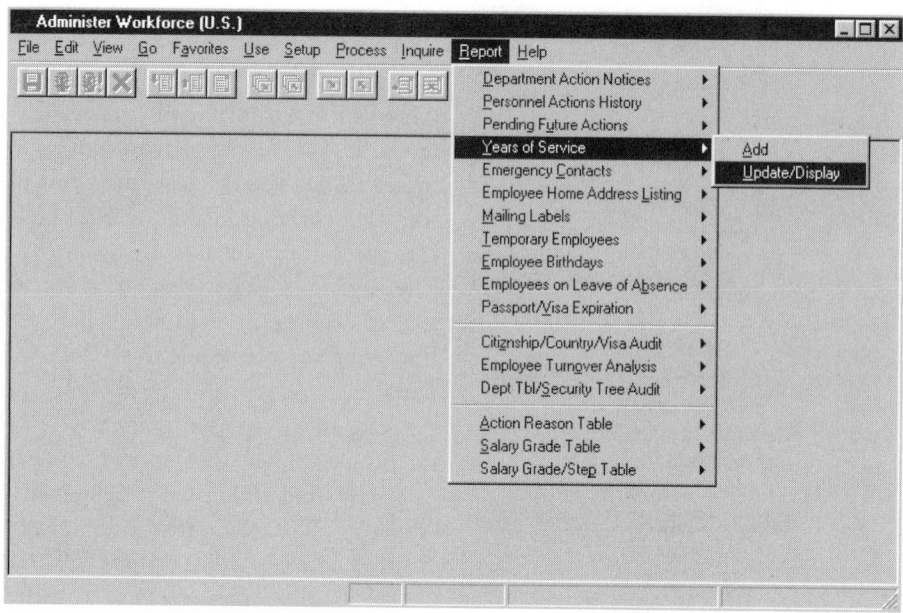

Figure 25.19 **Displaying an existing application Run Control record**

After you press the OK button, the system displays the list of all available Run Control IDs (figure 25.20).

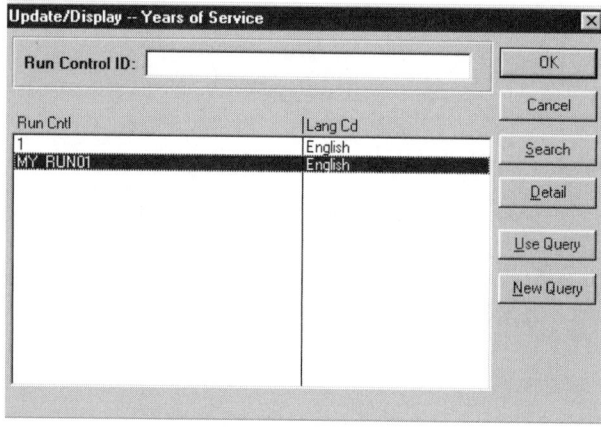

Figure 25.20
Run Control ID dialog

Select MY_RUN01, and the system displays the application Run Control panel with all process-specific parameter values (figure 25.21).

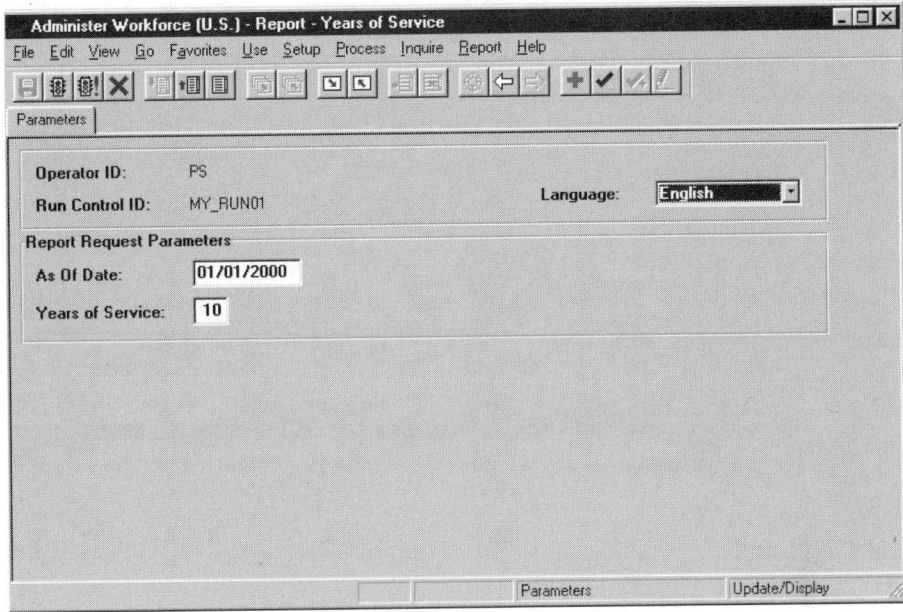

Figure 25.21   The application Run Control panel with process-specific parameters

Now you can see all previous parameter values and change some of these values if needed. In our case, there are two parameters, As Of Date and Years Of Service. Let's change the `As Of Date` parameter value from `01/30/1997` to `01/01/2000`. Click on the Traffic Light button to run the report. The system displays the next window, the Process Scheduler Request dialog shown in figure 25.22.

As you can see in figure 25.22, the Output Destination on this panel has been changed from `File` to `Printer`. If you run the report now, the system will use both the changed PeopleTools Run Control parameters and the changed application Run Control parameters.

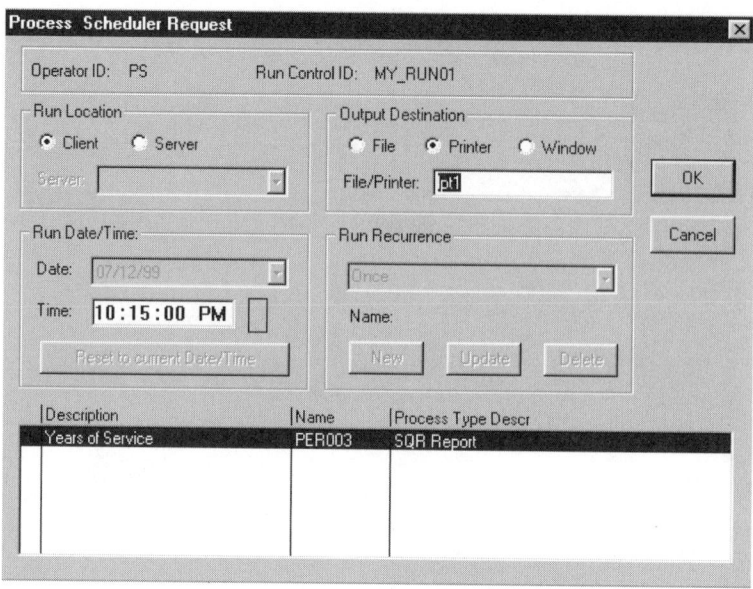

Figure 25.22   The Process Scheduler Request dialog with updated settings

1   PeopleSoft-delivered reports are usually executed from on-line panels and run with the help of the PeopleSoft Process Scheduler.

2   The Process Scheduler works with processes and job streams.

3   You can either run processes on your workstation or remotely on a server.

4   The Process Scheduler controls process executions with the help of the Run Control records: PeopleTools Run Control and the application Run Control. The Run Control ID along with the operator ID are the key fields in these records.

5   You can schedule a process execution at a specific date/time only if the process runs on a server.

6 The Process Monitor allows you to control your processes: you can view the process status or cancel, delete, or put processes on hold, depending on the status of your process.

7 You can view your report output if it were executed on the client via the Process Monitor panel.

8 The output destination of your report may go to File or Printer. Window output is available only for Crystal reports, not for SQR Reports.

C H A P T E R 2 6

Creating a custom SQR program

During the course of this book, we have been developing the Problem Tracking application. Our application would not be complete if we did not create reports for our users. Many reports are usually expected from Problem Tracking systems. Users may need to have a list of all open and not assigned incidents or all closed incidents listed by a particular date, by the project ID, by user, or by the person responsible to fix a problem. In this chapter, we will create a simple SQR program that will be able to support some of these functions.

We'll start with exercise 1:

> Create a Problem Tracking status report.

The report will list all reported incidents sorted by Problem Status and Incident Date. As a first step, we will create an SQR program that will not be attached to any

PeopleSoft menu and, therefore, will not be available for execution from the PeopleSoft Process Scheduler. In the following chapters, you will learn how to make this program run under PeopleSoft.

26.1   DESIGNING YOUR SQR PROGRAM

Navigation: Go → PeopleTools → Application Designer → Open → MY_PROJECT

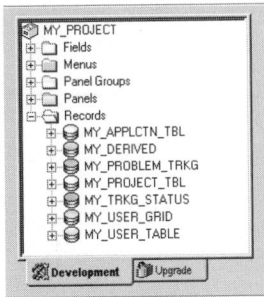

Let's take a look at the tables that we created in our Problem Tracking application and find the ones that can be used to produce our report.

As you can see from figure 26.1, the MY_PROJECT project contains all the Problem Tracking Application objects, including all the custom tables we created. Let's double-click on the MY_PROBLEM_TRKG record and examine all its fields (figure 26.2).

Figure 26.1   The MY_PROJECT Project

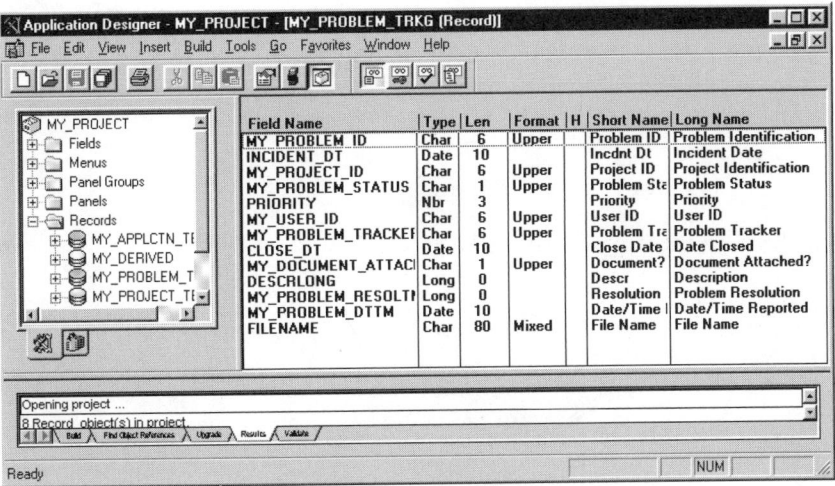

Figure 26.2   The MY_PROBLEM_TRKG record definition

When designing SQR programs, understanding your data model and building the right selection logic is a crucial part of any development process. As you can see from figure 26.2, the MY_PROBLEM_TRKG table can be used in our report since it contains all information about the incidents entered into the system via our custom online application. In addition, our report probably needs information such as an application and a project description, a user name, and so forth. We can select this information from other tables created for this Application.

Let's create our SQR program:

Listing 26.1

MYPROB01.sqr

```
!Problem Status Report

#define problem_status_len  10
#define project_descr_len   30
#define date_len            10
#define priority_len         8
#define user_name_len       20
#define responsible_name    20
#define col_sep              2


!**************
Begin-Setup
!**************
Load-Lookup Name=Projects
   Rows  = 500
        Table = PS_MY_PROJECT_TBL
        Key   = MY_PROJECT_ID
        Return_Value=Descr

Load-Lookup Name=Users
   Rows  = 1000
        Table = PS_MY_USER_TBL
        Key   = MY_USER_ID
        Return_Value=Name

End-Setup


!****************
Begin-Heading   7
!****************
print 'Problem Status Report' (1,1) Center

page-number                      (0,100)   'Page No.  '
print 'Run Date '                (+1,100)
Print 'Problem Status: '         (+1,1)
Print $Stat                      ()
print '='                        (+1,        1,                     125) fill
print 'Project Description '     (+1,        1, {project_descr_len} )
print 'Incident       '          (  ,+{col_sep}, {date_len}         )
print 'Priority       '          (  ,+{col_sep}, {priority_len}     )
print 'User Name      '          (  ,+{col_sep}, {user_name_len}    )
print 'Responsible    '          (  ,+{col_sep}, {responsible_name} )
```

```
    print 'Close          '          (    ,+{col_sep}, {date_len}            )
    print '               '          (+1,            1, {project_descr_len} )
    print '   Date         '          (    ,+{col_sep}, {date_len}            )
    print '               '          (    ,+{col_sep}, {priority_len}        )
    print '               '          (    ,+{col_sep}, {user_name_len}       )
    print 'To Resolve     '          (    ,+{col_sep}, {responsible_name}    )
    print 'Date           '          (    ,+{col_sep}, {date_len}            )
    print '='                         (+1,            1,            125) fill

End-Heading

!**************
Begin-Program
!**************
Do Init-Report
Do Main
End-Program


!***************************
Begin-Procedure Init-Report
!***************************
 Do Ask-Input-Parameters
 Do Build-Where
 Do Load-Xlats

End-Procedure

!***********************************
Begin-Procedure Ask-Input-Parameters
!***********************************
!Get User's Input

 Input $AsOfDate Type=Date 'Please enter As Of Date'

 Let #Input=1
 While #Input = 1
   Input $Problem_Status Type=Char 'Please Enter Problem Status
(1=Initiated, 2=Assigned,  3=Progress, 4=Testing, 5=Resolved,6=Void) or
press Enter for All' Status=#Input_Status
   If $Problem_Status     = ''
     Let #Input  = 0
   Else
     If $Problem_Status  > '0' and $Problem_Status < '7'
        show 'Problem Status Entered = ' $Problem_Status
        Let #Input        = 0
     Else
        Show 'Invalid Input, Re-Entry Required'
     End-If
   End-If
 End-While

End-Procedure
```

```
!****************************
Begin-Procedure Build-Where
!****************************
!Build Where Clause based on user's Input
 If $Problem_Status     = ''
   Let $Where_status = ''
 Else
   Let $Status=Rtrim($Problem_Status,' ')
   Let $Where_status = 'And A.My_Problem_Status = '|| ''''||$Status||''''
   Show $Where_status
 End-If

End-Procedure

!*************************
Begin-Procedure Load-Xlats
!*************************
 Let $Where_Xlat1 = 'FIELDNAME=''MY_PRIORITY'''
               ||' and X.EFFDT = (Select max(Effdt) from XLATTABLE '
               ||'Where Fieldname=X.Fieldname And FieldValue=X.FieldValue'
               ||' And Effdt <= Sysdate and Language_Cd = 'ENG') '

 Load-Lookup Name=Priority
   Rows  = 10
        Table = 'XLATTABLE X'
        Key   = FIELDVALUE
        Return_Value=XLATSHORTNAME
        Where=$Where_Xlat1

 Let $Where_Xlat2 = 'FIELDNAME=''MY_PROBLEM_STATUS'''
               ||' and S.EFFDT = (Select max(Effdt) from XLATTABLE '
               ||'Where Fieldname=S.Fieldname And FieldValue=S.FieldValue'
               ||' And Effdt <= Sysdate)'

 Load-Lookup Name=Status
   Rows  = 20
        Table = 'XLATTABLE S'
        Key   = FIELDVALUE
        Return_Value=XLATSHORTNAME
        Where=$Where_Xlat2
End-Procedure

!******************
Begin-Procedure Main
!******************
Begin-Select
A.My_Problem_Status    ()      on-break Print=Never After=Page-Break
Save=$Status_Cur
A.My_Project_ID
A.Incident_DT
A.Priority
A.My_User_ID
```

```
A.My_Problem_Tracker
A.Close_Dt
    Do Print-Line
From PS_MY_PROBLEM_TRKG A
Where A.Incident_Dt <= $AsOfDate
[$Where_status]
order by A.My_Problem_Status
End-Select
End-Procedure

!*************************
Begin-Procedure Print-Line
!*************************
 Lookup Projects &A.My_Project_ID $Descr
 Print $Descr                               (+1,          1, {project_descr_len}
)
 Print &A.Incident_DT                       (  ,+{col_sep}, {date_len}
)
 Lookup Priority &A.Priority $Priority_Descr
 Print $Priority_Descr                      (  ,+{col_sep}, {priority_len}
)
 Lookup Users &A.My_User_ID $User_Name
 Print $User_Name                           (  ,+{col_sep}, {user_name_len}
)
 Lookup Users &A.My_Problem_Tracker $Problem_Tracker_Name
 Print $Problem_Tracker_Name                (  ,+{col_sep}, {responsible_name}
)
 Print &A.Close_Dt                          (  ,+{col_sep}, {date_len}
)

End-Procedure

!*************************
Begin-Procedure Page-Break
!*************************
Lookup Status $Status_Cur $Stat
new-page
End-Procedure

!*****************************
```

As you can see from listing 26.1, our SQR program consists of the following sections:
Setup, Heading, Program, and several Procedure sections.

In the Setup section we loaded two tables, PS_MY_PROJECT_TBL and
PS_MY_USER_TBL, into the program memory with the help of the SQR
Load-Lookup command. This technique is used to speed up the data lookups per-
formed for every selected row in the Print-Line procedure.

In the Heading section we print our report header information.

In the Program section we call the Init-Report and Main procedures.

The purpose of the Init-Report procedure in our program is to prepare for our main reporting logic. We call the Ask-Input-Parameters procedure and, based on the results received from the user's input, call the Build-Where procedure to dynamically construct the WHERE clause for our main Select.

Ask-Input-Parameters interacts with users to obtain the input parameters: As Of Date and Problem Status. It also verifies a user's input and prompts again if the input is incorrect. Note that, when entering the problem status, users have an option to simply press Enter when they want to select records with all problem statuses.

Take a look at the Build-Where procedure. We are building a dynamic WHERE clause here. First, we check to see if our users entered any Problem Status or if they left this value blank (Null) to select all problems. If the value in the input variable is Null, we initialize the $Where_status string with Null. Otherwise, we build the WHERE clause by concatenating the column name with the status enclosed in quotes. Note that we use four quotes here. This is because we have two outside quotes to indicate the beginning and the end of a string as well as a double quote (instead of one) to tell SQR that this is a special character. You will see later that using this technique of building the dynamic parts of SQL helps us to create an efficient program.

The Load_Xlats procedure is designed to load lookup tables with value descriptions for the MY_PRIORITY and MY_PROBLEM_STATUS fields, thus saving on costly database operations. Why didn't we place this Load-Lookup into the Setup section along with the others? Because the Let statement is not allowed in the Setup section. Of course, other methods do exist for reading from the Translate table. PeopleSoft, for example, delivered a special include file READXLAT.sqc, which can also be used for this purpose.

The Select statement in the Main procedure selects the requested information. Its WHERE clause consists of two parts. The first one restricts the selection to the records with an Incident Date that is less then or equal to the input prompt date. The second part of the WHERE clause is stored in the string variable $Where_status that we built earlier in the Build_Where procedure. With this little trick, we can always select the required rows based on user's input. Another, simpler option would be to exclude Status variable from the WHERE clause and instead use the SQR procedural logic (If-Then) to check the selected rows one by one and compare the values in the column MY_PROBLEM_STATUS with the input variable. Our technique is clearly more efficient because we do not select unnecessary rows only to drop them later.

The Print-Line procedure is called from the Main Select. It is executed for each selected row. We perform several Lookup commands to get some field values from the Lookup arrays that we loaded into memory earlier. We then print the values. Here we use substitution variables (defined at the beginning of the program) which specify the print positions. If you need to change the layout of your report, you just have to modify these variables once where they were defined.

26.2 EXECUTING YOUR *SQR* PROGRAM

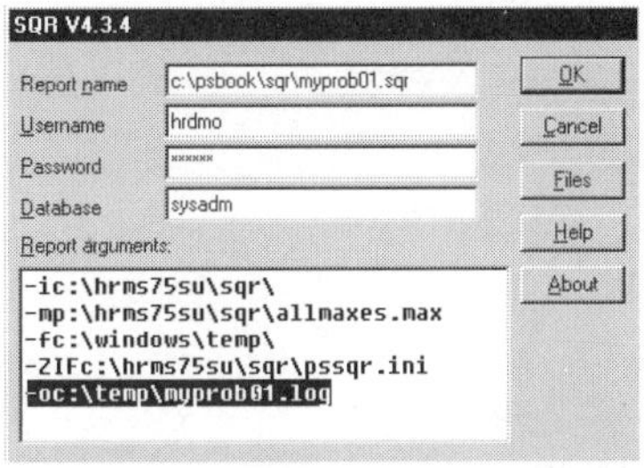

Figure 26.3 Submitting the SQR program via the SQRW dialog box

An SQR program can be invoked in different ways. You can start your program from the SQR dialog box in the Windows environment. You can also execute SQR programs from the operating system command line or call them from other programs. As an alternative, SQR programs can be run in batch mode under VAX/VMS, MVS, UNIX, MS-DOS, Windows, or OS/2 using DCL (VAX/VMS), JCL (MVS), shell scripts (UNIX), or batch files (MS-DOS, WINDOWS, OS/2).

At this point we execute our program from the SQRW dialog box. Let's fill in the SQRW dialog box as shown in figure 26.3 and submit our program.

After pressing the OK button, our program is submitted for execution. We are then prompted for our program's input parameters (figure 26.4):

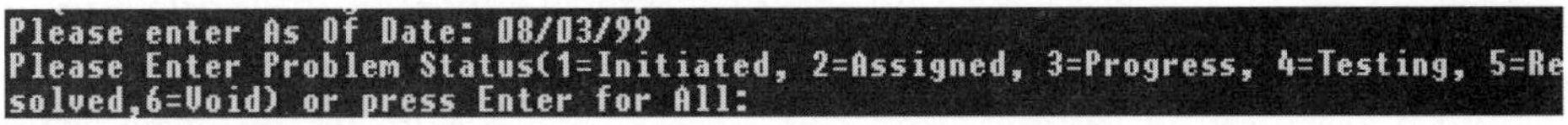

Figure 26.4 Prompt for input parameters

As you can see, we entered `08/03/99` as our `As Of Date` parameter value and pressed Enter to select records with all statuses. When all entries are accepted, our program runs to the end.

26.3 EXAMINING THE *SQR* PROGRAM OUTPUT FILES

Our program created two output files: the report file myprob01.lis and the log file myprob01.log. Let's take a look at the log file first. As you may already know, the log file contains information that is displayed by the `Display` or `Show` commands from our program. In addition, it may have some system information, such as the number of records loaded for the lookup table, Input command prompt, and so on. Our log file is shown in figure 26.5.

As you can see in figure 26.5, the information in this log file is printed by the SQR engine. The information about load lookup tables is useful, especially in the testing stage since it shows you how many rows were loaded. You can easily spot a problem using this information.

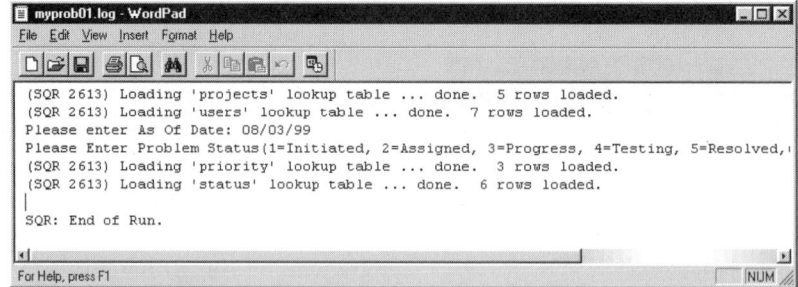

Figure 26.5 Myprob01.sqr log file

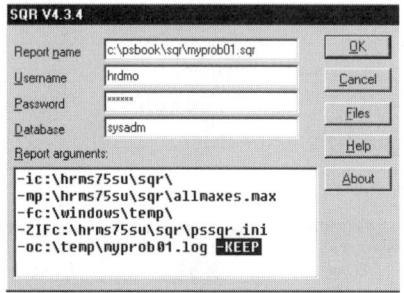

Figure 26.6 Creating an SPF file output along with a .lis file

Let's now take a look at our report output. The .lis file is intended to be printed and usually has formatting lines with information about the report layout, fonts, and such. You can still display the output file, but in order to test your report output, you need to print it. If you want to work with your report online, you should create an .spf file by using the –KEEP or –ZIV command line flags when submitting your program for execution. If we execute our report with the –KEEP flag, we would be able to see both: the .lis file and the .spf file output.

Figure 26.7 shows the output MYPROB01.lis file.

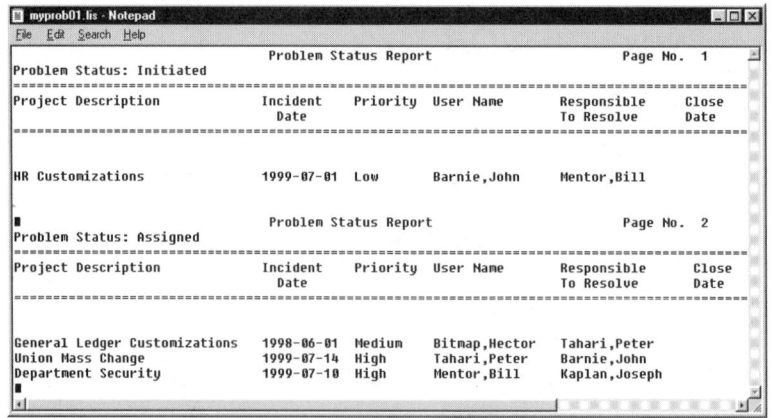

Figure 26.7 LIS file output

In order to see the SPF file, just double-click on C:\Windows\temp\myprob01.spf, and the SPF Viewer displays the file in a convenient online format (figure 26.8).

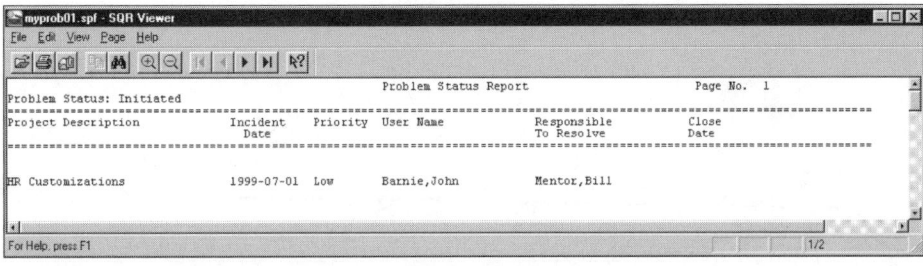

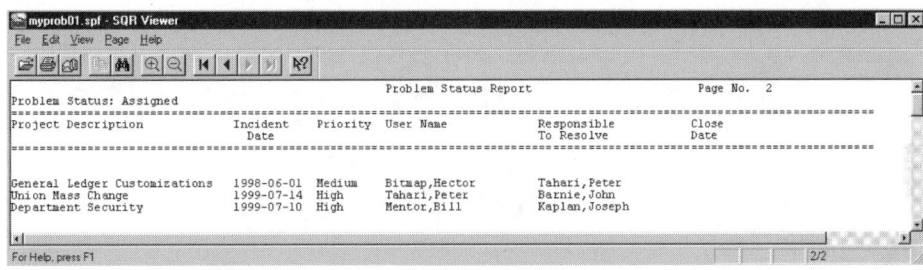

Figure 26.8   Using SQR Viewer to view SPF file output

KEY POINTS

1   In order to design an SQR program, you should be familiar with your database.

2   Dynamic SQL techniques help create more efficient programs.

3   An SQR program can be invoked from the SQR Dialog Box in the Windows environment or from the operating system command line. You can also call an SQR program from other programs or batch scripts.

4   If you would like to view your report online, you can create an .SPF file by using the –KEEP or –ZIV command line flags when submitting your program for execution.

C H A P T E R   2 7

Attaching SQR to the Process Scheduler

27.1   SELECTING A RUN CONTROL RECORD

PeopleSoft, which delivers a number of standard reports, records, panels, and menus, has always recommended that the best way to add new functionality is to clone already developed similar application objects. We will be using this commonly accepted approach in attaching custom reports to PeopleSoft.

   In PeopleSoft, the Application Run Control records are used to save the input parameters for processes. PeopleSoft developed a number of Application Run Control records that can be used if these records have the necessary fields for your program. For example, the Years of Service report uses the `As Of Date` and `Years of Service` as input parameters. Let's take a closer look at this report and find out what

Run Control record is used in the report. First, we need to find the name of the panel to which this report is attached.

Navigation: GO → Administer Workforce → Administer Workforce (U.S.) → Report → Years of Service

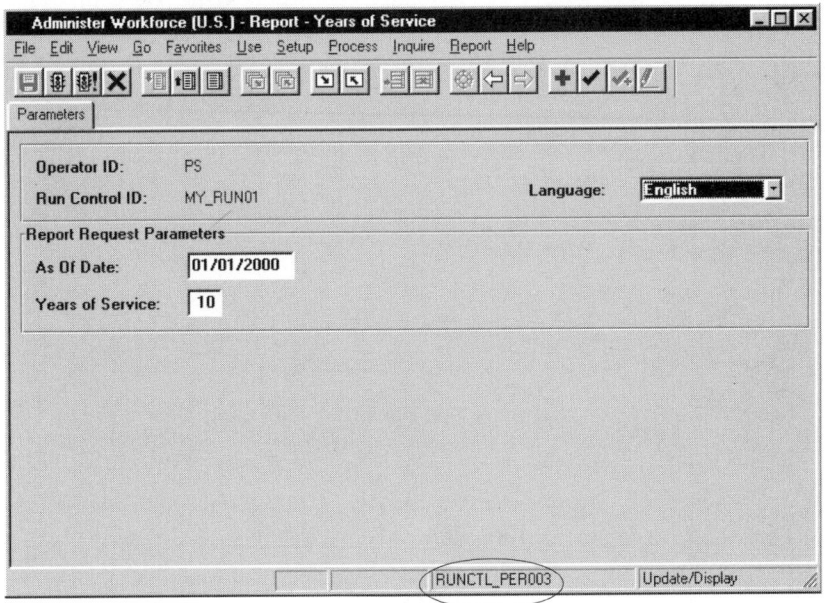

Figure 27.1   The Run Control panel for Years of Service report

We select View → Panel Name from the Administer Workforce (U.S.) menu, which allows us to see the panel name used for this report.

As you can see from figure 27.1, the panel name is RUNCTL_PER003.

TIP   You can select most of the delivered Run Control panels by typing 'RUNCTL_' in the Application Designer. They are a good source from which to clone.

Open this panel in the Application Designer to ascertain what record is used as its Run Control record.

When the panel is opened, select Layout → Order from the Application Designer menu (figure 27.2).

Navigation: Go → PeopleTools → Application Designer → Open → Panel →
 RUNCTL_PER003

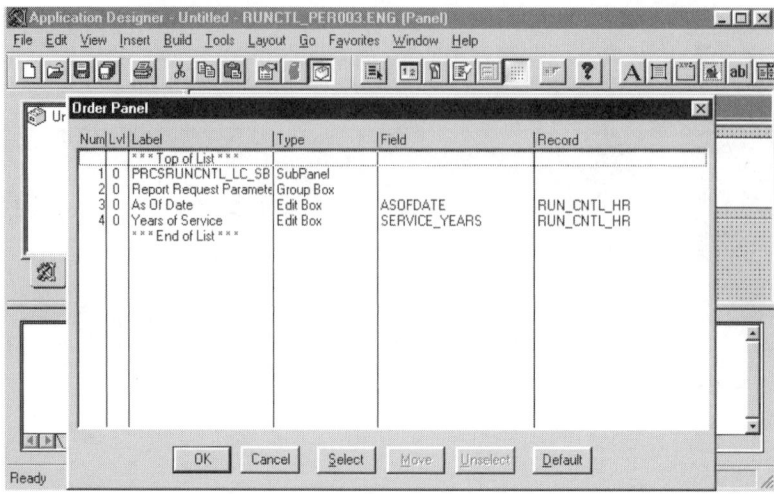

Figure 27.2   The RUN_CNTL_HR record is used as report's Run Control record

This report uses an application Run Control record named RUN_CNTL_HR. The structure of this record is shown in figure 27.3.

Field Name	Type	Len	Format	H	Short Name	Long Name
OPRID	Char	8	Mixed		Operator	Operator Id
RUN_CNTL_ID	Char	30	Mixed		Run Cntl	Run Control ID
FROMDATE	Date	10			From Date	From Date
THRUDATE	Date	10			Thru Date	Thru Date
ASOFDATE	Date	10			As Of	As Of Date
LANGUAGE_CD	Char	3	Upper		Lang Cd	Language Code
CALENDAR_YEAR	Nbr	4			Year	Calendar Year
SERVICE_YEARS	Nbr	2			YrsService	Years of Service
POSITION_NBR	Char	8	Num		Position	Position Number
POS_ACTIVE_OPTION	Char	1	Upper		Active Opt	Pos Active,Inactive,Both Optn
POS_ACTIVE	Char	1	Upper		PosnActive	Position Active
POS_INACTIVE	Char	1	Upper		PosnInact	Position Inactive
POS_REPORT_LEVEL	Nbr	2			Rpt Lvl	Pos Hierarchy Report Level
POS_VACANT_REQUEST	Char	1	Upper		Vacant Rqt	Request for Vacant Pos Report
POS_EXCEPT_OVRRIDE	Char	1	Upper		Exe/Ovrrid	Position Exception Override
JOB_REQUISITION#	Char	6	Num		Job Req #	Job Requisition #
RQMTS_SRCH#	Char	6	Num		Rqmt Srch#	Requirements Search #
JOBCODE	Char	6	Upper		Job Code	Job Code
DEPTID	Char	10	Upper		DeptID	Department
REPORT_CHOICE	Char	1	Upper		Rpt Choice	Output Report Choice
POPULATION	Char	1	Upper		Srch-Skill	Search Population-Skill Match
EE_REPORT_YEAR	Nbr	4			EE Year	Empl Equity Reporting Year
BUDGET_START_DT	Date	10			Start Dt	Budget Period Start Date
SAL_ADMIN_PLAN	Char	3	Upper		Sal Plan	Salary Administration Plan
INCR_START_DT	Date	10			Start Dt	Start Date for Step Increments
INCR_END_DT	Date	10			End Dt	End Date for Step Increments
JOB_EFFDT	Date	10			Job EffDt	Job Effective Date
COMPANY	Char	3	Upper		Co	Company
PAYGROUP	Char	3	Upper		Group	Pay Group
PERCENTCHG	Nbr	5.2			Change%	Percent of Salary Change
AMOUNTCHG	Nbr	5.2			Amt Chng	Amount of Salary Change
EMPLID	Char	11	Upper		ID	EmplID

Figure 27.3   The RUN_CNTL_HR Run Control record

As you can see from the figure 27.3, this record contains not just the fields necessary for our report. It is also used as a placeholder for most HRMS report input parameters. This does not mean, of course, that all record fields have to be used in every single report. If you know that your report input parameters are among the fields in this record, you can safely use the record as your report application Run Control record.

Let's see if we can use the RUN_CNTL_HR record for our Problem Tracking Status report program. Our program accepts two parameters: As Of Date and Problem Status. The first one, As Of Date, is present in the RUN_CNTL_HR record. The second parameter is our custom field, therefore, we won't find it in the delivered record. We can possibly use any other character type field as a placeholder for our Problem Status field, but if we want to do specific field edits to verify the proper entries, we would be better off creating our own custom Run Control record. Later on, we may want to add other fields to this record and use the record for other custom reports.

The safest way to create our own custom Run Control record is, of course, to clone an existing one. Since the RUN_CNTL_HR record is too big, and, if cloned, will require some effort in deleting all unused fields, let's rather use another record as a template, the PRCSRUNCNTL. This is a PeopleSoft-delivered record used for reports with no application-specific input parameters (figure 27.4).

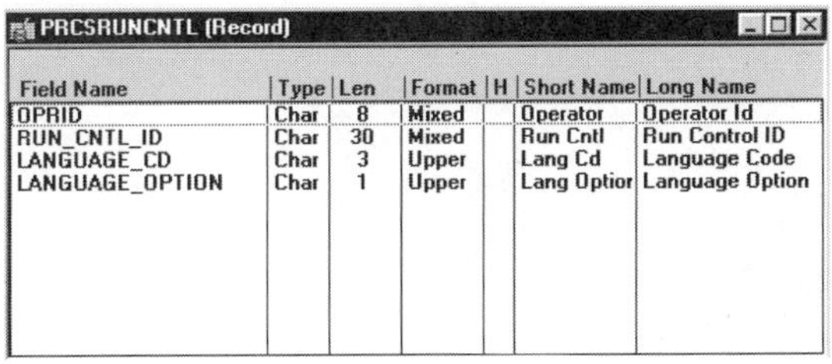

PRCSRUNCNTL (Record)

Field Name	Type	Len	Format	H	Short Name	Long Name
OPRID	Char	8	Mixed		Operator	Operator Id
RUN_CNTL_ID	Char	30	Mixed		Run Cntl	Run Control ID
LANGUAGE_CD	Char	3	Upper		Lang Cd	Language Code
LANGUAGE_OPTION	Char	1	Upper		Lang Option	Language Option

Figure 27.4
The PRCSRUNCNTL record is used for reports with no application specific input parameters

The fields OPRID and RUN_CNTL_ID are the PRCSRUNCNTL record key fields. The LANGUAGE_CD and LANGUAGE_OPTION fields are used in global development projects. The default value of the LANGUAGE_CD field depends on your operator ID. The LANGUAGE_OPTION tells the system if you are allowed to change the LANGUAGE_CD field.

After saving this record as MY_RUN_CNTL, deleting the LANGUAGE_CD and LANGUAGE_OPTION fields, and adding the fields that we need as our report input parameters, the record will look like that in figure 27.5.

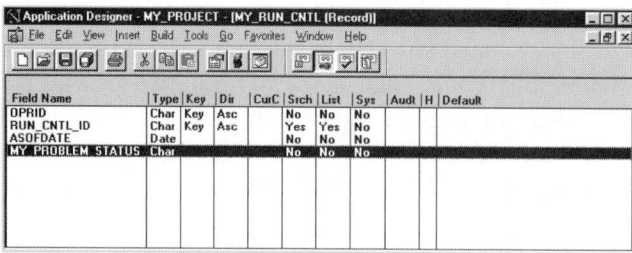

Figure 27.5
Creating a custom Run
Control record:
MY_RUN_CNTL

Since we've created our own record, we should not forget to add a description to identify the customizations.

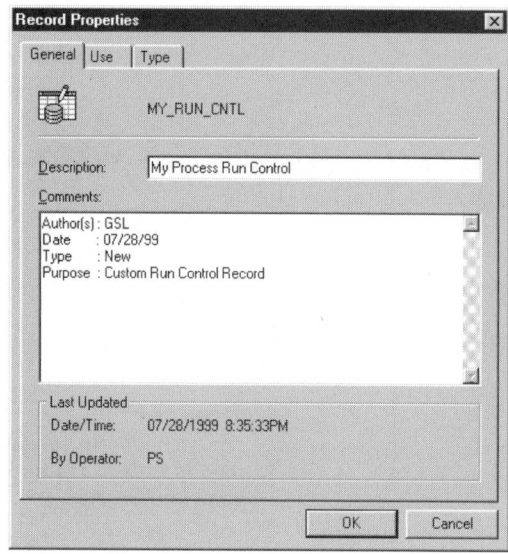

Figure 27.6
Entering record properties

After saving the record again, let's execute the Build option to create the database level table (figure 27.7).

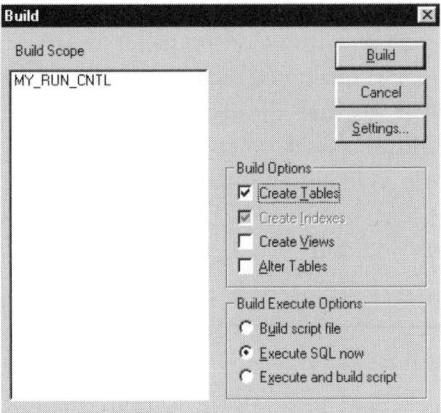

Figure 27.7
Building our custom Run Control record

As soon as the record is saved, it is automatically added to our project.

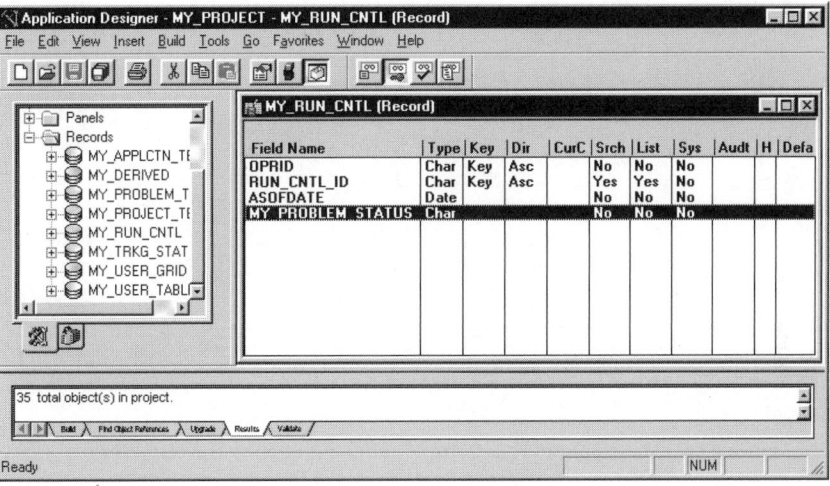

Figure 27.8   MY_RUN_CNTL Run Control record is added to a project

Now we can save the project and go to the next step of creating a Run Control panel.

27.2   CREATING A RUN CONTROL PANEL

PeopleSoft delivers many Run Control panels along with its applications. Therefore, if your report is using the same parameters as one of the PeopleSoft-delivered reports, it makes perfect sense to re-use the delivered panel. Since our report uses custom fields as input parameters, we create a new Run Control panel for it.

As we discussed in parts 2 and 4 of this book, each panel should have at least one record linked to it. In our particular case, we already know what record we are supposed to link to the Run Control panel since we just created it: it's our MY_RUN_CNTL record, which will hold all input parameters for our report.

Just as we did for the record creation, let's clone the Run Control panel that does not accept any parameters, then add our two fields to it. The panel name is PRCSRUNCNTL.

Let's check the panel structure in the Application Designer.

Navigation: Go → PeopleTools → Application Designer → File → Open.

Enter Panel as an object type, and PRCSRUNCNTL as a panel name. Press ENTER. You will see the panel that appears in figure 27.9.

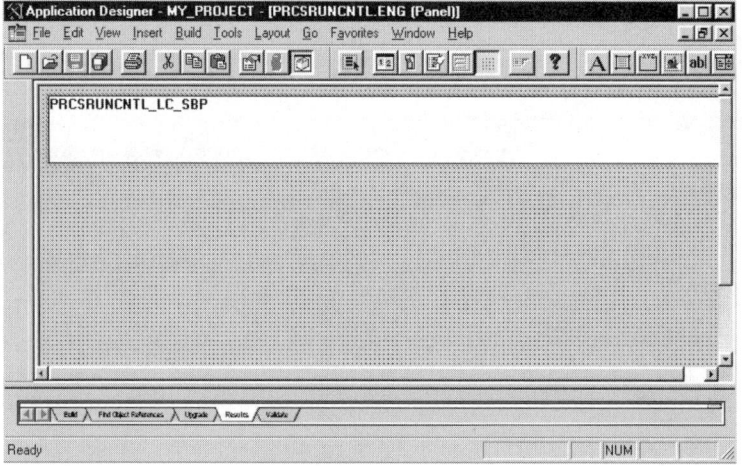

Figure 27.9   The standard Run Control panel with no input parameters

The panel contains a subpanel named PRCSRUNCNTL_LC_SBP. All the PRCSRUNCNTL panel fields are located inside of this subpanel. If you select Layout, Test Mode, or click on the Test Mode button 🔟 , you can see all the panel fields (figure 27.10).

CHAPTER 27   ATTACHING SQR TO THE PROCESS SCHEDULER

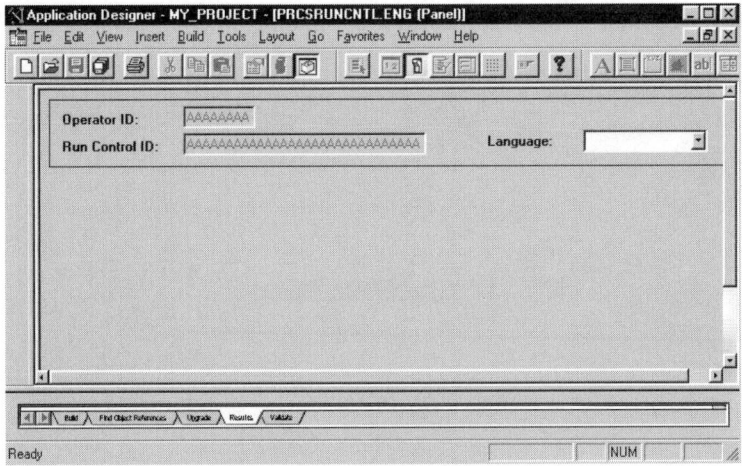

Figure 27.10   The PRCSRUNCNTL panel in test mode

Of the three fields in the panel, operator ID and the Run Control ID are the key fields automatically populated from the operator ID and the Run Control ID you entered. The third field, Language, is optional. If the operator does not select any Language from a prompt, it defaults to the operator's default language.

Since we are using this panel as a basis for cloning, we first save it as MY_RUN_CNTL_PRB01 panel and then modify it (figure 27.11).

After pressing the OK button, we add our custom fields to the panel under construction. This time we use our project to speed up the development. Double-click on the MY_RUN_CNTL record from the project workspace window. You can see all the fields in our record. Click on the As Of Date field and drag it to the panel space. Drop the field on the panel where you want the field to be placed. Repeat the same procedure for the MY_PROBLEM_STATUS field. Figure 27.12 shows our new panel.

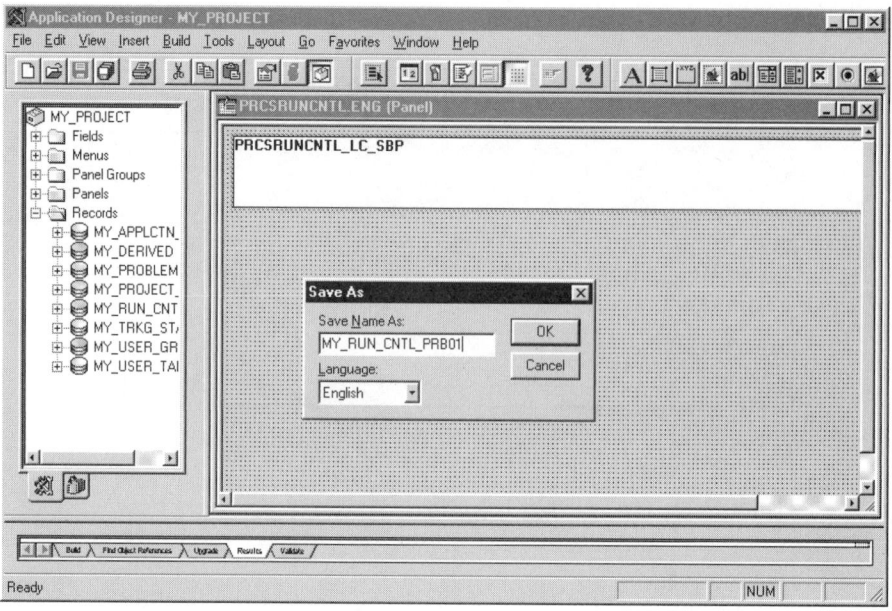

Figure 27.11 Cloning the PRCSRUNCNTL panel

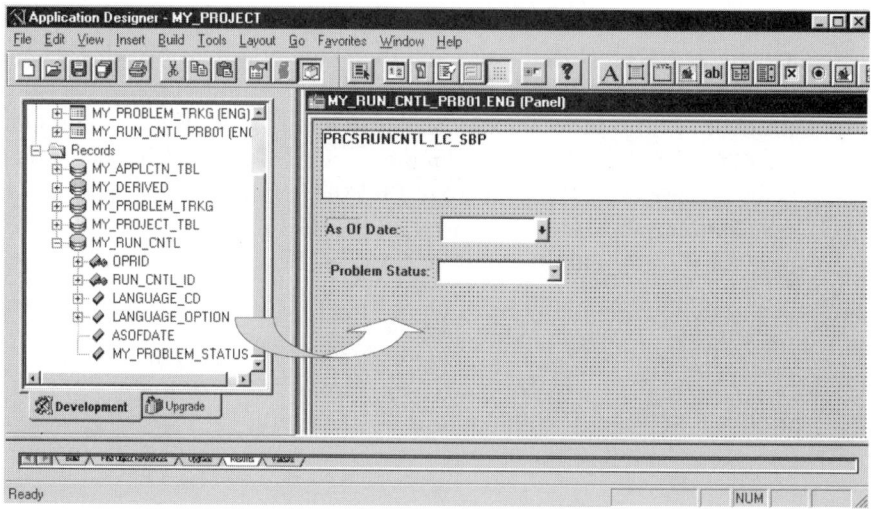

Figure 27.12 Dragging fields from the project to the panel

Since we modified our panel, let's not forget to save it.

Let's check the panel's layout. Select Layout → Order (figure 27.13).

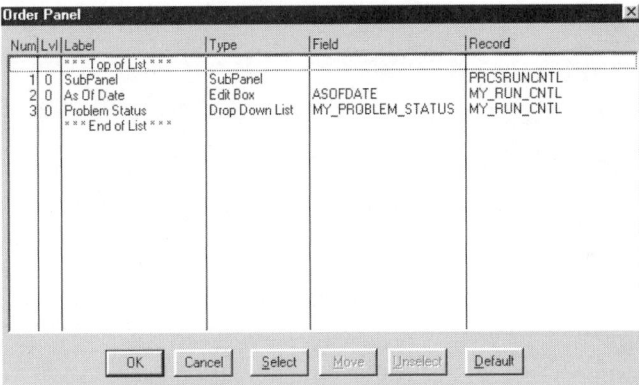

**Figure 27.13
Verifying the panel's
layout**

Our simple Run Control panel has only Level 0 fields. The standard subpanel is linked to the PRCSRUNCNTL record that has the same keys as our MY_RUN_CNTL record. Our two fields are in the correct order and belong to our custom record. The last thing we need to do is to update the Panel's properties.

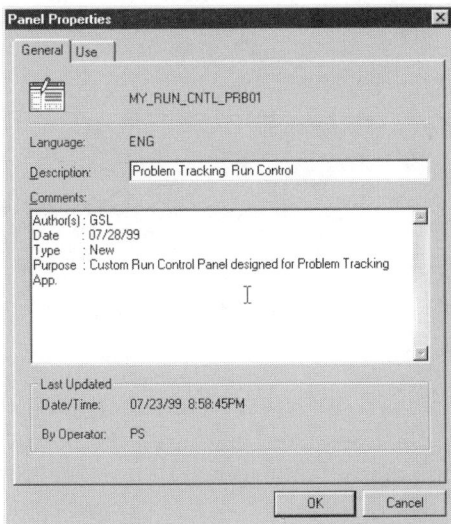

**Figure 27.14
Specifying panel's properties**

Our panel design is complete. In order to place it in a menu, we need to create a panel group.

27.3 CREATING A PANEL GROUP

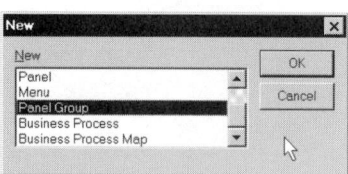

Figure 27.15 Creating a new Panel Group

After a panel is selected or created, it must be added to a panel group before you can attach it to a menu. A panel group is actually a link between the panel and the menu. Multiple panels may exist within a single panel group.

Let's create a new panel group by selecting File, New (in the Application Designer menu), and double-clicking on Panel Group in the New dialog (figure 27.15).

The Application Designer Panel Group screen appears (figure 27.16).

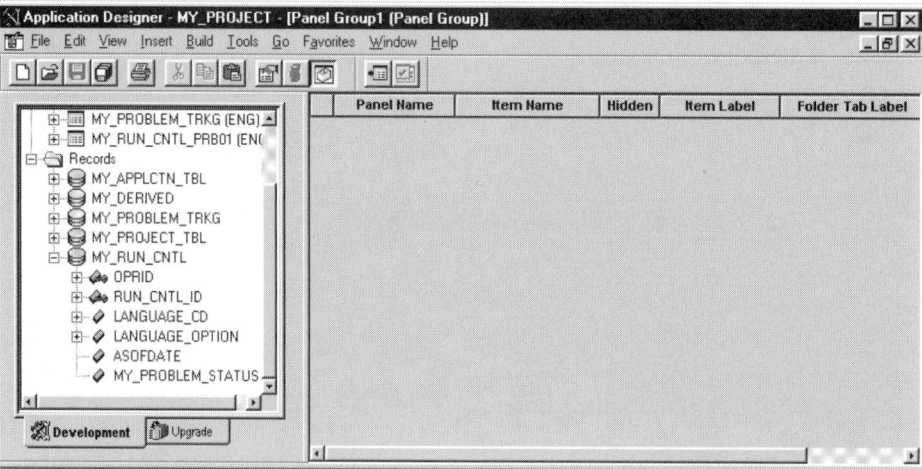

Figure 27.16   The Panel Group panel

We now need to add our panel (MY_RUN_CNTL_PROB01) to the panel group. To do this, you can either click on the Insert Panel button ▣ on the toolbar, or select Insert, Panel into Group, or use the drag-and-drop technique from the project window.

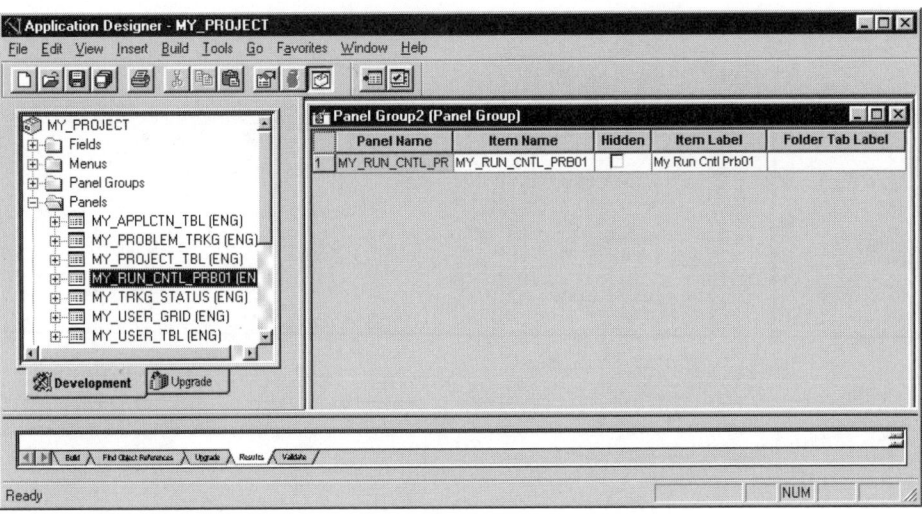

Figure 27.17 Dragging a panel from a project workspace to a panel group

Each panel in a group has a set of properties. The MY_RUN_CNTL_PRB01 panel has been added to the panel group with its properties set to their default values. Let's change these values to make them more meaningful.

The Item Name is used for informational purposes only, but it must be unique within the panel group. We'll specify our own name as Problem_Tracking.

The next property column is Hidden. You only check this value On if you need the panel to be hidden from the user's view. We'll leave the value of this column Off. You can have several panels in a panel group with the Hidden value set to Off and one or more panels with the value set to On. This technique is used when you need to bring to the buffer certain fields from some panels, but you don't want to display these panels to users.

The Item Label column is your panel name as it will appear on the menu. It will also be displayed at the bottom of the panel and as the default Folder tab label. Right now, it is named RUN CNTL PRB01, which is not very meaningful. Let's call it Problem Status Report.

The Folder Tab Label is used to identify the Folder tab when the Panel Group is selected. Let's name it Problem Status for our task.

After we enter all the values, our panel group definition looks like that shown in figure 27.18.

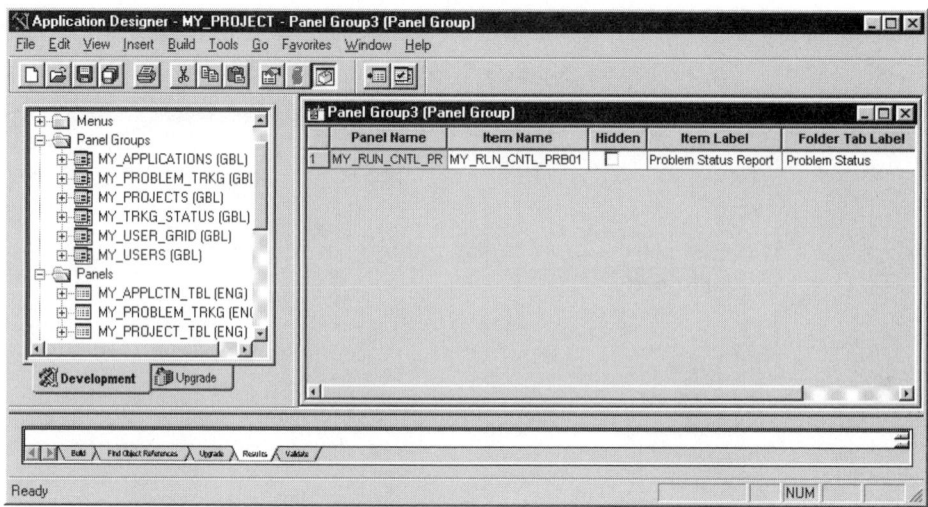

Figure 27.18   Setting panel group properties

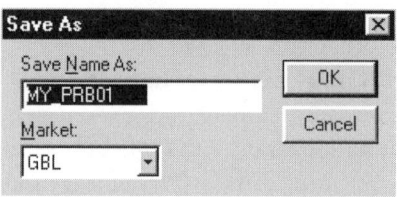

Figure 27.19   Saving a panel group

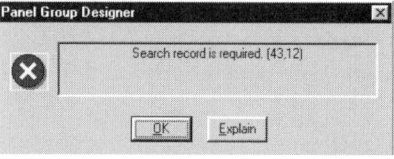

Figure 27.20   Panel group error window

Now, let's try to save our panel group.

After clicking on the OK button, an error message pops up (figure 27.20).

The Panel Group designer reminds us that we cannot save our panel group yet. We have not completed the design. We need to set the properties for the entire panel group, including search records, update and data entry actions, and detail panel information.

As we discussed in part 4, in order to allow our users access to the panels, the Search record has to be attached to the panel group. The search record that you select should contain all the keys that your user needs in order to retrieve rows displayed on the panel. Based on the actions that the user selects (Add, Update/Display), the Application Processor creates a prompt dialog box, which contains all the key fields in the search record. In our case, since we are defining a search record for a Run Control panel, the key fields are the operator ID and the Run Control ID. When the user selects an action to run a report, he/she is usually presented with two options: Add and Update/Display. When the Update/Display option is selected, the report is run under an existing Run Control ID. If the Add option is selected, a new Run Control ID is created to be used with the report. And, since the dialog box for operator should contain only the Run Control ID, you can always specify the standard PRCSRUNCNTL record as a search record for your report's panel group, no matter what application-specific parameters are defined for your report. This greatly simplifies the task of creating a panel group for reports.

PeopleSoft-delivered reports use the same search record: PRCSRUNCNTL.

Let's get back now to figure 27.20. After clicking on the OK button, the Panel Group Properties window appears. Let's fill in the Use tab as well as the General tab with the panel group description.

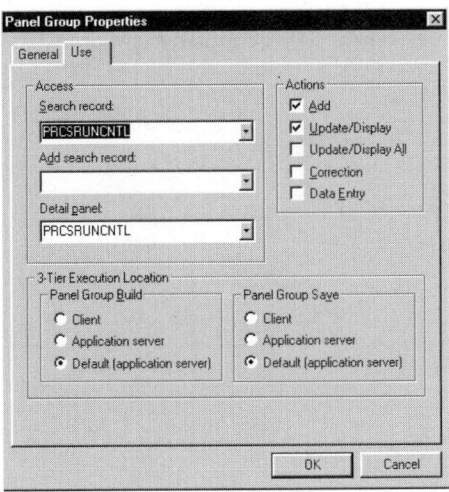

Figure 27.21
The Panel Group Properties

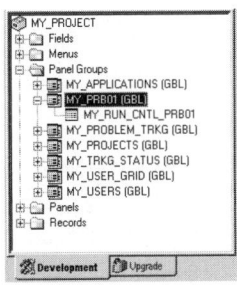

After all information is entered in the two tabs of Panel Group Properties, we can save our panel group. Select File, Save, and enter the new panel group name as MY_PROB01. Our panel group is automatically added to the project (figure 27.22).

Figure 27.22 Saving the MY_PROB01 panel group automatically adds it to our project

27.4 SELECTING A MENU FOR YOUR REPORT

The next decision you must make concerns the menu under which you will run your report. During the course of developing our Problem Tracking application, we already created a separate menu item named Problem Tracking. Let's open this menu item and add another item, Reports, to the menu bar. In order to do so, just click on the empty rectangle (figure 27.23), and specify the new Bar Item properties.

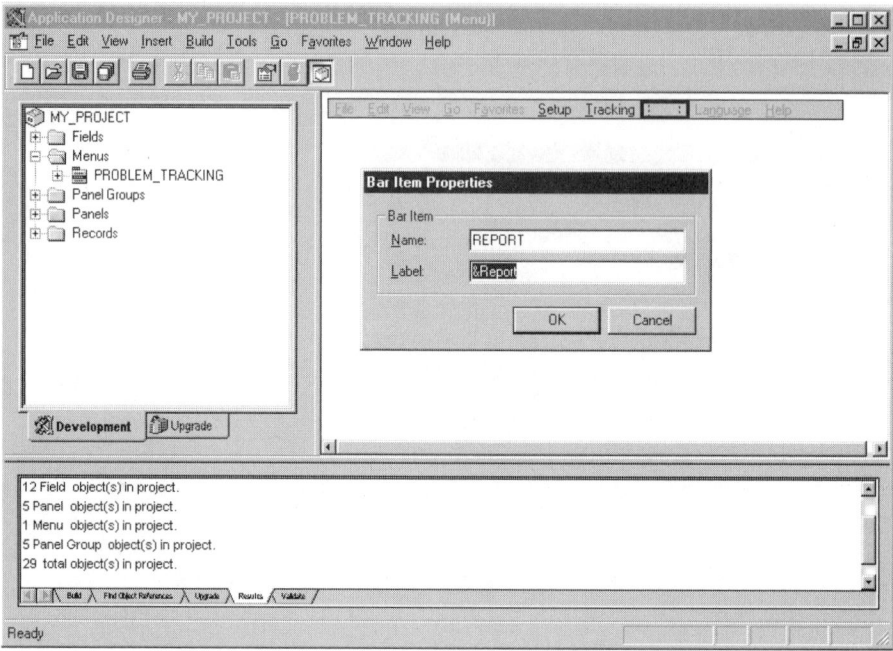

Figure 27.23 Adding a new bar item to the menu

Next we add a new menu item named Status Report to the Problem Tracking menu under the Report menu bar.

To create a new menu item, double-click on the empty rectangle on the menu. The Menu Item Properties dialog appears (figure 27.24).

On the panel shown in figure 27.24, click on Select and add our MY_PROB01 panel group to the Status Report menu item.

After the new menu item is created, you have to decide who will be able to access it. Only users who belong to the proper operator class should be granted access to the new menu item.

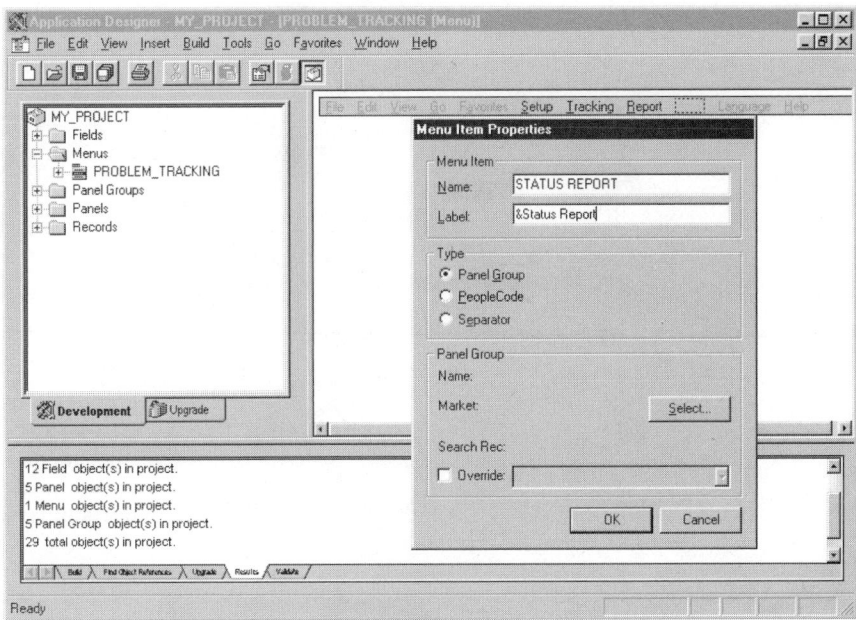

Figure 27.24   Adding a new menu item to the Report menu bar

27.5 *Granting security access*

Since we created a new menu item, we have to allow certain users to access it.

First, you need to grant access to the ALLPANLS operator class, which will be used in testing your application. Select File, Open and enter ALLPANLS as shown on the screen in figure 27.25.

Press OK and click on the Menu Items icon to display the list of all available menus for this operator class (figure 27.26).

Navigation: Go → PeopleTools → Security Administrator.

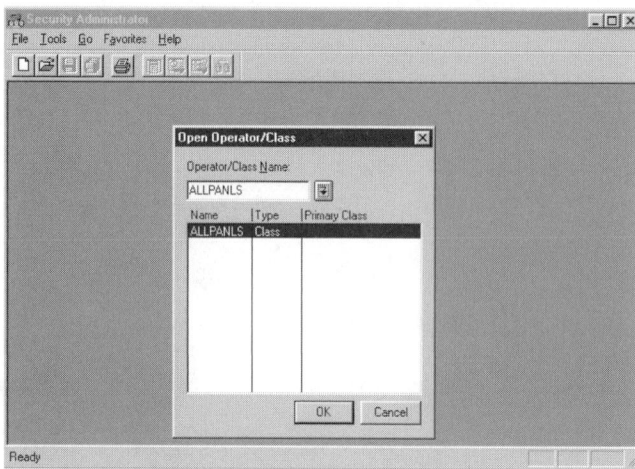

Figure 27.25
Opening the security panel for ALLPANLS operator class

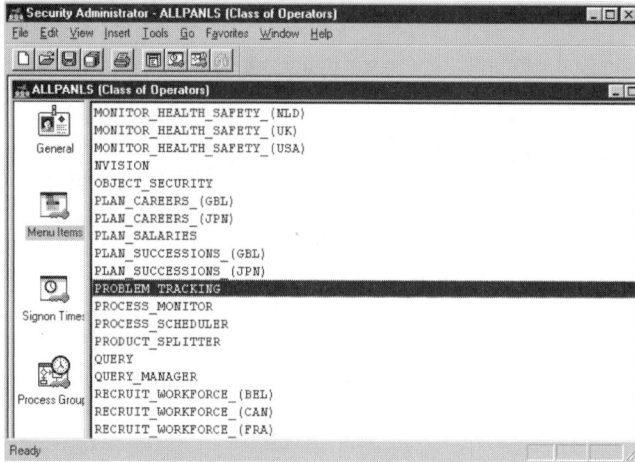

Figure 27.26
Menu Items to which ALLPANLS has access

We placed our new menu item under the Problem Tracking menu. In order to see all menu items under this menu, let's double-click on Problem Tracking. The system returns a list of all available menu items under the Problem Tracking menu (figure 27.27).

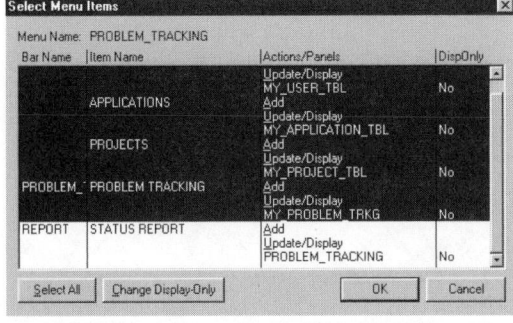

Figure 27.27
Selecting the Problem Tracking
menu from all menus available to the
ALLPANLS class

The newly created menu bar Report and the item Status Report are not highlighted and, therefore, not available to any operator from the ALLPANLS operator class.

Let's highlight all three lines that belong to the Status Report item by clicking on each line. Press OK to make our new menu item available for the ALLPANLS operator class.

27.6 TESTING YOUR CHANGES

So far in this chapter we created the following new objects:

- Run Control record, MY_RUN_CNTL
- Run Control panel, MY_RUN_CNTL_PRB01
- panel group, MY_PRB01
- menu bar, Report
- menu item, Status Report

Remember, our goal was to allow users to execute our SQR report from the online panels via PeopleSoft Process Scheduler. Is this all we need to do? If you recall all the steps we went through in this chapter, you'll note that our SQR report was never linked to any of our new objects. We prepared a Run Control record to hold the input parameters; we created a panel to accept these parameters online; and we even created a menu from which to display the panel. The last step is to create a process definition in order to attach our SQR to the panel group. We will discuss all the steps of creating a process definition in the following subchapter. Before we do this, we can test all the objects we developed without executing our SQR. It is important to make certain that our online components work properly.

Figure 27.28 shows the new menu item.

Our new menu bar and menu item look as we planned. Let's select the Add action and make sure that our new panel group and panel are working as well. After entering a new Run Control ID, MY_STATUS_01, the system displays the panel shown in figure 27.29.

Navigation: GO → Problem Tracking → Report → Status Report

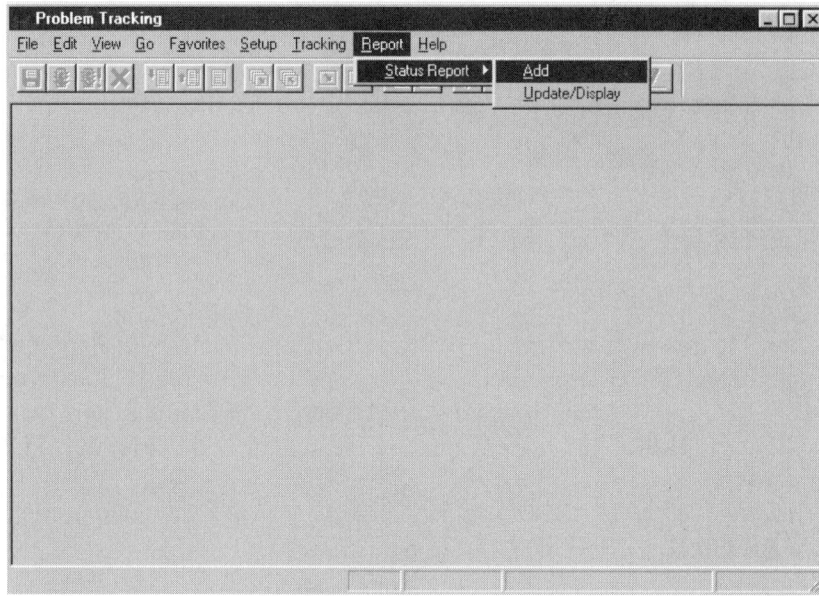

Figure 27.28   The newly added menu bar Report and menu item Status Report

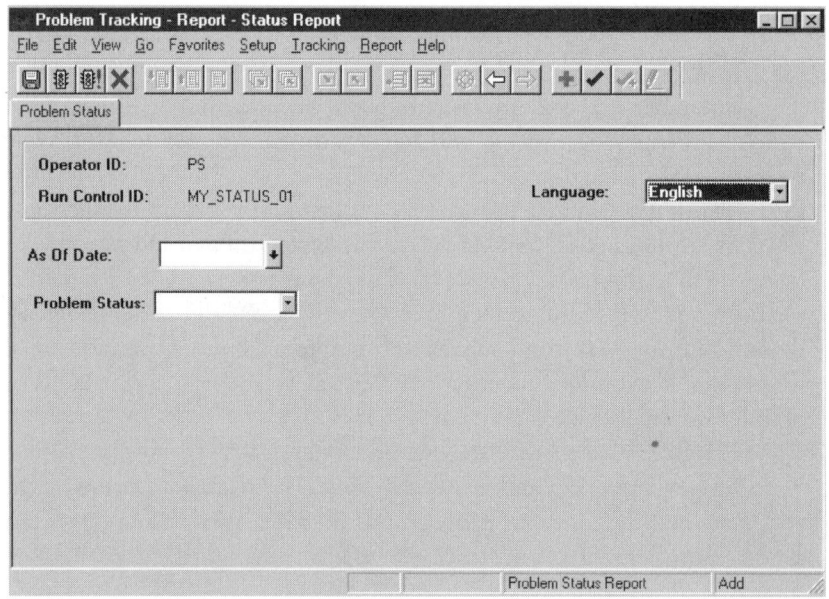

Figure 27.29   Invoking the Status Report panel

CHAPTER 27   ATTACHING SQR TO THE PROCESS SCHEDULER

If you click on the As Of Date field, the date selection calendar should pop up, since this field was defined as a date. Let's test this field first.

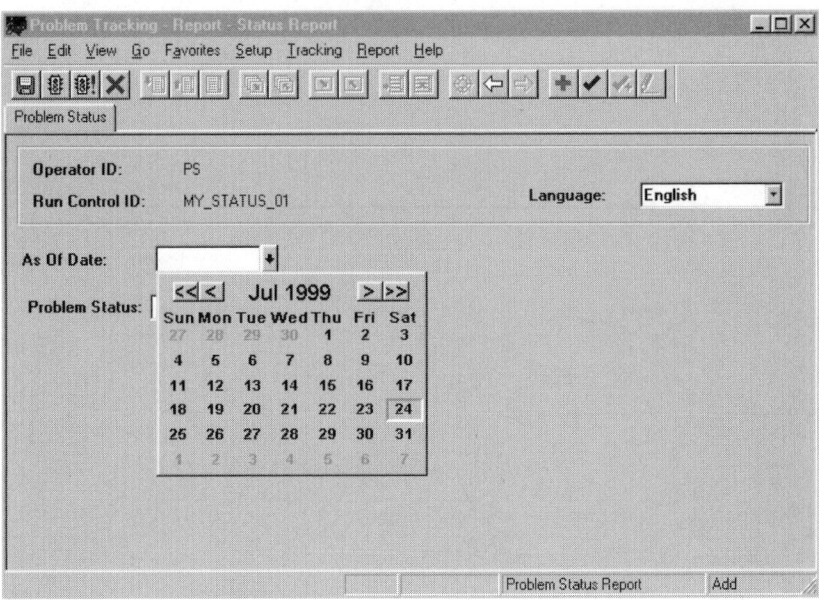

Figure 27.30   Selecting the date in As Of Date field from the pop-up calendar

As you can see, we can select any date from the pop-up panel. Let's click on the 24th of July. After the As Of Date is entered, move on to test our next field, the Problem Status (figure 27.31).

The Problem Status field prompts us to select from any of the values in the edit box. Let's select Initiated and save our selections. Where will the values be kept? The system saves all the panel's values in the record attached to this panel. In our case, that record is the MY_RUN_CNTL record that we created for this purpose. You can use your database-specific native SQL tools to select data from this table in order to be sure that our panel is working properly.

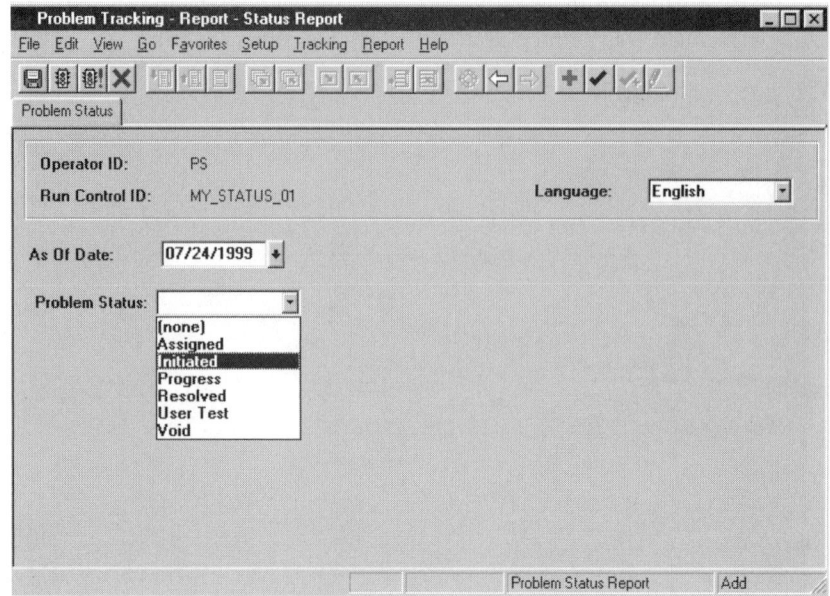

Figure 27.31   Selecting the Problem Status value for our report

Figure 27.32 shows the selected row from our Run Control table PS_MY_RUN_CNTL. (Remember, you have to add the prefix 'PS' to the tables when accessing them via your database native SQL tools.) All the fields we entered are properly saved. It is a good idea to always verify your Run Control tables when creating new panels to make sure they are populated correctly.

And now we are ready to create a process definition for our SQR report.

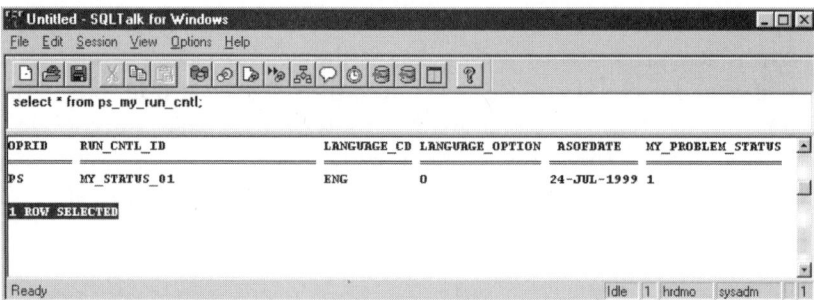

Figure 27.32   Selecting the Run Control information

27.7 CREATING A PROCESS DEFINITION FOR THE PROBLEM STATUS REPORT

Every process run under the PeopleSoft Process Scheduler needs a process definition to specify the process attributes and link the process to the appropriate panel group. We will go through all the steps of creating a process definition for our Problem Status report.

The system displays the Process Definition dialog box (figure 27.33).

Navigation: Go → PeopleTools → Process Scheduler → Use → Process Definitions → Process Definitions → Add

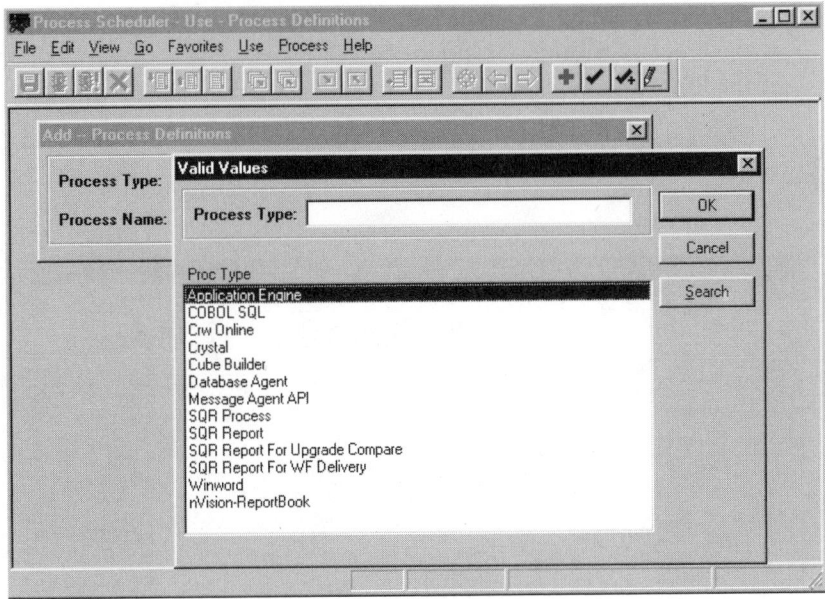

Figure 27.33   Assigning a type to your process

As you can see from the dialog box, we have to select the appropriate process type for our process. Please note that the valid type for our process is SQR Report, not SQR Process.

NOTE   If you select SQR Process instead of SQR Report for the Process Type, the Process Scheduler will not pass the operator ID and Run Control ID to your program, and the program will not work correctly, unless you specify operator ID and Run Control ID as additional parameters.

The process name must be the same as your program name: MYPROB01. Please note that no SQR extension is needed (figure 27.34).

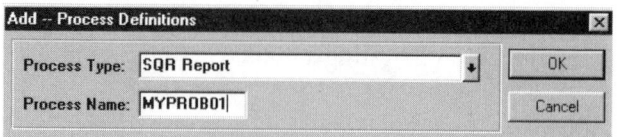

Figure 27.34
No extension is needed when entering the program name

After you press OK, the system displays the Process Scheduler Process Definitions panel group (figure 27.35). This panel group consists of the following three panels:

- the Process Definitions panel
- the Process Definitions Options panel
- the Panel Transfers panel.

The Process Definitions panel tab is the only one you have to fill in; the other two tabs in this panel group are optional.

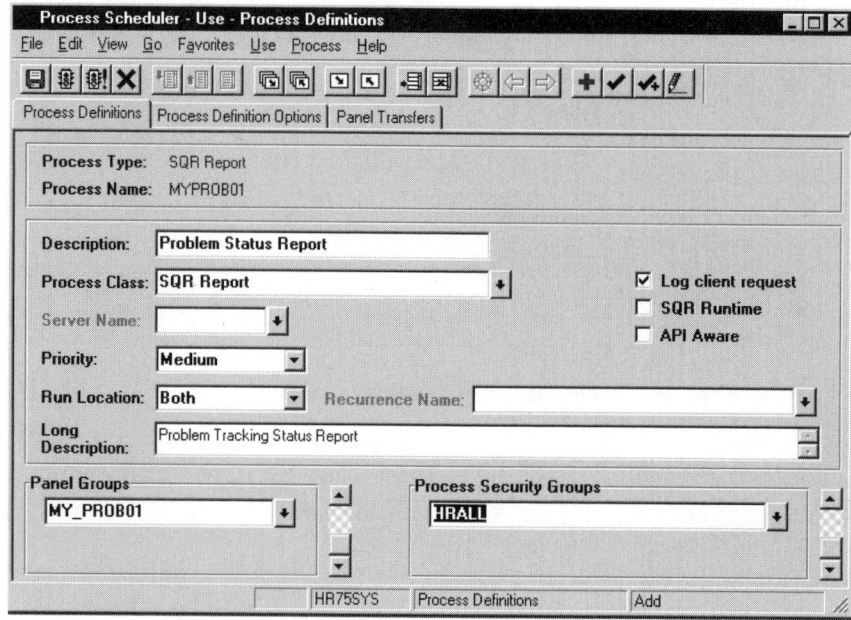

Figure 27.35   The Process Definitions panel

27.7.1 The Process Definitions panel

In the Process Definitions panel, you have to enter information about your process. Let's look at all the fields on the panel shown in figure 27.35.

- The *Description* will be displayed along with your process name on the Process Request panel, so make it meaningful.
- The *Process Class* must be a valid process class from the selection list. In our case, it is SQR Report.
- The *Server Name* (Optional) is specified if you plan to always run your process on a particular server. Otherwise, leave it blank. If, for example, you have both the Unix Server and the NT Server available to run your process, and you do not specify the server name on this panel, users will be able to select the server of their choice on the Process Request panel. If a user leaves the server name blank on the Process Request panel, the system will automatically find the first available server that can process the request for this process class.

> **TIP** The server name can be specified only if the run location is Server.

- The *Priority* can be set to Low, Medium, or High. If several processes are queued on a particular server, the system will be using this selection to decide which process should be initiated first. This parameter is applicable for processes that run on a server only.
- The *Run Location* (Optional) can be Server, Client, or Both. If either Server or Client is selected, it specifies the run location for your process request. If set to Both, the process is initiated on the Run Location set in the Process Scheduler Request panel. Note that this selection takes precedence over the Process Scheduler Request specification. This means that, if you select Server here, the process will be scheduled to run on the server only, regardless of what the user specifies in the Process Scheduler Request dialog box.
- The *Recurrence Name* (Optional) can be selected only for processes that run on a server. The recurrence definitions are created in the Process Request dialog. All previously created recurrence definitions are shown in the drop-down list for the Recurrence Name field. Note, if you specify the Recurrence Name here, this does not mean that the process will automatically start and run according to the specified recurrence definition.

> **TIP** In order to schedule your process for recurrent execution it has to be started manually from the Process Request Dialog Panel for the first time.

(Please see more about using run recurrences for your process in chapter 30.)

- The *Long Description* (Optional) is used for your process description.

- An *API Aware* process is a process that updates the Process Request table (PSPRCSRQST) with the process run status (`Error`, `Success`, and such), completion code, message set, and message number. This allows the system to perform a `Commit` or a `Rollback`, depending on the run status. Based on the process execution results, the system displays a standard or custom message on the Process Monitor's Process Request Detail panel. Not every program is API Aware. You have to add certain logic to your SQR program to make it API Aware.

WARNING Turning the API Aware flag On does not automatically make the process API Aware.

We'll discuss the process of making an SQR program API Aware in detail in the next chapter, but please note that, if your program is not API Aware, the flag must be turned Off.

As you can see, we turned this flag off for MYPROB01 process definition, since we did not place any special code to make our program API Aware—yet. (We'll do this in the next chapter.)

- If *Log Client Request* is on, the system logs the request on the Process Request table every time the process is run on the client. This is useful as an audit trail. Note that, for all server run requests, logging is always performed. By default, it is turned On for all API Aware processes.
- The *SQR Runtime* is checked when you want the system to append the .sqt extension to the process name (used for precompiled SQR programs). It will use the SQT working directory. For our Problem Status program, this option should be turned off.
- The *Panel Group* is used to specify the panel group from which you want to run your process.

In our case, the panel group is MY_PROB01 because we created this panel group to run the Status Report. Note that, in order to link your process to a panel group, this panel group must be created prior to creating the process definition.

TIP Make sure you enter the correct panel group name. PeopleSoft does not edit this field. If you misspell it, users will not be able to run your process.

To avoid the problem, click on the panel group and press CNTL + F4. The system will display a list of all available panel groups.

Optionally, you can specify more than one panel group for your process by inserting additional rows in the Panel Groups box. In this case, the process will appear on all selected panel groups.

- The *Process Security Groups* define operator classes or operators that have permission to submit this process. At least one process security group must be specified. You can allow multiple process security groups to run your process. You have to specify the process security groups that belong to your user's operator class. If you specify a security group here, but do not give permissions to some operators to use this group, the process will not be visible to those operators.

  Let's make certain that the HRALL process security group belongs to the ALL-PANLS class. Switch to the Security Administrator panel, click on the Process Groups icon within the panel, and check if the operators who belong to the ALL-PANLS class are allowed to use the HRALL process group. HRALL must be among other process security groups under the ALLPANLS class (figure 27.36).

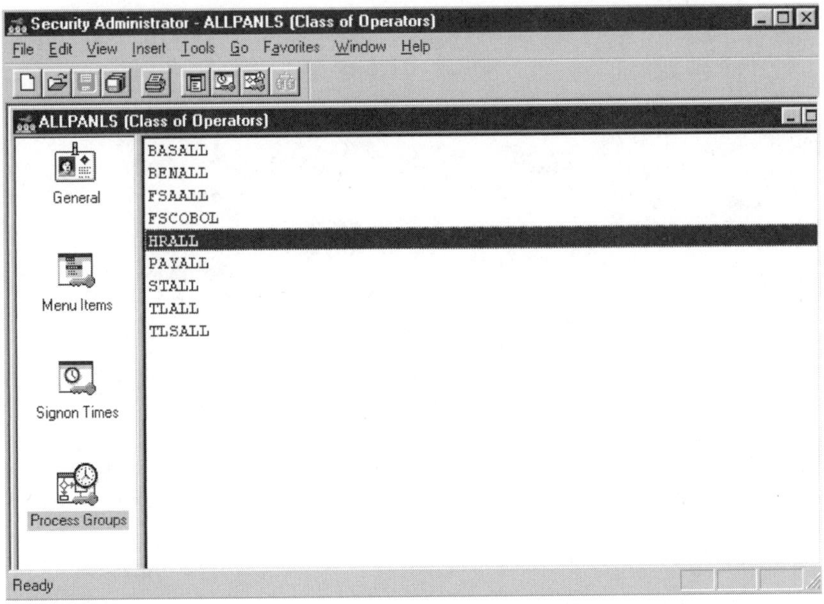

Figure 27.36   The authorized Process Groups for the ALLPANLS operator class

27.7.2 Process Definition Options panel

The second panel of the Process Scheduler panel group, the Process Definition Options panel, (figure 27.37) is optional.

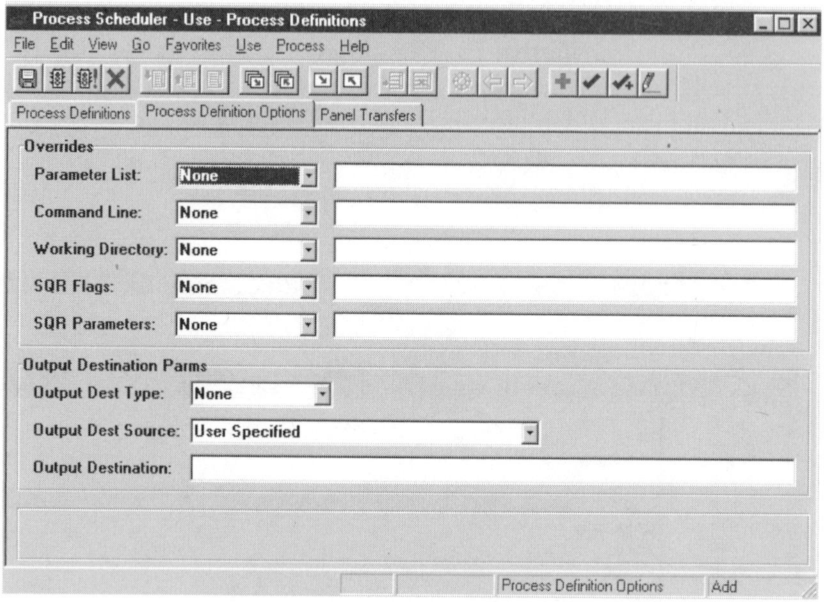

Figure 27.37 The Process Definitions Options panel for our process definition

This panel is used to modify the process parameter list, command line, working directory, and SQR flags and parameters. It is also used to change the Output Destination parameters.

The drop-down lists for each parameter allow you to preface, append, or override each parameter for your process. Suppose you want to invoke the SPF Viewer after generating your program.spf file. All you need to do is append the –ZIV flag to your SQR Flags parameter in your Process Definition Options panel (figure 27.38).

To illustrate another useful example (figure 27.38), we appended two parameters to the standard parameter list: MY_DERIVED.MY_USER_ID and MY_USER_TABLE.NAME. This is a simple and efficient technique that allows you to pass the parameters directly from your panel to the SQR program. The parameters are coded in the form of Record.Field. Please note that the SQR program must issue two additional input commands in this case to accept these two parameters.

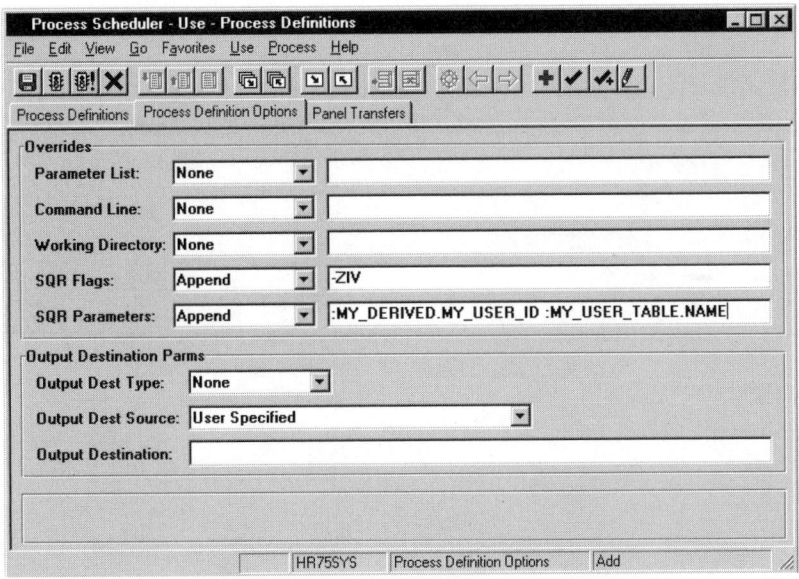

Figure 27.38 **An example of the Process Definitions Options panel with additional parameters**

| TIP | When appending additional SQR parameters via the Process Definitions Options panel, your SQR program should contain the Input commands to accept these additional parameters. |
| TIP | For SQR programs, Output Dest Source must be set to User Specified. |

For our process we won't be using any of the panel fields.

27.7.3 Panel Transfers panel

The Panel Transfers panel is a part of PeopleSoft Workflow. Also optional, it allows you to transfer to the specified panel from the Process Monitor after your process is successfully completed. You can specify directions of transfer and menu actions in this panel.

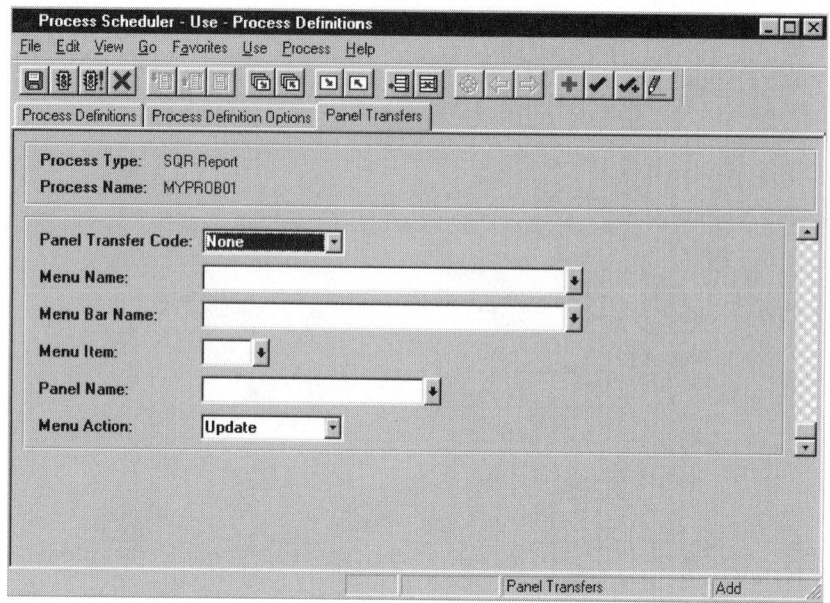

Figure 27.39   The Panel Transfers panel

For our sample program, we will leave this panel unchanged.

27.8   SPECIFYING THE PROGRAM DIRECTORY

Your last task is to place your program into the right directory so that the Process Scheduler will be able to find it. How do we know where the Process Scheduler expects to find the program? Let's take a look at the PeopleSoft System Configuration Manager.

Navigation: Edit → Preferences → Configuration → Process Scheduler

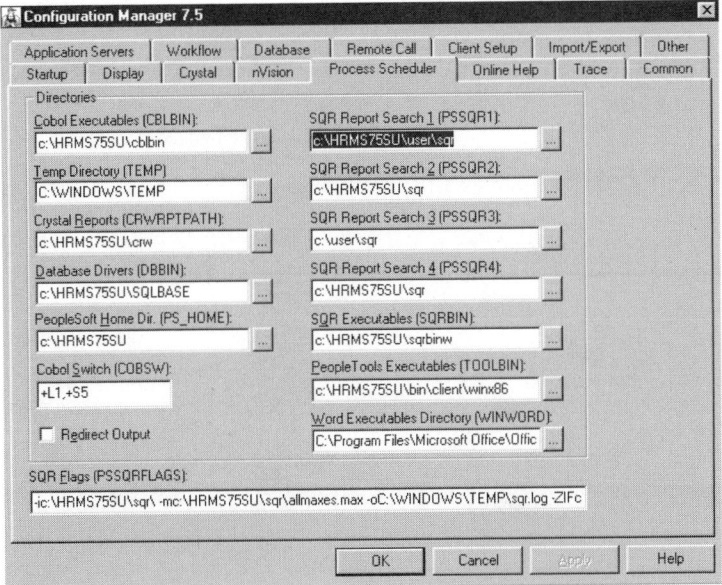

Figure 27.40 The PeopleSoft System Configuration panel

You have to ensure that your SQR program is in the path specified by either `PSSQR1`, `PSSQR2`, `PSSQR3`, or `PSSQR4` search path variables. Let's copy the MYPROB01.sqr program into c:\hrms75su\user\sqr.

27.9 *Testing Your Process Definition*

Now, we are ready to run our SQR program.

Select the Status Report from the Problem Tracking Menu. The system displays a Run Control prompt as shown in figure 27.41.

Note that this time we select the `Update/Display` option since we already created our Run Control record and therefore can reuse it. Let's select the `MY_STATUS_01` Run Control ID.

The system displays the Run Control panel shown in figure 27.42.

Navigation: Go → Problem Tracking → Report → Status Report → Update/Display

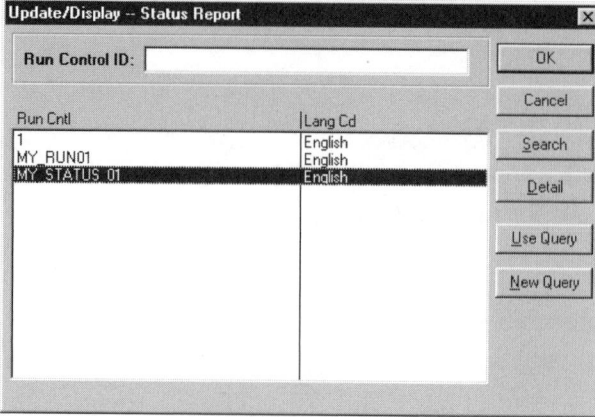

Figure 27.41
Run Control prompt

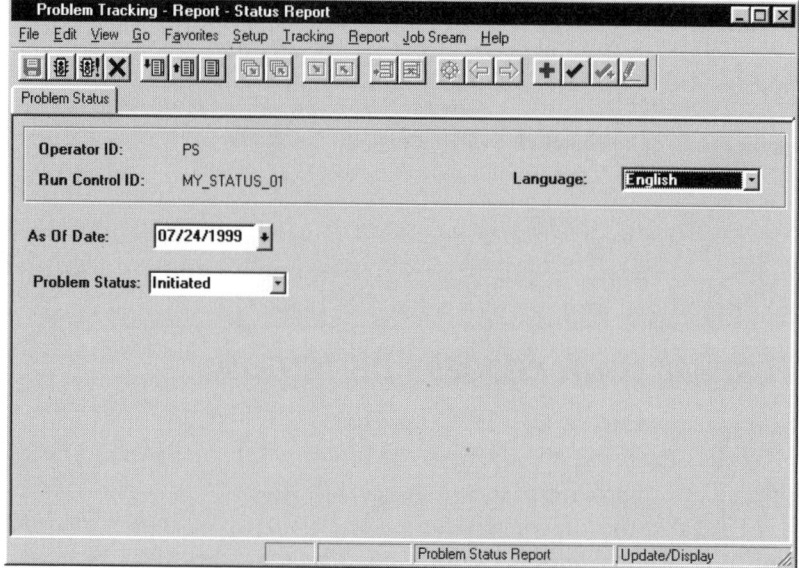

Figure 27.42 The Problem Status Report Run Control panel

As you can see from figure 27.42, all the parameters in this panel are already set up. This is because the information is retrieved from our Run Control record that is attached to this panel. We are ready to execute our program for the first time from the online panel. Click on the Traffic Light, and you will be presented with the process request panel (figure 27.43).

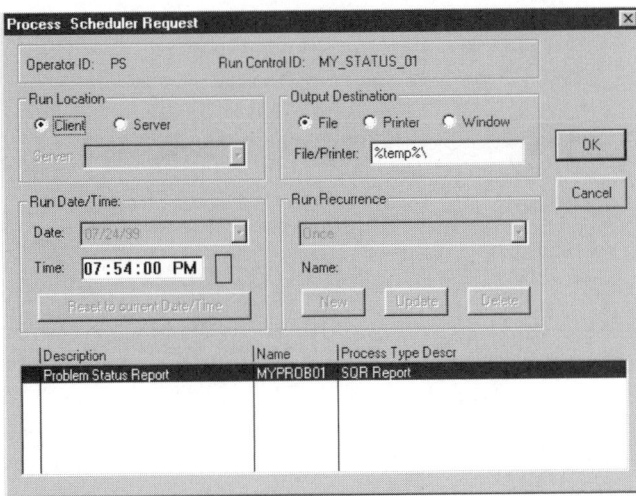

**Figure 27.43
The Process Request
panel for the Problem
Status report**

On the lower portion of the Process Scheduler Request panel, you can see that MYPROB01 is displayed as a program name. This means that the process definition that we created earlier correctly attached our SQR program to the panel group.

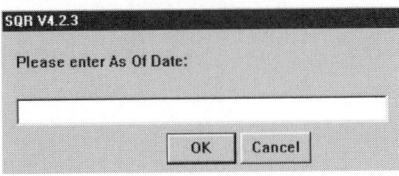

**Figure 27.44   SQR Prompts for the As Of
Date value**

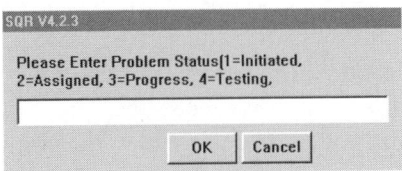

**Figure 27.45   SQR Prompts for the
Problem Status value**

Let's click OK and start testing our program. The program should run to the end without any problems.

Our program displays the first input prompt (figure 27.44).

After entering a valid date, we see another prompt (figure 27.44) for the problem status value.

Once we enter the problem status value, the program runs to the end. You may be asking yourself a question: "Why do we need to enter the same input information in both the Run Control panel and the prompt boxes?" The reason for this strange behavior is that our program does not know that it runs under the Process Scheduler. If the program is called for execution from the Process Scheduler, it should accept the input parameters from the online Run Control panels; otherwise, it should prompt the user to enter the input parameters via the Input command. In our next chapter, we will discuss this in detail, and will modify our SQR program to work correctly no matter under what environment it runs.

Let's verify the process execution status on the Process Monitor panel (figure 27.46).

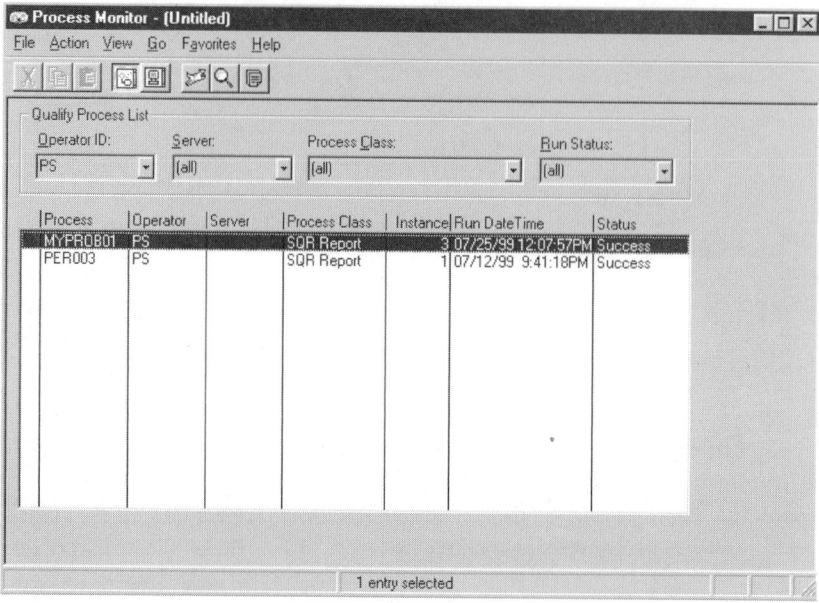

Figure 27.46   The Process Monitor panel

The status of the MYPROB01 process on the Process Monitor panel shows Success. This sounds good, but it does not mean that your project is finished. Even if our program fails, the Process Monitor has no idea of the program execution status. Remember that we just took an SQR program developed with no PeopleSoft interface code and plugged it into the PeopleSoft Process Scheduler. This allowed us to initiate and run the program from the PeopleSoft panel. The Status Report output has been created, but the Process Monitor's process status has not been updated. Therefore, PeopleSoft has no idea about the return code of the process. In the next chapter, you will learn how to solve the problem by making your program API Aware.

1 Any Run Control record must have the operator ID and the Run Control ID as its key fields.

2 A Run Control record may contain additional fields not used in your program.

3 A Run Control panel should be made specific to your application and should contain (or display) only the necessary fields.

4 A process definition must be created to link to the panel(s) from which it will be run.

5 You can add your SQR Program to an existing menu item or create a new one.

6 The appropriate security access must be granted to all operator classes that will be allowed to see the new menu item.

7 In order to inform the Process Monitor about the status of your program, you have to modify the program to make it API Aware.

Communicating with the Process Scheduler

In most cases, SQR programs that run under PeopleSoft need certain changes. While any SQR program can be executed under the Process Scheduler, only programs that include special code are capable of communicating their status back to the Process Scheduler. In order to allow the Process Monitor to reflect your program status, you have to make your program API Aware.

28.1 USING PEOPLESOFT-DELIVERED SQC FILES

PeopleSoft provides a number of routines that handle the communication between SQR programs and the Process Scheduler. In order to make your SQR program API Aware, you have to add the PeopleSoft-delivered program files (SQC files) that contain these routines to your program. At a minimum, you need to include the STDAPI.sqc and SETENV.sqc files to your program. The STDAPI.sqc, in turn, uses the nested #Include operators that refer to other important API files (figure 28.1). Let's look at two of these files: PRCSDEF.sqc and PRCSAPI.sqc.

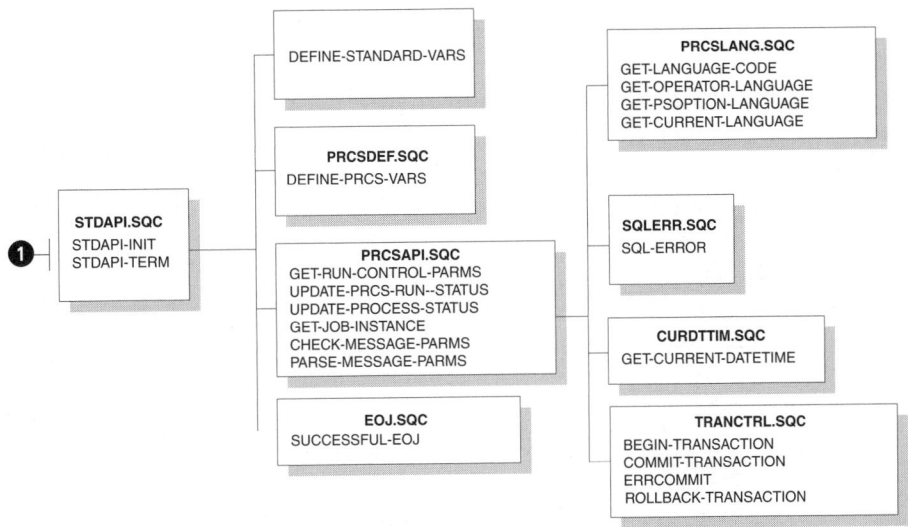

Figure 28.1   The Process Scheduler API SQC files and procedures

❶ These 2 procedures are called from every API Aware SQR Program.

The PRCSDEF.sqc file includes the `Define-Prcs-Vars` procedure. This procedure initializes all the fields used in API. The PRCSAPI.sqc file includes two important procedures: `Get-Run-Control-Parms` and `Update-Prcs-Run-Status`. The first procedure, `Get-Run-Control-Parms`, retrieves the input parameters (`Process Instance`, `Operator ID`, and `Run Control ID`) and updates the run status of the process request to `Processing`. The PRCSAPI.sqc, `Update-Prcs-Run-Status` procedure, is designed to update the Process Request table (PSPRCSRQST) upon program completion.

When you run your program from the Process Scheduler, the control parameters that identify your process (the process instance, the operator ID, and the Run Control ID) are passed as a part of the command line. The application-specific input parameters are not passed to the program—these parameters are saved in the Run Control table. When you run the same program from the SQR dialog box or from the command line, the `Get-Run-Control-Parms` API procedure does not detect any input values from the Process Scheduler and instead identifies the process as being run from outside the Process Scheduler.

Figure 28.1 lists PeopleSoft-delivered API SQC files and procedures and also shows the location of each API procedure and SQC file.

28.2 EXERCISE 2: MAKE YOUR SQR PROGRAM API AWARE

Making an SQR program API Aware involves adding program code to update the Process Request table (PSPRCSRQST) with the program run status (`Error`, `Success`, and so on), completion code, error message set, and error message number.

28.2.1 Incorporating SQC files into your program

Let's add the SQC files we just discussed to our Status Report. (The updated program will be called MYPROB02.sqr). To save space, we will show only the modified parts of the program.

```
!MYPROB02.SQR
!Problem Status Report

#include 'setenv.sqc'

!...
!**************
Begin-Program
!**************
do Init-DateTime
do Init-Number
Do Init-Report
Do Main
Do Stdapi-Term

End-Program


!****************************
Begin-Procedure Init-Report
!****************************
  Do Stdapi-Init
  Do Ask-Input-Parameters
  Do Build-Where
  Do Load-Xlats
End-Procedure
!...
!****************************
#include 'stdapi.sqc'      !Routines to Update Run Status
#Include 'datetime.sqc'    !Routines for date and time formatting
#Include 'number.sqc'      !Routines to format numbers
#include 'askaod.sqc'      !Ask As Of Date input
```

The `Stdapi-Term` procedure in `Stdapi.sqc` calls the `Successful-Eoj` procedure from EOJ.sqc which updates the run status to `'Successful'`

The `Stdapi-Init` procedure in `Stdapi.sqc` call `Define-Prcs-Vars` and `Get-Run-Control-Parms` to initialize API variables, gets control parameters and updates the run status to `'Processing'`

STDAPI.SQC includes all necessary API code

At the program start, the Stdapi-Init procedure is invoked. This procedure is a part of the PeopleSoft-delivered SQC file STDAPI.sqc. Stdapi-Init invokes two more procedures in turn. The first one, `Define-Prcs-Vars`, is located in PRCSAPI.sqc. Its job is to initialize all API variables. The second procedure, `Get-Run-Control-Parms`, determines whether the program is called from the Process Scheduler and, if so, promotes the run status from `Initiated` to `Processing`.

Let's see how the `Get-Run-Control-Parms` procedure knows that the program is invoked from the Process Scheduler. Take a look at the procedure source code shown in the following example:

```
!The Get-Run-Control-Parms procedure
Begin-Procedure Get-Run-Control-Parms
   Input $prcs_process_instance
   'Please press ENTER (Do not input a value)'
   if not isnull($prcs_process_instance)
       let #prcs_process_instance = to_number($prcs_process_instance)
       input $prcs_oprid 'Please press ENTER (Do not input a value)'
       let $prcs_oprid = upper($prcs_oprid)
       input $prcs_run_cntl_id  'Please press ENTER (Do not input a value)'
   else
       let #prcs_process_instance = 0
   end-if
   if #prcs_process_instance > 0
       let #prcs_run_status = #prcs_run_status_processing
       do Update-Prcs-Run-Status
       let #prcs_run_status = #prcs_run_status_successful
   end-if
end-procedure
```

> The first Input command is used to check where the program was called from

As you can see, the procedure code begins with the Input command. If the program is invoked from the regular SQR dialog window (which usually happens during the program's testing) or from the SQR command line, the operator receives the prompt `'Please press ENTER (Do not input a value)'`. After the operator presses the ENTER key, the `$prcs_process_instance` variable remains set to NULL, and the procedure logic can easily detect this.

If the program is invoked from the Process Scheduler, the `$prcs_process_instance` variable receives its value from the parameter list passed from the Process Scheduler. The parameter list, besides the Process Instance value, also includes the operator ID, and the process run ID. Figure 28.2 shows the Process Request Detail panel for the Status Report. For this particular program run, the Process Instance is equal to 4, the Operator ID is PS, and the Process Run ID is MY_STATUS_01.

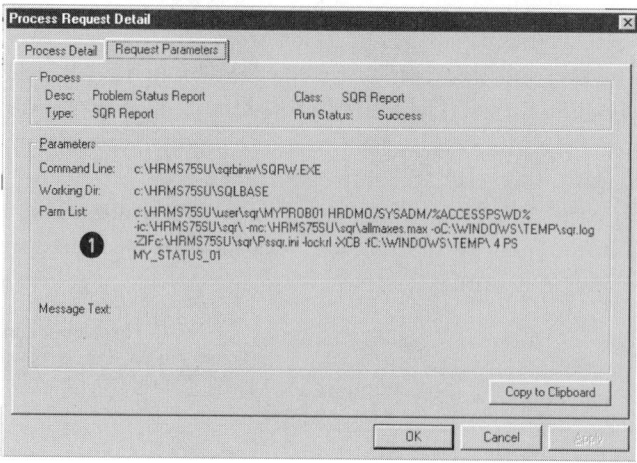

Figure 28.2   Run Control parameters passed to an SQR program

❶ The three Run Control parameters passed to an SQR program from the Process Scheduler.

Let's return to myprob02.sqr. At the end of the main section, the program calls the Stdapi-Term procedure, which is a part of STDAPI.sqc. The purpose of this procedure is to update the PSPRSCRQST table with process run status, the message parameters, and the return code. The chart in figure 28.3 will help you to figure out

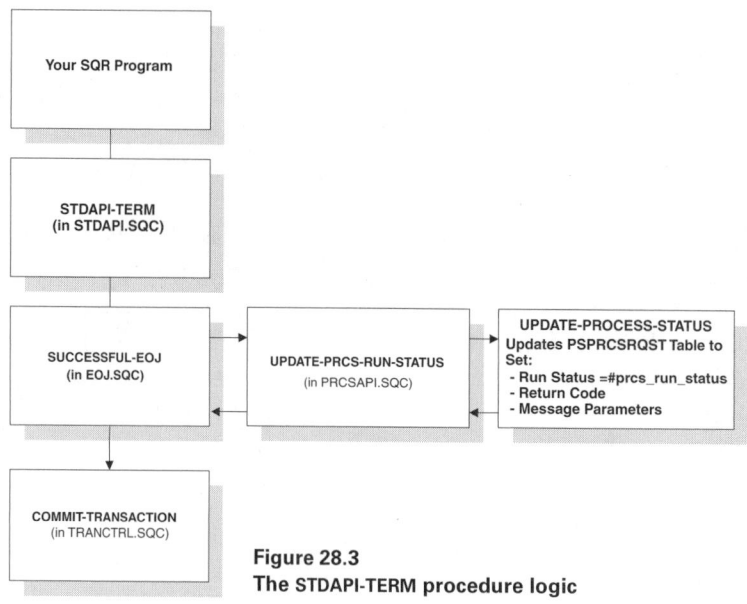

Figure 28.3
The STDAPI-TERM procedure logic

how the `Stdapi-Term` procedure communicates the program status to the Process Scheduler.

As you can see, the run status in the PSPRCSRQST table is updated based on the `#prcs_run_status` variable value. This variable determines the run status, which you see on the Process Monitor panel.

28.2.2   Communicating errors back to the Process Scheduler

It is important to remember that, in case of an error, the value of the `#prcs_run_status` variable must be updated by the application program. In a normal run, PeopleSoft promotes the process run status in the following order: `Queued`, `Initiated`, `Processing`, `Success`.

Please note that `#prcs_run_status` is a numeric variable. It cannot be assigned the above text values directly. The PRCSDEF.sqc file includes a number of predefined numeric status variables that can be used to assign the right status value to the `#prcs_run_status` variable.

As soon as your program is scheduled to run, the Process Scheduler sets the run status on the Process Monitor to `Queued`. Next, if all parameters in the process definition are resolved and the system resources are available to run the process, the Process Scheduler changes the status to `Initiated`. If your program fails to get through the compilation stage, the status on the Process Monitor panel remains `Initiated` if your program runs on Client. If it runs on the Server, the status will be changed to `Error` by the SQR invocation script.

The `Stdapi-Init` procedure (which must be called in the beginning of every API Aware program) changes the status to `Processing` and updates the PSPRCSRQST table. At this moment, you can see the status set to `Processing` on the Process Monitor panel. The `Stdapi-Init` procedure then sets the `#prcs_run_status` variable to `Success` (`#prcs_run_status_successful`) in the program memory only, but holds back from updating the PSPRCSRQST table until either the `Stdapi-Term` or `SQL-Error` procedure is called. Therefore, you will still see the `Processing` status on the Process Monitor panel.

If your SQR program runs to the end, then calls the `Stdapi-Term` procedure as shown in figure 28.3, this procedure updates the process status to `Success`. In case of an error, it is your program's responsibility to call a PeopleSoft-delivered error-handling routine `SQL-Error` or code a similar logic in your program. Otherwise, the status on the Process Monitor either remains set to `Processing` if your program aborted during execution or, worse yet, is set to `Success` if the program ran to the end and called `Stdapi-Term` regardless of the error situation.

If your program uses a PeopleSoft-delivered error handling routine (part of which is shown in the following example), you do not have to worry about updating the API variables in an error situation. If, however, your program uses its own error-processing logic, the program must include a code to set all API variables to the proper values and update the Process Request table PSPRCSRQST. Following is an example of the PeopleSoft-delivered SQL error-handling procedure:

```
!A part of the SQL Error                This procedure is usually referenced in the
!procedure in SQLERR.SQC            ◄─┘  On-Error parameter of the Begin-Sql
if #prcs_process_instance > 0
  let #prcs_message_set_nbr = #prcs_msg_set_nbr
  let #prcs_message_nbr = #prcs_msg_nbr_sql_error
  let #prcs_run_status = #prcs_run_status_error     Updating the API
  let #prcs_rc = #sql-status                        variables
  let $prcs_message_parm1 = $sql-error
  let #prcs_continuejob = 0
  do Rollback-Transaction
  if $prcs_in_update_prcs_run_stat <> 'Y'
    do Update-Prcs-Run-Status
    do Commit-Transaction                           Updating the
  end-if                                            PSPRCSRQST table
end-if
#ifndef VMS
  let #return-Status = 1
#end-if
stop
```

As you can see, the error-processing logic in an API Aware program should include updating a set of API variables and calling the Update-Prcs-Run-Status procedure that updates the Process Request table for your program. After the Process Request table is updated, the Commit-Transaction function makes this table change permanent.

28.3 CREATING A NEW PROCESS DEFINITION FOR AN API AWARE PROGRAM

Since our program name has changed from myprob01.sqr to myprob02.sqr, a new process definition has to be created. Remember that a process definition must have exactly the same name as your SQR program. If we modify our SQR program without changing its name, we can just update the API Aware flag in the MYPROB01 process definition.

In our case, we create a new one. We repeat the same steps that we performed in chapter 27. Just remember that, this time our process must be marked as an API Aware process (figure 28.4).

After you save the panel in figure 28.4, the MYPROB02 process definition is created. It has the same characteristics as MYPROB01, except that the API Aware flag is now turned on. Also, we attached it to the same panel group, MY_PROB01. Will this present any problems? How will the Process Scheduler know which program to execute? Let's find out the answers to our questions by performing a simple test. Select Status Report from the Problem Tracking menu and press the Traffic Light tool bar button.

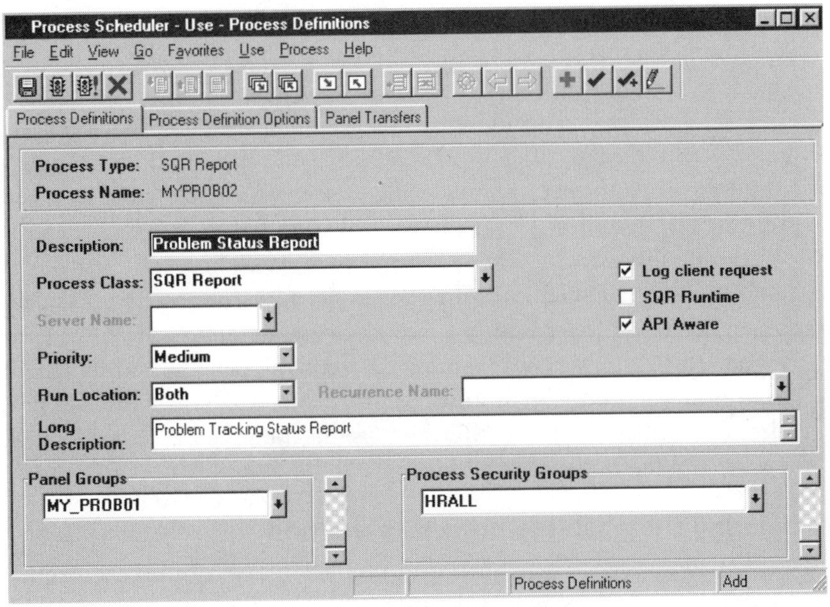

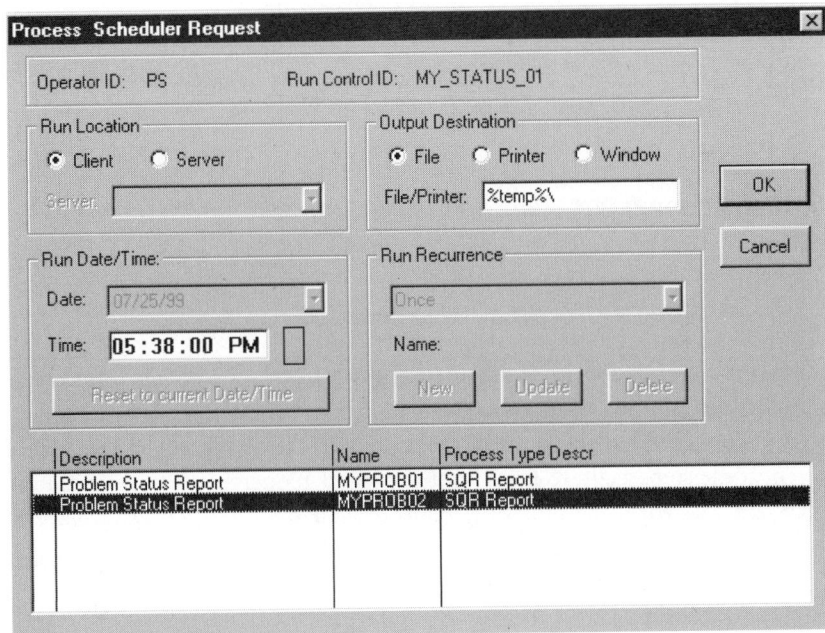

Figure 28.4   Creating a new process definition for an API Aware SQR program

Figure 28.5   Two SQR programs are available to run from the Process Scheduler

As you can see from figure 28.5, two SQR programs are available now for execution from the Process Scheduler. Sometimes, it is a good and economical solution to have several programs under the same roof (attached to the same panel group). For example, if you have a detail report and a summary report, and you need to give your users a way to execute either one of the two, you can place them together. In this case, your users would have to highlight the process which they need to execute, and then press the OK button.

In our situation, however, there is no need to keep the first report. It was not designed to be executed from the Process Scheduler in the first place, and, therefore, the report did not have any API interface code to communicate with API functions. We can either disconnect this program from the panel group by deleting the panel group from its process definition, or, using our database-specific SQL tools, we can delete the obsolete process definition from the tools tables. Let's use the second option in order to keep our system clean.

28.3.1   Deleting the obsolete process definition

We have to use a trick here. Presently, PeopleSoft does not have any online tools available to delete obsolete process definitions from the database. Using our knowledge of the PeopleSoft system (tools) tables, and with the help of the native SQL, we can create a simple cleanup script:

```
delete from ps_prcsdefn
where prcsname='MYPROB01' and prcstype = 'SQR Report';
delete from ps_prcsdefngrp
where prcsname='MYPROB01' and prcstype = 'SQR Report';
delete from ps_prcsdefnpnl
where prcsname='MYPROB01' and prcstype = 'SQR Report';
delete from ps_prcsdefnxfer
where prcsname='MYPROB01' and prcstype = 'SQR Report';
delete from psprcsrqst
where prcsname='MYPROB01' and prcstype = 'SQR Report';
delete from pspnlfield
where prcsname='MYPROB01' and prcstype = 'SQR Report';
```

After the `Delete` script is executed, log out from your PeopleSoft system, delete your cache files, and log back on to PeopleSoft.

To verify that the script we executed actually gave us the result we expected, we repeat the steps again to bring up the process request with Problem Status report. We can see that this time only one report is available for execution (figure 28.6)

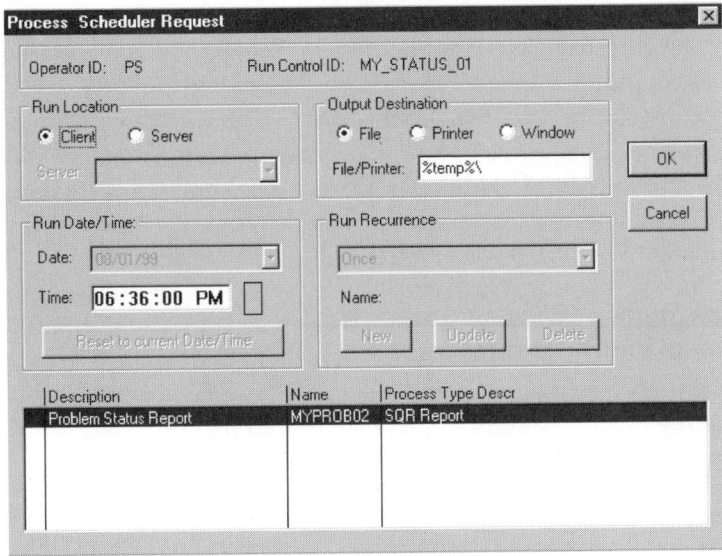

Figure 28.6 Only one report is available now for execution

We can click on the OK button and execute our report now, but, if you remember, we have one more important problem to address. Our program does not currently accept any parameters from the online panel that we created. Let's first discuss what tools PeopleSoft offers to simplify the task of obtaining the input parameters, then implement this in our program.

28.4 EXERCISE 3: ACCEPT THE AS OF DATE AND PROBLEM STATUS PARAMETERS FROM AN ON-LINE PANEL

Our task now is to modify MYPROB02.sqr so that it knows when it is being executed from the PeopleSoft online panel and accepts the parameters without further prompting. The program should also retain the functionality of the Input prompt when it is executed outside the Process Scheduler.

We have already done most of the work: we've developed the Run Control record and panel and made sure that the online part of this project is working properly. We were able to enter our parameters and to save them in the record. Let's do the rest now.

28.4.1 Using application-specific SQC files to obtain input parameters

PeopleSoft delivers a number of application-specific SQC files that are used to read input parameters from Application Run Control records. Usually, two SQC files are involved in reading the parameters: one file selects the input parameters, while another one formats the selected parameters and moves them to the designated SQR program variables. You can either use the PeopleSoft-delivered SQC files or develop your own, depending on the parameters your SQR program needs to accept.

Let's first learn how PeopleSoft-delivered SQR programs work with input parameters. Later, you will learn how to use a similar approach in your program. Since you have already become familiar with the PeopleSoft-delivered Years of Service report, let's examine how this program works. We know that this program accepts two input parameters: As Of Date and Years of Service.

28.4.2 How the Years of Service program accepts its input parameters

The name of the program that generates the Years of Service report is PER003.sqr. If you open the PER003.sqr, and scroll down to the end of the program code, you can see that it uses the following SQC files:

```
!SQC files that are used to obtain input parameters in the
!Years of Service program
#include 'hrrnctl1.sqc'  !Get Run Control parameter values
#include 'hrgetval.sqc'  !Get values mask routines
#include 'askaod.sqc'    !Ask As Of Date input
#include 'asksrvyr.sqc'  !Years Of Service input
```

This is how the input parameter read section of PER003.sqr appears:

```
!Procedures used in reading input parameters in PER003.sqr
begin-procedure Init-Report

  move 'PER003' to $ReportID
  do Delete-Worktable
  do Stdapi-Init
  if $prcs_oprid=''
     display ''
     display 'REPORT CAN NOT BE EXECUTED OUTSIDE OF PEOPLESOFT, PLEASE USE
PROCESS SCHEDULER.'
     display ''
     goto last1
  end-if

  do Sqr-Param

  if $prcs_process_instance = ''       ⟵  Check to see if run from the
    do Ask-As-Of-Date                      Process Scheduler. If yes, call
    do Ask-Years-Of-Service                Select-Parameters.
  else
    do Select-Parameters
  end-if
  do Init_Printer
  do Init_Report_Translation ($ReportID, $language_cd)
  do Append_Report_Translation ('HR')
```

```
last1:

end-procedure

begin-procedure Get-Values
    let $language_cd = $PRCS_LANGUAGE_CD
    do Get-As-Of-Date
    do Get-Years-Of-Service

end-procedure
```

> **This procedure is called from the `Select-Parameters` procedure.**

In the previous subchapter, we found that the `Stdapi-Init` procedure initializes API variables and obtains the Process Scheduler command-line parameters (if any). Next, the program determines the method of its invocation. The program may be initiated by the Process Scheduler or invoked some other way (submitted via the SQR dialog box, executed from the command line, or called by another application). Based on this check result, the program calls the proper subroutine to obtain the application-specific input parameters.

If the program is not run under the Process Scheduler, the `$prcs-process-instance` variable remains empty and the regular SQR Input command is used in the `Ask-As-Of-date` and `Ask-Years-Of-Service` subroutines to read the input parameters from user input. The `Ask-As-Of-date` code is located in the ASKAOD.sqc file, and the `Ask-Years-Of-Service` is located in the ASKSRVYR.sqc file.

If the program is invoked by the Process Scheduler, the `$prcs-process-instance` variable is assigned the process instance number value, and the `Select-Parameters` subroutine is called to retrieve the input parameters from a specific application Run Control table. In terms of the Years of Service report, the program is designed to work with the Run Control table named PS_RUN_CNTL_HR, but the procedure logic is a typical example of the communication between an SQR program and a PeopleSoft online panel.

Let's examine the `Select-Parameters` procedure. The procedure code is located in the HRRNCTL1.sqc file:

```
!A typical input parameters read procedure in HRRNCTL1.SQC
begin-procedure select-parameters
BEGIN-SELECT
RUN_CNTL_HR.OPRID
RUN_CNTL_HR.RUN_CNTL_ID
RUN_CNTL_HR.ASOFDATE
RUN_CNTL_HR.FROMDATE
RUN_CNTL_HR.THRUDATE
RUN_CNTL_HR.CALENDAR_YEAR
RUN_CNTL_HR.SERVICE_YEARS
RUN_CNTL_HR.AD_STEP
RUN_CNTL_HR.AD_STEP_ENTRY_DT
RUN_CNTL_HR.AD_COMPRATE
```

```
RUN_CNTL_HR.AD_HOURLYRT
RUN_CNTL_HR.AD_MONTHLYRT
RUN_CNTL_HR.AD_ANNUALRT
  !...
  !...
RUN_CNTL_HR.AD_CHANGEAMT
RUN_CNTL_HR.AD_CHANGEPCT
RUN_CNTL_HR.EEO_REPORT_TYPE
  do Get-Values
from PS_RUN_CNTL_HR RUN_CNTL_HR
where RUN_CNTL_HR.OPRID = $prcs_oprid
  and RUN_CNTL_HR.RUN_CNTL_ID = $prcs_run_cntl_id
end-select
end-procedure
```

> **If your program includes the HRRNCTL1.sqc file, a procedure named Get-Values should be coded withing your program.**

In the previous procedure developed by PeopleSoft, the application-specific input parameters are selected from the PS_RUN_CNTL_HR table for a given combination of operator ID ($prcs_oprid) and Run Control ID ($prcs_run_cntl_id). As you learned in the previous chapter, these two variables come from the Process Scheduler parameter list. An important and not-to-be-missed part of the Select-Parameters procedure is a call to the Get-Values procedure. This procedure moves and edits the selected input parameter values to the designated variables in an SQR program. If your program uses the HRRNCTL1.sqc file, the name of the input parameter edit subroutine must be Get-Values. If you code the input parameter retrieval logic yourself, the name of this subroutine (if any) can be different.

In the Years of Service report, a subroutine named Get-Values is a part of the Per003.sqr code. You can see this subroutine in our previous example explaining procedures used to read input parameters. Because the Per003.sqr program accepts the Language Code and two application-specific parameters, As Of Date and Years of Service, the Get-Values subroutine in this case is simple. It moves the Language Code value to its designated program variable and then calls the Get-As-Of-Date and Get-Years-Of-Service procedures to format these two variables and to move them to their respective designated variables:

```
begin-procedure Get-Values
   let $language_cd = $PRCS_LANGUAGE_CD
   do Get-As-Of-Date
   do Get-Years-Of-Service

end-procedure
```

28.4.3 Accepting input parameters in your SQR program

Now that you have learned how a PeopleSoft-delivered program retrieves its application-specific input parameters, let's apply this knowledge to the applicable Problem Status report.

Our program has two input parameters: As Of Date and Problem Status. We want to create our own include (SQC) files, which will help us in selecting and reformatting input parameters for our program.

28.4.4 Creating your own SQC files

Please note that you do not have to place all input parameter retrieval and reformatting logic into SQC files. This is just a convenient and modular way to read the input parameters. It also gives you an advantage when you want to re-use this code for other programs. Another way of working with your input parameters is to place this logic directly in the application program.

In order to create new application-specific SQC files, we will be using our preferred technique of cloning the existing SQC files. You already know that you need to have one SQC file to select the input parameter values from the appropriate Run Control record and another one to format the selected values and move them to designated variables in your program. Bearing in mind that your application program should retain an ability to be executed from either the SQR dialog box or the command line, you must also provide the code to prompt the user for input parameters.

28.4.5 Creating an SQC file to select parameters from the Run Control record

To create a new input parameter retrieval SQC file, we'll clone the existing HRRNCTL1.sqc file. Let's bring this file in, save it as MYRUNCTL.sqc and change it to make it work with the MY_RUN_CNTL Run Control record:

```
!The modified Select-Parameters procedure in MYRUNCTL.sqc
Begin-Procedure Select-Parameters
Begin-Select
OPRID
RUN_CNTL_ID
ASOFDATE
MY_PROBLEM_STATUS
     Do Get-Values
From    PS_MY_RUN_CNTL
Where OPRID = $prcs_oprid
And     RUN_CNTL_ID = $prcs_run_cntl_id
End-Select
End-Procedure
```

28.4.6 Creating an SQC file to format selected input parameters

We use the existing HRGETVAL.sqc file as a basis when creating the new input parameter formatting file MYGETVAL.sqc. All you need to do is delete the commands that format unused input parameters, and add logic to format your parameters. The changed program, MYGETVAL.sqc, is listed as follows:

```
!*****************************************
! MYGETVAL.SQC:
!*****************************************
Begin-Procedure Get-As-Of-Date
!*****************************************
  Let $AsOfDate = RTRIM(&Asofdate, ' ')
  If $AsOfDate = ''
    Move $AsOfToday to $AsOfDate
  End-if
End-Procedure
!*****************************************
Begin-Procedure Get-Problem-Status
!*****************************************
Let $Problem_Status = RTRIM(&MY_PROBLEM_STATUS, ' ')
End-Procedure
```

As you can see, the modified program includes the Get-As-Of-Date procedure for
the As Of Date column variable. In addition, a new Get-Problem-Status procedure is added to get the additional parameter, MY_PROBLEM_STATUS.

After your SQC file is created, it should be saved in the directory specified in the
Configuration Manager panel under the Process Scheduler tab, in the SQR Flags
parameter for Client program execution.

28.4.7 Integrating the SQC files with your program

Let's make a few modifications to the Problem Status report to make it work with the
newly created Run Control record and to include the new SQC files MYRUNCTL.sqc
and MYGETVAL.sqc. This time we list the entire program (listing 28.1):

Listing 28.1

```
!MYPROB02.SQR
!Problem Status Report

#include 'setenv.sqc'

#define problem_status_len 10
#define project_descr_len  30
#define date_len           10
#define priority_len        8
#define user_name_len      20
#define responsible_name   20
#define col_sep             2


!*************
Begin-Setup
!*************
Load-Lookup Name=Projects
      Rows  = 500
      Table = PS_MY_PROJECT_TBL
```

```
                Key    = MY_PROJECT_ID
                Return_Value=Descr

        Load-Lookup Name=Users
                Rows  = 1000
                Table = PS_MY_USER_TBL
                Key   = MY_USER_ID
                Return_Value=Name

        End-Setup

        !****************
        Begin-Heading  7
        !****************
        print 'Problem Status Report' (1,1) Center

        page-number                    (0,100)  'Page No. '
        print 'Run Date '              (+1,100)
        print $ReportDate              ()
        print 'Run Time '              (+1,100)
        print $ReportTime              ()

        Print 'Problem Status: '       (,1)
        Print $Stat                    ()


        print '='                      (+1,        1,              125) fill
        print 'Project Description '   (+1,        1, {project_descr_len} )
        print 'Incident       '        (   ,+{col_sep}, {date_len}          )
        print 'Priority       '        (   ,+{col_sep}, {priority_len}      )
        print 'User Name      '        (   ,+{col_sep}, {user_name_len}     )
        print 'Responsible    '        (   ,+{col_sep}, {responsible_name}  )
        print 'Close          '        (   ,+{col_sep}, {date_len}          )

        print '               '        (+1,        1, {project_descr_len} )
        print '   Date        '        (   ,+{col_sep}, {date_len}          )
        print '               '        (   ,+{col_sep}, {priority_len}      )
        print '               '        (   ,+{col_sep}, {user_name_len}     )
        print 'To Resolve     '        (   ,+{col_sep}, {responsible_name}  )
        print 'Date          '         (   ,+{col_sep}, {date_len}          )
        print '='                      (+1,        1,              125) fill

        End-Heading

        !**************
        Begin-Program
        !**************
        do Init-DateTime
        do Init-Number
        Do Init-Report
        Do Main
        Do Stdapi-Term
```

```
End-Program

!***************************
Begin-Procedure Init-Report          Check to see if run from the Process
!***************************          Scheduler; If yes, call Select- Parameters;
 Do Stdapi-Init                       otherwise, call Ask-Input-Parameters
 If $prcs_process_instance = '' ◁─┘
   Do Ask-Input-Parameters
 Else
   Do Select-Parameters       ◁─┐  Located in MYRUNCTL.sqc
 End-if
 Do Build-Where
 Do Load-Xlats
End-Procedure


!***************************
Begin-Procedure Get-Values           Call the Get-As-Of-Date and
!***************************          Get-Problem-Status
 Do Get-As-Of-Date            ◁─┐  procedures from MYGETVAL.sqc
 Do Get-Problem-Status

End-Procedure


!*************************
Begin-Procedure Load-Xlats
!*************************
 Let $Where_Xlat1 = 'FIELDNAME=''MY_PRIORITY'''
                ||' and X.EFFDT = (Select max(Effdt) from XLATTABLE '
                ||'Where Fieldname=X.Fieldname And FieldValue=X.FieldValue'
                ||' And Effdt <= Sysdate and Language_Cd = 'ENG') '

 Load-Lookup Name=Priority
        Rows  = 10
        Table = 'XLATTABLE X'
        Key   = FIELDVALUE
        Return_Value=XLATSHORTNAME
        Where=$Where_Xlat1

 Let $Where_Xlat2 = 'FIELDNAME=''MY_PROBLEM_STATUS'''
                ||' and S.EFFDT = (Select max(Effdt) from XLATTABLE '
                ||'Where Fieldname=S.Fieldname And FieldValue=S.FieldValue'
                ||' And Effdt <= Sysdate)'

 Load-Lookup Name=Status
        Rows  = 20
        Table = 'XLATTABLE S'
        Key   = FIELDVALUE
        Return_Value=XLATSHORTNAME
        Where=$Where_Xlat2
End-Procedure
```

```
!**********************************
Begin-Procedure Ask-Input-Parameters
!**********************************
!Get User's Input
```

Call PeopleSoft-delivered function to get As-Of-Date prompt.

```
 Do Ask-As-Of-Date                !in askaod.sqc        ←

 Let #Input=1
 While #Input = 1
    Input $Problem_Status Type=Char 'Please Enter Problem Status(1=Initi-
ated, 2=Assigned, 3=Progress, 4=Testing, 5=Resolved,6=Void) or press Enter
for All' Status=#Input_Status
    If $Problem_Status     = ''
       Let #Input   = 0
    Else
       If $Problem_Status  > '0' and $Problem_Status < '7'
          show 'Problem Status Entered = ' $Problem_Status
          Let #Input       = 0
       Else
          Show 'Invalid Input, Re-Entry Required'
       End-If
    End-If
 End-While

End-Procedure


!**************************
Begin-Procedure Build-Where
!**************************
!Build Where Clause based on user's Input
 If $Problem_Status     = ''
   Let $Where_status = ''
 Else
   Let $Status=Rtrim($Problem_Status,' ')
   Let $Where_status = 'And A.My_Problem_Status = '|| ''''||$Status||''''
   Show $Where_status
 End-If

End-Procedure


!*****************
Begin-Procedure Main
!*****************
Begin-Select
A.My_Problem_Status     ()      on-break Print=Never After=Page-Break
Save=$Status_Cur
A.My_Project_ID
A.Incident_DT
A.My_Priority
A.My_User_ID
A.My_Problem_Tracker
A.Close_Dt
```

```
     Do Print-Line
From PS_MY_PROBLEM_TRKG A
Where A.Incident_Dt <= $AsOfDate
[$Where_status]
order by A.My_Problem_Status
End-Select

End-Procedure


!**************************
Begin-Procedure Print-Line
!**************************
 Lookup Projects &A.My_Project_ID $Descr
 Print $Descr                      (+1,         1, {project_descr_len} )
 Print &A.Incident_DT          (   ,+{col_sep}, {date_len}             )
 Lookup Priority &A.My_Priority $Priority_Descr
 Print $Priority_Descr         (   ,+{col_sep}, {priority_len}         )
 Lookup Users &A.My_User_ID $User_Name
 Print $User_Name              (   ,+{col_sep}, {user_name_len}        )
 Lookup Users &A.My_Problem_Tracker $Problem_Tracker_Name
 Print $Problem_Tracker_Name   (   ,+{col_sep}, {responsible_name}     )
 Print &A.Close_Dt             (   ,+{col_sep}, {date_len}             )

End-Procedure


!**************************
Begin-Procedure Page-Break
!**************************
Lookup Status $Status_Cur $Stat
new-page
End-Procedure


!*****************************

#include 'stdapi.sqc'      !Routines to Update Run Status
#Include 'datetime.sqc'    !Routines for date and time formatting
#Include 'number.sqc'      !Routines to format numbers        The custom SQC
#include 'askaod.sqc'      !Ask As Of Date input              files are added to
#include 'myrunctl.sqc'    !Get Run Control parameters        the program.
#include 'mygetval.sqc'    !Format Run Control parameters
```

In listing 28.1, the code of the Status Report was changed to include the
MYRUNCNTL.sqc and MYGETVAL.sqc files. Also, we added a code to the
Init-Report and Get-Values procedures to reflect the new SQC functionality.

28.5 TESTING YOUR CHANGES

Before we start testing, let's list all the modifications that were made to make the
Problem Status report API Aware and to enable it to accept input parameters from the
Process Scheduler:

- The `Stdapi-Init` and `Stdapi-Term` procedure calls were added to the MYPROB02.sqr program. The STDAPI.sqc include file was incorporated into our program.
- The MYRUNCTL.sqc file was created to select input parameters from the MY_RUN_CNTL record.
- The MYGETVAL.sqc file was created to format the selected parameters and to move them to the designated program variables.
- The MYRUNCNTL.sqc and MYGETVAL.sqc files were included in the program.
- The `Init-Report` and `Get-Values` procedures in MYPROB02.sqr were modified to call the new `Select-Parameters`, `Get-As-Of-Date`, and `Get-Process-Status` procedures.

Let's execute our program, then verify the program output report.

Since we already created a Run Control ID, `MY_STATUS_01`, we can re-use it. Once displayed, we can change its input parameters. Let's enter `08/03/1999` in the `As Of Date` field, and select `Assigned` as our problem status (figure 28.7).

Navigation: Go → Problem Tracking → Report → Status Report → **Update/Display**

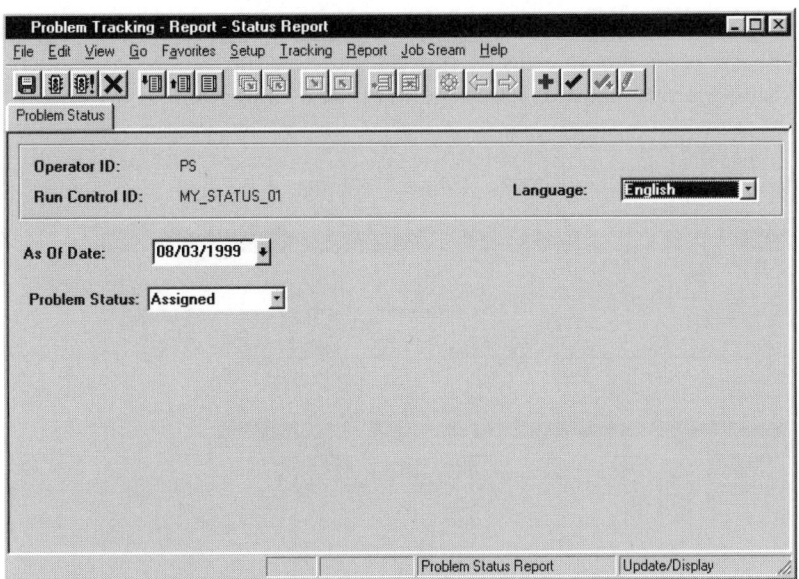

Figure 28.7   Executing the Problem Status report

When all parameters are entered, click on the traffic light to bring in the Process Request panel.

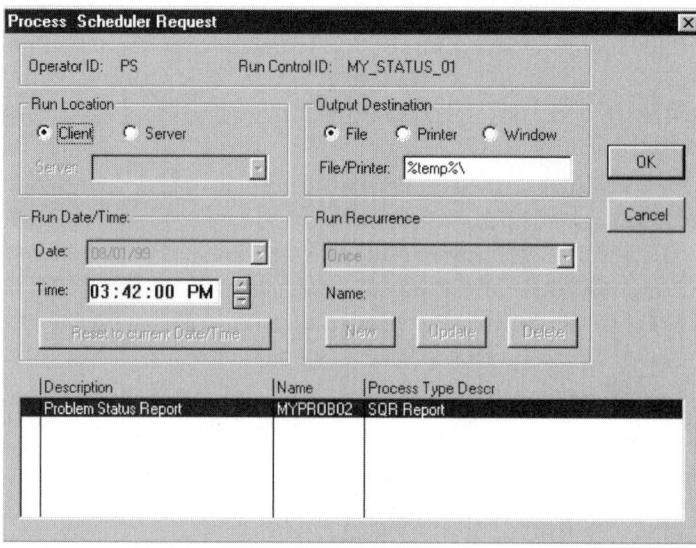

Figure 28.8   Process Request for MYPROB02.sqr

Let's click on the OK button and run the program. Since we made our program API Aware, it should send its process status to the Process Scheduler. The Process Monitor screen helps us to see the status of our program.

Navigation: Go → PeopleTools → Process Monitor

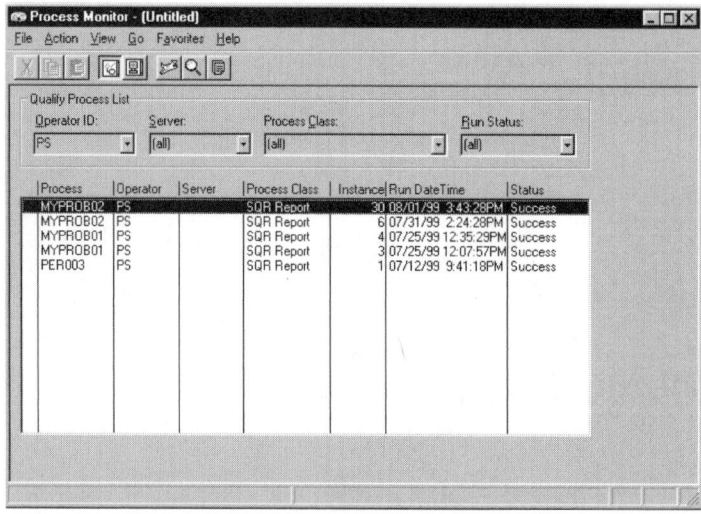

Figure 28.9   Examining the status of our program execution

CHAPTER 28   THE PROCESS SCHEDULER

Our program executed successfully. Let's verify the output report. First, double-check the destination of our output report. In order to find this, double-click on the process name of our process (MYPROB02) in the Process Monitor screen, then go to the second tab, Request Parameters.

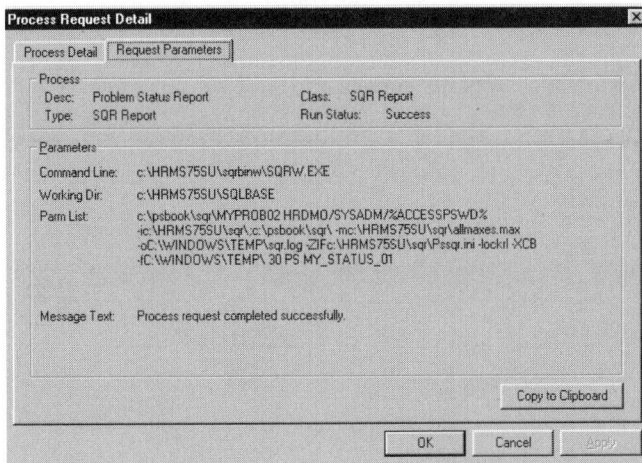

Figure 28.10
Verifying the output file destination

Take a look at the Parm list in figure 28.10. The report output file is specified with the –f flag. Therefore, we look for our .lis file in the c:\windows\temp directory.

TIP   An SQR program produces its output file only if there were at least one detail output record. If your program ran to success, but you cannot find your output report, check the following:

- Are you looking at the right directory?
- Are your input parameters correctly specified?
- Do you have data in the database?
- Is your selection criteria correct?

In our case, we received the report, shown in figure 28.11.

As you can see, our program ran successfully and produced the report which shows only the assigned incidents. Let's do one more test and see how our program handles the situation when we do not enter a specific problem status. We want to print all incidents entered into the system as of 08/03/99 in our report.

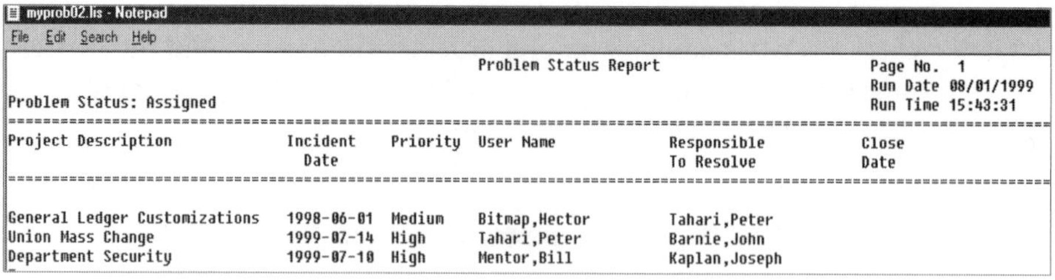

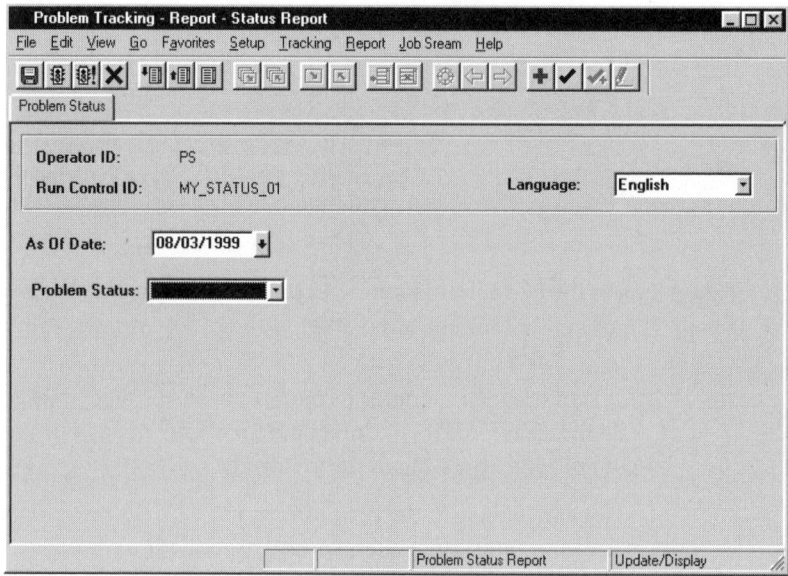

Figure 28.11   The output of MYPROB02.sqr report

Let's enter our parameters (figure 28.12).

Figure 28.12   Entering an empty Problem Status to select all incidents as of 08/03/1999 date

After our program executes, let's again examine the output report: MYPROB02.lis.

```
                                    Problem Status Report           Page No.   1
                                                                    Run Date 08/01/1999
Problem Status: Initiated                                           Run Time 17:50:34
========================================================================================
Project Description        Incident    Priority  User Name        Responsible    Close
                           Date                                    To Resolve     Date
========================================================================================

HR Customizations          1999-07-01  Low       Barnie,John      Mentor,Bill
```

```
                                    Problem Status Report           Page No.   2
                                                                    Run Date 08/01/1999
Problem Status: Assigned                                            Run Time 17:50:34
========================================================================================
Project Description           Incident    Priority  User Name     Responsible    Close
                              Date                                 To Resolve     Date
========================================================================================
General Ledger Customizations 1998-06-01  Medium   Bitmap,Hector  Tahari,Peter
Union Mass Change             1999-07-14  High     Tahari,Peter   Barnie,John
Department Security           1999-07-10  High     Mentor,Bill    Kaplan,Joseph
```

Figure 28.13   Problem Status report output that includes all problems grouped by Problem Status

As you can see from figure 28.13, the program produced several pages of the report. Therefore, our break logic as well as our parameter selection logic works. To confirm the test results, it is a good habit to use your native SQL tool and select records from the database to verify your report output. We can also use the online panels of our Problem Tracking application, and compare the report results. In addition, the report has to be tested on the Server to make certain that it runs correctly on both platforms. You should never assume that if your report works correctly on one platform, it runs without problems on another.

1 An API Aware process is a process that updates the Process Request table (PSPRCSRQST) with the process run status (`Error`, `Success`, and so on), completion code, message set, and message number.

2 To accept input parameters from PeopleSoft online panels, you can either use the existing PeopleSoft-delivered SQC files or develop your own, depending on the parameters your SQR program needs to accept.

3 Your program should support both types of input parameter retrieval logic: retrieving the parameters from the Process Scheduler, and accepting them from the SQR Dialog Box or the command line.

4 Usually, there are two SQC files involved in accepting program input parameters from a PeopleSoft online panel. One file should contain a procedure to select all required fields from the proper Run Control record. Another one should include procedures to edit the selected fields and place them into designated SQR variables.

5 Your SQR program must be changed to include the proper SQC files and a code to call the input parameter retrieval procedures.

6 A Run Control panel which contains all the input parameters should be developed, or an existing panel should be used or customized.

7 The changed SQR program must be thoroughly tested on both Client and Server to make sure that the input parameters are passed and accepted correctly.

CHAPTER 29

Implementing security in SQR

29.1 OVERVIEW OF THE PEOPLESOFT SECURITY LAYERS

Most of PeopleSoft-delivered applications work with important and sensitive information. Therefore, implementing and maintaining data security is usually a high priority task.

Before we start a discussion of different methods of implementing security in your SQR programs, let's review the online security functionality provided by PeopleSoft. Please be aware that, while comprehensive online Security Administration is not in the scope of this book (refer to PeopleSoft technical documentation for details), we will show you in great detail how to implement security in your SQR programs.

As we already discussed in the previous parts of this book, PeopleSoft provides you with layers of security to help protect your data from unauthorized access.

When accessing a PeopleSoft application in a networked environment, you have to pass through network security, database security, and PeopleSoft online security.

Network security typically includes the following components:

- an assigned ID and password for user verification
- an authorized sign-on time
- file access rights

In order to execute an SQR program, for example, users need to have appropriate access to the directory where the SQR executable resides and to the delivered or custom SQR programs. They also need to have access to the produced reports and input/output files (if any).

Database security is comprised of RDBMS (Relational Database Management System) security and PeopleSoft online security, which work together. The RDBMS security typically controls the database logon, database tables access and manipulations, and system administration activities.

PeopleSoft Online security includes *Operator Security* and *Object Security*. PeopleSoft provides you with utilities to maintain these two types of security. (Please refer to chapter 3.)

Row-Level security is used to control the user's access to specific rows of data from the database tables. PeopleSoft delivers applications with row-level security. PeopleSoft uses security search view records to provide online row-level security.

The *Field-Level* security can be implemented by using PeopleCode. For example, if you allow your operator to see a certain panel but would like to hide some fields in this panel, you can add logic to check the Operator ID, and either hide or show sensitive fields.

PeopleSoft also provides you with powerful tools to manage and enhance security based on your specific needs and applications. Using PeopleTools, you can design your own *Row-Level* and *Field-Level* security.

In the following subchapters, we are going to show you how to implement Row-Level security in batch SQR programs. Let's see first how Row-Level security works in PeopleSoft online programs. We will use similar approaches in batch SQR programs.

29.2 ROW-LEVEL SECURITY IN PEOPLESOFT ONLINE APPLICATIONS

PeopleSoft delivers a special way of controlling online access to your specific data rows by the means of security search records. These records are, in fact, regular SQL views designed with security in mind. You can either design your own security search records or use the PeopleSoft-delivered ones. After a view is created to be used as a security search record, PeopleTools lets you attach the view to the corresponding PeopleSoft table and panel group. PeopleSoft delivers different security search mechanisms based on the application. For example, the built-in Department security is delivered with PeopleSoft HRMS package, while PeopleSoft Financial applications secure financial transactions by business units and ledgers. We will be using the HRMS application to review the online security features delivered by PeopleSoft.

If you look at any of your application core record's properties, you can see how PeopleSoft attaches these views to the record definition. Let's display, for example, the property window of the JOB record.

After the record definition is displayed, press ALT/ENTER to display the record's properties, and switch to the Use tab (figure 29.1).

Navigation: GO → Application Designer → Open → Record → JOB

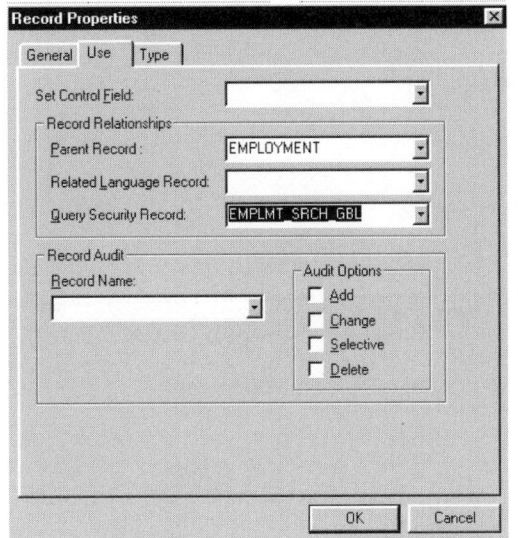

Figure 29.1
EMPLMT_SRCH_GBL is a query security record for the JOB record

As you can see from figure 29.1, the search view EMPLMT_SRCH_GBL is specified as a query security record for the JOB record. This lets the PeopleSoft system know what security record should be used to restrict the user's query access to the Job table.

Different tables may have the same or different query security records, depending on the table structure and the key fields it contains. For example, the PERSONAL_DATA table has the PERS_SRCH_QRY as its query security record, and the EMPLOYMENT table has the same search record as JOB. If you look at these view definitions, you can see that they are designed to restrict operator access to employee rows based on the department security that was set up for an operator.

29.2.1 Row-Level security in the PeopleSoft Query tool

In chapter 24, we discussed the nature of the EMPLMT_SRCH_US security record. If you open the EMPLMT_SRCH_GBL record in the Application Designer, you can see that this record is similar to the US record. In fact, the security mechanism is absolutely the same. Since we already learned how the record is built (and even took a brave attempt to modify it), we will show here how it's designed to work with the online QUERY tool.

Let's go to the Query tool and select the JOB record.

Navigation: Go → PeopleTools → Query

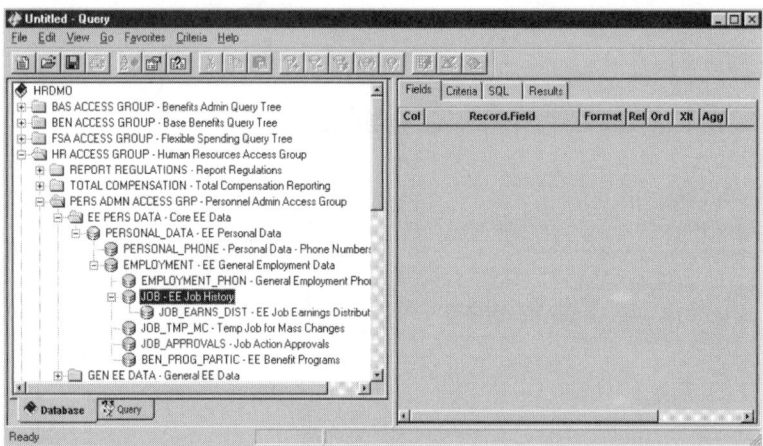

Figure 29.2   Selecting data from the JOB table via the Query tool

Double-click on the JOB record and select a few fields from this record. Take a look at the SQL statement by clicking on SQL tab on the right side of the Query panel.

What we see in figure 29.3, is an SQL statement that PeopleSoft generated on our behalf, based on the requirements it received from us. It contains the selection of the PS_JOB table columns that we specified. In addition, it joined the PS_JOB table with the PS_EMPLMT_SRCH_GBL table.

Now we can see how the security view limits the PS_JOB table row selection based on the previously defined security level. The join returns only rows defined in the security view PS_EMPLMT_SRCH_GBL. PeopleSoft joins the PS_JOB table with the Query Security record that we specified in the JOB's record definition.

CHAPTER 29   IMPLEMENTING SECURITY IN SQR

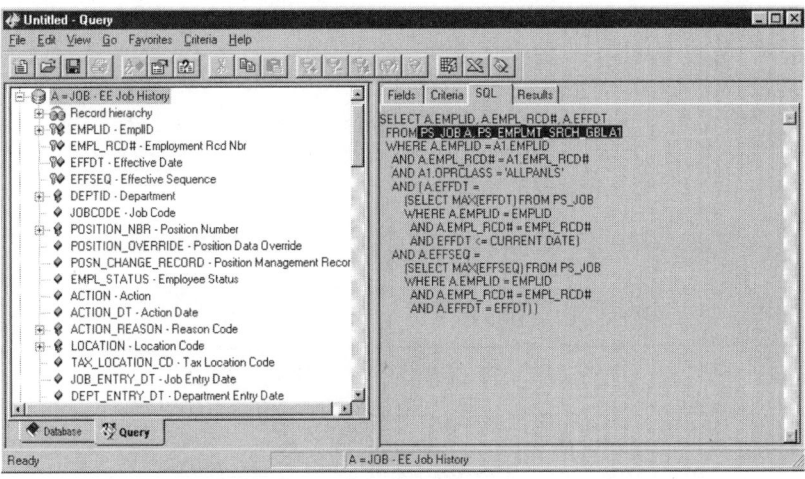

Figure 29.3 PeopleSoft generated SQL statement

What if we have to select data from two or more tables? Let's take a look at the SQL statement that PeopleSoft generates when we ask it to join our JOB table with the PERSONAL_DATA table (figure 29.4).

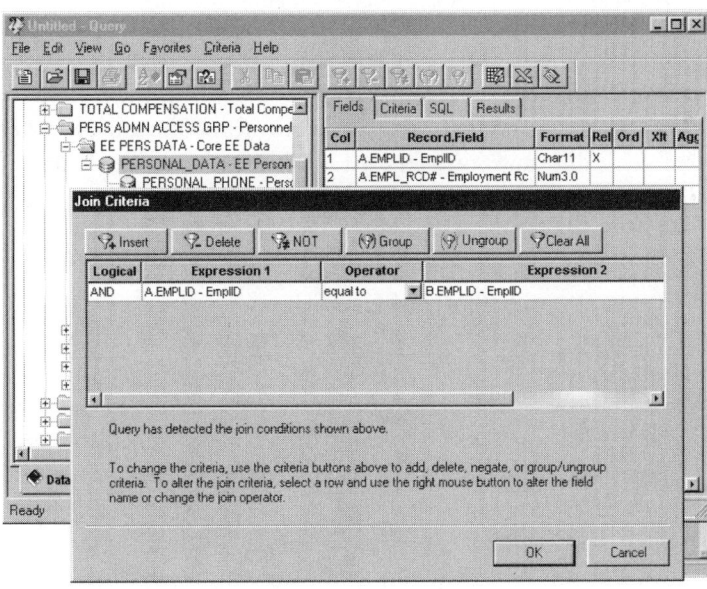

**Figure 29.4
Adding the
PERSONAL_DATA
table to the Query**

We examine the SQL statement now by switching to the SQL tab.

As you can see from the SQL statement in figure 29.5, in addition to joining PS_JOB with the PS_PERSONAL_DATA table, PeopleSoft also joins these two tables with the PS_EMPLMT_SRCH_GBL and PS_PERS_SRCH_QRY security search views. Therefore, when two records are joined with different security search records, PeopleSoft automatically joins the corresponding security views.

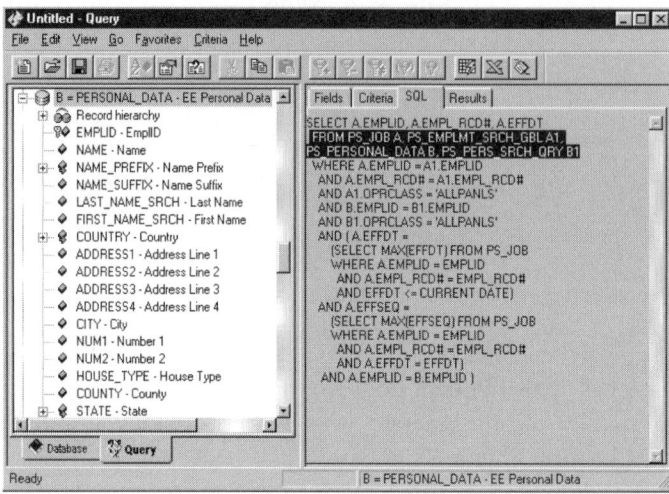

Figure 29.5   The PERSONAL_DATA table is joined with the Job table

Let's see one more example. Suppose we want to add the EMPLOYMENT table to our query. This table (and you can easily verify it) has the same security search view as the JOB table. Will PeopleSoft add the EMPLOYMENT table along with its security view or will it take the table alone? Let's check this out.

If you look again at the SQL statement that PeopleSoft generated, you see that the EMPLOYMENT table is joined without an additional security view. PeopleSoft is smart enough to recognize that the EMPLMT_SRCH_GBL is already present in the query.

Now that we learned that PeopleSoft automatically joins its tables with their respective security views, it's clear that the user's selection is controlled based on the view definition and the security setup. As we mentioned in the beginning of this part, the goal of our Security overview is to show the PeopleSoft security functionality that is relevant to our task of implementing security in SQR. The Security administration is a complex topic. In our examples, we only showed you how PeopleSoft joins its tables with their security views. The views themselves would never work without the proper Department security setup and administration. Each operator's security must be set up in conjunction with their business needs in order to gain appropriate access.

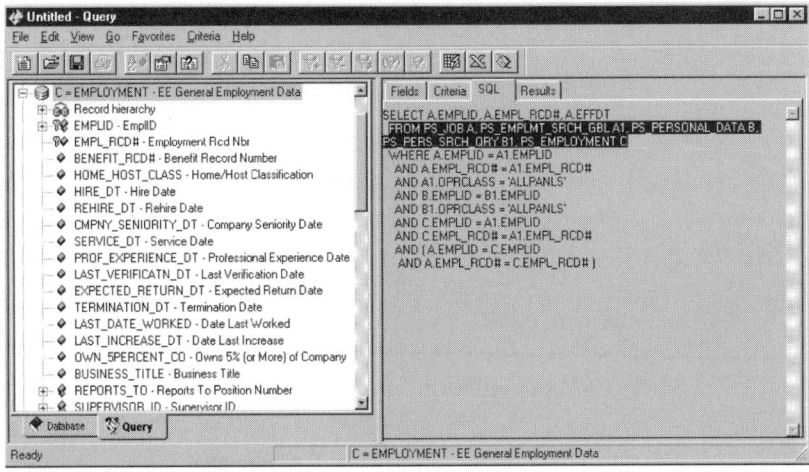

Figure 29.6   Adding the EMPLOYMENT table to our query

In addition to using the Query tool in PeopleSoft, data may also be selected from online panels. Let's take a closer look how PeopleSoft manages security in this case.

29.2.2   Row-Level security in online Panels

As an example, let's open the JOB_DATA panel group (figure 29.7).

Navigation: Go → PeopleTools → Application Designer → Open → Panel Group → JOB_DATA

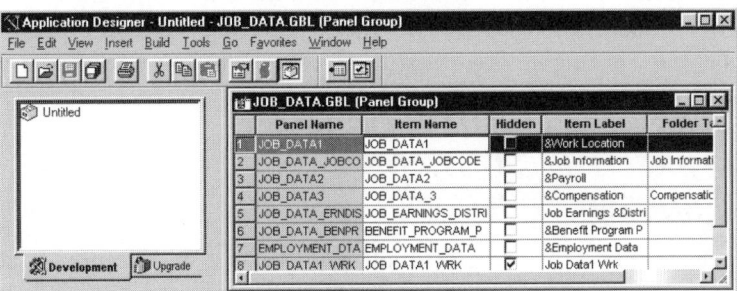

Figure 29.7   The JOB_DATA panel group

If you press ALT/ENTER, you can see the Properties Panel (figure 29.8).

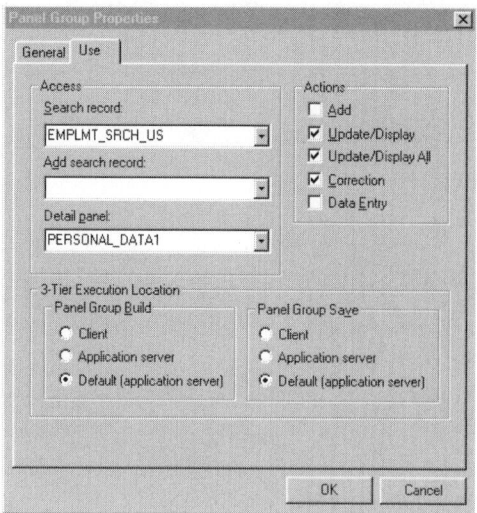

Figure 29.8
The EMPLMT_SRCH_US search record is used for the JOB_DATA panel group

As you can see from figure 29.8, the EMPLMT_SRCH_US search record is used for the JOB_DATA panel group. What that means is that this view is responsible for bringing up the Selection dialog box with all rows that correspond to both the user's criteria and the security criteria. For example, if the user specified a partial name search as "Smith," not all rows from the database with the name starting with "Smith" will be returned, only the ones to which the user has access based on the department security setup. In chapter 24 of this book, we ran a trace to learn exactly what PeopleSoft is doing behind the scenes when the search criteria has been entered. As we saw in chapter 24 when the user specifies the search criteria, PeopleSoft builds the SQL statements to select from the Access Search record specified for a particular panel group.

29.3 *PREVENTING AN SQR PROGRAM FROM EXECUTING OUTSIDE THE PROCESS SCHEDULER*

As we discussed, in online PeopleSoft processing, data selection is controlled by PeopleSoft Security. This is not necessarily true when you execute your batch processes. You know that SQR programs in PeopleSoft can be submitted in several different ways—from the Process Scheduler, from the SQRW dialog box, or from the command line.

If you're running your SQR programs through the Process Scheduler, their execution is controlled by levels of PeopleSoft Security. First, you must be an authorized PeopleSoft user to login to the PeopleSoft system. Second, menu security is in place to prevent unauthorized access to a particular menu or panel. Third, when creating a process definition, you must specify authorized process security groups, thus restricting the execution of a particular program to a specific group or groups. However, if a user is authorized to execute a program, the system in most cases will run the SQR as "SYSADM," which means that your program will have full, unrestricted access to data. In order to prevent this, you need to implement the Row-Level security in your SQR program.

If your SQR program is not run from the Process Scheduler, your security is at much bigger risk; the database access password alone is not sufficient to maintain the proper security.

In order to prevent SQR execution outside of PeopleSoft Process Scheduler, PeopleSoft (starting from PeopleSoft release 7.5) offers a simple and efficient solution. This technique is used in most of the PeopleSoft-delivered SQR programs for HRMS application. Since we are already familiar with the Years of Service report, let's look at this program:

```
!Part of PER003.SQR with a code that restricts the SQR execution outside of
the Process Scheduler
….
begin-procedure Init-Report

  move 'PER003' to $ReportID
  do Delete-Worktable

  do Stdapi-Init            PeopleSoft does not allow the report
  if $prcs_oprid=''         to run outside the process Scheduler
    display ''
    display 'REPORT CAN NOT BE EXECUTED OUTSIDE OF PEOPLESOFT,PLEASE USE
PROCESS SCHEDULER.'
    display ''
    goto last1
  end-if

  do Sqr-Param

  if $prcs_process_instance = ''
    do Ask-As-Of-Date
    do Ask-Years-Of-Service
  else
    do Select-Parameters
  end-if
  do Init_Printer
  do Init_Report_Translation ($ReportID, $language_cd)
  do Append_Report_Translation ('HR')
last1:
end-procedure
….
```

As you can see from the Init-Report procedure of the PER003.sqr, the program checks the $prcs_oprid variable, which is populated by the API code (in the Get-Run-Control-Parms procedure), only if the report were initiated from the

Process Scheduler. If the value of $prcs_oprid is Null, SQR displays an error message and exits the program.

This simple code can be easily implemented in any custom program, thus ensuring program execution only from the PeopleSoft Process Scheduler.

TIP   If you need to bypass this security check during your testing stage you can enclose the bolded code in the #ifdef/#endif statements.

29.4   *INCORPORATING ROW-LEVEL SECURITY IN SQR*

In release 7.5, PeopleSoft incorporated the Row-Level security for its HRMS application. This implementation consists of both the online and batch modifications. The online changes are performed by using PeopleTools, and once implemented, they will apply to all programs in the HRMS application. The batch modifications are done on a program-to-program basis.

Take a look at this feature in the INSTALLATION table.

Open the Third Party panel from the Installation Table panel group (figure 29.9).

Navigation: Go → Define Business Rules → Define General Options → Setup
→ Installation Table

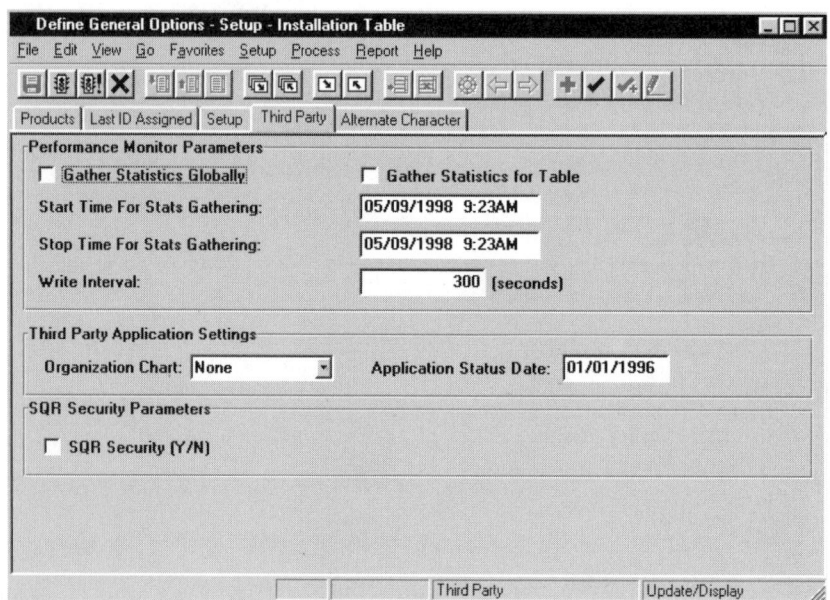

Figure 29.9 **SQR Security flag is added to the Installation Table**

As you can see from figure 29.9, the SQR Security flag is added to the Third Party panel. This is currently delivered for the PeopleSoft HRMS application. If you want to activate SQR Security, you should set the flag ON. If flag is not on, the system will not be using SQR Security features.

WARNING   In order to use the SQR Security delivered by PeopleSoft you should also implement the PeopleSoft's Fast Security to populate the security views that are used in the delivered SQR programs.

Let's see now how SQR Security is implemented in PER003.sqr

Listing 29.1

PER003.sqr

```
begin-report
  do Init-DateTime
  do Init-Number
  Move 1 to $Year4
  do Init-Report
  if $prcs_oprid=''
  goto last2
end-if
  if $scrty_flag='Y'                If Security is Activated, execute
  do Process-Main-Scrty             Process-Main-Scrty, otherwise
  else                              execute Process-Main
  do Process-Main
  end-if
  do Reset
  do Stdapi-Term
last2:
end-report

....

begin-procedure Init-Report

  move 'PER003' to $ReportID
  do Delete-Worktable
  do Stdapi-Init
  if $prcs_oprid=''
    display ''
    display 'REPORT CAN NOT BE EXECUTED OUTSIDE OF PEOPLESOFT,PLEASE USE
PROCESS SCHEDULER.'
    display ''
  goto last1
  end-if                           The Sqr-Param procedure
                                   selects Security flag value
  do Sqr-Param                     from the Installation table.
```

```
        if $prcs_process_instance = ''
          do Ask-As-Of-Date
          do Ask-Years-Of-Service
        else
          do Select-Parameters
        end-if
        do Init_Printer
        do Init_Report_Translation ($ReportID, $language_cd)
        do Append_Report_Translation ('HR')
last1:
end-procedure


....

begin-procedure Process-Main

  move '1' to $Year4
  move '-' to $DDelimiter
  do Format-DateTime($AsOfDate, $AsOf_YMD, {DEFYMD}, '', '')
  do Data-Selection
  do Create-Report
  do Delete-Worktable

end-procedure

begin-procedure Process-Main-Scrty

  move '1' to $Year4
  move '-' to $DDelimiter
  do Format-DateTime($AsOfDate, $AsOf_YMD, {DEFYMD}, '', '')
  do Data-Selection-Scrty
  do Create-Report
  do Delete-Worktable

end-procedure
...

#include 'hrsecty.sqc'    !Get SQR Security parameters
```

HRSECTY.sqc contains the SQR-Param procedure

As you can see in the above excerpt from PER003.sqr program, the program calls the SQR-Param procedure at the beginning. This procedure is located in the HRSECTY.sqc file. Its only job is to select the Security flag from the INSTALLATION table. Based on the selection, the program either uses the security features or ignores them. That's why, when PeopleSoft modified the old version of this program to incorporate the security features, it duplicated the data selection procedure leaving intact the old ones to be able to run the program in two modes—with and without security. Take a look at the Process-Main-Scrty procedure. It's a clone of the Process-Main, the only difference being that it calls another data selection procedure: Data-Selection-Scrty.

Let's compare two routines—Data-Selection and Data-Selection-Scrty—and see how PeopleSoft incorporated the row-level security.

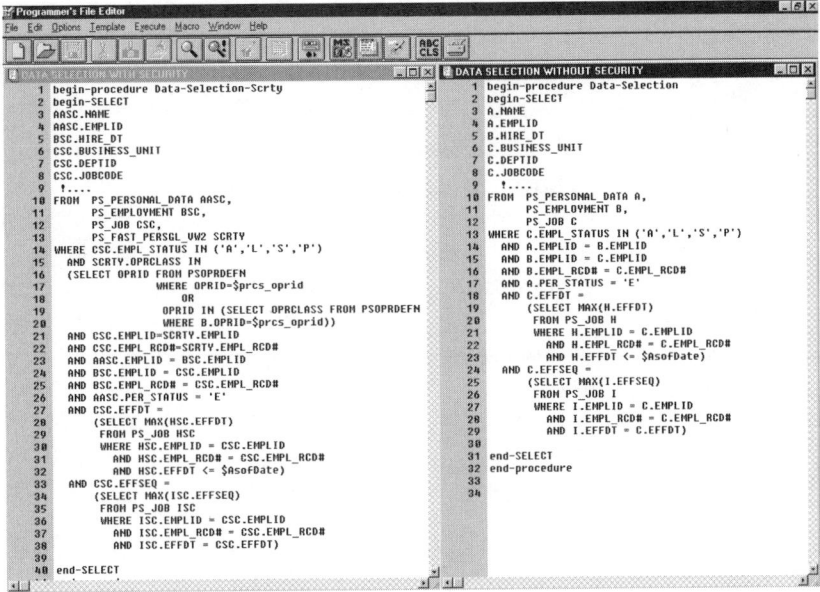

Figure 29.10   Data-Selection and Data-Selection-Scrty

Take a closer look at the two procedures displayed in figure 29.10. The one on the left is the new data selection with security, while the other on the right, is the procedure without security. For visibility purposes and to simplify the comparison, all irrelevant SQR statements between the last selected column and the FROM keyword were deleted from both procedures since they were absolutely identical.

The procedure with security has all the functionality of the one without security, plus more. Take a look at line number 13 on the left side. You can see that a new table, PS_FAST_PERSGL_VW2, is added to the SQL join. This is a fast department security view that plays the same role as the Query Security view that we discussed earlier in this chapter. This view is joined with the PS_JOB table by EMPLID and EMPL_RCD#. In addition (see line number 15) OPRCLASS, which is a key field in the security view, is matched with the $prcs_oprid. In other words, the Select statement only selects the records of the employees that the operator ($prcs_oprid) is authorized to access.

The fast security view PS_FAST_PERSGL_VW2 is an alternate fast search record for PS_PERS_SRCH_GBL. In order to use this view, the Fast Security delivered by PeopleSoft must be implemented. Fast Security uses the Application Engine to populate a special security table that was created to support search views with faster performance. Note that you do not have to use fast security search records in order to implement security in your SQR programs. Instead of the PS_FAST_PERSGL_VW2 record, the PS_PERS_SRCH_QRY search record could be used. If you have already implemented Fast Security, you can take advantage of both batch and online fast security access.

Let's summarize now what we have learned about implementing security in SQR and what practical steps have to be undertaken to support this security.

!!! Practical steps necessary to implement security in SQR for HRMS applications:

- make certain that SQR Security flag is checked ON in Installation table
- include the hrsecty.sqc file in your SQR program
- add code to your program to make sure your SQR program is executed from the Process Scheduler by verifying the `$prcs_oprid` variable
- call the SQR-Param procedure to select the SQR security flag from the Installation table
- check if SQR security Flag is On or Off and call the corresponding procedure (with or without security)
- create an additional data selection procedure that will be called if the SQR security flag is ON. Add a security search record to this procedure to restrict access to non-authorized data

---

TIP   When OPRCLASS is retrieved based on OPRID in a sub-select statement (figure 29.10, lines 16-20) the SQL performance is impacted negatively, because the sub-select is executed for every selected row. To improve performance, obtain OPRCLASS only once outside of the main select procedure. Then use the retrieved OPRCLASS in the main select.

Now, that we know how simple it is to implement security in SQR, can we go ahead and incorporate it in all our custom programs? The process may not always be that straight-forward. You need to know your data and choose a correct search record for your data selection procedure. If your goal is to limit the employee selection to authorized operators only based on the department security implemented in your system, you can use either the fast security record or query security records. Both these views utilize the department security. If your SQR program selects neither employees nor departments, you need to come up with some other alternatives. In the next section, we will show how you can limit selection at the Run Control panel level without changing your SQR program.

29.5   USING RUN CONTROL RECORDS FOR SQR SECURITY

When executing SQR programs from the Process Scheduler, users are often asked to enter parameters online via a Run Control panel. These parameters are saved in the corresponding Run Control records and then passed to your SQR. Of course, not all SQR programs accept input parameters. We will consider a case when parameters are entered from an online Run Control panel and will show you how you can implement a simple security system by using PeopleTools.

Let's consider, for example, a typical Payroll task—running a Paysheets report.

Figure 29.11 shows a standard Run Control panel used in most Payroll batch processes. In order to run a process (in this case it is the Paysheets report), the operator has to either specify a pay run ID or enter the three parameters on the right of the panel: Company, Pay Group, and Pay End Date. Let's use the second method and enter the parameters into the panel. Click on the Company field and you can see the list of all available companies (figure 29.12). When Company is selected, click on Pay Group, and you can see all the paygroups for the selected Company (figure 29.13).

Navigation: Go → Compensate Employees → Manage Payroll Process → Report 2 → Paysheets

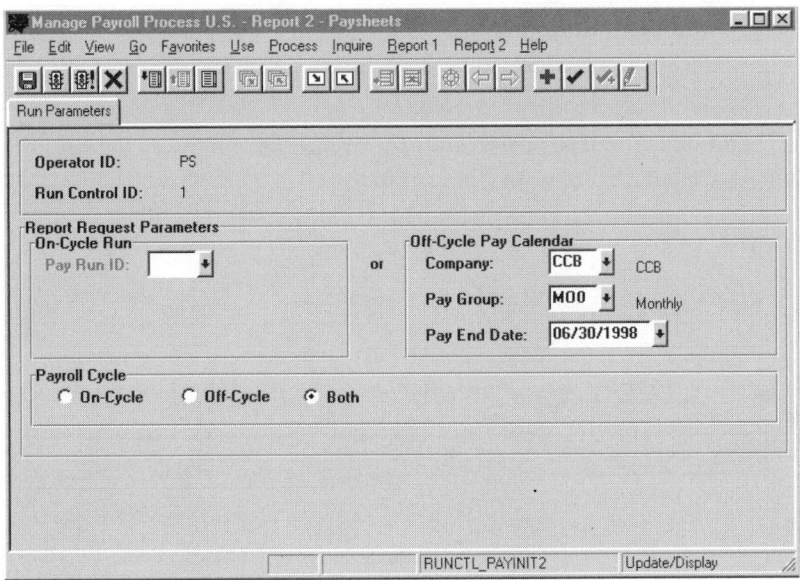

Figure 29.11   A Typical Run Control Panel for a Payroll Process

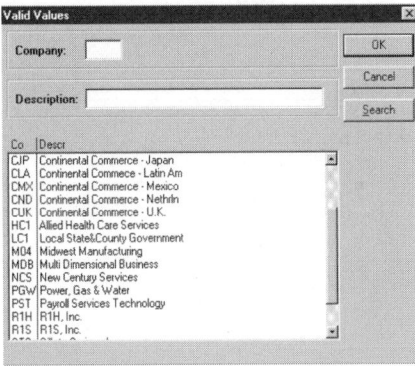

Figure 29.12   The Company Prompt

As you can see, an operator can select any Company/Paygroup combination available from the prompt. What if we make Company and Paygroup selection dependent on operator class? This will facilitate implementation of the online Company/Paygroup security.

1   Create a Company/Paygroup Security table to control data access for operators (operator classes) based on Company/Paygroup combinations.

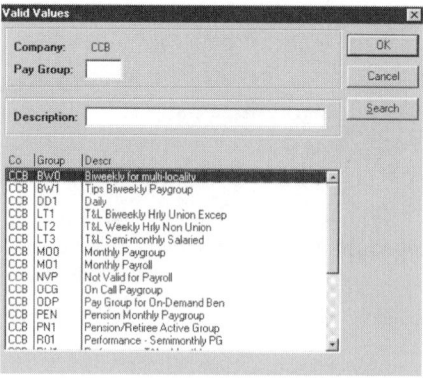

Figure 29.13 The Paygroup Prompt

2 Create a panel for online control of Company/Paygroup Security.

3 Create the company, paygroup, and run ID views to be used as online prompt tables for Company and Paygroup in all records related to any Payroll Process run. This will limit the process execution to operator classes that have access to authorized Company/Paygroups.

4 Modify the Run Control record definition to use the new prompt records.

Our objective is to demonstrate how the online security can be implemented. Following are the highlights of the Company/Paygroup security implementation.

Step 1

Creating Company/Paygroup Security table, MY_COMP_PAYGRP (figure 29.14).

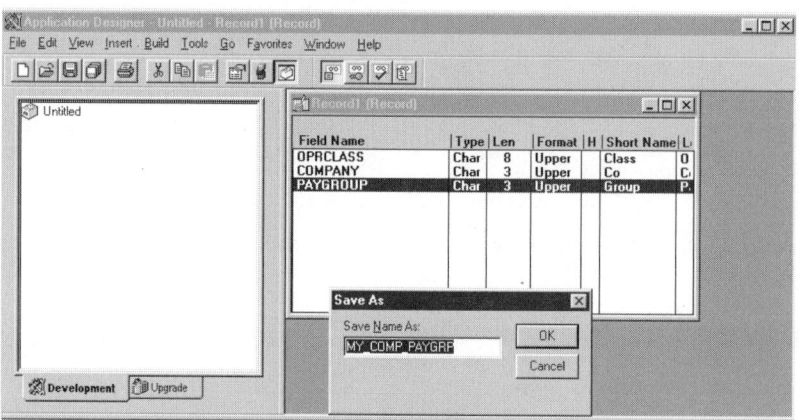

Figure 29.14 Creating Company/Paygroup Security table

Step 2

Creating Company/Paygroup Security Maintenance panel (figure 29.15).

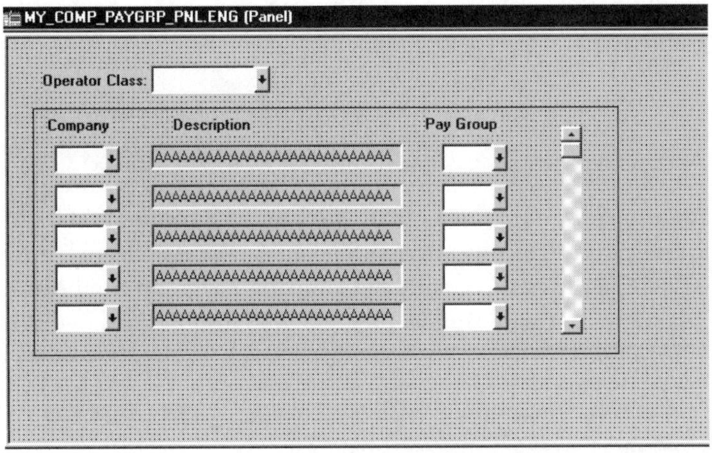

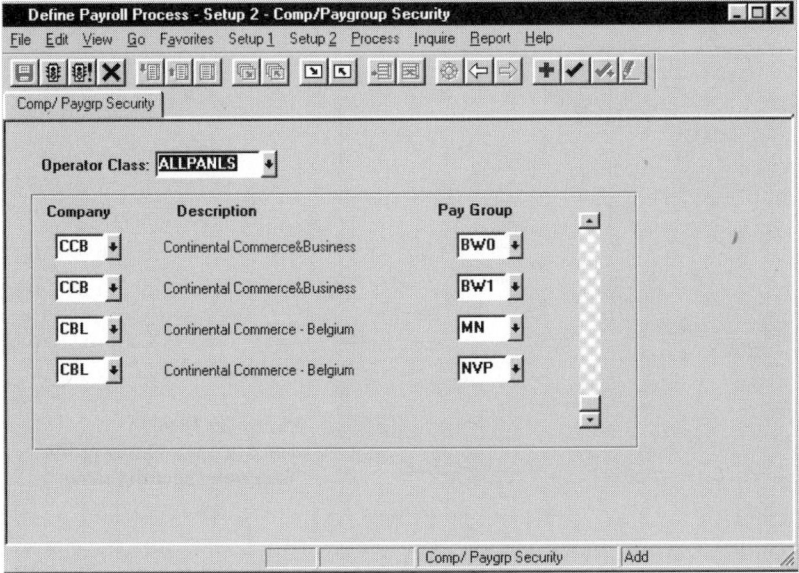

Figure 29.15 Company/Paygroup Security panel

After creating a panel group and adding it to the setup menu, we can populate the Company/Paygroup Security panel with the appropriate information. For each operator class, users must enter all combinations of Company and Paygroups a particular operator class can access. Figure 29.16 shows how the maintenance of the Company/Paygroup Security is performed.

Figure 29.16 Assigning companies and paygroups to the ALLPANLS operator class

Let's get back to our development. We need to create the necessary views for our prompt records.

Step 3

Creating the company, paygroup, and run ID views.

We need to create three views that may be used as prompt tables for Company, Paygroup, and Run ID respectively. Since we already created a security table (MY_COMP_PAYGRP) that contains all Company/Paygroup combinations per operator class, the view creation is simple. Figures 29.17 thru 29.22 show each of the views with their definitions.

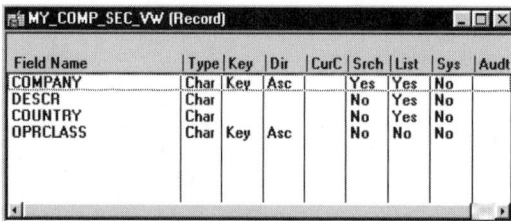

Figure 29.17
The Company security view

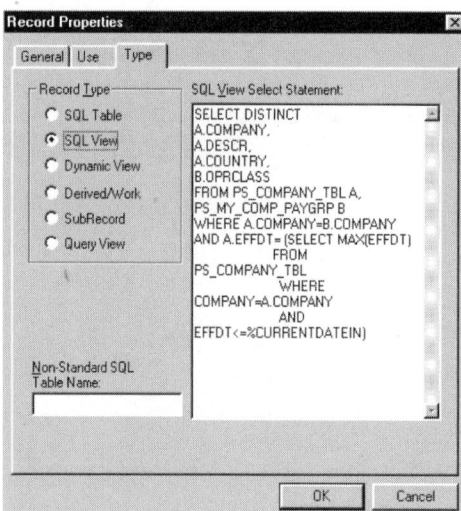

Figure 29.18
The SQL statement for the
Company security view

CHAPTER 29   IMPLEMENTING SECURITY IN SQR

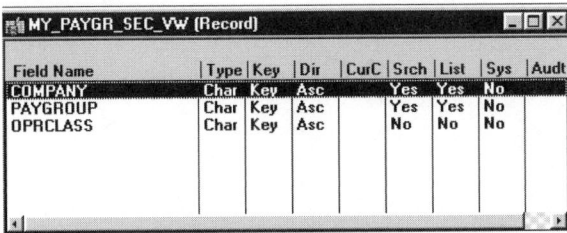

Figure 29.19
The Paygroup Security view

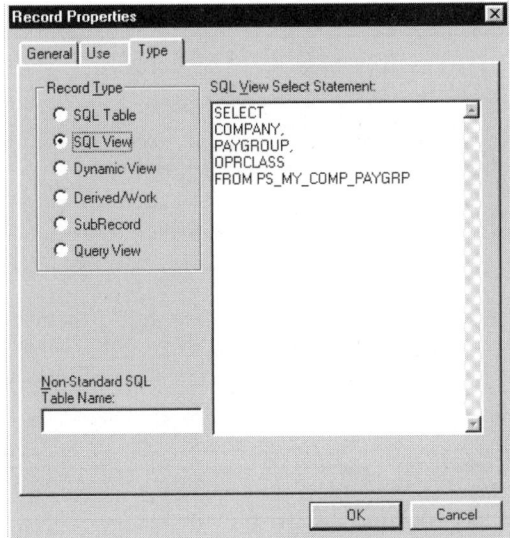

Figure 29.20
The SQL statement for the
Paygroup Security view

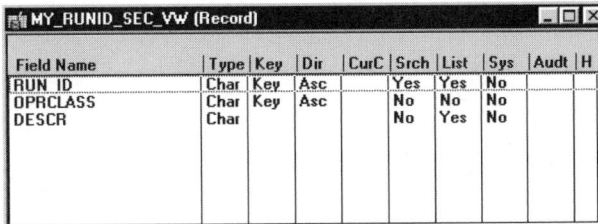

Figure 29.21
The Run ID Security view

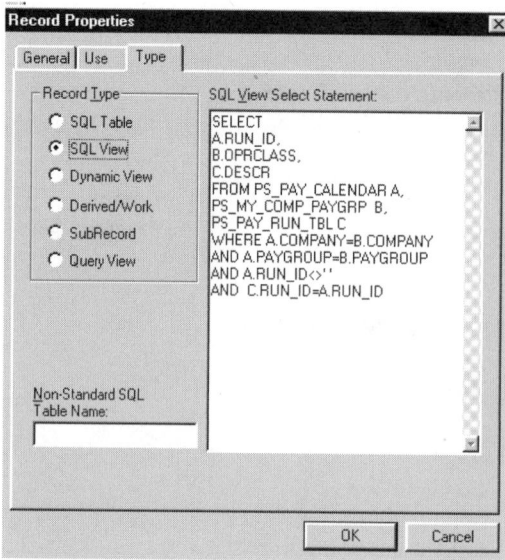

Figure 29.22
The SQL statement for the run ID security view

Our views have been created. We should, of course, build them on a database level. After all is done, we can move on to the next step.

Step 4

Modifying Run Control record definitions.

In the first three steps, we prepared a basis for our security. Now, we need to replace the current prompt tables with the new views we just created. Since we already discussed the Paysheets report, let's find the Run Control record used for this report, then modify this record.

Take a look at the Order panel for the RUNCTL_PAYINIT2 panel used in the Paysheets report (figure 29.23).

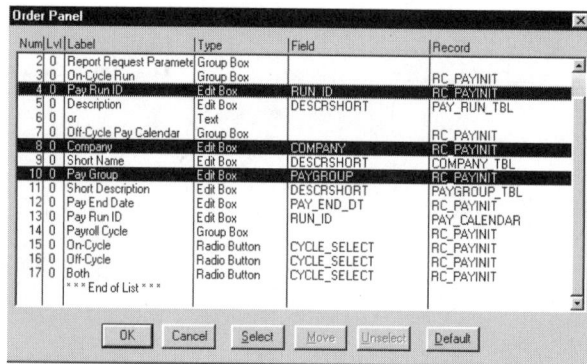

Figure 29.23
The RC_PAYINIT Run Control record used for the paysheets report

To implement this customization we have two alternatives:

- Customize the existing RC_PAYINIT record.
- Save this record as MY_RC_PAYINIT, then customize it. In addition, all panels that are linked to the RC_PAYINIT record and the corresponding panel groups must be cloned as well.

Generally, we do not recommend modifying PeopleSoft-delivered records, but our modifications in this case are not structural and, therefore, do not require the corresponding database level alterations. All panels that use this record with no modifications will benefit from the Company/Paygroup based security. During the upgrade process, the Compare and Report process will recognize the difference in the RC_PAYINIT record.

The second alternative requires more objects to be modified.

Therefore, selecting the first alternative, our customization of the RC_PAYINIT record is limited to replacing the prompt tables with our custom views.

Let's open the record and modify it by replacing the values for prompt tables in Run_ID, Company, and Paygroup fields with the newly created prompt tables (figure 29.24).

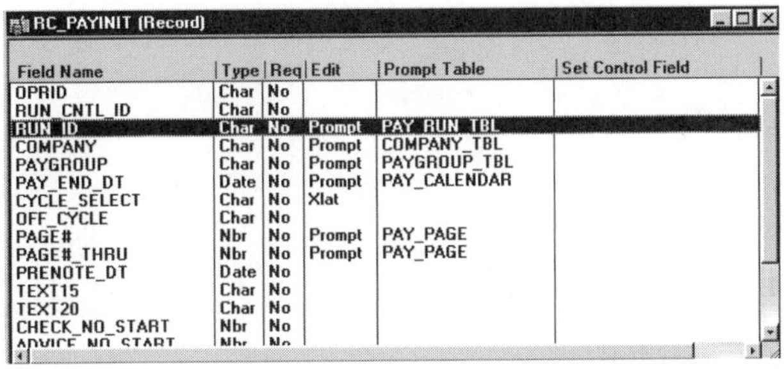
RC_PAYINIT (Record)

Field Name	Type	Req	Edit	Prompt Table	Set Control Field
OPRID	Char	No			
RUN_CNTL_ID	Char	No			
RUN_ID	Char	No	Prompt	PAY_RUN_TBL	
COMPANY	Char	No	Prompt	COMPANY_TBL	
PAYGROUP	Char	No	Prompt	PAYGROUP_TBL	
PAY_END_DT	Date	No	Prompt	PAY_CALENDAR	
CYCLE_SELECT	Char	No	Xlat		
OFF_CYCLE	Char	No			
PAGE#	Nbr	No	Prompt	PAY_PAGE	
PAGE#_THRU	Nbr	No	Prompt	PAY_PAGE	
PRENOTE_DT	Date	No			
TEXT15	Char	No			
TEXT20	Char	No			
CHECK_NO_START	Nbr	No			
ADVICE_NO_START	Nbr	No			

Figure 29.24
The Prompt tables that are currently used in RC_PAYINIT record

After replacing the prompt tables for Company, Paygroup, and Run_ID, our table looks like that in figure 29.25.

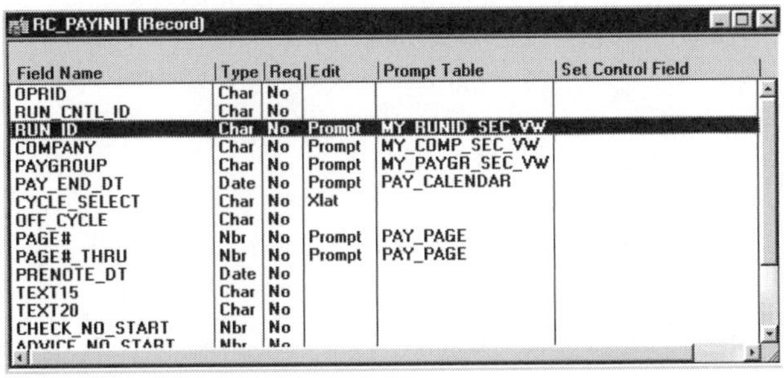
RC_PAYINIT (Record)

Field Name	Type	Req	Edit	Prompt Table	Set Control Field
OPRID	Char	No			
RUN_CNTL_ID	Char	No			
RUN_ID	Char	No	Prompt	MY_RUNID_SEC_VW	
COMPANY	Char	No	Prompt	MY_COMP_SEC_VW	
PAYGROUP	Char	No	Prompt	MY_PAYGR_SEC_VW	
PAY_END_DT	Date	No	Prompt	PAY_CALENDAR	
CYCLE_SELECT	Char	No	Xlat		
OFF_CYCLE	Char	No			
PAGE#	Nbr	No	Prompt	PAY_PAGE	
PAGE#_THRU	Nbr	No	Prompt	PAY_PAGE	
PRENOTE_DT	Date	No			
TEXT15	Char	No			
TEXT20	Char	No			
CHECK_NO_START	Nbr	No			
ADVICE_NO_START	Nbr	No			

Figure 29.25
The RC_PAYINIT record with the new prompt tables

The only step remaining is to test everything together. As you may remember, after the Company/Paygroup security table and maintenance panel were created, we just associated the ALLPANLS operator class with four combinations of two companies and two paygroups for each company (figure 29.16). This means that, if we try to select the company, paygroup, or Run Control ID values, from the modified Run Control record, we should only be able to select these values. Let's give this a try (figure 29.26).

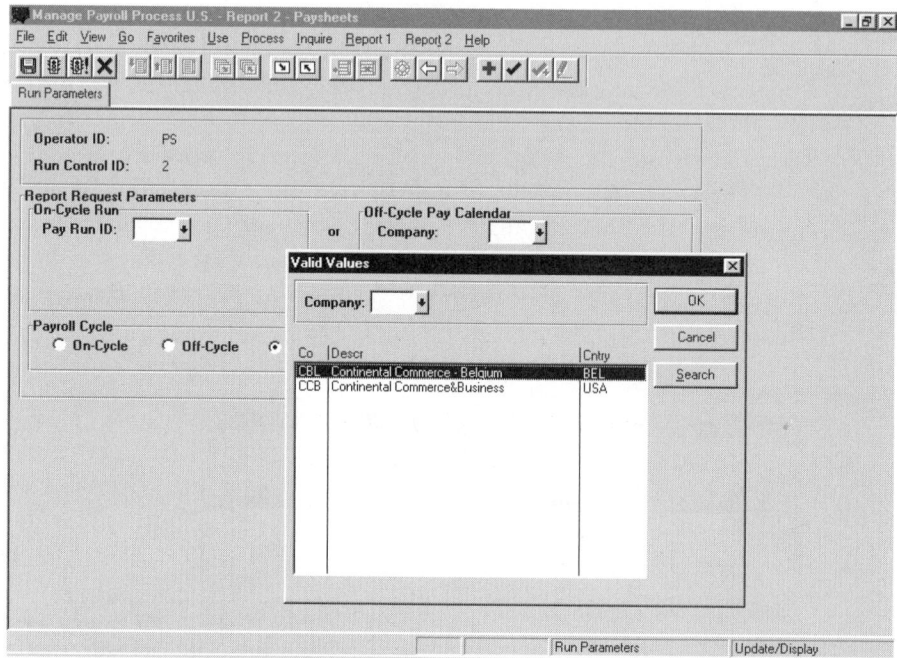

Figure 29.26   The prompt in Company field only shows two companies to which the ALLPANLS has access to

After selecting the Company value, let's select the Paygroup (figure 29.27).

We can also verify if our run ID prompt view works. Let's select another Run Control and, this time, enter the values on the left portion of the panel (figure 29.28).

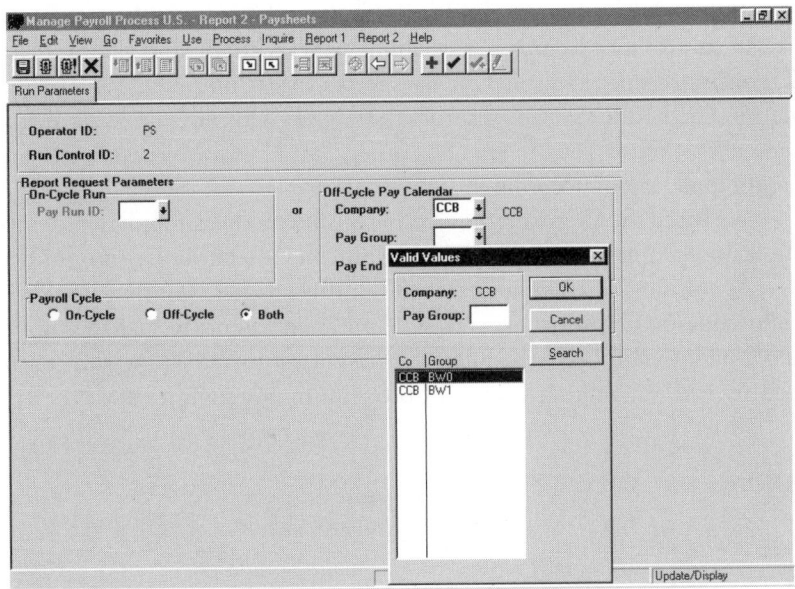

Figure 29.27   The prompt in the Paygroup field only allows to select from two paygroups

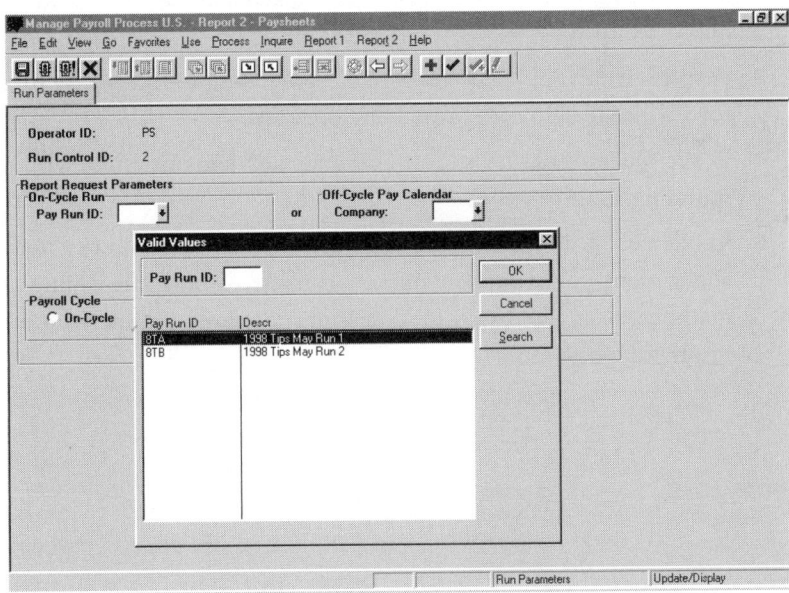

Figure 29.28   The prompt in the Run ID field only shows the run IDs that are valid for the company/paygroup to which we have access

As you can see, all our modifications are working. With this simple customization we can control user security via an online panel without changing your programs. We demonstrated this change for the Paysheets process, but in fact, any program that uses the modified Run Control record RC_PAYINIT will now be secured from unauthorized execution. If your report uses other Run Control records, you need to modify the prompt records accordingly.

We based the Company/Paygroup security on the combination of these two fields but a similar approach can be used to implement security based on other key fields.

As you can see from our examples in this chapter, you may need to make only a slight code modification in your SQR program to ensure that the program will run only under the Process Scheduler. We have demonstrated how you control your SQR security without altering your SQR program in any significant way.

KEY POINTS

1 PeopleSoft provides you with layers of online security to help protect your data from unauthorized access.

2 When accessing a PeopleSoft application in a networked environment, you have to pass through network security, database security, and PeopleSoft online security.

3 PeopleSoft delivers a special way of controlling online access to your data rows with the help of security search records.

4 In the Query tool, PeopleSoft automatically joins its tables with the corresponding security views.

5 In release 7.5, PeopleSoft incorporated the row-level security for its HRMS applications. This implementation consists of both the online and batch modifications. The batch modifications are done routinely on a program-to-program basis.

C H A P T E R   3 0

Additional Process Scheduler topics

During the course of this book, we've discussed the execution of both PeopleSoft-delivered and custom processes with the help of the PeopleSoft Process Scheduler. We demonstrated how to create a process definition to execute SQR programs and how to monitor the process execution status. You also learned how to communicate with the Process Scheduler via API programs. However, there are some other important aspects of the PeopleSoft Process Scheduler that we did not cover.

30.1 SCHEDULING PROGRAMS FOR EXECUTION ON A RECURRING BASIS

When you execute your programs on the Server, you can schedule them to run at pre-defined intervals. A special recurrence definition has to be created and assigned to the process. When the recurrence definition is created, it may be assigned to the process through its process definition or from the Process Request Dialog panel at runtime.

Let's see how we can schedule our custom program, MYPROB02.sqr for execution every Sunday at 8:00 A.M.

Navigation: Go → Problem Tracking → Report → Status Report → Add

Figure 30.1
Adding Run Control ID for every Sunday 8 A.M. run

TIP   Give each Run Control a meaningful name and use it for one process only.

The next screen is our Run Control panel. Since we are planning to schedule the Status Report for execution every Sunday, we have to supply the appropriate parameters to our SQR program every time the program runs. When the program is executed manually, users enter the parameters when they submit the process for execution. We need to find a way to automatically fill in our Run Control table. You can use several methods, depending on your business needs. The simplest method is to use the system date as the As Of Date parameter. The standard method is to make your program default to system date if the date in the Run Control record is blank. If you take a look at our MYGETVAL.sqc, you can see that this is exactly what we did. If the system date technique is not applicable to your process, you must develop your own custom method to automatically supply the correct date to your program at each program execution. The second parameter, Problem Status, can be entered only once, and the Run Control record retains its value for all the subsequent runs.

Suppose, we are going to use the system date as the As Of Date parameter and a blank to indicate that we need the status report of all the problem statuses. In this case, our Run Control panel is saved as shown in figure 30.2.

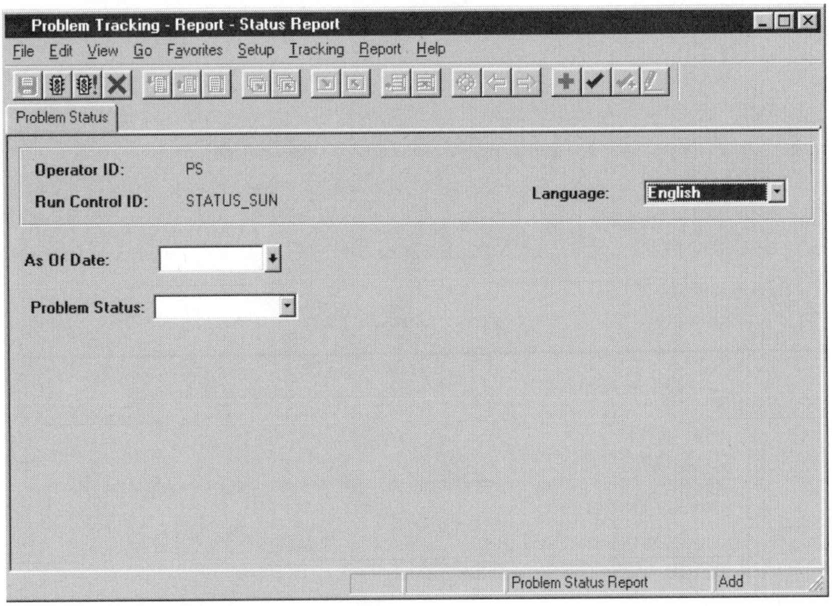

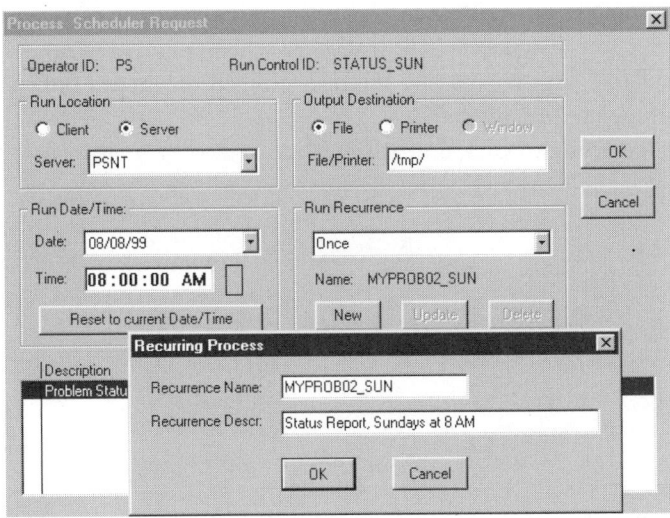

Figure 30.2   Leaving blank values in both parameters to use the system date as As of Date and to make the program report all problem statuses

Click on the Traffic Light to go to the Process Request panel, make sure that the process Run Location is Server, and start creating a new recurrence definition, by clicking on the New button in the Run Recurrence box.

**Figure 30.3
Creating a new Run
Recurrence**

After clicking on the OK button, we need to specify our new recurrence information (figure 30.4).

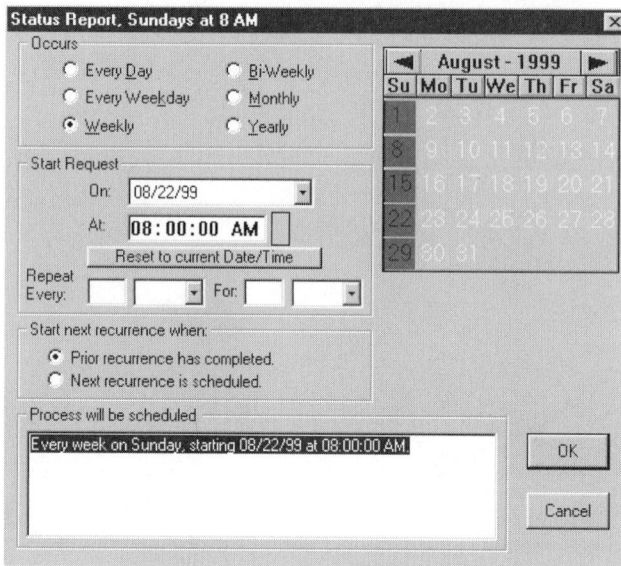

Figure 30.4
Specifying the recurrence information

In the panel shown in figure 30.4, we clicked on Weekly to specify the occurrence frequency, then we selected the starting day and time of the cycle. We also clicked on Su (Sunday), and the system automatically selected all Sundays in the calendar. Based on our selections, the system created a meaningful description in the lower box of the panel. You should always verify this description to make sure that all schedule parameters are correct. We also selected the option to schedule the next run when the prior run has completed. This means that the next job will be queued only when the previous job is completed successfully.

Now we are ready to click on the OK button.

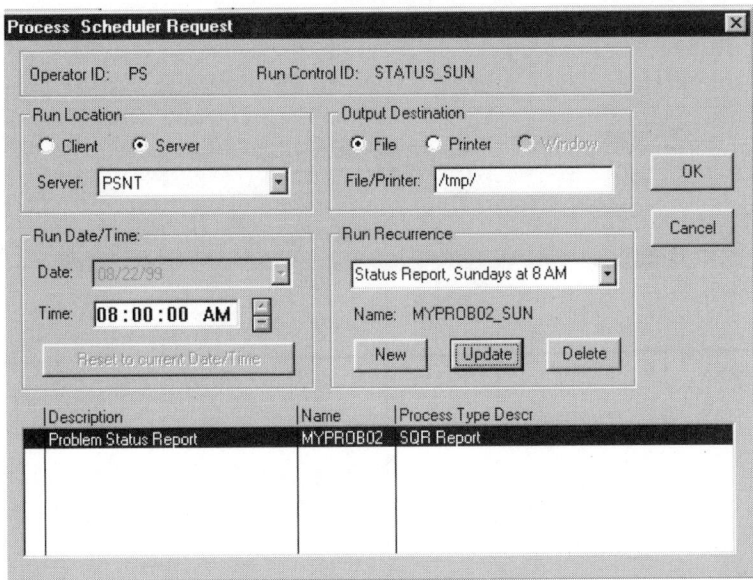

Figure 30.5   The MYPROB02 process is about to be scheduled

Note that, even though we are not planning to execute the process now, we must hit the OK button to schedule our process for recurrent executions. So far, we have created a process recurrence definition where we have specified all the parameters for our process scheduling, but we have not yet scheduled the process. We need to do it manually the first time in order to make the scheduling take place. After that, the Process Scheduler will do the job.

Let's click on the OK button again and verify the process status on the Process Monitor panel.

As you can see in figure 30.6, our process is queued and is scheduled for execution at 8 A.M. on 08/22/1999. As soon as this process has successfully executed, the next occurrence of this process will be scheduled automatically by the Process Scheduler in accordance with your process recurrence definition.

WARNING   When scheduling another process for recurring processing, be very careful if you decide to reuse an existing recurrence definition. Changing any parameters in the recurrence definition may result in taking the first process out of the scheduler.

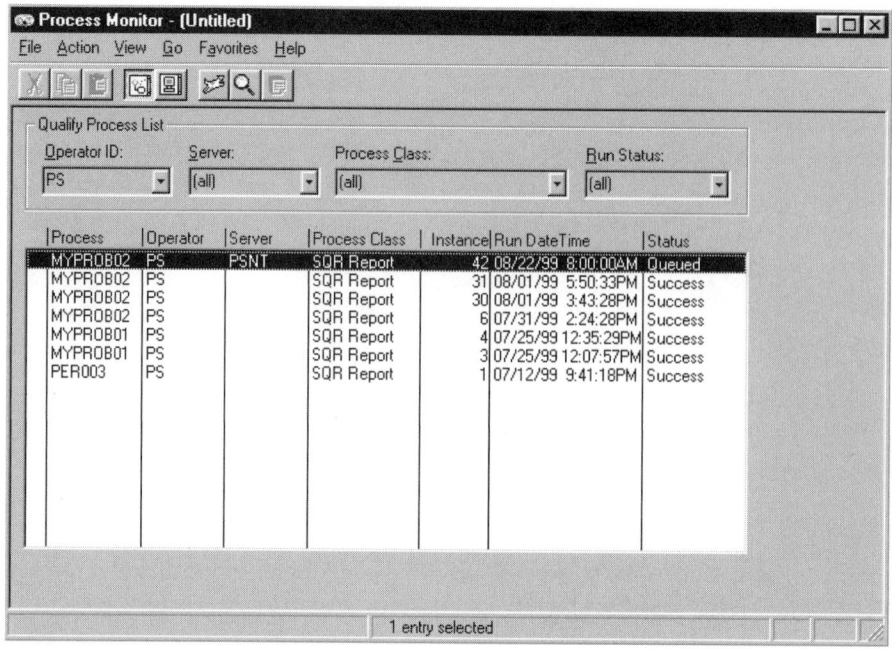

Figure 30.6   MYPROB02 is scheduled for execution

30.2   USING JOB STREAMS

So far we have been executing and scheduling single processes from the PeopleSoft Process Scheduler. Oftentimes, your business requires the execution of multiple processes one after another or in parallel. PeopleSoft allows you do this if you run your processes on Server. The job definition is used to accomplish this task.

A job (or job stream) in PeopleSoft usually consists of two or more processes. You can combine your SQR and COBOL programs into one Job to be executed in a parallel or serial mode. When scheduling your job to run in a serial mode, all processes within the job will be executed sequentially, one after another. Otherwise, they will be executed in a parallel mode without any specific order. As with an individual process, you can schedule a job to run at a later time or on a recurring basis. It is always a good approach to combine all processes, which should be executed at a specific time (for example, nightly), into a job stream and schedule this job stream to be executed at predefined time intervals (for example, every night at 10 PM).

In the following examples, we will create a job stream and schedule it for execution.

Exercise 1

Execute the Refresh Employees process (PER099.sqr) and the problem status report (MYPROB02.sqr) in a job stream every night at 10 P.M.

In order to schedule any job for execution, a job definition has to be created. Since our exercise calls for the execution of two reports, we need to create a job definition that contains PER099.sqr and MYPROB02.sqr. As we already know, when we execute a process from the Process Scheduler, this process accepts its input parameters from online panels. A process definition is linked to a specific panel through a panel group. Like a process definition, a job definition also requires a panel group to be specified. Therefore, all processes in your job stream accept input parameters from this particular panel group, which may consist of several panels. To illustrate this point, let's create a panel group for our job stream.

30.2.1 Creating a panel group for a job stream

Since the processes we are going to include in our job stream are already designed to run under the Process Scheduler, our task is simple. We just need to combine their Run Control panels into one panel group.

Let's find out what the components are for our new panel group. In order to do so, we take a look at the process definitions for PER099.sqr and MYPROB02.sqr (figure 30.7). We start with PER099.sqr.

Navigation: Go → Administer Workforce → Administer Workforce (U.S.) → Process → Refresh Employees Table → Update/Display

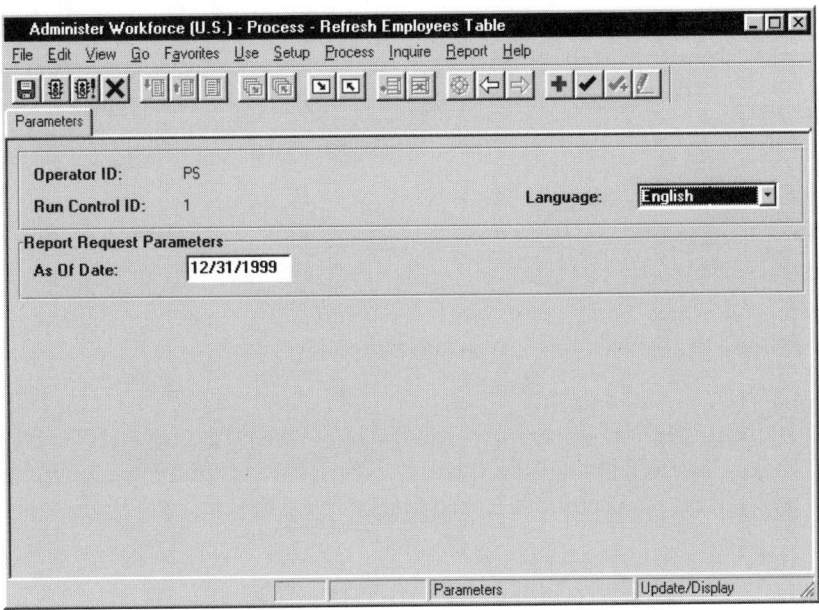

Figure 30.7   Finding the name of the Run Control panel for the Refresh Employees Table process

The Run Control panel used to run the Refresh Employees Table process is RUNCTL_ASOFDATE. When scheduling this program for execution in a job stream, we obviously want to preserve all the functionality of the job's components, including the input parameters processing. Therefore, we include this panel into our new panel group.

We know from the previous chapter that the name of the Run Control panel for our problem status report is MY_RUN_CNTL_PRB01.

Let's now create a new panel group.

Navigation: Go → PeopleTools → Application Designer → New → Panel Group

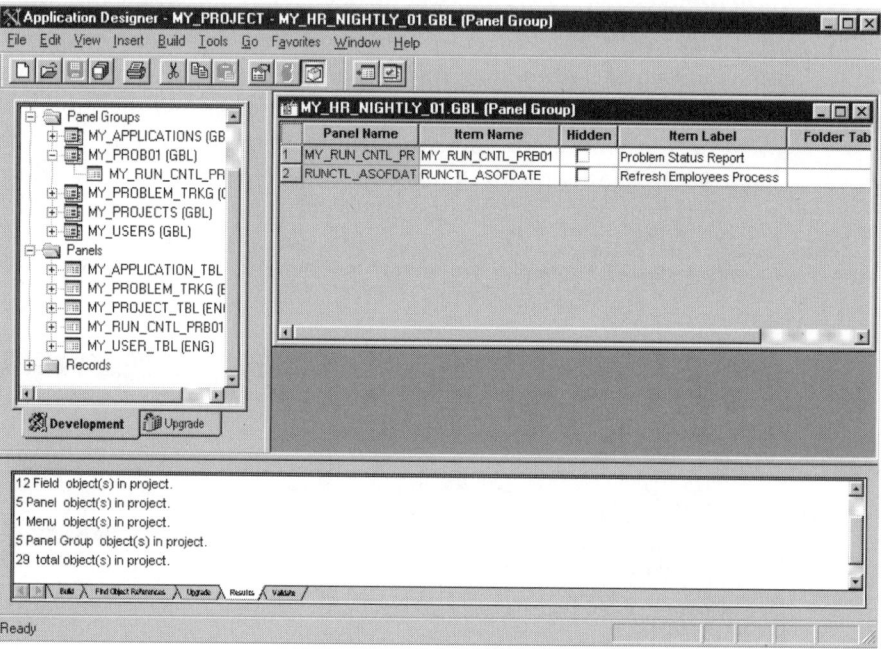

Figure 30.8   Creating a new panel group for a job stream

Our new panel group includes both the MY_RUN_CNTL_PRB01 and the RUNCTL_ASOFDATE Run Control panels. After putting meaningful labels for each panel in the panel group, we need to specify the Panel Group Properties (figure 30.9).

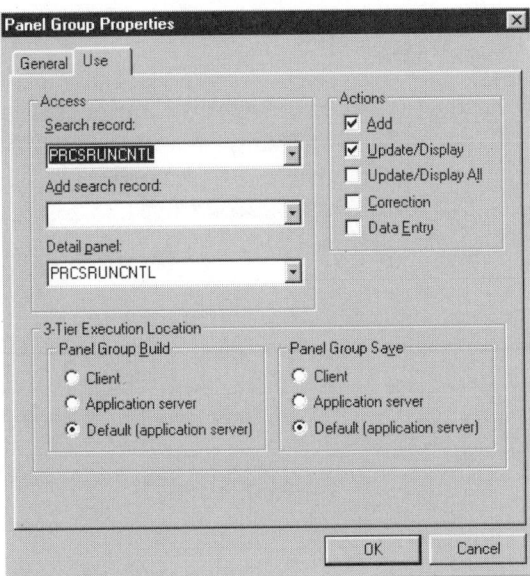

Figure 30.9
Specifying panel group properties
for our job stream

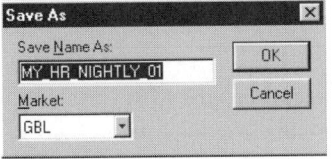

Figure 30.10 Saving panel group for new job stream

The Search record and the Detail panel for our Run Control panel group should be the same as the one for a panel group in a single process.

Now, we save the new object as MY_HR_NIGHTLY_01 (figure 30.10).

After clicking on the OK button, we are ready to add our job to a menu.

30.2.2 Creating a Menu Item for our new job stream

As usual, in order for our users to access a Run Control panel, we need to attach this panel to an appropriate menu item via a panel group. Let's create a new menu bar, Job Stream, and use it for our new job stream menu item and for all future job streams.

As we can see in figure 30.11, we created a new menu bar, Job Stream. Then, just by clicking on an empty rectangle under this menu bar, we created a new menu item, HR Nightly, and linked our MY_HR_NIGHTLY_01 panel group to this menu item.

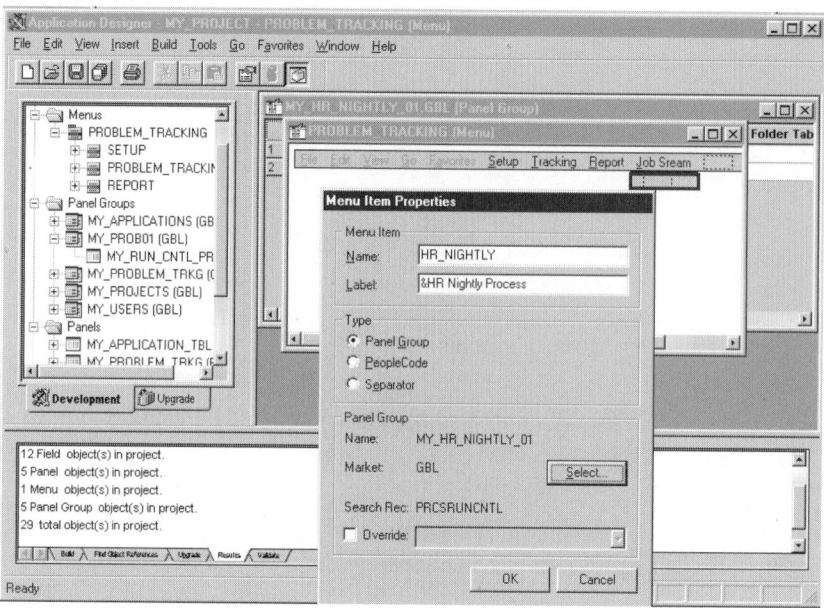

Figure 30.11   Creating a new menu bar and menu item

After clicking on the OK button, we can modify the Operator's Security to allow the ALLPNLS operator group access to our new menu item. Now, we can test the menu (figure 30.12).

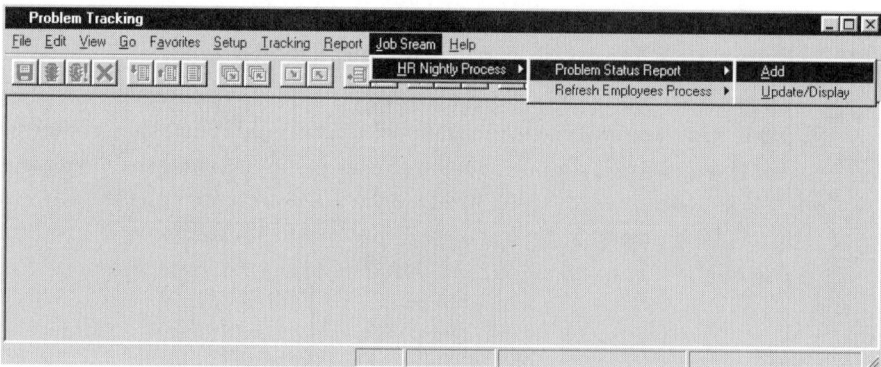

Figure 30.12   New menu bar and menu item are created for our job stream

Are we ready to run our job? Not yet. We need to create a job definition first.

30.2.3   Creating a job definition

Unlike a process definition creation, when adding a new job definition, the process job name does not have to match any of your processes. You can give any name to your job.

Navigation: Go → PeopleTools → Process Scheduler → Use → Job Definitions → Job Definitions → Add

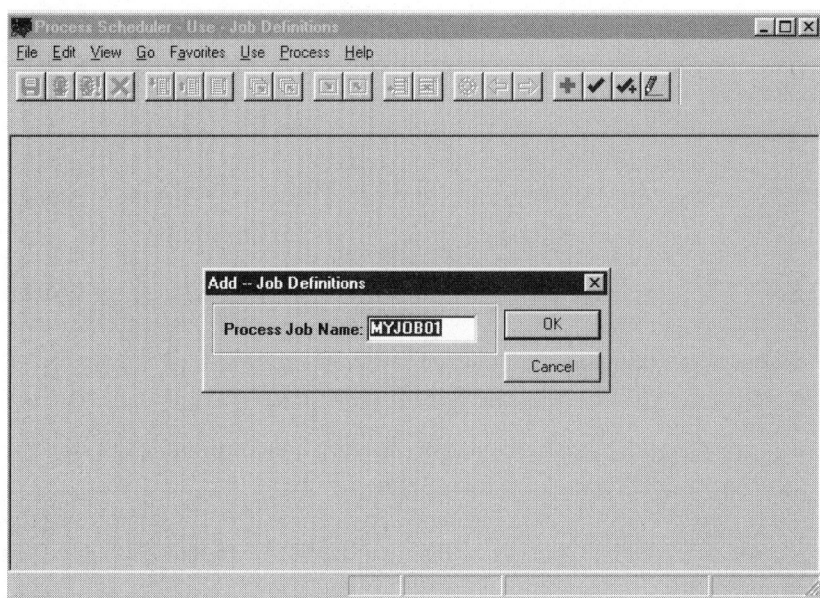

Figure 30.13   Specifying a job definition name

The process of creating a job definition is similar to that of creating a process definition. Let's take a close look at what is involved in this process and discuss the meaning of each field in the job definition.

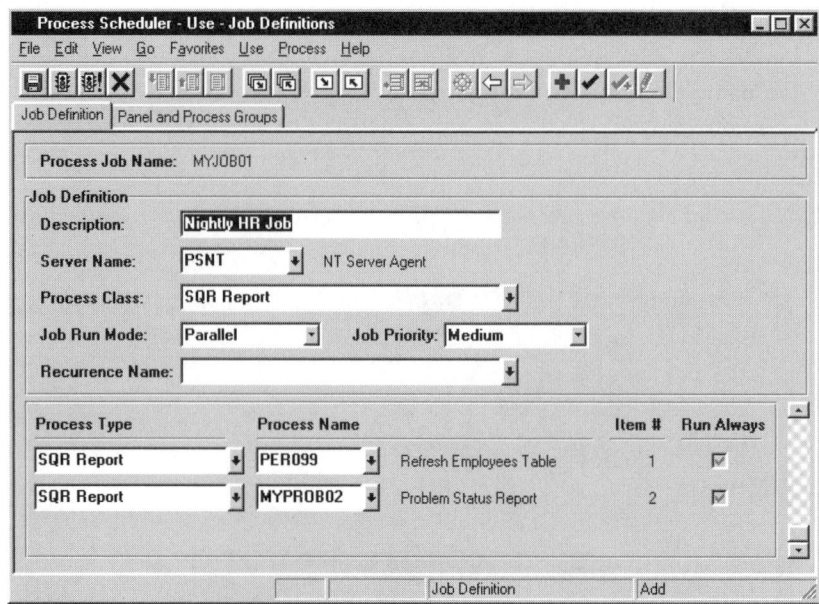

Figure 30.14 Creating a job definition

In the *Job Description*, you specify the job definition description that will be displayed on the Process Scheduler Request panel.

The *Server Name* should be specified only if you want to restrict your Job execution to a specific server. If you leave it blank, the system will find an available server based on the Process class.

You can specify a new *Process Class* by entering a unique process class name, or you can select it from a drop-down list. Usually if all the processes included in your job stream are SQR programs, you would select SQR Report as your process class.

TIP   If you include both SQR programs and other programs such as COBOL, or programs written in Application Engine, you need to select Programs as the Process class.

In our case, since we are executing two SQR programs, we select SQR Report.

The *Job Run Mode* can be either `Serial` or `Parallel`. If you want your processes to be executed sequentially, you select `Serial` mode, otherwise, use `Parallel`. We will run our processes in a parallel mode since the second report does not depend on the first process execution.

The *Job Priority* could be `High`, `Medium`, or `Low`. This information is used by the Process Scheduler to initiate jobs with higher priorities first. We'll specify a `Medium` priority for our job.

The *Recurrence Name* is used to specify a recurrence schedule that you previously set up. This parameter is optional and can be defined for your JOB on the Process Scheduler Request panels.

In the lower portion of your job definition panel, specify the processes you want to include in the job. If you've selected a `Serial` mode, your processes have to be listed in the order in which they will be executed. In prior releases, you had to number each item sequentially with no gaps. Release 7.5 takes care of the numbering automatically. It also re-numbers the processes when you need to add a new item between existing ones or change the order of processes in your job.

You should turn on the *Run Always* flag if you want your processes to be executed, even if one of the previous processes failed. Suppose, for example, you selected the mode as `Serial` and did not turn on the Run Always flag for any of your processes. Let's assume that your job contains three processes: Process1, Process2, and Process3. If your Process2 fails, you will see the following process statuses in the Process Monitor screen (assuming that you clicked on the job's "+" sign to see the individual processes):

Process	Status
- MyJob	Error
Process1	Success
Process2	Error
Process3	Hold

After you check the error messages in the log file and fix the problem, you need to restart your JOB from Process2. Currently, PeopleSoft Process Scheduler does not have capability to restart the Job from a specific point. You could either re-execute the entire Job or execute Process2 and Process3 as individual processes. Be careful. It's not always safe to execute certain processes again because your processes may be updating the database.

In the second panel of the JOB Definitions panel group, you specify the Process Security Groups for the users to whom you would like to give permissions to run your job. You also specify the panel group to which your job should be attached. For our job, we specify the name of the panel group that we created to run this Job.

Our job definition is created. Let's save it and see how we can schedule our job to run reccurently.

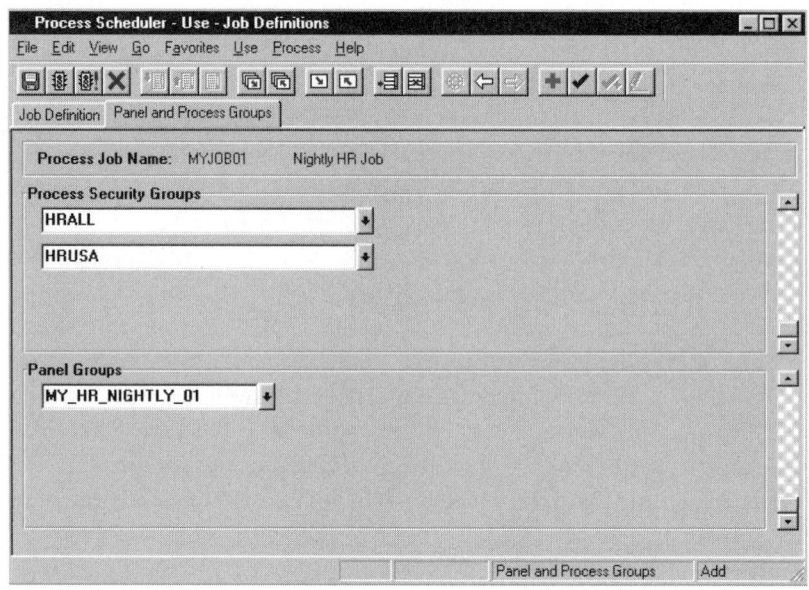

Figure 30.15   Specifying the Process Security Groups and the panel group for our job

30.2.4   Scheduling a job for recurrent execution

Navigation: Go → Problem Tracking → Job Stream → HR Nightly Process → Add

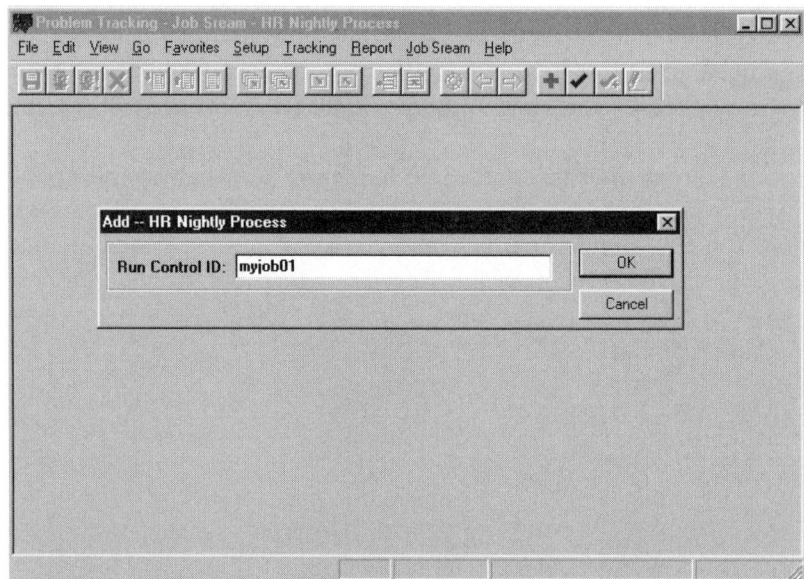

Figure 30.16   Adding a new Run Control record for job's execution

Let's add a new Run Control ID, myjob01, and click on the OK button. The Run Control panel group appears (figure 30.17).

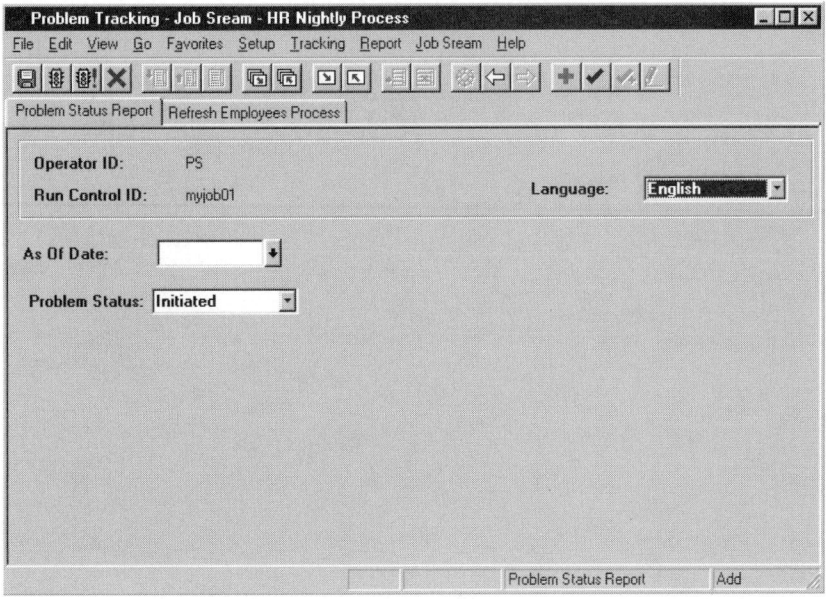

Figure 30.17 Entering input parameters

As shown in figure 30.17, our panel group contains two panels. The first one is the Problem Status Report panel, and the second one is the Refresh Employees Process panel. Does this mean that, if you have ten processes in your job definition, you need ten panels in your Run Control panel group? Not necessarily. Some of your processes may not require any input parameters and, therefore, do not need additional panels. Others may need the same input parameters. In that case, one panel may be used for several processes. It all depends on the Run Control records which your processes use to get the input parameters.

TIP You need to make sure that all Run Control records used by the processes in your job are present in the panel group.

Let's take, for example, the Years of Service program. It accepts two parameters: As Of Date and Years of Service. If you have one job that includes this program and another one that only needs As of Date as its input parameter—for example, the Pending Future Actions report—you can use the same panel to run both reports. This is all, of course, under condition that both programs are using the same Run Control record.

In the second panel of our panel group, the Refresh Employees Process Run Control panel (figure 30.18), we also use the `As Of Date` input parameter, but since the Run Control records for both our processes are different, we have to include both panels in our panel group.

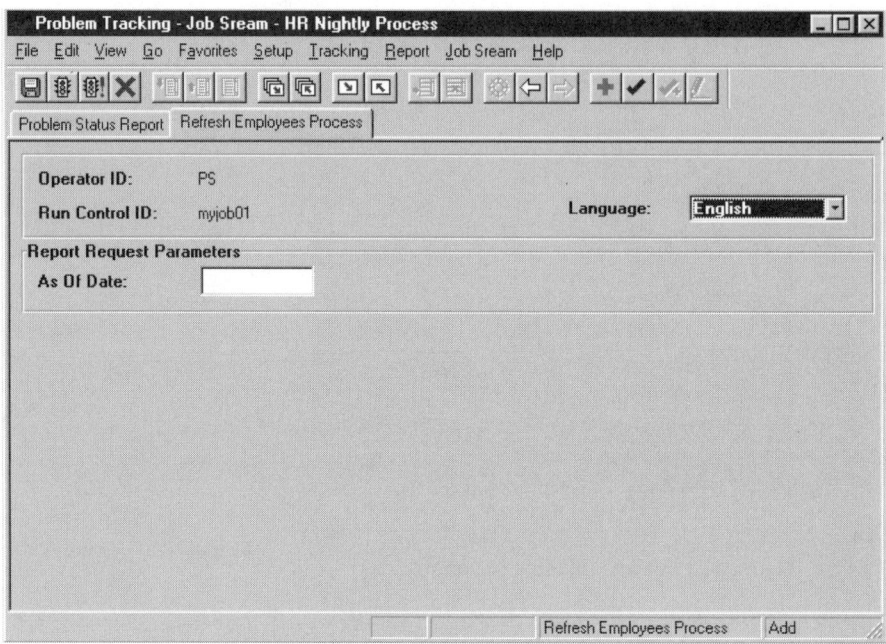

Figure 30.18   The Refresh Employees Run Control panel

Since we are planning to schedule our job to be executed on a recurrent basis, we leave the `As Of Date` field blank to force the process to use the system date instead. This way, we make our scheduling much simpler.

After all parameters in the Run Control panels have been entered, we are ready to schedule our job for execution. Let's click on the Traffic Light.

As you can see in figure 30.19, we specified the Run Location as `Server`, and we also selected a specific Server name from the Server drop-down list. Please note that jobs can only be scheduled on `Server`. On the bottom of the panel, you can see our job name displayed. If you click on the plus sign to the left of the job, as we did, both the processes that make up the job will be shown. When scheduling the job for execution, select the Nightly HR Job (figure 30.19).

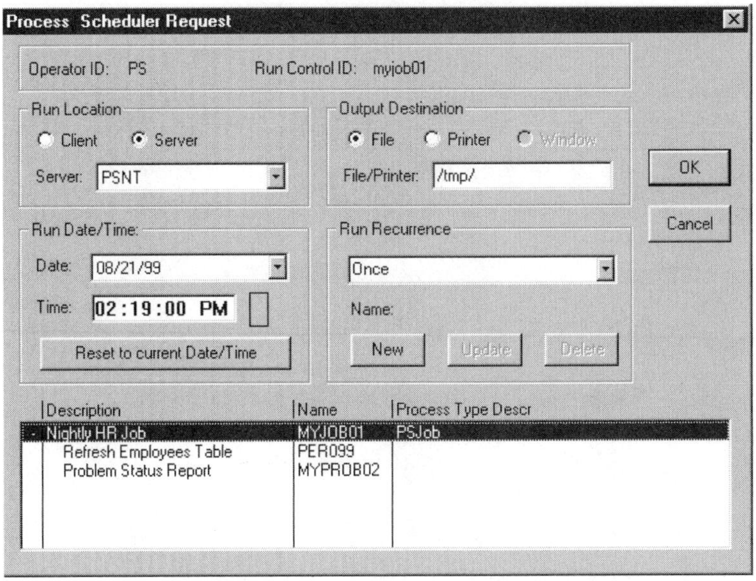

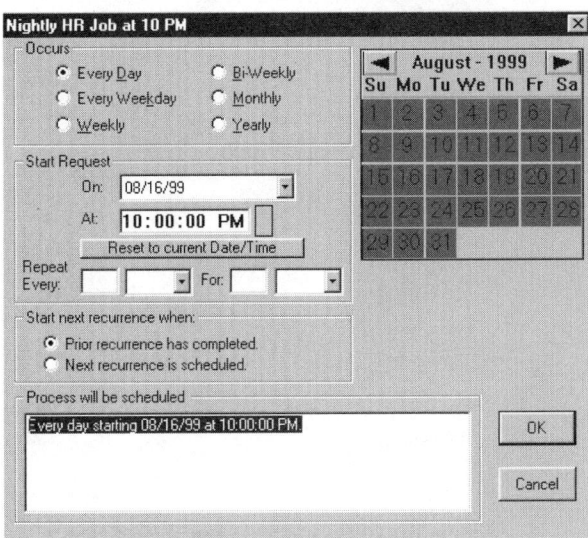

Figure 30.19 Process Scheduler Request panel for MYJOB01 job stream

Let's now create a new Run Recurrence based on the user's request to run this job daily at 10 P.M. To do so, click on the New button in the Run Recurrence group box.

Figure 30.20 shows the parameters we set for our new recurrence definition. Let's click on the OK button and give our recurrence definition a meaningful name.

Figure 30.20
Creating a new definition

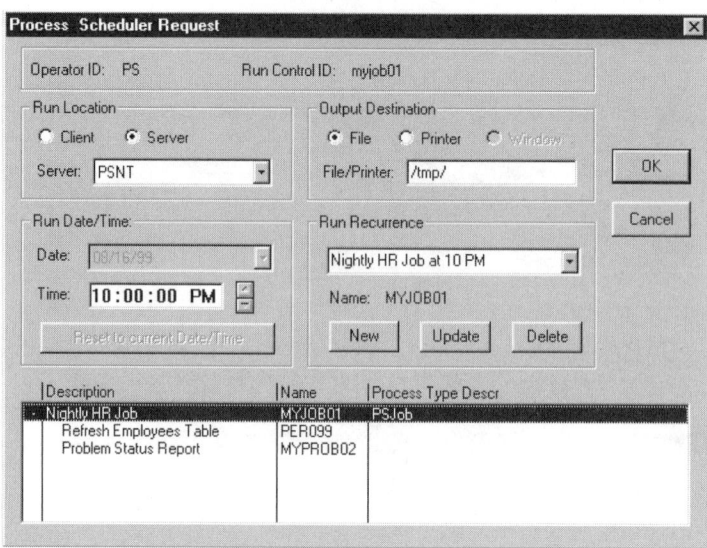

Figure 30.21   Process Scheduler Request with Run Recurrence

Our job is ready for execution. We click on the OK button to schedule the job to run for the first time (figure 30.22).

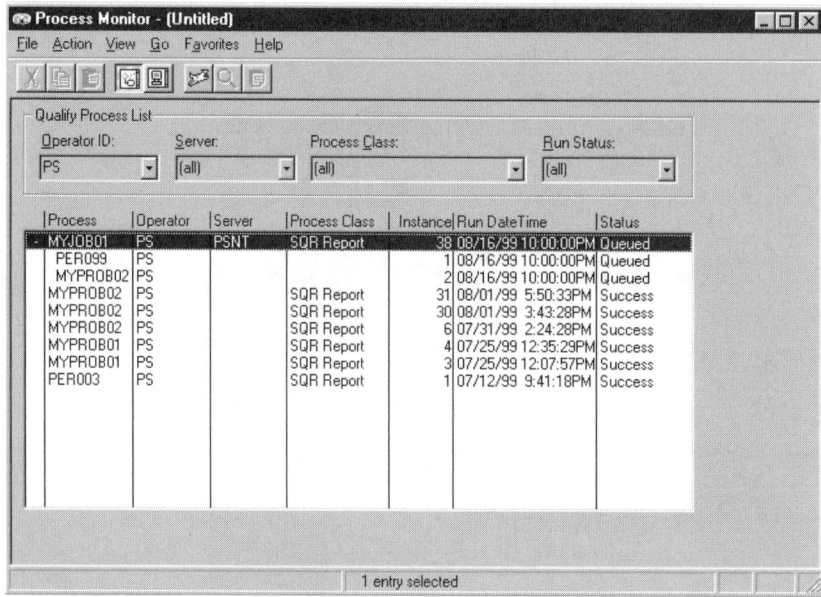

Figure 30.22   MYJOB01 is scheduled for execution on 08/16/99 at 10 P.M.

CHAPTER 30   ADDITIONAL PROCESS SCHEDULER TOPICS

As you can see from figure 30.22, our job MYJOB01 includes two processes, PER099 and MYPROB02. Its status is Queued, and it is scheduled for execution on 08/16/99 at 10 P.M. As soon as the job is executed successfully, the system will automatically schedule MYJOB01 for execution on the next day, 08/17/99 at 10 P.M.

KEY POINTS

1 You can schedule programs that run on the Server for execution on a recurring schedule.

2 A job (or job stream) may include more than one process.

3 In order to schedule a job for execution, a job definition has to be created. Similar to a process definition, a job definition also needs to be associated with a panel group.

4 You can include processes of different types (SQR program, COBOL, Application Engine) into one job.

5 Make sure that all Run Control records used by the processes in your job are present in the panel group.

6 If you want processes to be executed sequentially, you should select the Serial mode on your job definition panel; otherwise, routinely use the Parallel mode.

C H A P T E R   3 1

SQR and Process Scheduler—PeopleSoft 8

PeopleSoft introduced a number of new and enhanced features in PeopleTools 8. These features improve the way in which SQR programs and other processes interact with the PeopleSoft Process Scheduler. PeopleSoft delivered enhancements in the following areas:

- Process Scheduler terminology
- process definitions
- Process Scheduler Request Dialog
- output options
- Process Scheduler security
- recurrence definitions
- Process Scheduler PeopleCode support

Let's take a quick tour of these modifications in PeopleTools release 8.

31.1 PROCESS SCHEDULER TERMINOLOGY

PeopleSoft modified its terminology to avoid confusion and simplify the Process Scheduler usage for application developers, system administrators, and end-users. The Process Scheduler tool contains the following components:

- Process Scheduler Manager
- Process Scheduler Request Dialog
- Process Request Monitor
- Process Scheduler Server Agent

Each of these components has a specific task and, depending on your role in the PeopleSoft world, you may or may not work with all the tools. Nonetheless, the knowledge of when to use a particular tool is essential. Therefore, the new names that PeopleSoft introduced are extremely helpful.

Table 31.1 Modified Process Scheduler terminology

Release 7.5	Release 8
Process Scheduler	Process Scheduler Manager
Process Monitor	Process Request Monitor
Process Types	Process Type Definitions
Process Servers	Server Definitions
Process System	System Settings

As you can see from table 31.1, the Process Scheduler has been renamed to the Process Scheduler Manager. You use the Process Scheduler Manager to create and maintain process types and process and job definitions. You access it by selecting Go → PeopleTools → Process Scheduler Manager.

Similarly, the Process Monitor has been renamed to the Process Request Monitor. It is accessed by selecting Go → PeopleTools → Process Request Monitor.

The menu items, Process Types, Process Servers, and Process System, have been renamed to Process Type Definitions, Server Definitions, and System Settings, respectively. You can find these menu items under the Process Scheduler Manager → Use menu.

31.2 PROCESS DEFINITIONS

The Process Definitions panel group now consists of four panels. The existing panels have been redesigned as well.

Do you remember that the Process name you enter in this add box should be your SQR name without the .sqr extension? Have you ever tried to enter a name of a non-existing SQR program? Before release 8 such a blunder was possible. You could easily create a process definition for a program that was never written. Starting from release 8, PeopleSoft only allows you to specify programs that can be found in the

Navigation: Go → PeopleTools → Process Scheduler Manager → Use →
 Process Definition → Add

Figure 31.1   Adding a Process Definition

Configuration Manager's SQRW search path parameter. This is a great step toward
making the system more secure.

As you can see in figure 31.2, the Process Definition panel group has an additional tab, Override Options.

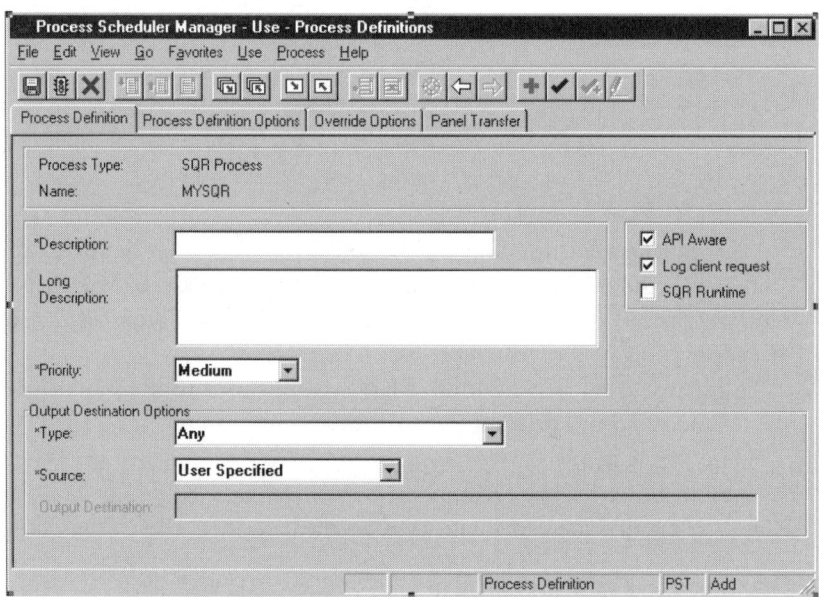

**Figure 31.2   The Process Definition panel group in the Process Scheduler
       Manager menu**

Let's take a closer look at the Process Definition panel. If you compare this panel
to that in release 7.5, you will notice that the panel, too, has changed. The Output
Destination options has been moved from the Process Definitions Options panel to

this panel. The types of output available for selection are Printer, Window, Email, File, or Any. The option Any allows a user to specify any valid option.

The Source should still be selected as User Specified for SQR programs.

The Output Destination is only available when the Source is selected as the process definition, which means that this request will default to the output destination specified by the process definition.

Let's switch to the Override Options tab (figure 31.3).

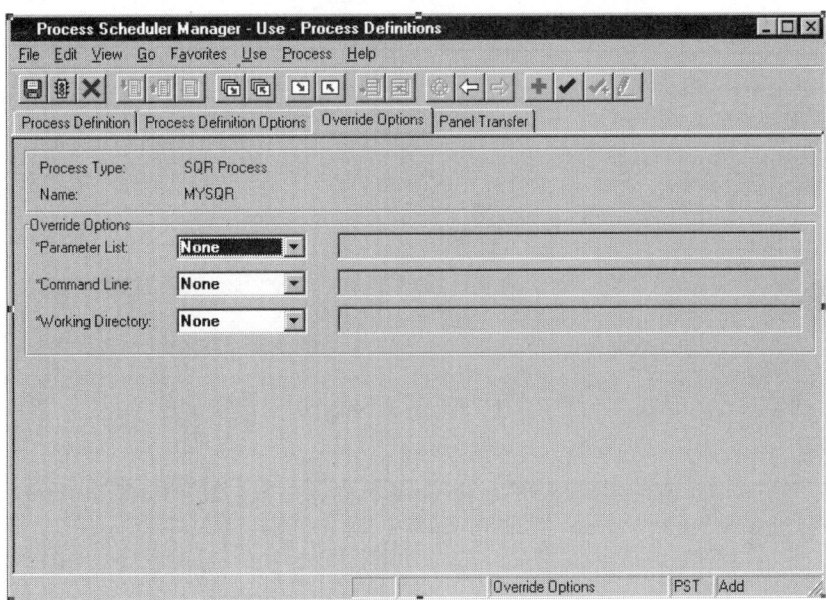

Figure 31.3   The Override Options tab

This panel is actually a simplified version of the old Process Definition Options. It allows you to specify the Override Options for the Parameter List, Command Line, and Working Directory.

How many times have you had your Process Scheduler definitions created incorrectly? Now, with release 8 tools, you will be able to run the SysAudit process to display incorrect Process Scheduler definitions.

31.3 PROCESS SCHEDULER REQUEST DIALOG

The Process Scheduler Request dialog box has been modified to simplify the end-user's run requests. Let's examine the panel in figure 31.4.

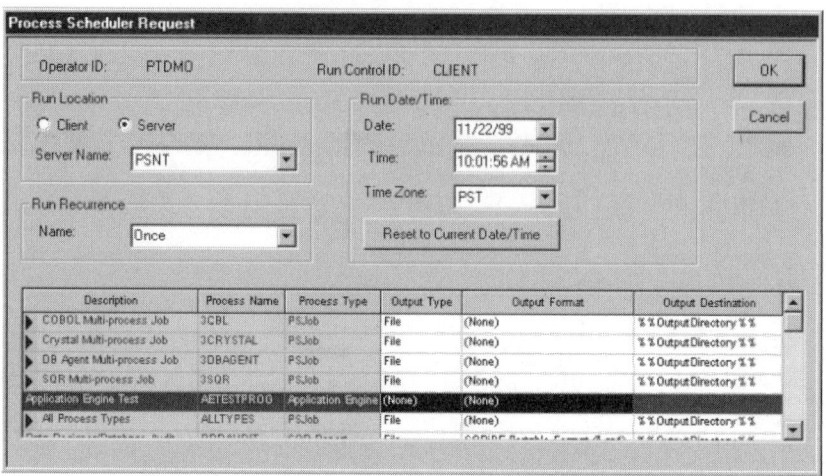

Figure 31.4   The Process Scheduler Request dialog in release 8.0

What makes release 8 exciting is that with it you are able to specify a different Output Type, Output Format, and Destination at the individual process level (including for each process within a job).

Release 8 also brought in some preventive measures that help identify problems before a process is submitted. For example, the Process type "PSJob" is disabled if you have `Client` set as the run location. Available output types and formats depend on particular process types. We'll discuss new output types later in this chapter.

Notice that even though the Run Recurrence box is still in the new panel, the end-user will not be able to update the recurrence definition from the Process Scheduler Request dialog panel. The end-user can select the necessary run recurrence from the list of recurrences previously set up. In release 8, Recurrence definitions are created through the Process Scheduler Manager → Use menu item. The new Recurrence Definition panel is shown in figure 31.5.

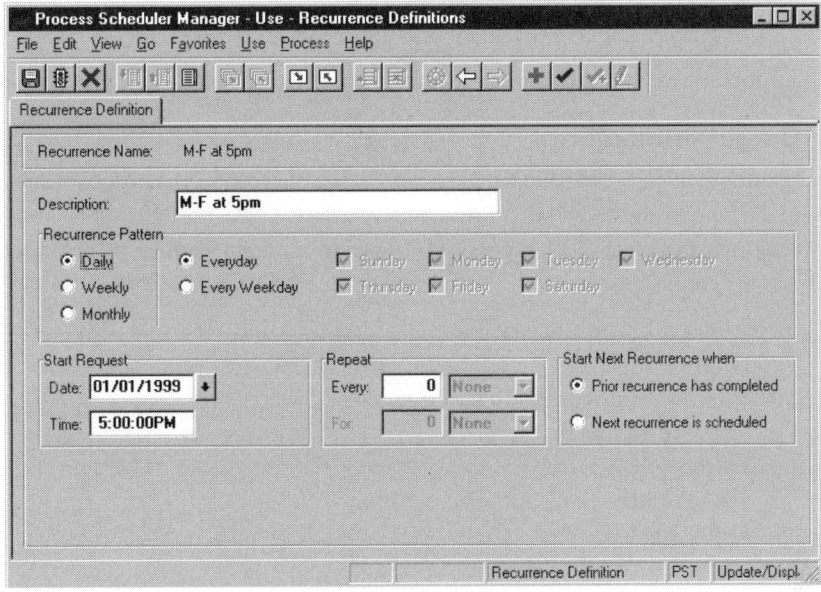

Figure 31.5   The Recurrence Definition panel in release 8.0

31.4   *OUTPUT OPTIONS*

Let's get back to figure 31.4. As you can see in the lower portion of the Process Request dialog panel, you can now specify the Output Type, the Output Format, and the Output Destination for each process. PeopleSoft introduced new output types and formats in release 8. To avoid any confusion in terminology, let's describe these three output options.

31.4.1   **Output types**

The output type tells the PeopleSoft Process Scheduler where the output of your process should go.

The following table shows the output types available in release 8.

Table 31.2   Output types

Output Type	Description	Available on Client	Available on Server
Window	Directs the process output to a DOS window.	Yes	No
File	Allows you to write the output to the file specified in Output Destination	Yes	Yes
Printer	Sends the output to the specified printer	Yes	Yes
Email	Sends the output to the predefined email list	No	Yes

As you can see from table 31.2, the long-awaited email file output is delivered as a new output type. You will be able to specify email addresses through the Security Administrator and send your output via email for applications executed on the Server.

31.4.2 Output formats

In addition to the output types, you will be able to select an appropriate Output Format, depending on what process type you have selected. If, for example, you select the process type as SQR Process, you have the following output format options:

- Acrobat(.pdf)
- Comma Delimited (.csv)
- HP format (.lis)
- HTML documents format (.htm)
- Line Printer Format (.lis)
- Postscript (.lis)
- SQR Portable Format (.spf)
- Other (.lis)

For *Crystal Reports* Process type the following formats will be available for your selection:

- Crystal Report (.rpt)
- HTML Document (.htm)
- Lotus 1-2-3 files (.wks)
- Microsoft Excel (.xls)
- Rich Text File (.rft)
- Text Files (.txt)

31.4.3 Output Destination

You can select an appropriate Output Destination depending on the Output Type and whether you run your process on Client or Server.

Table 31.3 shows the available options:

Table 31.3 Output Destination options

Output Type	Description	Client Output Destination	Server Output Destination
File	Directory output	Default Value: `%OutputDirectory%` defined in the Configuration Manager	Default Value: `%%OutputDirectory%%` defined in PSADMIN
Printer	Default printer	Printer defined for a Workstation	Printer defined for a Server
Email	Sends the output to a predefined email list	No	Email address

You can also enter the custom values for your file or printer output destinations if you have the proper security access.

In release 8, you will be able to select a printer from a list of installed printers in the Process Request Dialog panel.

You can also preset your process output type and output destination in the process definition. The values you specify will be reflected in the Process Request Dialog panel.

31.5 PROCESS SCHEDULER SECURITY

With Tools 8, the Security Administrator tool is also enhanced and allows you to access and set up the Process Profiles and Process Groups via a separate tab (figure 31.6).

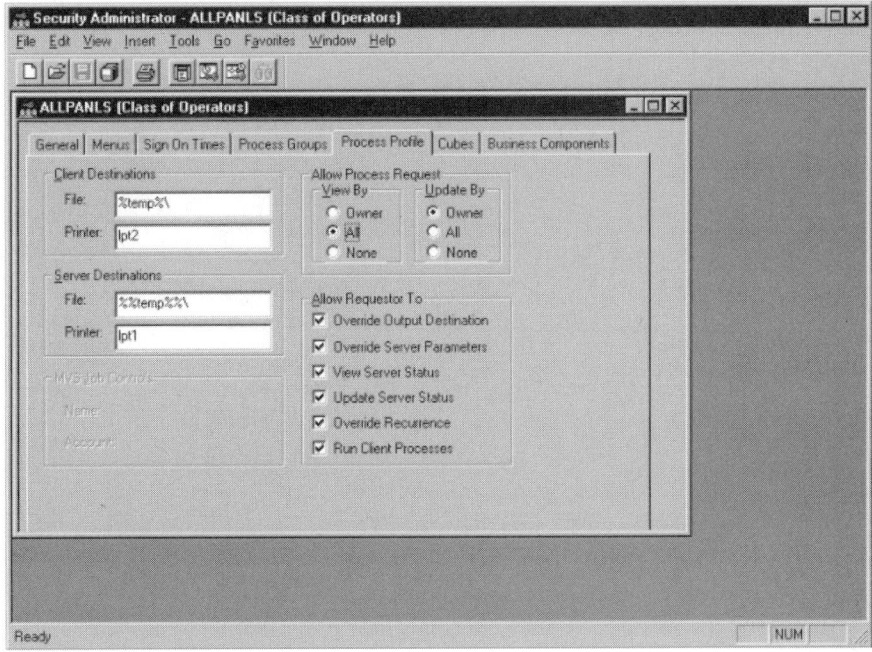

Figure 31.6   Security Administrator, Process Profile tab in release 8

Pay attention to the bottom checkbox in the Allow Requester To group box. By popular demand, PeopleSoft added an option to restrict certain classes of operators from running batch processes on their workstation.

In addition, the following changes were made to improve security in scheduling and executing processes:

- allowing the changing of an Operator/Access password after a process request is scheduled to run

- creating a "Super User" to monitor process requests via the Process Monitor
- offering an option to restrict users from scheduling recurring processes

31.6   PROCESS SCHEDULER PEOPLECODE SUPPORT

If you want to schedule your process from a PeopleCode script, PeopleSoft introduces a new Process Request PeopleCode Class. The goal is to make scheduling processes from PeopleCode easier. The `ScheduleProcess()` PeopleCode function is still supported in release 8, but it will be phased out in future releases.

The ProcessRequest class is used in release 8 for invoking processes through the Process Scheduler using PeopleCode. You can design a ProcessRequest PeopleCode program that can be triggered from a push button, a Save panel, or a field change event.

Using this new feature, you can schedule processes or jobs for immediate execution or in the future. It also supports the scheduling of recurring processes and jobs to run automatically at user-defined intervals.

31.7   SQR AND PEOPLETOOLS 8

As SQRiBe/Brio continues to improve its SQR application, PeopleSoft also integrates new SQR features to work smoothly with PeopleTools.

We already discussed in this chapter how PeopleSoft 8 improved the Process Request Dialog panel to incorporate Output Types, Output Formats, and Output Destinations. The SQR Output Formats now also include the PDF and CSV formats.

In addition, PeopleSoft 8 now supports the multiple report outputs.

31.7.1   Unique names for file output and logs

PeopleSoft 8 improved the naming of the output files and the log files. If a report is executed from the Process Scheduler the filenames will be:

< SQR Program Name>_<Instance>.xxx.

For example, if we executed the MYPROB01.sqr from the Process Scheduler and the Process Instance is 33876, the output filename will be MYPROB_33876.lis, and the log file name, MYPROB01_33876.log.

If the process instance is not available, the filenames are

<SQR Program Name>_<timestamp>.xxx

31.7.2   PSSQR shell

PeopleTools 8 delivers a new shell or SQR wrapper: the PSSQR executable. The PSSQR is an ANSI-C function consistent across different platforms. It replaces the script file that was previously used on Unix. This shell allows PeopleTools 8 to support output to HTML and PDF formats.

PSSQR also improves the delivery of reports to printers by employing a different technique of dealing with file outputs.

31.7.3 New printer setup SQCs

Since SQR output is processed differently in release 8, PeopleSoft developed new printer-independent versions of SETUPxx.sqc files. In order to use the new file output formats, you need to use either PTSET01.sqc or PTSET02.sqc files. The PTSET01.sqc was developed to replace PTPSP160.sqc, SETUP31.sqc, and SETUP01.sqc (whichever was used). The PTSET02.sqc is a replacement for PTPSL177.sqc, SETUP32.sqc, and SETUP02.sqc.

31.7.4 Additional features

PeopleTools 8 enhanced its support for the Global Time Zone and launched support of the Unicode.

Files will continue to be the primary way of integration. Release 8 brings in a simpler way of working with files. The File layout is now an object. It supports a graphical description of files. New robust file support features are added to PeopleCode as well. All this makes it easy for a third party to manipulate and exchange file layouts.

PART 6

Understanding PeopleSoft COBOL

Many of PeopleSoft's major business processes are written in COBOL. PeopleSoft documentation usually includes a section called "Before You Customize," which cautions against making any modifications to the delivered COBOL processes. This is generally good advice. There are many issues to consider, including development cost, version upgrades, and continued PeopleSoft support. Regardless of whether or not one decides to customize, it's good practice to understand how the COBOL applications work. Undoubtedly situations will arise when an analysis of the COBOL programs will be required. The purpose of this section is to provide the reader with a basic understanding of PeopleSoft's COBOL techniques and how they are used to access the database. All database activity is processed through the use of a called module named PTPSQLRT. Because no direct SQL execution exists (outside of the PTPSQLRT module), the program structure and approach is consistent across all database platforms. This is one of the key ingredients to PeopleSoft's success as a provider of packaged solutions. As we discover how PeopleSoft COBOL is used, we can apply what we've learned by making a sample customization to a delivered application. Additional topics covered include the Process Scheduler API, Configuration Manager, and trace files.

What's the difference?

32.1 *CONVENTIONAL COBOL PROGRAMMING*

COBOL is often used in the client/server world. In fact, it is used just about everywhere! Mainframes, Unix systems, personal computers—all can utilize applications written in COBOL. COBOL is a portable programming language with little variance in the "core" language itself. Theoretically, the same program can be compiled successfully on different platforms with varying elements that can be utilized depending upon the platform you're using. For example, some COBOL compilers have built-in functions (for running on a client-workstation) for keyboard handling, screen I/O (cursor control), and so forth. The main difference between conventional COBOL programming and PeopleSoft COBOL lies in the manner used in accessing the database. Instead of directly embedding your SQL statements, PeopleSoft uses a highly structured approach. All database access is controlled by calls to a delivered module called PTPSQLRT. SQL statements are stored in a database table and executed by passing the statement name and associated parameters to the PTPSQLRT module. We are going to explore how PeopleSoft uses this module to perform a variety of functions, including connecting to the database, selecting, updating, inserting, and deleting records; and disconnecting from the database.

Before we dive into PeopleSoft's method of database access, let's take a quick look at how we access the database using embedded SQL in a conventional COBOL program.

32.1.1 Using SQL in COBOL programs

Many COBOL compilers allow you to embed SQL within the program. The following example uses Pro*COBOL. The SQL directives are identified by the EXEC SQL and END-EXEC commands, and the SQL communication area and working storage section are defined:

```
*       SQL Communications Area
        EXEC SQL INCLUDE SQLCA
        END-EXEC.
**********************************************************************
*****    Declare Host Variables                                *****
**********************************************************************
        EXEC SQL BEGIN DECLARE SECTION
        END-EXEC.
        ...
 01  WS-SQL-WORK-AREAS.
     05  WS-USERID-PASSWD.
         10  USERNAME                PIC X(10).
         10  PASSWD                  PIC X(10).
     05  EMPLID-LAST-EMPL            PIC S9(08) COMP.
     ...
     EXEC SQL INCLUDE PSTABLES
     END-EXEC.
     ...


     ...
     EXEC SQL END DECLARE SECTION
     END-EXEC.
```

In the sample below we set a default error-handling routine. When any SQL error is encountered, the procedure Z999-SQL-ERROR is performed:

```
        EXEC SQL WHENEVER SQLERROR
                DO PERFORM Z999-SQL-ERROR
        END-EXEC.
```

It is a good practice to prompt the user for a user ID and password instead of hard-coding them. Once the user ID and password are entered, a CONNECT command is executed:

```
        DISPLAY 'Enter Username: ' WITH NO ADVANCING.
        ACCEPT USERNAME.
        DISPLAY 'Password       : ' WITH NO ADVANCING.
        ACCEPT PASSWD  WITH NO-ECHO.
```

```
EXEC SQL CONNECT
     :USERNAME IDENTIFIED BY :PASSWD
END-EXEC.
```

Following we select the column EMPLID_LAST_EMPL from the table PS_INSTALLATION and place the data into the bind variable EMPLID-LAST-EMPL, defined in the data division of the program:

```
EXEC SQL SELECT  EMPLID_LAST_EMPL
         INTO :EMPLID-LAST-EMPL
       FROM PS_INSTALLATION
END-EXEC.
```

The table PS_INSTALLATION is updated using the bind variable EMPLID-LAST-EMPL to populate the column EMPLID_LAST_EMPL:

```
EXEC SQL UPDATE PS_INSTALLATION
         SET  EMPLID_LAST_EMPL = :EMPLID-LAST-EMPL
END-EXEC.
```

Any updates are then committed to the database:

```
EXEC SQL COMMIT WORK
         RELEASE
END-EXEC.
```

As you can see, all SQL access is controlled by the programmer. The structure is free form and can vary by developer. PeopleSoft uses a far different approach, one that may seem cumbersome at first. Once you discover the secret to PeopleSoft's methodology, however, you'll find it much easier to analyze and, if necessary, modify PeopleSoft-delivered COBOL processes.

32.2 PEOPLESOFT STRUCTURED PROGRAMMING

All PeopleSoft COBOL programs use the same structured approach. There is no direct database access using embedded SQL. All SQL statements to be executed must reside in a database table called PS_SQLSTMT_TBL. PeopleSoft COBOL modules requiring database access through SQL are accompanied by a Data Mover script that contains all the SQL statements used by the module. The SQL statement table is populated by running the Data Mover script. This is how the SQL statements are initially loaded. Any modifications or additions to stored SQL statements should be made to the script and loaded using Data Mover. The key behind PeopleSoft's structured approach is the use of a main database activity module called PTPSQLRT. This module ensures consistency from one PeopleSoft program to another regardless of database platform or operating system.

To demonstrate the functionality of the PTPSQLRT module, let's use one of PeopleSoft's less complex processes—the process to delete obsolete monthly payroll balances (called PSPDLBAL)—as an example:

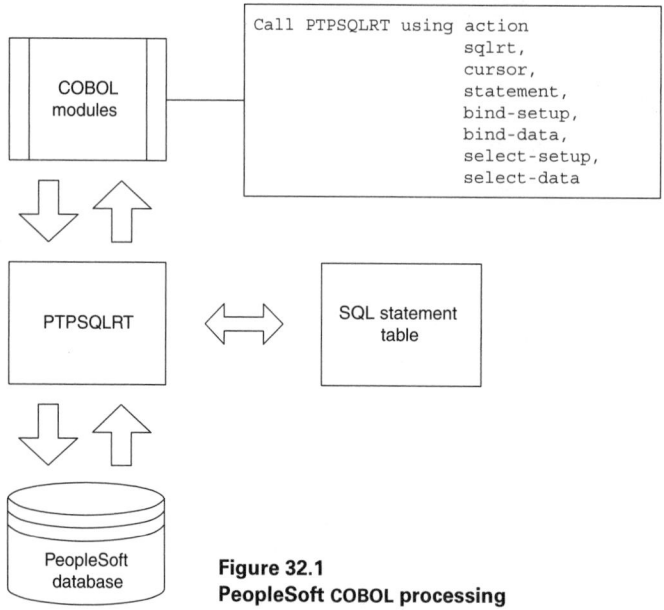

Figure 32.1
PeopleSoft COBOL processing

Figure 32.1 illustrates the overall design of PeopleSoft COBOL processing. Calls to PTPSQLRT are used to perform all database access functions. Stored SQL statements are retrieved from the SQL statement table and processed.

32.2.1 Stored SQL statements

First, let's take a quick look at the stored SQL statement table.

SQLSTMT_TBL	Stored SQL Statement Table
PGM_NAME	Program Name
STMT_TYPE	Statement Type
STMT_NAME	Statement Name
STMT_TEXT	Statement Text

Each COBOL program that calls a stored SQL statement has at least one entry. In our upcoming example, we'll access SQL statements with a PGM_NAME of PSPDLBAL. The statements are also qualified by a STMT_TYPE, which designates the type of SQL statement. The valid types are S (Select), U (Update), I (Insert), and

D (Delete). Finally, the STMT_NAME field is used to assign a unique statement name. The actual statement text is stored in the STMT_TEXT column. This statement text will be retrieved and compiled by PTPSQLRT.

32.2.2   Storing SQL statements from Data Mover scripts

The PSPDLBAL COBOL process comes with a Data Mover script (PSPDLBAL.DMS) which is loaded into the table PS_SQLSTMT_TBL. Let's look at a portion of this script:

```
STORE PSPDLBAL_S_RUNCTL
SELECT COMPANY,
       BALANCE_ID,
       BALANCE_YEAR,
       BALANCE_PERIOD
  FROM PS_PAY_DBAL_RUNCTL
 WHERE OPRID            = :1
   AND RUN_CNTL_ID      = :2
;
```

Our first line contains a Data Mover STORE command. This is used to store the subsequent text in the STMT_TEXT column of the stored SQL statement table. The STORE command parameter PSPDLBAL_S_RUNCTL is used to identify the key elements. The parameter is a consolidated form of the SQL statement table keys. They are then broken down by Data Mover into the PGM_NAME, STMT_TYPE, and STMT_NAME columns of the SQL statement table. When we discuss the PTPSQLRT module in detail, you'll discover the SQL statements are accessed using the same consolidated method of identifying the statement.

The SQL statement text following the STORE command is placed in the SQL statement table. Notice the use of bind variables :1 and :2. All bind variables are entered in this manner. When the statement is retrieved, the bind variable is resolved and the statement processed.

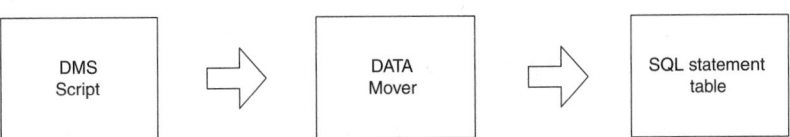

Figure 32.2   Data Mover processes DMS script (stores SQL statements)

Figure 32.2 depicts the Data Mover process of loading stored SQL statements. The DMS script contains all the stored SQL statements. Data Mover loads the SQL statements into the SQL statement table where they can then be utilized by the COBOL processes through calls to PTPSQLRT.

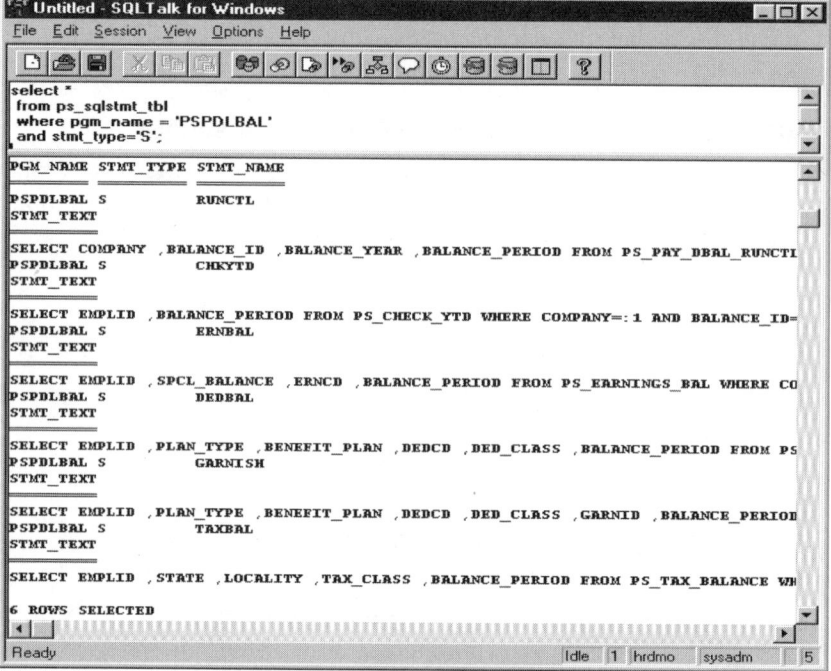

Figure 32.3 Viewing stored SQL statements using SQLTalk

Once the DMS script has executed, the stored SQL statement table can be queried using a simple Select statement. Figure 32.3 shows the results of a Select when using SQLTalk for Windows. All Select statement types for program PSPDLBAL are returned. The COBOL program uses a similar method to retrieve the SQL statement text.

Keep in mind that no need exists to query the stored SQL statements. This is informational only and demonstrates how the SQL statements are stored in the database.

32.3 *THE PTPSQLRT MODULE*

The module PTPSQLRT performs a variety of functions:

- executes Select statements
- fetches rows from the database
- processes SQL updates—Update, Delete, Insert statements
- performs commits and rollbacks
- connects to database
- disconnects from database
- disconnects cursors
- performs error handling

32.3.1   Calling PTPSQLRT

When calling PTPSQLRT from a COBOL program, the following format is used:

```
CALL 'PTPSQLRT' USING action,
                     sqlrt,
                     cursor,
                     statement,
                     bind-setup,
                     bind-data,
                     select-setup,
                     select-data
```

The preceding parameters are positional and must be passed in the precise order shown. The number of parameters passed to PTPSQLRT can range from two to eight, depending upon the particular Action being executed. For example, an error handling action only requires the first two parameters, while all eight are required when performing an Action that selects data from the database. Once we describe each of the parameters, the requirements for each particular Action will be explained.

32.4   *PARAMETER DESCRIPTIONS*

We'll now examine each of the parameters that may be passed to the PTPSQLRT module.

32.4.1   Parameter 1—ACTION

A one-character code is used to specify the action to be performed. These codes are already defined in a copybook called PTCSQLRT and should be used when interfacing with PTPSQLRT:

```
02   ACTION-SELECT          PIC X      VALUE 'S'.
02   ACTION-FETCH           PIC X      VALUE 'F'.
02   ACTION-UPDATE          PIC X      VALUE 'U'.
02   ACTION-COMMIT          PIC X      VALUE 'C'.
02   ACTION-ROLLBACK        PIC X      VALUE 'R'.
02   ACTION-DISCONNECT      PIC X      VALUE 'D'.
02   ACTION-DISCONNECT-ALL  PIC X      VALUE 'A'.
02   ACTION-CONNECT         PIC X      VALUE 'N'.
02   ACTION-ERROR           PIC X      VALUE 'E'.
02   ACTION-CLEAR-STMT      PIC X      VALUE 'L'.
02   ACTION-TRACE           PIC X      VALUE 'T'.
02   ACTION-START-BULK      PIC X      VALUE 'X'.
02   ACTION-STOP-BULK       PIC X      VALUE 'Y'.
02   ACTION-FLUSH-BULK      PIC X      VALUE 'Z'.
02   ACTION-DML-COUNT       PIC X      VALUE 'M'.
```

Here's how we specify Action as the first parameter in a parameter list:

```
CALL 'PTPSQLRT' USING ACTION-SELECT OF SQLRT
                    <additional parameters>
```

32.4.2 Parameter 2—SQLRT (Communication Area)

SQLRT is the communication area required by PTPSQLRT. Information about the database and the current run is stored here and passed to PTPSQLRT. The database platform, user ID, password, process instance, and job instance are some examples of data stored here. When control is passed back from PTPSQLRT to the calling module, a return code, which is also found within the PTCSQLRT copybook, is set. This code should be evaluated to determine if the operation were successful:

```
CALL 'PTPSQLRT' USING ACTION-SELECT OF SQLRT
                      SQLRT
                      <additional parameters>

IF RTNCD-ERROR OF SQLRT
   <error handling>
END-IF
```

Here are a few guidelines for using the PTCSQLRT copybook:

SQLRT should be defined as a 01-level item in the working storage section of the main module. A Copy statement should immediately follow, designating PTCSQLRT.

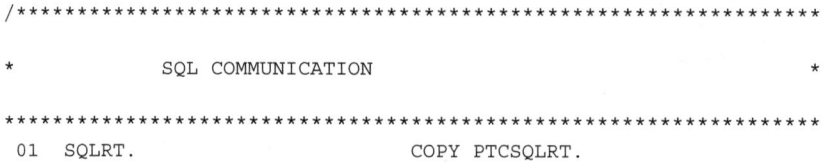

```
/****************************************************************

*               SQL COMMUNICATION                              *

****************************************************************
01  SQLRT.                    COPY PTCSQLRT.
```

The SQLRT communication area must be passed to all called modules. This ensures the same communication area is used:

```
CALL 'PSPDCWS1' USING   SQLRT
                        PSLCT
                        DARRY
```

All called modules must have SQLRT defined as a 01-level item in the programs linkage section. A COPY statement should immediately follow designating PTCSQLRT:

```
LINKAGE SECTION.
```

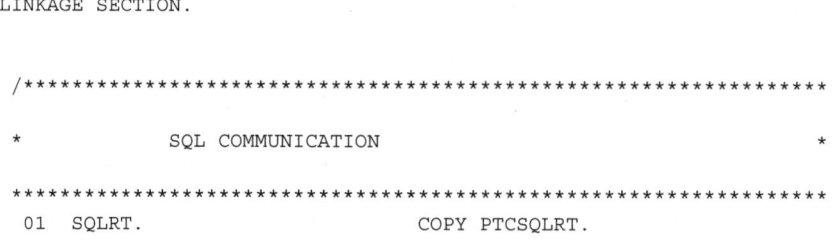

```
/****************************************************************

*               SQL COMMUNICATION                              *

****************************************************************
01  SQLRT.                    COPY PTCSQLRT.
```

The procedure division of the called program must accept the SQLRT parameter:

```
PROCEDURE DIVISION USING     SQLRT
                             PSLCT
                             DARRY
                               .
```

32.4.3   Parameter 3—CURSOR

Some actions require the use of a database cursor. This is defined as a four-digit computational number. If you don't need to re-use the cursor, the SQL-CURSOR-COMMON variable, which is found in the PTCSQLRT copybook, may be used. If you need to re-use the cursor, a dedicated variable will need to be defined. A cursor is also referred to as a resource connection unit:

```
CALL 'PTPSQLRT' USING ACTION-SELECT OF SQLRT
                      SQLRT
                      SQL-CURSOR-COMMON OF SQLRT
                      <additional parameters>
```

Here is a brief explanation on what it means to re-use a cursor: If you are selecting from a table only one time in your program, you don't need to dedicate a cursor variable. For example, when you select parameters from a Run Control record, you specify the cursor as SQL-CURSOR-COMMON in your Select and immediately fetch the row of data for the same cursor. You can then re-use the SQL-CURSOR-COMMON variable for other re-useable cursors. Please note that this is simply a convention used by PeopleSoft to make programming easier. It would be unnecessary to define a distinct cursor variable for every SQL function executed only one time.

A dedicated cursor is required when you perform a Select and fetch rows multiple times in the COBOL program. Between each fetch from the assigned cursor, you could perform SQL tasks on other open cursors. By dedicating a cursor, you can fetch a row of data at any time in your COBOL program without regard to any other cursors that may currently be open.

32.4.4   Parameter 4—SQL statement name

An SQL statement name is the consolidated name of the stored SQL statement. As we mentioned in our description of the stored SQL statement table, the table keys PGM_NAME, STMT_TYPE, and STMT_NAME must be passed as one string separated by underscores. An example of an SQL statement name is PSPDLBAL_S_RUNCTL. PeopleSoft commonly stores this statement name in a variable called SQL-STMT. The SQL-STMT variable is grouped under a 01-level item with all other components required for the call to PTPSQLRT. This may include Bind Setup/Data, Select Setup/Data, and SQL Cursor elements.

The SQL-STMT variable in the following example is part of the 01-level item called S-RUNCTL:

```
CALL 'PTPSQLRT' USING ACTION-SELECT OF SQLRT
                      SQLRT
```

```
                 SQL-CURSOR-COMMON OF SQLRT
                 SQL-STMT OF S-RUNCTL
                 <additional parameters>
```

32.4.5   Parameter 5—Bind Setup

The fifth and sixth parameters, the `Bind Setup` and `Bind Data` parameters, are used together to pass bind variable information. These define the format of the bind variable and the actual bind variable values. The number of bind variables must match that of the stored SQL statement which is designated as `:1`, `:2`, etc. The `Bind Setup` area is a group of picture clauses defined as `FILLER`, which represents the format of the corresponding bind data. This is known as a setup list. We will discuss this in detail following the parameter descriptions. Let's specify `Bind Setup` as the fifth parameter in a parameter list.

```
CALL 'PTPSQLRT' USING ACTION-SELECT OF SQLRT
                      SQLRT
                      SQL-CURSOR-COMMON OF SQLRT
                      SQL-STMT OF S-RUNCTL
                      BIND-SETUP OF S-RUNCTL
                      <additional parameters>
```

32.4.6   Parameter 6—Bind Data

The sixth parameter is the Bind Data list, which holds the bind variable values used in the stored SQL statement. Each bind data value in the list has a matching bind setup value. Some examples of where bind variables are used are in `WHERE` clauses or in the values list of an `Insert` statement:

```
CALL 'PTPSQLRT' USING ACTION-SELECT OF SQLRT
                      SQLRT
                      SQL-CURSOR-COMMON OF SQLRT
                      SQL-STMT OF S-RUNCTL
                      BIND-SETUP OF S-RUNCTL
                      BIND-DATA OF S-RUNCTL
                      <additional parameters>
```

32.4.7   Parameter 7—Select Setup

The seventh and eighth parameters are used together to define the Select area. This Select area is used by the `Fetch` action to return the selected row of data elements. The `Select Setup` list is similar to the `Bind Setup` list. Both use the setup list format, which will be described in detail shortly:

```
CALL 'PTPSQLRT' USING ACTION-SELECT OF SQLRT
                      SQLRT
                      SQL-CURSOR-COMMON OF SQLRT
                      SQL-STMT OF S-RUNCTL
                      BIND-SETUP OF S-RUNCTL
                      BIND-DATA OF S-RUNCTL
```

```
SELECT-SETUP OF S-RUNCTL
<additional parameter>
```

32.4.8 Parameter 8—Select Data

The eighth and final parameter is the `Select Data` list, which holds the returned values from a `Fetch` action. The number of `Select Setup` and `Select Data` entries corresponds to the number of Select columns in the stored SQL statement:

```
CALL 'PTPSQLRT' USING ACTION-SELECT OF SQLRT
                      SQLRT
                      SQL-CURSOR-COMMON OF SQLRT
                      SQL-STMT OF S-RUNCTL
                      BIND-SETUP OF S-RUNCTL
                      BIND-DATA OF S-RUNCTL
                      SELECT-SETUP OF S-RUNCTL
                      SELECT-DATA OF S-RUNCTL
```

Notice the `S-RUNCTL` designated by the COBOL designator `OF` for the parameters `SQL-STMT`, `BIND-SETUP`, `BIND-DATA`, `SELECT-SETUP`, and `SELECT-DATA`. `S-RUNCTL` is a 01-level item that contains all of these parameters. Using `OF` tells the COBOL compiler to qualify the variable names with the 01-level item. This feature allows duplicate variable names to be used. Generally speaking, each 01-level item used to access the database utilizes the same variable names for the desired `PTPSQLRT` parameters.

32.5 SETUP LISTS

The setup list is used to define the attributes of an accompanying list of data elements. The length of each setup item matches the length of its data item counterpart. The setup item contains a string of characters which designate the data type and, when applicable, the number of decimal places. With the exception of decimal numbers (COMP-3), two codes exist for each data type. If the same data types are defined one after the other, the setup list alternates between the two codes (table 32.2).

Table 32.1   PeopleSoft's Setup List table

Data types	Codes	Length	Data list picture
Character	C, H	1 to 255	X(1) through X(255)
Date	D, A	10	X(10)
Time	T, E	26	X(26)
Small integer	S, M	2	[S]999 or [S]9999 COMP
Large integer	I, N	4	[S]9(8) or [S]9(9) COMP

Table 32.1   PeopleSoft's Setup List table (continued)

Data types	Codes	Length	Data list picture
Decimal number	d[P...]	1 to 8	[S]9(w)[V9(d)] COMP-3
			Example 1: S9(5)V9(2) COMP-3 => 2PPP
			Example 2: 999V99 COMP-3 => 2PP
			Example 3: S9(11)V999 COMP-3 => 3PPPPPPP
END OF LIST	Z	1	All setup and data areas must be terminated with the character 'Z'.

Note that all `Bind-Setup`, `Bind-Data`, `Select-Setup`, and `Select-Data` areas must end with the termination character of 'Z.' If there are no bind data values, as in the case of an unconditional `Select` or `Update`, a single 'Z' termination character must exist in the `Bind-Setup/Bind-Data` areas.

Let's elaborate briefly on the decimal number setup (COMP-3). Look at the three examples used in the Decimal Number section of the Setup List table (table 32.1). The first example requires a string defined as `PIC X(4)` with a value of `2PPP`. This represents the number of decimal places along with the total length of the data field. A field defined as `S9(5)V99 COMP-3` takes up four bytes. The trailing 'P' character simply fills the remainder of the field after the number of decimal places. The second example would use a string defined as `PIC X(3)` with a value of `2PP`, which represents two decimals and a total length of three bytes. The data field in example 2 is defined as `999V99` which takes up three bytes. The last example uses a `PIC X(8)` string with a value of `3PPPPPPP`. This designates three decimal places and a total length of eight bytes. The data field defined as `S9(11)V999 COMP-3` takes up eight bytes in storage.

Let's take a look at an actual working storage area that includes a setup list. This section was taken from the PSPDLBAL module. Notice the stored SQL statement definition, `Bind Setup/Data`, and `Select Setup/Data` areas:

```
01   S-RUNCTL.
     02   SQL-STMT                   PIC X(18)    VALUE
                                                  'PSPDLBAL_S_RUNCTL'.

     02   BIND-SETUP.
          03   FILLER                PIC X(8)     VALUE ALL 'C'.
          03   FILLER                PIC X(30)    VALUE ALL 'H'.
          03   FILLER                PIC X        VALUE 'Z'.

     02   BIND-DATA.
          03   OPRID                 PIC X(8).
          03   BATCH-RUN-ID          PIC X(30).
          03   FILLER                PIC X        VALUE 'Z'.
```

```
02   SELECT-SETUP.
     03   FILLER              PIC X(10)   VALUE ALL 'C'.
     03   FILLER              PIC XX      VALUE ALL 'H'.
     03   FILLER              PIC XX      VALUE ALL 'S'.
     03   FILLER              PIC XX      VALUE ALL 'M'.
     03   FILLER              PIC X       VALUE 'Z'.


02   SELECT-DATA.
     03   COMPANY             PIC X(10).
     03   BALANCE-ID          PIC XX.
     03   BALANCE-YEAR        PIC 9999              COMP.
     03   BALANCE-PERIOD      PIC 999               COMP.
     03   FILLER              PIC X       VALUE 'Z'.
```

The preceding example shows a good sample of contiguous setup list strings. Let's examine the Bind-Setup and Bind-Data areas. The Bind-Data area is for the OPRID and BATCH-RUN-ID, which are both character fields. The Bind-Setup uses the character 'C' for the OPRID setup list string while the character 'H' is used for the BATCH-RUN-ID setup list string. You can also see that the character 'Z' terminates each setup and data area. This produces an image that will be recognized by the PTPSQLRT module to determine the position of the two fields.

If both fields use 'C' in the setup list string, the PTPSQLRT module interprets this as one thirty-eight character field with the second field missing. This produces an error in the COBOL program.

Let's also look at the stored SQL statement that will be executed. The following displays the portion of the DMS script containing the statement text:

```
STORE PSPDLBAL_S_RUNCTL
SELECT COMPANY,
       BALANCE_ID,
       BALANCE_YEAR,
       BALANCE_PERIOD
  FROM PS_PAY_DBAL_RUNCTL
 WHERE OPRID              = :1
   AND RUN_CNTL_ID        = :2
;
```

The Bind Setup/Data area in working storage contains the OPRID and BATCH-RUN-ID and will be used as the criteria for the Select. PTPSQLRT substitutes these for bind variables :1 and :2. The Select Setup/Data area will be used to store the results of the Select statement. COMPANY, BALANCE_ID, BALANCE_YEAR, and BALANCE_PERIOD will be stored in the format specified in the Select Setup. It is the developers responsibility to ensure that the datatypes are compatible. The Select Data elements are now populated and can be used by the COBOL program.

32.6 ACTION REQUIREMENTS

Let's review some of the basic actions found in PeopleSoft COBOL and the required parameters for each.

CONNECT— connects to the database.

```
CALL 'PTPSQLRT' USING ACTION-CONNECT OF SQLRT
                      SQLRT
                      SQL-CURSOR-COMMON OF SQLRT

IF RTNCD-ERROR OF SQLRT
   <Error Handling>
END-IF
```

CONNECT uses three parameters: The Action, SQL communication area, which is the minimum requirement for all actions, and a reuseable cursor which is required to connect. The return code is checked to determine whether or not the connect action was successful.

DISCONNECT— disconnects a cursor from database.

DISCONNECT uses three parameters. Notice the following example specifies a dedicated cursor, defined within the S-PYGRP 01-level of working storage.

```
CALL 'PTPSQLRT' USING ACTION-DISCONNECT OF SQLRT
                      SQLRT
                      SQL-CURSOR OF S-PYGRP

IF RTNCD-ERROR OF SQLRT
   <Error Handling>
END-IF
```

DISCONNECT ALL— disconnects all cursors from database.

```
CALL 'PTPSQLRT' USING ACTION-DISCONNECT-ALL OF SQLRT
                      SQLRT

IF RTNCD-ERROR OF SQLRT
   <Error Handling>
END-IF
```

DISCONNECT ALL uses two parameters. All cursors are disconnected. You will find this immediately before the end of the program.

ERROR—is the error handling routine.

```
CALL 'PTPSQLRT' USING  ACTION-CONNECT OF SQLRT
                       SQLRT
                       SQL-CURSOR-COMMON OF SQLRT
```

```
IF RTNCD-ERROR OF SQLRT

   MOVE 'SELECT-RUNCTL(CONNECT)'  TO  ERR-SECTION OF SQLRT
   PERFORM ZZ000-SQL-ERROR
END-IF

...

ZZ000-SQL-ERROR SECTION.
ZZ000.

CALL 'PTPSQLRT' USING   ACTION-ERROR OF SQLRT
                        SQLRT
```

ACTION-ERROR—uses two parameters: the Action and SQL communication area. This Action provides a consistent means of error handling. The PTCSQLRT copybook contains a field called ERR-SECTION. The section which caused the error should be placed in the ERR-SECTION field. The previous example shows both the controlling section, which may cause an error, and the ZZ000-SQL-ERROR section, which executes the `Action-Error` process. The error handling procedure displays the section which caused the error and also halts further processing. The user can see that the error occurred in the SELECT-RUNCTL section while trying to connect to the database.

COMMIT—performs a commit.

```
CALL 'PTPSQLRT' USING   ACTION-COMMIT OF SQLRT
                        SQLRT
                        SQL-CURSOR-COMMON OF SQLRT
IF RTNCD-ERROR OF SQLRT

   MOVE 'COMMIT'  TO  ERR-SECTION OF SQLRT
   PERFORM ZZ000-SQL-ERROR
END-IF
```

ACTION-COMMIT—uses three parameters: The Action, SQL Communication Area, and a database cursor. The SQL-CURSOR-COMMON variable (found in PTCSQLRT) may be used for reuseable cursors. When executed, all work will be committed since the latest commit (or rollback).

ROLLBACK—performs a Rollback.

```
CALL 'PTPSQLRT' USING   ACTION-ROLLBACK OF SQLRT
                        SQLRT
                        SQL-CURSOR-COMMON OF SQLRT
IF RTNCD-ERROR OF SQLRT

   MOVE 'ROLLBACK'  TO  ERR-SECTION OF SQLRT
   PERFORM ZZ000-SQL-ERROR
END-IF
```

ACTION-ROLLBACK—uses three parameters: The Action, SQL Communication Area, and a database cursor. When executed, all work completed since the last commit will be rolled back.

SELECT—selects and formats data from the database.

```
MOVE OPRID        OF SQLRT  TO  OPRID        OF S-RUNCTL
MOVE BATCH-RUN-ID OF SQLRT  TO  BATCH-RUN-ID OF S-RUNCTL

CALL 'PTPSQLRT' USING   ACTION-SELECT OF SQLRT
                        SQLRT
                        SQL-CURSOR-COMMON OF SQLRT
                        SQL-STMT OF S-RUNCTL
                        BIND-SETUP OF S-RUNCTL
                        BIND-DATA OF S-RUNCTL
                        SELECT-SETUP OF S-RUNCTL
                        SELECT-DATA OF S-RUNCTL

IF RTNCD-ERROR OF SQLRT

   MOVE 'SELECT-RUNCTL(SELECT)'  TO  ERR-SECTION OF SQLRT
   PERFORM ZZ000-SQL-ERROR
END-IF
```

ACTION-SELECT—uses all eight available parameters. The primary function of ACTION-SELECT is to create a result set of data from the database. Once created, the rows may be retrieved one-at-a-time using a Fetch action which we'll explain next. The example above is used to select Run Control information and is using a reuseable cursor. Before the call to PTPSQLRT, the OPRID and BATCH-RUN-ID are moved to the Bind-Data area within the S-RUNCTL 01-level area. The Bind Data is used as the Where clause criteria in the SQL statement. Let's look at some of the parameter definitions in working storage:

```
01  S-RUNCTL.
    02  SQL-STMT               PIC X(18)   VALUE
                                           'PSPDLBAL_S_RUNCTL'.

    02  BIND-SETUP.
        03  FILLER             PIC X(8)    VALUE ALL 'C'.
        03  FILLER             PIC X(30)   VALUE ALL 'H'.
        03  FILLER             PIC X       VALUE 'Z'.

    02  BIND-DATA.
        03  OPRID              PIC X(8).
        03  BATCH-RUN-ID       PIC X(30).
        03  FILLER             PIC X       VALUE 'Z'.

    02  SELECT-SETUP.
        03  FILLER             PIC X(10)   VALUE ALL 'C'.
```

```
       03    FILLER                 PIC XX        VALUE ALL 'H'.
       03    FILLER                 PIC XX        VALUE ALL 'S'.
       03    FILLER                 PIC XX        VALUE ALL 'M'.
       03    FILLER                 PIC X         VALUE 'Z'.

  02   SELECT-DATA.
       03    COMPANY                PIC X(10).
       03    BALANCE-ID             PIC XX.
       03    BALANCE-YEAR           PIC 9999              COMP.
       03    BALANCE-PERIOD         PIC 999               COMP.
       03    FILLER                 PIC X         VALUE 'Z'.
```

We can see the working storage definitions used in the ACTION-SELECT example. Notice the last five parameters in the call are grouped together under the same 01-level item called S-RUNCTL. If a dedicated cursor were required, it would also be defined in the S-RUNCTL area. This is a very structured and consistent approach used throughout PeopleSoft COBOL. Any analysis or modifications may be carried out with relative ease due to this structure.

Let's take a closer look at the SQL-STMT parameter. This contains the consolidated key of the SQL statement stored in the SQL statement table. Let's look at the SQL statement text retrieved by PTPSQLRT when the ACTION-SELECT is performed:

```
SELECT COMPANY,
       BALANCE_ID,
       BALANCE_YEAR,
       BALANCE_PERIOD
  FROM PS_PAY_DBAL_RUNCTL
 WHERE OPRID       =:1
   AND RUN_CNTL_ID =:2
```

The bind data OPRID and BATCH-RUN-ID are substituted for the bind variables :1 and :2. The statement is executed, and Select Data will be used to accept the data. An ACTION-FETCH needs to be performed to physically retrieve each row in the result set created by ACTION-SELECT.

FETCH—fetches a single row from result set created by Select:

```
MOVE OPRID        OF SQLRT  TO  OPRID        OF S-RUNCTL
MOVE BATCH-RUN-ID OF SQLRT  TO  BATCH-RUN-ID OF S-RUNCTL

CALL 'PTPSQLRT' USING    ACTION-SELECT OF SQLRT
                         SQLRT
                         SQL-CURSOR-COMMON OF SQLRT
                         SQL-STMT OF S-RUNCTL
                         BIND-SETUP OF S-RUNCTL
                         BIND-DATA OF S-RUNCTL
                         SELECT-SETUP OF S-RUNCTL
                         SELECT-DATA OF S-RUNCTL
```

```
IF RTNCD-ERROR OF SQLRT

   MOVE 'SELECT-RUNCTL(SELECT)'  TO  ERR-SECTION OF SQLRT
   PERFORM ZZ000-SQL-ERROR
END-IF

INITIALIZE SELECT-DATA OF S-RUNCTL

CALL 'PTPSQLRT' USING   ACTION-FETCH OF SQLRT
                        SQLRT
                        SQL-CURSOR-COMMON OF SQLRT

IF RTNCD-ERROR OF SQLRT

   IF RTNCD-END OF SQLRT

      DISPLAY 'Delete Balances Run Control Missing.'
      DISPLAY ' for Operator ID  ' OPRID OF S-RUNCTL
      DISPLAY ' and Batch Run ID ' BATCH-RUN-ID OF S-RUNCTL
      SET RTNCD-USER-ERROR OF SQLRT  TO  TRUE
      PERFORM ZZ000-SQL-ERROR
   ELSE
      MOVE 'SELECT-RUNCTL(FETCH)'  TO  ERR-SECTION OF SQLRT
      PERFORM ZZ000-SQL-ERROR
   END-IF
ELSE
   PERFORM DD000-RUNCTL-ACCEPTED
END-IF
```

ACTION-FETCH—uses three parameters. When the Fetch is performed, the data are placed in the Setup Data area defined in the ACTION-SELECT for the designated cursor. Notice that the ACTION-SELECT above utilizes the SQL-CURSOR-COMMON reusable cursor. The ACTION-FETCH uses the same cursor and all associated characteristics including the Select Data area. Upon returning from the Fetch, the return code is tested. If there is no error, a row has been successfully returned. If there is an error, it could be due to an end-of-data condition. An error message is displayed if there is no data (Missing Run Control). Any other database errors are handled as well with a simple 'SELECT-RUNCTL(FETCH)' message.

Our example was very straightforward. Since we are selecting a Run Control record, we are expecting one row to be returned. If multiple rows were processed, a loop would be required. The rows would be fetched one at a time with an end-of-data test used to break out of the loop. The Select Data area would be updated with each fetched row and utilized accordingly by the program.

UPDATE—performs an Insert, Update, or Delete.

```
MOVE OPRID        OF SQLRT  TO  OPRID        OF D-RUNCTL
MOVE BATCH-RUN-ID OF SQLRT  TO  BATCH-RUN-ID OF D-RUNCTL
```

```
CALL 'PTPSQLRT' USING   ACTION-UPDATE OF SQLRT
                        SQLRT
                        SQL-CURSOR-COMMON OF SQLRT
                        SQL-STMT OF D-RUNCTL
                        BIND-SETUP OF D-RUNCTL
                        BIND-DATA OF D-RUNCTL

IF RTNCD-ERROR OF SQLRT

   MOVE 'RUNCTL-ACCEPTED(DELETE)'  TO  ERR-SECTION OF SQLRT
   PERFORM ZZ000-SQL-ERROR
END-IF

PERFORM ZA000-COMMIT
```

ACTION-UPDATE—uses six parameters. This function is used to execute Inserts, Updates, and Deletes. The Select Setup and Data areas are omitted. The Bind Setup and Data areas are used to pass WHERE clause criteria, Update values and Insert values. The order of the Bind Setup/Data lists must match the order of the bind variables (:1, :2, :3, etc.) in the stored SQL statement. Now, let's have a look at the working storage section:

```
01  D-RUNCTL.
       02  SQL-STMT              PIC X(18)   VALUE
                                             'PSPDLBAL_D_RUNCTL'.

       02  BIND-SETUP.
           03  FILLER            PIC X(8)    VALUE ALL 'C'.
           03  FILLER            PIC X(30)   VALUE ALL 'H'.
           03  FILLER            PIC X       VALUE 'Z'.

       02  BIND-DATA.
           03  OPRID             PIC X(8).
           03  BATCH-RUN-ID      PIC X(30).
           03  FILLER            PIC X       VALUE 'Z'.
```

We see the 01-level item D-RUNCTL, which is the area used in our ACTION-UPDATE example. Notice the name of the SQL-STMT, 'PSPDLBAL_D_RUNCTL'. The middle character indicates that this is a Delete statement. The only bind variables utilized by a Delete are in the WHERE clause. We now know that the criteria for the Delete is OPRID and BATCH-RUN-ID. This statement will delete the Run Control record for the process we're running.

```
DELETE                              Bind variables :1 and :2 serve
   FROM PS_PAY_DBAL_RUNCTL    ◄┐    as the WHERE clause criteria in
WHERE OPRID        =:1         │    a DELETE
   AND RUN_CNTL_ID =:2
```

If you look in the DMS script (PSPDLBAL.DMS) or query the SQL statement table itself, you find the SQL statement displayed previously. The OPRID and BATCH-RUN-ID values in the Bind Data area are substituted for the :1 and :2 bind variables. The Delete SQL statement is then compiled and executed, and the Run Control record is deleted (if all goes well). Notice the error handling in our example as well as the Commit routine, which is performed if the Action were successful.

Let's look at a sample of an Update and Insert statement. We'll examine the working storage area and the portion of the DMS script which contains the SQL statement text. These examples can be found in the program PAPPPYMT.CBL and the DMS script PAPPPYMT.DMS:

```
01   U-RUNCNTL.
     05   SQL-CURSOR              PIC S9(4)    VALUE 0      COMP.
     05   SQL-STMT                PIC X(18)    VALUE
                                               'PAPPPYMT_U_RUNCNTL'.
     05   BIND-SETUP.
          10   FILLER             PIC X(11)    VALUE ALL 'C'.
          10   FILLER             PIC X(8)     VALUE ALL 'H'.
          10   FILLER             PIC X(30)    VALUE ALL 'C'.
          10   FILLER             PIC X(01)    VALUE 'Z'.
     05   BIND-DATA.
          10   EMPLID             PIC X(11)    VALUE SPACE.
          10   OPRID              PIC X(8).
          10   RUN-CNTL-ID        PIC X(30).
          10   FILLER             PIC X(01)    VALUE 'Z'.
```

The preceeding example displays a typical working storage area used in an Update action. Depending on the SQL statement, the bind data can be any combination of Update values or WHERE clause criteria. The bind data may be all Update values with criteria hard-coded in the SQL statement itself (or no criteria at all for a mass update). The bind data may be made up entirely of WHERE clause criteria with the Update value hard-coded in the SQL statement. There may not be any bind data values at all! Consider the statement, 'UPDATE PS_INSTALLATION SET EMPLID_LAST_EMPL = 0'. There are no bind data values and no WHERE clause values. The SQL statement requires no bind data at all. The bind data and bind setup lists would still be required. A single termination character of 'Z' would reside in both lists, and the statement would be executed without bind values.

```
STORE PAPPPYMT_U_RUNCNTL
UPDATE PS_PA_RUN_CNTL
     SET EMPLID        = :1     | Bind variable :1 is used as an UPDATE
   WHERE OPRID         = :2     | value while :2 and :3 are used as
     AND RUN_CNTL_ID   = :3     | WHERE clause criteria.
```

The bind data values in our (Update) working storage example correspond to the bind variables :1, :2, and :3 in the SQL statement text depicted above. Once again, the order and datatype of the bind data should match that of the bind variables in the SQL statement text.

Now let's look at a typical working storage area used in an `Insert` action. The bind values `EMPLID`, `BENEFIT_PLAN`, `EFFDT`, and `PENSION-STATUS` will be inserted into the table contained in the SQL statement:

```
01  I-PENSTAT.
    05  SQL-CURSOR              PIC S9(4)    VALUE 0      COMP.
    05  SQL-STMT               PIC X(18)    VALUE
                                            'PAPPPYMT_I_PENSTAT'.
    05  BIND-SETUP.
        10  FILLER             PIC X(11)    VALUE ALL 'C'.
        10  FILLER             PIC X(6)     VALUE ALL 'H'.
        10  FILLER             PIC X(10)    VALUE ALL 'D'.
        10  FILLER             PIC X(3)     VALUE ALL 'C'.
        10  FILLER             PIC X(01)    VALUE 'Z'.
    05  BIND-DATA.
        10  EMPLID             PIC X(11).
        10  BENEFIT-PLAN       PIC X(6).
        10  EFFDT              PIC X(10).
        10  PENSION-STATUS     PIC X(3).
        10  FILLER             PIC X(01)    VALUE 'Z'.
```

The bind variables `:1` thru `:4` will be replaced by the bind data values in the previous working storage definition. As you know, the order and datatype of the bind variables and bind data must match exactly to be executed successfully:

```
STORE PAPPPYMT_I_PENSTAT
INSERT INTO PS_PA_EMP_PEN_STAT
     (EMPLID
     ,BENEFIT_PLAN
     ,EFFDT
     ,PENSION_STATUS)
     VALUES (:1, :2, :3, :4)
```

Bind variables `:1` thru `:4` must be accounted for properly in the Bind Setup and Bind Data areas of the COBOL program

1 It is always wise to avoid COBOL customizations whenever possible. Make sure all possible solutions are investigated before deciding to modify delivered COBOL processes.

2 Even if you don't plan on modifying COBOL programs, become familiar with PeopleSoft COBOL techniques. There will surely be times when you need to browse the COBOL source code when troubleshooting.

3 The PTPSQLRT module regulates all database activity required by the COBOL process. Since it is one encapsulated routine, it remains consistent across all database platforms.

4 All SQL statements are stored in a database table and retrieved by the COBOL process where they are compiled and executed.

5 The SQL statements are loaded into the stored SQL statement table using Data Mover scripts. Any required modifications should be made to the scripts so they may be reloaded.

6 PTPSQLRT performs database functions as well as error handling. These functions are referred to as actions. Up to eight positional parameters may be passed, depending on the action requested.

7 The eight parameters are the `Action`, the SQL communication area, an SQL `cursor`, the SQL statement name reference, the `Bind Setup/Data` areas and the `Select Setup/Data` areas.

8 The copybook PTCSQLRT contains the SQL communication area used by the PTPSQLRT module and must be included in all COBOL modules. The Main module must define the SQLRT area as an 01-level item in working storage and must pass this area as a parameter to other called modules. All called or subordinate modules must define the SQLRT area as an 01-level item in the linkage section and the procedure division must accept the SQLRT parameter. This insures the same SQLRT area is used by all modules.

9 Setup lists are used to define the `Bind` and `Setup` areas in working storage. Each datatype has a pair of corresponding setup codes. The codes are alternated when two consecutive fields with the same datatype are used. This allows the PTPSQLRT module to parse the incoming bind data and outgoing select data properly.

Modifying PeopleSoft COBOL

33.1   DEFINING A MODIFICATION

To demonstrate how to modify a PeopleSoft COBOL program, we need to define a task. We'll continue to use the program PSPDLBAL as a model. As we mentioned earlier, this process is used in PeopleSoft Payroll to delete obsolete balances from the system. Let's take a closer look at this process before we decide on a sample customization.

33.1.1   Delivered functionality

In short, the PSPDLBAL process deletes obsolete balances from the following tables:

- YTD Check Balances (CHECK_YTD)
- YTD Earnings Balances (EARNINGS_BAL)

- YTD Deduction Balances (DEDUCTION_BAL)
- YTD Garnishment Balances (GARN_BALANCE)
- YTD Tax Balances (TAX_BALANCE)

The Run Control record contains the parameters:

- `Company`
- `Balance Year`
- `Balance ID`
- `Balance Period`

Any obsolete balances in the tables for the `Company` and `Balance ID` that were before (or equal to) the period defined by the `Balance Year` and `Balance Period` will be removed. All five tables will be checked and updated where necessary.

33.1.2 A simple modification

Let's say that I would like to have the ability to delete balances from all of the tables (as delivered) OR only one of the tables if I so choose. To accomplish this, I'm going to add the field `RECNAME` to the Run Control record. If no `recname` is specified on the Run Control panel, then all five tables will be processed. If the `RECNAME` is not blank, then I'll only process the record specified. The valid values are `CHECK_YTD`, `EARNINGS_BAL`, `DEDUCTION_BAL`, `GARN_BALANCE`, and `TAX_BALANCE`.

If a value is entered that is not blank or not one of these five tables, an error message should be produced and the process halted.

Please note that we'll skip the steps to add the `RECNAME` field to the Run Control record and panel. A full description of adding fields to records and panels using Application Designer has been given earlier in this book. We'll assume these changes have been implemented during our modification example.

33.2 MAKING OUR MODIFICATIONS

Let's take a look at the AA000-MAIN section following the PROCEDURE DIVISION. This is where the routine for each individual table is unconditionally called and will be one of the sections we'll modify. Before each of these routines is performed, we're going to test the `RECNAME` parameter passed on the Run Control record. If it is blank or matches the tablename, then the routine will be performed:

```
/*****************************************************************
*                                                               *
  PROCEDURE DIVISION.
*                                                               *
******************************************************************
*                                                               *
  AA000-MAIN SECTION.
  AA000.
*                                                               *
```

```
*********************************************************************

        COPY PTCLIBFX.
        COPY PSCVERSN.

        SET PAYROLL-STEP-DLTBALNC OF PSLCT  TO   TRUE
        PERFORM DA000-SELECT-RUNCTL

        ACCEPT TIME-OUT OF W-WK  FROM  TIME
        INSPECT TIME-OUT OF W-WK CONVERTING SPACE TO ':'
        INSPECT TIME-OUT OF W-WK CONVERTING '/' TO '.'
        DISPLAY 'Delete Balances started for Company: '
             COMPANY OF S-RUNCTL
        DISPLAY '                    Calendar Year: '
             BALANCE-YEAR  OF S-RUNCTL
        DISPLAY '                         Month: '
             BALANCE-PERIOD OF S-RUNCTL
        DISPLAY ' at ' TIME-OUT OF W-WK '.'

        PERFORM GA000-PURGE-CHECK-YTD
        PERFORM IA000-PURGE-EARNINGS-BAL
        PERFORM KA000-PURGE-DEDUCTION-BAL        Each PURGE routine is
        PERFORM MA000-PURGE-GARN-BALANCE         called unconditionally
        PERFORM OA000-PURGE-TAX-BALANCE
        PERFORM SA000-TERM

        COPY PSCRTNCD.

        .
    MAIN-EXIT.
        STOP RUN.
```

Let's also take a look at the working storage area used when selecting data from the Run Control record:

```
/*******************************************************************
*           PAY_DBAL_RUNCTL BUFFER AND STMT                       *
*******************************************************************
 01  S-RUNCTL.
     02   SQL-STMT               PIC X(18)    VALUE
                                              'PSPDLBAL_S_RUNCTL'.

     02   BIND-SETUP.
          03   FILLER            PIC X(8)     VALUE ALL 'C'.
          03   FILLER            PIC X(30)    VALUE ALL 'H'.
          03   FILLER            PIC X        VALUE 'Z'.

     02   BIND-DATA.
          03   OPRID             PIC X(8).
          03   BATCH-RUN-ID      PIC X(30).
```

```
      03   FILLER                PIC X       VALUE 'Z'.

02   SELECT-SETUP.
      03   FILLER                PIC X(10)   VALUE ALL 'C'.
      03   FILLER                PIC XX      VALUE ALL 'H'.
      03   FILLER                PIC XX      VALUE ALL 'S'.
      03   FILLER                PIC XX      VALUE ALL 'M'.
      03   FILLER                PIC X       VALUE 'Z'.

02   SELECT-DATA.
      03   COMPANY               PIC X(10).
      03   BALANCE-ID            PIC XX.
      03   BALANCE-YEAR          PIC 9999              COMP.
      03   BALANCE-PERIOD        PIC 999               COMP.
      03   FILLER                PIC X       VALUE 'Z'.
```

Take a close look at the Select Setup and Data areas as presented. We need to modify both of these areas to accept our new field RECNAME. Let's do it now:

```
/********************************************************************
*            PAY_DBAL_RUNCTL BUFFER AND STMT                       *
********************************************************************
01  S-RUNCTL.
    02   SQL-STMT               PIC X(18)   VALUE
                                            'PSPDLBAL_S_RUNCTL'.

    02   BIND-SETUP.
         03   FILLER            PIC X(8)    VALUE ALL 'C'.
         03   FILLER            PIC X(30)   VALUE ALL 'H'.
         03   FILLER            PIC X       VALUE 'Z'.

    02   BIND-DATA.
         03   OPRID             PIC X(8).
         03   BATCH-RUN-ID      PIC X(30).
         03   FILLER            PIC X       VALUE 'Z'.

    02   SELECT-SETUP.
         03   FILLER            PIC X(10)   VALUE ALL 'C'.       RECNAME
         03   FILLER            PIC XX      VALUE ALL 'H'.       picture string
         03   FILLER            PIC XX      VALUE ALL 'S'.       added to
         03   FILLER            PIC XX      VALUE ALL 'M'.       Select
         03   FILLER            PIC X(15)   VALUE ALL 'C'.  ⊲  Setup list
         03   FILLER            PIC X       VALUE 'Z'.

    02   SELECT-DATA.
         03   COMPANY           PIC X(10).
         03   BALANCE-ID        PIC XX.
         03   BALANCE-YEAR      PIC 9999              COMP.      RECNAME
         03   BALANCE-PERIOD    PIC 999               COMP.      added to Select
         03   RECNAME           PIC X(15).                  ⊲  Data list
         03   FILLER            PIC X       VALUE 'Z'.
```

The preceding example shows the changes we've made to the Select Setup and Data area. The RECNAME field length is fifteen characters. We've added the string 'CCCCCCCCCCCCCCC' as filler to the setup list. We've also added the field RECNAME to the data list. We're now ready to accept the additional parameter RECNAME on the Run Control record. We still have one important step to complete if we're going to pass an additional Run Control parameter. We need to update the DMS script to select the new field:

```
STORE PSPDLBAL_S_RUNCTL
SELECT
 COMPANY
,BALANCE_ID
,BALANCE_YEAR
,BALANCE_PERIOD
FROM PS_PAY_DBAL_RUNCTL
WHERE OPRID=:1
  AND RUN_CNTL_ID=:2
```

Now we can see the portion of the DMS script in its delivered form. We still need to add the new RECNAME column to the select list. It needs to be the last field contained in the SELECT list so it matches the order used in the Select Setup and Data areas in working storage. Let's change it now:

```
STORE PSPDLBAL_S_RUNCTL
SELECT
COMPANY
,BALANCE_ID
,BALANCE_YEAR
,BALANCE_PERIOD         RECNAME column added
,RECNAME            ◁┘  to SELECT list
FROM PS_PAY_DBAL_RUNCTL
WHERE OPRID=:1
  AND RUN_CNTL_ID=:2
```

We can see that the new column RECNAME has been added to the end of the Select list in the DMS script. Data Mover should be used to execute the DMS script so the stored SQL statement table will have the modified version of the SQL statement. Let's now make some programming changes to the delivered process:

Listing 33.1

Main section of PSPDLBAL.cbl after modifications

```
/*****************************************************************
*                                                               *
  PROCEDURE DIVISION.
*                                                               *
 *****************************************************************
```

```
*                                                                          *
 AA000-MAIN SECTION.
 AA000.
*                                                                          *
********************************************************************

     COPY PTCLIBFX.
     COPY PSCVERSN.

     SET PAYROLL-STEP-DLTBALNC OF PSLCT    TO    TRUE
     PERFORM DA000-SELECT-RUNCTL

     ACCEPT TIME-OUT OF W-WK    FROM    TIME
     INSPECT TIME-OUT OF W-WK CONVERTING SPACE TO ':'
     INSPECT TIME-OUT OF W-WK CONVERTING '/' TO '.'
     DISPLAY 'Delete Balances started for Company: '
             COMPANY OF S-RUNCTL
     DISPLAY '                      Calendar Year: '
             BALANCE-YEAR   OF S-RUNCTL
     DISPLAY '                             Month: '
             BALANCE-PERIOD OF S-RUNCTL
     DISPLAY ' at ' TIME-OUT OF W-WK '.'

*    Modification - Validate RECNAME Parameter

     IF   RECNAME OF S-RUNCTL NOT EQUAL SPACE
     AND RECNAME OF S-RUNCTL NOT EQUAL 'CHECK_YTD'
     AND RECNAME OF S-RUNCTL NOT EQUAL 'EARNINGS_BAL'
     AND RECNAME OF S-RUNCTL NOT EQUAL 'DEDUCTION_BAL'
     AND RECNAME OF S-RUNCTL NOT EQUAL 'GARN_BALANCE'
     AND RECNAME OF S-RUNCTL NOT EQUAL 'TAX_BALANCE'

         DISPLAY 'Invalid RECNAME: '
                 RECNAME OF S-RUNCTL
         MOVE 'MAIN(RECNAME)' TO ERR-SECTION OF SQLRT
         PERFORM ZZ000-SQL-ERROR

     END-IF

*    Modification - Conditionally perform each routine

     IF RECNAME OF S-RUNCTL = SPACE
     OR RECNAME OF S-RUNCTL = 'CHECK_YTD'
        PERFORM GA000-PURGE-CHECK-YTD
     END-IF

     IF RECNAME OF S-RUNCTL = SPACE
     OR RECNAME OF S-RUNCTL = 'EARNINGS_BAL'
        PERFORM IA000-PURGE-EARNINGS-BAL
     END-IF

     IF RECNAME OF S-RUNCTL = SPACE
```

Simple validation routine added. If RECNAME **is not one of six valid values, an error message is produced, and the process is halted.**

```
      OR RECNAME OF S-RUNCTL = 'DEDUCTION_BAL'
         PERFORM KA000-PURGE-DEDUCTION-BAL
      END-IF

      IF RECNAME OF S-RUNCTL = SPACE
      OR RECNAME OF S-RUNCTL = 'GARN_BALANCE'
         PERFORM MA000-PURGE-GARN-BALANCE
      END-IF

      IF RECNAME OF S-RUNCTL = SPACE
      OR RECNAME OF S-RUNCTL = 'TAX_BALANCE'
         PERFORM OA000-PURGE-TAX-BALANCE
      END-IF

      PERFORM SA000-TERM

      COPY PSCRTNCD.

           .
   MAIN-EXIT.
      STOP RUN.
```

Conditional logic has been added to control the execution of each of the five purge routines. They will be performed if the `RECNAME` is not entered (`SPACE`) or matches the table updated by each particular routine.

Consider the programming modifications we've implemented. The changes, although not elegant by any means, effectively produce the results we want. The validation of the RECNAME parameter could have been performed within the DA000-Select-Runctl section. We placed this validation within the AA000-Main section to keep things simple. After all, the focus of this exercise is on accessing an additional field in the database, not on creating the ideal placement of standard COBOL code.

A series of simple IF statements controls the execution of each of the Purge routines. As you can see, the changes required to access the new field RECNAME have been minimal. Let's review the basic steps required to implement our change:

1 Add RECNAME field to the Run Control record and panel using Application Designer.

2 Add RECNAME column to the Select list in the DMS script. Run Data Mover to update the stored SQL statement table with the new version of the SQL statement.

3 Update the Select Setup and Data areas in the working storage section to accept the new RECNAME parameter.

4 Add any required programming logic that utilizes the new RECNAME field. In our example, this includes validating parameters along with controlling the balance updates using the new parameter.

33.2.1   One important note

Because of PeopleSoft's structured technique, it isn't necessary to modify the routine that actually selects the Run Control information. In our example, this routine is called DA000-Select-Runctl. The only modification required within the program to accept an additional field is to the Select Setup and Select Data areas. Because the call to PTPSQLRT uses both Select Setup and Select Data as input parameters, the new field automatically is included. Let's look at the Run Control access routine:

Listing 33.2

DA000-SELECT-RUNCTL section (no modifications required)

```
/*********************************************************************
*                                                                    *
 DA000-SELECT-RUNCTL SECTION.
 DA000.
*                                                                    *
 *********************************************************************

     CALL 'PTPSQLRT' USING    ACTION-CONNECT OF SQLRT
                              SQLRT
                              SQL-CURSOR-COMMON OF SQLRT
     IF RTNCD-ERROR OF SQLRT

        MOVE 'SELECT-RUNCTL(CONNECT)'  TO  ERR-SECTION OF SQLRT
        PERFORM ZZ000-SQL-ERROR
     END-IF

     IF PROCESS-INSTANCE OF SQLRT  NOT =  ZERO

        PERFORM DB000-SET-RUN-STAT-PROCESSING
        MOVE PROCESS-INSTANCE OF SQLRT
                  TO   PROCESS-INSTANCE-ERRMSG OF PSLCT
     ELSE

        CALL 'PTPRUNID' USING    SQLRT
                                 PROCESS-INSTANCE-ERRMSG
                                     OF W-PRC-INSTANCE
        MOVE PROCESS-INSTANCE-ERRMSG OF W-PRC-INSTANCE
                  TO   PROCESS-INSTANCE-ERRMSG OF PSLCT
     END-IF

     MOVE OPRID OF SQLRT  TO  OPRID OF S-RUNCTL
     MOVE BATCH-RUN-ID OF SQLRT  TO  BATCH-RUN-ID OF S-RUNCTL

     CALL 'PTPSQLRT' USING    ACTION-SELECT OF SQLRT
                              SQLRT
                              SQL-CURSOR-COMMON OF SQLRT
                              SQL-STMT OF S-RUNCTL
                              BIND-SETUP OF S-RUNCTL
                              BIND-DATA OF S-RUNCTL
                              SELECT-SETUP OF S-RUNCTL
                              SELECT-DATA OF S-RUNCTL

     IF RTNCD-ERROR OF SQLRT
```

RECNAME is added within Select-Setup and Select-Data areas in working storage. RECNAME has been implicitly accounted for in the Select routine.

```
            MOVE 'SELECT-RUNCTL(SELECT)'  TO  ERR-SECTION OF SQLRT
            PERFORM ZZ000-SQL-ERROR
      END-IF

      INITIALIZE SELECT-DATA OF S-RUNCTL

      CALL 'PTPSQLRT' USING   ACTION-FETCH OF SQLRT
                              SQLRT
                              SQL-CURSOR-COMMON OF SQLRT

      IF RTNCD-ERROR OF SQLRT

         IF RTNCD-END OF SQLRT

            DISPLAY 'Delete Balances Run Control Missing.'
            DISPLAY ' for Operator ID  ' OPRID OF S-RUNCTL
            DISPLAY ' and Batch Run ID ' BATCH-RUN-ID OF S-RUNCTL
            SET RTNCD-USER-ERROR OF SQLRT  TO  TRUE
            PERFORM ZZ000-SQL-ERROR
         ELSE
            MOVE 'SELECT-RUNCTL(FETCH)'  TO  ERR-SECTION OF SQLRT
            PERFORM ZZ000-SQL-ERROR
         END-IF
      ELSE
         PERFORM DD000-RUNCTL-ACCEPTED
      END-IF


  SELECT-RUNCTL-EXIT.
```

■

1 Modifying the delivered COBOL process to accept an additional Run Control parameter requires:

- defining the modification requirements
- modifying the DMS script to include our new Run Control field in the `Select` statement, and once modified, loading the new Run Control field into the SQL statement table using Data Mover.
- adding our new Run Control field to both the `Select Setup` and `Select Data` areas.
- placing logic in the Main section of the COBOL program, which determines which `Purge` routines to execute based on the contents of our new Run Control field.
- no explicit coding is required in the procedure to select the Run Control parameters. The routine itself requires no modifications due to the methodology used by PeopleSoft.

C H A P T E R   3 4

Additional topics

Chapters 32 and 33 described the key aspect of PeopleSoft's particular flavor of COBOL: the manner in which the database is accessed. Numerous books have been written about the COBOL language itself. When you purchase the MicroFocus compiler, you receive documentation that may appear to be a small library! While this book does not make any attempt to explain standard COBOL material, we do want to cover some additional topics in COBOL that relate specifically to PeopleSoft.

34.1 PROCESS SCHEDULER API

This section deals with interfacing with the Process Scheduler through PeopleSoft COBOL. When a process is submitted, you can view the job status through Process Monitor. The COBOL program needs to update the run status information on the Process Monitor panel so you will know if the program is processing successfully or if it has encountered an error. To illustrate how the run status information is updated, we'll monitor a COBOL process and point out the code required to update the run status information.

34.1.1 The PTCUSTAT copybook and PTPUSTAT module

The best place to start is with the PTCUSTAT.CBL copybook, which contains the Process Scheduler interface structure. This copybook must exist as an 01-level item in your program.

```
/*******************************************************************
*              PROCESS SCHEDULER REQUEST STATUS INTERFACE          *
*******************************************************************
 01  USTAT.                      COPY PTCUSTAT.
```

The following shows an 01-level item called USTAT that includes the PTCUSTAT copybook:

Let's look at the field definitions that comprise the Process Scheduler interface structure. Values may be assigned to the fields in the copybook. This is how the run information is communicated to the Process Monitor:

```
03  PROCESS-INSTANCE         PIC S9(10)   VALUE ZERO   COMP-3.
03  RUN-STATUS               PIC 9(4)     VALUE ZERO   COMP.
    88  RUN-STATUS-CANCEL                 VALUE 1.
    88  RUN-STATUS-DELETE                 VALUE 2.
    88  RUN-STATUS-ERROR                  VALUE 3.
    88  RUN-STATUS-HOLD                   VALUE 4.
    88  RUN-STATUS-QUEUED                 VALUE 5.
    88  RUN-STATUS-INITIATED              VALUE 6.
    88  RUN-STATUS-PROCESSING             VALUE 7.
    88  RUN-STATUS-CANCELLED              VALUE 8.
    88  RUN-STATUS-SUCCESSFUL             VALUE 9.
    88  RUN-STATUS-UNSUCCESSFUL           VALUE 10.
03  RUN-STATUS-MSGSET        PIC S9(5)    VALUE ZERO   COMP.
    88  MSGSET-PRCS-SCHED                 VALUE 65.
03  RUN-STATUS-MSGID         PIC S9(5)    VALUE ZERO   COMP.
    88  MSGID-SUCCESSFUL                  VALUE 35.
    88  MSGID-UNSUCCESSFUL                VALUE 43.
03  RC                       PIC S9(4)    VALUE ZERO   COMP.
    88  RC-SUCCESSFUL                     VALUE 0.
03  RC-CHAR                  REDEFINES RC
                             PIC X(2).
03  MESSAGE-PARM1            PIC X(30)    VALUE SPACE.
```

```
03  MESSAGE-PARM2              PIC X(30)    VALUE SPACE.
03  MESSAGE-PARM3              PIC X(30)    VALUE SPACE.
03  MESSAGE-PARM4              PIC X(30)    VALUE SPACE.
03  MESSAGE-PARM5              PIC X(30)    VALUE SPACE.
03  CONTINUE-JOB               PIC 9(4)     VALUE ZERO   COMP.
    88  CONTINUE-JOB-NO                     VALUE 0.
    88  CONTINUE-JOB-YES                    VALUE 1.

03  PRUNSTATUS-RC              PIC S9(4)    VALUE ZERO   COMP.
    88  PRUNSTATUS-RC-OK                    VALUE ZERO.

03  CALLING-PROGRAM           PIC X(8)     VALUE SPACE.
    88  CALLED-FROM-PTPUPRCS                VALUE 'PTPUPRCS'.
```

A call to the delivered module PTPUSTAT performs the actual update:

```
INITIALIZE USTAT
MOVE PROCESS-INSTANCE OF SQLRT  TO   PROCESS-INSTANCE OF USTAT
SET RUN-STATUS-PROCESSING OF USTAT  TO   TRUE

CALL 'PTPUSTAT' USING   SQLRT
                        USTAT
```

The sample call displayed sets the run status to 'Processing'. First, the entire interface structure denoted by the 01 group level item USTAT is initialized. The process instance of the current program is then assigned along with the desired run status. The PTPUSTAT module updates the PSPRCSRQST entry for the process instance specified in the PROCESS-INSTANCE field, and Process Monitor displays the information contained in the PSPRCSRQST table.

Let's take a look at the Process Monitor panel after a process has completed.

Figure 34.1 shows the Process Monitor panel after a COBOL process is completed successfully. By double-clicking on the highlighted line, we can examine some additional details about the run.

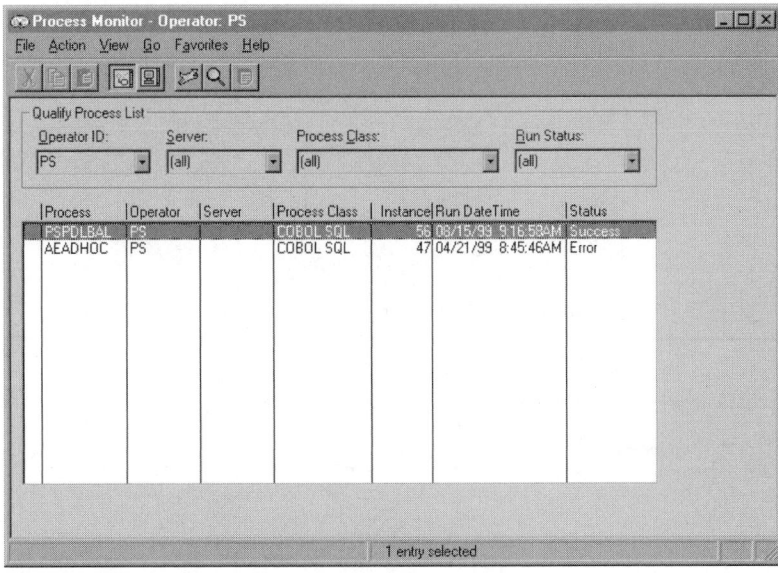

Figure 34.1   The Process Monitor panel

A panel with two folder tabs appears. The first folder tab, called "Process Detail" (figure 34.2), contains information on the run such as operating system, database type, and beginning and ending times.

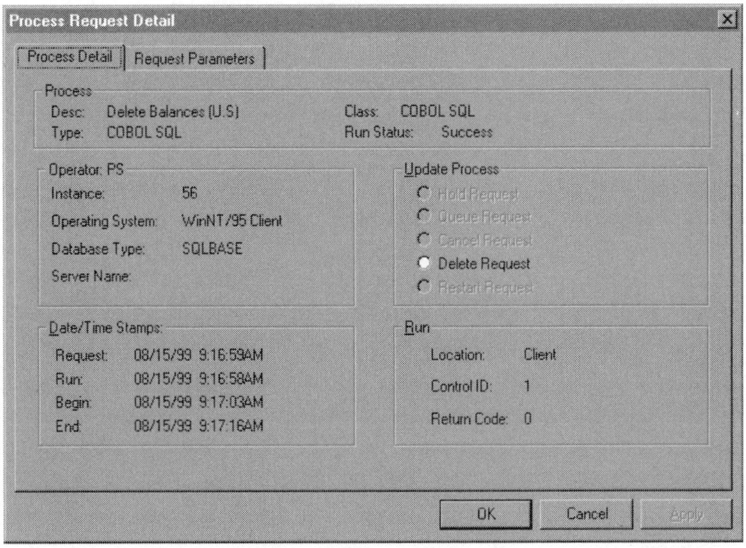

Figure 34.2   The Process Monitor Details folder tab

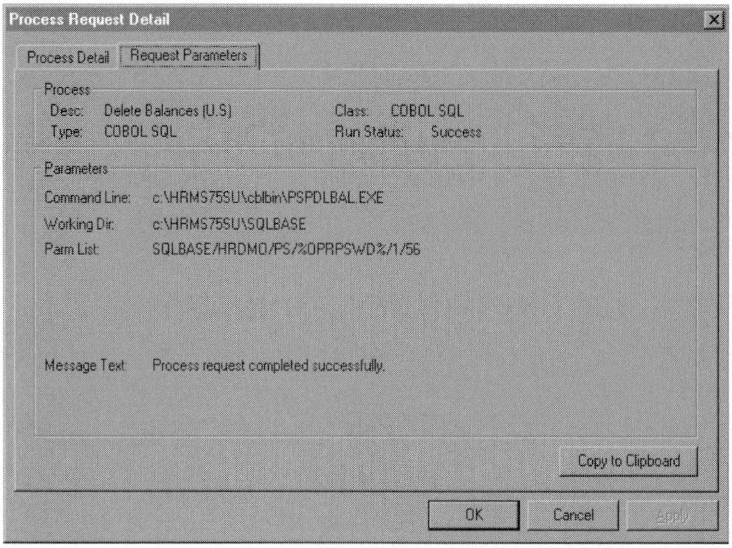

Figure 34.3   The Process Monitor Request Parameters folder tab

The second folder tab, "Request Parameters," displays additional run information such as the COBOL execution string, the working directory, and the parameters passed to the program.

Take special note of the parameter list passed to the COBOL program. It consists of the database type, the database name, the operator ID, the password, the Run Control ID, and the process instance. If a COBOL process is submitted through the process scheduler, a process instance is assigned. If it is submitted outside of PeopleSoft and the Process Scheduler, the process instance is set to zero. A COBOL process can be executed in its native environment through, for example, the MS-DOS prompt or Unix command line. In that case, the parameters are entered by the user through a series of prompts. The process instance may be entered if you are restarting an aborted COBOL process. Otherwise, the default of zero is used. Before any updates to the Process Monitor are made, the process instance needs to be interrogated to determine if the Process Monitor is being utilized.

```
IF PROCESS-INSTANCE OF SQLRT  NOT =  ZERO

    PERFORM SD000-SET-RUN-STAT-SUCCESSFUL
END-IF
```

If the process instance does not equal zero, then any updates to the run information may be executed. The preceeding code performs the `SD000-SET-RUN-STAT-SUCCESSFUL` only if a valid process instance is used.

Let's take a look at a real life example. Once again, we'll use the process to delete obsolete payroll balances called PSPDLBAL.

34.1.2   A real life example

We're going to execute the COBOL process to delete obsolete payroll balances. We'll fill in the required Run Control parameters first.

Once the Run Control panel is set with the parameters (figure 34.4), it is then saved. Click on the Traffic Light to initiate the run request.

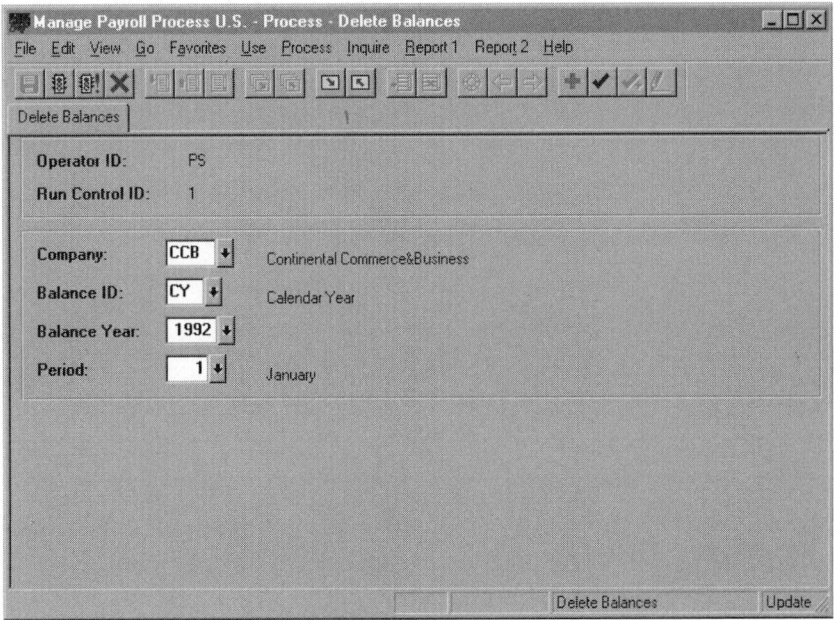

Figure 34.4   Setting the Run Control parameters

The Process Request screen appears (figure 34.5). Select the correct process from the attached list (in our case, the U.S. balance process). If the Run Location and Output Destination are correct, click the OK button to execute the PSPDLBAL process.

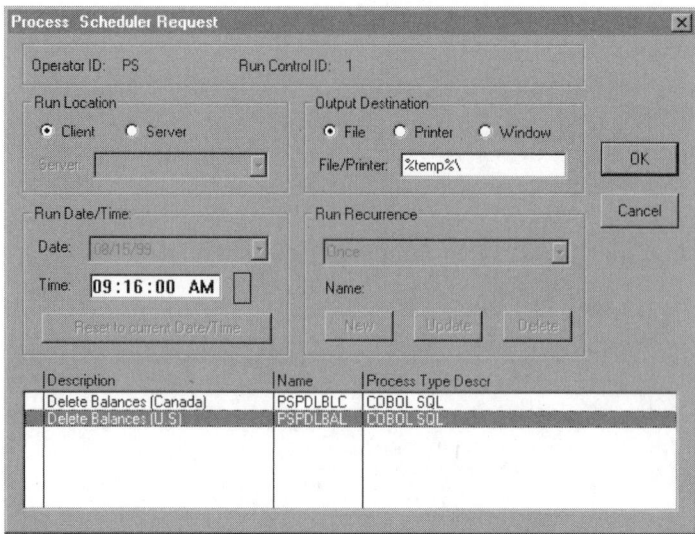

Figure 34.5   Executing a Process Scheduler request

If we were to immediately view the Process Monitor screen, we would see the status is set to 'Initiated' (figure 34.6), the default status before the COBOL program has started. Once the COBOL process takes over, it should set the run status to 'Processing'.

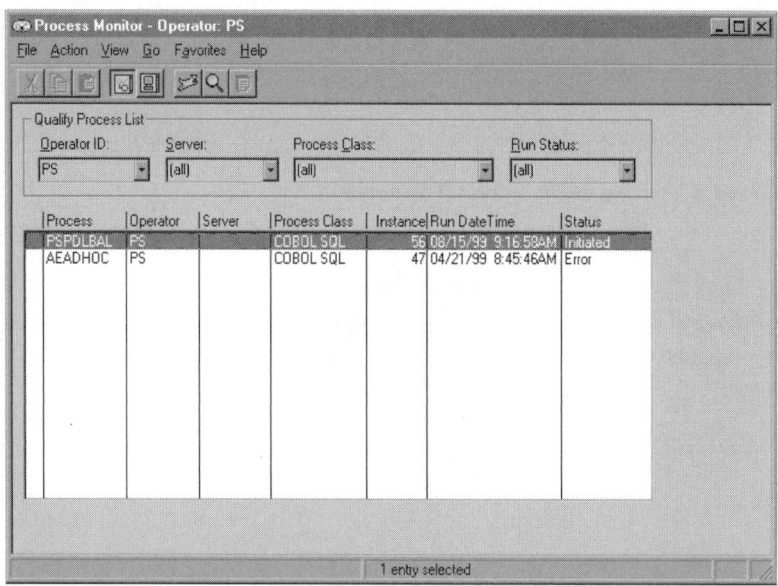

Figure 34.6   PSPDLBAL process in Initiated phase

CHAPTER 34   ADDITIONAL TOPICS

The run status shown in figure 34.7 is now set to `Processing`. This was controlled by the COBOL process by changing the Run Status field and calling the PTPUSTAT module.

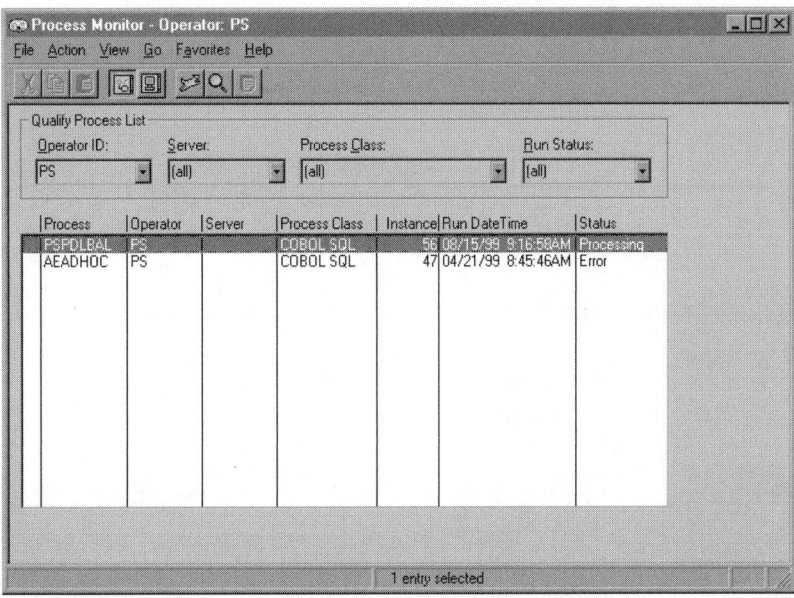

Figure 34.7   PSPDLBAL status moved to Processing

Let's look at a common method of determining whether the process was run through Process Scheduler. If not, an alternate method is used to select the Run Control parameters.

```
IF PROCESS-INSTANCE OF SQLRT  NOT =  ZERO

    PERFORM DB000-SET-RUN-STAT-PROCESSING
    MOVE PROCESS-INSTANCE OF SQLRT
            TO  PROCESS-INSTANCE-ERRMSG OF PSLCT
ELSE

    CALL 'PTPRUNID' USING   SQLRT
                            PROCESS-INSTANCE-ERRMSG
                                OF W-PRC-INSTANCE
    MOVE PROCESS-INSTANCE-ERRMSG OF W-PRC-INSTANCE
            TO  PROCESS-INSTANCE-ERRMSG OF PSLCT
END-IF
```

Now, let's look at the steps required to set the run status to `Processing`. First, the USTAT interface area is initialized. This must be done the first time *only*. The Process

Instance and Run Status fields are assigned. A call to PTPUSTAT is performed followed by the appropriate error handling.

```
INITIALIZE USTAT
MOVE PROCESS-INSTANCE OF SQLRT  TO  PROCESS-INSTANCE OF USTAT
SET RUN-STATUS-PROCESSING OF USTAT  TO  TRUE

CALL 'PTPUSTAT' USING    SQLRT
                         USTAT
IF RTNCD-ERROR OF SQLRT

    MOVE 'SET-RUN-STAT-PROCESSING(PTPUSTAT)'
         TO  ERR-SECTION OF SQLRT
    PERFORM ZZ000-SQL-ERROR
END-IF
```

Figure 34.8 shows the MS-DOS box that appears while the program is running. This may appear for only a few seconds if there isn't much processing to be performed. Any DISPLAY commands in the COBOL program will appear here.

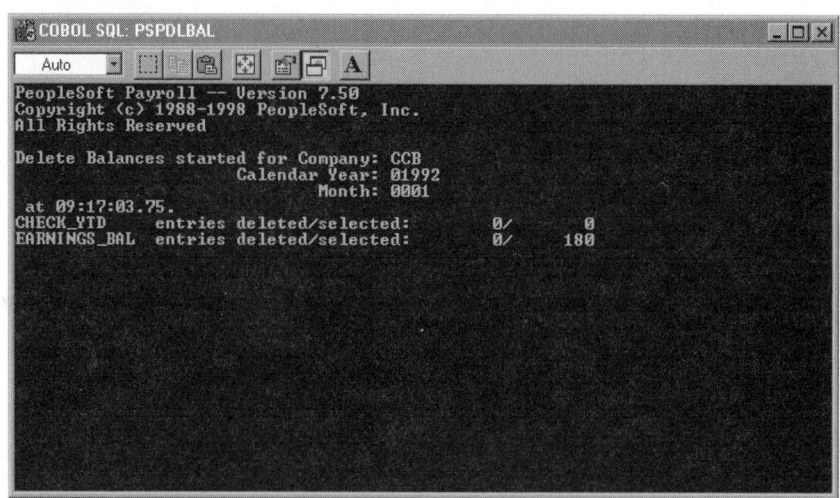

Figure 34.8 PSPDLBAL process executing (MS-DOS Box)

Looking at the Run Status field in figure 34.9, you can see our process ended successfully. Note the process below PSPDLBAL had some problems. The status has been set to Error.

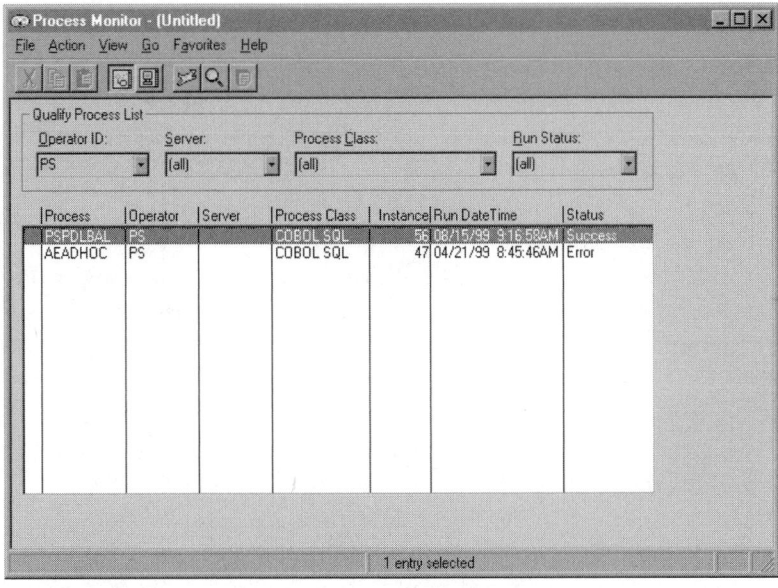

Figure 34.9   Viewing the results using Process Monitor

The following code sets the run status to `'Success'`. First the new Run Status field is assigned, then the PTPUSTAT module performs the update.

```
SET RUN-STATUS-SUCCESSFUL OF USTAT   TO   TRUE

CALL 'PTPUSTAT' USING   SQLRT
                        USTAT
IF RTNCD-ERROR OF SQLRT

    MOVE 'SET-RUN-STAT-SUCCESSFUL(PTPUSTAT)'
         TO   ERR-SECTION OF SQLRT
    PERFORM ZZ000-SQL-ERROR
END-IF
```

The following code sets the run status to `'Error'`. Once again, the new run status is set and the call to PTPUSTAT performs the update.

```
SET RUN-STATUS-ERROR OF USTAT   TO   TRUE

CALL 'PTPUSTAT' USING   SQLRT
                        USTAT
IF RTNCD-ERROR OF SQLRT

    MOVE 'SET-RUN-STAT-ERROR(PTPUSTAT)'
         TO   ERR-SECTION OF SQLRT
    PERFORM ZZ000-SQL-ERROR
END-IF
```

34.2 USING TRACE FILES

Ultimately, the goal of updating the Process Status is to enable the user to monitor the progress of their application. This is a very high-level method of monitoring. To actually determine what is happening within the program, a trace file may be generated. This is used primarily by the technical staff to debug problems or perform performance-tuning functions. Some highly skilled functional or "power" users may also use trace files to become more familiar with processes.

Configuration Manager is a PeopleTool that allows you to update PeopleSoft registry entries. Updates are made through a GUI interface that is much easier to use than the Windows Registry editor (regedit). A series of folder tabs groups each set of entries by category or function. Some of these include Startup, Process Scheduler, and Client Setup parameters. Trace settings may be turned on using Configuration Manager.

Click on the Trace folder tab to designate the desired tracing level. Three sections exist within the Trace panel: One section controls trace settings for PeopleCode; another controls the Message Agent trace; the third group of Trace settings, under the label "SQL Trace," controls the Trace settings for online activity and COBOL processes. Online activity is defined as all SQL activity generated by the Panel Processor. We're interested in the COBOL Trace settings. The checkboxes indicate the Trace level combinations you would like to use.

You can see the Configuration Manager trace settings in figure 34.10. Notice the Online Trace File edit box. Normally, this is used to redirect your trace file output. COBOL trace file output cannot be redirected using this field.

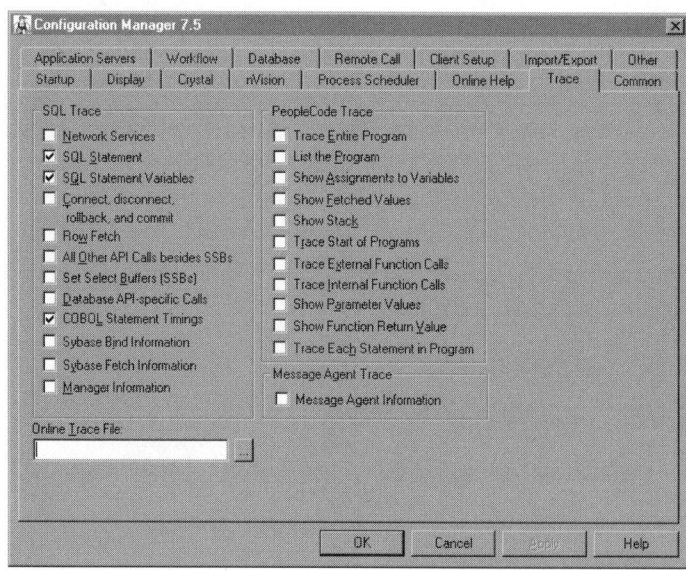

Figure 34.10   Configuration Manager trace settings

The COBOL trace file is written to the following directory:

For Windows: `%TEMP%\ps\<database_name>`
For Unix: `$PS_HOME/log/<database_name>`

The filename has the following format:

COBSQL[_progname]{_processinstance | _MMDDHHMMSS}.TRC

Depending on the COBOL process, the trace filename may vary. Special coding exists in each program that dictates the trace filename to use. The sample COBOL process we've been using (PSPDLBAL) writes the trace file as COBSQL_<process_instance>.TRC when run through Process Scheduler. When it is executed outside of PeopleSoft (MS-DOS prompt), it uses the format COBSQL_<MMDDHHMMSS>.TRC since no process instance is provided.

34.2.1 Trace settings

Each trace setting checkbox has a unique value. The combination of selected trace setting values are added and stored in the windows registry via Configuration Manager. Let's take a closer look at the trace values and how they are stored.

Table 34.1 SQL Trace values

Trace function	Decimal value	Binary value
SQL statement	1	0000 0000 0000 0001
SQL statement Variables	2	0000 0000 0000 0010
Connect, Disconnect, Rollback and Commit	4	0000 0000 0000 0100
Row Fetch	8	0000 0000 0000 1000
All other API calls besides SSBs	16	0000 0000 0001 0000
Set Select Buffers (SSBs)	32	0000 0000 0010 0000
Database API-specific calls	64	0000 0000 0100 0000
COBOL statement timings	128	0000 0000 1000 0000
Sybase Bind information	256	0000 0001 0000 0000
Sybase Fetch information	512	0000 0010 0000 0000
N/A	1024	0000 0100 0000 0000
Network services	2048	0000 1000 0000 0000
Manager information	4096	0001 0000 0000 0000

The individual trace setting values are shown in table 34.1. For each trace level, the decimal value and binary equivalent are presented. When your trace settings are applied, the values are added and stored in the Windows Registry.

The registry address (or key) is

My Computer\HKEY_CURRENT_USER\Software\PeopleSoft\
PeopleTools\Release7.5\Trace

The registry field (or subkey) is:

```
TraceSQL
```

Let's take a look at the Windows Registry after we apply the trace settings used in figure 34.10. In this particular example, we have selected the checkboxes to turn on the SQL statement, SQL statement variable, and COBOL statement timing levels. The corresponding values for these are 1, 2, and 128. The TraceSQL registry field (also referred to as a subkey) contains the total value of the selected checkboxes, which is 131 (1 + 2 + 128).

Using the Windows Registry Editor (regedit.exe), we can open the PeopleSoft Configuration Manager key and look at the TraceSQL subkey contents. The Registry Editor can be found in the Windows directory. Notice the key value in the Registry Editor window on the bottom of the screen. This is the full path key that leads to the TraceSQL subkey. You can see it contains the total of the selected trace values (131). The data in the subkey is displayed as a hexadecimal value (x'83') with the decimal equivalent in parentheses. Take special caution when using the Windows Registry editor. Incorrectly set values or transferred subkeys may cause serious problems with the Windows operating system.

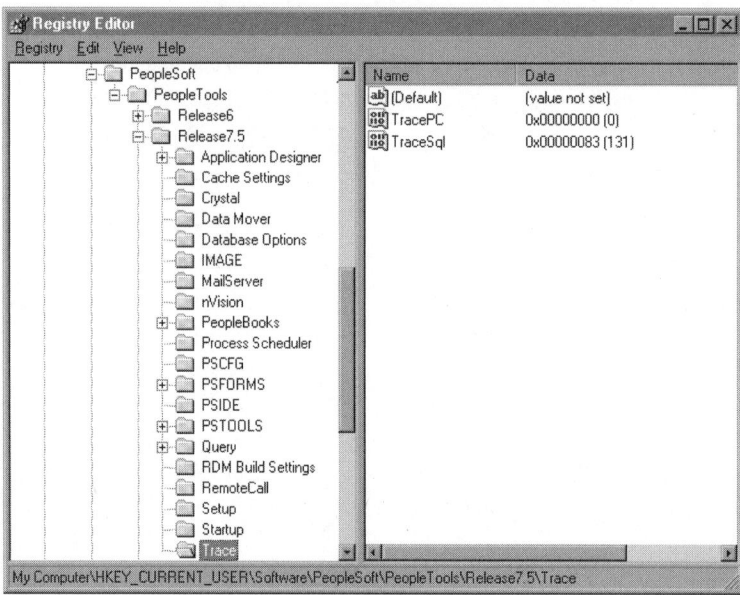

Figure 34.11   PeopleSoft registry entries

34.2.2 Tracing a COBOL process

Now let's see the COBOL Trace in action. We'll trace the PSPDLBAL process we've been using throughout this chapter (Delete Obsolete Balances). We'll use the same trace values as shown in figure 34.10 (SQL statement, SQL statement variable, and COBOL statement timings). Since we've already set these, we can move directly to the Run Control panel and initiate the process.

Once we fill in the parameters for our run (figure 34.12), we click on the Traffic Light to initiate the process. The COBOL process detects that the trace levels have been set through the Windows Registry subkey `TraceSQL` and produces the trace file in the default directory.

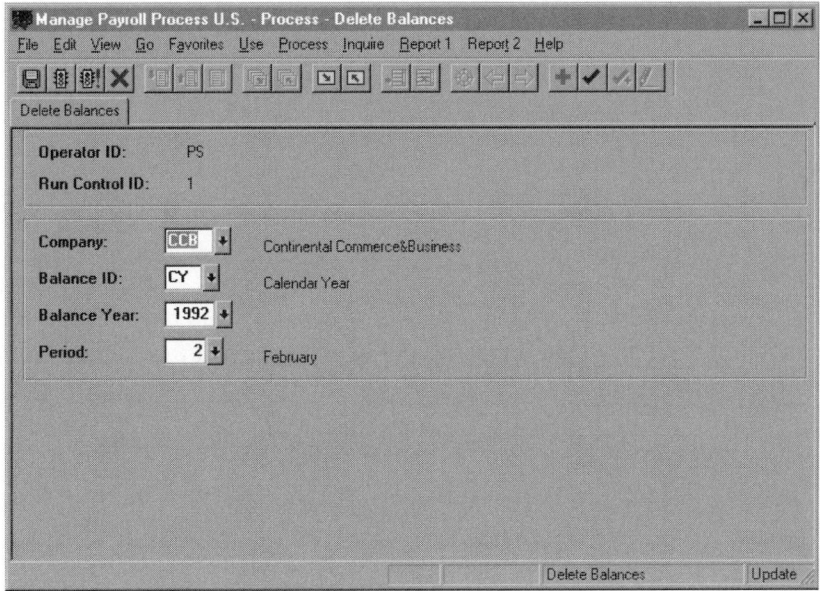

Figure 34.12   Setting the Run Control parameters

Figure 34.13 displays the results on the Process Monitor. Our run was successful. The process instance for our run was `61`. Let's take a look at the trace file generated during this run.

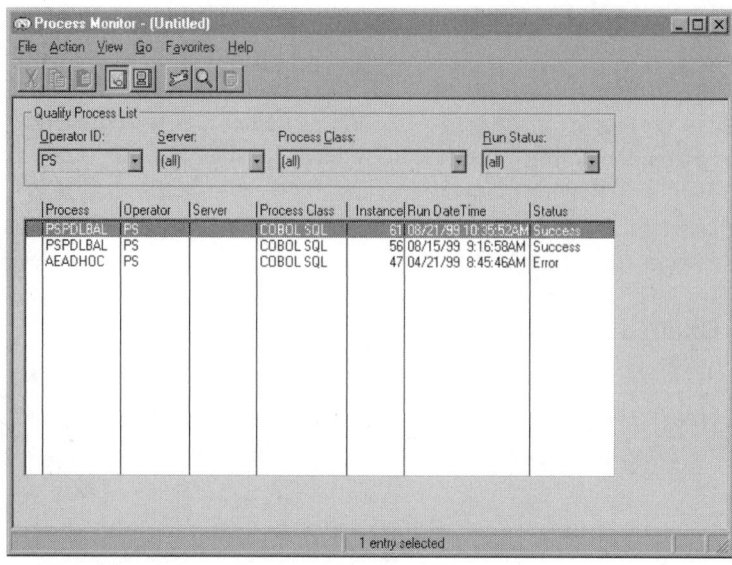

Figure 34.13   The process PSPDLBAL has ended successfully

Figure 34.14 shows the COBOL trace file as it appears in Windows Explorer. The directory is C:\WINDOWS\TEMP\PS\HRDMO, and the trace filename is COBSQL_61.TRC. This adheres to the naming conventions we spoke of earlier.

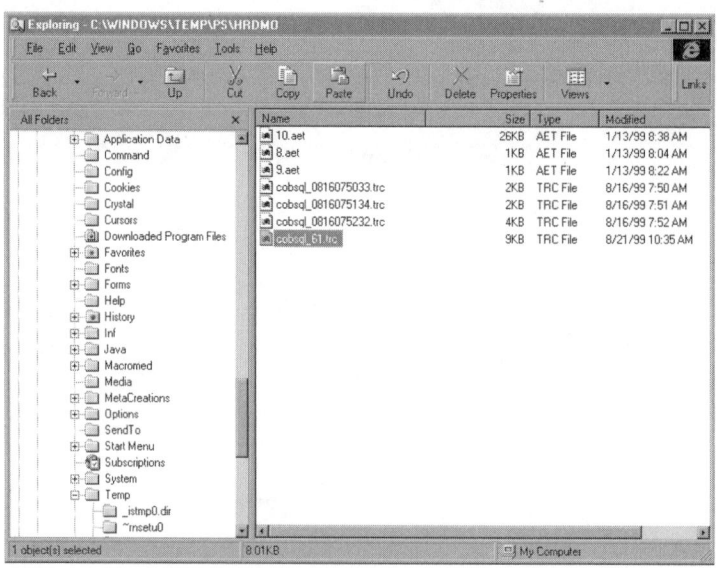

Figure 34.14   Locating the COBOL trace file

34.2.3   Examining the trace file contents

We can view the trace file contents using an editor or word processor. Let's take a look at the trace output now.

Since our trace file is relatively small, we can open and view it using Notepad (figure 34.15). Take a look at the highlighted area. The first highlighted line shows the word GETSTMT followed by the stored SQL statement retrieved by the PTPSQLRT module. The name of it is PSPDLBAL_D_RUNCTL. Once retrieved, the next line displays the SQL statement text to be compiled within the COBOL process. Notice the :1 and :2 bind variables used in the criteria of the SQL statement. The third and fourth highlighted lines show the data used when resolving the :1 and :2 bind variables. If you recall from earlier chapters, the bind variables are defined within the Bind Setup and Bind Data areas for each stored SQL statement called. The :1 bind variable is used for the OPRID which is set to the value 'PS'. The :2 bind variable is used for the RUN_CNTL_ID and has been set to 1. You can verify these values by looking at the Run Control panel in figure 34.12. All other stored SQL statements and the SQL statement variables appear in the trace file. This is because we have specifically checked them using Configuration Manager.

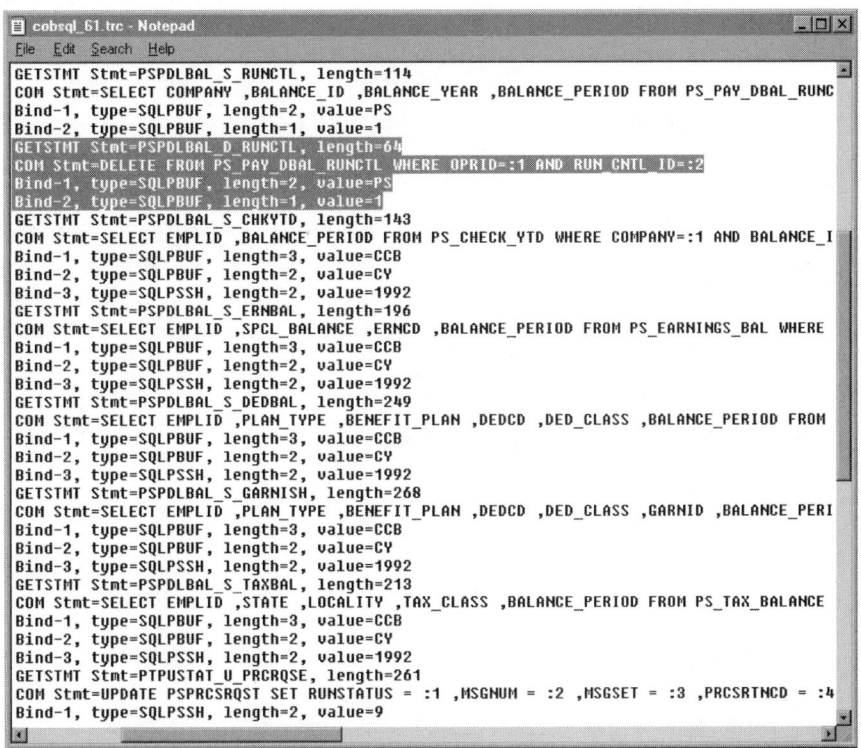

Figure 34.15   Viewing a portion of the trace file

We also selected the COBOL statement timings checkbox. At the end of the trace file, we can see the COBOL statement timings (figure 34.16). The checkbox shows statistics for each stored SQL statement processed by the COBOL program. This can be used for performance tuning functions.

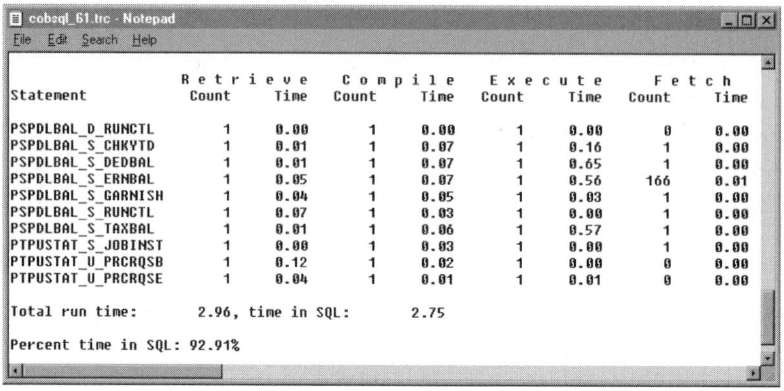

Statement	Retrieve Count	Retrieve Time	Compile Count	Compile Time	Execute Count	Execute Time	Fetch Count	Fetch Time
PSPDLBAL_D_RUNCTL	1	0.00	1	0.00	1	0.00	0	0.00
PSPDLBAL_S_CHKYTD	1	0.01	1	0.07	1	0.16	1	0.00
PSPDLBAL_S_DEDBAL	1	0.01	1	0.07	1	0.65	1	0.00
PSPDLBAL_S_ERNBAL	1	0.05	1	0.07	1	0.56	166	0.01
PSPDLBAL_S_GARNISH	1	0.04	1	0.05	1	0.03	1	0.00
PSPDLBAL_S_RUNCTL	1	0.07	1	0.03	1	0.00	1	0.00
PSPDLBAL_S_TAXBAL	1	0.01	1	0.06	1	0.57	1	0.00
PTPUSTAT_S_JOBINST	1	0.00	1	0.03	1	0.00	1	0.00
PTPUSTAT_U_PRCRQSB	1	0.12	1	0.02	1	0.00	0	0.00
PTPUSTAT_U_PRCRQSE	1	0.04	1	0.01	1	0.01	0	0.00

Total run time: 2.96, time in SQL: 2.75

Percent time in SQL: 92.91%

Figure 34.16 Viewing the COBOL statement timings

NOTE Once you have produced the trace output, make certain you turn off the trace options. If you don't, all subsequent activity will continue to be traced, which can greatly affect performance.

A simple batch program can be written to automatically deactivate the trace options when you restart Windows. Simply place the batch program in the Startup directory on the workstation. Here is an example, using a language called WinBatch (You can find information about WinBatch at http://www.windowware.com):

```
ErrorMode(@OFF)

Rpath = "Software\PeopleSoft\PeopleTools\Release75\Trace"
Rkey  = RegOpenKey(@REGCURRENT, Rpath)
Rerr  = LastError()

if Rerr == 0

   TraceFile = ''
   TracePC   = 0
   TraceSQL  = 0

   RegSetValue(Rkey, "[TraceFile]", TraceFile)
```

```
        RegSetDword(Rkey, "[TraceSQL]",  TraceSQL)
        RegSetDword(Rkey, "[TracePC]",   TracePC)

        RegCloseKey(Rkey)

endif

ErrorMode(@CANCEL)
```

The preceeding sample WinBatch script simply opens the key node of the registry and updates the subkeys with NULL or zeroes. The NULL is used for the `TraceFile` output subkey, and the zeroes will override the SQL Trace (Online/COBOL) and PeopleCode Trace subkey settings. Finally, the key node is closed. When the user signs on to PeopleSoft, the trace values will no longer be set.

34.3 CROSS REFERENCE FILES

PeopleSoft provides Cross-Reference report files, which accompany the delivered COBOL processes and help explain how they work. Some .xrf files list the programs and the modules they call. Others list the stored SQL statements or the database tables referenced by the SQL statements.

An example of a delivered Cross-Reference report is found in figure 34.17. It lists the COBOL processes and a tree listing of the modules called. Notice the highlighted area, which shows the sample COBOL process we have been using (PSPDLBAL). You can see that the PSPDLBAL module called three other modules: PTPRUNID, PTPSQLRT, and PTPUSTAT.

All of the delivered Cross-Reference reports are static. If any COBOL process is modified, they cannot be reproduced to reflect the latest version. The Cross-Reference listings may need to be tracked and updated manually (assuming it is being used as actual documentation for all updates).

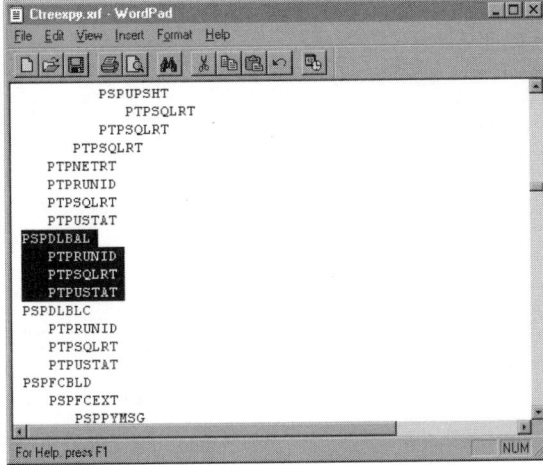

Figure 34.17
Delivered Call Structure
Cross-Reference report

In part 7, "Using Application Engine," we will discuss an SQR utility that can be downloaded and used to flowchart Application Engine programs. The same site contains utilities that produce an updated COBOL Call Structure listing (similar to the static Cross-Reference report) and a utility that flowcharts the actual COBOL perform structure (COBOL Analyzer). Both can be found on the site:

http://www.sqrtools.com.

The COBOL Analyzer produces a nested process flowchart of all the performed sections within a program. This can be extremely useful when looking through some of the larger processes such as those in PeopleSoft Payroll.

Let's look as a sample of the COBOL Analyzer output listing:

```
Report ID:  TDCBL02           COBOL ANALYZER              Page No.  6
                                                  Run Date 06/12/1999
   Program:  c:\src\pipcmpar.cbl                  Run Time 10:26:34
=======================================================================
   Process Flowchart
=======================================================================


       AA000-MAIN
          XA000-LOAD-FILE-DEFN
             <CALL>.PIPUTLTY
             XA100-SET-STOP-DATE
          XW000-GET-START-TIME
          XZ000-GET-CLOCK-TIME
          DA000-BUILD-PARTIC-LIST
          DD000-INSERT-PIPRT
             DE000-SELECT-PARTIC-CURRENT
                ZM000-MESSAGE
                   <CALL>.PSPPYMSG
             DF000-FETCH-PARTIC-CURRENT
                ZM000-MESSAGE <R>
             DG000-SELECT-PARTIC-PRIOR
                ZM000-MESSAGE <R>
             DH000-FETCH-PARTIC-PRIOR
                ZM000-MESSAGE <R>
             DI000-INSERT-PARTIC-DATA
                ZM000-MESSAGE <R>
             DF000-FETCH-PARTIC-CURRENT <R>
```

The first section above is AA000-MAIN. All subsequent sections appear in execution order. If the program is modified, either through customizations or upgrade patches, the analyzer can be run again and a new listing generated.

1 PeopleSoft COBOL programs interface with Process Scheduler using the PTPUSTAT module and the PTCUSTAT copybook. Specific COBOL code is called to update Process Monitor fields.

2 Set the SQL Trace levels using Configuration Manager. The trace values are stored in the Windows Registry. Make sure you turn the trace off when you're done. Since the online panels use the same trace settings as COBOL, system performance can be greatly affected.

3 You can use the trace to view the SQL statements executed along with the resolved bind variable contents. You may use several other trace options when troubleshooting.

4 PeopleSoft delivers Cross-Reference reports for their COBOL processes. You can also find additional downloadable utilities for COBOL processes at http://www.sqrtools.com.

PART 7

Using Application Engine

Application Engine (A/E), a PeopleTool introduced in version 5.0, offers an alternative to conventional structured programming. Application Engine programs are created using a series of online panels which allow you to define your application along with any section, step, and statement components. You can use radio buttons, checkboxes, and drop-down lists to designate execution options in your program. SQL statements are entered on the statement panel in an edit box. All of this information is saved within the database and utilized by the Application Engine driver program PTPEMAIN. Because Application Engine is not an intuitive development tool, we follow our introduction to Application Engine with a "hands-on" approach, presenting a series of exercises in a tutorial designed to illuminate the differences between A/E and conventional structured programming. As a prerequisite to part 7, the user should be well-versed in PeopleTools, particularly Application Designer. A good understanding of SQR programming (as well as SQL) would also be helpful. We end the section with an overview of new Application Engine features in release 8.0.

CHAPTER 35

What is Application Engine?

35.1 ABOUT APPLICATION ENGINE

Application Engine (A/E) is a PeopleTool that allows you to create and execute Batch SQL programs. SQL statements are entered online and processed by the PeopleSoft COBOL program PTPEMAIN. Applications can be broken into smaller pieces called Sections and within these Sections are Steps. Each Step either executes SQL statements, another Section, a COBOL program, or a Mass Change program. In structured programming languages such as SQR, variables are used to store information throughout the life of the program. In Application Engine, a Cache record is used to store values so they may be utilized by subsequent steps in the AE program. As your program proceeds through its Sections/Steps, messages may be written, which are stored in the Message Log tables. These messages may be viewed through the Application Engine Messages panel.

35.2 ADVANTAGES/DISADVANTAGES

Application Engine offers both advantages and disadvantages:

35.2.1   Advantages

- All Application Engine components reside within the database itself. All application development and testing is done within PeopleTools.
- Application Engine programs are considered multi-platform. Database-specific sections can be utilized using a database platform directive that matches your particular installation.
- PeopleSoft Meta-SQL is supported within Application Engine.
- Changes to the PeopleSoft data dictionary are global. No modifications to Application Engine programs are normally required when a field attribute is changed
- Application Engine programs use effective-dating for each section (or procedure). A history of modifications can be easily maintained instead of overlaid.
- Extremely efficient programs can be created using set processing techniques.

35.2.2   Disadvantages

- Application Engine panels are not intuitive: It can be confusing scrolling through a maze of checkboxes, radio buttons, and folder tabs.
- It is difficult to visualize the flow of an Application Engine program. Sections are stored and displayed in alphabetical order in the list box instead of a more logical order.
- Even the simplest of modifications to Application Engine programs can be a harrowing experience. Some more complex programs need to use temporary tables to pass information from one step to another. The dependencies on these temporary tables by other sections need to be carefully analyzed.

35.3 SET PROCESSING CONCEPTS

The most efficient Application Engine programs use set processing techniques whenever possible. In fact, Application Engine was designed with this technique in mind. Large groups of data with the same criteria can be processed at once instead of individually (or row-by-row). Depending on the volume of data processed, set processing can dramatically improve the overall performance of your program.

The set processing SQL concept has been around for many years. It is used extensively when updating the database using native SQL tools such as SQL*Plus or SQL*Talk. Set processing can also be referred to as a mass update. These mass updates may be split into several SQL statements to accommodate different sets of update criteria for each group of data. Let's look at a simplified example of set processing before we move on to Application Engine Basics. We'll use basic SQR routines to demonstrate set processing in comparison to row by row processing.

35.3.1 Set processing vs. row by row processing

For our example, let's assume we have a record called MY_TABLE. Many fields exist in the table including MY_KEY, DEPTID, and ACCT_TYPE. MY_KEY will serve as the unique table key. Also included is a field called BUSINESS_UNIT, which is not populated. Based on the ACCT_TYPE value, we need to perform two different methods of deriving the BUSINESS_UNIT using the DEPTID field.

If the ACCT_TYPE has a value of 'A', BUSINESS_UNIT will be extracted from a table called MY_CONV_A. If ACCT_TYPE has a value of 'B', the BUSINESS_UNIT will be extracted from a table called MY_CONV_B.

35.3.2 Example of row by row processing

First, we'll use the row-by-row processing technique to derive the business unit:

```
...

begin-select

u.my_key
u.deptid
u.acct_type

  let $NEW_business_unit = ''

  if &u.acct_type  = 'A'
     do Select-Conv-A
  else
     do Select-Conv-B
  end-if

  if not isnull($NEW_business_unit)
     do Update-My-Table
  end-if

 from ps_my_table
where u.acct_type in ('A','B')

end-select

...
```

The main Select, as indicated, fetches a row from MY_TABLE one by one. Only rows with ACCT_TYPE of 'A' or 'B' are selected. If ACCT_TYPE is equal to 'A', then the Select-Conv-A routine is performed. If ACCT_TYPE is not equal to 'A', then the Select-Conv-B routine is performed by default. If a BUSINESS_UNIT is found in either of these tables, then the routine Update-My-Table is performed. This process will continue until all rows with ACCT_TYPE equal to 'A' or 'B' have been processed.

Let's look at the `Select-Conv-A` routine. If there is a matching entry in the MY_CONV_A table for the `DEPTID`, then the `$NEW_business_unit` variable will be set to the BUSINESS_UNIT value in the table:

```
begin-procedure Select-Conv-A

begin-select

a.business_unit

 let $NEW_business_unit = &a.business_unit

 from ps_my_conv_a   a
where a.deptid       = &u.deptid

end-select

end-procedure
```

Let's look at the `Select-Conv-B` routine. If there is a matching entry in the MY_CONV_B table for the `DEPTID`, then the `$NEW_business_unit` variable will be set to the BUSINESS_UNIT value in the table:

```
begin-procedure Select-Conv-B

begin-select

b.business_unit

 let $NEW_business_unit = &b.business_unit

 from ps_my_conv_b   b
where b.deptid       = &u.deptid

end-select

end-procedure
```

Finally, let's have a look at the routine that updates MY_TABLE with the new BUSINESS_UNIT value (if a matching entry were found):

```
begin-procedure Update-My-Table

begin-sql

update ps_my_table
   set business_unit = $NEW_business_unit
 where my_key        = &u.my_key

end-sql

end-procedure
```

Depending on the volume of data that will be processed, the row by row approach may be fine. At a minimum, each row selected from MY_TABLE must perform a Select to retrieve the Business Unit. If it exists, an Update statement is performed. Imagine if the number of rows affected by this process were over 100,000. Maybe even 500,000 or more! This means the Select against a conversion table would be executed that many times. The Update routine could potentially execute the same amount of times! That's a lot of database activity that could be avoided! Network traffic, which could yield the greatest degradation in performance, needs to be considered.

We can implement optimization techniques in our row by row processing example to improve performance. For example, we can order the main Select by ACCT_TYPE and DEPTID. We then perform a Conversion Lookup only when a change to one of these fields occurs. We store and utilize the results based on the changing combination of these two fields in our update routine. Even with these improvements, performance can still be poor when processing large amounts of data one row at a time.

35.3.3   Example of set processing

Our set processing example is much simpler and much more efficient. The improvement in performance increases with the volume of transactions processed. Let's perform the set processing Update using the MY_CONV_A table:

```
. . .

begin-sql

update ps_my_table              u
   set u.business_unit          =
       (select z.business_unit
          from ps_my_conv_a      z
         where z.deptid         = u.deptid)
 where u.acct_type              = 'A'
   and exists
       (select 'X'
          from ps_my_conv_a      x
         where x.deptid         = u.deptid);

commit;

end-sql

. . .
```

The WHERE clause limits the Update to all rows in MY_TABLE that have ACCT_TYPE equal to 'A' and an existing entry in the MY_CONV_A table equal to the DEPTID on the row. This one Update statement populates all the rows that match this criteria at once. Now let's perform the set processing `Update` using the MY_CONV_B table:

```
...

begin-sql

update ps_my_table            u
   set u.business_unit         =
       (select z.business_unit
          from ps_my_conv_b     z
          where z.deptid       = u.deptid)
 where u.acct_type            = 'B'
   and exists
       (select 'X'
          from ps_my_conv_b     x
          where x.deptid       = u.deptid);

commit;

end-sql

...
```

The `WHERE` clause limits the `Update` to all rows in MY_TABLE that have an ACCT_TYPE equal to `'B'` and an existing entry in the MY_CONV_B table equal to the DEPTID on the row. This one update statement also populates all the rows that match this particular criteria at once.

TIP   It's a good idea to `COMMIT` frequently during set processing operations. Large amounts of data may be updated at once, causing more system resources to be utilized.

The set processing examples executed two SQL `Updates`. No further database activity was required, and there was no network traffic at all. The `Updates` were entirely at the database level.

Always keep set processing in mind when you're developing with Application Engine, and try to use it whenever possible to achieve the maximum performance in your programs.

35.4 *THE MAIN COMPONENTS OF APPLICATION ENGINE*

Application Engine contains the following main components:

APPLICATION   The highest level of an Application Engine program comprised of one or more sections.

SECTION Equivalent to an SQR procedure or COBOL paragraph comprised of one or more steps. An Application Engine program always begins with a section called MAIN.

STEP Can be considered the actual work component of an Application Engine program. In most cases, it is used to execute an SQL statement or call another section. It can also call a COBOL program or a Mass Change program.

STATEMENTS An SQL statement attached to a step. Several statement types are used to qualify a statement: `Select`, `Update/Insert/Delete`, `DO Select`, `DO When`, `DO Until`, `DO While`, and `Comment`. The `Update/Insert/Delete` statement type is used not only to update the database but also to insert messages into the message log.

35.5 A/E DEFINITION TABLES

All Application Engine development is done within the database itself. Just as a record or panel definition is created and stored in the database, the same can be said of Application Engine. Using the Application Engine panels, the application is defined and stored in an application table. Next a section is defined and stored in the section table. The same occurs for each step and each statement. Four definition tables are used to store Application Engine programs along with the relationship to one another (table 35.1 through table 35.5).

Table 35.1

AE_APPL_TBL	AE_SECTION_TBL	AE_STEP_TBL	AE_STMT_TBL
AE_PRODUCT	AE_PRODUCT	AE_PRODUCT	AE_PRODUCT
AE_APPL_ID	AE_APPL_ID	AE_APPL_ID	AE_APPL_ID
	AE_SECTION	AE_SECTION	AE_SECTION
	DB_PLATFORM	DB_PLATFORM	DB_PLATFORM
	EFFDT	EFFDT	EFFDT
		AE_STEP	AE_STEP
			AE_STMT_TYPE

We will now briefly describe some of the more important fields stored in each of these tables.

Table 35.2

AE_APPL_TBL	Application Definition Table
AE_PRODUCT	Product
AE_APPL_ID	Application Name
AE_VERSION	Version Number

Table 35.2   (continued)

AE_APPL_TBL	Application Definition Table
DESCR	Description
AE_CACHE_RECNAME	Cache Record Name
MESSAGE_SET_NBR	Message Set Number
AE_DEBUG_MODE	Debug Application
AE_TRACE	Trace Application Steps

Table 35.3

AE_SECTION_TBL	Section Definition Table
AE_PRODUCT	Product
AE_APPL_ID	Application Name
AE_SECTION	Section
DB_PLATFORM	Database Platform
EFFDT	Effective Date
EFF_STATUS	Effective Status
DESCR	Description

Table 35.4

AE_STEP_TBL	Step Definition Table
AE_PRODUCT	Product
AE_APPL_ID	Application Name
AE_SECTION	Section
DB_PLATFORM	Database Platform
EFFDT	Effective Date
AE_STEP	Step Name
AE_SEQ_NUM	Step Sequence Number
EFF_STATUS	Effective Status
PROGRAM_NAME	COBOL Program
MC_DEFN_ID	Mass Change Definition
AE_DO_PRODUCT	DO Product
AE_DO_APPLID	DO Application
AE_DO_SECTION	DO Section
AE_SQL_UPDATE	Edit SQL
AE_SQL_SELECT	Select Present
AE_DO_WHEN	When
AE_DO_WHILE	While
AE_DO_UNTIL	Until

Table 35.4   (continued)

AE_STEP_TBL	Step Definition Table
AE_DO_SELECT	Select
AE_SELECT_END_DO	Select Ends the DO
AE_DO_SELECT_TYPE	Type of DO Select

Table 35.5

AE_STMT_TBL	Statement Definition Table
AE_PRODUCT	Product
AE_APPL_ID	Application Name
AE_SECTION	Section
DB_PLATFORM	Database Platform
EFFDT	Effective Date
AE_STEP	Step Name
AE_STMT_TYPE	Statement Type
AE_STMT	SQL Statement

Be aware there is an additional table called AE_STMT_B_TBL, which is a Statement Chunk Table. This is used to store the SQL statements entered in AE_STMT_TBL into smaller pieces or chunks once you save the definitions using the online panels. When an Application Engine program is executed, the chunks are selected and pieced together to form the original statement entered. This alleviates any incompatibility problems using Long datatypes in other databases. The synchronization between the AE_STMT_TBL and AE_STMT_B_TBL may become corrupted. An option does exist on the Application Definition panel which rebuilds the chunked statements. We'll identify this option in the pages ahead. Keep in mind that the breakdown of the SQL statements is done in the background.

As you begin constructing your Application Engine program through the online panels, the fields in each of these tables will be populated based on the selections you make. For example, a statement type of DO When sets the AE_DO_WHEN indicator in the AE_STEP_TBL. You have to fill in the name of your application, sections, and steps along with the descriptions. The statements themselves must also be filled in manually. Most of the remaining options are selected using radio buttons, drop-down lists, and checkboxes.

35.6   A/E DEFINITION PANELS

The Application Engine Definitions for each application, section, step, and statement are entered through a series of panels. You can navigate freely through these panels using the folder tabs at the top or through some strategically placed push buttons. Let's take a look at the panels for each of the A/E categories (figures 35.1-35.4).

35.6.1 Application definition panel

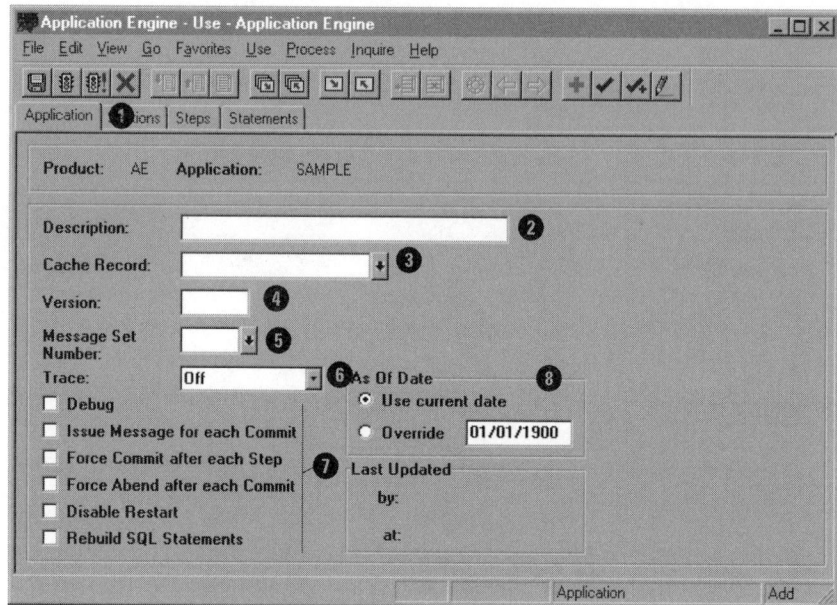

Figure 35.1 Application definition panel

❶ application folder tab, navigates through the four A/E panels

❷ description of application

❸ cache record used by application to store and pass values from one step to another

❹ version number (information only)

❺ default message set number, writes messages as our program progresses

❻ Trace options are used to create a trace file. Options are

Off NO trace file produced

Steps Only Each executed step is displayed on trace file showing time, section, step, and statement type.

SQL In addition to Steps Only, the executed SQL is displayed on the trace file.

Abend Trap Same information on trace file as SQL option. The trace file output is appended to any prior output for the same run rather than creating a new version. This creates a historical trace file that shows when an application prematurely aborted and was restarted.

CHAPTER 35   WHAT IS APPLICATION ENGINE?

❼ Processing checkboxes are used to control the behavior of Application Engine.

> *Debug* puts the application in interactive debugging mode. This allows you to set breakpoints, view the cache record contents, execute one step at a time, and issue commits and rollbacks.
>
> *Issue Message for each commit* writes a message for each executed commit. It is recommended to use the trace option instead due to the volume of messages that may be produced by this feature.
>
> *Force Commit after each step* instructs Application Engine to commit each step as the default method. Each section and step can override this if need be.
>
> *Force Abend after each commit* is used for testing purposes. This is used to test your application restart capability. You can continually execute and restart the application until it is completed. If this cannot be done successfully, the program will need to be corrected.
>
> *Disable Restart* allows you to restart your application from the beginning even if an abend occurs. Under normal circumstances a restart would be required. Use caution when using this option.
>
> *Rebuild SQL Statements* is used to repopulate the Statement Chunk table (AE_STMT_B_TBL). When you create an SQL statement, it is stored in chunks. If you believe your chunked statements are out of sync with the statements entered, you can use this option to rebuild them.

❽ The default date is used when filling in the effective date for each section. Sections are effective-dated. If development is spread out over several days, it's convenient to have the same effective date used when creating each new section.

35.6.2   Section definition panel

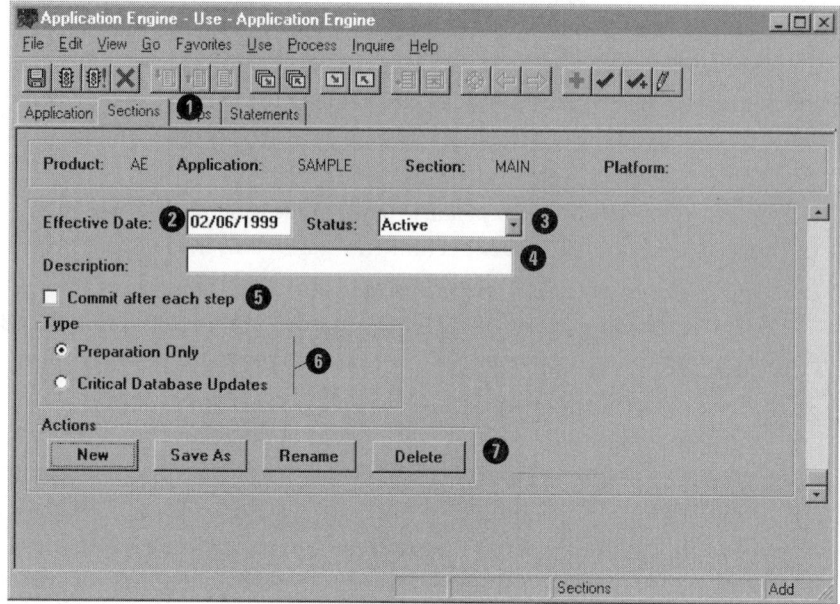

Figure 35.2   Section definition panel

❶ section folder tab, navigates through the four A/E panels

❷ effective date of the section

❸ effective status of the section

❹ description of application

❺ commit after each step within the section (This overrides the default setting.)

❻ Type option, used to designate the type of update being performed by the section

Critical Database Update should be used when a section could affect the integrity of the database in the event of an abend. A restart would be mandatory under these circumstances. Application Engine uses this indicator to update a column called AE_CRITICAL_PHASE in the AE_RUN_CONTROL table. This column will be set to 'Y' and can be used to determine if a restart is necessary.

Preparation Only simply means the section does not perform any critical database updates.

NOTE When trying to determine if a restart is necessary you can't rely totally on the AE_CRITICAL_PHASE indicator. If it is set to 'Y', you should definitely restart. If it does not equal 'Y', you may still need to restart your application. A prior step may have had critical database updates that need to be propagated in subsequent steps not yet executed. Extreme caution should be used to prevent integrity problems.

❼ The action buttons manage your section development:

New adds a new section.

Save As can be used to copy the current section to a new name.

Rename renames the current section.

Delete deletes the current section.

35.6.3 Step definition panel

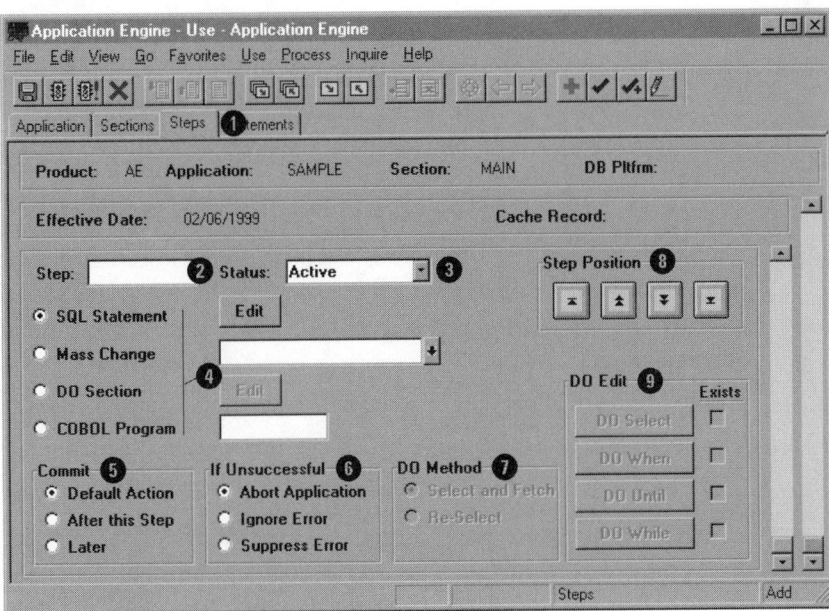

Figure 35.3   Step definition panel

❶ step folder tab, navigates through the four A/E panels

❷ the name of your step

❸ effective status of the step

❹ type of step

SQL Statement is used to perform an SQL or Application Engine statement entered in the Statements Panel. To access the Statements panel, press the SQL Statement Edit push button OR click on the Statement folder tab.

Mass Change allows you to execute a Mass Change program. The Mass Change definition ID can be selected from the drop-down list.

DO Section allows you to call another section. The called section can exist in your current application or an entirely different application. Sections can also be called dynamically at run time. Click on the DO Section Edit push button to access the DO Section properties dialog box. Here you will enter the DO section attributes.

COBOL Program allows a COBOL program to be called.

❺ Commit override attributes for the current step

❻ Error handling instructions

Abort Application performs a rollback and stops the process.

Ignore Error writes a message log entry and continues processing.

Suppress Error continues processing without any messages.

❼ DO Method for DO Select statement types

The *Select and Fetch* method executes the DO Select statement once and fetches the rows one at a time. For each row fetched, the DO section is executed until all the rows have been processed.

The *Re-Select* method executes the DO Select statement and processes the first row fetched. After the first row is fetched, the DO section is executed. Upon returning, the DO Select statement is executed again, and if another row is returned, the DO section is executed again. This process continues until no rows are remaining.

❽ step position buttons allow you to rearrange the order of steps in the section

❾ alternate method to access DO Select statement types on the Statements panel

35.6.4   Statement definition panel

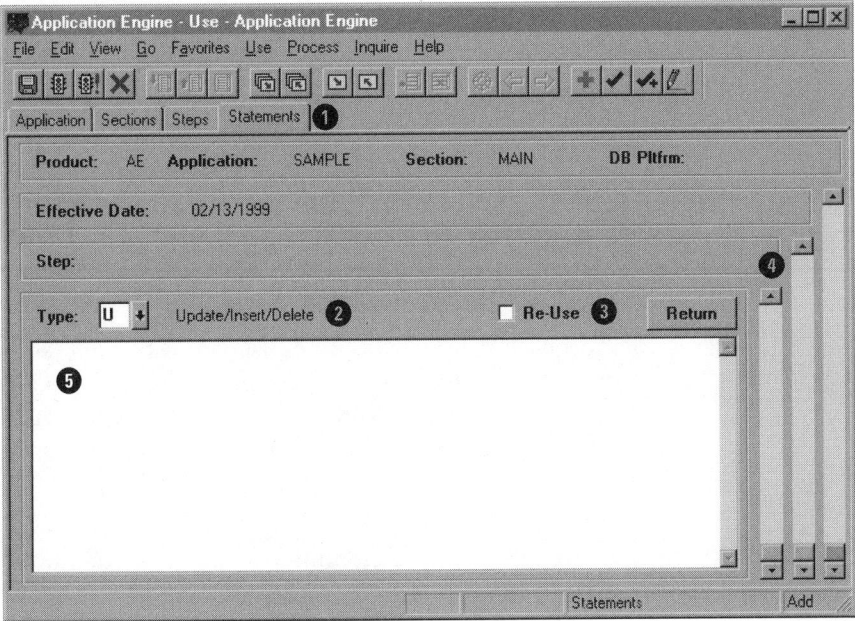

Figure 35.4   Statement definition panel

❶ Statement folder tab, navigates through the four A/E panels

❷ The type of statement to perform:

Comments is used to enter information about the step or to temporarily de-activate an executable statement.

Select is used to extract information and load it into your cache record.

Update statement types are used when executing SQL Updates, Inserts, or Deletes. It is also used when using the &MSG statement to write to the message log.

DO Select unconditionally executes a DO section for each row returned by the select SQL statement.

DO When conditionally executes a DO section. A Select statement is entered which will either return a row (representing a TRUE condition) or no rows (representing a FALSE condition). The DO section is executed when the condition is TRUE.

DO Until is used to break out of a DO Select. The DO section is performed and then the DO Until condition is evaluated. If a row is returned by the DO

Until Select statement, the DO section is no longer performed. If no rows are returned, the DO section is repeated.

DO While is similar to an SQR or COBOL while function. As long as the DO While Select statement returns a row (representing a TRUE condition), the DO section is performed. The DO While Select is executed again after the DO section has completed. This process continues until the DO While Select returns a FALSE condition (no rows returned).

❸ To convert &BIND cache fields into true bind variables, use the Re-Use checkbox. A true bind variable means those designated by :1, :2, etc. You may have seen these in PeopleCode's SQLExec functions or stored SQL statements in COBOL.

NOTE   The PeopleSoft documentation does not provide a full explanation of this feature. It is used to improve performance by compiling the statement once and re-executing it with updated bind variable values. When using this feature, make sure the application is adequately tested with the desired results produced.

---

❹ Click Return to go back to the Step Definition panel OR click on the Step folder tab.

❺ Enter your SQL or Application Engine statements here.

No validation is performed on the SQL or Application Engine statement text entered. Any syntax errors will be identified at runtime. Proper testing is required for each step.

35.7   A/E SECTION/STEP RELATIONSHIP

All Application Engine programs begin with a section called MAIN. This can be considered the parent section when viewed in a hierarchical manner as depicted in figure 35.5. MAIN.STEP1 executes a section called LEVEL2A. This level has three steps. Once all three steps have been completed, control is passed back to MAIN, and MAIN.STEP2 is executed. This performs the LEVEL2B section. In turn, LEVEL2B.STEP1 performs LEVEL3. All called sections are performed in this manner until the last step in the MAIN section has been completed.

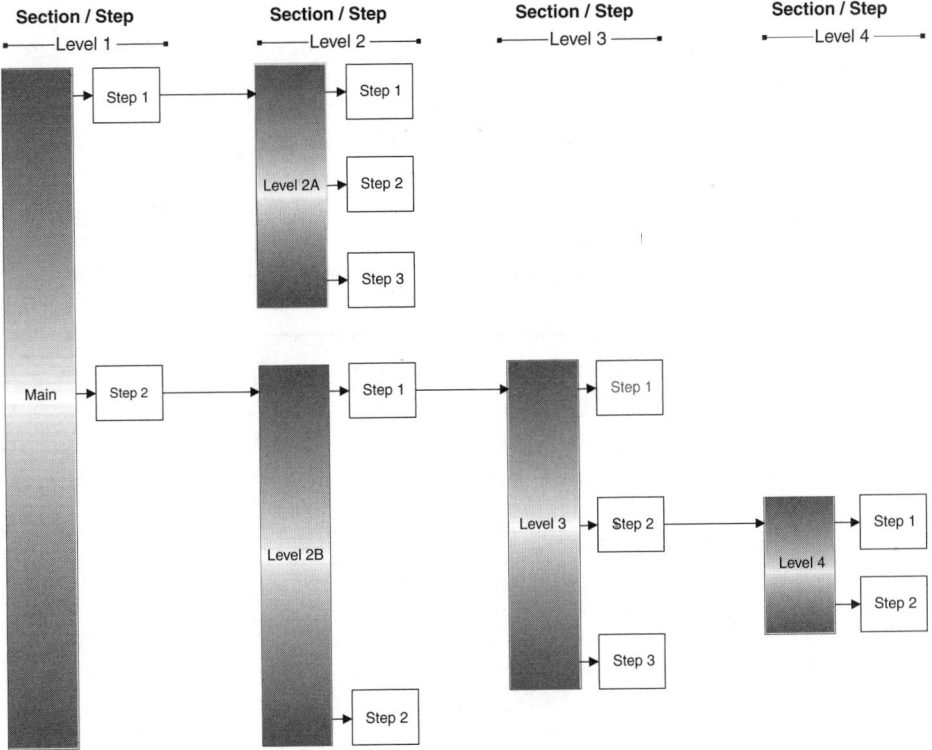

Figure 35.5   Section/step relationship

Let's take a look at the process flow (using the example in figure 35.5) as it would appear on a trace file listing. Each line represents a step executed within a section using the SECTION.STEP format:

```
MAIN.STEP1
   LEVEL2A.STEP1
   LEVEL2A.STEP2
   LEVEL2A.STEP3
MAIN.STEP2
   LEVEL2B.STEP1
      LEVEL3.STEP1
      LEVEL3.STEP2
         LEVEL4.STEP1
         LEVEL4.STEP2
      LEVEL3.STEP3
   LEVEL2B.STEP2
```

This is the basic execution structure of an Application Engine program. Visualizing the process in this manner will help tremendously when creating a new program or modifying an existing one.

35.8 APPLICATION ENGINE: THE BIG PICTURE

If you look at the "big picture" in figure 35.6 you will see the heart of the Application Engine is the COBOL process PTPEMAIN. This is what controls each action being performed. When a process request is submitted, the PTPEMAIN program is called. It reads any parameters that may be assigned and automatically updates the cache record of your application. It reads and processes the A/E definitions you have created (application, sections, steps, statements). It compiles and executes SQL statements against the PeopleSoft tables specified. It inserts messages into the message log. The PTPEMAIN process also maintains a special Run Control record called AE_RUN_CONTROL which tracks the last committed step for restart purposes. PTPEMAIN handles all processing of Trace Files.

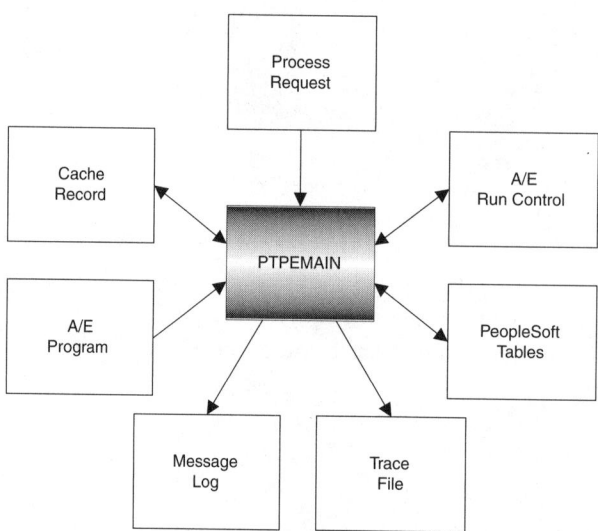

Figure 35.6   PTPEMAIN is the "heart" of Application Engine

C H A P T E R   3 6

Build your first application

36.1   BEFORE WE BEGIN:
AN INTRODUCTION TO OUR TUTORIAL

As discussed earlier, two of the elements of an Application Engine program are the message catalog and the cache record. It's not necessary to build these from scratch. Any predefined cache record within PeopleSoft can be used as can any existing message set. You can also modify the existing cache record or message set to support your particular requirements. For our purposes, we'll create a new cache record and a new message set.

36.2 ADDING MESSAGE CATALOG ENTRIES

Before we begin developing any custom applications, let's create our own custom message set in the Message Catalog table. The message set number will be linked to our Application Engine programs.

Navigation: Go → PeopleTools → Utilities → Message Catalog → Add

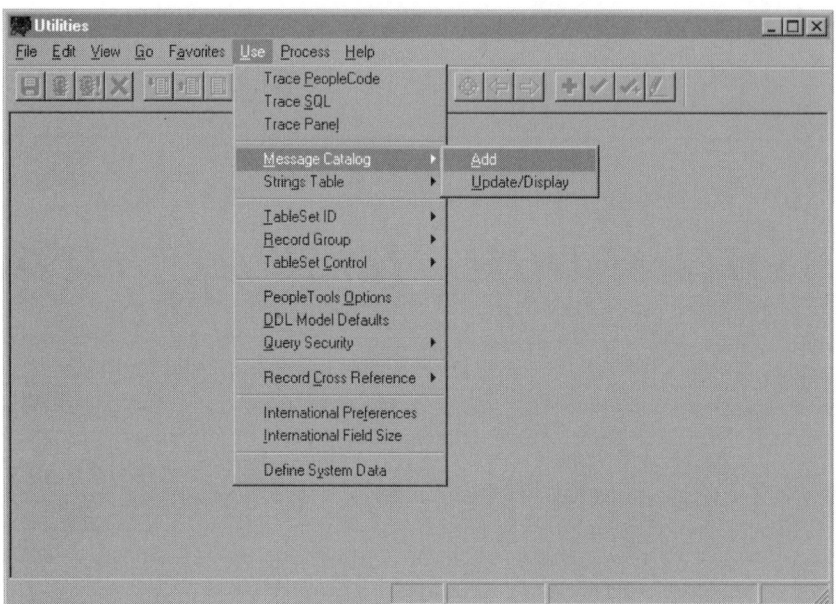

Figure 36.1   Adding a message catalog entry

Note that PeopleSoft reserves message set numbers up to 20000. When adding a custom message set, utilize any available number after 20000. This will make upgrades go much smoother. For our custom message set number, we'll be using 20001. English will be the language code for our custom applications (figure 36.2).

Figure 36.2   Adding Message Set Number 20001

We'll use the description "User Messages" for the 20001 message set. For each message we add to the message set, we'll assign a sequential number starting from 1 (figure 36.3). This is the message number we'll use to specify which message text and parameter format to use.

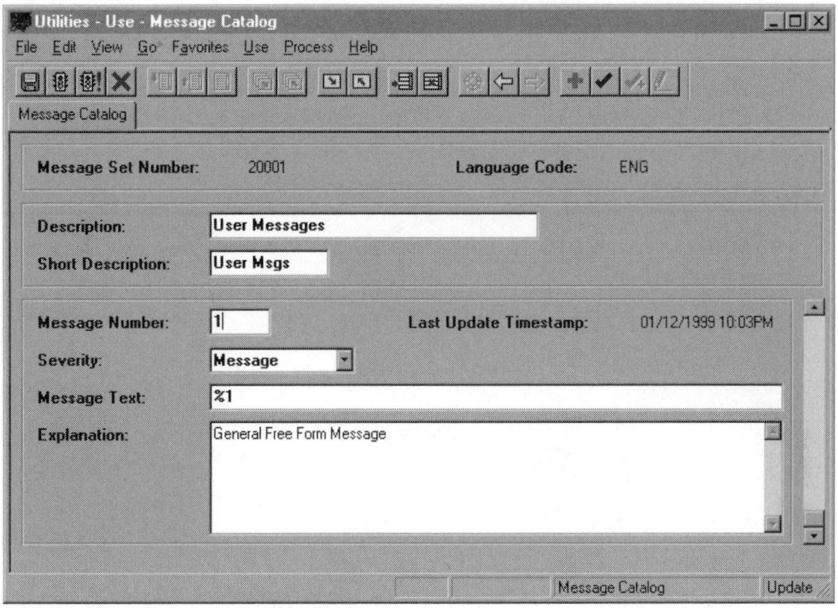

Figure 36.3   Message 1 definition

The %1 in the body of the message text indicates a value will be passed as a parameter and substituted in its place. We will use this in our first application we create. We are also adding two more messages to the message set that we'll be using in subsequent exercises. To add more messages, place the cursor in the message number edit box and press the F7 key to insert a new row. Use the scroll bar to view the messages in the message set.

Message Number 2 of our message set contains two input parameters %1 and %2 (figure 36.4).

Message Number 3 has two input parameters as well as actual text in the body of the message text area (figure 36.5). As you may have guessed by the Text and Explanation, we will be writing an application to select a table and display the number of rows.

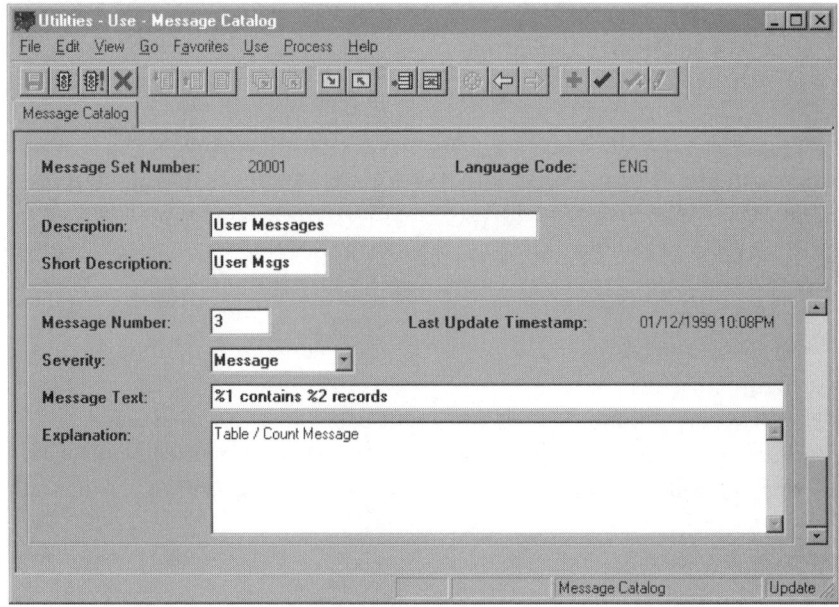

Figure 36.4   Message 2 definition

Figure 36.5   Message 3 definition

36.3 CREATING A CUSTOM CACHE RECORD

A cache record is no different than any other PeopleSoft record (or work record) you create in Application Designer. A couple of simple rules must be followed: there can only be one key field, and that key field has to be PROCESS_INSTANCE. When your Application Engine program is executed, a process instance is assigned by the Process Scheduler. This process instance is used to store the cache fields for your job, as opposed to someone else's (which has its own process instance).

Navigation: Go → PeopleTools → Application Designer → File → New...

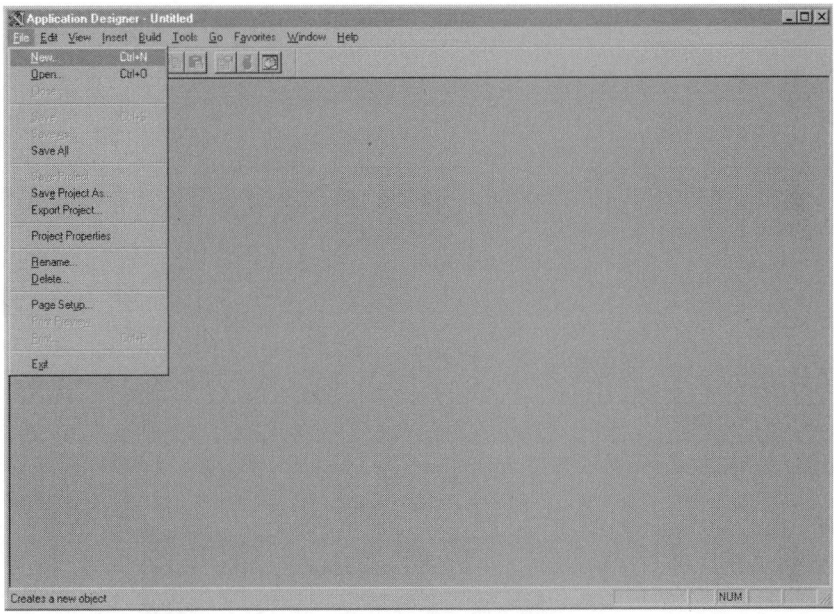

Figure 36.6   Creating a new object using Application Designer

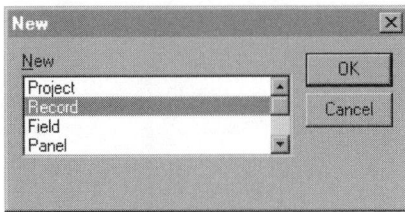

Figure 36.7
Creating a new record object

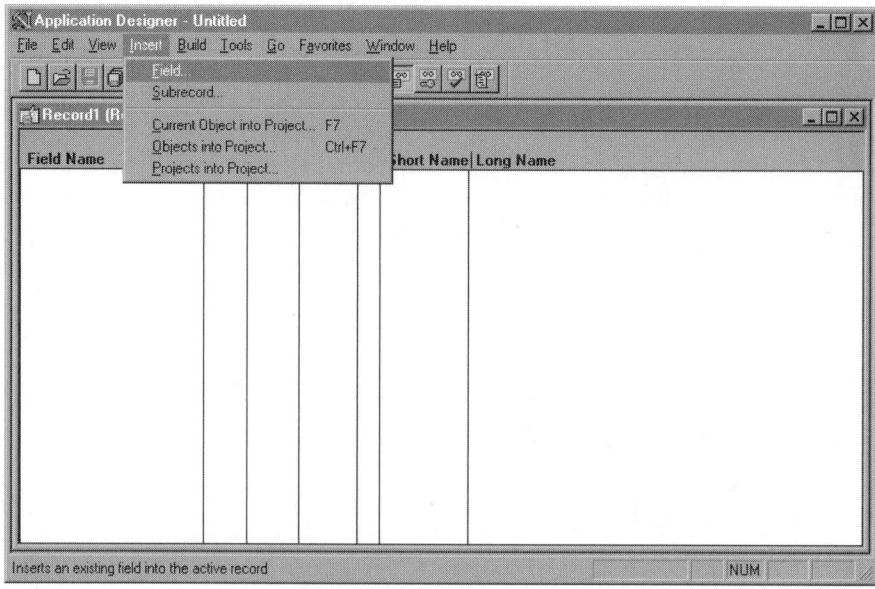

Figure 36.8   Inserting existing fields into the new record

Now we're going to add the following fields to our custom cache record: PROCESS_INSTANCE (Process Instance), COUNTER (Generic Counter), RECNAME (Record (Table) Name), FIELDNAME (Field Name), and AE_DECIDE (Decision Switch).

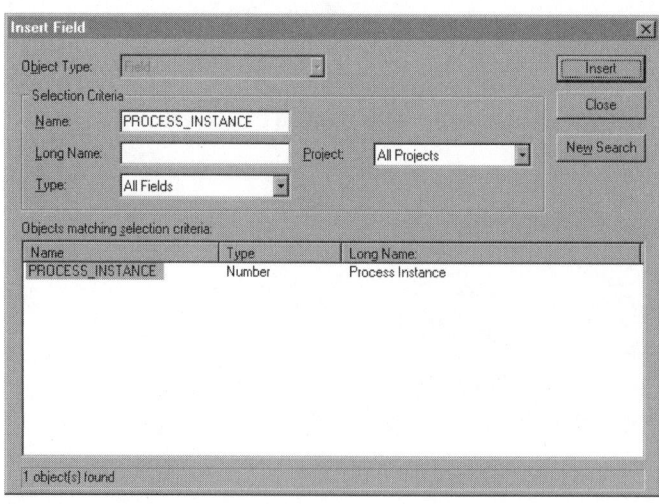

Figure 36.9   Inserting the process instance field object

The purpose of these fields will become evident as we build our applications.

NOTE   Only one key field can exist on a cache record—PROCESS_INSTANCE!

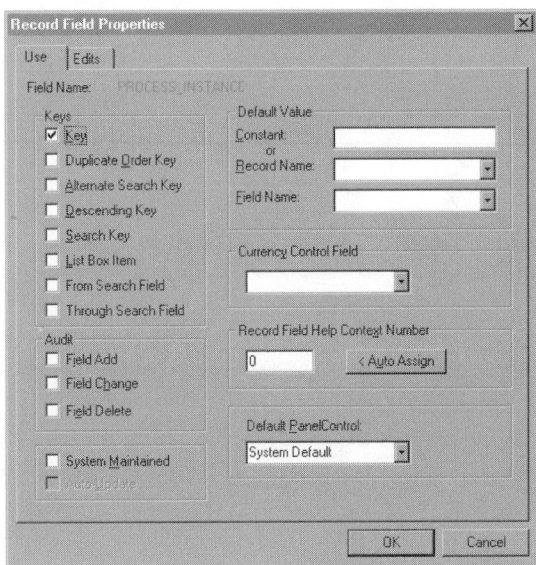

Figure 36.10
Assigning the primary key

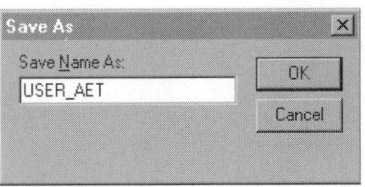

Figure 36.11   Saving the record

Once the fields have been added and the primary key (PROCESS_INSTANCE) assigned (figure 36.10), we can save the record (figure 36.11).

We'll call our custom cache record USER_AET.

Now, we need to create the table within the database itself using SQL*Create. This isn't necessary if the cache record is a work record. For the purposes of this book, we will use a physical SQL table for the cache record. When a work record is used, the cache values are lost if the program ends or aborts. You will not be able to restart an aborted process using a work record, therefore, it is a good practice to avoid them and use a physical SQL table.

While the USER_AET record is still open, click on the Build menu item, then click on Current Object (figure 36.12).

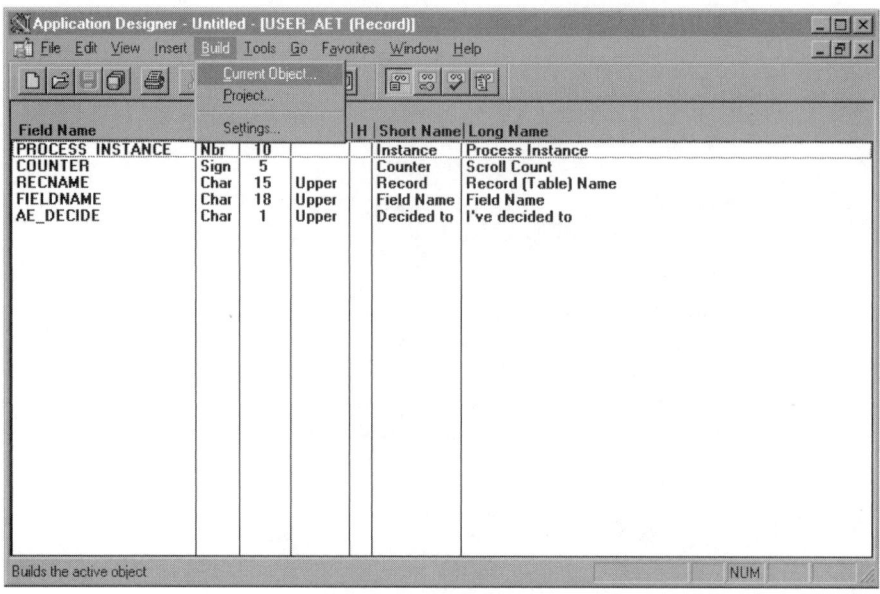

Figure 36.12   Building the current object in the database

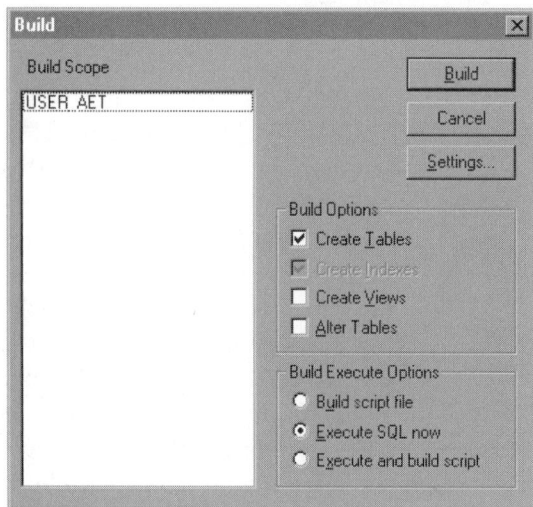

Figure 36.13
Executing SQL table creation

The Build screen appears with our current object, USER_AET, in the selection box. Click on the Create Tables checkbox and the Execute SQL now radio button. Now click on the Build push button to create the USER_AET table at the database level.

Our cache record is complete. We're ready for our first Application Engine program.

36.4 BEGINNING OUR TUTORIAL

Our first application isn't original but will clearly demonstrate basic Application Engine functionality. In many books about programming languages, it's customary to begin with an exercise that displays the short phrase "Hello world." This book is no exception. Let's begin.

36.5 EXERCISE 1: HELLO WORLD!

36.5.1 Creating an SQR version

Let's start by writing a simple SQR that displays "Hello World" on the log file:

```
! USER001.SQR
begin-program
do Main-Step1
end-program
begin-procedure Main-Step1
show 'Hello World'
end-procedure
```

After execution the SQR.log looks like this:

```
Hello World
```

Now, let's create a version of the program using Application Engine.

36.5.2 Defining the application

Navigation: Go → PeopleTools → Application Engine → Use → Application Engine
→ Application → Add

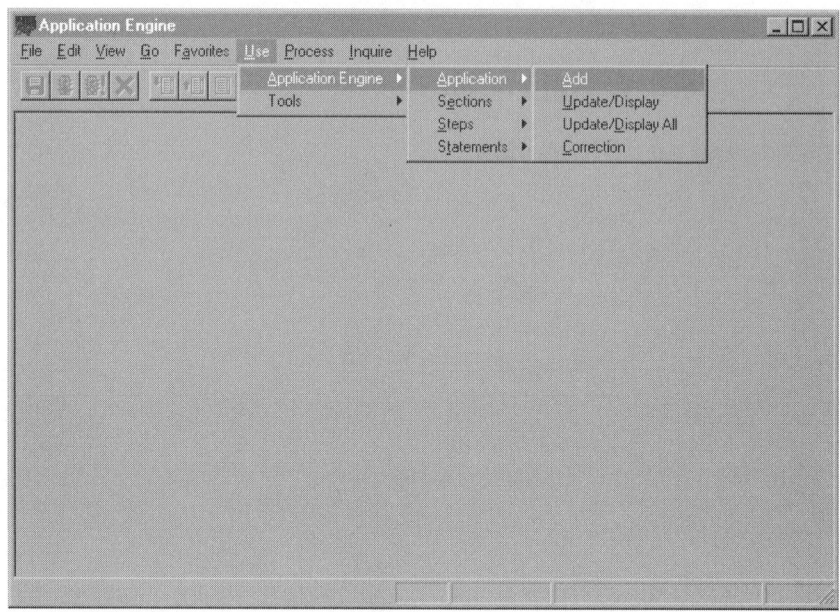

Figure 36.14   Creating a new application

Our first step here is to add a fully qualified program name. Application Engine programs are identified by *product* and *application*. Some examples of products are HR, Accounts Receivable, and General Ledger. Product categories are used to logically group your Application Engine programs.

Let's select the Application Engine Product type (PS/AE). We'll call our first application USER001 (figure 36.15). Remember, all Application Engine programs must begin with a section called MAIN. Additional sections may be added if necessary. Since we don't plan on using any database specific functionality, we can leave database platform blank.

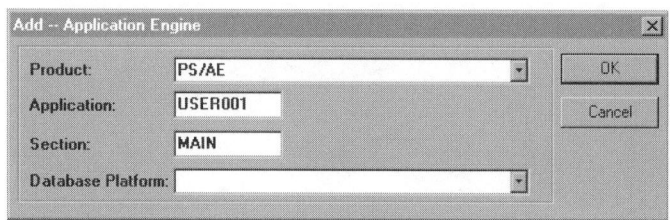

**Figure 36.15
Naming the
application**

The screen in figure 36.16 shows the Application Definition screen for our new program USER001. Notice the cache record and message set number edit boxes. We'll use our custom cache record USER_AET and custom message set 20,001. We can also document the program version using the Version edit box.

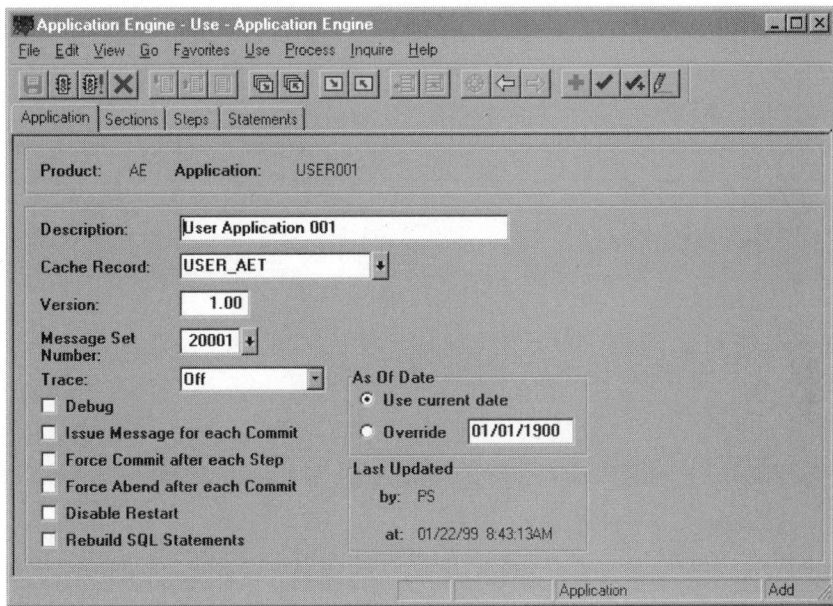

Figure 36.16   Defining our application

Take note of the group box As Of Date. It is set to use the current date when adding any new sections. When program development is spread out over several days, it's a good idea to override the current date with a common date for all sections.

We can now move to the Section MAIN definition.

TIP   Application Engine requires a section called MAIN in every program. The MAIN section is always executed first.

36.5.3 Creating sections, steps, and statements

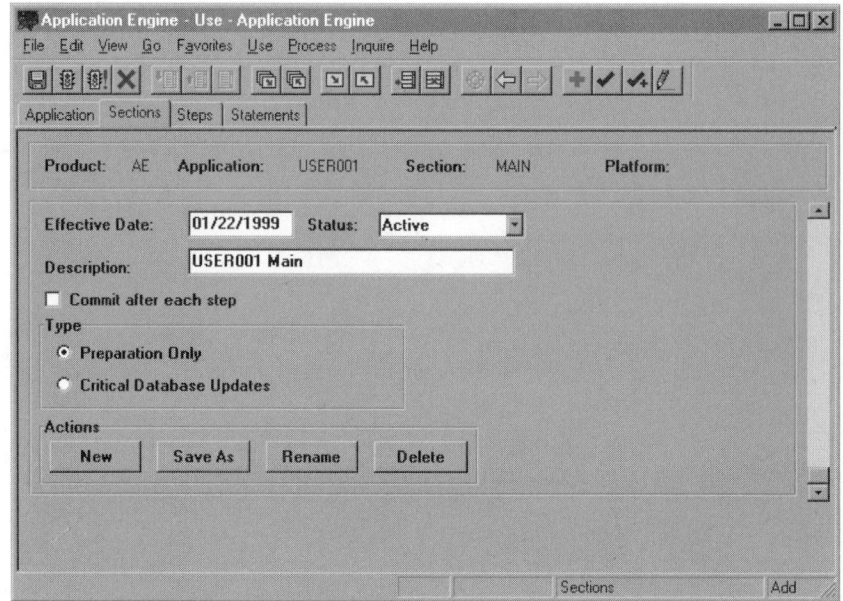

Figure 36.17   Defining section MAIN

The only additional piece of information we need to include on the section MAIN definition is the description. We're ready to add a step to our application.

Our first and only step of the application will be called STEP1 (figure 36.18). Since the objective of this step is to write a message, we use the SQL statement type. The message function of Application Engine comes under the SQL statement category. Notice the additional step options. In some cases, a Mass Change program, another A/E Section, or a COBOL program can be used instead of an SQL statement.

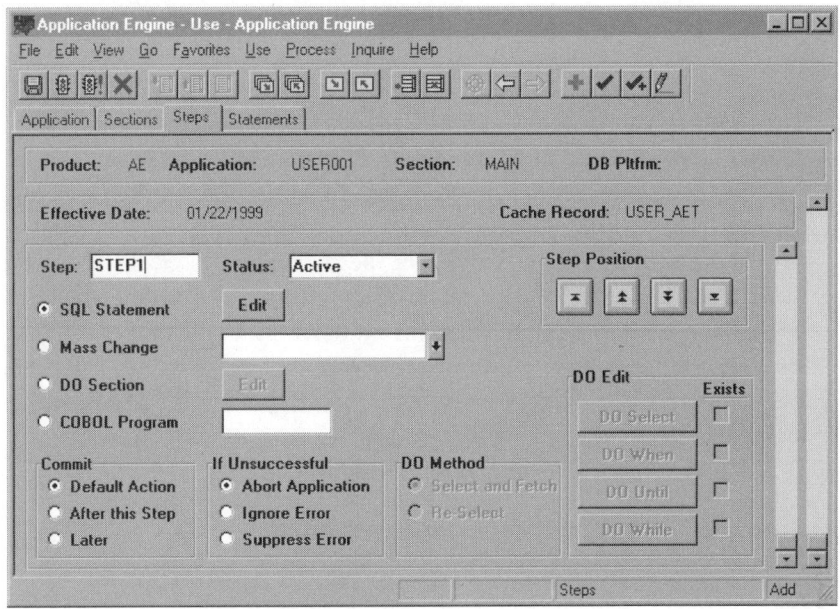

Figure 36.18   Defining our first step

36.5.4   Introducing the &MSG function

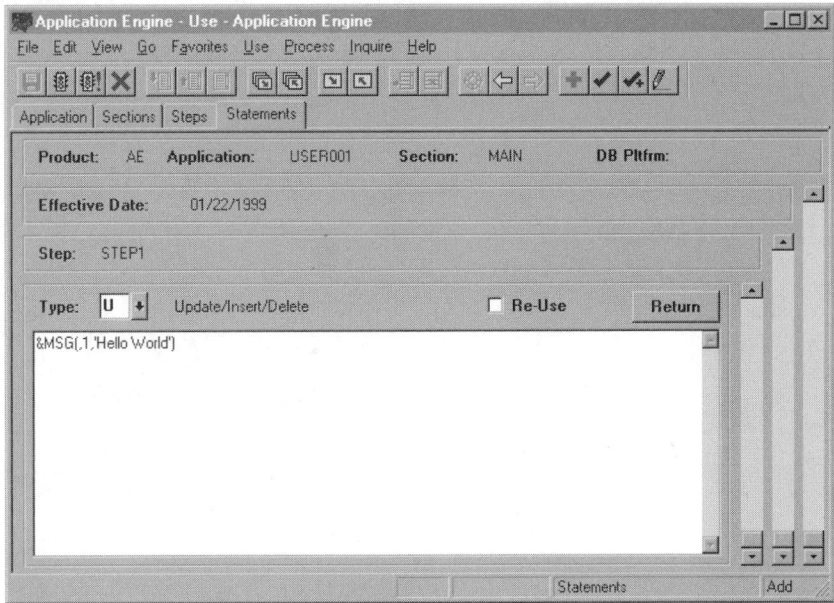

Figure 36.19   Defining our first statement

The &MSG function writes a message to the Message Log using the following format:

```
&MSG( [Message_Set_Number], Message_Number, [Parm_1],…. [Parm_n] )
```

The &MSG function always uses an SQL statement type of UPDATE and must be the first and only function or command in the statement.

For more information on the &MSG function refer to the function reference in appendix F.

In our &MSG function, we do not specify a message set, thereby defaulting to the 20001 message set we've defined on the application definition. The message number is 1, which you may recall consisted of a lone %1 input parameter. The "Hello World" text is the input parameter we are passing. We have completed our first Application Engine program! If all goes as planned, the "Hello World" phrase will appear in the message log.

We're ready to test the USER001 Application.

36.5.5 Running an Application Engine program

Navigation: Go → PeopleTools → Application Engine → Process → Request → Request → Add

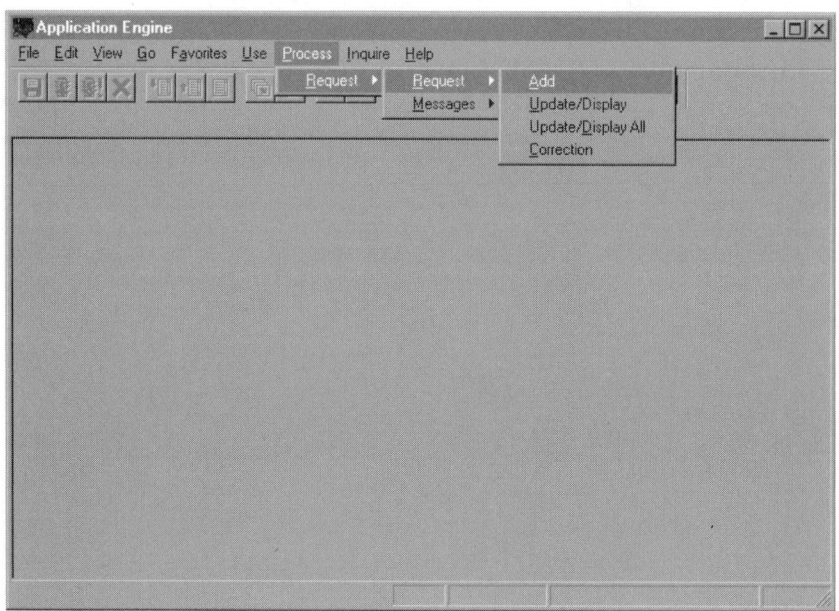

Figure 36.20 Adding a Process Request

We can test our Application Engine program through the Process Request panel. This provides a means to test without having to set up individual Run Control panels for each program we create. We also don't have to create any Process Scheduler definitions. Simply enter a Run Control ID and execute your program!

In figure 36.21, we assign a Run Control ID of #USER001.

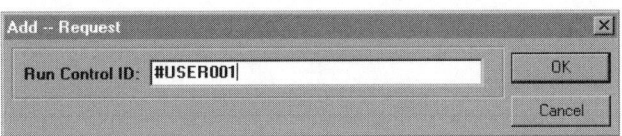

Figure 36.21
Assigning a Run Control ID

On the Process Request panel, we enter the product and application of our program (figure 36.22). The bottom half of the screen is used to initialize fields on the cache record. We'll discuss these in a future exercise. Our first application doesn't utilize any cache fields directly.

Once the Process Request panel is populated correctly, click on Traffic Signal to initiate a Process Scheduler request.

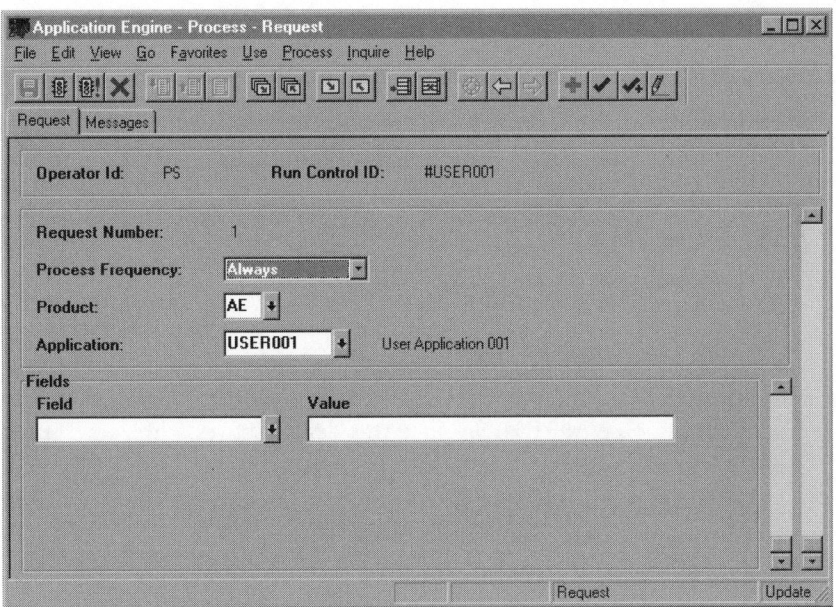

Figure 36.22   Defining a Process request

Highlight the Application Engine AEADHOC Process, and click the OK button to start (figure 36.23).

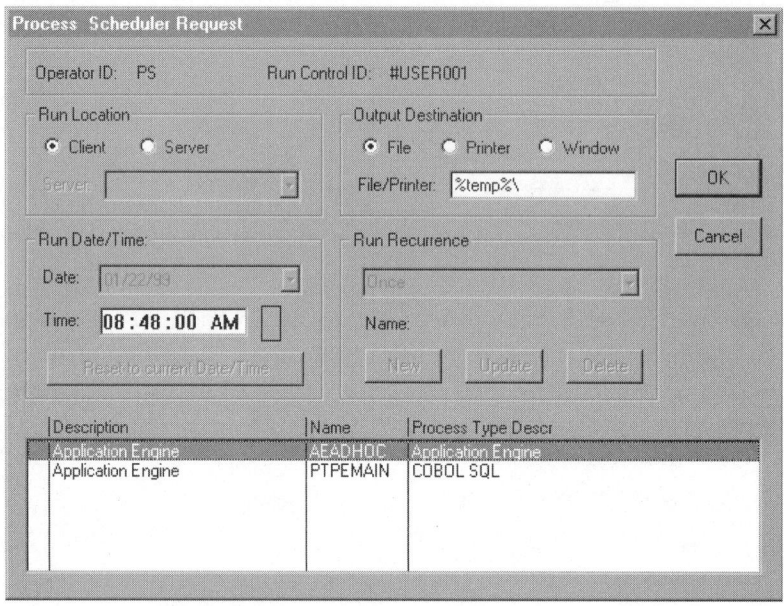

Figure 36.23   Submitting a Process Scheduler request

NOTE   You may find two process definitions in the Process Scheduler Request panel. Both AEADHOC and PTPEMAIN are linked to the Process Request panel.

Because AEADHOC is defined as an Application Engine process type, it will call the PTPEMAIN program by default. We could choose either to test our application. For purposes of this book, we'll use the same process definition throughout our exercises. We'll choose AEADHOC since this demonstrates a link to PTPEMAIN, which we'll also create in our last exercise.

Although you can run Application Engine processes on both the client and server, we will run on the client throughout this book.

36.5.6   Reviewing Application Engine messages

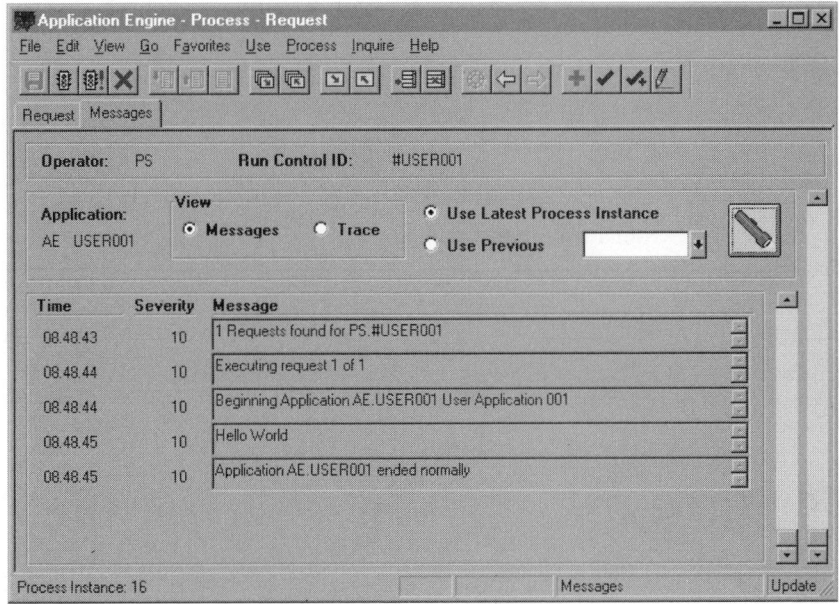

Figure 36.24   Reviewing Process Request messages

To view the message log, click on the Message folder tab. Set the View Messages radio button and the Use Latest Process Instance radio button. Click on the Flashlight to display the Latest Process Instance Message Log which happens to be our first run. At precisely 08.48.45, the "Hello World" message was displayed (figure 36.24). Our first program was successful!

36.6   *SQR/APPLICATION ENGINE COMPARISON*

Let's take a look at the logical structure of both our programs.

SQR: Application Engine:

Begin-Program
Main-Step1

USER001
MAIN.STEP1

Both programs follow the same structure: a step which writes a message, is performed. This comparison should prove to be beneficial as our exercises become more complex.

1 Two important elements of an Application Engine program are the message catalog and the cache record.

2 A cache record can have only one key, the process instance. The cache record will be used to store and retrieve values similar to using variables in conventional programs.

3 A cache record is assigned to your A/E program. The cache record is used to store and pass values from one step to another.

4 All Application Engine programs begin with a section called MAIN. Sections are similar to procedures in COBOL or SQR.

5 Each unit of work is broken down into a step. A step can call other sections, a COBOL program, a mass change program, or an SQL statement within the step itself.

6 Statements can be native SQL statements or Application Engine functions (or in some cases a combination of the two).

7 The &MSG function allows you to monitor the progress of your program by writing messages to the message log.

8 You can test your Application Engine programs using the Process Request panel.

9 The Process Request Messages panel allows you to view the messages generated during the run. Some messages are due to the &MSG function in your program while others are written by the PTPEMAIN process automatically.

C H A P T E R   3 7

Using cache fields

Variables do not exist in an Application Engine. Values are stored in a cache field and utilized by subsequent steps. Our next exercise demonstrates the use of cache fields.

37.1 EXERCISE 2: HOW MANY ROWS IN PERSONAL_DATA?

Our next exercise is also a basic one. We're going to select the number of rows in the PERSONAL_DATA table and store the count in the cache record. The next step will utilize the cached value and display the results in the message log.

PERSONAL_DATA is a core table in the PeopleSoft HRMS application. You may substitute any table for this exercise. For example, if you're running PeopleSoft Accounts Receivable you may want to use the CUSTOMER table instead.

37.1.1 Creating an SQR version

We'll begin this exercise by displaying the SQR version of this program:

```
! USER002.SQR

begin-program

do Main-Step1
do Main-Step2

end-program

begin-procedure Main-Step1

let #counter = 0

begin-select

count(*)          &counter

 let #counter = &counter

 from ps_personal_data

end-select

end-procedure

begin-procedure Main-Step2

show 'PERSONAL_DATA Record Count: ' #counter

end-procedure
```

The first procedure, Main-Step1, populates the variable #counter with the number of rows in the PERSONAL_DATA table. The second procedure, Main-Step2, displays the results.

After execution, the SQR.log looks like this:

```
PERSONAL_DATA Record Count: 347.000000
```

Now, let's create a version of the program using Application Engine.

Our second Application Engine program (figure 37.1) is called USER002, and, as we've learned, must begin with the section MAIN.

Navigation: Go → PeopleTools → Application Engine → Use → Application Engine
→ Application → Add

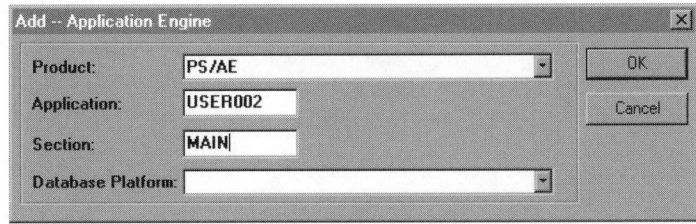

**Figure 37.1
Naming the
application**

Once again, we use the USER_AET cache record and the 20001 message set number (figure 37.2).

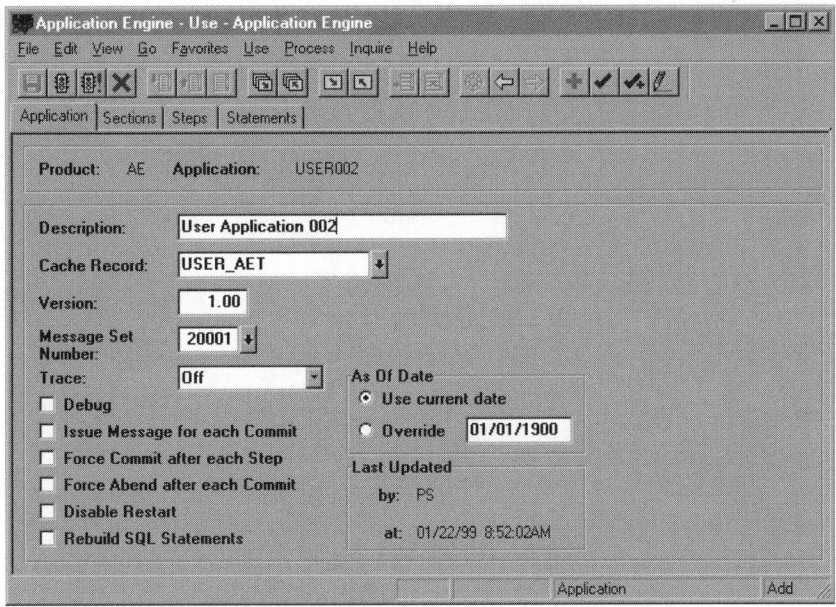

Figure 37.2   Defining our application

Figure 37.3 shows the section definition for MAIN.

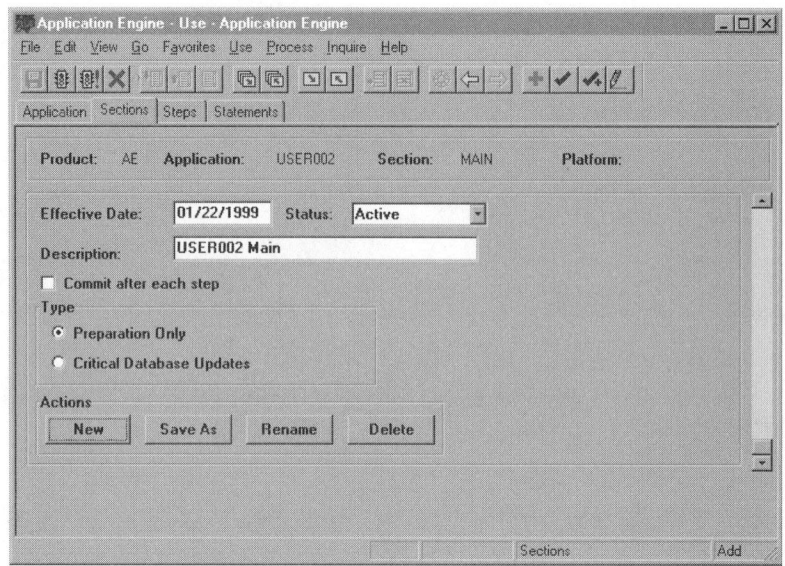

Figure 37.3 Defining section MAIN

Our first step is called STEP1 (figure 37.4). It consists of one SQL statement, which selects the number of rows in the PERSONAL_DATA table and stores the result in our cache field COUNTER.

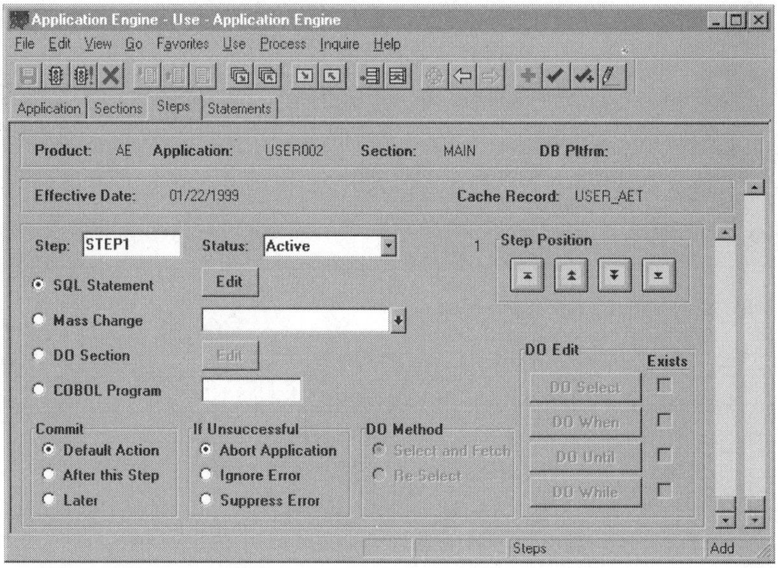

Figure 37.4 Defining STEP1

37.1.2   Assigning cache fields values with &SELECT

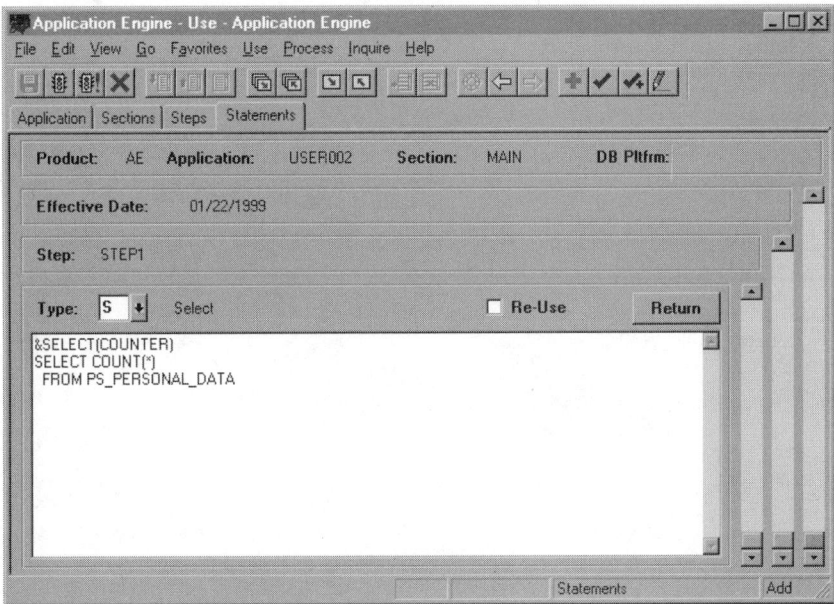

Figure 37.5   Entering the SQL statement text

We begin our statement definition by assigning a statement type of SELECT. Our statement text looks like this:

```
&SELECT(COUNTER)

SELECT COUNT(*)

  FROM PS_PERSONAL_DATA
```

The first line uses the Application Engine function &SELECT. This function updates the cache field with the value assigned by the corresponding SQL SELECT statement. The &SELECT function has the following format:

```
&SELECT(cache_field_1 [,cache_field_2] [,cache_field_x] )
SELECT field_1 [,field_2] [,field_x] )
```

&SELECT is immediately followed by an SQL Select statement.

The number of cache fields must match the number of fields in the SQL Select.

The datatypes of corresponding cache and Select fields must match.

If NO rows are returned by the SQL Select statement, the cache fields are assigned a value of zero or blank, depending on the datatype.

For more information on the &SELECT statement, refer to the function reference in appendix F.

37.1.3 Defining multiple steps within a section

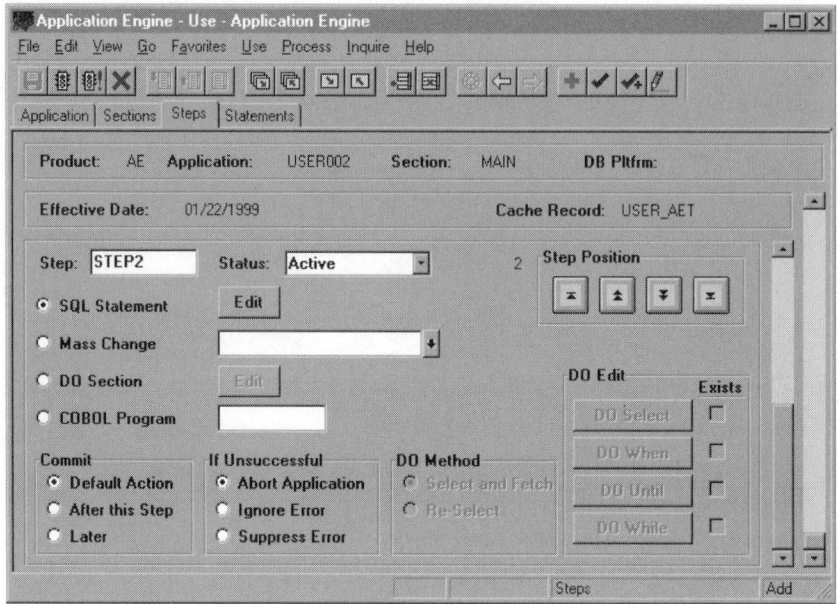

Figure 37.6 Defining STEP2

Our second step, STEP2, accesses the cache field COUNTER and displays the results in the message log. To create the new step, place the cursor in the step edit box and press the F7 key to insert a new row. When the step panel is complete, press the statement folder tab to enter our statement.

37.1.4 Retrieving cache field values with &BIND

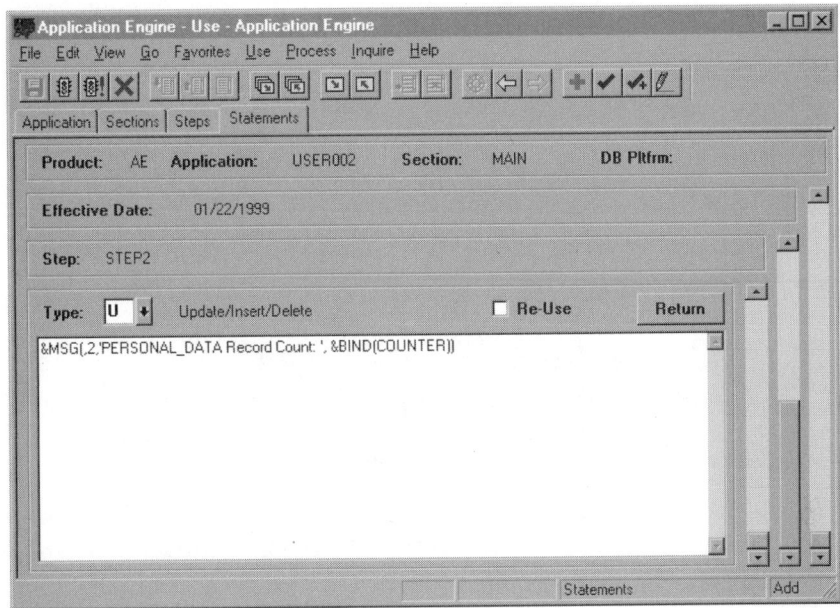

Figure 37.7 Entering &MSG statement text

As we did in exercise 1, we utilize the &MSG Application Engine function to write to the message log. We're not specifying a message set, so we default to the 20001 message set we've defined on the Application Definition panel. Message 2 was defined using two input parameters, %1 and %2. The first parameter we're passing is the string 'PERSONAL_DATA Record Count: '. The second parameter is the value stored in our cache field COUNTER. To retrieve the assigned cache field value, we use another Application Engine function called &BIND. This function has the following format:

```
&BIND(cache_field [,NOQUOTES] [,NOWRAP] [,STATIC])
```

The &BIND function follows these rules:

- The &BIND function can be used almost anywhere in an SQL statement. It cannot be used in a SELECT statement result set field list.
- A character field is returned enclosed in quotation marks unless the optional NOQUOTES parameter is used.
- Date fields will be automatically enclosed (or "wrapped") within the %DATEIN or %DATEOUT Meta-SQL functions unless the optional NOWRAP parameter is specified.

- When the STATIC parameter is specified, Application Engine will resolve the &BIND variable before compiling the SQL statement. This is useful when creating Dynamic SQL statements.

We'll discuss Dynamic SQL in the next exercise. Also, you can refer to the function reference in appendix F for more information on the &BIND function.

We're now ready to test USER002.

We test our new application using the Process Request Panel. We'll use '#USER002' as our Run Control ID (figure 37.8).

Navigation: Go → PeopleTools → Application Engine → Process → Request → Request → Add

Figure 37.8
Assigning a Run Control ID

Simply fill in the PRODUCT/APPLICATION without any cache field values. Click on Traffic Signal to initiate a Process Scheduler request.

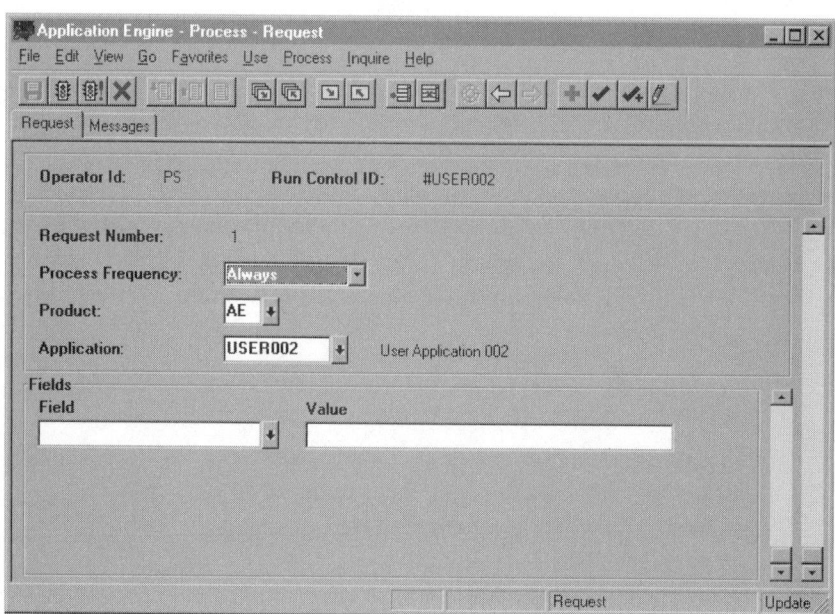

Figure 37.9   Defining a process request

Highlight the Application Engine AEADHOC process and click the OK button to start (figure 37.10).

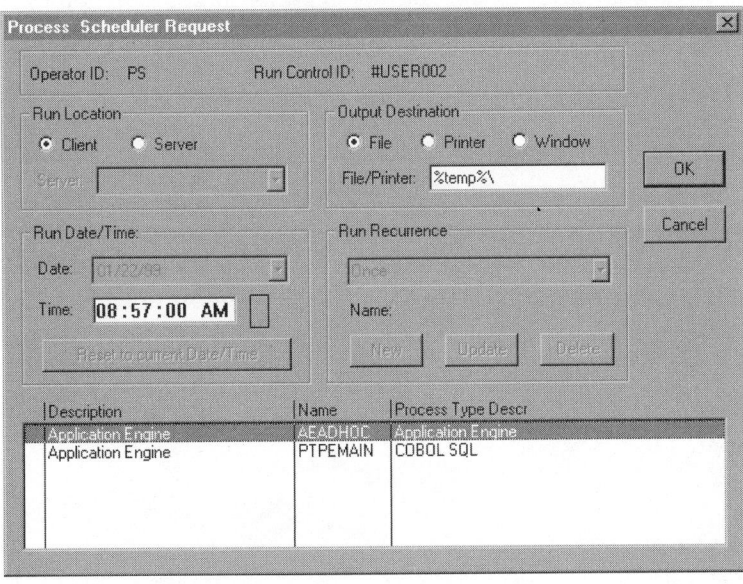

Figure 37.10   Submitting a Process Scheduler request

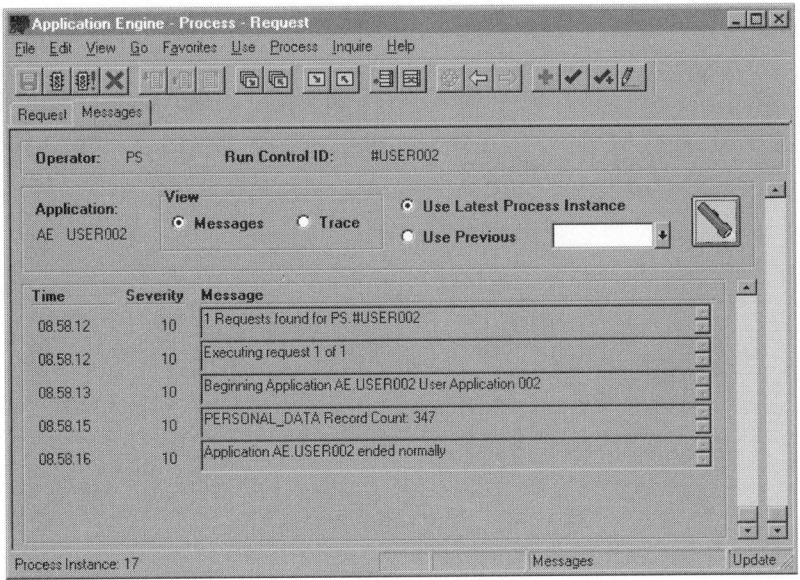

Figure 37.11   Reviewing process request messages

To view the message log, click on the Message Folder tab. Set the View Messages radio button and the Use Latest Process Instance radio button. Click on the Flashlight to display the Latest Process Instance Message Log for the current run. Our message appears in the log with the same record count as our SQR version of the program. Another success!

37.2   SQR/APPLICATION ENGINE COMPARISON

Let's take a look at the logical structure of both our programs:

SQR: Application Engine:

```
Begin-Program                    USER002
        Main-Step1                       MAIN.STEP1
        Main-Step2                       MAIN.STEP2
```

Once again, the structures are the same. Step 1 in both programs retrieves the number of rows in PERSONAL_DATA and displays the results in step 2.

KEY POINTS

Exercise 2 demonstrated some key features in Application Engine:

1   Multiple Steps may be defined within a section.

2   The &SELECT function is used in tandem with an SQL Select to assign values to cache record fields.

3   Cache record field values are retrieved with the &BIND function. The &BIND function can be used within SQL statements as bind variables or to create dynamic SQL.

Dynamic SQL statements

38.1   EXERCISE 3: HOW MANY ROWS IN ANY TABLE?

In our previous exercise, we determined the number of rows in PERSONAL_DATA.

In this exercise, we display the number of rows in ANY table. When we created our USER_AET cache record, we included the field RECNAME. This cache field is populated on the Process Request Panel with the name of the record we want to utilize. Using the RECNAME value, we select and store the resulting count in the cache record. The next step will utilize the cached value and display the results in the message log as we did in the prior exercise.

38.1.1   Creating an SQR version

We begin this exercise by displaying the SQR version of this program:

Listing 38.1

USER003.sqr

```
! USER003.SQR

begin-program

input $recname 'Enter RECNAME' maxlen=15

do Main-Step1
do Main-Step2

end-program

begin-procedure Main-Step1

let $table   = 'ps_' || $recname
let #counter = 0

begin-select

count(*)        &counter

 let #counter = &counter

 from [$table]

end-select

end-procedure

begin-procedure Main-Step2

show ' '

show $recname ' Record Count: ' #counter

end-procedure
```

The user is prompted for a record name using the INPUT statement. Note there is no validation on the entered value. We are assuming valid input to keep the program simple. The first procedure Main-Step1 populates the variable #counter with the number of rows in the table specified by the user (SQR also supports Dynamic SQL). The second procedure Main-Step2 displays the results. For our example, we use the JOB table as our RECNAME value.

After execution the SQR.log looks like this:

```
Enter RECNAME: JOB

JOB Record Count: 1685.000000
```

Now, let's create a version of the program using Application Engine.

Navigation: Go → PeopleTools → Application Engine → Use → Application Engine → Application → Add

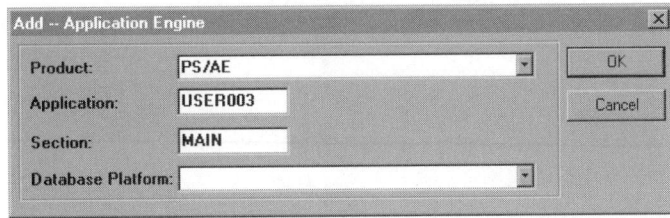

Figure 38.1
Naming the application

Our third Application Engine program is called 'USER003' and starts with section MAIN.

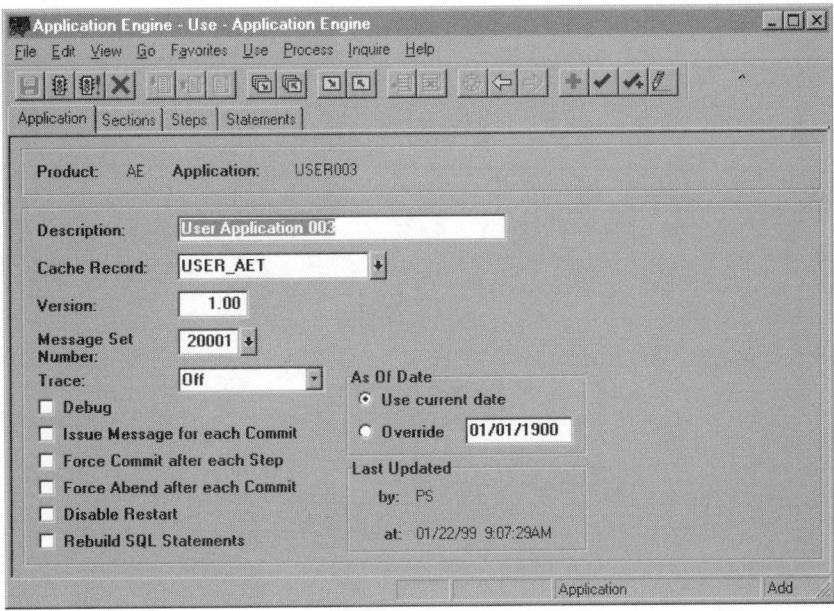

Figure 38.2   Defining the application

We'll continue to use the USER_AET cache record as well as the 20,001 message set. We'll fill in the description of our section (figure 38.3) and proceed with the first step.

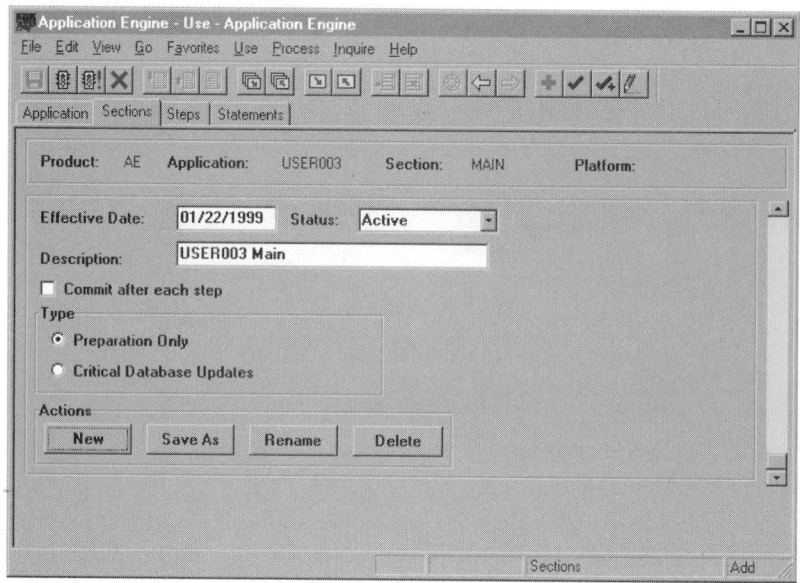

Figure 38.3   Defining section MAIN

We'll call our first step STEP1 (figure 38.4) and move to the Statement Definition panel.

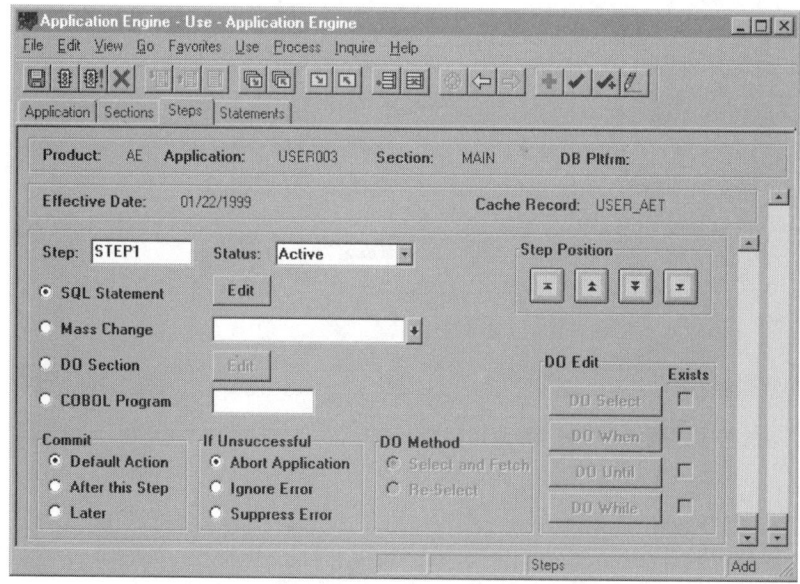

Figure 38.4   Defining STEP1

38.1.2 Using &BIND parameters NOQUOTES and STATIC

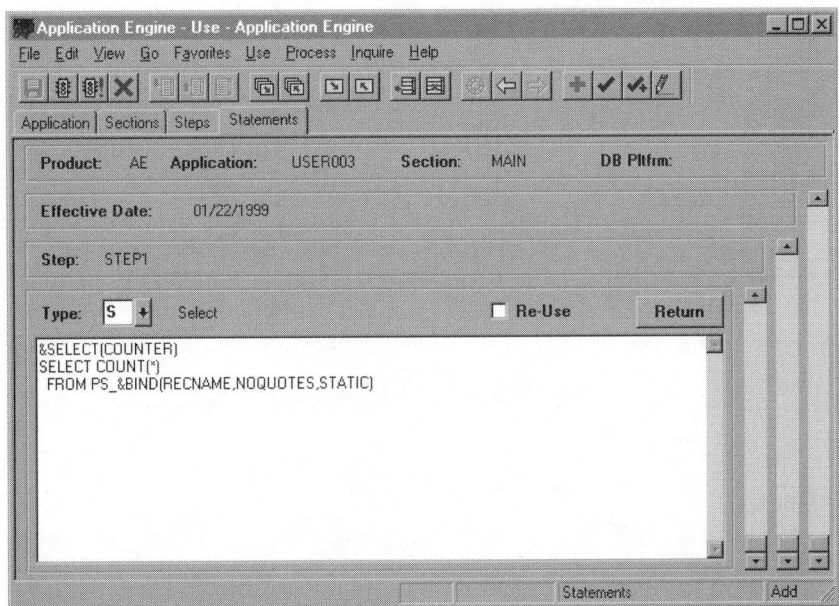

Figure 38.5 Entering the statement text

Notice the third line of the `Select` statement text:

```
&SELECT(COUNTER)

SELECT COUNT(*)

  FROM PS_&BIND(RECNAME,NOQUOTES,STATIC)
```

Remember, when we run this program through the Process Request panel we initialize the cache field RECNAME with the name of our table. In our test, we use JOB. Using the &BIND function Application Engine compiles the following SQL statement:

```
SELECT COUNT(*)
  FROM PS_JOB
```

Notice the RECNAME value JOB is prefixed by PS_. This is the standard PeopleSoft convention. The SQR version concatenates the PS_ with the entered RECNAME as well. Let's look at the &BIND value a little closer. RECNAME has a character datatype. If the NOQUOTES parameter was omitted, the resulting value would be JOB enclosed in quotation marks or 'JOB'. Since we are binding this value to the prefix PS_, the SQL would attempt to select from PS_'JOB', which is not valid and would cause an error condition. The STATIC parameter tells Application Engine to resolve the &BIND value before the SQL statement is compiled.

The row count from the JOB table is stored in the cache field COUNTER.

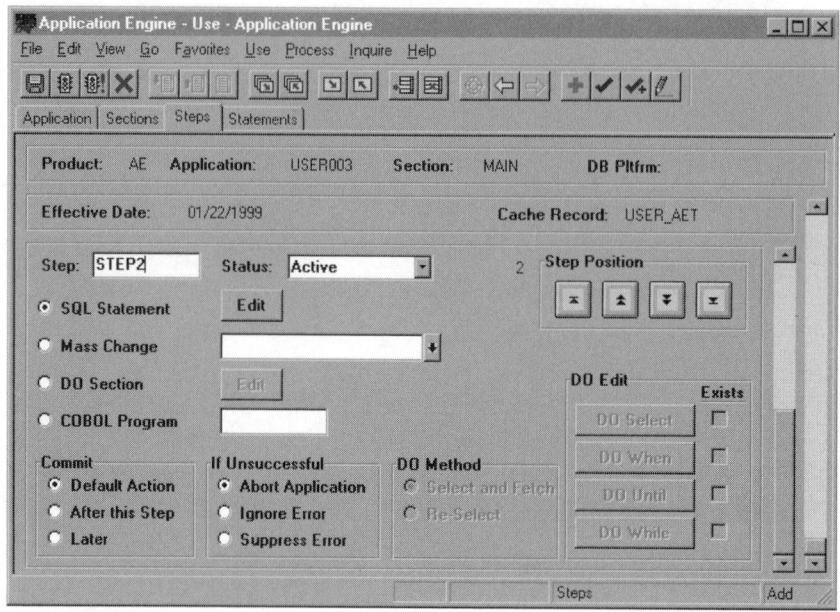

Figure 38.6   Defining STEP2

Figure 38.6 shows the completed Step Definition panel for STEP2. Let's move to the statement panel next.

38.1.3   Multiple &BIND parameters in a &MSG function

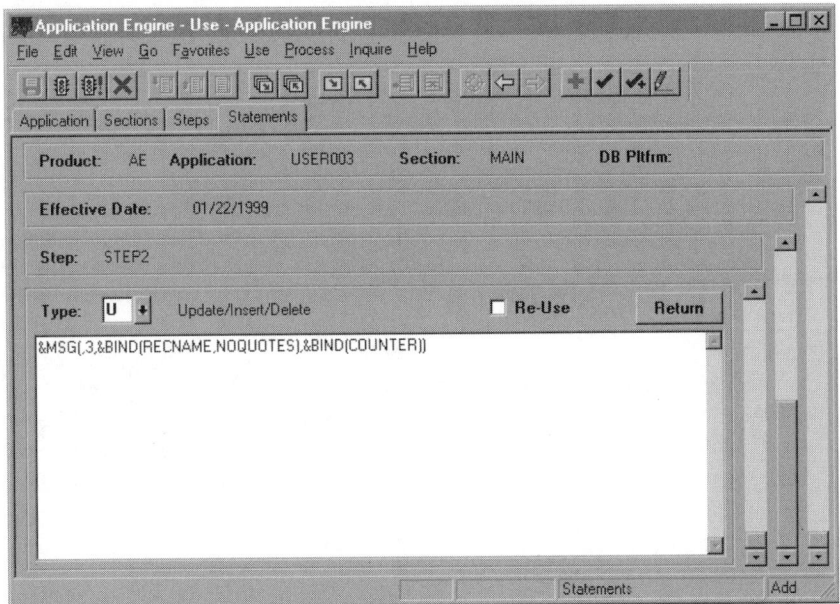

Figure 38.7   Entering &MSG statement text

Step 2 produces a message that includes two of our cache fields: the RECNAME initially entered by the user, and the COUNTER that's populated with the number of rows. We're using message number 3 of the default Message Set (20,001) which we entered as

%1 contains %2 records

Here is our &MSG function:

&MSG(,3,&BIND(RECNAME,NOQUOTES),&BIND(COUNTER))

The RECNAME value will be inserted into the first parameter or %1 of the message text.

The COUNTER value will be inserted into the second parameter or %2 of the message text.

We can now test the USER003 Application using the Process Request panel.

38.1.4 Assign initial cache values on the Process Request panel

Assign a Run Control ID—#USER003 (figure 38.8).

Navigation: Go → PeopleTools → Application Engine → Process → Request → Request → Add

**Figure 38.8
Assigning the
Run Control ID**

Once we fill in the Product (AE) and Application (USER003), we can assign an initial value to any cache fields included in the cache record. Simply click on the cache field 'Down Arrow' to display the drop-down list box. Figure 38.9 shows the drop-down list with all of the cache fields on the USER_AET cache record. We included the field RECNAME when we built our cache record for the purpose of this exercise. Select the RECNAME cache field.

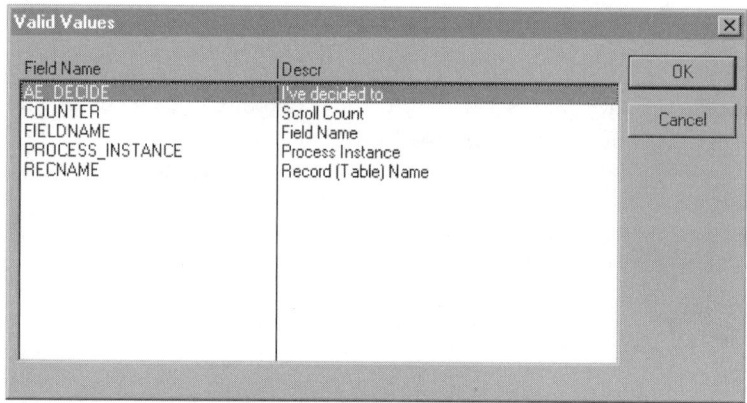

Figure 38.9   The cache field drop-down list box

Now assign the value JOB to our RECNAME cache field. Our application will substitute the value JOB in our Dynamic SQL Select statement.

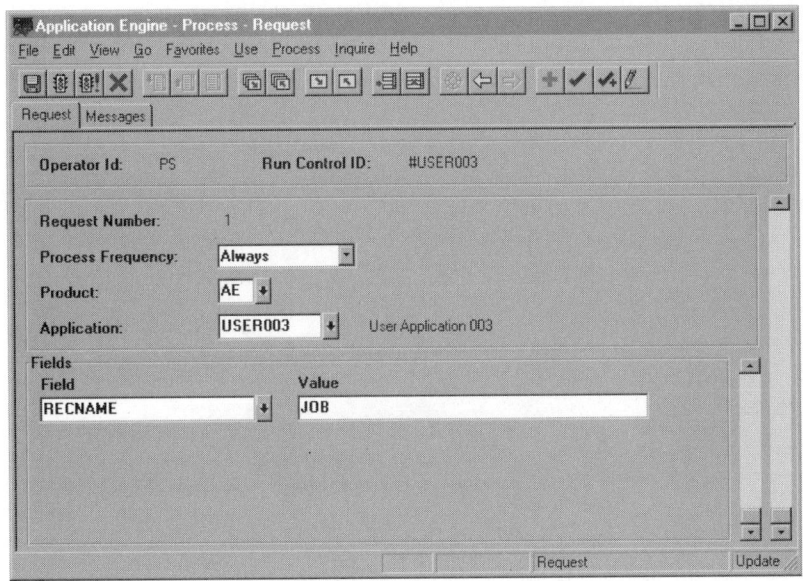

Figure 38.10　Assigning an initial value to the cache field

Once again, highlight the AEADHOC process and click OK.

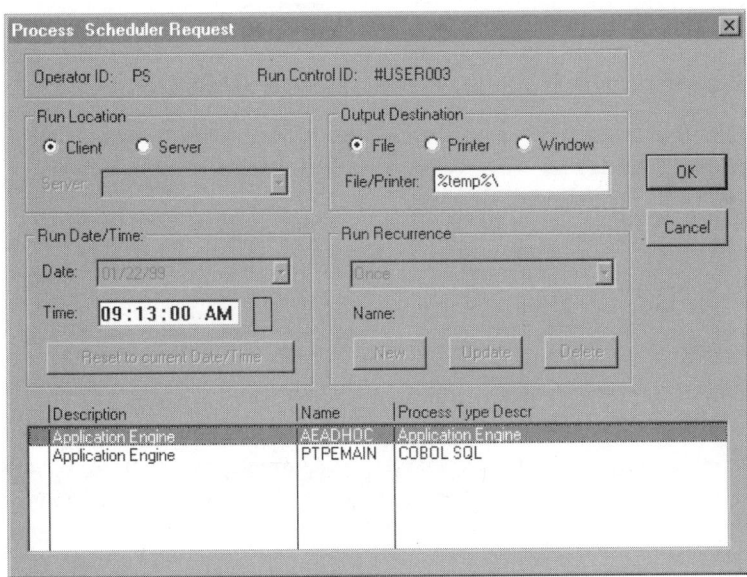

Figure 38.11　Submitting a Process Scheduler request

As the message log indicates, the USER003 program was successful. The Job record was dynamically called, and the correct number of rows were selected. Our totals match those generated by the USER003 SQR program (1685 rows).

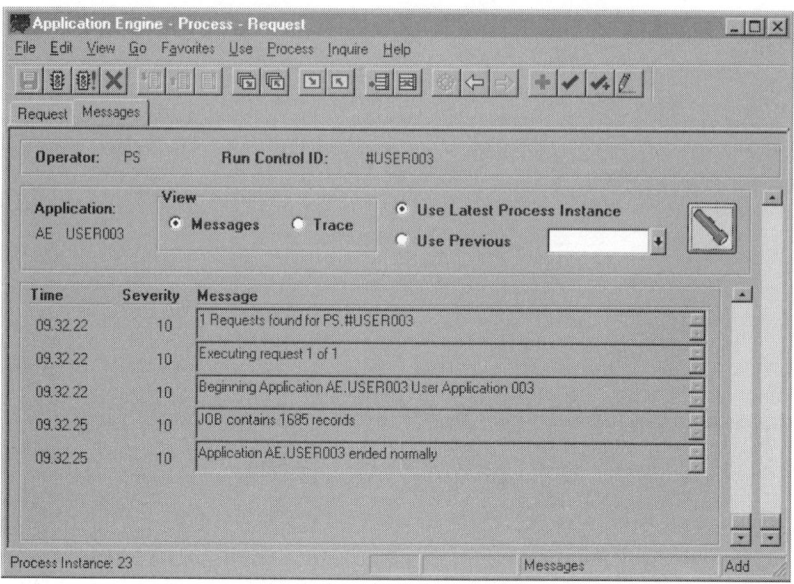

Figure 38.12   Reviewing Process Request messages

38.2   SQR/APPLICATION ENGINE COMPARISON

Now, let's look at the logical structure of both our programs:

SQR: Application Engine:

```
Begin-Program                    USER003
      User prompted                   Cache assignment
      Main-Step1                      MAIN.STEP1
      Main-Step2                      MAIN.STEP2
```

The structures are once again identical. The only exception lies in the method of entering the RECNAME. The SQR structure used an input prompt while the A/E program used the Process Request cache field assignment. Please note that a Run Control panel can be created for the SQR process, and values may be assigned in the same manner as the A/E program.

CHAPTER 38   DYNAMIC SQL STATEMENTS

1 The &BIND function can create dynamic SQL statements.

2 The &BIND parameters NOQUOTES and STATIC are used to format the bind value within the SQL statement.

3 Multiple &BIND parameters are permitted in a &MSG function.

4 The Process Request panel allows us to assign initial cache field values. This allows us to test our application engine programs without having to build a Run Control panel.

C H A P T E R   3 9

Selecting multiple rows

In our last two exercises, we selected one row of data and displayed a message. We will now learn how to process multiple rows returned by our Select. Also, we have been using one section only—the MAIN section. We will introduce multiple sections in this next exercise. The additional sections will give us increased flexibility and control in our Application Engine program.

39.1 EXERCISE 4: PROCESSING MULTIPLE ROWS

In the last exercise, we selected and displayed the number of rows from a record entered by the user. We'll add a little bit more complexity in this next exercise. The user will now enter a FIELDNAME. We are going to select the number of rows in EACH record containing this field. A message will be generated for each record as well. We will access the PeopleTools table PSRECFIELD to determine which record(s) to select based on the field entered by the user.

39.1.1 Creating an SQR version

We begin this exercise by displaying the SQR version of this program:

Listing 39.1

USER004.sqr

```
! USER004.SQR

begin-program
input $fieldname 'Enter FIELDNAME' maxlen=18

do Main-Step1

end-program

begin-procedure Main-Step1

begin-select
a.recname

  let $recname    = &a.recname

  do Count-Step1
  do Count-Step2

 from psrecfield    a,
      psrecdefn     b
where a.recname   = b.recname
  and a.fieldname = $fieldname
  and b.rectype   = 0
order by a.recname
end-select

end-procedure

begin-procedure Count-Step1

let $table    = 'ps_' || $recname
let #counter = 0
begin-select
```

```
count(*)          &counter
 let #counter = &counter
 from [$table]
end-select

end-procedure

begin-procedure Count-Step2

show ' '
show $recname ' Record Count: ' #counter

end-procedure
```

The user is prompted for a field name using the Input statement. Once again, we are not concerned with the validation of the user input. In our example, we use the field PAY_END_DT. Any record that has the PAY_END_DT field is selected and processed by the program.

Consider a portion of the SQR.LOG produced by the run:

```
Enter FIELDNAME: PAY_END_DT

BEN_PLAN_DATA Record Count: 0.000000
BOND_LOG Record Count: 471.000000
DED_CALC Record Count: 90.000000
DED_LINE Record Count: 29.000000
DED_MESSAGE Record Count: 0.000000
DED_WORK Record Count: 0.000000
ESPP_RUNCTL Record Count: 2.000000
GL_GEN_HISTORY Record Count: 0.000000
GP_CAL_BLD Record Count: 0.000000
GP_CRT_GER_AET Record Count: 0.000000
IMP_ADJUST Record Count: 0.000000
IMP_CALC Record Count: 0.000000
PAYROLL_ACCRUAL Record Count: 0.000000
PAY_CALC_RUNCTL Record Count: 0.000000
PAY_CALENDAR Record Count: 1170.000000
PAY_CALENDR_NLD Record Count: 241.000000
PAY_CAL_BAL_ID Record Count: 911.000000
PAY_CBLD_RUNCTL Record Count: 1.000000
PAY_CHECK Record Count: 7385.000000

Etc...
```

If you were to view each of these record definitions in Application Designer, you would see that each of the records listed above contains the field PAY_END_DT.

Now, let's duplicate this functionality in our Application Engine program.

Navigation: Go → PeopleTools → Application Engine → Use → Application Engine → Application → Add

Figure 39.1
Naming the application

We'll begin by adding the USER004 Application name and the section MAIN. Set the description, cache record, version and message set number for our application (figure 39.2).

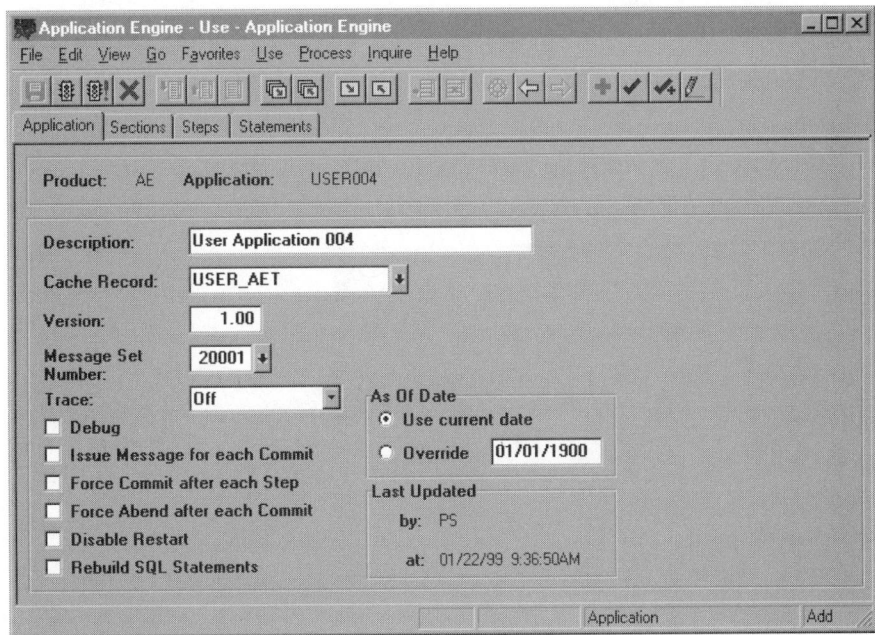

Figure 39.2   Defining the application

Now set the description on the section MAIN panel (figure 39.3).

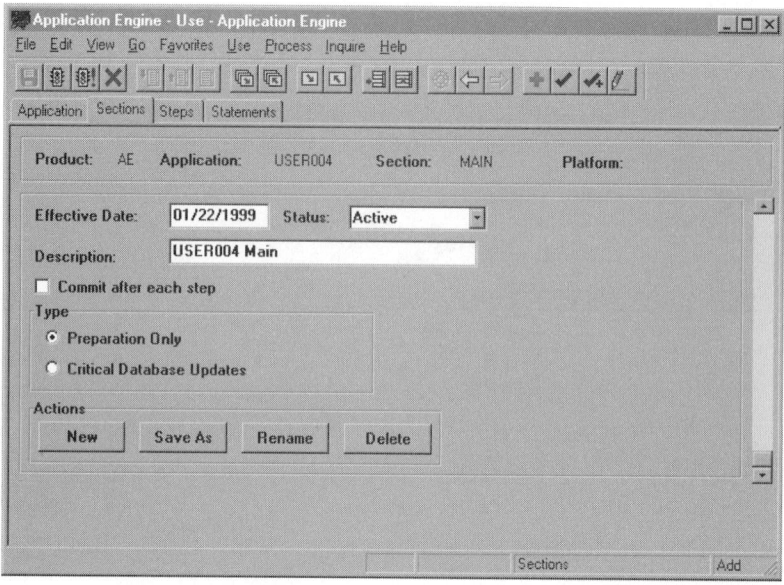

Figure 39.3 Defining section MAIN

We'll now proceed with STEP1. There hasn't been much variation in our exercises so far; this will change very soon.

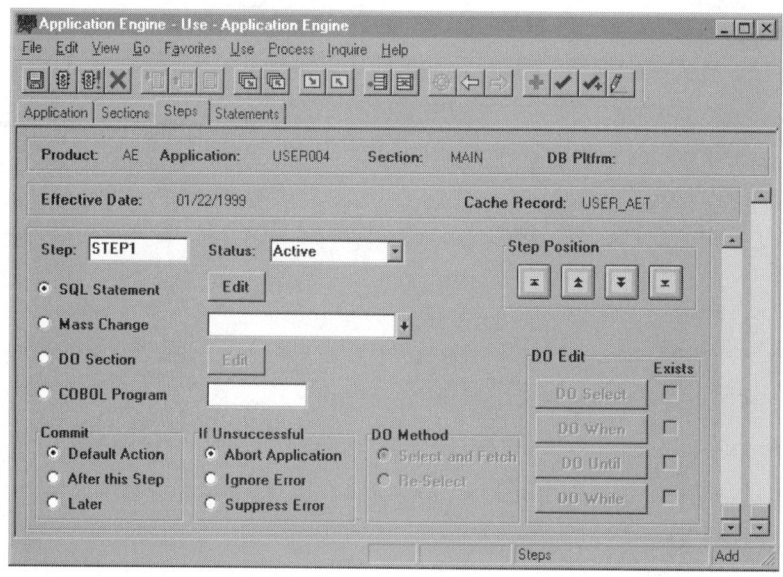

Figure 39.4 Defining STEP1

CHAPTER 39 SELECTING MULTIPLE ROWS

39.1.2 Using the DO Select statement type

In this exercise, we use a different statement type called a `Do Select`. For each row returned by the SQL `Select`, we perform or "DO" another section using the RECNAME value. Using the `DO Select` statement type tells Application Engine to call a "specified" subordinate section to process each returned row. Our new section uses this RECNAME value to dynamically select the number of rows, assign the number of rows to the cache field COUNTER, and once again display a message with the results.

Click on the Statements Folder tab. Figure 39.5 shows the statement type along with the SQL statement text we're going to use.

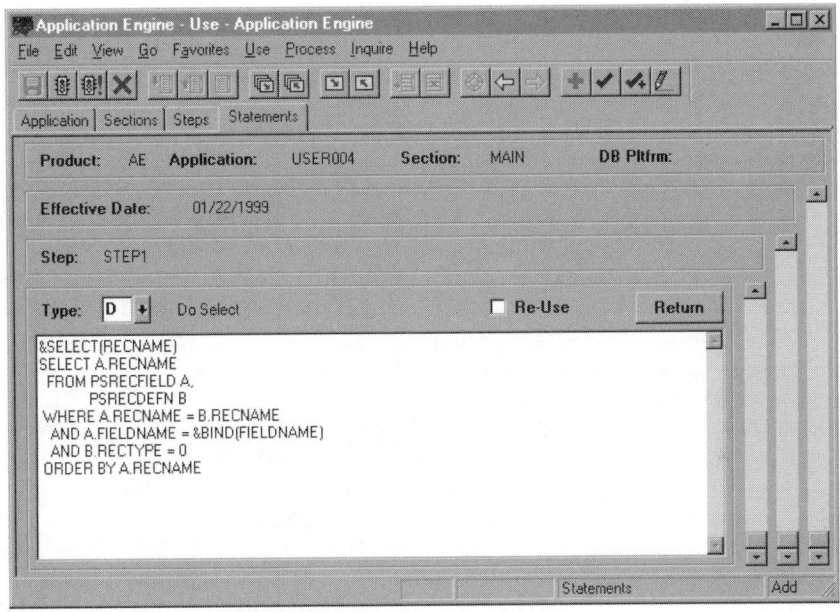

Figure 39.5 Entering DO Select statement text

Let's examine our SQL statement closer:

```
&SELECT(RECNAME)
SELECT A.RECNAME
   FROM PSRECFIELD   A,
        PSRECDEFN    B
  WHERE A.RECNAME    = B.RECNAME
    AND A.FIELDNAME  = &BIND(FIELDNAME)
    AND B.RECTYPE    = 0
  ORDER BY A.RECNAME
```

First of all, we are using two PeopleTools tables. PSRECFIELD stores all the record definitions created in Application Designer. We are selecting all RECNAME values that have the FIELDNAME value we've input on the Process Request screen. We're joining the PSRECFIELD table to another PeopleTools table called PSRECDEFN. This table is used to hold information about the record itself. The RECTYPE indicator is set to 0 if it is a physical SQL table. If it's not zero, it could be a type of view, work record or subrecord definition. Since the ultimate goal of our program is to determine the number of rows in each table, we need to make sure we're only selecting SQL table record definitions.

The &BIND function retrieves the cache field FIELDNAME. Remember, we're using the field PAY_END_DT in our example. We're using the FIELDNAME value as part of our selection criteria. The SQL criteria using &BIND is translated to:

AND A.FIELDNAME = 'PAY_END_DT'

Click back on the steps folder tab to return to the step definition panel (figure 39.6).

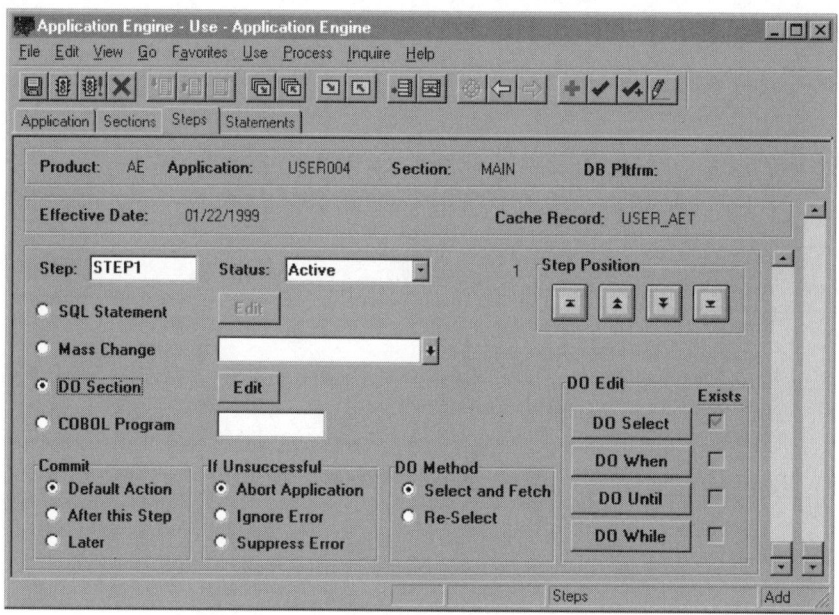

Figure 39.6 Using the DO section radio button

Notice the DO section radio button has been set. We controlled this by assigning the DO Select statement. Let's see what happens when we try to save our work (figure 39.7).

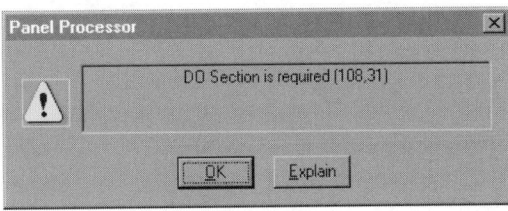

Figure 39.7
Error message—
DO section is required

An error message is produced. We click on the Explain button for further information (figure 39.8).

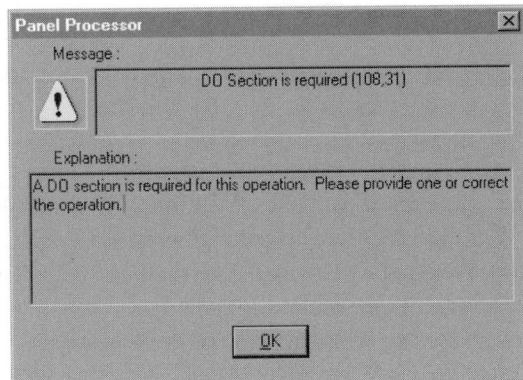

Figure 39.8
Same error message with explanation

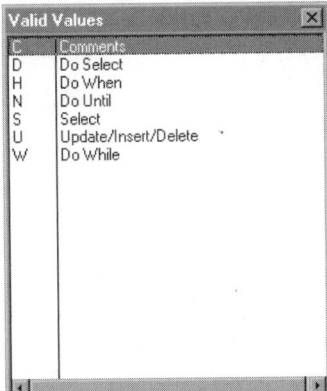

Figure 39.9 Statement type drop-down list box

Because we've used a statement type of DO Select, a DO section is required. This presents a problem because we haven't created the new section yet. We have to temporarily set the radio button back to SQL statement instead of Do Section. We can also set the statement type to Comments by clicking on the Edit push button (next to SQL statement) or by clicking on the Statements folder tab. The Statement panel has a drop-down box for statement types. Let's set the statement type to Comments for now.

You can use this statement type to add descriptions to your program. In our case, we use it to alleviate the problem we're having. We can now save our record. Once we create our new section, we can go back and change the statement type to Do Select. At that point, we'll link our new section to our program.

Please note that PeopleSoft will allow you to save the record without setting the statement type to Comments. In this particular case, it's a good practice to de-activate the DO Select since a DO section is not yet attached. Let's create the new section now.

39.1.3 Creating and using additional sections

Navigation: Go → PeopleTools → Application Engine → Use → Application Engine →
Section → Add

Figure 39.10
Adding a new section

When the Add edit box appears, we use the same product and application (figure 39.10). This is the first time we are adding a section name. Up until now, the first section has always been filled in for us. Remember the first section is always MAIN. We call our new section COUNT. It's an appropriate name since we'll determine the count of each REC-NAME passed to this section and display the results to the message log.

On the section definition screen, we enter a simple description.

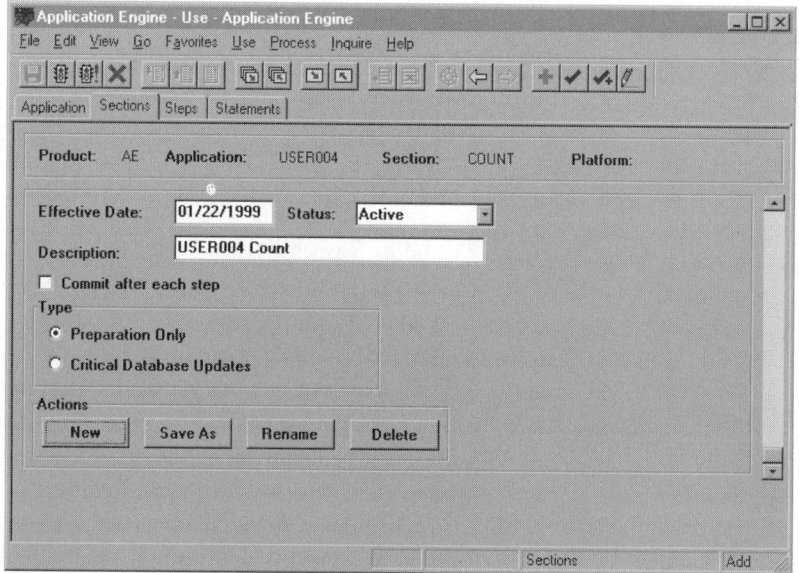

Figure 39.11   Defining section COUNT

Since we are in a new section, we can once again call our step STEP1. After all, this is the first step of the COUNT section. Now let's move to the statement definition panel.

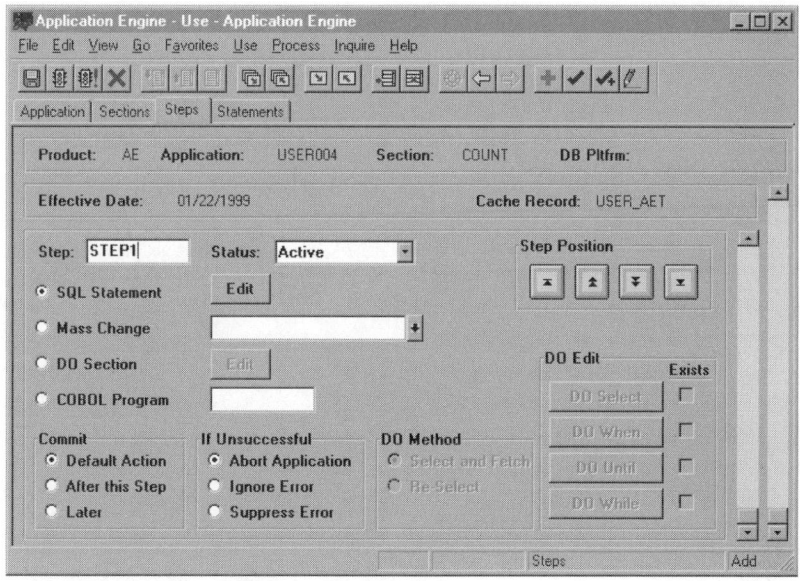

Figure 39.12   Defining STEP1 of COUNT section

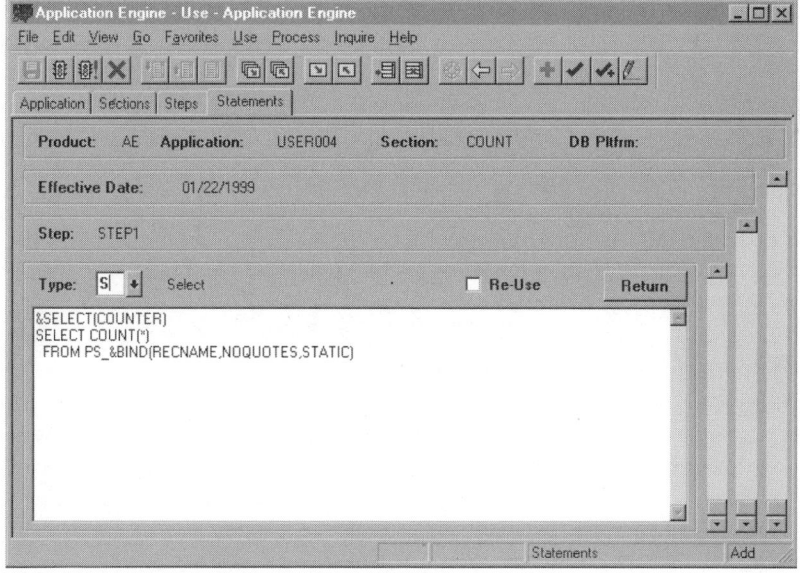

Figure 39.13   Adding Select statement text

You may have noticed this statement is identical to STEP1 in exercise 3. The reason is simple: We have a table determined by retrieving the value in the cache field RECNAME. The purpose of this step is to select the number of rows from that table. That purpose hasn't changed. In exercise 3, the cache field RECNAME was assigned through the Process Request Panel. In this exercise, the RECNAME value is assigned by the calling step MAIN.STEP1. We'll demonstrate the reuseability of applications/ sections at the end of this exercise.

We'll now enter the second step of the COUNT section which produces our message log entry (figure 39.15).

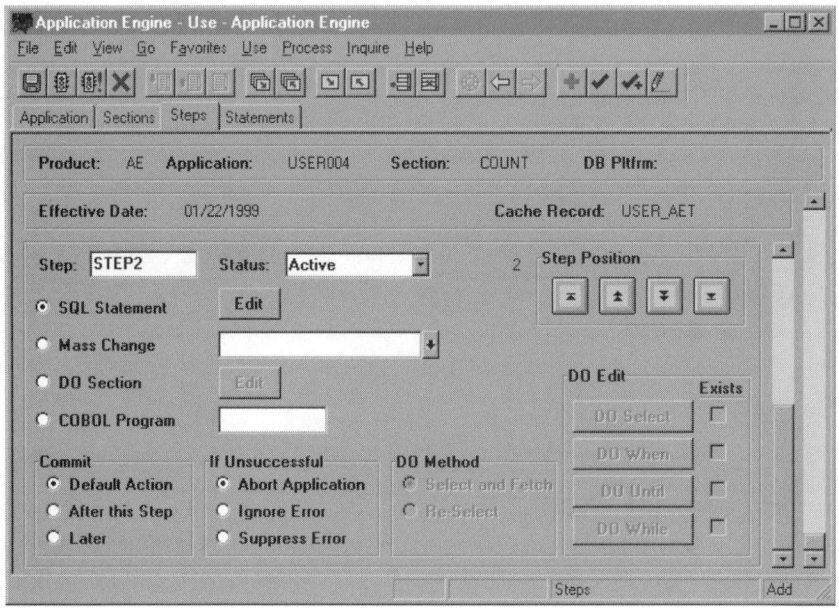

Figure 39.14   Defining STEP2 of section COUNT

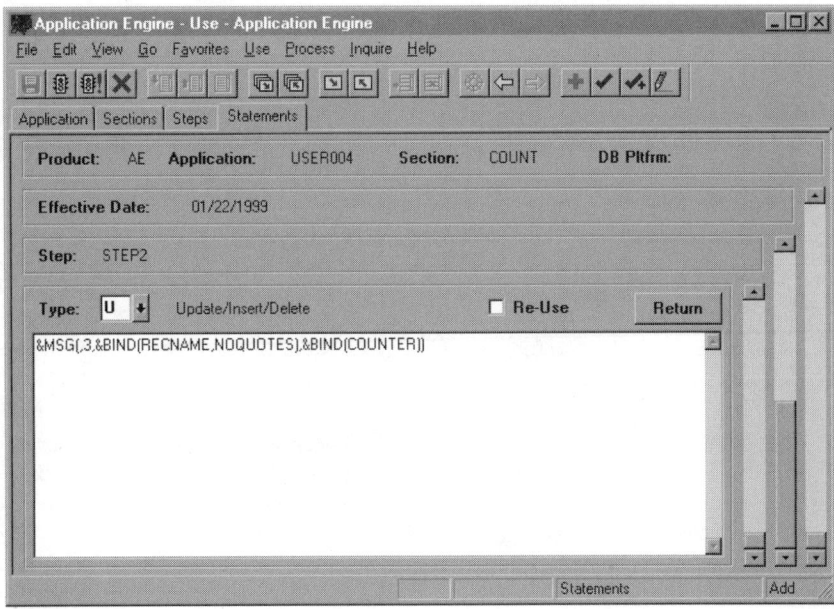

Figure 39.15 Adding &MSG statement text

As in step1, the STEP2 portion is identical to that of our prior exercise. Once we save the new section, we're ready to link it to our MAIN section.

We go back to the MAIN section using Correction Mode. Enter the product we're using (PS/AE), and click on the Search push button. You can see all of the applications and sections we've defined in our exercises. Select the MAIN section of the USER004 application (figure 39.16). Once we link our new section, we are ready to test.

Navigation: Go → PeopleTools → Application Engine → Use → Application Engine →
Application → Correction

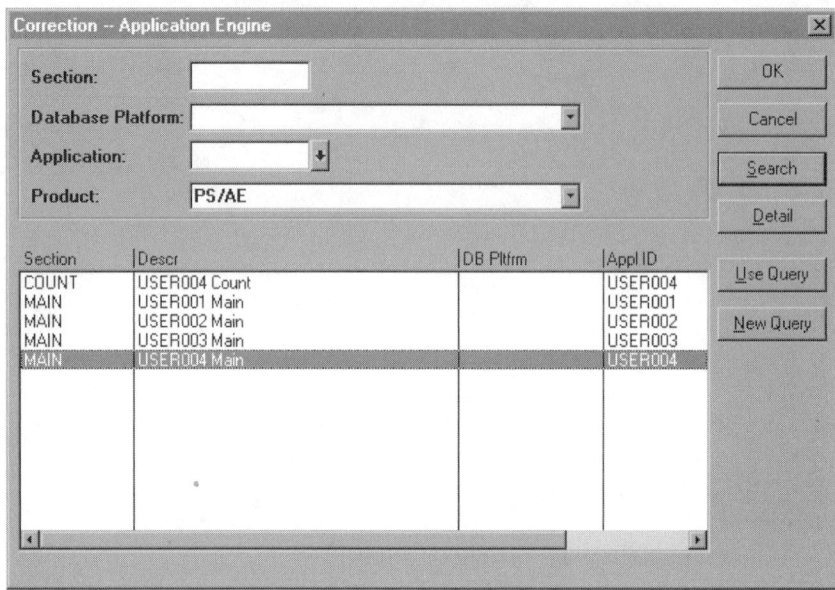

Figure 39.16   Application/section list box for all of our PS/AE exercises to date

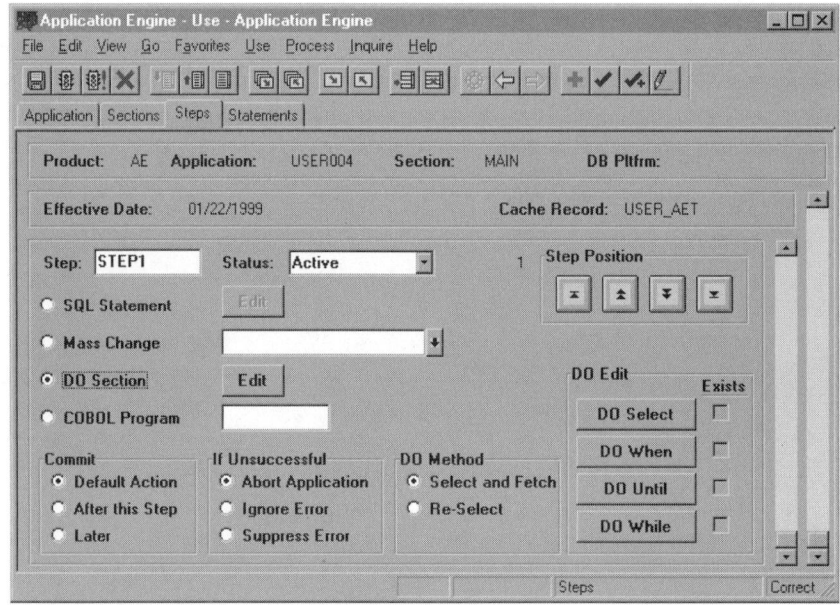

Figure 39.17   Resetting the DO section radio button

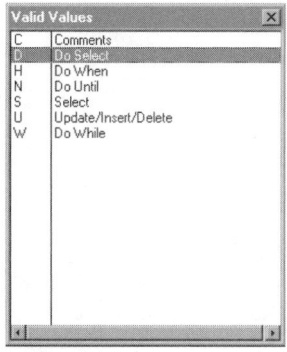

Figure 39.18 Statement type drop-down list box

Return to the statement definition by clicking on the Statements folder tab. Once we change our statement type back to DO Select (figure 39.18), we can proceed with linking our new section COUNT. Remember we deactivated the step by assigning a Comment statement type.

The DO section radio button should now be set. Click on the Edit button to link our new section.

Set the product and application and then click on the section drop-down box.

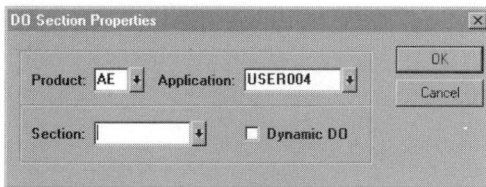

Figure 39.19 DO Section Properties dialog box

You'll see the valid choices for the AE.USER004 program. Our new section COUNT is in the drop-down list. Select the COUNT section (figure 39.20).

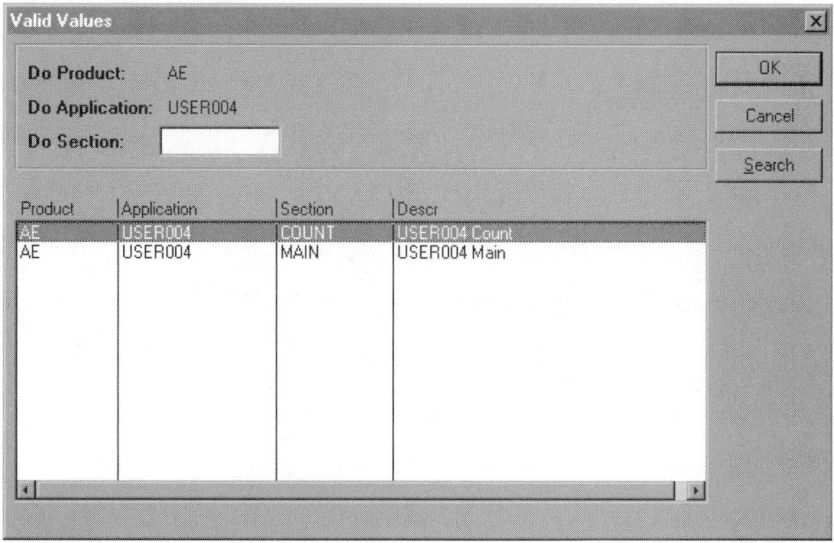

Figure 39.20 Selecting the DO section

Once selected, we return to the DO Section Properties box with our section COUNT filled in. Click the OK button.

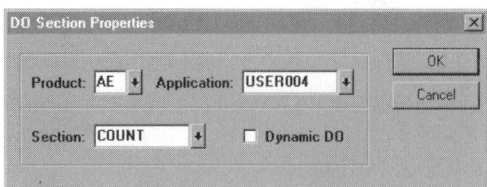

Figure 39.21
**The completed DO Section
Properties dialog box**

When we return to the Step Definition screen, we see the COUNT section displayed to the right of the DO section radio button. For each row returned by the STEP1 DO Select statement, the COUNT section will be executed. Save your work. Let's test our new program.

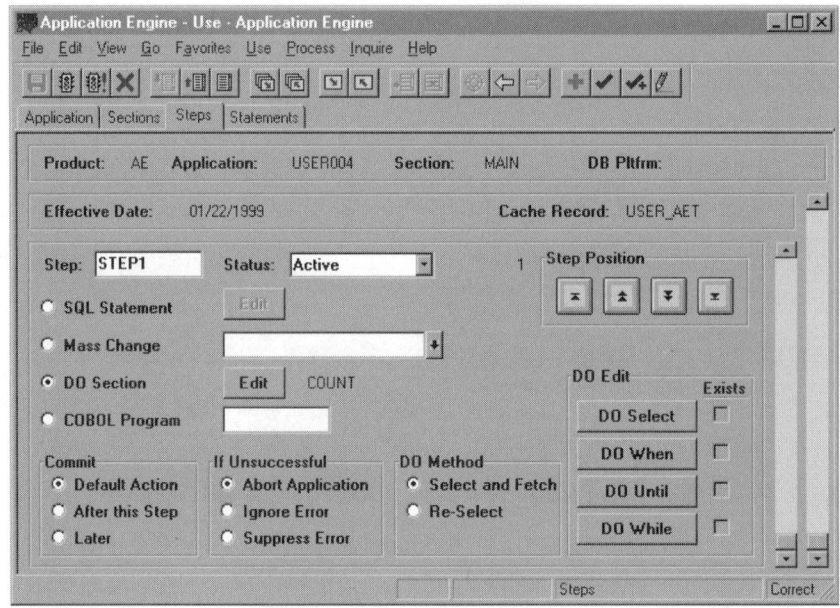

Figure 39.22   The DO Section has been completed

Return to the Process Request Panel and add the Run Control ID #USER004 (figure 39.23). Now, click the OK button.

Navigation: Go → PeopleTools → Application Engine → Process → Request → Request → Add

Figure 39.23
Assign the Run Control ID

When the Process Request panel appears, click on the Fields edit box and highlight the FIELDNAME cache field. Click OK to proceed (figure 39.24).

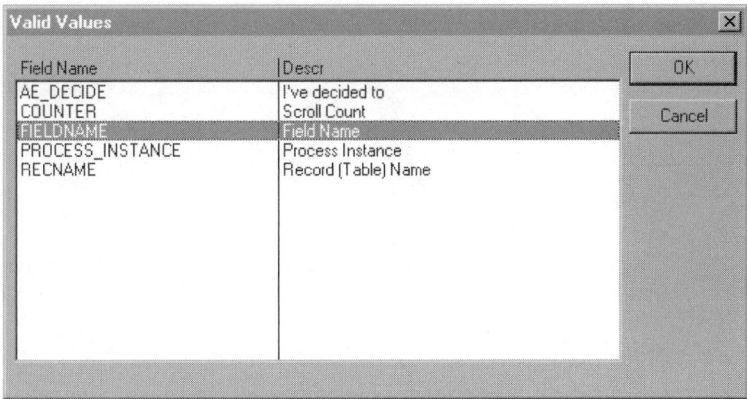

Figure 39.24   The cache field drop-down list box

We assign the value PAY_END_DT to our cache field (figure 39.25). Our Application Engine program now displays the number of rows in every table that has the field PAY_END_DT.

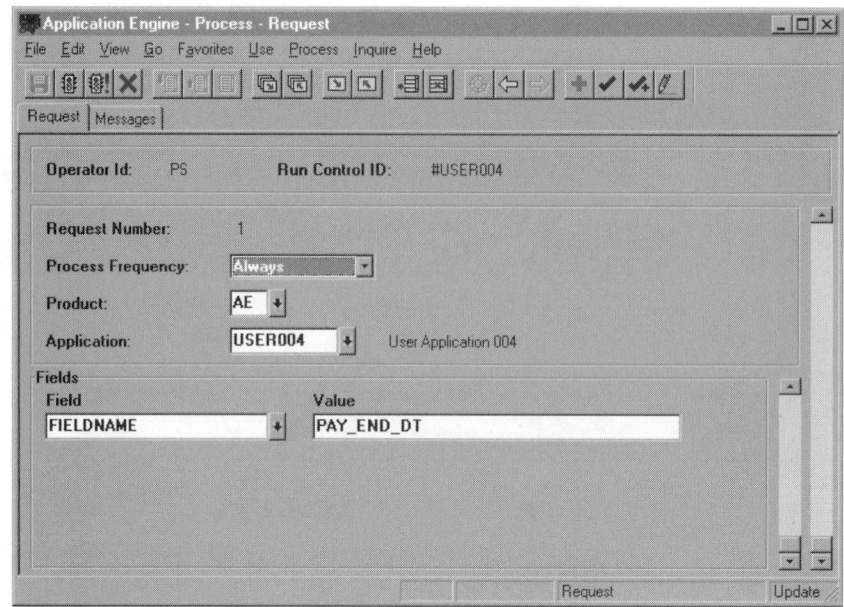

Figure 39.25   Assigning an initial value to the cache field

Once again, highlight the AEADHOC process and click OK.

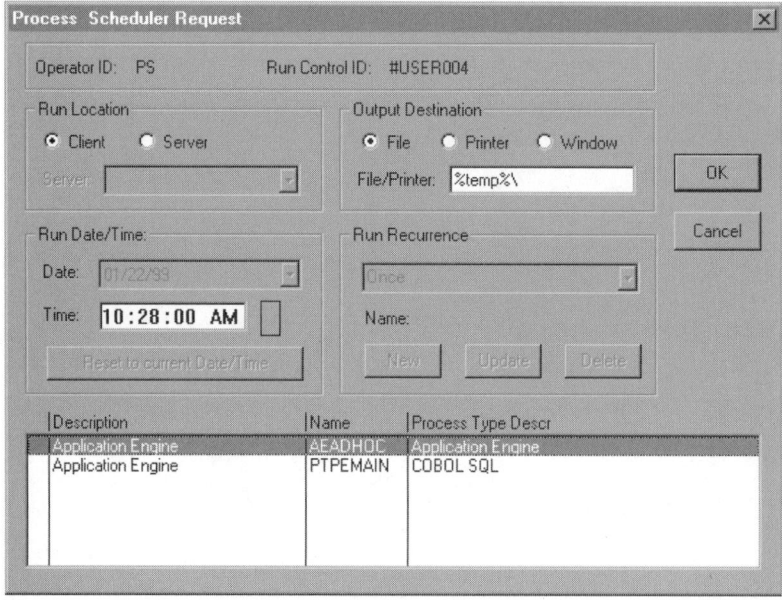

Figure 39.26   Submitting a Process Scheduler request

When running on the client, you may notice an MS-DOS box appear (figure 39.27). You may have missed it in earlier exercises since they processed much quicker. This screen shows the steps as they execute along with any messages generated. You can see our process seems to be working. The records are being displayed with the row counts. When the process ends, we'll look at the Message Log panel.

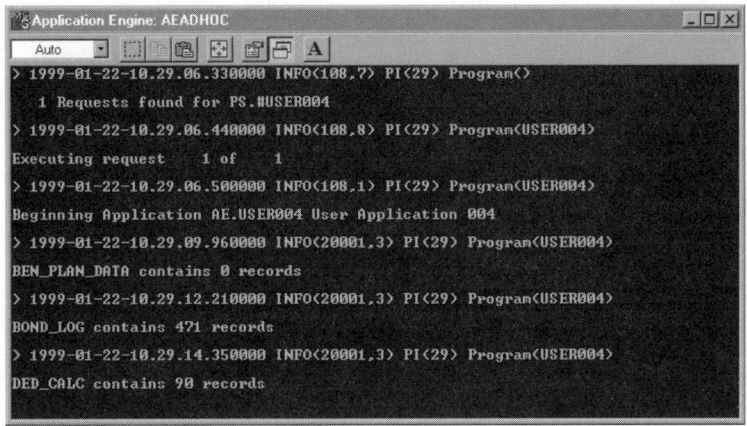

Figure 39.27   AEADHOC MS-DOS box

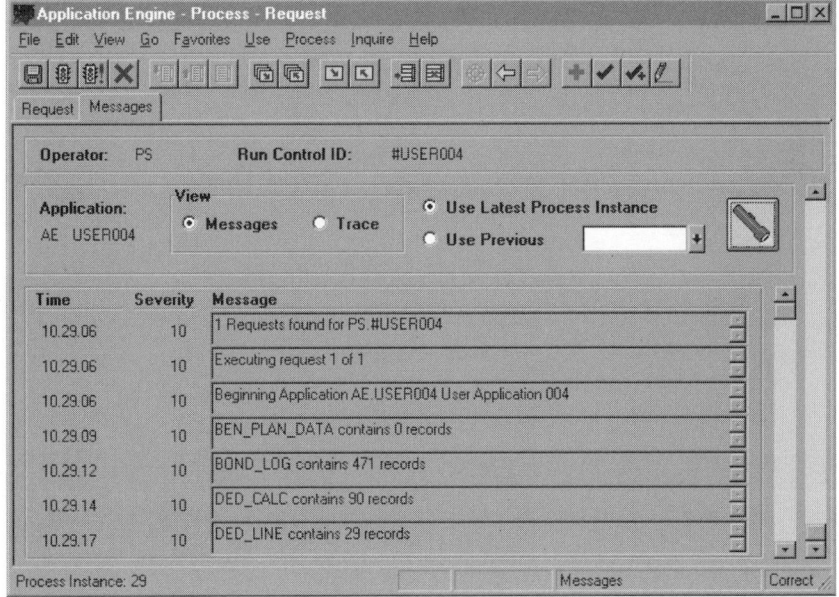

Figure 39.28   Reviewing Process Request messages

Another successful run! The message log output matches that of our SQR version. Before we end this exercise, let's talk about reuseability. During the creation of the COUNT section, we noticed it was identical to the USER003 program we created in exercise 3. Instead of creating a new section, we could routinely have called the USER003.MAIN section to accomplish the same task.

Let's give it a try.

39.1.4   Section reusability

Return to the Step Definition panel in our MAIN Section for STEP1. Click on the Edit button next to the DO section radio button. Instead of linking to Application USER004 section COUNT, link to Application USER003 Section MAIN (figure 39.29). Click the OK button.

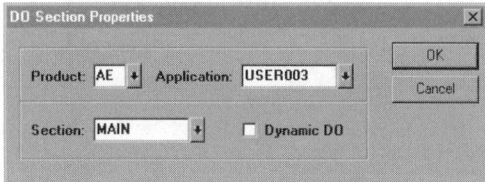

Figure 39.29
DO Section Properties reassignment

We are now linked to a different DO section (figure 39.30). AE.USER003.MAIN will now be performed instead of COUNT. Notice the fully qualified section name indicating product, application, and section. This allows you to borrow routines from other Application Engine programs. Let's test our changes.

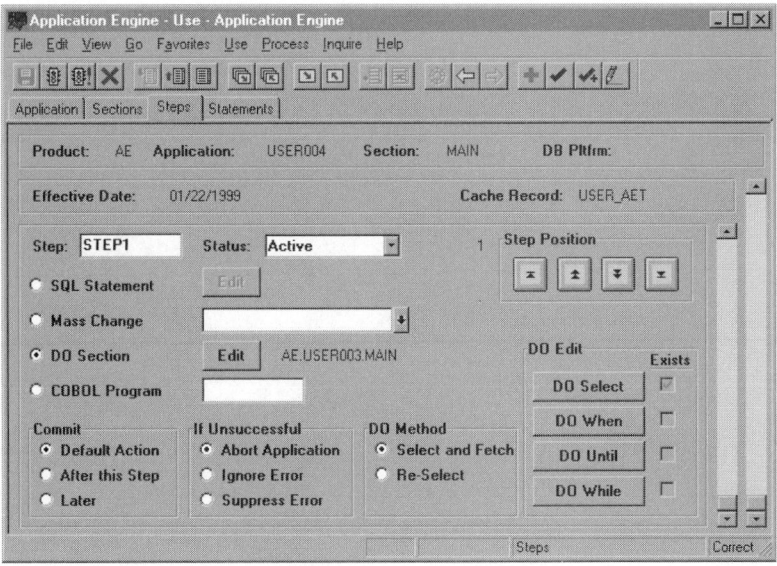

Figure 39.30 Revised DO section

Use the Process Request panel to execute the program. We can now examine the results on the Messages panel (figure 39.31).

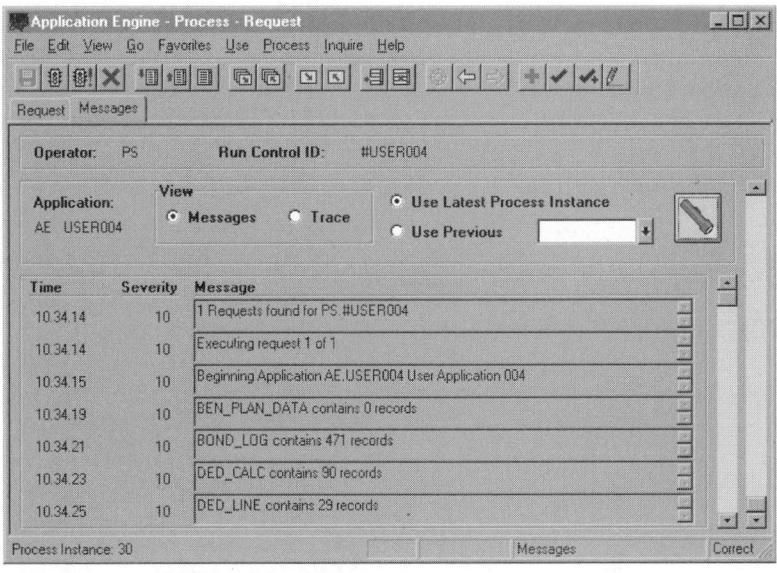

Figure 39.31 Review Process Request messages

Our results are the same as before. This demonstrates the reuseabilty of Application Engine sections.

39.2 SQR/Application Engine comparison

Once again, let's take a look at the logical structure of both our programs:

SQR: Application Engine:

```
Begin-Program                          USER003
        User prompted                          Cache assignment
        Main-Step1                             MAIN.STEP1
                Count-Step1                            COUNT.STEP1
                Count-Step2                            COUNT.STEP2
```

The structure is identical. The Main Step selects the record names that have the field name entered by the user. For each record selected, the COUNT section is processed. Step 1 selects the number of rows, and step 2 generates a message showing the results.

KEY POINTS

1   Multiple Rows may be processed one at a time using a `DO Select` statement.

2   Create and use additional sections to process each row.

3   Application Engine sections are reuseable. This means a section that exists in one application engine program can be called from another. Sections which perform common tasks can be created and used by multiple programs.

CHAPTER 40

Incorporating decision logic

In any programming language, the most vital function is the ability to make decisions and act accordingly. The purpose of this next chapter is to demonstrate the decision-making capability within Application Engine.

40.1 EXERCISE 5: ONLY PROCESS TABLES WITH ROWS

Exercise 4 selected a group of records, determined the number of rows in each, and displayed a message with the results. If you look at the message log, you'll notice many tables have zero rows. To demonstrate the decision-making capability of Application Engine, we're going to produce the messages only for tables that have rows of data.

40.1.1 Creating an SQR version

We'll begin this exercise by displaying the SQR version of this program:

Listing 40.1

USER005.sqr

```
! USER005.SQR

begin-program

input $fieldname 'Enter FIELDNAME' maxlen=15

do Main-Step1

end-program

begin-procedure Main-Step1

begin-select

a.recname

  let $recname    = &a.recname

  do Count-Step1

 from psrecfield    a,
      psrecdefn     b
where a.recname    = b.recname
  and a.fieldname = $fieldname
  and b.rectype    = 0
order by a.recname

end-select

end-procedure

begin-procedure Count-Step1

let $table    = 'ps_' || $recname
let #counter = 0

begin-select

count(*)         &counter

 let #counter = &counter

 if  #counter > 0
     do Msg-Step1
 end-if
```

```
      from [$table]

end-select

end-procedure

begin-procedure Msg-Step1

show ' '
show $recname ' Record Count: ' #counter

end-procedure
```

Once more the user is prompted for a fieldname using the Input statement again. For each table containing the fieldname, a record count is determined. If the record count is greater than zero, a message is produced.

Below is a portion of the SQR.log produced by the run:

```
Enter FIELDNAME: PAY_END_DT

BOND_LOG Record Count: 471.000000
DED_CALC Record Count: 90.000000
DED_LINE Record Count: 29.000000
ESPP_RUNCTL Record Count: 2.000000
PAY_CALENDAR Record Count: 1170.000000
PAY_CALENDR_NLD Record Count: 241.000000
PAY_CAL_BAL_ID Record Count: 911.000000
PAY_CBLD_RUNCTL Record Count: 1.000000
PAY_CHECK Record Count: 7385.000000
PAY_DEDUCTION Record Count: 45710.000000
PAY_DISTRIBUTN Record Count: 975.000000
PAY_EARNINGS Record Count: 13943.000000
PAY_GARNISH Record Count: 262.000000
PAY_GARN_OVRD Record Count: 2.000000
PAY_INS_EARNS Record Count: 8331.000000
PAY_LINE Record Count: 5104.000000
PAY_MESSAGE Record Count: 1.000000

Etc…
```

Notice, no tables are displayed with zero rows.

Now, let's duplicate this functionality in our Application Engine program.

We begin by adding the USER005 application name and the section MAIN (figure 40.1).

Navigation: Go → PeopleTools → Application Engine → Use → Application Engine → Application → Add

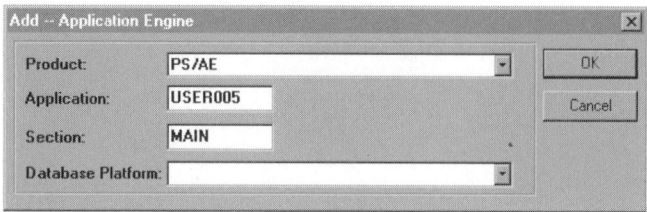

Figure 40.1
Naming the application

Set the description, cache record, version and message set number for our application (figure 40.2).

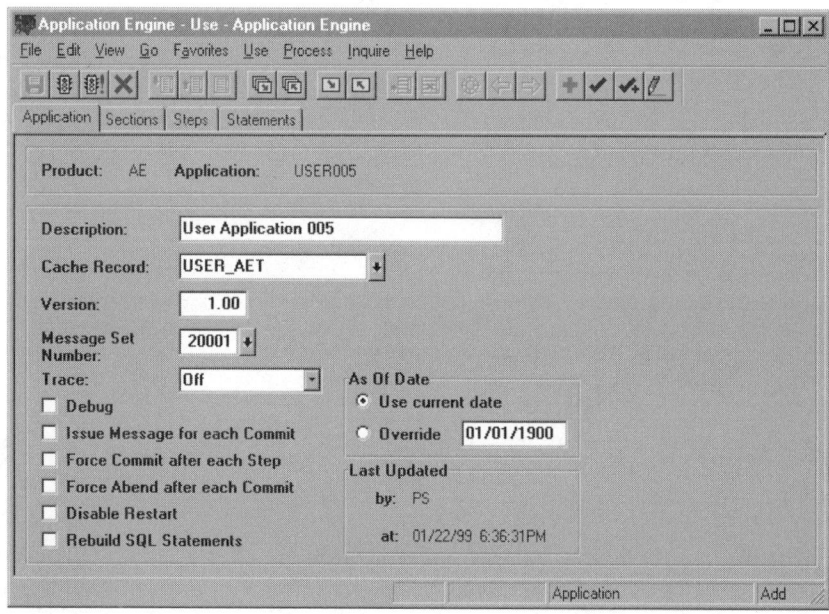

Figure 40.2 Defining the application

Now, set the description on the section MAIN panel.

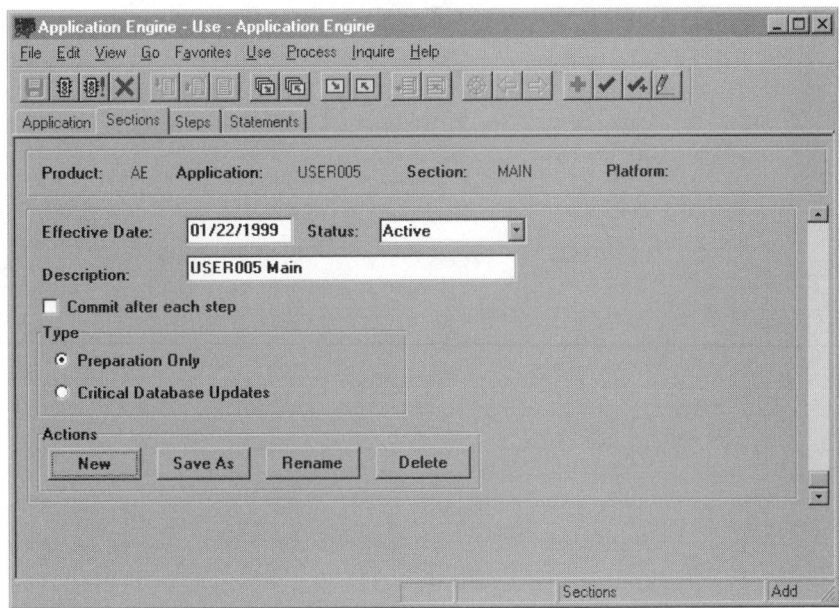

Figure 40.3   Defining section MAIN

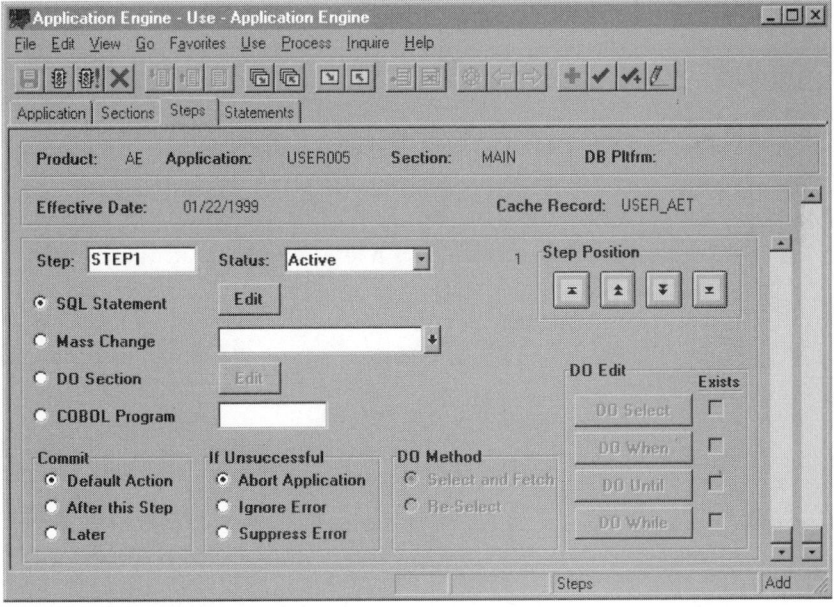

Figure 40.4   Defining STEP1

Step1 of our MAIN section in this exercise is identical to Step1 of the MAIN section of exercise 4. We did learn a small lesson in the last exercise. When using a DO Select statement type, a DO section needs to be defined in order to save the record. We need to create the new section. For now, let's change the statement type to Comment (figure 40.5). Now, save your work.

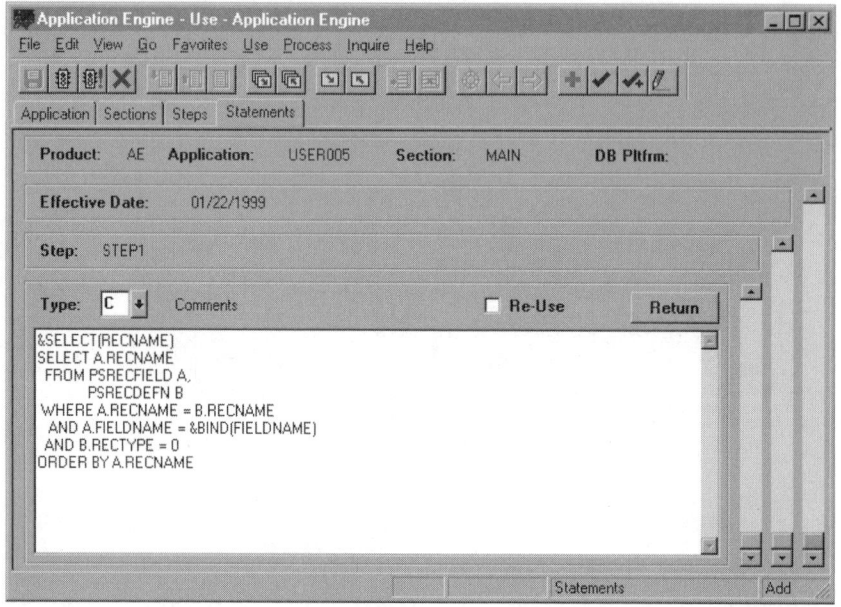

Figure 40.5   DO Select statement with Comment statement type

---

NOTE   The MAIN section does not have to be created first. If you carefully plan the structure of your program before you actually begin building it, you can start with the subordinate sections and work your way backward. We'll demonstrate this approach in exercise #7 found in chapter 42 (Using Run Controls).

Once again, we add a section called COUNT to our application (figure 40.6).

CHAPTER 40   INCORPORATING DECISION LOGIC

Navigation: Go → PeopleTools → Application Engine → Use → Application Engine → Section → Add

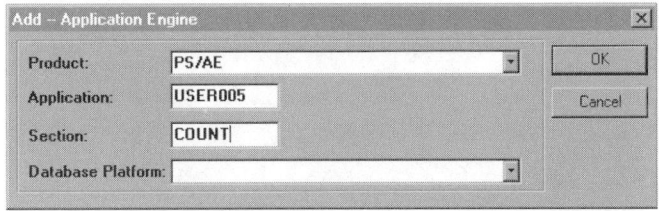

Figure 40.6
Adding a new section

Enter a brief description for the section COUNT.

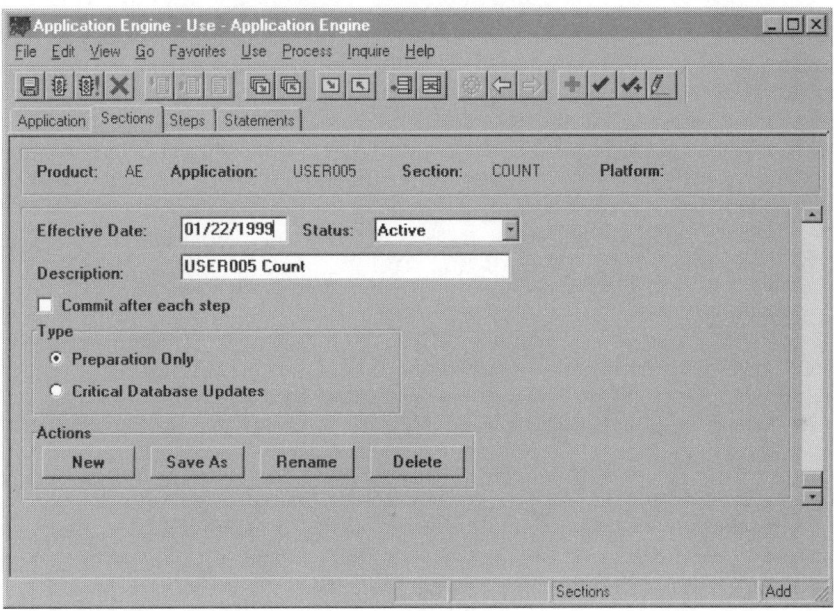

Figure 40.7   Defining section COUNT

We call the first step in our COUNT section STEP1.

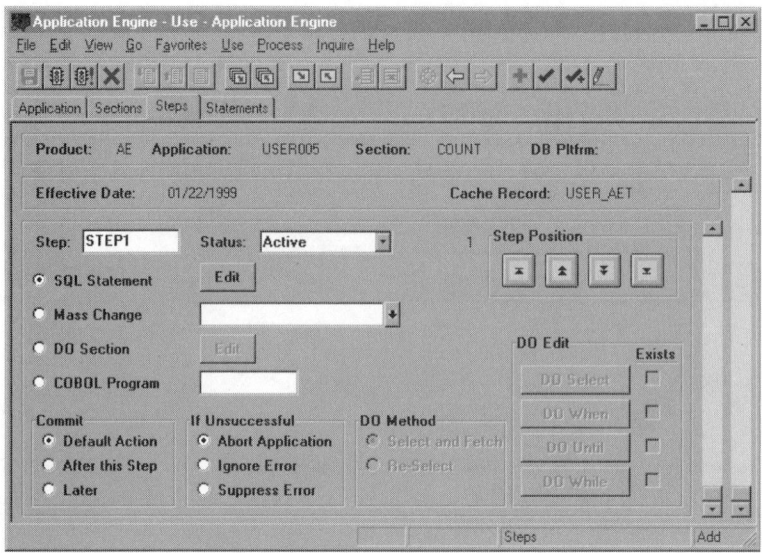

Figure 40.8   Defining STEP1 of section COUNT

Our `Select` statement hasn't changed since our last exercise. The cache field COUNTER is assigned the number of rows in the table. We'll revisit this after we create another section to display a message.

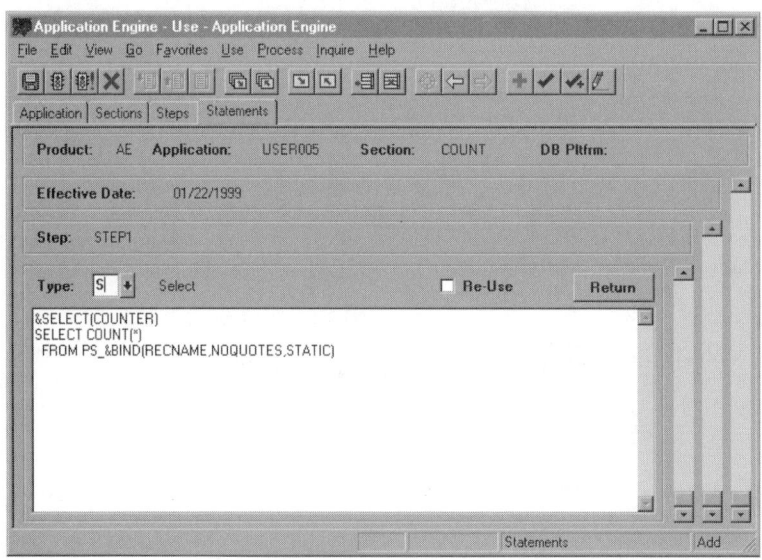

Figure 40.9   Adding Select statement text

We create a new section called MSG. The purpose of this routine is simply to display the table and number of rows in the table (figure 40.10).

Navigation: Go → PeopleTools → Application Engine → Use → Application Engine → Section → Add

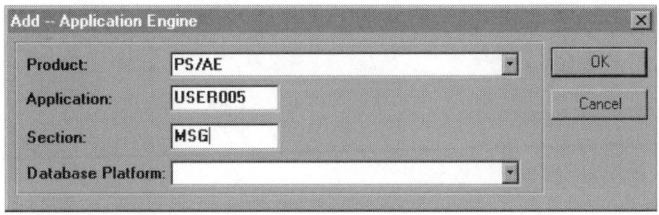

Figure 40.10
Adding another section

Once again a brief description would be appropriate (figure 40.11).

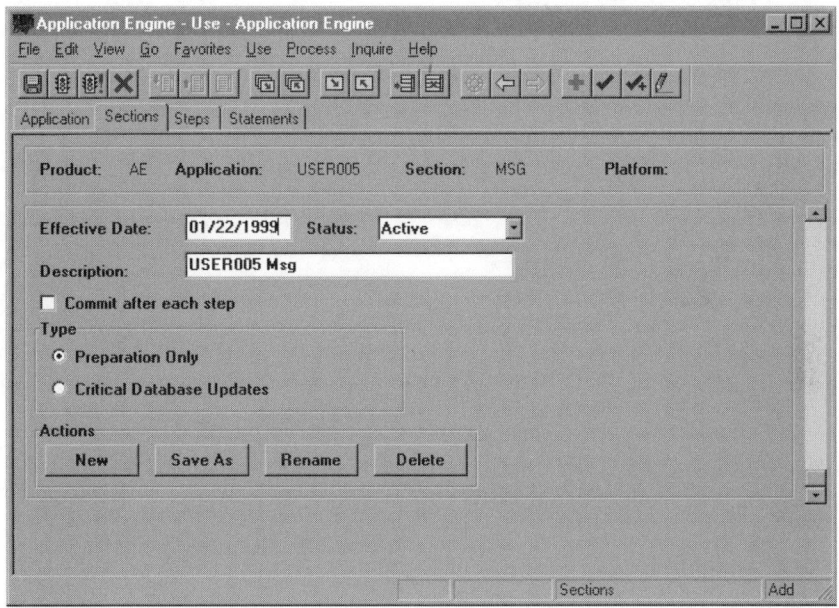

Figure 40.11   Defining section MSG

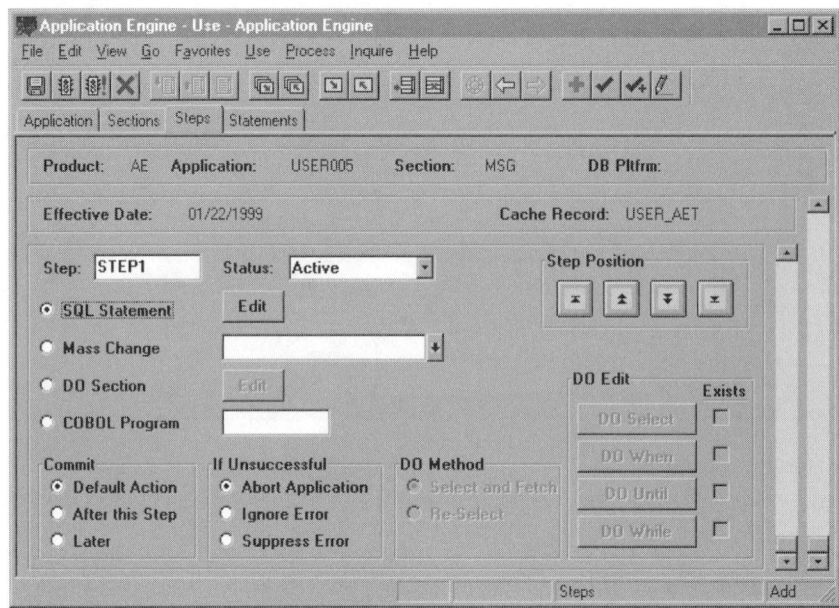

Figure 40.12 Defining STEP1 of section MSG

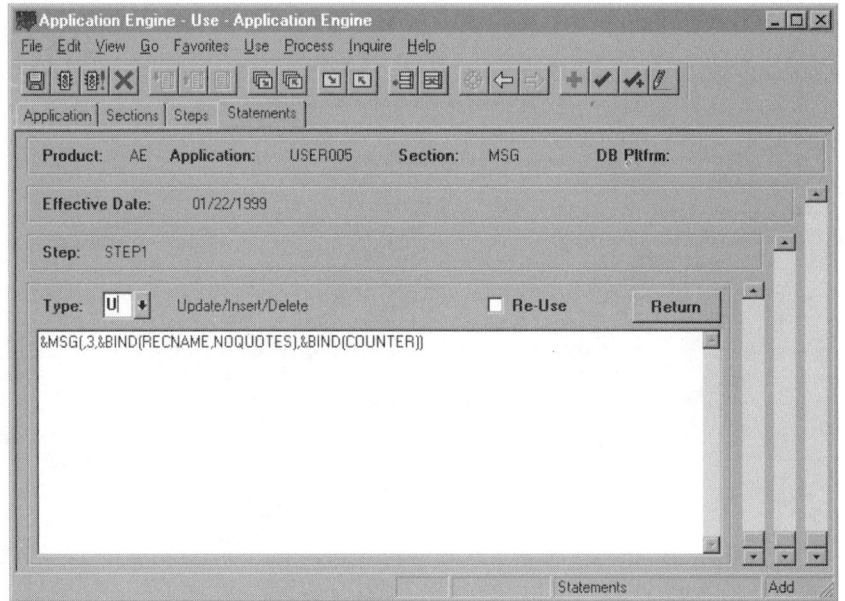

Figure 40.13 Adding the &MSG statement text

CHAPTER 40 INCORPORATING DECISION LOGIC

The &MSG function hasn't changed from the last exercise either. One main difference exists between this exercise and the last. In exercise 4, the message was included in a step immediately following the first step. The message step was executed unconditionally. In this exercise, we've place the message step in an entirely new section called MSG. The MSG section will only be performed if the row count is greater than zero. We now return to our MAIN section to link the COUNT section to our application (figure 40.14).

NOTE   Remember the &MSG function only works if the statement type is set to "U".

Navigation: Go → PeopleTools → Application Engine → Use → Application Engine → Application → Correction

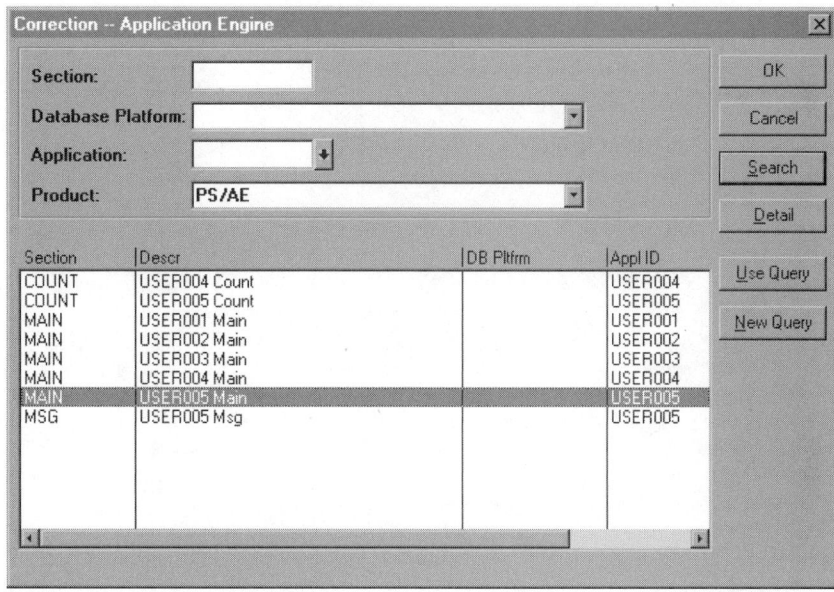

Figure 40.14   Application/section list box for all of our PS/AE exercises to date

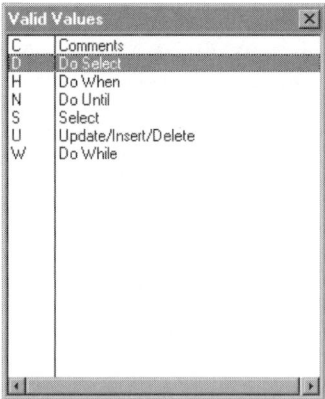

Figure 40.15 Statement type drop-down list box

Return to the MAIN section of our application (USER005) in Correction mode. Remember to enter the product we're using (PS/AE), and click on the Search push button. You'll see all of the applications and sections we've defined in our exercises. Select the MAIN section of the USER005 application.

Return to the statement definition by clicking on the Statements folder tab. Once we change our statement type back to DO Select, we can proceed with linking our section COUNT (figure 40.15).

The SQL statement type is set to DO Select. Now click on the DO section edit button (figure 40.16).

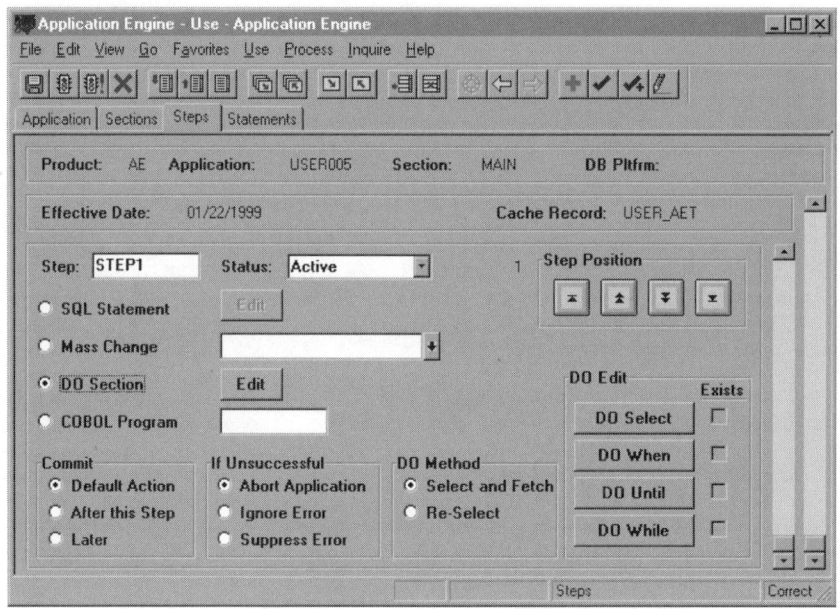

Figure 40.16 Setting the DO section radio button

Set the product and application and then click on the section drop-down box (figure 40.17).

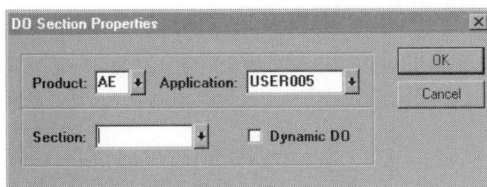

Figure 40.17
DO Section Properties dialog box

Along with our MAIN section, you can see the other two sections we've created. We need to link the COUNT section to our MAIN `Select`. Click on the COUNT section.

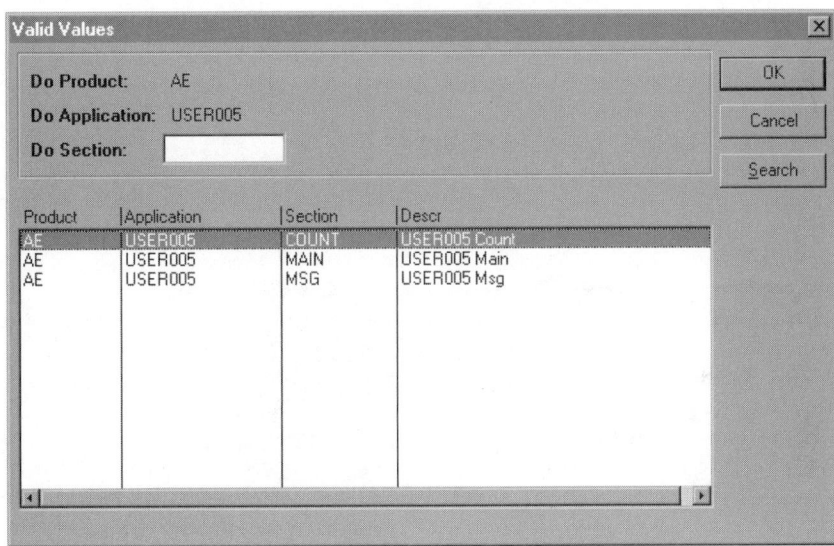

Figure 40.18   Selecting the DO section

Once selected, we return to the DO Section Properties Box with our section COUNT filled in. Click the OK button.

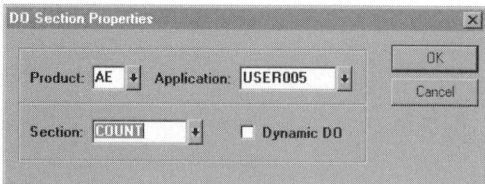

Figure 40.19
The completed DO Section dialog box

When we return to the Step Definition screen we see the COUNT section displayed to the right of the DO section radio button (figure 40.20). For each row returned by the STEP1 DO `Select` statement the COUNT section will be executed. We'll now return to the COUNT section.

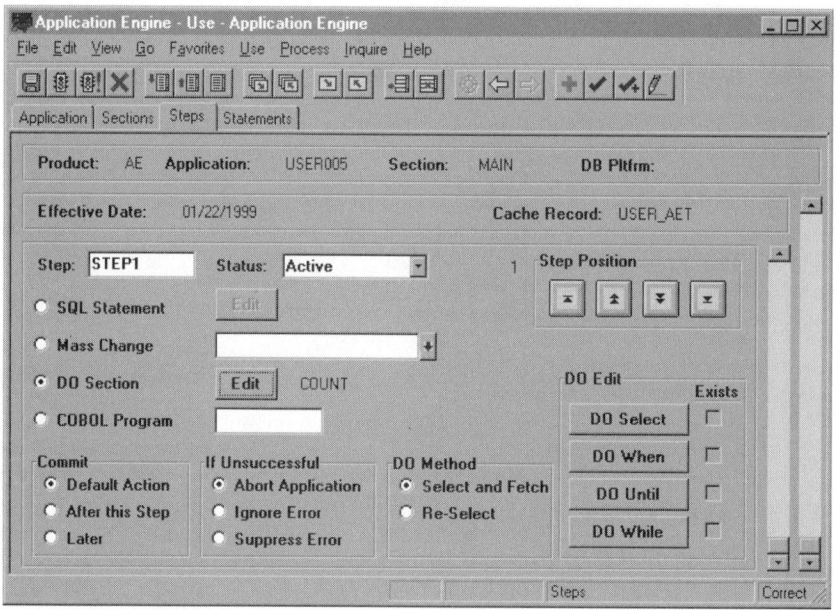

Figure 40.20   The DO Section has been completed

Return to the COUNT Section of our Application (USER005) in Correction Mode. Once again set the Product to PS/AE and click on the Search push button. Select the COUNT section of our USER005 application.

Navigation: Go → PeopleTools → Application Engine → Use → Application Engine → Application → Correction

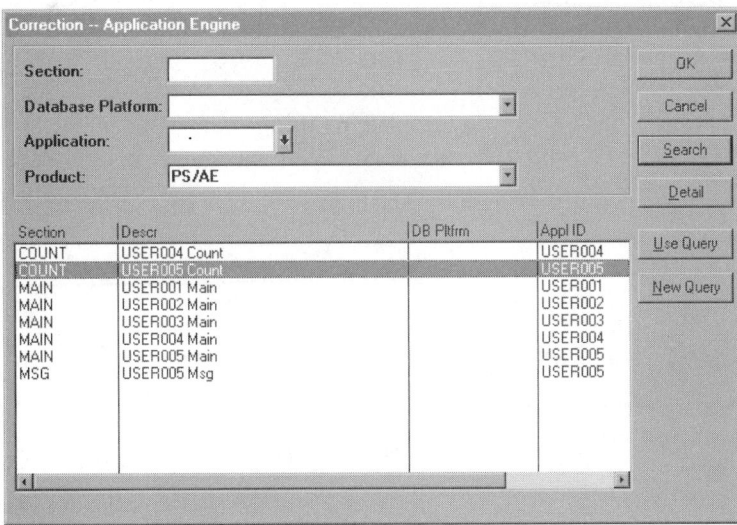

Figure 40.21   Application/section list box again

Add a second step called STEP2 to our COUNT section (figure 40.22). You can use the F7 Key to insert a new row.

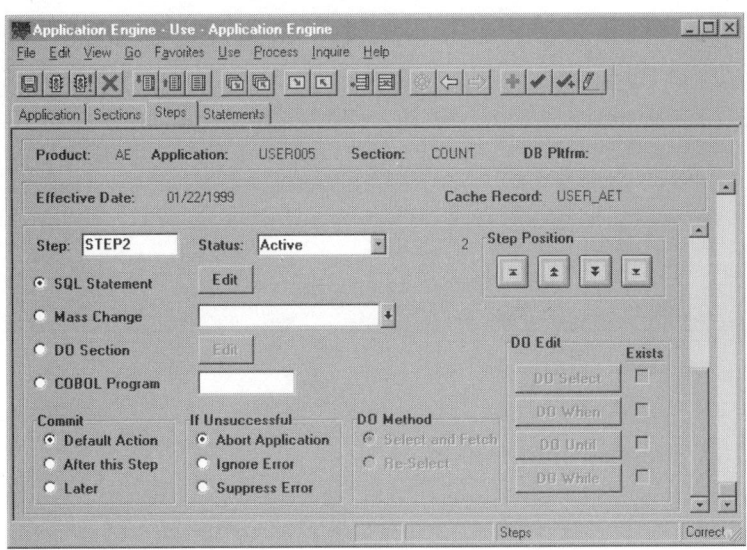

Figure 40.22   Creating STEP2 in section COUNT

40.1.2   Introducing the DO When statement type

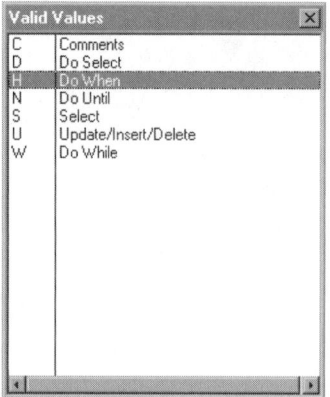

Use the Statements folder tab to define the statement. Click on the Statement Type edit box.

Select the DO When statement type in the drop-down list box shown in figure 40.23.

We're using a new statement type called DO When (figure 40.24). A DO section will be performed based on the results of a True or False Select statement. In our case we are evaluating the cache field COUNTER.

Figure 40.23   Select the DO When statement type

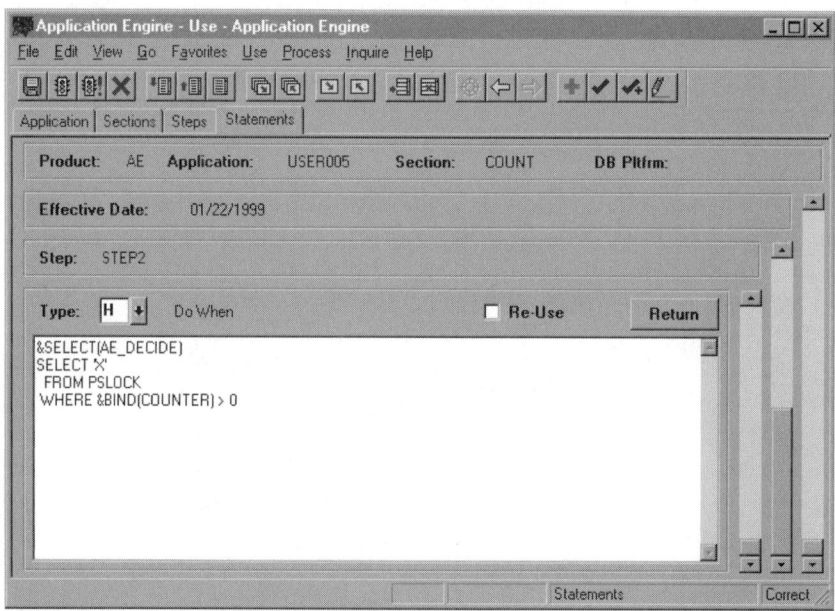

Figure 40.24   DO When statement text

40.1.3   PSLOCK and decision making

We are using a PeopleSoft-delivered table called PSLOCK which consists of one row. We're going to use the PSLOCK table as a placeholder instead of actually selecting data from the table itself. If you are an Oracle user, you may be familiar with this technique against the DUAL table. Although the main function of the PSLOCK table has little to do with Application Engine, it is ideal for decision-making functions such as this. You will find this frequently in PeopleSoft A/E processes. Let's take a closer look at our statement text:

```
&SELECT(AE_DECIDE)
SELECT 'X'
  FROM PSLOCK
WHERE &BIND(COUNTER) > 0
```

First, let's look at the SQL Select statement. If the cache field COUNTER has a value greater than zero, a single row with the character 'X' will be returned. This value will then be assigned to the cache field AE_DECIDE using the &SELECT function. If the COUNTER value is not greater than zero, the AE_DECIDE cache field will have a default value of blank, and no rows will be returned by the Select statement.

If a DO When Select statement returns rows, the DO section will be performed. This is a simple but effective decision-making tool. Now, we need to link our MSG Section to this step.

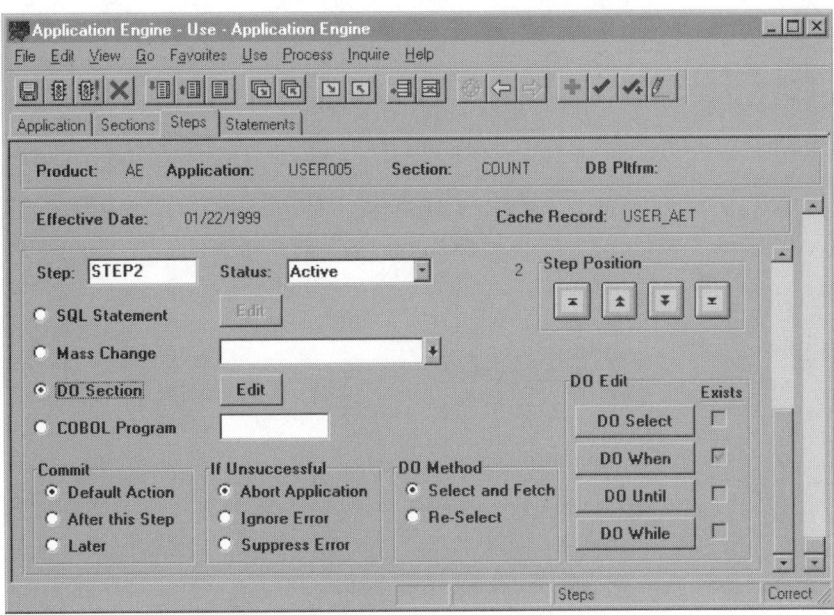

Figure 40.25 Setting the DO section for our DO When statement type

Click on the DO section edit box.. You may have noticed the DO Edit group box on the lower right side of the panel. Because we're using the DO When statement type, the Exists checkbox is automatically filled in next to the DO When push button. Pressing the DO When push button has the same affect as clicking on the Statements folder tab. It's simply an alternate method of navigation.

Set the product and application and then click on the section drop-down box (figure 40.26).

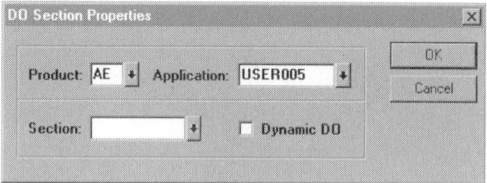

Figure 40.26
DO section properties dialog box

Highlight and click on the MSG section (figure 40.27).

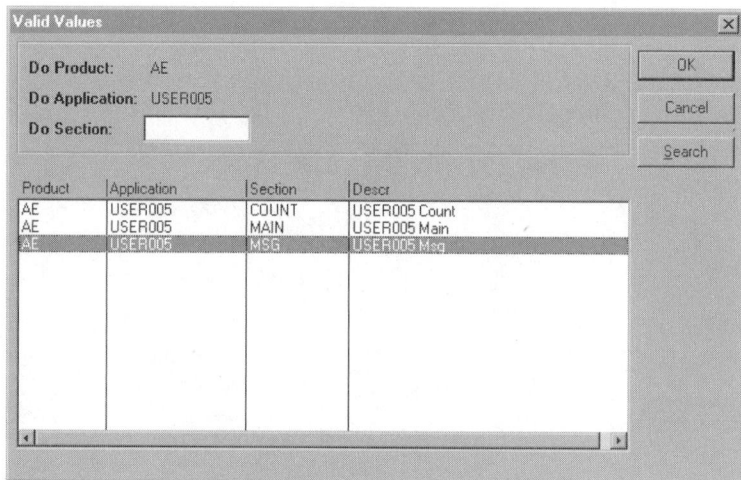

Figure 40.27   Selecting the DO section

Once selected, we return to the DO Section Properties box with our section MSG filled in (figure 40.28). Click the OK button.

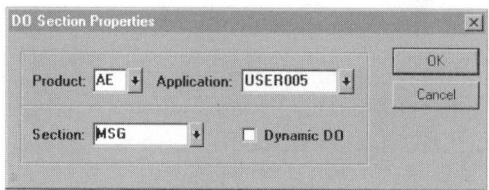

Figure 40.28
The completed DO Section
Properties dialog box

When we return to the Step Definition screen, we see the MSG section displayed to the right of the DO section radio button. For each row returned by the STEP2 DO When statement, the MSG section will be executed. This means only tables with a row count greater than zero will be displayed in the message log. We're ready to test our program.

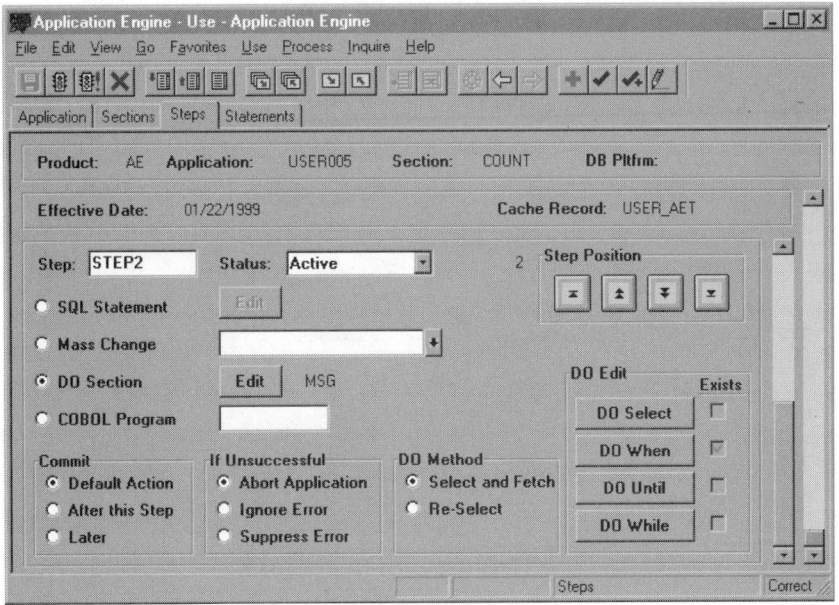

Figure 40.29 The DO section has been completed

Return to the Process Request panel and add the Run Control ID #USER005. Click the OK button.

Navigation: Go → PeopleTools → Application Engine → Process → Request → Request → Add

Figure 40.30
Adding the Run Control ID

When the Process Request panel appears, click on the Field edit box and enter the cache field FIELDNAME. Now, enter the value PAY_END_DT (figure 40.31). Save the record and click on the Traffic Signal to initiate the process request.

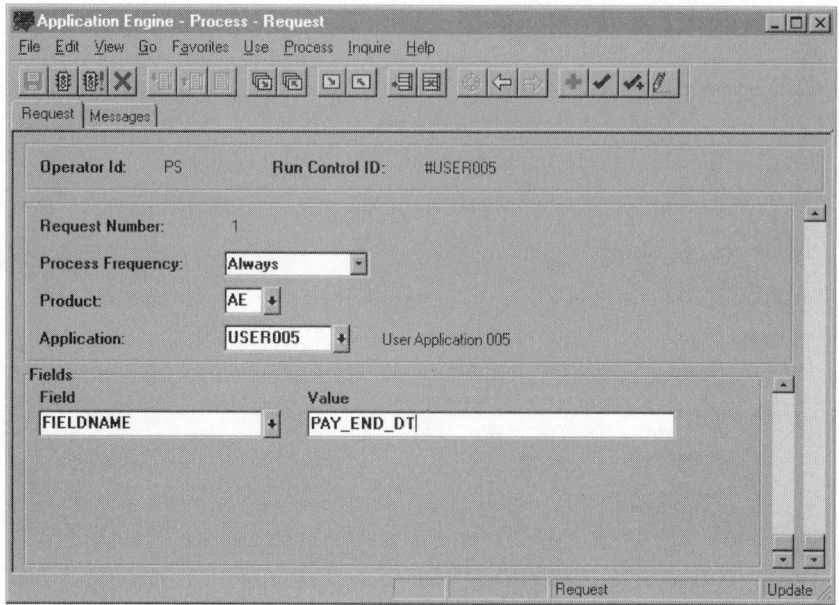

Figure 40.31   Assigning an initial value to the cache field

Once again, highlight the AEADHOC process (figure 40.32) and click OK.

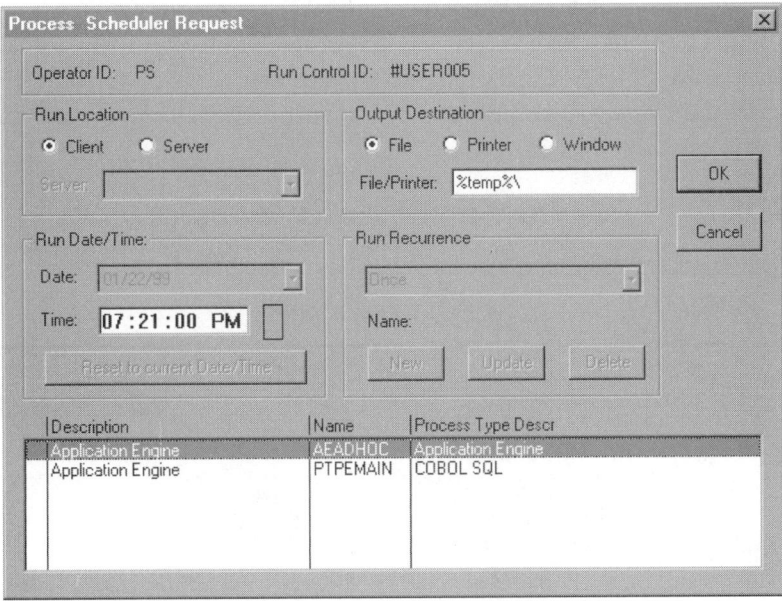

Figure 40.32 Submitting a Process Scheduler request

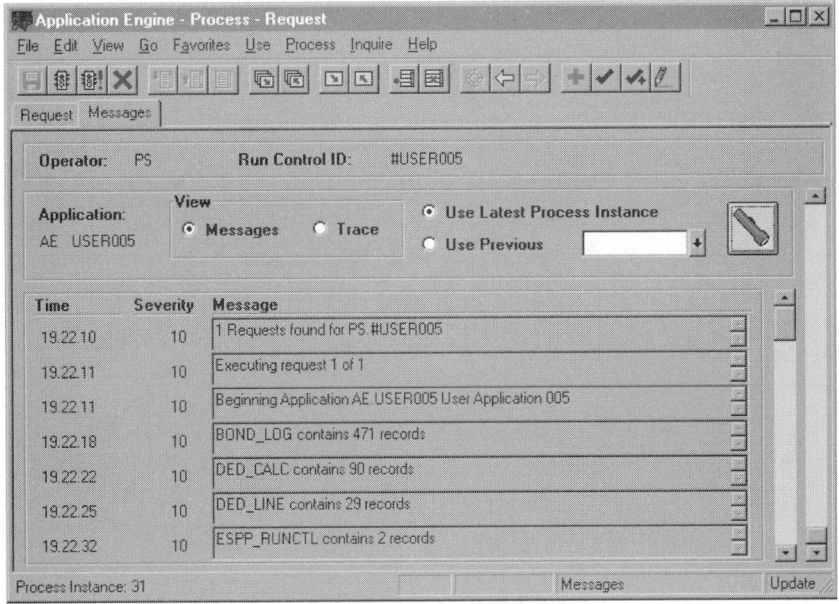

Figure 40.33 Reviewing Process Request messages

We are once again successful! The message log output matches that of our SQR version. Only tables that contain rows of data are displaying. Using the DO When construct, we've filtered out all tables with a zero row count. Two additional statement types—the DO Until and DO While statement types—control section execution in a similar fashion.

40.2 SQR/APPLICATION ENGINE COMPARISON

Once again, let's take a look at the logical structure of both our programs:

SQR:

```
Begin-Program
        User prompted
        Main-Step1
                Count-Step1
                        Msg-Step1
```

Application Engine:

```
USER003
        Cache assignment
        MAIN.STEP1
                COUNT.STEP1
                COUNT.STEP2
                        MSG.STEP1
```

This time the structures are slightly different. The SQR program doesn't need an additional step to perform a decision. A simple IF statement is used to determine if the Msg-Step1 procedure should be performed. Application Engine requires the additional step to build a DO When condition. Based on the results, the MSG section is performed.

KEY POINTS

1   You can control the processing logic using a DO When, DO While, or DO Until statement. This adds decision-making capability to your program and can regulate which sections are performed.

2   The PSLOCK table is often used as a dummy table to evaluate &BIND data values. It can be used in the same manner as the DUAL table is used in Oracle.

CHAPTER 41

Dynamic sections

An Application Engine program has the ability to call a section dynamically. This is a very powerful feature. Sections may be created and, based on certain conditions, a particular section may be executed. Let's begin.

41.1 EXERCISE 6: CALLING DYNAMIC SECTIONS

Our exercise is simple. We are going to dynamically call a section that either writes the message "Hello World" or "Goodbye." Dynamic sections are called based on the contents of the cache field AE_SECTION. This field must exist in the cache record we've designated for our application. We'll populate this field on the Process Request panel with the name of the section we'd like to perform. We begin by displaying a simple SQR that prompts the user for their choice of messages to display. Keep in mind the SQR version isn't dynamic—it simply performs the routine based on user selection—but it will demonstrate the logic flow as if it were dynamic.

41.1.1   Creating an SQR version

```
! USER006.SQR

begin-program

input $choice 'Enter Section# (1=Hello 2=Goodbye)' maxlen=1

evaluate $choice
   when = '1'
      do Hello-Step1
   when = '2'
      do Goodbye-Step1
end-evaluate

end-program

begin-procedure Hello-Step1
show 'Hello World'
end-procedure

begin-procedure Goodbye-Step1
show 'Goodbye'
end-procedure
```

If the user enters a '1', the SQR.log looks like this:

```
Hello World
```

If the user enters a '2', the SQR.log looks like this:

```
Goodbye
```

Let's create a version of the program using Application Engine.

We begin by adding the USER006 application name and section MAIN (figure 41.1).

Navigation: Go → PeopleTools → Application Engine → Use → Application Engine → Application → Add

Figure 41.1
Naming the application

CHAPTER 41   DYNAMIC SECTIONS

Fill in the description, version, and message set number as we've done in the past exercises. We're going to use a different cache record called AE_TESTAPPL_AET. This is a delivered PeopleSoft record. The field AE_SECTION is contained in this record so it's perfectly suited for our dynamic section exercise. We could have added this field to our USER_AET cache record, but I wanted to demonstrate the cache record assignment. There is no need to create additional cache records if one exists that meets your requirements.

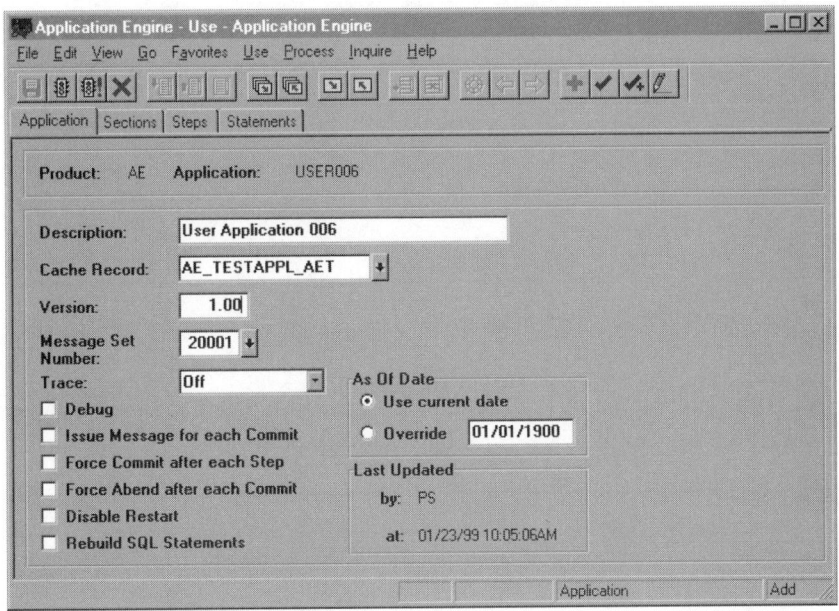

Figure 41.2 Defining the application

We add our section MAIN description (figure 41.3).

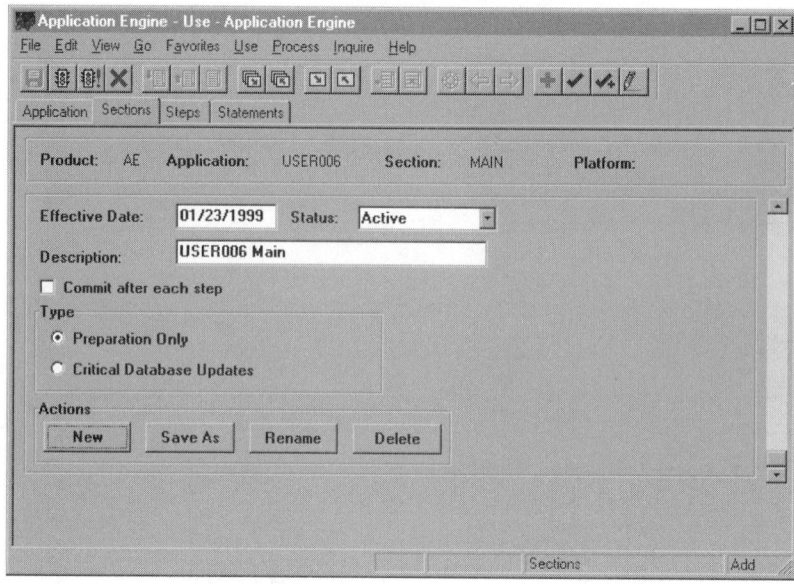

Figure 41.3   Defining section MAIN

We call our step STEP1 and click on the DO section radio button. Next, you click on the Edit button to indicate the section to perform.

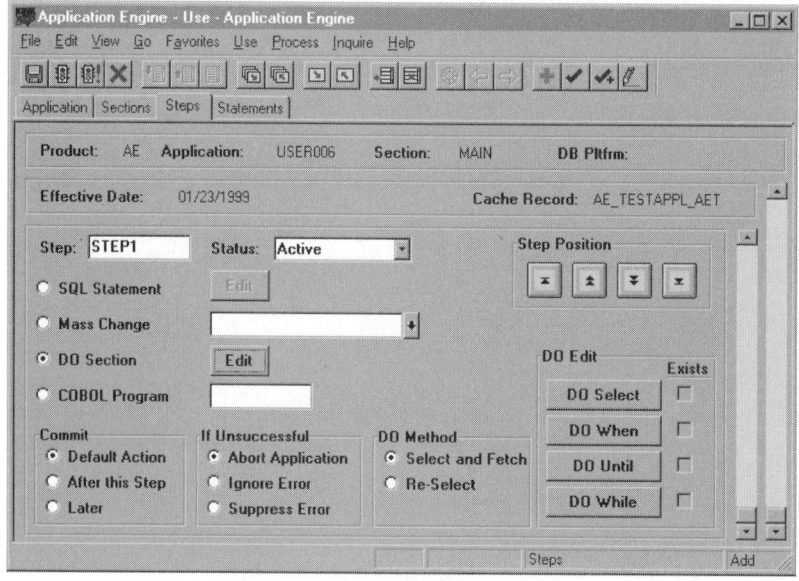

Figure 41.4   Defining STEP1

41.1.2 The &SECTION symbolic

When the DO Section Properties box appears, click on the dynamic DO checkbox (figure 41.5). Notice the &SECTION symbolic appears. You can also notice the product, application, and section edit boxes have been grayed out. This means the section you want to perform must exist within your Application Engine program. You cannot dynamically call a section from another Application Engine program.

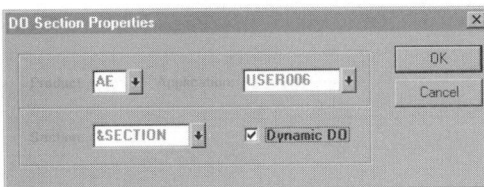

Figure 41.5
Designating dynamic section on DO Section Properties

When you return to the Step Definition panel, you'll notice the section being called is set to (DYNAMIC). When this step is executed, the DO section is determined by substituting the contents of the AE_SECTION cache field.

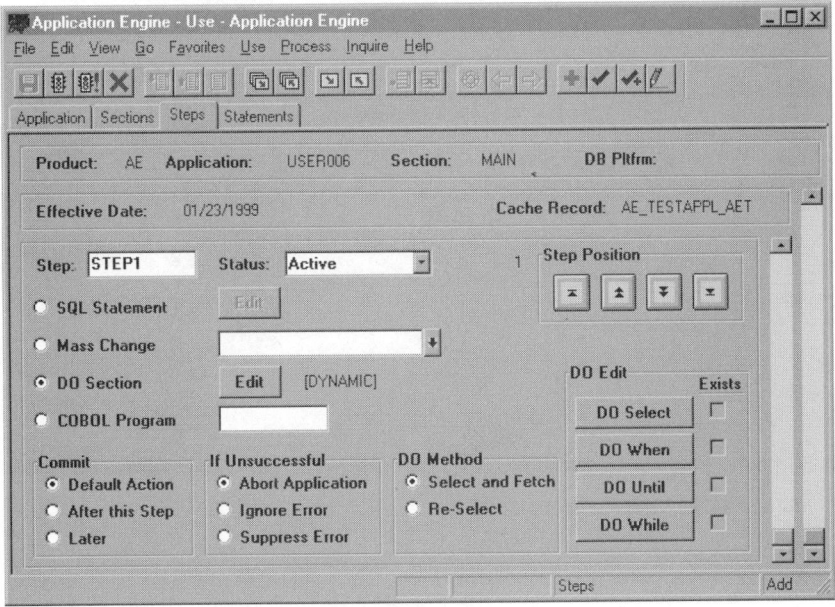

Figure 41.6   The DO section has been completed

We'll now add another section, called HELLO, to our application (figure 41.7).

Navigation: Go → PeopleTools → Application Engine → Use → Application Engine → Section → Add

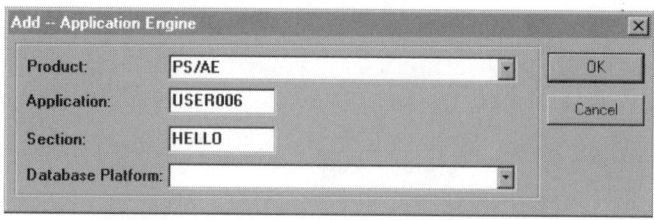

Figure 41.7
Adding another section
called HELLO

Fill in the description for the HELLO section (figure 41.8).

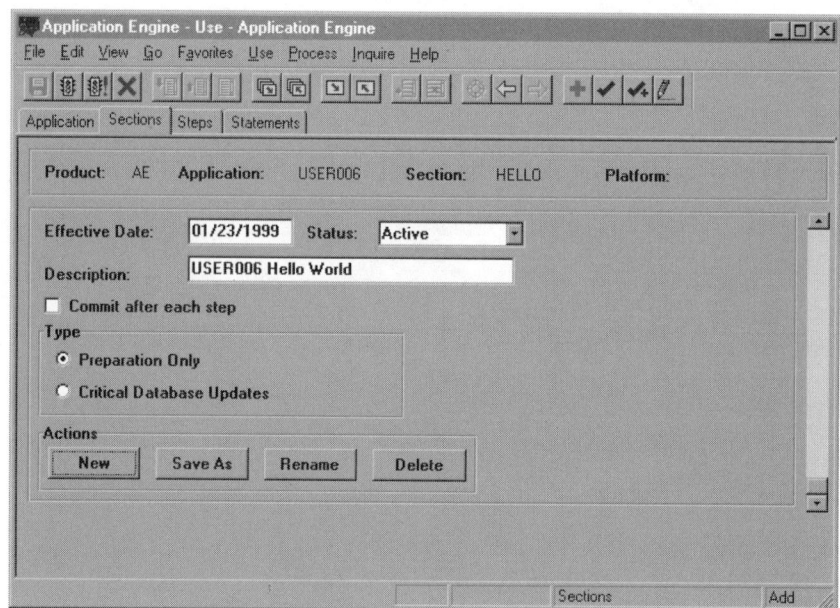

Figure 41.8   Defining section HELLO

We call the first step of the HELLO section STEP1 (figure 41.9).

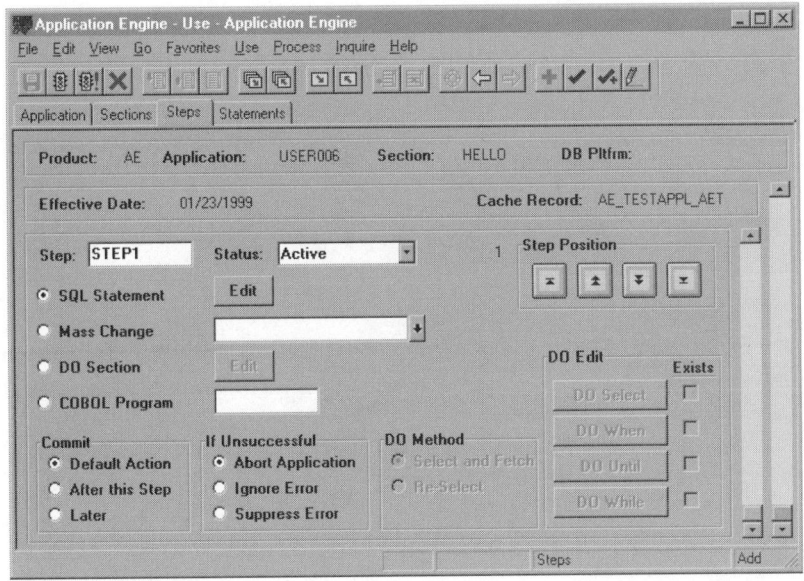

Figure 41.9 Defining STEP1 of section HELLO

We use the &MSG function to display "Hello World" on the message log (figure 41.10).

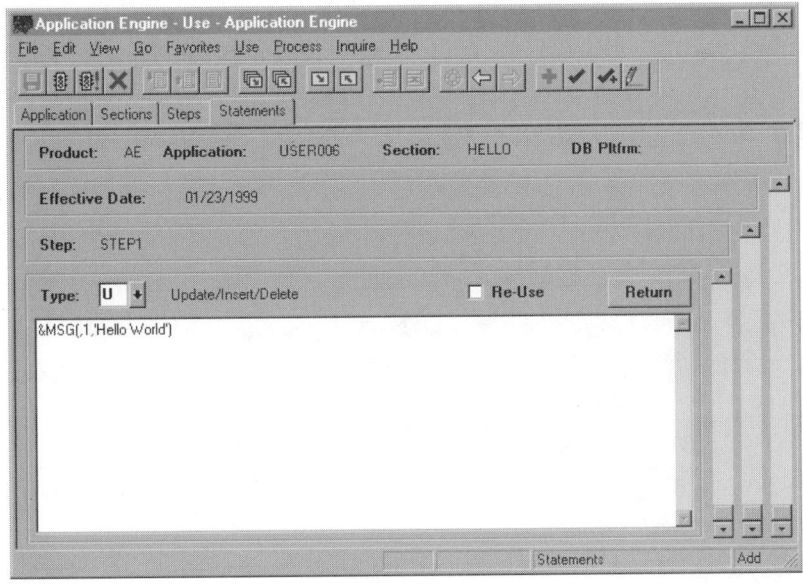

Figure 41.10 Adding the &MSG statement text

We'll now add another section to our application called GOODBYE (figure 41.11).

Navigation: Go → PeopleTools → Application Engine → Use → Application Engine → Section → Add

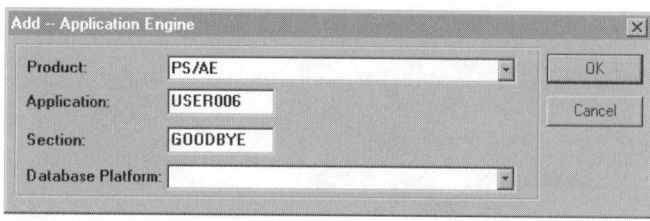

Figure 41.11 Adding another section called GOODBYE

Fill in the description for the GOODBYE section (figure 41.12).

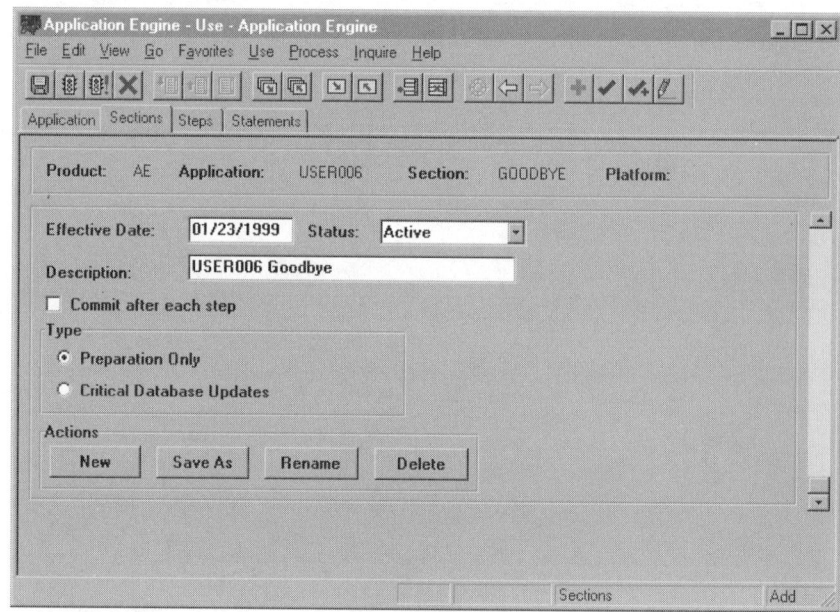

Figure 41.12   Defining section GOODBYE

We call the first step of the GOODBYE section STEP1 (figure 41.13).

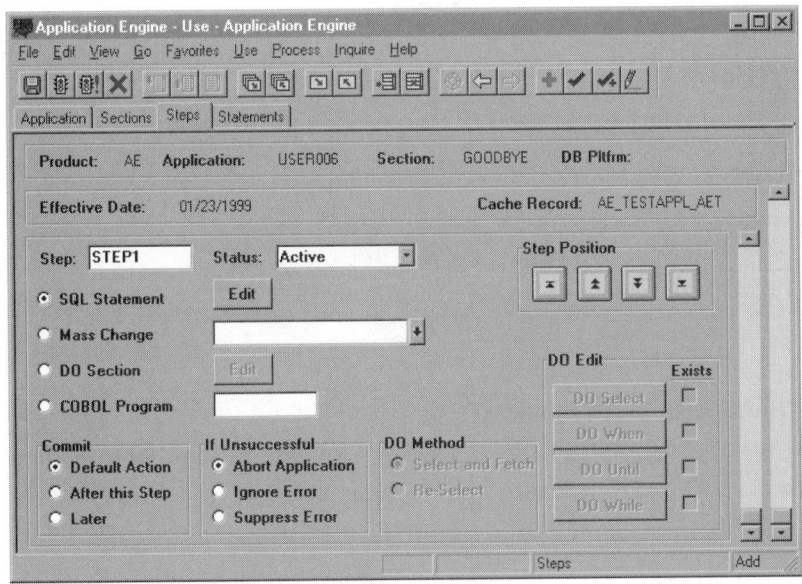

Figure 41.13   Defining STEP1 of section GOODBYE

We use the &MSG function to display "Goodbye" on the message log (figure 41.14).

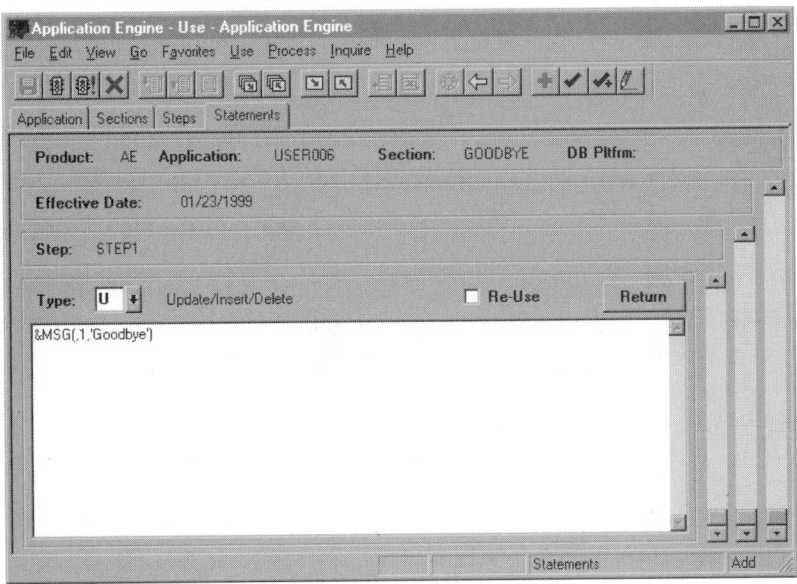

Figure 41.14   Adding the &MSG statement text

We're ready to test the USER006 application.

Return to the Process Request panel and add the Run Control ID #USER006. Click the OK button.

Navigation: Go → PeopleTools → Application Engine → Process → Request → Request → Add

Figure 41.15
Adding the Run Control ID

41.1.3   The AE_SECTION cache field

When the Process Request panel appears, click on the Field edit box. and scroll through the field list (figure 41.16). Select the cache field AE_SECTION.

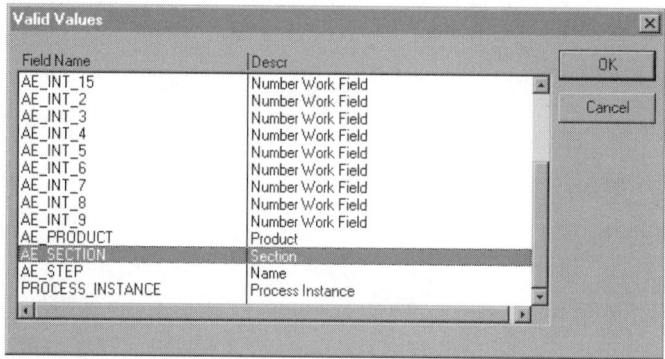

Figure 41.16   The cache field drop-down list box

We can now enter the name of the section which we'd like to perform. For the AE_SECTION cache field, we assign a value of HELLO. Our USER006 Application Engine program substitutes the section HELLO when it processes the &SECTION symbolic. Once the Process Request panel is populated correctly, click on the Traffic Signal to initiate a Process Scheduler request.

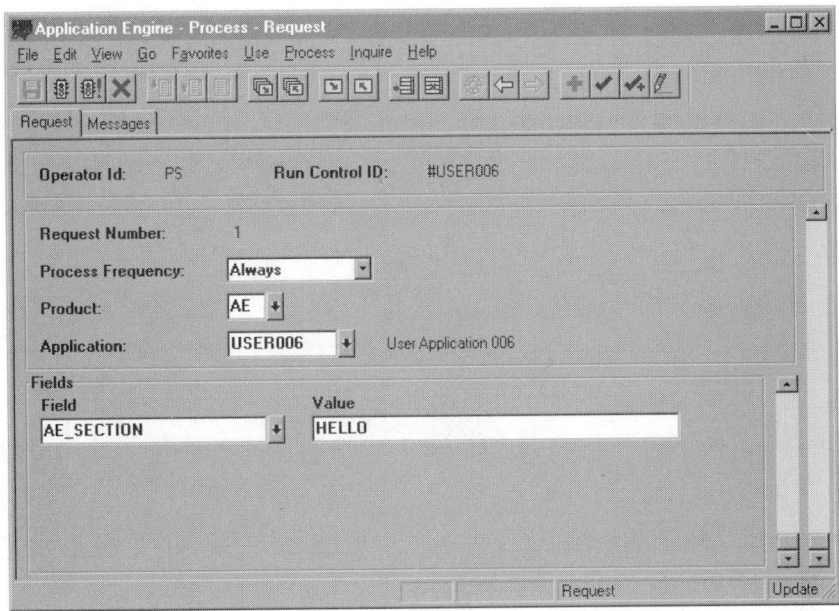

Figure 41.17   Assigning the dynamic section field the section HELLO

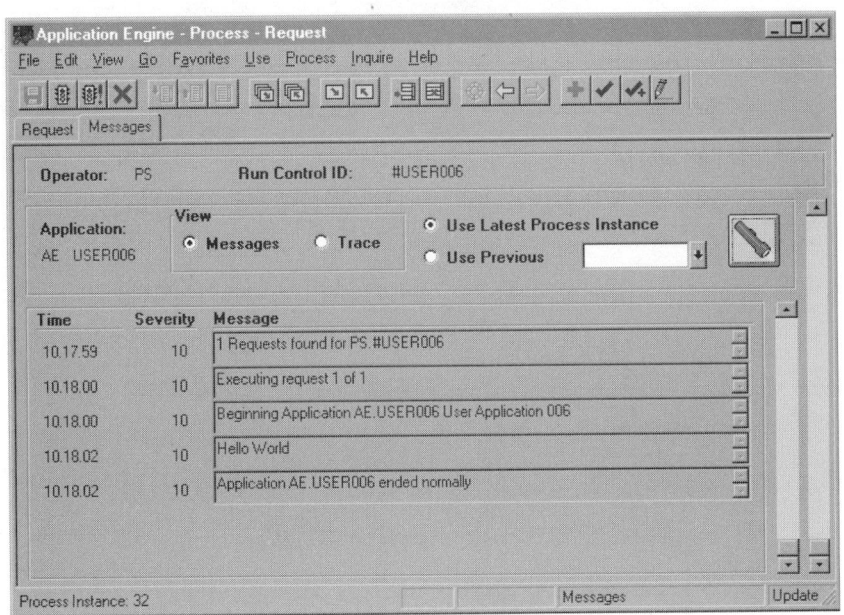

Figure 41.18   Reviewing process request messages

After examining the message log, you can see the HELLO section was performed. This was caused by populating the AE_SECTION cache field with the section which you'd like to perform.

Let's test our program again using another section. Return to the Process Request panel and assign the value GOODBYE to the AE_SECTION cache field (figure 41.19). Execute the program again and go to the message log to view the results.

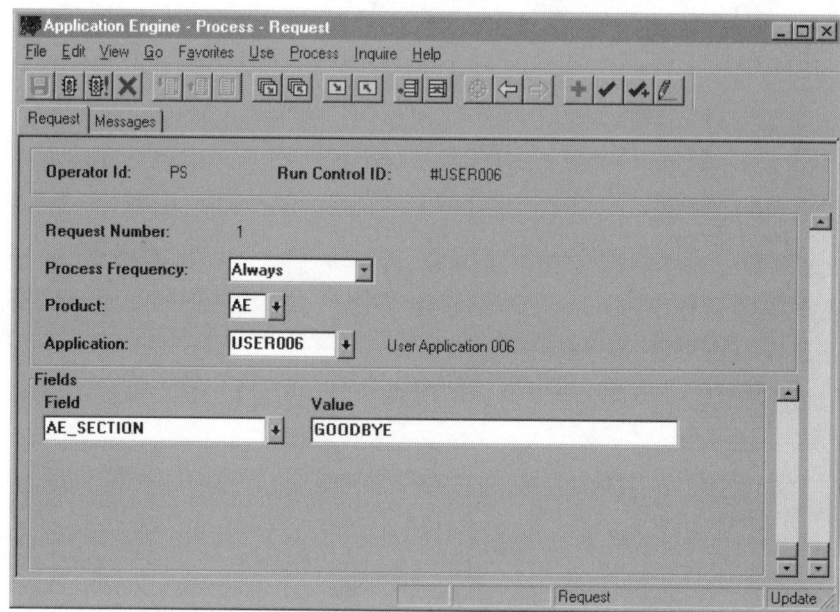

Figure 41.19   Assigning the dynamic section field the section GOODBYE

This time the GOODBYE section was performed (figure 41.20).

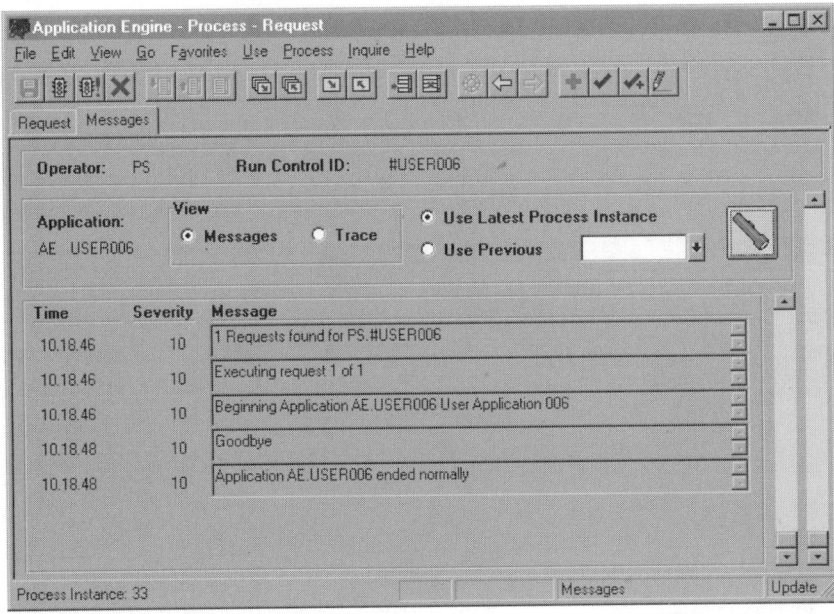

Figure 41.20   Reviewing process request messages

41.1.4   Multiple process requests

Let's try another quick experiment. We can use the Process Request panel to run multiple requests at once. We could have easily run the HELLO and GOODBYE versions of our exercise one after the other in the same run request.

Let's start by creating a new process request under a new Run Control ID.

Since we're running multiple requests, we use the Run Control ID 'MULTIPLE' (figure 41.21). Now we need to populate the Process Request panel.

Navigation: Go → PeopleTools → Application Engine → Process → Request → Request → Add

**Figure 41.21
Adding the Run Control ID**

So far nothing seems different (figure 41.22). The dynamic section HELLO will be executed. Take a look at the outermost scroll bar on the right. Each process request we enter can be viewed using the outer scroll bar. We can add another process request by placing the cursor in one of the outer scroll fields (process frequency, product, or application) then pressing the F7 key to insert a new row.

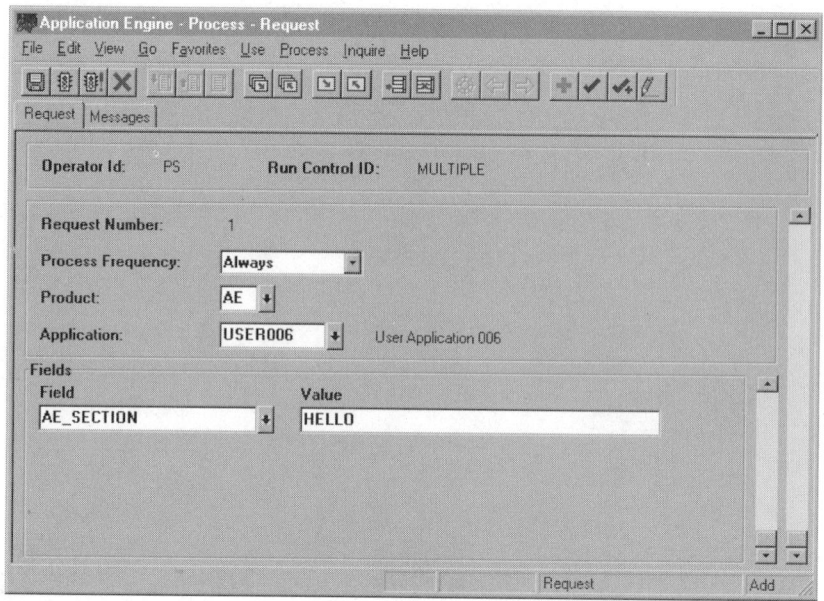

Figure 41.22 Adding Request Number 1 using the HELLO dynamic section

After pressing the F7 key, a new row can be filled in with our second set of run parameters. In figure 41.23, we have selected the dynamic section GOODBYE. Notice the request number for the GOODBYE section is incremented to 2. When we submit our request, the HELLO request will be executed followed by the GOODBYE request. Let's run the request and look at the message log.

Figure 41.24 displays the Messages panel. The first line shows that two requests were found for our run. The first request is executed (1 of 2) and displays the "Hello World" message. The second request is then executed (2 of 2) and displays the "Good-bye" message (though not visible in the screen shot). We could have executed all of our exercises consecutively in one process request run.

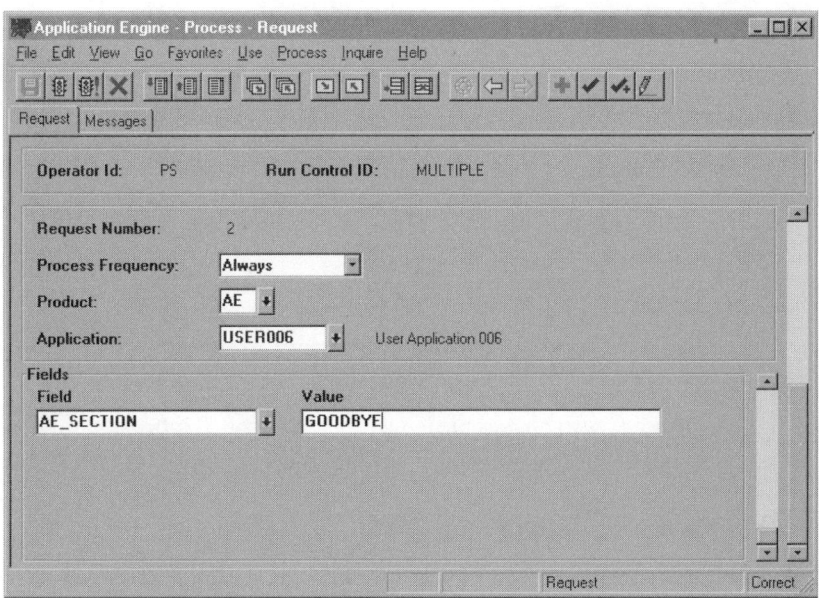

Figure 41.23   Adding Request Number 2 using the GOODBYE dynamic section

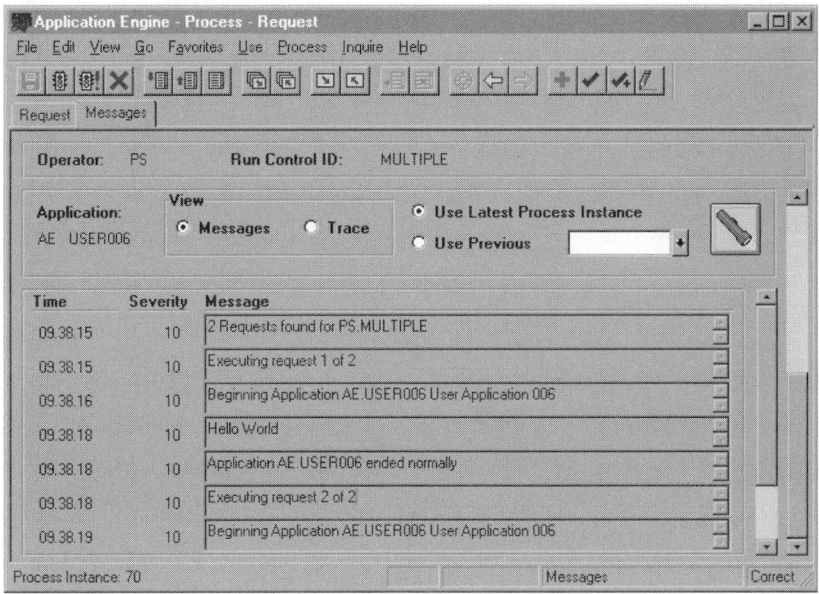

Figure 41.24   Examining the message log for the multiple request run

41.2 SQR/APPLICATION ENGINE COMPARISON

If we look at the logical structure of both our programs now

SQR: Application Engine:

```
Begin-Program                          USER001
      User prompted                          Cache assignment
      Main-Step1                             MAIN.STEP1
      When 1                                      MAIN.&SECTION
            Hello-Step1
      When 2
            Goodbye-Step1
```

We can see the Application Engine program is much more streamlined. The section is assigned on the Process Request panel and used in place of the &SECTION symbolic.

41.3 DYNAMIC SECTIONS IN PEOPLESOFT

You may be wondering where you can find an example of dynamic sections in an existing PeopleSoft application. A perfect example would be the payment predictor process, called PREDICT, found in Accounts Receivable. Its purpose is to match incoming payments with the associated items (or invoices). Several delivered sections or algorithms exist that can be selected to match payments based on certain criteria. A special payment predictor setup table is used to store the algorithm name to be used. When PREDICT is run, the setup information is retrieved. The algorithm is assigned to the AE_SECTION cache field and substituted for the &SECTION symbolic. Using dynamic sections in this manner provides a great deal of flexibility.

KEY POINTS

1 Sections are called dynamically when the value found in the AE_SECTION bind variable is substituted as the section represented by the &SECTION symbolic.

2 Dynamic sections can be found in several PeopleSoft Applications such as Payment Predictor. The use of dynamic sections allows the user to tailor programs to meet their own business requirements.

3 Multiple process requests can be submitted in one execution run. This is useful when you would like processes to run consecutively.

Using Run Controls— part A

The exercises we have completed thus far were designed to demonstrate the capabilities of Application Engine. You may not have a need to display a message saying "Hello World." You may not need any of the programs we've created! The important thing is that you've learned the concepts behind Application Engine development. We're now ready to produce something of value. In chapter 28, we mentioned that PeopleSoft does not provide a tool to delete obsolete process definitions. You can only delete these outside of PeopleSoft using your native SQL tools. Let's create a utility to accomplish this using Application Engine. This is the perfect opportunity to introduce Run Control records in Application Engine. In order to implement this utility, we're going to go through the complete cycle of program development. Let's get started.

42.1   EXERCISE 7: DELETE PROCESS DEFINITIONS

Let's refresh our memory first. In chapter 28, we listed the SQL statements necessary to clean up the process definition tables.

Let's look at the SQL statements used to remove the MYPROB01 SQR Report process definition from all associated tables:

```
DELETE
  FROM PS_PRCSDEFN
 WHERE PRCSNAME = 'MYPROB01'
   AND PRCSTYPE = 'SQR Report';

DELETE
  FROM PS_PRCSDEFNGRP
 WHERE PRCSNAME = 'MYPROB01'
   AND PRCSTYPE = 'SQR Report';

DELETE
  FROM PS_PRCSDEFNPNL
 WHERE PRCSNAME = 'MYPROB01'
   AND PRCSTYPE = 'SQR Report';

DELETE
  FROM PS_PRCSDEFNXFER
 WHERE PRCSNAME = 'MYPROB01'
   AND PRCSTYPE = 'SQR Report';

DELETE
  FROM PSPRCSRQST
 WHERE PRCSNAME = 'MYPROB01'
   AND PRCSTYPE = 'SQR Report';

DELETE
  FROM PSPNLFIELD
 WHERE PRCSNAME = 'MYPROB01'
   AND PRCSTYPE = 'SQR Report';
```

In our new process, we'll allow the user to enter the PRCSNAME and PRCSTYPE on a new Run Control panel. The Application Engine process we develop will remove the process definition from the six tables listed. Notice the first four tables use the standard prefix 'PS_' while the last two tables do not. We'll make our program interesting by accounting for this in our program.

Before we proceed, let's take a look at the development requirements. When developing applications, this is a critical and often overlooked step. Let's go over the steps we need to take to produce our application:

42.1.1   Application development steps

- create a custom Run Control record
- add PeopleCode to the Run Control record
- create a custom panel
- create a custom panel group
- attach the panel group to a menu
- assign operator security to the menu item
- create a process definition for our Application Engine program
- create the Application Engine program
- test our new application

We have a lot of work ahead of us. Fortunately, this will be a fairly easy task using PeopleTools.

One thing I'd like to resolve now is the name of our Application Engine program. This means the combination of product and application ID. We will use the product A/E (as we've done in all our exercises) and the name of the application is going to be MYPRCSDL.

Let's start by building a new Run Control record.

42.2   BUILD A NEW RUN CONTROL RECORD

Application Engine programs use a primary Run Control record called AE_REQUEST. You may not have realized it at the time, but this is the underlying Run Control record we've been using when testing our applications in exercises 1 through 6. We're going to create a new custom Run Control record that will be linked (as a child record) to the AE_REQUEST record. We start by cloning the AE_REQUEST record (figure 42.1).

Our Run Control record only needs five fields. Of course, the record needs the standard AE_REQUEST keys, which are OPRID, RUN_CNTL_ID, and REQUEST_NBR. In addition, we want the user to enter the process type and process name. We'll now clone the AE_REQUEST record for our purposes. Open the record AE_REQUEST and remove all fields except OPRID, RUN_CNTL_ID and REQUEST_NBR. Next, add the fields PRCSTYPE and PRCSNAME. The result should look like figure 42.1. Be careful not to save the record using the AE_REQUEST name! We save it under a new name: MY_RUN_CNTL_AE.

Navigation: Go → PeopleTools → Application Designer → File → Open → Record → AE_REQUEST

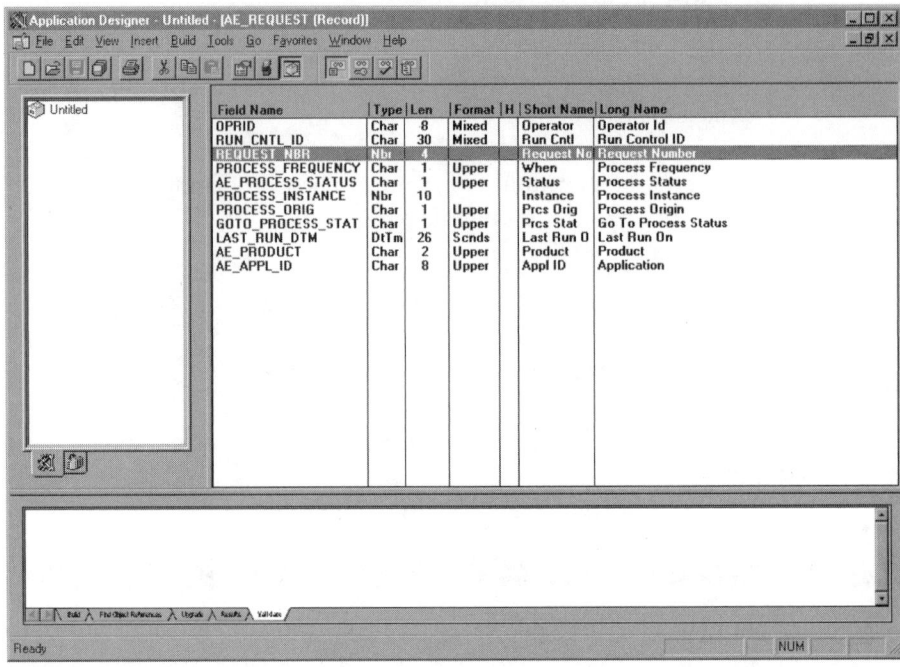

Figure 42.1   Cloning the AE_REQUEST Run Control record

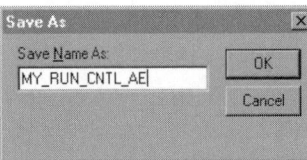

Figure 42.2   Saving our Run Control record

Use File → Save As to save the record under a new name. Figure 42.2 shows the prompt box filled in with our new name. Let's add some underlying edit prompts for our two new fields.

Figure 42.3 displays the record in Edit View. We've added the PRCSTYPE_VW and PRCSDEFN records as edit tables for the PRCSTYPE and PRCS-NAME fields. This allows the user to select the process type and process name on the Run Control panel using drop-down lists.

Also, note the record keys for our new Run Control record are OPRID, RUN_CNTL_ID, and REQUEST_NBR. The key attributes were copied when we saved the AE_REQUEST record under our new record name.

Because we plan to integrate our Run Control record with the AE_REQUEST record, we have to resolve a couple of issues. This will become clearer when we create the panel. For now, let's look at the required fields on the AE_REQUEST record.

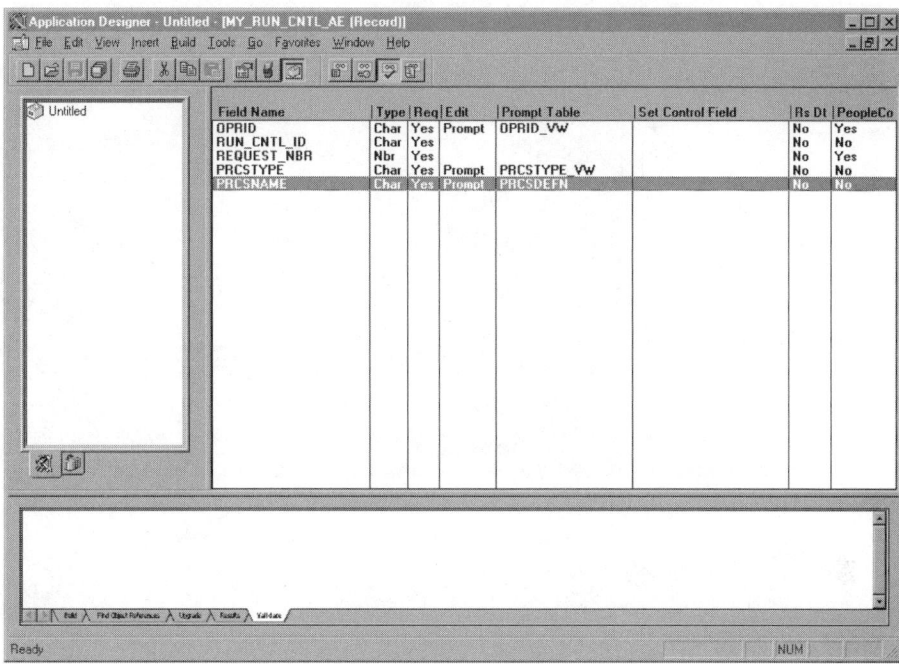

Figure 42.3   Adding edit prompts to the process type and process name fields

Figure 42.4 displays the required fields on the AE_REQUEST record. The first three are the record keys and will be filled in with the OPRID, RUN_CNTL_ID, and REQUEST_NBR. The last two fields, AE_PRODUCT and AE_APPL_ID, are also required. We plan to use the AE_REQUEST record as the primary record on our panel with our new custom record placed in the panel as a child record. We will not be able to save the record without a product or application ID. This is an easy customization using PeopleCode. We'll simply initialize these two fields with the product and application ID we're going to use. We've already decided to use AE.MYPRCSDL as the product and application ID. Let's add some PeopleCode.

Figure 42.5 shows the PeopleCode to populate the required fields AE_PRODUCT and AE_APPL_ID in the AE_REQUEST record.

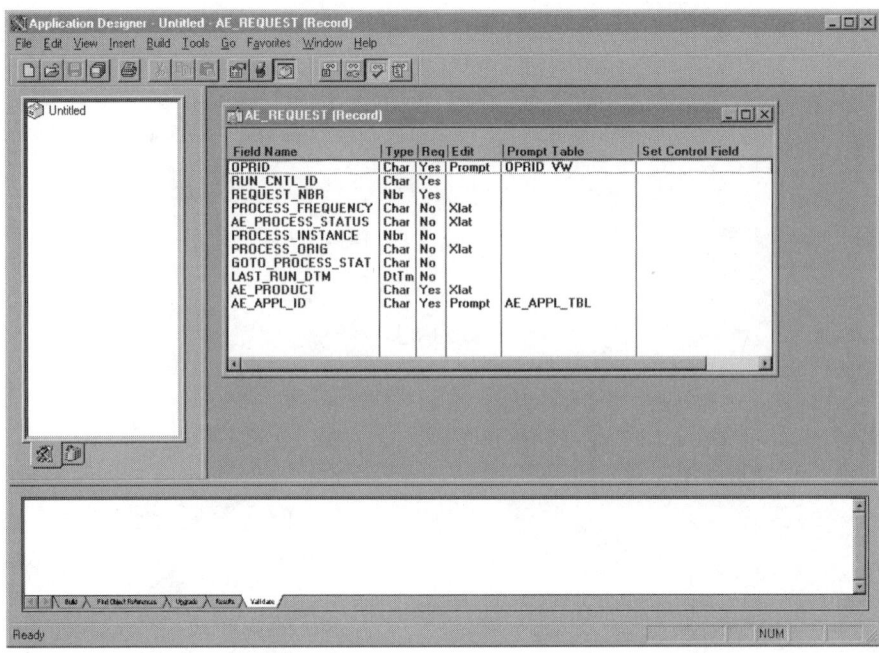

Figure 42.4 Looking at the AE_REQUEST required fields

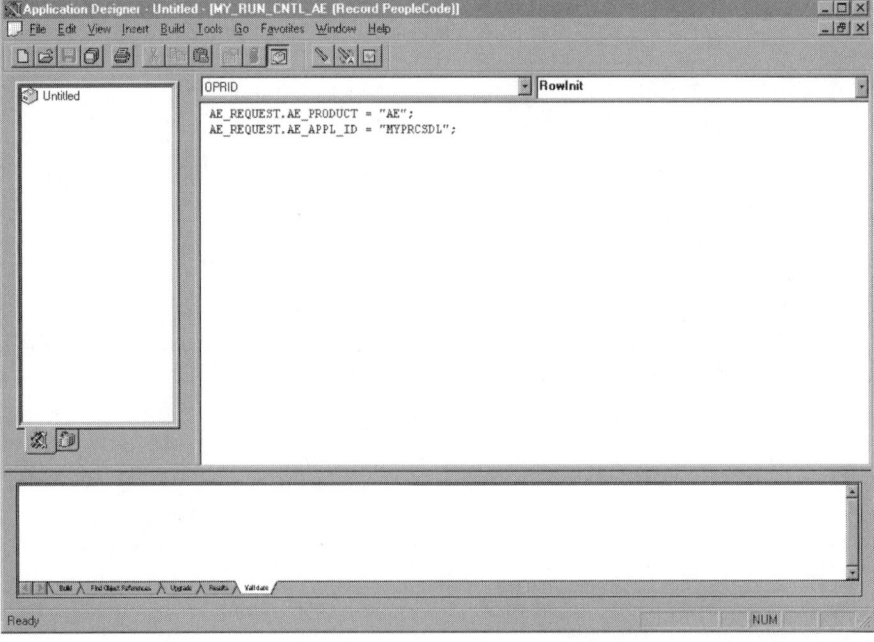

Figure 42.5 Updating AE_REQUEST record with our product and application ID

Build the current object using SQL create. This will create the table at the database level. We'll now make some modifications to our cache record, USER_AET.

42.2.1   Modify our existing cache record

The cache record USER_AET is the same record we've used for most of our exercises. We can re-use this by adding the additional fields we need for our application. We need to add the process type and process name fields passed from the Run Control record. We'll also add the AE_SECTION field to allow us to execute sections dynamically. We'll explain this as we develop the application.

Figure 42.6 shows the modifications we've made to the USER_AET cache record. As you can see, the three fields have been added. Now, we need to build the current record object using SQL create. We can now build the Run Control panel.

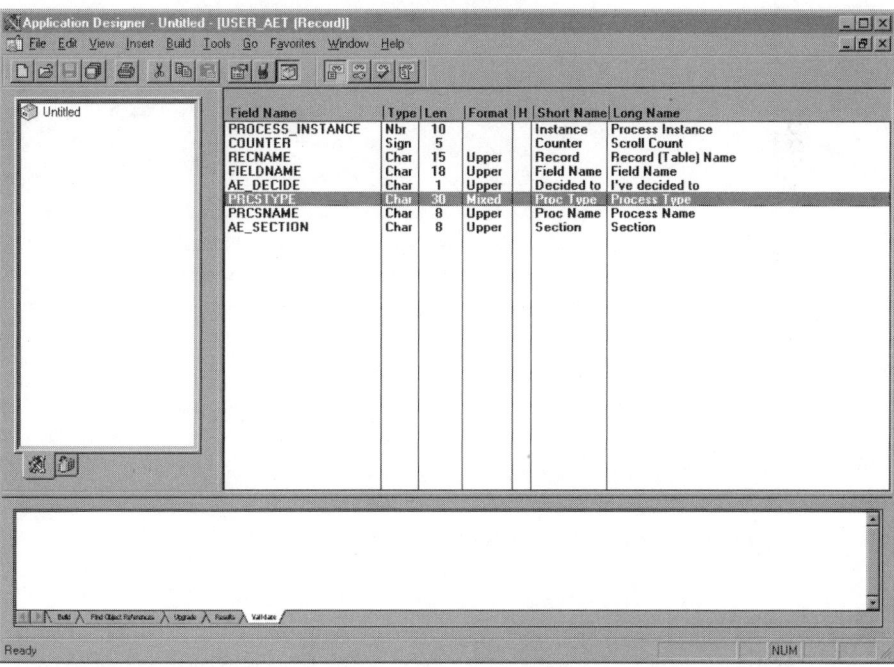

Figure 42.6   Modifying the USER_AET cache record

42.3   *BUILDING THE RUN CONTROL PANEL*

We can clone an existing panel used specifically for Application Engine. The panel name is AE_REQUEST. We used this panel when testing our applications from previous exercises. We're going to remove most of the fields on the panel, then add the new ones from our custom Run Control record.

Figure 42.7 shows the AE_REQUEST panel with all the fields intact. Let's remove all fields except operator ID, Run Control ID, and request number. We also will keep the rightmost scroll bar. Then we'll add the Process Type and Process Name fields from our custom Run Control record. We'll make a few slight adjustments that may seem a bit odd at first, but we'll explain as we go.

Navigation: Go → PeopleTools → Application Designer → File → Open → Panel
            → AE_REQUEST

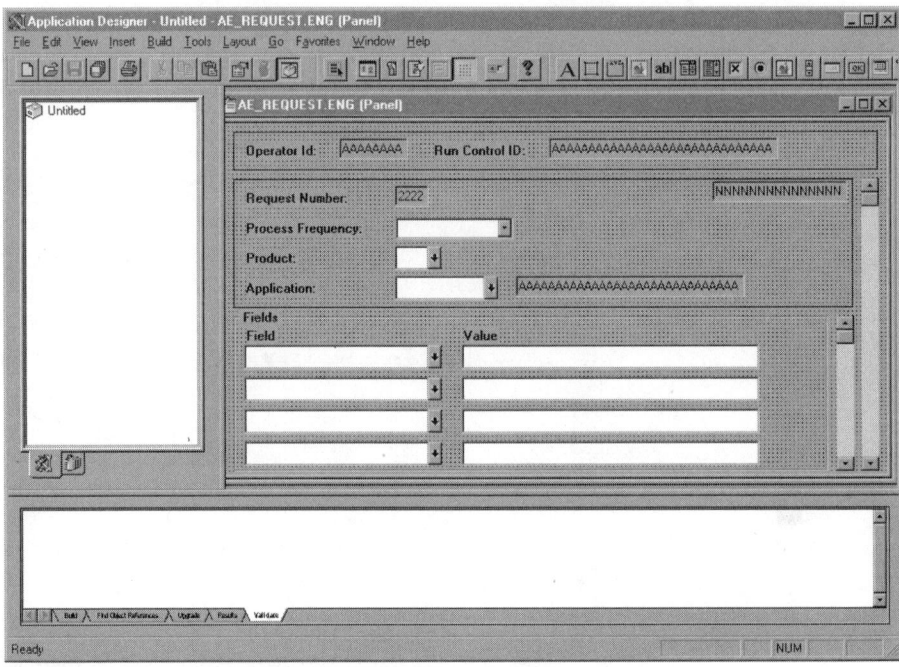

Figure 42.7 Cloning the AE_REQUEST panel

Let's save the panel using the name MY_RUN_CNTL_AE (figure 42.8).

Our panel is now complete.

Figure 42.8 Saving the panel with our new name

NOTE When cloning, make sure you don't inadvertently save the object under its original name. This is true for all cloned objects—records, panels, and so on.

Figure 42.9 shows the completed panel named MY_RUN_CNTL_AE. We've made some cosmetic adjustments as well. We moved the process request number into the top frame. We also surrounded the user fields Process Type and Process Name with a group box and labeled it "Processing Parameters." Also, notice the inner scroll bar. This contains the fields for our custom record. We had no choice in this matter. PeopleSoft does not allow you to place multiple records under the same scroll bar. We are going to change the inner scroll bar properties so it is not visible to the user.

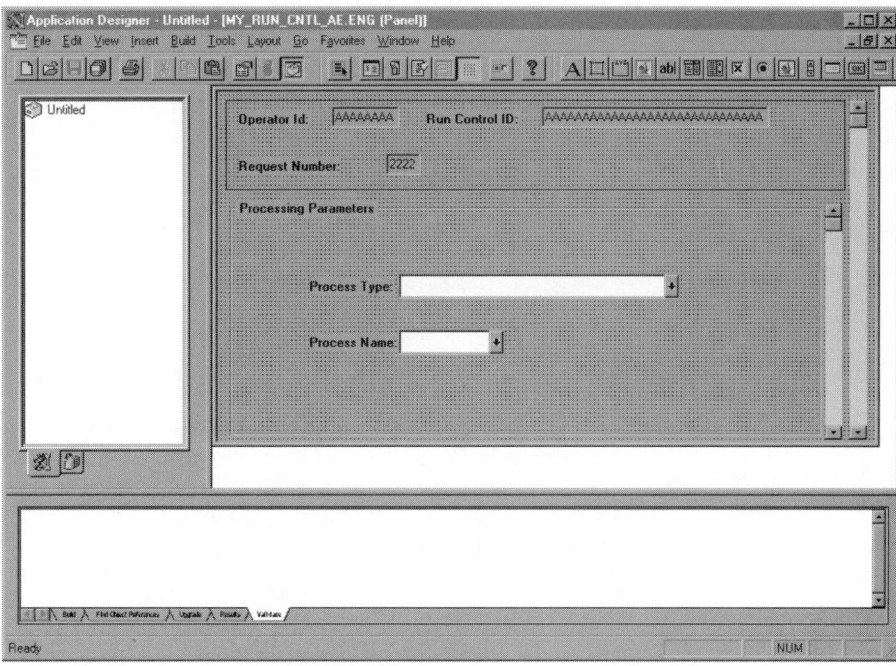

Figure 42.9   Our new Run Control panel is complete

In our previous exercise, we demonstrated the ability to submit multiple process requests. This is one of the features of the AE_REQUEST panel (which we cloned). For our purposes, we do not want to allow multiple process requests. Deleting process definitions can be considered a dangerous function. Restricting this function to delete one process definition at a time is a wise decision.

Because the only remaining fields within the outer scroll are "Display Only," we cannot insert an additional process request. This is the desired effect. We could have set the outer scroll properties to restrict rows from being inserted and to also make the scroll bar invisible. We'll leave the outer scroll bar properties as they are. Because the inner scroll bar has data entry fields, we have to modify the inner scroll bar properties.

Figure 42.10 displays the inner scroll bar properties we've set. The Occurs count is 1 so only one row may exist as a child of the AE_REQUEST record. The scroll bar will be invisible. The user will not be able to insert or delete rows within the inner scroll bar (via F7 and F8).

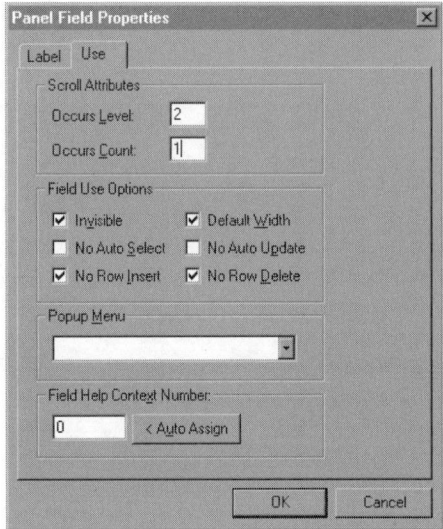

Figure 42.10
Inner scroll bar properties

Figure 42.11 shows the panel elements that make up the entire panel. You can access this screen by selecting Layout → Order on the Application Designer menu bar. Make sure your panel entries match those in figure 42.11.

Num	Lvl	Label	Type	Field	Record
		*** Top of List ***			
1	0	Frame	Frame		
2	1	Request Scroll Bar	Scroll Bar		
3	1	Operator Id	Edit Box	OPRID	AE_REQUEST
4	1	Run Control ID	Edit Box	RUN_CNTL_ID	AE_REQUEST
5	1	Request Number	Edit Box	REQUEST_NBR	AE_REQUEST
6	2	Scroll Bar (Request Option	Scroll Bar		
7	2	Processing Parameters	Group Box		MY_RUN_CNTL_AE
8	2	Process Type	Edit Box	PRCSTYPE	MY_RUN_CNTL_AE
9	2	Process Name	Edit Box	PRCSNAME	MY_RUN_CNTL_AE
		*** End of List ***			

OK   Cancel   Select   Move   Unselect   Default

Figure 42.11   The MY_RUN_CNTL_AE panel elements

42.4 CREATE A NEW PANEL GROUP

Now, let's create a panel group for our new Application Engine process.

Figure 42.12 shows the panels we've added to our new panel group. Of course, the custom Run Control panel has been added. We've also added the panel AE_MESSAGE_LOG. You've seen this panel during our exercises to look at Application Engine messages. We'll attach it to our panel group so we have a convenient means of viewing messages. We've also entered a descriptive label for each panel in the Item Label column.

Navigation: Go → PeopleTools → Application Designer → File → New → PanelGroup

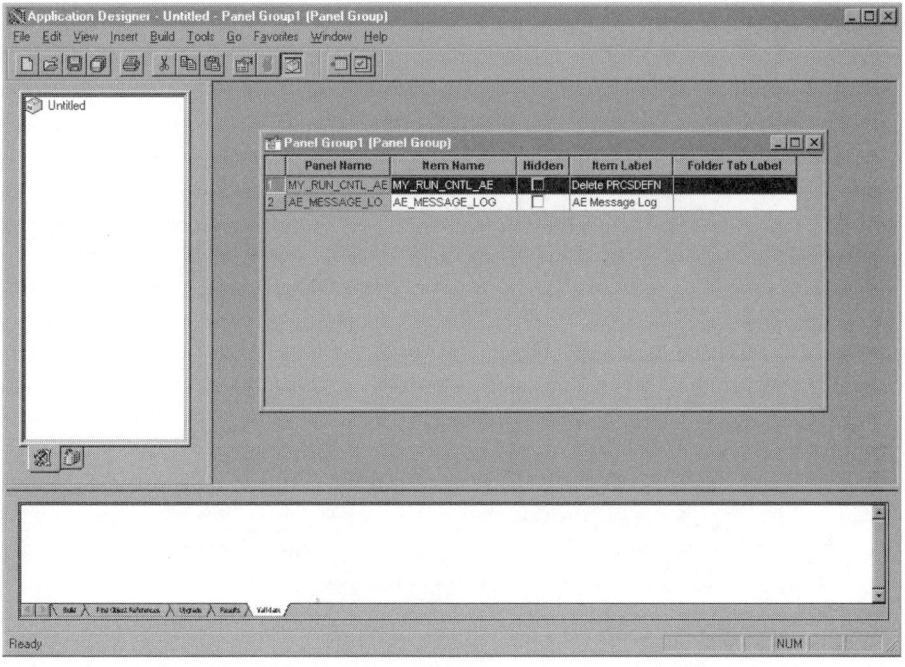

Figure 42.12 Creating the new panel group

NOTE	Much of the synchronization between the AE_REQUEST record and our MY_RUN_CNTL_AE record was made in anticipation of adding the AE_MESSAGE_LOG panel to our new panel group. It's always a nice touch to give the user access to Application Engine messages from the same panel group.

Before we can save the panel group, we need to enter the panel group properties. You can access the properties by clicking the right mouse button or pressing ALT-ENTER. Figure 42.13 shows the description added for our panel group.

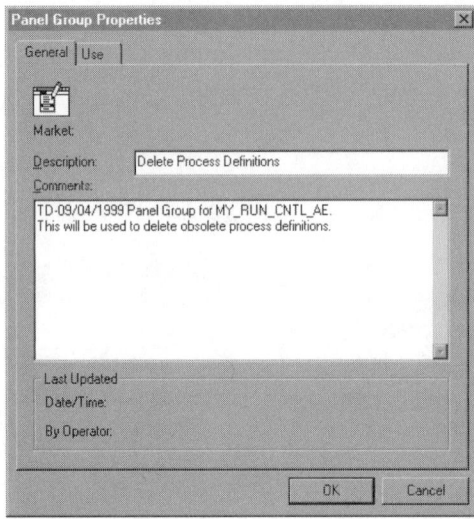

Figure 42.13
Adding a description to the
Panel Group Properties

We've added AE_REQUEST as the search record in figure 42.14. We've also checked the Add and Update/Display actions. We're ready to save our panel group.

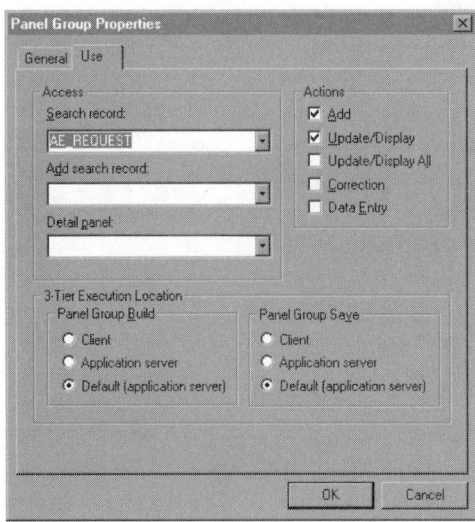

Figure 42.14
Adding a search record to the
Panel Group Properties

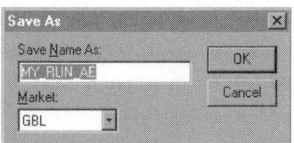

Figure 42.15 Saving our new panel group

Figure 42.15 shows the panel group as it's being saved. We'll use the name MY_RUN_AE.

Our next step is to add the panel group to an existing menu. Let's take a step back and review what our process actually does. When the user enters a process type and process name, the application will physically remove all references to it without a trace. If the wrong process type/name is entered it will be deleted! A menu with limited authorization would be suitable. Only a select few should be running this process. Since this can be considered a PeopleTools utility, it seems logical to add this to the delivered PeopleTools utility menu.

42.5 ATTACHING THE PANEL GROUP TO A MENU

Let's attach the panel group to the PeopleTools utility menu.

Figure 42.16 shows the utilities menu. The column labeled "Process" is a perfect place for our new panel group. Let's update the menu item properties for the next available menu item position (the open rectangle).

Navigation: Go → PeopleTools → Application Designer → File → Open → Menu → UTILITIES

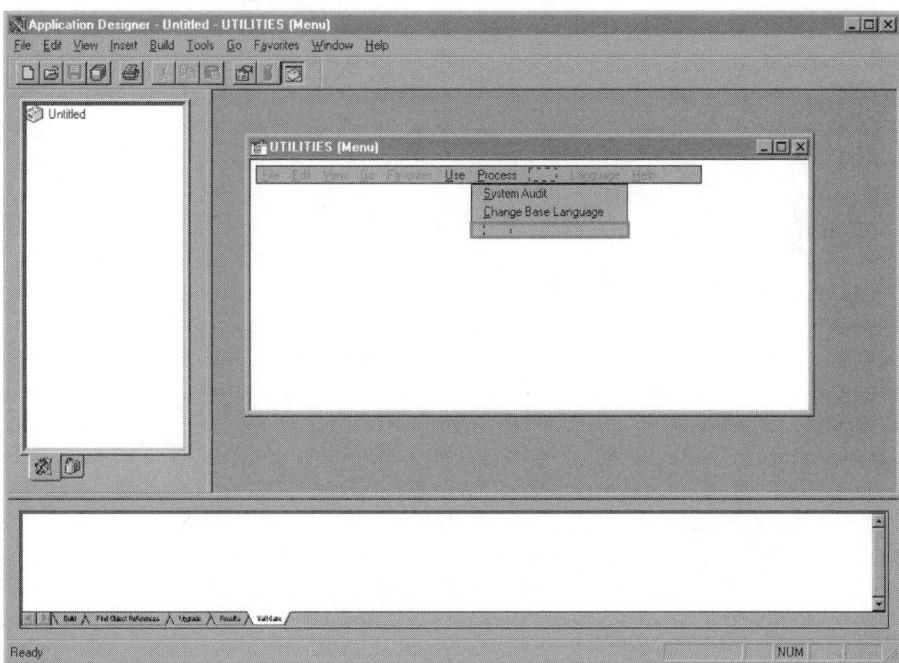

Figure 42.16 Adding the panel group to the Utilities menu

Enter the menu item properties as shown in figure 42.17 using the new panel group MY_RUN_AE. Use descriptive text for the menu item label. "Delete Process Definition" is a good choice.

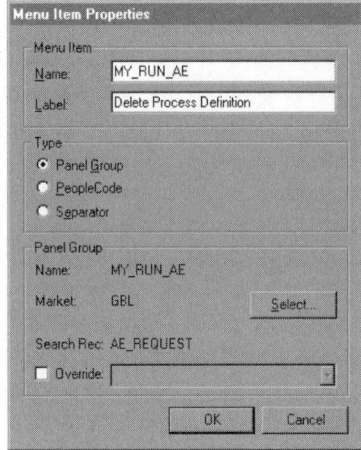

Figure 42.17
Entering the menu item properties

Now, click OK and save the utilities menu. Our next step is to assign security to the new menu item.

42.6   *ASSIGNING OPERATOR SECURITY*

We'll assign access to the operator class ALLPANLS. Remember, this process should be limited to a small group of people.

Figure 42.18 shows the security administrator panel. The UTILITIES menu is highlighted for the ALLPANLS operator class. Double-click the UTILITIES Menu to access our new menu item.

Navigation: Go → PeopleTools → Security Administrator → File → Open → ALLPANLS → Menu Items → UTILITIES

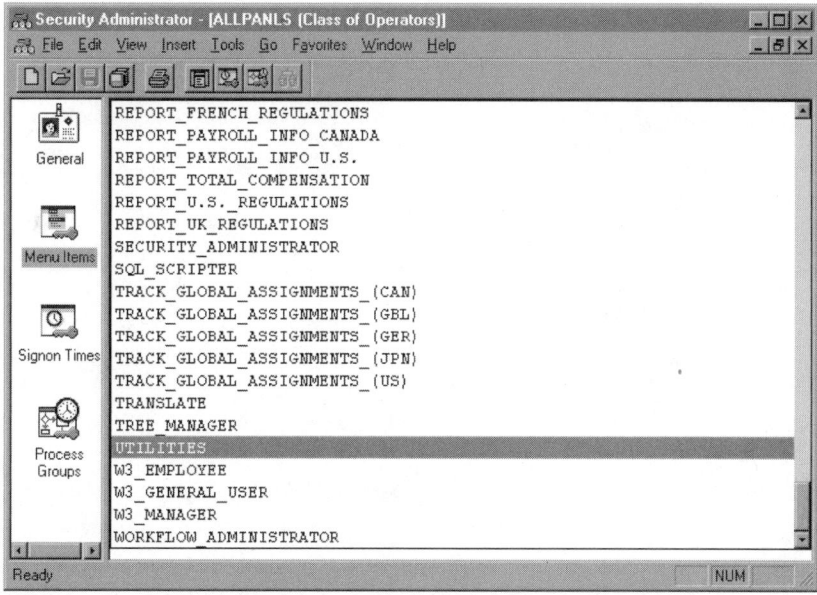

Figure 42.18   Assigning security to the ALLPANLS operator class

You can see our new menu item in figure 42.19. To assign security access to the ALLPANLS class, simply click on the associated MY_RUN_AE items. These are the last four items that appear. Once all four items are highlighted, click on the OK button.

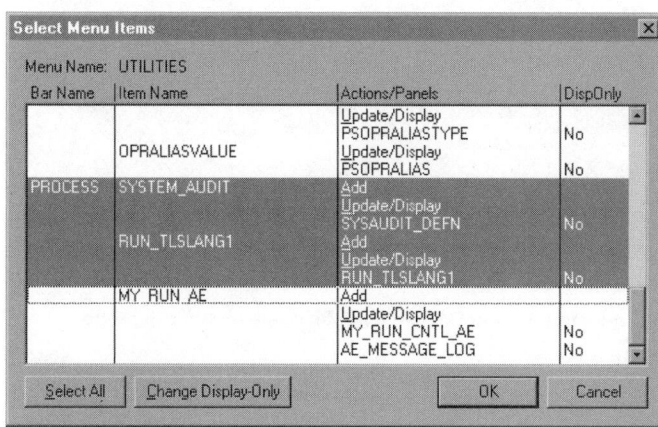

**Figure 42.19
Our new menu item
(MY_RUN_AE) as it ap-
pears in the menu**

Now, save the new operator class settings (File → Save).

Let's sign off PeopleSoft and log back on so that our new security goes into effect.

42.7 TESTING THE NEW PANEL

Let's test the modifications we've made. We haven't actually created the Application Engine program yet, but we can see if our Run Control panel is behaving correctly.

We can immediately tell that our operator security changes were successful: the panel does appear in the menu. Using a test Run Control ID (MYTEST), we can successfully select any process type and process name from the drop-down lists (figure 42.20). An important test would be saving the Run Control record. In our case, the record was saved without a problem. Part of the reason for our successful result was due to the PeopleCode we put in place to populate the AE_PRODUCT and AE_APPL_ID fields in the AE_REQUEST record. This alleviated the required field constraint found on the AE_REQUEST record.

Navigation: Go → PeopleTools → Utilities → Process → Delete Process Definition → Add → MYTEST

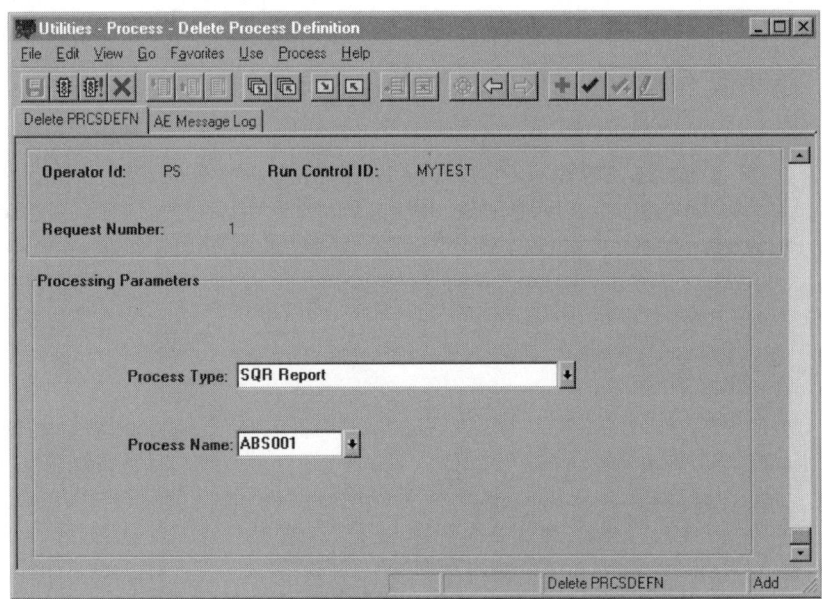

Figure 42.20   Our new menu item (MY_RUN_AE) as it appears in the menu

We can verify that the rows in both tables are being saved correctly using the database's query tool. Figure 42.21 shows the results of queries made against both tables.

Notice the second query has the product and application ID populated correctly. This was assigned by the PeopleCode we placed in the MY_RUN_CNTL_AE record. Everything seems to be working as planned.

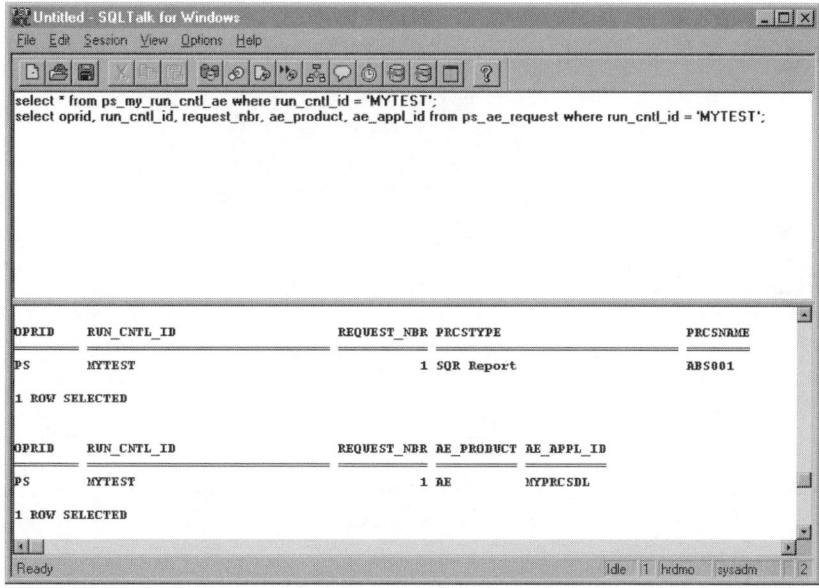

Figure 42.21   Looking at the resulting rows using SQL*Talk

Our next step is to create a process definition for our application.

42.8   CREATING OUR PROCESS DEFINITION

We'll now create the process definition for our application. The process type is Application Engine. The name of our application is MYPRCSDL.

We've added the process type and process name (figure 42.22). Let's enter the process definition information into Process Scheduler.

Navigation: Go → PeopleTools → Process Scheduler → Use → Process Definitions → Process Definitions → Add

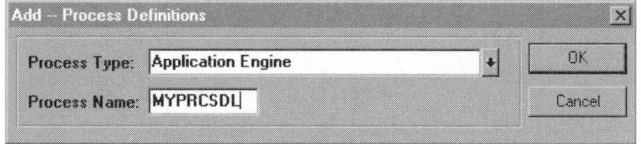

**Figure 42.22
Adding our process
definition**

Figure 42.23 shows the process definition information we need to add. We've added our new MY_RUN_AE panel group to the definition screen along with additional items such as descriptive text and process security groups. The process class of Application Engine programs is COBOL SQL.

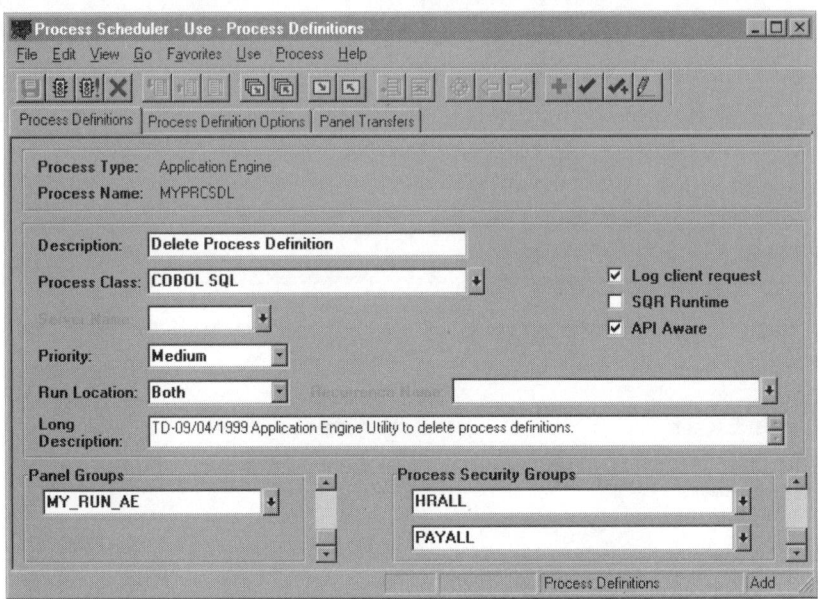

Figure 42.23   Adding process definition details

Our process definition is complete.

42.8.1   Create a DUMMY process definition for testing

While we're in Process Scheduler, let's create a dummy process definition that we'll use to test our application. We don't want to delete any existing process definitions. Let's add the dummy definition. We'll load random information since it's going to be deleted by our process.

Figure 42.24 shows a sample definition of a DUMMY process. We added a random panel group and process security groups. We'd like to see if our new application will delete process definition entries from a variety of tables. This panel will now contain DUMMY entries for the tables PRCSDEFN, PRCSDEFNPNL, and PRCSDEFNGRP.

We've also added some random panel transfer information for our DUMMY process definition. This will create a DUMMY entry in the table PRCSDEFNXFER.

Now, all that's left to do is create the actual Application Engine program!

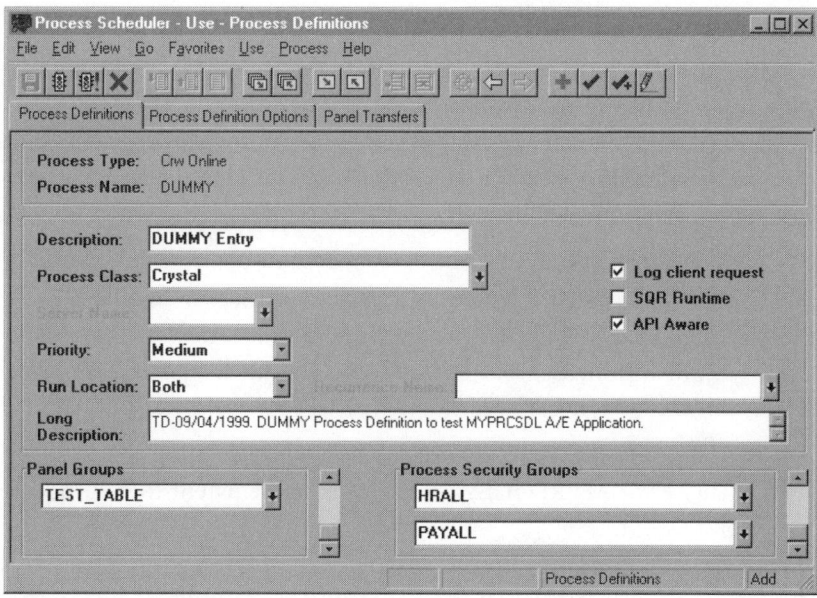

Figure 42.24   Adding a dummy process definition to test our application

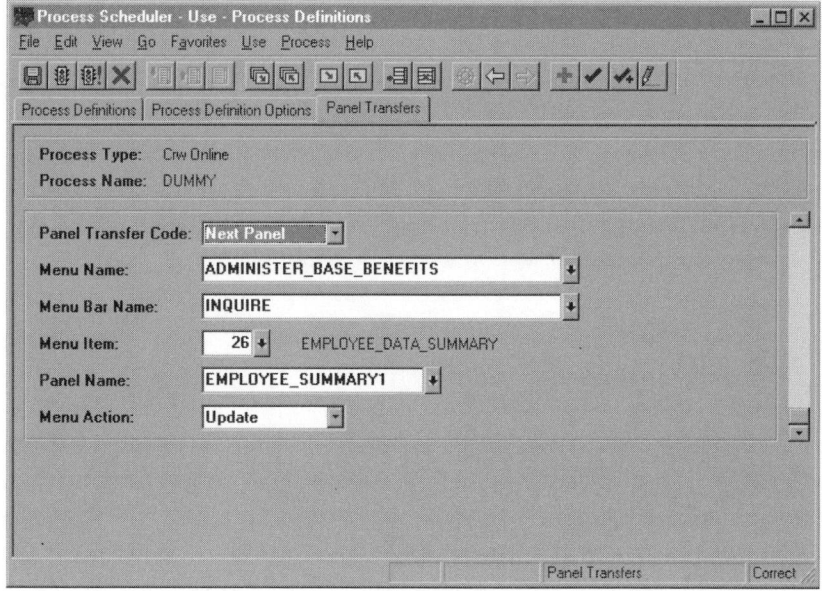

Figure 42.25   Adding a DUMMY process definition (Transfers)

1 The development life cycle for Application Engine programs is identical to that of SQR or COBOL development. The only difference is the Application Engine program itself.

2 When creating a Run Control record for Application Engine programs, use the AE_REQUEST record as a shell. Application Engine always uses the AE_REQUEST record so it's a good idea to integrate your new Run Control record with it. Use RowInit PeopleCode to assign your program name to the AE_PRODUCT and AE_APPL_ID fields in the AE_REQUEST record.

3 Also clone the AE_REQUEST panel when creating a new Run Control panel. The AE_REQUEST record will be the parent to your new Run Control record.

4 When creating the new panel group, add the AE_MESSAGE_LOG panel after your new Run Control panel This gives the user easy access to the message log entries for the completed run. The search record for your new panel group will be AE_REQUEST.

CHAPTER   4 3

Using Run Controls—
part B

The Run Control panel for our new utility program is complete. We can access the new panel on the menu and even enter Run Control parameters. That's as far as we can go at the moment. If we click on the Traffic Light to initiate the process, an error will occur. That's because we haven't created the Application Engine program yet. This chapter will concentrate on the development of the Application Engine program. Once created, we can initiate the process through the Run Control panel. Some careful planning must be made to structure our program properly. Once complete, we can begin using our new tool to delete obsolete process definitions.

43.1 CREATE THE APPLICATION ENGINE PROGRAM

We're ready to begin developing our Application Engine program. It may be helpful to give a brief overview of our program structure:

```
MAIN.STEP1              Obtain Run Control Parameters
MAIN.STEP2              Display Run Control Parms on Message Log
MAIN.STEP3              Fetch Table One by One (DO Select)

  DYNSECTN.STEP1        Dynamically call PROCESS1 or PROCESS2

    PROCESS1.STEP1      Determine Number of Rows
    PROCESS1.STEP2      Process if exists (DO When > 0)
      DELETE1.STEP1     Delete Process Definition from table
    PROCESS1.STEP3      Call Message Routine
      MESSAGE.STEP1     Display Message

    PROCESS2.STEP1      Determine Number of Rows
    PROCESS2.STEP2      Process if exists (DO When > 0)
      DELETE2.STEP1     Delete Process Definition from table
    PROCESS2.STEP3      Call Message Routine
      MESSAGE.STEP1     Display Message
```

We need to make two key points. Consider the structure of our Application Engine program. The first key point has to do with the MAIN.STEP3 line. This step will select each of the six tables and process them one by one. Early in this chapter, we pointed out that four of the process definition tables are prefixed with "PS_", and two are not. We'll use two separate processes (PROCESS1 and PROCESS2) to handle both types. They will be called dynamically based on the table being processed. The step DYNSECTN.STEP1 will call either PROCESS1 or PROCESS2.

The second point has to do with the processing steps we have chosen. Some readers may think we have taken the long way in performing our task. This may be true depending on the database you are using. For instance, if you're an Oracle user, you certainly don't need to determine if the row exists before deleting it. This is not true for all databases though. In DB2, you may receive an error if you try to delete a row that doesn't exist. We would then need to add additional error-handling steps. We could also use the DB platform field to code individual routines based on your particular database. This would hardly seem practical for the purposes of this book. Let's move on now.

We'll begin developing our program from the minor routines on up. Since we've established the program hierarchy, we can work backward and not worry about step dependencies we would encounter by going forward.

43.1.1 Building the MESSAGE section

We'll create the section MESSAGE first.

Navigation: Go → PeopleTools → Application Engine → Use → Application Engine → Application → Add

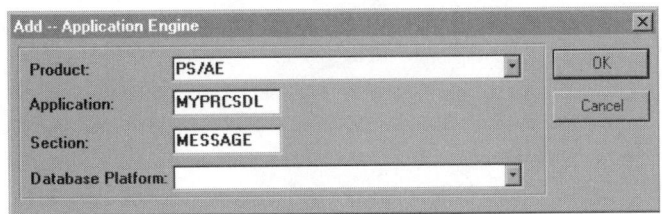

**Figure 43.1
Creating the
MESSAGE section**

First tab over to the application definition (figure 43.2). Fill in the description, cache record, version, and message set number. We'll be using our updated cache record (USER_AET) and message set from prior exercises. Also, set the trace parameter to SQL. After we test our application, we'll examine the trace file.

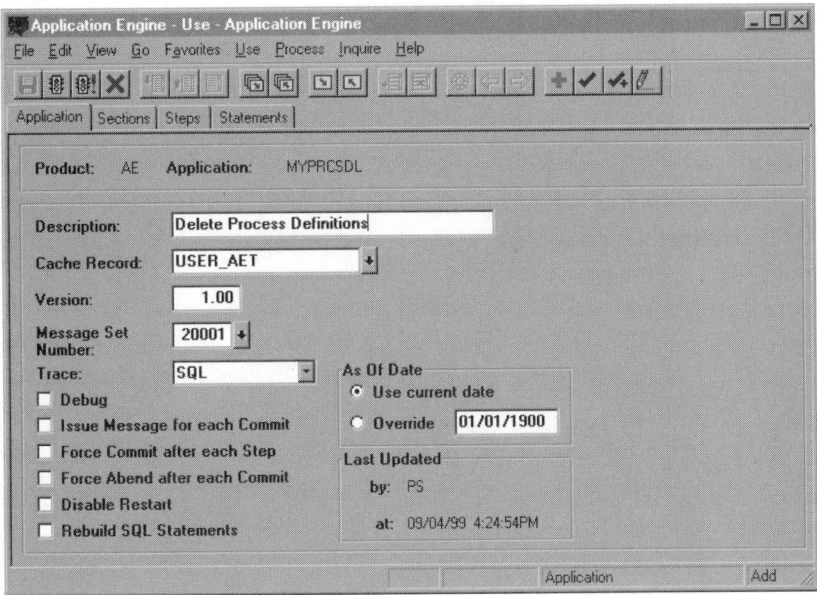

Figure 43.2   Defining our application MYPRCSDL

Fill in the description of the MESSAGE section (figure 43.3). This section simply writes a message to the message log.

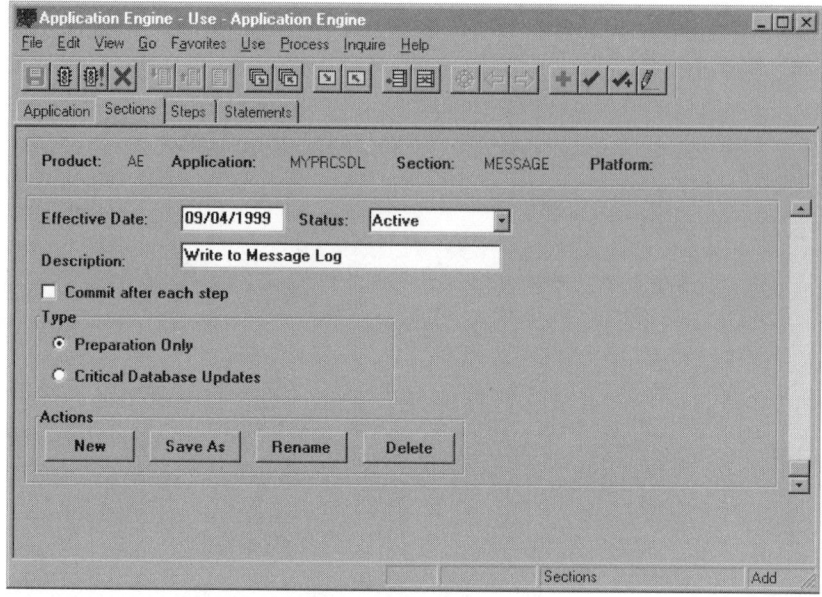

Figure 43.3 Defining the MESSAGE section

The only parameter you need to fill in for the first (and only) step of the MESSAGE section is the step name. We call it STEP1 (figure 43.4).

Figure 43.5 shows the message statement we use. This is similar to prior exercises. We pass the record name (RECNAME) and number of rows (COUNTER) to the message log.

We're done with the MESSAGE section.

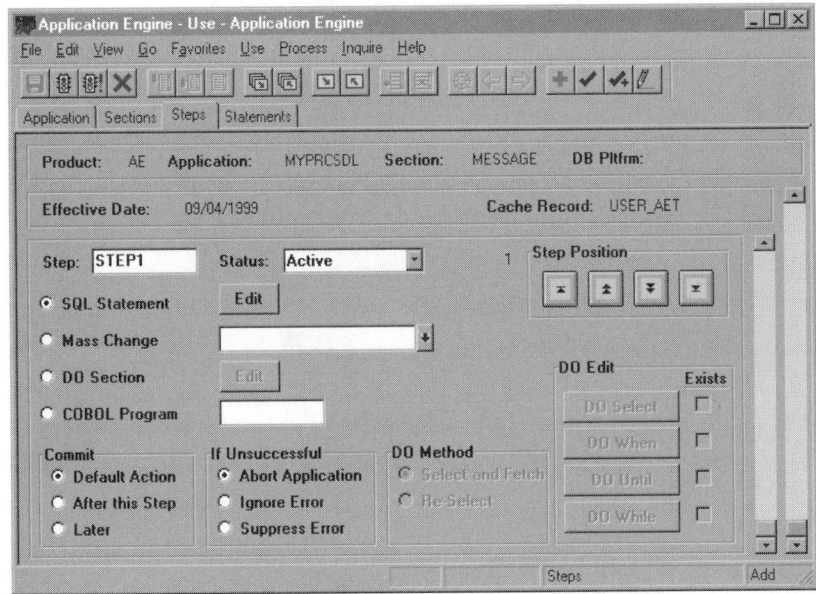

Figure 43.4   Defining STEP1 of the MESSAGE section

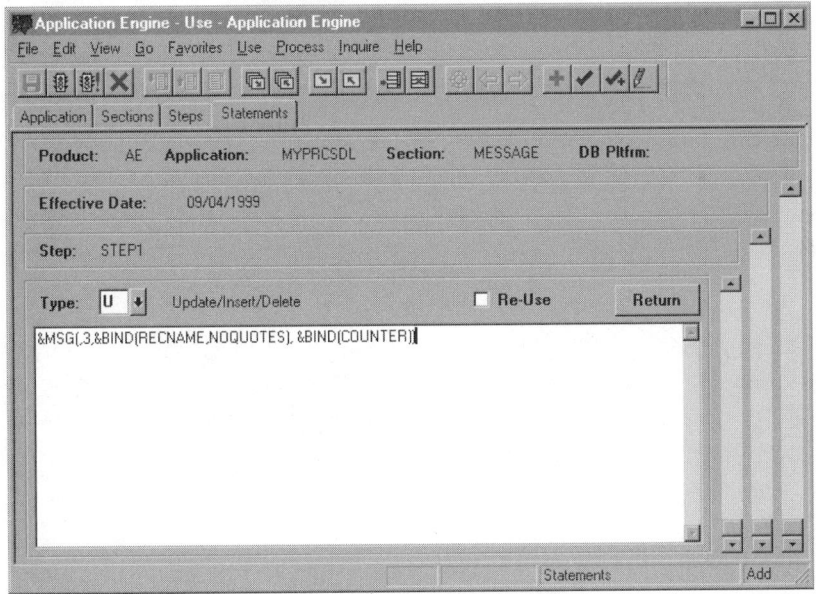

Figure 43.5   Adding our message statement

43.1.2   Building the DELETE1 section

We now add the DELETE1 section (figure 43.6), which performs the Delete against the process definition tables that have the standard 'PS_' prefix.

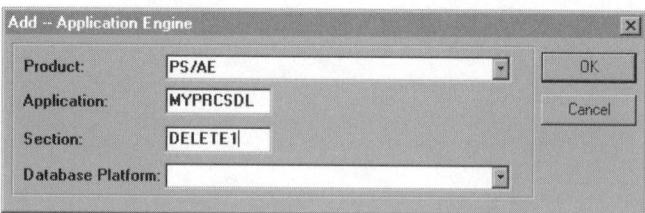

Figure 43.6
Adding the DELETE1
section

The only thing we need to add is the description. 'Delete Table with PS_' is a fairly accurate description (figure 43.7).

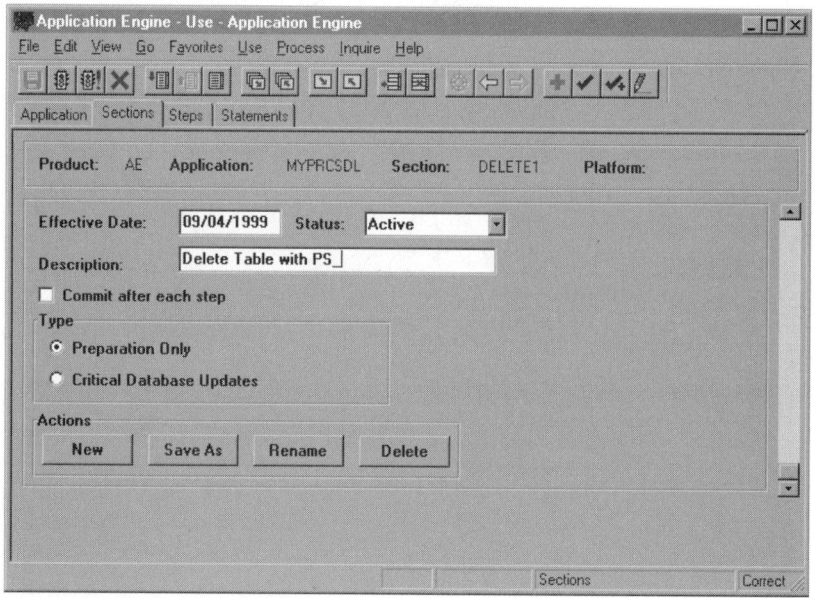

Figure 43.7   Defining the DELETE1 section

We call this first (and only) step of the DELETE1 section STEP1 (figure 43.8).

We've added the SQL statement to Delete a row from the table specified by the RECNAME cache field (figure 43.9). Notice the table name is in the same dynamic format used in prior exercises. The DELETE1 section will be part of the process that handles records with the PS_ prefix.

The DELETE1 section is complete.

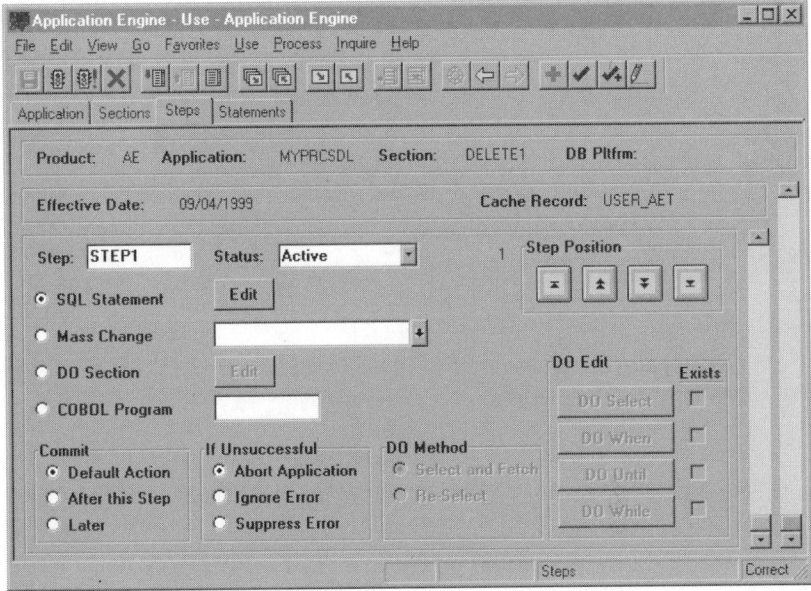

Figure 43.8   Defining STEP1 of the DELETE1 section

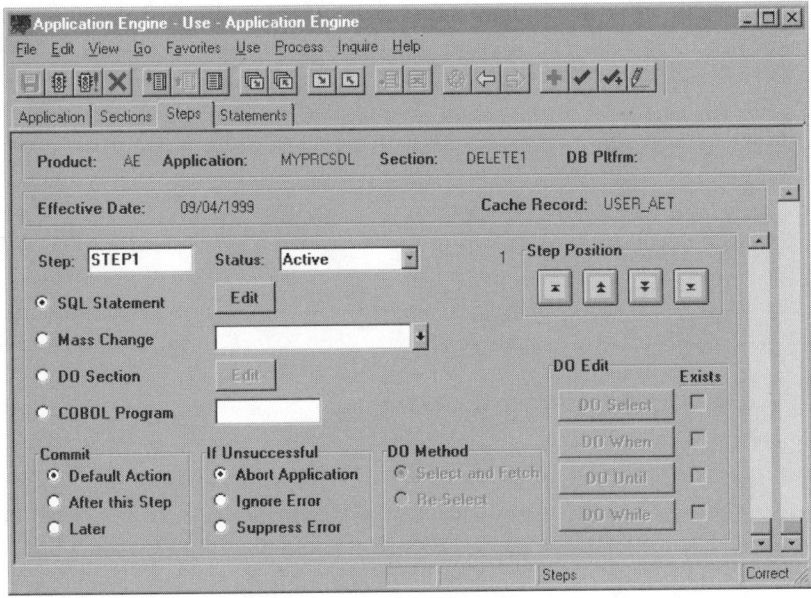

Figure 43.9   Defining STEP1 of the DELETE1 section

43.1.3 Building the DELETE2 section

We add the DELETE2 section (figure 43.10). This section performs the `Delete` against the process definition tables that DO NOT utilize the standard PS_ prefix.

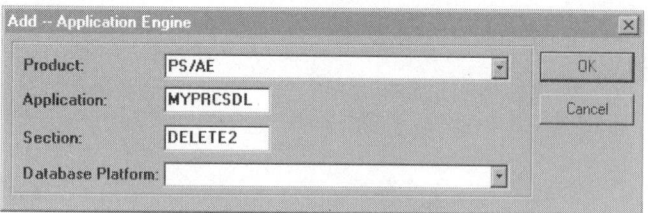

Figure 43.10 Adding the DELETE2 section

Once again, the only thing we need to add is the description. `'Delete Table without PS_'` is perfect for our section (figure 43.11).

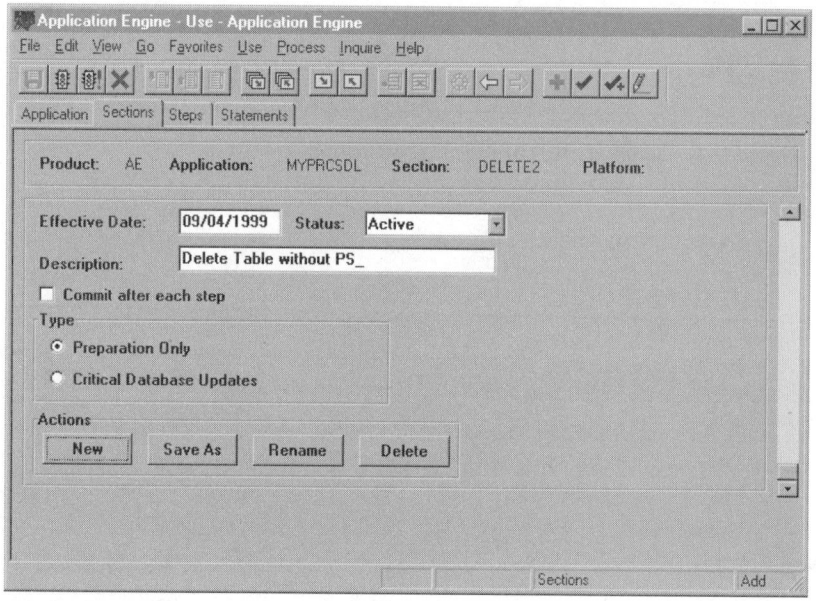

Figure 43.11 Defining the DELETE2 section

TIP   Existing sections can be "cloned" using the Save As button on the Section Definition panel. We can then modify the new section as needed. In the case of the DELETE1 and DELETE2 sections, the modifications are minimal. For purposes of these exercises, we'll create each section manually.

Let's call this first (and only) step of the DELETE2 section STEP1 (figure 43.12).

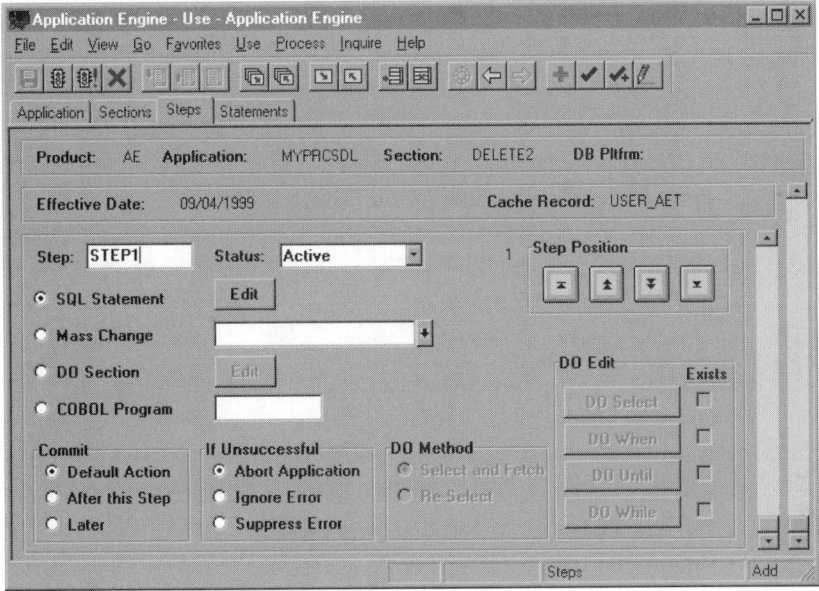

Figure 43.12   Defining STEP1 of the DELETE2 section

The delete statement in figure 43.13 is almost identical to the one in the DELETE1 section. The only difference is the absence of the PS_ prefix.

The DELETE2 section is complete.

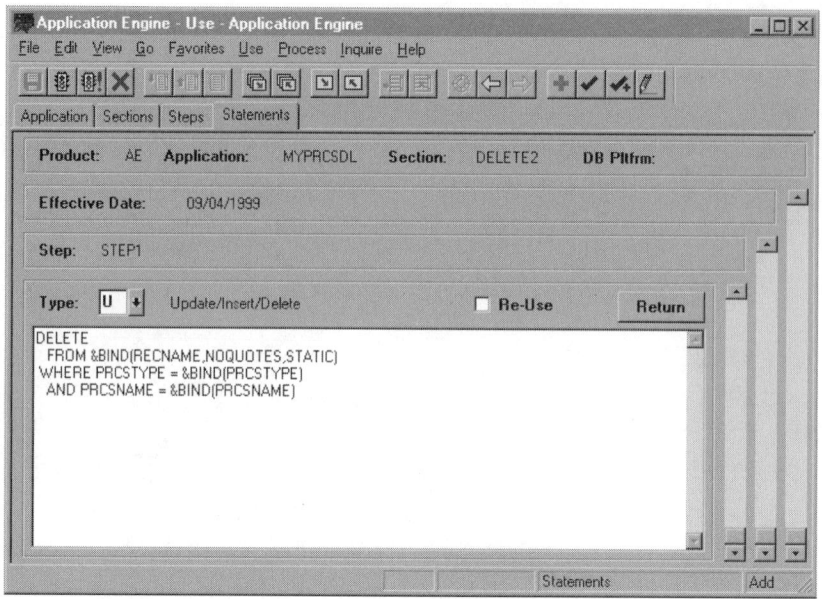

Figure 43.13   The Delete statement for DELETE2.STEP1

43.1.4   Building the PROCESS1 section

Next, let's develop the PROCESS1 section. This section will handle all process defini-tion tables that require the PS_ prefixed to the RECNAME. Add the PROCESS1 sec-tion now (figure 43.14).

**Figure 43.14
Adding the PROCESS1
section**

Fill in the description for the PROCESS1 section. 'Process Table with PS_' is the description we'll use for our section (figure 43.15).

Our first step in this section determines the number of rows in the particular process definition table, which is stored in the RECNAME cache field. The only parameter we need to enter in the Step Definition panel is the name of our step. We'll call it STEP1 (figure 43.16).

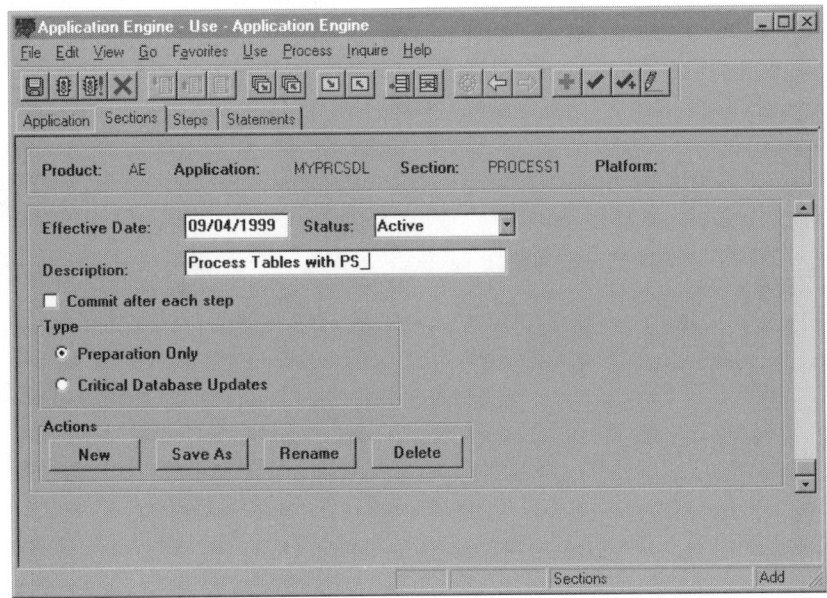

Figure 43.15   Defining the PROCESS1 section

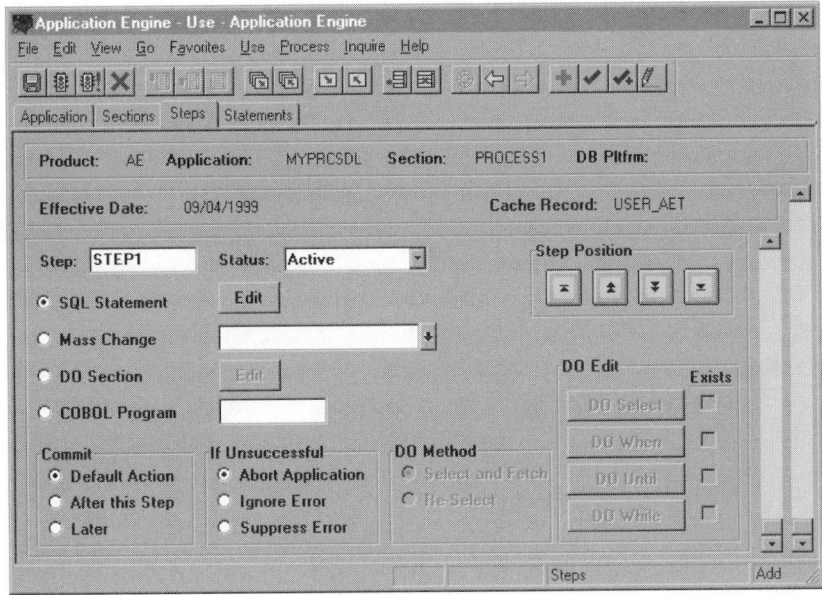

Figure 43.16   Adding STEP1 to the PROCESS1 section

We add a simple `Select` statement to retrieve the number of rows in the table (specified in RECNAME) and populate the COUNTER cache field.

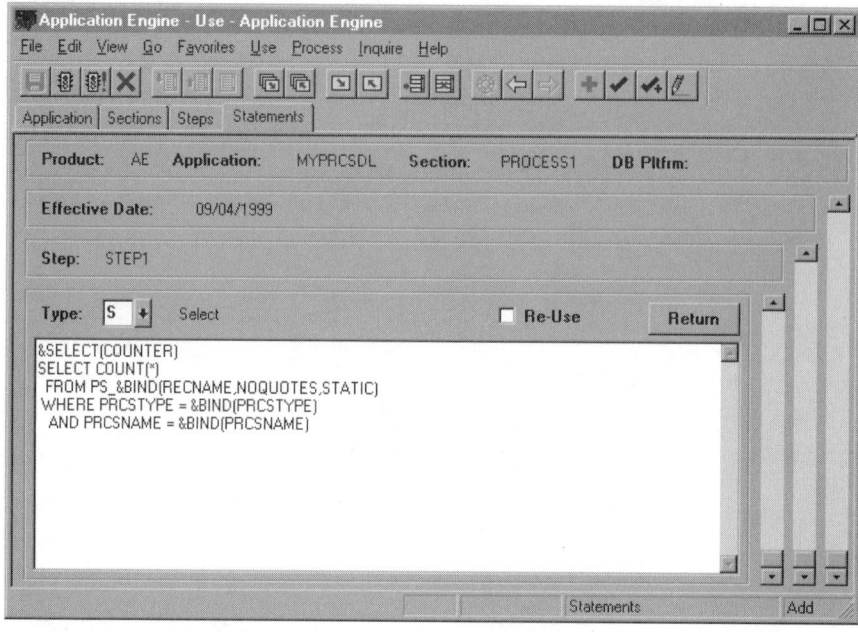

Figure 43.17   Adding the Select statement to PROCESS1.STEP1

Let's add another step to the PROCESS1 section. Click on the Steps Folder tab to return to the Step Definition panel. Place the cursor in the Step field and press the F7 key to insert a new row. Our next step will be named STEP2 (figure 43.18). Click on the DO section radio button then click on the corresponding edit button. Add the DELETE1 section when the DO section dialog box appears. You can see the DELETE1 section name next to the DO section edit button when you return. Our next step is to populate the statement panel with a `DO When` statement. The DELETE1 section is performed only if there are rows in the table containing the process definition from the Run Control record. Let's add the `DO When` statement now.

This is the same statement we've used in previous exercises. If the COUNTER cache field contains a value greater than zero, a `True` condition is returned, and the section DELETE1 is performed. If the COUNTER cache field contains a value of zero, a `False` condition is returned, and the DELETE1 section is not performed.

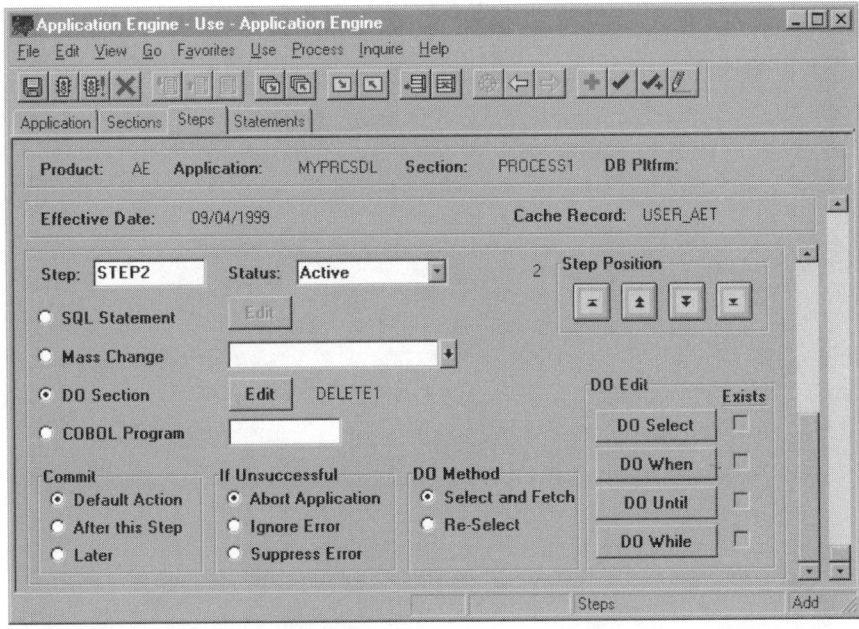

Figure 43.18   Adding STEP2 to the PROCESS1 section

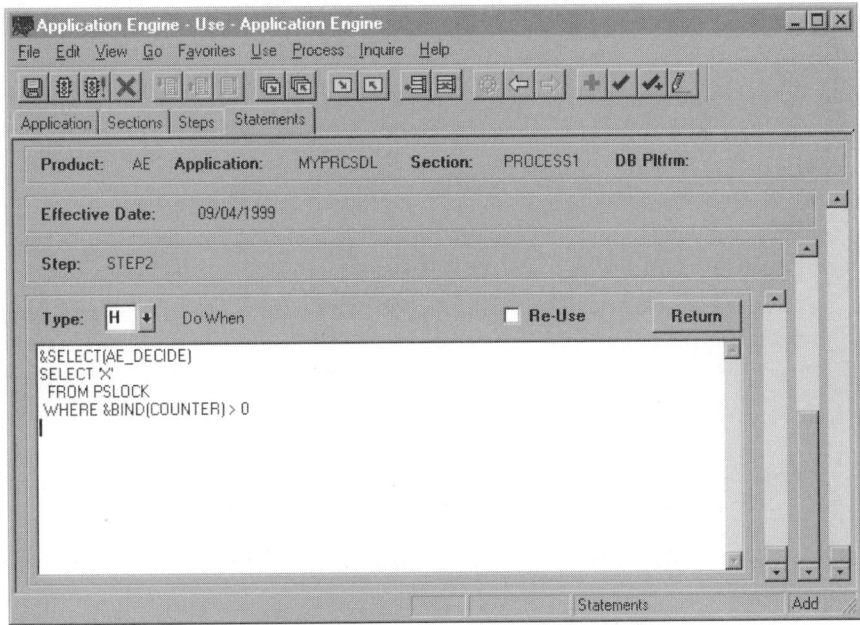

Figure 43.19   Adding the DO When statement to PROCESS1.STEP2

Use the F7 key again to insert a new step in the PROCESS1 section. Let's call it STEP3 (figure 43.20). Its function is to call the MESSAGE section we've created. Use the DO section radio button and edit box to set the section to MESSAGE. The MESSAGE section simply writes a message log entry containing the record name and number of rows processed.

The PROCESS1 section is complete.

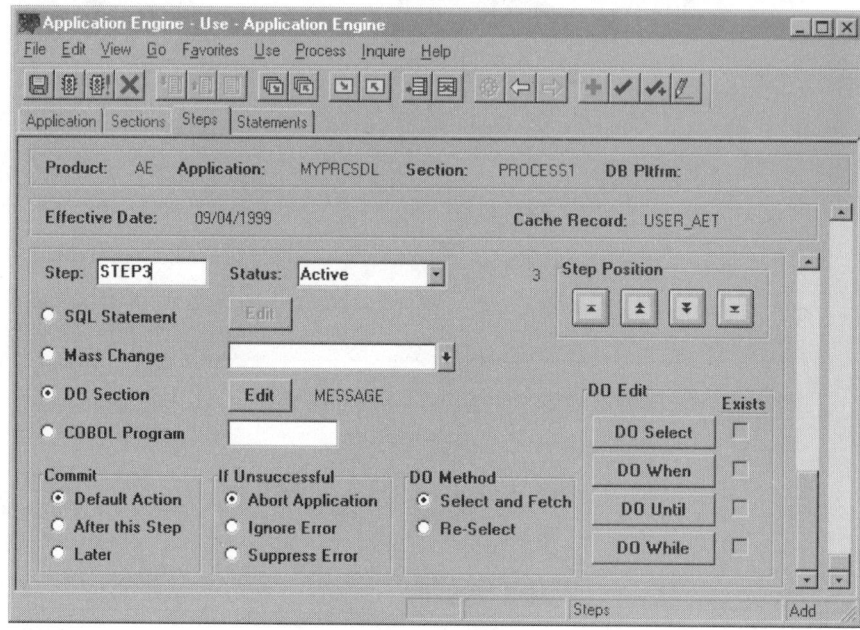

Figure 43.20   Adding STEP3 to the PROCESS1 section

43.1.5   Building the PROCESS2 section

Next, let's develop the PROCESS2 section. This section handles all process definition tables that do not require the PS_ prefix to the RECNAME. The PROCESS2 section is almost identical to the PROCESS1 section. Add the PROCESS2 section now (figure 43.21).

Figure 43.21
Adding the PROCESS2 section

Fill in the description for the PROCESS2 section. `Process Table without PS_` is the description we'll use for our section (figure 43.22).

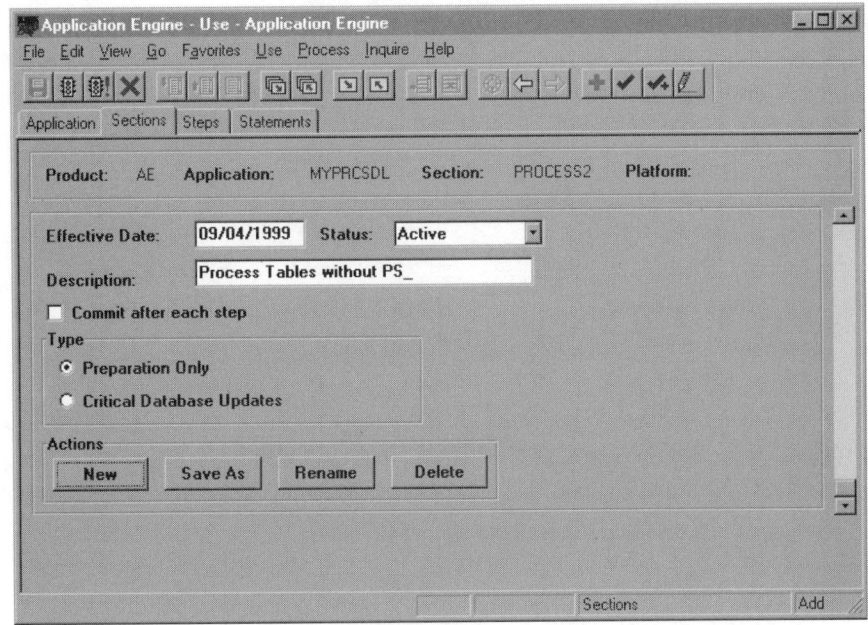

Figure 43.22   Defining the PROCESS2 Section

TIP   You can try cloning the PROCESS1 section to produce the new section PROCESS2 using the 'Save As' button. Make the alterations to the statements as you would if you had created the PROCESS2 section manually.

Our first step in this section determines the number of rows in the particular process definition table stored in the RECNAME cache field. The only parameter we need to enter in the Step Definition panel is the name of our step. We'll call it STEP1 (figure 43.23).

Next, we add a simple `Select` statement to retrieve the number of rows in the table (specified in RECNAME) and populate the COUNTER cache field. It is nearly identical to the `Select` statement found in STEP1 of the PROCESS1 section, the difference being the absence of the PS_ prefix preceding the table name.

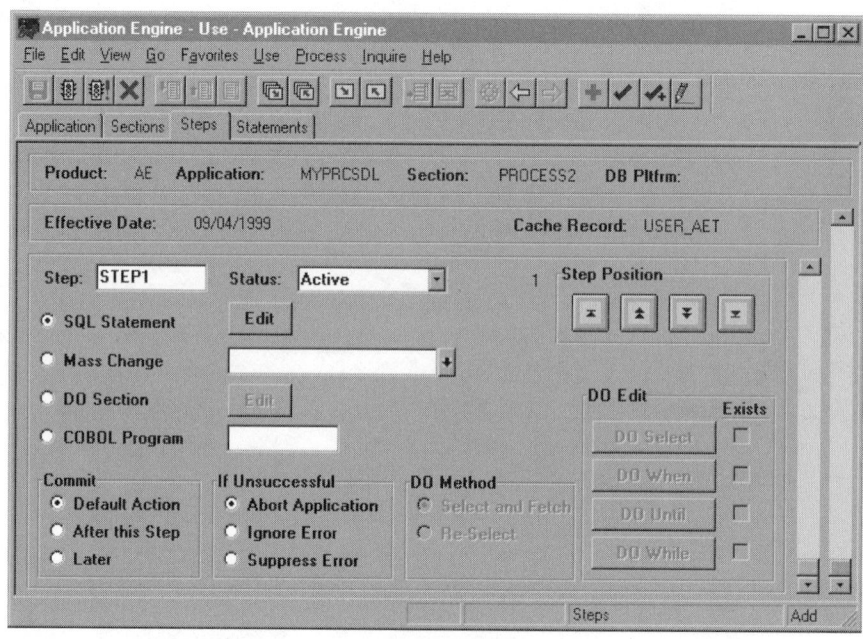

Figure 43.23   Adding STEP1 to the PROCESS2 section

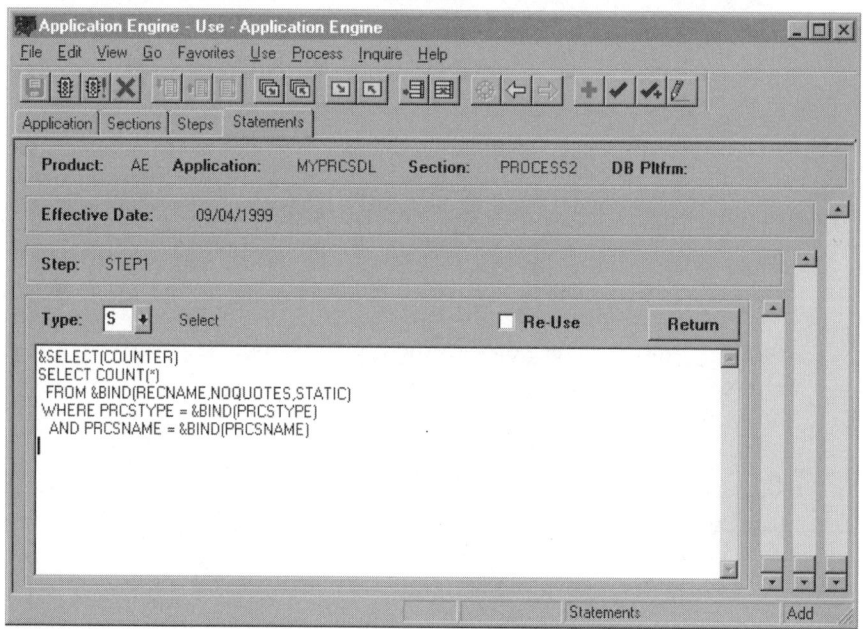

Figure 43.24   Adding the Select statement to PROCESS2.STEP1

Let's add another step to the PROCESS2 section. Click on the Step Folder tab to return to the Step Definition panel. Place the cursor in the Step field and press the F7 key to insert a new row. Our next step is named STEP2 (figure 43.25). Click on the DO section radio button, then on the corresponding edit button. Add the DELETE2 section when the DO section dialog box appears. You can see the DELETE2 section name next to the DO section edit button when you return. Our next step is to populate the statement panel with a DO When statement. The DELETE2 section is performed only if there are rows in the table containing the process definition from the Run Control record. Let's add the DO When statement now.

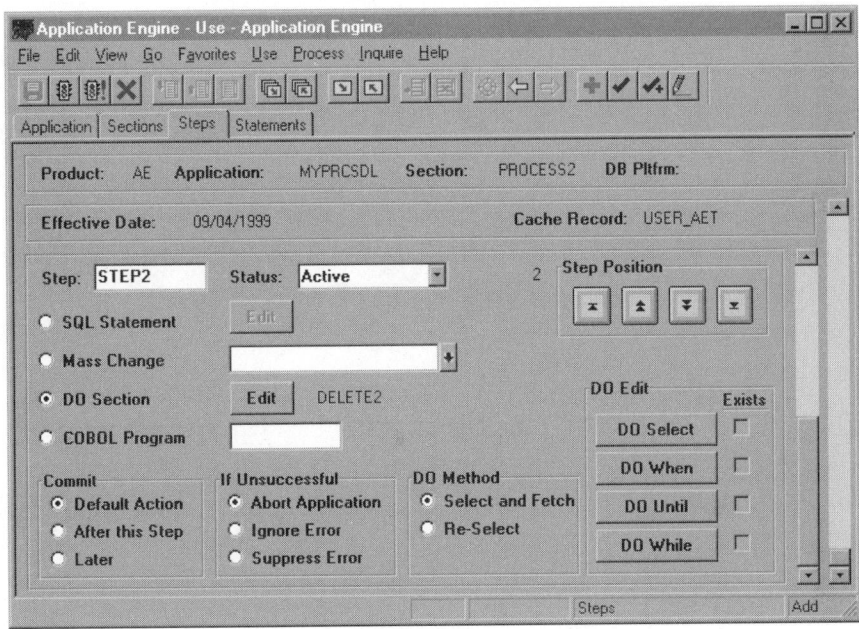

Figure 43.25   Adding STEP2 to the PROCESS2 section

Our DO When statement (figure 43.26) is the same as before. If the COUNTER cache field contains a value greater than zero, a True condition is returned, and the section DELETE1 is performed. IF the COUNTER cache field contains a value of zero, a False condition is returned, and the DELETE2 section is not performed.

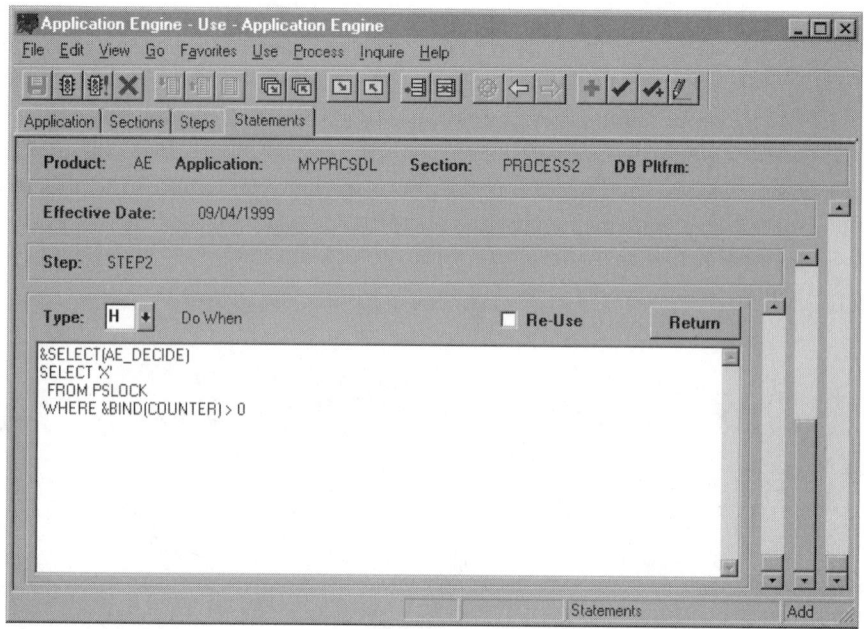

Figure 43.26 Adding the DO When statement to PROCESS2.STEP2

Use the F7 key again to insert a new step in the PROCESS2 section. Let's call it STEP3 (figure 43.27). Its function is to call the MESSAGE section we've created. Use the DO section radio button and edit box to set the section to MESSAGE. As stated in the creation of STEP3 in the PROCESS1 section, the MESSAGE section simply writes a message log entry containing the record name and number of rows processed.

The PROCESS2 section is complete.

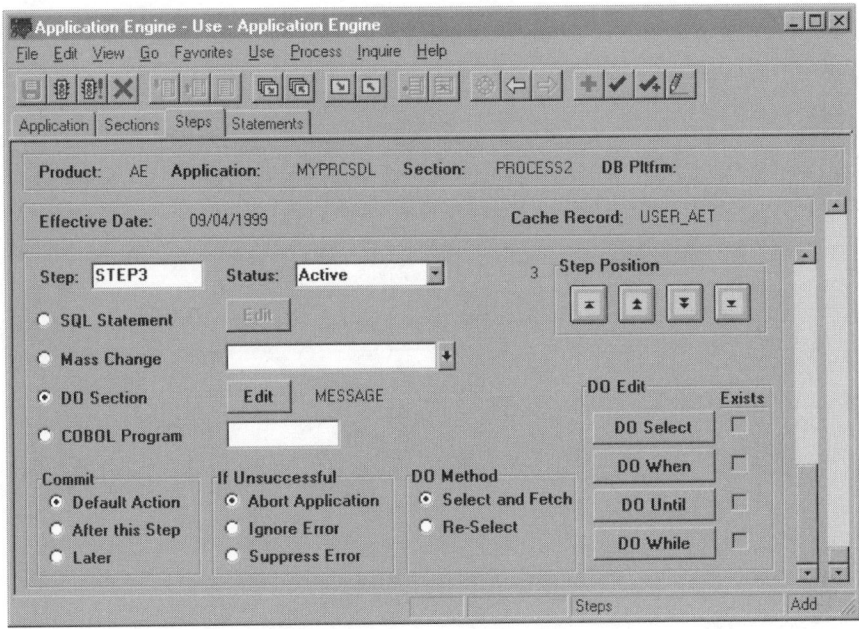

Figure 43.27   Adding STEP3 to the PROCESS2 section

43.1.6   Building the DYNSECTN section

Add a new section called DYNSECTN (figure 43.28). The purpose of this routine is to dynamically call either PROCESS1 or PROCESS2.

Figure 43.28
Adding the DYNSECTN
section

First, add the description for the DYNSECTN section (figure 43.29).

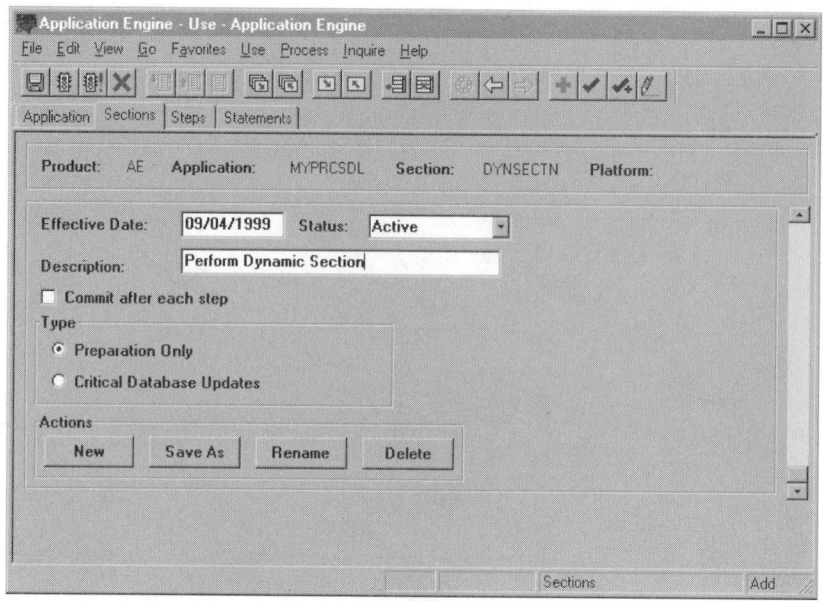

Figure 43.29 Defining the DYNSECTN section

On the Step Definition panel fill in the step name with STEP1 (figure 43.30).

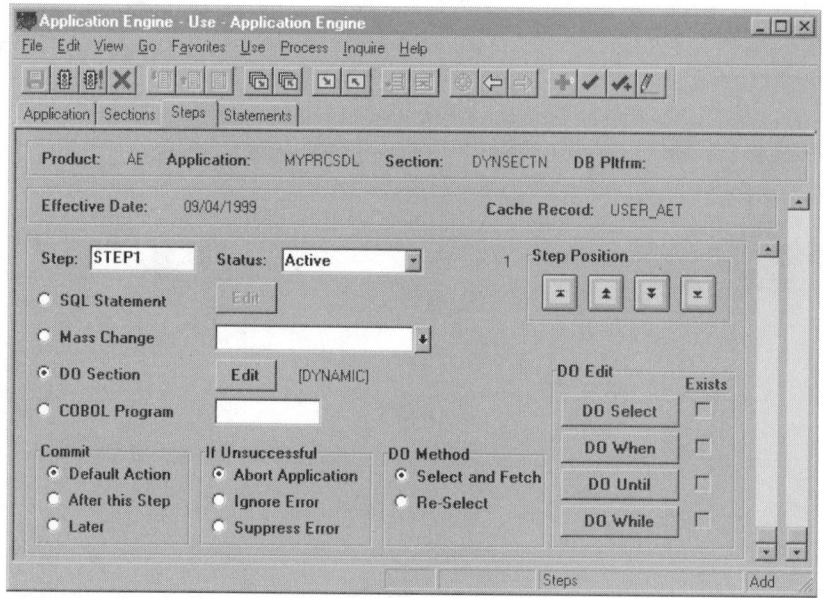

Figure 43.30 Adding STEP1 to the DYNSECTN section

Next, click on the DO section radio button and press the corresponding edit button. When the DO section dialog box appears, click on "Dynamic Section." Notice the literal DYNAMIC (in brackets) next to the DO section edit button (discussed in chapter 41). The symbolic parameter &SECTION is placed in the AE_DO_SECTION column in the AE_STEP_TBL. This is the table that's populated by your Step Definition panel entries. When the step is executed, the value of the AE_SECTION cache field will be used in place of the &SECTION symbolic. Our next and final section, MAIN, populates the AE_SECTION cache field with the value PROCESS1 or PROCESS2. The DYNSECTN section then performs PROCESS1 or PROCESS2.

The DYNSECTN section is complete.

43.1.7 Building the MAIN section

As we've discussed, all Application Engine programs must begin with a section called MAIN. Let's add the MAIN section now (figure 43.31).

Figure 43.31
Adding the MAIN section

The Section Definition panel is displayed in figure 43.32. We added a simple description of the MAIN section: Delete Process Definitions.

We'll call the first step of the MAIN section STEP1 (figure 43.33). The purpose of this step is to obtain the processing parameters from our Run Control record.

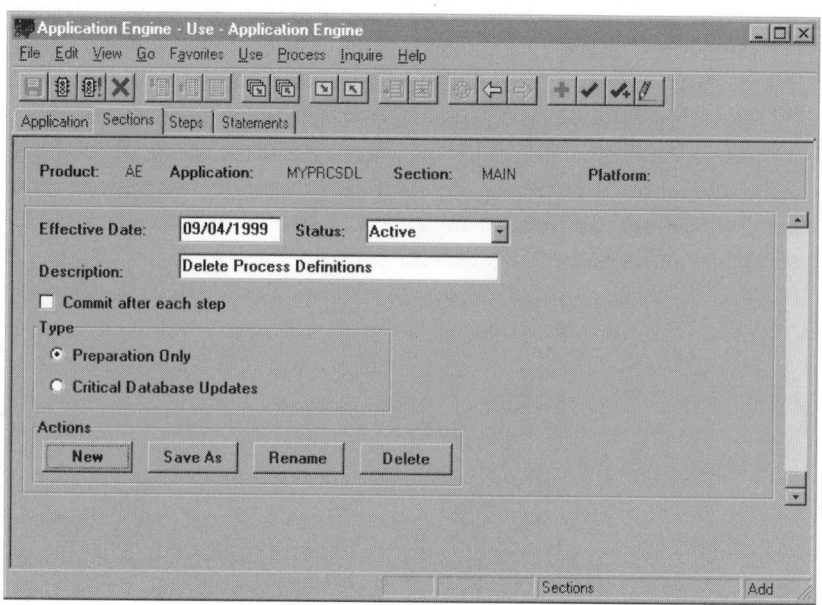

Figure 43.32 Defining the MAIN section

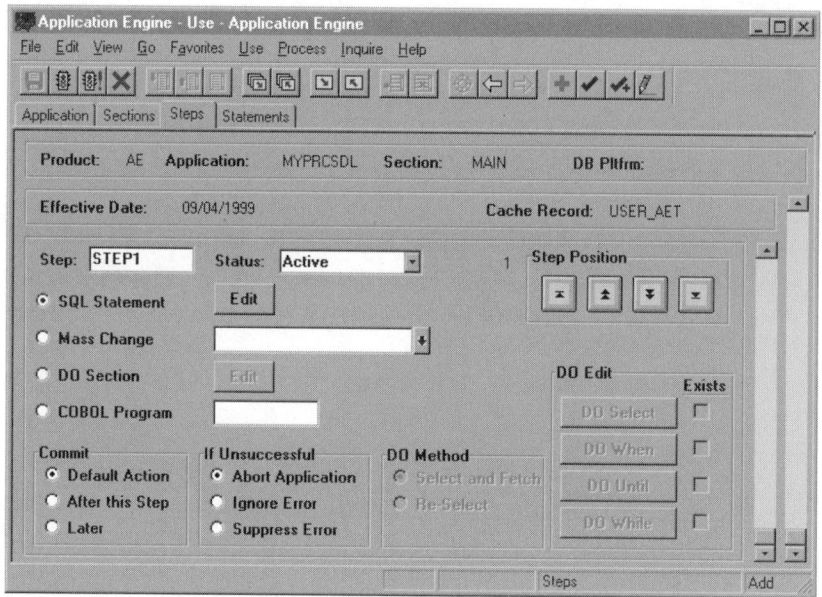

Figure 43.33 Adding STEP1 To the MAIN section

Figure 43.34 shows the `Select` statement for MAIN.STEP1. To retrieve our run parameters, we need to join our Run Control record (MY_RUN_CNTL_AE) to the Application Engine Run Control record called AE_RUN_CONTROL. The AE_RUN_CONTROL record discussed earlier in the book is used by Application Engine to hold run information such as PROCESS_INSTANCE, OPRID, RUN_CNTL_ID, and REQUEST_NBR. It also stores information about each run such as the last step committed, used when restarting an Application Engine program that may have terminated due to errors.

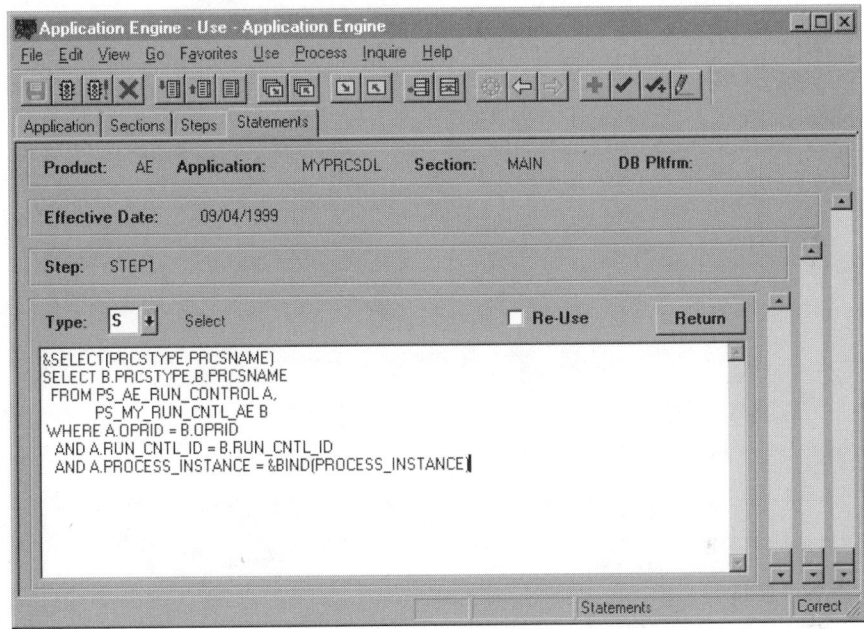

Figure 43.34   Select statement to retrieve our Run Control parameters

The records MY_RUN_CNTL_AE and AE_RUN_CONTROL are joined by the OPRID and RUN_CNTL_ID fields. The AE_RUN_CONTROL record is selected for the appropriate PROCESS_INSTANCE assigned by the Process Scheduler. The `&SELECT` statement stores the `PRCSTYPE` and `PRCSNAME` Run Control parameters in our cache record. We now have access to the process parameters entered on the Run Control panel. We'll display them on the message log in our next step.

Return to the Step Definition panel by clicking the Steps Folder tab. Place the cursor in the step field and press F7 to insert a new row. We'll call the new step STEP2 (figure 43.35). Now, click on the Statements Folder tab.

We write a simple message to the message log displaying the process type (`PRCSTYPE`) and process name (`PRCSNAME`) taken from the Run Control record. You can see the &MSG syntax in figure 43.36. Remember, the &MSG function only works with a statement Type of "U" (Update/Insert/Delete).

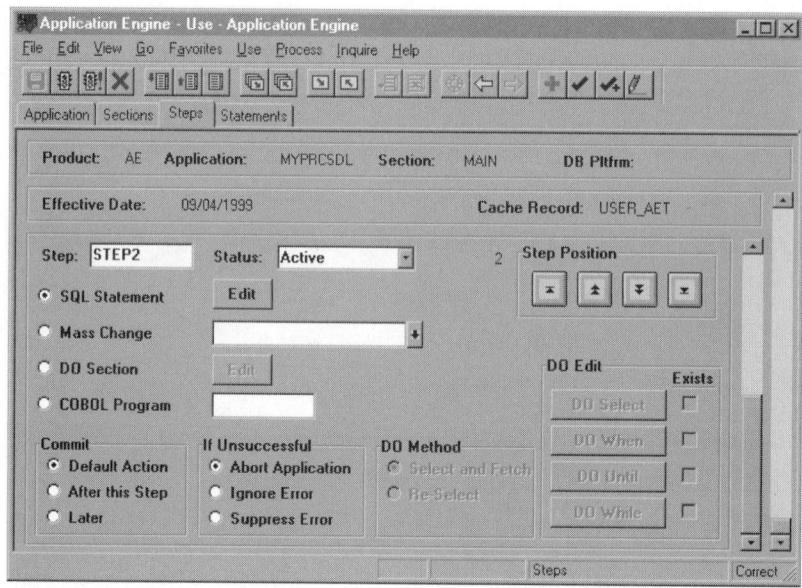

Figure 43.35   Adding STEP2 to the MAIN section

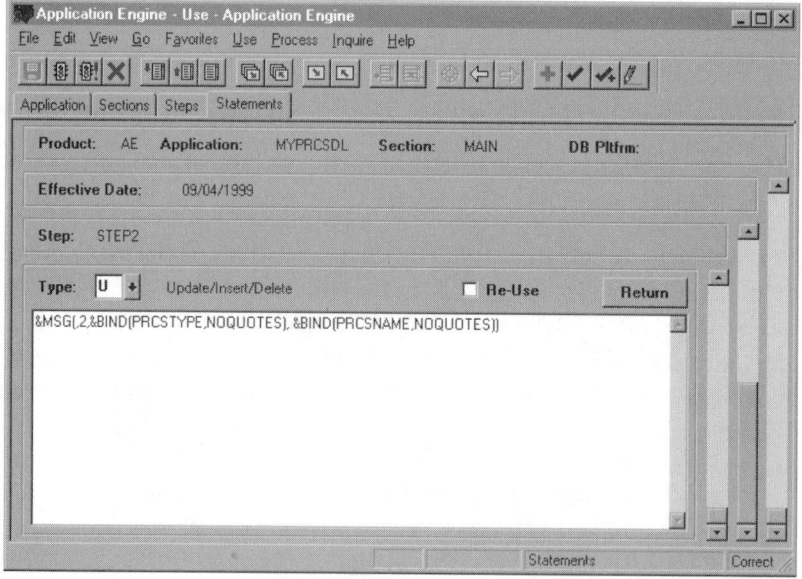

Figure 43.36   Run Control parameters are written to the message log

On the Step Definition panel, press F7 to insert another step. We'll call it STEP3 (figure 43.37). Click on the DO section radio button and the corresponding edit button. When the DO section dialog box appears, enter the section DYNSECTN. This is the section that handles the dynamic call of either PROCESS1 or PROCESS2. Let's code the DO Select statement for STEP3 in our MAIN section.

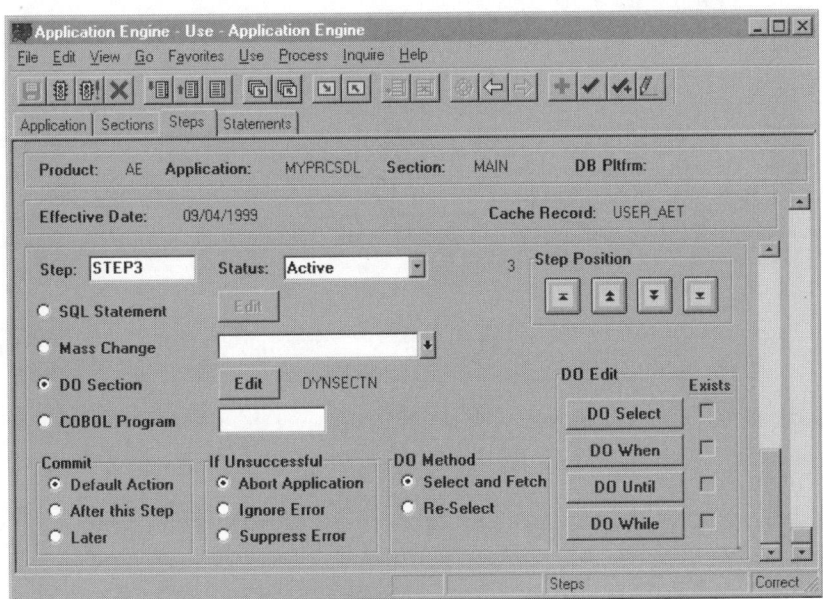

Figure 43.37   Adding STEP3 to the MAIN section

Figure 43.38 shows the DO Select statement that controls the processing of the six Process Definition tables. Let's take a closer look at the statement and describe what's happening:

```
&SELECT(AE_SECTION,RECNAME)          ◁── Assign cache field values
SELECT 'PROCESS1', RECNAME           ◁── Select process definition tables that require the
  FROM PSRECDEFN                          PS_ prefix. Each row selected returns two columns
 WHERE RECNAME = 'PRCSDEFN'               – 'PROCESS1' and RECNAME. 'PROCESS1'
    OR RECNAME = 'PRCSDEFNGRP'            populates the AE_SECTION cache field.
    OR RECNAME = 'PRCSDEFNPNL'
    OR RECNAME = 'PRCSDEFNXFER'

UNION                                ◁── Using a UNION, select process definition
                                          tables that do not use the PS_ prefix. The
SELECT 'PROCESS2', RECNAME                rows returned will have the columns
  FROM PSRECDEFN                          'PROCESS2' and RECNAME. 'PROCESS2' will
 WHERE RECNAME = 'PSPRCSRQST'             be stored in the AE_SECTION cache field.
    OR RECNAME = 'PSPNLFIELD'
 ORDER BY 1,2
```

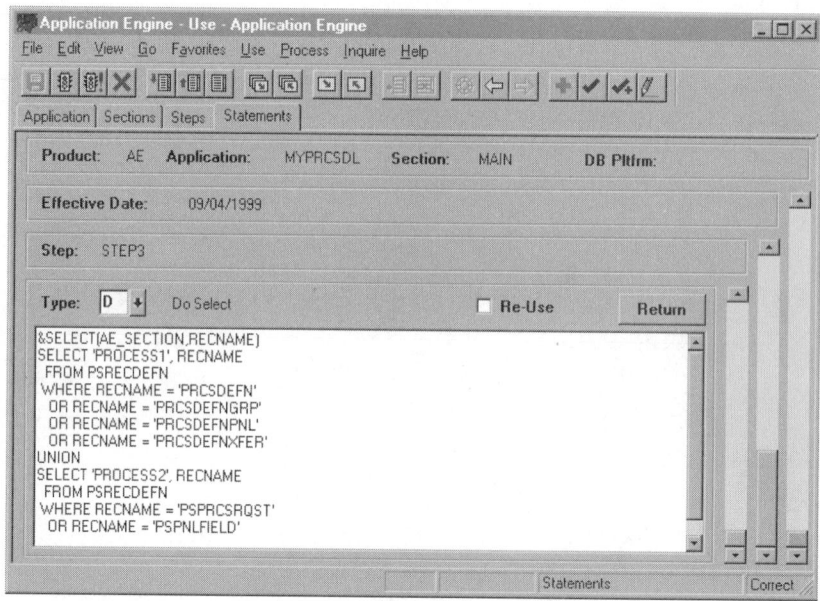

Figure 43.38   The DO Select statement to process the six process definition tables

The SQL DO Select statement above may appear strange at first. Let's talk about what we're trying to accomplish. Our goal is to delete any process definitions that match the process type and process name entered on the Run Control panel. There are six process definition tables that may contain the process definition entered. We're going to produce a result set that contains the record name (RECNAME) for each of the six tables along with the name of the dynamic section to use. Each row returned will then be processed by the appropriate section. PROCESS1 handles the tables with the PS_ prefix, and PROCESS2 handles the tables without the PS_ prefix. Let's test our statement using a database tool outside of PeopleSoft, SQL*Talk in this example.

Figure 43.39 shows the Select statement results using SQL*Talk. The first four tables use the PROCESS1 section while the last two tables use the PROCESS2 section. For each of these rows, the cache fields AE_SECTION and RECNAME are updated. The section DYNSECTN is performed for each row, which in turn calls either the PROCESS1 or PROCESS2 sections dynamically, based on the contents of the AE_SECTION cache field.

Our Application Engine program is finally complete! We can test our new utility to delete obsolete process definitions. It's perfectly normal to feel a bit nervous or excited before testing your work. We've put considerable effort into this application, and now we'll see if it has paid off. Let's begin our test.

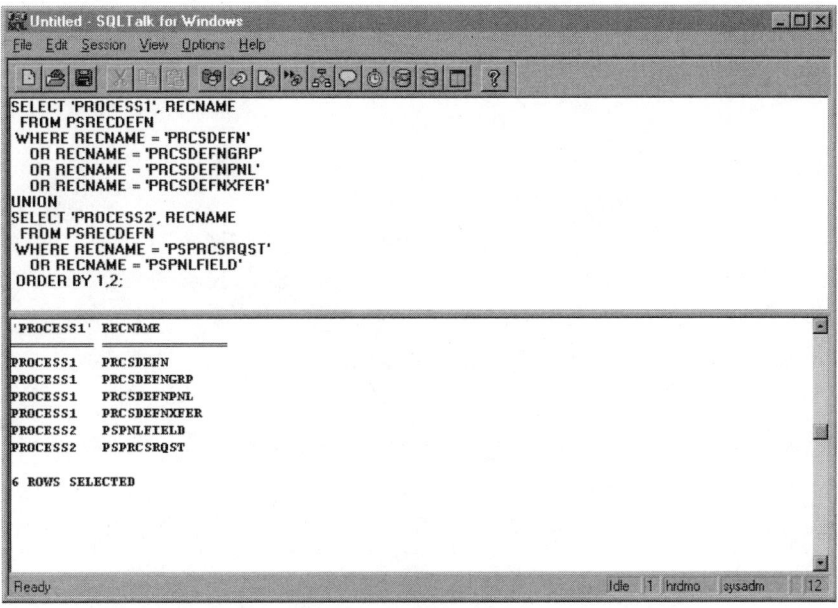

Figure 43.39   Testing our statement using SQL*Talk

43.2   TESTING THE COMPLETED APPLICATION

Figure 43.40 shows the navigation to our new utility panel. Add a new Run Control ID. I'm going to use a Run Control ID called "DUMMY" since we're going to delete the DUMMY process definition we created earlier in this chapter.

Navigation: Go → PeopleTools → Utilities → Process → Delete Process Definition →
Delete PRCSDEFN → Add

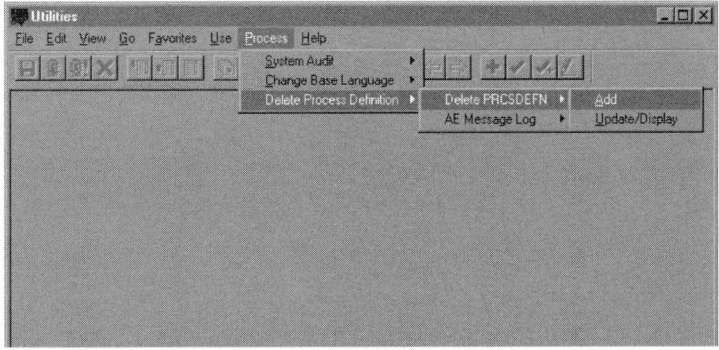

Figure 43.40   Accessing the Delete Process Definition panel

We've entered the process type and process name used for our DUMMY definition (figure 43.41). Remember, we created a DUMMY definition to test our process. We don't want to delete a "real" process definition.

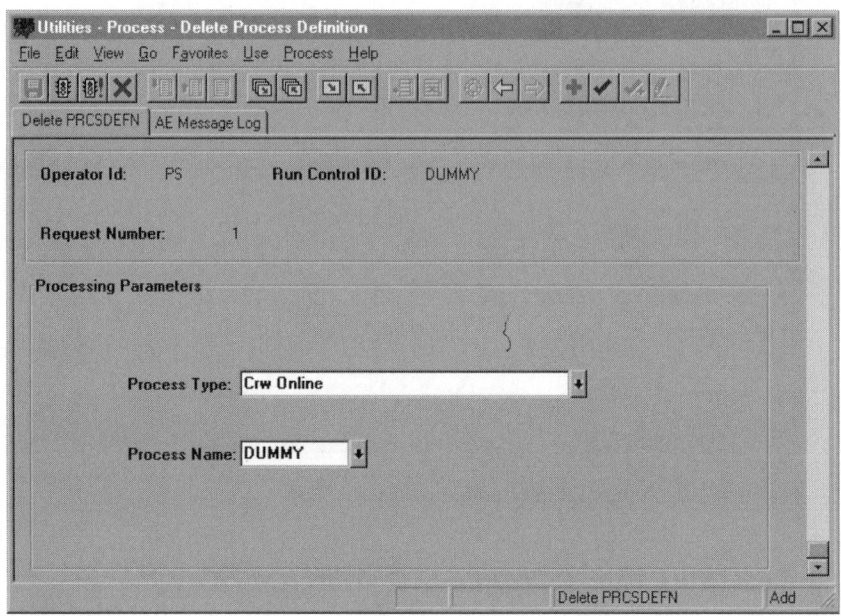

Figure 43.41   Assigning parameter values on the Run Control panel

Save the record and click on the Traffic Light to initiate a Process Scheduler request.

Figure 43.42 shows the Process Request panel. Our Application Engine program (MYPRCSDL) appears in the panel. Our process definition for MYPRCSDL appears to be functioning correctly, so click OK to initiate the process within Process Scheduler.

This is a good sign! You may notice the MS-DOS box appears when running on the client (figure 43.43). The lines displayed may move very quickly on the screen. Figure 43.43 shows some of the lines displayed in the MS-DOS box. Near the top of the screen, I can see our processing parameters in the Run Control record. Near the bottom, we see the first record (PRCSDEFN) had one row with our DUMMY process definition. Also notice the dynamic section PROCESS1 was performed as planned.

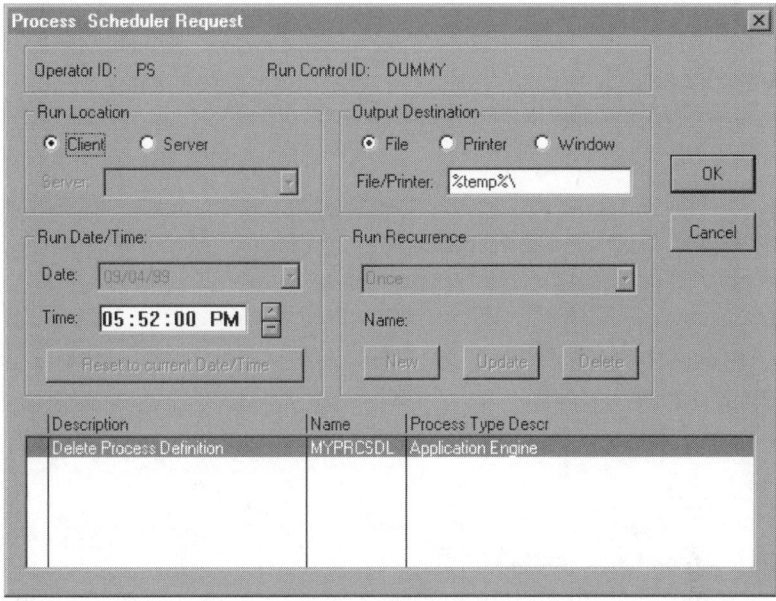

Figure 43.42   Submitting the Process Scheduler request

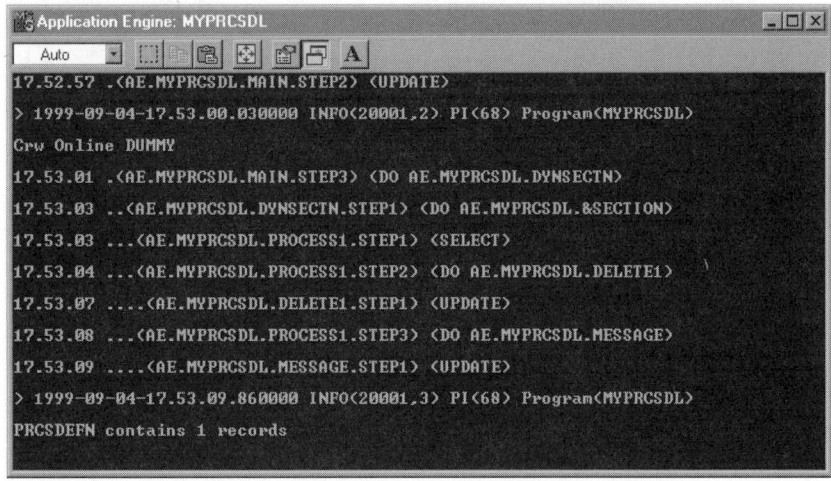

Figure 43.43   The MS-DOS box appears for our process

We still need to verify that the process functioned correctly, especially when a Delete statement is being executed. When the process has completed, we'll click on the A/E Message Log Folder tab to view the message log.

Figure 43.44 shows the Message Log panel. Click on the flashlight to view the messages from the latest run. We see the Run Control parameters (Crw Online DUMMY) and each table with the number of rows processed. Let's use our database query tool again to see if the rows have been deleted.

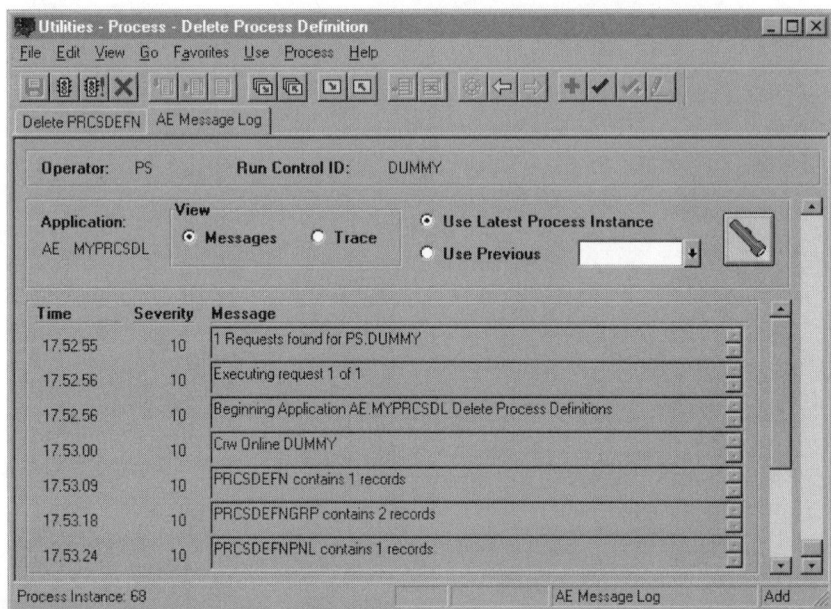

Figure 43.44   Reviewing the message log

43.2.1   Verifying our results

We verified that the DUMMY process definition rows were removed from the process definition tables using SQL*Talk (figure 43.45). Each Select returned zero rows. We can also examine the trace file for a more detailed look at the results.

You'll find the trace file in the %TEMP%/ps/<databasename> directory. The filename <process_instance>.aet will be used. In our particular case that translates to

```
C:\windows\temp\ps\hrdmo\68.aet
```

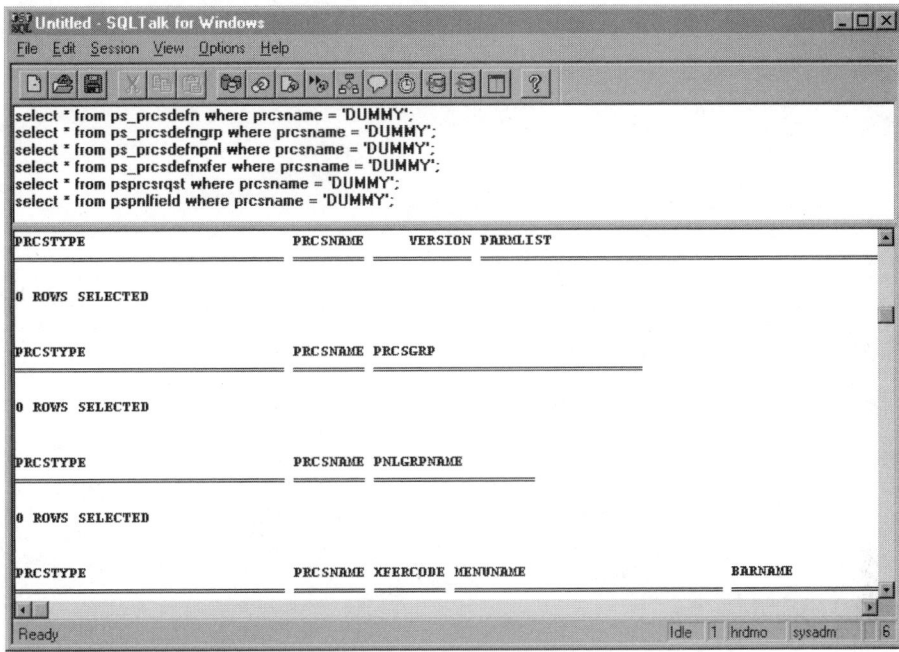

Figure 43.45   Verifying our test results using SQL*Talk

43.2.2   Examining the trace file

Let's take a look at the trace file contents:

Listing 43.1

The trace file

```
17.52.56 1999-09-04 PeopleTools 7.5 Application Engine
17.52.56 Tracing request PS.DUMMY
17.52.56 Starting application AE.MYPRCSDL Delete Process Definitions
/
INSERT INTO PS_USER_AET ( PROCESS_INSTANCE,COUNTER,RECNAME,FIELDNAME,
AE_DECIDE,PRCSTYPE,PRCSNAME,AE_SECTION  )
 VALUES (        68,0,' ',' ',' ',' ',' ',' '  )
/
COMMIT
/
17.52.56 .(AE.MYPRCSDL.MAIN.STEP1) (SELECT)
/
SELECT B.PRCSTYPE,B.PRCSNAME
  FROM PS_AE_RUN_CONTROL A,              PS_MY_RUN_CNTL_AE B
 WHERE A.OPRID = B.OPRID
   AND A.RUN_CNTL_ID = B.RUN_CNTL_ID
   AND A.PROCESS_INSTANCE = 68
```

```
/
17.52.57 .(AE.MYPRCSDL.MAIN.STEP2) (UPDATE)
17.53.01 .(AE.MYPRCSDL.MAIN.STEP3) (DO AE.MYPRCSDL.DYNSECTN)
/
SELECT 'PROCESS1', RECNAME
  FROM PSRECDEFN
 WHERE RECNAME = 'PRCSDEFN'
    OR RECNAME = 'PRCSDEFNGRP'
    OR RECNAME = 'PRCSDEFNPNL'
    OR RECNAME = 'PRCSDEFNXFER'
  UNION
 SELECT 'PROCESS2', RECNAME
  FROM PSRECDEFN
 WHERE RECNAME = 'PSPRCSRQST'
    OR RECNAME = 'PSPNLFIELD'
  ORDER BY 1, 2
/
17.53.03 ..(AE.MYPRCSDL.DYNSECTN.STEP1) (DO AE.MYPRCSDL.&SECTION)
17.53.03 ...(AE.MYPRCSDL.PROCESS1.STEP1) (SELECT)
/
SELECT COUNT(*)
  FROM PS_PRCSDEFN
 WHERE PRCSTYPE = 'Crw Online'
   AND PRCSNAME = 'DUMMY'
/
17.53.04 ...(AE.MYPRCSDL.PROCESS1.STEP2) (DO AE.MYPRCSDL.DELETE1)
/
SELECT 'X'
  FROM PSLOCK
 WHERE 1 > 0
/
17.53.07 ....(AE.MYPRCSDL.DELETE1.STEP1) (UPDATE)
/
DELETE
  FROM PS_PRCSDEFN
 WHERE PRCSTYPE = 'Crw Online'
   AND PRCSNAME = 'DUMMY'
/
17.53.08 ...(AE.MYPRCSDL.PROCESS1.STEP3) (DO AE.MYPRCSDL.MESSAGE)
17.53.09 ....(AE.MYPRCSDL.MESSAGE.STEP1) (UPDATE)
17.53.11 .(AE.MYPRCSDL.MAIN.STEP3) (DO FETCH)
17.53.11 ..(AE.MYPRCSDL.DYNSECTN.STEP1) (DO AE.MYPRCSDL.&SECTION)
17.53.12 ...(AE.MYPRCSDL.PROCESS1.STEP1) (SELECT)
/
SELECT COUNT(*)
  FROM PS_PRCSDEFNGRP
 WHERE PRCSTYPE = 'Crw Online'
   AND PRCSNAME = 'DUMMY'
/
17.53.14 ...(AE.MYPRCSDL.PROCESS1.STEP2) (DO AE.MYPRCSDL.DELETE1)
/
SELECT 'X'
  FROM PSLOCK
```

```
  WHERE 2 > 0
/
17.53.15 ....(AE.MYPRCSDL.DELETE1.STEP1) (UPDATE)
/
DELETE
  FROM PS_PRCSDEFNGRP
 WHERE PRCSTYPE = 'Crw Online'
   AND PRCSNAME = 'DUMMY'
/
17.53.17 ...(AE.MYPRCSDL.PROCESS1.STEP3) (DO AE.MYPRCSDL.MESSAGE)
17.53.17 ....(AE.MYPRCSDL.MESSAGE.STEP1) (UPDATE)
17.53.19 .(AE.MYPRCSDL.MAIN.STEP3) (DO FETCH)
17.53.19 ..(AE.MYPRCSDL.DYNSECTN.STEP1) (DO AE.MYPRCSDL.&SECTION)
17.53.19 ...(AE.MYPRCSDL.PROCESS1.STEP1) (SELECT)
/
SELECT COUNT(*)
  FROM PS_PRCSDEFNPNL
 WHERE PRCSTYPE = 'Crw Online'
   AND PRCSNAME = 'DUMMY'
/
17.53.21 ...(AE.MYPRCSDL.PROCESS1.STEP2) (DO AE.MYPRCSDL.DELETE1)
/
SELECT 'X'
  FROM PSLOCK
 WHERE 1 > 0
/
17.53.22 ....(AE.MYPRCSDL.DELETE1.STEP1) (UPDATE)
/
DELETE
  FROM PS_PRCSDEFNPNL
 WHERE PRCSTYPE = 'Crw Online'
   AND PRCSNAME = 'DUMMY'
/
17.53.23 ...(AE.MYPRCSDL.PROCESS1.STEP3) (DO AE.MYPRCSDL.MESSAGE)
17.53.23 ....(AE.MYPRCSDL.MESSAGE.STEP1) (UPDATE)
17.53.25 .(AE.MYPRCSDL.MAIN.STEP3) (DO FETCH)
17.53.25 ..(AE.MYPRCSDL.DYNSECTN.STEP1) (DO AE.MYPRCSDL.&SECTION)
17.53.26 ...(AE.MYPRCSDL.PROCESS1.STEP1) (SELECT)
/
SELECT COUNT(*)
  FROM PS_PRCSDEFNXFER
 WHERE PRCSTYPE = 'Crw Online'
   AND PRCSNAME = 'DUMMY'
/
17.53.27 ...(AE.MYPRCSDL.PROCESS1.STEP2) (DO AE.MYPRCSDL.DELETE1)
/
SELECT 'X'
  FROM PSLOCK
 WHERE 1 > 0
/
17.53.28 ....(AE.MYPRCSDL.DELETE1.STEP1) (UPDATE)
/
```

```
DELETE
  FROM PS_PRCSDEFNXFER
 WHERE PRCSTYPE = 'Crw Online'
   AND PRCSNAME = 'DUMMY'
/
17.53.29 ...(AE.MYPRCSDL.PROCESS1.STEP3) (DO AE.MYPRCSDL.MESSAGE)
17.53.30 ....(AE.MYPRCSDL.MESSAGE.STEP1) (UPDATE)
17.53.31 .(AE.MYPRCSDL.MAIN.STEP3) (DO FETCH)
17.53.31 ..(AE.MYPRCSDL.DYNSECTN.STEP1) (DO AE.MYPRCSDL.&SECTION)
17.53.32 ...(AE.MYPRCSDL.PROCESS2.STEP1) (SELECT)
/
SELECT COUNT(*)
  FROM PSPNLFIELD
 WHERE PRCSTYPE = 'Crw Online'
   AND PRCSNAME = 'DUMMY'
/
17.53.42 ...(AE.MYPRCSDL.PROCESS2.STEP2) (DO AE.MYPRCSDL.DELETE2)
/
SELECT 'X'
  FROM PSLOCK
 WHERE 0 > 0
/
17.53.43 ...(AE.MYPRCSDL.PROCESS2.STEP3) (DO AE.MYPRCSDL.MESSAGE)
17.53.44 ....(AE.MYPRCSDL.MESSAGE.STEP1) (UPDATE)
17.53.45 .(AE.MYPRCSDL.MAIN.STEP3) (DO FETCH)
17.53.45 ..(AE.MYPRCSDL.DYNSECTN.STEP1) (DO AE.MYPRCSDL.&SECTION)
17.53.46 ...(AE.MYPRCSDL.PROCESS2.STEP1) (SELECT)
/
SELECT COUNT(*)
  FROM PSPRCSRQST
 WHERE PRCSTYPE = 'Crw Online'
   AND PRCSNAME = 'DUMMY'
/
17.53.47 ...(AE.MYPRCSDL.PROCESS2.STEP2) (DO AE.MYPRCSDL.DELETE2)
/
SELECT 'X'
  FROM PSLOCK
 WHERE 0 > 0
/
17.53.48 ...(AE.MYPRCSDL.PROCESS2.STEP3) (DO AE.MYPRCSDL.MESSAGE)
17.53.48 ....(AE.MYPRCSDL.MESSAGE.STEP1) (UPDATE)
17.53.49 .(AE.MYPRCSDL.MAIN.STEP3) (DO FETCH)
/
DELETE
  FROM PS_USER_AET
 WHERE PROCESS_INSTANCE = 0000000068
/
17.53.50 Application AE.MYPRCSDL ended normally
/
COMMIT
/
17.53.50 Application Engine ended normally
```

In this entire trace file for the run, you can see each section and step as it was executed as well as the compiled SQL statements. Take special note of the dynamic sections PROCESS1 and PROCESS2. Also, notice the resolved bind variables used in the run.

Our Application Engine development is complete. There is always a great feeling of accomplishment that accompanies the successful completion of an application. I would suggest taking a nice long break before moving on to chapter 44 (Additional topics). You deserve some relaxation after a job well done!

KEY POINTS

1 You should always determine the program structure before creating your program. Building the lower (subordinate) sections first and working backward will alleviate any step dependencies you may encounter.

2 Validate your program results thoroughly using your database query tool and the trace file output. Pay close attention to the resolved bind variables.

3 You may not have realized it, but you've taken some huge strides in learning one of PeopleSofts' up-and-coming tools, Expand your knowledge and experience by creating custom Application Engine programs to perform a variety of different tasks.

Additional topics

So far, we've covered the basics of Application Engine, and we can surely begin developing batch processes. But what if your program does not yield the desired results? Or, worse yet, what if the process aborts unexpectedly. In this chapter, we'll discuss the use of trace files and learn how to restart an aborted process. In addition, we'll provide tips on tackling large, often cumbersome Application Engine programs. An SQR utility to help analyze A/E programs will be covered as well.

44.1 USING TRACE FILES

In chapter 35, we discussed the options available on the Application Definition panel. One of the options controls the creation of a trace file. The option indicates levels of detail to be included in the trace file. NO trace file is generated when the Trace option is set to Off. The trace filename is set to <process_instance>.AET and is placed in the current working directory. The trace file is simply an ASCII text file that displays each step as it is executed. Generated SQL may be written to the trace file.

Figure 44.1 shows the Application Definition panel. The Trace file option is turned OFF. The other trace options available are SQL and Steps Only. SQL displays all the steps executed along with the associated SQL statements. The Steps Only option only displays the steps executed. (No SQL statements are written to the trace file.)

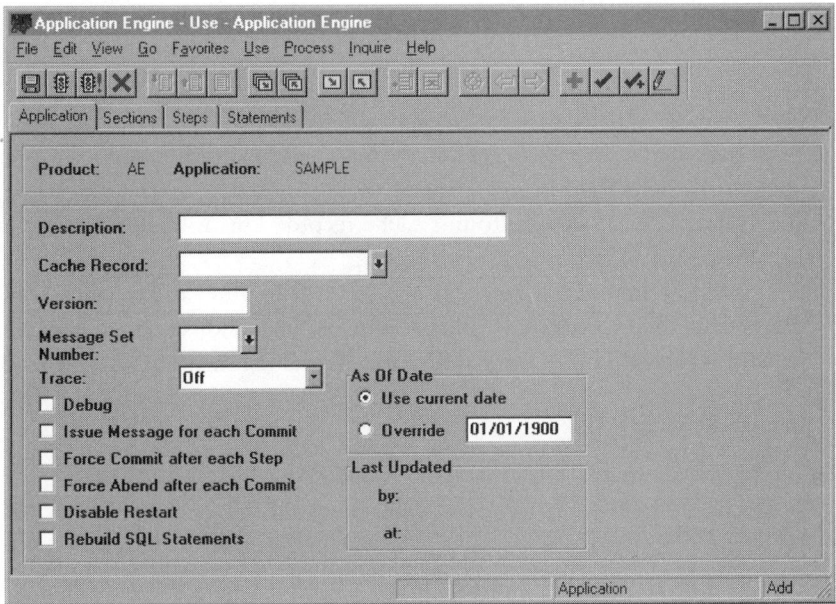

Figure 44.1   Trace options on Application Definition panel

44.1.1   Sample trace file

This sample trace file was generated during an execution of our exercise 5 application (called AE.USER005). The trace option was set to SQL, which displays all the steps and SQL statements processed. You can see some of the SQL statements are controlled by the PTPEMAIN process:

```
08.28.54 1999-01-13 PeopleTools 7.5 Application Engine
08.28.54 Tracing request PS.#USER005
08.28.54 Starting application AE.USER005 User Application 005
```

```
/
INSERT INTO PS_USER_AET ( PROCESS_INSTANCE,COUNTER,RECNAME,FIELDNAME,
AE_DECIDE  )
 VALUES (         10,0,' ',' ',' '  )
/
```

The `Insert` statement immediately preceding is an example of a PTPEMAIN-controlled statement. It initializes the cache record we specified on the Application Definition panel. Fields are initialized depending on their datatype. PROCESS_INSTANCE is always set to the process instance of our program. The field, COUNTER, is initialized to zero since it is numeric. The remaining fields in the cache record are initialized to blank since they are character datatypes.

```
UPDATE PS_USER_AET
   SET FIELDNAME = 'PAY_END_DT'
 WHERE PROCESS_INSTANCE = 0000000010
/
COMMIT
/
```

The statement above is also generated by PTPEMAIN. Remember, we initialized the cache field FIELDNAME to a value of `'PAY_END_DT'` on the Process Request panel. The value is then loaded into our cache record. This is how process request parameters are passed to the program.

The step in the code below selects `RECNAME` values and for each row returned (or fetched) executes a section called COUNT. The resolved bind variable for FIELD-NAME is displayed in the trace file, and the value is set to `'PAY_END_DT'`.

```
08.28.55 .(AE.USER005.MAIN.STEP1) (DO AE.USER005.COUNT)
/
SELECT A.RECNAME
  FROM PSRECFIELD     A,
       PSRECDEFN      B
 WHERE A.RECNAME    = B.RECNAME
   AND A.FIELDNAME = 'PAY_END_DT'
   AND B.RECTYPE   = 0
  ORDER BY A.RECNAME
/
```

The RECNAME passed to COUNT.STEP1 (in this instance) is BEN_PLAN_DATA:

```
08.28.58 ..(AE.USER005.COUNT.STEP1) (SELECT)
/
SELECT COUNT(*)
  FROM PS_BEN_PLAN_DATA
/
08.29.00 ..(AE.USER005.COUNT.STEP2) (DO AE.USER005.MSG)
/
SELECT 'X'
```

```
    FROM PSLOCK
 WHERE 0 > 0
/
```

Notice all &BIND() variables have been resolved in the SQL. STEP1 selects the row count for the BEN_PLAN_DATA table. COUNT.STEP2, as you may recall, performs a DO When statement. If the number of rows is greater than zero, the section MSG is performed. The WHERE clause against the PSLOCK table may look odd at first. In our statement definition, the WHERE clause was defined as WHERE &BIND(COUNTER) > 0. Since the cache field COUNTER contains a value of zero, the statement was compiled as WHERE 0 > 0. This returns NO rows, and the MSG section is not executed. Control once again is passed to MAIN.STEP1, and another row is fetched:

```
08.29.02 .(AE.USER005.MAIN.STEP1) (DO FETCH)
08.29.03 ..(AE.USER005.COUNT.STEP1) (SELECT)
/
SELECT COUNT(*)
  FROM PS_BOND_LOG
/
08.29.05 ..(AE.USER005.COUNT.STEP2) (DO AE.USER005.MSG)
/
SELECT 'X'
  FROM PSLOCK
 WHERE 471 > 0
/
08.29.07 ...(AE.USER005.MSG.STEP1) (UPDATE)
```

This time a RECNAME value of BOND_LOG is passed to the COUNT section. There were 471 rows in the table. The DO When criteria once resolved reads as WHERE 471 > 0. This returns a row from PSLOCK, which designates a TRUE condition. The section MSG is then executed:

```
08.29.09 .(AE.USER005.MAIN.STEP1) (DO FETCH)
08.29.10 ..(AE.USER005.COUNT.STEP1) (SELECT)
/
SELECT COUNT(*)
  FROM PS_DED_CALC
/
08.29.13 ..(AE.USER005.COUNT.STEP2) (DO AE.USER005.MSG)
/
SELECT 'X'
  FROM PSLOCK
 WHERE 90 > 0
/
08.29.15 ...(AE.USER005.MSG.STEP1) (UPDATE)
/
```

This process continues until no rows remain. We'll skip the rest and proceed to the end of the trace file:

```
/
08.38.24 .(AE.USER005.MAIN.STEP1) (DO FETCH)
/
DELETE
  FROM PS_USER_AET
 WHERE PROCESS_INSTANCE = 0000000010
/
08.38.24 Application AE.USER005 ended normally
/
COMMIT
/
08.38.25 Application Engine ended normally
```

The last DO FETCH returned no rows, so the COUNT section was no longer executed. Our defined program has completed, and PTPEMAIN does some final cleanup by deleting the cache record row we've been using.

44.2   RESTARTING AN A/E PROCESS

During the execution of your A/E program, an unexpected error may cause it to abort. There are numerous reasons why this may occur: for example, an SQL error, system resource problem, or syntax errors in your A/E statement. A critical process could be near completion when the error occurs, and starting the process over from the beginning may not be a feasible solution. Application Engine maintains an entry in the AE_RUN_CONTROL table, which holds restart information in the event of an abend. This restart information is refreshed at every commit point. When restarting, the process takes over from the last commit point and continues. You cannot submit an aborted process from the beginning using the same OPRID and RUN_CNTL_ID. The AE_RUN_CONTROL holds it in a suspended status so it may be restarted properly.

Only applications run on the server through Process Scheduler can be restarted using Process Monitor by highlighting the failed process and clicking on Action → Restart. All other applications must execute PTPEMAIN.exe manually on the client or server when restarting. PTPEMAIN.exe should reside in the CBLBIN subdirectory attached to the PSVER directory (PSVER standing for the PeopleSoft version assigned as the high-level directory name). Simply type PTPEMAIN on the command line. You will then be prompted for the database type, database name, username (OPRID), password, Run Control ID, and process instance. The process will then resume where it left off.

There are times when you may wish to start the process from the beginning. If so, you'll have to delete the AE_RUN_CONTROL row for the OPRID and RUN_CNTL_ID you're using. You may also have to delete the cache record for the process instance. Only then can you restart the process from the beginning. You may also disable the restart capability on the Application Definition panel. Please make certain that no data corruption can occur as a result of not restarting properly.

44.3   ANALYZING A/E PROGRAMS

Analyzing large Application Engine programs can be tedious. One section can call a multitude of other sections. Since all components are stored within the database, you'll have to toggle back and forth between sections using the online panels. You can, however, take several steps that will make your analysis a little easier:

- Read any documentation on the process beforehand.
- Print a listing of the cache record used by the A/E program. This identifies all fields used to pass values from one step to another.
- Start with the section MAIN. Identify all steps within the MAIN section and treat each step as a separate process. Breaking the process down into smaller logical sections will help put things in perspective.
- Keep track of everything that's happening, not just the relationship between sections but also the tables being affected. Make a list of permanent tables and temporary tables. The temp tables can pass large amounts of data to subsequent sections or steps.
- After running the process, look at the trace file produced. One method of trace execution I've seen used allows you to sort the lines in the trace file using an ASCII editor (or import the lines into Excel or Access and then sort them). To do so, you remove any lines that don't have the time-stamp on it. You are then left with the time and name of all the steps performed in execution order. Be wary of processes that run beyond midnight. You'll have to manipulate the file in your editor to correct the sequencing. The resulting data will look like this:

```
08.28.54 1999-01-13 PeopleTools 7.5 Application Engine
08.28.54 Starting application AE.USER005 User Application 005
08.28.54 Tracing request PS.#USER005
08.28.55 .(AE.USER005.MAIN.STEP1) (DO AE.USER005.COUNT)
08.28.58 ..(AE.USER005.COUNT.STEP1) (SELECT)
08.29.00 ..(AE.USER005.COUNT.STEP2) (DO AE.USER005.MSG)
08.29.02 .(AE.USER005.MAIN.STEP1) (DO FETCH)
08.29.03 ..(AE.USER005.COUNT.STEP1) (SELECT)
08.29.05 ..(AE.USER005.COUNT.STEP2) (DO AE.USER005.MSG)
08.29.07 ...(AE.USER005.MSG.STEP1) (UPDATE)
08.29.09 .(AE.USER005.MAIN.STEP1) (DO FETCH)
08.29.10 ..(AE.USER005.COUNT.STEP1) (SELECT)
08.29.13 ..(AE.USER005.COUNT.STEP2) (DO AE.USER005.MSG)
08.29.15 ...(AE.USER005.MSG.STEP1) (UPDATE)
```

We'll skip the middle part of the trace and go to the end.

```
08.38.19 .(AE.USER005.MAIN.STEP1) (DO FETCH)
08.38.20 ..(AE.USER005.COUNT.STEP1) (SELECT)
08.38.22 ..(AE.USER005.COUNT.STEP2) (DO AE.USER005.MSG)
08.38.24 .(AE.USER005.MAIN.STEP1) (DO FETCH)
08.38.24 Application AE.USER005 ended normally
08.38.25 Application Engine ended normally
```

This method gives you a good idea of the execution flow of the program but it's not one hundred percent accurate. The first three lines were all processed at 08.28.54, but they are not in execution order. The third line, "Tracing request PS.#USER005," should come before the "Starting application...." line. Any lines with the same time-stamp will then sort alphabetically. When analyzing a specific portion of the program, this may not be a factor.

- A simple SQR program can be written to extract the time-stamped lines from the trace file. This would be more effective than manipulating the file in Excel or Access. Basic SQR skills would be required.

- When using a trace file, remember a trace file only displays the steps based on certain conditions met at the time. Running the process two different times could follow two different execution paths. The trace files are simply "after the fact." PeopleSoft does not provide a mechanism to produce an indented "tree-formatted" flowchart of an entire A/E process. The next portion of this chapter deals with a custom SQR utility I developed to analyze an Application Engine program. The cache record is listed; each step is listed with all of its defined attributes; and, finally, an indented process flowchart is produced which illustrates the full execution flow of the process. I have named this utility (appropriately) "Application Engine Analyzer."

44.4   APPLICATION ENGINE ANALYZER

I developed this SQR utility to extract all the required information to analyze an A/E program. Once the program is identified through user-entered prompts, several functions are performed. The cache record is listed; the steps are printed with their attributes; and an indented process flowchart is produced.

When running the SQR utility, make sure the communication box is visible by using the –CB option (figure 44.2). This displays additional information before each prompt.

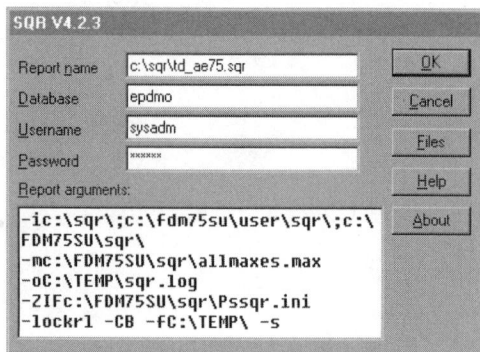

Figure 44.2
Running the SQR utility

The basic prompts are product, application ID and database platform. Figure 44.3 shows an example of the prompts issued when running the Application Analyzer utility. The product entered is AR, which is the product ID for Accounts Receivable. The application ID is PREDICT, the Payment Predictor process found in Accounts Receivable. This example was run under SQLBASE, so I entered the SQL-BASE code of "1" for the database platform prompt. When a step has a SQLBASE-specific version, the utility substitutes that in place of the generic one. This is how Application Engine processes steps as well. An additional prompt creates an A/E statement file, which produces a temporary file that can be imported into Word, formatted, and printed. It includes extracted A/E statements also in execution order. This is extremely valuable information put in an organized fashion. Only use this feature when absolutely necessary—the output can be very large, slowing the process down.

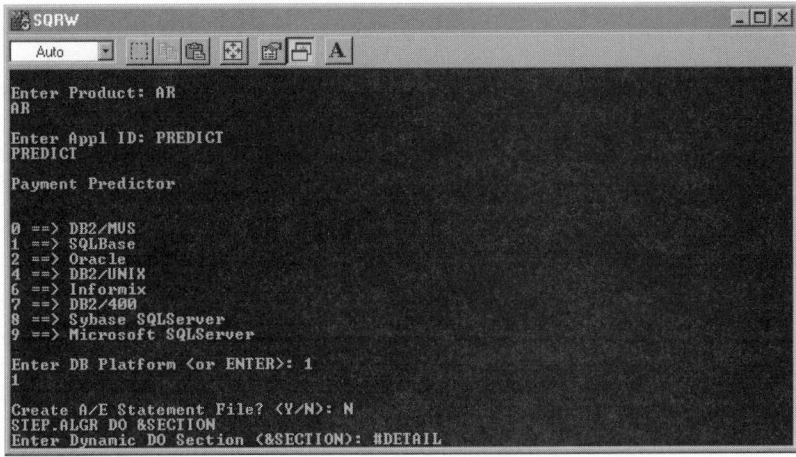

Figure 44.3   SQR utility prompts for user information

The user is also prompted when a dynamic DO section (&SECTION) is encountered. By entering the section #DETAIL, the dynamic DO is resolved and included in the process. #DETAIL is a payment predictor matching algorithm that may be called dynamically when running the payment predictor process. You may substitute any valid algorithm for the &SECTION substitution variable.

Let's now examine some sample output which has been condensed for the book:

```
Report ID:  TD_AE75          APPLICATION ENGINE ANALYZER
    Phase:  1
  Program:  AR/PREDICT        Cache Record: PP_AET
================================================================================
Fieldname              Key    Type   Len    Dec    LongName
================================================================================


PROCESS_INSTANCE       Y      Nbr    10            Process Instance
OPRID                  N      Char   8             Operator Id
RUN_CNTL_ID            N      Char   30            Run Control ID
SETID                  N      Char   5             SetID
PP_METHOD              N      Char   15            Payment Predictor Method
EFFDT                  N      Date   10            Effective Date
PP_SEQ_NUM             N      Nbr    3             Sequence
PP_USAGE               N      Char   1             Usage
PP_SORT_SEQ_NUM        N      Nbr    3             Sorting Sequence number
```

The AR.PREDICT Application Engine program (known as Payment Predictor) uses a cache record called PP_AET. The first portion of the utility prints each field in PP_AET along with the field attributes.

The second portion lists each step in the A/E program with the MAIN section listed first. Additional attributes, such as DO section, Step Information, DO types, DB Platform, and so forth, are listed:

```
Report ID:  TD_AE75          APPLICATION ENGINE ANALYZER
    Phase:  2
  Program:  AR/PREDICT
================================================================================
Section  Step      Do        Activity          Type Update Select DO_When
================================================================================


MAIN     INIT      INIT      (DO INIT)         D    N      N      N
MAIN     PREP      PREP      (DO PREP)         D    N      N      Y
MAIN     SBLD      SBLD      (DO SBLD)         D    N      N      Y
MAIN     UPDM      UPDM      (DO UPDM)         D    N      N      Y
MAIN     DOC_SEQ   DOCSEQ    (DO DOCSEQ)       D    N      N      N
MAIN     REALGAIN  REALGAIN  (DO REALGAIN)     D    N      N      N
MAIN     PGEN      PGEN      (DO PGEN)         D    N      N      Y
MAIN     PUPD      PUPD      (DO PUPD)         D    N      N      Y
MAIN     TERMINAT  TERMINAT  (DO TERMINAT)     D    N      N      N
```

Let's look at steps that execute a COBOL process and a dynamic DO section. Notice the &SECTION has been resolved with the user-entered section #DETAIL.

```
DOC-CBL   FTPDOCAE              (COBOL: FTPDOCAE)      C   N    N    N

STEP      ALGR    #DETAIL       (DO &SECTION:#DETAIL)  D   N    N    Y
```

The process flow portion of the SQR utility begins with the section MAIN and flow-charts all steps in execution order. If a section has already been analyzed, the literal <Repeated Section> appears after it. There is no need to drill-down a second time:

```
Report ID:   TD_AE75            APPLICATION ENGINE ANALYZER
   Phase:    3
 Program:    AR/PREDICT
================================================================================
Process Flowchart
================================================================================


....(MAIN.INIT)   (DO INIT)
........(INIT.STARTMSG)   (UPDATE)
........(INIT.ROUNDSET)   (SELECT)
........(INIT.ROUNDIN3)   (DO ROUNDIN3)
............(ROUNDIN3.DECIMAL3)   (SELECT)
........(INIT.REQUESTS)   (UPDATE)
........(INIT.CNT)   (SELECT)
........(INIT.MSG)   (UPDATE)
........(INIT.NONE)   (DO MSG_NONE)
............(MSG_NONE.MESSAGE)   (UPDATE)
....(MAIN.PREP)   (DO PREP)
........(PREP.CLEARTMP)   (DO CLEARTMP)
............(CLEARTMP.PAYMENT)   (UPDATE)
............(CLEARTMP.CUST)   (UPDATE)
............(CLEARTMP.ITEM)   (UPDATE)
............(CLEARTMP.ITEM2)   (UPDATE)
............(CLEARTMP.MATCH)   (UPDATE)
........(PREP.MESSAGE)   (UPDATE)
........(PREP.PAYMENTS)   (UPDATE)
........(PREP.DOC_SEQ)   (UPDATE)
........(PREP.SET_REF)   (UPDATE)
........(PREP.ID_ITEM)   (DO ID_ITEM)
............(ID_ITEM.CUSTMP1)   (UPDATE)
............(ID_ITEM.DUPE1)   (DO DUPECUST)
................(DUPECUST.DEL_DUPE)   (UPDATE)
................(DUPECUST.COPYTMP2)   (UPDATE)
................(DUPECUST.CLEANUP)   (UPDATE)
............(ID_ITEM.CUSTMP2)   (UPDATE)
............(ID_ITEM.DUPE2)   (DO DUPECUST)        <Repeated Section>
```

Here is the portion of the process flowchart where the dynamic DO is encountered. The #DETAIL section entered by the user has been substituted and included in the listing:

```
..........(STEP.ALGR)  (DO &SECTION:#DETAIL)
...............(#DETAIL.ALGO_1)  (SELECT)
...............(#DETAIL.ADJUST)  (DO ADJUST)
....................(ADJUST.INIT)  (UPDATE)
....................(ADJUST.ADJ_OVER)  (UPDATE)
....................(ADJUST.ADJ_UNDR)  (UPDATE)
....................(ADJUST.NAMEOVER)  (DO AUTO_ADJ)  <Repeated Section>
....................(ADJUST.NAMEUNDR)  (DO AUTO_ADJ)  <Repeated Section>
....................(ADJUST.COPYTMP2)  (DO COPYTMP2)  <Repeated Section>
..............(#DETAIL.MATCHTMP)  (UPDATE)
..............(#DETAIL.ALGR_B1)  (DO DUPES)
...................(DUPES.DUPES)  (DO ALGR_DUP)
.........................(ALGR_DUP.GET_ONE)  (SELECT)
.........................(ALGR_DUP.DEL_REST)  (UPDATE)
..............(#DETAIL.ALGR_C1)  (DO PYSTATUS)
```

Let's look at how the COBOL section appears in the process flowchart. The developer can easily identify any COBOL or Mass Change sections:

```
....(MAIN.DOC_SEQ)  (DO DOCSEQ)
........(DOCSEQ.DOC_SEQ)  (DO DOC_SEQ)
............(DOC_SEQ.CHK_SEQ)  (DO DOC-CBL)
................(DOC-CBL.FTPDOCAE)  (COBOL: FTPDOCAE)
............(DOC_SEQ.SETID)  (SELECT)
............(DOC_SEQ.GET_TYPE)  (SELECT)
............(DOC_SEQ.UPD_BU)  (UPDATE)
............(DOC_SEQ.GET_SEQ)  (DO DOC-CBL)        <Repeated Section>
....(MAIN.REALGAIN)  (DO REALGAIN)
```

44.4.1   Application Engine Analyzer source code—TD_AE75.SQR

The Application Engine Analyzer program processes sections and steps in the same manner as the PTPEMAIN process. The complete source code may be downloaded from the website http://www.sqrtools.com (under Utilities).

This process has been tested under Oracle, SQLBase, and DB2, but it may work with other databases as well. Additional updates may be posted to SQRTOOLS.COM, which may include compatibility with non-compliant databases.

Versions prior to Application Engine 7.5 are supported as well. Simply deactivate the substitution variable AE_75. This will bypass all references to the columns AE_DO_PRODUCT and AE_DO_APPLID. A major (and quite useful) enhancement in version 7.5 was the ability to call sections outside of the current application. The two aforementioned columns allow a called section to be qualified with the product and application ID, if necessary.

1 Use the Trace option to generate trace files for the Application Engine program. The trace file will show you the steps performed along with the SQL statements and resolved bind variables.

2 You can restart an Application Engine program so it picks up at the last commit point before it failed. This helps maintain system integrity when a process aborts.

C H A P T E R   4 5

Application Engine— PeopleSoft 8

As we have proceeded through each Application Engine chapter, we've covered more concepts of Application Engine development. As an SQL processing tool, A/E can be used to create efficient batch processes. A/E's many useful features include decision capability and loop control, dynamic section calling, and messaging functionality. Other nice features in the current release are the trace file generation and the Commit/Restart logic (when a process terminates abnormally). All said, A/E is an extremely useful and well-conceived tool.

45.1 APPLICATION ENGINE "WISH LIST"

Although Application Engine is undeniably a tribute to creativity and resourcefulness, one can't help but think of enhancements that might still be made to the existing product. For instance, Application Engine exclusively acts on data that resides in the database itself. Imagine if Application Engine had the capability to read or write external files. This would make Application Engine an ideal choice for interface and conversion applications.

The Application Engine Definition panels are adequate for developing your programs, but a more intuitive graphical interface would be more suitable. The ability to view your program as a tree structure with each section and step in execution order would be a tremendous help.

There are times when updating a simple cache field value may seem cumbersome. Using the &SELECT function against the PSLOCK table (or any other single row table) is an ingenious solution, but is a bit convoluted. It also requires an additional call to the database where an alternative method may not need to do so. Application Engine could also use a mechanism to handle complex IF-THEN-ELSE expressions.

The ability to add Application Engine components to a project would be a welcome enhancement. Customizations could then be managed the same as other PeopleTool objects. Also, having Change Control in effect to lock your Application Engine programs would prevent other users from concurrently updating your program.

The types of enhancements I've mentioned here would elevate Application Engine to a much higher level, making it difficult to ignore the batch-processing capability that Application Engine provides. Let's now take a look at some of the great features implemented in release 8, some of which are nothing short of spectacular.

45.2 PEOPLESOFT RELEASE 8

Release 8 of PeopleSoft contains all of our "wish list" enhancements plus many additional features that can make Application Engine the tool of choice for many business processes. The single most important feature is Application Engines' complete integration with Application Designer. All Application Engine components are now objects. This means they can be placed into projects just as a record or panel definition would. You can also utilize the Change Control functionality to lock and unlock the Application Engine objects you're working on. Application Engine is now written entirely in C++. COBOL is no longer used to execute A/E programs.

When creating or modifying Application Engine objects, you will encounter a new graphical interface. It is much more intuitive than prior versions and behaves in a fashion similar to PeopleTool object interfaces. The Application Engine program is displayed in Definition or Program Flow view. The Program Flow view allows you to view your Application Engine program as a tree structure with each section and step displayed as a tree node. You can click on the "+" or "-" to expand or collapse a node. Any object type actions within a step are also displayed. Object types include SQL

Selects (DO types), SQL objects, other A/E sections, Message Log, and PeopleCode objects. Yes, that's correct—PeopleCode! Application Engine can now invoke PeopleCode and share many common business functions with online PeopleCode. A/E can be used to update fields in a state record (formerly referred to as a cache record). Any complex IF-THEN-ELSE expressions can be written in PeopleCode as well.

A new set of PeopleCode functions and classes have been added to support Application Engine. Some allow the reading and writing of external files. A new PeopleCode File class has been created that allows a variety of file handling operations to take place. You can even define a file layout with the new file layout definition in Application Designer and utilize it in your program.

Application Engine functions and macros have been replaced with Meta-SQL and a new set of macros. The Meta-SQL set has been expanded for greater functionality. For example, system (Meta) variables, which serve as text substitution variables, have been introduced. An example of a Meta-Variable would be %ProcessInstance, which contains the process instance of the run. %RunControl contains the Run Control ID used for the run. Prior versions of Application Engine required a database call against the A/E Run Control table to retrieve these values.

Temporary tables used in Application Engine programs have also increased functionality. Application Designer allows you to specify if a table is temporary. If so, you may designate the number of temporary table instances. For example, if you have a record called MY_TEMP, defined as a temporary table with three instances, the following physical SQL tables are created: PS_MY_TEMP, PS_MY_TEMP01, PS_MY_TEMP02, and PS_MY_TEMP03. During the execution of the Application Engine program, a specific instance of the temporary table can be utilized. This can greatly improve efficiency when running parallel processes.

Another interesting feature added is the Access checkbox on the section properties. If the section is designated as Public, all external Application Engine programs may call the section. If it is not Public, then the section is not available to any other programs. This is an excellent security measure that will prevent sensitive and potentially destructive SQL statements from being executed inadvertently.

The Application Engine debugger is also introduced in PeopleSoft release 8. While using the debugger, you can set break points, step through the code, view and edit state record fields, and even switch to the PeopleCode debugger when executing PeopleCode actions. This is a great feature that will make testing and debugging your Application Engine programs much easier than in the past.

Let's take a quick tour of some of the Application Engine features in PeopleSoft release 8.

45.2.1 Application Designer—Creating

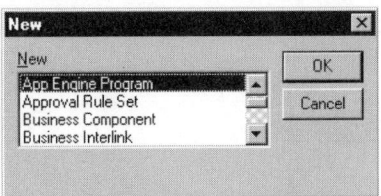

Figure 45.1 Creating a new Application Engine program

As mentioned previously, the Application Engine Designer Interface is accessed through Application Designer. You can create an Application Engine program by selecting File → New... and then selecting the Application Engine Program object in the drop down list (figure 45.1).

Once you select the new or existing Application Engine program, you can view or modify the program properties. Figure 45.2 shows the Program Properties panel. You can add a description and comments on the General folder tab.

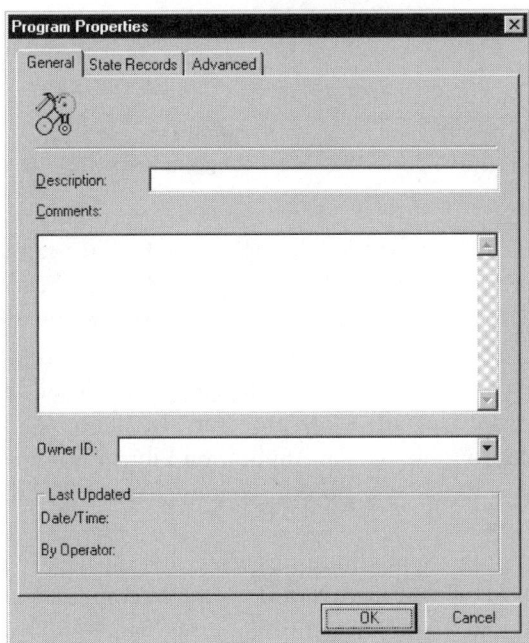

Figure 45.2
Program Properties—General

The State Record folder tab allows you to enter the State record(s) used by your Application Engine program. Multiple state records may be utilized by the program. You set the default state record by clicking on the Default State Record checkbox (figure 45.3). Note that the state record was formerly known as a cache record. The state record must still end with the suffix _AET as in prior versions.

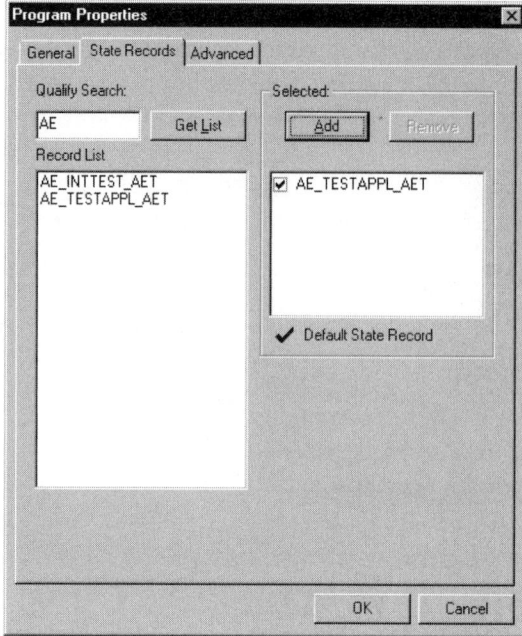

Figure 45.3
Program Properties—State Record

State records have much more functionality in release 8. They can now be used globally. The same state record can be used by both the calling and called program. Parameters can easily be passed from one program to another when sharing the same state record.

The Advanced folder tab (figure 45.4) lets you specify the default Message Set, Disable Restart, and designate Upgrade Only programs. In addition, your program can be defined as an Application Library. An Application Library is not an executable Application Engine program but a collection of sections that can be called by other Application Engine programs.

You make your actual program modifications using the Application Engine Definition interface. Two tabs allow you to view your program components: the definition view and the program flow view. The definition view (figure 45.5) allows you to create sections, steps, and actions, which are displayed as nodes. You can collapse and expand the nodes to drill down into each section. The sections in the definition view are not displayed in the order they are executed. You need to click on the Program Flow tab to view the execution order of the program.

Pay close attention to the Project Workspace window in figure 45.5. The Application Engine object has been inserted into the project. As you can see, Application Engine is fully integrated with PeopleTools in release 8.

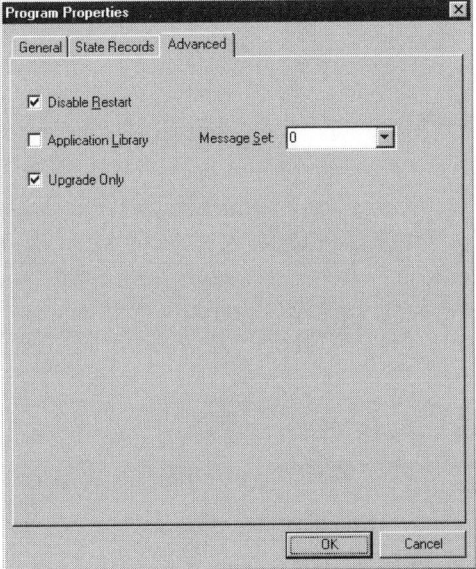

Figure 45.4
Program Properties—Advanced

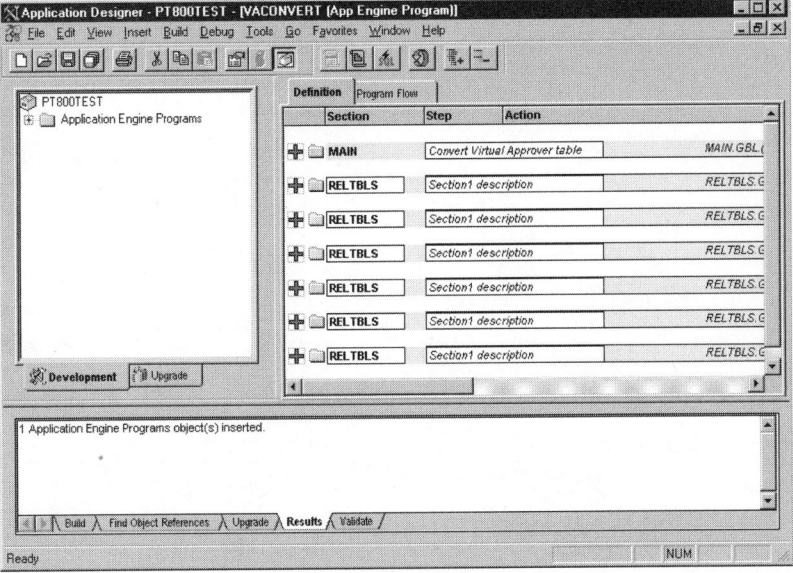

Figure 45.5   Application Engine Definition view

You can access the section properties by clicking on the section node and then clicking the right mouse button. Notice the Access checkbox in the section properties (figure 45.6). You can make the section `Public` by clicking the checkbox. Another

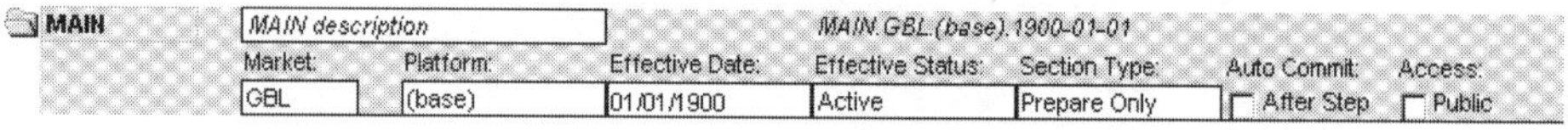

MAIN	MAIN description			MAIN.GBL (base).1900-01-01			
Market:	Platform:	Effective Date:	Effective Status:	Section Type:	Auto Commit:		Access:
GBL	(base)	01/01/1900	Active	Prepare Only	☐ After Step		☐ Public

Figure 45.6   Viewing section properties

new feature is the Market designation. You can define your section as Global (GBL) or use a market code such as USA or JPN to make your section market specific.

The Application Engine Program Flow View (figure 45.7) displays the program as a tree structure with each node in its logical execution sequence. This feature should aid developers by providing a graphical representation of their Application Engine program.

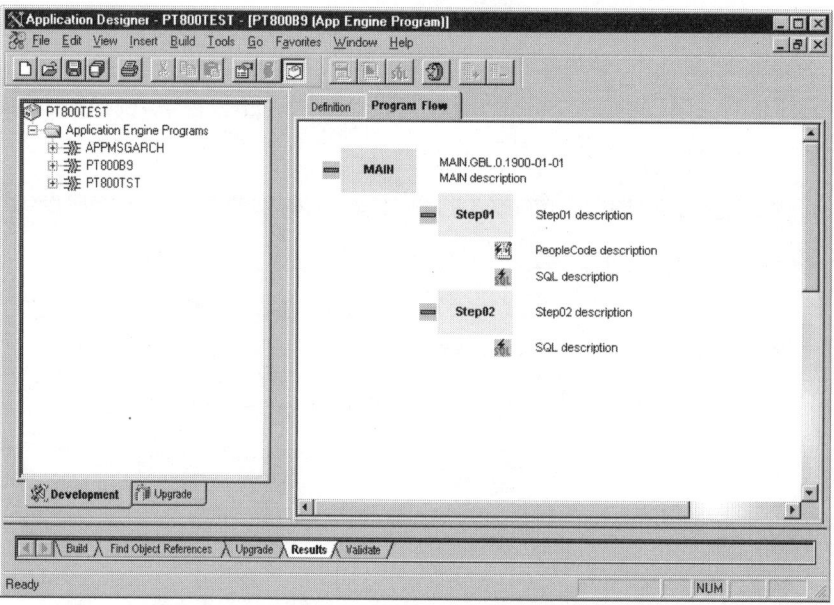

Figure 45.7   Application Engine Program Flow view

Notice the PeopleCode node under Step01 (figure 45.7). You can insert People-Code actions (in Definition view) within a step. You use the PeopleCode Editor to write the PeopleCode program.

You can invoke the PeopleCode Editor by double-clicking on the PeopleCode node (Figure 45.8). SQL actions can be inserted the same way within a step and modified using something called the SQL Editor. Each Action Type, viewed as a node, will have a particular set of action type properties.

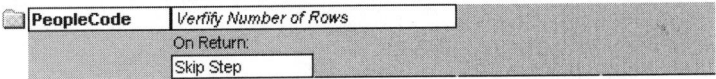

Figure 45.8   Accessing a PeopleCode program in Definition view

Figure 45.9 shows two action type nodes. The Do Select action type displays the description, Reuse statement, and Do Select type properties. The Call Section action type displays the description, section name, program ID, and dynamic section properties.

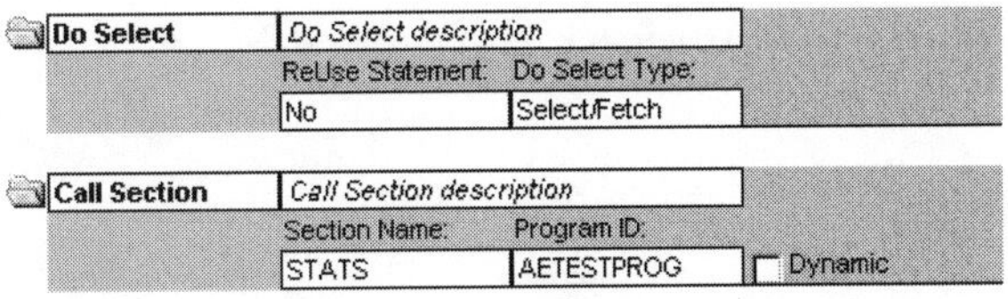

Figure 45.9   Action types and action type properties

45.2.2   Action types

Table 45.1 shows the possible action types along with the object type, the available properties, and the corresponding editor used to create the code behind the action. COBOL and Mass Change programs can no longer be called through the action properties. You can still call a COBOL program, but it must be invoked using PeopleCode and the RemoteCall() function. Mass Change programs are no longer supported—alternatives, such as the Application Engine Mass Change program, can be used instead. The message action is used in place of the &MSG function. The Message properties contain the same parameters as the &MSG function.

Table 45.1   Action types and associated properties

Action Type	Object Type	Properties	Editor
DO When	SQL Select	ReUse Statement	SQL Editor
DO While	SQL Select	ReUse Statement	SQL Editor
DO Until	SQL Select	ReUse Statement	SQL Editor
DO Select	SQL Select	ReUse Statement DO Select Type	SQL Editor
PeopleCode	PeopleCode	On Return	PeopleCode Editor
SQL	SQL Statement	ReUse Statement No Rows	SQL Editor

Table 45.1 Action types and associated properties (continued)

Action Type	Object Type	Properties	Editor
Call Section	A/E Section	Section Name Program ID Dynamic Section	N/A
Message	Message Log	Message Set Message Set Number Message Parameters	N/A

45.2.3   Meta-SQL

Application Engine now supports Meta-SQL such as `%DateIn` and `%DateOut`. Application Engine Meta-SQL constructs have been added.

Table 45.2

Function	Description
`%Bind`	Retrieves a value from the State record.
`%ExecuteEdits`	Supports data dictionary edits in batch mode. This includes any field defined with edit types of `Required`, `Yes/No`, `DateRange`, `Prompt Table`, or `Translate Table`. Meta-Variables `%Edit_Required`, `%Edit_YesNo`, `%Edit_DateRange`, `%Edit_PromptTable`, and `%Edit_TranslateTable` are used to specify the particular Edit(s) required. These Meta-Variables can be added together to produce combination edits on a field.
`%Select`	Selects fields and updates State Record values. If the SQL `select` returns no rows, the state record fields are untouched.
`%SelectInit`	Selects fields and updates state record values. If no rows are returned, the state record fields are initialized.
`%SQL`	Allows an SQL object to be utilized in Application Engine SQL statements or PeopleCode regardless of differences in bind variable syntax between the two.
`%Table`	Returns the SQL table name for the record name specified. This eliminates the need to prefix certain tables with PS_ before accessing them. If the table is defined as a temporary table, the appropriate temporary table instance number is appended to the returned SQL table name (i.e., PS_MY_TEMPnn where nn is the instance number).
`%TruncateTable`	Depending on the database, either a `TRUNCATE TABLE` or `DELETE FROM` (without a `WHERE` clause) is generated.
`%UpdateStats`	Generates a platform-specific statement to update the system catalog tables for use in optimization procedures.

45.2.4 Application Engine macros

Some macros in release 8 look familiar. Some of the differences are in syntax only. The &&RECORD macro is no longer used.

Table 45.3   Application Engine macros

Macro	Description
%ClearCursor	recompiles re-used statements. Resets any STATIC %Bind variables
%Execute	execute database-specific commands such as PL/SQL Blocks
%Next	increments a sequence value
%Previous	decrements a sequence value
%RoundCurrency	rounds an amount to proper currency precision when using the Multi-Currency option

45.2.5 System Meta-Variables

Application Engine now provides useful Meta-Variables that eliminate unnecessary calls to the database to retrieve fields such as the Run Control ID and process instance. The SQL syntax is also simpler when using the Meta-Variables. %Bind is not needed to retrieve the values from the state record.

Table 45.4   Application Engine System Variables

Meta-Variable	Description
%AeProgram	current Application Engine program name (in quotes)
%AeSection	current Application Engine section name (in quotes)
%AeStep	current Application Engine step name (in quotes)
%JobInstance	Process Scheduler job instance number
%ProcessInstance	Process Instance
%ReturnCode	return code of last SQL statement
%RunControl	current Run Control ID (in quotes)
%AsOfDate	As-Of-Date of the current process (in quotes)
%Comma	character substitution— comma
%LeftParen	character substitution—left parenthesis
%RightParen	character substitution—right parenthesis
%Space	character substitution—space
%SQLRows	number of rows affected by SQL statement. Select statements return a value of 0 or 1 (to represent no rows or some rows, respectively).

45.2.6 Application Engine PeopleCode

The use of PeopleCode is one of the most powerful enhancements to Application Engine. You can update state records directly, perform complex IF-THEN-ELSE expressions, and process file input/output records. When you attach a PeopleCode

Action to a step, you may also specify the On-Return property, which is either `Abort`, `Break`, or `Skip Step`. The On-Return property is initiated when the PeopleCode program issues a `Non-Zero` or `True` return code. If no return code is assigned by the PeopleCode program, then zero is used as the default. `Abort` halts processing of the entire program. `Break` exits the entire section currently executing. `Skip Step` processes no additional actions attached to the current step—the next step is processed immediately.

Let's examine a few examples, drawing comparisons with PeopleSoft 7.5 when possible.

You can see that a database call is required in PeopleSoft 7.5 to update a single cache field value:

```
&SELECT(AE_SECTION)
SELECT 'PROCESS1'
  FROM PSLOCK
```

In the direct updating of the state record field using PeopleCode (PeopleSoft 8.0), no additional database call is required. Also, note the absence of a return code assignment which defaults to zero:

```
AE_SECTION = "PROCESS1";
```

Let's consider `IF-THEN-ELSE` logic now. Imagine that we need to execute a Mass `SQL Insert` only if the table into which we're inserting is empty. For this example, we assume the row count of our table into which has been determined and is contained in the field COUNTER (either in the cache or state record).

In PeopleSoft 7.5, a `DO When` statement type is used to execute an additional section, depending on the "SQL Select" results. If the COUNTER cache field is zero (meaning the table is empty), the `DO When` section specified (which performs the SQL Insert) is executed. If the COUNTER is not zero, the `DO When` section is not performed:

```
&SELECT(AE_DECIDE)
SELECT 'X'
  FROM PSLOCK
 WHERE &BIND(COUNTER) = 0
```

Look at the PeopleSoft 8 version using PeopleCode:

```
If USER_AET.COUNTER > 0
   Exit(1)
End-if;
```

The state record field COUNTER is interrogated directly. If the COUNTER field is greater than zero, the return code is set to 1 (or TRUE), and the On Return property of the PeopleCode action becomes effective. Let's assume the On Return property is set to Skip Step. Any additional actions for the current step are now bypassed including the SQL action for our Insert statement. If the COUNTER is zero, the subsequent SQL action for the step is executed. (The Return Code defaults to zero in our PeopleCode action.)

PeopleSoft 8 enables file operations within Application Engine through PeopleCode. This is made possible by the new object classes now available. We'll demonstrate how PeopleCode actions can use these object classes to write records to a flat file. The output file will be created using a file layout definition. By changing the File-Layout property of our file object, we can switch file layouts whenever necessary.

We can now perform a simple demonstration for a typical outbound interface program. The sample PeopleCode program creates a flat file based on the contents of the table MY_TABLE. Let's assume this table was created during preceding steps of the Application. The columns are selected using a temporary SQL object created dynamically at run time. A Meta-SQL function (%Selectall) is used to build the Select statement. The SQL Object uses the Fetch method to retrieve each row one at a time. The file object (our output file) uses the file layout definition MY_LAYOUT:

```
Ln#  PeopleCode
---  -------------------------------------------------------------
 1   Local Record &MY_REC;
 2   Local File    &MY_FILE;
 3   Local SQL     &MY_SQL;
 4
 5   &MY_FILE = GetFile("myoutput.txt", "W");
 6
 7   if &MY_FILE.IsOpen Then
 8      if &MY_FILE.SetFileLayout(FILELAYOUT.MY_LAYOUT) Then
 9         &MY_REC = CreateRecord(RECORD.MY_TABLE);
10         &MY_SQL = CreateSQL("%Selectall(:1)", &MY_REC);
11         While &MY_SQL.Fetch(&MY_REC)
12            &MY_FILE.WriteRecord(&MY_REC);
13         End-While;
14      End-If;
15   End-If;
16
17   &MY_FILE.Close();
18
```

Our program is displayed above with line numbers (for reference only). Let's take a closer look at each line in the PeopleCode program.

Lines 1 through 3 create temporary object variables: &MY_REC is a record object; &MY_FILE is a file object; and &MY_SQL is an SQL object. Each of these temporary variables has a set of properties unique to its own object type. We can now perform some simple manipulations to accomplish our task.

Line 5 uses the GetFile function to associate a file to our file object &MY_FILE. The GetFile function also opens "myoutput.txt" in Write Mode.

Line 7 tests to see if the file associated with &MY_FILE was opened successfully (evaluating the IsOpen property using dot notation).

Line 8 sets the FileLayout property of the &MY_FILE file object to our file layout definition (MY_LAYOUT).

Line 9 uses the CreateRecord function to pass the MY_TABLE attributes to the &MY_REC record object. Now MY_TABLE and &MY_REC have equivalent attributes.

Line 10 dynamically creates the SQL for the &MY_SQL object using the CreateSQL function. %Selectall(:1) is a Meta-SQL construct that creates the Select statement based on the record passed as a parameter. Since we passed the &MY_REC record object as the parameter, the record MY_TABLE is used. (Remember, &MY_REC now has the same attributes as MY_TABLE.)

Lines 11 through 13 perform a Do While loop. A Fetch method is performed using the SQL object we created (&MY_SQL). This selects each row one by one. The WriteRecord method for the &MY_FILE object is used with the &MY_REC object to write lines to the output file. The records are then written as directed by the file layout definition currently used.

The operations being performed may be considered complex, but the PeopleCode that is actually produced by the developer couldn't be much simpler. Also, note any changes to the original record or file layout definitions do not affect the PeopleCode program.

45.2.7 Application Engine debugger

Another exciting enhancement in release 8 is the Application Engine debugger. You must enable the debugger through Configuration Manager or as a command line option. You must also enable the PeopleCode debugger if you want to debug any PeopleCode actions in the Application Engine program. Debug mode is easy to use. Here's a glimpse of the Application Engine debugger Help menu:

```
PeopleTools 8.0 - Application Engine
Copyright (c) 1988-1999 PeopleSoft, Inc.
All Rights Reserved

Application Engine Debugger - enter command or type ? for help.

AEMYPRCSDL.MAIN.STEP1> ?
Debug Commands:

        (Q)uit           Rollback work and end program
     E(X)it              Commit work and end program (valid between steps)
        (C)ommit         Commit work (valid between steps)
        (B)reak          Set or remove a break point
        (L)ook           Examine state record fields
        (M)odify         Change a state record field
        (W)atch          Set or remove a watch field
        (S)tep over      Execute current step or action and stop
   Step (I)nto           Go inside current step or called section and stop
```

```
Step (O)ut of          Execute rest of step or called section and stop
     (G)o              Resume execution
     (R)un to commit   Resume execution and stop after next commit
```

As you can see, the Application Engine debugger contains an extensive set of debug commands. The descriptions of the commands on the Help menu do not need much more elaboration, but I'd like to review a couple of commands.

The BREAK command allows you to set, and subsequently unset, breakpoints in your program. There is also an option to list the currently active breakpoints.

Let's consider how to set a breakpoint with the Set option. The user is prompted for the program, section, and step to which the breakpoint should be set:

```
AEMYPRCSDL.MAIN.STEP1> b
(S)et, (U)nset, or (L)ist? s
Program [AEMYPRCSDL]:
Section [MAIN]: DYNSECTN
Step    [STEP1]: STEP1

Breakpoint set at AEMYPRCSDL.DYNSECTN.STEP1
```

Now, let's look at the use of the Unset option. A list of active breakpoints is displayed along with a corresponding sequence number. The user must enter the sequence number of the breakpoint to remove it from the active breakpoint list. The List option displays the active breakpoint list without any additional options.

```
AEMYPRCSDL.MAIN.STEP1> b
(S)et, (U)nset, or (L)ist? u

Active Breakpoints:
(1) AEMYPRCSDL.MAIN.STEP2
(2) AEMYPRCSDL.DYNSECTN.STEP1

Remove which breakpoint? 1
```

The LOOK, MODIFY, and WATCH commands allow you to view and modify state record fields and designate watch fields. Once you set a watch field, the program stops when the value of the field changes.

```
Record Name [USER_AET]:
Field Name [*]:
USER_AET:
  PROCESS_INSTANCE    = 50
  COUNTER             = 1685
  RECNAME             = 'JOB'
  FIELDNAME           = ' '
  AE_DECIDE           = ' '
```

In our LOOK command, the record name selected was USER_AET (the default for this Application Engine program). All the fields in USER_AET are listed with their current values.

Consider now the results of our MODIFY command. We selected the COUNTER state record field and changed the value from 1685 to 0. The MODIFY command is a useful tool when testing conditions in your Application Engine program:

```
AEUSER003.MAIN.STEP2> m
Record Name [USER_AET]:
Field Name [none]: COUNTER

Current value:  USER_AET.COUNTER = 1685

Enter new value (do not use quotes around text strings):
0
```

The field RECNAME is selected as a watch field using the Set option of the WATCH command. The program will stop each time the value of this field changes. You can Unset and List watch fields in a similar manner as breakpoints.

```
Set or remove a watch field
AEUSER004.MAIN.STEP1> w
(S)et, (U)nset, or (L)ist? s
Record Name [USER_AET]:
Field Name [none]: RECNAME
```

If enabled, the PeopleCode debugger is invoked when a PeopleCode action is encountered. Many new features exist in the PeopleCode debugger such as Hover Inspect, where a pop-up displays the value of simple variables and fields simply by hovering over it with the mouse. The variable display window allows you to drill down on the properties of each object by expanding/collapsing the corresponding node. As you can see, the PeopleTools development team has been busy. The features I've mentioned in this chapter are just a small sampling of the next generation of PeopleTools!

Some readers may have come directly to this chapter to read about some of the great new Application Engine features in the PeopleSoft 8 release. If you have no familiarity with the PeopleSoft 7.5 version of Application Engine, I would suggest going through the tutorial in the preceeding chapters. The examples there will give you the opportunity to develop a good understanding of Application Engine concepts without being bombarded with terminology such as object classes, meta-this, meta-that, and such. The PeopleSoft 8 version of Application Engine builds and improves upon the concepts previously discussed. In this ever-changing world of technology, it's a good idea to take advantage of every learning opportunity you can.

APPENDIX A

Problem Tracking application

All objects used to build our Problem Tracking application are listed in this appendix. The readers can develop these objects as they read this book. The readers should not be limited to the objects in the appendix. They can further enhance the application and develop other objects by using the techniques described in this book.

Let us look at an ERD diagram of all the record definitions used to develop the Problem Tracking application. All columns which are in bold and underlined are part of the primary key. All columns in bold alone are alternate keys.

Problem Tracking—Record Definitions

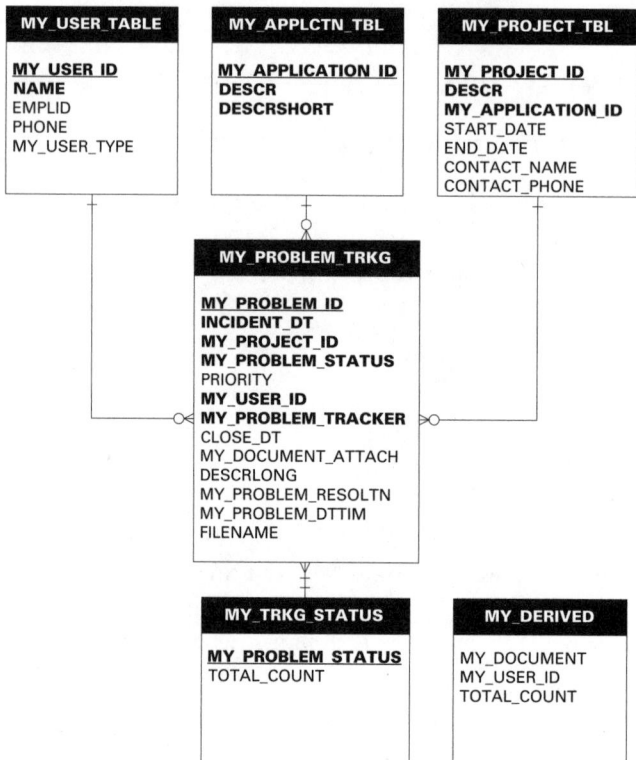

MY_USER_TABLE

MY USER ID
NAME
EMPLID
PHONE
MY_USER_TYPE

MY_APPLCTN_TBL

MY APPLICATION ID
DESCR
DESCRSHORT

MY_PROJECT_TBL

MY PROJECT ID
DESCR
MY_APPLICATION_ID
START_DATE
END_DATE
CONTACT_NAME
CONTACT_PHONE

MY_PROBLEM_TRKG

MY PROBLEM ID
INCIDENT_DT
MY_PROJECT_ID
MY_PROBLEM_STATUS
PRIORITY
MY_USER_ID
MY_PROBLEM_TRACKER
CLOSE_DT
MY_DOCUMENT_ATTACH
DESCRLONG
MY_PROBLEM_RESOLTN
MY_PROBLEM_DTTIM
FILENAME

MY_TRKG_STATUS

MY PROBLEM STATUS
TOTAL_COUNT

MY_DERIVED

MY_DOCUMENT
MY_USER_ID
TOTAL_COUNT

Figure A.1
**Problem Tracking Application—
record definitions**

Let us list all the record definitions showing the different views. New fields start with a prefix of MY_. These fields have to be created in the system before the record definitions are built.

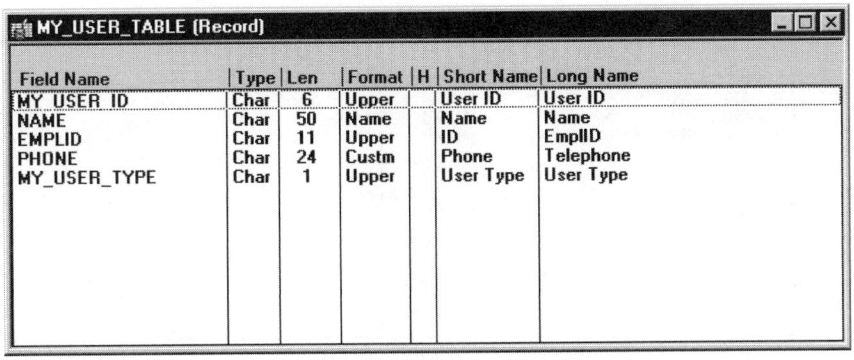

MY_USER_TABLE (Record)

Field Name	Type	Len	Format	H	Short Name	Long Name
MY_USER_ID	Char	6	Upper		User ID	User ID
NAME	Char	50	Name		Name	Name
EMPLID	Char	11	Upper		ID	EmplID
PHONE	Char	24	Custm		Phone	Telephone
MY_USER_TYPE	Char	1	Upper		User Type	User Type

Figure A.2   MY_USER_TABLE Table—Field Display

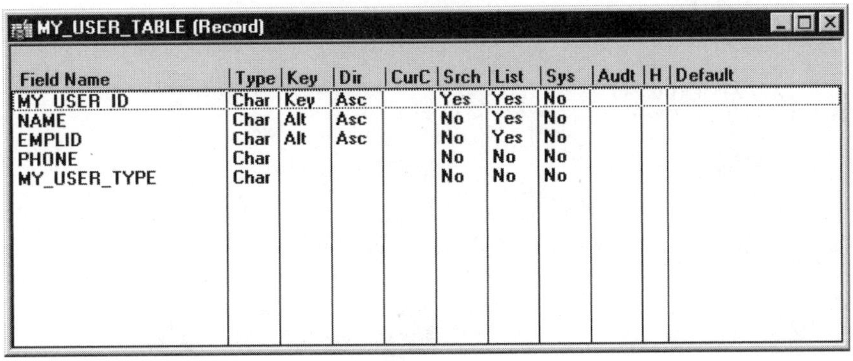

MY_USER_TABLE (Record)

Field Name	Type	Key	Dir	CurC	Srch	List	Sys	Audt	H	Default
MY_USER_ID	Char	Key	Asc		Yes	Yes	No			
NAME	Char	Alt	Asc		No	Yes	No			
EMPLID	Char	Alt	Asc		No	Yes	No			
PHONE	Char				No	No	No			
MY_USER_TYPE	Char				No	No	No			

Figure A.3   MY_USER_TABLE Table—Use Display

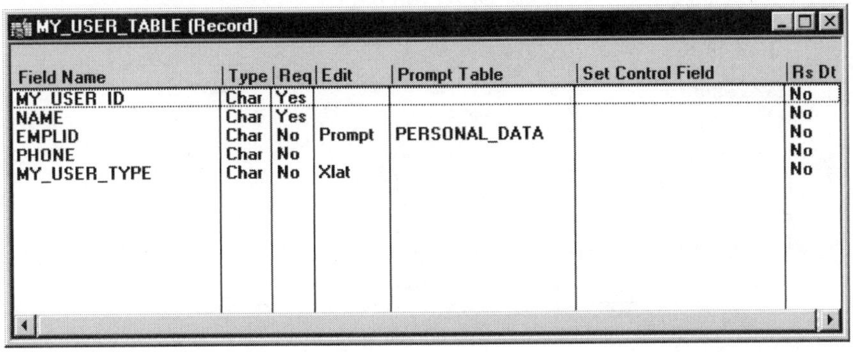

MY_USER_TABLE (Record)

Field Name	Type	Req	Edit	Prompt Table	Set Control Field	Rs Dt
MY_USER_ID	Char	Yes				No
NAME	Char	Yes				No
EMPLID	Char	No	Prompt	PERSONAL_DATA		No
PHONE	Char	No				No
MY_USER_TYPE	Char	No	Xlat			No

Figure A.4   MY_USER_TABLE Table—Edits Display

MY_USER_TABLE stores all the users reporting problems in our application.

MY_APPLCTN_TBL (Record)

Field Name	Type	Len	Format	H	Short Name	Long Name
MY_APPLICATION_ID	Char	3	Upper		Application	Application Identification
DESCR	Char	30	Mixed		Descr	Description
DESCRSHORT	Char	10	Mixed		Short Desc	Short Description

Figure A.5   MY_APPLCTN_TBL Table—Field Display

MY_APPLCTN_TBL (Record)

Field Name	Type	Key	Dir	CurC	Srch	List	Sys	Audt	H	Default
MY_APPLICATION_ID	Char	Key	Asc		Yes	Yes	No			
DESCR	Char	Alt	Asc		No	Yes	No			
DESCRSHORT	Char				No	No	No			

Figure A.6   MY_APPLCTN_TBL Table—Use Display

MY_APPLCTN_TBL (Record)

Field Name	Type	Req	Edit	Prompt Table	Set Control Field	Rs Dt
MY_APPLICATION_ID	Char	Yes				No
DESCR	Char	Yes				No
DESCRSHORT	Char	Yes				No

Figure A.7   MY_APPLCTN_TBL Table—Edits Display

MY_APPLCTN_TBL stores all applications that are tracked in our system.

MY_PROJECT_TBL (Record)

Field Name	Type	Len	Format	H	Short Name	Long Name
MY_PROJECT_ID	Char	6	Upper		Project ID	Project Identification
DESCR	Char	30	Mixed		Descr	Description
MY_APPLICATION_ID	Char	3	Upper		Application	Application Identification
START_DATE	Date	10			Start Date	Start Date
END_DATE	Date	10			End Date	End Date
CONTACT_NAME	Char	50	Mixed		Name	Contact Name
CONTACT_PHONE	Char	12	Phone		Phone	Contact Phone

Figure A.8 MY_PROJECT_TBL **Table—Field Display**

MY_PROJECT_TBL (Record)

Field Name	Type	Key	Dir	CurC	Srch	List	Sys	Audt	H	Default
MY_PROJECT_ID	Char	Key	Asc		Yes	Yes	No			
DESCR	Char	Alt	Asc		No	Yes	No			
MY_APPLICATION_ID	Char	Alt	Asc		No	Yes	No			
START_DATE	Date				No	No	No			
END_DATE	Date				No	No	No			
CONTACT_NAME	Char				No	No	No			
CONTACT_PHONE	Char				No	No	No			

Figure A.9 MY_PROJECT_TBL **Table—Use Display**

MY_PROJECT_TBL (Record)

Field Name	Type	Req	Edit	Prompt Table	Set Control Field	Rs Dt
MY_PROJECT_ID	Char	Yes				No
DESCR	Char	Yes				No
MY_APPLICATION_ID	Char	No	Prompt	MY_APPLCTN_TBL		No
START_DATE	Date	No				No
END_DATE	Date	No				No
CONTACT_NAME	Char	No				No
CONTACT_PHONE	Char	No				No

Figure A.10 MY_PROJECT_TBL **Table—Edits Display**

MY_PROJECT_TBL stores all projects that are tracked in our application.

MY_PROBLEM_TRKG (Record)

Field Name	Type	Len	Format	H	Short Name	Long Name
MY_PROBLEM_ID	Char	6	Num		Problem ID	Problem Identification
INCIDENT_DT	Date	10			Incdnt Dt	Incident Date
MY_PROJECT_ID	Char	6	Upper		Project ID	Project Identification
MY_PROBLEM_STATUS	Char	1	Upper		Problem Sta	Problem Status
PRIORITY	Nbr	3			Priority	Priority
MY_USER_ID	Char	6	Upper		User ID	User ID
MY_PROBLEM_TRACKEF	Char	6	Upper		Problem Tra	Problem Tracker
CLOSE_DT	Date	10			Close Date	Date Closed
MY_DOCUMENT_ATTACI	Char	1	Upper		Document?	Document Attached?
DESCRLONG	Long	0			Descr	Description
MY_PROBLEM_RESOLTI	Long	0			Prob.Resolt	Problem Resolution
MY_PROBLEM_DTTIM	DtTm	26	Scnds		Date/Time	Date/Time Reported
FILENAME	Char	80	Mixed		File Name	File Name

Figure A.11   MY_PROBLEM_TRKG Table—Field Display

MY_PROBLEM_TRKG (Record)

Field Name	Type	Key	Dir	CurC	Srch	List	Sys	Audt	H	Default
MY_PROBLEM_ID	Char	Key	Asc		Yes	Yes	No			
INCIDENT_DT	Date	Alt	Asc		No	Yes	No			
MY_PROJECT_ID	Char	Alt	Asc		No	Yes	No			
MY_PROBLEM_STATUS	Char	Alt	Asc		No	Yes	No			'1'
PRIORITY	Nbr				No	No	No			
MY_USER_ID	Char	Alt	Asc		No	Yes	No			
MY_PROBLEM_TRACKEF	Char	Alt	Asc		No	Yes	No			
CLOSE_DT	Date				No	No	No			
MY_DOCUMENT_ATTACI	Char				No	No	No			
DESCRLONG	Long				No	No	No			
MY_PROBLEM_RESOLTI	Long				No	No	No			
MY_PROBLEM_DTTIM	DtTm				No	No	No			
FILENAME	Char				No	No	No			

Figure A.12   MY_PROBLEM_TRKG Table—Use Display

MY_PROBLEM_TRKG (Record)

Field Name	Type	Req	Edit	Prompt Table	Set Control Field	Rs Dt
MY_PROBLEM_ID	Char	Yes				No
INCIDENT_DT	Date	Yes				Yes
MY_PROJECT_ID	Char	No	Prompt	MY_PROJECT_TBL		No
MY_PROBLEM_STATUS	Char	No	Xlat			No
PRIORITY	Nbr	No				No
MY_USER_ID	Char	No	Prompt	MY_USER_TABLE		No
MY_PROBLEM_TRACKEF	Char	No	Prompt	MY_USER_TABLE		No
CLOSE_DT	Date	No				No
MY_DOCUMENT_ATTACI	Char	No	Y/N			No
DESCRLONG	Long	No				No
MY_PROBLEM_RESOLTI	Long	No				No
MY_PROBLEM_DTTIM	DtTm	No				No
FILENAME	Char	No				No

Figure A.13   MY_PROBLEM_TRKG Table—Edits Display

MY_PROBLEM_TRKG stores all incidents tracked in our application.

MY_TRKG_STATUS (Record)

Field Name	Type	Len	Format	H	Short Name	Long Name
MY_PROBLEM_STATUS	Char	1	Upper		Problem Sta	Problem Status
TOTAL_COUNT	Nbr	7			Total Cnt	Total Count

Figure A.14   MY_TRKG_STATUS View—Field Display

MY_TRKG_STATUS (Record)

Field Name	Type	Key	Dir	CurC	Srch	List	Sys	Audt	H	Default
MY_PROBLEM_STATUS	Char	Key	Asc		No	No	No			
TOTAL_COUNT	Nbr				No	No	No			

Figure A.15   MY_TRKG_STATUS View—Use Display

MY_TRKG_STATUS (Record)

Field Name	Type	Req	Edit	Prompt Table	Set Control Field	Rs Dt
MY_PROBLEM_STATUS	Char	No	Xlat			No
TOTAL_COUNT	Nbr	No				No

Figure A.16   MY_TRKG_STATUS View—Edits Display

MY_TRKG_STATUS is an SQL view that represents data from MY_PROBLEM_TRKG table.

Record Properties
General
Use
Type
Record Type
SQL Table
SQL View
Dynamic View
Derived/Work
SubRecord
Query View
SQL View Select Statement:
select
my_problem_status,
count(*)
from ps_my_problem_trkg
group by my_problem_status
Non-Standard SQL
Table Name:
OK
Cancel

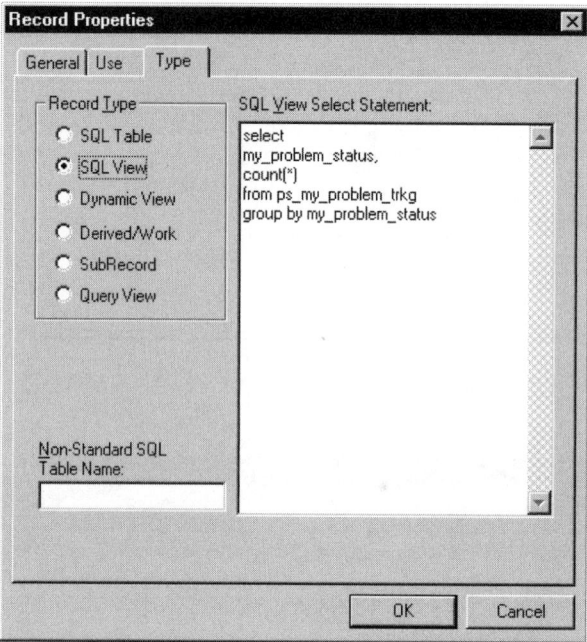

Figure A.17 MY_TRKG_STATUS **View—**SQL **Select Statement**

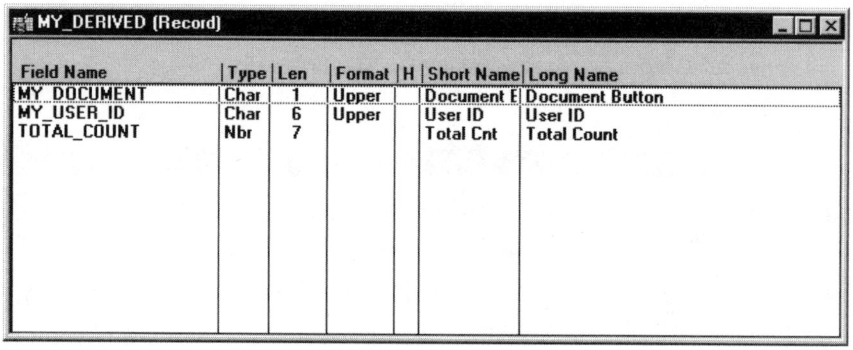

MY_DERIVED (Record)
Field Name | Type | Len | Format | H | Short Name | Long Name
MY_DOCUMENT | Char | 1 | Upper | | Document E | Document Button
MY_USER_ID | Char | 6 | Upper | | User ID | User ID
TOTAL_COUNT | Nbr | 7 | | | Total Cnt | Total Count

Figure A.18 MY_DERIVED **Work Record—Field Display**

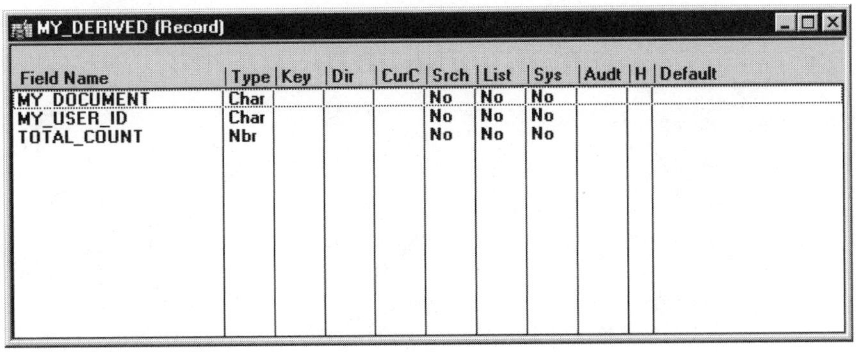

MY_DERIVED (Record)

Field Name	Type	Key	Dir	CurC	Srch	List	Sys	Audt	H	Default
MY_DOCUMENT	Char				No	No	No			
MY_USER_ID	Char				No	No	No			
TOTAL_COUNT	Nbr				No	No	No			

Figure A.19 MY_DERIVED **Work Record—Use Display**

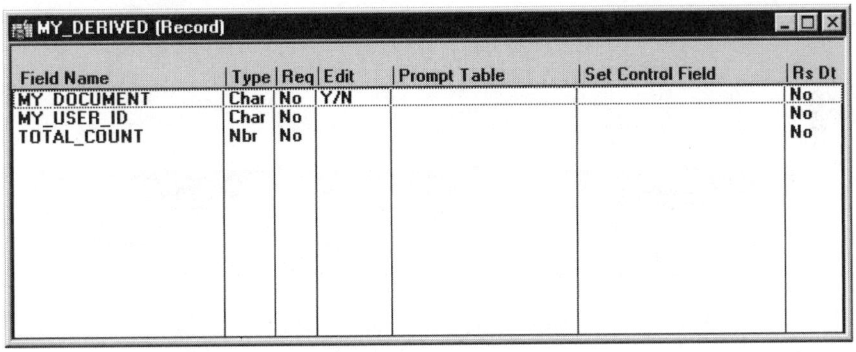

MY_DERIVED (Record)

Field Name	Type	Req	Edit	Prompt Table	Set Control Field	Rs Dt
MY_DOCUMENT	Char	No	Y/N			No
MY_USER_ID	Char	No				No
TOTAL_COUNT	Nbr	No				No

Figure A.20 MY_DERIVED **Work Record—Edits Display**

MY_DERIVED is a derived record that holds three fields which are used as work fields in our application.

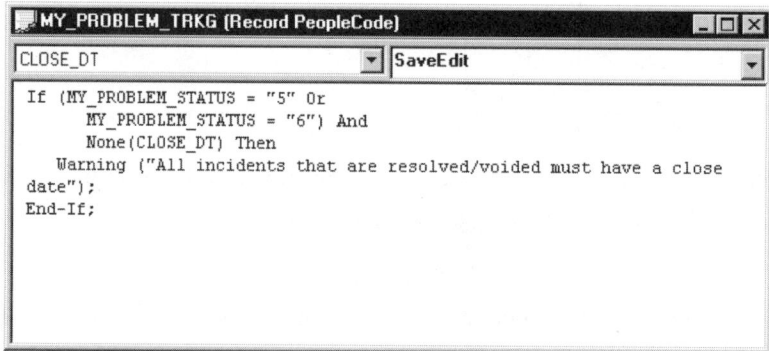

```
MY_PROBLEM_TRKG (Record PeopleCode)                         _ □ ×
MY_PROBLEM_ID                        ▼  FieldDefault                    ▼

SQLExec("select max(my_problem_id) from ps_my_problem_trkg",
&MAX_PROBLEM_ID);
If All(&MAX_PROBLEM_ID) Then
   &NEXT_PROBLEM_ID = LTrim(&MAX_PROBLEM_ID, "0");
   &NEXT_PROBLEM_ID = &MAX_PROBLEM_ID;
   &NEXT_PROBLEM_ID = &NEXT_PROBLEM_ID + 1;
   &NEXT_ID_STRING = String(&NEXT_PROBLEM_ID);
   &ID_LENGTH = Len(&NEXT_ID_STRING);
   &ID_DIFF = 6 - &ID_LENGTH;
   If &ID_DIFF > 0 Then
      MY_PROBLEM_ID = Rept("0", &ID_DIFF) | &NEXT_ID_STRING;
   Else
      MY_PROBLEM_ID = &NEXT_ID_STRING;
   End-If;
Else
   MY_PROBLEM_ID = "000001";
End-If;
```

Figure A.21   MY_PROBLEM_TRKG.MY_PROBLEM_ID.FieldDefault

```
MY_PROBLEM_TRKG (Record PeopleCode)                         _ □ ×
CLOSE_DT                             ▼  SaveEdit                        ▼

If (MY_PROBLEM_STATUS = "5" Or
      MY_PROBLEM_STATUS = "6") And
      None(CLOSE_DT) Then
   Warning ("All incidents that are resolved/voided must have a close
date");
End-If;
```

Figure A.22   MY_PROBLEM_TRKG.CLOSE_DT.SaveEdit

The first PeopleCode program automatically increments the MY_PROBLEM_ID field to the next one. The second PeopleCode program performs an edit to ensure that the CLOSE_DT field is entered when incidents are resolved or voided.

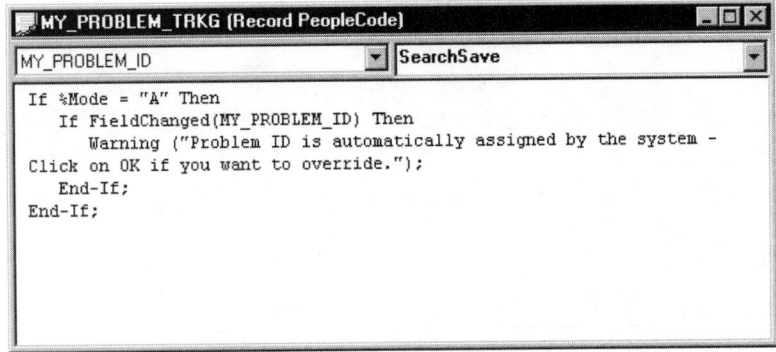

Figure A.23   MY_PROBLEM_TRKG.MY_PROBLEM_ID.SearchSave

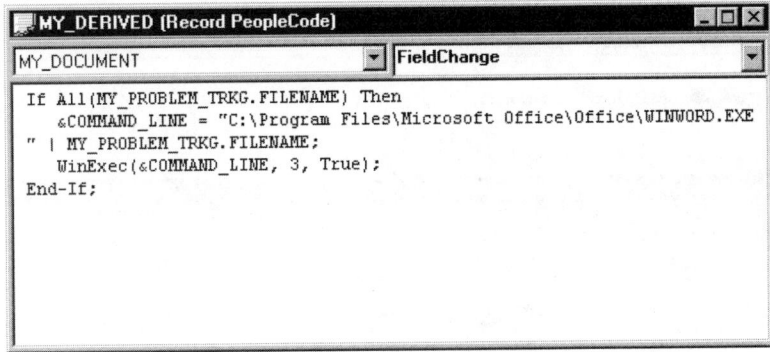

Figure A.24   MY_DERIVED.MY_DOCUMENT.FieldChange

The first PeopleCode program prevents the user from assigning a value to the MY_PROBLEM_ID field when new incidents are added using our application. The second PeopleCode program opens a Microsoft Word document explaining an incident in our application.

MY_USER_TBL.ENG (Panel)
User ID:
NNNNNN
EmplID:
Name:
Phone:
(eg. 914-555-1212)
User Type:

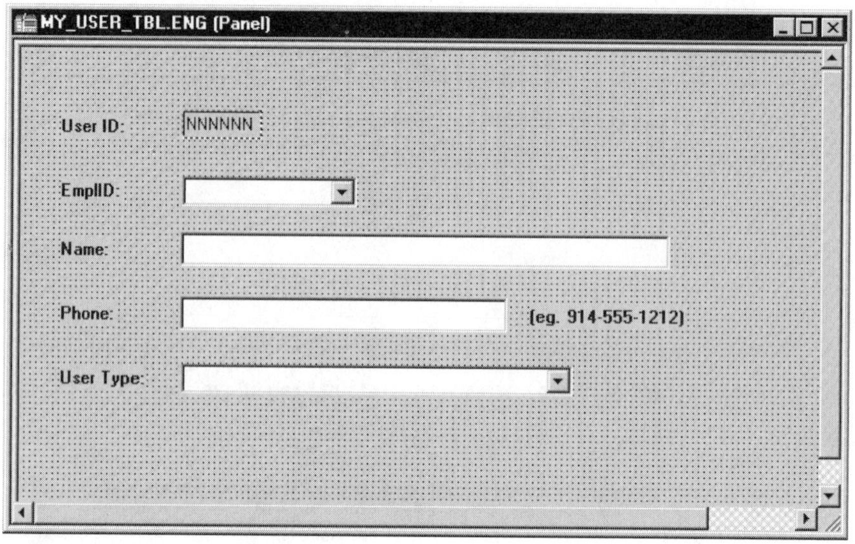

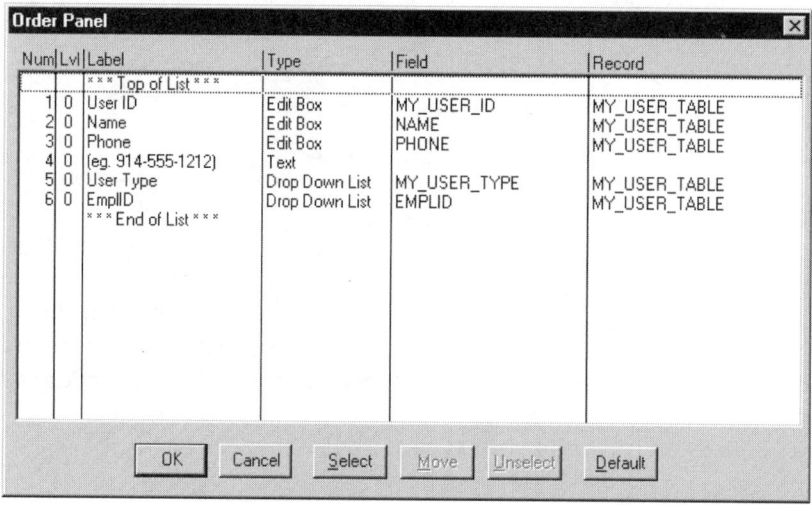

Figure A.25 MY_USER_TBL panel

Order Panel
Num Lvl Label Type Field Record
*** Top of List ***
1 0 User ID Edit Box MY_USER_ID MY_USER_TABLE
2 0 Name Edit Box NAME MY_USER_TABLE
3 0 Phone Edit Box PHONE MY_USER_TABLE
4 0 (eg. 914-555-1212) Text
5 0 User Type Drop Down List MY_USER_TYPE MY_USER_TABLE
6 0 EmplID Drop Down List EMPLID MY_USER_TABLE
*** End of List ***
OK
Cancel
Select
Move
Unselect
Default

Figure A.26 MY_USER_TBL panel layout

MY_USER_TBL panel is used to enter user information on our application.

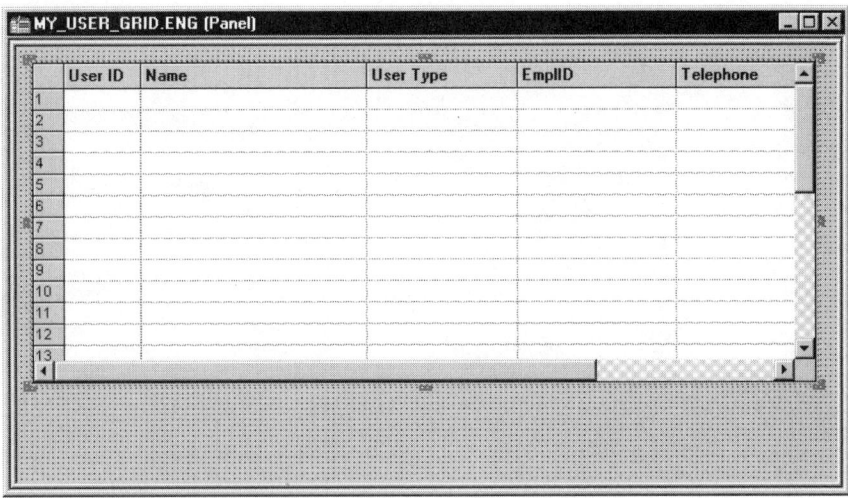

Figure A.27 MY_USER_GRID panel

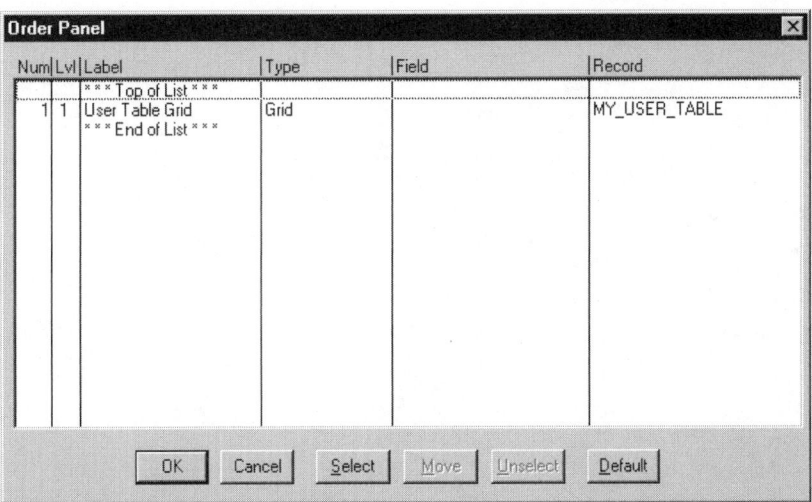

Figure A.28 MY_USER_GRID panel layout

MY_USER_GRID panel is used to enter user information in a grid format.

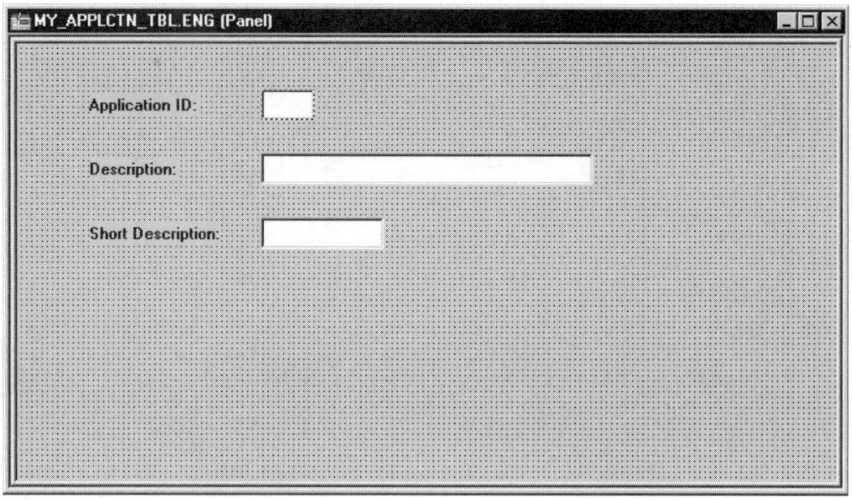

Figure A.29   MY_APPLCTN_TBL panel

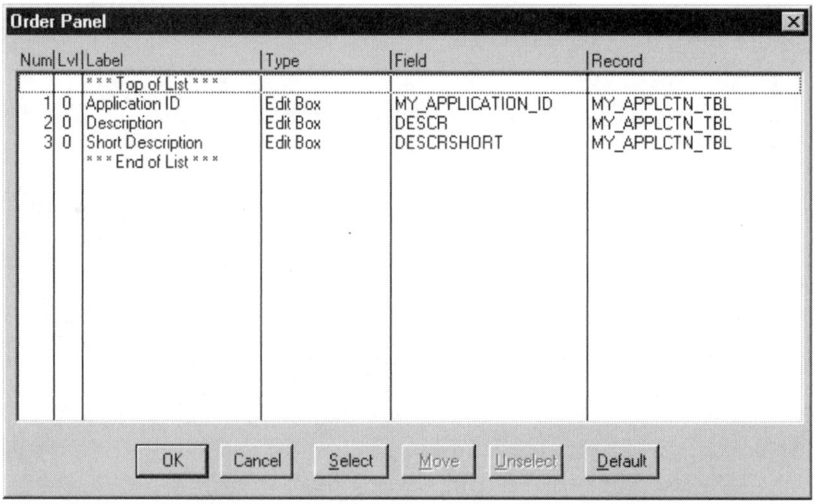

Figure A.30   MY_APPLCTN_TBL panel layout

MY_APPLCTN_TBL panel is used to set up applications that are tracked through our Problem Tracking application.

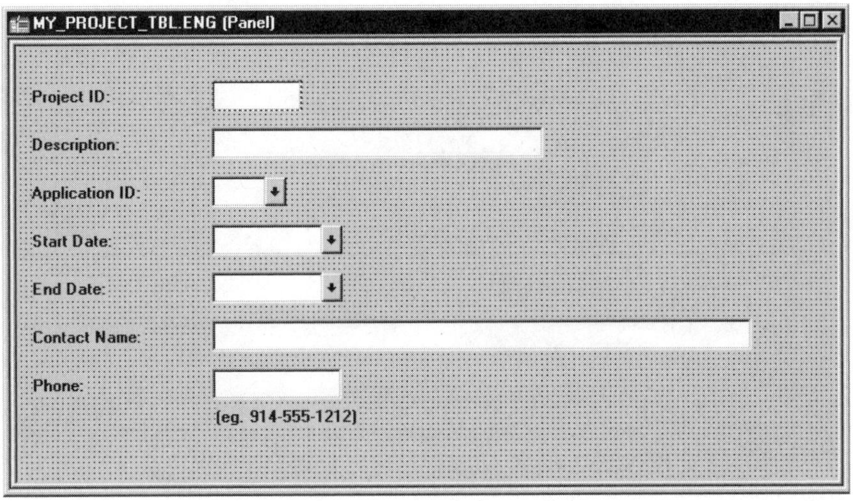

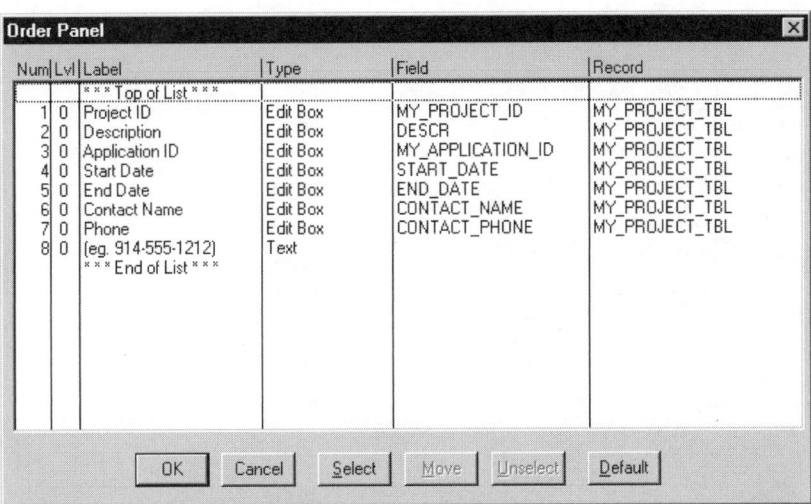

Figure A.31   MY_PROJECT_TBL panel

Num	Lvl	Label	Type	Field	Record
		* * * Top of List * * *			
1	0	Project ID	Edit Box	MY_PROJECT_ID	MY_PROJECT_TBL
2	0	Description	Edit Box	DESCR	MY_PROJECT_TBL
3	0	Application ID	Edit Box	MY_APPLICATION_ID	MY_PROJECT_TBL
4	0	Start Date	Edit Box	START_DATE	MY_PROJECT_TBL
5	0	End Date	Edit Box	END_DATE	MY_PROJECT_TBL
6	0	Contact Name	Edit Box	CONTACT_NAME	MY_PROJECT_TBL
7	0	Phone	Edit Box	CONTACT_PHONE	MY_PROJECT_TBL
8	0	(eg. 914-555-1212)	Text		
		* * * End of List * * *			

Figure A.32   MY_PROJECT_TBL panel layout

MY_PROJECT_TBL panel is used to enter project information in our application.

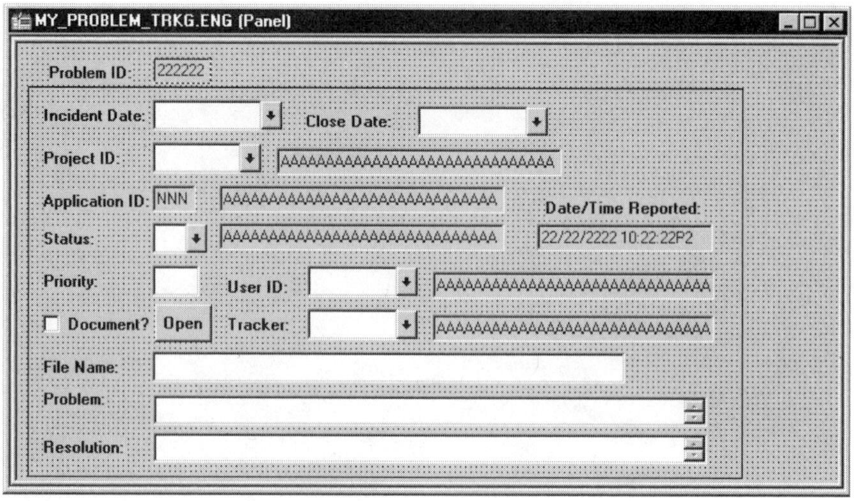

Figure A.33   MY_PROBLEM_TRKG panel

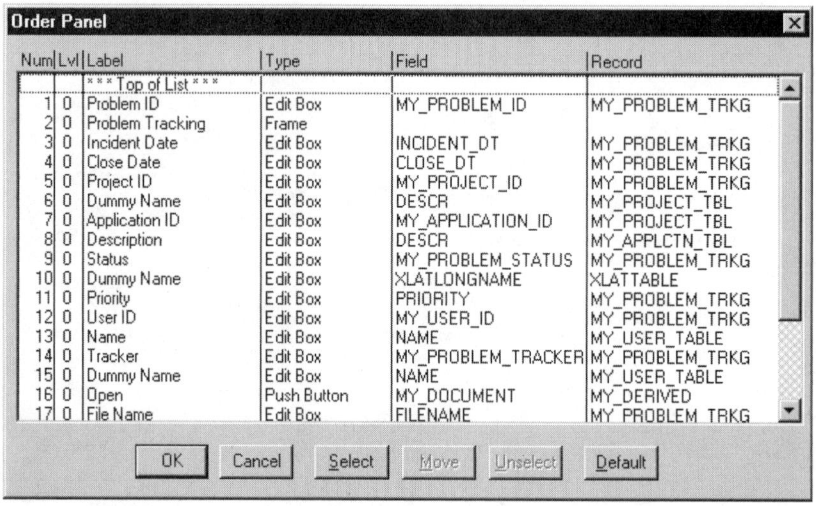

Figure A.34   MY_PROBLEM_TRKG panel layout

MY_PROBLEM_TRKG panel is used to enter incidents and resolutions through our Problem Tracking application.

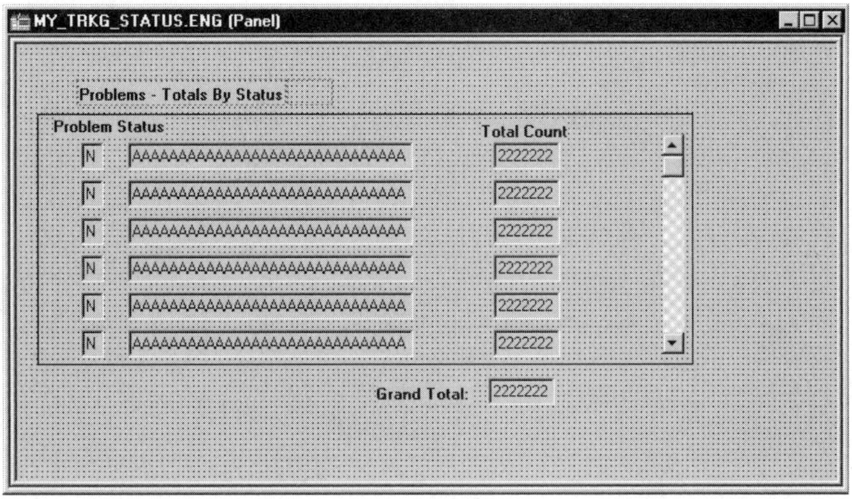

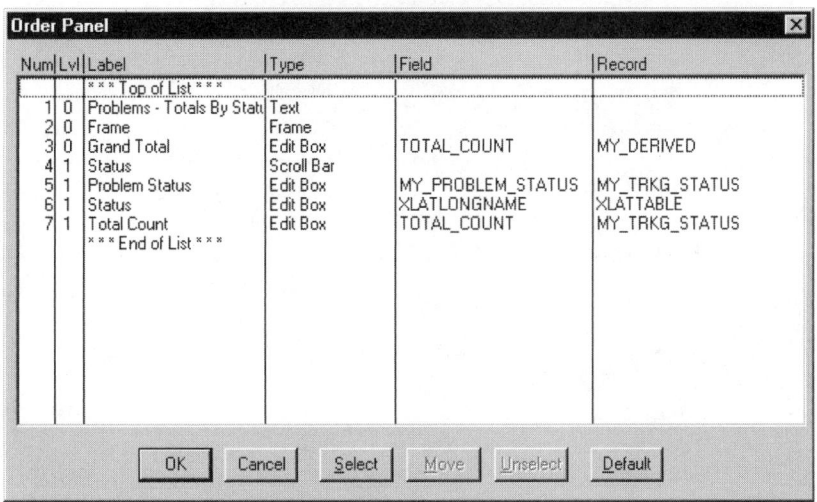

Figure A.35   MY_TRKG_STATUS panel

Figure A.36   MY_TRKG_STATUS panel layout

MY_TRKG_STATUS panel is used to view totals of all incidents/problems tracked using our application.

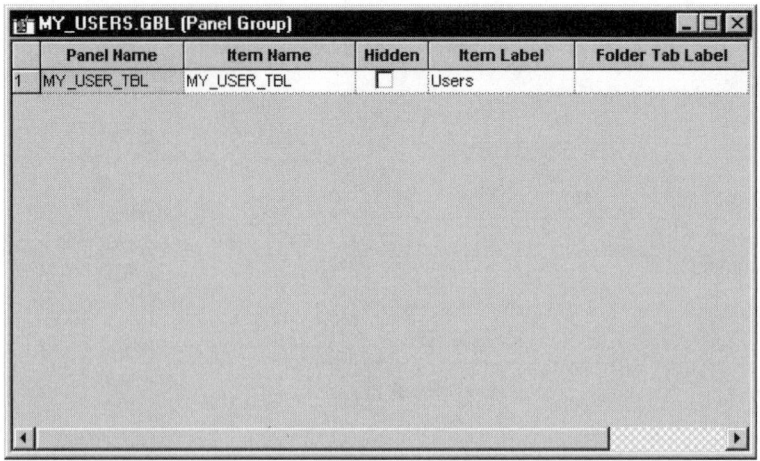

Figure A.37   MY_USERS panel group

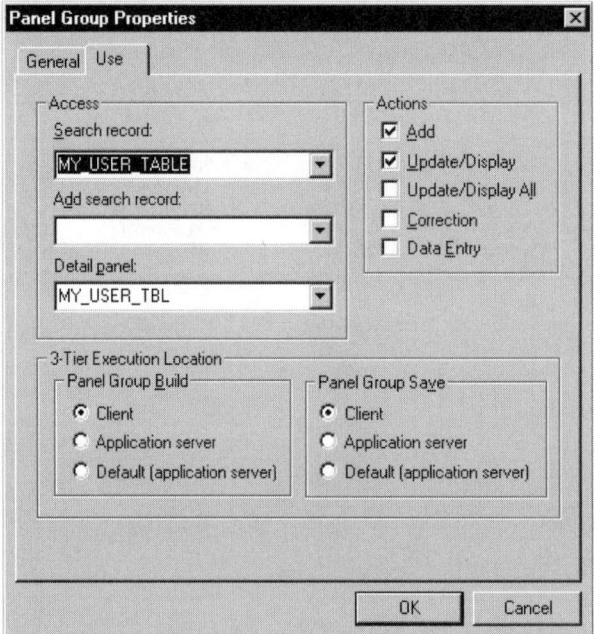

Figure A.38   MY_USERS panel group properties

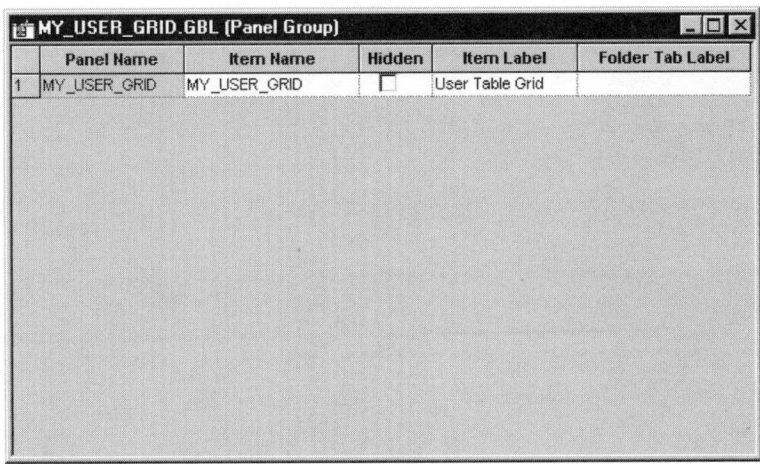

Figure A.39   MY_USER_GRID panel group

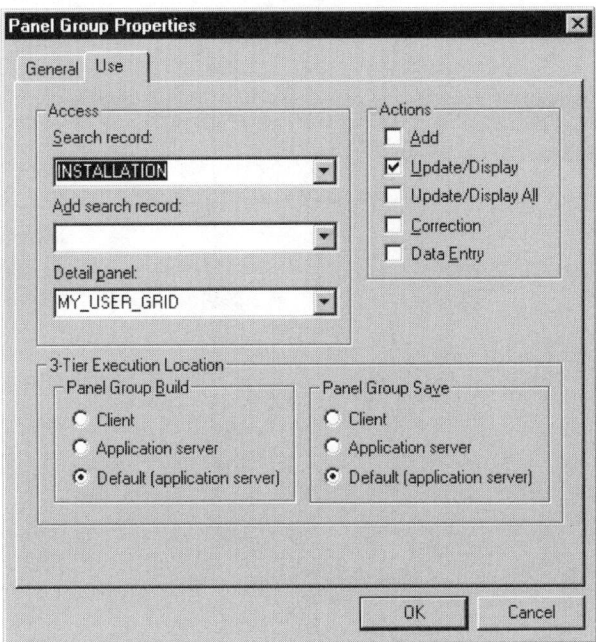

Figure A.40   MY_USER_GRID panel group properties

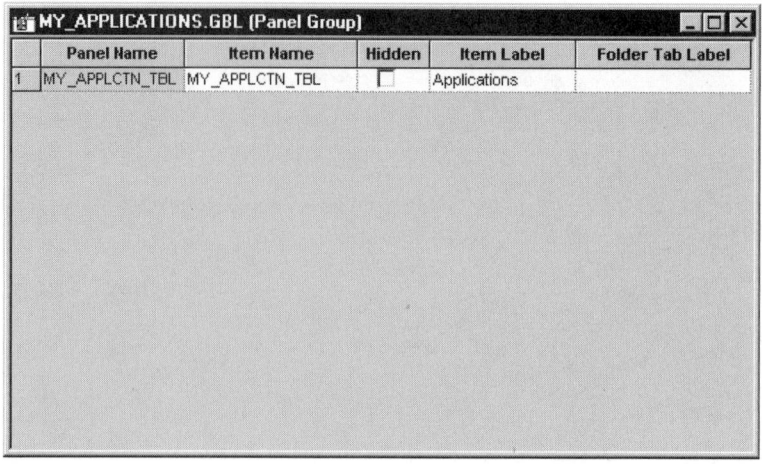

Figure A.41   MY_APPLICATIONS panel group

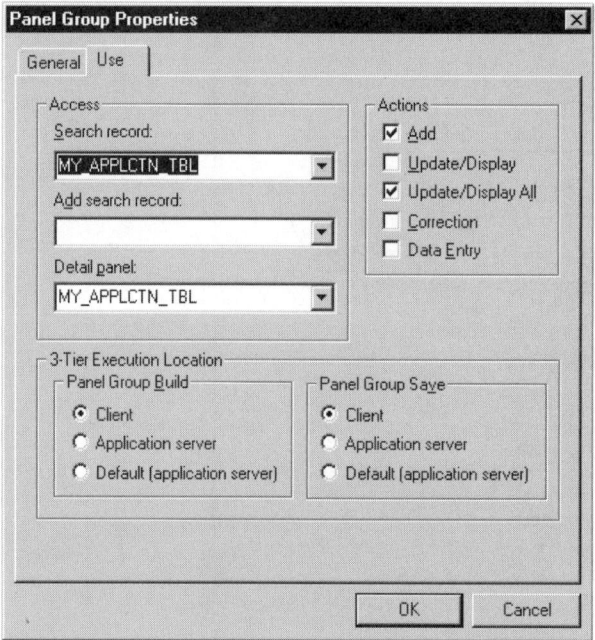

Figure A.42   MY_APPLICATIONS panel group properties

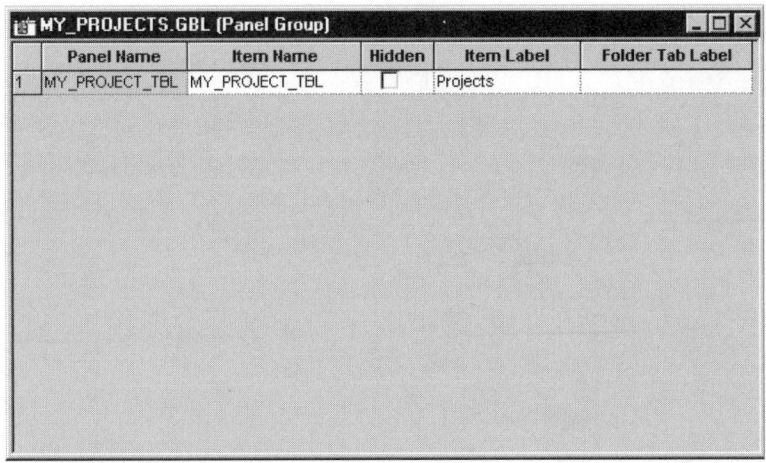

Figure A.43   MY_PROJECTS panel group

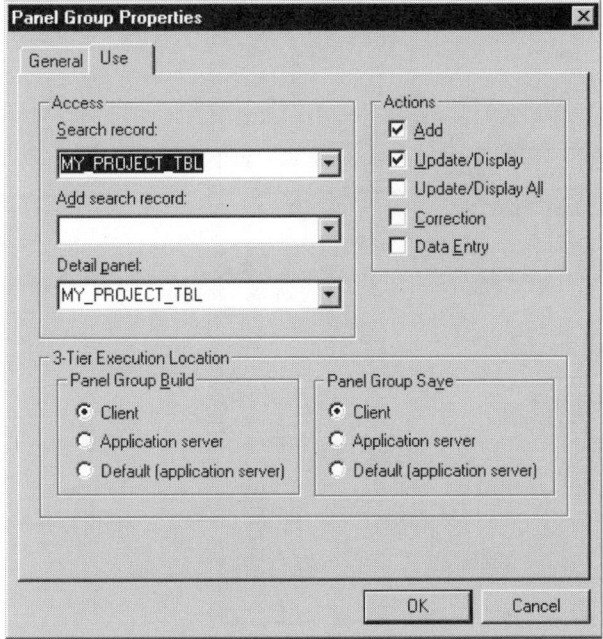

Figure A.44   MY_PROJECTS panel group properties

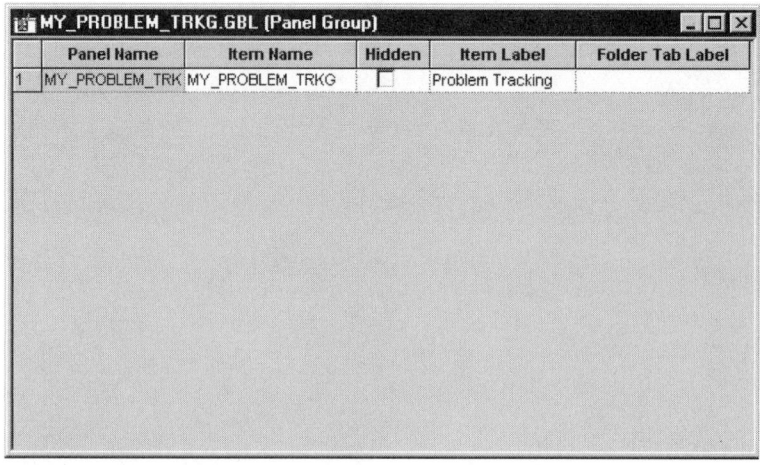

Figure A.45   M_PROBLEM_TRKG panel group

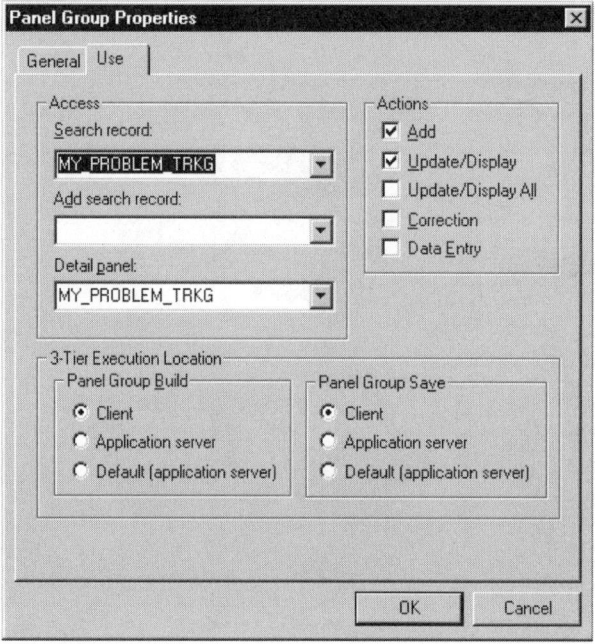

Figure A.46   M_PROBLEM_TRKG panel group properties

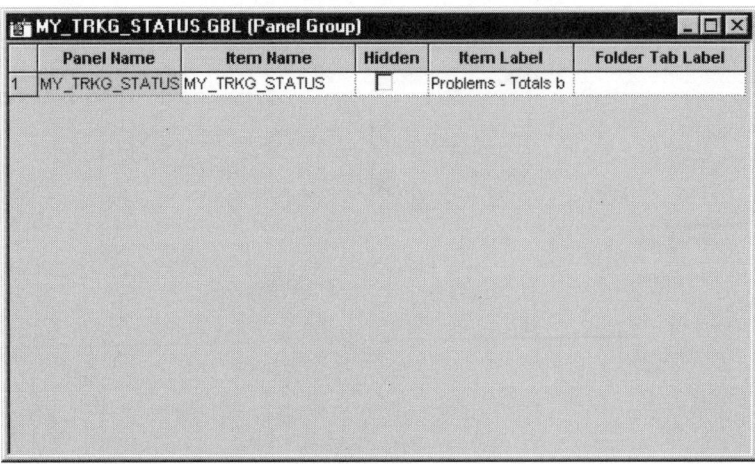

Figure A.47   MY_TRKG_STATUS panel group

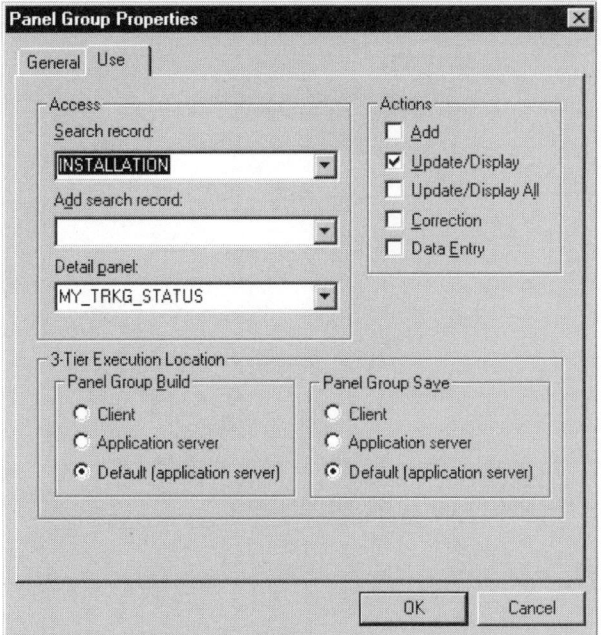

Figure A.48   MY_TRKG_STATUS panel group properties

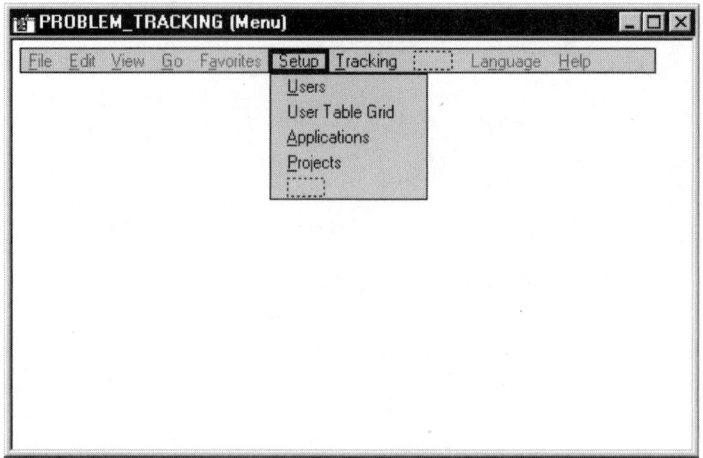

Figure A.49   Problem Tracking menu—setup bar items

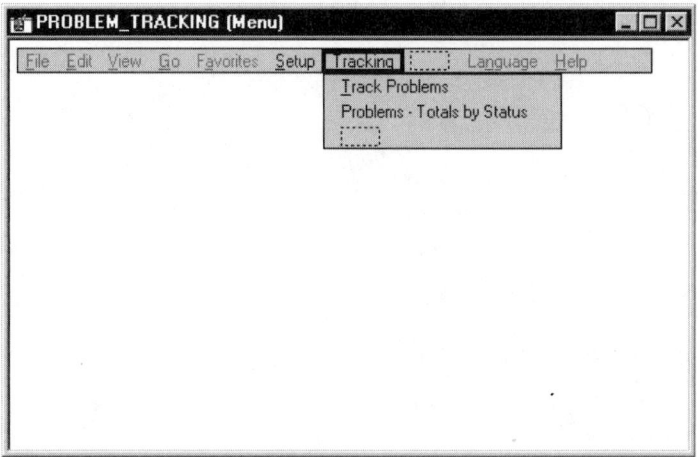

Figure A.50   Problem Tracking menu—tracking bar items

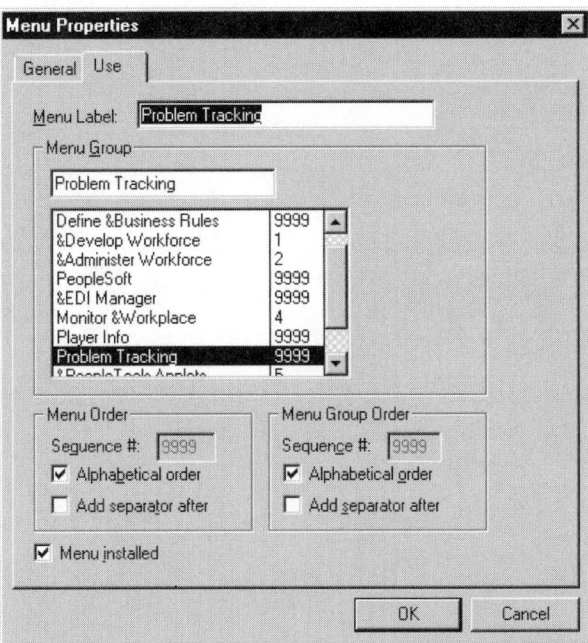

Figure A.50   Problem Tracking menu properties

Operator Class/Locations

The Operator Class and Employee Locations application links PeopleSoft operator classes to office locations. Employees currently working out of these office locations can be linked to the Operator Class/Location for security and reporting purposes.

The application is comprised of three main records, two views, and a Derived/Work record which stores the PeopleCode statements. The application is used primarily to demonstrate the use of scroll-related functions.

The records are:
MY_LOCATION_HDR
MY_LOCATIONS
MY_LOCATION_EMP

The two Views are:
MY_LOC_OPR_VW
MY_LOC_EMPL_VW

The Derived/Work record is:
MY_DERIVED

Figure B.1 graphically illustrated the records, the views, and the Derived/Work record for this Applet.

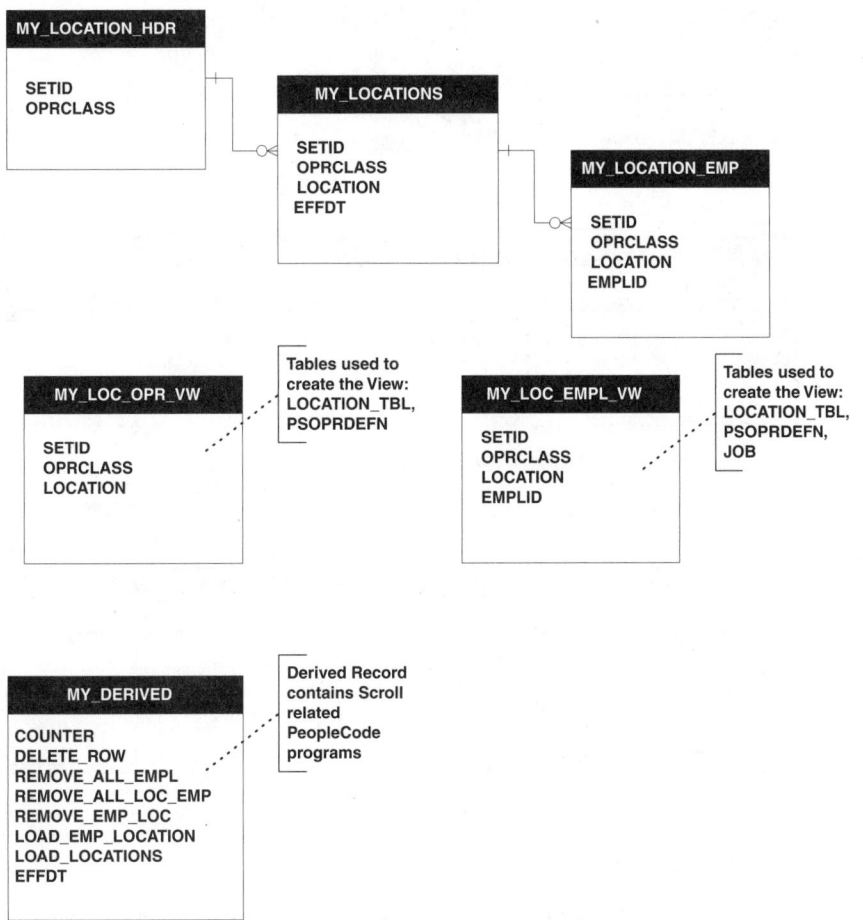

Figure B.1 Operator Classes linked to Employee Locations. Records, Views and Derived/Work

Field Name	Type	Key	Dir	CurC	Srch	List	Sys	Audt	H	Default
SETID	Char	Key	Asc		Yes	Yes	No			OPR_DEF_TBL_HR.SETID
OPRCLASS	Char	Key	Asc		Yes	Yes	No			

Figure B.2 MY_LOCATION_HDR record

MY_LOCATIONS (Record)

Field Name	Type	Key	Dir	CurC	Srch	List	Sys	Audt	H	Default
SETID	Char	Key	Asc		Yes	Yes	No			OPR DEF TBL HR.SETID
OPRCLASS	Char	Key	Asc		Yes	Yes	No			
LOCATION	Char	Key	Asc		Yes	No	No			
EFFDT	Date				No	No	No			%Date

Figure B.3   MY_LOCATIONS record

MY_LOCATION_EMP (Record)

Field Name	Type	Key	Dir	CurC	Srch	List	Sys	Audt	H	Default
SETID	Char	Key	Asc		Yes	Yes	No			OPR DEF TBL HR.SETID
OPRCLASS	Char	Key	Asc		Yes	Yes	No			
LOCATION	Char	Key	Asc		Yes	No	No			
EMPLID	Char	Key	Asc		No	No	No			

Figure B.4   MY_LOCATION_EMP record

MY_LOC_OPR_VW (Record)

Field Name	Type	Key	Dir	CurC	Srch	List	Sys	Audt	H	Default
SETID	Char	Key	Asc		Yes	Yes	No			
OPRCLASS	Char	Key	Asc		Yes	Yes	No			
LOCATION	Char	Key	Asc		Yes	No	No			

Figure B.5   MY_LOC_OPR_VW view

MY_LOC_EMPL_VW (Record)

Field Name	Type	Key	Dir	CurC	Srch	List	Sys	Audt	H	Default
SETID	Char	Key	Asc		Yes	Yes	No			
OPRCLASS	Char	Key	Asc		Yes	Yes	No			
LOCATION	Char	Key	Asc		Yes	No	No			
EMPLID	Char	Key	Asc		No	No	No			

Figure B.6   MY_LOC_EMPL_VW view

The PeopleCode associated with this application resides primarily in the Derived/ Work record MY_DERIVED as illustrated in figure B.7. Refer to part 3 for PeopleCode illustrations related to scroll processing.

MY_DERIVED (Record)

Field Name	Type	FDe	FEd	FCh	FFo	RIn	RIs	RDe	RSe	SEd	SPr	SPo	Srl	SrS	Wrk	PPr
COUNTER	Sign					Yes										
OPRCLASS	Char					Yes				Yes						
DELETE_ROW	Char			Yes						Yes						
REMOVE_ALL_EMPL	Char			Yes												
REMOVE_ALL_LOC_EMP	Char			Yes												
REMOVE_EMP_LOC	Char			Yes												
LOAD_EMP_LOCATION	Char			Yes												
LOAD_LOCATIONS	Char			Yes												Yes
EFFDT	Date			Yes												

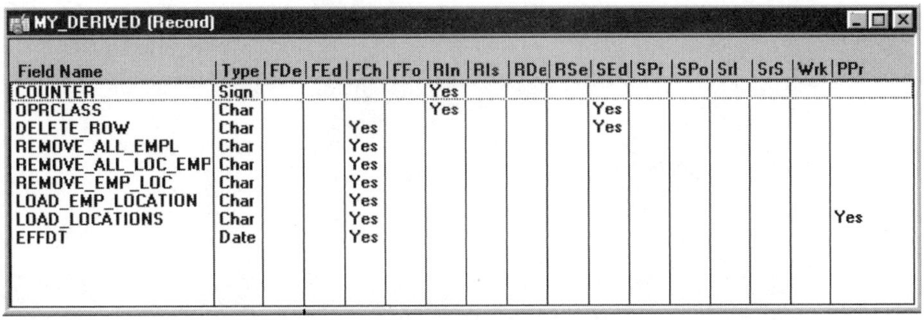

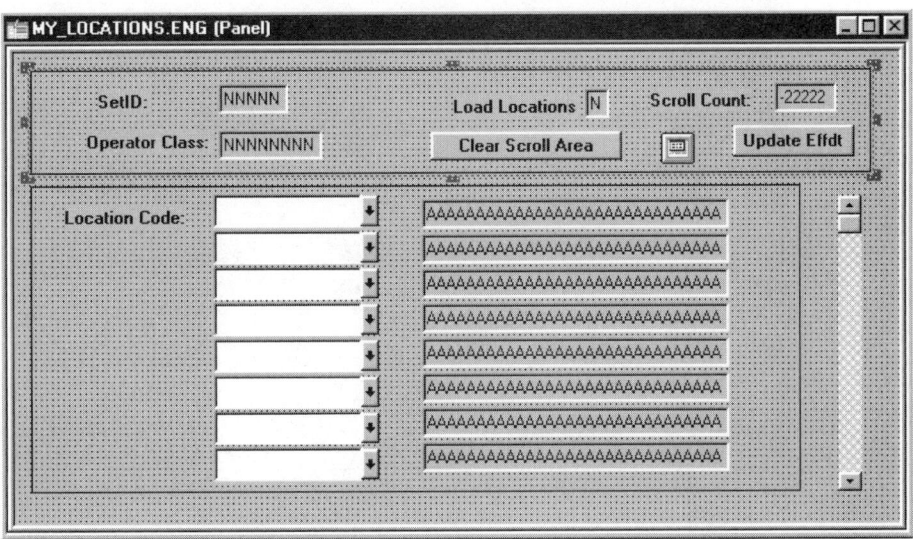

Figure B.7 MY_DERIVED Derived/Work record

Panels used include those shown in figure B.8 through B.16.

Figure B.8 MY_LOCATIONS Panel

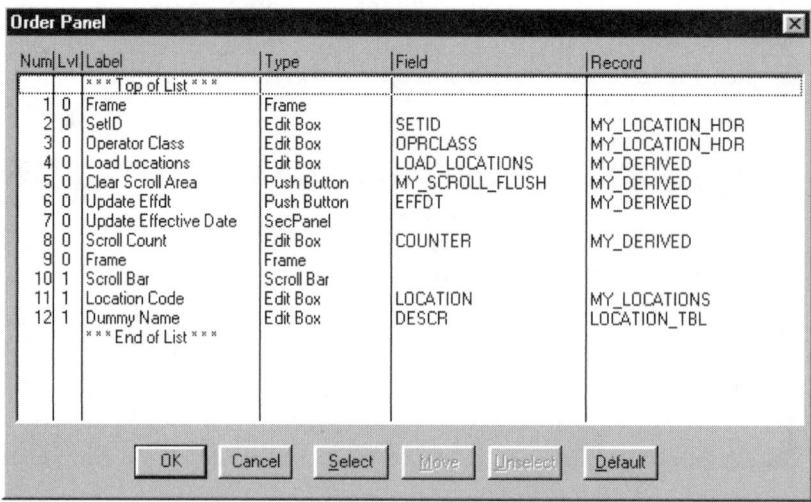

Figure B.9 MY_LOCATIONS order of Panel

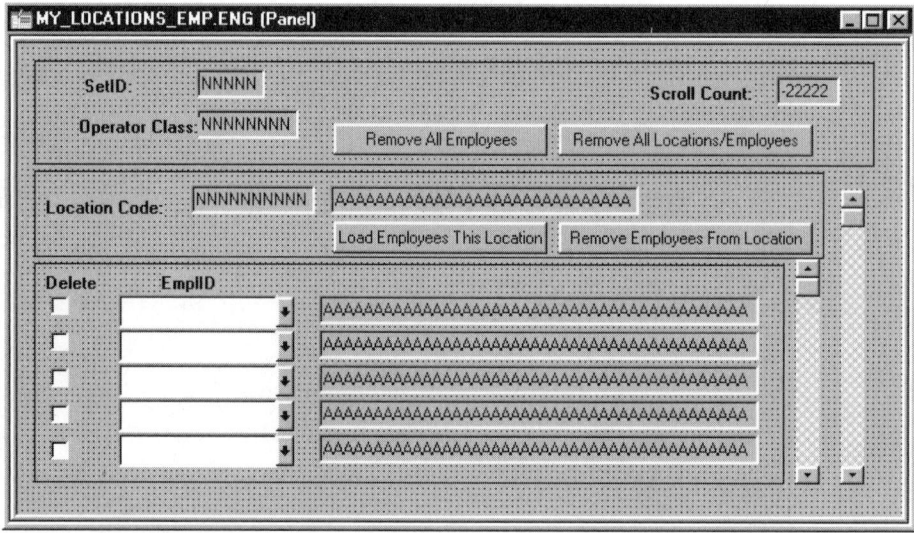

Figure B.10 MY_LOCATIONS_EMP Panel

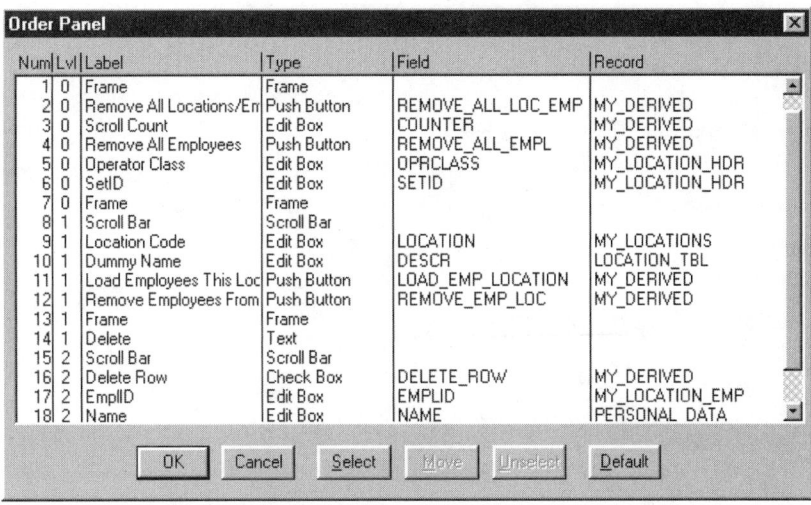

Figure B.11   MY_LOCATIONS_EMP Order of Panel

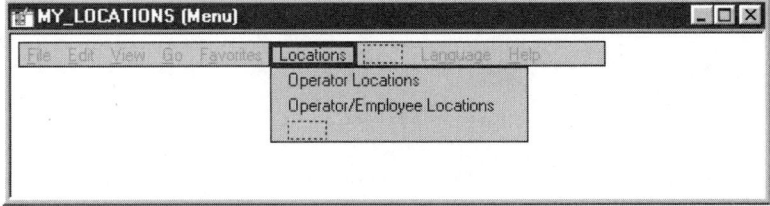

Figure B.12   Operator/Class & Employee Locations Panel Group

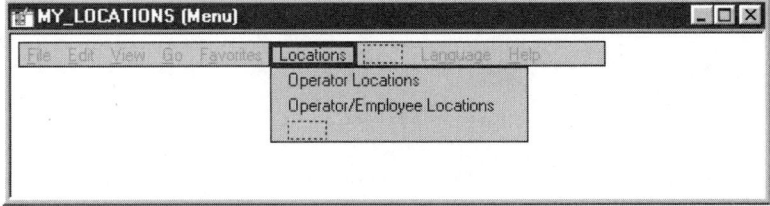

Figure B.13   Operator/Class & Employee Locations Menu

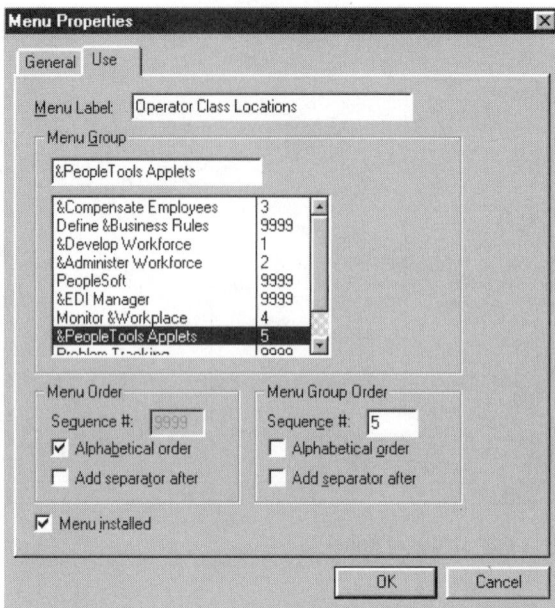

Figure B.14
Operator/Class & Employee
Locations Menu Properties

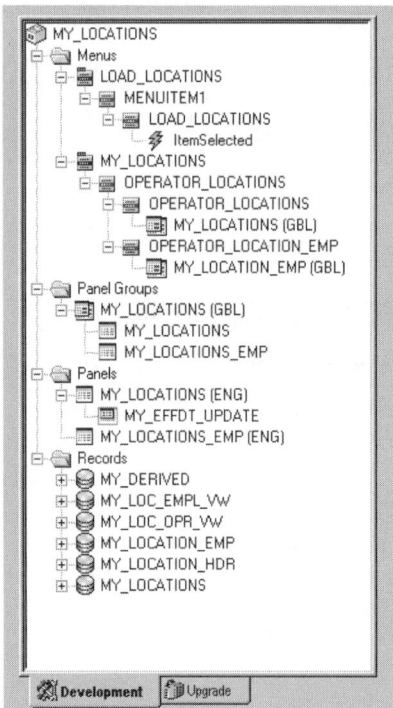

Figure B.15
Operator/Class Employee Location
Project Workspace

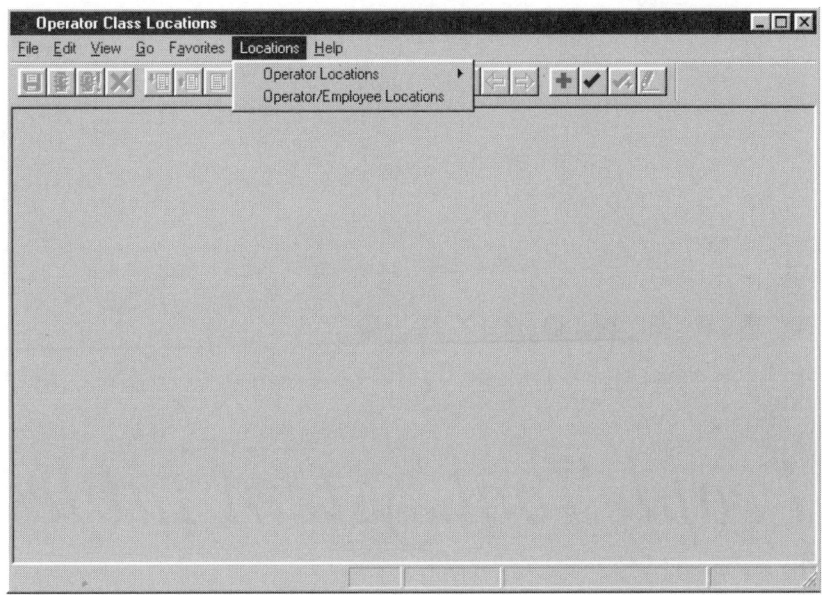

Figure B.16   Operator/Class & Employee Locations Applet as implemented

PeopleTool system tables

In this appendix you can find names and descriptions of the underlying PSTOOLS System tables. Some system tables have been omitted such as those that support Workflow and EDI Manager. The most common tables are listed by Tools Category.

Application Engine

AE_APPL_TBL	Application Definitions
AE_REQUEST	AE Request
AE_RUN_CONTROL	AE Run Control
AE_SECTION_TBL	Application Sections
AE_STEP_TBL	Section Steps
AE_STMT_B_TBL	AE Statement Chunk Table
AE_STMT_TBL	AE Statement Table

Change Control

PSCHGCTLHIST	Change Control History Table
PSCHGCTLLOCK	Change Control Locked Objects

Field Definition

PSDBFIELD	Database Field

Record Definition

PSDDLDEFPARMS	DDL Model Parameter

PSDDLMODEL	DDL Model Statement
PSIDXDDLPARM	Index DDL Parameters
PSINDEXDEFN	Index Definition
PSKEYDEFN	Key in Index Definition
PSPROGNAME	Record Field PeopleCode
PSRECDDLPARM	Record DDL Parameter
PSRECDEFN	Record Definition
PSRECFIELD	Record Field
PSSPCDDLPARM	Space DDL Parameters
PSVIEWTEXT	SQL View Text
XLATTABLE	Translate Value

Panel Definition

PSCOLORDEFN	Color Definition
PSPNLDEFN	Panel Definition
PSPNLFIELD	Panel Field
PSPNLTREECTRL	Panel Tree Control
PSSTYLEDEFN	Style Definition
PSTOOLBARDEFN	Toolbar Definition
PSTOOLBARITEM	Toolbar Item

Panel Group

PSPNLGROUP	Panel Group
PSPNLGRPDEFN	Panel Group Definition

Menu Definition

PSMENUDEFN	Menu Definition
PSMENUITEM	Menu Item
PSXFERITEM	Pop-up Menu Item Transfer Defns

Operator Definition

ACCESS_GRP_TBL	Tree Access Groups
PSACCESSPRFL	Access Profile
PSAUTHITEM	Authorized Menu Item
PSAUTHPRCS	Authorized Process
PSAUTHSIGNON	Authorized Signon Period
PSOBJGROUP	Object Group
PSOPRALIAS	Operator Alias
PSOPRALIASTYPE	Operator Alias Types
PSOPRCLS	Operator classes per operator
PSOPRDEFN	Operator Definition

PSOPROBJ	Operator Object Group	
PSPRCSPRFL	Process Profile	
PSPRCSRUNCNTL	Process Run Control	
SCRTY_ACC_GRP	Access Group Security	
SCRTY_QUERY	PS/Query Profile	

Tree Definition

PSTREEDEFN	Tree Definition
PSTREELEAF	Tree Leaf
PSTREELEVEL	Tree Level
PSTREENODE	Tree Node
PSTREESTRCT	Tree Structure
TREE_LEVEL_TBL	Sample/Default Tree Level Tbl
TREE_NODE_TBL	Tree Nodes

Query Definition

PSQRYBIND	Query Prompt
PSQRYCRITERIA	Query Criteria
PSQRYDEFN	Query Definition
PSQRYDEL	Query Definition
PSQRYEXPR	Query Expression
PSQRYFIELD	Query Field
PSQRYRECORD	Query Record
PSQRYSELECT	Query Select

NVision Definition

NVS_REPORT	PS/nVision Report Requests
NVS_SCOPE	PS/nVision Scope
NVS_SCOPE_FIELD	PS/nVision Scope Field
NVS_SCOPE_VALUE	PS/nVision Scope Values
PSTREESELCTL	Tree Selection Control
PSTREESELNUM	Tree Select Control Number
PSTREESELECTxx	Tree Select Work-Size (01 thru 30)

PeopleCode Definition

PSPCMNAME	PeopleCode Reference
PSPCMPROG	PeopleCode Program

Utilities (Messages/Tablesets)

MESSAGE_CATALOG	Message Catalog
MESSAGE_SET_TBL	Message Sets

REC_GROUP_REC	Record Group Records
REC_GROUP_TBL	Record Groups
SETID_TBL	TableSet IDs
SET_CNTRL_GROUP	TableSet Record Groups
SET_CNTRL_REC	TableSet Record Detail
SET_CNTRL_TBL	TableSet Controls
SET_CNTRL_TREE	TableSet Tree Controls

Import Definitions

PSIMPFIELD	Import Field
PSIMPDEFN	Import Definition

Upgrader Definition

PSOBJCHNG	Object Change
PSPROJECTDEFN	Project Definition Table
PSPROJECTITEM	Project Item Table
PSPROJECTMSG	Project Messages
PSRELEASE	Release Table
PST_PNLFIELDS	Upgrader Panel Work

Process Scheduler

PRCSDEFN	Process Definitions
PRCSDEFNGRP	Process Definition Groups
PRCSDEFNPNL	Process Definition Panelgroups
PRCSDEFNXFER	Process Definition Transfers
PRCSJOBDEFN	Process Job Definitions
PRCSJOBGRP	Process Job Groups
PRCSJOBITEM	Process Job Items
PRCSJOBPNL	Process Job Panel Groups
PRCSRUNCNTL	Process Run Control Template
PRCSSAMPLER	Process Scheduler Example
PRCSSYSTEM	Process System Table
PRCSTYPEDEFN	Process Type Definitions
PSPRCSLOCK	Process Scheduler Lock Table
PSPRCSRQST	Process Request
PSPRCSRQSTXFER	Process Request Transfer
PSRECURDEFN	Process Recurrence Definition
PSSERVERSTAT	Process Server Statistics
SERVERCLASS	Server Classes
SERVERDEFN	Process Server Definition

COBOL Definition

MESSAGE_LOG	Message Log Table
MESSAGE_LOGPARM	Message Parameter Log
SQLSTMT_TBL	Stored SQL Statements

Mass Change

MC_DATA_TBL	Mass Change SQR Datatypes
MC_DEFN	Mass Change Definition
MC_DEFN_CRIT	Mass Change Defn Criteria
MC_DEFN_CRIT_VL	Mass Change Defn Crit Values
MC_DEFN_DEFAULT	Mass Change Defn Defaults
MC_DEFN_DESCR	Mass Change Defn Description
MC_DEFN_PT	Mass Change Defn PeopleTools
MC_DEFN_SQL	Mass Change Defn SQL
MC_DEFN_SQL_LN	Mass Change Defn SQL Line
MC_DEFN_STMNT	Mass Change Defn Statement
MC_DTTM_PARMS	Mass Change Datetime Parms
MC_GROUP	Mass Change Defn Group
MC_GROUP_LN	Mass Change Defn Group Line
MC_HIST_CRIT	Mass Change History Criteria
MC_HIST_CRIT_VL	Mass Change History Crit Value
MC_HIST_DEFAULT	Mass Change History Defaults
MC_HIST_STMNT	Mass Change History Statement
MC_OPRID	Mass Change Operator Security
MC_OPR_SECURITY	Mass Change Operator Security
MC_PROMPTS	Mass Change Prompt Table Setup
MC_RUN_CNTL	Mass Change Run Control
MC_TEMPLATE	Mass Change Template
MC_TEM_CRITERIA	Mass Change Template Criteria
MC_TEM_DEFAULTS	Mass Change Template Defaults
MC_TEM_DESCR	Mass Change Template Descr
MC_TEM_STMNT	Mass Change Template Statement
MC_TYPE	Mass Change Type
MC_TYPE_DESCR	Mass Change Type Description
MC_TYPE_FIELD	Mass Change Type Field
MC_TYPE_JOIN	Mass Change Type Join Table
MC_TYPE_RECORD	Mass Change Type Record
MC_TYPE_SQL	Mass Change Type SQL Statement
MC_TYPE_STMNT	Mass Change Type Statement
MC_TYPE_WHERE	Mass Change Type Where Clause

International Tables

COUNTRY_TBL	Countries
CURRENCY_CD_TBL	Currency Codes

System Tables

PSASOFDATE	SQR Request Dates
PSCLOCK	Database Clock Access
PSCOLORDEFN	Color Definition
PSFMTDEFN	Format Definition Table
PSFMTITEM	Format Item Table
PSLOCK	PeopleTools System Control
PSOPTIONS	PeopleTools System Options
PSSTYLEDEFN	Style Definition
RUN_CNTL_SYSAUD	SysAudit Control Table
STRINGS_TBL	Strings Table

Application Engine examples

In this appendix you can find the Application Engine source code used in our exercises. Each section/step is listed along with the statement type and the statement text used (if any). Any called sections appear next to the statement type (in the case of DO Select, DO When, or DO section types).

Exercise #1—Application USER001

Section/Step	MAIN.STEP1
Statement Type	Update
Statement Text	&MSG(,1,'Hello World')

Exercise #2—Application USER002

Section/Step	MAIN.STEP1
Statement Type	Select
Statement Text	&SELECT(COUNTER) SELECT COUNT(*) FROM PS_PERSONAL_DATA

Section/Step	MAIN.STEP2
Statement Type	Update
Statement Text	&MSG(,2,'PERSONAL_DATA Record Count ', &BIND(COUNTER))

Exercise #3 — Application USER003

Section/Step	MAIN.STEP1
Statement Type	Select
Statement Text	&SELECT(COUNTER)

```
SELECT COUNT(*)
    FROM PS_&BIND(RECNAME,NOQUOTES,STATIC)
```

Section/Step	MAIN.STEP2
Statement Type	Update
Statement Text	&MSG(,3,

```
        &BIND(RECNAME,NOQUOTES),&BIND(COUNTER))
```

Exercise #4 — Application USER004

Section/Step	MAIN.STEP1
Statement Type	DO Select (Calls Section COUNT)
Statement Text	&SELECT(RECNAME)

```
SELECT A.RECNAME
  FROM PSRECFIELD        A,
     PSRECDEFN           B
  WHERE A.RECNAME       = B.RECNAME
   AND A.FIELDNAME      = &BIND(FIELDNAME)
   AND B.RECTYPE        = 0
  ORDER BY A.RECNAME
```

Section/Step	COUNT.STEP1
Statement Type	Select
Statement Text	&SELECT(COUNTER)

```
SELECT COUNT(*)
    FROM PS_&BIND(RECNAME,NOQUOTES,STATIC)
```

Section/Step	COUNT.STEP2
Statement Type	Update
Statement Text	&MSG(,3,

```
        &BIND(RECNAME,NOQUOTES),&BIND(COUNTER))
```

Exercise #5 — Application USER005

Section/Step	MAIN.STEP1
Statement Type	DO Select (Calls Section COUNT)
Statement Text	&SELECT(RECNAME)

```
SELECT A.RECNAME
    FROM PSRECFIELD        A,
         PSRECDEFN         B
    WHERE A.RECNAME       = B.RECNAME
```

```
                              AND A.FIELDNAME    = &BIND(FIELDNAME)
                              AND B.RECTYPE      = 0
                          ORDER BY A.RECNAME
```

Section/Step	COUNT.STEP1
Statement Type	Select
Statement Text	`&SELECT(COUNTER)`
	`SELECT COUNT(*)`
	`  FROM PS_&BIND(RECNAME,NOQUOTES,STATIC)`

Section/Step	COUNT.STEP2
Statement Type	Do When (Calls Section MSG)
Statement Text	`&SELECT(AE_DECIDE)`
	`SELECT 'X'`
	`  FROM PSLOCK`
	`WHERE &BIND(COUNTER) > 0`

Section/Step	MSG.STEP1
Statement Type	Update
Statement Text	`&MSG(,3,`
	`    &BIND(RECNAME,NOQUOTES),&BIND(COUNTER))`

Exercise #6—Application USER006

Section/Step	MAIN.STEP1
Statement Type	DO Section (Calls Dynamic Section —HELLO or GOODBYE)
Statement Text	No Statement Text

Section/Step	HELLO.STEP1
Statement Type	Update
Statement Text	`&MSG(,1,'Hello World')`

Section/Step	GOODBYE.STEP1
Statement Type	Update
Statement Text	`&MSG(,1,'Goodbye')`

Exercise #7—Application MYPRCSDL

Section/Step	MAIN.STEP1
Statement Type	Select
Statement Text	`&SELECT(PRCSTYPE,PRCSNAME)`
	`SELECT B.PRCSTYPE,B.PRCSNAME`
	`  FROM PS_AE_RUN_CONTROL    A,`
	`       PS_MY_RUN_CNTL_AE    B`
	`WHERE A.OPRID            = B.OPRID`

```
                  AND A.RUN_CNTL_ID      = B.RUN_CNTL_ID
                  AND A.PROCESS_INSTANCE =
                          &BIND(PROCESS_INSTANCE)
```

Section/Step	MAIN.STEP2
Statement Type	Update
Statement Text	`&MSG(,2,&BIND(PRCSTYPE,NOQUOTES),`
	`  &BIND(PRCSNAME,NOQUOTES))`

Section/Step	MAIN.STEP3
Statement Type	DO Select (Calls Section DYNSECTN)
Statement Text	`&SELECT(AE_SECTION,RECNAME)`

```
                  SELECT 'PROCESS1, RECNAME
                    FROM PSRECDEFN
                   WHERE RECNAME = 'PRCSDEFN'
                       OR RECNAME = 'PRCSDEFNGRP'
                       OR RECNAME = 'PRCSDEFNPNL'
                       OR RECNAME = 'PRCSDEFNXFER'
                   UNION
                  SELECT 'PROCESS2', RECNAME
                    FROM PSRECDEFN
                   WHERE RECNAME = 'PSPRCSRQST'
                       OR RECNAME = 'PSPNLFIELD'
                  ORDER BY 1,2
```

Section/Step	DYNSECTN.STEP1
Statement Type	DO Section (Calls Dynamic Section —PROCESS1 or PROCESS2)
Statement Text	No Statement Text

Section/Step	PROCESS1.STEP1
Statement Type	Update
Statement Text	`&SELECT(COUNTER)`

```
                  SELECT COUNT(*)
                    FROM PS_&BIND(RECNAME,NOQUOTES,STATIC)
                   WHERE PRCSTYPE = &BIND(PRCSTYPE)
                     AND PRCSNAME = &BIND(PRCSNAME)
```

Section/Step	PROCESS1.STEP2
Statement Type	DO When (Calls Section DELETE1)
Statement Text	`&SELECT(AE_DECIDE)`

```
                  SELECT 'X'
                    FROM PSLOCK
                   WHERE &BIND(COUNTER) > 0
```

Section/Step	PROCESS1.STEP3
Statement Type	DO Section (Calls Section MESSAGE)
Statement Text	No Statement Text

Section/Step	DELETE1.STEP1
Statement Type	Update
Statement Text	DELETE

```
  FROM PS_&BIND(RECNAME,NOQUOTES,STATIC)
 WHERE PRCSTYPE = &BIND(PRCSTYPE)
   AND PRCSNAME = &BIND(PRCSNAME)
```

Section/Step	PROCESS2.STEP1
Statement Type	Update
Statement Text	&SELECT(COUNTER)

```
SELECT COUNT(*)
   FROM &BIND(RECNAME,NOQUOTES,STATIC)
  WHERE PRCSTYPE = &BIND(PRCSTYPE)
    AND PRCSNAME = &BIND(PRCSNAME)
```

Section/Step	PROCESS2.STEP2
Statement Type	DO When (Calls Section DELETE2)
Statement Text	&SELECT(AE_DECIDE)

```
SELECT 'X'
   FROM PSLOCK
  WHERE &BIND(COUNTER) > 0
```

Section/Step	PROCESS2.STEP3
Statement Type	DO Section (Calls Section MESSAGE)
Statement Text	No Statement Text

Section/Step	DELETE2.STEP1
Statement Type	Update
Statement Text	DELETE

```
     FROM &BIND(RECNAME,NOQUOTES,STATIC)
    WHERE PRCSTYPE = &BIND(PRCSTYPE)
      AND PRCSNAME = &BIND(PRCSNAME)
```

Section/Step	MESSAGE.STEP1
Statement Type	Update
Statement Text	&MSG(,3,&BIND(RECNAME,NOQUOTES),

```
     &BIND(COUNTER))
```

Built-in functions

FREQUENTLY USED BUILT-IN FUNCTIONS

The following section lists frequently used built-in functions. Examples of these functions are also illustrated throughout the book.

PeopleCode built-in functions can be grouped into functional categories. Some of the more frequently used categories are:

- Conversion
- Date/Time
- Effective Date/Sequence
- Logical
- Math
- Message Catalog/Display
- Panel Buffer
- Panel Control
- Process Scheduler
- Save/Cancel
- Scroll functions
- SQL
- String
- Trace control
- Transfers

Conversion functions

Char

Description   Converts a numeric value to a character based on the character set in use

Syntax
```
Char (n)
```

Rules   Accepts one byte value only and not multiple values.

Returns   Returns a string value based on the corresponding number passed to the function statement.

Example
```
&CHAR_VALUE = Char(70);
```

Code

Description   Examines the first character passed in a text string and returns the corresponding numeric code

Syntax
```
Code(str)
```

Rules   Double-byte characters are returned as numeric codes representing both bytes

Returns   A number equal to the character set in use

Example
```
&NUMERIC_CODE = Code(&MY_STRING);
```

ConvertChar

Description   Converts the characters identified in the source string to the target character code

Syntax
```
ConvertChar(source_str, source_str_category, output_str, target_char_code)
```

where:

    `source_str` identifies the source string to be converted
    `source_str_category` the language classification of the source string
    `output_str` represents the converted string
    `target_char_code` numeric value identifying the conversion character type

Rules Allows for conversion between character sets such as Japanese Hankaku Katakana, Zenkaku Katakana, and Hiragana. These character sets can also be converted to ASCII single-byte representation.

Source and target character code sets not supported by `ConvertChar` are processed by the function without alteration. The 0 and 1 characters are processed without conversion. A value of -1 is returned when `ConvertChar` cannot determine the placement of source and target characters. A -2 is returned when the characters in the source string can be partially converted. The characters that can be converted and the characters that cannot be converted are sent to the target string as they appear in the source string.

Returns A return code of 1 indicates the string was converted successfully and a 0 indicates the string was not converted. A -1 indicates an unknown condition.

Example
```
&RETURN_CODE = ConvertChar(&KANJI_STRING, 5, ASCII_STRING, 0);
```

String

Description Takes a value stored in a non-string type and converts it to a string

Syntax
```
String(val)
```

Rules `String` can be used when field comparisons require the specific use of string data. Object data types cannot be converted using the `String` function.

Returns A string representation of the value passed to the function

Example
```
&MY_STRING = String(&NUMBER_FIELD);
```

Date/Time functions

Date

Description Converts a number formatted as YYYYMMDD and returns a DATE value

Syntax
```
Date (date_number)
```

Rules The input format must be a number.

Returns A DATE data type value

Example
```
&DATE_FIELD = Date(20000101);
```

DatePart

Description   Returns part of an input DateTime value

Syntax
```
DatePart(datetime_value)
```

Rules   The input value is a `DateTime` data type.

Returns   Returns the date value portion

Example
```
&DATE_PORTION = DateTimeValue("01/01/00 06:30:25 AM");
&DATE_PORTION = DatePart(&DATE_PORTION);
```

DateValue

Description   Converts a date string that is in the Windows standard date setting and returns a date type

Syntax
```
DateValue(date_str)
```

Rules   When the input date value is in the YY/MM/DD format and Windows regional date setting is MM/DD/YY, the panel processor returns an invalid date function error message.

Returns   Returns values based on the Windows regional date setting

Example
```
/* Date format is mm/dd/yy */
&DATE_FIELD = DateValue("01/01/00");
/* Date format is yy/mm/dd */
&DATE_FIELD = DateValue("00/12/31");
```

AddToDate

Description   Accepts a date and three additional parameters representing number of years, months, and days. The specified values are added to the date.

Syntax
```
AddToDate (date, num_years, num_months, num_days)
```

Rules   The function accounts for leap years and will subtract from the specified date when negative values are passed.

Returns   A date representing the date passed and +/- the number of years, months and days.

```
/* Subtracts five years from current date, then adds six months and two days
*/
```

Example
```
&CALCULATED_DATE = AddToDate(%Date, -5, 6, 2);
```

Effective Date/Sequence functions

CurrEffdt

Description   Identifies and returns a value representing the current effective date for the record at the current scroll level

Syntax
```
CurrEffDt(level_number)
```

Rules   When a level is not specified, the effective date of the current scroll level is returned.

Returns   The return value is a Date type. When used in a scroll area that does not contain an effective dated record in the primary scroll, the function returns a number.

Example
```
&EFFDT = CurrEffDt(2);
```

CurrEffSeq

Description   Returns the effective sequence of a specified scroll area

Syntax
```
CurrEffSeq(level_num)
```

Rules   When a level is not specified, the effective sequence returned is that of the current scroll level.

Returns   A number data type representing the effective sequence of the scroll area

Example
```
If CurrEffSeq(CurrentLevelNumber()) <> &PREVIOUS_EFFSEQ Then
   SetDefault(JOB.ACTION);
   SetDefault(JOB.ACTION_REASON);
End-If;
```

CurrEffRowNum

Description   Returns the effective row number of the current specified scroll area

Syntax
```
CurrEffRowNum(level_number)
```

Rules   When a level is not specified, the effective row number returned is that of the current scroll level.

Returns   A number data type representing the effective row number of the scroll area

Example
```
&ROW_NUMBER = CurrEffRowNum(2);
```

NextEffDt

Description   Returns the value of the specified record field that exists in the next effective-dated row

Syntax
```
NextEffDt(record_field)
```

Rules   Works only with effective dated records. When a next record does not exist, the statement is bypassed.

Returns   An Any data type containing the field in the next effective-dated record

Example
```
If JOB.DEPTID = NextEffdt(JOB.DEPTID) Then
     Gray(JOB.PAYGROUP);
End-If;
```

PriorEffDt

Description   Works with effective-dated records and is a contrast to NextEffDt. It returns the contents of the field passed to the function statement that appear in the prior effective-dated row

Syntax
```
PriorEffdt(record_field)
```

Rules   Works only with effective dated records. When there is no prior record, the statement is bypassed by the Application Processor.

Returns   An Any data type containing the field from the prior effective-dated record

Example
```
If JOB.COMPRATE < PriorEffdt(JOB.COMPRATE) Then
   Error ("New Compensation Rate cannot be < previous rate");
End-If;
```

Logic functions

All

Description   Determines whether one or more fields contain a value. The `All` function is useful in the `SaveEdit` PeopleCode event if we wish to verify that one or more fields have been entered.

Syntax
```
All(fieldlist)
```

Rules   fieldlist represents one or more field names. They can be specified as
```
[recordname.] fieldname1 [, [recordname.] fieldname2]
```

Returns   A Boolean. If all the fields contain a value, then the function returns `True`. If one or more fields do not contain a value, the function returns `False`.

Example
```
If All(MY_PROBLEM_RESOLTN, CLOSE_DT) Then
   Gray(MY_PROBLEM_STATUS);
End-If;
```

AllOrNone

Description   This function is a combination of the `All` and `None` functions. The function returns a Boolean `True` when all the fields contain values or if none of the fields contain values. `False` is returned when there is a combination of fields containing values and fields that do not contain values.

Syntax
```
AllOrNone(FieldList)
```

Rules   A character field containing blanks or a numeric field containing a zero is categorized as a `null` field value.

Returns   `True` when all fields contain values or none of the fields contain values.

Example
```
If AllOrNone(CLOSE_DT, MY_PROBLEM_RESOLTN) Then
   &RETURN = MyAuditFunction();
End-If;
```

None

Description   Verifies a character field contains blanks or a numeric field contains zero

Syntax
```
None(FieldList)
```

Rules   A character field containing blanks or a numeric field containing a zero is categorized as a null field value.

Returns   Returns `True` if the field or list of fields do not contain a value. A `False` is returned if one or more fields contain a value.

Example

```
If MY_PROBLEM_STATUS = "5" Then
   If None(CLOSE_DT) Then
      Error ("Close date is required for resolved issues");
   End-If;
End-If;
```

Math functions

Round

Description   Rounds up the number passed to the specified number of decimal positions.

Syntax

```
Round (decimal, precision)
```

Rules   The value represented by a decimal must be of a number data type.

Returns   Returns a decimal number rounded up to the number of decimal positions in precision.

Example

```
&ANNUAL_RT = Round(JOB.COMPRATE, 3);
```

Int

Description   Removes the decimal positions from a number and returns an integer value.

Syntax

```
Int(decimal_number)
```

Rules   Int does not round the input value; it only truncates the decimal positions.

Returns   Returns a whole number value.

Example

```
&HOURLY_RATE = 12.675;
&NEW_RATE = Int(&HOURLY_RATE);
/*  Value of &New_rate is now 12 */
```

Truncate

Description Removes the specified number of digits from a decimal value.

Syntax
```
Truncate (decimal_number, digits)
```

Rules Does not perform any rounding. When the parameter identified by digits contains a zero, all numbers to the right of the decimal point are removed.

Returns Returns a number value.

Example
```
  &COMPENSATION_RATE = 2375.67895;
  &NEW_RATE = Truncate(&COMPENSATION_RATE, 3);
/* Value of &New_Rate is 2375.678 */
  &COMPENSATION_RATE = 2375.67895;
  &NEW_RATE = Truncate(&COMPENSATION_RATE, 0);
/* Value of &New_Rate is 2375 */
```

Message Catalog/Display functions

MessageBox

Description Creates and displays a message box window.

Syntax
```
MessageBox(style, title, message_set, message_num,
default_txt [, paramlist])
```

where

> `style` Enables the message box window to be tailored with a blend of icons and push buttons.

> `title` The message box title.

> `message_set` message_set of the message catalog. Message sets 1 through 19,999 are reserved for PeopleSoft applications.

> `message_num` The message number within the message set.

> `default_txt` Text that is displayed in the message box when the cataloged message set is not available or message set is represented by zero.

> `parmlist` List of parameters that are displayed in the text string. They can be represented as `%1`, `%2` and so on.

Rules The function return value can be interpreted if necessary. With the style parameter, two or more buttons can be included in the message box, but their use is limited to certain PeopleCode events. When the style parameter is left out or style contains more than one button, the function becomes user think-time, which indicates the button action returns a value back to the function. As a result of awaiting a reply, the Application Processor suspends the PeopleCode program until the user clicks on one of the buttons contained in the message.

Returns A number value indicating which button was pressed. See table E.1 for a list of return value descriptions. A return value of zero indicates there was insufficient memory to construct the `MessageBox`.

Example
```
If MY_PROBLEM_STATUS = "2" Then
   MessageBox(289, "Incorrect Data", 20012, 1, "Project ID %1 is invalid",
MY_PROJECT_ID);
End-If;
```

Table E.1 Message return values

Returns	Description
0	Insufficient memory
-1	Warning
1	OK button was pressed
2	Cancel
3	Abort
4	Retry
5	Ignore
6	Yes
7	No

WinMessage

Description `WinMessage` is used to display information in a message box.

Syntax
```
WinMessage (message [, style] [, title]
```

> message A text string displayed in the message box. When `WinMessage` is used as a debugging tool, a text string provides valuable information by including field contents as parameters. Utilizing `WinMessage` to assist while debugging does not require the use of `MsgGet` and `MsgGetText` functions.
>
> style This parameter is optional.
>
> title The message box title.

Rules From a debugging perspective, `WinMessage` can be used to display field contents and allow us to "inch" through PeopleCode statements if necessary.

Returns When the style parameter is passed, `WinMessage` returns a number indicating which button was pressed. See table E.1 for a list of return value descriptions.

A return value of zero indicates there is insufficient memory to construct the message box.

When the style parameter is not included, a Boolean value is returned. True indicates the OK button is pressed.

Example

```
/* This example does not use style or title */
WinMessage("A message with no style!");

/* This message has style and returns a value based on button pressed */
WinMessage("Close date cannot be less than the reported incident date", 289,
"Invalid Date");
```

Error

Description   Is used to display an error message and stop processing of the active panel. Error works with messages stored in the Message Catalog or with a text string supplied to the function.

Syntax
```
Error (String)
```

Rules   The value contained in string can be a literal text message or a message stored in the message catalog. The stored message must be retrieved using the MsgGet or MsgGetText functions. This is important when using translated text messages. Error terminates the PeopleCode program and prevents further statements from being executed. Error, however, produces varying results from one PeopleCode event to another. The events in which Error is commonly used include FieldEdit and SaveEdit. When executed in these events, the message is displayed and processing is halted. In FieldEdit, the field that contains the PeopleCode event is highlighted; in SaveEdit, no fields are highlighted. One manner in which to work around this in the SaveEdit event is to use the SetCursorPos function for the field, prior to calling Error. RowDelete is another PeopleCode event in which the Error function is sometimes used. When Error is called in RowDelete, the message is displayed and the row is not deleted.

Returns   Does not return a value

Example

```
/* Implemented with a message string */
   Error ("All field values are required");

/* Used with a cataloged message */
   Error MsgGet(20010, 1, "All field values are required");
```

Warning

Description   Warning is used to display a message. Warning differs from Error because it does not halt processing. The user is presented with OK and Explain buttons, then has the opportunity to correct or change data.

Syntax
```
Warning (String)
```

Rules   Warning works with messages stored in the message catalog or a text string supplied to the function. The stored message must be retrieved using the MsgGet or MsgGetText function. When executed, the Warning statement terminates the PeopleCode program and prevents further statements from being executed. Warning produces varying results from one PeopleCode event to another. The events in which Warning is commonly used include FieldEdit and SaveEdit. When used in FieldEdit, the message is displayed and the field that contains the PeopleCode is highlighted. Placing Warning in SaveEdit displays the message but does not highlight fields. One manner in which to work around this in the SaveEdit event is to use the SetCursorPos function for the field prior to Warning. RowDelete is another PeopleCode event in which Warning is sometimes used. When Warning is called in RowDelete the message is displayed with OK and Cancel buttons. The user then has the option to delete the row by pressing OK or to back out of the delete by pressing Cancel.

Returns   Does not return a value

Example
```
/* This message enables the user to continue after pressing OK */

  Warning("Incident status has been assigned");
```

MsgGet

Description   MsgGet retrieve messages from the message catalog and, when necessary, substitutes the value of each parameter contained in the message text identified by %1, %2, %3.

Syntax
```
MsgGet (message_set, message_num,
  default_msg_text [, paramlist] )
```

Rules   When a message set number less than 1 is passed, or if the message is not in the catalog, the default message text is substituted.

MsgGet is not a separate function. It is used in conjunction with MessageBox, WinMessage, Error, and Warning.

Returns Retrieves stored message and substitutes parameter in a paramlist, but does not return a value

Example
```
Warning (MsgGet(20011, 1, "Number of rows deleted is %1",
  &COUNT));
```

MsgGetText

Description MsgGetText retrieve messages from the Message Catalog and when necessary substitutes the value of each parameter contained in the message text identified by %1, %2, %3.

Syntax
```
MsgGetText (message_set, message_num,
  default_msg_text [, paramlist] )
```

Rules MsgGetText is almost identical to MsgGet except that the function displays the message without displaying a message set and message number.

Returns Retrieves stored message and substitutes parameter in a paramlist, but does not return a value

Example
```
Error (MsgGetText(20012, 1, "Data cannot be saved until all fields are
entered"));
```

Panel Buffer functions

DeleteRecord

Description Works on a level zero scroll record and is used to remove the parent and any corresponding child records from the database

Syntax
```
DeleteRecord (level_zero_recfield)
```

Rules Marks records to be deleted. During save processing, the row is deleted from the database. The DeleteRecord function cannot be executed from a Save-PostChange or WorkFlow PeopleCode event because database updates are performed at the conclusion of the Workflow event.

Returns An optional Boolean value is returned following the completion of the function

Example
```
  &RETURN_VALUE = DeleteRecord(MY_PROJECT_ID);
```

FieldChanged

Description   Is used to verify if one or more specified fields have been changed. A field can be changed on a panel or by a PeopleCode program.

Syntax   There are two methods of implementing `FieldChanged`, and they are based on how the field is referenced. When the field is referenced in a scroll path, the syntax is

```
FieldChanged(scrollpath, target_row,
   [recordname.] fieldname)
```

When the field is referenced by context:

```
FieldChanged( [recordname.] fieldname)
```

Rules   When performed from a record definition that is not the same as the record name, then the recordname prefix is required.

Returns   Returns `True` when the contents of the Record.Fieldname have been changed since being retrieved from the database

Example

```
If FieldChanged(PRIORITY) Then
    &RETURN = MyAuditFunction();
  End-If;
```

InsertRow

Description   Inserts a new row of data into the scroll buffer. The operation is followed by the `RowInsert` PeopleCode event.

Syntax

```
InsertRow (scrollpath, target_row [, turbo])
```

Rules   This function performs the same steps as if the F7 key were pressed. The `InsertRow` function is immediately followed by the `RowInsert` PeopleCode event. The remaining PeopleCode events then follow `RowInsert`. For effective-dated scrolls, the new row is inserted before the target row. When a non-effective-dated record is inserted, the new row is inserted after the row identified in the function. For effective-dated rows, the Effdt field is set to the current date, and the values that exist in the previous row are copied to the newly inserted row.

Returns   An optional Boolean value is returned following the completion of the function.

Example

```
InsertRow(RECORD.MY_LOCATIONS,
CurrentRowNumber(), RECORD.MY_LOCATION_EMP);
```

PriorValue

Description   Returns the prior value of a buffer field

Syntax
```
PriorValue(fieldname)
```

Rules   To expect correct results, this function should be used in the `FieldEdit` and `FieldChange` events for the buffer field where `PriorValue` is called. When the value of a field is `'1'` during panel startup, and the value is then changed by the user to a `'2'` and then to `'3'`, the PriorValue function returns `'2'` when executed after the second change. The value will not be the initial `'1'`.

Returns   Returns an `Any` data type

Example
```
If PriorValue(DESCRLONG) = " " Then
    CLOSE_DT = %Date;
End-If;
```

RecordChanged

Description   Indicates whether a row has been modified since being retrieved from the database

Syntax
```
Contexual Reference:  RecordChanged(RECORD.target_recname)
```

When the PeopleCode program executing is on the same record, we can use
```
            RecordChanged(recordname.fieldname)
```

Rules   Can be used during save processing to identify updates based on changes made during a panel session

Returns   Returns `True` if the record was changed by a user panel or changed from within a PeopleCode program

Example
```
If RecordChanged(MY_USER_TABLE.NAME) Then
    &RETURN = MyAuditFunction();
End-If;
```

RecordDeleted

Description   Can be used to identify rows marked for deletion as a result of an operator F8 delete or a program `DeleteRow` function call

Syntax   There are two methods of implementing the `RecordDeleted` function, and they are based on how the row is referenced. When the row is referenced in a scroll path, the syntax is

```
RecordDeleted(scrollpath, target_row)
```

When the row is referenced by context

```
RecordDeleted(RECORD.target_recordname)
```

Rules   Deleted rows are removed from the buffer during save processing, which enables the `RecordDeleted` function to be used in most events up to and including `SavePostChg`.

Returns   Returns a Boolean `True` when a row has been marked for deletion

Example

```
If RecordDeleted(RECORD.MY_LOCATIONS,
CurrentRowNumber(),        RECORD.MY_LOCATIONS_EMP) Then
   MY_DERIVED.COUNTER = ActiveRowCount(RECORD.MY_LOCATIONS,
   CurrentRowNumber(), RECORD.MY_LOCATION_EMP);
End-If;
```

RecordNew

Description   Used during save processing to determine if a row is new to the database

Syntax   Can be used in two ways based on how the row is referenced. When the row is referenced in a scroll path, the syntax is

```
RecordNew(scrollpath, target_row)
```

When the row is referenced by context

```
RecordNew(RECORD.target_recordname)
```

Rules   In previous releases of PeopleCode this could be written as Record-New(Recordname.Fieldname)

Returns   Returns a Boolean True when the record is new to the panel buffer.

Example

```
/* Using scrollpath */
If RecordNew(RECORD.MY_LOCATIONS, CurrentRowNumber(),
RECORD.MY_LOCATION_EMP) Then
   &RETURN = MyAuditFunction();
End-If;
/* Using contextual reference) */
If RecordNew(RECORD.MY_LOCATIONS) Then
   &RETURN = MyAuditFunction();
End-If;
```

Panel Control functions

Gray

Description   Sets a field on a panel so that it is display only and cannot be changed

Syntax
```
Gray(fieldname)
```

Rules   The `Gray` function is commonly used in the `RowInit` event and can appear in other events such as `FieldChange`.

Returns   Returns a Boolean that can be used to determine if the function was successful

Example
```
If MY_PROBLEM_STATUS = "5" Then
   Gray(CLOSE_DT);
End-If;
```

Hide

Description   Hides a field on a panel making it invisible to the user

Syntax
```
Hide (fieldname)
```

Rules   `Hide` can be used in a `RowInit` event, but can also appear in events such as `FieldChange` when fields are hidden based on changes made to corresponding data elements.

Returns   Returns a Boolean, which can be used to determine if the function was successful

Example
```
If MY_PROBLEM_STATUS <> "5" Then
   Hide(MY_PROBLEM_RESOLTN);
End-If;
```

UnHide

Description   `UnHide` makes a panel field visible again.

Syntax
```
UnHide(fieldname)
```

Rules   Fields that are hidden based on the Panel Field Properties-Use-Invisible tab are not made visible because `UnHide` has no impact on these fields.

Returns Returns a Boolean, which can be used to determine if the function was successful

Example
```
If PERSONAL_DATA.BIRTHCOUNTRY <> "USA" Then
   UnHide(PERSONAL_DATA.BIRTHSTATE);
End-If;
```

Ungray

Description Allows a previously non-editable field to be editable

Syntax
```
Ungray (fieldname)
```

Rules Used in events such as `RowInit`. Can also appear in `FieldChange` after the status of a field is impacted by changes to its value or other corresponding fields.

Returns Returns a Boolean, which can be used to determine if the function was successful

Example
```
If COMPANY = DEPT_TBL.COMPANY Then
   Hide(COMPANY, PAYGROUP);
End-If;
```

Process Scheduler functions

ScheduleProcess

Description The `ScheduleProcess` function stores a row in the Process Request table enabling the system to schedule a process or job.

Syntax
```
ScheduleProcess(process_type, process_name
[, run_location] [, run_cntl_id] [, process_instance]
[, run_dttm] [, recurrence_name] [, server_name])
```

where

process_type   A case-sensitive string that identifies the type of process to be run. SQR Report and Application Engine are examples of process types.

process_name   An eight-character string used to identify the process

run_location   A one character string that identifies if the process is run on the client ('1') or the server ('2')

run_cntl_id   Identifies the Run Control ID that links operator IDs to Run Controls `process_instance` The `ScheduleProcess` function receives this as a variable and assigns a unique number to identify each process requested.

`run_dttm` A process or job can be scheduled for some future time by passing a `DateTime` value in this parameter. The `%DateTime` system variable can also be passed for immediate scheduling.

`recurrence_name` Identifies the name of a recurring job or process

`server_name` Identifies the server on which the process or job will be run

Rules process_type and process_name are the only required parameters necessary to schedule a process.

When a call to `ScheduleProcess` is made from a program running on an application server, the run_location parameter cannot be passed as `'1'` (client). Doing so generates an error and subsequent cancellation of the request.

Any process involving COBOL or SQR scheduled from a program on an application server must also be run on the server. When the PeopleCode program containing `ScheduleProcess` is run on a client, the COBOL or SQR process is not restricted and can run on either the client or server.

The parameter list can accept strings in the form of bind variables or a Meta-SQL string.

Returns A successful process returns zero. A non-zero return indicates an error was encountered.

Example
```
If ScheduleProcess("SQR Report", &REPORT_NAME,
   &RUN_LOCATION, &RUN_CNTL_ID) = 0 Then
   WinMessage("SQR Report successfully scheduled");
End-If;
```

Save/Cancel functions

DoCancel

Description Used to cancel activity on a panel. The function mimics the ESC key and the Cancel toolbar icon.

Syntax
```
DoCancel( )
```

Rules For the current panel group, all PeopleCode programs are terminated except for those executing in the following events:

```
SaveEdit
SavePreChg
SavePostChg
```

Returns   Does not return a value

Example
```
If &RETURN_CODE <> 0 Then
    DoCancel();
End-If;
```

DoSave

Description   Performs save processing at the conclusion of the current PeopleCode program in the `FieldEdit`, `FieldChange`, and `MenuItemSelect` events.

Syntax
```
DoSave ( )
```

Rules   PeopleCode programs containing `DoSave` continue processing until the remaining statements are executed. The panel is saved at the conclusion of the program. Save processing includes the following events:
```
SaveEdit
SavePreChg
SavePostChg
WorkFlow
```

Returns   Does not return a value

Example
```
If &RETURN_CODE = 0 Then
    DoSave();
End-If;
```

DoSaveNow

Description   Works similar to `DoSave`, however, the panel is immediately saved without waiting for the PeopleCode program to conclude.

Syntax
```
DoSaveNow ( )
```

Rules   After the panel is saved, any remaining PeopleCode statements that follow `DoSaveNow` are executed.

DoSaveNow is only valid from the `FieldEdit` and `FieldChange` events.

A common use of `DoSaveNow` is when remote calls are involved. When using `RemoteCall`, `DoSaveNow` can be used to save information to the database before a remote process is called.

Returns   Does not return a value

Example
```
If &RETURN_CODE = 0 Then
   DoSaveNow();
   If ScheduleProcess("SQR Report", &REPORT_NAME,
&RUN_LOCATION, &RUN_CNTL_ID) = 0 Then
      &RETURN = MyAuditFunction();
   End-If;
End-If;
```

WinEscape

Description   Used to cancel activity on a panel. WinEscape mimics the ESC key.

Syntax
```
WinEscape ( )
```

Rules   Changes made to the panel since the previous save are revoked

Returns   An optional Boolean value is returned if required.

Example
```
/* This example cancels the panel when fields are missing */
If None(MY_PROBLEM_STATUS, PRIORITY, MY_USER_ID) Then
   WinEscape();
End-If;
```

Scroll functions

ScrollSelect

Description   Selects records from a table and loads them into the scroll buffer area of a panel. Inserts child rows under the next higher level row.

Syntax
```
ScrollSelect (levelnum, [RECORD.level1_recname,
[RECORD.level2_recname,]] RECORD.target_recname,
RECORD.sel_recname
[, sqlstr [, bindvars]]
[, turbo])
```

where

    levelnum   The level number of the target scroll area. This value can be 1, 2, or 3.

    RECORD.level1_recname   Represents the path to the target scroll area. When the target record is on scroll level 2, this parameter must precede target_recordname.

    RECORD.level2_recname   Represents the path to the target scroll area. When the target record is on scroll level 3, the target_recordname must be preceded by RECORD.level1_recname and RECORD.level2_recname.

`RECORD.target recordname` The target scroll area where the selected data are loaded. When the target scroll is on level 3, specify the level 1 and level 2 records first followed by the level 3 target scroll.

`RECORD.sel_recordname` Specifies the record or view to retrieve data from. The sel_recordname can be the same as target_recordname. One characteristic of this parameter is that it enables target rows to be loaded into a buffer with only those fields used in the scroll area, in addition to key fields. When selecting rows from a large table such as JOB (in HRMS) and the target scroll area only uses five fields, specifying a smaller target reduces the amount of data loaded into system buffers.

`sqlstr [, bindvars]` The optional SQL string parameter can contain an SQL `WHERE` and `ORDER BY` clause. One or both can be specified. The `WHERE` clause enables us to limit the number of rows loaded into the scroll area. The `ORDER BY` clause can be used to sort the rows before being loaded into the target scroll area. The SQL string can accept bind variables that are used as part of the `WHERE` or `ORDER BY` clause. Bind variables can be regular bind or inline bind variables. SQL string can include Meta-SQL functions.

`turbo` When specified, improves performance of the `ScrollSelect` function. The parameter is passed as a Boolean `True`.

Rules Allows for the specification of the target scroll area, a source record from which to select rows, and an optional SQL string. Keys on the select record must be the same as on the target scroll record. A record can be used as both select and scroll record. Select record must be defined and created using Application Designer. Select record cannot be a Derived/Work record.

Returns Does not return a value

Example
```
/* Selects data into level 2 using a target record with limited fields */
   ScrollSelect(2, RECORD.MY_LOCATIONS,
     RECORD.MY_LOCATION_EMP, RECORD.MY_LOC_EMPL_VW, True);
```

ScrollSelectNew

Description Resembles `ScrollSelect`, except that `ScrollSelectNew` marks records as new when they are loaded into the scroll area. During save processing, these records are automatically added to the database.

Syntax
```
ScrollSelectNew (levelnum,
[RECORD.level1_recname, [RECORD.level2_recname,]]
RECORD.target_recname, RECORD.sel_recname
[, sqlstr [, bindvars]]
[, turbo])
```

where

levelnum Represents the level number of the target scroll area. This value can be 1, 2, or 3.

RECORD.level1_recname Represents the path to the target scroll area. When the target record is on scroll level 2, this parameter must precede the target_recordname.

RECORD.level2_recname Represents the path to the target scroll area. When the target record is on scroll level 3, the target_recordname must be preceded by RECORD.level1_recname and RECORD.level2_recname.

RECORD.target recordname The target scroll area where the selected data are loaded. When the target scroll is on level 3, we need to specify the level 1 and level 2 records first, followed by the record at target scroll level 3.

RECORD.sel_recordname Specifies the record or view to retrieve data from. The sel_recordname can be the same as target_recordname. One characteristic of this parameter is that it allows target rows to be loaded into a record with only those fields used in the scroll area in addition to key fields.

sqlstr [, bindvars] The optional SQL string parameter can contain an SQL WHERE and ORDER BY clause. One or both can be specified. The WHERE clause enables us to limit the number of rows loaded into the scroll area. The ORDER BY clause can be used to sort the rows before they are loaded into the target scroll area. The SQL string can accept bind variables that are used as part of the WHERE or ORDER BY clause. Bind variables can be regular or inline bind variables. The SQL string can include Meta-SQL functions.

turbo Improves performance of the ScrollSelectNew function. The parameter is passed as a Boolean True when Turbo is used.

Rules Keys on the select record must be the same as on the target scroll record. A record can be used as both select and scroll record. Select record must have been defined and created using Application Designer and cannot be a Derived/Work record.

Returns Does not return a value

Example
```
/*Load Location data into scroll level 1 */
  ScrollSelectNew(1, RECORD.MY_LOCATIONS,
    RECORD.MY_LOC_OPR_VW, True);
```

ScrollFlush

Description Removes records from a target scroll area

Syntax
```
ScrollFlush (scrollpath)
ScrollPath defined as
[RECORD.level1_recname,    level1_row,]
[RECORD.level2_recname,]   level2_row,]
 RECORD.target_recname
```

where

> RECORD.level1_recname   Represents the path to the target scroll area. When the target record is on scroll level 2, this parameter must precede the target_recordname. The level1_recname requires the RECORD prefix.

> level1_row   The level 1 row to flush. The value is an integer and can be a variable or a constant. The parameter must be specified when ScrollFlush is targeted at scroll levels 2 or 3.

> RECORD.level2_recname   Represents the path to the target scroll area. When the target record is on scroll level 3, the target_recordname must be preceded by a RECORD.level1_recname and RECORD.level2_recname.

> level2_row   Indicates the scroll level 2 to flush. The value is an integer and can be a variable or a constant. The parameter must be specified when Scroll-Flush is targeted at scroll level 3.

> Target recordname   The target scroll area where rows to remove are located. When the target scroll is on level 3, specify the level 1 and level 2 records first, then the record at target level 3. The target record name must be prefixed by RECORD.

Rules   Rows flushed from the target scroll area are not removed from the database

Returns   Does not return a value

Example
```
ScrollFlush(RECORD.MY_LOCATIONS, CurrentRowNumber(),
 RECORD.MY_LOCATION_EMP, RECORD.MY_LOC_EMPL_VW);
```

ActiveRowCount

Description   Identifies the sum of active rows in a given scroll area

Syntax
```
ActiveRowCount (Scrollpath)
ScrollPath defined as:
[RECORD.level1_recname,    level1_row,]
[RECORD.level2_recname,]   level2_row,]
 RECORD.target_recname
```

where

RECORD.level1_recname Represents the path to the target scroll area. When the target record is on scroll level 2 this parameter must precede the target_recordname. The leve1_recname requires the RECORD prefix.

level1_row Identifies the record at scroll level 1. The value is an integer and can be a variable or a constant. The parameter must be specified when ActiveRowCount is used to return the number of active rows at scroll level 2 or 3.

RECORD.level2_recname Represents the path to the target scroll area. When the target record is on scroll level 3, the target_recordname must be preceded by a RECORD.level1_recname and RECORD.level2_recname.

level2_row Identifies the record at scroll level 2. The value is an integer and can be a variable or a constant. The parameter must be specified when ActiveRowCount is used to return the number of active rows at scroll level 3.

Target recordname Record in the target scroll area. The target record name must be prefixed by RECORD. The target record may be on scroll level 1, 2, or 3

Rules Records marked as deleted are not included in the count.

Returns Returns a number representing the number of active rows in a scroll area

Example
```
&NUMBER_OF_ROWS = ActiveRowCount(RECORD.MY_LOCATIONS,
CurrentRowNumber(), RECORD.MY_LOCATION_EMP);
```

CurrentRowNumber

Description CurrentRowNumber is used when it is necessary to identify the row number of the current row in a scroll area.

Syntax
```
CurrentRowNumber ( [level] )
```

or
```
CurrentRowNumber()
```

where
    level Identifies the scroll level where the row number is retrieved

Rules When the level parameter is not specified, the function uses the current scroll level from where the function is called as the default level. CurrentRowNumber is sometimes used with ActiveRowCount to limit program loops to the number of active rows.

Returns   A number representing the current row number on the specified scroll level

Example
```
/*The return value can be used in ActiveRowCount*/
   &COUNT = ActiveRowCount(RECORD.MY_LOCATIONS, &ROW_NUMBER,
   RECORD.MY_LOCATION_EMP);

/*CurrentRowNumber can also be specified explicitlty */
   &COUNT = ActiveRowCount(RECORD.MY_LOCATIONS,
   CurrentRowNumber(1), RECORD.MY_LOCATION_EMP);
```

DeleteRow

Description   DeleteRow enables rows to be deleted from a PeopleCode program. The function triggers the RowDelete event, which mimics the F8/Delete Row operation.

Syntax
```
DeleteRow (Scrollpath, target_row )
```

ScrollPath defined as:
```
[RECORD.level1_recname, level1_row,  ]
[RECORD.level2_recname,] level2_row,  ]
RECORD.target_recname
```

where

> RECORD.level1_recname   Represents the path to the target scroll area. When the target record is on scroll level 2, this parameter must precede the target_recordname. The leve1_recname requires the RECORD prefix.

> level1_row   Identifies the record at scroll level 1. The value is an integer and can be a variable or a constant. The parameter must be specified when DeleteRow is used to delete rows at scroll level 2 or 3.

> RECORD.level2_recname   Represents the path to the target scroll area. When the target record is on scroll level 3, the target_recordname must be preceded by a RECORD.level1_recname and RECORD.level2_recname.

> level2_row Identifies the record at scroll level 2. The value is an integer and can be a variable or a constant. The parameter must be specified when DeleteRow is used to delete the number of rows at scroll level 3.

> Target recordname The target scroll area to delete. The target record may be on scroll level 1, 2, or 3 and must be prefixed by RECORD.

> target_row Identifies the row number to be deleted

Rules   When `DeleteRow` is used in a loop, the operation must begin with the highest row and work downwards. Each time a row is deleted the system renumbers all remaining rows.

Returns   Returns an optional Boolean value

Example
```
For &I = ActiveRowCount(RECORD.PERS_DATA_EFFDT)
   To 1 Step - 1
   DeleteRow(RECORD.PERS_DATA_EFFDT, &I);
End-For;
```

FetchValue

Description   Retrieves the value of a field from a row stored in the panel buffer of a scroll area and places it into a variable or fieldname

Syntax
```
FetchValue (Scrollpath, target_row,
[recordname.] fieldname )
```

ScrollPath is defined as:
```
RECORD.level1_recname, level1_row,  ]
[RECORD.level2_recname,] level2_row,  ]
RECORD.target_recname
```

where

> `RECORD.level1_recname`   Represents the path to the target scroll area. When the target record is on scroll level 2, this parameter must precede the target_recordname. The level1_recname requires the RECORD prefix.

> `level1_row`   Indicates the scroll level 1 row. The value is an integer and can be a variable or a constant. The parameter must be specified when fields from rows at level 2 or 3 are fetched.

> `RECORD.level2_recname`   Represents the path to the target scroll area. When the target record is on scroll level 3, the target_recordname must be preceded by a RECORD.level1_recname and RECORD.level2_recname.

> `level2_row`   Represents the scroll level 2 row to be referenced. The value is an integer and can be a variable or a constant. The parameter must be specified when `FetchValue` is targeted at scroll level 3.

> `Target recordname`   Represents the target scroll area containing the row where data are to be fetched from. The target record name must be prefixed by RECORD. The target record may be on scroll level 1, 2. or 3.

> `target_row`   Identifies the row number in the target scroll area where buffer field contents we will be retrieved.

[recordname.] fieldname   The name of the field that references the value to be loaded. The record name is used when the function call is made from a record definition that is not the same as recordname. The fieldname can reside on scroll level 1, 2, or 3.

Rules   In many instances `FetchValue` may not be necessary if the contents of a field are accessible to a program by using the [recordname].fieldname syntax. `FetchValue` can be used when a value is not within context.

Returns   Returns an ANY data type value.

Example
```
&EMPLID = FetchValue(RECORD.MY_LOCATIONS,
CurrentRowNumber(), RECORD.MY_LOCATION_EMP, &I,
MY_LOCATION_EMP.EMPLID);
```

HideRow

Description   HideRow is used to hide a specific row and any child rows in subordinate scroll levels.

Syntax
```
HideRow (Scrollpath)
[, target_row]
```

ScrollPath defined as:
```
[RECORD.level1_recname, level1_row, ]
[RECORD.level2_recname,] level2_row, ]
RECORD.target_recname
```

where

RECORD.level1_recname   Represents the path to the target scroll area. When the target record is on scroll level 2, this parameter must precede the target_recordname. The level1_recname requires the RECORD prefix.

level1_row   This parameter indicates the scroll level 1 row. The value is an integer and can be a variable or a constant. The parameter must be specified when fields from rows at level 2 or 3 are to be hidden.

RECORD.level2_recname   Represents the path to the target scroll area. When the target record is on scroll level 3, the target_recordname must be preceded by a RECORD.level1_recname and RECORD.level2_recname.

level2_row   This parameter represents data at scroll level 2. The value is an integer and can be a variable or a constant. The parameter must be specified when `HideRow` is targeted at scroll level 3.

Target recordname   The target record to hide. The target record may be on scroll level 1, 2, or 3 and must be prefixed by RECORD.

`target_row`   Identifies the row number to be hidden

Rules   When a row at a higher scroll level is hidden, any associated child rows are hidden as well. When the `HideRow` function is used, the target row is hidden but there is no impact to the underlying database tables.

Returns   A Boolean indicating the success (`True`) or failure (`False`) of the call

Example
```
If MY_LOCATIONS.EFFDT < &TARGET_DATE Then
   HideRow(RECORD.MY_LOCATIONS, CurrentRowNumber(),
RECORD.MY_LOCATION_EMP, &I);
End-If;
```

HideScroll

Description   This function is similar to `HideRow` except that rather than hiding a row, the complete scroll area is hidden including all data in the scroll and the scroll bar.

Syntax
```
HideScroll (Scrollpath)
```

ScrollPath is defined as:
```
[RECORD.level1_recname, level1_row, ]
[RECORD.level2_recname,] level2_row,  ]
 RECORD.target_recname
```

where

   `RECORD.level1_recname`   Represents the path to the target scroll area. When the target record is on scroll level 2, this parameter must precede the target_recordname. The level1_recname requires the RECORD prefix.

   `level1_row`   This parameter indicates data at scroll level one. The value is an integer and can be a variable or a constant. The parameter must be specified when hiding scroll areas at level 2 or 3.

   `RECORD.level2_recname`   Represents the path to the target scroll area. When the target record is on scroll level 3, the target_recordname must be preceded by a RECORD.level1_recname and RECORD.level2_recname.

   `level2_row`   This parameter represents data at scroll level 2. The value is an integer and can be a variable or a constant. The parameter must be specified when hiding a scroll at level 3.

   `Target recordname`   The target scroll area to hide. The target record may be on scroll level 1, 2, or 3 and must be prefixed by RECORD.

Rules   `HideScroll` is usually implemented in the `RowInit` and `FieldChange` events.

Returns   A Boolean indicating the success (`True`) or failure (`False`) of the call.

Example
```
If %Mode = "U" Then
   If ActiveRowCount(RECORD.MY_LOCATIONS) = 0 Then
      HideScroll(RECORD.MY_LOCATIONS);
   End-If;
End-If;
```

RowScrollSelect

Description   `RowScrollSelect` uses the select record parameter to read data and place it into a scroll specified for a particular parent row. This function is similar to `ScrollSelect`. The difference between `ScrollSelect` and `RowScrollSelect` is that `ScrollSelect` uses the key hierarchy of the parent keys and automatically places child rows under their corresponding parent data within the scroll buffer. `RowScrollSelect` does not do this and requires that the SQL string be used to limit the rows loaded into the scroll to those of the parent row keys.

Syntax
```
RowScrollSelect (levelnum, scrollpath,
RECORD.sel_recname
[, sqlstr [, bindvars]]
[, turbo])
```

ScrollPath is defined as:
```
[RECORD.level1_recname, level1_row,
[RECORD.level2_recname, level2_row]]
RECORD.target_recname
```

where

    `levelnum`   Represents the level number of the target scroll area. This value can be 1, 2, or 3.

    `RECORD.level1_recname`   Represents the path to the target scroll area. When the target record is on scroll level 2, this parameter must precede the target_recordname. The level1_recname requires the RECORD prefix.

    `level1_row`   Specifies the scroll level 1 row. The value is an integer and can be a variable or a constant. The parameter must be specified when the target record name is on scroll level 2.

    `RECORD.level2_recname`   Represents the path to the target scroll area. When the target record is on scroll level 3, the target_recordname must be preceded by a RECORD.level1_recname and RECORD.level2_recname.

    `level2_row`   This parameter represents data at scroll level 2. The value is an integer and can be a variable or a constant. The parameter must be specified when the target record name is on scroll level 3.

target recordname   Target record name appears at the lowest scroll level. The target record name must be prefixed by RECORD. Target record may be on scroll level 1, 2, or 3. When the target record is on scroll level 2, the target record name must be prefixed with the RECORD.level1_recname, level1_row parameter. When the target is on scroll level 3, the target record name must be prefixed with the RECORD.level1_recname, level1_row and the RECORD.level2_recname, level2_row.

RECORD.sel_recordname   Specifies the record or view from which data can be retrieved. Sel_recordname can be the same as target_recordname. One characteristic of this parameter is that it enables target rows to be loaded into a record with only those fields required in the scroll area in addition to key fields.

sqlstr [, bindvars]   The SQL string parameter requires the SQL WHERE and an optional ORDER BY clause. The WHERE clause is used to limit any child keys read to those of the parent row key. The ORDER BY clause can be used to sort the rows before data are loaded into the target scroll area. The SQL string can accept bind variables that can be used as part of the WHERE or ORDER BY clause. Bind variables can be regular or inline bind variables. The SQL string can include Meta-SQL functions.

turbo   Improves performance of the RowScrollSelect function. The parameter is passed as a Boolean True when Turbo RowScrollSelect is used.

Rules   RowScrollSelect does not arrange child rows under their related parent row keys. It is up to the WHERE clause in the SQL string to limit child rows to the parent record key. Select record should be defined and created using Application Designer and cannot be a Derived/Work record.

Returns   Does not return a value

Example
```
/* Loads the Direct Deposit Distribution record for the current Emplid */
   For &I = 1 To ActiveRowCount(RECORD.DIRECT_DEPOSIT);
      RowScrollSelect(2, RECORD.DIRECT_DEPOSIT, &I,
      RECORD.DIR_DEP_DISTRIB, "WHERE EMPLID = :1
      ORDER BY EFFDT", PERSONAL_DATA.EMPLID, True);
   End-For;
```

RowScrollSelectNew

Description   RowScrollSelectNew resembles RowScrollSelect, except that RowScrollSelectNew marks records as New when they are loaded into the scroll area. RowScrollSelectNew does not automatically place child rows under their corresponding parent key within the scroll buffer. It requires that the SQL string be used to limit the rows loaded into the scroll to those of the parent key.

Syntax

```
RowScrollSelectNew (levelnum, scrollpath,
RECORD.sel_recname
[, sqlstr [, bindvars]]
[, turbo])
```

ScrollPath is defined as:

```
[RECORD.level1_recname, level1_row,
[RECORD.level2_recname, level2_row]]
RECORD.target_recname
```

where

> `levelnum` Represents the level number of the target scroll area. This value can be 1, 2, or 3.

> `RECORD.level1_recname` Represents the path to the target scroll area. When the target record is on scroll level 2, this parameter must precede the target_recordname. The level1_recname requires the RECORD prefix.

> `level1_row` Indicates the scroll level 1 row. The value is an integer and can be a variable or a constant. The parameter must be specified when the target record name is on scroll level 2.

> `RECORD.level2_recname` Represents the path to the target scroll area. When the target record is on scroll level 3, the target_recordname must be preceded by a RECORD.level1_recname and RECORD.level2_recname.

> `level2_row` Represents data at scroll level 2. The value is an integer and can be a variable or a constant. The parameter must be specified when the target record name is on scroll level 3.

> `target recordname` The target record name appears at the lowest scroll level. The target record name must be prefixed by RECORD. The target record may be on scroll level 1, 2, or 3. When the target record is on scroll level 2, the target record name must be prefixed with the RECORD.level1_recname, level1_row parameter. When the target is on scroll level 3, the target record name must be prefixed with the RECORD.level1_recname, level1_row, and the RECORD.level2_recname, level2_row.

> `RECORD.sel_recordname` Specifies the record or view from which data can be retrieved. sel_recordname can be the same as target_recordname. One characteristic of this parameter is that it enables target rows to be loaded into a record with only those fields required in the scroll area in addition to key fields.

> `sqlstr [, bindvars]` The SQL string parameter requires the SQL WHERE and an optional ORDER BY clause. The WHERE clause is used to limit any child keys read to those of the parent row key. The ORDER BY clause can be used to sort the rows before data are loaded into the target scroll area. The SQL string can accept bind variables that can be used as part of the WHERE or ORDER BY

clause. Bind variables can be regular or inline bind variables. The SQL string can include Meta-SQL functions.

`turbo`   Improves performance of the `RowScrollSelectNew` function. The parameter is passed as a Boolean `True`.

Rules   `RowScrollSelectNew` does not arrange child rows under their related parent row keys. It is up to the `WHERE` clause in the SQL string to limit child rows to the parent record key. Select record should be defined and created using Application Designer and cannot be a Derived/Work record.

Returns   Does not return a value

Example
```
RowScrollSelectNew(2, RECORD.MY_LOCATIONS,
RECORD.MY_LOCATION_EMP, RECORD.MY_LOC_EMPL_VW,
"WHERE SETID = :1 AND OPRCLASS = :2 AND LOCATION = :3",
MY_LOCATIONS.SETID, MY_LOCATIONS.OPRCLASS,
MY_LOCATIONS.LOCATION, True);
```

RowFlush

Description   Used at the row level to remove a particular row of data from a scroll

Syntax
```
RowFlush(scrollpath, target_row)
```

ScrollPath is defined as:
```
[RECORD.level1_recname, level1_row,
[RECORD.level2_recname, level2_row]]
RECORD.target_recname
```

where

   `RECORD.level1_recname`   Represents the path to the target scroll area. When the target record is on scroll level 2, this parameter must precede the target_recordname. The level1_recname requires the RECORD prefix.

   `level1_row`   Indicates the scroll level 1 row. The value is an integer and can be a variable or a constant. The parameter must be specified when the target record name is on scroll level 2.

   `RECORD.level2_recname`   Represents the path to the target scroll area. When the target record is on scroll level 3, the target_recordname must be preceded by a RECORD.level1_recname and RECORD.level2_recname.

   `level2_row`   This parameter represents data at scroll level 2. The value is an integer and can be a variable or a constant. The parameter must be specified when the target record name is on scroll level 3.

target recordname   The target record name appears at the lowest scroll level. The target record name must be prefixed by RECORD. The target record may be on scroll level 1, 2, or 3. When the target record is on scroll level 2, the target record name must be prefixed with the RECORD.level1_recname, level1_ row parameter. When the target is on scroll level 3, the target record name must be prefixed with the RECORD.level1_recname, level1_row, and the RECORD.level2_recname, level2_row.

target_row   Identifies the row number to be removed from the specified target scroll area

Rules   RowFlush does not remove rows from the database; it only removes them from the panel scroll buffer. To remove records from the panel scroll buffer as well as from the database, the DeleteRow function can be used because it performs both operations.

Returns   Does not return a value

Example
```
If EMPLID <> PERSONAL_DATA.EMPLID Or
    EFFDT <> DIRECT_DEPOSIT.EFFDT Then
  RowFlush(RECORD.DIRECT_DEPOSIT, CurrentRowNumber(),
 RECORD.DIR_DEP_DISTRIB, CurrentRowNumber());
End-If;
```

UpdateValue

Description   UpdateValue is commonly used in a scroll area to update the value of a field using a value parameter.

Syntax
```
UpdateValue (Scrollpath, target_row,
 [recordname.] fieldname, value )
```

ScrollPath is defined as:
```
[RECORD.level1_recname, level1_row,
[RECORD.level2_recname, level2_row]]
RECORD.target_recname
```

where

RECORD.level1_recname   Represents the path to the target scroll area. When the target record is on scroll level 2, this parameter must precede the target_recordname. The level1_recname requires the RECORD prefix.

level1_row   Indicates the scroll level 1 row. The value is an integer and can be a variable or a constant. The parameter must be specified when the target record name is on scroll level 2.

RECORD.level2_recname   Represents the path to the target scroll area. When the target record is on scroll level 3, the target_recordname must be preceded by a RECORD.level1_recname and RECORD.level2_recname.

level2_row   This parameter represents data at scroll level 2. The value is an integer and can be a variable or a constant. The parameter must be specified when the target record name is on scroll level 3.

target recordname   The target record name appears at the lowest scroll level. The target record name must be prefixed by RECORD. The target record may be on scroll level 1, 2, or 3. When the target record is on scroll level 2, the target record name must be prefixed with the RECORD.level1_recname, level1_ row parameter. When the target is on scroll level 3, the target record name must be prefixed with the RECORD.level1_recname, level1_row, and the RECORD.level2_recname, level2_row.

target_row   Identifies the row number in the specified target scroll area be to updated

[recordname.] fieldname   The name of the field to be updated on the target row. Recordname is used when the function call is made from a record definition that is not the same as the recordname. Fieldname can reside on scroll level 1, 2, or 3.

Value   Identifies the variable, constant, or record field that is moved to the corresponding target record

Rules   The data type of the value parameter must be of a type compatible with the record field. The UpdateValue function updates the value of the field in the scroll. If the panel is canceled, no changes are written to the database.

Returns   Does not return a value

Example
```
&NEW_DATE = %Date;
If EFF_STATUS <> "A" Then
   For &I = ActiveRowCount(RECORD.DIRECT_DEPOSIT)
      To 1 Step - 1;
        UpdateValue(RECORD.DIRECT_DEPOSIT, CurrentRowNumber(),
        RECORD.DIR_DEP_DISTRIB, &I,
        DIR_DEP_DISTRIB.LAST_UPDATE_DATE, &NEW_DATE);
   End-For;
End-If;
```

TotalRowCount

Description   Produces the aggregate number of rows in a scroll area including deleted rows

Syntax
```
TotalRowCount (Scrollpath)
```

ScrollPath is defined as:
```
[RECORD.level1_recname, level1_row,
[RECORD.level2_recname, level2_row]]
RECORD.target_recname
```

where

`RECORD.level1_recname`   Represents the path to the target scroll area. When the target record is on scroll level 2, this parameter must precede the target_recordname. The level1_recname requires the RECORD prefix.

`level1_row`   Indicates the scroll level 1 row. The value is an integer and can be a variable or a constant. The parameter must be specified when the target record name is on scroll level 2.

`RECORD.level2_recname`   Represents the path to the target scroll area. When the target record is on scroll level 3, the target_recordname must be preceded by a RECORD.level1_recname and RECORD.level2_recname.

`level2_row`   This parameter represents data at scroll level 2. The value is an integer and can be a variable or a constant. The parameter must be specified when the target record name is on scroll level 3.

`target recordname`   The target record name appears at the lowest scroll level. The target record name must be prefixed by RECORD. The target record may be on scroll level 1, 2, or 3. When the target record is on scroll level 2, the target record name must be prefixed with the RECORD.level1_recname, level1_row parameter. When the target is on scroll level 3, the target record name must be prefixed with the RECORD.level1_recname, level1_row, and the RECORD.level2_recname, level2_row.

Rules   TotalRowCount is similar to ActiveRowCount except that TotalRowCount includes deleted rows. Rows that are marked as deleted remain in the buffer until all system updates have been performed.

Returns   A number that includes active as well as deleted rows.

Example
```
/* To obtain total number of rows at level 1 */
   &TOTAL_ROWS = TotalRowCount(RECORD.MY_LOCATIONS);
/* Total number of rows at level 2 */
   &TOTAL_ROWS_LEVEL2 = TotalRowCount(RECORD.MY_LOCATIONS,
   CurrentRowNumber(), RECORD.MY_LOCATION_EMP);
```

SQL functions

SQLExec

Description   Executes an SQL command passed as a string from a PeopleCode program. The SQL string can contain bind variables, subselects, and joins. Data elements appearing in a `Select` statement are returned to the PeopleCode program as output and can be stored in variables or record fields.

Syntax
```
SQLExec (sqlcmd, bindvars, output)
```

> `sqlcmd`   Represents an SQL string passed by the PeopleCode program. It can contain references to both regular and inline bind variables.
>
> `bindvars` Bind variables are the data elements referenced in the SQL string. There are two types of bind variables, regular and inline. When regular bind variables are used, each requires a corresponding variable name that replaces the :n reference in the SQL string. These variables appear outside the double quotes as
>
> variable-1 [, variable-2, variable-3 …]
>
> When inline bind variables are used, the variables are enclosed within the SQL string as
>
> [:recordname1.]fieldname1 [, [recordname2.]fieldname2] …
>
> `output` Represents the column name (s) populated as a result of a `Select` statement. The output can be placed into variables or record fields. Each column selected requires a corresponding output variable or record field separated by commas. The two forms include
>
> variable-1 [, variable-2, variable-3] …
>
> or
>
> [:recordname1.]fieldname1 [, [recordname2.]fieldname2] …

Rules   SQLExec is one function where unpredictable results can occur if rules are not followed. Because SQLExec bypasses the Application Processor and heads directly to the database, no evaluation of the SQL string contained within quotes is performed. Record fields used as inline bind variables or output variables are evaluated by the Application Processor when they are not contained in the SQL string. When PeopleCode containing SQLExec statements are entered into the PeopleCode editor, any undefined record fields are represented by an error message during the syntax check or save operation. SQLExec statements containing inline bind variables are the exception. Because an inline bind variable is enclosed in quotes, an SQL statement which contains incorrect inline bind variables generates a runtime error message. A previously undefined output variable is created at runtime and does not generate an error.

A SQLExec Select statement retrieves one row of data only. When multiple rows are selected, only the first row is actually returned.

The maximum number of output variables when using Select is 64.

With SQLExec, Updates, Inserts and Deletes can be performed but can only be done in the following events:

```
SavePreChg
WorkFlow
SavePostChg
```

Application records referenced in a SQLExec statement require the PS_ prefix.

Returns   Returns an optional Boolean. A True indicates the function ran successfully.

Example
```
/* Using UPDATE with a regular bind variable */
SQLExec("Update PS_MY_LOCATIONS SET EFFDT = %1",
MY_LOCATIONS.EFFDT);

/* Using an inline bind variable */
SQLExec("Update PS_MY_LOCATIONS SET EFFDT =
:MY_LOCATIONS.EFFDT");
```

String functions

Lower

Description   Converts the uppercase characters of the field or variable to lower case and returns them as a String data type

Syntax
```
Lower (string)
```

Rules   Numeric, punctuation and other non-letter values are not changed

Returns   A lowercase string

Example
```
&MY_STRING = "THIS STRING BECOMES LOWER CASE";
&NEW_STRING = Lower(&MY_STRING);
```

LTrim

Description   Function is used to remove any leading characters identified in string2 from string1

Syntax
```
Ltrim (string1 [, string2])
```

Rules   When string2 is not supplied, all leading blanks from string1 are removed. When string2 is supplied, the function is terminated when characters found in string1 do not match those found in string2.

Returns   A string with leftmost characters in string2 removed or blanks when string2 is not supplied.

Example
```
&STREET_ADDRESS = ",##@&100 Main Street";
&STREET_ADDRESS = LTrim(&MY_STRING, ",.#@&");
/* &STREET_ADDRESS Now contains 100 Main Street */
```

RTrim

Description   Function is used to remove any rightmost characters identified by trim_str from the source string

Syntax
```
RTrim (source_str, [, trim_str] )
```

Rules   Works from right to left removing trailing characters defined in trim_str. When trim_str is not supplied, any rightmost blanks are removed.

Returns   A string with leftmost characters in string2 removed or blanks when string2 is not supplied.

Example
```
&DEPARTMENT_DESCR = "Software development & Web
Services,,,,,,";
&DEPARTMENT_DESCR = RTrim(&DEPARTMENT_DESCR, ",");
```

Upper

Description   Converts the characters appearing in a text string to upper case values

Syntax
```
Upper (string)
```

Rules   Characters such as numeric, punctuation, and other non-letter values are not changed

Returns   Returns a string containing uppercase values.

Example
```
&LAST_NAME = "picard";
&LAST_NAME_SRCH = Upper(&LAST_NAME);
/* Value of &LAST_NAME_SRCH = PICARD */
```

Trace Control functions

SetTracePC

Description   Controls PeopleCode Trace based on parameter values passed.

Syntax
```
SetTracePC (n)
```

Rules   Takes one parameter, which represents the trace settings used in producing the output trace file. When multiple trace options are required, each option number is added, and the sum is passed to the function. The options available to SetTracePC are shown in table E.2.

By default SetTracePC produces a file named DBG1.TMP in the Windows Temp directory. A unique file name can be specified if necessary, and this can be done from within the configuration manager trace option.

Returns   Does not return a value

Table E.2   SetTracePC options

Option #	Description
1	This option traces the program that is executed. It includes options 64, 128 and 256 specified below.
2	Lists the entire program.
4	Displays the outcomes of assignments made to variables.
8	Identifies the values retrieved for all variables.
16	Identifies the contents used in the internal stack.
64	This trace option identifies when each program is started.
128	Identifies the calls made to external PeopleCode routines.
256	Identifies the calls made to internal PeopleCode routines.
512	Displays the value of parameters passed to a function.
1024	This option displays the values of parameters at the conclusion of a function call.

Transfer functions

SetNextPanel

Description   SetNextPanel identifies a panel name that will be transferred control to when the operator activates the F6 or presses the NextPanel toolbar icon.

Syntax
```
SetNextPanel (panelname)
```

Rules   Verifies that the panel identified by panelname is available on the current active menu

Returns   Returns an optional Boolean value based on the success or failure of the function call

Example

```
If &RETURN_CODE = 0 Then
    SetNextPanel("MY_APPLCTN_TBL");
Else
    SetNextPanel("MY_USER_TBL");
End-If;
```

TransferPanel

Description   Transfers control to the next panel in the panel group, the panel name supplied to the function, or to the panel identified by a previous `SetNextPanel` function.

Syntax

```
TransferPanel ( [panel_name] )
```

or

```
TransferPanel ( )
```

Rules   The panel transferred to must exist in the current panel group. When the function is called from events outside of save processing (`SavePreChg`, `SavePostChg`), any PeopleCode statements following the `TransferPanel` function are not executed and processing is halted.

Returns   Returns an optional Boolean value based on the success or failure of the function call.

Example

```
If &RETURN_CODE = 0 Then
    SetNextPanel("MY_APPLCTN_TBL");
Else
    SetNextPanel("MY_USER_TBL");
End-If;
TransferPanel();

/* Can also be written */

If &RETURN_CODE = 0 Then
    &NEXTPANEL = "MY_APPLCTN_TBL";
Else
    &NEXTPANEL = "MY_USER_TBL";
End-If;
TransferPanel(&NEXTPANEL);
```

META-SQL FUNCTIONS

Meta-SQL functions are used in SQL strings. They expand in these strings to become platform-specific parameters in the SQL statements. SQL strings are used in the SQLExec as well as scroll functions that accept an SQL string. Meta-SQL can also be implemented when constructing dynamic views or Application Engine statements.

Table E.3 Selected Meta-SQL functions

Function	Description
%CurrentDateIn	This is an In function that becomes a platform-specific SQL string. The string can be used to represent current date in a Select, Update, or Insert statement.
%CurrentDateOut	An Out function that can be used as the current date in the Select clause of an SQL string
%CurrentDateTimeIn	An In function that becomes a platform-specific SQL string. The string can be used as a DateTime value in a Select, Update, or Insert statement.
%CurrentDateTimeOut	%CurrentDateTimeOut is an out function that can be used as the current DateTime value in the Select clause of an SQL string.
%CurrentTimeIn	This is an In function that becomes a platform-specific SQL string. The string is used as current time in a Select, Update, or Insert statement.
%CurrentTimeOut	An Out function that can be used as the current time in the Select clause of an SQL string
%DateAdd	Returns a date after adding the add_days parameter to date_from. syntax: %DateAdd (date_from, add_days) add_days is an integer that can have a negative value and is added to date_from.
%DateDiff	Identifies the difference between two dates syntax: %DateDiff (date_from, date_to) The difference between date_from and date_to is returned as an integer value. When a date literal is used, it must be passed as a %DateIn. Example &Difference = %DateDiff(INCIDENT_DT, CLOSE_DT); &Difference = %DateDiff (CLOSE_DT, %DateIn('1999-05-31'));
%DateIn	An In function that becomes a platform-specific SQL string. The function accepts a date value parameter or a date literal in the format YYYY-MM-DD. %DateIn is used in SQL statements such as Select, Insert, and Update that require a date bind variable or date literal. syntax %DateIn(date)
%DateOut	An Out function that can be used as the date in the Select clause of an SQL string syntax: %DateOut(date)
%TimeIn	This is an In function that becomes a platform-specific SQL string. The string is used as the time value in a Select, Update, or Insert statement. The time parameter passed can be a time variable or a literal in the form hh:mm:ss.ssssss [{AM|PM}].

Table E.3   Selected Meta-SQL functions (continued)

Function	Description
%TimeOut	An Out function that can be used as the time in the Select clause of an SQL string
%Substring	This function references only the portion of the string identified by source_str. The starting position is identified by start and is relative to 1. Length represents the number of characters to be referenced. %Substring can be used to extract or compare a selected area of a string. syntax %Substring (source_str, start, length)
%TrimSubstr	This function is similar to %Substring and can be used to extract or compare a selected area of a string. The difference is that any trailing blanks in the string referenced by source are removed from the target substring. syntax %TrimSubstr (source_str, start, length)

Application Engine functions

Eight basic functions or macros can be utilized in Application Engine statements: &BIND, &CLAUSE, &CLEARCURSOR, &EXECUTE, &MSG, &&RECORD, &ROUND, and &SELECT. We've already covered the most common functions in our exercises (&BIND, &MSG, and &SELECT). The only macro is &&RECORD.

&BIND

Purpose   Retrieves an individual field value from the cache record.

Syntax
&BIND(cache_field [,NOQUOTES] [,NOWRAP] [,STATIC])

Rules   The &BIND function can be used almost anywhere in an SQL statement. It cannot be used in a Select statement Result Set field list.

A character field is returned enclosed in quotes unless the optional NOQUOTES parameter is used.

Date fields are automatically enclosed (or "wrapped") within the %DATEIN or %DATEOUT Meta-SQL functions unless the optional NOWRAP parameter is specified.

When the STATIC parameter is specified, Application Engine resolves the &BIND variable before compiling the SQL statement. This is useful when creating dynamic SQL statements.

Example
```
&SELECT(COUNTER)
SELECT COUNT(*)
  FROM PS_&BIND(RECNAME,NOQUOTES,STATIC)
```

The example is the same used in exercise #3 of our tutorial. When using a RECNAME of JOB, the following SQL statement is compiled:
```
SELECT COUNT(*) FROM PS_JOB
```

The value of JOB is not enclosed in quotes due to the NOQUOTES parameter and can therefore be concatenated properly with the PS_ prefix. The STATIC parameter tells Application Engine to resolve the &BIND variable before compiling the statement.

The &SELECT portion of this statement is described in the &SELECT section.

&CLAUSE

Purpose Similar to a COBOL copybook (or #Include in SQR). When used in a statement it is replaced with the contents of the Application Engine statement specified in the &CLAUSE function. One of the main uses of the &CLAUSE function is retrieving predefined column lists and substituting them in the calling statement. This is useful for Select lists or Insert statements. There are several parameters that can be used with &CLAUSE to increase its' flexibility.

Syntax
```
&CLAUSE(product, application, section, step, type [,parm1] …
 [,parm9])
```

Rules &CLAUSE must point to a valid statement designated by the fully qualified Application Engine statement name of product, application, section, step, and type. No validation is performed. Any errors will be recognized at run-time.

The actual clause section that's retrieved may have optional &P(n) parameter variables embedded within it. A parameter value must be passed to it with the &CLAUSE function. Up to nine parameters may be passed. Several symbolic parameters may be used in an &CLAUSE function:

&COMMA Since a physical comma (or ',') would not be interpreted as an actual parameter, the &COMMA symbolic can be used.

&SPACE This symbolic represents a blank or space. If the retrieved clause section uses &P(n) but isn't required a space can be passed to resolve them using &SPACE.

&RPAREN A right parenthesis may be passed to the specified "clause section." Once again, the symbolic must be used. A physical right parenthesis would not be interpreted as a parameter that needs to be passed.

One of the primary uses of parameters in a &CLAUSE function is to pass a synonym to be used as a column prefix.. The table synonym must be passed with a period like 'A.' or 'B.' —without the quotes. The &CLAUSE function would then return the columns with the desired prefixes to your current statement.

Example   Assuming we defined a "clause section" for product = AE, Appl ID = SAMPLE, section = COMMON, step = CITYINFO, and statement type = S. The column list is entered in the statement text box as follows:

```
&p(1)CITY
,&p(1)STATE
,&p(1)ZIP
```

The &CLAUSE function allows us to substitute the above column list anywhere in our program. Using parameters, we can tailor the column list to our particular needs with prefixes. You'll notice the &P(n) prefix variable contains a '1' for all three columns. This means the first parameter passed in the &CLAUSE function is used as the prefix for all three columns. Using &p(n), the n represents the nth parameter passed in the &CLAUSE.

```
INSERT INTO ps_user_cityinfo
( &CLAUSE(AE, SAMPLE, COMMON, CITYINFO, S, &SPACE) )
SELECT &CLAUSE(AE, SAMPLE, COMMON, CITYINFO, S, A.)
  FROM ps_temp_cityinfo A
```

The &CLAUSE is used twice: Once for the Insert Column list, which doesn't allow prefixes, and once for the Select Column list, which in this case uses a prefix of 'A'. When the SQL statement is resolved, it appears as:

```
INSERT INTO ps_user_cityinfo
(CITY, STATE, ZIP)
SELECT A.CITY, A.STATE, A.ZIP
  FROM ps_temp_cityinfo A
```

Also, see the &&RECORD macro for similar functionality.

&CLEARCURSOR

Purpose   A re-used statement may need to be recompiled during execution of the program. The &CLEARCURSOR function accomplishes this and resets any &BIND variables in the statement that use the STATIC option.

Syntax
```
&CLEARCURSOR([product, ] [application, ] section, step,
 type)
```

Rules   This function must be located at the start of the statement. There may be no other functions or commands in the statement.

Example
```
&CLEARCURSOR(BI, BIIVC000, DUEDATE, SETDATE, D)
```

This recompiles the DO Select statement in the SETDATE step. The step is found in the DUEDATE section of the billing application BIIVC000.

NOTE   Refer to the section describing the Statement Definition panel in appendix F for an explanation of re-used statements.

&EXECUTE

Purpose   Database-specific commands may be executed with this function. Generally, this means any SQL statement that cannot be executed directly using the Update/Insert/Delete SQL statement type.

Syntax
```
&EXECUTE ( [/] )
   command_1 {; | /} ...
   command_n {; | /}
```

Rules   The Update/Insert/Delete statement type must be used. This function must be located at the start of the statement. No other functions or commands may exist in the statement.

Application Engine expects each command within the &EXECUTE function to be delimited with a semi-colon. The optional forward slash (/) parameter overrides this convention and allows the use of a procedural language such as Oracle's PL/SQL to be used. Since the commands within a PL/SQL block are normally terminated by a semi-colon, the forward slash override avoids any conflict. The forward slash would then be required at the end of the &EXECUTE statement.

Example
```
&EXECUTE (/)
declare
   ctr    integer:= 0;
begin
   while ctr = 0 loop
      ctr   = ctr + 1;
      update ps_installation_ar    set st_id_num = ctr;
   end loop;
end;
/
```

The forward slash (/) tells Application Engine to execute the entire PL/SQL block. No conflicts result due to the semi-colon.

&MSG

Purpose   The &MSG function writes a message to the message log.

Syntax
```
&MSG( [Message_Set_Number], Message_Number, [Parm_1],....
 [Parm_n] )
```

Rules   The &MSG function always uses an SQL statement type of Update and must be the first and only function or command in the statement.

Example
```
&MSG(,1,'Hello World')
```

The example is the same as that used in exercise #1. Since the Message Set Number is excluded, it defaults to the Message Set Number specified on the Application Engine definition panel. Message Number 1 is passed a string value of "Hello World". This string value is used in place of the %1 substitution variable defined in the message catalog entry.

&&RECORD

Purpose   The &&RECORD macro inserts all the field names of the specified record into your statement. The optional parameter can be used to assign a column synonym when the entire record is required in your statement(s). This is a quick alternative to the &CLAUSE function.

Syntax
```
&&RECORD(record [, parm_1] )
```

Rules   You must use a valid RECNAME.

Example
```
INSERT INTO ps_customer_tao
SELECT &&RECORD(CUSTOMER)
  FROM ps_customer
```

Using &&RECORD, the Select statement uses all the columns in the Customer record as they exist in Application Designer. This example assumes the CUSTOMER_TAO record matches the Customer record exactly.

&ROUND

Purpose   When Multi-Currency is activated, this function can be used to round numeric fields to the currency precision specified under Define General Options.

Syntax
```
&ROUND(field)
```

Rules   The Multi-Currency option must be specified.

To set the Multi-Currency option

Go → PeopleTools → Utilities → Use → PeopleTools Options

To set the currency precision:

Go → Define Business Rules → Define General Options → Use A-D → Currency Code

Example
```
UPDATE ps_user_tmp
   SET USER_AMT1 = &ROUND(USER_AMT1)
```

This example updates the table with the USER_AMT1 value rounded to the appropriate currency precision.

&SELECT

Purpose   Updates the cache field with the value assigned by the corresponding SQL `Select` statement

Syntax
```
&SELECT(cache_field_1 [,cache_field_2] [,cache_field_x] )
SELECT field_1 [,field_2] [,field_x]
```

Rules   &SELECT is used in tandem with an SQL `Select` statement immediately following.

- The number of cache fields must match the number of fields in the SQL `Select`.
- The datatypes of corresponding cache and SELECT fields must match.
- If NO rows are returned by the SQL `Select` statement, the cache fields are assigned a value of `zero` or `blank`, depending on the datatype.

Example
```
&SELECT(COUNTER)
SELECT COUNT(*)
  FROM PS_PERSONAL_DATA
```

The example is the same as that used in exercise #2. The record count is selected from the PERSONAL_DATA table (lines 2 and 3). The &SELECT function (line 1) assigns the record count to the cache field COUNTER.

index